WileyPLUS

The next generation of WileyPLUS gives you the freedom of mobility and provides a clear path to your course material and assignments, helping you stay engaged and on track.

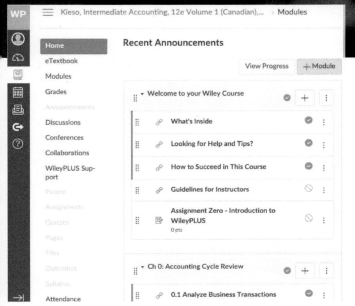

When course materials are presented in an organized way, you are more likely to stay focused, develop mastery, and participate in class. WileyPLUS provides you a clear path through the course material.

Starting with Wiley's quality curated content and adaptive practice questions, you can quickly access material most relevant to your course and understand topics that are most challenging to you. This easy-to-use, intuitive interface saves you time, helps you stay on track, and keeps you motivated throughout your course.

Customized Content

Your course has been customized with videos, documents, pages, and relevant links to keep you motivated.

Interactive eTextbook

You can easily search content, highlight and take notes, access instructor's notes and highlights, and read offline.

Adaptive Practice Questions

Quickly identify areas that are most challenging for you and then focus on material most relevant to your needs.

Linear Design and Organization

Course modules organized by learning objective include eTextbook content, videos, animations, interactives, and practice questions.

Calendar

The course calendar syncs with other features—like assignments and syllabus —so any updates from your instructor will immediately appear.

Student App

You can view due dates, submit assignments, read material, and communicate with your instructor all from your phone.

Wileyplus.com/student-register

WILEY

Intermediate Accounting

Twelfth Canadian Edition

DONALD E. KIESO, Ph.D., CPA

KPMG Peat Marwick Emeritus
Professor of Accounting
Northern Illinois University
DeKalb, Illinois

JERRY J. WEYGANDT, Ph.D., CPA

Arthur Andersen Alumni Professor
of Accounting
University of Wisconsin
Madison, Wisconsin

TERRY D. WARFIELD, Ph.D.

PwC Professor in Accounting
University of Wisconsin
Madison, Wisconsin

IRENE M. WIECEK, FCPA, FCA

Professor of Accounting, Teaching Stream
University of Toronto
Toronto, Ontario

BRUCE J. McCONOMY, Ph.D., CPA, CA

Professor and KPMG Foundation Fellow
in Accounting
Wilfrid Laurier University
Waterloo, Ontario

WILEY

VICE PRESIDENT, EDUCATION	Tim Stookesberry
DIRECTOR, BUSINESS, ACCOUNTING, AND FINANCE	Michael McDonald
SENIOR EDITOR	Emily Marcoux
EDITORIAL ASSISTANT	Kirsten Loose
ASSOCIATE PRODUCT DESIGNER	Daleara Hirjikaka
PRODUCT DESIGN MANAGER	Karen Staudinger
SENIOR MARKETING MANAGER	Anita Osborne
SENIOR CONTENT MANAGER	Dorothy Sinclair
PRODUCTION EDITOR	Rachel Conrad
DESIGN	Wiley
COVER DESIGN	Joanna Vieira/Wiley
COVER PHOTOGRAPHS	© Vadim Petrov/123RF

This book was set in 9.5/12 STIX Two Text by Aptara, Inc. Printed and bound by Quad Graphics. This book is printed on acid-free paper. ∞

Founded in 1807, John Wiley & Sons, Inc. has been a valued source of knowledge and understanding for more than 200 years, helping people around the world meet their needs and fulfill their aspirations. Our company is built on a foundation of principles that include responsibility to the communities we serve and where we live and work. In 2008, we launched a Corporate Citizenship Initiative, a global effort to address the environmental, social, economic, and ethical challenges we face in our business. Among the issues we are addressing are carbon impact, paper specifications and procurement, ethical conduct within our business and among our vendors, and community and charitable support. For more information, please visit our website: www.wiley.com/go/citizenship.

ISBN 978-1-119-49633-5 (E-Pub); 978-1-119-49649-6 (LLPC)

The inside back cover will contain printing identification and country of origin if omitted from this page. In addition, if the ISBN on the cover differs from the ISBN on this page, the one on the cover is correct.

References to the *CPA Canada Handbook—Accounting* are reprinted (or adapted) with permission from Chartered Professional Accountants of Canada. All rights reserved by the copyright owner.

Questions adapted from the Uniform Final Evaluation and the Financial Accounting: Assets (FA2) Exams or Financial Accounting: Liabilities & Equities (FA3) Exams are reproduced with permission from CPA Canada, Toronto, Canada. Any changes to the original material are the sole responsibility of the author (and/or publisher) and have not been reviewed or endorsed by CPA Canada.

This publication and course contains copyright material of the IFRS® Foundation in respect of which all rights are reserved. Reproduced by John Wiley & Sons Canada, Limited with the permission of the IFRS Foundation. No permission granted to third parties to reproduce or distribute. For full access to IFRS Standards and the work of the IFRS Foundation please visit http://eifrs.ifrs.org

The International Accounting Standards Board, the IFRS Foundation, the authors and the publishers do not accept responsibility for any loss caused by acting or refraining from acting in reliance on the material in this publication, whether such loss is caused by negligence or otherwise.

Printed in the United States of America

V10007942_020419

Dedication

Dedicated to our students, who, as graduates and professional accountants, will ably lead us through the next few decades, a period which promises to be an exciting one, with technological advancements accelerating the pace of change.

About the Authors

Canadian Edition

IRENE M. WIECEK, FCPA, FCA, is a Professor of Accounting, Teaching Stream at the University of Toronto, where she is cross-appointed to the Institute for Management & Innovation and the Joseph L. Rotman School of Management. She has taught financial reporting in various programs, including the Commerce Program (Accounting Specialist) and the CPA-accredited Master of Management & Professional Accounting Program (MMPA). The Director of the MMPA Program (previously Associate Director), she co-founded (in 2004) and was Director of the CPA/Rotman Centre for Innovation in Accounting Education, which supported and facilitated innovation in accounting education until 2018. Irene has been involved in professional accounting education for over 25 years, sitting on various provincial and national professional accounting organization committees as well as developing and directing the CICA IFRS Immersion Programs for practising accountants. She was appointed a member of the E&Y Academic Resource Center, where she helped to author a new IFRS curriculum for the Americas. In the area of standard setting, she has chaired the CAAA Financial Reporting Exposure Draft Response Committee and is currently a member of the IFRS Discussion Group (IDG). Irene co-authored the *IFRS Primer: International GAAP Basics* (Canadian and U.S. editions) and was the co-editor and contributor for the books *Leveraging Change—The New Pillars of Accounting Education* and *Educating Professionals: Ethics and Judgment in a Changing Learning Environment.* She co-authored the *Guide to IFRS in Canada* series, which is published by CPA Canada. Irene is on the editorial board of *Accounting Perspectives.*

BRUCE J. McCONOMY, Ph.D., CPA, CA, is a Professor of Accounting and a KPMG Foundation Fellow in Accounting at the Lazaridis School of Business and Economics at Wilfrid Laurier University in Waterloo, Ontario. He was a Senior Audit Manager with Deloitte before returning to Queen's University to obtain his Ph.D. in accounting. Bruce is Director of the Graduate Diploma in Accounting program at Laurier and was Director of the CPA Ontario Centre for Capital Markets and Behavioural Decision Making, and its predecessor Centre, from 2005–2018. He has been teaching intermediate financial accounting since the late 1990s in Laurier's B.B.A. and M.B.A. programs, and also teaches in Laurier's Ph.D. in Management program. Bruce has published articles in *Contemporary Accounting Research, Journal of Accounting, Auditing and Finance, Journal of Business, Finance and Accounting, Accounting, Auditing & Accountability Journal, Canadian Journal of Administrative Sciences*, and *Accounting Perspectives*. He has also published cases in *Issues in Accounting Education,*

Canadian Financial Accounting Cases—2nd edition, Accounting Perspectives, and *Journal of Accounting Case Research.* Bruce is an Associate Editor and is on the Advisory Committee of *Accounting Perspectives* and is on the Editorial Advisory Board of the *International Journal of Accounting & Information Management.*

U.S. Edition

DONALD E. KIESO, Ph.D., CPA, received his bachelor's degree from Aurora University and his doctorate in accounting from the University of Illinois. He has served as chair of the Department of Accountancy and is currently the KPMG Emeritus Professor of Accountancy at Northern Illinois University. He has public accounting experience with Price Waterhouse & Co. (San Francisco and Chicago) and Arthur Andersen & Co. (Chicago) and research experience with the Research Division of the American Institute of Certified Public Accountants (New York). He has done post-doctorate work as a Visiting Scholar at the University of California at Berkeley and is a recipient of NIU's Teaching Excellence Award and four Golden Apple Teaching Awards. Professor Kieso is the author of other accounting and business books and is a member of the American Accounting Association, the American Institute of Certified Public Accountants, and the Illinois CPA Society. He is the recipient of the Outstanding Accounting Educator Award from the Illinois CPA Society, the FSA's Joseph A. Silvoso Award of Merit, the NIU Foundation's Humanitarian Award for Service to Higher Education, the Distinguished Service Award from the Illinois CPA Society, and in 2003 received an honorary doctorate from Aurora University.

JERRY J. WEYGANDT, Ph.D., CPA, is Arthur Andersen Alumni Professor of Accounting at the University of Wisconsin-Madison. He holds a Ph.D. in accounting from the University of Illinois. His articles have appeared in *Accounting Review, Journal of Accounting Research, Accounting Horizons, Journal of Accountancy*, and other academic and professional journals. Professor Weygandt is the author of other accounting and financial reporting books and is a member of the American Accounting Association, the American Institute of Certified Public Accountants, and the Wisconsin Society of Certified Public Accountants. He has been actively involved with the American Institute of Certified Public Accountants and has been a member of the Accounting Standards Executive Committee (AcSEC) of that organization. He also served on the FASB task force that examined the reporting issues related to accounting for income taxes. He is the recipient of the Wisconsin Institute of CPAs' Outstanding Educator's Award and the Lifetime Achievement Award. In 2001, he received the American Accounting Association's Outstanding Accounting Educator Award.

TERRY D. WARFIELD, Ph.D., is the PwC Professor in Accounting at the University of Wisconsin-Madison. He received a B.S. and M.B.A. from Indiana University and a Ph.D. in accounting from the University of Iowa. Professor Warfield's area of expertise is financial reporting, and prior to his academic career, he worked for five years in the banking industry. He served as the Academic Accounting Fellow in the Office of the Chief Accountant at the U.S. Securities and Exchange Commission in Washington, D.C., from 1995–1996. Professor Warfield's primary research interests concern financial accounting standards and disclosure policies. He has published scholarly articles in *The Accounting Review, Journal of Accounting and Economics, Research in Accounting Regulation*, and *Accounting Horizons*, and he has served on the editorial boards of *The Accounting Review, Accounting Horizons*, and *Issues in Accounting Education*. Professor Warfield has served on the Financial Accounting Standards Committee of the American Accounting Association (Chair 1995–1996) and the AAA-FASB Research Conference Committee. He currently serves on the Financial Accounting Standards Advisory Council of the Financial Accounting Standards Board. Professor Warfield has received teaching awards at both the University of Iowa and the University of Wisconsin, and he was named to the Teaching Academy at the University of Wisconsin in 1995. Professor Warfield has developed and published several case studies based on his research for use in accounting classes. These cases have been selected for the AICPA Professor-Practitioner Case Development Program and have been published in *Issues in Accounting Education*.

Preface

As we present the twelfth edition of this course, we note that over the years, so much has changed in the accounting profession. We adopted International Financial Reporting Standards (IFRS) in Canada as well as Accounting Standards for Private Enterprises (ASPE), both starting in 2011—moving us into a multiple GAAP environment. In addition, we saw a merger of the three main legacy accounting bodies (representing Chartered Accountants, Certified Management Accountants, and Certified General Accountants), resulting in one unified group: the Chartered Professional Accountants of Canada (CPA Canada). From an educational perspective, the outcome was a new CPA Canada Competency Map with a broader curriculum, newly formatted professional examinations with a changed emphasis (Common Final Examinations), and a new roadmap for accredited programs and educational pathways into the CPA profession.

The body of knowledge seems to have swelled as a result of these changes. We have been striving to navigate these new waters as well as thinking about how the different technical areas interrelate. As we have found out, "more" is not always better. Our curricula seem to be ever expanding. Many of us, as accounting educators, feel that the more we add to the curriculum, the less students learn (and retain). So what do we do?

It is important to emphasize that students must continue to learn the technical material (both quantitative and qualitative). This is the foundation of who we are as accountants. But students must also learn to think through unstructured problems, especially given the impact of new technologies on emerging industries and business models. How do we get there? We all need to clear time and space for working through messy problems and for subsequent reflection—not an easy task when there is so much foundational material that needs to be learned.

This edition reaffirms the need for foundational, technical knowledge but it also reaffirms the need to help students deal with complicated problems. Part of the key to the latter is reflection. Who uses financial statements and why? How do accounting standards help provide useful information? Our hope is to help produce capable decision-makers who are thoughtful and able to continue to grow and evolve even when things keep changing. We encourage students to reflect and to think about things a little more deeply. This can be surprisingly fruitful in developing insights and lasting knowledge. By continually going back to the basics of decision-making in the accounting environment, we can start the reflection process.

It is a good time to do this because IFRS and ASPE are, for the moment, fairly stable (after a flurry of new standards affecting financial instruments, measurement, revenue recognition and leases (IFRS 9, 13, 15, and 16)). Many of the larger, more complex accounting topics have been studied with new accounting standards produced and put in place. We are now looking at how these are being implemented. We note that the standard setters seem to be going back to basics as well,

continuing to refine the conceptual framework, working on the principles of disclosure framework, and rethinking performance measures. So as you work your way through the material in this course, think about two things: foundations and reflection. We have added some new features to help with this.

Engaging Students Digitally

Intermediate Accounting, Twelfth Canadian Edition, is completely integrated with *WileyPLUS*, featuring a suite of teaching and learning resources. *WileyPLUS* allows you to create a personalized study plan, assess your progress along the way, and access the content and resources needed to master the material. *WileyPLUS* provides immediate insight into your strengths and problem areas with visual reports that highlight what's most important for both the instructor and student.

Many dynamic resources are integrated into the course to help you build your knowledge and understanding, stay motivated, and prepare for decision making in a real-world context. *WileyPLUS* also includes Orion, an integrated adaptive practice that helps you build proficiency and use your study time most effectively. Additional features of the *WileyPLUS* course include:

Chapter 0 Accounting Cycle Review

This section offers you adaptive review and practice for essential accounting topics necessary to master Intermediate Accounting. Built to serve as a refresher of introductory accounting content, this chapter includes reading content, algorithmic practice, and interactive tutorials built to improve your performance.

New Solution Walkthrough Lightboard Videos

These videos feature the authors working through more than fifty end-of-chapter problems. In these videos, we work through numerous problems to help you gain a deeper understanding of various technical and conceptual issues. You can watch these multiple times if needed, in order to master the material. These will help you not only to master technical materials, but also to pause and think about the issues. Many of these videos anchor and reinforce the foundations of accounting. In addition to the Lightboard videos, the *WileyPLUS* course also offers approximately sixty additional solution walkthrough videos offering just-in-time homework assistance and problem-solving techniques. Questions that are accompanied by videos are identified by a ▶ **Video** word mark.

Excel Templates and Excel Function Videos

These videos provide you with step-by-step examples of how to use Excel Functions. Excel templates are also available for selected end of chapter questions.

New Module on Data Analytics

A new accounting-specific data analytics module with interactive lessons, case studies, and videos has been prepared using industry-validated content to help you develop the professional competencies needed for the Common Final Examination (CFE) and the changing workforce.

New and Continuing Features

New Practice Problems

We have included a Practice Problem at the end of each chapter that reviews some of the key material from the chapter, together with the related solution. As a first step after reading the chapter, you will find these problems a jumping-off point to working through the end-of-chapter material.

New Examples

Each chapter has been rewritten and reformatted to provide specific examples within the chapter illustrating key concepts. Each example has a fact set, instructions, and a solution. Highlighting the examples and structuring them in a consistent manner means that you will be able to test your knowledge and to quickly identify examples in any chapter. The numerous examples are easily searchable and reinforce the basics as well as covering nuances and explaining reasoning.

New Emphasis on Data Analytics

With the advent of new technologies, more data are being created and collected. How do companies use this explosion of data to make accounting and other decisions? We have highlighted the exciting developments in the growing field of data analytics in vignettes and in chapter topics. The `Data Analytics` word mark calls the reader's attention to this new addition. These additions will allow you to begin to think about emerging issues and their impact on accounting. Selected chapters include an Analytics in Action question that allows you to apply the information derived from the analysis of "big" data to various real-life accounting scenarios. You will find the data sets and detailed instructions accompanying these questions in your *WileyPLUS* course.

Emphasis on Integration with Related Areas

We have included integration word marks (such as `Finance` and `Audit`) in each chapter to help identify key areas of integration, including integration of accounting with finance, law, economics, managerial accounting, auditing, strategy and governance, and taxation. Many of our end-of-chapter questions have an integration aspect. For those problems that most directly focus on integration, we also include integration word marks so that they are easily identified. By integrating accounting knowledge with knowledge in related areas, you will gain a deeper understanding of things. We continue with our Office Hour Video feature developed for the eleventh edition, focusing on integration-related topics in most chapters.

CPA Competency Map Integration

At the start of each chapter, we provide a chart linking that chapter's Learning Objectives with the related requirements of CPA Canada's Competency Map. This information will help those of you planning to obtain their Advanced Certificate in Accounting and Finance (ACAF) or write the CFE to link the coverage of intermediate accounting topics to the CPA educational requirements. We have also mapped the content against the Competency Map and Knowledge Supplement. These appear in Appendix D. In addition, the material in *WileyPLUS* has been more comprehensively mapped.

Emphasis on Business

The focus of many of the feature stories that start each chapter in this edition is on the business models of various companies and industries, along with accounting issues that affect them. The first section of most chapters focuses on **Understanding the Business**, which introduces the accounting topic in the context of everyday business. Many chapters have a **business transactions example box**. In most business transactions, you give something up and receive something. These boxes are meant to help you understand what has been given up and what has been received in the transaction. This is tremendously helpful when you are trying to decide how to account for a transaction or economic event. We have added some new feature stories dealing with current issues relating to new technologies.

Emphasis on IFRS and ASPE

`IFRS` `ASPE` Individual IFRS and ASPE word marks call attention to items treated differently by the two sets of standards. When the IFRS and ASPE word marks appear side by side this indicates a direct comparison between the two approaches. **Side-by-side** journal entries are used to illustrate differences in treatment between IFRS and ASPE, and help with analytical thinking. The end-of-chapter charts that identify the major differences between IFRS and ASPE include a column with cross-references to relevant examples, illustrations, and brief exercises that describe the differences outlined in the comparison chart. The chapter's Looking Ahead feature alerts you to upcoming changes to accounting standards.

Emphasis on Professional and Ethical Behaviour

Ethics Rather than featuring ethics coverage and problem material in isolation, we use an ethics word mark to highlight ethical issues as they are discussed within each chapter. This word mark also appears beside exercises, problems, or cases where ethical issues must be dealt with in relation to all kinds of accounting situations.

Emphasis on Readability

The readability of the material has been improved by using fewer abbreviations, plainer language, shorter sentences, numbered lists, and clearer headings. A **glossary** provides definitions of key terms highlighted in all the chapters and appendices. **Alternative Terminology** notes within the chapter familiarize you with other commonly used terms. As noted earlier, we have structured the **examples** in each chapter to make them more accessible.

Grounding in Accounting Research and Theory

Theory We have always emphasized concepts and principles, including those that span other disciplines, such as law and finance. In addition to this, the **Accounting Theory** word mark calls attention to accounting theory that underpins much of the accounting body of knowledge, introducing you to an accounting research perspective.

Real World Emphasis

Real World Emphasis Because intermediate accounting is a course in which you must understand the application of accounting principles and techniques in practice, we strive to include a wide variety of real-world examples in each chapter. Real companies are highlighted in colour the first time that they are mentioned.

Reinforcement of the Concepts

Throughout each chapter, you are asked **"What Do the Numbers Mean?"** and are presented with discussions applying accounting concepts to business contexts. This feature builds on the opening feature stories in making the accounting concepts relevant to you. Through current examples of how accounting is applied, you will be better able to relate to and understand the material. The **Underlying Concept** notes in each chapter alert you to remember that the issue under discussion draws on concepts identified in Chapter 2 as part of the conceptual framework. More emphasis has been placed on measuring fair values using the IFRS 13 standard. In addition, an Analysis section is present in most chapters. This section discusses the effect on the financial statements of many of the accounting choices made by corporate management, alerting you to look behind the numbers. Finally, the accounting equation appears in the margin next to key journal entries to help you understand the impact of each transaction on the company's financial position and cash flows.

Helping You Practise

The end-of-chapter material is comprehensive. Brief exercises, exercises, and problems focus on quantitative material. **Excel** End-of-chapter material includes questions that provide you with pre-populated Excel spreadsheets to help you prepare solutions. We also continued our emphasis on having you evaluate the differences in solutions prepared using IFRS versus ASPE. Case material allows you to analyze business transactions and apply both IFRS and ASPE, with attention to integration being provided by Integrated Case questions. Research and Analysis questions allow you to explore the nature of GAAP differences and understand how different accounting standard setters can arrive at different solutions in terms of standards.

A summary of the Case Primer guiding you through the case study method appears in Appendix E. The complete Case Primer appears in *WileyPLUS* and the Student Website. The Case Primer provides a framework for case analysis to help you structure your response to case situations.

Analysis doesn't have to be just part of the cases. Our **Digging Deeper** feature asks you to look more closely at the results you obtain in the problems and exercises and to reflect. For instance, you might be asked to comment on results or determine how things might be different if one of the original variables were to change.

We have included end-of-chapter material that is in a format similar to questions used in the CPA Professional Education program. Task-Based Simulations after Chapters 5, 9, 12, 15, 17, and 23 combine material from the current chapter with previous chapters and present it in a hands-on format. This allows you to become familiar with the CPA PEP format while getting a sense of how the various concepts fit together.

Currency and Accuracy

Significant Change As in past editions, we have endeavoured to make this edition the most current and accurate available. Where there has been a significant change in an accounting standard or how it is applied, it has been highlighted with a Significant Change word mark. Where change is on the horizon, we have noted this at the end of each chapter in the Looking Ahead section. We are also committed to issuing brief update supplements on *WileyPLUS* when new standards are issued.

The following list outlines the revisions and improvements made to the chapters in Volume 1.

Chapter 2 Conceptual Framework Underlying Financial Reporting

- We have introduced a three-step method to help learners ensure both fundamental characteristics of useful information are present (relevance and representational faithfulness).

- We have incorporated material from the new IFRS conceptual framework as follows:

  - updated discussions on conservatism and prudence

- new definitions of financial statement elements
- new material on unit of account
- the fact that recognition criteria no longer include a probability criterion
- added discussion relating to the notions of existence uncertainty and measurement uncertainty including the introduction of outcome uncertainty
- new material on current values (including value in use)
- guidance on effective communication
- A brief overview of ongoing projects on materiality, primary financial statements, and disclosures has been added.

Chapter 3 Measurement

- The opening story focuses on big data and data analytics in helping accountants to estimate fair values.
- The revised chapter now focuses solely on measurement since this issue is becoming more prominent and is now foundational knowledge.
- Material on preparation of financial statements and the accounting information system has been moved to a separate appendix (Appendix C). Because this material is extensively covered in introductory accounting courses, students and instructors can choose how much (or little) review of the basics is needed. Similarly, Chapter 0 is available on *WileyPLUS* for additional review of the basics in preparation for Intermediate Accounting studies.
- We have added a section on disclosures relating to measurement uncertainty as well as on the IASB post-implementation review of IFRS 13. This material will help you reflect upon measurement and how new standards are being applied.

Chapter 4 Reporting Financial Performance

- The chart relating to Other Comprehensive Income has been updated, highlighting whether those items are to be recycled or not.
- New examples relating to discontinued operations and quality of earnings have been added. Material on quality of earnings helps develop deeper understanding of how financial statements provide useful information.
- Updated examples and financial statement disclosures have been added.

Chapter 5 Financial Position and Cash Flows

- Chapter 5 now includes an example of the direct method of preparing the statement of cash flows. In addition, the end-of-chapter material now includes problems that compare and contrast the direct and indirect methods of preparing the statement of cash flows.
- Appendix 5A includes several additional ratios, such as "gross profit margin" and "free cash flow to operating cash flow".

Chapter 6 Revenue Recognition

- Chapter 6 has been streamlined and reorganized since IFRS 15 became effective January 1, 2018, and there has been more exposure to the standard.
- The detailed discussion of upfront fees, warranties, volume discounts, and returns has been relocated to earlier in the chapter (within the five-step discussion) to enhance the flow.
- Comments about ASPE have been incorporated within the five-step method, thus integrating the discussion and helping users to reflect upon differences.
- IFRS/ASPE differences for volume discounts and sales returns have been included in greater specificity. These side-by-side examples help develop critical thinking.
- Additional discussion, illustrations, and/or examples have been added relating to material rights (loyalty points, initiation fees, and gift cards), warranties, series of goods that are substantially the same, royalties, licensing, fulfillment costs, zero profit method (new learning objective), onerous contracts (new learning objective), and different types of long-term contracts. There are now over 40 examples in the chapter (including the appendix) due to the complexity of the material. Since accounting for revenues is foundational, the examples are very important to ensure deeper understanding of the material.
- Commentary on the use of the gross and net methods of accounting for discounts has been added.

Chapter 7 Cash and Receivables

- To reflect a new emphasis under IFRS, for sales returns we discuss use of the Refund Liability account, while retaining the discussion of the use of an allowance account under ASPE.
- A data analytics example has been included that discusses the use of "predictive analytics" by some companies to assess the collectibility of their accounts receivable.
- Similar to other chapters, we separate out examples from illustrations. The impact of this change was more significant for this chapter because it has 17 examples in the main chapter and one in the appendix.

Chapter 8 Inventory

- Content has been reworked to more closely align with Chapter 6 (from the purchasing side of the transaction) by:
  - making terminology more consistent between chapters (e.g., repurchase agreements, volume rebates) and
  - removing duplication (relating to sales returns and delayed payments).
- Chapter material has been simplified by:
  - removing material on purchase/cash discounts since they are covered in introductory accounting courses;
  - streamlining discussion of the retail method, removing non-GAAP alternatives (the conventional method);

- reducing key terms where necessary and adding a few new ones dealing with biological assets; and
  - streamlining learning objectives and headings.
- Examples and financial statement disclosures have been updated and refreshed.
- The opening story features the use of new technologies in collecting large amounts of data to assist with inventory count procedures and subsequent analyses.

Chapter 9 Investments

- Chapter 9 has been reorganized and simplified. We have:
  - restructured the main headings to coincide with learning objectives;
  - standardized journal entries (sale, dividend income, revaluations);
  - moved the summary of methods to the end of the chapter; and
  - removed references to IAS 39, since IFRS 9 is now fully in effect.
- The recording of premium/discounts on bonds under the FV-NI model is no longer identified as an IFRS/ASPE difference in the chapter. Examples reflect recording of premium/discount amortization separately in journal entries since, under IFRS, companies may capture the information in this manner (similar to the ASPE treatment).
- We have added some commentary on why the standards are different to help learners with critical thinking and reflection.

Chapter 10 Property, Plant, and Equipment: Accounting Model Basics

- A more detailed discussion of the full cost and successful efforts methods of accounting for natural resource properties is now included.
- The revaluation method described in Appendix 10B (the proportionate method) was reworked and includes an additional column to better illustrate how the amounts in the journal entries are calculated.
- We updated the Looking Ahead section for recent and upcoming changes relating to IAS 16 for property, plant, and equipment and IFRS 6 (on mineral resources).

Chapter 11 Depreciation, Impairment, and Disposition

- The Looking Ahead section was updated to discuss some changes being considered in relation to goodwill impairment and a related Discussion Paper/Exposure Draft being considered by the IASB.
- A data analytics example has been added examining how companies use predictive analytics to track baseline asset performance, machinery failure, the impact of things like weather conditions on assets that are exposed to the

elements, and other items to help assess the maintenance and impairment requirements.

Chapter 12 Intangible Assets and Goodwill

- The Looking Ahead section was updated to discuss some changes being considered in relation to goodwill impairment and a related Discussion Paper/Exposure Draft being considered by the IASB.
- A data analytics example has been included that discusses the use of "Big Data" by bricks and mortar and online retailers to enhance their customers' shopping experience.
- The discussion of the most valuable brands in Canada, and the world, was updated to reflect the rise in high technology firms internationally.

Appendix C The Accounting Information System

- The prior Chapter 3 (from the eleventh edition) has been split into two parts for ease of use and flexibility.
- The overview and review of accounting transactions, journal entries, and other aspects of the accounting cycle has been moved to Appendix C (after Chapter 12) for instructors who prefer to have this as a review and reference tool for students (rather than something that they will teach in class).
- For instructors who prefer to have an in-class review of the accounting information system material, they can still do so because the chapter material (including the 10-column work sheet approach to assist with financial statement presentation) is retained in the self-contained Appendix. Extensive exercise and problem material has also been retained as part of Appendix C.

Other Special Student Supplements by Wiley

The Intermediate Accounting Simulation Practice Set by Fred Pries will help students see how the individual topics they study in intermediate accounting are related to the accounting systems of an organization and to the financial statements as a whole. Students play the role of a newly hired accountant for Woodlawn Engineering, an owner-managed company, and prepare a full set of financial statements starting from an unadjusted trial balance. Each module of the simulation is linked to a particular topic covered in the intermediate accounting course and introduces new information. Students analyze this information, recommend what adjustments are needed to the books and financial statements of the company, and write reports to the chief financial officer explaining the basis for their recommendations.

Canadian Financial Accounting Cases by Camillo Lento and Jo-Anne Ryan provides additional cases at the intermediate level that may be used either for assignment purposes or for in-class discussion. The cases are keyed to various topics covered by the two volumes of *Intermediate Accounting* and have been developed using IFRS and ASPE.

Acknowledgements

We thank the users of our eleventh edition, including the many instructors, faculty, and students who contributed to this revision through their comments and instructive criticism.

Appreciation is also extended to colleagues at the University of Toronto and the Lazaridis School of Business and Economics, Wilfrid Laurier University, who provided input, suggestions, and support, especially Peter Thomas and Allan Foerster, for their professionalism and wisdom. A special thanks to Nicola Young, who devoted her time and significant energies to reviewing much of the material.

It takes many people and coordinated efforts to get an edition off the ground. Many thanks to the team at John Wiley & Sons, who are superb: Emily Marcoux, Senior Editor; Daleara Hirjikaka, Product Designer; Karen Staudinger, Product Design Manager, who has been an integral part of the last seven editions; Rachel Conrad, Production Editor; Deanna Durnford, Supplements Coordinator; and Anita Osborne, Senior Marketing Manager. Their enthusiasm and support have been invaluable. The editorial contributions of Laurel Hyatt, Zofia Laubitz, Denise Showers, and Belle Wong are also very much appreciated.

Because this was our first time doing Solution Lightboard Videos, we especially thank Paul Chen, Lisa Holloway, Eric Hurst, and Caitlyn Flowers, who helped and guided us during a very busy and productive three days of studio recording time. Megan Garvin was very helpful in terms of setting up the slides and formatting as well as keeping us on track.

We appreciate the suggestions offered by the following participants who attended our focus groups:

Megan Costiuk	University of Regina
Catherine Duffy	Humber College
Joseph Faello	Mississippi State University - Meridian
Arsineh Garabedian	Simon Fraser University /Douglas College
Wenxia Ge	University of Manitoba
Irene Herremans	Simon Fraser University
Karel Hrazdil	Simon Fraser University
Sandra Iacobelli	York University
Camillo Lento	Lakehead University
Sarah Magdalinski	Northern Alberta Institute of Technology
Ana Marques	Nova School of Business and Economics
Deborah Mortimer	University of Winnipeg
Elizabeth Peltier	Concordia University
Wendy Schultz	University of Manitoba
Wendy Wilson	Northern Alberta Institute of Technology

We are grateful to the following reviewers for their valuable insights and feedback:

Peter Alpaugh	George Brown College
Darrin Jay Ambrose	University of Calgary
Robert Bruce	Capilano University/University of British Columbia
Megan Costiuk	University of Regina
Kevin deWolde	University of Fraser Valley
Robert Ducharme	University of Waterloo
Catherine Duffy	Humber College
Kathy Falk	University of Toronto
Camillo Lento	Lakehead University
Marie Madill-Payne	George Brown College
Cameron Morrill	University of Manitoba
Flora Niu	Wilfrid Laurier University
Jeffrey O'Leary	McMaster University
Laura Simeoni	York University

We are particularly grateful to Cécile Laurin and Maria Belanger for all their help with the end-of-chapter material and solutions. Thanks also go to Laura Cumming, Ilene Gilborn, Chris Leduc, Debra Lee-Hue, Ross Meacher, Marisa Morriello, Joel Shapiro, and Marie Sinnott, who contributed so much to the related supplements and the accuracy of the course.

We thank CPA Canada and the IFRS Foundation for allowing us to quote from their materials.

We appreciate the opportunity to reach out to so many colleagues and students through this course. Your conversations and input have greatly helped shape the content and made it all it can be. We are thankful to be part of a group of such dedicated educators! Let's keep the conversation going.

Suggestions and comments are always appreciated. We have striven to produce error-free content, but if anything has slipped through the variety of checks undertaken, please let us know so that corrections can be made to subsequent printings.

IRENE M. WIECEK
Toronto, Ontario
wiecek@rotman.utoronto.ca

BRUCE McCONOMY
Waterloo, Ontario
bmcconomy@wlu.ca

October 2018

Brief Contents

VOLUME ONE

PREFACE   vi

1   The Canadian Financial Reporting Environment   1-1

2   Conceptual Framework Underlying Financial Reporting   2-1

3   Measurement   3-1

4   Reporting Financial Performance   4-1

5   Financial Position and Cash Flows   5-1

6   Revenue Recognition   6-1

7   Cash and Receivables   7-1

8   Inventory   8-1

9   Investments   9-1

10   Property, Plant, and Equipment: Accounting Model Basics   10-1

11   Depreciation, Impairment, and Disposition   11-1

12   Intangible Assets and Goodwill   12-1

APPENDIX A   Time Value of Money Tables   AP-1

APPENDIX B   Specimen Financial Statements   AP-6

APPENDIX C   The Accounting Information System   AP-27

APPENDIX D   CPA Competency Map Coverage   AP-76

APPENDIX E   A Summary of the Case Primer   AP-79

GLOSSARY   G-1

COMPANY INDEX   I-1

SUBJECT INDEX   I-2

VOLUME TWO

13   Non-Financial and Current Liabilities   13-1

14   Long-Term Financial Liabilities   14-1

15   Shareholders' Equity   15-1

16   Complex Financial Instruments   16-1

17   Earnings Per Share   17-1

18   Income Taxes   18-1

19   Pensions and Other Post-Employment Benefits   19-1

20   Leases   20-1

21   Accounting Changes and Error Analysis   21-1

22   Statement of Cash Flows   22-1

23   Other Measurement and Disclosure Issues   23-1

APPENDIX A   Time Value of Money Tables

APPENDIX B   Specimen Financial Statements

APPENDIX C   The Accounting Information System (Online content only)

APPENDIX D   CPA Competency Map Coverage

APPENDIX E   A Summary of the Case Primer

GLOSSARY

COMPANY INDEX

SUBJECT INDEX

Contents

1 The Canadian Financial Reporting Environment 1-1

Financial Statements and Financial Reporting 1-3
Accounting and Capital Allocation 1-4
Stakeholders 1-5
Objective of Financial Reporting 1-7
Information Asymmetry 1-9
Standard Setting 1-12
Need for Standards 1-12
Parties Involved in Standard Setting 1-12
Generally Accepted Accounting Principles 1-17
GAAP Hierarchy 1-17
Professional Judgement 1-19
Challenges and Opportunities for the Accounting Profession 1-19
Oversight in the Capital Marketplace 1-19
Centrality of Ethics 1-20
Standard Setting in a Political Environment 1-21
Principles versus Rules 1-22
Impact of Technology 1-23
Integrated Reporting 1-24
Conclusion 1-25

2 Conceptual Framework Underlying Financial Reporting 2-1

Conceptual Framework 2-3
Rationale for a Conceptual Framework 2-3
Development of the Conceptual Framework 2-3
Information Asymmetry Revisited 2-5
Objective of Financial Reporting 2-5
Qualitative Characteristics of Useful Information 2-6
Fundamental Qualitative Characteristics 2-6
Enhancing Qualitative Characteristics 2-10
Trade-Offs 2-11
Elements of Financial Statements 2-12
Assets 2-12
Liabilities 2-13
Equity 2-15
Revenues/Income 2-15
Expenses 2-15
Gains/Losses 2-15
Foundational Principles 2-16
Recognition/Derecognition 2-17
Measurement 2-23
Presentation and Disclosure 2-29

Financial Reporting Issues 2-31
Principles-Based Approach 2-32
Financial Engineering 2-32
Fraudulent Financial Reporting 2-33
IFRS/ASPE Comparison 2-34
Looking Ahead 2-34

3 Measurement 3-1

Measuring Financial Statement Elements 3-2
Valuation Techniques 3-3
Value in Use Measurements 3-7
Disclosures Relating to Measurement 3-9
Measuring Fair Value Using IFRS 13 3-9
Present Value Concepts 3-13
The Nature of Interest 3-13
Fundamental Variables in Present Value Calculations 3-14
Different Ways to Perform the Calculations 3-16
Some Additional Calculations 3-25
IFRS/ASPE Comparison 3-27
A Comparison of IFRS and ASPE 3-28
Looking Ahead 3-28

4 Reporting Financial Performance 4-1

Performance 4-3
Business Models and Industries 4-3
Communicating Information about Performance 4-7
Quality of Earnings/Information 4-7
Measurement of Income 4-12
Discontinued Operations 4-14
Component of an Enterprise 4-14
Assets Held for Sale 4-15
Measurement and Presentation 4-16
The Statement of Income and the Statement of Comprehensive Income 4-20
Presentation 4-21
The Statement of Retained Earnings and the Statement of Changes in Equity 4-32
Presentation of the Statement of Retained Earnings 4-32
Presentation of the Statement of Changes in Equity 4-34
Disclosure and Analysis 4-35
Disclosure 4-35
Analysis 4-35
Non-GAAP Measures 4-36

Other Key Measures 4-37
IFRS/ASPE Comparison 4-38
A Comparison of IFRS and ASPE 4-38
Looking Ahead 4-39
Appendix 4A: Application of the Cash and Accrual Bases of Accounting 4-39
Differences Between Cash and Accrual Bases 4-39
Conversion from Cash Basis to Accrual Basis 4-41
Theoretical Weaknesses of the Cash Basis 4-44

5 Financial Position and Cash Flows 5-1

Usefulness of the Statements of Financial Position and Cash Flows from a Business Perspective 5-3
Analyzing a Statement of Financial Position 5-4
Assessing Earnings Quality 5-4
Assessing the Creditworthiness of Companies 5-4
Usefulness and Limitations of the Statement of Financial Position 5-4
Usefulness 5-5
Limitations 5-6
Classification in the Statement of Financial Position 5-7
Monetary versus Nonmonetary Assets and Liabilities 5-7
Financial Instruments 5-8
Elements of the Statement of Financial Position 5-8
Preparation of the Classified Statement of Financial Position (Balance Sheet) 5-10
Current Assets 5-10
Non-current Investments 5-15
Property, Plant, and Equipment 5-15
Intangible Assets and Goodwill 5-17
Other Assets 5-17
Current Liabilities 5-18
Long-Term Debt and Liabilities 5-18
Owners' Equity 5-20
Statement of Financial Position Format 5-21
Other Required Disclosures 5-22
Contingencies and Provisions 5-22
Accounting Policies 5-23
Contractual Situations 5-23
Additional Detail 5-24
Subsequent Events 5-24
Techniques of Disclosure 5-24
Parenthetical Explanations 5-24
Notes 5-25
Cross-References and Contra Items 5-25
Supporting Schedules 5-26
Terminology 5-26
Purpose, Content, and Format of a Statement of Cash Flows 5-26
Preparation of the Statement of Cash Flows 5-29
Usefulness of the Statement of Cash Flows 5-34
Financial Liquidity 5-35
Financial Flexibility 5-35
Perspectives 5-35
IFRS/ASPE Comparison 5-37
A Comparison of IFRS and ASPE 5-37
Looking Ahead 5-38
Appendix 5A: Ratio Analysis: A Reference 5-39
Business Risks 5-39
Financial Ratios 5-40

6 Revenue Recognition 6-1

Understanding the Nature of Sales Transactions from a Business Perspective 6-4
Economics of Sales Transactions 6-4
Legalities of Sales Transactions 6-9
Information for Decision-Making 6-10
The Asset-Liability Approach to Revenue Recognition: An Overview of the Five-Step Process 6-10
Identifying the Contract with Customers—Step 1 6-13
Basic Accounting 6-14
Contract Modifications 6-15
Identifying Separate Performance Obligations—Step 2 6-16
Material Rights 6-17
Warranties 6-18
Upfront Fees 6-19
Series of Goods and Services That Are Substantially the Same 6-20
Determining the Transaction Price—Step 3 6-21
Variable Consideration 6-21
Time Value of Money 6-25
Non-cash Consideration 6-27
Consideration Paid or Payable to Customers 6-27
Allocating the Transaction Price to Separate Performance Obligations—Step 4 6-28
Recognizing Revenue When (or As) Each Performance Obligation Is Satisfied—Step 5 6-32
Earnings Approach to Revenue Recognition 6-35
Selling Goods 6-36
Selling Services 6-37
Measurability and Collectibility 6-38
Other Revenue Recognition Issues 6-38
Repurchase Agreements 6-38
Bill-and-Hold Arrangements 6-39
Principal-Agent Relationships 6-39
Consignments 6-40
Summary of Other Revenue Recognition Issues 6-42
Presentation and Disclosure 6-42
Presentation 6-42
Disclosure 6-45
IFRS/ASPE Comparison 6-47
A Comparison of IFRS and ASPE 6-47

Looking Ahead   **6-48**

Appendix 6A: Long-Term Contracts   6-49

Percentage-of-Completion Method   6-49

Measuring the Progress Toward
   Completion   **6-50**

Zero-Profit Method   6-55

Completed-Contract Method   6-56

Losses on Long-Term Contracts   6-57

Loss in Current Period on a Profitable Contract   **6-57**

Loss on an Unprofitable Contract   **6-58**

7   Cash and Receivables   7-1

Understanding Cash and Accounts Receivable   7-3

How Do Companies Manage and Control Cash?   **7-4**

What Types of Companies Have Extensive Accounts
   Receivable?   **7-4**

What Are the Types of Accounts Receivable?   **7-4**

How Do Companies Manage Accounts Receivable?   **7-5**

Cash   7-6

What Is Cash?   **7-6**

Reporting Cash   **7-7**

Summary of Cash-Related Items   **7-9**

Receivables   7-9

**Recognition and Measurement of Accounts
   Receivable   7-11**

Trade Discounts   **7-12**

Cash Discounts (Sales Discounts)   **7-12**

Sales Returns and Allowances   **7-12**

Nonrecognition of Interest Element   **7-13**

Measurement of Accounts Receivable
   after Acquisition   **7-14**

Impairment of Accounts Receivable   7-14

Estimating Uncollectible Trade
   Accounts Receivable   **7-14**

Allowance Method   **7-16**

Effects on Accounts   **7-18**

Direct Write Off Method   **7-20**

Notes and Loans Receivable   7-20

Recognition and Measurement of Short-Term Notes
   and Loans Receivable   **7-21**

Recognition and Measurement of Long-Term Notes
   and Loans Receivable   **7-22**

Derecognition of Receivables   7-30

Secured Borrowings   **7-31**

Sales of Receivables   **7-31**

Securitized Receivables-Transparency   **7-36**

**Presentation, Disclosure, and Analysis
   of Receivables   7-37**

Presentation and Disclosure   **7-37**

Analysis   **7-39**

IFRS/ASPE Comparison   7-40

A Comparison of IFRS and ASPE   **7-40**

Looking Ahead   **7-41**

Appendix 7A: Methods for Controlling Cash   7-42

Management and Control of Cash   **7-42**

Using Bank Accounts   **7-42**

The Imprest Petty Cash System   **7-43**

Physical Protection of Cash Balances   **7-44**

Reconciliation of Bank Balances   **7-45**

8   Inventory   8-1

Understanding Inventory   8-4

What Types of Companies Have Inventory?   **8-4**

Inventory Categories   **8-4**

Inventory Planning and Control   **8-5**

Information for Decision-Making   **8-5**

Recognition of Physical Goods Included in Inventory   8-7

Accounting Definition of Inventory   **8-7**

Goods Included in Inventory   **8-8**

Inventory Errors   8-13

Ending Inventory Misstated   **8-14**

Purchases and Inventory Misstated   **8-15**

Measurement of Inventory—Costs Included   8-16

Volume Rebates   **8-17**

Product Costs   **8-18**

Measurement and Inventory Accounting Systems   8-20

Perpetual System   **8-21**

Periodic System   **8-21**

Comparing Perpetual and Periodic Systems   **8-22**

Supplementary System—Quantities Only   **8-23**

Measurement and Cost Formulas   8-23

Specific Identification   **8-24**

Weighted Average Cost   **8-26**

First-In, First-Out (FIFO)   **8-27**

Choice of Cost Formula   **8-29**

Last-In, First-Out (LIFO)   **8-29**

**Measurement and the Lower of Cost and Net Realizable
   Value (LC&NRV) Principle   8-30**

What Is Net Realizable Value?   **8-31**

Application of the LC&NRV Principle   **8-31**

Evaluation of the LC&NRV Principle   **8-35**

**Exceptions to Lower of Cost and Net Realizable
   Value   8-35**

Inventories Measured at Net Realizable Value   **8-35**

Inventories Measured at Fair Value Less
   Costs to Sell   **8-36**

Measuring Inventory Using Estimates   8-40

The Need for Estimates   **8-40**

Gross Profit Method   **8-41**

Presentation, Disclosure, and Analysis   8-43

Presentation and Disclosure of Inventories   **8-43**

Analysis   **8-44**

IFRS/ASPE Comparison   8-45

A Comparison of IFRS and ASPE   **8-45**

Looking Ahead **8-47**
Appendix 8A: The Retail Inventory Method of Estimating Inventory Cost **8-47**
Retail Method Terminology **8-48**
Special Items **8-50**
Evaluation of Retail Inventory Method **8-51**
Appendix 8B: Accounting Guidance for Specific Inventory **8-51**

9 Investments **9-1**

Understanding Investments **9-3**
Types of Investments **9-3**
Types of Companies That Have Investments **9-5**
Information for Decision-Making **9-7**
Measurement: Overview **9-7**
Measurement—Cost/Amortized Cost Model **9-9**
Investments in Shares of Other Entities **9-9**
Investments in Debt Instruments of Other Entities **9-11**
Measurement—Fair Value Through Net Income (FV-NI) Model **9-15**
Measurement—Fair Value Through Other Comprehensive Income (FV-OCI) Model **9-20**
Investments in Shares of Other Entities **9-21**
Investments in Debt Instruments of Other Entities **9-23**
Measurement—Impairment Models **9-26**
Incurred Loss Impairment Model **9-26**
Expected Loss Impairment Model **9-27**
Fair Value Loss Impairment Model **9-31**
Summary of Impairment Models **9-31**
Strategic Investments—Investments in Associates **9-32**
Significant Influence **9-32**
Equity Method **9-33**
Summary of Accounting Standards for Associates **9-37**
Strategic Investments—Investments in Subsidiaries **9-38**
Presentation, Disclosure, and Analysis **9-39**
Presentation and Disclosure **9-40**
Analysis **9-44**
IFRS/ASPE Comparison **9-44**
A Comparison of IFRS and ASPE **9-45**
Looking Ahead **9-48**

10 Property, Plant, and Equipment: Accounting Model Basics **10-1**

Definition and Recognition of Property, Plant, and Equipment **10-4**
Property, Plant, and Equipment—Business Perspective **10-4**
Property, Plant, and Equipment—Characteristics **10-4**

Cost Elements **10-6**
Self-Constructed Assets **10-7**
Borrowing Costs **10-8**
Dismantling and Restoration Costs **10-9**
Measurement of Cost for Nonmonetary Exchange **10-10**
Cash Discounts Not Taken **10-10**
Deferred Payment Terms **10-11**
Lump-Sum Purchases **10-12**
Nonmonetary Exchanges **10-13**
Contributed Assets and Government Grants **10-18**
Measurement of Costs Associated with Specific Assets **10-19**
Land **10-20**
Buildings **10-20**
Leasehold Improvements **10-20**
Equipment **10-21**
Investment Property **10-21**
Natural Resource Properties **10-21**
Biological Assets **10-22**
Measurement after Acquisition **10-23**
Cost and Revaluation Models **10-23**
Fair Value Model **10-27**
Costs Incurred after Acquisition **10-29**
Additions **10-30**
Replacements, Major Overhauls, and Inspections **10-30**
Rearrangement and Reinstallation **10-33**
Repairs **10-33**
IFRS/ASPE Comparison **10-34**
A Comparison of IFRS and ASPE **10-34**
Looking Ahead **10-36**
Appendix 10A: Capitalization of Borrowing Costs **10-37**
Qualifying Assets **10-37**
Capitalization Period **10-38**
Avoidable Borrowing Costs **10-38**
Disclosures **10-42**
Appendix 10B: Revaluation: The Proportionate Method **10-42**

11 Depreciation, Impairment, and Disposition **11-1**

The Importance of Depreciation, Impairment, and Disposition from a Business Perspective **11-3**
Depreciation **11-4**
Factors Considered in the Depreciation Process **11-5**
Depreciation—Methods of Allocation and Calculation **11-7**
Straight-Line Method **11-9**
Diminishing Balance Method **11-10**
Activity Methods **11-11**
Other Methods **11-12**
Depletion of Mineral Resources **11-13**
Pattern of Depletion **11-13**

Estimating Recoverable Reserves   **11-14**
Liquidating Dividends   **11-15**
Other Depreciation Issues   11-16
Depreciation and Partial Periods   **11-16**
Revision of Depreciation Rates   **11-18**
Impairment   11-19
Indicators of Impairment   **11-20**
Impairment—Recognition
   and Measurement Models   **11-21**
Asset Groups and Cash-Generating Units   **11-25**
Held for Sale and Derecognition   11-27
Long-Lived Assets to Be Disposed of by Sale   **11-27**
Derecognition   **11-28**
Presentation, Disclosure, and Analysis   11-30
Presentation and Disclosure   **11-30**
Analysis   **11-32**
IFRS/ASPE Comparison   11-35
A Comparison of IFRS and ASPE   **11-35**
Looking Ahead   **11-36**
Appendix 11A: Depreciation and Income Tax   11-37
Capital Cost Allowance Method   **11-37**

12 Intangible Assets and Goodwill   12-1

**The Business Importance and Characteristics
   of Goodwill and Intangible Assets   12-3**
Characteristics of Goodwill   **12-4**
Characteristics of Intangible Assets   **12-5**
**Recognition and Measurement of Intangible Assets
   at Acquisition   12-6**
Purchased Intangibles   **12-6**
Intangibles Purchased in a Business Combination   **12-7**
Prepayments   **12-7**
**Recognition and Measurement of Internally
   Developed Intangible Assets   12-9**
Identifying Research and Development
   Phase Activities   **12-9**
Accounting for Research Phase Costs   **12-10**
Accounting for Development Phase Costs   **12-10**
Costs Included and Excluded   **12-11**
**Recognition and Measurement of Intangible Assets
   after Acquisition   12-12**
Limited-Life Intangibles   **12-14**
Indefinite-Life Intangibles   **12-15**
Specific Intangibles   12-16
Marketing-Related Intangible Assets   **12-16**
Customer-Related Intangible Assets   **12-17**
Artistic-Related Intangible Assets   **12-18**
Contract-Based Intangible Assets   **12-18**
Technology-Based Intangible Assets   **12-19**
Impairment and Derecognition   12-21
Impairment of Limited-Life Intangibles   **12-21**
Impairment of Indefinite-Life Intangibles   **12-23**

Derecognition   **12-24**
Goodwill—Recognition and Measurement   12-24
Internally Generated Goodwill   **12-24**
Purchased Goodwill   **12-24**
Bargain Purchase   **12-26**
Valuation after Acquisition   **12-27**
Goodwill—Impairment   12-27
Presentation, Disclosure, and Analysis   12-30
Presentation and Disclosure   **12-30**
Analysis   **12-34**
IFRS/ASPE Comparison   12-35
A Comparison of IFRS and ASPE   **12-35**
Looking Ahead   **12-37**
Appendix 12A: Valuing Goodwill   12-37
Excess-Earnings Approach   **12-37**
Total-Earnings Approach   **12-41**
Other Valuation Methods   **12-42**

APPENDIX A   **Time Value of Money Tables   AP-1**

APPENDIX B   **Specimen Financial Statements   AP-6**

APPENDIX C   **The Accounting Information System   AP-27**
Accounting System Overview   AP-28
Basic Terminology and Double-Entry Rules   **AP-28**
Accounting Equation   **AP-30**
The Accounting Cycle and the Recording Process   AP-31
Identifying and Recording Transactions
   and Other Events   **AP-31**
Journalizing   **AP-31**
Posting   **AP-33**
Preparing the Trial Balance   **AP-34**
Adjusting Entries   AP-34
Adjusting Entries for Prepayments   **AP-36**
Alternative Method for Adjusting Prepayments   **AP-39**
Adjusting Entries for Accruals   **AP-40**
Adjusting Entries for Estimated Items   **AP-43**
Unrealized Holding Gains or Losses
   (FV-NI and FV-OCI)   **AP-44**
Financial Statements and Ownership Structure   AP-45
The Closing Process   AP-46
Preparing Closing Entries   **AP-47**
Reversing Entries   **AP-48**
Using a Work Sheet   AP-50
Work Sheet Columns   **AP-51**
Completing the Work Sheet   **AP-51**
Preparing Financial Statements from a Work Sheet   **AP-53**

APPENDIX D   **CPA Competency Map Coverage   AP-76**

APPENDIX E   **A Summary of the Case Primer   AP-79**

GLOSSARY   **G-1**

COMPANY INDEX   **I-1**

SUBJECT INDEX   **I-2**

CHAPTER 1

The Canadian Financial Reporting Environment

Capitalizing on Financial Reporting

Every business—from the lawn-mowing service you may have operated in high school to a multinational corporation—needs capital to survive. You may have borrowed money from your parents to buy a weed trimmer, while the corporation issued millions of shares to raise capital from the public. But what about new businesses or those trying to branch into emerging markets? How do they get money to grow?

Large public corporations generally issue shares on a large stock exchange such as the Toronto Stock Exchange. But the fees, reporting requirements, and other regulations could be a barrier to smaller companies. To offer a less expensive and less stringent alternative, the Canadian Securities Exchange (CSE) was launched in 2004. "We seek to facilitate the lowest cost of public capital for these companies, principally by providing a very streamlined listings process, and then once the company is listed to provide cost certainty in the form of fixed fees, regardless of how active the company is in secondary financings, changing its business, making acquisitions and other activities," said the CEO of CSE, Richard Carleton. In 2017, the value of shares traded among the CSE's 300 listed companies was $7.8 billion—more than four times the value of the previous year.

In 2017, companies related to cannabis accounted for eight of the top 10 firms in terms of overall value traded. Fifty-six of the CSE's 300 issuers were cannabis-related and made up nearly two-thirds of the total market capitalization—the value of all shares traded. The other two top 10 companies by trading value were firms in the financial technology industry specializing in blockchain, a way of verifying transactions in cryptocurrencies such as bitcoin.

The cannabis and financial technology industries were both undergoing rapid growth in 2017, and the value of their trading reflected that. They were boosted by the expectation of Canada legalizing recreational marijuana in mid-2018 and by the exploding popularity of cryptocurrencies.

Companies trading on the CSE work in other emerging fields. One example is Global UAV Technologies, which manufactures drones, or unmanned aerial vehicles (UAVs), that do land surveying for mining, construction, engineering, and agricultural firms. The Vancouver-based company used to be called Alta Vista Ventures Ltd. and owned mining properties in Mexico. In fiscal 2015, a market downturn and lack of activity at the properties caused the company to write down its land value to zero. In mid-2017, it changed its name to Global UAV and moved into aerial surveying by acquiring existing UAV technology companies. Global UAV earned nearly $600,000 in net income on sales of more than $1 million for its year ended October 31, 2017.

What does raising capital have to do with financial reporting? No matter how big the company, no matter how it raises money, it needs to present its financial information to

Logorilla/Getty Images

potential investors and other stakeholders accurately and consistently with financial reporting standards—using a common "language" that investors understand.

Sources: John Harrington, "Global UAV Technologies: Pure Play Drone Sector Exposure with Earnings Just Starting to Take Off," *Public Entrepreneur* (Canadian Securities Exchange), April 4, 2018; Hamish Khamisa, "Interview with Canadian Securities Exchange CEO Richard Carleton: Year-End Review 2017," CSE website, January 5, 2018; Armina Ligaya, The Canadian Press, "Canadian Securities Exchange Trades Record $7.81 Billion in 2017, Thanks to Pot, Block-chain Buzz," *The Financial Post*, January 4, 2018; Canadian Securities Exchange corporate website, http://thecse.com; Global UAV Technologies 2017 annual report; Global UAV Technologies corporate website, www.globaluavtech.com.

LEARNING OBJECTIVES	CHAPTER OUTLINE	CPA COMPETENCIES
After studying this chapter, you should be able to:	The chapter headings related to the learning objective are:	Competencies addressed by each learning objective are as follows:
1. Understand the financial reporting environment.	**Financial Statements and Financial Reporting** • Accounting and capital allocation • Stakeholders • Objective of financial reporting • Information asymmetry	**1.1.1, 1.1.2, 1.2.1, 5.2.3**
2. Explain the need for accounting standards and identify the major entities that influence standard setting and financial reporting.	**Standard Setting** • Need for standards • Parties involved in standard setting	**1.1.1, 1.1.2**
3. Explain the meaning of generally accepted accounting principles (GAAP) and the significance of professional judgement in applying GAAP.	**Generally Accepted Accounting Principles** • GAAP hierarchy • Professional judgement	**1.1.1, 1.1.2, 1.2.1**
4. Discuss some of the challenges and opportunities for accounting.	**Challenges and Opportunities for the Accounting Profession** • Oversight in the capital marketplace • Centrality of ethics • Standard setting in a political environment • Principles versus rules • Impact of technology • Integrated reporting • Conclusion	**1.1.1, 1.1.2, 1.1.4, 1.2.1, 1.3.1**

Preview of Chapter 1

North American financial reporting systems are among the best in the world. Our commitment to keeping our financial reporting systems strong is as intense as ever, because in this changing business world, information must be relevant and reliable for our capital markets to work efficiently.

This chapter explains the environment of financial reporting and the many factors that affect it. It provides the theory and concepts underpinning the topics covered in the rest of the chapters, giving you the foundation to exercise professional judgement in the many issues that require it.

Financial Statements and Financial Reporting

LEARNING OBJECTIVE 1
Understand the financial reporting environment.

Like other human activities and disciplines, accounting is largely a product of its environment. This environment includes conditions, constraints, and influences that are social, economic, political, and legal—all of which change over time. As a result, accounting theory and practices have always evolved and need to continue to evolve in order to remain relevant.

Over the past decade or two, the accounting landscape has changed dramatically, being shaped by many things—some good and some not so good. These include:

- spectacular business failures, including WorldCom Inc., Enron, and Arthur Andersen;
- capital market failures, including the subprime lending crisis and bank failures;
- near bankruptcies of several countries;
- globalization of capital and other markets;
- globalization of financial reporting standards;
- increasing use of more sophisticated technology; and
- increasing access to information.[1]

All of these factors, as well as many others, provide accountants with great challenges but also great opportunities!

Accounting is defined best by describing its three essential characteristics. Accounting is (1) the identification, measurement, and communication of financial information (2) about economic entities (3) to interested persons.

Financial accounting (financial reporting) is the process that culminates in the preparation of financial reports that cover all of the enterprise's business activities and that are used by both **internal and external** parties. Users of these financial reports include investors, creditors, and others. In contrast, managerial accounting is the process of identifying, measuring, analyzing, and **communicating financial information** to **internal** decision-makers. This information may take varied forms, such as cost-benefit analyses and forecasts that management uses to plan, evaluate, and control an organization's operations. This textbook focuses on financial accounting, while managerial accounting is covered in other courses.

Financial statements are the principal way of communicating financial information to those who are outside an enterprise. These statements give the firm's history, quantified in terms of money. The most frequently provided financial statements are the:

1. **statement of financial position**,
2. **statement of income/comprehensive income**,
3. **statement of cash flows**, and
4. **statement of changes in equity**.

See **Alternative Terminology 1.1**.

> **Alternative Terminology 1.1**
> These financial statements are also sometimes called:
>
> 1. balance sheet,
> 2. income statement, and
> 3. cash flow statement.
>
> Under Accounting Standards for Private Enterprises, a statement of retained earnings is generally prepared instead of a statement of changes in equity.

---

[1] Julia Christensen Hughes and Joy Mighty, in their book entitled *Taking Stock* (Queen's School of Policy Studies, Kingston, 2010), refer to this as the ubiquity of information, meaning that information is now more freely, openly, and readily available. In the book, Christensen Hughes and Mighty discuss the impact of this phenomenon on education; however, it applies equally to the capital marketplace.

In addition, **note disclosures** are an important part of each financial statement. Some financial information cannot be expressed in the financial statements or is better expressed through other means. Examples include the president's letter and supplementary schedules in the corporate annual report, prospectuses, reports filed with government agencies, news releases, management forecasts, and descriptions of an enterprise's social or environmental impact. Such information may be required by a pronouncement by an authority, or a regulatory rule[2] or custom, or because management wants to disclose it voluntarily. The main focus of this textbook is the basic financial statements (including notes).

Accounting and Capital Allocation

Because **resources** are limited, people try to conserve them, use them effectively, and identify and encourage those who can make efficient use of them. Through an **efficient use of resources**, our standard of living increases.

 Finance 5.2.3 Markets, free enterprise, and competition determine whether a business will succeed and thrive. The accounting profession has the important responsibility of **measuring company performance** accurately and fairly on a timely basis. The information provided by accounting enables investors and creditors to **compare** the income and assets of companies and thus **assess the relative risks and returns** of different investment opportunities. Based on their assessments, investors and creditors can then channel their resources (that is, invest in these companies or lend them money) more effectively. **Illustration 1.1** shows the process of capital allocation.

ILLUSTRATION 1.1

Capital Allocation Process

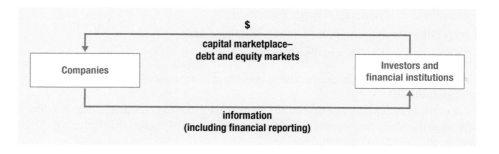

In Canada, the primary exchange mechanisms for allocating resources are **debt and equity markets**,[3] as well as **financial institutions** such as banks.[4] The debt and equity marketplace includes both public stock markets/exchanges and private sources.

Illustration 1.2 shows the sources of capital in Canada for various stages of company growth.

Providing an effective system to facilitate capital allocation is critical to a healthy economy. Efficient capital markets promote productivity, encourage innovation,

---

[2] All public companies must disclose certain information under provincial securities law. This information is collected by the provincial securities commissions under the Canadian umbrella organization, the Canadian Securities Administrators (CSA), and is available electronically at www.sedar.com.

[3] The largest, most senior equity market in Canada is the Toronto Stock Exchange (TSX). The junior market—the TSX Venture Exchange (TSXV, formerly called the CDNX Stock Market)—was created in 2001 to handle start-up companies and the Canadian Securities Exchange (CSE), another junior market, was launched in 2004. The Montreal Exchange (MX), known also as the Canadian Derivatives Exchange, is the main market for derivatives and futures trading. In 2014, the TMX Group, which operates the TSX, launched a new market to help private companies raise capital (called TSX Private Markets).

[4] According to Bloomberg in an article entitled "Big 5 Canadian Banks Now Big 3 as Assets Diverge" on July 7, 2014, what were previously known as the "Big 5"—the Royal Bank of Canada, Toronto Dominion Bank, Bank of Nova Scotia, Bank of Montreal, and Canadian Imperial Bank of Commerce—have now become the "Big 3" with the first three listed being the largest.

ILLUSTRATION 1.2 Sources of Capital

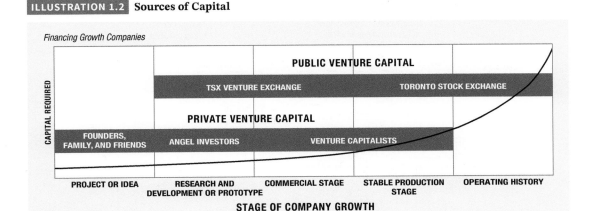

© TSX Inc., 2018. All rights reserved.

and provide a platform for buying and selling securities and obtaining and granting credit.[5] Unreliable and irrelevant information leads to **poor capital allocation**, which hurts the securities markets and economic growth. The accounting numbers that companies report affect the **transfer of resources** among companies and individuals. Consider the fact that stock prices generally rise when positive news (including financial information) is unexpectedly released. In addition, **credit rating agencies** use accounting and other information to rate companies' financial stability.[6] This gives investors and creditors **additional independent information** to use when making decisions. For companies, a good rating can mean greater access to capital and at lower costs.

Stakeholders

Stakeholders are parties who have something at risk in the financial reporting environment, such as their salary, job, investment, or reputation. Key stakeholders in the financial reporting environment include **traditional users** of financial information as well as others. In the stakeholder context, **users** may be more broadly defined to include not only parties who are relying directly on the financial information for resource allocation (such as investors and creditors) but also others who help in the efficient allocation of resources (such as financial analysts and regulators).

The broader definition of users includes anyone who **prepares**, **relies on**, **reviews, audits, or monitors financial information**. It includes investors, creditors, analysts, managers, employees, customers, suppliers, industry groups, unions, government departments and ministers, the public in general (such as consumer groups), regulatory agencies, other companies, and standard setters, as well as auditors, lawyers, and others. Illustration 1.3 shows the relationships among these stakeholders.

Various stakeholders have specific functions in the financial reporting environment. Company management **prepares** the financial statements. It has the best insight into the business and therefore knows what should be included in the financial statements. The statements are then **audited** by auditors, who may discuss with management how economic events and transactions have been communicated in the financial statements. The value that auditors add to the statements lies in the auditors' independence. They act on behalf of the shareholders to ensure that management is accounting properly for the economic transactions. The auditors also **review** the information to ensure that it reflects sound accounting practices.

---

[5]AICPA Special Committee on Financial Reporting, "Improving Business Reporting: A Customer Focus," supplement in *Journal of Accountancy* (October 1994).

[6]For example, institutions such as Dominion Bond Rating Service, Moody's Investor Services (Moody's), and Standard & Poor's rate issuers of bonds and preferred shares in the Canadian and global marketplaces.

Selected Key Stakeholders in the Financial Reporting Environment

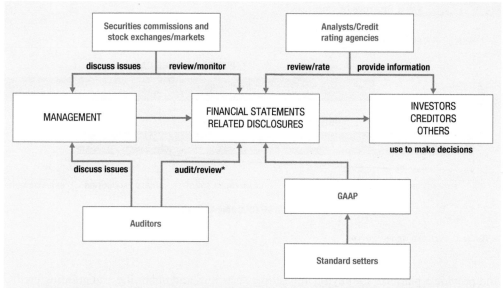

* Not all financial statements are required to be audited. In general, all companies whose shares or debt is **publicly traded** must have an audit and therefore comply with generally accepted accounting principles (GAAP). Private companies may decide not to have an audit but must have unanimous shareholder consent according to the Canada Business Corporations Act. For private companies, the decision to have an audit or not may depend on whether the statements' users would find audited GAAP statements more useful.

Law   Investors and creditors **rely on** the financial statements to make decisions. It is up to these parties to carefully examine the information given. Standard setters set **generally accepted accounting principles (GAAP)**. Securities commissions and stock exchanges **monitor** the financial statements to ensure full and plain disclosure of material information and to determine whether the companies may continue to list their shares on stock exchanges. Finally, the credit rating agencies and analysts **monitor and analyze** the information produced by the company, looking for signs of change; that is, an improved or weakened financial condition.

Illustration 1.4 identifies what is at stake for each stakeholder. This is not meant to be a complete list. Rather, it identifies the major stakeholder groups.

What Is at Stake for Each Stakeholder

Stakeholder	What Is at Stake
Investors/creditors	Investment/loan
Management	Job, bonus, reputation, salary increase, access to capital markets by company
Securities commissions and stock exchanges	Reputation, effective and efficient capital marketplace
Analysts and credit rating agencies	Reputation, profits
Auditors	Reputation, profits (companies are their clients)
Standard setters	Reputation
Others	Various

As noted in Illustration 1.3, the system provides **checks and balances** to ensure that the people with capital—the investors and creditors—have good information to use when deciding where best to invest or allocate their capital. The system does not always work, however. Because the system involves people, human behaviour is often a key unpredictable variable. People often act in their own **self-interest** rather than in the **best interest of the capital marketplace, and by extension, the economy**. See What Do the Numbers Mean? 1.1.

| What Do the Numbers Mean? 1.1 |

Consider the much-publicized crisis that arose when large numbers of borrowers with lower-quality, "subprime" mortgages defaulted, which was partly responsible for destabilizing the capital markets and the economy, starting in 2007. What was this all about and how did it trigger a global recession? Much has to do with individuals and entities acting in their own self-interest and a lack of transparency or lack of understanding of the true risks involved.

Financial institutions regularly securitize pools of assets in order to access the cash that is tied up in the assets. As a general rule, the securitization involves selling the assets to a separate entity, often for cash. The entity then sells units or shares in the pool of assets to investors. The following are the steps in a normal securitization of mortgage assets:

1. Lender lends money to customers to buy homes.
2. Lender sells pool of mortgage assets from the above loans to a separate entity (often referred to as a special purpose entity or SPE).
3. SPE sells units or shares in the pool of mortgages to investors.

Ethics There is nothing inherently wrong with this structure and it can work very well for all parties as long as they understand the risks involved. It is good for borrowers because it makes funds more accessible. It is good for lenders because they are able to get their cash out of the mortgage assets. It is good for SPEs because they earn interest on the pool of assets. Finally, it is good for investors because they earn a return on their investment. What went wrong in the subprime lending situation, then?

First, the lenders or their designated mortgage brokers loaned money aggressively, in the hopes of higher profits, to borrowers who may not have been creditworthy.

Second, many of the loans were adjustable-rate notes, which meant that, initially, the interest rates were low—often below the prime lending rate, which is where the term "subprime" comes from. But afterward, the rates reset themselves according to the loan agreement, often becoming significantly higher. Therefore, even though the borrowers may have been able to afford the loan payments initially, many could no longer afford them once the interest rates became higher. The borrowers borrowed the funds anyway because they wanted to buy houses, even though they knew or should have known that they might not be able to keep up with the loan payments in future.

Third, many investors in the SPE did not understand the risks they were taking on by investing in this type of pool of assets, which was systemically risky due to the creditworthiness of the borrowers and the mortgages' interest rate reset feature.

Things began to unwind when the mortgages' interest rates were set higher. This caused many borrowers to default on their mortgages and lose their homes. These homes were repossessed and flooded the market, driving house prices down. Many borrowers found that the amounts of their mortgages were now higher than the value of their homes and they walked away from their debt, causing more homes to go on sale in an already depressed market. The investors in the SPE suffered large losses due to the defaulted loans. All this contributed to a depressed housing market and economy.

From a financial reporting perspective, a few lessons were learned:

1. Many capital market participants act in their own self-interest to the potential harm of others.
2. The amount and nature of risk are not always properly communicated to investors.
3. Investors do not always understand what they are investing in.

Stakeholders in the capital marketplace continue to work to ensure that this type of situation does not happen again. For instance, the International Accounting Standards Board has declared that it intends to make better communication in financial reporting an underlying theme in its work over the next few years.

Objective of Financial Reporting

What is the **objective of financial reporting**? The objective of **general-purpose financial statements** is to **provide financial information about the reporting entity that is useful to present and potential equity investors, lenders, and other creditors in making decisions in their capacity as capital providers**.[7] (This is referred to as the **decision-usefulness approach** to financial reporting.) Information that is decision-useful to capital providers may also be useful to other users of financial reporting who are not investors and creditors. Let's examine each of the elements of this objective.

Theory As part of the objective of general-purpose financial reporting, an **entity perspective** is adopted. Using this perspective, companies are viewed as separate and distinct from their owners (present shareholders). The assets of incorporated entities such as companies listed on stock exchanges are viewed as assets of the company and not of a specific creditor or shareholder. Investors and creditors have claims on a company's assets in the form of equity or liability claims. The entity perspective is common today, because most companies that report their financial information have substance distinct from their investors (both shareholders and creditors). Thus,

---

[7]IASB Conceptual Framework, Chapter 1. Copyright © IFRS Foundation. All rights reserved. Reproduced with permission. Reprinted/adapted with permission from the *CPA Canada Handbook—Accounting* © 2018, Part II, Section 1000.12, by Chartered Professional Accountants of Canada. All rights reserved by the copyright owner.

the perspective that financial reporting should be focused only on the needs of shareholders—often referred to as the **proprietary perspective**—is not considered appropriate.

As mentioned earlier, investors are interested in assessing (1) the company's ability to generate net cash inflows and (2) management's ability to protect and enhance the capital providers' investments. Financial reporting should therefore help investors assess the amounts, timing, and uncertainty of prospective cash inflows from dividends or interest, and the proceeds from the sale, redemption, or maturity of securities or loans. In order for investors to make these assessments, they must understand an enterprise's economic resources, the claims to those resources, and the changes in them. Financial statements and related explanations should be a primary source for determining this information.

The emphasis on "assessing cash flow prospects" does not mean that the cash basis is preferred over the accrual basis of accounting. Information based on accrual accounting generally better indicates a company's present and future ability to generate favourable cash flows than does information limited to the financial effects of cash receipts and payments. Recall from your first accounting course the objective of **accrual-basis accounting**. It ensures that a company records events that change its financial statements in the periods in which the events occur, rather than only in the periods in which it receives or pays cash. Using the accrual basis to determine net income means that a company recognizes revenues when it provides the goods or services rather than when it receives cash. Similarly, it recognizes expenses when it incurs them rather than when it pays them. Under accrual accounting, a company generally recognizes revenues when it makes sales. The company can then relate the revenues to the economic environment of the period in which they occurred. Over the long run, trends in revenues and expenses are generally more meaningful than trends in cash receipts and disbursements.

Providing information that is useful to users is a challenging task because they have **different needs and levels of knowledge**. **Institutional investors**,[8] such as the Canada Pension Plan (see **What Do the Numbers Mean? 1.2**), hold an increasing percentage of equity

What Do the Numbers Mean? 1.2

The Canada Pension Plan (CPP) is one of the 10 largest retirement funds in the world according to its website. Over 20 million Canadians participate in the plan. The plan is managed by the Canada Pension Plan Investment Board (CPPIB), which decides how to invest the CPP funds. Its mandate is to "maximize returns without undue risk of loss."

The chart below (based on the CPPIB 2017 Annual Report) shows where the money is invested by type of asset and region.

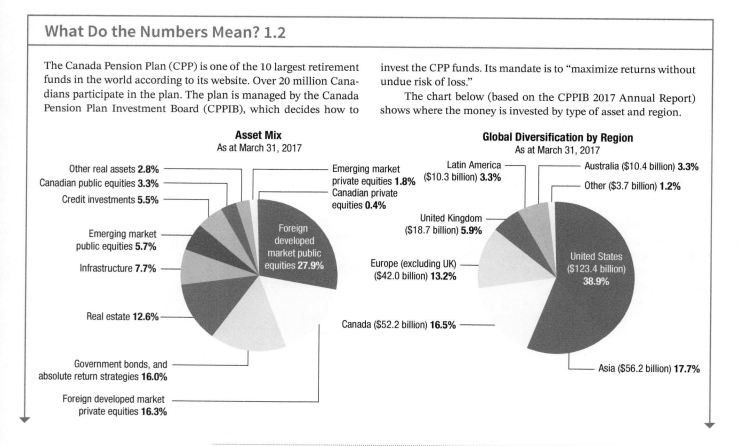

Asset Mix
As at March 31, 2017

- Other real assets **2.8%**
- Canadian public equities **3.3%**
- Credit investments **5.5%**
- Emerging market public equities **5.7%**
- Infrastructure **7.7%**
- Real estate **12.6%**
- Government bonds, and absolute return strategies **16.0%**
- Foreign developed market private equities **16.3%**
- Emerging market private equities **1.8%**
- Canadian private equities **0.4%**
- Foreign developed market public equities **27.9%**

Global Diversification by Region
As at March 31, 2017

- Latin America ($10.3 billion) **3.3%**
- Australia ($10.4 billion) **3.3%**
- Other ($3.7 billion) **1.2%**
- United Kingdom ($18.7 billion) **5.9%**
- Europe (excluding UK) ($42.0 billion) **13.2%**
- United States ($123.4 billion) **38.9%**
- Canada ($52.2 billion) **16.5%**
- Asia ($56.2 billion) **17.7%**

[8]Institutional investors are corporate investors such as insurance companies, pension plans, mutual funds, and others. They are considered a separate class of investors because of their size and financial expertise, and the large size of the investments that they hold in other companies. In general, for these reasons, institutional investors have greater power than the average investor.

The fund stood at $316.9 billion as at March 31, 2017 and experienced an 11.8% rate of return for 2017. As you can see in the following diagram, the composition of types of assets has shifted from primarily fixed income to primarily equities—including shares in publicly traded corporations as well as private companies.

CPPIB has increasingly expanded its investment in real assets including real estate, infrastructure, agricultural land, energy, and natural resources. As a large institutional investor with substantial equities holdings, the CPP is a significant stakeholder in terms of how publicly traded companies report their financial information.

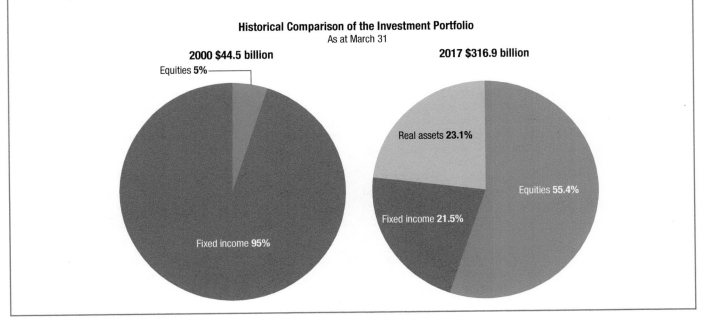

Historical Comparison of the Investment Portfolio
As at March 31

2000 $44.5 billion

Equities **5%**

Fixed income **95%**

2017 $316.9 billion

Real assets **23.1%**

Fixed income **21.5%**

Equities **55.4%**

shareholdings and generally put a lot of their resources into managing their investment portfolios. Can those who prepare financial information therefore assume that the average individual investor has the same needs and knowledge level as an institutional investor when it comes to business and financial reporting? Likely not.[9] We will discuss this issue further in Chapter 2.

Information Asymmetry

Ideally, to facilitate the flow of capital in the most efficient and effective manner, all stakeholders should have equal access to all relevant information. In other words, there should be symmetry of access to information (**information symmetry**). This is nice in theory but it does not always work in practice. Management may feel that disclosure of too much information may hurt the company's competitive advantage or position. For instance, if the company were in the middle of a lawsuit, management would want to be careful about how much information was disclosed because it might affect the outcome of the lawsuit. In cases such as this, the company must weigh the costs and benefits of sharing information. On the one hand, if the company is known to be open and forthright, revealing information may facilitate the flow of capital to the company and perhaps lower the cost of capital. On the other hand, if the company is too open, it might give away proprietary information that might cause profits to fall. For this reason, perfect information symmetry does not exist and, as a general rule, management rightly has access to more or better information than others because they run the company. In other words, there is **information asymmetry**. (See **What Do the Numbers Mean? 1.3** for a discussion on how the Internet is changing information asymmetry.)

---

[9]The Canadian Coalition for Good Governance (CCGG) is a group of institutional investors that manages over $3.0 trillion in investments (including investments in private and public equities and bonds). Its members include many significant pension funds in Canada, such as the Alberta Teachers' Retirement Fund, Ontario Teachers' Pension Plan, OPSEU Pension Trust, and Ontario Municipal Employees Retirement System, as well as many significant mutual funds and financial institutions, such as Mackenzie Financial Corp., RBC Global Asset Management Inc., and TD Asset Management Inc. According to its website (www.ccgg.ca), CCGG was started in 2002 "to represent Canadian institutional shareholders in the promotion of corporate governance practices that best align the interests of boards and management with those of the shareholder." As a comparison point, the total market capitalization of the TSX is estimated at $2.8 trillion (as at March 2017).

What Do the Numbers Mean? 1.3

In their book *Freakonomics*, Levitt and Dubner acknowledge that it is very common in most transactions for one party to have more or better information than the other. Often, in a transaction, one party is an expert and the other not. In the capital marketplace, experts, including accountants, bankers, institutional investors, and company managers, all have more and better information than the average consumer or investor. Levitt and Dubner go on to argue, however, that the Internet allows information to pass very freely from experts to non-experts. They argue that the Internet has "vastly shrunk the gap between experts and the public."

Shifting to another discipline, for example, consider your own relationship with your family doctor. Several decades ago, if something was wrong with you, you would have made an appointment and sat passively in the doctor's office while he or she analyzed your symptoms and made a diagnosis. At that time, the doctor might have shared the analysis and diagnosis with you and might have handed you an illegible prescription to fill. The Internet

has changed this. Now, most people do a bit of research before they go to the doctor. By doing a quick search on the Internet, patients are able to get information so that they know what questions to ask and what options might be available for treatment. Patients can now freely access information about side effects and new drugs. Many people keep their own medical histories. Doctors understand that their role is to help their patients navigate the significant amount of information that is available, not necessarily (only) to dictate a diagnosis and treatment.

Returning to the business world, the real question is: As people turn more and more to the Internet and the information there becomes more and more robust, what is the role of experts in the capital marketplace and how will the issue of information asymmetry evolve?

Source: Steven Levitt and Stephen Dubner, *Freakonomics*, HarperCollins Publishers, New York, 2005.

As well as the above, there are other reasons why information asymmetry exists in the marketplace. This might be due to the way the markets operate or to human nature. Some issues are as follows:

1. Capital markets such as stock exchanges are not necessarily fully efficient; that is, not all information is incorporated into the stock prices of companies. The problem, of course, is that the prices may not reflect hidden or insider information. This may be due to the reasons noted above, or other reasons in point 2 below.

2. Human behaviour sometimes results in individuals and companies acting in ways that will maximize their own well-being at the cost of other capital market participants. For instance, management may wish to show only positive information about a company in order to ensure access to capital markets or maximize their own personal bonuses.

Accounting and economic theory tries to help us understand these issues. The **efficient markets hypothesis** proposes that market prices reflect all publicly available information about a company.[10]

Theory In addition to researching whether market mechanisms are efficient or not, accounting theorists look at the issue of information asymmetry from other perspectives. There are two common types of information asymmetry problems that are studied by academics. These are identified and briefly explained below. Basically these theories argue that information asymmetry results in a suboptimal or inefficient capital marketplace. In markets where this phenomenon is observed, investors may discount share prices, require higher returns on investment (as a penalty for having to deal with the lack of information), or choose not to invest in the market. In the extreme, information asymmetry may interfere with a company's ability to access capital and/or minimize the cost of capital.

We will refer back to these concepts throughout the text. Because these concepts are also studied in other disciplines, the examples below look at them from a financial reporting and capital marketplace perspective.

Adverse selection—Basically, this means that, where information asymmetry exists, the marketplace may attract the wrong types of market participants (including buyers and sellers as well as investors). If buyers cannot assess the quality of the product they are buying, they may decide not to buy anything or to buy at a discount. Sellers, knowing this, will therefore

---

[10]There are three forms of the efficient markets hypothesis: (1) the weak form (market prices incorporate all historic publicly available information), (2) the semi-strong form (market prices incorporate all public information), and (3) the strong form (market prices incorporate all information whether public or not). Historically, economists have argued that North American markets are less than perfectly efficient and that they are efficient in the semi-strong form only. This hypothesis has come under attack in recent years. Many feel that we have put too much faith in the belief that markets are efficient and may need other mechanisms to deal with information asymmetry.

put only inferior products up for sale; thus the market could contain only companies with poor products or it could fail. In addition, companies with higher-quality products may choose not to enter the capital marketplace knowing that share prices may be discounted due to the existence of information asymmetry that does not allow investors to separate high-quality firms from "lemons" that produce low-quality products.

Moral hazard—This is the concept that people will often shirk their responsibilities if they think that no one is watching. For instance, a manager of a pharmaceutical company may choose not to work as hard, if investors cannot tell the level of effort being made due to information asymmetry. Similarly, he (or she) may choose not to disclose negative information about ongoing drug trials, knowing that it will result in a decline in share prices and perhaps his bonus. In addition, he may engage in greater risk-taking. Accountants sometimes refer to this as management bias. Managers may decide to downplay the negative and focus on the positive (referred to as aggressive accounting). This bias might take the form of overstated assets and/or net income, understated liabilities and/or expenses, or carefully selected note disclosures that emphasize only positive events.[11] Conservative accounting would be the opposite.[12] Any bias in financial reporting results in less useful information.

There are many reasons why management may present biased information in the financial statements. Illustration 1.5 examines these possible motivations. We will revisit the issue of bias in Chapter 2 and throughout the text.

ILLUSTRATION 1.5 **Possible Motivations for Management Bias**

Motivation to Bias Information	Explanation
Evaluation of management performance	Financial statements provide evidence to investors about how management has discharged its stewardship function. Stewardship is how well management has looked after the money invested in the company. Ideally, they at least maintained the capital and hopefully increased it.
Compensation structures	Management remuneration may be based on financial statements directly (for example, bonus based on net income) or indirectly (stock options based on the value of the shares that may be affected by reported net income).
Access to capital markets and meeting financial analysts' expectations	There is a strong desire to meet financial analysts' expectations because this may affect a company's cost of capital or access to capital markets.[13] In addition, there may be a concern that share prices and therefore management compensation may drop.
Contractual obligations	Many lending agreements and contracts require that certain financial benchmarks be met, and these often relate to financial stability or liquidity. For instance, a debt covenant (a term in a loan agreement) may state that the company must maintain certain minimum financial ratios or the loan may be called (demanded to be repaid).

[11]This is not a new problem. David Brown, then-chairman of the Ontario Securities Commission (OSC), spoke at length on this topic in a speech in 1999 entitled "Public Accounting at a Crossroads." Arthur Levitt, then-chair of the U.S. Securities and Exchange Commission (SEC), discussed his concerns over this issue in "Numbers Game," a major address to New York University in 1998. Both the OSC and the SEC review financial statements and financial reporting practices to ensure that investors have "full and plain disclosure" of all material facts that are needed to make investment decisions. In their speeches, Mr. Brown and Mr. Levitt both cited specific cases where they felt that financial reporting practices were problematic.

[12]As noted earlier, conservative accounting would generally result in ensuring that assets and income are not overstated and that all relevant information is disclosed.

[13]Financial analysts monitor earnings announcements carefully and compare them with their earlier expectations. They and others (including certain stock markets) post what they refer to as earnings surprises each day on their websites. Earnings surprises occur when a company reports net income figures that are different from what the market expected. The focus is on net income or earnings. If net income is higher than expected, this is a positive earnings surprise. If net income is lower than expected, this is a negative earnings surprise, and the market will generally react unfavourably, resulting in declining share prices. For instance, for quarterly earnings numbers released on August 17, 2017, the NASDAQ website noted that there were 10 positive earnings surprises and eight negative earnings surprises. Positive earnings surprises included Alibaba Group Holdings Limited and Wal-Mart Stores, Inc. Selected negative earnings surprises noted for the same day included LSI Industries Inc. and Lancaster Colony Corporation.

Standard Setting

Need for Standards

LEARNING OBJECTIVE 2
Explain the need for accounting standards and identify the major entities that influence standard setting and financial reporting.

Accounting standards help reduce the information asymmetry problem in financial reporting. They do this by requiring that transactions and events be recognized, measured, presented, and disclosed in a specific way. But the main controversy in financial reporting is this: Whose rules should we play by, and what should they be? The answer is not immediately clear. This is because the users of financial statements have both similar and conflicting needs for information of various types.

Accounting professions in various countries have tried to develop a set of standards that are generally accepted and universally practised. Without these standards, each enterprise would have to develop its own standards, and readers of financial statements would have to become familiar with every company's particular accounting and reporting practices. It would be almost impossible to prepare statements that could be compared.

This common set of standards and procedures is called generally accepted accounting principles (GAAP). The term "generally accepted" means either that an authoritative rule-making body in accounting has created a reporting principle in a particular area or that, over time, a specific practice has been accepted as appropriate because it is used universally.[14] Although principles and practices have resulted in both debate and criticism, most members of the financial community recognize them as the standards that over time have proven to be most useful. A more detailed discussion of GAAP is presented later in this chapter.

Parties Involved in Standard Setting

Before 1900, single ownership was the most common form of business organization in our economy. Financial reports emphasized **solvency and liquidity** and were only for **internal use** or for banks and other lending institutions to examine. From 1900 to 1929, the growth of large corporations and their absentee ownership led to **increasing investment and speculation** in corporate stock. When the stock market crashed in 1929, this contributed to the Great Depression. These events emphasized the need for **standardized and increased corporate disclosures** that would allow shareholders to make informed decisions.

Several organizations play a role in developing financial reporting standards in Canada. The major standard-setting organizations are:

1. Canadian **Accounting Standards Board (AcSB)**: *www.frascanada.ca*
2. **International Accounting Standards Board (IASB)**: *www.ifrs.org*
3. The **Financial Accounting Standards Board (FASB)**: *www.fasb.org;* and the U.S. **Securities and Exchange Commission (SEC)**: *www.sec.gov*
4. **Provincial securities commissions** such as the **Ontario Securities Commission (OSC)**: *www.osc.gov.on.ca*

Illustration 1.6 shows how these organizations influence GAAP for Canadian entities. We will discuss each in greater detail below.

---

[14]The terms "principle" and "standard" are used interchangeably in practice and throughout this textbook.

ILLUSTRATION 1.6 **Various Entities Responsible for GAAP**

Standard-Setting Body	GAAP Development	How GAAP Applies to Canadian Entities
AcSB	GAAP for Canadian private companies (referred to as **Accounting Standards for Private Enterprises** or **ASPE**), pension plans, and not-for-profit entities	ASPE became effective for periods beginning on or after January 1, 2011. Not-for-profit entities in the public sector may have to follow public sector GAAP, which is the responsibility of the Public Sector Accounting Board (PSAB).
IASB	GAAP for public companies, referred to as **International Financial Reporting Standards (IFRS)**	IFRS became effective for periods beginning on or after January 1, 2011. Private companies and not-for-profit entities may choose to use IFRS.
FASB	GAAP for U.S. entities (referred to as U.S. GAAP)	Canadian public companies may choose to follow U.S. GAAP.
Securities commissions	Not responsible for GAAP but often require additional disclosures for public companies	The Ontario Securities Commission requires that public companies follow IFRS or U.S. GAAP (where public companies list on U.S. stock exchanges or markets and choose to follow U.S. GAAP instead of IFRS) for periods beginning on or after January 1, 2011.

Canadian Accounting Standards Board (AcSB)

The first official recommendations on standards of financial statement disclosure were published in 1946 by the **Canadian Institute of Chartered Accountants (CICA)**. The CICA was one of the predecessor organizations of **Chartered Professional Accountants of Canada (CPA Canada)**. Today, the Accounting Standards Board (AcSB) has primary responsibility for setting GAAP in Canada. The AcSB produces a variety of authoritative material, including the most important source of GAAP, the *CPA Canada Handbook*.[15] The *CPA Canada Handbook* was originally published in 1968[16] and now consists of several volumes of accounting and assurance guidance.[17]

The objectives of the AcSB are as follows:

a. To establish financial reporting standards that improve the quality of information reported by Canadian entities with due consideration for the costs and the benefits to the preparers and users of financial statements, and changes in the economic environment;

b. To facilitate the capital allocation process in both the business and not-for-profit sectors through improved information;

c. To participate with other standard setters in the development of a single set of high-quality internationally accepted financial reporting standards; and

d. To support the implementation of financial reporting standards and the resolution of emerging application issues.[18]

---

[15]The Canada Business Corporations Act and Regulations (CBCA), Part XIV Financial Disclosure and Part 8 (paras. 70 and 71), as well as provincial corporations' acts, require that most companies incorporated under these acts prepare financial statements in accordance with Canadian GAAP. This textbook usually refers to this document as the *CPA Canada Handbook* or just the *Handbook*.

[16]The *Handbook* is also available to students and members online. With the rapid pace of change in standard setting, most members use the online version as their main source of GAAP.

[17]Technically, IFRS is considered to be part of the Canadian *CPA Canada Handbook—Accounting* for legal reasons. However, the *CPA Canada Handbook* as it relates to IFRS will exactly mirror the IASB standards as long as the AcSB continues to officially accept any updates or changes into Canadian GAAP. This was done because many Canadian laws refer to Canadian GAAP.

[18]AcSB Terms of Reference (www.frascanada.ca).

Two basic premises underlie the process of establishing financial accounting standards:

1. The AcSB should **respond to the needs and viewpoints** of the **entire economic community**, not just the public accounting profession.
2. The AcSB should **operate in full public view** through a **due process** system that gives interested persons enough opportunity to make their views known.

The **Accounting Standards Oversight Council (AcSOC)** oversees AcSB activities. Its duties include providing input to AcSB activities and reporting to the public, among other things. Members of the AcSB and the AcSOC come from a wide range of groups that are interested or involved in the financial reporting process.[19]

The AcSB is responsible for setting standards for public and private entities as well as not-for-profit entities (including some profit-oriented government entities). As noted in Illustration 1.6, from 2011 onward, the AcSB has been responsible for developing standards for private enterprises, not-for-profit entities, and pension plans only. Standards for publicly accountable entities (public companies) are developed by the International Accounting Standards Board even though they are still adopted into Canadian GAAP by the AcSB. This approach makes sense for a number of reasons, including the following:

1. Public companies often operate globally and may raise funds in global capital markets; therefore, it makes sense to have a common language for reporting financial position and performance so that users can compare companies internationally.
2. Private companies often operate locally and have less complex business models and fewer users, who are often close to the company and can gain other information about the business first-hand. Therefore, it makes sense to have a separate GAAP that is less complicated, has fewer disclosures, and is geared toward fewer users who have access to additional information about the company.

Note that there are some private companies that are global and complex. These entities have the option to use IFRS. Private entities that are planning to go public may find it easier to follow IFRS right from the beginning.[20]

The AcSB has created a subcommittee called the **IFRS Discussion Group (IFRS DG)**. The IFRS DG meetings create a public forum, allowing for discussion of issues arising in Canada as a result of implementing IFRS. The group's mandate is to raise awareness of these issues and to make recommendations to the AcSB for referral to the International Accounting Standards Board and its subcommittees.

International Accounting Standards Board (IASB)

Most countries agree that more uniform standards are needed. As a result, the International Accounting Standards Committee (IASC) was formed in 1973 to try to lessen the areas of difference among countries' own standards. The IASC's objective in standard setting was to work generally to improve and harmonize regulations, accounting standards, and procedures relating to the presentation of financial statements. Eliminating differences is not easy: the financial reporting objectives in each country are different, the institutional structures are often not comparable, and there are strong national tendencies in most countries. Nevertheless, much progress has been made since the IASC's early days. In 2001, a new International Accounting Standards Board (IASB) was created, replacing the IASC.

According to the IASB website: "Our mission is to bring transparency, accountability and efficiency to financial markets around the world by developing IFRS Standards. Our work

---

[19]AcSOC membership consists of senior members from business, finance, government, academe, the accounting and legal professions, regulators, and the financial analyst community. The members have a broad perspective on the complex issues facing standard setters. The goal is to achieve full representation across the spectrum of stakeholders (www.frascanada.ca).

[20]Actually, there are at least seven sets of GAAP in Canada. The *CPA Canada Handbook—Accounting* is divided into five parts: Part I—IFRS (for publicly accountable enterprises), Part II—Accounting Standards for Private Enterprises, Part III—Accounting Standards for Not-for-profit Organizations, Part IV—Accounting Standards for Pension Plans, and Part V—Pre-changeover Canadian GAAP (pre-2011). In addition, the *Public Sector Accounting Standards Handbook* contains GAAP for governments. Finally, as mentioned earlier, the Ontario Securities Commission allows Canadian public companies that are U.S. reporting issuers to use U.S. GAAP.

serves the public interest by fostering trust, growth and long-term financial stability in the global economy."[21]

Illustration 1.7 shows the IASB's governing structure. The **IFRS Foundation** monitors, reviews the effectiveness of, appoints members to, and funds the IASB. The IASB is supported by the **IFRS Advisory Council** (which is composed of various user groups) and the **Accounting Standards Advisory Forum** (which is composed of national standard setters). Both groups provide guidance and advice to the Board. The **IFRS Interpretations Committee (IFRIC)** studies issues where guidance in IASB is insufficient or non-existent. If necessary, it produces additional guidance in the form of IFRIC interpretations, which are part of IFRS.

ILLUSTRATION 1.7

How the IASB Is Set Up[22]

Illustration 1.8 shows the various stages in producing an international standard.

ILLUSTRATION 1.8

Evolution of a New or Revised IFRS[23]

---

[21]According to the IFRS Foundation Constitution: www.ifrs.org. Note that the IASB also establishes standards for small and medium-sized private entities (referred to as IFRS for SMEs). Since the AcSB produces separate standards for Canadian private entities, Canadian companies do not follow IFRS for SMEs. Copyright © IFRS Foundation. All rights reserved. Reproduced with permission.

[22]*Pocket Guide to IFRS Standards: The Global Financial Reporting Language*, 2017, p. 20. Copyright © International Financial Reporting Standards Foundation. Copyright © IFRS Foundation. All rights reserved. Reproduced with permission.

[23]*Pocket Guide to IFRS Standards: The Global Financial Reporting Language*, 2017, p. 21. Copyright © International Financial Reporting Standards Foundation. Copyright © IFRS Foundation. All rights reserved. Reproduced with permission.

The process is very similar to the Canadian and U.S. processes. One difference is the increased and more common use of discussion papers (DPs). DPs are often the predecessors of exposure drafts (EDs). When IFRS are being formulated, the IASB may issue a DP and ask for comment letters just as it does for EDs. Therefore, by the time the proposed standard gets to the ED stage, many key decisions have already been made.[24]

The IASB is a dominant global standard-setting body. As of April 2017, over 139 countries required or allowed the use of IFRS (with 126 of these countries requiring IFRS for all or most domestic-listed companies).[25]

Financial Accounting Standards Board and the Securities and Exchange Commission

In the United States, the Financial Accounting Standards Board (FASB) is the major standard-setting body, although it does not have final authority over standards—instead, the Securities and Exchange Commission (SEC) does. (Note that the SEC is a national body, whereas in Canada, the securities commissions are provincial.) The SEC has confirmed its support for the FASB by stating that financial statements that conform to FASB standards will be presumed to have substantial authoritative support. The SEC has also indicated in its reports to the U.S. government that it continues to believe that the private sector (for example, the FASB) should stay responsible for establishing and improving accounting standards, although the commission must oversee any changes. Like the Canadian securities commissions, the SEC also indicates its position on various financial reporting issues through what it calls financial reporting releases.

U.S. GAAP has and will continue to have a significant impact on GAAP in Canada for several reasons. First, because Canadian GAAP is based on principles and is fairly open to interpretation, **accounting professionals have often (in the past) relied on the more prescriptive, specific guidance** provided in U.S. GAAP.

Second, many Canadian companies are also listed on U.S. stock markets and exchanges, such as NASDAQ (National Association of Securities Dealers Automated Quotation) and the NYSE (New York Stock Exchange). To be listed on a U.S. exchange, these companies must follow U.S. GAAP[26] or IFRS.[27] As we move toward international harmonization in accounting standards, the U.S. standards will continue to influence Canadian and international standards due to the significant capital pool of these markets.

This brings us to the third point, which concerns the fact that the United States has not adopted IFRS. In October 2002, the FASB and IASB signed an agreement (the Norwalk Agreement) that formalized their commitment to converge U.S. and international accounting standards. In 2008, the FASB and IASB reaffirmed their commitment to continue to work together, although it is not clear whether this relationship will continue. In addition, the SEC issued a document known as the "Roadmap"[28] outlining issues regarding the convergence initiative. More recently, the United States has been examining how moving to IFRS might work from a practical perspective, if at all. It is uncertain whether the FASB will proceed with IFRS.

---

[24]For instance, the IASB issued a DP for revenue recognition, financial statement presentation, and fair value measurement and received 221, 227, and 136 comment letters, respectively. These comment letters were used to draft the subsequent ED and the final standard.

[25]www.iasplus.com, "Use of IFRS Standards by Jurisdiction." A complete up-to-date list is on the website. Some of these countries allow companies to alter IFRS (that is, not follow certain standards or follow alternative standards). The IASB has also done an analysis, which may be found at www.ifrs.org under "Analysis of IFRS Jurisdictional Profiles."

[26]The make-up of U.S. GAAP is discussed in What Do the Numbers Mean 1.4.

[27]Before 2007, Canadian companies that were listed on U.S. exchanges could use IFRS or pre-changeover Canadian GAAP but had to reconcile their reporting to U.S. GAAP. This reconciliation was difficult and cumbersome and many Canadian entities decided to just use U.S. GAAP for their U.S. filings. The OSC allows Canadian reporting issuers that list on U.S. stock exchanges or markets to use U.S. GAAP or IFRS according to Canadian Securities Administrators National Instrument 52-107. Note that many non-U.S. companies that list on U.S. exchanges use IFRS. According to the *Pocket Guide to IFRS Standards: The Global Financial Reporting Language* (published by the IFRS Foundation in 2017, p. 21), there are 500 foreign firms that file in the United States, with a total market capitalization of U.S. $7 trillion.

[28]SEC, *Roadmap for the Potential Use of Financial Statements Prepared in Accordance with International Financial Reporting Standards by U.S. Issuers*, November 2008.

Provincial Securities Commissions

Law Provincial securities commissions[29] oversee and monitor the capital marketplace in their jurisdiction. They ensure that participants in the capital markets (including companies, auditors, brokers and dealers, and investors) respect securities law and legislation so that, ultimately, the marketplace is fair. For instance, the British Columbia Securities Commission (www.bcsc.bc.ca) states that its mission is to protect and promote the public interest by fostering:

- a securities market that is fair and warrants public confidence and
- a dynamic and competitive securities industry that provides investment opportunities and access to capital.

As part of ensuring that investors have access to the information that they need in order to make informed decisions, securities law and legislation require that companies that issue shares to the public and whose shares trade on a Canadian stock exchange or stock market produce GAAP financial statements.

Ontario is home to the largest stock exchange in Canada, the **Toronto Stock Exchange (TSX)**, and most large Canadian public companies are therefore registered with the Ontario Securities Commission (OSC). The OSC reviews and monitors the financial statements of companies whose shares are publicly traded on the TSX so that it can judge whether the statements present the financial position and results of operations of these companies fairly.[30] It also issues its own Management Discussion and Analysis disclosure requirements.[31] Stock exchanges, as well as securities commissions, can fine a company and/or delist the company's shares from the stock exchange, which removes a company's access to capital markets.

Generally Accepted Accounting Principles

LEARNING OBJECTIVE 3

Explain the meaning of generally accepted accounting principles (GAAP) and the significance of professional judgement in applying GAAP.

GAAP includes **not only specific rules, practices, and procedures** for particular circumstances but also **broad principles and conventions that apply generally**, including underlying concepts.

GAAP Hierarchy

The **GAAP hierarchy** identifies the sources of GAAP and lets users know which ones should be consulted first in asking the question: What is GAAP?

---

[29]In Canada, securities regulation is carried out by each province, with each of the 10 provinces and three territories being responsible for the companies in its jurisdiction. Many critics feel that this is cumbersome and costly, and are therefore lobbying for a national securities commission. There has been some movement in this direction. The provincial and territorial regulators have formed the Canadian Securities Administrators (CSA). The CSA is mainly responsible for developing a harmonized approach to securities regulation across the country (www.securities-administrators.ca). For now, the CSA collects and archives all filings that are required under the securities regulations of each province and territory (www.sedar.com).

[30]The OSC has a Continuous Disclosure Team that regularly reviews public companies' financial statements and other regulatory filings. The team plans to review each company at least every four years. Results of the review are published on the OSC website.

[31]For instance, in 2016, CSA Staff Notice 52-306 (Revised) on "Non-GAAP Earnings Measures" was issued.

ASPE Under ASPE, GAAP is divided into **primary sources** and **other sources**. Based on the *CPA Canada Handbook*, Part II, Section 1100, the **primary** sources of GAAP (in descending order of authority) are as follows:

- *Handbook* Sections 1400 to 3870, including Appendices; and
- **Accounting guidelines**, including Appendices.

Other sources of GAAP noted in Section 1100 include:

- **Background information and basis for conclusion documents issued by the AcSB**
- **Pronouncements** by accounting standard-setting bodies in other jurisdictions, although it is not necessary to comply with guidance in IFRS or other GAAP in order to comply with Canadian GAAP for private entities[32]
- **Approved drafts of primary sources** of GAAP where no primary sources apply (such as exposure drafts)
- **Research studies**
- **Accounting textbooks, journals, studies, and articles**
- Industry practice (as long as it is consistent with the concepts in Section 1000)

In general, primary sources must be looked at **first** for how to treat an issue. If primary sources do not deal with the specific issue, the entity should use accounting policies that are **consistent with the primary sources**. The policies should also be developed through the use of professional judgement in accordance with the concepts in Section 1000, which is the **conceptual framework**. (The conceptual framework is the foundation of financial reporting and is examined in greater detail in Chapter 2.) As business is constantly changing and new business transactions and contracts are regularly being entered into, the other listed sources are also important sources of GAAP.

IFRS Under IFRS, GAAP incorporates the following, which include guidance that is integral to the standard:[33]

- IFRS
- International Accounting Standards (IAS) (standards that were issued by the IASB's predecessor)[34]
- Interpretations (IFRIC or the former Standards Interpretation Committee [SIC])

What happens when a company has an accounting issue but the above do not specifically apply? In that case, management uses professional judgement, considering the conceptual framework and the applicability of similar IFRS in similar situations, as long as the resulting information is relevant and reliable. The following sources would be considered, in descending order:

- Pronouncements of other standard-setting bodies
- Other accounting literature
- Accepted industry practices

In essence, although the wording is different, both hierarchies are similar, as follows:

- They provide guidance that helps answer the question "What is GAAP?"
- They rank sources and consider certain sources as more important.
- They are grounded in the conceptual framework.
- They establish the value of and expect the use of professional judgement.

---

[32]*CPA Canada Handbook—Accounting*, Part II, Section 1100.20.

[33]IAS 8. Copyright © IFRS Foundation. All rights reserved. Reproduced with permission.

[34]The IASB decided to retain the old numbering system for these standards for familiarity and to signal that these standards are older and originated from the IASB's predecessor, the IASC.

Professional Judgement

Professional judgement plays an especially important role in ASPE and IFRS.[35] This is due to the basic philosophy of Canadian and international accountants on standard setting: **there cannot be a rule for every situation**. ASPE and IFRS are therefore based primarily on **general principles** rather than **specific rules**. The basic premise is that professional accountants with significant education and experience will be able to apply these principles appropriately to any situation.

In a principles-based standard-setting system, the conceptual framework underlies the standards. Therefore, accountants either apply specific standards that are based on the conceptual framework, or, if no specific standard exists, the accountant uses the conceptual framework and professional judgement to reason through to an answer, as noted previously as part of the GAAP hierarchy.[36]

Challenges and Opportunities for the Accounting Profession

LEARNING OBJECTIVE 4

Discuss some of the challenges and opportunities for accounting.

During 2001 and 2002, the future of the capital market system was challenged by several major corporate scandals and business failures, as mentioned earlier in this chapter. This was followed by the subprime lending and banking crisis starting in 2007, which triggered a period of significant global economic instability. The resulting turmoil has given stakeholders a chance to re-examine their roles in the capital marketplace and to question if and how they add value to the system. Advancements in technology and the way we view information are also having a profound impact on accounting. It is useful to continually review the role accountants play in the capital markets in light of constant change. Are we doing what we should? Can we do better? Do others understand what we do?

Oversight in the Capital Marketplace

`Ethics` `Law` While most stakeholders fulfill their roles in the capital marketplace in a very positive and productive manner, some do not. Should the markets be self-regulating? Accounting scandals at companies such as Enron, Cendant, Sunbeam, Rite-Aid, and Livent have prompted governments to increase regulation in the capital marketplace. In the United States, the Sarbanes-Oxley Act **(SOX)**, enacted in 2002, gave more resources to the SEC to fight fraud and poor business practices.[37] The SEC was able to increase its policing efforts and approve new auditor independence rules and materiality guidelines for financial reporting. In addition, SOX introduced sweeping changes to the institutional structure of the accounting profession. The following are some of the legislation's key provisions:

- An **accounting oversight board** was established and given oversight and enforcement authority. It was mandated to establish auditing, quality control, and independence standards and rules, and is known as the **Public Company Accounting Oversight Board (PCAOB)**.

---

[35]As mentioned earlier, U.S. GAAP is often said to be more prescriptive, and provides significantly more detailed guidance than IFRS and ASPE.

[36]Neither ASPE nor IFRS is a perfect principles-based system. The conceptual frameworks for both were written after many of the other standards were written. Therefore, there may be inconsistencies. Standard setters are working to get rid of these inconsistencies in the standards.

[37]Sarbanes-Oxley Act of 2002, H. R. Rep. No. 107-610 (2002).

- Stronger **independence rules** were made for auditors. Audit partners, for example, are required to rotate every five years.
- Chief executive officers (CEOs) and chief financial officers (CFOs) are required to **certify** that the financial statements and company disclosures are appropriate and fairly presented. They must **forfeit bonuses and profits** if there is a restatement of their companies' accounting disclosures.
- Company management must **report on the effectiveness of the financial reporting internal control systems** and the auditors must assess and report on these internal controls.
- Audit committees must be comprised solely of **independent members** and companies must disclose whether at least one member is a "financial expert" and if not, why not.
- Companies must disclose whether they have a **code of ethics** for their senior financial officers.

Stakeholders in Canada were faced with the question of whether similar reforms should be put in place in our capital markets. Companies that issue shares in the United States are bound by SOX[38] and these companies therefore have no choice. Many stakeholders felt that unless Canada matched the standard set by SOX, Canadian capital markets would be seen as inferior. As a result, many of the SOX requirements have now been put in place in Canada, as follows:

- The **Canadian Public Accountability Board (CPAB)**[39] was formed to look after similar issues to the PCAOB.
- The **Canadian Securities Administrators** (CSA) issued rules that, among other things, require company management to take **responsibility for the appropriateness and fairness of the financial statements**, public companies to have **independent audit committees**, and public accounting firms to be subject to the CPAB.[40]
- The **CSA** issued a harmonized statement that requires much **greater disclosures**, including ratings from rating agencies, payments by companies to stock promoters, legal proceedings, and details about directors, including their previous involvement with bankrupt companies.[41]
- The **Province of Ontario** made amendments to its Securities Act.

The impact of these reforms on North American capital markets has been to put more emphasis on government regulation and less on self-regulation. Do we have the balance right? At a minimum, there is greater understanding of the roles that the various stakeholders play. However, stakeholders should be doing things because they are the right things to do, not just because they must do so by law.

Centrality of Ethics

Ethics   Accountants play significant roles in the capital marketplace. Illustration 1.3 shows that they are part of every stakeholder group, including preparers, auditors, regulators, investors, and others. They are therefore central in making the capital marketplace efficient and effective. However, decision-making is a complicated and human process. In accounting, as in other areas of business, ethical dilemmas are common. Some of these dilemmas are simple and easy to resolve. Many, however, are complex, and solutions are not obvious. Management biases—either internally prompted (by the desire to maximize bonuses, for example) or

---

[38]Sarbanes-Oxley Act of 2002, Section 106 (2002).

[39]www.cpab-ccrc.ca.

[40]CSA Multilateral Instrument 52-109, 52-110, and 52-108. A multilateral instrument is an instrument that has been adopted by one or more CSA jurisdictions.

[41]CSA revised National Instrument 51-102, "Continuous Disclosure Obligations." A national instrument is an instrument that has been adopted by all CSA jurisdictions.

externally prompted (by the desire to meet analysts' earnings expectations, for example)—are the starting point of many ethical dilemmas. These biases sometimes lead to an emphasis on short-term results over long-term results and place accountants (both inside and outside the company) in an environment of conflict and pressure. Basic questions such as "Is this way of communicating financial information transparent?", "Does it provide useful information?", and "What should I do in this circumstance?" cannot always be answered by simply following GAAP or the rules of the profession. Technical competence is not enough when decisions have an ethical side.

Doing the **right thing** and making the right decision are not always easy. What is right is not always evident and the pressures to "bend the rules," "play the game," or "just ignore it" can be considerable. In these cases, self-interest must be balanced with the interests of others. The decision is more difficult because no consensus has emerged among business professionals as to what constitutes a comprehensive ethical system.

This process of **ethical sensitivity** and choosing among alternatives can also be complicated by time pressures, job pressures, client pressures, personal pressures, and peer pressures. Throughout this textbook, ethical considerations are presented to make you aware of the types of situations that you may encounter in your professional responsibility. Many believe that accountants play the role of a conscience in the capital marketplace. That is our challenge and opportunity. Throughout the text, we will refer to specific ethics-related issues with an ethics icon. The cases at the end of each chapter focus on professional judgement and accounting policy choices. They also include ethical considerations.

Standard Setting in a Political Environment

When it comes to influencing the development of accounting standards, the most powerful force may be the stakeholder. **Accounting standards result as much from political action as they do from careful logic or research findings.** As part of their mandate, standard setters include stakeholders as members, giving them a **formal voice** in the process. Furthermore, through due process, interested parties can comment on proposed changes or new standards. This is generally a good thing.

However, stakeholders may want particular economic events to be accounted for or reported in a particular way, and they may fight hard to get what they want. They know that the most effective way to influence the standards that dictate accounting practice is to participate in formulating them or to try to influence or persuade the formulator. This is not necessarily optimal since the stakeholders who make themselves heard the loudest may get their way, to the detriment of others.

Should politics play a role in setting financial accounting and reporting standards? The AcSB and IASB do not exist in isolation. Standard setting is part of the real world, and it cannot escape politics and political pressures. That is not to say that politics in standard setting is necessarily bad. Since many accounting standards do have economic consequences,[42] it is not surprising that special interest groups become vocal and critical (some supporting, some opposing) when standards are being formulated. Given this reality, a standard-setting body must pay attention to the economic consequences of its actions; at the same time, however, it should not issue pronouncements that are motivated mainly by politics. While paying attention to their constituencies, standard setters should base their standards on sound research and a conceptual framework that is grounded in economic reality. Work done by the European Financial Reporting Advisory Group has resulted in some widely supported conclusions that standard setters should undertake an analysis of the impact of potential changes during the standard-setting process.

The standard-setting process is difficult enough when a standard setter is a national one such as the AcSB. The political nature of standard setting has increased as more and more

---

[42]"Economic consequences" in this context means the impact of accounting reports on the wealth positions of issuers and users of financial information and the decision-making behaviour resulting from that impact. The resulting behaviour of these individuals and groups could have harmful financial effects on the providers of the financial information (enterprises). For a more detailed discussion of this phenomenon, see Stephen A. Zeff, "The Rise of Economic Consequences," *Journal of Accountancy* (December 1978), pp. 56–63.

countries have adopted IFRS. The IASB, for instance, has 14 members from many countries. It must consider the needs of all users when creating or changing standards. These user needs become more diverse as we consider the different political, cultural, economic, social, and legal settings of an increasing number of countries.

One political factor is how the standard-setting bodies are financed. The IASB has committed to four principles to ensure that the nature and amount of funding for standard setting do not result in politicization of the process. The principles are as follows per the IASB website.

Funding should be:

1. **Broad-based:** It should not rely on one or a few sources.
2. **Compelling:** Constituents should not be allowed to benefit from the standards without contributing to the process of standard setting.
3. **Open-ended:** Financial commitments for funding should not be contingent upon any particular outcomes that may infringe upon independence in the standard-setting process.
4. **Country-specific:** Funding should be shared by the major economies on a proportionate basis.[43]

The challenge for standard setters is to find a balance between letting stakeholders have a voice while not bowing to undue political pressures. You might find it very interesting to follow along as a standard is being set. Information such as IASB minutes, presentations to the IASB, exposure drafts, discussion papers, and comment letters are all available on the IASB website (www.ifrs.org). You will see that some spirited discussion takes place and there are many dissenting views.

Principles versus Rules

As mentioned in this chapter, Canadian, U.S., and international accounting standards are becoming increasingly interrelated. All parties are committed to converging toward a high-quality set of standards, but there are still many issues that standard setters must deal with. One key issue is the **principles versus rules** debate regarding GAAP.

U.S. GAAP has historically been more prescriptive (even though it is based on principles) and thus has leaned toward the rules-based approach. **In a rules-based approach— much like the Canadian tax system**—there is a rule for most things (even though the rule may be based on a principle). The result is that the body of knowledge in a rules-based approach is significantly larger than that in a principles-based approach. There is also a tendency for companies to interpret the rules literally. Many companies take the view that, if there is no rule for a particular situation, they are free to choose whatever treatment they think is appropriate (within reason). Similarly, many believe that as long as they comply with a rule, even in a narrow sense, they are in accordance with GAAP. Some accountants, auditors, lawyers, and companies favour a GAAP body of knowledge that is more prescriptive because it may be easier to **defend** how to account for a particular item.

Unfortunately, the rules-based approach does not always emphasize the importance of communicating the **best** information for users. Just because a practice is defensible does not mean it provides the best information. This particular issue is a significant one for the United States as it continues to debate whether to adopt IFRS. (See **What Do the Numbers Mean? 1.4.**)[44]

---

[43]These principles were established in 2006. The IASB's 2016 revenue, including contributions and revenues from sale of products, was £30.5 million. Twenty percent of this was from sale of products and the majority of the remainder was from stakeholder contributions.

[44]Note that adoption of IFRS is not necessarily the same as convergence with IFRS. Under convergence, the two sets of standards might still exist side by side and have differing aspects.

What Do the Numbers Mean? 1.4

Will the United States migrate to IFRS? That is a big question. As mentioned previously, there is a significant difference philosophically between IFRS, which is a high-level, principles-based system, and U.S. GAAP, which is a more detailed, prescriptive system of GAAP. While IFRS consists of between 2,000 and 3,000 pages, before 2009, U.S. GAAP had more than 2,000 separate standards, many containing multiple pages. The bodies of knowledge are different in size and level of detailed guidance. The FASB has since restructured the U.S. body of knowledge, reorganizing the separate standards into one large set of U.S. GAAP. This initiative is known as the codification project and it brings all of U.S. GAAP under one roof. This is a giant move forward in helping to make U.S. GAAP more accessible and user-friendly.

Before the codification, the FASB surveyed more than 1,400 people who use U.S. GAAP. Some 80% felt it was confusing and 85% felt the required level of research to determine how to account for something was excessive.

While the codification project makes U.S. GAAP more user-friendly, it is still fundamentally different from IFRS. For a number of years, the FASB and the IASB have been working together to harmonize various specific standards so that they are worded essentially the same. Moving from a prescriptive, detailed body of knowledge to a more high-level, principles-based body of knowledge may not be so easy, however. In a speech in December 2010, the deputy chief accountant of the SEC, Paul Beswick, was asked what a reasonable approach would be for the United States to move over to IFRS. Mr. Beswick proposed what he called a "condorsement" approach: part endorsement and part convergence. Under this approach, U.S. GAAP would continue to exist and the FASB would continue to work through each IFRS standard to ensure it was suitable for the U.S. capital market. (This is the convergence aspect.) In addition, the FASB would consider new IASB standards and make a decision whether to endorse them or not. Whether U.S. companies will ever be allowed to use IFRS remains to be seen.

Currently, the FASB has implemented a three-part strategy for seeking greater comparability in accounting standards internationally:

1. Develop high-quality GAAP standards.
2. Actively participate in the development of IFRS.
3. Enhance relationships and communications with other national standard setters.

There are significant divergent views between the IASB and FASB in the areas of impairment of financial instruments, accounting for certain lease contracts, and treatment of insurance contracts. The list of areas where the two standard-setting bodies differ in their views is growing. Thus it seems less and less likely that the United States will adopt IFRS for U.S. companies.

Source: Financial Accounting Foundation, FASB Accounting Standards Codification, 2011, and the FASB website, http://fasb.org/home.

IFRS and ASPE are more principles-based. The body of knowledge is smaller and the idea is that one or more principles form the basis for decision-making in many differing scenarios. In addition, professional judgement is fundamental. There is less emphasis on right and wrong answers. Rather, the financial reporting is a result of carefully reasoned application of the principle to the business facts. In a principles-based body of knowledge, bright-line tests are minimized. **Bright-line tests** are often numeric benchmarks for determining accounting treatment. For instance, when determining how to account for a lease under Section 3065 (ASPE), there is a test that looks at whether the lease term is greater than or equal to 75% of the economic life of the asset. The trouble with bright-line tests is that they create a distinctive threshold that is either met or not. Reality is not so clear-cut.

The challenge for standard setters is to ensure that the body of knowledge:

1. rests on a cohesive set of principles and a conceptual framework that are consistently applied,
2. is sufficiently flexible to be of use in many differing business situations and industries, and
3. is sufficiently detailed to provide good guidance but not so big as to be unwieldy.

Throughout the text, we will focus on the development of professional judgement within a principles-based GAAP system (IFRS and ASPE). The cases at the end of each chapter are particularly good for helping you understand how to apply GAAP and deal with choice and ambiguity.

Impact of Technology

As **providers of information**, accountants **identify, measure, and communicate useful information to users**. Technology affects this process in many profound ways. Information is becoming increasingly abundant and available through technology. Companies now file required disclosures electronically with securities commissions. Investors can tap into conversations, including earnings calls, briefings with analysts, and interviews with senior management and market regulators. This gives stakeholders easy access to a significant amount of very timely company information. The Internet allows users to quickly find related information about a company. Companies can disclose more detail online, which the user can then aggregate and analyze. From the company's perspective, providing information over the Internet gives it access to a much larger group of users. Information can also be targeted to specific users, and costs are greatly reduced as well.

Some of the main drawbacks of technology concern accessibility: Will all users have the knowledge and ability to access the information? Equal access is certainly important to ensure fairness for all stakeholders. Another issue is the quality and reliability of the information, especially since the information may not be audited. Are certain sites and content more reliable than others? Finally, will making increasing amounts of information available in this way leave companies open to information theft or manipulation?

As technology advances at a dramatic pace, will this lead to online real-time and/or continuous reporting with access for all users? The industry is moving toward the use of extensible business reporting language (XBRL). This system allows a company to tag its information so that users can more easily extract it for analyzing and other use. The CSA has launched a voluntary filing program, encouraging companies to use XBRL when filing their financial information with securities regulators.

In addition, the IASB has created what is known as the IFRS taxonomy. A taxonomy is a system for classifying things such as financial statement elements and amounts. In 2014, the IASB put together the IFRS Taxonomy Consultative Group. The group provides a technical advisory and review forum to keep abreast of the issues and keep the IFRS taxonomy up to date and relevant.

With XBRL and the IFRS taxonomy, companies can streamline financial information collecting and reporting, while consumers of financial data such as investors, analysts, financial institutions, and regulators can find, receive, compare, and analyze data more quickly and efficiently.

The challenge is to embrace technological opportunities without losing the quality and content of traditional financial reporting.

Integrated Reporting

Financial performance is rooted in a company's business model (that is, the earnings process, how companies finance the process, and what resources companies invest in). Historically, this has not always been the focus of financial accounting. However, a company's ability to articulate its strategic vision and carry out that vision does affect financial performance. The accounting information system is also part of a larger system of information management—a system that contains a significant amount of non-financial information.

Institutional investors are increasingly looking for more information about how a company deals with environmental, social, and governance issues.[45]

The **International Integrated Reporting Committee (IIRC)** has been established to look at this broader view of reporting and includes in its membership corporations, investors, accountants, regulators, academics, standard setters, and others. Its goal is to work toward a more integrated framework for business reporting that includes management information, governance and compensation, and financial and sustainability reporting.[46]

The opportunity is to view financial reporting as part of a larger integrated "ecosystem" and not in isolation.

---

[45]In March 2014, CPA Canada and the TMX Group (which operates the Toronto Stock Exchange) issued a publication entitled "A Primer for Environmental & Social Disclosure." It is available online (www.tsx.com).

[46]See the publication entitled "The International IR Framework," published by the IIRC (December 2013) (available at http://integratedreporting.org). The IIRC is now completing what it calls its "breakthrough phase" during which its goal was to shift companies toward early adoption of the IR framework. It will shortly enter what it refers to as its "global adoption phase."

Conclusion

Financial reporting is standing at the threshold of some significant changes. Is the accounting profession up to the challenge? We believe that the profession is reacting responsibly and effectively to correct the shortcomings that have been identified and to move forward with a new vision. Because of its great resources and expertise, the profession should be able to develop and maintain high standards. This is and will continue to be a difficult process that requires time, logic, and diplomacy. Through a well-chosen mix of these three ingredients, however, the accounting profession will continue to be a leader on the global business stage.

Review and Practice

Summary of Learning Objectives

1 Understand the financial reporting environment.

Accounting provides reliable, relevant, and timely information to managers, investors, and creditors so that resources are allocated to the most efficient enterprises. Accounting also provides measurements of efficiency (profitability) and financial soundness.

Investors, creditors, management, securities commissions, stock exchanges, analysts, credit rating agencies, auditors, and standard setters are some of the major stakeholders. Illustration 1.4 explains what is at stake for each one.

The objective of financial reporting is to communicate information that is useful to key decision-makers such as investors and creditors in making resource allocation decisions (including assessing management stewardship) about the resources and claims to resources of an entity and how these are changing.

Ideally, all stakeholders should have access to the same information in order to ensure that good decisions are made in the capital marketplace. This is known as information symmetry. However, this is not the case—there is often information asymmetry. Of necessity, management has access to more information so that it can run the company. It must also make sure that it does not give away information that might harm the company, such as in a lawsuit where disclosure might cause the company to lose. Aside from this, information asymmetry exists because of management bias whereby management acts in its own self-interest, such as wanting to maximize management bonuses. This is known as moral hazard in accounting theory. Information asymmetry causes markets to be less efficient. It may cause stock prices to be discounted or costs of capital to increase. In addition, it might restrict good companies from raising capital in a particular market where relevant information is not available (referred to as adverse selection in accounting theory). The efficient markets hypothesis is felt to exist only in a semi-strong form, meaning that publicly available information is assimilated into stock prices.

2 Explain the need for accounting standards and identify the major entities that influence standard setting and financial reporting.

The accounting profession has tried to develop a set of standards that is generally accepted and universally practised. This is known as GAAP (generally accepted accounting principles). Without this set of standards, each enterprise would have to develop its own standards, and readers of financial statements would have to become familiar with every company's particular accounting and reporting practices. As a result, it would be almost impossible to prepare statements that could be compared. In addition, accounting standards help deal with the information asymmetry problem.

The Canadian Accounting Standards Board (AcSB) is the main standard-setting body in Canada for private companies, pension plans, and not-for-profit entities. Its mandate comes from the Canada Business Corporations Act and Regulations as well as provincial acts of incorporation. For public companies, GAAP is International Financial Reporting Standards (IFRS) as established by the International Accounting Standards Board (IASB). Public companies are required to follow GAAP in order to access capital markets, which are monitored by provincial securities commissions. The U.S. Financial Accounting Standards Board (FASB) is also important because it influences IFRS standard setting. Private companies may choose to follow IFRS. Public companies that list on U.S. stock exchanges may choose to follow U.S. GAAP.

3 Explain the meaning of generally accepted accounting principles (GAAP) and the significance of professional judgement in applying GAAP.

Generally accepted accounting principles are either principles that have substantial authoritative support, such as the *CPA Canada Handbook*, or those arrived at through the use of professional judgement and the conceptual framework.

Professional judgement plays an important role in Accounting Standards for Private Enterprises (ASPE) and IFRS since much of GAAP is based on general principles, which need to be interpreted.

4 Discuss some of the challenges and opportunities for accounting.

Some of the challenges facing accounting are oversight in the capital markets, centrality of ethics, standard setting in a political environment, principles- versus rules-based standard setting, the impact of technology, and integrated reporting. All of these require the accounting profession to continue to strive for excellence and to understand how accounting adds value in the capital marketplace.

Practice Problem

At the completion of Bloom Ltd.'s audit, the president, Judy Bloom, asks about the meaning of the phrase "in conformity with IFRS" that appears in your audit report on the management's financial statements. Judy observes that the meaning of the phrase must include something more and different than what she thinks of as "standards." Judy is curious about the pronouncements that are encompassed in IFRS and asks, "if there are different types of pronouncements, which are more authoritative than others?"

Instructions

a. Describe the pronouncements that comprise IFRS.

b. Explain to Judy how a company determines which type of pronouncement takes precedence when deciding the recognition, valuation, and disclosure related to a particular program.

Solution

a. International Financial Reporting Standards are the standards and interpretations issued by the IASB and its predecessor body, the IASC:

1. International Financial Reporting Standards (IFRS)

2. International Accounting Standards (IAS)

3. International Financial Reporting Committee Interpretations (IFRIC)

4. Statements of the Interpretations Committee (SIC)

5. While the underlying Conceptual Framework for Financial Reporting underlies all these pronouncements, the Conceptual Framework itself is not an IFRS accounting standard.

b. The IASB sets out a hierarchy of sources that make up IFRS generally accepted accounting principles (GAAP). These are, in descending order:

1. When there is a specific standard that applies (use those listed in [a] above).

2. If there is no specific IFRS standard, then management applies professional judgement in determining what is GAAP, considering the conceptual framework and accounting standards used for similar transactions and events.

3. Other sources might be referred to. These include, for example, pronouncements of other standard-setting bodies that use a similar conceptual framework, the accounting literature and accepted industry practices.

Any company indicating that it is preparing its financial statements in conformity with IFRS must comply with all these standards and interpretations.

Key Terms

Accounting Standards Advisory Forum, p. 1-15

Accounting Standards Board (AcSB), p. 1-12

Accounting Standards for Private Enterprises (ASPE), p. 1-13

Accounting Standards Oversight Council (AcSOC), p. 1-14

accrual-basis accounting, p. 1-8

adverse selection, p. 1-10

aggressive accounting, p. 1-11

bright-line tests, p. 1-23

Canadian Institute of Chartered Accountants (CICA), p. 1-13

Canadian Public Accountability Board (CPAB), p. 1-20

capital allocation, p. 1-4

Chartered Professional Accountants of Canada (CPA Canada), p. 1-13

conservative accounting, p. 1-11

CPA Canada Handbook, p. 1-13

decision-usefulness approach, p. 1-7

due process, p. 1-14

efficient markets hypothesis, p. 1-10

entity perspective, p. 1-7

ethical dilemmas, p. 1-20

financial accounting, p. 1-3

Financial Accounting Standards Board (FASB), p. 1-12

financial reporting, p. 1-3

financial statements, p. 1-3

GAAP hierarchy, p. 1-17

generally accepted accounting principles (GAAP), p. 1-6

general-purpose financial statements, p. 1-7

IFRS Advisory Council, p. 1-15

IFRS Discussion Group (IFRS DG), p. 1-14

IFRS Foundation, p. 1-15

information asymmetry, p. 1-9

information symmetry, p. 1-9

institutional investors, p. 1-8

International Accounting Standards Board (IASB), p. 1-12

IFRS Interpretations Committee (IFRIC), p. 1-15

International Financial Reporting Standards (IFRS), p. 1-13

International Integrated Reporting Committee (IIRC), p. 1-24

management bias, p. 1-11

managerial accounting, p. 1-3

moral hazard, p. 1-11

objective of financial reporting, p. 1-7

Ontario Securities Commission (OSC), p. 1-12

professional judgement, p. 1-19

proprietary perspective, p. 1-8

provincial securities commissions, p. 1-12

Public Company Accounting Oversight Board (PCAOB), p. 1-19

Securities and Exchange Commission (SEC), p. 1-12

stakeholders, p. 1-5

stewardship, p. 1-11

Toronto Stock Exchange (TSX), p. 1-17

Assignment Material

Note: **Enabling Competencies** Completion of this end-of-chapter material will help develop CPA enabling competencies (such as ethics and professionalism, problem-solving, and decision-making and communication) and technical competencies. We have highlighted selected items with a specific integration word mark and material in *WileyPLUS* has been linked to the competencies. All cases emphasize integration, especially of the enabling competencies. The brief exercises, exercises, and problems generally emphasize problem-solving and decision-making.

Brief Exercises

BE1.1 (LO 1) How does accounting help the capital allocation process?

BE1.2 (LO 1) Identify at least three major stakeholders that use financial accounting information and briefly explain how these stakeholders might use the information from financial statements.

BE1.3 (LO 1) What are the major objectives of financial reporting?

BE1.4 (LO 1) Describe what is meant by information asymmetry.

BE1.5 (LO 1) How does information asymmetry hurt investors in the capital marketplace?

BE1.6 (LO 2) What is the value of having a common set of standards in financial accounting and reporting?

BE1.7 (LO 1) What is the likely limitation on "general-purpose financial statements"?

BE1.8 (LO 2) What are some of the developments or events that occurred between 1900 and 1930 that helped bring about changes in accounting theory or practice?

BE1.9 (LO 2) Which organization is currently dominant in the world for setting accounting standards? Explain.

BE1.10 (LO 2) Explain the role of the Canadian Accounting Standards Board (AcSB) in establishing generally accepted accounting principles.

BE1.11 (LO 2) What is the role of the Ontario Securities Commission (OSC) in standard setting?

BE1.12 (LO 2) What are some possible reasons why another organization, such as the OSC or the Securities and Exchange Commission (SEC), should not issue financial reporting standards?

BE1.13 (LO 2) What are the sources of pressure that change and influence the development of accounting principles and standards?

BE1.14 (LO 3) Some individuals have argued that all Canadian companies should follow the same set of accounting principles. Explain why there are multiple sets of standards in Canada.

BE1.15 (LO 3) If you were given complete authority to decide this, how would you propose that accounting principles or standards be developed and enforced?

BE1.16 (LO 3) If you had to explain or define "generally accepted accounting principles," what essential characteristics would you include in your explanation?

BE1.17 (LO 3) Explain the difference between primary and other sources of GAAP.

BE1.18 (LO 4) The chair of the Financial Accounting Standards Board (FASB) at one time noted that "the flow of standards can only be slowed if (1) producers focus less on quarterly earnings per share and tax benefits and more on quality products, and (2) accountants and lawyers rely less on rules and law and more on professional judgement and conduct." Explain his comment.

BE1.19 (LO 4) Some individuals have argued that the AcSB and the International Accounting Standards Board (IASB) need to be aware of the economic consequences of their pronouncements. What is meant by "economic consequences"? What are some of the dangers if politics play too much of a role in the development of financial reporting standards?

BE1.20 (LO 4) What is the difference between principles-based and rules-based accounting standards? In which category does IFRS belong? ASPE? Explain.

BE1.21 (LO 4) One writer recently noted that 99.4% of all companies prepare statements that are in accordance with GAAP. Why then is there such concern about fraudulent financial reporting?

BE1.22 (LO 4) Some foreign countries have reporting standards that are different from standards in Canada. What are some of the main reasons why reporting standards are often different among countries?

BE1.23 (LO 4) How are financial accountants pressured when they need to make ethical decisions in their work? Is having technical mastery of GAAP enough to practise financial accounting?

BE1.24 (LO 4) What are some of the major challenges facing the accounting profession?

BE1.25 (LO 4) The Sarbanes-Oxley Act was enacted to combat fraud and curb poor reporting practices. What are some key provisions of this legislation? Are these provisions in effect in Canada?

Cases

Refer to the Case Primer on the Student Website and in WileyPLUS *to help you answer these cases.*

CA1.1 Sherry Tsang has just started up a small corporation that produces clothing. She has applied for and received a government grant. The grant will automatically be renewed as long as the business shows a profit at year end. Because she is trying to control costs, Sherry will prepare the financial statements. The bank has lent Sherry money and is also waiting for the year-end statements. It will decide whether to renew the loan or not.

Instructions

a. **Ethics** Discuss the ethical issues of Sherry preparing her own financial statements.

b. Which GAAP should she follow? Explain.

CA1.2 **Ethics** When the AcSB issues new standards, the implementation date is usually 12 months after the issue date, but early implementation is encouraged. In this case, Paula Prentice, controller, is discussing with her financial vice-president the need for early implementation of a standard that would result in a fairer presentation of the company's financial condition and earnings. When the financial vice-president determines that early implementation of the standard will lower the reported net income for the year, he discourages Prentice from implementing the standard until it is required.

Instructions

Discuss the ethical issues of the financial VP's request.

(CMA adapted)

CA1.3 Verity Retail Limited was a private company that experienced cash flow difficulties and hired new management to turn the company around. The company then went public and the shares sold at $15 per share. Within months, however, the share price plummeted and Beatle Clothing Inc. acquired the company for $1 per share when Verity was on the threshold of bankruptcy.

Instructions

a. Which GAAP should the company have followed when it went public? Explain.

b. Who were the stakeholders in this situation?

c. Explain what was at stake and why and how stakeholders were affected when the share price plummeted.

CA1.4 **Finance** The National Credit Rating Agency downgraded the credit rating of Grand Limited by two levels from BB to B+. The credit rating agency was concerned about the company's ability to refinance portions of its debt. Both BB and B+ are considered "junk" bonds and are below the BBB− category, which is the lowest grade that many pension and mutual funds are allowed to hold.

Financial statement analysts said the company's financial profile had weakened due to tight debt covenants and resulting cash flow restrictions.

Instructions

a. Discuss whether the credit rating agency is a stakeholder from Grand Limited's perspective.

b. **Ethics** Discuss any bias that Grand might have when it issues its financial statements.

CA1.5 Save the Trees (STT) is a not-for-profit organization whose mandate is to keep our cities green by planting and looking after trees. STT is primarily funded by government grants and must comply with a significant number of criteria in order to obtain additional funds. One such requirement is that the entity prepare financial statements in accordance with GAAP.

Instructions

a. Identify who the stakeholders are in this case and explain why they are stakeholders.

b. Which GAAP should the entity follow and why?

Research and Analysis

RA1.1 Standardized versus Voluntary Disclosure

Some critics argue that having different organizations establish accounting principles is wasteful and inefficient. Instead of mandating accounting standards, each company could voluntarily disclose the type of information it considered important. In addition, if an investor wanted additional information, the investor could contact the company and pay to receive the desired information.

Instructions

Comment on the appropriateness of this viewpoint.

RA1.2 Politicization of Standard Setting

Some accountants have said that the development and acceptance of generally accepted accounting principles (that is, standard setting) is undergoing a "politicization." Some use the term "politicization" in a narrow sense to mean the influence by government agencies, particularly the securities commissions, on the development of generally accepted accounting principles. Others use it more broadly to mean the compromise that results when the bodies that are responsible for developing generally accepted accounting principles are pressured by interest groups (securities commissions, stock exchanges, businesses through their various organizations, financial analysts, bankers, lawyers, and so on).

Instructions

a. What are the arguments in favour of the politicization of accounting standard setting?

b. What are the arguments against the politicization of accounting standard setting?

(CMA adapted)

RA1.3 Accounting Standard-Setting Models

Three models for setting accounting standards follow:

1. The purely political approach, where national legislative action decrees accounting standards

2. The private, professional approach, where financial accounting standards are set and enforced by private, professional actions only

3. The public/private mixed approach, where standards are set by private-sector bodies that behave as though they were public agencies and the standards are mostly enforced through government agencies

Instructions

a. Which of these three models best describes standard setting in Canada? Explain your choice.

b. Why are companies, financial analysts, labour unions, industry trade associations, and others actively interested in standard setting?

c. Cite an example of a group other than the AcSB that tries to establish accounting standards. Speculate on why such a group might want to set its own standards.

RA1.4 Continuous Reporting Model

The increased availability and accessibility of information has had a major impact on the process of financial reporting. Most companies have websites and make available to stakeholders a significant amount of financial information, including annual reports and other financial data. This has sparked the question of whether companies should use a continuous reporting model instead of the current discrete model where financial statements are generally issued only quarterly and annually. Under a continuous reporting model, the company would make more information available to users in real time or perhaps on a "delayed" real-time basis (such as weekly).

Instructions

What are the pros and cons of a continuous reporting model? Consider the various stakeholders in the capital marketplace.

RA1.5 **Fair Presentation**

Nortel Networks Inc., the former Canadian telecommunications giant, was accused of misstating its financial statements. The auditors for the company signed audit reports in which they stated that Nortel's financial statements were fairly presented.

Instructions

How is it possible that a company can misrepresent its financial statements and still receive a "clean" audit opinion from its auditors?

RA1.6 **Government Regulation**

As mentioned in the chapter, the capital marketplace's reaction to recent corporate failures has been to increase the amount of government regulation.

Instructions

a. Identify what steps Canada and the United States have taken to increase government regulation of the capital marketplace.

b. What other options to strengthen the capital marketplace might have been available to stakeholders?

c. What are the strengths and weaknesses of government regulation in this area?

RA1.7 **Disclosures**

Hans Hoogervorst, Chair of the IASB, has spoken of issues related to the IASB's disclosure initiative, particularly corporate reporting of non-GAAP measures and the need for professional judgement when making disclosure decisions.

Instructions

Access one of Mr. Hoogervorst's speeches dealing with non-GAAP measures and IAS 1 *Presentation of Financial Statements* on the IASB website (www.ifrs.org).

a. What is meant by "non-GAAP measures"? Explain Mr. Hoogervorst's position on such measures and why they are a concern to the IASB.

b. What disclosure issues does Mr. Hoogervorst identify that require professional judgement? What does he mean by "boilerplate" disclosures? What is meant by professional judgement?

c. Review the requirements of IAS 1 and identify three requirements where preparers of the financial statements would need to exercise professional judgement.

RA1.8 **Stakeholder Information Needs**

Financial statements can be a valuable tool for many parties interested in a company's performance. Consider a public company in Alberta that drills for oil and sells it to refineries in the United States. The company prepares its financial statements using IFRS and publishes the statements on its website.

Instructions

a. Who are the stakeholders who would be interested in the company's financial reporting?

b. What information would be most relevant to these stakeholders?

RA1.9 **Limits on Disclosure**

There are many situations in which management of a company may want to disclose more or less information about its operations. Consider a manufacturer that is preparing for the launch of a new product line. The information available to management may include the product's projected release date, the associated costs, the price at which the product will be sold, and the results of any market research performed as to the expected sales.

Instructions

Ethics Why might management want to share the information above with the public? Why might they try to keep this information private? Also consider the impact of management's decision on those outside of the organization.

RA1.10 Disclosure Decision

It is a goal of standard setters to develop accounting standards that will provide comparability across organizations and over time. However, there are instances when professional judgement must be used in determining the correct amount of disclosure. Assume the role of the ethical accountant working as an advisor for ABC Inc., a toy manufacturer. ABC Inc. has received reports that a particular toy may have led to children's injuries. At this time, the information available is inconclusive as to whether the toy actually caused the injury or whether it was a result of user error. Management must now decide whether to communicate the potential malfunction to the public or to wait for additional information.

Instructions

a. Describe the reasons for management to await additional information before making a public statement about the toy's safety.

b. Describe the reasons management might communicate the potential defect to the public immediately.

c. **Ethics** In your role as the ethical accountant, what course of action would you recommend and why?

RA1.11 Users of Integrated Reporting

The integrated reporting initiative discussed in this chapter focuses on extending the disclosure of financial statements to include more information about a company and its objectives and performance.

Instructions

Discuss what type of financial statement users would be in favour of the additional disclosure required for integrated reporting.

RA1.12 Funding Principles

The IASB has instituted four principles related to its funding to ensure that funding does not lead to politicization of standard setting. The standards specify that funding should be broad-based, compelling, open-ended, and country-specific. This differs from the funding processes for the AcSB and FASB.

Instructions

a. Discuss these four principles and what impact they have on the standard-setting process.

b. What issues might arise if these principles did not exist?

c. The AcSB and FASB do not have the same funding principles in place. Why might the same principles not work for the AcSB and FASB?

RA1.13 Materiality

Materiality has always been an elusive concept in IFRS. It is defined in a general sense, but, in the past, there has been little guidance to help preparers and others apply the concept. For this reason, the IASB decided it was important to issue a Practice Statement on materiality (in late 2015) as part of its disclosure initiative. In 2017, the IASB revised the Practice Statement, which is called Practice Statement 2.

While a Practice Statement does not form an authoritative part of IFRS, it has been subject to due process, having received public exposure and input. It falls somewhere between educational guidance and implementation guidance as far as its authority is concerned.

Instructions

Read Practice Statement 2 on materiality and respond to the following questions:

a. What was the reason for undertaking the project on materiality?

b. How is materiality defined?

c. What general guidance is provided on how to apply the materiality concept to financial reporting decisions?

RA1.14 IASB

Michael Sharpe, then-deputy chairman of the International Accounting Standards Committee, made the following comments before the Financial Executives International 63rd Annual Conference:

There is an irreversible movement toward the harmonization of financial reporting throughout the world. The international capital markets require an end to:

1. The confusion caused by international companies announcing different results depending on the set of accounting standards applied. Recent announcements by Daimler-Benz (now DaimlerChrysler) highlight the confusion that this causes.

2. Companies in some countries obtaining unfair commercial advantages from the use of particular national accounting standards.

3. The complications in negotiating commercial arrangements for international joint ventures caused by different accounting requirements.

4. The inefficiency of international companies having to understand and use myriad accounting standards depending on the countries in which they operate and the countries in which they raise capital and debt. Executive talent is wasted on keeping up to date with numerous sets of accounting standards and the never-ending changes to them.

5. The inefficiency of investment managers, bankers, and financial analysts as they seek to compare financial reporting drawn up in accordance with different sets of accounting standards.

6. Failure of many stock exchanges and regulators to require companies subject to their jurisdiction to provide comparable, comprehensive, and transparent financial reporting frameworks giving international comparability.

7. Difficulty for developing countries and countries entering the free market economy, such as China and Russia, in accessing foreign capital markets because of the complexity of and differences between national standards.

8. The restriction on the mobility of financial service providers across the world as a result of different accounting standards.

Clearly, eliminating these inefficiencies by having comparable high-quality financial reporting used across the world would benefit international businesses.

Instructions

Research the issue using the Internet and answer the following questions:

a. What is the International Accounting Standards Board and what is its relationship with the International Accounting Standards Committee?

b. Which stakeholders might benefit from the use of international accounting standards?

c. What do you believe are some of the major obstacles to harmonization?

RA1.15 Real World Emphasis   Canadian Coalition for Good Governance (CCGG)

The Canadian Coalition for Good Governance (www.ccgg.ca) was formed in 2002 and represents a significant number of institutional investors in Canada.

Instructions

a. What is the purpose of the CCGG?

b. How does an institutional investor differ from other investors?

c. In your opinion, what impact would the presence of a large number of institutional investors have on management's financial reporting decisions?

d. Identify three current members of the CCGG. Go to these member companies' websites and identify some of their most significant investments. What total dollar value of investments does each have under management?

RA1.16 SOX and the CPAB

In 2002, the Sarbanes-Oxley Act (SOX) was passed in the United States to strengthen the capital marketplace. In the following year, there were many debates in Canada about whether the securities commissions here should adopt the same regulations. In the end, Canada did adopt a similar level of regulation with the introduction of the Canadian Public Accountability Board (CPAB).

Instructions

a. Why was the Sarbanes-Oxley Act issued and what are its key components?

b. What impact do you think the Act had on the U.S. capital marketplace?

c. What was the major spillover effect in the Canadian regulatory environment?

d. Since SOX and the CPAB have been in place, continuing pressure has been felt in a number of areas relating to auditor independence requirements. Identify three current and emerging issues the CPAB has studied and reported on. What is the CPAB's position?

RA1.17 Convergence of IASB and FASB GAAP

From the IFRS website (www.ifrs.org), locate reports relating to the convergence between U.S. GAAP and IFRS. These reports provide a picture of the extent to which convergence is being achieved on significant accounting and reporting issues. Some of the significant differences between U.S. GAAP and IFRS are related to the perceived rules-based approach taken by the United States compared with the principles-based approach of IFRS.

Instructions

Review the reports and respond to the following questions:

a. In your own words, state the differences between a rules-based approach and a principles-based approach.

b. Refer to the updates related to the revenue standard. What are the reasons provided for needing convergence on this standard? Have the differences been resolved in the converged revenue standard?

c. Refer to the updates on the work undertaken on the impairment model within the financial instruments standard. Identify whether the proposed amendments resulted in a converged impairment standard.

d. Refer to the updates on the leases project. What are the reasons provided for needing convergence on this standard? Have the differences been resolved in a converged lease standard?

RA1.18   Real World Emphasis   Financial Reporting Pressures

What follows is part of the testimony from Troy Normand in the case of WorldCom, the U.S. telecommunications company that filed for bankruptcy in 2002 after an accounting scandal. He was a manager in the corporate reporting department and is one of five individuals who pleaded guilty to various fraud-related charges. He testified in the hope of receiving no prison time when he was ultimately sentenced.

Q: Mr. Normand, if you could just describe for the jury how the meeting started and what was said during the meeting?

A: I can't recall exactly who initiated the discussion, but right away Scott Sullivan acknowledged that he was aware we had problems with the entries, David Myers had informed him, and we were considering resigning.

He said that he respected our concerns but that we weren't being asked to do anything that he believed was wrong. He mentioned that he acknowledged that the company had lost focus quite a bit due to the preparations for the Sprint merger, and that he was putting plans in place and projects in place to try to determine where the problems were, why the costs were so high.

He did say he believed that the initial statements that we produced, that the line costs in those statements could not have been as high as they were, that he believed something was wrong and there was no way that the costs were that high.

I informed him that I didn't believe the entry we were being asked to do was right, that I was scared, and I didn't want to put myself in a position of going to jail for him or the company. He responded that he didn't believe anything was wrong, nobody was going to be going to jail, but that if it later was found to be wrong, that he would be the person going to jail, not me.

He asked that I stay, don't jump off the plane, let him land softly, that's basically how he put it. And he mentioned that he had a discussion with Bernie Ebbers asking Bernie to reduce projections going forward and Bernie had refused.

Q: Mr. Normand, you said that Mr. Sullivan said something about don't jump out of the plane. What did you understand him to mean when he said that?

A: Not to quit.

Q: During this meeting, did Mr. Sullivan say anything about whether you would be asked to make entries like this in the future?

A: Yes, he made a comment that from that point going forward we wouldn't be asked to record any entries, high-level late adjustments, that the numbers would be the numbers.

Q: What did you understand that to mean, the numbers would be the numbers?

A: That after the preliminary statements were issued, with the exception of any normal transactions, valid transactions, we wouldn't be asked to be recording any more late entries.

Q: I believe you testified that Mr. Sullivan said something about the line cost numbers not being accurate. Did he ask you to conduct any analysis to determine whether the line cost numbers were accurate?

A: No, he did not.

Q: Did anyone ever ask you to do that?

A: No.

Q: Did you ever conduct any such analysis?

A: No, I didn't.

Q: During this meeting, did Mr. Sullivan ever provide any accounting justification for the entry you were asked to make?

A: No, he did not.

Q: Did anything else happen during the meeting?

A: I don't recall anything else.

Q: How did you feel after this meeting?

A: Not much better actually. I left his office not convinced in any way that what we were asked to do was right. However, I did question myself to some degree after talking with him wondering whether I was making something more out of what was really there.

Instructions

Answer the following questions:

a. What appears to be the ethical issue in this case?

b. Was Troy Normand acting improperly or immorally?

c. What would you do if you were Troy Normand?

d. Who are the major stakeholders in this case?

RA1.19 **Prudence**

In 2012, Hans Hoogervorst, Chairman of the IASB, gave a speech at the FEE Conference on Corporate Reporting of the Future entitled "The Concept of Prudence: Dead or Alive?" This speech was in answer to many who opposed the elimination of "prudence" from the recently revised qualitative characteristics of useful financial statement information. The speech can be found on the IFRS website at www.ifrs.org. Subsequently, in the May 2015 Exposure Draft "Conceptual Framework for Financial Reporting," the notion of "prudence" was reintroduced into the conceptual framework, with an explanation in the basis for conclusions that accompanied the Exposure Draft. The concept has since been adopted in the revised conceptual framework.

Instructions

a. Mr. Hoogervorst indicated in his 2012 speech that there are many instances that demonstrate that IFRS implementation has not led to a loss of prudence. Discuss some specific examples he provides in which the revised conceptual framework of IFRS continues to instill the concept of prudence, in financial reporting.

b. Why was the idea of prudence originally removed from the earlier version of the qualitative characteristics of the conceptual framework? Why was the concept reintroduced in the 2015 Exposure Draft?

c. How does professional judgement affect the application of the concept of prudence? Will it be applied any differently than it was originally?

RA1.20 Data Analytics **Big Data, Data Analytics, and Artificial Intelligence**

In the past two decades, our access to information has grown exponentially. With innovative technologies, we can access the Internet quickly and cheaply, and storage and computing capabilities continue to increase.

As accountants, we must ask ourselves what this means to us as a profession.

Instructions

Terms such as Big Data, data analytics, and artificial intelligence are being used with increased frequency as the discussion around information and the Internet continues.

a. Define each of these terms by doing a quick search on the Internet.

b. How may each of these concepts be used in accounting?

c. What opportunities do each of these concepts present to the profession? What are the challenges?

CHAPTER 2

Conceptual Framework Underlying Financial Reporting

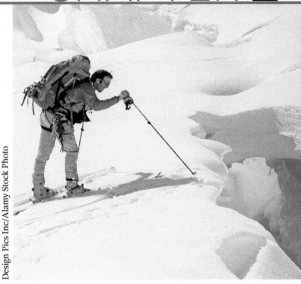

Design Pics Inc/Alamy Stock Photo

A "Prudent" Approach to Financial Reporting Concepts

The accounting profession relies on the conceptual framework to underpin financial reporting standards and to guide accountants' judgement when applying these standards. And the profession relies on the standard setters to get the conceptual framework right.

So when the International Accounting Standards Board (IASB) changed the conceptual framework for International Financial Reporting Standards (IFRS) in 2010 and removed the concept of conservatism, or what the IASB calls prudence, some in the profession cried foul. Conservatism is the principle that net assets and net income should not be overstated. The pre-2010 conceptual framework stated that prudence is using some caution when exercising judgements to make estimates in cases of uncertainty. But the IASB removed the term in the 2010 framework because it feared that it would be misunderstood as being inconsistent with the notion of information neutrality. The Board felt that in exercising prudence, accountants could introduce bias.

When the IASB issued a Discussion Paper in 2013 to revise the conceptual framework, it again left out the idea of prudence. But many who responded to comments wanted it put back. Some argued that prudence is one of the most important tenets of accounting. When the IASB released its new framework in 2018, it once again referred to prudence.

The IASB said it was persuaded by arguments that prudence can actually help achieve neutrality when selecting and applying accounting policies. Some stakeholders wanted the Board to adopt the idea of "asymmetric prudence," where there needs to be more persuasive evidence to recognize income or assets than to recognize expenses or liabilities, or to choose measurement methods that recognize losses earlier than gains. The Board did not adopt asymmetric prudence because it felt that it could sometimes conflict with the conceptual framework's two fundamental characteristics of useful information: that it is relevant and that it provides a faithful representation of a company's financial information.

Instead, in 2018, the IASB reintroduced the term "prudence," describing it in the new conceptual framework as "cautious prudence," which it says is "the exercise of caution when making judgements under conditions of uncertainty." The Board hoped that would satisfy stakeholders. "The previous conceptual framework led a lot of people to believe that the Board did not think prudence to be important," said Hans Hoogervorst, IASB Chair. "And I think in the new conceptual framework, that confusion will be gone."

Sources: "IFRS Conceptual Framework Feedback Statement: Conceptual Framework for Financial Reporting," IASB, March 2018; video of Hans Hoogervorst to accompany the news release "IASB Completes Revisions to its Conceptual Framework," IASB, March 29, 2018; Peter Hogarth, "Dear Prudence," PricewaterhouseCoopers blog, http://pwc.blogs.com/ifrs/2015/06/dear-prudence.html, June 3, 2015.

LEARNING OBJECTIVES After studying this chapter, you should be able to:	CHAPTER OUTLINE The chapter headings related to the learning objective are:	CPA COMPETENCIES Competencies addressed by each learning objective are as follows:
1. Indicate the usefulness and describe the main components of a conceptual framework for financial reporting.	**Conceptual Framework** • Rationale for a conceptual framework • Development of the conceptual framework • Information asymmetry revisited • Objective of financial reporting	**1.1.1, 1.2.1, 1.2.2**
2. Identify the qualitative characteristics of accounting information.	**Qualitative Characteristics of Useful Information** • Fundamental qualitative characteristics • Enhancing qualitative characteristics • Trade-offs	**1.1.2, 1.2.1, 1.2.2, 3.1.3, 4.3.4**
3. Define the basic elements of financial statements.	**Elements of Financial Statements** • Assets • Liabilities • Equity • Revenues/income • Expenses • Gains/losses	**1.2.1, 1.2.2**
4. Describe the foundational principles of accounting.	**Foundational Principles** • Recognition/derecognition • Measurement • Presentation and disclosure	**1.2.1, 1.2.2, 1.2.3, 6.1.1, 6.2.1**
5. Explain the factors that contribute to choice and/or bias in financial reporting decisions.	**Financial Reporting Issues** • Principles-based approach • Financial engineering • Fraudulent financial reporting	**1.2.1, 1.2.2, 2.3.2, 4.3.5**
6. Discuss current trends in standard setting for the conceptual framework.	**IFRS/ASPE Comparison** • Looking ahead	**1.1.4**

Preview of Chapter 2

Users of financial statements need relevant and reliable information. To help develop this type of financial information, accountants use a conceptual framework that guides financial accounting and reporting. The conceptual frameworks developed by the AcSB and IASB are not considered to be accounting standards and therefore they do not override any of the ASPE or IFRS that specifically deal with accounting for certain transactions and events. In addition, there may be some inconsistencies between the newer conceptual frameworks and the older accounting standards (in both ASPE and IFRS) since the older standards may have been created using an older conceptual framework (or none at all).

Conceptual Framework

LEARNING OBJECTIVE 1

Indicate the usefulness and describe the main components of a conceptual framework for financial reporting.

A **conceptual framework** is like a constitution: it is a "coherent system of interrelated objectives and fundamentals that can lead to consistent standards and that prescribes the nature, function, and limits of financial accounting and financial statements."[1] Many observers believe that the real contribution of standard-setting bodies, and even their continued existence, depends on the quality and usefulness of the conceptual framework.

Rationale for a Conceptual Framework

Why is a conceptual framework necessary? First, to be useful, **standard setting should build on an established body of concepts and objectives**. Having a soundly developed conceptual framework as their starting point, standard setters are then able to issue additional **useful and consistent** standards over time. The result is a **coherent** set of standards and rules, because they have all been built upon the same foundation. It is important that such a framework **increase** financial statement users' **understanding** of and **confidence** in financial reporting, and that it **enhance the comparability** of different companies' financial statements.

Second, by referring to an existing framework of basic theory, it should be possible to solve **new and emerging practical problems** more quickly. It is difficult, if not impossible, for standard setters to quickly state the proper accounting treatment for highly complex situations. Practising accountants, however, must solve such problems on a day-to-day basis. By using **good judgement**, and with the help of a **universally accepted conceptual framework**, it is hoped that accountants will be able to decide against certain alternatives quickly and to focus instead on a logical and acceptable treatment.

Development of the Conceptual Framework

Over the years, many organizations, committees, and interested individuals have developed and published their own conceptual frameworks, but no single framework has been universally accepted and relied on in practice. Realizing there was a need for a generally accepted

---

[1]"Conceptual Framework for Financial Accounting and Reporting: Elements of Financial Statements and Their Measurement," FASB discussion memorandum (Stamford, CT: FASB, 1976), p. 1 of the "Scope and Implications of the Conceptual Framework Project" section.

framework, in 1976 the Financial Accounting Standards Board (FASB) issued a three-part discussion memorandum entitled "Conceptual Framework for Financial Accounting and Reporting: Elements of Financial Statements and Their Measurement." It stated the major issues that would need to be addressed in establishing a conceptual framework for setting accounting standards and resolving financial reporting controversies. Based on this, six Statements of Financial Accounting Concepts were then published. A seventh statement, on accounting measurement, was added in 2000. The AcSB and IASB followed the FASB's example and issued their own respective frameworks.

Illustration 2.1 shows an overview of a conceptual framework.[2] At the first level, the objectives identify accounting's **goals and purposes**: these are the conceptual framework's building blocks. At the second level are the **qualitative characteristics** that make accounting information useful and the elements of financial statements (assets, liabilities, equity, revenues, expenses, gains, and losses).[3] At the third and final level are the **foundational principles** used in establishing and applying accounting standards.

ILLUSTRATION 2.1

Conceptual Framework for Financial Reporting

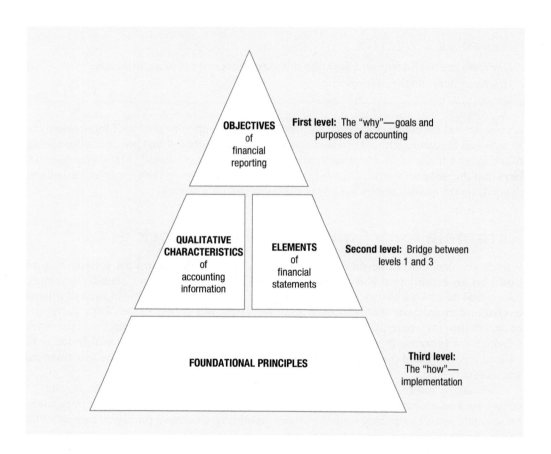

Significant Change As mentioned in the chapter-opening story, a new framework was issued by the IASB in March 2018. It deals with the objective of general-purpose financial reporting, qualitative characteristics of useful information, financial statements and the reporting entity, the elements of financial statements, recognition and derecognition, measurement, presentation and disclosure, and concepts of capital and capital maintenance. There are some

---

[2]Adapted from William C. Norby, "Accounting for Financial Analysis," *The Financial Analysts Journal*, March/April 1982, p. 22.

[3]IFRS does not define other comprehensive income as a separate element of the financial statements because it simply contains other elements, such as income and expenses. It is considered to be a subclassification of the income statement (statement of financial performance).

significant changes. This chapter incorporates ideas from this new framework. The AcSB has signalled that it will likely adopt the framework for private entities as well.

It is important to note that, in practice, applying the new conceptual framework may not necessarily change how things are presently accounted for, since the conceptual framework does not override specific IFRS, as we noted earlier. The new conceptual framework is effective January 1, 2020, for those financial statement preparers developing accounting policies. Having said that, the IASB planned to start using the conceptual framework immediately after it was issued.

Information Asymmetry Revisited

Theory As discussed in Chapter 1, investors and creditors need information in order to make sound resource allocation decisions. However, information in the capital marketplace is not always evenly accessible or available to investors and creditors. Stock markets and regulators go to great lengths to ensure information symmetry for all capital market participants so that no one is at a disadvantage. Despite this, various stakeholders often do not have the same information. This can be a problem because stakeholders may make suboptimal decisions because they are lacking good or complete information.

Financial statements play a large part in helping to ensure that investors, creditors, and others have access to information they need to make decisions. However, because of **adverse selection** and/or **moral hazard** (see Chapter 1), problems may arise. The moral hazard issue is worse where certain stakeholders such as accountants and owner-managers have expert knowledge that the rest of the capital marketplace does not. They may use this expertise to act in their own self-interest to the detriment of other capital marketplace participants such as investors.

A well-written conceptual framework based on sound principles may help address these information asymmetry concerns.

Objective of Financial Reporting

According to the conceptual framework, the objective of financial reporting is to communicate information that is **useful** to investors, creditors, and other users. Financial information is useful in making decisions about how to **allocate resources** (including assessing management stewardship). For example, a bank may need information in order to decide whether to lend a company money or call a loan. Similarly, an investor may need information about a company's profitability in order to decide whether to invest in it or divest. Management stewardship is how well management is using entity resources to create and sustain value.

Consequently, companies should provide information about their financial position, changes in financial position, and performance. They should also show how efficiently and effectively management and the board of directors have discharged their responsibilities to use the entity's resources wisely.[4]

Companies provide this information to users of financial statements through generalpurpose financial statements. These are basic financial statements that give information that meets the needs of **key users**.[5] The statements are intended to provide the most **useful information possible in a manner whereby benefits exceed costs** to the different kinds of users.

---

[4]IASB *IFRS Conceptual Framework*, Chapter 1. Copyright © IFRS Foundation. All rights reserved. Reproduced with permission.

[5]Investors and creditors are assumed to be the primary or key users. For not-for-profit entities, key users include members and contributors rather than investors.

Qualitative Characteristics of Useful Information

LEARNING OBJECTIVE 2
Identify the qualitative characteristics of accounting information.

Choosing an acceptable accounting method, the amount and types of information to be disclosed, and the format in which information should be presented involves determining **which alternative gives the most useful information for decision-making purposes** (decision usefulness). The conceptual framework's second level has identified the qualitative characteristics of accounting information that distinguish information that is better (more useful) for making decisions from information that is inferior (less useful). These characteristics are explained next.

Fundamental Qualitative Characteristics

Relevance and representational faithfulness (sometimes called faithful representation) are fundamental qualities that make accounting information useful for decision-making. Above all else, these two characteristics must be present.

Relevance

To be relevant, accounting information must be capable of **making a difference in a decision**. If a piece of information has no impact on a decision, it is irrelevant to that decision. Care should be taken to ensure that relevant information is included in financial reporting. Relevant information helps users make predictions about the final outcome of past, present, and future events; that is, it has predictive value. For example, separating income from continuing operations from that of operations that have been discontinued may help users predict future income. Relevant information also helps users confirm or correct their previous expectations; it has feedback/confirmatory value. For instance, providing information about rental income and the value of the investment in rental properties might help users assess how well management is managing the investment in rental properties.

When discussing relevance, we often hear about the notion of materiality. Materiality refers to how important a piece of information is. It is generally thought to be material if it would make a difference to the decision-maker. For instance, a major product defect would be of interest to a potential investor. Material information is relevant and should be included in the financial statements. When determining whether something is material or not, the amount in question is often compared with the entity's amounts of other revenues and expenses, assets and liabilities, or net income.

It is hard to give firm guidelines to decide when an item is or is not material because materiality depends on both a relative amount and relative importance. Example 2.1 looks at materiality calculations.

Example 2.1 | Materiality Comparison

Facts   The two sets of numbers below show relative size.

	Company A	Company B
Sales	$10,000,000	$100,000
Expenses	9,000,000	90,000
Income from operations	1,000,000	10,000
Unusual gain	20,000	5,000

During the particular period, the revenues and expenses, and therefore the net incomes, of Company A and Company B are proportional. That is, the amounts for Company A are 10 times larger than those for Company B. Each has an unusual gain.

Instructions   Is the unusual gain material?

Solution   In looking at the abbreviated income figures for Company A, it does not appear significant whether the amount of the unusual gain is presented separately or is merged with the regular operating income. It is only 2% of the operating income and, if merged, would not seriously distort the income figure. Company B has had an unusual gain of only $5,000, but it is relatively much more significant than the larger gain recognized by A. For Company B, an item of $5,000 amounts to 50% of its operating income. Obviously, including such an item in ordinary operating income would affect the amount of that income materially. In this example, we can therefore see the importance of an item's relative size in determining its materiality.

Audit & Assurance   4.3.4 Current auditing standards (CAS 320.A7) define what is material by using benchmark examples from different types of organizations. This standard considers 5% of pre-tax income from continuing operations for manufacturing companies and 1% of revenues for not-for-profit entities to be material. This is not a definitive rule and is a fairly simplistic view of materiality. We need to consider the item's impact on other factors, such as on key financial statement ratios and management compensation; in other words, on **any sensitive number on the financial statements**. In addition, both **quantitative** and **qualitative** factors must be considered in determining whether an item is material.

Qualitative factors might include illegal acts, failure to comply with regulations, or inadequate or inappropriate description of an accounting policy. Materiality is also a factor in a large number of internal accounting decisions. Judgements should be determined based on reasonableness and practicality with, for example:

- the amount of classification required in a subsidiary expense ledger,
- the degree of accuracy required in prorating expenses among the departments of a business, and
- the extent to which adjustments should be made for accrued and deferred items.

In other words, we must sensibly apply the materiality constraint. Only by exercising good judgement and professional expertise can we find reasonable and appropriate answers. **What Do the Numbers Mean? 2.1** explores the issue of materiality in auditing.

What Do the Numbers Mean? 2.1

As noted earlier, the concept of materiality is used in financial reporting to help determine if the way something is accounted for would influence decisions made by users of financial statements. How is this concept used in auditing? The overall objective of the audit is to determine whether the financial statements are materially misstated or not. The auditor must complete audit procedures to gain this assurance.

An auditor would use the concept of materiality as follows:

1. In the planning stages: to help decide how many and what type of audit procedures to perform on particular transactions or balances. More work would be done on balances and transactions that are thought to be material.

2. During the audit: to refine the amount and type of audit procedures being done, given the findings. For instance, in the planning stages, the auditor might not think something is material but when the audit is being performed, some new information might come to light.

3. In assessing whether the financial statements are materially misstated and whether they can give an unmodified audit opinion, which states that the financial statements are fairly presented. The auditor will generally find things that need adjusting in the financial statements and must decide whether these adjustments have to be made or not. As long as the financial statements are not materially misstated, an unmodified opinion may be given.

Below is an excerpt from the audit report for **Air Canada**. Note the reference to materiality. PwC (the external auditors) gave Air Canada an unmodified audit opinion.

Opinion

In our opinion, the consolidated financial statements present fairly, in all material respects, the financial position of Air Canada and its subsidiaries as at December 31, 2017 and December 31, 2016 and their financial performance and their cash flows for the years then ended in accordance with International Financial Reporting Standards as issued by the International Accounting Standards Board.

Montreal, Quebec
February 15, 2018

Representational Faithfulness

Accounting information is representationally faithful to the extent that it faithfully reflects or represents the underlying economic substance of an event or transaction, not just its legal form. Although the legal form may be the starting point in terms of understanding the nature of a transaction, it is often necessary to look behind the legal form. Companies sometimes structure transactions a certain way from a legal perspective in order to manage risk, protect the company from lawsuits, or minimize income taxes. Thus, the legal form of the transaction may be quite complex and may differ from the economic substance or intent. Where this happens, the conceptual framework requires that the financial statements reflect the economics of the transaction notwithstanding the legal structure. We will refer back to this notion of **economic substance over legal form** throughout the text as we begin to look at more complex transactions.

This notion of representing economic reality is sometimes called transparency. If financial statement users read the financial statements, can they see what lies beneath the numbers? This is critical since the statements are meant to tell a story about the business. Is this a risky business? Is it a mature business? Is it capital-intensive?

How do we ensure that this information is appropriately presented? Information that is representationally faithful is **complete, neutral**, and **free from error**. In addition, highly uncertain estimates affect representational faithfulness. For instance, where the only information about an amount (such as the estimated potential loss on a lawsuit) is highly uncertain, perhaps additional disclosure may be necessary to explain this. We will return to the issue of measurement later in this chapter and again throughout the text.

Completeness is the idea that the statements should include all information needed to portray the underlying events and transactions. Care must be taken to ensure that pertinent information is included since it is possible to misrepresent something by not including all pertinent information. Often this is a question of the amount of details to be presented. For instance, it is important to note the nature of capital assets that an entity has under its control, including property, plant, and equipment. But presenting the amortized cost of such investments might not be sufficient if some of these assets are leased. The presumption about most property, plant, and equipment that is reported on a statement of financial position is that the company has legal title to the property. Therefore, if this is not the case—in other words, the assets are leased—this additional information should be presented.

Neutrality means that information should not be selected to **favour one set of interested parties over another**. The information should not be manipulated in any way. Factual, truthful, unbiased information needs to be the overriding consideration when preparing financial information. **What Do the Numbers Mean? 2.2** examines how neutrality fits with conservatism, which was mentioned in our feature story.

What Do the Numbers Mean? 2.2

How does the concept of **neutrality** fit with the notion of conservatism? Few conventions in accounting are as misunderstood as conservatism. In situations involving uncertainty and professional judgement, historically, the concept of conservatism has meant that **net assets and net income would not be overstated**. Conservatism acknowledges a **pre-existing tendency** of companies to overstate net assets and net income and it acts to counterbalance this tendency.

Users of financial statements are more tolerant of understated net assets and net income than overstated balances. Does the use of conservatism represent a bias? Many believe that it does. The concept of conservatism was originally downplayed in the 2015 IASB Exposure Draft relating to the conceptual framework in favour of neutrality. Having said that, there are many existing standards, both in IFRS and ASPE, where conservatism is embedded. For instance, where cost is used as a measurement basis

(as opposed to fair value), accountants feel quite justified and even compelled to override the historical cost principle and write down the carrying value of an impaired asset. However, accountants are not always so quick to recognize an increase in the asset's value. After much consultation, the IASB decided to reintroduce the concept of conservatism in the new IASB conceptual framework, noting that caution should be exercised when uncertainty exists. The IASB calls this prudence. The concept is more even-handed, however, since in defining the word "prudence," the conceptual framework notes that care should be taken to ensure, for instance, that assets and income are not overstated but not understated either.

The AcSB includes the concept of conservatism in its conceptual framework, noting that conservatism affects the concept of neutrality in an acceptable way. Thus these two notions (neutrality and conservatism) are not necessarily in conflict with each other.

As noted above, neutrality is supported by the concept of conservatism/prudence. In practice, management needs to use many assumptions because of uncertainty in financial reporting, such as uncertainty caused by accrual accounting. For instance, revenues are recorded when earned and not necessarily when cash is received. Thus, companies must estimate the amount of revenue that will be realized or eventually collected. When choosing these assumptions, management must use its best estimates (**management best estimate**) in order to portray the economic reality. Management best estimate assumptions are supposed to be unbiased, and involve management making diligent efforts to obtain and use all information that it has access to in order to come up with the best-quality information.

Ethics Producing financial statements with biased information can have significant negative consequences, not only for investors and creditors, but also for financial statement preparers and company management.

There is another aspect to neutrality: neutrality in standard setting. Some observers argue that standards should not be issued if they cause undesirable economic effects on an industry or company. (This is the **economic consequences argument**, which we mentioned in Chapter 1.) Standards must be free from bias, however, or we will no longer have **credible financial statements**. Standard setters should therefore choose the best standards regardless of economic consequences. If the accounting results in users changing their decisions, then by definition, the information is decision-relevant.[6]

Freedom from error means that the information must be reliable. The task of converting economic events (which are constantly changing and difficult to measure) to numbers in a set of financial statements is complex. Management must make estimates and use judgement in determining how to portray events and transactions. This does not mean that information must be "**perfectly accurate in all respects**."[7] Often, there is no correct or single right way to portray economic reality. For instance, how does a company portray the impact of a major ecological disaster such as an oil spill? Significant assumptions must be made about cleanup activities in order to estimate potential costs and liabilities.

How much effort should be put into obtaining information? Do we need to incur costs such as hiring engineers to help estimate? When is a mismeasurement an error? Information is more useful if it is free from material error, so every attempt should be made to achieve this. Companies must ensure that they invest in good information systems so that they can capture necessary information and must also have strong internal controls to ensure that errors and omissions are minimized.

In order to ensure that both fundamental characteristics of useful information (relevance and representational faithfulness) are present, the following three steps should be taken:

1. **Identify the economic event or transaction.** For instance, assume that an investment in shares of a publicly traded company has increased in value. This is an economic event.

2. **Identify the type of information about that transaction or event that would be relevant and can be faithfully represented.** The type of information that would be relevant might be the fair value of the investment.

3. **Assess whether the information is available and can be faithfully represented.** Since the shares are publicly traded, fair value is available and could easily be presented faithfully in the financial statements.[8]

---

[6]As a matter of fact, when the IASB issued its standard on joint arrangements in July 2011, it produced a document that assessed the effects of the standard (*IASB Effect Analysis*). In the document, the IASB noted the following: "We expect our standards to have economic effects, and we expect those effects to be beneficial for some entities and detrimental to others. For example, a change in financial reporting requirements might affect the cost of capital for individual entities by changing the absolute or relative level of information asymmetry associated with those entities."

[7]IASB, *IFRS Conceptual Framework*, 2.18. All references to the Conceptual Framework are to the new version that was issued by the IASB on March 29, 2018. Copyright © IFRS Foundation. All rights reserved. Reproduced with permission.

[8]IASB, *IFRS Conceptual Framework*, 2.21. Copyright © IFRS Foundation. All rights reserved. Reproduced with permission.

Enhancing Qualitative Characteristics

Enhancing qualitative characteristics include **comparability**, **verifiability**, **timeliness**, and **understandability**.

Comparability

Information that has been measured and reported in a similar way (both company to company and consistently from year to year) is considered comparable. Comparability enables users to **identify the real similarities and differences in economic phenomena** because these have not been obscured by accounting methods that cannot be compared. For example, the accounting for inventory is different under IFRS and U.S. GAAP. U.S. GAAP allows the use of last-in, first-out (LIFO) accounting, for instance, whereas IFRS does not. The result is that, in times of rising prices, companies using LIFO, such as Walmart Inc., will have a net income that is lower than companies not using LIFO, such as Loblaw Companies Limited.

It is important to remember that **resource allocation decisions involve evaluations of alternatives** and it is easier to make a valid evaluation if comparable information is available. Although it is not a substitute for comparable information, a full disclosure of information sometimes allows users to overcome inconsistencies in how information is presented.

Verifiability

Verifiability exists when knowledgeable, independent users achieve similar results or reach consensus regarding the accounting for a particular transaction. Some numbers are more easily verified than others; for example, cash can be verified by confirming with the bank where the deposit is held. Other numbers—such as accruals for pension liabilities—are more difficult (although not necessarily impossible) to verify, as many assumptions are made to arrive at an estimate. Numbers that are easy to verify with a reasonable degree of accuracy are often called "hard" numbers. Those that are more difficult to measure are called "soft" numbers.

Timeliness

Timeliness is also important. Information should be available to decision-makers before it loses its ability to influence their decisions. Quarterly reporting (issuing financial information every three months) provides information on a more timely basis. Thus, users have information throughout the year instead of having to wait until after the year end for the annual financial statements.

Understandability

Users need to have **reasonable knowledge** of business and financial accounting matters in order to understand the information in financial statements. However, financial information must also be of sufficient quality and clarity that it allows reasonably informed users to see its significance. This is the information's understandability. In addition, standard setters assume that users have the responsibility to review and analyze the information with reasonable diligence. This point is important: it means that the onus to prepare understandable statements and to be able to understand them rests with both the financial statement preparer and the user. This characteristic affects both how information is reported and how much is reported.

Where the underlying transactions or economic events are more complex (such as in the case highlighted in What Do the Numbers Mean? 2.3), the assumption is that users will seek the aid of an advisor. The preparer must also have a clear understanding of the legalities and economics of transactions in order to be able to portray them in the most meaningful way to users.[9]

---

[9]IASB, *IFRS Conceptual Framework*, 2.36. This represents a subtle shift in the level of knowledge required. Before the joint IASB/FASB conceptual framework project, users were expected to have only a reasonable understanding of business and a willingness to study the statements.

What Do the Numbers Mean? 2.3

An excerpt follows from the notes to the financial statements of **Enron Corp.** for the year ended December 31, 2000 (all figures are in U.S. dollars). The complexity of the business arrangements makes it difficult to understand the nature of the underlying transactions. It contributes to a set of financial statements that lack transparency. The choice of words also makes the note difficult to read.

> In 2000 and 1999, Enron sold approximately $632 million and $192 million, respectively, of merchant investments and other assets to Whitewing. Enron recognized no gains or losses in connection with these transactions. Additionally, in 2000, ECT Merchant Investments Corp., a wholly owned Enron subsidiary, contributed two pools of merchant investments to a limited partnership that is a subsidiary of Enron. Subsequent to the contributions, the partnership issued partnership interests representing 100% of the beneficial, economic interests in the two asset pools, and such interests were sold for a total of $545 million to a limited liability company that is a subsidiary of Whitewing. See Note 3. These entities are separate legal entities from Enron and have separate assets and liabilities. In 2000 and 1999, the Related Party, as described in Note 16, contributed $33 million and $15 million, respectively, of equity to Whitewing. In 2000, Whitewing contributed $7.1 million to a partnership formed by Enron, Whitewing, and a third party. Subsequently, Enron sold a portion of its interest in the partnership through a securitization. See Note 3.[10]

The IASB is currently working on a project to create a framework for disclosures in order to ensure that information presented is decision-useful including being understandable. More information is presented in the Looking Ahead section at the end of the chapter.

Trade-Offs

In general, preparers of financial information should identify all **relevant** information, then consider how best to ensure that the financial statements are presented such that they reflect the economic substance **(representational faithfulness)**. Both characteristics must be present in order to ensure the information is decision-relevant.

However, it is not always possible for financial information to have all the enhancing qualities of useful information. Trade-offs may exist. For instance, in the interest of providing more relevant information, a new standard may be applied prospectively. In this case, comparability (or **consistency** year to year) is temporarily sacrificed for better information in the future.

The accounting profession is constantly striving to produce financial information that meets all of the qualitative characteristics of useful information.

Too often, users assume that information is a cost-free commodity. But preparers and providers of accounting information know this is not true. This is why the **cost-benefit relationship** must be considered: the costs of providing the information must be weighed against the benefits that can be had from using the information. In order to justify requiring a particular measurement or disclosure, the costs must be justified by the benefits. In other words, the benefits must outweigh the costs.

Management Accounting 3.1.3 The difficulty in cost-benefit analysis is that the costs and, especially, the benefits are not always evident or measurable. There are several kinds of costs, including the costs of:

- Collecting and processing
- Distributing
- Auditing
- Potential litigation
- Disclosure of proprietary information to competitors
- Analysis and interpretation

The benefits are enjoyed by both preparers (in terms of greater management control and access to capital) and users (in terms of allocation of resources, tax assessment, and rate regulation). Benefits are generally more difficult to quantify than costs.

The AcSB has taken some steps to reduce the cost of providing information by developing separate standards for private entities that are less onerous and costly. This model allows

---

[10]Consolidated financial statements of Enron Corp. for the year ended December 31, 2000.

these companies to follow a simplified version of GAAP based on cost-benefit considerations. In many cases, the shareholders and creditors of private companies have greater access to information and do not necessarily rely solely on the external financial statements. In addition, for smaller private companies, the business and business model are not as complicated and therefore less complex accounting standards are required. Private entities have the option to use IFRS if they wish.

Elements of Financial Statements

LEARNING OBJECTIVE 3
Define the basic elements of financial statements.

Accounting uses many terms that have specific meanings. These terms make up the **language of accounting and business**. There are many **elements** that users expect to find on the financial statements, including **assets**, **liabilities**, **equity**, **revenues/income**, **expenses**, and **gains/losses**. In addition, within each of these categories, there are many subcategories, such as current and non-current assets, cash, inventory, and so on. The conceptual framework defines the basic elements so that users have a common understanding of the main items presented on the financial statements.

The basic elements of financial statements that are most directly related to measuring an enterprise's performance and financial status are listed below. First we will examine the characteristics of each element. Then we will look at criteria for recognition of elements in the financial statements. Finally, we will review bases for measurement and principles for presentation and disclosure (assuming that recognition criteria are met). Just because something meets the definition of an element does not mean that it is recognized. This is an important point to remember. We will revisit the elements in later chapters.[11]

Assets

Significant Change Assets have three essential characteristics:

1. They represent a **present economic resource**—a **right** that has the potential to produce economic benefits.
2. The entity has **control** over that resource.
3. The resource results from a **past transaction or event**.[12]

Control is evidenced by the company's ability to decide how to use the asset and receive economic benefits.[13] For instance, consider a manufacturing plant that is owned by a company. The plant is a present economic resource because it gives the company the right to receive the cash flows that the plant has the potential to generate. **According to the conceptual framework, the asset is actually the right as opposed to the physical asset.**[14] The

---

[11]The elements are defined in the respective conceptual frameworks under IFRS and ASPE and, even though the wording differs, they are essentially very close in meaning. In practice, the different wording would generally not result in different accounting.

[12]*CPA Canada Handbook—Accounting*, Part II, Section 1000.25 and IFRS *Conceptual Framework* 4.3-4.5. Copyright © IFRS Foundation. All rights reserved. Reproduced with permission.

[13]IASB *IFRS Conceptual Framework* 4.20.

[14]IASB *IFRS Conceptual Framework* 4.4 and 4.5.

entity has access to (control over) the resource through **legal ownership** of the property itself (a tangible asset), thus allowing the company to decide whether to sell it or use it in order to generate cash flows. The transaction giving rise to the resource would have been the acquisition of the asset.

An asset may also be represented by a contractual or other right. Example 2.2 gives examples of contractual or other rights.

Example 2.2 | Contractual or Other Rights

Facts   Fredrich Inc. purchases a much sought-after patent for a manufacturing process during the year. In addition, it signed a contract to lease a machine for its useful life of five years.

Instructions   Do these transactions represent assets?

Solution   The purchased patent has value because it gives the holder the right to receive future cash flows from the sale of the patented product. The lease contract gives the company contractual right to use (through **possession**) the asset even though the company does not have legal title to the machine. In both cases, the purchase and signing of the contract represents the **past event** and gives the company **control** over the **rights to potential future economic benefits**. Thus they both represent assets.

Note that, in order to meet the definition of an asset, the right only needs to have the **potential to produce economic benefits**, even if the likelihood of future benefits is uncertain. For instance, assume the acquisition of the patent in a business combination gives the holder the right to future cash flows from use of the patent. The criterion for an asset is met even if it is not probable that future benefits will flow to the entity. The next step is to determine if the asset should be recognized and if so, how it should be measured.

In cases such as legal disputes, it may not be possible to determine whether an asset exists, so we look to the recognition criteria to help decide whether to recognize anything in the financial statements.[15] If the asset has uncertain potential to produce economic benefits, then we consider this when we look at recognition criteria and measurement.

When determining if an economic resource exists, we must take care to review not only items such as inventory, cash, land, and patents (which represent both tangible and intangible properties) but also contractual and other rights (such as forward contracts, insurance, and others).

Liabilities

Liabilities have three essential characteristics:

1. They represent a **present duty or responsibility** (there is **no practical ability to avoid them**).
2. The duty or responsibility obligates the entity to **transfer an economic resource**.
3. The obligation results from a **past transaction or event**.[16]

Similar but opposite to an asset, a liability has a negative economic value and requires the entity to give up economic resources to settle the obligation. Example 2.3 looks at a potential liability.

---

[15]IASB *IFRS Conceptual Framework* 4.13.

[16]*CPA Canada Handbook—Accounting*, Part II, Section 1000.29 and *IFRS Conceptual Framework* 4.26 and 4.27.

Example 2.3 | Contractual Obligations

Facts Assume that a company hires employees and agrees to pay them a salary for services provided.

Instructions Is this a liability?

Solution Once the employee accepts the offer of employment and starts to provide services (**both "past events"**), a liability is created. The company has a **duty** to pay the salary according to the predetermined employment arrangement with the employee once the employee has rendered services. The entity must pay the salary; otherwise there will be negative consequences. For example, the employee will quit and may sue the company for unpaid wages and/or damages. Therefore, the company has **no practical ability to avoid paying**.

Liabilities may arise through contractual obligations, as noted in Example 2.3, or through statutory requirements, such as for illegally polluting. In addition, they may arise through other means, including constructive and equitable obligations.

> **Law** **Constructive obligations** are obligations that arise through past or present practice that signal that the company acknowledges a potential economic burden. **Example 2.4** looks at a constructive obligation.

Example 2.4 | Constructive Obligations

Facts Crestco produces cooking ovens. On its website, it notes that it stands behind its product. It states that the ovens are high quality and, if by some chance there is a problem, the company will fix it at no cost to the customer. There is otherwise no written warranty or contract stating this.

Instructions Does the note on the website create a constructive obligation?

Solution The expectation is that the entity will fix or replace any defective ovens because of the statement that it stands behind its products. This expectation creates a **duty** to fix any problems. Therefore, the company has **no practical ability to avoid** the obligation because there will be negative economic repercussions. The **past events** are the sale of the oven to the customer and the statement on the website.

> **Law** **Equitable obligations** arise due to moral or ethical considerations. **Example 2.5** looks at equitable obligations.

Example 2.5 | Equitable Obligations

Facts Addition Limited is downsizing and is selling or closing all of its international operations. Many employees are being laid off. The company would like to retrain those employees who have been with the company for many years so that they can find another job. At this point, Addition Limited has not yet told the employees this.

Instructions Does the desire to retrain the employees create an obligation?

Solution The desire to retrain does not necessarily create an obligation since it has not yet been communicated. There is no expectation on the part of the employees. Therefore, the company **may be able to avoid** the retraining assuming it has not yet promised anything to the employees being laid off.

Care should be taken to ensure that all obligations are identified and properly accounted for. Sometimes, however, it may be unclear as to whether an obligation actually exists—for instance, in a lawsuit against the company. The company (or its lawyers) may not yet know if there was any wrongdoing or how the law applies (if at all).[17] We will look at recognition and measurement in the next section.

Liabilities may be further categorized by standard setters as either financial (as defined in IAS 32 regarding contractual obligations to deliver cash or other financial assets) or non-financial (everything else).[18]

Liabilities will be discussed further in subsequent chapters, including Chapters 13, 14, and 16.

Equity

Equity is a **residual interest** in an entity that remains after deducting its liabilities from its assets. This is also known as its net worth. In a business enterprise, the equity is the **ownership** interest.[19] Equity would normally consist of common or ordinary shares, preferred shares, retained earnings, and, under IFRS, accumulated other comprehensive income.

Revenues/Income

ASPE Under ASPE, **revenues** are increases in economic resources, either by inflows or other enhancements of an entity's assets or by settlement of its liabilities, which result from an entity's **ordinary activities**. For instance, assume that a real estate company owns 10 buildings and leases them out under long-term leases. For this company, revenues would include rental income.

IFRS Under IFRS, **income** is defined as increases in assets or decreases in liabilities other than those relating to contributions from shareholders.

Expenses

Expenses are decreases in economic resources, either by outflows or reductions of assets or by the incurrence of liabilities that result from an entity's **ordinary revenue-generating activities**. For instance, for the real estate company above, expenses would include heating and property taxes. IFRS does not make a distinction between ordinary revenue-generating activities and losses.

Gains/Losses

Gains are increases in equity (net assets) from an entity's **peripheral or incidental transactions** and from all other transactions and other events and circumstances affecting the entity during a period, except those that result from revenues or investments by owners.[20]

---

[17]IASB *IFRS Conceptual Framework* 4.35.

[18]The terms "financial" and "non-financial" are somewhat vague and are meant to draw a line between liabilities that represent financial instruments (financial liabilities) and all other liabilities. Therefore, the term "non-financial" includes items such as contractual nonmonetary performance obligations (such as warranties to fix assets or provide services) and non-contractual monetary obligations (such as lawsuits).

[19]The IASB and FASB are currently looking at the definition of "equity" because the line between liabilities and equity is not well defined for complex financial instruments and business structures.

[20]Under IFRS, revenues and gains are grouped together under the heading of Income in the framework. Similarly, expenses and losses are grouped together under the heading of Expenses. Thus, although acknowledging the existence of and the potential for separate disclosure of gains and losses, IFRS defines fewer elements in the conceptual framework. For instance, when property, plant, and equipment are disposed of, IAS 16.68 notes that any gains or losses should be recognized and that gains shall not be classified as revenues. ASPE defines these items separately. In practice, they would not result in different accounting.

Losses are decreases in equity (net assets) from an entity's **peripheral or incidental transactions** and from all other transactions and other events and circumstances affecting the entity during a period, except those that result from expenses or distributions to owners.

For the same real estate company, these might include gains and losses on the sale of the buildings. As noted in the above example, the company's business model includes purchasing buildings and renting them out on a long-term basis, not buying and selling buildings.

Significant Change   The financial statements include the following items:[21]

1. Statement of financial performance
   - May be two statements (statement of profit or loss and statement of comprehensive income) or combined as one
2. Statement of financial position
3. Statement of changes in shareholders' equity
4. Statement of cash flows

The term comprehensive income is a relatively new income concept and includes more than the traditional notion of net income. It includes net income and other comprehensive income (OCI; all other changes in equity except for owners' investments and distributions). Other comprehensive income is made up of revenues, expenses, gains, and losses that, in accordance with primary sources of GAAP, are recognized in comprehensive income, but excluded from net income. For example, the following would be included as other comprehensive income in the comprehensive income statement:

- Unrealized holding gains and losses on certain securities (such as fair value-OCI investments)
- Changes in the revaluation surplus when using the revaluation method to account for capital assets
- Certain gains and losses related to the translation of foreign operations, and cash flow hedges
- Certain gains and losses related to remeasurement of defined benefit plans and liabilities measured at fair value

IFRS   ASPE   Note that IFRS does not require companies to use the terms "comprehensive income" or "other comprehensive income." We will discuss this further in Chapter 4. Under ASPE, the statement of financial performance is generally called the income statement and the statement of financial position is called the balance sheet. Instead of a statement of changes in shareholders' equity, there is a statement of retained earnings. The concepts of comprehensive income and other comprehensive income do not exist under ASPE. Items would be booked through net income.

Foundational Principles

LEARNING OBJECTIVE 4

Describe the foundational principles of accounting.

The conceptual framework's third level consists of **foundational principles** that implement the basic objectives of the first level. These concepts help explain which, when, and how financial elements and events should be **recognized**, **measured**, and **presented/disclosed** by the accounting system. They act as guidelines for developing rational responses

---

[21]IASB *IFRS Conceptual Framework* 3.3.

to controversial financial reporting issues. They have evolved over time, and the specific accounting standards issued by standard setters are based on these concepts in a fundamental way.

It is important to decide at which level these concepts will be applied when recognizing and measuring **rights** (assets) and **obligations** (liabilities). This is called the unit of account. For example, the owner of a building has the **right** to use, **right** to pledge, and **right** to sell. These rights would be grouped together and recognized as one asset: property, plant, and equipment. The building is therefore the unit of account. We will refer back to the unit of account as we move through subsequent chapters. The accounting standard itself determines the unit of account. For instance, when depreciating an asset, we divide the cost of the total asset into its component parts and depreciate each component separately. An airplane would have numerous components, including the engine, body, and cabin interior equipment. It is acceptable to use one unit of account for recognition purposes and another for measurement purposes, as shown in the airplane depreciation example where the airplane itself is broken down into smaller parts for depreciation purposes (measurement).

Basic **foundational principles** underlying the financial accounting structure also include assumptions and conventions. It is often difficult to put a label onto the items noted below and accounting practices vary, and so we have grouped them together. The label is not important—it is the substance of the concept and how it provides a solid foundation for accounting standard setting that is important.

We will discuss the 10 foundational principles and assumptions under the groupings of recognition/derecognition, measurement, and presentation and disclosure, as shown in **Illustration 2.2**.

ILLUSTRATION 2.2

Ten Foundational Principles and Assumptions

Recognition/Derecognition	Measurement	Presentation and Disclosure
1. Economic entity assumption	**5.** Periodicity assumption	**10.** Full disclosure principle
2. Control	**6.** Monetary unit assumption	
3. Revenue recognition and realization principles	**7.** Going concern assumption	
	8. Historical cost principle	
4. Matching principle	**9.** Fair value principle and value in use	

Recognition/Derecognition

Recognition is the act of including something on the entity's statement of financial position or income statement. At a macro level, decisions need to be made about whether to consolidate investments in other entities. At a micro level, decisions need to be made about whether and when to include assets, liabilities, revenues, expenses, gains, and losses in the financial statements. For instance, executory contracts are agreements between two or more parties under which the parties to the contract have not yet performed. A contract to buy inventory from a supplier is generally seen to be an executory contract as long as neither party has performed under the contract. Should these contracts be recognized in the financial statements? Most purchase orders are not recognized because the seller has not yet shipped the goods and the purchaser has not yet paid for them. That is, neither party has performed. We will revisit this when we look at inventory in greater detail in Chapter 8.

The conceptual framework provides general recognition and measurement criteria, and in the absence of specific guidance under IFRS and ASPE, underlying principles may be used to justify whether something should be reflected in the financial statements or not.

Historically, elements of financial statements have been recognized when they:

- meet the definition of an element (for example, a liability),
- are probable, and
- are reliably measurable.

ASPE This is still the case under ASPE. For instance, an entity must use all information to make a neutral decision as to whether the liability or asset exists or not (that is, whether the definition is met). It must then decide whether it is probable that an outflow or inflow of resources will occur and whether it is measurable.

Significant Change Under the new IFRS conceptual framework, the recognition criteria are different.[22] In order to be recognized, the element must do the following:

1. meet the definition of the element, and
2. provide users with relevant information that faithfully represents the underlying transaction or event.

In other words, there are no additional special recognition criteria. The principle is to recognize an element in the financial statements if the information is **useful** (and therefore has the **fundamental qualities** associated with useful information).[23]

Note that there is no probability criterion under IFRS, nor is there a measurability criterion. Having said that, where there is **significant** uncertainty as to existence or measurement, or there is a **low probability of occurrence**, information may not be as useful. For instance, in a lawsuit against the company, it might be very difficult to determine if the company was at fault (existence uncertainty) and therefore, there is a low probability of having to make a payment. Existence uncertainty, under IFRS, is the question as to whether something exists or not (in this case, the liability). Because the company does not really know if it was at fault, information about a lawsuit might not be **relevant** until more information is available. It is therefore inappropriate to recognize the lawsuit until this is determined. Even if fault is established, it might similarly be difficult to measure the expected damages to be paid (measurement uncertainty). As noted earlier, we will revisit the notion of measurement uncertainty in greater detail later in this chapter.

The representational faithfulness criteria may not be met, for instance, where there is insufficient information available, which would be needed for users to understand the transaction or event. Perhaps the only information available is biased information. In the case of the lawsuit, the company might take the position that it was not at fault, but this is biased information and therefore might not faithfully represent the situation. Involving the use of experts, such as lawyers who represent both sides, might bridge the gap and help establish more neutral information.

Derecognition is the act of taking something off the statement of financial position or income statement. For assets, this occurs when control is given up. For liabilities, this occurs when the obligation is extinguished.[24]

Several additional underlying principles help determine whether something should be recognized or not. We discuss these next.

Economic Entity Assumption and Control

The economic entity assumption (or entity concept) allows us to **identify an economic activity** with a particular **unit of accountability** (for example, a company, a part of a company such as a division, or an individual). If all the economic events that occur could not be

---

[22]Even though the criteria for recognition differ under IFRS and ASPE, in practice, this may not result in large differences, especially where there is specific GAAP dealing with a transaction or event (which is mostly the case). The conceptual framework comes into play only where there is otherwise no specific IFRS or ASPE standard or where a new standard is being developed.

[23]IASB *IFRS Conceptual Framework* 5.7.

[24]IASB *IFRS Conceptual Framework* 5.26. As we will see later in the text, derecognition is linked with how we define the entity, especially where the entity is transferring or selling assets to another entity that it may control. For instance, if an entity transfers investments to another entity that it controls, there is essentially no derecognition since the entity will end up consolidating the combined entity and the entity is just seen to be transferring things between the two related entities. The new IFRS conceptual framework provides a fair bit of guidance on derecognition. Because of the complexity often associated with many transactions involving derecognition (for example, factoring and restructuring), we will deal with these more complex transactions in subsequent chapters.

separated in a meaningful way, there would be no basis for accounting. This concept helps accountants determine what to include or recognize in a particular set of financial statements (as well as what not to recognize). As you may have learned in your introductory financial accounting course, companies are organized in many different ways. The organizational structure is often driven by tax and legal factors.

Taxation 6.1.1, 6.2.1 Three common forms of organization are sole proprietorship, partnership, and corporation. **Illustration 2.3** looks at some pros and cons of each type of business structure.

ILLUSTRATION 2.3   **Some Common Forms of Business Organization**

	Brief Description	Pros	Cons
Proprietorship	Small business owned and run by one person (sole proprietor)	– Simple to set up and maintain records – Does not have to file a separate tax return since the income is treated as income of the owner for tax purposes	– Not a separate legal entity and therefore any lawsuits against the business would be directed against the sole proprietor – Personal assets may be required to pay off business debts
Partnership	Business usually owned and/or run by more than one person (the partners)	– A basic partnership is simple to set up and for maintaining records – Does not have to file separate tax returns because the income is treated as income of the partners for tax purposes	– Not a separate legal entity and therefore any lawsuits against the business would be directed against the partners – Personal assets may be required to pay off business debts
Corporation	Business is incorporated as a separate legal entity	– Limited liability protection – Any obligations are the obligations of the corporation and not the owners	– More complex to set up and for maintaining records – Separate tax returns must be completed and filed for the corporation – Covered by the Canada Business Corporations Act or provincial corporations act—legal requirements for reporting and maintaining records

What Do the Numbers Mean? 2.4 looks at additional forms of business.

What Do the Numbers Mean? 2.4

There are two additional types of organizational structures that are used by professionals in Canada: professional corporations and limited liability partnerships (LLPs). These have evolved for two main reasons:

1. for tax planning, and
2. to limit liability of the partners for negligence by other partners.

According to CPA Canada:

> The LLP legislation provides that a partner is not personally liable for any debts, obligations or liabilities of the LLP that arise

from any negligent act by another partner or by any person under that partner's direct supervision and control. The law does not reduce or limit the liability of the Firm. All of the Firm's assets and insurance protection remain at risk. In addition, all partners of an LLP remain personally liable for their own actions and for the actions of those they directly supervise and control.

Note that the partners are still held accountable for their own actions—just not those of the other partners.

Professional corporations may allow for greater flexibility in tax planning than limited liability partnerships.

Taxation 6.1.1 This text deals mostly with corporations. We will revisit issues relating to unincorporated businesses in Chapter 23. For tax and legal purposes, the **legal entity** is the relevant unit for an incorporated company. Tax returns are filed and taxes are paid based on taxable income for each corporation. Lawsuits pertaining to the business are generally filed against the corporation since it is a separate legal entity (although the shareholders and management may also be sued as individuals).

GAAP, however, considers a broader definition when preparing consolidated financial statements. A parent company and its subsidiaries may be separate **legal entities** (such as separate corporations), but merging their activities for accounting and reporting purposes gives more meaningful information. Thus, the consolidated financial statements are prepared from the perspective of the **economic entity**. This allows the company to recognize and group together the assets, liabilities, and other financial statement elements that are under the parent's control into one set of statements. Several separate corporations may therefore be grouped together to produce the consolidated financial statements.

Historically, for most situations, the definition of control has been anchored in the number of common shares held. That is, control existed where the entity held more than 50% of the voting common shares of another entity.[25] However, the concept has been changing as business practices have been changing.[26] As noted earlier, control is an important part of deciding whether something meets the definition of an asset.

IFRS IFRS 10 notes that an investor has **control** over an investee when it has the following:

1. power over the investee;
2. exposure, or rights, to variable returns from its involvement with the investee; and
3. the ability to use its power over the investee to affect the amount of the investors' returns.

This standard is principles-based and broadens the concept so that control is assessed not only through ownership of common shares but through other means, including exposure to the risks and rewards of the entity. Since IFRS 10 specifically deals with consolidation, it overrides the more general definition of control in the IFRS conceptual framework.

ASPE Under ASPE, control is defined as the continuing power to determine strategic decisions without the co-operation of others—a similarly broad concept.[27] For the most part, ASPE standards are similar where the company owns voting common shares in another company. However, in some situations (for instance, when dealing with sales of financial instruments to certain trusts or other legal entities), the ASPE standards are significantly different. ASPE focuses more on whether the other entity is "demonstrably distinct" from the company. In assessing this, the company looks at the following (as well as other factors):

- whether the entity in question can be unilaterally dissolved by the company, and
- whether others have more than a 10% ownership interest.[28]

Consolidation of financial statements is generally covered in advanced accounting courses so we will not deal with that further here. It is important, however, to have a high-level view of which entities are included as part of the economic entity for financial reporting purposes (such as special purpose entities, discussed in **What Do the Numbers Mean? 2.5**). As mentioned earlier, this will also have an impact on accounting for derecognition of financial instruments in situations where assets are transferred.[29]

---

[25]That is, if the parent owns more than 50% of the (voting) common shares, it can exercise voting control.

[26]For example, it is now harder to define the boundaries of companies. There are public companies with multiple public subsidiaries, each with joint ventures, licensing arrangements, and other affiliations and strategic alliances. Increasingly, loose affiliations of enterprises in joint ventures or customer-supplier relationships are formed and dissolved in a matter of months or weeks. These virtual companies raise accounting issues about how to account for the entity.

[27]*CPA Canada Handbook—Accounting*, Part II, Section 1591.03. Copyright © IFRS Foundation. All rights reserved. Reproduced with permission.

[28]See *CPA Canada Handbook—Accounting*, Part II, Section 3856.B14 and B15. The 10% test is an example of a bright-line test discussed in Chapter 1. The IASB is, in principle, trying to purge bright-line tests from IFRS due the fact that, in most cases, the "line drawn" is an arbitrary one.

[29]For instance, this may be the case where entity A transfers an asset to entity B and entity A controls entity B. Entity A may be able to derecognize the asset and perhaps recognize a gain/loss, but when the consolidated statements are prepared, the asset will be included in the consolidated financial statements and any gain/loss eliminated.

> ### What Do the Numbers Mean? 2.5
>
> Many companies use what are known as special purpose entities (SPEs). SPEs are sometimes called variable interest entities or structured entities. They are often separate legal entities (for instance, they could be a limited partnership or corporation) set up for a specific purpose, such as to hold leases, pension funds, or perhaps certain investments, or to create investment opportunities for investors. Are SPEs part of the economic entity for consolidated financial reporting purposes? This was the centre of much of the controversy surrounding the Enron scandal. Enron created many SPEs that it did not consolidate. It sold assets to these SPEs, often
>
> at a profit. As it turned out, Enron should have consolidated them since the liabilities and losses of these SPEs ended up being liabilities and losses of Enron. In other words, Enron was exposed to the risks of ownership.
>
> Enron's accounting had the impact of understating liabilities and overstating income in its consolidated financial statements. Under revised accounting standards, SPEs that were not previously included may now be included in the consolidated financial statements. Similarly, some may be excluded since the detailed guidance has changed.

Revenue Recognition and Realization Principles

A crucial question for many enterprises is when revenue should be recognized. This is governed loosely by what is known as the **revenue recognition principle**. Although this is a principle in transition, historically, revenue has generally been recognized when the following three conditions are met:

1. **risks and rewards** have passed and/or the **earnings process is substantially complete (significant acts have been performed and there is no continuing involvement)**;
2. **the revenue is measurable**; and
3. **the revenue is collectible** (realized or realizable).[30]

ASPE This is an **income statement approach** in that it focuses more on the earnings process. ASPE continues to follow this.

Significant Change **IFRS** The new IFRS 15 standard *Revenue from Contracts with Customers* is effective for fiscal years beginning on or after January 1, 2018. This new standard follows a five-step approach in determining when revenue is recognized:

1. Identify the contract with the customer.
2. Identify the performance obligations in the contract (promises to transfer goods and/or services that are distinct).
3. Determine the transaction price.
4. Allocate the transaction price to each performance obligation.
5. Recognize revenue when each performance obligation is satisfied.

This new IFRS approach is a **balance sheet approach**, which recognizes that a transaction has occurred when the entity enters into a contract. The entity has rights and performance obligations under the contract. Collectible revenues are recognized when **performance obligations** are settled (when control over goods or services passes to the customer). There is a presumption that the contract is measurable. We will examine this in greater detail in Chapter 6.

Revenues are **realized** when products (goods or services), merchandise, or other assets are **exchanged** for cash. Revenues are **realizable** if the assets received or held can be readily converted into cash or claims to cash. Assets are readily convertible if they can be sold or interchanged in an active market at prices that are readily determinable and there is no significant additional cost.

Matching Principle

Assets such as property, plant, and equipment contribute to a company's ability to generate revenues. Therefore, accounting attempts to match these costs with the revenues that they

---

[30]*CPA Canada Handbook—Accounting*, Part II, Section 3400.04-.06.

produce. This practice is called **matching** because it dictates that effort (expenditures) be matched with accomplishment (revenues) whenever this is reasonable and can be done. It also illustrates the **cause and effect relationship** between the money spent to earn revenues and the revenues themselves.

It may be difficult to establish exactly how much of a contribution is made to each period, however, so often an estimation technique must be used. GAAP requires that a **rational and systematic** allocation policy be used that will approximate the asset's contribution to the revenue stream. Selection of a rational and systematic allocation technique involves making assumptions about the benefits that are being received as well as the costs associated with those benefits. The cost of a long-lived asset, for example, must be allocated over all accounting periods during which the asset is used because the asset contributes to revenue generation throughout its useful life.

Assets such as inventory similarly contribute to a company's ability to generate revenues, but in a different way. While property, plant, and equipment are normally used up in generating revenues, inventory is sold to generate revenues. Operating expenditures incurred during the year are often classified into two groups depending on whether they are seen to be part of the inventory production process or not. These two groups are labelled **product costs** and **period costs**.

Product costs such as material, labour, and overhead attach to the product and are carried into future periods as inventory (if not sold) because they are seen to be part of the inventory production process and because inventory meets the definition of an asset. Period costs such as officers' salaries and other administrative expenses are recognized immediately—even though the benefits associated with these costs occur in the future. This is because they are not seen as part of the production process and therefore are not inventory costs, and because the costs do not meet the definition of an asset by themselves. Period costs are seen to be a normal ongoing annual expense of running the business as opposed to part of the inventory production process. This same analysis occurs for self-constructed or internally generated assets other than inventory. The following discussion deals with allocation of costs. See **What Do the Numbers Mean? 2.6**.

What Do the Numbers Mean? 2.6

Ethics **Livent Inc.** was a Canadian company that produced and presented large Broadway-style musicals. The company followed the policy of deferring pre-production costs for the creation of each separate show until the show opened. The company felt that this was acceptable because it was creating an asset: the show. On opening night, the show would start to produce revenues and then the costs were amortized and matched with those revenues. Such costs included advertising, publicity and promotions, set construction, props, costumes, and salaries paid to the cast, crew, musicians, and creative workers during rehearsal. In short, anything to do with the production was deferred.

On the one hand, one might argue that this was aggressive. One could also argue that this treatment was acceptable because of the direct and incremental nature of these costs in terms of future production revenues. The trouble began when Livent started to reclassify some of these costs as fixed assets and also to reallocate these costs to different and unrelated shows that had higher revenue. The company even had spreadsheets to keep track of actual results as compared with those that were publicly reported.[31] There was more going on than a simple accounting policy choice. In the end, senior management was tried and convicted of fraud. The auditors were found to be negligent and fined. The case was appealed in the Court of Appeal for Ontario in 2016 as well as the Supreme Court of Canada in 2017 where the ruling was upheld although the damages ended up being reduced.

While in the past, it may have been acceptable to capitalize certain costs on the basis of matching, there are no grounds for recognizing assets and liabilities that do not specifically meet the definitions of these elements under the conceptual framework. If a cost or expenditure does not meet the definition of an asset, it is expensed (matching notwithstanding). Care should also be taken to ensure that only costs directly related to the creation of assets such as inventory or property, plant, and equipment are included. Similarly, there are no grounds for deferral of revenues as liabilities based exclusively on matching.[32]

---

[31]OSC Notice of Hearing and Statement of Allegations concerning Livent Inc., July 3, 2001.

[32]Many would argue that accounting standard setters are migrating toward a balance sheet emphasis. Thus the concept of matching is not as central as it would be if the statement of comprehensive income were the main focus. In addition, the use of fair value in measuring assets renders the concept of matching—as historically defined—much less useful.

Measurement

Once we decide whether something meets the definition of an element, we then decide whether we recognize the element and then we must decide how to measure it.

Because **accrual accounting** is followed, many estimates must be used when preparing financial statements. Most numbers on a statement of financial position and income statement are in fact quite "soft" and inexact. In order to communicate information about economic events, accountants must convert the economic events into the language of business: numbers. Some things are easy to measure, such as cash in the bank. Others are not so easy to measure. For instance, how do you measure the potential cost of selling what proves to be a dangerous product?

Measurability is a big issue for many financial statement elements and it is an even greater issue in certain types of companies or industries. For instance, in the pharmaceutical industry it is very challenging to measure the cost of a newly developing drug. When a company cannot objectively identify a value (for instance, the value of a share that is not publicly traded) and therefore it must estimate the value, the resulting imprecision is called measurement uncertainty. Measurement uncertainty affects faithful representation. Accountants are continually working to develop and make use of **measurement tools** such as option pricing and discounted cash flow models. When observable values are not available, these models or tools are used as a way of dealing with measurement uncertainty.

Significant Change   As noted earlier in this chapter, **existence uncertainty** may complicate the decision as to whether to recognize an asset or liability and if so, how to measure it. There is one more uncertainty and that is outcome uncertainty. Outcome uncertainty is the uncertainty surrounding future inflows and outflows for assets and liabilities. For instance, outcome uncertainty exists when trying to determine cash inflows for a particular asset such as a hotel. Where the range of possible outcomes is large or probabilities extremely difficult to determine, for example, then this contributes to outcome uncertainty.

Both outcome uncertainty and existence uncertainty may contribute to measurement uncertainty (but they do not necessarily do so). **Example 2.6** looks at this.

Example 2.6 | Types of Uncertainty in Recognizing and Measuring Financial Statement Elements

Facts   Genco has just invested $1,000 in a small start-up company through an initial token offering. In return for paying cash to the new company, Genco receives 10 tokens. The tokens give Genco rights to a percentage of revenues from specific products that Genco will sell in future. Sometimes tokens such as these end up trading on a cryptocurrency market. That is not the case here.

Instructions   Is the investment an asset? Why? What types of uncertainties exist in terms of deciding how to account for the investment?

Solution   Genco **controls** the tokens, which result from the payment of cash to the start-up company (**the transaction**). The tokens give Genco the **rights** to future cash flows from future sales. Therefore, there is **no existence uncertainty** (at least initially) and the transaction represents an asset.

Since the company is a start-up and the sales of specific products have not yet happened, there is **outcome uncertainty**. Perhaps there will be no future sales. Alternatively, the company could be very successful and there could be significant future sales. The outcome uncertainty contributes to measurement uncertainty. The transaction itself establishes a value at the date of the investment (that is, Genco invested $1,000). Since there is no market for the tokens, the company will have to estimate the value going forward and also evaluate whether an asset still exists. There will be significant **measurement uncertainty** in estimating the value because this is a start-up company with no established sales record. There is a significant risk that the $1,000 may have to be written down.

It may be worthwhile to summarize the types of uncertainty mentioned so far. **Illustration 2.4** looks at the three types of uncertainty we have discussed in this chapter.

ILLUSTRATION 2.4

Types of Uncertainty and Their Impact on Measuring Financial Statement Elements

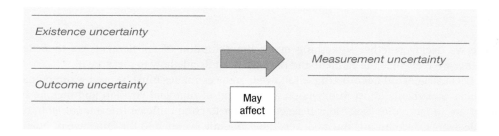

Which model or tool should be used? It depends on the nature of the transaction or balance (including whether related cash flows are variable), the sensitivity to market forces such as interest rates, and the nature of the business/industry.[33] Sometimes multiple models may be used.

Accountants must also choose which **measurement basis** should be used. Common choices are historical cost (including amortized cost), value in use, and fair value. How do we determine which measurement basis should be used? In many cases, IFRS and ASPE specify which basis should be used. For instance, inventory is generally recorded at cost unless it is obsolete or the value is impaired. As a general principle, the choice should result in the most useful information. Measurement bases must provide relevant information that faithfully represents the event or transaction.[34]

Significant Change The new IFRS conceptual framework articulates that measurement bases reflect either **historical costs** or **current values**. Historic costs are often more readily available; however, there can be complexities including estimating depreciation, useful life, impairment, and other things. Current values are relevant and easy to determine where market values exist; however, this is not always the case, and therefore estimating current values can be very subjective. Three current value measurement bases are identified in the framework:

1. **fair value**,
2. **value in use** for assets and **fulfilment value** for liabilities, and
3. **current cost**.[35]

There is a trade-off with uncertainty. As noted earlier under "Recognition," too much uncertainty (existence, outcome, or measurement) may make it inappropriate to recognize a financial statement element because it undermines the usefulness of the financial statements. Estimates with high measurement uncertainty provide information that is less relevant for decision-making than those with low measurement uncertainty. However, if the element is not recognized at all in the financial statements, then some relevant information has not been included and the statements are incomplete. A compromise is to measure and recognize the elements in the body of the financial statements and to disclose the measurement uncertainty and its significance in the notes to the financial statements.

We will now discuss a few underlying concepts, such as periodicity, unit of measure, and going concern. Then we will look at some commonly used measurement bases such as historical cost, fair value, and value in use.

---

[33]The IFRS conceptual framework also notes that we must consider measurement inconsistency. Measurement inconsistency occurs where there is an accounting mismatch. We will look at accounting mismatches later in the text when we review hedging (Chapter 16).

[34]The IFRS conceptual framework provides significant guidance on selecting a measurement basis that provides most useful information. The optimal choice depends on the facts and circumstances of the company.

[35]IASB *IFRS Conceptual Framework* 6.11. Note that, previously, detailed discussion on measurement was not included as part of the IFRS conceptual framework. Having said this, the measurement bases articulated above have been in use for quite a while and are reflected in specific IFRS and ASPE standards. The value of including them in the conceptual framework lies in the fact that, going forward, when accounting policies and new standards are established, it provides a framework to ensure consistency. Current cost reflects the amount an entity is willing to pay to acquire an equivalent asset (or receive to take on an equivalent liability). Current cost is not often used. Fulfilment value is the amount of resources required to be transferred upon fulfilling an obligation (*IFRS Conceptual Framework* 6.17). We will focus on fulfilment costs in subsequent chapters, including Chapter 6. Copyright © IFRS Foundation. All rights reserved. Reproduced with permission.

The key for accountants is to:

1. **Determine an acceptable level of uncertainty.**
2. Use **measurement tools** that help deal with the uncertainty (such that useful information is produced).
3. **Disclose enough information** to signal the uncertainty.

Chapter 3 looks at measurement models, tools, and bases (including current values) in greater detail.

Periodicity Assumption

The most accurate way to measure the results of an enterprise's activity would be to do the measurement at the time of the enterprise's eventual liquidation. At that point, there is complete certainty about all of the company's cash flows. Business, government, investors, and various other user groups, however, cannot wait that long for such information. Users need to be informed about performance and economic status on a **timely basis** so that they can evaluate and compare firms. For this reason, information must be reported periodically. The periodicity assumption (or time period assumption) implies that an enterprise's economic activities can be divided into **artificial time periods**. These time periods vary, but the most common are one month, one quarter, and one year.

The shorter the time period, the more difficult it becomes to **determine the proper net income** for the period. A month's results are usually less reliable than a quarter's results, and a quarter's results are likely less reliable than a year's results. This is because more estimates are needed to accrue costs and revenues in accrual accounting when the time period is shorter. Investors want and demand information that has been processed and distributed quickly, yet the more quickly the information is released, the more likely errors become.

The question of what time period is appropriate is becoming more serious because product cycles are shorter and products become obsolete more quickly. Many observers believe that, given the advances in technology, more online, **real-time financial information** needs to be provided to ensure that relevant information is available. The issue of continuous financial reporting was introduced in Chapter 1.

Monetary Unit Assumption

The monetary unit assumption means that money is the common denominator of economic activity and is an appropriate **basis for accounting measurement** and analysis. This assumption implies that the monetary unit is the most effective way of expressing to interested parties changes in capital and exchanges of goods and services. The monetary unit is relevant, simple, universally available, understandable, and useful. Applying this assumption depends on the even more basic assumption that **quantitative data** are useful in communicating economic information and in making rational economic decisions.

`IFRS` In Canada and the United States, accountants have generally chosen to ignore the phenomenon of **price-level change** (inflation and deflation) by assuming that the unit of measure, the dollar, remains reasonably **stable**. This assumption about the monetary unit has been used to justify adding 1970 dollars to today's dollars without any adjustment. Only if circumstances change dramatically (such as if Canada or the United States were to experience extremely high inflation) would the standard setters consider "inflation accounting." IAS 29 deals with hyperinflation. There is no comparable standard under ASPE.

Going Concern Assumption

Most accounting methods are based on the going concern assumption. This is the assumption that a business enterprise will **continue to operate for the foreseeable future**; that is, it will not be forced to end its operations. Although there are many business failures, experience indicates that companies do have a fairly high continuance rate. While accountants do not believe that business firms will last indefinitely, they do expect them to last long enough to fulfill their commitments. Management must assess the company's ability to continue as a going concern and take into account all available information, looking out at least 12 months from the date of the statement of financial position.

The implications of this assumption are profound. Measuring financial statement elements at historical cost would have limited usefulness if **liquidation** were assumed to be likely. Under a liquidation approach, for example, asset values are better stated at **net realizable value** (sales price less costs of disposal) than at **acquisition cost**. Amortization and amortization policies are justifiable and appropriate only if we assume some permanence to the enterprise; this is what justifies allocating the costs of the amortized assets to future periods to match them against future revenues. If a liquidation approach were adopted, the **current versus non-current classification** of assets and liabilities would lose much of its significance. Labelling anything a **fixed or long-term** asset would be difficult to justify. Indeed, listing liabilities according to their likely liquidation date would be more reasonable.

The going concern assumption applies in most business situations. The only time when the assumption does not apply is when **there is intent to liquidate the company's net assets and cease operations or cease trading in the company's shares or when the company has no realistic alternative but to liquidate or cease operations**. In these cases, a total revaluation of assets and liabilities can provide information that closely approximates the entity's **net realizable value**. The accounting problems that arise when an enterprise is in liquidation are presented in advanced accounting courses.

How do we measure things when we assume the entity is a going concern? Management must continually assess the likelihood of outcomes (such as whether the company will lose a lawsuit) based on history and supporting evidence. Often, companies rely on specialists such as lawyers and engineers for help with such assessments.

Historical Cost Principle

Transactions are initially measured at the amount of cash (or cash equivalents) that was paid or received or the fair value that was ascribed to the transactions when they took place. This is often called the historical cost principle. The historical cost principle has three underlying assumptions that support its value and usefulness:

1. It represents a value at a **point in time**.
2. It results from a reciprocal exchange (in other words, a two-way exchange).
3. The exchange includes **an outside arm's-length party**.

Initial Recognition   For non-financial assets, the value includes any laid-down costs; that is, any cost that is incurred to get the asset ready (whether for sale or for generating income by using it). Inventory, for instance, might include the **cost of material, labour, and a reasonable allocation of overhead**. Similarly, for a self-constructed asset, cost would include any expenditure made to get the asset **ready for its intended use**, including transportation and installation costs.

Sometimes it is not possible or not appropriate to determine a value using the historical cost principle. Transactions that have some or all of the following characteristics present challenges:

- Nonmonetary or barter transactions where **no cash or monetary consideration** is exchanged. Here it may be more difficult to determine the value of the assets exchanged.

- Nonmonetary, non-reciprocal transactions where there is **no exchange**, such as donations.

- Related party transactions where the parties to the transaction are not acting at arm's length (in other words, there is **no outside party**). In these cases, the exchange price may not reflect the true value of the assets exchanged.

As a default, an attempt may be made to estimate the **fair value** if possible, and this may become the cost basis going forward.

The historical cost principle also applies to financial instruments. Bonds, notes, and accounts payable and receivable are issued by a business enterprise in exchange for assets, or perhaps services. This price, established by the exchange transaction, is the "cost" of the financial instrument and gives the figure at which the instrument should be recognized in the financial statements as long as it is equal to the fair value of the financial instrument issued. Where the instruments are issued in exchange for cash, the cost is straightforward but where they are issued for goods or services, the value may be more difficult to determine. Measurement techniques such as discounting are used to measure the transaction.

Subsequent Remeasurement   Historical cost has an important advantage over other valuation methods. Because it generally comes from an **arm's-length transaction** or exchange, it represents a bargained, fairly arrived-at value at a specific point in time. When it is first recognized, cost usually represents fair value. Over time, however, it often becomes irrelevant in terms of **predictive value**.

Later remeasurements also have limitations, however. They can be based on different measurement values, such as fair value, and give information that is more relevant, but they often involve **measurement uncertainty**. Furthermore, because there is often no external exchange (exchange with an outside party), the values may be **subjective**. Despite these limitations, the trend is toward an increasingly **mixed valuation model**. What used to be primarily a **historical cost-based model**, modified by the application of conservatism (that is, revaluations occurred if the asset's value declined below cost), is moving more toward a **market valuation model**. We discuss the use of fair value below.

Fair Value Principle and Value in Use

IFRS   IFRS has increasingly called for the use of standardized fair value measurements in the financial statements. This is an emerging principle that we will call the fair value principle. Fair value information may be more useful than historical cost for certain types of assets and liabilities and in certain industries. For example, companies report many financial instruments, including derivatives, at fair value. Brokerage houses and mutual funds prepare their financial statements using fair value.

Fair value is defined under IFRS as "the price that would be received to sell an asset or paid to transfer a liability in an orderly transaction between market participants at the measurement date."[36] Accordingly, fair value is an exit price. Exit price is a selling price, as opposed to an "entry price," which reflects the entity's purchase price. According to the definition, fair value is also a **market-based measure**, as opposed to an entity-specific measure. As such, it is meant to be more objective. An **entity-specific value** represents how the company might value the item in question. This is often called value in use and reflects the present value of the future cash flows the entity expects to receive from use of the asset. It is not necessarily the same as a market-based value. A **market-based value** seeks to determine value by looking at how market participants would value the item in question. It does not look at value from the perspective of the entity itself and as such it does not consider company-specific synergies.[37]

Illustration 2.5 shows the various ways to define "value" or price.

---

[36]IFRS 13.9 and the *IFRS Conceptual Framework* 6.12. The term "market" refers to any mechanism whereby parties objectively determine price, usually through bargaining and supply and demand. IFRS 13 includes the following as examples: exchange markets (such as the London Stock Exchange), dealer markets (such as commodities markets and used-equipment markets), brokered markets (such as real estate markets), and others. The definition of fair value has now been incorporated into the IFRS conceptual framework. Copyright © IFRS Foundation. All rights reserved. Reproduced with permission.

[37]This is different from the way accountants have historically viewed fair values, which often considered the value from the entity's perspective, including any company-specific synergies. The objective of moving to a market-based fair value measure is to reduce subjectivity. For instance, an entity may believe that the asset is worth more than the market thinks it is worth and often attributes this to past entity-specific synergies, which are difficult to prove.

ILLUSTRATION 2.5
Defining Value or Price

Example 2.7 looks at fair value versus value in use.

Example 2.7 | Fair Value Versus Value in Use

Facts   Assume that a restaurant has a fully integrated industrial kitchen, and the grills are built-in but are now broken.

Instructions   How should it value the kitchen?

Solution   The restaurant may attribute a higher value to the grills since they are an integrated part of the kitchen and already in place. This value represents an entity-specific value (value in use). Market participants might view the value of broken, used equipment as being lower—perhaps at scrap value—especially if the grills are too costly to fix. This latter value is the fair value under IFRS. Where a liquid market does not exist, the entity may use a model such as a discounted cash flow model to estimate fair value.

Which value is better for use in the financial statements? Good question. There is a trade-off. Entity-specific value may be more relevant for operating assets where the entity plans to hold on to them and use them to produce revenues, but it may be more subjective. As noted above, the market-based view is more objective and verifiable and thus, where fair value is called for under IFRS, the market-based view must be applied.

At initial acquisition, historical cost generally equals fair value. In subsequent periods, as market and economic conditions change, historical cost, value in use, and fair value often diverge. Current value measures or estimates often provide more relevant information about the expected cash flows related to the asset or liability. For example, when a long-lived asset declines in value, value in use and/or fair value measures may be used to help determine a potential impairment loss.

In order to encourage increased use of fair value and to simplify accounting, standard setters have given companies the option to use fair value for most financial instruments (such as non-strategic investments) as an accounting policy choice. This is called the **fair value option** under both IFRS and ASPE. Standard setters feel that fair value is more relevant for most financial instruments because it reflects the current cash equivalent value. In addition, markets exist for many financial instruments, thereby providing independent, objective evidence of value. Under the fair value option, financial instruments are measured at fair value with gains and losses being booked to income. IFRS requires certain criteria be met in order for the fair value option to be used.

IFRS **ASPE**   Certain standards under IFRS explicitly allow the use of fair value for some non-financial assets (such as investment properties and property, plant, and equipment) or require it for others (such as certain biological assets). ASPE does not refer to the use of fair value for these items, although it does acknowledge that fair value measures might be used in certain industries, including agriculture and mining.[38] Note that ASPE has defined fair value as the "amount of consideration that would be agreed upon in an arm's length transaction between knowledgeable, willing parties who are under no compulsion to act."[39]

There are some subtle differences here, including the fact that the ASPE definition does not refer to an orderly market, nor does it stipulate that the price is an exit price.

We will expand upon the use of the fair value principle and value in use in future chapters, including Chapter 3.

Presentation and Disclosure

Full Disclosure Principle

Accountants follow the general practice of providing information that is important enough to influence an informed user's judgement and decisions. This is called the **full disclosure principle**. The principle recognizes that the nature and amount of information in financial reports reflects a series of judgemental trade-offs. These trade-offs aim for information that is:

- **detailed enough** to disclose matters that make a difference to users, but
- **condensed enough** to make the information understandable, and also appropriate in terms of the costs of preparing and using it.

More information is not always better. Too much information may result in the user being unable to digest or process it. This is called **information overload**. Information about a company's financial position, financial performance, cash flows, and investments can be found in one of three places:

1. The **main body of financial statements**
2. The **notes to the financial statements**
3. Supplementary information, including the **Management Discussion and Analysis (MD&A)**

The financial statements are a **formalized, structured way of communicating financial information**. Disclosure is not a substitute for proper accounting.[40] Certain numbers, such as earnings per share, send signals to the capital marketplace. For example, cash basis accounting for cost of goods sold is misleading, even if accrual-based amounts have been disclosed in the notes to the financial statements. As we mentioned in Chapter 1, the market watches and listens for signals about earnings in particular and does not usually react well to negative earnings surprises.

The **notes to financial statements** generally **amplify or explain** the items presented in the main body of the statements. If the information in the main body of the statements gives an incomplete picture of the enterprise's performance and position, additional information that is needed to complete the picture should be included in the notes.

Information in the notes does not have to be quantifiable, nor does it need to qualify as an element. Notes can be partially or totally narrative. Examples of notes are:

- **Descriptions** of the accounting policies and methods used in measuring the elements reported in the statements
- **Explanations** of uncertainties and contingencies
- **Details** that are too voluminous to include in the statements

---

[38]*CPA Canada Handbook—Accounting*, Part II, Section 3031.04. The standard acknowledges that certain assets may be held at net realizable value or fair value less cost to sell. These assets are excluded from the requirements of Section 3031, which essentially requires the use of historical cost for unimpaired inventory.

[39]*CPA Canada Handbook—Accounting*, Part II, various sections, including sections 1582, 3055, 3063, 3064, 3065, and 3462.

[40]According to GAAP, recognition means including an item in one or more individual statements and does not mean disclosure in the notes to the financial statements. Some critics might argue, however, that if markets are assumed to be efficient, then as long as the information is disclosed, the market will absorb and use the information in pricing the shares. Whether the markets are fully efficient or not is a question that researchers seek to answer. There is evidence that efficient markets exist at least in a semi-strong form.

The notes are not only helpful in understanding the enterprise's performance and position, they are essential.

Significant Change The new IFRS conceptual framework provides general guidance on what constitutes effective communication in the financial statements as follows:

1. Entity-specific information is most useful as opposed to general information.
2. Duplication of information inhibits the usefulness of information.[41]

Supplementary information may include details or amounts that present a different perspective from what appears in the financial statements. They may include quantifiable information that is high in relevance but low in reliability, or information that is helpful but not essential. One example of supplementary information is the data and schedules provided by oil and gas companies: typically, they give information on proven reserves as well as the related discounted cash flows.

Supplementary information also includes management's explanation of the financial information and a discussion of its significance in the **MD&A**. CPA Canada's publication *MD&A: Guidance on Preparation and Disclosure* lays out six general disclosure principles.

The MD&A should:

1. enable readers to view the entity through management's eyes;
2. supplement and complement the information in the financial statements;
3. provide fair, complete, and balanced information that is material to the decision-making needs of users;
4. outline key trends, risks, and uncertainties that are likely to affect the company in the future and provide information about its quality of earnings and cash flows;
5. explain management's plan for accomplishing short-term and long-term goals; and
6. be understandable, relevant, comparable, verifiable, and timely.[42]

Thus, the MD&A is a step toward a more broadly based business reporting model that also contains forward-looking information. The guidance also includes a framework that identifies five key elements that should be included in the MD&A:

1. core businesses,
2. objectives and strategy,
3. capability to deliver results,
4. results and outlook, and
5. key performance measures and indicators.

It is hoped that these additional disclosures will give financial information users a greater insight into a company's business.[43]

IFRS We discuss the content, arrangement, and display of financial statements, along with other facets of full disclosure, specifically in Chapters 4, 5, and 23, and more generally throughout the text. Note that under IFRS there is a general trend toward increased disclosures in a bid for greater transparency.

Illustration 2.6 presents the conceptual framework discussed in this chapter. It is similar to Illustration 2.1, except that it gives additional information for each level. We cannot overemphasize the usefulness of this conceptual framework in helping to understand many of the problem areas that are examined in later chapters.

---

[41]IASB *IFRS Conceptual Framework* 7.6.

[42]CPA Canada's Canadian Performance Reporting Board (2014), *MD&A: Guidance on Preparation and Disclosure*. This material is part of the CPA Canada Standards and Guidance Collection.

[43]Although MD&A disclosures are mandated for public companies, the *CPA Canada Guidance*, in its executive summary, notes that the MD&A can also be used by other organizations to communicate more effectively.

ILLUSTRATION 2.6 **Expanded Conceptual Framework for Financial Reporting**

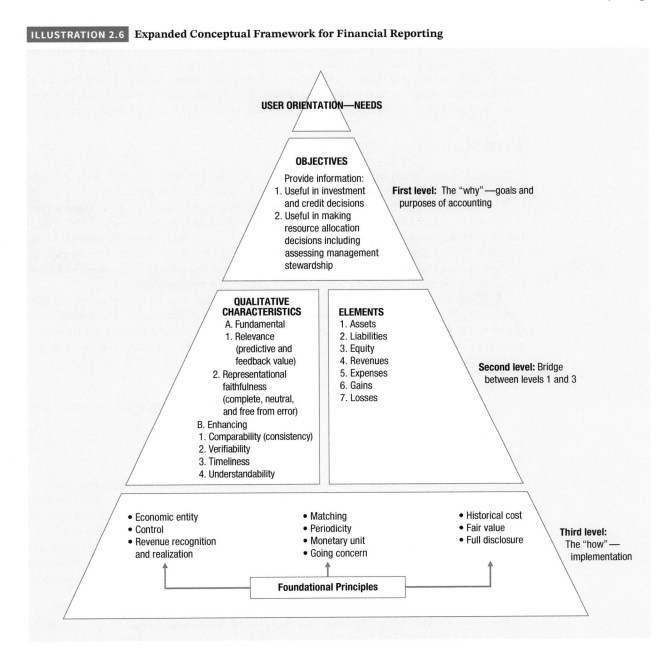

Financial Reporting Issues

LEARNING OBJECTIVE 5

Explain the factors that contribute to choice and/or bias in financial reporting decisions.

Making financial reporting decisions is complex. This section examines the factors that make this process challenging. As mentioned earlier in the chapter, the main objective of financial reporting is to **provide reliable, decision-relevant financial information** to users so that they can make well-informed capital allocation decisions. Capital that is invested in good investments fuels the economy and encourages job growth and wealth creation. To achieve this objective, well-judged choices must be made between alternative accounting concepts, methods, and means of disclosure. Accounting principles and rules must be **selected and interpreted and professional judgement must be applied**.

As mentioned, accounting is **influenced by its environment**—in many cases in a negative way. It is also influenced by decisions made by individuals who often act in **self-interest** or in the interests of the company (at the expense of other stakeholders). Because of this, it is unrealistic to believe that the financial reporting system will always work properly. Instead of wealth creation in the capital markets and the economy, financial reporting decisions sometimes lead to wealth and value destruction. Bias may exist and this is not a good thing.

Principles-Based Approach

IFRS and ASPE are **principles-based**; that is, they are based on a few foundational principles and concepts like those in the conceptual framework noted earlier in the chapter.

The benefit of this approach is that all decisions should theoretically be **consistent** if they start from the same foundational reasoning. Another benefit is that principles-based GAAP is **flexible**. The most appropriate accounting for any new situation or novel business transaction may be arrived at through reason by going back to these principles (sometimes called first principles). However, principles-based GAAP is sometimes criticized for being too flexible. Some critics feel that it allows too much choice and therefore results in **lack of comparability**.

Ethics Care should therefore be taken to ensure that this flexibility is not abused. The key foundational concept of **neutrality** is of the greatest importance. **The conceptual framework described in this chapter is the anchor that should ground all financial reporting decisions.** In the absence of specific GAAP guidance, an entity should adopt accounting policies that are:

1. consistent with specific GAAP guidance, and
2. **developed** through exercising professional judgement and applying the conceptual framework.

Financial Engineering

A practice known as financial engineering became more visible during the past three decades. Financial engineering is the process of legally structuring a business arrangement or transaction so that it meets the company's financial reporting objective (such as maximizing earnings or minimizing a debt to equity ratio). This is often done by creating complex legal arrangements and financial instruments. These arrangements and instruments are created so that the resulting accounting meets the desired objective within GAAP. For example, a company that is raising debt financing might want the instrument structured so that it meets the GAAP definition of equity rather than debt. In this way, the debt to equity ratio is not negatively affected.

Many financial institutions develop and market these financial instruments to their clients. These arrangements are often called **structured financings**. Since Enron, this practice has been reduced. Are financial engineering and the practice of structured financings ethically acceptable? Financial engineering has moved from being an accepted practice and commodity to a potentially fraudulent activity.

Ethics Illustration 2.7 looks at the various shades of grey in accounting for transactions.

ILLUSTRATION 2.7

Choice in Accounting Decision-Making

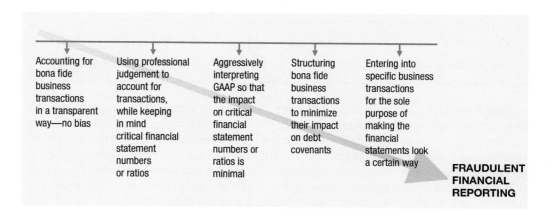

| Accounting for bona fide business transactions in a transparent way—no bias | Using professional judgement to account for transactions, while keeping in mind critical financial statement numbers or ratios | Aggressively interpreting GAAP so that the impact on critical financial statement numbers or ratios is minimal | Structuring bona fide business transactions to minimize their impact on debt covenants | Entering into specific business transactions for the sole purpose of making the financial statements look a certain way |

FRAUDULENT FINANCIAL REPORTING

Fraudulent Financial Reporting

The role of accountants who are responsible for preparing a company's financial records is to capture business and economic events and transactions as they occur and communicate them to interested parties. They should not use the financial statements to portray something that is not there. Similarly, good financial reporting should be a result of **well-reasoned and supported analysis** that is grounded in a conceptual framework. It should not be influenced by external pressures. Pressures in the capital marketplace are everywhere, however, and their potentially negative impact on financial reporting must be acknowledged. Pressures may arise from various sources, including the ones discussed below.

Economic or Business Environment

Ethics Sometimes a company experiences sudden drops in revenue or market share. The underlying reason may be unique to the company and due to some poor strategic and business decisions or it may result from an industry or economic downturn. This may put pressure on a company to "prop up" its revenues. There may be pressure to recognize revenues before they should be recognized or to defer the recognition of some expenses.

Strategy & Governance 2.3.2 Some companies use an industry or economic downturn as an opportunity to "clean up" their financial statements and generally take large write-downs on assets such as inventory or goodwill.

The markets expect a loss and the company's share price is therefore not overly affected in a negative way. This "purging" of the statement of financial position has the positive impact of making future earnings look better.

Other Pressures

Budgets put tremendous pressure on company management. Since bonuses and even jobs may depend on meeting budget targets, sometimes this negative influence leaks inappropriately into accounting decisions. Other pressures were discussed in Chapter 1.

Audit & Assurance 4.3.5 Ethics If these and other pressures are not monitored and controlled properly, they are a major problem (see **What Do the Numbers Mean? 2.7**). In order to lessen the chances of fraudulent financial reporting, a company may put in place various controls and a solid governance structure. These could include:

- Vigilant, knowledgeable top management
- An independent audit committee
- An internal audit function
- Strong internal control systems

What Do the Numbers Mean? 2.7

The U.S.-based Committee of Sponsoring Organizations of the Treadway Commission (COSO) is composed of professional accounting organizations such as the American Accounting Association, the American Institute of Certified Public Accountants, Financial Executives International, the Institute of Internal Auditors, and the National Association of Accountants (now the Institute of Management Accountants). COSO's mandate, according to its website (www.coso.org), is as follows:

> . . . to provide thought leadership through the development of comprehensive frameworks and guidance on enterprise risk management, internal control and fraud deterrence designed to improve organizational performance and governance and to reduce the extent of fraud in organizations.

In 2010, COSO released a report entitled *Fraudulent Financial Reporting: 1998–2007*. The report updated a prior report that it had released looking at fraud for the period 1987 to 1997. The 2010 report found that there were 347 alleged cases of fraud that were investigated by the U.S. Securities and Exchange Commission (SEC) from 1998 to 2007 (as compared with 294 cases for the prior 10-year period). COSO calculated the amount of the misappropriations to be around U.S. $120 billion.

The most common area of fraud involved revenue recognition (alleged in 61% of the frauds). This was followed by overstatement of assets including overcapitalization of expenses (51% of the cases). Understatement of liabilities was much lower (31% of the cases). Approximately 26% of the firms allegedly involved in fraud changed auditors. The average period the alleged frauds took place was 31 months.

Although the report stated that more study was needed to determine why the frauds were committed, it noted that the SEC identified in its proceedings the following motivations for fraud:

- the need to meet internal or external earnings expectations,
- an attempt to conceal the company's deteriorating financial condition,
- the need to increase the stock price,
- the need to bolster financial performance for pending equity or debt financing, or

- the desire to increase management compensation based on financial results.

Standard setters are continually updating and rewriting accounting standards to make sure that they capture relevant information faithfully, but as noted above, it is often behavioural factors that result in fraudulent reporting.

Source: M.S. Beasley, J. V. Carcello, D. R. Hermanson, and T. L. Neal, *Fraudulent Financial Reporting: 1998–2007, An Analysis of U.S. Public Companies*, Committee of Sponsoring Organizations of the Treadway Commission, 2010.

IFRS/ASPE Comparison

LEARNING OBJECTIVE 6
Discuss current trends in standard setting for the conceptual framework.

IFRS and ASPE are fundamentally similar since they are both principles-based. We have noted some differences throughout the chapter but we will look at these in more detail in subsequent chapters.

Looking Ahead

The IASB has issued an Exposure Draft on the definition of materiality. It was hoping to standardize the definition, which now appears in several places throughout IFRS, including the conceptual framework. In late 2017, the IASB also issued a Practice Statement on applying materiality. The purpose of the Practice Statement is to help apply materiality; however, it is not part of IFRS and is therefore not mandatory.

The IASB continues to work on its Primary Financial Statements Project. It is currently in discussions and is hoping to issue either a Discussion Paper or Exposure Draft in 2019.

In March 2017, the IASB issued a Discussion Paper relating to disclosures. The comment period ended in October 2017. The IASB hopes to identify and develop a set of disclosure principles. In the process of writing the Discussion Paper, the IASB performed significant outreach activities, consulting with financial statement users and preparers. It found that people were concerned about disclosure on three dimensions:

1. not enough relevant information,
2. too much irrelevant information, and
3. ineffective communication.

The disclosure problem is identified in the Discussion Paper and an excerpt is in **Illustration 2.8**.

As a starting point, the IASB developed some basic principles of effective communication. It then looked at where to disclose information, the use of performance measures, and the disclosure of accounting policies. Finally, it proposed some principles to improve disclosures. An excerpt from the paper is in **Illustration 2.9**. Discussions are currently ongoing on this project.

The Disclosure Problem		
1. Not enough relevant information	**2. Irrelevant information**	**3. Ineffective communication of the information provided**
Information is relevant if it is capable of making a difference in the decisions made by the primary users of financial statements. If financial statements do not provide enough relevant information, their users might make inappropriate investing or lending decisions.	Irrelevant information is undesirable because: • it clutters the financial statements so that relevant information might be overlooked or hard to find, making financial statements difficult to understand; and • it can add unnecessary ongoing cost to the preparation of the financial statements.	If information is communicated ineffectively, it makes the financial statements hard to understand and time-consuming to analyse. Additionally, users of the financial statements may overlook relevant information or fail to identify relationships between pieces of information in different parts of the financial statements.

Information should be:

a. entity-specific, since information tailored to an entity's own circumstances is more useful than generic, 'boilerplate' language or information that is readily available outside the financial statements;

b. described as simply and directly as possible without a loss of material information and without unnecessarily increasing the length of the financial statements;

c. organised in a way that highlights important matters—this includes providing disclosures in an appropriate order and emphasising the important matters within them;

d. linked when relevant to other information in the financial statements or to other parts of the annual report (see Section 4 *Location of information*) to highlight relationships between pieces of information and improve navigation through the financial statements;

e. not duplicated unnecessarily in different parts of the financial statements or the annual report;

f. provided in a way that optimises comparability among entities and across reporting periods without compromising the usefulness of the information; and

g. provided in a format that is appropriate for that type of information–for example, lists can be used to break up long narrative text, and tables may be preferable for data-intensive information, such as reconciliations, maturity analysis, etc.

Review and Practice

Summary of Learning Objectives

1 Indicate the usefulness and describe the main components of a conceptual framework for financial reporting.

A conceptual framework is needed to (1) create standards that build on an established body of concepts and objectives, (2) provide a framework for solving new and emerging practical problems, (3) increase financial statement users' understanding of and confidence in financial reporting, and (4) enhance comparability among different companies' financial statements.

The first level of the framework deals with the objective of financial reporting. The second level includes the qualitative characteristics of useful information and elements of financial statements. The third level includes foundational principles and conventions.

2 Identify the qualitative characteristics of accounting information.

The overriding criterion by which accounting choices can be judged is decision usefulness; that is, the goal is to provide the information that is the most useful for decision-making. Fundamental characteristics include relevance and faithful representation. These two characteristics must be present. Enhancing characteristics include comparability, verifiability, timeliness, and understandability. There may be trade-offs.

3 Define the basic elements of financial statements.

The basic elements of financial statements are (1) assets, (2) liabilities, (3) equity, (4) revenues/income, (5) expenses, and (6) gains/losses. IFRS has fewer elements defined.

4 Describe the foundational principles of accounting.

(1) Economic entity: the assumption that the activity of a business enterprise can be kept separate and distinct from its owners and any other business unit. (2) Control: the entity has the power to make decisions and reap the benefits or be exposed to the losses (which are variable). (3) Revenue recognition: revenue is generally recognized when it is (a) earned, (b) measurable, and (c) collectible (realizable) under ASPE and when performance obligations are satisfied (control passes) under IFRS. (4) Matching: the assumption assists in the measurement of income by ensuring that costs (relating to long-lived assets) incurred in earning revenues are booked in the same period as the revenues earned. (5) Periodicity: the assumption that an enterprise's economic activities can be divided into artificial time periods to facilitate timely reporting. (6) Monetary unit: the assumption that money is the common denominator by which economic activity is conducted, and that the monetary unit gives an appropriate basis for measurement and analysis. (7) Going concern: the assumption

that the business enterprise will have a long life. (8) Historical cost principle: existing GAAP requires that many assets and liabilities be accounted for and reported based on their acquisition price. (9) Fair value principle and value in use: assets and liabilities are valued at fair value—that is, an exit price—and viewed from a market participant perspective. (10) Full disclosure principle: accountants follow the general practice of providing information that is important enough to influence an informed user's judgement and decisions.

5 Explain the factors that contribute to choice and/or bias in financial reporting decisions.

Choice is the result of many things, including principles-based standards, measurement uncertainty, and increasingly complex business transactions. The conceptual framework is the foundation that GAAP is built on. If there is no primary source of GAAP for a specific decision, then professional judgement must be used, making sure that the accounting policies chosen are consistent with the primary sources of GAAP and the conceptual framework.

Financial engineering is the process of legally structuring a business arrangement or transaction so that it meets the company's financial reporting objective. This can be a dangerous practice since it often results in biased information.

Fraudulent financial reporting often results from pressures on individuals or the company. These pressures may come from various sources, including worsening company, industry, or economic conditions; unrealistic internal budgets; and financial statement focal points related to contractual, regulatory, or capital market expectations. Weak internal controls and governance also contribute to fraudulent financial reporting.

6 Discuss current trends in standard setting for the conceptual framework.

The IASB is currently working on the primary financial statement project, a framework for disclosure as well as a consistent definition of materiality.

Practice Problem

Meadow Limited has hired you to review its accounting records prior to the closing of the revenue and expense accounts as at December 31, the end of the current fiscal year. The company follows IFRS. The following information comes to your attention.

1. During the current year, Meadow Limited changed its policy in regard to expensing purchases of small tools. In the past, it had expensed these purchases because they amounted to less than 2% of net income. Now, the president has decided that the company should follow a policy of capitalization and subsequent depreciation. It is expected that purchases of small tools will not fluctuate greatly from year to year.

2. The company built a warehouse at a cost of $1 million. It had been depreciating the asset on a straight-line basis over 10 years. In the current year, the controller doubled depreciation expense because the replacement cost of the warehouse had increased significantly.

3. When the statement of financial position was prepared, the preparer omitted detailed information as to the amount of cash on deposit in each of several banks. Only the total amount of cash under a caption "Cash in banks" was presented.

4. On July 15 of the current year, Meadow purchased an undeveloped tract of land at a cost of $320,000. The company spent $80,000 in subdividing the land and getting it ready for sale. An

appraisal of the property at the end of the year indicated that the land was now worth $500,000. Although none of the lots were sold, the company recognized revenue of $180,000, less related expenses of $80,000, for a net income on the project of $100,000.

5. For a number of years, the company used the FIFO method for inventory valuation purposes. During the current year, the president noted that all the other companies in the industry had switched to the average-cost method. The company decided not to switch to average-cost because net income would decrease by $830,000.

Instructions

State whether you agree or disagree with the decisions made by Meadow in each of the five items above. Support your answers with reference, whenever possible, to the conceptual framework.

Solution

1. From the facts, it is difficult to determine whether to agree or disagree. Consistency, of course, is violated in this situation although its violation may not be material. Furthermore, the change of accounting policies regarding the treatment of small tools cannot be judged good or bad but would depend on the circumstances. In this case, it seems that the result will be approximately the same whether the company capitalizes and expenses, or simply expenses each period, since the purchases are fairly uniform. Perhaps from a cost standpoint (expediency), it might be better to continue the present policy rather than become involved in detailed depreciation schedules, assuming that purchases remain fairly uniform. On the other hand, the president may believe there is a significant unrecorded asset that should be shown on the statement of financial position. If such is the case, capitalization and subsequent depreciation would be more appropriate.

2. Disagree. At the present time, accountants do not recognize price level or current value adjustments in the accounts. Therefore, unless the controller is proposing the use of revaluation accounting for all warehouses (IAS 16), it is misleading to deviate from the historical cost principle because conjecture or opinion can take place. Also, depreciation is not so much a matter of valuation as it is a means of cost allocation. Assets are not depreciated on the basis of a decline in their fair value. Rather, they are depreciated on the basis of a systematic charge of expired cost against revenues.

3. Agree. The full disclosure principle recognizes that reasonable condensation and summarization of the details of a company's operations and financial position are essential to readability and comprehension. Therefore, in determining what is full disclosure, the accountant must decide whether leaving something out will mislead readers of the financial statements. Generally, companies present only the total amount of cash on a statement of financial position unless some special circumstance is involved (such as a possible restriction on the use of the cash). In most cases, however, the company's presentation would be considered appropriate and in accordance with the full disclosure principle.

4. Disagree. The historical cost principle indicates that companies account for assets and liabilities on the basis of cost. If sales value were selected, for example, it would be extremely difficult to establish an appraisal value for the given item without selling it. Note, too, that the revenue recognition principle provides guidance on when revenue should be recognized. Revenue should be recognized when the performance obligation is satisfied. In this case, the revenue was not recognized because the critical event for satisfying the performance obligation, "sale of the land with transfer to the buyer," had not occurred. This assumes that the property is not an investment property under IAS 40, in which case, the revaluation to fair value is acceptable.

5. From the facts, it is difficult to determine whether to agree or disagree with the president. The president's approach is not a violation of any principle. Consistency requires that entities give accountable events the same accounting treatment from period to period for a given business enterprise. It says nothing concerning consistency of accounting principles among business enterprises. From a comparability viewpoint, it might be useful to report the information on an average cost basis. But, as indicated above, there is no requirement to do so.

Key Terms

assets, p. 2-12
basic elements, p. 2-12
comparability, p. 2-10
completeness, p. 2-8

comprehensive income, p. 2-16
conceptual framework, p. 2-3
conservatism, p. 2-8
consistency, p. 2-11

constructive obligations, p. 2-14
control, p. 2-12
cost-benefit relationship, p. 2-11
decision usefulness, p. 2-6

derecognition, p. 2-18
economic entity assumption, p. 2-18
economic substance, p. 2-8
elements of financial statements, p. 2-4
equitable obligations, p. 2-14
equity, p. 2-15
executory contract, p. 2-17
existence uncertainty, p. 2-18
exit price, p. 2-27
expenses, p. 2-15
fair value option, p. 2-28
fair value principle, p. 2-27
feedback/confirmatory value, p. 2-6
financial engineering, p. 2-32
first principles, p. 2-32
freedom from error, p. 2-9
full disclosure principle, p. 2-29
gains, p. 2-15
general-purpose financial statements, p. 2-5
going concern assumption, p. 2-25
historical cost principle, p. 2-26

income, p. 2-15
information overload, p. 2-29
laid-down costs, p. 2-26
liabilities, p. 2-13
losses, p. 2-16
management best estimate, p. 2-9
management stewardship, p. 2-5
matching, p. 2-22
materiality, p. 2-6
measurement uncertainty, p. 2-23
monetary unit assumption, p. 2-25
neutrality, p. 2-8
nonmonetary/barter transactions, p. 2-26
nonmonetary, non-reciprocal transactions,
    p. 2-26
notes to financial statements, p. 2-29
objective of financial reporting, p. 2-5
other comprehensive income, p. 2-16
outcome uncertainty, p. 2-23
performance obligation, p. 2-21
periodicity assumption, p. 2-25

predictive value, p. 2-6
prudence, p. 2-9
qualitative characteristics, p. 2-6
realizable (revenue), p. 2-21
realized (revenue), p. 2-21
reciprocal exchange, p. 2-26
recognition, p. 2-17
related party transactions, p. 2-26
relevance, p. 2-6
representational faithfulness, p. 2-6
revenue recognition principle, p. 2-21
revenues, p. 2-15
supplementary information, p. 2-30
timeliness, p. 2-10
transparency, p. 2-8
understandability, p. 2-10
unit of account, p. 2-17
value in use, p. 2-27
verifiability, p. 2-10

Assignment Material

Note: **Enabling Competencies** Completion of this end-of-chapter material will help develop CPA-enabling competencies (such as ethics and professionalism, problem-solving and decision-making, and communication) and technical competencies. We have highlighted selected items with a specific integration word mark and material in *WileyPLUS* has been linked to the competencies. All cases emphasize integration, especially of the enabling competencies. The brief exercises, exercises, and problems generally emphasize problem-solving and decision-making.

Brief Exercises

BE2.1 (LO 2) Indicate the qualitative characteristic of financial information being described in each item below:

   a. Financial statements should include all information necessary to portray the underlying transactions.

   b. Financial information should make a difference in a user's decision-making.

   c. Financial information should not favour one user or stakeholder over another.

   d. Financial information should reflect the economic substance of business events or transactions.

   e. Financial information should help users assess the impact of past, present, or future events.

   f. Financial information must be reliable and without errors or omissions.

   g. Financial information should help users confirm or correct their previous expectations.

   h. Financial information should be reported and measured in a similar way within a company and between different companies.

   i. Financial information should be of sufficient quality and clarity to permit reasonably informed users to assess the information's significance.

   j. Financial information should be available to users before it loses its ability to be decision-useful.

   k. Knowledgeable, independent users should be able to achieve similar results and consensus when accounting for a particular financial transaction.

BE2.2 (LO 2) Identify which specific qualitative characteristic of accounting information is best described in each item below.

   a. The annual financial reports of Treelivingo Corp. are audited by public accountants.

   b. Able Corp. and Mona Inc. both use the straight-line depreciation method.

c. Global Corp. issues its quarterly reports within five days after each quarter ends.

d. Filipo Inc. segregates information that relates to one of its two subsidiaries, which was disposed of in the year but was included in its consolidated statements for prior years.

e. The CFO of WebDesign stresses that factual, truthful, unbiased information is the overriding consideration when preparing WebDesign's financial information.

f. EB Energy Inc. realizes that financial information may be misrepresented or misinterpreted if all pertinent information is not included.

g. Wright Industries exercises due care and professional judgement in developing all estimates and assumptions used to prepare its financial information.

BE2.3 (LO 2) Presented below are four different transactions related to materiality. Explain whether you would classify these transactions as material.

a. Blair Inc. has reported a positive trend in earnings over the past three years. In the current year, it reduces its allowance for bad debts and corresponding bad debt expense recovery to ensure another positive earnings year. The impact of this adjustment is equal to 2% of net income.

b. Heney Limited has a gain of $3.1 million on the sale of plant assets and a $3.3-million loss on the sale of investments. It decides to net the gain and loss because the net effect is considered immaterial. Heney Limited's income for the current year was $10 million.

c. Manion Corp. expenses all capital equipment under $10,000 on the basis that it is immaterial. The company has followed this practice for a number of years.

d. Sidney Inc. decided that a note payable of a very small balance should be classified as non-current on its statement of financial position, although the maturity of the note was five months after the year end. The reason given by management was that the current ratio had to be maintained at a certain level to satisfy creditors and that the note would likely be refinanced at maturity.

BE2.4 (LO 2) Sider Corp. was recently sued by a competitor for patent infringement. Lawyers have determined that it is probable that Sider will lose the case, and will have to pay $250,000 in damages. Using the three-step analysis for determining whether the fundamental characteristics of useful information are present, determine what, if anything, should be recognized concerning this information in Sider's accounting records.

BE2.5 (LO 2) Bradford Construction Ltd. submitted a $14.5-million sealed bid for a fixed-price roads contract with the local municipality. Historically, Bradford is awarded 20% of the contracts on which it submits sealed bids. Using the three-step analysis for determining whether the fundamental characteristics of useful information are present, determine what, if anything, should be recognized concerning this information in Bradford's accounting records.

BE2.6 (LO 2) **Ethics** Refer to the information for Bradford Construction Ltd. in BE2.5. Assume that the sealed bid for the road contract was submitted on December 28, 2020, that Bradford has a calendar year end, and that the annual financial statements are issued in late February 2021. The bidding process closed on January 2, 2021, the award of the contract was announced on January 15, 2021, and the construction work will start in March 2021. Using the three-step analysis for determining whether the fundamental characteristics of useful information are present, determine what, if anything, should be recognized concerning this information in Bradford's December 31, 2020 financial statements under the following conditions. Be specific about the timing of any recognition.

a. Bradford is awarded the contract on January 15, 2021.

b. Bradford is not awarded the contract on January 15, 2021.

BE2.7 (LO 2) What principle(s) from the conceptual framework does Henday Limited use in each of the following situations?

a. Henday includes the activities of its subsidiaries in its financial statements.

b. Henday was involved in litigation with Kinshasa Ltd. over a product malfunction. This litigation is disclosed in the financial statements.

c. Henday allocates the cost of its tangible assets over the period when it expects to receive revenue from these assets.

d. Henday records the purchase of a new packaging machine at its cash equivalent price.

e. Henday prepares quarterly financial statements for its users.

f. In preparing its financial statements, Henday assesses its ability to continue to operate for the foreseeable future.

g. Henday records revenue when risks and rewards (control) are passed to the purchaser.

BE2.8 (LO 3) Discuss whether the following items would meet the definition of an asset using the IFRS definitions. If so, explain with reference to the appropriate criteria.

a. MBI Ltd. owns a corporate fleet of cars for senior management's use in performing work duties.

b. A franchisee has a licence to operate a Tim Hortons restaurant.

c. Customized manufacturing machinery can only be used for one product line and has a small and limited customer market.

d. The parent company has guaranteed the operating line of credit of its subsidiary, which resulted in the subsidiary obtaining a lower interest rate than it would otherwise receive. Is the guarantee an asset for the subsidiary?

e. FreshWater Inc. bottles and sells the spring water from a natural spring near its property. Is the natural spring an asset of the company?

f. Mountain Ski Resort Ltd. often has to use its snow-making machine to make snow for its hills and trails when there is not enough natural snowfall. Is the snow an asset for Mountain Ski?

BE2.9 (LO 3) Discuss whether the following items would meet the definition of a liability using the criteria under IFRS. If so, explain with reference to the appropriate criteria.

a. Environmental remediation when a chemical spill has occurred. This spill has violated an existing law and statute. Does a liability for cleanup exist?

b. Environmental remediation after a chemical spill has occurred. No existing law or statute has been broken. Does a liability for cleanup exist?

c. As part of its contract with the government, a logging company must replant one tree for each tree it cuts. Does a liability for replanting exist?

d. A logging company has a corporate policy of always replanting trees and it advertises this fact in its corporate and marketing brochures. Does a liability for replanting exist?

e. An airline collects cash for tickets issued for future charter flights to exotic locations.

BE2.10 (LO 3) Explain how you would decide whether to record each of the following expenditures as an asset or an expense. Assume all items are material.

a. Legal fees paid in connection with the purchase of land are $1,500.

b. Eduardo Inc. paves the driveway leading to the office building at a cost of $21,000.

c. A meat market purchases a meat-grinding machine at a cost of $3,500.

d. On June 30, the partnership Monroe and Moore, medical doctors, pays six months' office rent to cover the month of July and the next five months.

e. Smith's Hardware Ltd., a public company, pays $9,000 in wages to labourers for construction on a building to be used in the business.

f. Alvarez's Florists Ltd. pays wages of $2,100 for the month to an employee who serves as driver of their delivery truck.

BE2.11 (LO 3) Assets are the cornerstone of financial reporting; often it is unclear whether an expenditure is an asset or an expense. For each of the transactions described below, consider whether the expenditure should be recorded as an asset or as an expense. Be sure to discuss the specific criteria in your response. Assume all items are material.

a. Akamu Limited operates an oil change shop and buys windshield washer fluid to top up customers' reservoirs.

b. John & John Massage Therapists pay $600 to a receptionist for taking appointments and issuing receipts to clients.

c. On October 1, Alan & Cheng, Chartered Professional Accountants, pay $500 to a local snow removal service for the upcoming winter season.

d. Luca Inc. is a contractor that cuts trees for the local sawmill. Luca pays $1,000 for a chainsaw.

e. Pharma Inc. incurs legal fees of $5,500 for registering a patent for its product.

f. Delhi Florists pays $4,500 for shipping charges for the delivery of flowers.

g. Sports Starts Here Inc. spent $4,500 installing hardwood floors in its leased store located in a mall.

BE2.12 (LO 3) For each item that follows, indicate which element of the financial statements it belongs to:

a. Retained earnings

b. Sales revenue

c. Acquired goodwill

d. Inventory

e. Depreciation expense

f. Loss on sale of equipment

g. Interest payable

h. Dividends

i. Issuance of common shares

BE2.13 (LO 4) For each item that follows, identify the foundational principle of accounting that best describes it.

a. For its annual reports, Sumsong Corp. divides its economic activities into 12-month periods.

b. Sullivan, Inc. does not adjust amounts in its financial statements for the effects of inflation.

c. Kiran Ltd. reports current and non-current classifications in its statement of financial position.

d. In preparing its consolidated financial statements, Paddy Corporation assesses whether it has the power to direct the other entity's activities.

e. Jaspreet Corporation reports revenue in its income statement when it is earned, even if cash has not been collected.

f. Duong Enterprises normally includes business transactions in its general ledger when the item meets the definition of an element (as defined in the conceptual framework) and the item is measurable.

g. Gomez Inc. provides information about pending lawsuits in the notes to its financial statements.

h. D&H Farms reports land on its statement of financial position at the amount paid to acquire it, even though the estimated fair value is higher.

i. King Corporation uses fair value measurements for its financial instruments portfolio.

j. Magic Inc. assumes that it will continue to operate into the foreseeable future.

k. Donaldson Corp. operates a chain of restaurants and divides its fiscal year into 13 four-week accounting periods.

BE2.14 (LO 1, 2, 5) What is the objective of financial reporting? For each of the situations discussed below, explain the qualitative characteristics of financial information that help provide decision-useful information to users.

a. Marcus Corp. has a management bonus plan based on net income. Marcus records revenue only after the risks and rewards of ownership of the goods it sells have passed to the customer.

b. Beliveau Ltd. is a real estate company that holds land for eventual sale to developers. Beliveau provides fair value information on its property holdings to its users.

c. Mohawk Inc. has entered into a rental agreement that will eventually transfer ownership of the manufacturing equipment to Mohawk at the end of three years. Irrespective of the legal documentation, Mohawk will account for this transaction based on its economic impact to the company.

d. Standard setters must ensure that accounting standards do not favour one set of users over another or one industry over another.

Exercises

E2.1 (LO 1) **(Usefulness, Objective of Financial Reporting)** The conceptual framework has been created to make accounting information useful.

Instructions

Indicate whether the following statements about the conceptual framework are true or false. If false, provide a brief explanation supporting your position.

a. Accounting standards that rely on a body of concepts will result in useful and consistent pronouncements.

b. General-purpose financial reports are most useful to company insiders in making strategic business decisions.

   c. Accounting standards based on individual conceptual frameworks will generally result in consistent and comparable accounting reports.

   d. Capital providers are the only users who benefit from general-purpose financial reporting.

   e. Accounting reports should be developed so that users without knowledge of economics and business can become informed about the financial results of a company.

E2.2 (LO 2, 5) **(Qualitative Characteristics)** The conceptual framework identifies the fundamental and enhancing qualitative characteristics that make accounting information useful.

Instructions

Answer the following questions related to these qualitative characteristics.

   a. Which quality of financial information makes it possible for users to confirm or correct prior expectations?

   b. Identify some of the trade-offs and constraints in financial reporting.

   c. The U.S. Securities and Exchange Commission chairman once noted that, if it becomes accepted or expected that accounting principles are determined or modified in order to achieve goals that do not involve economic measurement, we risk a serious loss of confidence in the credibility of our financial information system. Which qualitative characteristic of accounting information should ensure that this situation will not occur?

   d. Milner Corp. chooses to account for a transaction based simply on its legal form. Is this acceptable?

   e. Companies in the mining industry defer losses on their properties because recognizing such losses immediately could have adverse economic consequences for the industry. Which qualitative characteristic of accounting information is not followed?

   f. Only Once Ltd. provides overly complicated descriptions and explanations in its statement notes and provides only aggregated totals on the face of its financial statements. Which qualitative characteristic of accounting information is not followed?

   g. Baskins does not issue its first-quarter report until after the second quarter's results are reported. Which qualitative characteristic of accounting information is not followed?

   h. Predictive value is an ingredient of which qualitative characteristic of useful information?

   i. Vittorio Inc. is the only company in its industry to depreciate its plant assets on a straight-line basis. Which qualitative characteristic is not present?

   j. Green Gable Corp. has tried to determine the replacement cost of its inventory. Three different appraisers arrive at substantially different amounts for this value. The president then decides to use the middle value for external reports. Which qualitative characteristic of information is lacking in these data? (Do not use representational faithfulness.)

   k. The controller at Owens Inc. noticed that a material transaction was not included in the year-end financial results. Which qualitative characteristic is not present?

E2.3 (LO 2) **(Qualitative Characteristics)** The qualitative characteristics that make accounting information useful include:

Relevance	Neutrality	Representational faithfulness
Verifiability	Completeness	Understandability
Freedom from error	Timeliness	Comparability
Feedback value	Consistency	Predictive value

Instructions

Identify the appropriate qualitative characteristic(s) to be used given the information provided below.

   a. The qualitative characteristic being employed when companies in the same industry are using the same accounting policies.

   b. Quality of information that confirms users' earlier expectations.

   c. Necessary for providing comparisons of a company from period to period.

   d. Ignores the economic consequences of a standard.

   e. Requires a high degree of consensus among individuals on a given measurement.

   f. Predictive value is an ingredient of this fundamental quality of information.

   g. Four qualitative characteristics that are related to both relevance and faithful representation.

   h. Neutrality is an ingredient of this fundamental quality of accounting information.

i. Two fundamental qualities that make accounting information useful for decision-making purposes.

j. Issuance of interim reports is an example of this enhancing quality of relevance.

E2.4 (LO 3) (Elements of Financial Statements) The elements that are most directly related to measuring an enterprise's performance and financial status follow:

Assets	Expenses	Liabilities
Gains	Equity	Revenues
Losses		

Instructions

a. Indicate which element is being described below. For any item that is an asset or liability, consider if the item qualifies according to the definitions under IFRS. For purposes of this exercise, consider revenues, expenses, gains, and losses separately.

1. Arises from peripheral or incidental transactions.

2. Obliges a transfer of resources because of a present, enforceable obligation.

3. Increases in the ownership interest through issuance of shares.

4. Cash dividends to owners (declared and paid).

5. An expenditure that has future economic benefit.

6. Decreases in assets during the period for the payment of income taxes.

7. Arises from income-generating activities that are the entity's ongoing major or central operations.

8. Is the residual interest in the enterprise's assets after deducting its liabilities.

9. Increases assets during the period through the sale of inventory.

10. Decreases assets during the period by purchasing the company's own shares.

b. Indicate which element listed above is being illustrated in the examples that follow.

1. Notes Co. has a written contract to receive money from the sale of copies of future recordings of music yet to be written.

2. ReadyMart Inc. has inventory out on consignment at a local retailer waiting for sale to the final customer.

3. Music Corp. has a written contract to deliver a percentage of future music revenues (royalties) from the sale of existing recordings.

E2.5 (LO 4) Law Taxation **(Forms of Organizations)**

Instructions

a. Identify three common forms of business organizations. Briefly outline the pros and cons of setting up a company using each form of organization.

b. Identify why accounting professionals use limited liability partnerships and professional corporations.

E2.6 (LO 4) (Foundational Principles) The foundational principles and assumptions of accounting are as follows:

Recognition/Derecognition	Measurement	Presentation and Disclosure
1. Economic entity	5. Periodicity	10. Full disclosure
2. Control	6. Monetary unit	
3. Revenue recognition and realization	7. Going concern	
4. Matching	8. Historical cost	
	9. Fair value and value in use	

Instructions

For each situation that follows, identify by its number the foundational principle above that is described.

a. Allocates expenses to revenues in the proper period.

b. Indicates that market value changes after the purchase are not recorded in the accounts unless impairment exists. (Do not use the revenue recognition principle.)

c. Ensures that all relevant financial information is reported.

d. Is why plant assets are not reported at their liquidation value. (Do not use the historical cost principle.)

e. Related to the economic entity principle, defines the entities that should be consolidated in the financial statements.

f. Indicates that personal and business record-keeping should be separately maintained.

g. Separates financial information into time periods for reporting purposes.

h. Permits the use of market valuation in certain specific situations.

i. Requires passing of risks and rewards, measurability, and collectibility before recording the transaction.

j. Assumes that the dollar is the measuring unit for reporting financial performance.

E2.7 (LO 4) **(Foundational Principles)** The following are operational guidelines and practices that have developed over time for financial reporting.

1. Price-level changes (inflation and deflation) are not recognized in the accounting records.

2. Sufficient financial information is presented so that reasonably prudent investors will not be misled.

3. Property, plant, and equipment are capitalized and depreciated over the periods that they benefit.

4. There is no intent to liquidate the company's operations or activities.

5. Market value is used by companies for the valuation of certain securities that are regularly bought and sold.

6. After initial acquisition, the entity values land at its original transaction price.

7. All significant post–balance sheet events are reported.

8. Revenue is recorded at the point of sale.

9. All important aspects of bond indentures are presented in financial statements.

10. The rationale for accrual accounting is stated.

11. The use of consolidated statements is justified.

12. Reporting must be done at defined time intervals.

13. An allowance for doubtful accounts is established.

14. Goodwill is recorded only at the time of a business combination and does not change unless the goodwill becomes impaired.

15. Sales commission costs are charged to expense in the period of the sale.

Instructions

Select the foundational principle that best justifies each of these procedures and practices.

E2.8 (LO 4) **(Foundational Principles)** ASPE and IFRS have differing criteria for whether an element should be recognized or not. Assume that Thatcher Inc. (TI) is the subject of a lawsuit. TI sells prepared food on a wholesale basis to supermarket chains (which resell the food at a retail level). The food is perishable and must be kept refrigerated. Recently, a customer purchased some of the food from a local supermarket and then was very ill. They have sued TI and the supermarket. The lawsuit has just been launched and has yet to go to court. It is unclear whether the food was tainted when it was sold to the supermarket or whether the supermarket failed to keep the food properly refrigerated before it was sold. TI has spoken with its lawyers and determined that there is more than a low probability that TI is at fault but is not sure at this point whether it is probable that it will lose the lawsuit.

Instructions

Using only the conceptual frameworks (and not other specific GAAP), complete the items below.

a. List the recognition criteria under ASPE and IFRS, noting how they differ.

b. Identify the three essential characteristics of a liability (the definition of a liability).

c. Discuss the terms "existence uncertainty," "outcome uncertainty," and "measurement uncertainty" as they relate to the recognition criteria.

d. Apply the recognition criteria under both ASPE and IFRS to the lawsuit.

E2.9 (LO 4) **(Foundational Principles)** Jasper Bakery Limited signed a purchase order to buy 50 kg of butter from a farmer over the next month at a fixed price. The butter is of exceptional quality and will be used in baked goods that will be sold in the bakery.

Instructions

a. Define the term "executory contract."

b. Is the contract to buy the butter an executory contract? Explain.

E2.10 (LO 2) **(Qualitative Characteristics)** The ASPE conceptual framework acknowledges the concept of conservatism.

Instructions

a. Define the term "conservatism."

b. IFRS introduced the term "prudence" in the new Conceptual Framework. Explain what this means.

c. Is conservatism and/or prudence in conflict with the concept of neutrality? Explain.

E2.11 (LO 1, 2, 4) **(Foundational Principles)** Examples of operational guidelines used by accountants follow.

1. The treasurer of Sweet Grapes Corp. would like to prepare financial statements only during downturns in the company's wine production, which occur periodically when the grape crop fails. He states that it is at such times that the statements could be most easily prepared. The company would never allow more than 30 months to pass without statements being prepared.

2. Tower Manufacturing Ltd. decided to manufacture its own widgets because it would be cheaper than buying them from an outside supplier. In an attempt to make its statements comparable with those of its competitors, Tower charged its inventory account for what it felt the widgets would have cost if they had been purchased from an outside supplier. (Do not use the revenue recognition principle.)

3. Cargo Discount Centres buys its merchandise by the truckload and train carload. Cargo does not include any transportation costs in calculating the cost of its ending inventory. Such costs, although they vary from period to period, are always material in amount.

4. Quick & Healthy, a fast-food company, sells franchises for $100,000, accepting a $5,000 down payment and a 25-year note for the remainder. Quick & Healthy promises to assist in site selection, building, and management training for three years. Quick & Healthy records the full $100,000 franchise fee as revenue when the contract is signed.

5. Kalil Corp. faces a possible government expropriation (that is, takeover) of its foreign facilities and possible losses on amounts that are owed by various customers who are almost bankrupt. The company president has decided that these possibilities should not be noted on the financial statements because Kalil still hopes that these events will not take place.

6. Maurice Norris, owner of Rare Bookstore Inc., bought a computer for his own use. He paid for the computer by writing a cheque on the bookstore chequing account and charged the Office Equipment account.

7. Brock Inc. decides that it will be selling its subsidiary, Breck Inc., in a few years. Brock has excluded Breck's activities from its consolidated financial results.

8. Wilhelm Corporation expensed the purchase of new manufacturing equipment.

9. A large lawsuit has been filed against Mahoney Corp. Mahoney has recorded a loss and related estimated liability that is equal to the maximum possible amount that it feels it might lose. Mahoney is confident, however, that either it will win the suit or it will owe a much smaller amount.

Instructions

a. Discuss the usefulness of a conceptual framework.

b. For each of the situations above, list the foundational principle or qualitative characteristic of financial information that has been violated.

E2.12 (LO 2) **(Qualitative Characteristics)** In general, financial information should include all relevant information that faithfully represents the economic substance of business transactions.

Instructions

Discuss whether it is possible for financial information to have all of the qualitative characteristics.

E2.13 (LO 2, 3, 4) **(Conceptual Framework—Comprehensive)** The following are transactions recorded by Trimm Corporation during the current year.

1. Ordinary operating maintenance on equipment was recorded as follows:

| Equipment | 2,500 | |
| Accounts Payable | | 2,500 |

2. Trimm received an advance on a custom order for merchandise that will be shipped during the next accounting year.

| Cash | 8,000 | |
| Sales Revenue | | 8000 |

3. Trimm Corporation is holding inventory on consignment for Rubber Ltd. Trimm will only pay Rubber when a sale is made to a customer. Trimm made the following entry when it received the inventory:

Inventory	15,000	
Accounts Payable		15,000

4. On the last day of the accounting period, a 12-month insurance policy was purchased. The insurance coverage is for the next accounting year.

Insurance Expense	4,000	
Cash		4,000

Instructions

For each transaction, determine which component of the conceptual framework (that is, qualitative characteristic, element, or principle) was violated, if any, and give the entry that should have been recorded if there was a violation.

E2.14 (LO 4, 5) **(Full Disclosure Principle)** The following information is for Brittany Inc.

1. To be more concise, the company decided that only net income should be reported on the income statement. Details on revenues, cost of goods sold, and expenses were also omitted from the notes to the financial statements.

2. Equipment purchases of $270,000 were partly financed during the year by issuing a $110,000 note payable. The company offset the equipment against the note payable and reported plant assets at $160,000. No information has been provided in the notes.

3. During the year, an assistant controller for the company embezzled $50,000. Brittany's net income for the year was $2.3 million. Neither the assistant controller nor the money has been found. No information has been provided in the notes.

4. Brittany has reported its ending inventory at $2.7 million in the financial statements. No other information on inventories is presented in the financial statements and related notes.

5. The company changed its method of depreciating equipment from the double-declining balance to the straight-line method. This change is not mentioned anywhere in the financial statements or in the related notes.

Instructions

a. Explain the meaning and implications of the full disclosure principle and how such information may be provided to users.

b. For each of the situations above, discuss whether Brittany has followed acceptable accounting and disclosure practices.

E2.15 (LO 4) **(Going Concern Assumption)**

Instructions

a. Explain the meaning and implications of the going concern assumption in financial accounting.

b. If the going concern assumption did not apply in accounting, how would this affect the amounts shown in the financial statements for the following items?
   1. Equipment
   2. Unamortized bond premium
   3. Depreciation expense
   4. Inventory
   5. Prepaid insurance

E2.16 (LO 4, 5) **(Revenue Recognition Principle)** The following independent situations require professional judgement for determining when to recognize revenue from the transactions.

1. Air Yukon sells you an advance purchase airline ticket in September for your flight home at Christmas.

2. Better Buy Ltd. sells you a home theatre on a "no money down, no interest, and no payments for one year" promotional deal.

3. The Centurions baseball team sells season tickets to games online. Fans can purchase the tickets at any time, although the season doesn't officially begin until April. It runs from April through October.

4. River's End Ltd. sells you a sweater. In August, you placed the order using River's End's online catalogue. The sweater arrives in September and you charge it to your River's End credit card. You receive and pay the credit card bill in October.

Instructions

a. Explain when revenue is recognized in each of these situations under ASPE.

b. Identify when revenue should be recognized in each of the situations under the IFRS 15 model.

Problems

P2.1 Foundational principles of financial reporting may be grouped into four categories: recognition/derecognition, measurement, presentation, and disclosure.

Instructions

Briefly describe what is meant by these terms.

P2.2 Fusters Inc. provides audited financial statements to its creditors and is required to maintain certain covenants based on its debt to equity ratio and return on assets. In addition, management of Fusters receives a bonus partially based on revenues for the year. Information related to Fusters Inc. follows.

1. Depreciation expense on the building for the year was $45,000. Because the building was increasing in value during the year, the controller decided not to record any depreciation expense in the current year.

2. New legislation was discussed by the government that would require new pollution control technology for companies such as Fusters. Prior to this, Fusters had been complying with all current requirements and otherwise believed that it was acting in an environmentally responsible manner. In anticipation of this legislation being passed next year, Fusters expects it will need to upgrade its equipment and has booked the following entry:

Equipment	121,000	
Accounts Payable		121,000

3. During the year, the company sold certain equipment for $285,000, recognizing a gain of $45,000. Because the controller believed that new equipment would be needed in the near future, the controller decided to defer the gain and depreciate it over the life of the new equipment that would soon be purchased.

4. An order for $61,500 was received from a customer on December 29, for products on hand. This order was shipped f.o.b. shipping point on January 9, 2021. The company made the following entry for 2020:

Accounts Receivable	61,500	
Sales Revenue		61,500

Instructions

a. Discuss the reporting objectives of the users of Fusters' financial statements.

b. **Ethics** Comment on the appropriateness of Fusters' accounting procedures and their impact on the company's financial statement users, applying the conceptual framework.

c. Discuss whether there are alternatives available under IFRS to provide the reporting desired by Fusters' management.

P2.3 Transactions from Gravenhurst Inc.'s current year follow. Gravenhurst follows IFRS.

1. Gravenhurst Inc. thinks it should dispose of its excess land. While the carrying value is $50,000, current market prices are depressed and only $25,000 is expected upon disposal. The following journal entry was made:

Loss on Disposal of Land	25,000	
Land		25,000

2. Merchandise inventory that cost $630,000 was reported on the statement of financial position at $690,000, which is the expected selling price less estimated selling costs. The following entry was made to record this increase in value:

Inventory	60,000	
Sales Revenue		60,000

3. The company is being sued for $500,000 by a customer who claims damages for personal injury that was allegedly caused by a defective product. Company lawyers feel extremely confident that the company will have no liability for damages resulting from the situation. Nevertheless, the company decides to make the following entry:

Litigation Expense	450,000	
Litigation Liability		450,000

4. Because the general level of prices increased during the current year, Gravenhurst Inc. determined that there was a $15,000 understatement of depreciation expense on its equipment and decided to record it in its accounts. The following entry was made:

Depreciation Expense	15,000	
Accumulated Depreciation—Equipment		15,000

5. Gravenhurst Inc. has been concerned about whether intangible assets could generate cash in case of liquidation. As a result, goodwill arising from a business acquisition during the current year and recorded at $800,000 was written off as follows:

Retained Earnings	800,000	
Goodwill		800,000

6. Because of a "fire sale," equipment that was obviously worth $200,000 was acquired at a bargain price of $155,000. The following entry was made:

Equipment	200,000	
Cash		155,000
Gain		45,000

Instructions

Digging Deeper In each of the above situations, discuss the appropriateness of the journal entries in terms of generally accepted accounting principles. For the purposes of your discussion, assume that the financial statements, particularly net income, will be used by the court in a divorce settlement for the company president's spouse.

P2.4 Accounting information provides useful data about business transactions and events. The people who provide and use financial reports must often select and evaluate accounting alternatives. The conceptual framework that was discussed in this chapter examines the characteristics of accounting information that make it useful for decision-making. It also points out that various limitations that are part of the measurement and reporting process can make it necessary to trade off or sacrifice some of the characteristics of useful information.

Instructions

a. For each of the following pairs of qualitative characteristics, give an example of a situation in which one of the characteristics may be sacrificed for a gain in the other:

1. Relevance and verifiability
2. Relevance and comparability
3. Relevance and timeliness
4. Relevance and understandability

b. What criterion should be used to evaluate trade-offs between information characteristics?

P2.5 You are hired to review the accounting records of Sheridan Inc. (a public corporation) before it closes its revenue and expense accounts as at December 31, 2020, the end of its current fiscal year. The following information comes to your attention.

1. During the current year, Sheridan Inc. changed its shipment policy from f.o.b. destination to f.o.b. shipping point. This would result in an additional $50,000 of revenue being recorded for fiscal 2020.

2. The estimated remaining useful life of its manufacturing equipment was reviewed by management and increased by five years. This reduced depreciation expense by $30,000 during fiscal 2020.

3. Due to the recent deterioration in the age of outstanding accounts receivable, Sheridan's controller changed the percentage of accounts receivable from 4.5% to 6% when arriving at the allowance for doubtful accounts for the year ended December 31, 2020. This revision in the percentage used was applied to the previous year and an additional $50,000 was recorded as bad debt expense for the year ended December 31, 2019.

4. The controller changed the classification of one expense on the comprehensive income statements for 2020 and 2019. The expense had been previously reported as a selling expense and is now re-classified as an administrative expense. The controller didn't agree with the treatment given in prior years. Nothing was mentioned in the financial statements concerning implementing this change as he reasoned that net income and any key financial ratios remained unaffected.

5. During the year, Sheridan had an opportunity to buy equipment at an auction when its competitor went bankrupt. The equipment had to be purchased as bundles. Some of the equipment in the bundle purchased could be used by Sheridan immediately. Some of the equipment in the bundle did not fit the company's operations and had to be held for resale. The resale was expected to take place early in 2021. The purchase price of the bundle of equipment was added to property, plant, and equipment and depreciated in 2020. The controller mentioned that the price paid for the equipment was such a bargain that any future gain or loss from the resale of equipment will not have any material effect on net income.

6. During fiscal 2020, new government legislation was passed requiring companies like Sheridan to install additional health and safety devices in their offices by 2025. Although Sheridan does not intend to retrofit the required new devices until 2025, an accrual for $375,500 has been established in the year-end financial statements for the future installation costs.

7. To maintain customer goodwill, Sheridan voluntarily recalled some products during the year. Sheridan has not established an accrual and is recording the sales returns as they happen.

Instructions

State whether or not you agree with each of the accounting decisions made by Sheridan Inc. Explain your reasoning and, wherever possible, support your answers by referring to the generally accepted accounting principles that apply to the circumstances.

P2.6 The following transactions fall somewhere in the continuum of choices in accounting decision-making that is shown in Illustration 2.7.

1. The company president approaches one of the company's creditors to ask for a modification of the repayment terms so that they extend beyond the current year. This would make the liabilities long-term rather than short-term and would improve the company's current ratio.

2. The controller determines that significant amounts of capital assets are impaired and should be written off. Coincidentally, the company is currently showing lower levels of net income but expects better results in the following years.

3. The company management decides to use FIFO as opposed to weighted average, since it more closely approximates the flow of costs.

4. The vice-president of finance decides to capitalize interest during the self-construction of its properties. This policy will increase net income and several profitability ratios.

5. The business owner enters into an arrangement with a business associate whereby they will buy each other's merchandise before year end. The merchandise will then be shipped to customers after year end from the holding company's warehouse.

6. The assets and liabilities of an investment have been consolidated into Maher Company's annual financial statements. Maher Company does not have the power to direct the investee's activities.

7. The corporate litigation lawyer representing the business in its defence against a patent infringement lawsuit is uncertain about the possible outcome of the case, as he has only recently been engaged in the matter. Although there is considerable work to be done to establish the merits of the case, management has decided to accrue in the current period half of the amount claimed under the lawsuit. Management is worried that the board of directors may declare dividends in the current year that will have to be reduced in a subsequent year, when the case is ultimately settled.

Instructions

Ethics For each situation, state where it falls in the continuum of choices in decision-making.

P2.7 A Special Committee on Financial Reporting proposed the following constraints related to financial reporting.

1. Business reporting should exclude information outside of management's expertise or for which management is not the best source, such as information about competitors.

2. Management should not be required to report information that would significantly harm the company's competitive position.

3. Management should not be required to provide forecast financial statements. Rather, management should provide information that helps users forecast for themselves the company's financial future.

4. Other than for financial statements, management need report only the information it knows. That is, management should be under no obligation to gather information it does not have, or does not need, in order to manage the business.

5. Companies should present certain elements of business reporting only if users and management agree they should be reported—a concept of flexible reporting.

Instructions

For each item, briefly discuss how the proposed constraint addresses concerns about the costs and benefits of financial reporting.

P2.8 Recently, your Uncle Warren, who knows that you always have your eye out for a profitable investment, has discussed the possibility of your purchasing some corporate bonds that he just learned of. He suggests that you may wish to get in on the ground floor of this deal. The bonds being issued by Jingle Corp. are 10-year debentures, which promise a 40% rate of return. Jingle manufactures novelty and party items.

You have told Uncle Warren that, unless you can take a look at Jingle's financial statements, you would not feel comfortable about such an investment. Thinking that this is the chance of a lifetime, Uncle Warren has obtained a copy of Jingle's most recent, unaudited financial statements, which are a year old. These statements were prepared by Mrs. Jingle. You look over these statements, and they are quite impressive.

The statement of financial position showed a debt to equity ratio of 1:10 and, for the year shown, the company reported net income of $2,424,240.

The financial statements are not shown in comparison with amounts from other years. In addition, there are no significant note disclosures about inventory valuation, depreciation methods, loan agreements, and so on.

Instructions

Write a letter to Uncle Warren explaining why it would be unwise to base an investment decision on the financial statements that he has given you. Refer to the concepts discussed in this chapter.

Cases

Refer to the Case Primer on the Student Website and in WileyPLUS *to help you answer these cases.*

CA2.1 **Real World Emphasis** **Bre-X Minerals,** a small Canadian mining company, announced in the early 1990s that it had discovered a fairly significant gold deposit in Indonesia. The company's shares skyrocketed from pennies a share to over $280 per share. Subsequently, it was discovered that the company had been "salting the samples" and that there was little, if any, gold there. This information was not disclosed to the market until long after it was discovered that there was no gold. Certain parties who had access to this information benefited; however, many investors lost a significant amount of money. For example, the Ontario Municipal Employees Retirement System and the Ontario Teachers' Pension Plan lost millions of dollars. Investors sued the company and its management for providing misleading information.

Instructions

Using the conceptual framework, identify and analyze the financial reporting issues.

CA2.2 **Ethics** Environmental Inc. operates in Canada and the United States. Its basic business is high-temperature treatment services for contaminated soil. In its 2020 financial statements, the company had a loss of $9.3 million (and an accumulated deficit of $43.7 million).

In the notes to the financial statements, the company stated that it deferred certain transportation costs and recorded them as assets. These costs relate to shipping contaminated materials to the treatment plant. They are reimbursable under the terms of the contract. Per Note 10, the company can only run efficiently when it operates continuously for extended periods; however, demand for the services is sporadic. Therefore, the company's business model is structured such that it shuts down operations and otherwise stockpiles inventory. These shutdown periods are followed by active periods during which it processes the stockpiled inventory. Revenues for 2020, a shutdown period, were $0.

In addition, the company received a subpoena from the U.S. Department of Justice regarding conspiracy to commit fraud with respect to the bidding process on a government project. During 2020, the courts stayed proceedings, essentially halting them for the time being.

Instructions

Assume that the financial statements must be issued prior to the resolution of the lawsuit. Discuss the financial reporting issues. The company's shares are publicly traded.

CA2.3 `Finance` The statement that follows about Timber Corporation appeared in a financial magazine:

> The land and timber holdings are now carried on the company's books at a mere $100 million (U.S.). The value of the timber alone is variously estimated at $1 billion to $3 billion and is rising all the time. The understatement is pretty severe, conceded company management, who noted, "We have a whole stream of profit nobody sees and there is no way to show it on our books."

Instructions

Act as an analyst and discuss the financial reporting issues. Use the principles noted in Chapter 2 (only) to analyze the issues.

Research and Analysis

RA2.1 `Real World Emphasis` **Teck Resources Limited**

Obtain the 2017 financial statements of Teck Resources Limited from SEDAR (www.sedar.com).

Instructions

a. Using the notes to the consolidated financial statements, determine the company's revenue recognition policy. Comment on whether the company uses an aggressive or conservative method for reporting revenue.

b. Give two examples where historical cost information is reported in the financial statements and related notes. Give two examples where fair value information is reported in either the financial statements or the related notes.

c. Did Teck implement any new pronouncements under IFRS ahead of the implementation deadlines? What were the reasons given for the adoption or non-adoption? From the perspective of a user of the financial statements, would you be in agreement with the treatment given by Teck?

RA2.2 `Real World Emphasis` **Air Canada**

In its 2017 financial statements (Note 3), Air Canada has disclosed its critical estimates and judgements used in preparing the financial statements.

Instructions

Access the 2017 audited annual financial statements for Air Canada for the year ended December 31, 2017, from the company's website or SEDAR (www.sedar.com). Read Note 3 and related notes and answer the following questions.

a. What are the main critical accounting estimates and judgements that the company discloses? Briefly outline each.

b. Why is it important that the company disclose these types of judgements? Consider this question from a user perspective.

c. How significant are the related financial statement elements?

RA2.3 Retrieval of Information on Public Company

There are several commonly available indexes and reference products to help find articles that have appeared in business publications and periodicals. Articles can generally be searched by company or by subject matter. Several common sources are Canadian Business and Current Affairs (CBCA Fulltext Business), Investex Plus, The Wall Street Journal Index, Business Abstracts (formerly the Business Periodical Index), EBSCO Business Source Premier, and ABI/Inform.

Instructions

Use one of these resources to find an article about a company that interests you. Read the article and answer the following questions. (*Note:* Your library may have hard-copy or CD-ROM versions of these sources or they may be available through your library's electronic database.)

a. What is the article about?

    b. What specific information about the company is included in the article?

    c. Identify any accounting-related issues that are discussed in the article.

RA2.4 Fair Values

Using fair values came under attack in light of the credit crunch of the last decade and the related financial crisis. Some have even accused fair value accounting of exacerbating the crisis. Access the following articles: "Discussing the Credit Crunch," *IASB INSIGHT Journal*, Q1 and Q2 (from www.ifrs.org), and "Fair Values: When the Engine Overheats, Don't Blame the Oil Light," by Paul Cherry and Ian Hague, *CA Magazine*, June/July 2009 (from http://www.cpacanada.ca/en/connecting-and-news/cpa-magazine/cpa-magazine-archives/CA-Magazine-archives). You can also access PricewaterhouseCoopers' report on Fair Value Measurements, Global Edition on its website at https://www.pwc.com/us/en/cfodirect/publications/accounting-guides/fair-value-measurements-asc-820.html.

Instructions

Using the articles and report, answer the following questions:

    a. What impact does using fair values to report assets and liabilities have on the financial statements?

    b. Why do some people believe that using fair values is not appropriate for financial reporting? Discuss this in light of the financial crisis that began in 2007.

    c. What are the arguments in support of using fair values in financial reporting?

    d. Do you think fair value accounting should be used in the preparation of financial statements?

    e. Does IFRS allow for greater use of fair values than ASPE? Discuss, giving examples.

RA2.5 Conservatism/Neutrality

Access the *Investor Perspectives* article written by Steve Cooper, a member of the IASB, in June 2015, entitled "A Tale of 'Prudence'?" (https://www.ifrs.org/-/media/feature/resources-for-investors/investor-perspectives/investor-perspective-jun-2015.pdf). Mr. Cooper states that two different meanings have been attributed to the term "prudence" when it is used as part of the conceptual framework of financial reporting.

Instructions

    a. What two meanings does Steve Cooper describe as having been attributed to the term "prudence"? Explain each briefly.

    b. Identify which meaning has been supported by the IASB in issuing a revised conceptual framework in 2018. What major arguments support the IASB's position?

RA2.6 Faithful Representation

In the IASB standard-setting conceptual framework, the word "reliability" has been replaced with "faithful representation." This has caused much discussion among preparers of financial information. The change has led to other implications related to substance over form, neutrality, conservatism, and the ability of entities to "override" a standard in very rare circumstances.

Instructions

Discuss the following questions. (You may find the IASB's *Basis for Conclusions on the Exposure Draft Conceptual Framework for Financial Reporting*, of May 2015 (https://www.ifrs.org/-/media/project/conceptual-framework/exposure-draft/published-documents/ed-conceptual-framework-basis-conclusions.pdf), and *Summary of the Discussion Paper: A Review of the Conceptual Framework for Financial Reporting*, of January 2015 (http://archive.ifrs.org/Current-Projects/IASB-Projects/Conceptual-Framework/Documents/Effect-of-Board-decisions-on-DP-January-2015.pdf), helpful in your discussion.)

    a. "Faithful representation" has replaced the term "reliability" as a fundamental qualitative characteristic of financial information. What does faithful representation mean and how does this differ from reliability? Why was the term "reliability" replaced?

    b. What does "substance over form" mean? Give examples of where this might be relevant.

RA2.7 Measurement Uncertainty

Bancroft Corporation (BC) has just completed its analysis of the income taxes that it believes it will have to pay to the government either this year or in future years. Although he feels that the final estimate of income taxes payable is probably fine, Jason Bacon, the controller, is a bit concerned, because some of the assumptions underlying the calculations required a fair bit of judgement. In one case, the company has deducted an item from taxable income, resulting in less taxes payable. The taxes payable amount is calculated as the dollar amount of the deduction times the tax rate. The controller is worried that if BC is audited by the Canada Revenue Agency, it may deny the deduction and BC would subsequently have to pay additional income taxes. The tax rates are not expected to change. Jason has reasonable tax knowledge but does not consider himself an expert.

Instructions

The chapter discusses several concepts relating to dealing with uncertainty. These include existence uncertainty, outcome uncertainty, and measurement uncertainty.

a. Define each of these terms.

b. Discuss how each of these terms relates to the measurement of the income tax liability.

RA2.8 **Data Analytics**   **Measurement Uncertainty and Artificial Intelligence/Big Data**

Refer to the scenario in RA2.7 regarding Bancroft Corporation (BC). Jason has been reading lately about artificial intelligence and big data. He notes during a quick Internet search that a company called **Blue J Legal** has created a product that scans and analyzes all prior court rulings on a particular legal or tax topic and helps predict whether the tax assumption made or position taken by a company is sound based on prior rulings. He notes that there are numerous other companies using artificial intelligence and "Big Data" to gather evidence, which is then analyzed. These tools do cost money, however.

Instructions

a. How might artificial intelligence and Big Data help Jason in dealing with the measurement uncertainty? (*Hint:* Go to Blue J Legal's website, or that of any similar company using artificial intelligence and Big Data).

b. As a potential investor in BC, how much time and expense do you think BC should go to in order to make sure that the tax liability measurement is representationally faithful?

Measurement

Big Data Has Big Accounting Potential

Data Analytics Chances are good that many of the transactions you make and movements you take every day are captured and stored in a database for some company or government to make use of. When you buy something online, pass in front of a video security camera, or pull up to a traffic light, those data might be gathered and used to market something to you or predict future economic trends. For example, a top U.S. finance executive waiting on the tarmac for his plane to take off sent a tweet to the airline, thanking them for playing his favourite song on the intercom. He got an instant tweet back. The airline would be collecting the data to use when planning future entertainment. In New Zealand, the ANZ bank uses traffic volume data to compile the "ANZ Truckometer," a set of two economic indicators that help forecast gross domestic product. In New Zealand, most freight is moved by road, so an increase in traffic can signal an increase in economic activity.

These examples are part of a phenomenon called Big Data, where corporations and governments collect billions of bytes of data to be analyzed for budgeting, marketing, and planning purposes. Walmart, for example, gathers more than 2.5 petabytes of information from customer transactions every hour—enough data to fill almost 4 million CD ROMs.

How can data analytics help with accounting? Among its many uses is in providing more accurate fair value estimates for items that don't have an available market price, such as investments in start-up companies that don't have shares traded on a public market. Accountants and other valuators use professional judgement to arrive at and report a fair value of these types of investments, but the amounts can vary widely. In the United States, the Securities and Exchange Commission has begun looking at the fact that different mutual funds with investments in the same private companies can report different values of those investments on the same day. Data analytics can help smooth out those estimates by tapping into Big Data on such things as consumer buying habits in a start-up's industry, and non-financial information such as customer reviews of a start-up's products on social media or how many people click through to a link in a promotional email.

Organizations that use data analytics to strengthen their fair value estimates can increase transparency for shareholders and reduce the risk of running afoul of securities regulators for having inaccurate asset valuations. Data analytics can also help companies uncover potential internal fraud by employees who might be inflating the value of assets to help them earn a bonus or promotion.

Data analytics doesn't just use more data: it collates scattered data to paint a bigger picture of trends and allow companies to search a database to get a more accurate valuation of assets similar to theirs. And Big Data includes such things as video and audio data, something traditional accounting systems have never been able to capture.

Sources: Zabihollah Rezaee and Jim Wang, "Big Data, Big Impact on Accounting," *A Plus* magazine, Hong Kong Institute of Certified Public Accountants, October 2017; Suresh Sood, "Big Data Accounting: The Predictive Accountant," *Acuity* magazine, Chartered Accountants Australia and New Zealand, March 6, 2017; Greg Forsythe, Erik Dilger, and Heather Harris, "Harness the Power: How Advanced Analytics in Valuation Is Driving Value," Deloitte Development LLC, 2016; David M. Katz, "Accounting's Big Data Problem," CFO.com, March 4, 2014.

LEARNING OBJECTIVES	CHAPTER OUTLINE	CPA COMPETENCIES
After studying this chapter, you should be able to:	The chapter headings related to the learning objective are:	Competencies addressed by each learning objective are as follows:
1. Use valuation techniques to measure financial statement elements.	**Measuring Financial Statement Elements** • Valuation techniques • Value in use measurements • Disclosures relating to measurement	**1.1.2, 1.1.3, 1.2.1, 1.2.2, 5.4.1, 5.4.2, 5.4.3**
2. Use IFRS 13 to measure fair value.	**Measuring Fair Value Using IFRS 13**	**1.1.2, 1.1.3, 1.2.1, 1.2.2, 1.2.3, 1.4.5, 5.4.1, 5.4.2, 5.4.3**
3. Understand and apply present value concepts.	**Present Value Concepts** • The nature of interest • Fundamental variables in present value calculations • Different ways to perform the calculations • Some additional calculations	**1.1.3, 1.2.2, 5.4.1, 5.4.2, 5.4.3**
4. Identify differences in accounting between ASPE and IFRS, and what changes are expected in the near future.	**IFRS/ASPE Comparison** • A comparison of IFRS and ASPE • Looking ahead	**1.1.4**

Preview of Chapter 3

How we measure financial statement elements affects income and key ratios significantly. Therefore, it is important to understand how companies measure and record transactions. This chapter presents the tools and techniques that will help you understand how financial statement elements are measured.

Similar to Chapter 2, Chapter 3 provides foundational knowledge that you will need in subsequent chapters.

Measuring Financial Statement Elements

LEARNING OBJECTIVE 1

Use valuation techniques to measure financial statement elements.

A significant part of accounting is measurement. As we discussed in Chapter 2, we have a mixed-attribute measurement model. That is, many items are measured based on historical cost (such as property, plant, and equipment, and inventory), but many are based on fair value (such as certain financial instruments). Some measurements fall in between: they are not quite fair value measurements but neither are they completely historical cost measurements. Determining an item's fair value is fairly straightforward when market prices are available. However, when a market price is not available, accountants must rely on valuation models to develop a fair value estimate.

Illustration 3.1 lists some examples of the three measurement categorizations.

ILLUSTRATION 3.1 **Measurement Categorizations and Some Examples of Each**

Cost-based measures (for example, historical cost)	Hybrid measures (for example, those that have some attributes of cost-based and current value)	Current value measures (for example, fair value measures)
Property, plant, and equipment carried at cost or net book value (depreciated cost) (under ASPE 3061 and IAS 16)	Impaired property, plant, and equipment measured at the recoverable amount (higher of the value in use and fair value less costs of disposal) (under IAS 36)	Financial instruments carried at fair value (under ASPE 3856 and IFRS 9)
Financial instruments carried at cost or amortized cost using the effective interest or straight-line methods to amortize premiums and discounts (under ASPE 3856 and IFRS 9)	Inventory measured at the lower of cost and net realizable value (under ASPE 3031 and IAS 2)	Biological assets (IAS 41)
Inventory using various cost flow assumptions, such as weighted average and FIFO (under ASPE 3031 and IAS 2)	Impaired notes receivable measured using management best estimates of revised cash flows discounted at the original historical discount rate (under IFRS 9)	Investment properties (option to measure at fair value under IAS 40)

In addition, we need to think about measurement on initial recognition of the asset, liability, or other element and then again subsequently (for instance, at subsequent financial reporting dates). It is generally easier to measure an initial exchange transaction—usually the transaction is measured at fair value on the transaction date as long as it is arm's length. However, it may be more difficult to determine the subsequent value. Valuation techniques may need to be used.

Historical cost measures, including depreciation and the effective interest method, have a long history and are well developed. We will discuss these further in subsequent chapters. The rest of this chapter will deal with some basic measurement techniques that are more rooted in economics and finance.

Valuation Techniques

Finance 5.4.1, 5.4.2, 5.4.3 Whether we are trying to come up with a cost-based measure, a current value measure, or something in between, there are many techniques that may be used to measure value.

Two common types of valuation techniques are noted below:[1]

1. **Income models:** These techniques convert future amounts (such as future cash flows to be generated by an asset) to current amounts (that is, amounts adjusted for the time value of money). Examples include discounted cash flows and option pricing models. Both of these use present value concepts. Present value concepts are very commonly

---

[1]These techniques are discussed in IFRS 13.62 and the related appendix to IFRS 13 in the context of fair value measurements. IFRS 13 mentions a third approach that may be used to measure fair value: the current cost model/approach. This approach is also mentioned in the newly issued IFRS Conceptual Framework and was discussed in Chapter 2.

used in measurement and we will revisit them later in this chapter and throughout the text.

2. **Market models:** These techniques use prices and other information generated from market transactions involving identical or similar transactions. An example is the earnings multiples model. Under this example, an investment in a privately owned company may be valued using publicly available earnings numbers for similar companies as well as multiples that are generated by comparing publicly available earnings numbers with share prices. We will look at earnings multiples in more detail in Chapter 4.

A measurement may be thought of as having three components: the inputs or assumptions, the model or technique, and the measurement itself. This is shown in **Illustration 3.2**.

ILLUSTRATION 3.2

Using Models to Measure Elements

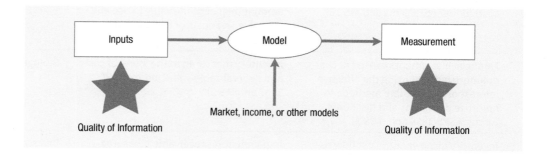

When measuring the value of a financial statement element, accountants must ask and answer three questions:

1. Which model or technique should be used?
2. Which inputs should be used?
3. Does the resulting measurement result in useful information?

Note that the quality of the measurement depends on the quality of the information used and the choice of the model. Certain measurements are seen to be of higher quality because they produce more useful information.

We will discuss each of these three questions below.

Which Model?

How do we decide which model to use? It depends on the item being measured. For instance, in measuring the impairment value of a unique manufacturing facility, it might make sense to use a discounted cash flow calculation (income model). It is likely that comparable market information would not be available for the manufacturing facility given its uniqueness. Thus a market model would not be a good choice. Management is likely able to determine cash flow projections and a suitable discount rate. Income models are frequently used in practice and we will therefore emphasize them in this and subsequent chapters. Many market models are beyond the scope of this text.

You were likely exposed to present value calculations in an introductory accounting or finance course. We have included an overview of basic present value concepts in the next section as a refresher.

Illustration 3.3 gives examples of measurements using present values and discounted cash flows. We will discuss many of these in greater detail in the following chapters. As you can see, present value concepts to measure financial statement elements are used in many situations, whether these are cost-based measures, current value measures, or something in between.

ILLUSTRATION 3.3 Some Present Value-Based Accounting Measurements

Financial statement elements	When present value may be used as a tool to help measure the financial statement element
Notes	Valuing non-current notes receivable and payable that carry no stated interest rate or a lower-than-market interest rate (see Chapters 7 and 14)
Investments	Valuing investments at amortized cost as well as impairment (see Chapter 9)
Derivatives	Valuing derivatives using various models, including option pricing models (see Chapter 16, including Appendix 16C)
Leases	Valuing assets and obligations to be capitalized under leases, calculating annual amortization of the lease obligation, or calculating interest rates and lease payments (see Chapter 20)
Pensions and other post-retirement benefits	Measuring service cost components relating to employers' post-retirement benefits expense and defined benefit obligations (see Chapter 19)
Tangible capital assets	Determining the value of assets acquired under deferred payment contracts and measuring impairment of assets (see Chapters 10 and 11)
Goodwill	Determining the value of goodwill in business combinations and for impairment purposes (see Chapter 12 and Appendix 12A)
Environmental liabilities	Determining the amount of future obligations for asset retirements (see Chapters 10, 11, and 13)

Which Inputs?

Which inputs to the various models are the best to use? Inputs and assumptions that are more reliable are better. For instance, a risk-free interest rate is generally available[2] whereas a risk-adjusted rate may be more difficult to determine and may be more subjective. Objectively determined information is generally more reliable.

Inputs to income models include the following:

1. **Estimates of cash flows:** Management makes its best estimates of expected cash flows incorporating contractual cash flows as well as other estimated cash flows. When valuing an asset, assumptions may need to be made about how the asset is used (which will affect the cash flows).

2. **Time value of money:** An interest rate is used to discount the cash flows. This rate may be the risk-free rate or it may be a risk-adjusted rate (see point 3 below). The choice of discount rate is a major issue and we will look at it frequently in subsequent chapters.

3. **Uncertainty or risk:** Since not all cash flows are the same in terms of amount, timing, and riskiness, discounted cash flow models reflect the risk or uncertainty by adjusting either the cash flows or the discount rate but generally not both in the same calculation. Uncertainty may be reflected in the numerator by applying probabilities to various cash flow scenarios. It may be incorporated in the discount rate by applying a risk premium such that the rate exceeds the risk-free rate.

[2]The rate of interest on Government of Canada bonds is published and freely available. It may be used in present value calculations as the risk-free rate.

Underlying Concept 3.1

Refer to Chapter 2, which discusses the qualitative characteristics of useful information.

What Is the Quality of the Measurement?

What is the resulting quality of the measurement? Does the measurement provide high-quality information to the users of the financial statements? For instance, is it relevant and does it faithfully represent the asset or liability being valued? Better quality information is obviously better for decision-making. (See Underlying Concept 3.1.) When measuring the value of financial statement elements, the goal is to provide the best information possible within the cost/benefit constraint. At some point, the cost of obtaining the information may outweigh the benefits, and so a judgement call must be made.

We will discuss quality of information further in Chapter 4.

A Closer Look at Discounted Cash Flows

The discounted cash flow model is a very robust, widely accepted tool for dealing with uncertainty and the time value of money.

Two approaches are generally accepted:[3]

1. **Traditional discounted cash flow approach:** The discount rate reflects all risks in the cash flows but the cash flows are assumed to be certain. This is sometimes called the "discount rate adjustment technique."

2. **Expected cash flow approach:** A risk-free discount rate is used to discount cash flows that have been adjusted for uncertainty. This is sometimes called the "expected present value technique."

Traditional Discounted Cash Flow Approach   Under the traditional discounted cash flow approach, the stream of contracted cash flows is discounted, and the discount rate is adjusted to accommodate the riskiness of the cash flows. This model is best used where the cash flows are otherwise fairly certain. For instance, if the company is trying to determine the value of a note receivable, it would adjust the discount rate for the credit risk posed by the party that is paying the cash flows to the company. This method is useful for instruments where the cash flows are specified in the contract, such as fixed interest and principal payments. It is not very useful for more complex instruments where the cash flows may be variable for other reasons than the credit risk.

Example 3.1 illustrates the traditional discounted cash flow approach.

Example 3.1 | Estimating a Bond Value Using the Traditional Discounted Cash Flow Approach

Facts   To illustrate the traditional discounted cash flow approach, let's assume that Company A has issued a 10% bond that is due in 10 years and has a face value of $100. Assume further that the risk-adjusted market rate that reflects the credit risk of Company A is 10%. This rate would be the rate that the market would demand of Company A, given the specific credit risk. The credit risk is the risk that the company will not be able to repay the bond. This would be influenced by factors such as the economy (whether things are good or bad), the company's business model (whether it is sustainable or not), and the company's cash position. If the market feels that the company is riskier, then the market will demand a premium.

Instructions   How would you calculate the present value of the bond (fair value)?

Solution   We would calculate the bond's present value as follows:

PV $1 at 10% × Principal (10 years) + PV of an annuity of $10 for 10 years at 10%
(All discounted at 10%) = $100

---

[3] These two approaches are discussed in IFRS 13 Appendix B in the context of fair value measurement and also in ASPE 3063 Appendix A in the context of impairment.

Expected Cash Flow Approach Under the expected cash flow approach, the discount rate is the risk-free rate and the cash flow uncertainty is dealt with by using probabilities. The projected cash flows reflect the uncertainty in terms of amount and timing using probability weighting. This model is more flexible and is useful where the element being measured has variable cash flows. Example 3.2 illustrates the expected cash flow approach.

Example 3.2 | Using the Expected Cash Flow Approach to Measure Lawsuits

Facts Data Analytics Assume that Al's Auto has several minor lawsuits outstanding. To determine the amount of liability to recognize on the December 31, 2019, statement of financial position, Al's Auto decides to use expected cash flow techniques.

Based on discussions with the company's lawyers, Al's Auto estimates the expected cash outflows associated with the lawsuits at the end of each year, as shown below.

	Cash Flow Estimate	×	Probability Assessment	=	Expected Cash Flow
2020	$3,800		20%		$ 760
	6,300		50%		3,150
	7,500		30%		2,250
			Total		$6,160
2021	$5,400		30%		$1,620
	7,200		50%		3,600
	8,400		20%		1,680
			Total		$6,900

Instructions Calculate the present value of the lawsuits.

Solution Applying expected cash flow concepts to these data, the company estimates cash outflows of $6,160 in 2020 and $6,900 in 2021. The present values of these cash flows at December 31, 2019, assuming a risk-free rate of 5% and cash flows occurring at the end of the year, are shown below. (See Table PV.1 on p. 3-19 for these factors.) Thus the potential cost of the lawsuit is estimated at $12,125.17.

Year	Expected Cash Flow	×	PV Factor, $i = 5\%$	=	Present Value
2020	$6,160		0.95238		$ 5,866.66
2021	6,900		0.90703		6,258.51
			Total		$12,125.17

Value in Use Measurements

We introduced the notion of **value in use** in Chapter 2. It is an **entity-specific measure** that values assets based on how the company (entity) plans to use them. This is different from a fair value measure under IFRS 13, which is based on a **market participant view** of the value. For instance, potential buyers in the market might decide to use the asset differently than the company is currently using it.

Companies are required to regularly determine whether the value of property, plant, and equipment has been impaired. Under IFRS, an asset is impaired if the carrying amount reported on the statement of financial position is greater than its recoverable amount. The recoverable amount is the **greater of the asset's fair value less costs to dispose and its value in use**. Present value techniques may be used to measure both value in use and fair value. Let's assume that the value in use and fair value are the same, although they would not necessarily be so if the market values the asset using different assumptions about its potential use.

Determining the **value in use** requires applying present value concepts. Value in use is calculated in two steps: (1) estimate the future cash flows, and (2) calculate the present value of these cash flows. **Example 3.3** looks at how to measure the value in use of the equipment.

Example 3.3 | Using Present Value Concepts to Measure Value in Use of Equipment

Facts   Assume JB Company owns a specialized piece of equipment used in its manufacturing process. JB needs to determine the asset's value in use to test for impairment.

Instructions   Calculate the value in use.

Solution   JB follows the two steps to determine value in use. First, JB's management estimates that the equipment will last for another five years and that it will generate the following future cash flows at the end of each year:

Year 1	Year 2	Year 3	Year 4	Year 5
$9,000	$10,000	$13,000	$10,000	$7,000

In the second step of determining value in use, JB calculates the present value of each of these future cash flows. Using a discount rate of 8%, the present value of each future cash flow is shown below. (See Table PV.1 for these factors.)

	Year 1	Year 2	Year 3	Year 4	Year 5
Future cash flows	$9,000	$10,000	$13,000	$10,000	$7,000
Present value factor[a]	0.92593	0.85734	0.79383	0.73503	0.68058
Present value amount	$8,333	$8,573	$10,320	$7,350	$4,764

[a]The appropriate interest rate to be used is based on current market rates according to IAS 36.30; however, adjustments for uncertainties related to the specific asset may be made. Further discussion on this topic is in more advanced texts.

The value in use of JB's specialized equipment is the sum of the present value of each year's cash flow, $39,340 ($8,333 + $8,573 + $10,320 + $7,350 + $4,764). If this amount is less than the asset's carrying amount, JB may be required to record an impairment loss.

The present value method of estimating the value in use of an asset can also be used for intangible assets. **Example 3.4** looks at how the concept of value in use is applied to intangible assets.

Example 3.4 | Using Present Value Concepts to Measure Value in Use of an Intangible Asset

Facts   Assume JB purchases a licence from Redo Industries for the right to manufacture and sell products using Redo's processes and technologies. JB estimates it will earn $6,000 per year from this licence over the next 10 years (at the end of each year).

Instructions   What is the value in use to JB of this licence?

Solution   Since JB expects to earn the same amount each year, **Table PV.2** is used to find the present value factor of the annuity after determining the appropriate discount rate. As pointed out in the previous example, JB should choose a rate based on current market rates; however, adjustments for uncertainties related to the specific asset may be required. Assuming JB uses 8% as the discount rate, the present value factor from Table PV.2 for 10 periods is 6.71008. The value in use of the licence is $40,260 ($6,000 × 6.71008).

Disclosures Relating to Measurement

Because of the judgements involved with measurement, note disclosure is extremely important. IAS 1 and ASPE 1505 and 1508 all require disclosure of sources of measurement uncertainty as well as accounting policies (including those relating to measurement). Companies must disclose information regarding assumptions made about the future and any other information relating to the "softness" of the numbers. The full disclosure principle supports these types of disclosures (both under IFRS and ASPE).

Some examples of sources of measurement uncertainty include assumptions about future cash flows when determining impairment of assets, the amount that is recoverable for potentially obsolete inventory, outcome of litigation settlements, interest rates, and other such determinations. This part of measurement is often the most difficult part since the company must look into the future and try to envision what might happen.

Illustration 3.4 is an excerpt from note 3 to the 2017 financial statements of Air Canada.

ILLUSTRATION 3.4

Excerpt from Note 3 of the 2017 Financial Statements of Air Canada Dealing with Critical Accounting Estimates and Judgements

3 Critical Accounting Estimates and Judgments

The preparation of financial statements in conformity with GAAP requires management to make estimates and assumptions that affect the amounts reported in these financial statements and accompanying notes. These estimates and associated assumptions are based on historical experience, future operating plans and various other factors believed to be reasonable under the circumstances, and the results of such estimates form the basis of judgments about carrying values of assets and liabilities. These underlying assumptions are reviewed on an ongoing basis. Actual results could differ materially from those estimates.

Significant estimates and judgments made in the preparation of these financial statements include, but are not limited to, the following areas, with further information contained in the applicable accounting policy or note:

Depreciation and amortization period for long-lived assets

- The Corporation makes estimates about the expected useful lives of long-lived assets and the expected residual value of the assets based on the estimated current and future fair values of the assets, the Corporation's fleet plans and the cash flows they generate. Changes to these estimates, which can be significant, could be caused by a variety of factors, including changes to maintenance programs, changes in jet fuel prices and other operating costs, changes in utilization of the aircraft, and changing market prices for new and used aircraft of the same or similar types. Estimates and assumptions are evaluated at least annually. Generally, these adjustments are accounted for on a prospective basis, through depreciation and amortization expense. For the purposes of sensitivity analysis on these estimates, a 50% reduction to residual values on aircraft with remaining useful lives greater than five years results in an increase of $13 to annual depreciation expense. For aircraft with shorter remaining useful lives, the residual values are not expected to change significantly.

Measuring Fair Value Using IFRS 13

LEARNING OBJECTIVE 2

Use IFRS 13 to measure fair value.

IFRS **Finance** 5.4.1, 5.4.2, 5.4.3 In Chapter 2, we introduced the fair value principle. This section delves a bit deeper in to this principle as presented in IFRS 13. According to IFRS 13, in order to measure fair value, an entity must determine (1) the item being measured; (2) how the item would be or could be used by market participants (for non-financial assets); (3) the market that the item would be (or was) bought and sold in; (4) and finally, if a model is being used to measure fair value, which model it is. Recall that the fair value measurement under IFRS is an exit price. So, for instance, when measuring the value of an asset, the fair value measurement would look at the value that potential buyers would attribute to the asset—in other words, the selling price from the company's perspective.

We'll look at these items in more detail below using tangible assets as an example.

1. **The particular asset being measured:** Consider the specific nature, condition, and location of the asset being measured. Is it old, damaged, obsolete?

2. **How the item would/could be used:** Many non-financial assets are used for different purposes. For instance, a building may be rented out, used as part of a manufacturing facility, or held for capital appreciation purposes. The perceived value of the building might be different depending on what the company might use it for. This is sometimes called the "valuation premise." Generally, the asset is valued based on what is known as its **highest and best use** in the market **regardless of how the entity is actually using the asset**.

   The highest and best use concept values the asset based on the highest value that the market would place on the asset, considering all possible uses that are **physically possible, legally permissible, and financially feasible**. In making these assessments, you would take into account physical characteristics of the asset (size, location, condition), any legal restrictions (such as zoning), and whether the use would yield sufficient positive cash flows to make it a financially acceptable option.

   As a practical expedient, the entity's current use of the asset may be presumed to reflect highest and best use unless there is specific evidence to the contrary.

   Example 3.5 looks at the concept of highest and best use.

Example 3.5 | Highest and Best Use

Facts   Suppose your company owns a piece of land that is zoned by the local municipality as residential, meaning that it can only be developed for residential purposes (including single dwellings, condominiums, and parks). There are no opportunities for rezoning. Assume you would like to determine the fair value of the land.

Instructions   What factors would you consider when determining highest and best use?

Solution   In trying to measure the land's fair value, you would have to first consider highest and best use. Therefore, you would look at what is physically possible, legally permissible, and financially feasible. In this case, the legal zoning is the limiting factor since the land is zoned as residential and there are no opportunities to rezone. You would **not** consider a value that assumed for instance that the land was zoned as a commercial property, because **legally**, only residential development is allowed at the measurement date. Depending on the law, the land could possibly have multiple uses given the residential zoning, including building condominiums, single dwellings, or parks. Building houses, condominiums, or parks are all **physically possible** alternatives. The **highest and best use** would consider the use that would yield the most economic benefit (**financial feasibility**). This might depend on factors such as location. In our example, if the piece of land were in a downtown area, condominiums would likely yield the highest economic benefit. Therefore, the highest and best use would be a condominium development and the next two steps would be determined on this basis (that is, market and valuation technique).

Illustration 3.5 provides some guidance in the form of a decision tree.

3. **The market:** The measurement would consider the value based on the market that the entity normally buys and sells in (called the **principal market**). This would usually also be the **most advantageous market**; that is, the market in which the price would be the highest. Many entities buy and sell in different markets so this concept looks at the

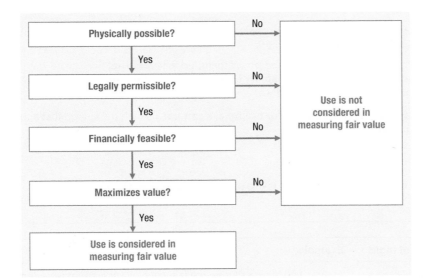

main market that the company deals in. For instance, if a company buys and sells shares for investment purposes through the TSX, then the company would use market values as quoted by the TSX.

4. **The valuation technique/model:** In many cases, a liquid market for the item being measured will be available and this best represents fair value. For example, when valuing common shares that trade on the TSX, the dollar amount that the shares are traded at (**market value**) would provide the best evidence of fair value. In other cases, however, we would use a **valuation technique or model** to value the item. Any time that pure market values are not used, you are essentially **estimating** the value using a model. Examples of models include those mentioned earlier in the "Valuation Techniques" section—**market** and **income** models—and one additional model: the **cost model**. The cost model attempts to reflect the amount that would be required to replace the asset's service capacity. The cost model is used to value older non-financial assets where there is no longer a market for the asset, perhaps because it is obsolete.

Because estimating a fair value using a model introduces measurement uncertainty, IFRS 13 attempts to offset this by ideally using good-quality input information. Inputs are classified into three categories depending on their quality: level 1 inputs, level 2 inputs, and level 3 inputs. Level 1 inputs are the highest-quality inputs and will produce the best-quality fair value measurement. Level 3 inputs are at the other end and are used where level 1 and/or 2 inputs are not available.

This categorization of **inputs** is often called the fair value hierarchy. Level 1 and 2 inputs are generally observable in various markets and are therefore more **objective**, whereas level 3 inputs are generally not observable and hence more **subjective**. Level 1 inputs require the existence of liquid markets that generate good information that may be used as the inputs.

Assets and liabilities are also categorized into one of the three levels based on the various levels of inputs. For instance, if the fair value of an impaired asset is calculated using level 3 inputs, the asset itself is categorized as a level 3 asset. A company must disclose information about which models and input levels are used. **The lower the level of input (for instance, level 3), the greater the required disclosures**. This gives additional information to financial statement users about the measurement uncertainty. Illustration 3.6 summarizes the inputs to the IFRS 13 valuation model.

[4]KPMG, *Fair Value Measurement, Questions and Answers, U.S. GAAP and IFRS,* December 2017. Copyright © 2017 KPMG LLP, a Delaware limited liability partnership and the US member firm of KPMG network of independent member firms affiliated with KPMG International Cooperative, a Swiss entity. All rights reserved.

ILLUSTRATION 3.6

Inputs to the IFRS 13
Valuation Model

Level 1: Observable inputs that reflect quoted prices for identical assets or liabilities in active markets.

Level 2: Inputs other than quoted prices included in level 1 that are observable for the asset or liability either directly or through corroboration with observable data.

Level 3: Unobservable inputs (for example, a company's own data or assumptions).

Least subjective

↓

Most subjective

Some examples of the various levels of inputs are in **Illustration** 3.7.

ILLUSTRATION 3.7

Examples of the Various Input
Levels under IFRS 13

Level of input	Example
Level 1 input	Assume you are measuring the fair value of a share that is traded on the TSX. A level 1 input would be the price for the exact class of share (as evidenced by the price it is being traded at currently on the TSX). You would categorize the shares as level 1 assets.
Level 2 input	Assume that you are measuring the fair value of a new issue of bonds. A level 2 input would be interest rates that are observable in the market (that is, for similar or identical bonds already trading in the market). You would categorize the bonds as level 2 assets (indicating greater measurement uncertainty).
Level 3 input	Assume you are trying to measure the fair value of a manufacturing division for purposes of impairment. A level 3 input would be the estimated cash flows. You would categorize the manufacturing division as a level 3 asset (and therefore greater disclosures would be required focusing on the increased measurement uncertainty).

Fair value measures may be calculated using any of these models and using different types of inputs. Assume we are trying to determine the fair value of a piece of machinery in order to decide if an impairment loss needs to be recognized. Which model should we use? As a rule of thumb, you should use the one that provides the **best-quality fair value measure**. This is a judgement call and depends on the characteristics of the asset itself and available information. In most cases, only one model may work, but in some cases, more than one may be used. **Example** 3.6 looks at which model provides the best-quality information.

Example 3.6 | Which Valuation Model?

Facts Restaurant Limited has some restaurant equipment that may be impaired for financial statement purposes.

Instructions Which valuation technique or model should the company use to measure fair value less cost to sell when determining impairment?

Solution If the machinery is older and obsolete, the market model will not work because you will likely not be able to get any market information for the exact or a similar machine, especially if the machines are no longer produced. Nor would it make sense for management to try to estimate market values for the exact or a similar machine, because too much judgement is involved. In this case, you might use an income model or, alternatively, a cost model (which looks at valuing the cost to replicate or replace the service capacity as opposed to the asset). Inputs from various levels might be needed to do the calculation. As noted above, the lower the level of the inputs (for instance, level 3), the greater the disclosures required.

However, if you are valuing a company that is planning on going public, you may be able to use both the market and income models. You might use the income model to measure the value by focusing on the discounted cash flows. Alternatively, you might look at recent market transactions for similar companies (or perhaps earnings multiples).

There is no perfect answer, just better or worse information. If you are able to measure fair value by using more than one model, this will help because you can compare the estimates to see if they are both reasonable or not. However, keep in mind that using more than one model requires more effort, so the costs might exceed the benefits.

Due to the complexity involved with fair value measurements, IFRS 13 requires significant disclosures (see **What Do the Numbers Mean? 3.1**). Since many of the disclosures relate to financial instruments, we will revisit this topic in Chapter 16.

What Do the Numbers Mean? 3.1

IFRS 13 was issued in May 2011 and implemented for years beginning on or after January 1, 2013. As a result, it has now been incorporated into the financial statements of companies for several years. Preparers, auditors, investors, and other stakeholders have had a chance to evaluate the standard and its usefulness.

As part of its post-implementation review of IFRS 13, the IASB has solicited feedback from various stakeholders as to whether the standard is working as envisaged or needs to be adjusted. According to its phase 1 outreach feedback document dated January 2017, the IASB noted that the standard appears to be working quite well overall. Stakeholders stated that the standard has helped improve financial reporting by increasing consistency in the way fair value measurements are done and improving disclosures in general. There were some areas of concern expressed, however, and the IASB issued a Request for Information, asking stakeholders to send in comment letters noting more specific concerns.

Some issues raised in the comment letters received thus far note that the disclosures, while better than before, tend to be boilerplate, lacking entity-specific information. Others noted the difficulty with the concept of highest and best use. As stated earlier in this chapter, IFRS 13 allows the company to presume that highest and best use reflects the company's current use of the asset unless there are other factors that suggest otherwise. In particular, accounting firm Deloitte asked how much evidence would be needed to prove that the company's current use of the asset might not reflect highest and best use. Accountants Ernst & Young noted similar concerns, stating that the "assessment of highest and best use, and the related concept of valuation premise can be challenging and is not well understood." Feedback such as this is very important in helping the IASB in its standard-setting mandate.

The Board decided to feed the findings into its other projects on Principles of Disclosure and Primary Financial Statements and to continue to liaise with the valuations profession. As such, the fair value standard will hopefully continue to evolve in a positive way, improving financial reporting.

Present Value Concepts

LEARNING OBJECTIVE 3
Understand and apply present value concepts.

Time value concepts are widely used by accountants when preparing financial statements under both IFRS and ASPE. We looked at a few examples earlier in this chapter when reviewing income models. This section will go back to the basics that you must be aware of to understand related topics in this text. It will also serve as a foundation for doing more complex measurement calculations. Finally, it will give some basic examples of how time value concepts are incorporated into financial statement measurements while briefly touching on different tools available for doing present value calculations, including formulas, present value tables, calculators, and spreadsheets.

The Nature of Interest

Finance 5.4.1, 5.4.2, 5.4.3 You are no doubt familiar with the concept of interest, but what exactly does it represent? Interest is recognition of the fact that the value of one dollar today is not equal to the value of one dollar in the future. There is some utility in having the dollar "in hand" today versus waiting until the end of the year. For instance, if a company borrows money from a bank today, the bank will expect to be repaid this amount plus some additional amount (interest) for the use of the funds and to reflect the fact that the dollar today is worth more than the dollar in the future, because of the time value of money. The company that borrows money incurs interest expense, while the company that lends the money receives interest revenue.

Example 3.7 illustrates the nature of interest.

Example 3.7 | Basic Interest Calculations

Facts   Assume that Corner Bank lends Hillfarm Company $10,000 with the understanding that Hillfarm will repay $11,500.

Instructions   Calculate the interest rate.

Solution   The excess of the repayment amount ($11,500) over $10,000 (the amount loaned) is equal to $1,500 and represents interest expense for Hillfarm and interest revenue for Corner Bank.

The lender generally states the amount of interest as a rate over a specific period of time. For example, if Hillfarm borrowed $10,000 for one year before repaying $11,500, the rate of interest is 15% per year ($1,500 ÷ $10,000). The custom of expressing interest as a percentage rate is an established business practice. In fact, business managers make investing and borrowing decisions based on the rate of interest involved, rather than on the actual dollar amount of interest to be received or paid.

How is the interest rate determined? One important factor is the level of credit risk (risk of non-payment) involved. Other factors being equal, the higher the credit risk, the higher the interest rate. Low-risk borrowers can probably obtain a loan at or slightly below the average market rate of interest. However, a bank would probably charge the neighbourhood delicatessen several percentage points above the prime or base interest rate, if granting the loan at all. Macroeconomic factors also affect interest rates. For instance, when the government wants to encourage savings, it may decide to increase the prime interest rate. Similarly, when it wants to encourage spending, it may decrease interest rates.

Fundamental Variables in Present Value Calculations

Where money is borrowed or invested, interest is usually paid.[5] It reflects payment for the use of money. The amount of interest paid is a function of three variables:

1. **Principal (p):** the amount borrowed or invested.
2. **Interest rate (i):** a percentage of the outstanding principal. The rate of interest is generally stated as an annual rate and is sometimes called the nominal, stated or "coupon rate" on a bond or the "contractual rate."
3. **Time or number of periods (n):** the number of years or fractional portion of a year that the principal is outstanding.

Thus, the following three relationships apply:

1. The larger the principal amount, the larger the dollar amount of interest.
2. The higher the interest rate, the larger the dollar amount of interest.
3. The longer the time period, the larger the dollar amount of interest.

---

[5]Although, as we shall see in subsequent chapters, in some cases, such as in non–arm's-length transactions, interest is not always charged or paid.

Simple Interest

Companies calculate **simple interest** on the amount of the principal only. It is the return on (or growth of) the principal for one time period. The following equation in **Illustration 3.8** expresses simple interest.[6]

$$\text{Interest} = p \times i \times n$$

where

$p = \text{principal}$
$i = \text{rate of interest for a single period}$
$n = \text{number of periods}$

ILLUSTRATION 3.8

Simple Interest Formula

Example 3.8 illustrates simple interest.

Example 3.8 | Calculating Simple Interest

Facts   Assume that you borrow $1,000 for three years at a simple interest rate of 9% annually. Interest is paid at the end of each year.

Instructions   How much interest would you pay over the three years?

Solution   If you borrowed $1,000 for three years at a simple interest rate of 9% annually, you would pay $270 in total interest, calculated as follows:

$$\begin{aligned} \text{Interest} &= p \times i \times n \\ &= \$1,000 \times 9\% \times 3 \\ &= \$270 \end{aligned}$$

	Year 1		Year 2		Year 3		
	$90	+	$90	+	$90	=	$270

Compound Interest

Compound interest is the return on (or growth of) the principal for two or more time periods. Compounding calculates interest not only on the principal but also on the interest earned to date on that principal, assuming the interest is left on deposit (that is, added to the original principal amount).

Example 3.9 illustrates the difference between simple and compound interest.

Example 3.9 | Simple Versus Compound Interest

Facts   Assume that you deposit $1,000 in the Last Canadian Bank, where it will earn simple interest of 9% per year, and you deposit another $1,000 in the First Canadian Bank, where it will earn interest of 9% per year compounded annually. Also assume that in both cases you will not withdraw any interest until three years from the date of deposit.

Instructions   Calculate interest to be received and the accumulated year-end balances.

[6]Business mathematics and business finance textbooks traditionally state simple interest as I (interest) = P (principal) × R (rate) × T (time).

Solution The calculation of interest to be received and the accumulated year-end balances are shown below.

Last Canadian Bank			First Canadian Bank		
Simple Interest Calculation	Simple Interest	Accumulated Year-End Balance	Compound Interest Calculation	Compound Interest	Accumulated Year-End Balance
Year 1			Year 1		
$1,000.00 × 9%	$ 90.00	$1,090.00	$1,000.00 × 9%	$ 90.00	$1,090.00
Year 2			Year 2		
$1,000.00 × 9%	90.00	$1,180.00	$1,090.00 × 9%	98.10	$1,188.10
Year 3			Year 3		
$1,000.00 × 9%	90.00	$1,270.00	$1,188.10 × 9%	106.93	$1,295.03
	$270.00			$295.03	

$25.03 Difference

Note in Example 3.9 that simple interest uses the initial principal of $1,000 to calculate the interest in all three years. Compound interest uses the accumulated balance (principal plus interest to date) at each year end to calculate interest in the following year. This explains why your compound interest account is larger: you are earning interest on interest. For practical purposes, compounding assumes that unpaid interest earned becomes a part of the principal. The accumulated balance at the end of each year becomes the new principal on which interest is earned during the next year.

Assuming all else is equal (especially risk), if you had a choice between investing your money at simple interest or at compound interest, you would choose compound interest. In the example, compounding provides $25.03 of additional interest income.

Compound interest is used in most business situations. Simple interest is generally applicable only to short-term situations of one year or less.

Different Ways to Perform the Calculations

In the previous section on compound and simple interest, the initial principal was given. It was used to calculate the interest earned and the value of the investment at the end of three years. The initial principal, invested at the beginning of year one, is the present value of the investment. The value of the investment at the end of three years is the future value of the investment. The process of determining the present value is often referred to as **discounting the future cash flows**. The word "discount" has many meanings in accounting, each of which varies with the context in which it is used. Be careful not to confuse the use of this term.

There are many different ways to calculate present value, including using the following four tools:

1. Present value formulas
2. Present value tables
3. Financial calculators
4. Spreadsheets such as Excel

Calculating Present Value of a Single Future Amount Using Different Tools

In the following section, we will show four methods of calculating the present value of a single future amount, using each of the above four tools.

Example 3.10 looks at a timeline for a simple present value calculation. We will use this simple fact set in each of the four methods.

Example 3.10 | Timeline for Present Value of $1,000 Discounted for One Period at 5%

Facts Assume that you want to invest a sum of money at 5% in order to have $1,000 at the end of one year. The present value is $952.38.

Instructions Prepare a timeline to illustrate the present and future values.

Solution The amount that you would need to invest today is the present value of $1,000 discounted for one year at 5%. The variables in this example are shown in the time diagram below.

Present Value = $952.38   Future Amount = $1,000

$i = 5\%$

$n = 1$ year

Now   1 Year

The next section will show how to use the different tools to calculate the present values.

Present Value Formula The formula used to determine the present value for any interest (discount) rate (i), number of periods (n), and future amount (FV) is shown in **Illustration 3.9**.

$$\text{Present value } (PV) = \frac{\text{Future value } (FV)}{(1 + i)^n}$$
$$= FV \div (1 + i)^n$$

ILLUSTRATION 3.9

Present Value of a Single Future Amount Formula

Example 3.11 uses the present value formulas to calculate the present values for one and two periods.

Example 3.11 | Calculating the Present Value of $1,000 Discounted for One and Two Periods at 5% Using a Formula

Facts Assume the information in Example 3.10.

Instructions Calculate the present value using the present value formula.

Solution In applying this formula to calculate the present value (PV) for the above example, the future value (FV) of $1,000, the interest (discount) rate (i) of 5%, and the number of periods (n) of 1 are used as follows:

$$(PV) = \$1,000 \div (1 + 5\%)^1$$
$$= \$1,000 \div 1.05$$
$$= \$952.38$$

If the single future cash flow of $1,000 is to be received in two years and discounted at 5%, its present value is calculated as follows:

$$(PV) = \$1,000 \div (1 + 5\%)^2$$
$$= \$1,000 \div 1.1025 \text{ or } [\$1,000 \div (1.05 \times 1.05)]$$
$$= \$907.03$$

The time diagram below shows the variables used to calculate the present value when cash is received in two years.

Present Value = $907.03   Future Amount = $1,000

$$i = 5\%$$

$$n = 2 \text{ years}$$

Now   1 year   2 Years

Present Value Tables   The present value may also be determined through tables that show the present value of 1 for n periods for different periodic interest rates or discount rates. In Table PV.1, the rows represent the number of discounting periods and the columns the periodic interest or discount rates. The five-digit decimal numbers in the respective rows and columns are the factors for the present value of 1. **Example 3.12** looks at our basic example using tables.

Example 3.12 | Calculating the Present Value of $1,000 Discounted for One and Two Periods at 5% Using Present Value Tables

Facts   Assume the facts from Example 3.10.

Instructions   Calculate the present value using PV tables.

Solution   When present value tables are used, the present value is calculated by multiplying the future cash amount by the present value factor specified at the intersection of the number of periods and the discount rate. For example, if the discount rate is 5% and the number of periods is 1, Table PV.1 shows that the present value factor is 0.95238. Then the present value of $1,000 discounted at 5% for one period is calculated as follows:

$$(PV) = \$1,000 \times 0.95238$$
$$= \$952.38$$

For two periods at a discount rate of 5%, the present value factor is 0.90703. The present value of $1,000 discounted at 5% for two periods is calculated as follows:

$$(PV) = \$1,000 \times 0.90703$$
$$= \$907.03$$

Note that the present values in these two examples are identical to the amounts determined previously when using the present value formula. This is because the factors in a present value table have been calculated using the present value formula. The benefit of using a present value table is that it can be quicker than using the formula. If you are using a basic calculator (not a financial calculator) or doing the calculations by hand, there are more calculations involved as the number of periods increase, making it more tedious than using the present value tables.

Table PV.1 can also be used if you know the present value and wish to determine the future cash flow. The present value amount is divided by the present value factor specified at the intersection of the number of periods and the discount rate in Table PV.1. (An extract from Table A.2 is provided in Table PV.1. The full set of present value tables is in Appendix A at the end of the textbook.) For example, you can easily determine that an initial investment of $907.03 will grow to yield a future amount of $1,000 in two periods, at an annual discount rate of 5% ($1,000 = $907.03 divided by 0.90703).

TABLE PV.1   **Present Value of 1**

(n) periods	2%	2¹/₂%	3%	4%	5%	6%	7%	8%	9%	10%	11%	12%	15%
1	0.98039	0.97561	0.97087	0.96156	0.95238	0.94340	0.93458	0.92593	0.91743	0.90909	0.90090	0.89286	0.86957
2	0.96117	0.95181	0.94260	0.92456	0.90703	0.89000	0.87344	0.85734	0.84168	0.82645	0.81162	0.79719	0.75614
3	0.94232	0.92860	0.91514	0.88900	0.86384	0.83962	0.81630	0.79383	0.77218	0.75132	0.73119	0.71178	0.65752
4	0.92385	0.90595	0.88849	0.85480	0.82270	0.79209	0.76290	0.73503	0.70843	0.68301	0.65873	0.63552	0.57175
5	0.90583	0.88385	0.86261	0.82193	0.78353	0.74726	0.71299	0.68058	0.64993	0.62092	0.59345	0.56743	0.49718
6	0.88797	0.86230	0.83748	0.79031	0.74622	0.70496	0.66634	0.63017	0.59627	0.56447	0.53464	0.50663	0.43233
7	0.87056	0.84127	0.81309	0.75992	0.71068	0.66506	0.62275	0.58349	0.54703	0.51316	0.48166	0.45235	0.37594
8	0.85349	0.82075	0.78941	0.73069	0.67684	0.62741	0.58201	0.54027	0.50187	0.46651	0.43393	0.40388	0.32690
9	0.83676	0.80073	0.76642	0.70259	0.64461	0.59190	0.54393	0.50025	0.46043	0.42410	0.39092	0.36061	0.28426
10	0.82035	0.78120	0.74409	0.67556	0.61391	0.55839	0.50835	0.46319	0.42241	0.38554	0.35218	0.32197	0.24719
11	0.80426	0.76214	0.72242	0.64958	0.58468	0.52679	0.47509	0.42888	0.38753	0.35049	0.31728	0.28748	0.21494
12	0.78849	0.74356	0.70138	0.62460	0.55684	0.49697	0.44401	0.39711	0.35554	0.31863	0.28584	0.25668	0.18691
13	0.77303	0.72542	0.68095	0.60057	0.53032	0.46884	0.41496	0.36770	0.32618	0.28966	0.25751	0.22917	0.16253
14	0.75788	0.70773	0.66112	0.57748	0.50507	0.44230	0.38782	0.34046	0.29925	0.26333	0.23199	0.20462	0.14133
15	0.74301	0.69047	0.64186	0.55526	0.48102	0.41727	0.36245	0.31524	0.27454	0.23939	0.20900	0.18270	0.12289
16	0.72845	0.67362	0.62317	0.53391	0.45811	0.39365	0.33873	0.29189	0.25187	0.21763	0.18829	0.16312	0.10687
17	0.71416	0.65720	0.60502	0.51337	0.43630	0.37136	0.31657	0.27027	0.23107	0.19785	0.16963	0.14564	0.09293
18	0.70016	0.64117	0.58739	0.49363	0.41552	0.35034	0.29586	0.25025	0.21199	0.17986	0.15282	0.13004	0.08081
19	0.68643	0.62553	0.57029	0.47464	0.39573	0.33051	0.27651	0.23171	0.19449	0.16351	0.13768	0.11611	0.07027
20	0.67297	0.61027	0.55368	0.45639	0.37689	0.31180	0.25842	0.21455	0.17843	0.14864	0.12403	0.10367	0.06110

Financial Calculators   Present values can also be calculated using financial calculators. A financial calculator will perform the same calculation as a basic calculator, but it requires fewer steps and less input. Basically, with a financial calculator, you input the future value, the discount rate, and the number of periods, and then tell it to calculate the present value. Illustration 3.10 shows the required inputs for a present value calculation using a financial calculator.

PV	?	Yield ($952.38)
I	5%	
N	1	
FV	$1,000	
PMT	0	

ILLUSTRATION 3.10

Calculating the Present Value of a Single Future Amount Using a Financial Calculator

Where:

PV = present value
I = interest rate
N = number of periods
FV = future value

Details vary with different financial calculators; however, they generally ask for these variables.

You should know that the present value amounts calculated with a financial calculator can be slightly different than those calculated with present value tables. That is because the numbers in a present value table are rounded. For example, in Table PV.1 the factors are rounded to five digits. In a financial calculator, the final answer is rounded to the number of digits you have specified.

A major benefit of using a financial calculator is that you are not restricted to the interest rates or numbers of periods on a present value table. In Table PV.1, present value factors have been calculated for 13 interest rates (there are 13 columns in that table) and the maximum number of periods is 20. With a financial calculator you could, for example, calculate the present value of a future amount to be received in 25 periods using 5.75% as the discount rate. Later in this section, we will illustrate how to partly overcome this limitation of present value tables through a method called interpolation.

Spreadsheets   Using a spreadsheet is very similar to using financial calculators; however, many spreadsheets such as Excel are significantly more robust. Using Excel as an example to calculate the present value in our example, first select "Formulas," and then "Financial," and then, in the drop-down menu, select "PV." **Illustration 3.11** shows the variables that need to be input.

<table>
<tr><td>**ILLUSTRATION 3.11**

Calculating the Present Value of a Single Future Amount Using a Spreadsheet such as Excel</td><td></td></tr>
</table>

Where:

> PV = present value = amount to be calculated
> Rate = interest rate = 5% or .05
> Nper = number of periods = 1
> Pmt = payment = 0
> FV = future value = $1,000
> Type = type of annuity

In this case, since there are no additional payments aside from one interest payment and one principal payment, the amount included beside "Pmt" is 0. The section entitled "Type" relates to annuities and is not relevant here since this is a single payment. If you input 0 or leave it blank, this will suffice. We will cover annuities in the next section.

Regardless of the method used in calculating present values, a higher discount rate produces a smaller present value. For example, using an 8% discount rate, the present value of $1,000 due one year from now is $925.93 versus $952.38 at 5%. You should also recognize that **the further away from the present the future cash flow is, the smaller the present value**. For example, using the same discount rate of 5%, the present value of $1,000 due in five years is $783.53.

Calculating the Present Value of a Series of Future Cash Flows (Annuities) Using Different Tools

The preceding discussion was for the discounting of only a single future amount. Businesses and individuals frequently engage in transactions in which a series of equal dollar amounts are to be received or paid periodically. Examples of series of periodic receipts or payments are loan agreements, instalment sales, mortgage notes, lease (rental) contracts, and pension obligations. These series of periodic receipts or payments are called "annuities." When calculating the present value of an annuity, we need to know (1) the discount rate (i), (2) the number of discount periods (n), (3) the amount of the periodic receipts or payments (FV), and (4) when the payments are made (at the end of a period or the beginning). When dealing with payments at the end of a period, this is called an "ordinary annuity." When the payments are made at the beginning of a period, this is called an "annuity due" or "annuity in arrears."

Example 3.13 looks at a timeline for a three-year annuity.

Example 3.13 | Timeline for Present Value of an Annuity of $1,000 Discounted for Three Periods at 4%

Facts   Assume that you will pay $1,000 cash annually for three years (at the end of the year), and that the discount rate is 4%. The present value is $2,775.

Instructions   Prepare a timeline showing the payments and number of periods.

Solution   This situation is shown in the timeline below.

Now let's look at the calculation using the four tools.

Present Value Formula   One method of calculating the present value of this annuity is to use the present value formula to determine the present value of each of the three $1,000 payments and then add those amounts as shown in Example 3.14.

Example 3.14 | Present Value of an Annuity of $1,000 Discounted for Three Periods at 4% Using a PV of $1 Formula for Each Year

Facts   Assume the information as shown in Example 3.13.

Instructions   Calculate the present value using PV of $1 formulas.

Solution

$$PV = [\$1{,}000 \text{ divided by} (1 + 4\%)^1] + [\$1{,}000 \text{ divided by} (1 + 4\%)^2]$$
$$+ [\$1{,}000 \text{ divided by} (1 + 4\%)^3]$$
$$= \$961.54 + \$924.56 + \$889.00$$
$$= \$2{,}775.10$$

The same result is achieved by using present value factors from Table PV.1, as shown in Example 3.15.

Example 3.15 | Present Value of an Annuity of $1,000 Discounted for Three Periods at 4% Using a PV of $1 Table

Facts Assume the information as shown in Example 3.13.

Instructions Calculate the present value using a PV of $1 table (Table PV.1).

Solution

Future Value	×	Present Value of 1 Factor at 4%	=	Present Value
$1,000 (one year away)		0.96156		$ 961.56
1,000 (two years away)		0.92456		924.56
1,000 (three years away)		0.88900		889.00
		2.77512		$2,775.12

Determining the present value of each single future cash flow, and then adding the present values, is required when the periodic cash flows are not the same in each period. But when the future receipts are the same in each period, an annuity formula may be used to calculate present value. The annuity formula differs depending on whether it is an ordinary annuity (payments at the end of the period) or an annuity due (payments at the beginning of the period).

The present value of an ordinary annuity formula is shown in **Illustration 3.12**. Differences are due to rounding and are not significant.

ILLUSTRATION 3.12

Present Value of an Ordinary Annuity Formula

$$\text{Present value } (PV) = \text{Future value } (FV) \times \frac{1 - \frac{1}{(1+i)^n}}{i}$$

$$= \$1,000 \times [(1 - (1 \div (1 + 4\%)^3)) \div 4\%]$$
$$= \$1,000 \times [(1 - (1 \div (1 + 1.04)^3)) \div 0.04]$$
$$= \$1,000 \times [(1 - (1 \div 1.124864)) \div 0.04]$$
$$= \$1,000 \times [(1 - 0.888996359) \div 0.04]$$
$$= \$1,000 \times 2.77509$$
$$= \$2,775.09$$

The formula for an annuity due is shown at the top of Table PV.2.

Present Value Tables

The calculation may also be done using a present value of an ordinary annuity table. As illustrated in **Table PV.2**, which is an extract from Table A.4 in Appendix A: Time Value of Money. Tables PV.2 and the more extensive Table A.4 show the present value of 1 to be received periodically for a given number of periods. **Example 3.16** illustrates this.

Example 3.16 | Present Value of an Annuity of $1,000 Discounted for Three Periods at 4% Using a PV Table for an Annuity

Facts Assume the information as shown in Example 3.13.

Instructions Calculate the present value using a PV of an ordinary annuity table (Table PV.2).

Solution From Table PV.2, we can see that the present value factor of an ordinary annuity of 1 for three periods at 4% is 2.77509. This present value factor is the total of the three individual present value factors, as shown in Example 3.15 (subject to rounding). Applying this present value factor to the annual cash flow of $1,000 produces a present value of $2,775.09 ($1,000 × 2.77509). Recall that there is a separate present value table for annuity due/annuity in arrears.

TABLE PV.2   **Present Value of an Annuity of 1**

$$PV = 1 - \frac{\dfrac{1}{(1+i)^n}}{i}$$

(n) Periods	2%	2½%	3%	4%	5%	6%	7%	8%	9%	10%	11%	12%	15%
1	0.98039	0.97561	0.97087	0.96154	0.95238	0.94340	0.93458	0.92593	0.91743	0.90909	0.90090	0.89286	0.86957
2	1.94156	1.92742	1.91347	1.88609	1.85941	1.83339	1.80802	1.78326	1.75911	1.73554	1.71252	1.69005	1.62571
3	2.88388	2.85602	2.82861	2.77509	2.72325	2.67301	2.62432	2.57710	2.53130	2.48685	2.44371	2.40183	2.28323
4	3.80773	3.76197	3.71710	3.62990	3.54595	3.46511	3.38721	3.31213	3.23972	3.16986	3.10245	3.03735	2.85498
5	4.71346	4.64583	4.57971	4.45182	4.32948	4.21236	4.10020	3.99271	3.88965	3.79079	3.69590	3.60478	3.35216
6	5.60143	5.50813	5.41719	5.24214	5.07569	4.91732	4.76654	4.62288	4.48592	4.35526	4.23054	4.11141	3.78448
7	6.47199	6.34939	6.23028	6.00205	5.78637	5.58238	5.38929	5.20637	5.03295	4.86842	4.71220	4.56376	4.16042
8	7.32548	7.17014	7.01969	6.73274	6.46321	6.20979	5.97130	5.74664	5.53482	5.33493	5.14612	4.96764	4.48732
9	8.16224	7.97087	7.78611	7.43533	7.10782	6.80169	6.51523	6.24689	5.99525	5.75902	5.53705	5.32825	4.77158
10	8.98259	8.75206	8.53020	8.11090	7.72173	7.36009	7.02358	6.71008	6.41766	6.14457	5.88923	5.65022	5.01877
11	9.78685	9.51421	9.25262	8.76048	8.30641	7.88687	7.49867	7.13896	6.80519	6.49506	6.20652	5.93770	5.23371
12	10.57534	10.25776	9.95400	9.38507	8.86325	8.38384	7.94269	7.53608	7.16073	6.81369	6.49236	6.19437	5.42062
13	11.34837	10.98319	10.63496	9.98565	9.39357	8.85268	8.35765	7.90378	7.48690	7.10336	6.74987	6.42355	5.58315
14	12.10625	11.69091	11.29607	10.56312	9.89864	9.29498	8.74547	8.24424	7.78615	7.36669	6.98187	6.62817	5.72448
15	12.84926	12.38138	11.93794	11.11839	10.37966	9.71225	9.10791	8.55948	8.06069	7.60608	7.19087	6.81086	5.84737
16	13.57771	13.05500	12.56110	11.65230	10.83777	10.10590	9.44665	8.85137	8.31256	7.82371	7.37916	6.97399	5.95424
17	14.29187	13.71220	13.16612	12.16567	11.27407	10.47726	9.76322	9.12164	8.54363	8.02155	7.54879	7.11963	6.04716
18	14.99203	14.35336	13.75351	12.65930	11.68959	10.82760	10.05909	9.37189	8.75563	8.20141	7.70162	7.24967	6.12797
19	15.67846	14.97889	14.32380	13.13394	12.08532	11.15812	10.33560	9.60360	8.95012	8.36492	7.83929	7.36578	6.19823
20	16.35143	15.58916	14.87747	13.59033	12.46221	11.46992	10.59401	9.81815	9.12856	8.51356	7.96333	7.46944	6.25933

Financial Calculators   Recall that, when using a financial calculator, you must input the number of periods, the interest rate, and the amount of the annual payment. When using a financial calculator to calculate the present value of an annuity, you also need to specify if the annual cash flow is an ordinary annuity or an annuity due (in arrears). **Illustration 3.13** shows the inputs needed using a financial calculator. In this case, you do not need to enter a future amount because you are entering a payment value of $1,000, which will be paid at the end of each year.

PV	?	Yield $2,775.09
I	4%	
N	3	
PMT	–$1,000	
FV	0	
Type	0	

ILLUSTRATION 3.13

Calculating the Present Value of an Ordinary Annuity Using a Financial Calculator

Where:

PV = present value
I = interest rate
N = number of periods
PMT = the payment at the end of each period
FV = future value
Type = ordinary annuity (enter 0) or annuity due (enter 1)

Spreadsheets   Using Excel as an example to calculate the present value of an ordinary annuity in our example, first select "Formulas," and then "Financial," and then, in the drop-down menu, select "PV." **Illustration 3.14** shows the variables that need to be input.

Calculating the Present Value of an Ordinary Annuity Using a Spreadsheet Such as Excel

Where:

> PV = present value = amount to be calculated
> Rate = interest rate = 4% or .04
> Nper = number of periods = 3
> Pmt = −1000
> FV = future value = no need to input
> Type = 0

In this case, there is no need to input the FV since you are inputting a payment of $1,000, which is paid at the end of each of the three years. Since this is an ordinary annuity, the Type = 0. If it were an annuity due, the Type = 1.

Interest Rates and Time Periods

In the preceding calculations, the discounting has been done on an annual basis using an annual interest rate. There are situations where adjustments may be required to the interest rate, the time period, or both.

Using Time Periods of Less Than One Year

Discounting may be done over shorter periods of time than one year, such as monthly, quarterly, or semi-annually. When the time frame is less than one year, it is necessary to convert the annual interest rate to the applicable time frame. **Example 3.17** looks at the calculations.

Example 3.17 | Present Value of an Annuity of $500 Paid Semi-annually and Discounted for Six Periods at 2% Using PV Tables

Facts   Assume that an investor received $500 semi-annually for three years at 4% annual interest. The number of periods (n) becomes six (three annual periods × 2), and the discount rate (i) is 2% (4% × $^6/_{12}$ months).

Instructions   Calculate the present value using PV tables.

Solution   If present value tables are used to determine the present value, the appropriate present value factor from Table PV.2 is 5.60143. The present value of the future cash flows is $2,800.72 (5.60143 × $500). This amount is slightly higher than the $2,775 calculated in Example 3.15 and Illustration 3.12 because interest is calculated twice during the same year. Thus, interest is compounded on the first half-year's interest.

Interpolation   As previously discussed, one of the limitations of the present value tables is that the tables contain a limited number of interest rates. But in certain situations where the factor for a certain interest rate is not available, it can be deduced or interpolated from the tables. **Example 3.18** illustrates this.

Example 3.18 | Interpolation of 3½% Interest Rate Factor

Facts   Assume a $3^1/_2\%$ interest rate and five periods.

Instructions   Find the factor to determine the present value.

Solution   It would be difficult to use Table PV.1 to do so. Table PV.1 (or Table PV.2 for that matter) does not have a $3^1/_2\%$ interest rate column. We can, however, average the factors for the 3% and 4% interest rates to approximate the factor for a $3^1/_2\%$ interest rate, as shown below.

Factor, $n = 5$, $i = 3\%$		0.86261
Factor, $n = 5$, $i = 4\%$	+	0.82193
Sum of two factors	=	1.68454
Average two factors	÷	2
Factor, $n = 5$, $i = 3^1/_2\%$	=	0.84227

As previously mentioned, interpolation is only necessary when using present value tables. When using a financial calculator or spreadsheet, you can use any interest rate in the calculations.

Some Additional Calculations

Often you need to calculate the present value, but sometimes one of the other variables (such as interest rate or annuity payments) needs to be calculated. The next section looks at how this might be done.

Calculation of the Interest Rate

Many shoppers use credit cards to make purchases. When you receive the statement for payment, you may pay the total amount due or you may pay the balance in a certain number of payments. **Example 3.19** shows how to solve for the interest rate using a formula.

Example 3.19 | Solving for the Interest Rate

Facts   Assume you receive a statement from MasterCard with a balance due of $528.77. You may pay it off in 12 equal monthly payments of $50 each, with the first payment due one month from now.

Instructions   What rate of interest would you be paying?

Solution   The $528.77 represents the present value of the 12 ordinary annuity payments of $50 each at an unknown rate of interest. The time diagram below depicts this situation.

Recall from prior examples (including Example 3.10) that the present value is equal to the cash flows (payments or receipts) times a PV factor. We can use this formula where we know the present value and cash flows in order to determine the interest rate. You calculate the rate as follows:

$$\text{Present value of an ordinary annuity} = R(PVF - OA_{n,i})$$

$$\$528.77 = \$50(PVF - OA_{12,i})$$

$$(PVF - OA_{12,i}) = \frac{\$528.77}{\$50} = 10.57540$$

In the formula, R refers to payment. Referring to Table PV.2 and reading across the 12-period row, you find 10.57534 in the 2% column. Therefore, you are paying 2% per month. Obviously, you are better off paying the entire bill now if possible.

When using a spreadsheet such as Excel, you would select "Formula," then "Financial," and then "Rate." **Example 3.20** shows the factors that need to be input for both a spreadsheet and a financial calculator.

Example 3.20 | Solving for the Interest Rate Using a Spreadsheet or Financial Calculator

Facts   Assume the same facts as in Example 3.19.

Instructions   Calculate what rate of interest you would be paying using a spreadsheet and financial calculator.

Solution

Excel		Financial calculator	
Nper	12	N	12
Pmt	50	PMT	50
PV	−528.77	PV	−528.77
FV	0	FV	0
Type	0	Type	0

Where:

PV = present value
Nper or N = number of periods
Pmt or PMT = the payment at the end of each period
FV = future value
Type = ordinary annuity (enter 0) or annuity due (enter 1)

Note that if you have a situation whereby you know the present value and future value (and there are no payments) you input the future value amount as a negative amount.

Calculation of the Periodic Payment

Another very common calculation in accounting involves calculating a payment. **Example 3.21** looks at how to do this.

Example 3.21 | Calculating a Lease Payment Using a PV Table, Spreadsheet, and Financial Calculator

Facts   Assume that Norm Inc. is considering leasing a car from Jackie Inc. for a period of four years. The fair value of the car today is $36,000. The current market interest rate for financing such a vehicle is 4% compounded semi-annually.

Below is a time diagram of this situation.

Instructions Calculate the semi-annual lease payment assuming that the payment is made at the end of the period.

Solution Determining the answer by simply dividing $36,000 by eight payments is incorrect. Why? Because that ignores the impact of interest compounding. Thus, the amount of the payment is determined as follows.

$$\text{Present value of an ordinary annuity} = R(PVF - OA_{n,i})$$
$$\$36,000 = R(PVF - OA_{8,2\%})$$
$$\$36,000 = R(7.32548)$$
$$R = \$4,914.35$$

When using a spreadsheet such as Excel, you would select "Formula," then "Financial," and then "Pmt." Below are the factors that need to be input for both a spreadsheet and a financial calculator.

Excel		Financial calculator	
Rate	2%	I	2%
Nper	8	N	8
PV	36000	PV	36000
FV	0	FV	0
Type	0	Type	0

Where:

PV = present value
Nper or N = number of periods
Rate or I = the interest rate per period
FV = future value
Type = ordinary annuity (enter 0) or annuity due (enter 1)

We have covered off the basics of measurement in the chapter. There will be many more examples throughout the text. Feel free to revisit this chapter as you work through other chapters to ensure that you understand the foundations of measurement.

IFRS/ASPE Comparison

LEARNING OBJECTIVE 4

Identify differences in accounting between ASPE and IFRS, and what changes are expected in the near future.

The main difference in the accounting for measurement issues is that IFRS has a well-developed framework for measuring fair values (IFRS 13), whereas ASPE does not. While IFRS 13 lays out specific definitions and principles, the guidance relating to fair value is spread throughout the ASPE body of knowledge. Chapter 2 covers more general guidance as it relates to measurement, including fair values and historical cost.

A Comparison of IFRS and ASPE

Illustration 3.15 sets out the major differences between the accounting standards under IFRS and ASPE regarding the measurement of fair values.

ILLUSTRATION 3.15 **IFRS and ASPE Comparison Chart**

	IFRS—Conceptual Framework for Financial Reporting, IFRS 13	Accounting Standards for Private Enterprises (ASPE)— *CPA Canada Handbook, Part II*, Section 1000	Further Comments
Measurement of fair value	Guidance is concentrated in IFRS 13	Guidance is spread throughout the ASPE standards	The guidance in ASPE is not inconsistent with IFRS 13, although there is significantly less detail. Specific differences in measurement as they relate to financial statements and elements will be covered in subsequent chapters.

Looking Ahead

The IASB has issued a new conceptual framework. This conceptual framework has considerably increased coverage regarding measurement issues. More detail on this was included in Chapter 2 and in What Do the Numbers Mean? 3.1.

Review and Practice

Summary of Learning Objectives

1 Use valuation techniques to measure financial statement elements.

IFRS and ASPE incorporate a mixed-attribute measurement model including measurements that are cost-based (such as historical cost), those that are based on current value (such as fair value), and many hybrid measures that have attributes of both cost-based and current value measurements. Valuation techniques are used to help with measurement of financial statement elements. Common examples include market models and income models. Income models are widely used and include discounted cash flow methods and present value concepts. When using models, you must determine what inputs should be used. Common inputs include discount rates and cash flow estimates. The quality of these inputs affects the quality of the final measurement. Accountants often use probabilities to help deal with risk and uncertainty. Given the amount of judgement that goes into measuring financial statement elements, disclosures are very important.

2 Use IFRS 13 to measure fair value.

IFRS 13 establishes a fairly detailed body of knowledge relating to measurement of fair value. Fair value measurement under IFRS 13 is a market-based approach that incorporates the specific attributes of the asset or liability being measured, the valuation premise (how the asset or liability is to be used), the principal market, and the valuation

technique. Since market prices are not always available, valuation models are used to measure the value. Inputs to these models are either observable in the market or not. Observable inputs are most useful since they are more objective. The fair value hierarchy establishes three levels of inputs, with level 1 being the highest and best type of input (based on observable market prices). Because level 3 inputs are more subjective, additional disclosures are required.

3 Understand and apply present value concepts.

Present value concepts are used to acknowledge the time value of money. There are various techniques and tools to calculate present value, including formulas, tables, financial calculators, and spreadsheets. Inputs to the calculation include interest, payments, number of periods, and if the calculation involves an annuity, information about whether it is an ordinary annuity or an annuity due. Present value concepts are frequently used in measuring financial statement elements.

4 Identify differences in accounting between ASPE and IFRS, and what changes are expected in the near future.

The main difference is that IFRS contains specific guidance in IFRS 13 regarding fair value measurements. Under ASPE, guidance is spread throughout the body of knowledge and is less detailed.

Practice Problem

You are the controller of Kelowna Limited (KL) and are in the process of determining the value of several items to prepare the year-end financial statements. The company follows IFRS. The items are noted below.

1. KL owns a piece of manufacturing equipment that has outdated technology. You suspect that the machinery is impaired and would like to calculate the impairment loss, if any. The equipment will generate the following cash flows over the next three years (at the end of each year):

   Year 1: $10,000

   Year 2: $10,000

   Year 3: $5,000

   Assume that an appropriate discount rate is 5%. You plan to estimate the equipment's value in use as a first step. The carrying value before any adjustment is $30,000. Assume the fair value less costs of disposal is equal to the value in use.

2. KL has an investment in shares of Shore Limited. The shares trade on the national stock exchange.

3. KL has recently signed a lease agreement to lease a building for 10 years at a price of $1 million per year (paid at the end of the year). At the end of the lease, the building reverts to the lessor. The discount rate is 5%.

4. KL is planning to issue some bonds before year end. The 10-year bonds carry interest at 6% (paid annually) and have a face value of $100,000. The market interest rate is 5%. There are no identical bonds in the market.

Instructions

a. For the manufacturing equipment, calculate the value in use. Should KL recognize an impairment loss? Why or why not? Calculate the impairment loss (if any).

b. For the investment in shares, identify which level of the fair value hierarchy the asset would be categorized as. Explain why.

c. For the lease, calculate the present value using PV tables.

d. For the bonds, calculate the fair value of the bonds using PV tables. Which model would you use to estimate fair value and why? Which level would you categorize the bonds at in the fair value hierarchy?

e. For all four items, identify sources of measurement uncertainty that you may wish to highlight in the financial statements. *Hint:* Include any items that were given in the question that the company would have had to estimate.

Solution

a. The value in use is calculated by first estimating the future cash flows and then discounting them as follows:

Future cash flows	Discount rate per PV table	Discounted amount
$10,000	.95238	$ 9,524
10,000	.90703	9,070
5,000	.86384	4,319
		$22,913
	Carrying value	$30,000
	Loss	$ 7,087

The company should recognize an impairment loss of $7,087 since the value in use (which equals fair value) is less than the carrying value of $30,000.

b. The shares would be categorized as level 1 since they trade on the national stock exchange and therefore a market value is available.

c. The present value of the lease is $1,000,000 × 7.72173 = $7,721,730.

d. The fair value of the bond is as follows:

$$\$100,000 \times .61391 = \$ 61,391$$
$$\$6,000 \times 7.72173 = \underline{\quad 46,330}$$
$$\underline{\underline{\$107,721}}$$

The fair value would likely be calculated using an income model (present value) since identical bonds do not trade in the market. Therefore, the fair value must be estimated. Since the estimated cash flows and a discount rate are available, an income model makes sense. The bonds would be categorized as level 2 in the fair value hierarchy because there are no identical bonds that trade in the market.

e. Items relating to measurement uncertainty include the following:

- Equipment: estimated cash flows (amount and number of years) and discount rate. In addition, determining whether there is impairment at all adds an element of measurement uncertainty in terms of measuring the value of the equipment. If it is not impaired, then the value in the financial statements would be higher.

- Shares: None, since market value is readily available.

- Lease: discount rate. The payments and payment dates would be identified in the lease contract so there is no measurement uncertainty related to these cash flows initially.

- Bonds: discount rate. The payments of principal and interest would have been identified in the contract and so there is no measurement uncertainty related to these cash flows initially.

  (Note that estimating a "market rate" is often more complex than it might appear. The company must consider the risk-free rate plus any additional risk premiums.)

Key Terms

compound interest, p. 3-15	fair value hierarchy, p. 3-11	principal market, p. 3-10
discounted cash flow model, p. 3-6	highest and best use, p. 3-10	simple interest, p. 3-15
expected cash flow approach, p. 3-7	most advantageous market, p. 3-10	traditional discounted cash flow approach, p. 3-6

Assignment Material

Note: **Enabling Technology** Completion of this end-of-chapter material will help develop CPA-enabling competencies (such as ethics and professionalism, problem-solving and decision-making, and communication) and technical competencies. We have highlighted selected items with a specific integration word mark and material in *WileyPLUS* has been linked to the competencies. The brief exercises, exercises, and problems generally emphasize problem-solving and decision-making. For Chapter 3, since much of the end-of-chapter material dealing with measurement relates also to the finance technical competency area, we have highlighted only selected items relating to finance.

Brief Exercises

BE3.1 (LO 1) Below are some financial statement elements and their basis of measurement for a public company that follows IFRS. Complete the third column by noting whether the basis of measurement is a cost-based measure, a current-value measure, or a hybrid measure. Explain your choice.

Element	Basis of measurement	Measurement categorization
Building	Depreciated cost unless impaired	
Manufacturing inventory	Lower of cost and net realizable value	
Biological assets	Fair value less (estimated) costs to sell	
Bonds payable	Amortized cost	

BE3.2 (LO 1) In the chapter, there are two common types of valuation techniques noted. Explain the differences between these two models. Note when each of these techniques might be used in measuring financial statement elements.

BE3.3 (LO 1) Present value concepts are often used for measurement in financial reporting. List five situations where present value techniques are used to measure assets and explain how. List five situations where present value techniques are used to measure liabilities.

BE3.4 (LO 1) When using the discounted cash flow model, there are two approaches that are generally accepted. List these two approaches and explain when each might be used to measure a financial statement element.

BE3.5 (LO 1) Assume that Enter Inc. just issued a $1,000, 10-year bond bearing annual interest of 4%. The company would like to determine the amount that should be recognized on the financial statements. The bond carries a fixed interest rate of 4% (interest is payable annually), which is lower than the market interest rate of 5%. Identify and explain what inputs would be required in measuring the bond. Would you recommend using the traditional approach or the expected cash flow approach to measure this liability? Why?

BE3.6 (LO 1) Lucky Enterprises is using a discounted cash flow model. Identify which model Lucky might use to estimate the discounted fair value under each scenario, and calculate the fair value using factor Table PV.1:

Scenario 1: Cash flows are fairly certain
$100/year for five years
Risk-adjusted discount rate is 6%
Risk-free discount rate is 3%

Scenario 2: Cash flows are uncertain
75% probability that cash flows will be $100 in five years
25% probability that cash flows will be $75 in five years
Risk-adjusted discount rate is 6%
Risk-free discount rate is 3%

BE3.7 (LO 1) Chang Company must perform an impairment test on its equipment. The equipment will produce the following cash flows: Year 1, $35,000; Year 2, $45,000; Year 3, $55,000. The discount rate is 10%. What is the value in use for this equipment? Use factor Table PV.1 in your calculation.

BE3.8 (LO 1) Alpha Company signs a contract to sell the use of its patented manufacturing technology to Delta Corp for 15 years. The contract for this transaction stipulates that Delta Corp pays Alpha $18,000 at the end of each year for the use of this technology. Using a discount rate of 9%, what is the value in use of the patented manufacturing technology? To calculate, use (a) factor Table PV.1, (b) a financial calculator, or (c) Excel function PV.

BE3.9 (LO 1) Zang Services Inc. accounts for the lease of a truck. The lease includes a residual value guarantee at the end of the lease term of $16,000. Zang estimates that the likelihood that the residual value will be $16,000 has a 50% certainty. Zang feels that there is a 30% chance that the residual value will be $12,000 and a 20% chance that it will be $10,000. Calculate the probability-weighted value of the residual guarantee that needs to be included in the measurement of the lease payments liability recorded by Zang when the lease is signed.

BE3.10 (LO 2, 4) Assume that you are following IFRS 13 and measuring the fair value of a building. The building is currently being rented out. Under IFRS 13, the entity must determine the following: (a) how the item could be/is used, (b) the market, and (c) the valuation technique/model. Briefly explain each of these and note how they would apply to measuring the building. How would your analysis change under ASPE?

BE3.11 (LO 2, 4) Medici Patriarchs purchased the following investments during 2020:

a. 1,000 shares of Private Limited, a start-up company. The value of this investment was based on an internally developed model.

b. 5,000 shares of CIBC, a public company listed on the TSX.

c. $15,000 of corporate bonds. Although these bonds do not trade in an active market, their value closely reflects movements in the Bank of Canada bond rate.

Based on the IFRS 13 guidance, indicate at which level in the fair value hierarchy these investment values will fall (level 1, 2, or 3). Explain your choice. How would your analysis change under ASPE?

BE3.12 (LO 3) Determine the amount of interest that will be earned on each of the following investments:

	Investment	(*i*) Interest Rate	(*n*) Number of Periods	Type of Interest
a.	$100	5%	1	Simple
b.	$500	6%	2	Simple
c.	$500	6%	2	Compound

BE3.13 (LO 3) **Excel** Smolinski Company is considering an investment that will return a lump sum of $500,000 five years from now. What amount should Smolinski Company pay for this investment in order to earn a 4% return? Show calculations using all four methods: (a) formula, (b) factor Table PV.1, (c) financial calculator, and (d) Excel function PV.

BE3.14 (LO 3) **Excel** If Kerry Dahl invests $3,152 now, she will receive $10,000 at the end of 15 years. What annual rate of interest will Kerry earn on her investment? Round your answer to the nearest whole number. Show calculations using any of three methods: (a) factor Table PV.1, (b) a financial calculator, or (c) Excel function PV.

BE3.15 (LO 3) Kilarny Company is considering investing in an annuity contract that will return $25,000 at the end of each year for 15 years. What amount should Kilarny Company pay for this investment if it earns a 6% return? Show calculations using any of the following methods: (a) factor Table PV.2, (b) a financial calculator, or (c) Excel function PV.

BE3.16 (LO 3) For each of the following cases, indicate in the chart below the appropriate discount rate (*i*) or Rate and the appropriate number of periods (*n*) or Nper to be used in present value calculations. Show calculations. The first one has been completed as an example.

	Annual Interest Rate	Number of Years	Frequency of Payment	(*n*) or Nper Number of Periods	(*i*) or Rate Discount Rate
1.	8%	3	Quarterly	$3 \times 4 = 12$	$8\% \div 4 = 2\%$
2.	5%	4	Semi-annually		
3.	7%	5	Annually		
4.	4%	3	Quarterly		
5.	6%	6	Semi-annually		
6.	6%	15	Monthly		

BE3.17 (LO 3) Insert the appropriate discount factor into the table below for each of the situations given. These factors have to be interpolated from factor Tables PV.1 and PV.2.

	PV of 1 (Table PV.1)	PV of an Annuity of 1 (Table PV.2)
a. $n = 4, i = 4\frac{1}{2}\%$		
b. $n = 6, i = 6\frac{1}{2}\%$		

BE3.18 (LO 3) Cross Country Railroad Co. is about to issue $100,000 of 10-year bonds that pay a 5.5% annual interest rate, with interest payable semi-annually. The market interest rate is 5%. How much can Cross Country expect to receive for the sale of these bonds? To calculate, use (a) factor Tables PV.1 and PV.2, (b) a financial calculator, or (c) Excel function PV.

BE3.19 (LO 3) **Excel** Assume the same information as BE3.18, except that the market interest rate is 6% instead of 5%. In this case, how much can Cross Country expect to receive from the sale of these bonds? Show calculations using any of the following three methods: (a) factor Tables PV.1 and PV.2, (b) a financial calculator, or (c) Excel function PV.

BE3.20 (LO 3) **Excel** Caledonian Company receives a six-year, $50,000 note that bears interest at 8% (paid annually) from a customer at a time when the market interest rate is 6%. What is the present value of the note received by Caledonian? Show calculations using (a) factor Tables PV.1 and PV.2, (b) a financial calculator, or (c) Excel function PV.

BE3.21 (LO 3) **Excel** Hung-Chao Yu Company issues a six-year, 8% mortgage note on January 1, 2020, to obtain financing for new equipment. The terms provide for semi-annual instalment payments of $112,825. What were the cash proceeds received from the issue of the note? Show calculations using (a) factor Table PV.1, (b) a financial calculator, or (c) Excel function PV.

BE3.22 (LO 3) **Excel** You are told that a note has repayment terms of $4,000 per year for five years, with a stated interest rate of 4%. How much of the total payment is for principal, and how much is for interest? Show calculations using (a) financial calculator or (b) Excel function PV.

BE3.23 (LO 3) Assume the same information as in BE3.22 except that the note calls for quarterly instalment payments of $1,000. Before repeating the calculation, try to predict the outcome of the calculation and determine if the total interest will be higher or lower than with an annual payment. Show calculations using (a) financial calculator or (b) Excel function PV.

BE3.24 (LO 3) You would like to purchase a car with a negotiated price of $30,000, and the dealer offers financing over a five-year period at 8%. If repayments are to be made annually, what would be your annual payments? Show calculations using (a) factor Table PV.2, (b) a financial calculator, or (c) Excel function PMT.

BE3.25 (LO 3) Assume the same information as in BE3.24 except that the payments are made monthly, at the end of each month, instead of annually. What would be the monthly payments? Show calculations using (a) a financial calculator or (b) Excel function PMT.

BE3.26 (LO 3) Assume the same information as in BE3.24, except that you can afford to make annual payments of only $6,000. If you decide to trade in your current car to help reduce the amount of financing required, what trade-in value would you need to negotiate to ensure your annual payment is $6,000? Show calculations using (a) factor Table PV.2, (b) a financial calculator, or (c) Excel function PV.

BE3.27 (LO 3) As CFO of a small manufacturing firm, you have been asked to determine the best financing for the purchase of a new piece of equipment. If the vendor is offering repayment options of $10,000 at the end of each year for five years, or no payment for two years followed by one payment of $46,000, which option would you recommend? The current market rate of interest is 8%. To calculate each option, use (a) a financial calculator or (b) Excel function PV.

BE3.28 (LO 3) If the market rate of interest in BE3.27 were 10%, would you choose the same option? To calculate each option, use (a) a financial calculator or (b) Excel function PV.

BE3.29 (LO 3, 4) Assume the same information as in BE3.27. (a) Describe how the vendor arrived at the amounts of the two options. (b) What would have been the equivalent cash selling price? (c) Is the risk the same to the vendor as with a cash sale? (d) What, if any, would be the difference in the reporting on the financial statements under the two options? Would your answer change if the vendor were following ASPE?

Exercises

E3.1 (LO 1) (Discounted Cash Flow Models) Hoda Inc. owns 25% of the common shares of Willard Corp. The other 75% of the shares are owned by the Willard family. Hoda acquired the shares eight years ago through a financing transaction. Each year, Hoda has received a dividend from Willard. Willard has been in business for 60 years and continues to have strong operations and cash flows. Hoda must determine the fair value of this investment at its year end. Since there is no market on which the shares are traded, Hoda must use a discounted cash flow model to determine fair value.

Hoda management intends to hold the shares for five more years, at which time they will sell the shares to the Willard family under an existing agreement for $1 million. There is no uncertainty in this amount. Management expects to receive dividends of $80,000 for each of the five years, although there is a 20% chance that dividends could be $50,000 each year. The risk-free rate is 4% and the risk-adjusted rate is 6%.

Instructions

a. Identify some of the items Hoda will need to consider in determining the fair value of the investment.

b. Calculate the fair value of the investment in Willard using the traditional approach with factor Tables PV.1 and PV.2.

c. Calculate the fair value of the investment using the expected cash flow approach.

d. **Digging Deeper** In this case, which discounted cash flow model is the best? Why?

E3.2 (LO 2) (Fair Value Estimate) Killroy Company owns a trade name that was purchased in an acquisition of McClellan Company. The trade name has a book value of $3.5 million, but according to IFRS, it is assessed for impairment on an annual basis. To perform this impairment test, Killroy must estimate the fair value of the trade name (using IFRS 13). It has developed the following cash flow estimates related to the trade name based on internal information. Each cash flow estimate reflects Killroy's estimate of annual cash flows over the next eight years. The trade name is assumed to have no salvage value after the eight years. (Assume the cash flows occur at the end of each year.)

Video

Cash Flow Estimate	Probability Assessment
$380,000	20%
630,000	50%
750,000	30%

Instructions

a. What is the estimated fair value of the trade name? Killroy determines that the appropriate discount rate for this estimation is 8%. To calculate, use (1) factor Table PV.2, (2) a financial calculator, or (3) Excel function PV.

b. Is the estimate developed for part (a) a level 1, level 2, or level 3 fair value estimate? Explain.

c. Draft a short note to the financial statements noting any sources of measurement uncertainty.

E3.3 (LO 3) (Unknown Rate) HQ Ltd. purchased a used truck from Trans Auto Sales Inc. HQ paid a $4,000 down payment and signed a note that calls for 36 payments of $1,033.34 at the end of each month. The stated rate of interest in the note is 4%. As an incentive for entering into the contract, Trans has agreed to forgive the first two payments under the lease.

Instructions

a. What was the purchase price of the used truck excluding the incentive given? To calculate, use (1) a financial calculator or (2) Excel function PV.

b. What effect, if any, does the forgiveness of the first two payments have on the purchase price of the truck?

c. Calculate the present value of the 34 payments of $1,033.34 that will be made by HQ for payments 3 to 36 inclusive. You will need to perform two steps.

    1. Calculate the present value of the 34 payments as of the end of the second month following the purchase of the used truck. Use (a) a financial calculator or (b) Excel function PV.

    2. Take the result from the first calculation and calculate the present value as of the date of purchase. Use (a) a financial calculator or (b) Excel function PV.

d. What amount should HQ use to record the purchase of the truck?

e. What amount of interest should be accrued at the end of the first month following the purchase?

E3.4 (LO 3) **(Unknown Rate)** LEW Company purchased a machine at a price of $100,000 by signing a note payable, which requires a single payment of $123,210 in two years.

a. Assuming annual compounding of interest, what rate of interest is being paid on the loan? Use either a financial calculator or the Excel function Rate to calculate the rate.

b. What would be the purchase price of the machine had LEW negotiated a single payment of $120,000 in two years, using the same effective rate? To calculate, use (1) a financial calculator or (2) Excel function PV.

E3.5 (LO 3) **(Evaluation of Purchase Options)** Sosa Excavating Inc. is purchasing a bulldozer. The equipment has a price of $100,000. The manufacturer has offered a payment plan that would allow Sosa to make 10 equal annual payments of $16,274.53, with the first payment due one year after the purchase.

Instructions

a. How much total interest will Sosa pay on this payment plan?

b. Sosa could borrow $100,000 from its bank to finance the purchase at an annual rate of 9%. Should Sosa borrow from the bank or use the manufacturer's payment plan to pay for the equipment? *Hint:* Use factor Table PV.2, a financial calculator, or Excel function Rate to calculate the interest on the payment plan and then compare with the bank rate.

E3.6 (LO 3) **Finance** **(Analysis of Alternatives)** The Black Knights Inc., a manufacturer of low-sugar, low-sodium, low-cholesterol TV dinners, would like to increase its market share in Western Canada. In order to do so, Black Knights has decided to locate a new factory in Kelowna, B.C. Black Knights will either buy or lease a site, depending upon which is more advantageous. The site location committee has narrowed down the available sites to the following three buildings.

    Building A: Purchase for a cash price of $600,000, useful life 25 years.

    Building B: Lease for 25 years with annual lease payments of $69,000 being made at the beginning of the year.

    Building C: Purchase for $650,000 cash. This building is larger than needed; however, the excess space can be sublet for 25 years at a net annual rental of $7,000. Rental payments will be received at the end of each year. The Black Knights Inc. has no aversion to being a landlord.

Instructions

In which building would you recommend that The Black Knights Inc. locate, assuming a 12% cost of funds? For Buildings B and C, calculate using (a) factor Table PV.1, (b) a financial calculator, or (c) Excel function PV.

E3.7 (LO 3) **(Calculation of Bond Liability)** Viavélo Inc. manufactures cycling equipment. Recently, the company's vice-president of operations has requested construction of a new plant to meet the increasing demand for the company's bikes. After a careful evaluation of the request, the board of directors has decided to raise funds for the new plant by issuing $2 million of 11% term corporate bonds on March 1, 2020, due on March 1, 2034, with interest payable each March 1 and September 1. At the time of issuance, the market interest rate for similar financial instruments is 10%.

Instructions

a. As Viavélo's controller, determine the selling price of the bonds. Show calculations using (a) factor Tables A.2 and A.4 in Appendix A, (b) a financial calculator, or (c) Excel function PV.

b. What is the basis of measurement for the bonds?

c. Is there any measurement uncertainty that requires disclosure in Viavelo's financial statement notes?

E3.8 (LO 3) **(Calculation of Amount of Lease Payments)** Your client, Danyleyko Leasing Company, is preparing a contract to lease a machine to Souvenirs Corporation for a period of 25 years. Danyleyko has an investment cost of $365,755 in the machine, which has a useful life of 25 years and no salvage value at the end of that time. Your client is interested in earning an 11% return on its investment and has agreed to accept 25 equal rental payments at the end of each of the next 25 years.

Instructions

a. You are requested to provide Danyleyko with the amount of each of the 25 rental payments that will yield an 11% return on investment. Show calculations using (a) factor Table A.4 in Appendix A, (b) a financial calculator, or (c) Excel function PMT.

b. What valuation model is Danyleyko using in the measurement of this lease?

c. **Digging Deeper** Besides the interest return on this investment, what other risk factors would Danyleyko have considered in pricing this transaction? Do these risks involve measurement uncertainty that needs disclosure in the financial statements?

E3.9 (LO 1, 3) **(Expected Cash Flows)**

Instructions

For each of the following, determine the expected cash flows.

	Cash Flow Estimate	Probability Assessment
a.	$4,800	20%
	6,300	50%
	7,500	30%
b.	5,400	30%
	7,200	50%
	8,400	20%
c.	(1,000)	10%
	3,000	80%
	5,000	10%

E3.10 (LO 1, 3) **(Expected Cash Flows and Present Value)** Keith Nobrega is trying to determine the amount to set aside so that he will have enough money on hand in two years to overhaul the engine on his vintage used car. While there is some uncertainty about the cost of engine overhauls in two years, by conducting some research online, Keith has developed the following estimates.

Engine Overhaul Estimated Cash Outflow	Probability Assessment
$200	10%
450	30%
600	50%
750	10%

Instructions

How much should Keith deposit today in an account earning 6%, compounded annually, so that he will have enough money on hand in two years to pay for the overhaul?

Problems

P3.1 Langevin Ltd., which has a calendar year end, entered into an equipment lease on June 1, 2020, with GH Financing Limited. The lease term is two years and requires payments of $3,000 at the end of each month beginning September 30. The stated rate of interest in the lease is 6%. As an incentive for entering into the contract, GH has agreed to forgive the first three payments under the lease (June, July, and August).

Instructions

a. What effect, if any, does the forgiveness of the first three payments have on the measurement of the lease transaction on June 1, 2020?

b. Calculate the amount that Langevin should record for the lease obligation on June 1, 2020. Use a financial calculator or Excel functions in your calculation. *Hint:* Calculate the present value of the monthly payments as at September 1, 2020, and then discount this amount to June 1, 2020.

c. What is the amount of the interest accrual that Langevin will record on June 30, 2020, for the lease obligation?

d. Is there any measurement uncertainty that needs disclosure in the notes to Langevin's financial statements? *Hint:* Assume that GH is confident of collecting the lease payments under the lease contract.

P3.2 M&B Tooling Ltd. is assessing two available options for the purchase of new equipment with a negotiated cash price of $100,000. The manufacturer is willing to accept a down payment of 20% of the purchase price and an instalment note for the balance. The note would require quarterly fixed principal payments (plus interest) starting October 1, 2020, for a period of two years. M&B has a proposal from its bank for an instalment loan for two years that requires a fixed blended monthly payment (including both principal and interest) starting August 1, 2020. The loan would be for 80% of the equipment's purchase price. The current market rate of interest is 8%. Both contracts have an interest rate of 8%.

Instructions

a. Is there any measurement uncertainty in determining which option is best for M&B? Which discounted cash flow approach should be used in the comparison of the two alternatives?

b. Calculate the amount of the payments required of M&B under each alternative. Use either a financial calculator or Excel functions in your calculation.

c. Besides interest costs, what other considerations should M&B use in making a choice between the two alternatives?

d. Digging Deeper What financial ratios could be affected by M&B's choice?

P3.3 Khalfan Industries would like to determine the fair value of its manufacturing facility in London, Ontario. The facility consists of land, building, and manufacturing equipment.

Instructions

a. Identify some of the considerations that are involved in a fair value measurement.

b. Explain the various levels of input in the fair value hierarchy.

c. Using the fair value hierarchy, discuss the level 1, 2, and 3 types of inputs that Khalfan could use to value each asset as well as its facility altogether.

d. Draft a short note to the financial statements noting any sources of measurement uncertainty.

P3.4 Finance James Halabi is a financial executive with McDowell Enterprises. Although James has not had any formal training in finance or accounting, he has a "good sense" for numbers and has helped the company grow from a very small company ($500,000 in sales) to a large operation ($45 million in sales). With the business growing steadily, however, the company needs to make a number of difficult financial decisions in which James Halabi feels a little "over his head." He therefore has decided to hire a new employee with "numbers" expertise to help him. As a basis for determining whom to employ, he has decided to ask each prospective employee to prepare answers to questions relating to situations he has encountered recently.

The following are the facts for the first question asked of prospective employees.

In 2019, McDowell Enterprises negotiated and closed a lease contract for newly constructed truck terminals and freight storage facilities. On January 1, 2020, McDowell took possession of the leased property. The 20-year lease is effective for the period January 1, 2020, through December 31, 2039. Advance rental payments of $800,000 are payable to the lessor (owner of facilities) on January 1 of each of the first 10 years of the lease term. Advance payments of $400,000 are due on January 1 for each of the last 10 years of the lease term. McDowell has an option to purchase all the leased facilities for $1 on December 31, 2039. At the time the lease was negotiated, the fair value of the truck terminals and freight storage facilities was approximately $7.2 million. If the company had borrowed the money to purchase the facilities, it would have had to pay 10% interest. Should the company have purchased rather than leased the facilities?

Instructions

a. Calculate the present value of the payments required of McDowell Enterprises under the lease agreement. Use factor Tables PV.1 and PV.2, a financial calculator, or Excel functions in your calculation. Steps to be followed include:

1. Calculate the present value of the future cash flows for the advance rental payments of $800,000 for the period from January 1, 2020, through December 31, 2029. *Hint:* If using factor tables, because the lease payments are due at the beginning of each year, use the PV.2 regular annuity table for nine years and add the first payment of January 1, 2020, in your calculation.

2. Calculate the present value of the future cash flows for the advance rental payments of $400,000 for the 10-year period beginning January 1, 2030. *Hint:* If using factor tables, as in the first step, use the PV.2 regular annuity table for 10 years for the present value at January 1, 2029.

3. Take the calculation result of step 2 and arrive at the present value of that amount at January 1, 2020, by using nine years in your discount calculation.

4. Add the result of the first and third steps to arrive at the total cost of leasing.

b. Based on your analysis in part (a), should McDowell lease or buy the storage facilities?

P3.5 Assume the same information as in P3.4.

Instructions

Redo the analysis using Excel functions for an annuity due. Will the conclusion reached be the same as in P3.4?

P3.6 Assume the same role as described in P3.4.

The following are the facts for the second question asked of prospective employees.

Last year the company exchanged a piece of land for a non–interest-bearing note. The note is to be paid at the rate of $15,000 per year for nine years, beginning one year from the date of disposal of the land. An appropriate rate of interest for the note was 11% (market rate). At the time the land was originally purchased, it cost $90,000.

Instructions

a. Calculate the fair value of the note using IFRS 13 on the date of the exchange. Use (1) factor Table PV.2, (2) a financial calculator, or (3) Excel functions in your calculation. *Hint:* discount the payments at the market rate of interest to find the present value of the note.

b. Prepare the journal entry for the exchange.

c. Prepare the journal entry on the date of the first payment. Ignore any year-end accruals.

P3.7 Finance Dunn Inc. owns and operates a number of hardware stores in the Atlantic region. Recently, the company has decided to open another store in a rapidly growing area of Nova Scotia. The company is trying to decide whether to purchase or lease the building and related facilities. Currently, the cost of funds for Dunn Inc. is 10%.

Purchase: The company can purchase the site, construct the building, and purchase all store fixtures. The cost would be $1,850,000. An immediate down payment of $400,000 is required, and the remaining $1,450,000 would be paid off over five years with payments of $350,000 per year (including interest payments made at the end of the year). The property is expected to have a useful life of 12 years, and then it will be sold for $500,000. As the owner of the property, the company will pay $56,000 in occupancy expenses at the end of each year.

Lease: First National Bank has agreed to purchase the site, construct the building, and install the appropriate fixtures for Dunn Inc. if Dunn will lease the completed facility for 12 years. The annual payments would be $270,000. Dunn would have no responsibility related to the facility over the 12 years. The terms of the lease are that Dunn would be required to make 12 annual payments. (The first payment is to be made at the time the store opens and then one each following year.) In addition, a deposit of $100,000 is required when the store is opened. This deposit will be returned at the end of the twelfth year, assuming there is no unusual damage to the building structure or fixtures. Assume a 10% discount rate.

Instructions

a. Using factor tables, calculate the present value of the net cash flows required of Dunn Inc. for:

1. the purchase alternative and

2. the lease alternative. *Hint:* For the lease payments, use Table PV.2 for 11 years and add the first payment to convert a regular annuity to an annuity due.

Which of the two alternatives should Dunn Inc. adopt?

P3.8 Finance Use the information in P3.7.

Instructions

a. Using a financial calculator, calculate the present value of the net cash flows required of Dunn Inc. for:

1. the purchase alternative and

2. the lease alternative. *Hint:* For the annuity due for the lease payments, program your calculator to annuity due or calculate a regular annuity for 11 years and add the first payment to convert a regular annuity to an annuity due.

b. Which of the two approaches should Dunn Inc. adopt?

P3.9 **Finance** Use the information in P3.7.

Instructions

a. Using Excel functions, calculate the present value of the net cash flows required of Dunn Inc. for (1) the purchase alternative and (2) the lease alternative. *Hint:* For the annuity due for the lease payments, use type 1.

b. Which of the two alternatives should Dunn Inc. adopt?

Cases

Refer to the Case Primer on the Student Website and in WileyPLUS *to help you answer these cases.*

CA3.1 Branson Restaurants Limited is currently reviewing its financial operations for the past year. Specifically, it is looking to determine what is happening with one of its restaurants (which it owns – including the land). The following summary gives data about the restaurant in question.

Restaurant Orro:

- In business for five years.
- Serves Italian cuisine.
- Initially catered to a young set of patrons but over time this has changed such that the restaurant is attracting mainly tourists.
- Initially very successful and generated significant cash flows.
- In the past year, business has slowed down (cash flows have declined as a result).
- Feedback about the quality of the service has not been as positive lately although there is no consistent thing that the company can readily put its finger on in the comments.
- Other similar restaurants in the area are doing quite well although they do not serve Italian cuisine.
- The surrounding area is doing quite well economically and real estate prices have been rising.
- Many condominiums are being built around the restaurant (there have been numerous condominium developers purchasing land in the past year).
- Rezoning is not an issue (any purchaser will be able to get the land rezoned for condo development).

Branson has decided to sell the restaurant in question and is looking to determine a fair value. The company follows IFRS. It would likely remeasure the investment in the restaurant to fair value less costs to sell in the year-end financial statements (assuming the value is less than carrying value). This is acceptable treatment under IFRS as long as the asset is being held to sell (which it is). Branson is owned by several large investors who are deciding whether to dispose of their holdings in the company.

Instructions

You are the external auditor of the company. Discuss how fair value would be measured for purposes of revaluing the restaurant. *Hint:* Start with an analysis of the highest and best use.

CA3.2 Oil Company Limited (OCL) is in the oil and gas business and operates internationally. The company is public and lists on the National Stock Exchange. In the past two years, oil prices have been declining significantly. The company's Canadian operations are primarily located in Western Canada and consist of holdings in what are known as the "tar sands." Costs to extract the oil from these types of geological formations are fairly high. In some months in the past year, the cost to extract the oil has been higher than the market price.

OCL is worried that oil prices will continue to decline and has therefore decided to write down its productive asset. To this end, the company needs to calculate the value in use and fair value less costs to sell. The higher value will be used to measure the impairment loss and to revalue the property. Financial analysts who follow the company (and other companies in the oil and gas sector) understand that the lower oil and gas prices are negatively affecting share prices. The land otherwise has little market value.

Instructions

Adopt the role of OCL's controller and discuss how to measure the value in use and fair value for purposes of recording an impairment loss and the writedown of the Canadian operations. *Hint:* Start with an analysis of highest and best use.

Research and Analysis

RA3.1 **Real World Emphasis**   **Hudson's Bay Company**

The financial statements of the Hudson's Bay Company are presented at the end of the book. Complete the following instructions by referring to these financial statements and the accompanying notes.

Instructions

a. What is the company's basis of presentation for its financial statements?

b. Using Illustration 3.3 as an example, list the bases of measurement and measurement categorization of the major assets and liabilities.

c. What valuation technique does the Hudson's Bay Company use to measure impairment of property, plant, and equipment?

d. The company issued warrants in connection with the acquisition of Saks. These instruments are classified as financial liabilities and are accounted for on a fair value basis. What level of the fair value hierarchy is applied in determining the fair value of the warrants? How is the fair value determined?

e. The Hudson's Bay Company has various pension plans for its employees and employees of its subsidiaries. The information for its pension plans is disclosed in Note 15 to the financial statements. The note also discloses a sensitivity analysis of the impact of changes in assumptions underlying the pension needs of its employees. Changes in these assumptions could increase or decrease the defined benefit obligation, which could affect future pension expense. What would be the worst-case scenario of cumulative increases or decreases of assumptions on the defined benefit obligation? How much of a change does this represent as a percentage of the defined pension obligation?

RA3.2 **Real World Emphasis**   **Maple Leaf Foods Inc.**

Obtain the 2017 annual report for Maple Leaf Foods Inc. from the company's website or from SEDAR (www.sedar.com). The company's note disclosure (Note 2) on "Basis of preparation" for (d) Use of Estimates and Judgements, for its biological assets is reproduced below.

Biological Assets

Biological assets are measured at each reporting date, at fair value less costs to sell, except when fair value cannot be reliably measured. If fair value cannot be reliably measured, biological assets are measured at cost less depreciation and impairment losses. Although a reliable measure of fair value may not be available at the point of initial recognition, it may subsequently become available. In such circumstances, biological assets are measured at fair value less costs to sell from the point at which the reliable measure of fair value becomes available. Gains and losses that arise on measuring biological assets at fair value less costs to sell are recognized in the statement of net earnings in the period in which they arise. Costs to sell include all costs that would be necessary to sell the biological assets, including costs necessary to get the biological assets to market. Management uses estimates for some of the inputs into the determination of fair value. To the extent that actual values differ from estimates, biological assets, net earnings and comprehensive income will be affected in future periods.

The company also discloses the following information in Note 3: Significant Accounting Policies.

(i) Inventories

Inventories are valued at the lower of cost and net realizable value, with cost being determined substantially on a first-in, first-out basis. The cost of inventory includes direct product costs, direct labour, and an allocation of variable and fixed manufacturing overhead, including depreciation.

(j) Biological Assets

Biological assets consist of live hogs, poultry, and eggs. For the purposes of valuation, these assets are categorized as either parent stock or commercial stock. Parent stock represents animals held and bred for the purpose of generating commercial stock and to replace parent stock nearing the end of its productive cycle. Commercial stock is held for the purposes of further processing or eventual sale, at which point it becomes inventory. The fair value of commercial stock is determined based on market prices of livestock of similar age, breed, and generic merit, less costs to sell the assets, including estimated costs necessary to transport the assets to market. Where reliable market prices of parent stock are not available, they are valued at cost less accumulated depreciation and any accumulated impairment losses. No active market exists for parent stock as they are rarely sold. Hog parent stock is depreciated on a straight-line basis over two to three years after considering residual values, whereas poultry parent stock is depreciated on a straight-line basis over six to eight months.

Biological assets are transferred into inventory at fair value less costs to sell at the point of delivery.

Instructions

a. Discuss why, for hog and poultry stock, two different bases of measurement are used.

b. What category of input information (fair value hierarchy) do you believe Maple Leaf uses in determining the fair value of its biological assets? Discuss some of the factors the company uses in determining fair value of its commercial stock.

c. How is the gain or loss on changes in fair value of its commercial stock shown in the company's financial statements?

d. The company's accounting policy measures commercial stock at fair value. As the assets are processed, they become inventory, which is then measured at the lower of cost and net realizable value. How does commercial stock go from a fair value basis to a cost basis? Is there a contradiction in this change of measurement basis?

RA3.3 ┃ Real World Emphasis ┃   **Warranty Cost Measurement**

The "Internet of things" refers to physical devices such as phones, cars, cameras, fitness tracking devices, and other sensing devices that capture and track data through the Internet. Such devices collect a significant amount of data. For instance, most newer cars are likely part of the Internet of things, capturing and transmitting data. Car companies, such as Toyota, manufacturer of the Lexus brand, sell hybrid vehicles that include an internal combustion engine as well as an electric engine powered by a battery. According to the company's website, they warranty all hybrid and electrical components for up to 96 months or 100,000 miles. This means that, if the hybrid or electrical components fail during this period, the company will replace or fix them at no cost to the customer. The company must estimate the potential cost of this for financial statement preparation.

Instructions

How can data collected from the Internet of things help accountants measure potential warranty costs?

RA3.4 ┃ Real World Emphasis ┃ ┃ Data Analytics ┃   **Use of Data Analytics**

TripAdvisor Inc. describes itself as an online travel company, which empowers users to plan and book the perfect trip. Among other things, it allows users to post reviews of their visits including visits to restaurants.

You are currently a financial analyst and are covering the hospitality industry.

Instructions

How might you use the data generated from the TripAdvisor website to help determine the value of shares of companies in the hospitality industry?

CHAPTER 4

Reporting Financial Performance

MARTIN BUREAU/Staff/Getty Images

Making Money Out of Thin Air

How can a business make money in the accommodations industry without actually owning any property? Or make money in the taxi industry without owning any vehicles? Companies such as Airbnb and Uber do it by charging fees to match people who own assets—homes or cars—with people wanting to use them temporarily. These businesses are part of the "sharing economy," where individuals share their assets with others, tapping into the value of their assets that might otherwise go unused—like their homes when they're on vacation or their cars when they're not otherwise being used.

The trend to own fewer assets has been growing in the corporate world for years. For example, companies like Apple outsource their manufacturing instead of owning factories, some corporations have sold their headquarters and lease them back, and many airlines lease rather than own their aircraft. In fact, when the British budget airline Monarch went bankrupt in 2017, its biggest asset was not planes, but its rights to land at certain airports in the United Kingdom.

It's only been recently that consumers have gotten in on the act. More people are renting music and movies from streaming services like iTunes and Netflix rather than owning CDs or DVDs. On the flip side, consumers who own things like homes or cars are renting them out to earn extra cash.

How do firms in the sharing economy create value? Generally, their own assets are their websites, technology, and brand reputations. They earn money by charging fees to use their services. In the case of Airbnb, it charges homeowners 3% of the amount that they get from the guests who rent their rooms or homes. Launched in 2008, Airbnb now lists nearly 5 million properties in more than 191 countries. Airbnb's business model is the same as that for ride-sharing services like Uber and Lyft, which charge a fee for every transaction. Uber, which started in 2010, operates in more than 250 cities around the world.

Even though businesses in the sharing economy don't need a lot of assets to launch, if they want to grow they need to raise cash to spend on advertising, improving their apps, and trying to get bigger than competitors. Airbnb has raised more than U.S. $3 billion in several rounds of venture capital funding, while Uber in late 2017 got a U.S. $7.7-billion infusion of cash from a Japanese bank for a minority stake.

To get venture capital funding, these businesses would have had to show potential investors their financial statements to convince them that the business model of making money without any physical substance can work. Airbnb and Uber are privately held companies and so they don't publicly release their financial statements. However, one source expected Airbnb to have profits of U.S. $3 billion by 2020. Uber, meanwhile, was valued at U.S. $48 billion at the time of the Japanese investment.

Sources: Greg Bensinger and Liz Hoffman, "SoftBank Succeeds in Tender Offer for Large Stake in Uber," *Wall Street Journal*, December 28, 2017; Brooke Masters, "Winners and Losers in the Sharing Economy," *Financial Times*, December 28, 2017; Leigh Gallagher, "Airbnb's Profits to Top $3 Billion by 2020," *Fortune* magazine, February 15, 2017; Richard Koch, "How Uber Used a Simplified Business Model to Disrupt the Taxi Industry," *Entrepreneur* magazine, January 3, 2017; Airbnb corporate website, www.airbnb.com.

LEARNING OBJECTIVES	CHAPTER OUTLINE	CPA COMPETENCIES
After studying this chapter, you should be able to:	The chapter headings related to the learning objective are:	Competencies addressed by each learning objective are as follows:
1. Understand how firms create value, manage performance, and communicate useful information to users.	**Performance** • Business models and industries • Communicating information about performance	**1.1.1, 1.1.2, 1.2.1, 1.2.2, 1.2.3, 1.4.2, 1.4.4, 1.4.5, 2.3.1, 2.3.2, 2.3.3, 4.3.5, 5.1.1, 5.5.1**
2. Understand the concept of and be able to assess the quality of earnings/information.	**Quality of Earnings/Information**	**1.2.1, 1.2.2, 5.1.1**
3. Understand the differing perspectives on how to measure income.	**Measurement of Income**	**1.2.1, 1.2.2**
4. Measure and report results of discontinued operations.	**Discontinued Operations** • Component of an enterprise • Assets held for sale • Measurement and presentation	**1.2.1, 1.2.2, 1.3.1, 1.4.1**
5. Measure income and prepare the income statement and the statement of comprehensive income using various formats.	**The Statement of Income and the Statement of Comprehensive Income** • Presentation	**1.2.1, 1.2.2, 1.3.1, 1.3.2**
6. Prepare the statement of retained earnings and the statement of changes in equity.	**The Statement of Retained Earnings and the Statement of Changes in Equity** • Presentation of the statement of retained earnings • Presentation of the statement of changes in equity	**1.2.1, 1.2.2, 1.3.1, 1.3.2**
7. Understand how disclosures and analysis help users of financial statements assess performance.	**Disclosure and Analysis** • Disclosure • Analysis • Non-GAAP measures • Other key measures	**1.2.1, 1.2.2, 1.3.2, 1.4.2, 1.4.4, 1.4.5, 5.4.2**
8. Identify differences in accounting between IFRS and ASPE and potential changes.	**IFRS/ASPE Comparison** • A comparison of IFRS and ASPE • Looking ahead	**1.1.4**

After studying Appendix 4A, you should be able to:

9. Explain the differences between the cash basis of accounting and the accrual basis of accounting.	**Appendix 4A: Application of the Cash and Accrual Bases of Accounting** • Differences between cash and accrual bases • Conversion from cash basis to accrual basis • Theoretical weaknesses of the cash basis	1.2.1, 1.2.2

Preview of Chapter 4

The way items are reported in the statement of income/comprehensive income can affect how useful the statement is to users. Although the net income number (the bottom line) is a key focal point for many users, the other elements in the income statement have significant information value as well. This chapter examines the many different types of revenues, expenses, gains, and losses that are represented in the income statement and related information.

Performance

LEARNING OBJECTIVE 1
Understand how firms create value, manage performance, and communicate useful information to users.

`Significant Change` The **statement of income/earnings** has many names. Under ASPE, **income statement** is the term commonly used. But under IFRS, the statement is expanded to include other comprehensive income and may be shown as two separate statements (called the **statement of profit or loss** and **statement of comprehensive income**) or as a combined statement, newly named the **statement of financial performance**.[1]

Regardless of its name, it is the report that measures the success of a company's operations for a specific time period. It is a key statement. Not all income statements are the same, however. This is partly due to underlying differences in business models and/or industries, and partly because of how this information is communicated. We will look at business models and industries first.

Business Models and Industries

`Strategy & Governance` 2.3.1, 2.3.2, 2.3.3 `Finance` 5.5.1 The basic **business model** consists of getting cash, investing it in resources, and then using these resources to generate profits. This model can be broken down into three distinct types of activities:

1. **Financing:** Obtaining cash funding, often by borrowing, issuing shares, or (in established companies) retaining profits. Financing activities also involve the repayment of debt and/or repurchase of shares.

---

[1]The newly issued IASB *IFRS Conceptual Framework* has renamed the combined statement. Note that since IAS 1 still uses the old labelling, we will do so throughout the rest of the text.

2. **Investing:** Using the funding to buy assets and invest in people. Investing activities also include divestitures.

3. **Operating:** Using the assets to earn profits.

In performing these three types of activities, companies are exposed to different levels of **risk** and are given different **opportunities**. Some industries are riskier than others. Take, for instance, a small corner pizzeria, owned by a chef who makes fresh pizzas and sells them to the local neighbourhood, versus a big multinational chemical company that transports and sells chemicals. The biggest business risks the pizzeria has may be that the pizza ingredients are not fresh or that there are not sufficient cash flows. The multinational company faces many risks, including the risk of lawsuits due to pollution, the risk of fraud given the fact that many employees work for the company, the risk of workplace accidents, and many others.

Managing risks takes money. There is an area of study devoted to this called **risk management**. It involves identifying risks, deciding if and how to manage risks, and monitoring risks. Companies can use various techniques to manage risks, such as educating their employees, buying insurance, and installing safety equipment. This all costs money, however. So the riskier the business, the more decisions need to be made about how to manage the risks, keeping in mind that the decisions made will affect profits. The market demands a greater return when there is greater risk. This is called the **risk/return trade-off**.[2]

On the opportunities side, some industries have greater opportunities. Consider the potential for companies where there are emerging markets or technologies. Companies must make decisions about which opportunities to take and when. Value creation is central in any business model. It is the act of finding an optimal balance between managing risks and taking the right opportunities such that the firm's net assets and potential are maximized. Well-run companies develop strategies that will allow them to react to the best opportunities in order to maximize shareholder value and maintain risks at an acceptable level. See **Underlying Concept 4.1**.

Illustration 4.1 presents an overview of the business model.

> **Underlying Concept 4.1**
>
> The concept of representational faithfulness requires the financial statements to reflect the economic reality of running a business, including how it creates and sustains value.

ILLUSTRATION 4.1

An Overview of the Business Model

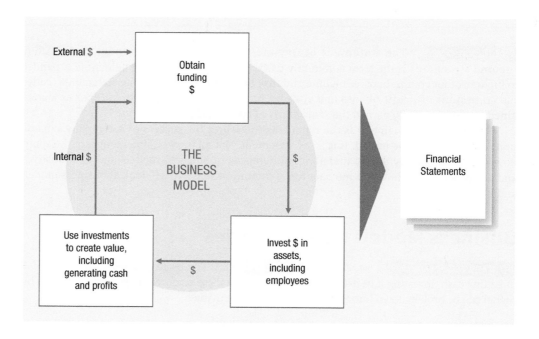

---

[2]For instance, if a risky company borrows from the bank, it will be charged a higher interest rate than a less risky company.

Different industries have different business models, and within industries different companies have different business models. Consider the two statements of income in **Illustration 4.2**. Partial statements have been presented to illustrate the differing business models. Walmart Stores Inc. is in the retail business. It buys large quantities of inventory in bulk wholesale and then sells them at the retail level through its stores at a markup. That is how it creates value for its investors. Canadian Natural Resources Limited (CNRL) is in the business of exploration, development, acquisition, and production of crude oil and natural gas. It sells the oil and gas that it discovers, usually after spending a significant amount of time, effort, and money to find and develop it. This is how CNRL creates value for its shareholders.

ILLUSTRATION 4.2

Consolidated Statements of Income—Walmart versus CNRL

Walmart
Consolidated Statements of Income

(Amounts in millions, except per share data)	Fiscal Years Ended January 31,		
	2017	2016	2015
Revenues:			
Net sales	**$481,317**	$478,614	$482,229
Membership and other income	**4,556**	3,516	3,422
Total revenues	**485,873**	482,130	485,651
Costs and expenses:			
Cost of sales	**361,256**	360,984	365,086
Operating, selling, general and administrative expenses	**101,853**	97,041	93,418
Operating income	**22,764**	24,105	27,147
Interest:			
Debt	**2,044**	2,027	2,161
Capital lease and financing obligations	**323**	521	300
Interest income	**(100)**	(81)	(113)
Interest, net	**2,267**	2,467	2,348
Income from continuing operations before income taxes	**20,497**	21,638	24,799
Provision for income taxes	**6,204**	6,558	7,985
Income from continuing operations	**14,293**	15,080	16,814
Income from discontinued operations, net of income taxes	**—**	—	285
Consolidated net income	**$ 14,293**	$ 15,080	$ 17,099

CNRL
Consolidated Statements of Earnings (Loss)

For the years ended December 31 (millions of Canadian dollars, except per common share amounts)	Note	**2017**	2016	2015
Product sales		**$17,669**	$11,098	$13,167
Less: royalties		**(1,018)**	(575)	(804)
Revenue		**16,651**	10,523	12,363
Expenses				
Production		**5,596**	4,099	4,726
Transportation, blending and feedstock		**2,917**	2,003	2,379
Depletion, depreciation and amortization	5, 6	**5,186**	4,858	5,483
Administration		**319**	345	390
Share-based compensation	11	**134**	355	(46)
Asset retirement obligation accretion	11	**164**	142	173
Interest and other financing expense	17	**631**	383	322
Risk management activities	18	**35**	33	(469)

(continued)

ILLUSTRATION 4.2

(*continued*)

For the years ended December 31 (millions of Canadian dollars, except per common share amounts)	Note	**2017**	2016	2015
Foreign exchange (gain) loss		**(787)**	(55)	761
Gain on acquisitions, disposition and revaluation of properties	5, 6, 7	**(379)**	(250)	(739)
(Gain) loss from investments	8, 9	**(38)**	(327)	50
		13,778	11,586	13,030
Earnings (loss) before taxes		**2,873**	(1,063)	(667)
Current income tax recovery	12	**(164)**	(618)	(261)
Deferred income tax (recovery) expense	12	**640**	(241)	231
Net earnings (loss)		**$ 2,397**	$ (204)	$ (637)

Finance 5.1.1 Because of these different business models and industries, CNRL's cost structure is different than Walmart's. We can see from the statements for Walmart that 75.0 cents out of every dollar of sales is for cost of goods sold ($361,256 ÷ $481,317). Its main cost is the inventory that it has sold. For CNRL, one of the largest costs is depletion and depreciation, which accounts for 31.1 cents out of every dollar of net sales ($5,186 ÷ $16,651). Its main cost is the depletion of its wells and natural resource properties.

Now let's look at another retailer, **Hudson's Bay Company (HBC)**. The partial statement of income for HBC is shown in **Illustration 4.3**.

ILLUSTRATION 4.3

Consolidated Statements of Income—HBC

HUDSON'S BAY COMPANY
CONSOLIDATED STATEMENTS OF LOSS
For the 53 weeks ended February 3, 2018 and January 28, 2017
(millions of Canadian dollars, except per share amounts)

	Notes	**February 3, 2018 (Fiscal 2017)**	January 28, 2017 (Fiscal 2016)
Retail sales		**14,349**	14,455
Cost of sales	9	**(8,514)**	(8,481)
Selling, general and administrative expenses ("SG&A")		**(5,794)**	(5,692)
Depreciation and amortization	5	**(687)**	(695)
Gain on sale of investments in joint ventures	12	**—**	45
Operating loss		**(646)**	(368)
Finance costs, net	6	**(228)**	(192)
Share of net loss in joint ventures	12	**(85)**	(158)
Dilution gains from investments in joint ventures	12	**10**	24
Loss before income tax		**(949)**	(694)
Income tax benefit	7	**368**	178
Net loss for the year		**(581)**	(516)

Strategy & Governance 2.3.1, 2.3.2, 2.3.3 Note that, even though HBC is in the same industry as Walmart (retail), its cost structure is a bit different. Only 59.3 cents out of every dollar goes toward cost of goods sold ($8,514 ÷ $14,349). What is the difference between HBC and Walmart? The numbers are different primarily because of a different business strategy. Walmart prices its goods lower to attract more customers and get higher volumes of sales. It follows what is known as a **low-cost/high-volume strategy**. HBC, on the other hand, is able to attract higher prices because it sells more unique and higher-end products. This is called a **cost differentiation strategy**. The purpose of this discussion is not to teach you everything you need to know about different industries, business models, and strategies. Rather, the goal is to introduce you to these ideas and get you thinking about how the financial statements might best reflect these factors in the interest of transparency. It is important to think about the nature of the industry as well as the business model and strategy when preparing and using financial statements. The statements should tell users about the business.

Audit & Assurance 4.3.5 Note that as an auditor, it is very important to have a good understanding of the business and industry in order to perform the audit (and determine whether the financial statements fairly present the entity's financial position and performance).

Communicating Information about Performance

There are several ways in which the income statement helps financial statement users decide where to invest their resources and evaluate how well management is using a company's resources.

For example, investors and creditors can use the information in the income statement to:

1. **Evaluate the enterprise's past performance and profitability.** By examining revenues, expenses, gains, and losses, users can see how the company (and management) performed and compare the company's performance with that of its competitors. (Statement of financial position information is also useful in assessing profitability, such as by calculating return on assets. See Appendix 5A for details on how to analyze financial statement data using various ratios.)

2. **Provide a basis for predicting future performance.** Information about business risk and past performance can be used to determine important trends that, if they continue, provide information about future performance. However, success in the past does not necessarily mean the company will have success in the future.

3. **Help assess the risk of not achieving future net cash inflows.** Information on the various components of income—revenues, expenses, gains, and losses—highlights the relationships among them and can be used to assess the risk of not achieving a particular level of cash flows in the future. For example, segregating a company's recurring **operating** income (results from continuing operations) from nonrecurring income sources (discontinued operations) is useful because **operations are usually the primary way to generate revenues and cash**. Thus, results from continuing operations usually have greater significance for predicting future performance than do results from nonrecurring activities.

> **Underlying Concept 4.2**
>
> A useful statement of income has both feedback and predictive value, which helps investors, creditors, and other users make decisions about stewardship and resource allocation.

In summary, a well-prepared statement of income/comprehensive income provides feedback and predictive value, which helps stakeholders understand the business. See **Underlying Concept 4.2**.

Quality of Earnings/Information

LEARNING OBJECTIVE 2

Understand the concept of and be able to assess the quality of earnings/information.

Finance 5.1.1 **Ethics** Not all information is created equal. Some information is high quality and some is poor quality. For instance, information that is complete and unbiased is better than incomplete and biased information. Financial statements can be of a higher or lower quality also. Some statements better represent the underlying business and industry than others and it is important to understand why. Let's look at some of the things that make a statement of income/comprehensive income less useful.

The statement of income/comprehensive income and other key financial statements are presented as a series of point estimates. For instance, in Illustration 4.3, the retail sales for HBC for the year ended in 2018 were presented as $14,349 million. It is important to understand that, even though the statements show elements such as retail sales as point estimates, revenues, expenses, gains, and losses are rarely exact dollar values. Rather, they represent a range of possible values. This is because the numbers included in financial statements are based on numerous assumptions.

By definition, accrual accounting requires **estimates** of such things as sales and expenses. The income statement includes a mix of **hard** numbers (which are easily measured with a reasonable level of certainty, such as cash sales) and **soft** numbers (which are more difficult to measure, such as a provision for bad debt). With soft numbers, there is significant measurement uncertainty.

Specifically, the statement of income/comprehensive income has the following shortcomings:

1. **Items that cannot be measured reliably are not reported in the income statement**. This is because the information would not be useful. See **Underlying Concept 4.3**. Currently, companies are not allowed to include certain items in the determination of income even though these items arguably affect an entity's performance from one point in time to another. For example, contingent gains cannot be recorded in income, because there is uncertainty about whether the gains will ever be realized. Note that if such items are material, in general, they should be disclosed in the notes.

2. **Income numbers are affected by the accounting methods that are used.** For example, one company may choose to depreciate its plant assets on an accelerated basis; another may choose straight-line depreciation. Assuming all other factors are equal, the first company's income will be lower even though the two companies are essentially the same. The result is that we are comparing "apples and oranges." GAAP requires that information about accounting methods be disclosed.

3. **Income measurement involves the use of estimates.** For example, one company may estimate in good faith that an asset's useful life is 20 years while another company uses a 15-year estimate for the same type of asset. Similarly, some companies may make overly optimistic estimates of future warranty returns and bad debt write offs, which would result in lower expenses and higher income. As mentioned above, when there is significant measurement uncertainty, the resulting numbers that are captured in the financial statements are sometimes called "soft numbers." GAAP requires that, where there is significant measurement uncertainty, additional disclosures be made. We looked at measurement in Chapters 2 and 3 and this will continue to be a focus throughout this textbook.

4. **Financial reporting bias.** Chapter 1 discussed the importance of ethics. Chapter 2 discussed how pressures on financial reporting can lead to financial engineering and fraud. Bias exists and it degrades the quality of the financial statements.

5. **GAAP.** Because the process of standard setting is political, GAAP is not always optimal. For instance, historically, most leases were not recorded on the statement of financial position. Similarly, certain pension surpluses and deficits were excluded as well. Although the standard setters are systematically working their way through the standards to fix issues such as these, care should be taken to look for items that may not be properly represented in the financial statements.

Let's look specifically at the concept of **quality of earnings**. Quality of earnings refers to how solid the earnings numbers are. The concept of quality of earnings is used by analysts and investors to assess how well the reported income reflects the underlying business and future potential. In other words, they look at the predictive value of the income. If the quality is assessed as low, then the usefulness of the numbers is discounted. If the quality is assessed as high, then the numbers are accepted as is. Users start with the statement of income/comprehensive income and supplement that information with the other statements, notes to the statements, and other facts that they know about the company (perhaps from company announcements, news reports, or information in the MD&A).

Underlying Concept 4.3

The conceptual framework, as discussed in Chapter 2, identifies all of the qualitative characteristics of useful information, including relevance, representational faithfulness, comparability, verifiability, timeliness, and understandability.

When analyzing the quality of earnings, two aspects are generally considered:

1. **Content**, which includes:
   a. the **integrity of the information**, including whether it is unbiased and reflects the underlying business fundamentals, and
   b. the **sustainability of the earnings**.
2. **Presentation**, which means the earnings are presented in a clear, concise manner that makes the information easy to use and understandable.

Since quality of earnings analysis is often done to assess future earnings potential, sustainability of income is important. Sustainability of income refers to whether the company is able to continue to generate or sustain these earnings in the future given its current business model, the industry, and the economy. This can be difficult to assess.

Note that well-prepared statements send a signal by attempting to segregate income that is recurring from income that is not. For instance, where a company has sold part of its operations, the income statement segregates earnings from the part of the business that has been sold. Acquisitions are disclosed in the notes.

The statements may reflect the nature and source of the income on a historical basis but they cannot and do not make any promises about the future. Even though the underlying business might be accurately and appropriately reflected in GAAP financial statements, the quality of the earnings might be judged to be low because the earnings are felt to be unsustainable.[3]

Higher-quality earnings provide higher-quality information, have a lower likelihood of potential misstatement, and have greater predictive value. See Underlying Concept 4.4. They are more representative of the underlying business and economic reality. The shares of companies with higher-quality earnings are valued higher in the capital markets, all other things being equal. Earnings that cannot be replicated and/or appear significantly biased are discounted by the markets.

Illustration 4.4 presents some attributes of high-quality earnings.

> **Underlying Concept 4.4**
> Higher-quality earnings have greater predictive value.

ILLUSTRATION 4.4

Some Attributes of High-Quality Earnings

High-quality earnings have the following characteristics:

1. Content
   - **Unbiased**, because numbers are not manipulated, and **objectively determined**. Consider the need to estimate, the accounting choices, and the use of professional judgement.
   - **Reflect the economic reality** because all transactions and events are appropriately captured.
   - **Reflect primarily the earnings generated from ongoing core business activities** instead of earnings from one-time gains or losses.
   - **Closely correlate with cash flows from operations.** Earnings that convert to cash more quickly provide a better measure of sustainable earnings because there is little or no uncertainty about whether they will be realized.
   - **Based on sound business strategy and business model.** Consider the riskiness of the business, business strategy, industry, and the economic and political environments. Identify the effect of these on earnings stability, volatility, and sustainability. Consider also the cost structure of the company, including fixed versus variable costs. (High fixed costs can make the company riskier in times of falling selling prices.)

2. Presentation
   - **Transparent**, because no attempt is made to disguise or mislead. It reflects the underlying business fundamentals.
   - **Understandable**

---

[3]In assessing whether earnings are sustainable, a strategic analysis of the company's positioning within the industry should be performed, as well as an assessment of the business model's viability. This is beyond the scope of this course.

Ethics Earnings management may be defined as the process of **targeting certain earnings levels** (whether current or future) or desired earnings trends and then **working backward to determine what has to be done to ensure that these targets are met**. This can involve the selection of accounting and other company policies, the use of estimates, and even the execution of otherwise unnecessary transactions. In many cases, earnings management is used to increase income in the current year by reducing income in future years. For example, companies may prematurely recognize sales before they are complete in order to boost earnings. Some companies may enter into transactions only so that the statements look better, and thus incur unnecessary transaction costs.

Theory Earnings management can also be used to decrease current earnings in order to increase future income. Reserves may be established by using aggressive assumptions to estimate items such as sales returns, loan losses, and warranty returns. These reserves can then be reduced in the future to increase income. Earnings management activities have a negative effect on the quality of earnings. As long as there is full disclosure, an efficient market should see through these attempts to mask the underlying economic reality. Unfortunately, companies do not always disclose all important information and markets do not always operate efficiently.

Although many users do not believe that management intentionally misrepresents accounting results, there is concern that much of the information that companies distribute is too promotional and that troubled companies take great pains to present their results in the best light. Preparers of financial statements must strive to present information that is of the highest quality. Users of this information should assess the quality of earnings before making their decisions. When companies manage earnings, it affects the quality of earnings. See **What Do the Numbers Mean? 4.1**.

What Do the Numbers Mean? 4.1   Four: The Loneliest Number

Managing earnings up or down adversely affects the quality of earnings. Why do companies engage in such practices? Research concludes that many companies tweak quarterly earnings to meet investor expectations. How do they do it? Research findings indicate that companies tend to nudge their earnings per share numbers up by a 10th of a cent or two. That lets them round results up to the highest cent, as illustrated in the following chart.

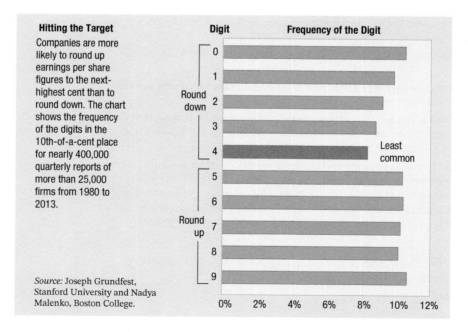

Hitting the Target

Companies are more likely to round up earnings per share figures to the next-highest cent than to round down. The chart shows the frequency of the digits in the 10th-of-a-cent place for nearly 400,000 quarterly reports of more than 25,000 firms from 1980 to 2013.

Digit

Frequency of the Digit

Round down — 0, 1, 2, 3, 4

4 — Least common

Round up — 5, 6, 7, 8, 9

0% 2% 4% 6% 8% 10% 12%

Source: Joseph Grundfest, Stanford University and Nadya Malenko, Boston College.

What the research shows is that the number "4" appeared less often in the 10th's place than any other digit and significantly less often than would be expected by chance. This effect is called "quadrophobia." For the typical company in the study, an increase of $44,000 in quarterly net income would boost earnings per share by a 10th of a cent.

Another recent study reinforces the concerns about earnings management. Based on a survey of 169 public-company chief financial officers (and with in-depth interviews of 12), the study concludes that high-quality earnings are sustainable when backed by actual cash flows and "avoiding unreliable long-term estimates." However, about 20% of firms manage earnings to misrepresent their economic performance. And when they do manage earnings, it could move EPS by an average of 10%.

Is such earnings management a problem for investors? It is if they cannot determine the impact on earnings quality. Indeed, the surveyed CFOs "believe that it is difficult for outside observers to unravel earnings management, especially when such earnings are managed using subtle unobservable choices or real actions." What's an investor to do? The survey authors say the CFOs "advocate paying close attention to the key managers running the firm, the lack of correlation between earnings and cash flows, significant deviations between firm and peer experience, and unusual behavior in accruals."

Sources: S. Thurm, "For Some Firms, a Case of 'Quadrophobia'," *Wall Street Journal* (February 14, 2010); and H. Greenberg, "CFOs Concede Earnings Are 'Managed'," *www.cnbc.com* (July 19, 2012). The study referred to is by I. Dichev, J. Graham, C. Harvey, and S. Rajgopal, "Earnings Quality: Evidence from the Field," Emory University Working Paper (July 2012).

Example 4.1 demonstrates a quality of earnings assessment.

Example 4.1 | Quality of Earnings Assessment

Facts   Rexine Limited is looking to acquire a small private company, Texine Inc. The acquisition will give Rexine more exposure to international markets. Rexine has hired a firm of investment bankers to put a value on Texine so that it can determine how much to offer to the current shareholders. Texine has made its audited financial statements available to the investment bankers, who note the following:

- Texine is the subject of several lawsuits, which have not yet been settled.
- The company has recently reorganized and has sold off a subsidiary that had accounted for 25% of its revenues.
- The company recently switched depreciation method from the double-declining method to a method that recognizes lower depreciation expense in the earlier years of the asset's life.
- Texine has recently switched its business model so that it is primarily selling through an online platform.

As a starting point for the valuation, the investment bankers have decided to do a quality of earnings analysis to determine if the financial statements have predictive value.

Instructions   What is the quality of earnings for Texine?

Solution   A quality of earnings analysis is complex and there is generally no right or wrong answer. In many cases, there are factors that might support a lower quality conclusion as well as factors that would support a higher quality conclusion.

Factors supporting lower quality:

- The lawsuits create uncertainty because they are as yet unresolved and, although an estimate of the potential losses will likely have been recorded, the number could change.
- The recent sale of a major subsidiary means that the historic financial statements may not have predictive value. The income relating to the subsidiary should be backed out in the valuation of the company.
- The switch in accounting method needs further analysis. Why was the change made? If there is a valid reason for the change, then this factor is not relevant. However, we should examine whether the change was made in order to increase net income.
- The change in business model to an online selling platform creates uncertainty. Will this model work? Will Texine be more profitable or less profitable? The valuation will have to take this into account.

Factors supporting higher quality:

- The financial statements have been audited. This adds assurance that the statements are fairly presented.

Because there are numerous factors supporting lower quality, the investment bankers would consider adjusting the reported income number before they use it in their valuation modelling exercise.

As mentioned at the beginning of the chapter, the main statement that gives information about performance is the statement of income/comprehensive income. The statement of retained earnings and the statement of changes in equity show the accumulated and retained income over time. We will first look at the statement of income/comprehensive income and then the statements of retained earnings and changes in equity.

Measurement of Income

LEARNING OBJECTIVE 3
Understand the differing perspectives on how to measure income.

The big question is: How do we measure income? Is it **net income** or is it comprehensive income or is it something else, such as operating income? This is very important since many users focus on income and treat it as one of the most important numbers on the income statement, if not **the** most important. Earnings per share (EPS) numbers are generally based on net income.

Net income represents revenues and gains less expenses and losses from both continuing and discontinued operations. **Comprehensive income** is net income plus/minus other comprehensive income/loss. The concept of **operating income** is not defined by GAAP but is generally seen to be ongoing revenues less expenses. See **Underlying Concept 4.5**. It represents a measure of regular income before any irregular items such as gains/losses, discontinued operations, and other comprehensive income.[4]

The concept of net income has been around for many years and therefore is well understood. ASPE currently uses this view of income.

More recently, the concept of comprehensive income has emerged in GAAP.[5] Essentially, this newer measure of income includes all changes in equity aside from shareholder transactions and is therefore more "comprehensive," as its name suggests. This notion of earnings is sometimes called the **all-inclusive approach** to measuring income. IFRS generally supports this view of income.

Some users support a **current operating performance approach** to income reporting. They argue that the most useful income measures are the ones that reflect only regular and recurring revenue and expense elements; that is, normalized, sustainable earnings. Irregular items do not reflect an enterprise's future earning power since, by definition, they are irregular and atypical or nonrecurring. Operating income supporters believe that including one-time items such as write offs and restructuring charges reduces the income measure's basic **predictive value**.

Theory In contrast, others warn that a focus on operating income potentially misses important information about a firm's performance. Any gain or loss that is experienced by the firm, whether it is directly or indirectly related to operations, contributes to the firm's long-term profitability. In other words, a gain or loss has **feedback value**. As a result, some non-operating items can be used to assess the riskiness of future earnings—and therefore they have **predictive value**. Furthermore, determining which items are (regular) **operating** items and which are **irregular** requires judgement and this could lead to differences in the treatment of irregular items and to possible manipulation of income measures.

IFRS Other comprehensive income (OCI) is made up of certain specific gains or losses, including unrealized gains and losses on certain securities, certain foreign exchange gains or losses, and other gains and losses as defined by IFRS.[6] Some items are "recycled" or

> **Underlying Concept 4.5**
>
> The conceptual framework provides definitions for the elements revenues, expenses, gains, and losses in Chapter 2.

---

[4]The term "irregular" is used for transactions and other events that come from developments that are outside the normal business operations.

[5]In actuality, this concept has its roots in **capital maintenance theory**, which says that as long as capital is maintained from year to year, the rest is assumed to be income. Capital may be defined as financial (in terms of amount of dollars invested in the business) or physical (earnings potential of the income-generating assets).

[6]We will discuss these items in greater detail in subsequent chapters.

reclassified. This means that they are recognized first in OCI and then reclassified later to net income. For instance, under IFRS 9, gains and losses on certain investments classified as fair value through other comprehensive income (FV-OCI) are first booked to OCI and then booked to net income later, when the investment is impaired or sold. We will examine this in Chapter 9. Some items—such as gains on revaluing property, plant, and equipment under the revaluation method—are not recycled. They are recognized once in OCI. We will revisit this in Chapter 10.

Significant Change The new *IFRS Conceptual Framework* added guidance on other comprehensive income, noting the following:

1. All items of income and expense should be included in net income except under exceptional circumstances.

2. In principle, all items should be recycled to net income in future periods as long as this treatment results in relevant information that is representationally faithful.

IFRS **ASPE** Illustration 4.5 shows some items included in OCI and notes how these are dealt with under ASPE. Under IFRS, the company must group items that will be reclassified and not reclassified and present them separately on the income statement.

ILLUSTRATION 4.5 How OCI Items Are Treated under IFRS and ASPE[7]

Items Defined as OCI under IFRS	ASPE Treatment
Changes in revaluation surplus under the revaluation method for property, plant, and equipment. Amounts are not recycled/reclassified.[8]	Revaluation method not allowed.
Gains and losses on remeasurement of defined benefit pension plans. Amounts are not recycled/reclassified.[9]	Recognized in net income under the immediate recognition approach.
Gains and losses arising from translating the financial statements of certain foreign operations. Amounts are recycled/reclassified.[10]	Recognized directly in equity.
Gains and losses for certain hedges. Amounts are recycled/reclassified if a cash flow hedge.[11]	Hedging instruments are generally not recognized until maturity, and related gains and losses are generally recognized in net income when the hedged item is recognized in net income.
Gains and losses on remeasuring FV-OCI investments. Amounts are recycled for debt instruments but not equity instruments.[12]	FV-OCI investment category not applicable. Investments either measured at cost/amortized cost or at fair value through net income (FV-NI).
Changes in fair value of certain liabilities measured at fair value through profit or loss relating to the liability's credit risk under IFRS 9. Amounts are not recycled/reclassified.[13]	Recognized in net income.
Certain income and expenses relating to insurance and reinsurance contracts.[14]	Recognized in net income.

----

[7]IAS 1.7.

[8]IAS 16.41.

[9]IAS 19.122

[10]IAS 21.32.

[11]IFRS 9.6.5.11. Note that there may be other amounts booked to OCI under more complex hedging arrangements but these are beyond the scope of this text.

[12]IFRS 9.5.7.10.

[13]IFRS 9.B5.7.9.

[14]Insurance accounting is beyond the scope of this text.

Other comprehensive income is closed out to a statement of financial position account that is often named **Accumulated Other Comprehensive Income**, which acts as a type of retained earnings account. Accumulated Other Comprehensive Income is an equity account on the statement of financial position. We will come back to this item later in the chapter.

Having these multiple views of income may confuse the marketplace. For instance, should EPS be based on comprehensive income instead of net income? Why does IFRS use the comprehensive income concept but ASPE does not? See **What Do the Numbers Mean? 4.2.**

What Do the Numbers Mean? 4.2

Analysts focus on EPS, which is based on net income. It raises the interesting question as to whether the analysts don't understand the concept of comprehensive income or whether they believe that the "real number" is net income. Some argue that OCI represents only unrealized gains and losses and this is why it should be segregated. Is this true? When looking at the items included in OCI, they generally include unrealized gains and losses. However, not all unrealized gains and losses are included in OCI. Many are included in net income. Consider for instance the revaluation of a U.S. dollar receivable or a provision for obsolete inventory. These unrealized gains and losses are booked to net income. So part of the problem is that it is unclear from a conceptual perspective why some items are included in OCI and others in net income. Similarly, what is the justification for deciding which items in OCI are reclassified and which are not?

Having said that, the idea of comprehensive income is a sound one because it takes an all-inclusive view of income, defining it as all changes in equity other than shareholder transactions. As reaffirmed by the conceptual framework (Chapter 2), it looks as though the concept of OCI is here to stay, at least for a while.

Discontinued Operations

LEARNING OBJECTIVE 4
Measure and report results of discontinued operations.

One of the most common types of irregular items is discontinued operations. Discontinued operations include separate **components of an enterprise** that have been **disposed of** (by sale, abandonment, or spinoff) or are classified as held for sale where:

1. they represent (or are part of a plan to dispose of) a **major line of business** or **geographical area**; or

2. they are a subsidiary acquired for resale.[15]

Discontinued operations are presented separately on the statement of income/comprehensive income and also on the statement of cash flows. They are shown net of tax.

Component of an Enterprise

The discontinued operation that is a component of an enterprise must have operations, cash flows, and financial elements that are clearly distinguishable from the rest of the enterprise.[16] It must generate its own net cash flows (sometimes called a cash-generating unit) and be operationally distinct. That is, it must operate as a separate unit with its own assets, liabilities, and cash flows. Separate financial information is critical so that the gain or loss from discontinued operations can be properly **measured**.

---

[15]IFRS 5.32. Copyright © IFRS Foundation. All rights reserved. Reproduced with permission. This excerpt is reprinted with permission from the *CPA Canada Handbook—Accounting* © 2018, Part II, Section 3475.03(e), by Chartered Professional Accountants of Canada. All rights reserved by the copyright owner.

[16]IFRS 5.31. Copyright © IFRS Foundation. All rights reserved. Reproduced with permission. Reprinted/adapted with permission from the *CPA Canada Handbook—Accounting* © 2018, Part II, Section 3475.03(e), by Chartered Professional Accountants of Canada. All rights reserved by the copyright owner.

Some examples of a component include a hotel, an apartment building, a division, a subsidiary, a restaurant, or a geographical area such as the European operations of a company. All of these examples would operate as a separate unit and would have cash flows that are specifically tied to the unit. For instance, a hotel would generate cash inflows from its guests and cash outflows relating to operating costs including things such as payroll and heat, light, and power.

In addition, a component is generally a **major line of business** or a **geographical area**. What does the word "major" mean and what is a separate line of business? In practice, there is no bright-line test for determining whether something is considered to be major or not. It is a matter of judgement. Example 4.2 illustrates the concept of a component for the purposes of presentation as discontinued operations.

Example 4.2 | Determination of a Component When Assessing Discontinued Operations

Facts Antics Productions Limited operates a string of theatres across Canada. Seventy-five percent of all revenues are derived from the sale of movie tickets, advertising in the theatre, and in-house food and beverage sales. The theatre division (as this part of the business is called) generates 90% of the company's profit. The other 10% of the profits (and 25% of the revenues) come from the live theatre division. The live theatre division produces and presents live theatre in three unique playhouses that are owned by the company. Antics disposed of the live theatre division at the end of the year.

Instructions Is the live theatre division a **component** for the purposes of determining whether this is a discontinued operation?

Solution In order to be considered a separate component for the purposes of presenting the business as a discontinued operation, it must be distinct (financially and operationally) and represent a major line of business (or geographical area). The live theatre division is distinct since it has its own unique costs and revenues from running the productions. In addition, it has its own separate playhouses. We might argue that it is a major line of business since it generates 25% of revenues and 10% of profits.

In this case, the operations are sufficiently big that they are considered to be major. In practice, the threshold could be lower. The determination is generally based on size but may also be made in terms of whether the presentation as discontinued operations would make a difference to decision-making. In other words, is it material to the users of the statements? We discussed materiality in Chapter 2.

Assets Held for Sale

If a discontinued operation that represents a component is not yet disposed of, an additional condition must be met before the transaction can be given "separate discontinued operations" presentation on the income statement. This condition is that the assets relating to the component must be considered to be held for sale by the company. Assets are considered to be held for sale when all of the following criteria are met:

- There is an **authorized plan** to sell.
- The asset is **available for immediate sale** in its current state.
- There is an **active program** to find a buyer.
- Sale is **probable** within one year.
- The asset is **reasonably priced** and actively marketed.
- **Changes** to the plan are **unlikely**.[17]

---

[17]IFRS 5.7 and .8. Copyright © IFRS Foundation. All rights reserved. Reproduced with permission. This excerpt is reprinted with permission from the *CPA Canada Handbook—Accounting* © 2018, Section 3475.08, by Chartered Professional Accountants of Canada. All rights reserved by the copyright owner.

In summary, for accounting purposes, assets may be considered as held for sale when there is a **formal plan** to dispose of the component. This ensures that only assets or asset groups for which management has a detailed, approved plan for disposal get measured and presented as held for sale.

Example 4.3 provides an analysis regarding whether an asset is considered to be held for sale.

Example 4.3 | Assets Held for Sale

Facts On November 1, 2020, top management of DeGrootes Corporation approved a detailed plan to discontinue its electronics division (a separate major line of business). DeGrootes has already hired an agent to help with the sale and hopes to sell the division within the year. The agent has determined the selling price (by looking at comparable sales of similar businesses). The business is available for sale immediately.

Instructions Do the facts meet the **held for sale** criteria? Explain.

Solution Because top management has approved the disposal and has stated which assets are to be disposed of and how, a **formal plan** exists. The company has already hired an agent to sell the business and a price has been set. They are looking to sell the business within the year. Therefore, the division meets the criteria and will be presented separately on the balance sheet and separately on the income statement as discontinued operations.

Measurement and Presentation

When an asset is held for sale, the asset is remeasured to the "lower of its carrying amount and fair value less its cost to sell".[18] Note that, if the value of an asset that has been written down later increases, the gain can be recognized up to the amount of the original loss. Once an asset has been classified as held for sale, no further depreciation is recognized.

IFRS **ASPE** Assets and related liabilities that are classified as held for sale are **presented** separately in the balance sheet (if material) and retain their original classification as assets (or liabilities) that are current or non-current under ASPE.[19] Under IFRS, assets held for sale are generally classified as current assets (and any related liabilities are shown separately as current liabilities).[20] Assets and liabilities are not offset.

Note that assets that are held for sale might not (and do not need to) meet the definition of discontinued operations. Where this is the case, these assets, as noted below, would be measured and presented in the same way (similar to discontinued operations) on the statement of financial position. However, any related gains or losses on remeasurement would be recorded as part of income from continuing operations on the statement of income/comprehensive income.[21] If the asset does not meet the definition of a discontinued operation, the writedown is treated like any other asset impairment charge on the statement of income/comprehensive income.

The results of discontinued operations are shown separately on the income statement, net of tax for both the current and prior periods. The entity must show the amount of gain or loss on disposal as well as the earnings or loss from discontinued operations. This can be shown either in the income statement or the notes, along with revenues, expenses, and pre-tax profit or loss. Comparative information is required for prior years on the income statement but not on the statement of financial position. In addition to the detail shown on the income

---

[18]IFRS 5.15. Copyright © IFRS Foundation. All rights reserved. Reproduced with permission. Reprinted/adapted with permission from the *CPA Canada Handbook—Accounting* © 2018, Part II, Section 3475.13, by Chartered Professional Accountants of Canada. All rights reserved by the copyright owner.

[19]These assets and liabilities would be classified as current only if they have been sold before the financial statements are complete and if the proceeds are expected to be received within the year. Reprinted/adapted with permission from the *CPA Canada Handbook—Accounting* © 2018, Part II, 3475.33-.35, by Chartered Professional Accountants of Canada. All rights reserved by the copyright owner.

[20]IFRS 5.3 and .8.

[21]The term "income from continuing operations" is a financial statement subtotal often used. Its use is not mandated nor required by GAAP but companies use it where there are discontinued operations.

statement, note disclosures including a description of the disposal are required. Finally, the net cash flows attributable to operating, investing, and financing activities would be shown separately in the statement of cash flows.[22]

Example 4.4 illustrates accounting concepts related to discontinued operations.

Example 4.4 | Measurement and Presentation of Discontinued Operations

Facts   Delman Inc. operates in two separate industries: retail groceries and restaurants. Each is operated as a separate division. The restaurants are located in company-owned buildings that are separate from the grocery store locations. On December 31, 2020, Delman decided to dispose of its restaurant division. Management has come up with a detailed plan to dispose of the business, which has been approved by the board of directors. Delman feels that it can dispose of the business and its assets at a loss of $500,000 (net of tax). During the current year, the restaurant division lost $300,000 (net of tax). The company has income of $3.5 million (net of tax) from the retail grocery division.

Instructions   Is the restaurant division a **discontinued operation**? If so, how should the division be **presented** on the income statement?

Solution   The restaurant division is a separate component because the grocery and restaurant businesses represent different industries. The restaurant business is **operationally and financially distinct** because it has its own separate buildings and its costs and revenues are separate from those of the retail industry. We might argue that it is a **major line of business** due to the size of the operations as well as the losses (10% of the income from the grocery division in absolute dollars). The company will have no continuing involvement in the restaurant division after it is sold.

The information would be shown as follows on the current year's annual statement of income/comprehensive income (assuming $3.5 million of income before discontinued operations).

Income from continuing operations		$3,500,000
Discontinued operations		
Loss from operation of discontinued		
restaurant division (net of tax)	$300,000	
Loss on disposal of restaurant division		
(net of tax)	500,000	800,000
Net income		$2,700,000

The company could also show a single amount on the statement of income/comprehensive income ($800,000) and show the detail in the notes. Delman would stop recording depreciation on the division's assets and, in the following year, would show any operating losses or profits and/or revised gain or loss on disposal as discontinued operations. Estimated future losses would not be included in the loss from operations because they would already be implied (and therefore included) in the fair value estimate of the assets held for sale or sold. The assets of the discontinued operations would be shown separately on the statement of financial position.

Illustration 4.6 shows how **Onex Corporation**, a diversified company that has operations in various industries, presented its discontinued operation in its 2017 statements. The consolidated statements of earnings and cash flows are supplemented by notes 1 and 8. All are reproduced in Illustration 4.6. By the end of 2017, the assets had been disposed of and therefore did not show up on the 2017 consolidated balance sheet. The company has chosen to show one line on the consolidated statement of income with a detailed breakdown in Note 8. In the excerpt from the cash flow statement, note the reference to discontinued operations at the bottom of the section relating to operating activities. There are similar one-line inclusions for the investing and financial sections of the statement.

[22]IFRS 5.33, .34, .41, 42, and *CPA Canada Handbook—Accounting*, Part II, Section 3475.30 and .36.

ILLUSTRATION 4.6

Presentation of a Discontinued Operation— Onex Corporation

CONSOLIDATED STATEMENTS OF EARNINGS (EXCERPTS)

Year ended December 31 *(in millions of U.S. dollars except per share data)*	2017	2016
Revenues	**$ 24,497**	$ 17,805
Cost of sales (excluding amortization of property, plant and equipment, intangible assets and deferred charges) (note 22)	**(17,921)**	(12,908)
Operating expenses (note 22)	**(4,220)**	(3,033)
Interest income	**376**	349
Amortization of property, plant and equipment (note 9)	**(642)**	(447)
Amortization of intangible assets and deferred charges	**(678)**	(518)
Interest expense of operating companies and credit strategies (note 23)	**(1,212)**	(882)
Increase in value of investments in joint ventures and associates at fair value, net (note 10)	**760**	180
Stock-based compensation expense (note 24)	**(178)**	(194)
Other gains (note 25)	**731**	36
Other expense (note 26)	**(707)**	(21)
Impairment of goodwill, intangible assets and long-lived assets, net (note 27)	**(187)**	(232)
Limited Partners' Interests charge (note 17)	**(1,350)**	(647)
Loss before income taxes and discontinued operations	**(731)**	(512)
Recovery of (provision for) income taxes (note 19)	**84**	(107)
Loss from continuing operations	**(647)**	(619)
Earnings from discontinued operations (note 8)	**3,042**	583
Net Earnings (Loss) for the Year	**$ 2,395**	$ (36)
Loss from Continuing Operations attributable to:		
Equity holders of Onex Corporation	**$ (715)**	$ (660)
Non-controlling Interests	**68**	41
Loss from Continuing Operations for the Year	**$ (647)**	$ (619)
Net Earnings (Loss) attributable to:		
Equity holders of Onex Corporation	**$ 2,394**	$ (130)
Non-controlling Interests	**1**	94
Net Earnings (Loss) for the Year	**$ 2,395**	$ (36)
Net Earnings (Loss) per Subordinate Voting Share of Onex Corporation (note 28)		
Basic and Diluted:		
Continuing operations	**$ (6.99)**	$ (6.36)
Discontinued operations	**30.46**	5.11
Net Earnings (Loss) per Subordinate Voting Share for the Year	**$ 23.47**	$ (1.25)

(continued)

Consolidated Cash Flow Statement (Excerpts)

ILLUSTRATION 4.6

(*continued*)

Year ended December 31 (in millions of U.S. dollars)	2017	2016
Operating Activities		
Loss for the year from continuing operations	$ **(647)**	$ (619)
Adjustments to loss from continuing operations:		
Provision for (recovery of) income taxes	**(84)**	107
Interest income	**(376)**	(349)
Interest expense of operating companies and credit		
strategies	**1,212**	882
Earnings before interest and provision for (recovery of)		
income taxes	**105**	21
Cash taxes paid	**(248)**	(152)
Items not affecting cash and cash equivalents:		
Amortization of property, plant and equipment (note 9)	**642**	447
Amortization of intangible assets and deferred charges	**678**	518
Increase in value of investments in joint ventures and		
associates at fair value, net (note 10)	**(760)**	(180)
Stock-based compensation expense	**120**	166
Other gains (note 25)	**(731)**	(36)
Foreign exchange loss	**74**	35
Impairment of goodwill, intangible assets and long-lived		
assets, net (note 27)	**187**	232
Limited Partners' Interests charge (note 17)	**1,350**	647
Change in carried interest	**(39)**	35
Change in provisions	**42**	103
Other	**254**	(326)
	1,674	1,510
Changes in non-cash working capital items:		
Accounts receivable	**(45)**	(380)
Inventories	**18**	(187)
Other current assets	**92**	(59)
Accounts payable, accrued liabilities and other current		
liabilities	**122**	548
Increase (decrease) in cash and cash equivalents due to		
changes in non-cash working capital items	**187**	(78)
Increase in other operating activities	**4**	14
Cash flows from operating activities of discontinued		
operations (note 8)	**10**	466
	1,875	1,912

Note 1 (Excerpts)

Assets held for sale and discontinued operations

An asset is classified as held for sale if its carrying amount will be recovered by the asset's sale rather than by its continuing use in the business, the asset is available for immediate sale in its present condition and management is committed to, and has initiated, a plan to sell the asset which, when initiated, is expected to result in a completed sale within 12 months. An extension of the period required to complete the sale does not preclude the asset from being classified as held for sale, provided the delay is for reasons beyond the Company's control and management remains committed to its plan to sell the asset. Assets that are classified as held for sale are measured at the lower of their carrying amount or fair value less costs to sell and are no longer depreciated. The determination of fair value less costs to sell involves judgement by management to determine the probability and timing of disposition and the amount of recoveries and costs.

(*continued*)

ILLUSTRATION 4.6
(*continued*)

A discontinued operation is a component of the Company that has either been disposed of, or satisfies the criteria to be classified as held for sale, and represents a separate major line of business or geographic area of operations, is part of a single coordinated plan to dispose of a separate major line of business or geographic area of operations, or is an operating company acquired exclusively with a view to its disposal.

8. DISCONTINUED OPERATIONS

The following tables show revenues, expenses and net after-tax results from discontinued operations. Carestream Health's sale of its Dental Digital business in September 2017 did not represent a separate major line of business and as a result has not been presented as a discontinued operation. The sale of Cicis in August 2016, as described in note 3(g), did not represent a separate major line of business and as a result has not been presented as a discontinued operation.

Year ended December 31	2017			2016				
	USI[a]	JELD-WEN[b]	Total	USI[a]	JELD-WEN[b]	Krauss-Maffei[c]	Sitel Worldwide[d]	Total
Revenues	$ 400	$ 1,393	$ 1,793	$ 1,048	$ 3,670	$ 420	$ –	$ 5,138
Expenses	(510)	(1,580)	(2,090)	(1,112)	(3,562)	(461)	–	(5,135)
Earnings (loss) before income taxes	(110)	(187)	(297)	(64)	108	(41)	–	3
Recovery of (provision for) income taxes	13	15	28	(31)	92	(4)	–	57
Gain, net of tax	1,797	1,514	3,311	–	–	500	23	523
Net earnings (loss) for the year	$1,700	$ 1,342	$ 3,042	$ (95)	$ 200	$ 455	$23	$ 583

a) USI

The operations of USI have been presented as discontinued in the consolidated statements of earnings and cash flows for the years ended December 31, 2017 and 2016, as described in note 2(e).

b) JELD-WEN

The operations of JELD-WEN have been presented as discontinued in the consolidated statements of earnings and cash flows for the years ended December 31, 2017 and 2016, as described in note 2(a).

c) KraussMaffei

The operations of KraussMaffei have been presented as discontinued in the consolidated statements of earnings and cash flows for the year ended December 31, 2016, as described in note 3(c).

d) Sitel Worldwide

In June 2016, the Company signed an agreement to settle the earn-out component from the sale of Sitel Worldwide that occurred in September 2015. A gain of $23 was recorded within discontinued operations during the second quarter of 2016, of which Onex' share was $21. The gain reflected the present value of the expected future payments under the agreement.

Underlying Concept 4.6

The business model should be transparent. This means that the financial statements should reflect the way that the company earns income and creates shareholder value.

Note 8 refers to the fact that some of the operations that were sold by Onex did not meet the size test required to be treated as discontinued operations because they did not represent a major line of business (Dental Digital business and Cicis). Thus they were not accounted for as discontinued operations.

See Underlying Concept 4.6.

The Statement of Income and the Statement of Comprehensive Income

LEARNING OBJECTIVE 5

Measure income and prepare the income statement and the statement of comprehensive income using various formats.

Presentation

There are many different ways to present performance information. Some involve formatting only and some involve signalling information about core ongoing operations versus peripheral or discontinued operations. Income can be further classified by customer, product line, nature, or function, or by operating and non-operating, continuing and discontinued, and regular and irregular categories. Recall that the objective of financial reporting is to communicate information to users about the company and give them the information that they need to make decisions. Items should not be offset except in very limited situations. For example, gains and losses should generally be shown separately and not as a net item.

We have already looked at discontinued operations and other comprehensive income as unique items. Next, let's look at items that are reflected in continuing operations on the statement of income/comprehensive income. We will then look at different ways to present the whole statement of income/comprehensive income.

Ordinary versus Peripheral Activities

What is the difference between revenues/expenses and gains/losses? Should they be shown separately? The importance of properly presenting these elements should not be underestimated. For many decision-makers, the parts of a financial statement may be more useful than the whole. From a business perspective, a company must be able to generate positive net cash flows from its normal ongoing core (regular) business activities (revenues minus expenses) in order to survive and prosper.[23] Having income statement elements shown in some detail and in a format that shows the data from prior years allows decision-makers to better assess whether a company does indeed generate cash flows from its normal ongoing core business activities and whether it is getting better or worse at it.

The **distinction** between revenues and gains (and expenses and losses) depends to a great extent on how the enterprise's **ordinary** or **typical business activities** are defined. It is therefore critical to understand an enterprise's typical business activities. For example, when McDonald's sells a hamburger, the selling price is recorded as **revenue**. However, when McDonald's sells a deep fryer machine, any excess of the selling price over the book value would be recorded as a **gain**. This difference in treatment results because the hamburger sale is part of the company's regular operations but the deep fryer sale is not. Only when a manufacturer of deep fryers sells a fryer, therefore, would the sale proceeds be recorded as **revenue**.

Unusual gains and losses are items that by their nature are not typical of everyday business activities or do not occur frequently. They include such items as writedowns of inventories and gains and losses from fluctuations of foreign exchange. However, they are generally presented as part of normal, recurring revenues, expenses, gains, and losses (as part of income from continuing operations). If they are not material in amount, they are combined with other items in the income statement. If they are material, they are disclosed separately. See Underlying Concept 4.7. This separate presentation allows for greater transparency because the users are able to see the cause of major gains and losses.

If the same types of gains/losses recur each year, then they are not really unusual and care must be taken to classify them with other gains and losses as normal transactions. Otherwise, it is misleading.

> **Underlying Concept 4.7**
>
> Any items that are material and/or relevant to understanding the financial performance should also be presented separately under the full disclosure principle.

Basic Presentation Requirements

IFRS **ASPE** Companies are required to include all elements in the financial statements (as long as they are measurable and probable under ASPE). In addition, the items in Illustration 4.7 are specifically required to be presented separately in the statement of income/comprehensive income. Judgement may be used to determine where additional items are best presented (that is, in the income statement or notes).[24]

---

[23]In addition, these cash flows should be sufficient to cover other things such as cost of capital.

[24]*CPA Canada Handbook—Accounting*, Part II, Section 1520.04 and IAS 1.97–.105. ASPE notes that, where these items may be set out "more readily" in the notes or in a schedule, this should be noted on the income statement.

ASPE per Section 1520	IFRS per IAS 1
• Revenue • Income from investments • Income tax expense (before discontinued operations) • Income or loss before discontinued operations • Results of discontinued operations • Net income or loss	• Revenue • Finance costs • Share of profit/loss for investments accounted for using the equity method • Tax expense • Results of discontinued operations • Profit or loss • Other comprehensive income classified by nature showing which will be recycled and which will not • Share of other comprehensive income of investments accounted for using the equity method • Total other comprehensive income • Profit or loss and comprehensive income attributable to noncontrolling interest and owners • Comprehensive income

Alternative Terminology 4.1

Note that a company is not required to use the terms "other comprehensive income" or "comprehensive income" under IFRS. Other terminology may be used, such as identifying the specific items included; for example, revaluation adjustment on property, plant, and equipment.

Combined Statement of Income/Comprehensive Income

Under IFRS, the statement of comprehensive income is presented either:[25]

1. in a single combined statement including revenues, expenses, gains, losses, net income, other comprehensive income, and comprehensive income; or

2. in two separate statements showing the traditional income statement in one and a second statement beginning with net income and displaying the components of other comprehensive income, as well as comprehensive income. See **Alternative Terminology 4.1**.

By providing information on the components of comprehensive income, the company communicates information about all changes in net assets. With this information, users will be better able to understand the quality of the company's earnings. This information should help users predict the amounts, timing, and uncertainty of future cash flows.

A separate statement of comprehensive income is shown for Onex Corporation in **Illustration 4.8**. Note the statement of income was shown in Illustration 4.6 (including discontinued operations). This statement starts off with net profit as presented on the statement of income. Recall from Illustration 4.5 that OCI items must be grouped and presented based on whether they will be recycled (reclassified to net income) or not. Note also that the comprehensive income attributable to shareholders is shown separately from that for noncontrolling interests, as required by IFRS. This split was also presented for net profit, as shown in Illustration 4.6.

A combined income statement format is shown in **Illustration 4.9** for **TELUS Corporation**, a Canadian company whose shares list on the TSX and NYSE.

By convention, income statements may be presented using a number of formats, including the single-step, multiple-step, and condensed formats. These are not GAAP-required formats. Companies choose which format they think best presents the performance information. In addition, expenses may be grouped in different ways, perhaps emphasizing activities or functions (such as selling, production, research, and development) versus the nature of the expense (payroll, depreciation, and so on). We will discuss these formats next.

---

[25]IAS 1.81A and B.

Onex Corporation

CONSOLIDATED STATEMENTS OF COMPREHENSIVE EARNINGS

Year ended December 31 (*in millions of U.S. dollars*)	2017	2016
Net earnings (loss) for the year	**$2,395**	$ (36)
Other comprehensive earnings (loss), net of tax		
Items that may be reclassified to net earnings (loss):		
Currency translation adjustments	375	(37)
Change in fair value of derivatives designated as hedges	45	5
Unrealized gains on available-for-sale financial assets	2	—
	422	(32)
Items that will not be reclassified to net earnings (loss):		
Remeasurements for post-employment benefit plans	6	13
Other comprehensive earnings from discontinued operations, net of tax (note 8)	174	8
Other comprehensive earnings (loss) for the year, net of tax	602	(11)
Total Comprehensive Earnings (Loss) for the Year	**$2,997**	$ (47)
Total Comprehensive Earnings (Loss) attributable to:		
Equity holders of Onex Corporation	**$2,951**	$(154)
Non-controlling Interests	46	107
Total Comprehensive Earnings (Loss) for the Year	**$2,997**	$ (47)

TELUS Corporation

CONSOLIDATED STATEMENTS OF INCOME AND OTHER COMPREHENSIVE INCOME

Years ended December 31 (millions except per share amounts)	Note	2017	2016
OPERATING REVENUES			
Service		**$12,478**	$12,000
Equipment		**724**	725
Revenues arising from contracts with customers		**13,202**	12,725
Other operating income	7	**102**	74
		13,304	12,799
OPERATING EXPENSES			
Goods and services purchased		**5,935**	5,631
Employee benefits expense	8	**2,595**	2,939
Depreciation	17	**1,617**	1,564
Amortization of intangible assets	18	**552**	483
		10,699	10,617
OPERATING INCOME		**2,605**	2,182
Financing costs	9	**573**	520
INCOME BEFORE INCOME TAXES		**2,032**	1,662
Income taxes	10	**553**	426
NET INCOME		**1,479**	1,236
OTHER COMPREHENSIVE INCOME	11		
Items that may subsequently be reclassified to income			
Change in unrealized fair value of derivatives designated as cash flow hedges		**19**	(20)

ILLUSTRATION 4.9

(*continued*)

Years ended December 31 (millions except per share amounts)	Note	**2017**	2016
Foreign currency translation adjustment arising from translating financial statements of foreign operations		**5**	5
Change in unrealized fair value of available-for-sale financial assets		**(11)**	—
		13	(15)
Item never subsequently reclassified to income			
Employee defined benefit plans re-measurements		**(172)**	—
		(159)	(15)
COMPREHENSIVE INCOME		**$ 1,320**	$ 1,221
NET INCOME ATTRIBUTABLE TO:			
Common Shares		**$ 1,460**	$ 1,223
Non-controlling interests		**19**	13
		$ 1,479	$ 1,236
COMPREHENSIVE INCOME ATTRIBUTABLE TO:			
Common Shares		**$ 1,297**	$ 1,206
Non-controlling interests		**23**	15
		$ 1,320	$ 1,221
NET INCOME PER COMMON SHARE	12		
Basic		**$ 2.46**	$ 2.06
Diluted		**$ 2.46**	$ 2.06
TOTAL WEIGHTED AVERAGE COMMON SHARES OUTSTANDING			
Basic		**593**	592
Diluted		**593**	593

Single-Step Income Statements

In reporting revenues, gains, expenses, and losses, a format known as the **single-step income statement** is often used. In the single-step statement, only two main groupings are used: **revenues** and **expenses**. Expenses and losses are deducted from revenues and gains to arrive at net income. The expression "single-step" comes from the single subtraction that is needed to arrive at net income before discontinued operations. Frequently, income tax is reported separately as the last item before net income before discontinued operations to show its relationship to income before income tax.

Illustration 4.10 shows the single-step income statement of Great Canadian Gaming Corporation, a company operating in the gaming, entertainment, and hospitality industry. We have reproduced only the profit and loss portion of the statement.

The single-step form of income statement is also widely used in financial reporting in smaller private companies. The **multiple-step** form described below is often used by public companies.

The main advantages of the single-step format are that the **presentation is simple** and **no one type of revenue or expense item is implied to have priority over any other**. Potential classification problems are thus eliminated. The main disadvantage of the single-step format is oversimplification and less detail.

Multiple-Step Income Statements

Some users argue that **presenting other important revenue and expense data separately** makes the income statement more informative and more useful. For instance, additional information is communicated if there is separation between the company's operating and non-operating activities such as **other revenues and gains** and **other expenses and losses**. These other categories include interest revenue and expense, gains or losses from sales of miscellaneous items, and dividends received.

GREAT CANADIAN GAMING CORPORATION

Consolidated Statements of Earnings and Other Comprehensive Income
(Expressed in millions of Canadian dollars, except for per share information)
For the years ended December 31,

		2017	2016
Revenues	Note 15	**$ 614.3**	$566.4
Expenses			
Human resources	Note 21	**218.3**	202.4
Property, marketing and administration		**175.8**	157.7
Share of profit of equity investments		**(1.0)**	(2.6)
Amortization		**58.3**	54.7
Share-based compensation	Note 14, 21	**8.1**	6.7
Impairment reversal of long-lived assets	Note 7, 8	**(0.9)**	—
Interest and financing costs, net	Note 11	**33.9**	34.9
Business acquisition, restructuring and other	Note 16	**1.5**	7.3
Foreign exchange gain and other		**—**	(0.3)
		494.0	460.8
Earnings before income taxes		**120.3**	105.6
Income taxes	Note 17	**34.6**	29.0
Net earnings		**$ 85.7**	$ 76.6
Net earnings attributable to:			
Shareholders of the Company		**$ 84.3**	$ 75.7
Non-controlling interests		**1.4**	0.9
		$ 85.7	$ 76.6

A **multiple-step income statement** separates **operating** transactions from **non-operating** transactions and **matches** costs and expenses with related revenues. It also highlights certain intermediate components of income that are used to calculate ratios for assessing the enterprise's performance (that is, gross profit margin).

To illustrate, **Cameco Corporation**'s multiple-step income statement is presented in **Illustration 4.11**. In this statement, there are three main subtotals that are presented that deal with operating activities: cost of sales, gross profit, and loss from operations. Note that

Cameco Corporation
CONSOLIDATED STATEMENTS OF EARNINGS

For the years ended December 31 ($Cdn thousands, except per share amounts)	**Note**	2017	2016
Revenue from products and services		$2,156,852	$2,431,404
Cost of products and services sold		1,390,233	1,596,235
Depreciation and amortization		330,345	371,689
Cost of sales		1,720,578	1,967,924
Gross profit		436,274	463,480
Administration		163,095	206,652
Impairment charges	8, 9	358,330	361,989
Exploration		29,933	42,579
Research and development		5,660	4,952
Other operating expense (income)	14	43	(34,075)
Loss on disposal of assets		6,947	23,168
Loss from operations		(127,734)	(141,785)
Finance costs	17	(110,608)	(111,906)
Gain on derivatives	24	56,250	34,407
Finance income		5,265	4,379
Other income (expense)	18	(30,410)	60,671
Loss before income taxes		(207,237)	(154,234)

(continued)

ILLUSTRATION 4.11

(*continued*)

For the years ended December 31 ($Cdn thousands, except per share amounts)	Note	2017	2016
Income tax recovery	19	(2,519)	(94,355)
Net loss		**$(204,718)**	**$ (59,879)**
Net earnings (loss) attributable to:			
Equity holders		(204,942)	(61,611)
Non-controlling interest		224	1,732
Net loss		**$(204,718)**	**$ (59,879)**
Loss per common share attributable to equity holders:			
Basic	20	$ (0.52)	$ (0.16)
Diluted	20	$ (0.52)	$ (0.16)

depreciation and amortization have been included as part of cost of sales. This would indicate that the related assets are directly used in producing the goods for sale.

The disclosure of revenue relating to the cost of products and services normally sold is useful because trends in revenue from continuing operations (typical business activities) should be easier to identify, understand, and analyze. Similarly, the reporting of gross profit provides a useful number for evaluating performance and assessing future earnings. A study of the trend in gross profits may show **how successfully a company uses its resources** (prices paid for inventory, costs accumulated, and wastage). It may also be a basis for **understanding how profit margins have changed** as a result of competitive pressure (which may limit the prices that the company is able to charge for its products and services). Gross profit percentage is a very important ratio in the retail business, for instance, and is regularly tracked by industry analysts, investors, and competitors. For Cameco, note that the gross profit percentage is increasing from 19% ($463,480 ÷ $2,431,404) to 20.2% ($436,274 ÷ $2,156,852) even though sales have declined.

Disclosing income or loss from operations **highlights the difference between regular and irregular or incidental activities**. Disclosure of operating earnings may help in comparing different companies and assessing their operating efficiencies. Income/losses from discontinued operations are by definition **nonrecurring** and therefore have **little predictive value**. They do, however, give **feedback value** on past decisions made by management. See Underlying Concept 4.8. Net income that consists mainly of income from continuing operations would be viewed as **higher quality**.

When a multiple-step income statement is used, some or all of the following sections or subsections shown in Illustration 4.12 may be presented.

Although the **content** of the operating section is generally the same, the **presentation** or organization of the material does not need to be as described above. Sometimes the expenses are grouped by nature instead of function.

This is discussed below.

> **Underlying Concept 4.8**
>
> Separate disclosure helps users recognize that incidental or irregular activities are unlikely to continue at the same level (in other words, it enhances predictive value).

ILLUSTRATION 4.12

Multiple-Step Income Statement Presentation

MULTIPLE-STEP INCOME STATEMENT SECTIONS

1. ***Continuing Operations***

    a. **Operating** section. A report of the **revenues and expenses** of the company's principal operations.

       i. **Sales or Revenue.** A subsection presenting sales, discounts, allowances, returns, and other related information. Its purpose is to arrive at the net amount of sales revenue.

       ii. **Cost of Goods Sold.** A subsection that shows the cost of goods that were sold to produce the sales.

       iii. **Selling Expenses.** A subsection that lists expenses resulting from the company's efforts to make sales.

       iv. **Administrative or General Expenses.** A subsection reporting expenses for general administration.

(*continued*)

   b. Non-Operating section. A report of revenues and expenses resulting from the company's secondary or auxiliary activities. In addition, special gains and losses that are infrequent and/or unusual are normally reported in this section. Generally these items break down into two main subsections:

   i. Other Revenues and Gains. A list of the revenues earned or gains incurred from non-operating transactions, and generally net of related expenses.

   ii. Other Expenses and Losses. A list of the expenses or losses incurred from non-operating transactions, and generally net of any related income.

   c. Income Tax. A short section reporting income taxes on income from continuing operations.

2. *Discontinued Operations.* Operating income or loss from operations that are discontinued plus gains or losses resulting from the disposition of a part of the business (net of taxes).

3. *Other Comprehensive Income.* Under IFRS, other gains/losses that are not required by primary sources of GAAP to be included in net income. This section includes all other changes in equity that do not relate to shareholder transactions (net of taxes).

> **Underlying Concept 4.9**
>
> Having less detail contributes to understandability because it reduces "information overload."

Usually, financial statements that are provided to external users have **less detail** than internal management reports. See Underlying Concept 4.9. The latter tend to have more expense categories, and they are usually grouped along lines of responsibility. This detail allows top management to judge staff performance.

Condensed Financial Statements

In some cases, it is impossible to present all the desired expense detail in a single income statement of convenient size. This problem is solved by including only the totals of expense groups in the statement of income and preparing **supplementary schedules** of expenses to support the totals. With this format, the income statement itself may be reduced to a few lines on a single page. In such instances, readers who want to study all the reported data on operations must give their attention to the supporting schedules. See Underlying Concept 4.10.

> **Underlying Concept 4.10**
>
> The use of supplementary schedules is an example of a trade-off between understandability and full disclosure.

Illustration 4.13 shows the statement of comprehensive income for Brick Brewing Company Limited. Note the high level of aggregation and also the numerous references

ILLUSTRATION 4.13

Condensed Statements of Comprehensive Income—Brick Brewing Company Limited

STATEMENTS OF COMPREHENSIVE INCOME
Years ended January 31, 2017 and 2016

	Notes	January 31, 2017	January 31, 2016
Revenue	7	$45,176,380	$37,609,568
Cost of sales	8	29,464,917	27,075,078
Gross profit		15,711,463	10,534,490
Selling, marketing and administration expenses	8	9,248,039	7,367,411
Other expenses	8,9	643,273	641,474
Finance costs	10	478,181	478,945
Gain on disposal of property, plant and equipment		—	(205,912)
Income before tax		5,341,970	2,252,572
Income tax expense	11	1,345,158	658,392
Net income and comprehensive income for the year		$ 3,996,812	$ 1,594,180
Basic earnings per share	18	$ 0.11	$ 0.05
Diluted earnings per share	18	$ 0.11	$ 0.05

to notes, which give more detail. An example of a supporting schedule, cross-referenced as Note 9 and detailing other expenses, is shown in Illustration 4.14.

Sample Supporting Schedule—
Brick Brewing Company
Limited

9. OTHER EXPENSES

The Company's other expenses consist of the following amounts:

	January 31, 2017	January 31, 2016
Depreciation of property, plant & equipment	$487,214	$500,222
Amortization of intangible assets	20,400	20,400
Other personnel-related expenses	120,214	32,945
Foreign exchange losses	15,445	87,907
	$643,273	$641,474

Deciding **how much detail** to include in the income statement is always a problem. On the one hand, a simple, summarized statement allows a reader to quickly discover important factors. On the other hand, disclosure of the results of all activities provides users with detailed relevant information. Earlier, we looked at the basic presentation requirements under GAAP. As long as these requirements are met, there is a significant amount of flexibility in how to present the information.

Nature versus Function

IFRS Whether the single-step or multiple-step method is used, consideration should be given to providing additional details about expenses. This helps ensure transparency. IFRS requires an entity to present an analysis of expenses based on either nature or function, as follows:

1. **Nature** refers to the type of expense (such as depreciation, purchases of materials, transport costs, and employee benefits). This method tends to be more straightforward since no allocation of costs is required between functions.

2. **Function** refers to business function or activity. Most businesses are structured around activities. For instance, a manufacturing business will have a production function, a selling function, and a head office function that supports the other two functions. Therefore, a statement that shows expenses by function for the manufacturing business would group costs by production, selling, and administration. These might be presented as cost of sales (production), distribution costs (selling), and administrative costs (administration). This method requires more judgement since costs such as payroll and amortization are allocated between functions. At a minimum, this method requires that cost of sales be presented separately from other costs. This presentation gives more insight into the various phases of operations (such as production and distribution).

Regardless of how the entity classifies the expenses (nature or function), it is encouraged to present the analysis in the statement of income/comprehensive income under IFRS; however, it may be presented elsewhere. Because information about the nature of expense is useful for predicting cash flows, additional information, including amortization, depreciation, and employee benefits expenses, must also be disclosed under IFRS when the income statement presents expenses by function.

ASPE Although ASPE does not mandate that companies present according to nature or function, an entity may choose to make such disclosures if it feels that the information is decision relevant.

Which method is better? That depends on the nature of the business and industry. For instance, as noted earlier, it is useful in the retail and manufacturing industries to focus on cost of sales and gross profit. Gross profit margins give important information about pricing and costs. Therefore, manufacturing and retail companies may wish to present costs by function. Similarly, entities that are heavily involved in research and development may wish to present costs by function to highlight this. Since research and development costs may be largely com-posed of payroll costs, they would otherwise be lumped with payroll or salary expenses if the expenses were presented by nature and not by function. Many public companies use a combi-nation of both approaches or group the majority of expenses by function.

Recall the (condensed) statements of comprehensive income shown for Brick Brewing Company Limited above. Those statements are presented primarily by function. Since the company derives most of its revenues by creating and selling a product, it makes sense to group and present the expenses by these activities. The statement shows cost of sales (production function) and selling, marketing, and administration expenses (selling and head office functions). Additional disclosures are shown in the accompanying notes to the company's financial statements (as required under IFRS), which provide details of the expenses by nature (Illustration 4.15).

ILLUSTRATION 4.15

Additional Disclosures Required under IFRS Where Expenses Are Presented Primarily by Function—Brick Brewing Company Limited

8. EXPENSES BY NATURE

Expenses relating to depreciation, amortization, impairment and personnel expenses are included within the following line items on the statements of comprehensive income:

	January 31, 2017	January 31, 2016
Depreciation of property, plant & equipment		
Cost of sales	$2,368,344	$2,462,649
Other expenses	487,214	500,222
Amortization of intangible assets		
Other expenses	20,400	20,400
Salaries, benefits and other personnel-related expenses		
Cost of sales	6,386,669	6,016,270
Selling, marketing and administrative expenses	3,934,754	3,048,498
Other expenses	120,214	32,945

Note how depreciation expense is recorded partly in cost of sales and partly in other expenses. Similarly salaries, benefits, and other personnel-related expenses are recorded in three separate lines: cost of sales; selling, marketing, and administrative expenses; and other expenses.

Illustration 4.16 shows the consolidated income statements for Torstar Corporation. The company shows its expenses mostly by nature. The publishing industry is transitioning from primarily print to online business models so this statement reflects this. You can see that the most significant expenses are salaries and benefits as well as other operating costs (presumably including such things as heat, light, and power). The restructuring cost involves payments to employees.

ILLUSTRATION 4.16

Consolidated Statement of Loss—Torstar Corporation; Classified Primarily by Nature

Torstar Corporation

Consolidated Statement of Loss

(*Thousands of Canadian Dollars except per share amounts*)

	Year ended December 31	
	2017	2016
Operating revenue	**$615,685**	$685,099
Salaries and benefits	**(245,906)**	(299,315)
Other operating costs	**(325,631)**	(356,192)
Amortization and depreciation (notes 9 and 10)	**(36,987)**	(44,020)
Restructuring and other charges (note 17)	**(17,512)**	(45,823)
Impairment of assets (note 12)	**(8,133)**	(800)

(*continued*)

ILLUSTRATION 4.16
(continued)

	Year ended December 31	
	2017	2016
Operating loss	**(18,484)**	(61,051)
Interest and financing costs (note 15)	**(2,213)**	(3,080)
Foreign exchange	**493**	298
Loss from joint ventures (note 7)	**(1,845)**	(5,532)
Loss from associated businesses (note 8)	**(6,824)**	(34,919)
Other income (note 23)	**3,935**	24,348
	(24,938)	(79,936)
Income and other taxes recovery (expense) (note 14)	**(5,700)**	3,900
Net loss from continuing operations	**(30,638)**	(76,036)
Income from discontinued operations (note 24)	**1,350**	1,200
Net loss	**$(29,288)**	$(74,836)
Attributable to:		
Equity shareholders	**$(29,171)**	$(74,750)
Minority interests	**$ (117)**	$ (86)
Net income (loss) attributable to equity shareholders per Class A (voting) and Class B (non-voting) share (note 20(c)):		
Basic and Diluted:		
From continuing operations	**$ (0.38)**	$ (0.94)
From discontinued operations	**$ 0.02**	$0.01
	$ (0.36)	$ (0.93)

As mentioned earlier, most companies use some combination of the nature and function presentations. While most items on the Torstar statement, for instance, are presented by nature, the restructuring charge could include many things, such as salaries, severance costs, or lease costs.

Intraperiod Tax Allocation

As previously noted, certain irregular items are shown on the income statement net of tax, which is a more informative disclosure to statement users. This procedure of allocating tax balances within a period is called **intraperiod tax allocation**. Intraperiod tax allocation relates the income tax expense or benefit of the fiscal period to the underlying income statement items and events that are being taxed. Intraperiod tax allocation is used for the following items: (1) income from continuing operations, (2) discontinued operations, and (3) other comprehensive income. Companies pay taxes at the federal and provincial level in Canada and rates are indicated by the Canada Revenue Agency.[26]

Example 4.5 looks at intraperiod tax allocation.

Example 4.5 | Allocating Tax Expense in the Income Statement

Facts Assume that Schindler Corp. has income before income tax and discontinued operations of $250,000 and a gain from the sale of one of its operations of $100,000. Assume the income tax rate is 25%.

Instructions How do you allocate tax expense to the various lines in the income statement?

Solution

Income before income tax and discontinued operations	$250,000
Income tax	62,500
Income before discontinued operations	187,500
Gain on sale of discontinued operations net of applicable taxes ($25,000)	75,000
Net income	$262,500

[26]Corporate tax rates in Canada have declined in the past decade.

The income tax of $62,500 ($250,000 × 25%) that is attributed to income before income tax and discontinued operations is determined from the revenue and expense transactions related to this income. In this income tax calculation, the tax consequences of items excluded from the determination of income before income tax and discontinued operations are not considered. The "gain on sale of discontinued operation" then shows a separate tax effect of $25,000.

IFRS IFRS allows a company to present items included as other comprehensive income either net of tax or before tax with one amount shown for taxes related to all other comprehensive income items. The amount of tax may be shown on the face of the statement or in the notes.

Earnings per Share

Typically, the results of a company's operations are summed up in one important figure: net income. As if this simplification were not enough, the financial world has widely accepted an even more distilled and compact figure as its most significant business indicator: **earnings per share (EPS)**. Many users focus primarily on the EPS number (rightly or wrongly) as a key indicator of the company's performance. While the EPS number yields significant information, it does not tell the whole story. This undue emphasis on EPS makes it a very sensitive number for companies. Note further that, when comprehensive income is presented, it raises the question of why EPS is not based on this more "comprehensive" measurement of income.

The calculation of basic earnings per share is usually straightforward. The calculation is:

Net income − Preferred dividends = Income available to common shareholders

$$\frac{\text{Income available to common shareholders}}{\text{Weighted average number of common shares outstanding}} = \text{EPS}$$

Example 4.6 looks at the EPS calculation.

Example 4.6 | Calculating EPS

Facts   Assume that Lancer Inc. reports net income of $350,000 and declares and pays preferred dividends of $50,000 for the year. The weighted average number of common shares outstanding during the year is 100,000 shares.

Instructions   What is the EPS for Lancer?

Solution   Earnings per share is $3.00.

$$\frac{\text{Net Income} - \text{Preferred Dividends}}{\text{Weighted Average Number of Common Shares Outstanding}}$$
$$= \text{Earnings per Share (EPS)}$$
$$= \frac{\$350,000 - \$50,000}{100,000}$$
$$= \$3.00$$

Note that the EPS figure measures the number of dollars earned by each common share, not the dollar amount paid to shareholders in the form of dividends.

"Net income per share" or "earnings per share" is a ratio that commonly appears in prospectuses, proxy material, and annual reports to shareholders. It is also highlighted in the financial press, by statistical services like Standard & Poor's, and by Bay Street securities analysts. Because of its importance, public companies are required to disclose EPS on the face of their income statements. In addition, a company that reports a discontinued operation must report EPS for income before discontinued operations as well as per-share amounts for discontinued operations either on the face of the income statement or in the notes to the financial statements.[27] Throughout the chapter, we have included numerous sample income statements that include EPS. Earnings per share information related to comprehensive income is not required.

Many corporations have simple capital structures that include only common shares. For these companies, a presentation such as earnings per common share is appropriate on the income statement. In many instances, however, companies' earnings per share are subject to dilution (reduction) in the future because existing contingencies allow future issues of additional common shares. These corporations would present both basic EPS and fully diluted EPS.[28]

In summary, the simplicity and availability of figures for per-share earnings mean that they are used widely. Because of the excessive importance that the public—even the well-informed public—attaches to EPS, this information should be made as meaningful as possible. Note that this area is of lesser relevance to private entities because most have shares that are closely held. Therefore, companies following ASPE are not required to include EPS.

The Statement of Retained Earnings and the Statement of Changes in Equity

---

LEARNING OBJECTIVE 6
Prepare the statement of retained earnings and the statement of changes in equity.

Net income is closed out to retained earnings at the end of the period. Retained earnings show the company's accumulated earnings (or deficit in the case of losses). Under ASPE, the **statement of retained earnings** shows this accumulated income (or deficit) as well as how much has been paid out as dividends.

Recall that OCI exists only under IFRS and that OCI is closed out to accumulated other comprehensive income (AOCI). Therefore, under IFRS we need an expanded statement that shows the changes in retained earnings and AOCI. Under IFRS, instead of a statement of retained earnings, we use a **statement of changes in equity** and show all changes in all equity accounts, including retained earnings and AOCI.

Presentation of the Statement of Retained Earnings

ASPE Retained earnings are affected by many variables and can be presented in many ways. Net income increases retained earnings and a net loss decreases retained earnings. Both cash and share dividends decrease retained earnings. Retrospectively applied changes in accounting policies and corrections of errors may either increase or decrease retained earnings. Information on retained earnings, including the changes they have undergone, can be shown in different ways. For example, companies following ASPE usually prepare a separate retained earnings statement, as shown in **Illustration 4.17.**

The reconciliation of the beginning to the ending balance in retained earnings provides information about why net assets increased or decreased during the year. The association of dividend distributions with net income for the period indicates what management is doing with earnings: it may be putting part or all of the earnings back into the business, distributing all current income, or distributing current income plus the accumulated earnings of prior

---

[27]IAS 33.68.

[28]We will cover earnings per share in significant detail in Chapter 17.

ILLUSTRATION 4.17

Retained Earnings Statement

STATEMENT OF RETAINED EARNINGS

For the Year Ended December 31, 2020

Balance, January 1, as reported		$1,050,000
Correction for understatement of net income in prior period		
(inventory error) (net of taxes of $12,000)		50,000
Balance, January 1, as adjusted		1,100,000
Add: Net income		360,000
		1,460,000
Less: Cash dividends	$100,000	
Less: Stock dividends	200,000	300,000
Balance, December 31		$1,160,000

years. Note that the retained earnings statement may be combined with the income statement by adding it to the bottom of the income statement.

ASPE Changes in accounting occur frequently in practice, because important events or conditions may be in dispute or uncertain at the statement date. One type of accounting change occurs when a different accounting principle is adopted to replace the one previously used. **Changes in accounting policy** would include, for example, a change in the method of inventory pricing from FIFO to average cost. Accounting policy changes are allowed only if they are required by a primary source of GAAP or if they result in reliable and more relevant information. Under ASPE, there are some exceptions to this principle. For instance, where ASPE allows a choice of accounting policies such as accounting for income taxes, significant influence investment, or development costs, an accounting policy change may be made without having to prove that the new policy is reliable and more relevant. This is because, in principle, ASPE is meant to be more flexible and adaptable.

Changes in accounting policy are generally recognized through **retrospective restatement**, which involves determining the effect of the policy change on the income of prior periods that are affected. See **Underlying Concept 4.11**. The financial statements for all prior periods that are presented for comparative purposes should be restated except when the effect cannot be determined reasonably. If all comparative years are not disclosed, a cumulative amount would instead be calculated and adjusted through the opening retained earnings amount.

Example 4.7 looks at how a retrospective change would be presented in the statement of retained earnings.

> **Underlying Concept 4.11**
>
> The retrospective application ensures consistency.

Example 4.7 | Retrospective Restatement and Presentation

Facts Assume Gaubert Inc. decided in March 2020 to change from the FIFO method of valuing inventory to the weighted average method. If prices are rising, cost of sales would be higher and ending inventory lower for the preceding period by $16,000. Assume a tax rate of 25% and that previously reported retained earnings were $120,000.

Instructions How would this change be presented in the statement of retained earnings? Prepare the adjusting journal entry.

Solution The change would be presented on a retrospective basis, thus affecting opening retained earnings.

Retained earnings, January 1, 2020, as previously reported	$120,000
Cumulative effect on prior years of retrospective application of new inventory costing method (net of $4,000 tax)	12,000
Adjusted balance of retained earnings, January 1, 2020	$108,000

The journal entry would be:

Income Tax Receivable	4,000	
Retained Earnings	12,000	
Inventory		16,000

A note describing the change and its impact would be required as well as comparative statements which were restated.

Another type of change is a change in accounting estimate that is accounted for prospectively with no catch-up adjustment. We will revisit accounting changes in Chapter 21.

Presentation of the Statement of Changes in Equity

IFRS The statement of changes in equity reports the changes in each shareholders' equity account and in total shareholders' equity during the year, including comprehensive income. The statement of shareholders' equity is often **prepared in columnar form** with columns for each account and for total shareholders' equity. This is a required statement under IFRS.

IFRS The following must be presented in the statement:

1. Total comprehensive income (showing amounts attributable to owners and noncontrolling interests)
2. For each component of equity: effects of retrospective application
3. For each component of equity: a reconciliation between the carrying amounts at the beginning and end of the period, including profit or loss, OCI, and transactions with owners.

The entity may disclose an analysis of OCI by item either in the statement or in the notes.

A statement of changes in equity for Cameco Corporation is shown in **Illustration 4.18**. Note that Cameco has chosen to present the analysis of OCI by item in this statement.

ILLUSTRATION 4.18 Presentation of Consolidated Statements of Changes in Equity—Cameco Corporation

Consolidated statements of changes in equity

($Cdn thousands)	Share capital	Contributed surplus	Retained earnings	Foreign currency translation	Available for-sale assets	Total	Non-controlling interest	Total equity
	Attributable to equity holders							
Balance at January 1, 2017	$1,862,646	$216,213	$3,019,872	$ 156,411	$3,229	$5,258,371	$ 157	$5,258,528
Net earnings (loss)	—	—	(204,942)	—	—	(204,942)	224	(204,718)
Other comprehensive income (loss)	—	—	(6,216)	(44,070)	5,837	(44,449)	(10)	(44,459)
Total comprehensive income (loss	—	—	(211,158)	(44,070)	5,837	(249,391)	214	(249,177)
Share-based compensation	—	13,960	—	—	—	13,960	—	13,960
Stock options exercised	6	(1)	—	—	—	5	—	5
Restricted and performance share units released	—	(5,360)	—	—	—	(5,360)	—	(5,360)
Dividends	—	—	(158,297)	—	—	(158,297)	—	(158,297)
Balance at December 31, 2017	$1,862,652	$224,812	$2,650,417	$ 112,341	$9,066	$4,859,288	$ 371	$4,859,659
Balance at January 1, 2016	$1,862,646	$209,115	$3,241,902	$ 233,918	$(561)	$5,547,020	$(1,741)	$5,545,279
Net earnings (loss)	—	—	(61,611)	—	—	(61,611)	1,732	(59,879)
Other comprehensive income (loss)	—	—	(2,109)	(77,507)	3,790	(75,826)	166	(75,660)
Total comprehensive income (loss)	—	—	(63,720)	(77,507)	3,790	(137,437)	1,898	(135,539)
Share-based compensation	—	14,101	—	—	—	14,101	—	14,101
Restricted and performance share units released	—	(7,003)	—	—	—	(7,003)	—	(7,003)
Dividends	—	—	(158,310)	—	—	(158,310)	—	(158,310)
Balance at December 31, 2016	$1,862,646	$216,213	$3,019,872	$ 156,411	$3,229	$5,258,371	$ 157	$5,258,528

The shareholders' equity section of Cameco's balance sheet is shown in Illustration 4.19.

	December 31, 2017	December 31, 2016
Shareholders' equity		
Share capital	1,862,652	1,862,646
Contributed surplus	224,812	216,213
Retained earnings	2,650,417	3,019,872
Other components of equity	121,407	159,640
Total shareholders' equity attributable to equity holders	4,859,288	5,258,371
Non-controlling interest	371	157
Total shareholders' equity	4,859,659	5,258,528
Total liabilities and shareholders' equity	**$7,778,727**	**$8,249,198**

Note that the company has chosen to present the account "Accumulated Other Comprehensive Income" as "Other Components of Equity." This is fine since IFRS does not mandate the use of specific headings for these items.

Disclosure and Analysis

LEARNING OBJECTIVE 7
Understand how disclosures and analysis help users of financial statements assess performance.

Disclosure

In addition to disclosures on the face of the financial statements, the notes to the financial statements are a great source of background and explanatory information. The notes supplement the main statements. They should be presented in a systematic manner and cross-referenced to the main financial statements. The notes should include the following:

1. accounting policies;
2. sources of estimation uncertainty;
3. information about the capital of the company (including how the company manages its capital and any changes); and
4. information including dividends, the legal form of the entity, its country of incorporation, description of the business name of the parent company, and information required under the full disclosure principle, including the basis of preparation where the financial statements were not prepared on a going concern basis.

Analysis

As noted earlier, **financial analysts and investors** assess quality of earnings and factor it into their resource allocation decisions.

Some attributes of high-quality earnings were expressed in Illustration 4.4. To assess the quality of earnings, you must look at the whole set of financial statements, including the notes. In addition, the MD&A provides valuable insights into the nature of the business and industry and what is happening. Newspaper articles and analysts' reports are also good sources of information. When analyzing the health of a company and its quality of earnings, look for and analyze the following:

- **Accounting policies**—aggressive accounting policies, soft numbers
- **Notes to financial statements**—unrecognized liabilities and asset overstatement
- **Measurement uncertainty**—how hard/soft are the numbers? How risky is the business?
- **Financial statements** as a whole—complexity of presentation or language (which may obscure the company's performance or financial position)
- **Income statement**—percentage of net income derived from ongoing operations, to see whether the company can produce profits mainly from its core business
- **Cash flow statement**—cash from operating activities versus net income, to get a sense of whether net income is backed by cash or not
- **Statement of financial position**—to see how the company is financed and what the revenue-generating assets are
- **Other**—environmental factors such as the industry and economy. How is the company doing compared with its competitors? How is it positioning itself to take advantage of opportunities and manage risk? Where is the industry going? Are current earnings likely to be repeated in the future?

Non-GAAP Measures

Companies often try to help users assess the results of operations and their financial position by providing modified GAAP information such as **non-GAAP earnings**. Non-GAAP earnings start with GAAP net income and add back or deduct nonrecurring or non-operating items to arrive at an adjusted net income number. Non-GAAP earnings are not bad as such. If the calculation of the non-GAAP earnings is **clearly disclosed and explained**, and is also reconciled to net income, it hopefully adds value to the decision-making process. The danger with these numbers is that there are no standards to ensure that the calculation is **consistently** prepared and **comparable** between companies.

The Ontario Securities Commission (OSC) has issued a Staff Notice on these disclosures.[29] Its concern is that the additional information presented may mislead people. The OSC has therefore set out certain principles.

The Staff Notice states that, specifically, an issuer should do the following:

1. Note that the non-GAAP financial measure does not have any standardized meaning prescribed by the issuer's GAAP and is therefore unlikely to be comparable.
2. Provide a name for the non-GAAP measure that distinguishes it from other information provided.
3. Explain why the non-GAAP measure provides useful information.
4. Present the most directly comparable measure calculated in accordance with the issuer's GAAP and presented in its financial statements.
5. Provide a clear quantitative reconciliation from the non-GAAP financial measure to the most directly comparable measure calculated in accordance with the issuer's GAAP and presented in its financial statements.
6. Make sure that adjustments are not described as non-recurring, infrequent or unusual if they are not.
7. Present the information consistently from year to year.

---

[29]OSC Staff Notice 52-306 (Revised in 2016).

It is interesting to see how the OSC has defined the term "unusual items" in the Staff Notice—that is, if an item is reasonably likely to occur in the next two years, it is recurring. The OSC regularly reviews disclosures and looks at items such as non-GAAP measures as part of this process. See **What Do the Numbers Mean? 4.3**.

What Do the Numbers Mean? 4.3

In a review of 50 companies in 2013, the OSC found deficiencies in 86% of the companies' disclosures. According to the report (OSC Staff Notice 52-722), the OSC looked at the following:

- where non-GAAP financial measures or additional GAAP measures were reported,
- calculations of non-GAAP financial measures or additional GAAP measures,
- presentations of non-GAAP financial measures or additional GAAP measures, and
- disclosure of non-GAAP financial measures or additional GAAP measures.

The OSC continues to monitor the use of non-GAAP measures and as noted above, revised its Staff Notice regarding this issue in 2016. In its 2016 review, non-GAAP measures were still an issue.

Other Key Measures

Finance 5.4.2 Chapters 5 (Appendix 5A) and 23 cover financial statement analysis in more detail but it is worthwhile to note a couple of common ratios here that are based on earnings. We have already looked at how to calculate EPS and will come back to this in Chapter 17.

The other key ratio mentioned in Appendix 5A is the price earnings ratio. This is a very common ratio and it (or a variant of the ratio) is often used in the valuation of shares and/or companies. The ratio as presented in Appendix 5A is as follows:

$$\frac{\text{Market price per share}}{\text{EPS}}$$

Example 4.8 looks at a calculation for a price earnings ratio.

Example 4.8 | Calculating a Price Earnings Ratio

Facts   Assume that the shares of Thinker Limited are trading at $120 per share. The earnings per share are $10.

Instructions   What is the price earnings ratio?

Solution   The price earnings ratio is calculated as follows:

$$\frac{\text{Market price per share}}{\text{EPS}} = \frac{\$120}{\$10} = 12$$

This means that investors are willing to pay $12 for every dollar of earnings. Conversely, for every dollar earned by the company, if we multiply that dollar by 12, then we should get the share value.

When we present the analysis in this way, it is sometimes called an **earnings multiple**. Analysts track and compare earnings multiples between companies and industries. There are many other ways to calculate multiples and they can be based on book values, market values, cash flows, or some variant of income. The above is a very simplistic overview of how earnings multiples are calculated and it is meant only as a very high-level introduction to show how important the EPS number can be when valuing companies. Multiples and price earnings ratios are generally covered in greater detail in finance texts.

IFRS/ASPE Comparison

> ### LEARNING OBJECTIVE 8
> Identify differences in accounting between IFRS and ASPE and potential changes.

A Comparison of IFRS and ASPE

Illustration 4.20 sets out the major differences between GAAP for private entities and international accounting standards for publicly accountable enterprises.

ILLUSTRATION 4.20 **IFRS and ASPE Comparison Chart**

	IFRS—IAS 1, 8, and IFRS 5	Accounting Standards for Private Enterprises (ASPE)—*CPA Canada Handbook*, Part II, Sections 1400, 1506, 1520, 1521, 3251, and 3475	References to related illustrations and select brief exercises
Required presentation on face of income statement	As noted earlier in the chapter, IFRS mandates a list of required items that must be presented.	Requirements are different in some respects under ASPE.	Illustrations 4.7 and 4.12
Guidance on how to classify expenses (nature versus function)	IFRS requires that the entity present an analysis of expenses based on either their nature or function.	There is no guidance on how or when to present expenses according to their nature or function. Entities are free, however, to present their income statements in a manner that is most transparent as long as they adhere to the required disclosures noted above.	Illustrations 4.14, 4.15, and 4.16
Discontinued operations	Held-for-sale assets and liabilities are reclassified as current assets/liabilities.	Held-for-sale assets and liabilities are classified as current or non-current depending on the nature of the assets/liabilities unless the assets were sold before the financial statements were completed.	Illustration 4.6 BE4.11
Other comprehensive income/comprehensive income	Certain items must be classified as either comprehensive income or net income. In addition, entities must prepare a statement of comprehensive income.	Not recognized. Transactions are either booked through net income or directly to a separate component of shareholders' equity (such as certain foreign currency gains/losses).	Illustration 4.5 BE4.8
Earnings per share	Basic and diluted EPS must be presented in the statements.	Not mentioned since many private entities have closely held shareholdings by definition.	Example 4.6, Illustrations 4.6, 4.9, 4.11, 4.13, and 4.16

(continued)

Statement of retained earnings versus statement of changes in shareholders' equity	The statement of changes in equity is a required statement.	The statement of retained earnings is one of the core financial statements. There is no requirement to present a statement of changes in shareholders' equity, although changes in shareholders' equity accounts must be disclosed.	Illustrations 4.17, 4.18, and 4.19
Accounting changes	For all accounting policy changes, new policy must be reliable and more relevant.	Certain accounting policy choice changes do not have to meet the "must be reliable and more relevant" test.	

Looking Ahead

The IASB has been working on its Primary Financial Statements Project and plans to issue either a Discussion Paper or an Exposure Draft in the first half of 2019.

The IASB was in the process of deciding its next steps on the disclosure project as well as the project on primary financial statements. Both were still in the research project stage.

Appendix 4A	# Application of the Cash and Accrual Bases of Accounting

> **LEARNING OBJECTIVE 9**
> Explain the differences between the cash basis of accounting and the accrual basis of accounting.

Differences Between Cash and Accrual Bases

Most companies use the **accrual basis** of accounting: they recognize revenue when it is earned and recognize expenses in the period when they are incurred, which means that the time when cash is received or paid is not a factor in recognizing the transaction. Some small enterprises and the average individual taxpayer, however, use a strict or modified cash basis approach. Under the **strict cash basis**, revenue is recorded only when the cash is received, and expenses are recorded only when the cash is paid. Income is determined based on the actual collection of revenues and payment of expenses, and the revenue recognition and matching principles are ignored. Consequently, cash basis financial statements do not conform with generally accepted accounting principles.

Example 4A.1 illustrates and contrasts cash basis versus accrual accounting.

Example 4A.1 | Cash Basis Versus Accrual Accounting

Facts   Quality Contractor signs an agreement to build a garage for $22,000. In January, Quality Contractor begins construction, incurs costs of $18,000 on credit, and by the end of January delivers a finished garage to the buyer. In February, Quality Contractor collects $22,000 cash from the customer. In March, Quality pays the $18,000 that is owed to the creditors.

Instructions   What would the income statement and balance sheets look like under the cash basis and accrual basis of accounting? Prepare separate statements for each month.

Solution The monthly income statements under cash basis accounting and accrual basis accounting, respectively, would be shown as follows.

Quality Contractor Income Statement—Cash Basis For the Month of				
	January	**February**	**March**	**Total**
Cash receipts	$-0-	$22,000	$ -0-	$22,000
Cash payments	-0-	-0-	18,000	18,000
Net income (loss)	$-0-	$22,000	$(18,000)	$ 4,000

Quality Contractor Income Statement—Accrual Basis For the Month of				
	January	**February**	**March**	**Total**
Revenues	$22,000	$-0-	$-0-	$22,000
Expenses	18,000	-0-	-0-	18,000
Net income	$ 4,000	$-0-	$-0-	$ 4,000

For the three months combined, total net income is the same under both cash basis accounting and accrual basis accounting; the difference is in the timing of net income. The balance sheet is also affected by the basis of accounting. For instance, if cash basis accounting were used, Quality Contractor's balance sheets at each month end would appear as follows:

Quality Contractor Balance Sheets—Cash Basis As at			
	Jan. 31	**Feb. 28**	**Mar. 31**
Assets			
Cash	$-0-	$22,000	$4,000
Total assets	$-0-	$22,000	$4,000
Liabilities and Owners' Equity			
Owners' equity	$-0-	$22,000	$4,000
Total liabilities and owners' equity	$-0-	$22,000	$4,000

The following shows what Quality Contractor's balance sheets at each month end would look like if accrual basis accounting were used.

Quality Contractor Balance Sheets—Accrual Basis As at			
	Jan. 31	**Feb. 28**	**Mar. 31**
Assets			
Cash	$ -0-	$22,000	$4,000
Accounts receivable	22,000	-0-	-0-
Total assets	$22,000	$22,000	$4,000
Liabilities and Owners' Equity			
Accounts payable	$18,000	$18,000	$ -0-
Owners' equity	4,000	4,000	4,000
Total liabilities and owners' equity	$22,000	$22,000	$4,000

Now let's compare and contrast the two approaches. **Example 4A.2** critically evaluates the cash basis in the context of IFRS/ASPE.

Example 4A.2 | Evaluation of the Cash Basis in the Context of IFRS/ASPE

Facts   Review the income statements and balance sheets from Example 4A.1.

Instructions   How is the cash basis inconsistent with IFRS/ASPE?

Solution   An analysis of the income statements and balance sheets from Example 4A.1 shows the following ways in which cash basis accounting is inconsistent with basic accounting theory under IFRS/ASPE:

1. The cash basis understates revenues and assets from the construction and delivery of the garage in January. It ignores the $22,000 of accounts receivable, which is a near-term future cash inflow.

2. The cash basis understates the expenses incurred with the construction of the garage and the liability outstanding at the end of January. It ignores the $18,000 of accounts payable, which is a near-term future cash outflow.

3. The cash basis understates owners' equity in January by not recognizing the revenues and the asset until February, and it overstates owners' equity in February by not recognizing the expenses and the liability until March.

   In short, cash basis accounting violates the theory underlying the elements of financial statements as noted in IFRS/ASPE.

The **modified cash basis**, a mixture of cash basis and accrual basis, is the method often followed by professional services firms (doctors, lawyers, accountants, consultants) and by retail, real estate, and agricultural operations. It is the pure cash basis of accounting with modifications that have substantial support, such as capitalizing and depreciating plant assets or recording inventory.[30]

Conversion from Cash Basis to Accrual Basis

Fairly often, a cash basis or a modified cash basis set of financial statements needs to be converted to the accrual basis so it can be presented to investors and creditors. In order to do this, cash received is converted to revenues or unearned revenues and cash outlays are converted to expenses or assets.

Revenue Calculation

To convert the amount of cash received to revenue on an accrual basis, changes in accounts receivable and unearned revenue during the year must be considered. Accounts receivable at the beginning of the year represent revenues earned last year that are collected this year. Ending accounts receivable indicate revenues earned this year that are not yet collected. Therefore, beginning accounts receivable are subtracted from cash received and ending accounts receivable added to arrive at revenue on an accrual basis. **Illustration 4A.1** summarizes this.

Cash receipts from customers	(− Beginning accounts receivable) (+ Ending accounts receivable)	=	Revenue on an accrual basis

ILLUSTRATION 4A.1

Conversion of Cash Receipts to Revenue—Accounts Receivable

---

[30]A cash or modified cash basis might be used in the following situations:
1. A company that is primarily interested in cash flows (for example, a group of physicians that distributes cash-basis earnings for salaries and bonuses)
2. A company that has a limited number of financial statement users (a small, closely held company with little or no debt)
3. A company that has operations that are relatively straightforward (small amounts of inventory, long-term assets, or long-term debt)

Using similar analysis, beginning unearned service revenue represents cash received last year for revenues earned this year. Ending unearned service revenue results from collections this year that will be recognized as revenue next year. Therefore, beginning unearned service revenue is added and ending unearned service revenue is subtracted to arrive at revenue on an accrual basis, as shown in **Illustration 4A.2**.

ILLUSTRATION 4A.2

Conversion of Cash Receipts to Revenue—Unearned Service Revenue

Cash receipts from customers	(+ Beginning unearned revenue) (− Ending unearned revenue)	=	Revenue on an accrual basis

Expense Calculation

To convert cash paid for operating expenses during the year to operating expenses on an accrual basis, you must consider changes in prepaid expenses and accrued liabilities during the year. Beginning prepaid expenses should be recognized as expenses this year. (The cash payment occurred last year.) Therefore, the beginning prepaid expenses balance is added to cash paid for operating expenses to arrive at operating expense on an accrual basis.

Conversely, ending prepaid expenses result from cash payments made this year for expenses to be reported next year. (The expense recognition is deferred to a future period.) As a result, ending prepaid expenses are deducted from cash paid for expenses. **Illustration 4A.3** summarizes this.

ILLUSTRATION 4A.3

Conversion of Cash Payments to Expenses—Prepaid Expenses

Cash paid for operating expenses	(+ Beginning prepaid expenses) (− Ending prepaid expenses)	=	Expenses on an accrual basis

Using similar analysis, beginning accrued liabilities result from expenses recognized last year that require cash payments this year. Ending accrued liabilities relate to expenses recognized this year that have not been paid. Beginning accrued liabilities, therefore, are deducted and ending accrued liabilities are added to cash paid for expenses to arrive at expenses on an accrual basis, as shown in **Illustration 4A.4**.

ILLUSTRATION 4A.4

Conversion of Cash Payments to Expenses—Accrued Liabilities

Cash paid for operating expenses	(− Beginning accrued liabilities) (+ Ending accrued liabilities)	=	Expenses on an accrual basis

Let's look at an example, shown in **Example 4A.3**.

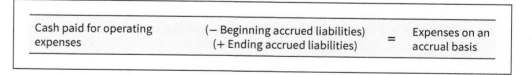

Example 4A.3 | Conversion from Cash Basis to Accrual Basis

Facts   Assume that Dr. Diane Windsor keeps her accounting records on a cash basis. In the year 2020, Dr. Windsor received $300,000 from her dental patients and paid $170,000 for operating expenses, resulting in an excess of cash receipts over disbursements of $130,000 ($300,000 − $170,000). At January 1 and December 31, 2020, she has the accounts receivable, unearned service revenue, accrued liabilities, and prepaid expenses shown below in the excerpt from the general ledger.

	Jan. 1, 2020	Dec. 31, 2020
Accounts receivable	$12,000	$9,000
Unearned revenue	–0–	4,000
Accrued liabilities	2,000	5,500
Prepaid expenses	1,800	2,700

Instructions   How would you convert the cash receipts and payments to revenues and expenses (accrual basis)?

Solution   Cash collected from customers is converted to service revenue on an accrual basis as shown below.

Cash receipts from customers		$300,000
Beginning accounts receivable	$(12,000)	
Ending accounts receivable	9,000	
Beginning unearned revenue	–0–	
Ending unearned revenue	(4,000)	(7,000)
Service revenue (accrual)		$293,000

Cash paid for operating expenses is converted to operating expenses on an accrual basis as shown below.

Cash paid for operating expenses		$170,000
Beginning prepaid expenses	$1,800	
Ending prepaid expenses	(2,700)	
Beginning accrued liabilities	(2,000)	
Ending accrued liabilities	5,500	2,600
Operating expenses (accrual)		$172,600

The chart below shows how this entire conversion can be presented in a work sheet.

Diane Windsor, D.D.S.
Conversion of Income Statement Data from Cash Basis to Accrual Basis
For the Year 2020

		Adjustments		
	Cash Basis	Add	Deduct	Accrual Basis
Collections from customers	$300,000			
– Accounts receivable, Jan. 1			$12,000	
+ Accounts receivable, Dec. 31		$9,000		
+ Unearned revenue, Jan. 1		–		
– Unearned revenue, Dec. 31			4,000	
Service revenue				$293,000
Disbursements for expenses	170,000			
+ Prepaid expenses, Jan. 1		1,800		
– Prepaid expenses, Dec. 31			2,700	
– Accrued liabilities, Jan. 1			2,000	
+ Accrued liabilities, Dec. 31		5,500		
Operating expenses				172,600
Excess of cash collections over disbursements—cash basis	$130,000			
Net income—accrual basis				$120,400

Using this approach, collections and disbursements on a cash basis are adjusted to revenue and expenses on an accrual basis to arrive at accrued net income. In any conversion from the cash basis to the accrual basis, depreciation or amortization expense is an expense in arriving at net income on an accrual basis.

Looking forward, this type of analysis is used (only in reverse) when preparing a cash flow statement. Often, when preparing a cash flow statement, the income statement is used as a starting point. Therefore, you are converting from an accrual basis to a cash basis.

Theoretical Weaknesses of the Cash Basis

The cash basis does report exactly when cash is received and when cash is disbursed. To many people, that information represents something solid, something concrete. Isn't cash what it's all about? Does it make sense to invent something, design it, produce it, market it, and sell it, if you aren't going to get cash for it in the end? If so, then what is the merit of accrual accounting?

Today's economy is based more on credit than cash. And the accrual basis, not the cash basis, recognizes all aspects of credit. Investors, creditors, and other decision-makers seek timely information about an enterprise's future cash flows. Accrual basis accounting provides this information by reporting the cash inflows and outflows associated with earnings activities as soon as these cash flows can be estimated with an acceptable degree of certainty. Receivables and payables are forecasters of future cash inflows and outflows. In other words, accrual basis accounting aids in predicting future cash flows by reporting transactions and other events with cash consequences at the time the transactions and events occur, rather than when the cash is received and paid. See Underlying Concept 4.12.

> **Underlying Concept 4.12**
>
> Accrual-based net income is a good predictor of future cash flows.

Review and Practice

Summary of Learning Objectives

1. Understand how firms create value, manage performance, and communicate useful information to users.

A business is based on a basic model of obtaining financing, investing in assets, and using those assets to generate profits. Different industries have different business models. Even within an industry, different businesses may have different strategies for generating revenues. Some businesses and industries are riskier than others. Companies must decide how and whether to manage these risks. Managing risks costs money, which reduces profits. Capital markets demand greater returns for riskier businesses.

Users use information about performance to evaluate past performance and profitability and to provide a basis for predicting future performance. They also use the information to help assess risk and uncertainty regarding future cash flows.

2. Understand the concept of and be able to assess the quality of earnings/information.

The concept of quality of earnings is used by analysts and investors to assess how well the reported income reflects the underlying business and future potential. When assessing quality of earnings, users must consider all information about a company. High-quality earnings have various attributes, as noted in Illustration 4.4. Where the information is biased, this degrades the quality.

3. Understand the differing perspectives on how to measure income.

There are various ways to measure income, including operating income, net income, and comprehensive income. IFRS recognizes the

concept of comprehensive income but this is not included under ASPE. Other comprehensive income consists of a set list of items identified under IFRS essentially dealing with certain unrealized gains/losses. Under IFRS, some of these items are recycled (reclassified) to net income and some are not.

4. Measure and report results of discontinued operations.

The gain or loss on disposal of a business component involves the sum of: (1) the income or loss from operations to the financial statement date, and (2) the gain or loss on the disposal of the business component. These items are reported net of tax among the irregular items in the income statement. Related assets are identified on the balance sheet where material. Under IFRS, non-current assets are reclassified to current assets.

5. Measure income and prepare the income statement and the statement of comprehensive income using various formats.

There are many ways to present the income statement and the statement of comprehensive income. GAAP lays out certain minimum requirements, but beyond that, a company has some leeway to present the information as it wishes. The goal is to ensure that the statements present information about performance in a transparent manner, including presenting items such that the users can see which are ordinary and which are peripheral activities. IFRS allows the statement of comprehensive income to be presented in a combined statement or two separate statements.

By convention, companies use what is known as a single-step method or a multiple-step method (or a variation of the two).

IFRS requires entities to provide information about either the nature or function of expenses. When information is presented using function, additional disclosures should be made regarding the breakdown of the nature of expenses because the latter has good cash flow predictive value. The entity should choose the method that best reflects the nature of the business and industry.

6. Prepare the statement of retained earnings and the statement of changes in equity.

The retained earnings statement should disclose net income (loss), dividends, prior period adjustments, and transfers to and from retained earnings (appropriations). This statement is required under ASPE.

The statement of changes in equity is a required statement under IFRS and takes the place of the statement of changes in retained earnings. It shows all changes in all equity accounts, including accumulated other comprehensive income.

7. Understand how disclosures and analysis help users of financial statements assess performance.

Disclosures include notes and supplementary information. They provide background and explanatory information needed to understand the business. Investors and analysts use quality of earnings analysis to help determine a company's value.

8. Identify differences in accounting between IFRS and ASPE and potential changes.

The chart in Illustration 4.20 outlines the major differences. The IASB was in the research project stages regarding financial performance reporting.

9. Explain the differences between the cash basis of accounting and the accrual basis of accounting.

Accrual basis accounting provides information about cash inflows and outflows associated with earnings activities as soon as these cash flows can be estimated with an acceptable degree of certainty. That is, accrual basis accounting aids in predicting future cash flows by reporting transactions and events with cash consequences at the time the transactions and events occur, rather than when the cash is received and paid. The cash basis focuses on when the cash is received or disbursed, and therefore it is not the best predictor of future cash flows if the company has irregular cash flow patterns.

Practice Problem

Presented below are income statement items from Braunfeld Limited for the year ended December 31, 2020. Assume Braunfeld follow IFRS.

Sales revenue	$2,700,000
Cost of goods sold	1,150,000
Interest revenue	15,000
Loss from abandonment of plant assets	45,000
Gain from extinguishment of debt	28,000
Selling and administrative expenses	480,000
Effect of change in estimated useful lives of fixed assets	35,000
Loss from earthquake	30,000
Gain on disposal of discontinued operation	50,000

Instructions

Using the information above, prepare a statement of financial performance. Assume a tax rate of 30% and 100,000 ordinary shares outstanding during 2020. Assume Braunfeld had an unrealized holding loss on FV-OCI securities of $12,000, net of tax.

Solution

Braunfeld Limited
Statement of Comprehensive Income
For the Year Ended December 31, 2020

Sales revenue		$2,700,000
Cost of goods sold		1,150,000
Gross profit		1,550,000
Selling and administrative expenses		480,000
		1,070,000
Other income and expense		
Interest revenue	$ 15,000	
Gain on debt extinguishment	28,000	
Loss from plant abandonment	(45,000)	
Loss from earthquake	(30,000)	(32,000)

(continued)

Braunfeld Limited
Statement of Financial Performance
For the Year Ended December 31, 2020 (*cont.*)

Income from operations		1,038,000
Income tax (30%)		311,400
Income from continuing operations		726,600
Discontinued operations		
Gain on disposal of discontinued operation	50,000	
Less: Applicable income tax	15,000	35,000
Net income		761,600
Unrealized holding loss on FV-OCI equity securities, net of tax		
(will not be subsequently reclassified)		12,000
Comprehensive income		$ 749,600
Earnings per ordinary share:		
Income from continuing operations		$ 7.27
From discontinued operations		0.35
Discontinued operations		$ 7.62

Key Terms

accrual basis, p. 4-39	function, p. 4-28	risk management, p. 4-4
all-inclusive approach, p. 4-12	held for sale, p. 4-15	risk/return trade-off, p. 4-4
business model, p. 4-3	income statement, p. 4-3	single-step income statement, p. 4-23
changes in accounting principle, p. 4-33	intraperiod tax allocation, p. 4-30	statement of changes in equity, p. 4-32
component of an enterprise, p. 4-14	modified cash basis, p. 4-41	statement of comprehensive income,
comprehensive income, p. 4-12	multiple-step income statement, p. 4-25	p. 4-3
current operating performance	nature, p. 4-28	statement of financial performance,
approach, p. 4-12	net income, p. 4-12	p. 4-3
discontinued operations, p. 4-14	non-GAAP earnings, p. 4-36	statement of income/earnings, p. 4-3
earnings management, p. 4-10	operating income, p. 4-12	statement of profit or loss, p. 4-3
earnings multiple, p. 4-37	other comprehensive income (OCI), p. 4-12	statement of retained earnings, p. 4-32
earnings per share (EPS), 4-31	quality of earnings, p. 4-8	strict cash basis, p. 4-39

Assignment Material

Note: All assignment material with an asterisk (*) relates to the appendix to the chapter.

Enabling Competencies Completion of this end-of-chapter material will help develop CPA-enabling competencies (such as ethics and professionalism, problem-solving and decision-making, and communication) and technical competencies. We have highlighted selected items with a specific integration word mark and material in *WileyPLUS* has been linked to the competencies. All cases emphasize integration, especially of the enabling competencies. The brief exercises, exercises, and problems generally emphasize problem-solving and decision-making.

Brief Exercises

BE4.1 (LO 1) Sunmart Inc. is a discount retailer with 1,000 stores across North America. Sunmart purchases bulk quantities of groceries and household goods, and then sells the goods directly to retail customers at a markup. Pharmedical Inc. is a pharmaceutical company that develops medications to prevent and treat diseases. Pharmedical develops, produces, and markets medications for purchase by patients of health care professionals and customers of retail pharmacies and stores. Referring to each company's business model, which company would have (a) a higher gross profit percentage, (b) a higher selling

expense as a percentage of sales, (c) a higher research and development expense as a percentage of sales, and (d) higher net income?

BE4.2 (LO 1) **Audit** Obtain the auditor's reports for TELUS Corporation. Identify and read the opinion paragraph. Explain why it is important for auditors to understand the business model and business environment (including the nature of the industry) before they can render an audit opinion. (*Hint:* Refer back to the discussion in Chapter 2.)

BE4.3 (LO 1) **Audit** What is the purpose of a financial audit? (*Hint:* Search "financial audit" on Wikipedia.)

BE4.4 (LO 1, 2) Several of Kimper Corporation's major customers experienced cash flow problems in 2020, mainly due to their increasing labour and production costs in 2019 and 2020. As a result, Kimper's accounts receivable turnover ratio (net sales revenue/average trade receivables [net]) decreased significantly in 2020. However, Kimper believes that its customers' cash flow problems are temporary. In estimating uncollectible accounts receivable as at December 31, 2020, Kimper decreased the estimated percentage of its outstanding accounts receivable that will become uncollectible. (A lower percentage was applied in 2020 than was applied in the previous five years.) Kimper's bad debt expense as a percentage of sales for the year ended December 31, 2020, was lower than the percentage reported in the previous five years, and no additional note disclosure regarding potentially higher risk of uncollectible accounts was reported. Based only on the information above, (a) evaluate the quality of information provided by Kimper and (b) show whether the earnings reported by Kimper will be discounted in the capital markets.

BE4.5 (LO 2) Environmental Corporation specializes in the production and sale of ecofriendly packaging. In 2020, Environmental reported net income (earnings) in excess of analyst expectations. This included a significant gain on disposal of investments in the year and lower depreciation expense due to the company's change from the declining-balance method (used by competitors) to the straight-line method for depreciating its equipment. Answer the following questions based only on the information provided. (a) From the perspective of an investor, does Environmental have high-quality earnings? (b) Will the earnings reported by Environmental be discounted in the capital markets?

BE4.6 (LO 2) **Ethics** Cyan Corporation is a manufacturer of paints and specialty coatings. In March 2020, Beck Inc. filed a lawsuit against Cyan Corporation for alleged patent infringement, claiming $1.1 million in damages. Cyan's lawyer disputed the claim, but in December 2020, Cyan's lawyer informed management that Cyan will likely lose the dispute and have to pay between $900,000 and $1.1 million. Dissatisfied with this estimate and its potential impact on 2020 net income, Cyan's management sought a second legal opinion in December 2020. The lawyer who provided the second opinion suggested that Cyan will likely have to pay between $400,000 and $600,000. In its financial statements for the year ended December 31, 2020, Cyan recorded a provision for a loss on the lawsuit and a liability in the amount of $500,000. Answer the following questions based only on the information provided. (a) Does Cyan have high-quality earnings? (b) Will the earnings reported by Cyan be discounted in the capital markets?

BE4.7 (LO 3) On January 1, 2020, Twist Corp. had cash and common shares of $60,000. At that date, the company had no other asset, liability, or shareholders' equity balances. On January 2, 2020, Twist paid $40,000 cash for equity securities that it designated as fair value through other comprehensive income (FV-OCI) investments. During the year, Twist received non-taxable cash dividends of $18,000 and had an unrealized holding gain of $25,000 (net of tax) on these securities. Determine the following amounts for 2020: (a) net income, (b) other comprehensive income, (c) comprehensive income, and (d) accumulated other comprehensive income (as at the end of 2020).

BE4.8 (LO 3, 8) Delray Inc. follows IFRS and has the following amounts for the year ended December 31, 2020: gain on disposal of FV-NI investments (before tax), $15,000; loss from operation of discontinued division (net of tax), $42,000; income from operations (before tax), $220,000; unrealized holding gain-OCI (net of tax), $12,000; income tax on income from continuing operations, $63,000; loss on disposal of discontinued division (net of tax), $75,000. The unrealized holding gain-OCI relates to investments that are not quoted in an active market. (a) Calculate income from continuing operations. (b) Calculate net income. (c) Calculate other comprehensive income. (d) Calculate comprehensive income. (e) How would your answers to parts (a) to (d) be different if Delray followed ASPE?

BE4.9 (LO 4) Billy's Burgers (BB) is a franchisor that operates several corporate-owned restaurants as well as several franchised restaurants. The franchisees pay 3% of their sales revenues to BB in return for advertising and support. During the year, BB sold its corporate-owned stores to a franchisee. BB continues to monitor quality in its franchised operations and franchisees must buy all products from it. The corporate-owned stores are not considered a separate major line of business. Would the sale qualify for discontinued operations treatment?

BE4.10 (LO 4, 8) Argon Noble Limited has approved a formal plan to sell its head office tower to an outside party. A detailed plan has been approved by the board of directors. The building is on the books at $50 million (net book value). The estimated selling price is $49 million. The company will continue to use the building until the construction of the new head office is complete. Construction has not yet started on the new building, but the company has begun to look for a buyer. (a) Should Argon Noble present its existing head office tower as held for sale? (b) Assume it is now two years later and construction of the new building is complete. The company has moved into the new building. How would the old building be presented on the income statement and statement of financial position under both ASPE and IFRS? The book value of the old building is now $45 million and the fair value is $42 million.

BE4.11 (LO 4, 8) Mega Inc.'s manufacturing division lost $100,000 (net of tax) for the year ended December 31, 2020, and Mega estimates that it can sell the division at a loss of $200,000 (net of tax). The division qualifies for treatment as a discontinued operation. (a) Explain how the discontinued operation would be measured and presented on the income statement and statement of financial position under ASPE. (b) Explain how your answer to part (a) would be different if Mega prepared financial statements in accordance with IFRS.

 BE4.12 (LO 5, 7) Sierra Corporation had sales revenue of $5,850,000 and investment revenue of $227,000 for the year ended December 31, 2020. Other items pertaining to 2020 were as follows:

Cost of goods sold	$4,610,000
Salaries and wages expense (sales)	368,000
Advertising expense	126,000
Entertainment expense	78,000
Selling expenses	572,000
Salaries and wages expense (administrative)	300,000
Rent expense	101,000
Utilities expense	44,000
Administrative expenses	445,000
Increase in value of company reputation	74,000
Unrealized gain on value of patents	36,000
Interest expense	160,000
Income tax expense	84,000

Sierra has 100,000 common shares outstanding throughout the year. Prepare a single-step income statement showing expenses by nature. Include calculation of EPS.

BE4.13 (LO 5, 7) (a) Use the information in BE4.12 to prepare a multiple-step income statement for Sierra Corporation, showing expenses by function. (b) Assume the average market price for the common shares is $66. What is Sierra's price-earnings ratio?

BE4.14 (LO 5, 7) The Blue Collar Corporation had income from continuing operations of $12.6 million in 2020. During 2020, it disposed of its restaurant division at a loss of $89,000 (net of tax of $38,000). Before the disposal, the division operated at a loss of $315,000 (net of tax of $135,000) in 2020. Blue Collar also had an unrealized gain-OCI of $43,000 (net of tax of $18,000) related to its FV-OCI equity investments. Blue Collar had 10 million common shares outstanding during 2020. Prepare a partial statement of financial performance for Blue Collar, beginning with income from continuing operations. Include calculation and disclosure of EPS.

BE4.15 (LO 5, 7) The Big and Rich Corporation had income from operations before tax for 2020 of $4.4 million. In addition, it suffered an unusual and infrequent loss of $1,060,000 from a tornado. Of this amount, $300,000 was insured. In addition, the company realized a loss from the disposal of a building amounting to $150,000. The corporation's tax rate is 30%. Prepare a partial income statement for Big and Rich, beginning with income from operations. The corporation had 2 million common shares outstanding during 2020. Include calculation and disclosure of EPS.

 BE4.16 (LO 6) Parfait Limited reported the following for 2020: sales revenue, $900,000; cost of sales, $750,000; operating expenses, $100,000; and unrealized gain on FV-OCI investments, $60,000. The company had January 1, 2020 balances as follows: common shares, $600,000; accumulated other comprehensive income, $250,000; and retained earnings, $900,000. The company did not issue any shares during 2020. On December 15, 2020, the board of directors declared a $300,000 dividend payable on January 31, 2021. Prepare a statement of changes in equity. Ignore income tax.

BE4.17 (LO 6) Global Corporation prepares financial statements in accordance with ASPE. At January 1, 2020, the company had retained earnings of $1,038,000. In 2020, net income was $335,000, and cash

dividends of $70,000 were declared and paid. Prepare a 2020 statement of retained earnings for Global Corporation.

BE4.18 (LO 6) Use the information in BE4.17 to prepare a statement of retained earnings for Global Corporation, assuming that in 2020, Global discovered that it had overstated 2017 depreciation by $40,000 (net of tax of $17,000).

BE4.19 (LO 7) Neon Limited had 40,000 common shares on January 1, 2020. On April 1, 8,000 shares were repurchased. On August 31, 12,000 shares were issued. Calculate the number of shares outstanding at December 31, 2020, and the weighted average number of shares for 2020.

BE4.20 (LO 7) In 2020, I & T Corporation reported net income of $8.6 million, and declared and paid preferred share dividends of $3.2 million. During 2020, I & T had a weighted average of 900,000 common shares outstanding. Calculate I & T's 2020 earnings per share.

***BE4.21 (LO 9)** In 2020, Renato Corp. had cash receipts from customers of $152,000 and cash payments for operating expenses of $97,000. At January 1, 2020, accounts receivable were $13,000 and total prepaid expenses were $17,500. At December 31, 2020, accounts receivable were $18,600 and total prepaid expenses were $23,200. Calculate (a) total service revenue and (b) total operating expenses.

Exercises

E4.1 (LO 3) (Comprehensive Income) Reach Out Card Company Limited reported the following for 2020: sales revenue, $1.2 million; cost of goods sold, $750,000; selling and administrative expenses, $320,000; gain on disposal of building, $250,000; and unrealized gain-OCI (related to FV-OCI equity investments with gains/losses not recycled), $18,000.

Instructions

Prepare a statement of comprehensive income. Ignore income tax and EPS. Assume investments are accounted for as FV-OCI equity investments, with gains/losses not recycled through net income.

E4.2 (LO 3, 8) (Comprehensive Income) Pike Corporation, a clothing retailer, had income from operations (before tax) of $375,000, and recorded the following before-tax gains/(losses) for the year ended December 31, 2020:

Gain on disposal of equipment	27,000
Unrealized (loss)/gain on FV-NI investments	(54,000)
(Loss)/gain on disposal of building	(68,000)
Gain on disposal of FV-NI investments	33,000

Pike also had the following account balances as at January 1, 2020:

Retained earnings	$410,000
Accumulated other comprehensive income (this was due to a revaluation surplus on land)	74,000
Accumulated other comprehensive income (this was due to gains on FV-OCI debt investments)	55,000

As at January 1, 2020, Pike had one piece of land that had an original cost of $142,000 that it accounted for using the revaluation model. It was most recently revalued to fair value on December 31, 2019, when its carrying amount was adjusted to fair value of $216,000. In January 2020, the piece of land was sold for proceeds of $216,000. In applying the revaluation model, Pike maintains the balance in the Revaluation Surplus (OCI) account until the asset is retired or disposed of.

In 2015, Pike purchased a portfolio of debt investments that the company intended to hold for the longer term and it classified the portfolio of investments as fair value through other comprehensive income (FV-OCI) with gains/losses recycled through net income. The investments in the portfolio are traded in an active market. Pike records unrealized gains and losses on these investments as OCI, and then books these gains and losses to net income when they are impaired or sold. The portfolio's carrying amount on December 31, 2019, was $110,000. The entire portfolio was sold in November 2020 for proceeds of $126,000.

Pike's income tax expense for 2020 was $99,000. Pike prepares financial statements in accordance with IFRS.

Instructions

a. Calculate net income for the year ended December 31, 2020.

b. Calculate retained earnings as at December 31, 2020.

c. Explain the change in accumulated other comprehensive income in 2020.

d. Calculate net income for the year ended December 31, 2020, and retained earnings as at December 31, 2020, if Pike prepares financial statements in accordance with ASPE. Assume that under ASPE, Pike's retained earnings at January 1, 2020, would be $465,000, and that Pike's income tax expense would not change.

e. Will the sum of the Accumulated Other Comprehensive Income and Retained Earnings under IFRS equal the balance of Retained Earnings under ASPE at December 31, 2020? Prepare a continuity schedule of the related accounts to demonstrate your answer.

E4.3 (LO 4, 8) **(Discontinued Operations)** Assume that Elrond Inc. decided to sell DemandTV Ltd., a subsidiary, on September 30, 2020. There is a formal plan to dispose of the business component, and the sale qualifies for discontinued operations treatment. Pertinent data on the operations of the TV subsidiary are as follows: loss from operations from beginning of year to September 30, $1.9 million (net of tax of $700,000); loss from operations from September 30 to end of 2020, $700,000 (net of tax of $250,000); estimated loss on disposal of net assets to December 31, 2020 (net of tax of $50,000), $150,000. The year end is December 31. Elrond prepares financial statements in accordance with IFRS.

Instructions

a. What is the net income/loss from discontinued operations reported in 2020?

b. Prepare the discontinued operations section of the income statement for the year ended 2020.

c. If the amount reported in 2020 as a gain or loss on disposal of the subsidiary becomes materially incorrect, when and how is the correction reported, if at all?

d. How would the discontinued operation be presented on the statement of financial position?

e. How would your answer to part (d) be different if Elrond prepared financial statements in accordance with ASPE?

 E4.4 (LO 4, 8) **(Discontinued Operations)** On October 5, 2020, Diamond in the Rough Recruiting Group Inc.'s board of directors decided to dispose of the Blue Division. A formal plan was approved. Diamond derives approximately 75% of its income from its human resources management practice. The Blue Division gets contracts to perform human resources management on an outsourced basis. The board decided to dispose of the division because of unfavourable operating results.

Net income for Diamond was $91,000 for the fiscal year ended December 31, 2020 (after a charge for tax at 30% and after a writedown for the Blue assets). Income from operations of the Blue Division accounted for $4,200 (after tax) of this amount.

Because of the unfavourable results and the extreme competition, the board believes that it cannot sell the business intact. Its final decision is to auction off the office equipment. The equipment is the division's only asset and has a carrying value of $25,000 at October 5, 2020. The board believes that proceeds from the sale will be approximately $5,000 after the auction expenses. Currently, the equipment's estimated fair value is $8,000. The Blue Division qualifies for treatment as a discontinued operation. Diamond prepares financial statements in accordance with ASPE.

Instructions

a. Prepare a partial income statement for Diamond in the Rough Recruiting Group and the appropriate footnote that relates to the Blue Division for 2020. The income statement should begin with income from continuing operations before income tax.

b. Explain how the assets would be valued and presented on the statement of financial position.

c. Explain how the assets would be valued and presented on the statement of financial position if Diamond prepared financial statements in accordance with IFRS.

d. **Digging Deeper** From the perspective of an investor, comment on Diamond's quality of earnings if Diamond presented the Blue Division as a discontinued operation but did not have a formal plan in place to dispose of the division.

E4.5 (LO 5) **(Calculation of Net Income)** The following are all changes in the account balances of Chili Lime Ltd. during the current year, except for Retained Earnings:

	Increase (Decrease)		Increase (Decrease)
Cash	$ 76,000	Accounts payable	$(64,000)
Accounts receivable (net)	59,000	Unearned revenue	18,000
Inventory	140,000	Bonds payable	69,000
Investments in FV-NI securities	(23,000)	Common shares	105,000
		Contributed surplus	63,000

Instructions

Calculate the net income for the current year, assuming that there were no entries in the Retained Earnings account except for net income and a dividend declaration of $16,000, which was paid in the current year.

E4.6 (LO 5) (Calculation of Net Income) Videohound Video Company, a sole proprietorship, had the following information for 2020:

Cash balance, January 1	$ 23,000	Total assets, December 31	$101,000
Accounts receivable, January 1	19,000	Cash balance, December 31	20,000
Collections from customers		Accounts receivable,	
during year	200,000	December 31	36,000
Capital account balance,		Merchandise taken for	
January 1	38,000	personal use	11,000
Total assets, January 1	75,000	Total liabilities, December 31	41,000
Cash investment by sole			
proprietor, July 1	5,000		

Instructions

Calculate the net income for 2020.

E4.7 (LO 5) (Income Statement Items) Certain account balances follow for Vincenti Products Corp., which follows ASPE:

Rent revenue	$ 8,500	Sales discounts	$ 17,800
Interest expense	2,700	Selling expenses	79,400
Beginning retained earnings	114,400	Sales revenue	490,000
Ending retained earnings	74,000	Income tax expense	100
Dividend revenue	91,000	Cost of goods sold	384,400
Sales returns and allowances	22,400	Administrative expenses	82,500

Instructions

Based on the balances, calculate the following:

a. Total net revenue

b. Net income or loss

c. Dividends declared during the current year

E4.8 (LO 5) (Multiple-Step and Single-Step—Periodic Inventory Method) Income statement information for Flett Tire Repair Corporation for the year 2020 follows:

General and administrative expenses:		Freight in	$ 14,000
Salaries and wages expense	$ 39,000	Purchase discounts	10,000
Depreciation expense—building	28,500	Dividend revenue	20,000
Office supplies expense	9,500	Inventory (beginning)	120,000
Inventory (ending)	137,000	Sales returns and allowances	15,000
Loss from flood damage	50,000	Service expenses:	
Gain on the disposal of equipment	5,500	Salaries and wages	71,000
Purchases	600,000	Depreciation expense—	
Sales revenue	930,000	garage equipment	18,000
Interest expense	9,000	Garage supplies expense	9,000

The effective tax rate on all income is 25%, and Flett follows ASPE.

Instructions

a. Prepare a multiple-step income statement for 2020, showing expenses by function.

b. Prepare a single-step income statement for 2020, showing expenses by nature.

c. Discuss the merits of the two income statements, compared with each other.

E4.9 (LO 5) **(Combined Single-Step)** The following information was taken from the records of Biscay Inc. for the year 2020:

Gain from expropriation	$300,000	Cash dividends declared	$ 220,000
Loss from operation of discontinued		Retained earnings,	
Rochelle Division	240,000	January 1, 2020	1,900,000
Administrative expenses	750,000	Cost of goods sold	2,680,000
Rent revenue	130,000	Selling expenses	950,000
Loss from flood damage	190,000	Sales revenue	6,000,000

The following additional information was also available: income tax applicable to income from continuing operations, $465,000; income tax recovery applicable to loss from operation of discontinued Rochelle Division, $60,000.

The company has elected to adopt ASPE.

Instructions

a. Prepare a single-step income statement for 2020, showing expenses by function.

b. Prepare a combined single-step income and retained earnings statement.

E4.10 (LO 5, 6, 8) **(Multiple-Step Statement, Statement of Comprehensive Income, and Statement of Changes in Equity)** The following is information for Gottlieb Corp. for the year ended December 31, 2020:

Sales revenue	$1,300,000	Loss on inventory due to decline in net	
Unrealized gain on FV-OCI		realizable value	$ 80,000
equity investments	42,000	Loss on disposal of equipment	35,000
Interest income	7,000	Depreciation expense related to	
Cost of goods sold	780,000	buildings omitted by mistake in 2019	55,000
Selling expenses	65,000	Retained earnings at December 31, 2019	980,000
Administrative expenses	48,000	Loss from expropriation of land	60,000
Dividend revenue	20,000	Dividends declared	45,000

The effective tax rate is 25% on all items. Gottlieb prepares financial statements in accordance with IFRS. The FV-OCI equity investments trade on the stock exchange. Gains/losses on FV-OCI investments are not recycled through net income.

Instructions

a. Prepare a multiple-step statement of financial performance for 2020, showing expenses by function. Ignore calculation of EPS.

b. Prepare the retained earnings section of the statement of changes in equity for 2020.

c. Prepare the journal entry to record the depreciation expense omitted by mistake in 2019.

d. How should Gottlieb account for the unrealized gain on FV-OCI investments if it prepares financial statements in accordance with ASPE? How would Gottlieb's retained earnings balance at December 31, 2019 be different if financial statements in all previous years had been prepared in accordance with ASPE?

E4.11 (LO 5) **(Single-Step Income Statement)** The financial records of Geneva Inc. were destroyed by fire at the end of 2020. Fortunately, the controller had kept the following statistical data related to the income statement:

1. The beginning inventory was $84,000 and it decreased by 20% during the current year.

2. There were 15,000 common shares outstanding for the entire year.

3. Interest expense was $35,000.

4. The income tax rate was 25%.

5. Cost of goods sold amounted to $420,000.

6. Administrative expenses were 20% of cost of goods sold but only 4% of gross sales.

7. Selling expenses were four fifths of cost of goods sold.

Instructions

Based on the available data:

a. Prepare a single-step income statement for the year ended December 31, 2020, including calculation of EPS. Expenses should be shown by function.

b. Assume the average market price for the common shares is $980. What is Geneva's price-earnings ratio?

E4.12 (LO 5, 7) `Excel` **(Multiple-Step and Single-Step)** Two accountants, Yuan Tsui and Sergio Aragon, are arguing about the merits of presenting an income statement in the multiple-step versus the single-step format. The discussion involves the following 2020 information for P. Bride Company (in thousands):

Administrative expenses		Selling expenses	
Officers' salaries	$ 4,900	Delivery	$ 2,690
Depreciation of office furniture		Sales commissions	7,980
and equipment	3,960	Depreciation of sales equipment	6,480
Cost of goods sold	60,570	Sales revenue	96,500
Rental revenue	17,230	Interest expense	1,860

Common shares outstanding for 2020 total 30,550. Income tax for the year was $9,070.

Instructions

a. Prepare an income statement for the year ended December 31, 2020, using the multiple-step format. Include calculation of EPS.

b. Prepare an income statement for the year ended December 31, 2020, using the single-step format. Include calculation of EPS.

c. `Digging Deeper` From the perspective of an investor who is interested in information about operating versus non-operating items and the various areas of the company's operations, which format is preferred? Explain why.

E4.13 (LO 5) **(Multiple-Step and Unusual Items)** The following balances were taken from the books of Quality Fabrication Limited on December 31, 2020:

Interest income	$ 70,000	Accumulated depreciation—equipment	$ 32,000
Cash	40,000	Accumulated depreciation—buildings	23,000
Sales revenue	1,120,000	Notes receivable	125,000
Accounts receivable	122,000	Selling expenses	160,000
Prepaid insurance	16,000	Accounts payable	140,000
Sales returns and allowances	118,000	Bonds payable	81,000
Allowance for doubtful accounts	6,000	Administrative expenses	80,000
Sales discounts	40,000	Unearned revenue	16,000
Land	80,000	Interest expense	50,000
Equipment	160,000	Notes payable	80,000
Buildings	115,000	Loss from storm damage	124,000
Cost of goods sold	504,000	Depreciation expense	50,000

Assume the total effective tax rate on all items is 25%.

Instructions

Prepare a multiple-step income statement showing expenses by function. Assume that 150,000 common shares were outstanding during the year. Quality Fabrication Limited follows ASPE but decides to disclose EPS on its income statement.

E4.14 (LO 5) **(Condensed Income Statement—Periodic Inventory Method)** The following are selected ledger accounts of Holland Rose Corporation at December 31, 2020:

Cash	$ 185,000	Entertainment expense	$ 69,000
Inventory (as at Jan. 1, 2020)	535,000	Office expense	33,000
Sales revenue	4,275,000	Insurance expense	24,000
Unearned revenue	117,000	Advertising expense	54,000
Purchases	2,786,000	Freight out	93,000
Sales discounts	34,000	Depreciation expense of office	
Purchase discounts	27,000	equipment	48,000
Salaries and wages expense		Depreciation expense of sales	
(sales)	284,000	equipment	36,000

(*continued*)

Salaries and wages expense		Telephone and Internet expense	
(administrative)	$346,000	(sales)	$17,000
Purchase returns and allowances	15,000	Utilities expense (administrative)	32,000
Sales returns and allowances	79,000	Miscellaneous expense	8,000
Freight in	72,000	Rental revenue	240,000
Accounts receivable	142,500	Loss on disposal of equipment	70,000
Sales commission expense	83,000	Interest expense	176,000
		Common shares	900,000

Holland Rose's effective tax rate on all items is 25%. A physical inventory shows that the ending inventory is $686,000. The number of common shares outstanding is 90,000.

Instructions

Prepare a multiple-step 2020 income statement for Holland Rose Corporation, showing expenses by function. Holland Rose follows ASPE but decides to disclose EPS on its income statement.

E4.15 (LO 6) `Excel` **(Statement of Retained Earnings)** Eddie Zambrano Corporation, a private company, began operations on January 1, 2017. During its first three years of operations, Zambrano reported net income and declared dividends as follows:

	Net income	Dividends declared
2017	$ 40,000	$ –0–
2018	125,000	50,000
2019	160,000	50,000

The following information is for 2020:

Income before income tax	$240,000
Correction of prior period error: understatement of 2018 depreciation expense (before tax)	25,000
Cumulative increase in prior years' income from change in inventory method (before tax)	35,000
Dividends declared (of this amount, $25,000 will be paid on January 15, 2021)	100,000
Effective tax rate	40%

Instructions

Prepare a 2020 statement of retained earnings for Eddie Zambrano Corporation. The company follows ASPE.

E4.16 (LO 6) (Comprehensive Income) Rainy Day Umbrella Corporation had the following balances at December 31, 2019 (all amounts in thousands): preferred shares, $3,375; common shares, $8,903; contributed surplus, $3,744; retained earnings, $23,040; and accumulated other comprehensive income, $2,568.

During the year ended December 31, 2020, the company earned net income of $7,320,000, generated an unrealized holding gain on FV-OCI investments of $585,000, sold common shares of $285,000, and paid out dividends of $30,000 and $20,000 to preferred and common shareholders, respectively.

Instructions

Prepare a statement of changes in equity for the year ended December 31, 2020, as well as the shareholders' equity section of the Rainy Day Umbrella Corporation statement of financial position as at December 31, 2020. Gains/losses on FV-OCI investments are not recycled through net income.

E4.17 (LO 7) (Earnings per Share) The shareholders' equity section of Cadmium Corporation as at December 31, 2020, follows:

8% cumulative preferred shares, 100,000 shares authorized, 80,000 shares outstanding	$ 4,500,000
Common shares, 10 million shares authorized and issued	10,000,000
Contributed surplus	10,500,000
	25,000,000
Retained earnings	177,000,000
	$202,000,000

Net income of $24 million for 2020 reflects a total effective tax rate of 25%. Included in the net income figure is a loss of $15 million (before tax) relating to the operations of a business segment that is to be discontinued.

Instructions

Calculate earnings per share information as it should appear in the financial statements of Cadmium Corporation for the year ended December 31, 2020.

E4.18 (LO 7) (Earnings per Share) At December 31, 2020, Tres Hombres Corporation had the following shares outstanding:

10% cumulative preferred shares, 107,500 shares outstanding	$10,750,000
Common shares, 4,000,000 shares outstanding	20,000,000

During 2020, the corporation's only share transaction was the issuance of 400,000 common shares on April 1. During 2020, the following also occurred:

Income from continuing operations before tax	$23,650,000
Discontinued operations (loss before tax)	3,225,000
Preferred dividends declared	1,075,000
Common dividends declared	2,200,000
Effective tax rate	30%

Instructions

Calculate earnings per share information as it should appear in the financial statements of Tres Hombres Corporation for the year ended December 31, 2020.

*E4.19 (LO 9) (Cash and Accrual Basis) In its first year of operations, 2020, Strats Corp. invoiced $172,000 in service revenue. Of that amount, $18,000 was still owing from customers at the end of year. In 2020, Strats incurred various operating expenses totalling $81,000, of which $77,500 was paid in cash. Salaries and wages paid to employees totalled $61,500 and $2,500 was still owing at the end of the year. In addition, Strats prepaid $4,000 for insurance coverage that covered the last half of 2020 and the first half of 2021. Strats estimates it will owe $9,000 in income tax when it files its corporate income tax return after its 2020 year end.

Instructions

a. Calculate the net income for 2020 under the accrual basis of accounting.

b. Calculate the net income for 2020 under the cash basis of accounting.

c. Which basis of accounting (accrual or cash) gives the most useful information for decision-makers? Explain.

*E4.20 (LO 9) (Cash and Accrual Basis) Canviar Corp. maintains its financial records using the cash basis of accounting. Because it would like to secure a long-term loan from its bank, the company asks you, as an independent CPA, to convert its cash basis income statement information to the accrual basis. You are provided with the following summarized data for 2018, 2019, and 2020:

	2018	2019	2020
Cash receipts from sales:			
On 2018 sales	$320,000	$160,000	$ 30,000
On 2019 sales	–0–	355,000	90,000
On 2020 sales	–0–	–0–	408,000
Cash payments for expenses:			
On 2018 expenses	185,000	67,000	25,000
On 2019 expenses	40,000[a]	135,000	55,000
On 2020 expenses	–0–	45,000[b]	218,000

[a]Prepayments of 2019 expenses
[b]Prepayments of 2020 expenses

Instructions

Using the information above, prepare abbreviated income statements for the years 2018 and 2019, using:

a. the cash basis of accounting and

b. the accrual basis of accounting.

Problems

P4.1 Ethics In recent years, Grace Inc. has reported steadily increasing income. The company reported income of $20,000 in 2017, $25,000 in 2018, and $30,000 in 2019. Several market analysts have recommended that investors buy Grace Inc. shares because they expect the steady growth in income to continue. Grace is approaching the end of its 2020 fiscal year, and it looks to be a good year once again. However, it has not yet recorded warranty expense.

Based on prior experience, this year's warranty expense should be around $5,000, but some members of top management have approached the controller to suggest that a larger, more conservative warranty expense should be recorded this year. Income before warranty expense is $43,000. Specifically, by recording an $8,000 warranty accrual this year, Grace could report an income increase for this year and still be in a position to cover its warranty costs in future years.

Instructions

a. What is earnings management?

b. What would be the effect of the proposed accounting in 2020? In 2021?

c. What is the appropriate accounting in this situation?

d. **Digging Deeper** Discuss the effect of the proposed accounting on a potential investor's decision to invest in the company.

P4.2 On November 1, 2019, Campbell Corporation management decided to discontinue operation of its Rocketeer Division and approved a formal plan to dispose of the division. Campbell is a successful corporation with earnings of $150 million or more before tax for each of the past five years. The Rocketeer Division, a major part of Campbell's operations, is being discontinued because it has not contributed to this profitable performance.

The division's main assets are the land, building, and equipment used to manufacture engine components. The land, building, and equipment had a net book value of $42 million on November 1, 2019.

Campbell's management has entered into negotiations for a cash sale of the division for $36 million (net of costs to sell). The sale date and final disposal date of the division is expected to be July 1, 2020. Campbell Corporation has a fiscal year ending May 31. The results of operations for the Rocketeer Division for the 2019–20 fiscal year and the estimated results for June 2020 are presented below. The before-tax losses after October 31, 2019, are calculated without depreciation on the building and equipment.

Period	Before-Tax Loss
June 1, 2019, to October 31, 2019	$(2,500,000)
November 1, 2019, to May 31, 2020	(1,600,000)
June 1 to 30, 2020 (estimated)	(300,000)

The Rocketeer Division will be accounted for as a discontinued operation on Campbell's financial statements for the year ended May 31, 2020. Campbell's tax rate is 25% on operating income and all gains and losses. Campbell prepares financial statements in accordance with IFRS.

Instructions

a. Explain how the Rocketeer Division's assets would be reported on Campbell Corporation's statement of financial position as at May 31, 2020.

b. Explain how the discontinued operations and pending sale of the Rocketeer Division would be reported on Campbell Corporation's income statement for the year ended May 31, 2020.

c. On July 5, 2020, Campbell Corporation disposes of the division's assets at an adjusted price of $40 million. Explain how the discontinued operations and sale of the Rocketeer Division would be reported on Campbell Corporation's income statement for the year ended May 31, 2021. Assume the June 2020 operating loss is the same as estimated.

d. **Digging Deeper** Assume that Campbell Corporation management was debating whether the sale of the Rocketeer Division qualified for discontinued operations accounting treatment under IFRS. List specific factors or arguments that management would use to suggest that the Rocketeer Division should be treated as a discontinued operation. Why might management have a particular preference about which treatment is given? From an external user's perspective, what relevance does the presentation of the discontinued operation have when interpreting the financial results?

P4.3 Information for 2020 follows for Rolling Thunder Corp.:

Retained earnings, January 1, 2020	$ 1,980,000
Sales revenue	36,500,000
Cost of goods sold	28,500,000
Interest income	170,000
Selling and administrative expenses	4,700,000
Unrealized gain on FV-OCI equity investments (gains/losses not recycled)	320,000
Loss on impairment of goodwill	520,000
Income tax on continuing operations for 2020 (assume this is correct)	797,500
Assessment for additional income tax for 2018 (normal, recurring, and not caused by an error)	500,000
Gain on disposal of FV-NI investments	110,000
Loss from flood damage	390,000
Loss on disposal of discontinued division (net of tax of $87,500)	262,500
Loss from operation of discontinued division (net of tax of $55,000)	165,000
Dividends declared on common shares	250,000
Dividends declared on preferred shares	70,000

Rolling Thunder decided to discontinue its entire wholesale division (a major line of business) and to keep its manufacturing division. On September 15, it sold the wholesale division to Dylane Corp. During 2020, there were 800,000 common shares outstanding all year. Rolling Thunder's tax rate is 25% on operating income and all gains and losses (use this rate where the tax provisions are not given). Rolling Thunder prepares financial statements in accordance with IFRS.

Instructions

Prepare a multiple-step statement of financial performance for the year ended December 31, 2020, showing expenses by function. Include calculation of EPS.

P4.4 **Excel** Wavecrest Inc. reported income from continuing operations before tax of $1,790,000 during 2020. Additional transactions occurring in 2020 but not included in the $1,790,000 were as follows:

1. The corporation experienced an insured flood loss of $80,000 during the year.

2. At the beginning of 2018, the corporation purchased a machine for $54,000 (residual value of $9,000) that has a useful life of six years. The bookkeeper used straight-line depreciation for 2018, 2019, and 2020, but failed to deduct the residual value in calculating the depreciable amount.

3. The sale of FV-NI investments resulted in a loss of $107,000.

4. When its president died, the corporation gained $100,000 from an insurance policy. The cash surrender value of this policy had been carried on the books as an investment in the amount of $46,000. (The gain is non-taxable.)

5. The corporation disposed of its recreational division at a loss of $115,000 before tax. Assume that this transaction meets the criteria for accounting treatment as discontinued operations.

6. The corporation decided to change its method of inventory pricing from average cost to the FIFO method. The effect of this change on prior years is to increase 2018 income by $60,000 and decrease 2019 income by $20,000 before taxes. The FIFO method has been used for 2020.

Instructions

a. Prepare an income statement for the year 2020, starting with income from continuing operations before income tax. Calculate earnings per share as required under IFRS. There were 80,000 common shares outstanding during the year. (Assume a tax rate of 30% on all items, unless they are noted as being non-taxable.)

b. Assume that beginning retained earnings for 2020 is $2,540,000 and that dividends of $175,000 were declared during the year. Prepare the retained earnings portion of the statement of changes in equity for 2020.

c. **Digging Deeper** Discuss how proper classification and disclosure of items on the income statement help users in making their investment and credit decisions.

P4.5 `Excel` The trial balance follows for Thompson Corporation at December 31, 2020:

Thompson Corporation
Trial Balance
December 31, 2020

	Debits	Credits
Purchase discounts		$ 10,000
Cash	$ 189,700	
Accounts receivable	105,000	
Rent revenue		18,000
Retained earnings		160,000
Salaries and wages payable		18,000
Sales revenue		1,100,000
Notes receivable	110,000	
Accounts payable		49,000
Accumulated depreciation—equipment		28,000
Sales discounts	14,500	
Sales returns and allowances	17,500	
Notes payable		70,000
Selling expenses	232,000	
Administrative expenses	99,000	
Common shares		300,000
Income tax expense	53,900	
Dividends	45,000	
Allowance for doubtful accounts		5,000
Supplies	14,000	
Freight in	20,000	
Land	70,000	
Equipment	140,000	
Bonds payable		100,000
Gain on disposal of land		30,000
Accumulated depreciation—buildings		19,600
Inventory	89,000	
Buildings	98,000	
Purchases	610,000	
Totals	$1,907,600	$1,907,600

A physical count of inventory on December 31 showed that there was $64,000 of inventory on hand.

Instructions

Prepare a condensed single-step income statement and a statement of retained earnings, assuming that Thompson is a private company that prepares financial statements in accordance with ASPE. Assume that the only changes in retained earnings during the current year were from net income and dividends.

P4.6 Hamza Khan, vice-president of finance for Dani Ipo Corp., has recently been asked to conduct a seminar for the company's division controllers. He would discuss the proper accounting for items that are large but do not typify normal business transactions (due to either the nature or the frequency of the transaction). Khan prepares the situations that follow to use as examples in the discussion. He understands that accounting standards mandate separate presentation of certain items, that these standards change over time, and that different standards may have different requirements. He has decided to focus on general principles.

1. An earthquake destroys one of the oil refineries owned by a large multinational oil company. Earthquakes are rare in this location.

2. A publicly held company has incurred a substantial loss in the unsuccessful registration of a bond issue. The company accesses capital markets very frequently.

3. A large portion of a farmer's crops is destroyed by a hailstorm. Severe damage from hailstorms is rare in this area.

4. A large diversified company sells a block of shares from its portfolio of investments. The shares are currently treated as FV-OCI investments (with gains/losses not recycled).

5. A company sells a block of common shares of a publicly traded company. The block of shares, which represents less than 10% of the publicly held company, is the only share investment that the

company has ever owned. The shares are accounted for as FV-OCI investments (with gains/losses not recycled).

6. A company that operates a chain of warehouses sells the extra land surrounding one of its warehouses. When the company buys property for a new warehouse, it usually buys more land than it needs for the warehouse because it expects the land to increase in value. Twice during the past five years, the company has sold excess land.

7. A textile manufacturer with only one plant moves to another location and incurs relocation costs of $725,000. Prior to the move, the company had been in the same location for 100 years.

8. A company experiences a material loss in the repurchase of a large bond issue that has been outstanding for three years. The company regularly repurchases bonds of this type.

9. A railroad experiences an unusual flood loss to part of its track system. Flood losses normally occur every three or four years. How would this be different if the company were to insure itself against this loss?

10. A machine tool company sells the only land it owns. The land was acquired 10 years ago for future expansion, but shortly after the purchase, the company abandoned all plans for expansion and decided to keep the land as an investment that would appreciate in value.

Instructions

For each situation, determine whether the item should be treated as unusual. Explain the reasons for your position. Assume that the company follows IFRS.

P4.7 The following financial statement was prepared by employees of Intellisys Corporation, which follows ASPE:

Intellisys Corporation
Income Statement
Year Ended December 31, 2020

Sales revenue	
Gross sales revenue, including sales taxes	$1,044,300
Less: Sales returns and allowances	56,200
Net sales revenue	988,100
Dividend revenue, interest income, and purchase discounts	30,250
Recoveries of accounts written off in prior years	13,850
Total revenues	1,032,200
Operating expenses	
Cost of goods sold	465,900
Salaries and wages expense	60,500
Rent expense	19,100
Freight in and freight out	3,400
Bad debt expense	27,800
Total operating expenses	576,700
Income before unusual items	455,500
Unusual items	
Loss on discontinued styles (Note 1)	37,000
Loss on disposal of FV-NI investments (Note 2)	39,050
Loss on disposal of warehouse (Note 3)	86,350
Tax assessments for 2019 and 2018 (Note 4)	34,500
Total unusual items	196,900
Net income	$ 258,600
Net income per common share	$ 2.30

Note 1: New styles and rapidly changing consumer preferences resulted in a $37,000 loss on the disposal of discontinued styles and related accessories.

Note 2: The corporation sold an investment in trading securities at a loss of $39,050. The corporation normally sells securities of this type.

Note 3: The corporation sold one of its warehouses at an $86,350 loss (net of taxes).

Note 4: The corporation was charged $34,500 for additional income taxes resulting from a settlement in 2020. Of this amount, $17,000 was for 2019, and the balance was for 2018. This type of litigation recurs frequently at Intellisys Corporation.

Instructions

Identify and discuss the weaknesses in classification and disclosure in the single-step income statement above. You should explain why these treatments are weaknesses and what the proper presentation of the items would be in accordance with recent professional pronouncements.

P4.8 The following account balances were included in the trial balance of Reid Corporation at June 30, 2020:

Sales revenue	$1,835,050	Telephone and Internet expense	
Cost of goods sold	1,071,770	(office)	$ 2,820
Salaries and wages expense (sales)	56,260	Salaries and wages (office)	7,320
Sales commission expense	97,600	Supplies expense (sales)	4,850
Advertising expense (sales)	28,930	Repairs and maintenance expense (office)	9,130
Freight out	21,400	Depreciation understatement due to	
Entertainment expense (sales)	14,820	error—2018 (net of tax of $3,300)	17,700
Telephone and Internet expense (sales)	9,030	Miscellaneous expense (office)	6,000
Depreciation of sales equipment	4,980	Dividend revenue	38,000
Repairs and maintenance expense		Interest expense	18,000
(sales)	6,200	Income tax expense	133,000
Miscellaneous expenses (sales)	4,715	Dividends declared on preferred	
Supplies expense (office)	3,450	shares	9,000
Depreciation expense on office		Dividends declared on common	
furniture and equipment	7,250	shares	32,000

During 2020, Reid incurred production salary and wage costs of $710,000, consumed raw materials and other production supplies of $474,670, and had an increase in work-in-process and finished goods inventories of $112,900. The Retained Earnings account had a balance of $292,000 at June 30, 2020, before closing. There are 180,000 common shares outstanding. Assume Reid has elected to adopt IFRS. (*Hint:* Production payroll and materials costs reduced by the increase in ending work-in-process and finished goods inventories = the cost of goods sold.)

Instructions

a. Prepare an income statement for the year ended June 30, 2020, using the multiple-step format and showing expenses by function.

b. Prepare the retained earnings portion of the statement of changes in equity for the year ended June 30, 2020.

c. Prepare an income statement for the year ended June 30, 2020, using the single-step format and showing expenses by nature.

d. Assume the average market price of the common shares outstanding was $31.70. What was Reid's price-earnings ratio?

P4.9 A combined single-step income statement and statement of retained earnings for California Tanning Salon Corp. follows for 2020 (amounts in thousands):

Net sales revenue		$640,000
Operating expenses		
Cost of goods sold		500,000
Selling, general, and administrative expenses		66,000
Other, net		17,000
		583,000
Income before income tax		57,000
Income tax expense		19,400
Net income		37,600
Retained earnings at beginning of period, as previously reported	141,000	
Adjustment required for correction of error	(7,000)	
Retained earnings at beginning of period, as restated		134,000
Dividends on common shares		(12,200)
Retained earnings at end of period		$159,400

Additional facts are as follows:

1. Selling, general, and administrative expenses for 2020 included a usual but infrequently occurring charge of $10.5 million for a loss on inventory due to a decline in net realizable value.

2. "Other, net" for 2020 included the results of an identified component of the business that management had determined would be eliminated from the future operations of the business ($9 million). If the decision had not been made to discontinue the operation, income tax for 2020 would have been $22.4 million instead of $19.4 million. The component has one asset, a piece of equipment with a carrying value of $3.2 million, which is included on the company's statement of financial position under property, plant, and equipment (and is equal to the fair value).

3. "Adjustment required for correction of an error" resulted from a change in estimate as the useful life of certain assets was reduced to eight years and a catch-up adjustment was made.

4. The company disclosed earnings per common share for net income in the notes to the financial statements. The company has elected to adopt ASPE.

Instructions

a. Discuss the appropriate presentation of the facts in the California Tanning Salon Corp. income statement and statement of retained earnings and discuss the theory that supports the presentation.

b. Prepare a revised combined statement of income and retained earnings for California Tanning Salon Corp.

P4.10 A combined statement of income and retained earnings for DC 5 Ltd. for the year ended December 31, 2020, follows. (As a private company, DC 5 has elected to follow ASPE.) Also presented are three unrelated situations involving accounting changes and the classification of certain items as ordinary or unusual. Each situation is based on the combined statement of income and retained earnings of DC 5 Ltd.

DC 5 Ltd.
Combined Statement of Income and Retained Earnings
For the Year Ended December 31, 2020

Sales revenue	$7,300,000
Cost of goods sold	3,700,000
Gross profit	3,600,000
Selling, general, and administrative expenses	2,300,000
Income before income tax	1,300,000
Income tax expense	390,000
Income before unusual item	910,000
Loss from tornado (net of taxes)	630,000
Net income	280,000
Retained earnings, January 1	1,250,000
Retained earnings, December 31	$1,530,000

Situation 1. In late 2020, the company discontinued its apparel fabric division. The loss on the disposal of this discontinued division amounted to $790,000. This amount was included as part of selling, general, and administrative expenses. Before its disposal, the division reported the following for 2020: sales revenue of $1.5 million; cost of goods sold of $750,000; and selling, general, and administrative expenses of $580,000.

Situation 2. At the end of 2020, the company's management decided that the estimated loss rate on uncollectible accounts receivable was too low. The loss rate used for the years 2019 and 2020 was 1.2% of total sales revenue, and owing to an increase in the write off of uncollectible accounts, the rate was raised to 2.6% of total sales revenue. The amount recorded in Bad Debt Expense under the heading Selling, General, and Administrative Expenses for 2020 was $87,600 and for 2019 it was $95,700.

Situation 3. On January 1, 2018, the company acquired machinery at a cost of $640,000. The company adopted the declining-balance method of depreciation at a rate of 30% for this machinery, and had been recording depreciation over an estimated life of 10 years, with no residual value. At the beginning of 2020, a decision was made to adopt the straight-line method of depreciation for this machinery to better match expenses to their related revenues. Depreciation for 2020, based on the straight-line method, was included in selling, general, and administrative expenses. (*Hint:* A change in depreciation method is considered a change in estimate, not a change in accounting policy.)

Instructions

For each of the three unrelated situations, prepare a revised combined statement of income and retained earnings for DC 5 Ltd. The company has a 30% income tax rate.

P4.11 Zephyr Corporation began operations on January 1, 2017. Recently the corporation has had several unusual accounting problems related to the presentation of its income statement for financial reporting purposes. The company follows ASPE.

You are the CPA for Zephyr and have been asked to examine the following data:

Zephyr Corporation
Income Statement
For the Year Ended December 31, 2020

Sales revenue	$9,500,000
Cost of goods sold	5,900,000
Gross profit	3,600,000
Selling and administrative expense	1,300,000
Income before income tax	2,300,000
Income tax expense (30%)	690,000
Net income	$1,610,000

This additional information was also provided:

1. The controller mentioned that the corporation has had difficulty collecting certain receivables. For this reason, the bad debt accrual was increased from 1% to 2% of sales revenue. The controller estimates that, if this rate had been used in past periods, an additional $83,000 worth of expense would have been charged. The bad debt expense for the current period was calculated using the new rate and is part of selling and administrative expense.

2. There were 400,000 common shares outstanding at the end of 2020. No additional shares were purchased or sold in 2020.

3. The following items were not included in the income statement:
   - Inventory in the amount of $112,000 was obsolete.
   - The company announced plans to dispose of a recognized segment. For 2020, the segment had a loss, net of tax, of $162,000.

4. Retained earnings as at January 1, 2020, were $2.8 million. Cash dividends of $700,000 were paid in 2020.

5. In January 2020, Zephyr changed its method of depreciating plant assets from the straight-line method to the declining-balance method to present more relevant information. The controller has prepared a schedule that shows what the depreciation expense would have been in previous periods if the declining-balance method had been used.

	Depreciation Expense under Straight-Line	Depreciation Expense under Declining-Balance	Difference
2017	$ 75,000	$150,000	$ 75,000
2018	75,000	112,500	37,500
2019	75,000	84,375	9,375
	$225,000	$346,875	$121,875

6. In 2020, Zephyr discovered that in 2019 it had failed to record $20,000 as an expense for sales commissions. The sales commissions for 2019 were included in the 2020 expenses.

Instructions

a. Prepare the income statement for Zephyr Corporation. The effective tax rate for past years was 30%. (*Hint:* A change in depreciation method is considered a change in estimate, not a change in accounting policy.)

b. Prepare a combined statement of net income and retained earnings.

c. **Digging Deeper** From the perspective of the reader of the financial statements, what is the purpose of intraperiod tax allocation for the statements of income and retained earnings?

P4.12 Joe Schreiner, controller for On Time Clock Company Inc., recently prepared the company's income statement and statement of changes in equity for 2020. Schreiner believes that the statements are a fair presentation of the company's financial progress during the current period, but he also admits that he has not examined any recent professional pronouncements on accounting.

On Time Clock Company Inc.
Income Statement
For the Year Ended December 31, 2020

Sales revenues		$358,675
Cost of goods sold		198,112
Gross profit		160,563
Selling expenses	41,850	
Administrative expenses	32,142	73,992
Income before income tax		86,571
Other revenues and gains		
Unrealized gain on FV-OCI equity investments		36,000
Dividend revenue		40,000
		162,571
Income tax expense		56,900
Net income		$105,671

On Time Clock Company Inc.
Excerpt from Statement of Changes in Equity
For the Year Ended December 31, 2020

Retained earnings, January 1, 2020			$216,000
Add:			
Net income for 2020	$105,671		
Gain on disposal of long-term investments	31,400	$137,071	
Deduct:			
Loss on expropriation	13,000		
Correction of mathematical error (net of tax)	17,186	(30,186)	106,885
Retained earnings, December 31, 2020			$322,885

Instructions

a. Assume that On Time Clock Company follows IFRS. Assume that investments are accounted for as FV-OCI equity investments with gains/losses not recycled through net income. Prepare a statement of financial performance showing expenses by function. Ignore calculation of EPS.

b. Prepare the retained earnings and accumulated other comprehensive income portion of the statement of changes in equity. Assume an opening balance of $120,000 in accumulated other comprehensive income.

c. **Digging Deeper** Will the sum of the Accumulated Other Comprehensive Income and Retained Earnings at December 31, 2020, using the revised financial statement equal the sum of the Accumulated Other Comprehensive Income and the Retained Earnings balance from the original draft of the financial statement prepared by the controller? If not, explain any differences.

P4.13 Faldo Corp. is a public company and has 100,000 common shares outstanding. In 2020, the company reported income from continuing operations before income tax of $2,710,000. Additional transactions not considered in the $2,710,000 are as follows:

1. In 2020, Faldo Corp. sold equipment for $140,000. The machine had originally cost $80,000 and had accumulated depreciation to date of $36,000.

2. The company discontinued operations of one of its subsidiaries during the current year at a loss of $290,000 before tax. Assume that this transaction meets the criteria for discontinued operations. The loss on operation of the discontinued subsidiary was $90,000 before tax. The loss from disposal of the subsidiary was $200,000 before tax.

3. The sum of $520,000 was received as a result of a lawsuit for a breached 2017 contract. Before the decision, legal counsel was uncertain about the outcome of the suit and Faldo had not established a receivable.

4. In 2020, the company reviewed its accounts receivable and determined that $54,000 of accounts receivable that had been carried for years appeared unlikely to be collected. No allowance for doubtful accounts was previously set up.

5. An internal audit discovered that amortization of intangible assets was understated by $35,000 (net of tax) in a prior period. The amount was charged against retained earnings.

Instructions

Analyze the above information and prepare an income statement for the year 2020, starting with income from continuing operations before income tax. Calculate earnings per share as it should be shown on the face of the income statement. (Assume a total effective tax rate of 25% on all items, unless otherwise indicated.)

P4.14 Amos Corporation was incorporated and began business on January 1, 2020. It has been successful and now requires a bank loan for additional capital to finance an expansion. The bank has requested an audited income statement for the year 2020 using IFRS. The accountant for Amos Corporation provides you with the following income statement, which Amos plans to submit to the bank:

Amos Corporation
Income Statement

Sales revenue		$850,000
Dividend revenue		32,300
Gain on recovery of earthquake loss (unusual)		27,300
Unrealized holding gain on FV-OCI equity investments		5,000
		914,600
Less:		
Selling expenses	$100,100	
Cost of goods sold	510,000	
Advertising expense	13,700	
Loss on inventory due to decline in net realizable value	34,000	
Loss on discontinued operations	48,600	
Administrative expenses	73,400	779,800
Income before income tax		134,800
Income tax expense		33,700
Net income		$101,100

Amos had 100,000 common shares outstanding during the year and has an effective tax rate of 25%. Gains/losses on FV-OCI equity investments are not recycled through net income.

Instructions

a. Show the deficiencies in the income statement as it currently is. Assume that the corporation prepares a single-step income statement.

b. Prepare a revised single-step statement of comprehensive income.

P4.15 The equity accounts of Good Karma Corp. as at January 1, 2020, were as follows:

Retained earnings, January 1, 2020	$257,600
Common shares	600,000
Preferred shares	250,000
Contributed surplus	300,000
Accumulated other comprehensive income	525,000

During 2020, the following transactions took place:

Adjustment to correct error in prior years (gain net of tax $20,000)	$ 48,000
Unrealized gains on FV-OCI equity investments (net of tax $34,000)	82,000
Dividends:	
Common shares	120,000
Preferred shares	62,000
Issue of equity:	
Common shares	300,000
Preferred shares	5,000
Net income	325,000

Instructions

Prepare a statement of changes in equity for the year ended December 31, 2020. The company follows IFRS. Assume that equity investments are accounted for as FV-OCI investments, with gains/losses not recycled through net income.

P4.16 The following is from a recent income statement for Graben Inc. (a public company):

Sales revenue	$21,924,000,000
Costs and expenses	20,773,000,000
Income from operations	1,151,000,000
Other income	22,000,000
Interest and debt expense	(130,000,000)
Earnings before income tax	1,043,000,000
Income tax expense	(287,000,000)
Net income	$ 756,000,000

It includes only five separate numbers, two subtotals, and the net earnings figure.

Instructions

a. Show the deficiencies in the income statement.

b. What recommendations would you make to the company to improve the usefulness of its income statement?

c. Digging Deeper Why do some businesses provide only a minimal disclosure of financial statement elements on their income statement?

*P4.17 On January 1, 2020, Caroline Lampron and Jenni Meno formed a computer sales and service enterprise in Montreal by investing $90,000 cash. The new company, Razorback Sales and Service, had the following transactions in January:

1. Paid $6,000 in advance for three months' rent of office, showroom, and repair space.

2. Purchased 40 personal computers at a cost of $1,500 each, six graphics computers at a cost of $3,000 each, and 25 printers at a cost of $450 each, paying cash on delivery.

3. Sales, repair, and office employees earned $12,600 in salaries during January, of which $3,000 was still payable at the end of January.

4. Sold 30 personal computers for $2,550 each, four graphics computers for $4,500 each, and 15 printers for $750 each. Of the sales amounts, $75,000 was received in cash in January and $30,750 was sold on a deferred payment plan.

5. Other operating expenses of $8,400 were incurred and paid for during January; $2,000 of incurred expenses were payable at January 31.

Instructions

a. Using the transaction data above, prepare (1) a cash basis income statement and (2) an accrual basis income statement for the month of January.

b. Using the transaction data above, prepare (1) a cash basis statement of financial position and (2) an accrual basis statement of financial position as at January 31, 2020.

c. Identify the items in the cash basis financial statements that make cash basis accounting inconsistent with the theory underlying the elements of financial statements.

*P4.18 Dr. Emma Armstrong, M.D., maintains the accounting records of the Blood Sugar Clinic on a cash basis. During 2020, Dr. Armstrong collected $146,000 in revenues and paid $55,470 in expenses. At January 1, 2020, and December 31, 2020, she had accounts receivable, unearned revenue, accrued liabilities, and prepaid expenses as follows (all long-lived assets are rented):

	January 1	December 31
Accounts receivable	$9,250	$16,100
Unearned revenue	2,840	1,620
Accrued liabilities	3,435	2,200
Prepaid expenses	2,000	1,775

Instructions

Last week, Dr. Armstrong asked you, her CPA, to help her determine her income on the accrual basis. Write a letter to her explaining what you did to calculate net income on the accrual basis. Be sure to state net income on the accrual basis and to include a schedule of your calculations.

Case

Refer to the Case Primer on the Student Website and in WileyPLUS *to help you answer this case.*

CA4.1 As a reviewer for the Ontario Securities Commission, you are reviewing the financial statements of public companies. The following items have come to your attention:

1. A merchandising company overstated its ending inventory two years ago by a material amount. Inventory for all other periods is correctly calculated.

2. An automobile dealer sells for $137,000 an extremely rare 1930 S-type Invicta, which it purchased for $21,000 10 years ago. The Invicta is the only such display item that the dealer owns.

3. During the current year, a drilling company extended the estimated useful life of certain drilling equipment from 9 to 15 years. As a result, depreciation for the current year was materially lowered.

4. A retail outlet changed its calculation for bad debt expense from 1% to 0.5% of sales because of changes in its clientele.

5. A mining company sells a large foreign subsidiary that does uranium mining, although the company continues to mine uranium in other countries.

6. A steel company changes from straight-line depreciation to accelerated depreciation in accounting for its plant assets, stating that the expected pattern of consumption of the future economic benefits has changed.

7. A construction company, at great expense to itself, prepares a major proposal for a government loan. The loan is not approved.

8. A water pump manufacturer has had large losses resulting from a strike by its employees early in the year.

9. Depreciation for a prior period was incorrectly understated by $950,000. The error was discovered in the current year.

10. A large sheep rancher suffered a major loss because the provincial government required that all sheep in the province be killed to halt the spread of a rare disease. Such a situation has not occurred in the province for 20 years.

11. A food distributor that sells wholesale to supermarket chains and to fast-food restaurants (two major classes of customers) decides to discontinue the division that sells to one of the two classes of customers.

Instructions

Discuss the financial reporting issues.

Integrated Cases

(*Hint:* If there are issues here that are new, use the conceptual framework to help you support your analysis with solid reasoning.)

IC4.1 Snow Spray Corp. (SSC) recently filed for bankruptcy protection. The company manufactures downhill skis and reports under ASPE. With the increased popularity of such alternative winter sports as snowboarding and tubing, sales of skis are sagging. The company has decided to start a new line of products that focuses on the growing industry surrounding snowboarding and tubing. At present, however, the company needs interim financing to pay suppliers and its payroll. It also needs a significant amount of cash so that it can reposition itself in the marketplace. Management is planning to go to the bank with draft financial statements to discuss additional financing. The company's year end is December 31, 2019, and it is now January 15, 2020. Current interest rates for loans are 5%, but because it is in bankruptcy protection, SSC feels that it will likely have to pay at least 15% on any loan. There is concern that the bank will turn the company down.

At a recent management meeting, the company decided to convert its ski manufacturing facilities into snowboard manufacturing facilities. It will no longer produce skis. Management is unsure if the company will be able to recover the cost of the ski inventory. Although the conversion will result in significant expenditures, the company feels that this is justified if SSC wants to remain a viable business. The shift in strategic positioning will not result in any layoffs, as most employees will work in the retrofitted plant. The remaining employees will be trained in the new business.

The conversion to snowboard manufacturing facilities would not require selling the ski manufacturing machines, as these machines can be used to produce snowboards. The company estimates the results and cash flows from its operation of selling skis to be a $20-million loss.

On December 15, 2019, the company entered into an agreement with Cashco Ltd. to sell its entire inventory in ski bindings to Cashco. Under the terms of the deal, Cashco paid $10 million cash for the inventory (its regular selling price at the time). The cost to SSC of this inventory was $6 million and so a profit of $4 million was booked pre-tax. In a separate deal, SSC agreed to buy back the inventory in January for $10,125,000.

Before filing for bankruptcy protection, the company was able to buy a large shipment of snow tubes wholesale for a bargain price of $7 million from a supplier that was in financial trouble. The value of the inventory is approximately $10 million. The inventory was sitting in the SSC manufacturing facility taking up a lot of space. Because the manufacturing facility was being renovated, SSC reached an agreement with its leading competitor, Alpine Gear Ltd. (AGL). According to the contract, AGL agreed to purchase the snow tubes from SSC for $8 million, and SSC shipped the inventory on December 31 to arrive on January 5. The inventory was shipped f.o.b. shipping point. SSC normally reimburses its customers if the inventory is damaged in transit. SSC has a tentative verbal agreement that it will repurchase the snow tubes that AGL does not sell by the time the renovations are complete (in approximately six months). The buyback price will include an additional amount that will cover storage and insurance costs.

Instructions

Adopt the role of Rachel Glover—the company controller—and discuss the financial reporting issues related to the preparation of the financial statements for the year ended December 31, 2019.

IC4.2 Brave Maven Inc. (BMI) operates in challenging economic times. It currently manufactures trucks and equipment used for construction, as well as off-road automobiles and automotive parts. During the year, net losses from off-road automobiles and parts totalled $1 million (net of tax). Future losses are expected to increase by an additional $1 million. BMI's management team is contemplating selling off this unprofitable business segment. In December, BMI's board of directors authorized a sale transaction.

Management would also like to expand the production of trucks and construction equipment. BMI's lenders are not willing to provide additional financing, so BMI will need to explore equity financing. Management is preparing the necessary documentation for an initial public offering.

The carrying value of the facility and equipment used to manufacture the automobiles and parts is $2 million. Two years ago, some modifications were made to the equipment. The equipment is now specialized for use by BMI, which would have to spend $500,000 to disassemble the previous modifications in order to sell the equipment. By year end, management had already hired a contractor to begin disassembling the equipment.

BMI has been in sale negotiations with one of its automotive parts suppliers interested in expanding its own automotive parts business. Negotiations are expected to continue, but the two companies are not able to agree on a price. The supplier has indicated it would only be willing to pay up to 90% of the asking price, as it would have to make its own modifications to the equipment first. The purchase would only go ahead if BMI completed the disassembly of the equipment's existing modifications and the supplier's engineer subsequently inspected and approved the equipment. Management feels that 90% of the asking price is just under what it would be willing to sell the assets at.

BMI is also in a dispute with one of its suppliers of truck parts. In order to get a discounted price, BMI had to commit to purchasing $500,000 of spare parts each year for three years. BMI recently upgraded its safety standards and consequently made modifications to its construction trucks in the current year. As a result, management did not accept delivery of the spare parts for the current year. There is a provision in the contract that stipulates an annual penalty of $250,000 for failure to take delivery. One more year remains in the contract. BMI's lawyers are reviewing the contract. They have suggested that BMI may qualify for exemption from the penalty for not taking delivery because its refusal resulted from a change in the safety specification for the part and not because of a change in sales demand. The supplier is willing to modify its spare parts to conform to BMI's new safety standard.

Just before year end, management purchased an additional building. BMI plans to use 50% of the building and move the current sales team to the new location. It does not plan to use the other 50% as part of its current operations. BMI's real estate agent looked at the property and believes the part of the building that BMI will not occupy can be sold or leased separately. Management does not want BMI to use fair value as its basis for measurement because it is concerned that changes in fair value will create too much volatility in the income statement. This may lower the price that BMI shares sell at in the future public offering.

Instructions

Audit It is now two months after year end. Assume the role of BMI's auditor and discuss the financial reporting issues.

Research and Analysis

RA4.1 **Real World Emphasis** **Kirkland Lake Gold Ltd.**

Locate the audited consolidated financial statements (including the accompanying notes) of Kirkland Lake Gold Ltd. for its year ended December 31, 2017 (available at www.sedar.com).

Instructions

Refer to the statements and notes to answer the following questions.

a. What type of income statement format does the company use: single- or multiple-step? Comment.

b. What business(es) is the company in during 2017? (*Hint:* Look at Note 1 to the financial statements.)

c. How are these businesses reflected in Kirkland Lake Gold's balance sheet and income statement?

d. Is the income statement presented by function or nature? Why?

e. Explain what makes up any reported amount for discontinued operations for the year ended December 31, 2017. Why is it important to disclose this information separately from other results for the year? The company also disclosed a loss on disposal of plant and equipment as part of Other Income, above "Earnings from continuing operations" and not included in the loss on disposition of discontinued operations. Why was this loss not included in the loss on discontinued operations?

f. What is included in other comprehensive income and what is the total of comprehensive income for the current year?

g. How has the EPS been calculated? How many EPS figures are presented and why? Where is the EPS disclosed?

RA4.2 **Real World Emphasis** **Royal Bank of Canada**

Obtain the 2017 annual report for the Royal Bank of Canada from the company's website or from SEDAR (www.sedar.com). Note that financial reporting for Canadian banks is also constrained by the Bank Act and monitored by the Office of the Superintendent of Financial Institutions.

Instructions

a. Revenues and expenses arise primarily from ordinary business activities. What are the bank's ordinary (core) business activities? What normal expenses must the bank incur in order to generate core revenues?

b. How are the core business activities and other income and expenses reflected in the bank's statement of income?

c. Calculate the percentage of the various revenue and income streams to total revenue and income. Discuss the trends from year to year. In other words, are these revenue and income streams increasing as a percentage of the total revenue and income or decreasing? What are the main sources of the revenue and income?

d. Describe the types of transactions that are included in the statement of changes in equity.

RA4.3 **Real World Emphasis** **Brookfield Office Properties Inc. and Mainstreet Equity Corp.**

Use the annual reports and/or the audited annual financial statements of Brookfield Office Properties Inc. for the year ended December 31, 2015, and of Mainstreet Equity Corp. for the year ended September 30, 2016, to answer the following questions. These reports are available on SEDAR (www.sedar.com) or the companies' websites.

Instructions

a. Look at the Management Discussion and Analysis and the annual report in general. What business are both companies in?

b. What type of income statement format(s) do these two companies use? Identify any differences in income statement format between the two companies. Are their income statements presented by function or by nature?

c. What are the main sources of revenues for both companies? Are these increasing or decreasing?

d. Is the nature of each business reflected in its balance sheet? (*Hint:* What is the main asset and what percentage of total assets does this asset account for?)

e. What types of items are included in other comprehensive income for each company?

RA4.4 Canadian Securities Administrators

The Canadian Securities Administrators (CSA), an umbrella group of Canadian provincial securities commissions, accumulates and publishes all documents that public companies are required to file under securities law. This database may be accessed from the SEDAR website (www.sedar.com).

Instructions

Visit the SEDAR website and find the company documents and financial reports for the Bank of Montreal and Royal Bank of Canada. Company financial statements and other information can also be accessed through the company websites (www.bmo.com and www.rbcroyalbank.com). Answer the following questions:

- **a.** What types of company documents can be found here that provide useful information for investors who are making investment decisions?
- **b.** Locate the annual information form. Explain the nature of the information that it contains. As a financial statement analyst, is this information useful to you? Why or why not?
- **c.** Who is the auditor of each bank?
- **d.** Which stock exchange(s) does each bank trade on?
- **e.** Go to the company websites directly. Look under Investor Relations. What type of information is on these websites and how is it different from what is found on the CSA website? Should these websites contain the same information as the CSA website?

RA4.5 Quality of Earnings Assessment

Quality of earnings analysis is a very important tool in assessing the value of a company and its shares. The chapter presents a framework for evaluating quality of earnings.

Instructions

Do an Internet search on the topic and write a critical essay discussing the usefulness of the quality of earnings assessment.

RA4.6 **Real World Emphasis**   BCE Inc.

An excerpt from Section 10.2 of the Management Discussion and Analysis in the 2017 annual report of BCE Inc. is shown below. The excerpt shows summarized financial information, including calculations of earnings before interest, tax, depreciation, and amortization (EBITDA), and adjusted net earnings—both non-GAAP earnings measures. The company provides information on these calculations, which is also shown.

Instructions

Read the excerpts below. Discuss the pros and cons of management's decision to report additional earnings numbers outside of the traditional audited financial statements. In the case of this company, in your opinion, do you think that this presentation provides good, useful information?

10.2 Non-GAAP financial measures . . .

This section describes the non-GAAP financial measures . . . we use in this MD&A to explain our financial results. It also provides reconciliations of the non-GAAP financial measures to the most comparable IFRS financial measures.

In Q1 2017, we updated our definition of adjusted net earnings and adjusted EPS to also exclude impairment charges as they may affect the comparability of our financial results and could potentially distort the analysis of trends in business performance. There was no impact to previously reported results as a result of this change.

Adjusted EBITDA and Adjusted EBITDA margin

The terms Adjusted EBITDA . . . do not have any standardized meaning under IFRS. Therefore, . . . [they] are unlikely to be comparable to similar measures presented by other issuers. **We use Adjusted EBITDA** . . . to evaluate the performance of our businesses as it reflects their ongoing profitability. We believe that certain investors and analysts use Adjusted EBITDA to measure a company's ability to service debt and to meet other payment obligations or as a common measurement to value companies in the telecommunications industry. We believe that certain investors and analysts also use Adjusted EBITDA . . . to evaluate the performance of our businesses. Adjusted EBITDA is also one component in the determination of short-term incentive compensation for all management employees.

Adjusted EBITDA . . . has no directly comparable IFRS financial measure. Alternatively, the following table provides a reconciliation of net earnings to Adjusted EBITDA.

	2017	2016
Net earnings	2,970	3,087
Severance, acquisition and other costs	190	135
Depreciation	3,037	2,877
Amortization	813	631
Finance costs		
Interest expense	955	888
Interest on post-employment benefit obligations	72	81
Other (income) expense	102	(21)
Income taxes	1,039	1,110
Adjusted EBITDA	9,178	8,788

Adjusted net earnings and Adjusted EPS

The terms Adjusted net earnings and Adjusted EPS do not have any standardized meaning under IFRS. Therefore, they are unlikely to be comparable to similar measures presented by other issuers.

We define Adjusted net earnings as net earnings attributable to common shareholders before severance, acquisition and other costs, net (gains) losses on investments, and early debt redemption costs. We define Adjusted EPS as Adjusted net earnings per BCE common share.

We use Adjusted net earnings and Adjusted EPS, and we believe that certain investors and analysts use these measures, among other ones, to assess the performance of our businesses without the effects of severance, acquisition and other costs, net (gains) losses on investments, and early debt redemption costs, net of tax and non-controlling interest (NCI). We exclude these items because they affect the comparability of our financial results and could potentially distort the analysis of trends in business performance. Excluding these items does not imply they are non-recurring.

The most comparable IFRS financial measures are net earnings attributable to common shareholders and EPS. The following table is a reconciliation of net earnings attributable to common shareholders and EPS to Adjusted net earnings on a consolidated basis and per BCE common share (Adjusted EPS), respectively.

	2017		2016	
	Total	Per Share	Total	Per Share
Net earnings attributable to common shareholders	2,786	3.12	2,894	3.33
Severance, acquisition and other costs	143	0.16	104	0.12
Net (gains) losses on investments	29	0.03	3	
Early debt redemption costs	15	0.02	8	0.01
Impairment charges	60	0.06		
Adjusted net earnings	3,033	3.39	3,009	3.46

RA4.7 `Data Analytics` Financial Reporting

In financial reporting, the goal is to provide useful information to users of the financial statements such as investors. Investors often use numbers from the financial statements (and other sources) to calculate financial statement ratios. For instance, in the retail or merchandising industry, the gross profit ratio is a key ratio. It shows information about pricing, purchases, shrinkage, and many other things.

Investors compare the ratios with prior years for the same company and with industry comparators so they can see what has changed or what is different. This can be done by accessing the financial statements of public companies through websites such as SEDAR (the System for Electronic Document Analysis and Retrieval; www.sedar.com). It is hosted by the Canadian Securities Administrators and was created in 1997, allowing public companies to electronically file all documents required under securities legislation in Canada. SEDAR houses a searchable database. In the United States, a similar site is hosted by the U.S Securities and Exchange Commission (SEC). It is referred to as EDGAR—the Electronic Data Gathering, Analysis, and Retrieval system (www.sec.gov). Companies also include their financial statements on their own websites.

Instructions

a. Access SEDAR and search the database, looking for all merchandising companies. How many companies are in this merchandising industry? Make a note of the number in each subcategory. Why do you think the companies are subcategorized this way?

b. For the companies in the wholesale distributors subcategory, calculate the gross profit for each. Are these numbers comparable between companies? Why or why not?

c. If you wanted to compare gross profit margins for all companies in this or a similar category around the world, how might you approach this research?

d. For a fee, companies such as Bloomberg give access to large amounts of data and analysis. These companies are sometimes called data aggregators. What are the pros and cons of using a service such as this as opposed to doing your own research?

CHAPTER 5

Financial Position and Cash Flows

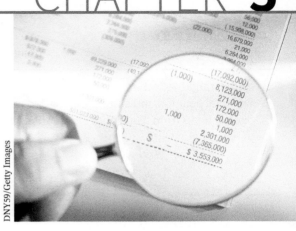

DNY59/Getty Images

Toward Better Disclosure

As you've seen in previous chapters, solid financial reporting underpins the capital marketplace. Investors, creditors, and other stakeholders need assurance that publicly traded companies are presenting an accurate and transparent picture of their financial information.

One way to increase this assurance is by the Canadian Securities Administrators (CSA), the umbrella group of provincial securities regulators, reviewing a sample of the financial statements issued by public companies (called "issuers") to check their compliance with disclosure requirements. The CSA examines company financial statements (such as the statement of financial position), management discussion and analysis reports, and other regulatory disclosure documents.

For the 2016 fiscal year, the CSA reviewed 902 issuers. Two thirds of the reviews were partial, focusing on particular issues. The CSA found that in 62% of the reviews, the filer was required to take action to improve its disclosure, or in the most extreme instances was referred to enforcement, ceased trading, or was placed on the default list (which could require it to refile its financial statements). The deficiencies the CSA found regarding financial statement measurement and disclosure included compliance with IFRS recognition, measurement, and disclosure requirements, including regarding impairment, accounting for acquisitions, revenue, and significant judgements.

Among the deficiencies found in some issuers' financial statements was how goodwill and intangible assets are recognized after mergers and acquisitions. "We continue to see issuers that allocate the entire purchase price to one intangible asset. However, the disclosure indicates the presence of other identifiable intangible assets or goodwill," the CSA said. However, it noted that IFRS 3 *Business Combinations* and IAS 38 *Intangible Assets* require that companies separately recognize intangible assets acquired in a business combination. As well, "Some issuers do not explain how they determined the useful lives for finite-lived intangible assets, or why an intangible asset has an indefinite useful life. Some issuers inappropriately determine an indefinite useful life for an intangible asset that has a finite useful life. Distinguishing the indefinite-lived intangible assets from those with a finite life, as well as determining the useful lives for finite-lived intangible assets, has an impact on the financial statements for the current period and for the subsequent periods."

The CSA also observed frequent problems with reporting operating segments. "Issuers often aggregate several operating segments into a single operating segment for reporting purposes. This is particularly prevalent in certain industries such as the retail industry, for example, where retailers have several different distinct operations that offer a broad range of products (for example, home furnishings, personal care, and clothing) that are all considered to be part of one operating segment for reporting purposes." This goes against IFRS 8 *Operating Segments*. "Issuers that aggregate operating segments into a single operating segment for reporting purposes must ensure that the aggregation criteria have been met. Issuers are required to disclose the judgments made by management in applying the aggregation criteria. Issuers are required to report separately specific information about an operating segment that meets certain quantitative thresholds."

Sources: Canadian Securities Administrators, "CSA Staff Notice 51-346 – Continuous Disclosure Review Program Activities for the Fiscal Year Ended March 31, 2016," Canadian Securities Administrators website, https://www.securities-administrators.ca/.

LEARNING OBJECTIVES	CHAPTER OUTLINE	CPA COMPETENCIES
After studying this chapter, you should be able to:	The chapter headings related to the learning objective are:	Competencies addressed by each learning objective are as follows:
1. Understand the statement of financial position and statement of cash flows from a business perspective.	**Usefulness of the Statements of Financial Position and Cash Flows from a Business Perspective** • Analyzing a statement of financial position • Assessing earnings quality • Assessing the creditworthiness of companies	1.1.1, 1.4.2, 1.4.4
2. Identify the uses and limitations of a statement of financial position.	**STATEMENT OF FINANCIAL POSITION** **Usefulness and Limitations of the Statement of Financial Position** • Usefulness • Limitations	1.1.1, 1.3.1. 5.1.1
3. Identify the major classifications of a statement of financial position.	**Classification in the Statement of Financial Position** • Monetary versus nonmonetary assets and liabilities • Financial instruments • Elements of the statement of financial position	1.1.1, 1.2.1, 1.2.2, 1.2.3, 1.3.1, 1.4.2
4. Prepare a classified statement of financial position.	**Preparation of the Classified Statement of Financial Position (Balance Sheet)** • Current assets • Non-current investments • Property, plant, and equipment • Intangible assets and goodwill • Other assets • Current liabilities • Long-term debt and liabilities • Owners' equity • Statement of financial position format	1.3.1, 1.4.2, 1.4.5, 2.3.1
5. Identify statement of financial position information that requires supplemental disclosure.	**Other Required Disclosures** • Contingencies and provisions • Accounting policies • Contractual situations • Additional detail • Subsequent events	1.3.1, 1.3.2, 1.4.1, 1.4.2
6. Identify major disclosure techniques for the statement of financial position.	**Techniques of Disclosure** • Parenthetical explanations • Notes • Cross-references and contra items • Supporting schedules • Terminology	1.1.1, 1.3.1, 1.3.2

7. Indicate the purpose and identify the content of the statement of cash flows.	**STATEMENT OF CASH FLOWS** **Purpose, Content, and Format of a Statement of Cash Flows**	**1.1.1, 1.2.1, 1.2.2, 1.3.1, 1.4.3**
8. Prepare a statement of cash flows using the indirect and direct methods.	**Preparation of the Statement of Cash Flows**	**1.3.1, 1.3.2, 1.4.2, 5.2.1**
9. Understand the usefulness of the statement of cash flows.	**Usefulness of the Statement of Cash Flows** • Financial liquidity • Financial flexibility • Perspectives	**1.1.1, 1.3.1, 1.4.2, 1.4.3, 5.1.1, 5.2.1**
10. Identify differences in accounting between IFRS and ASPE and identify the significant changes planned by the IASB for financial statement presentation.	**IFRS/ASPE Comparison** • A comparison of IFRS and ASPE • Looking ahead	**1.1.2, 1.1.4**

After studying Appendix 5A, you should be able to:

11. Identify the major types of financial ratios and what they measure.	**Appendix 5A: Ratio Analysis: A Reference** • Business risks • Financial ratios	**1.4.2, 1.4.4, 1.4.5, 5.1.1**

Preview of Chapter 5

The statement of financial position and statement of cash flows complement the statement of comprehensive income, offering information about the company's financial position and how the firm generates and uses cash. This chapter examines the many different types of assets, liabilities, and shareholders' equity items that affect the statement of financial position and the statement of cash flows.

Usefulness of the Statements of Financial Position and Cash Flows from a Business Perspective

LEARNING OBJECTIVE 1

Understand the statement of financial position and statement of cash flows from a business perspective.

It is important to understand how the users of financial statements use the statement of financial position and the statement of cash flows. For example, what might potential investors in a company focus on when analyzing a statement of financial position? What aspects of the statement of cash flows do financial analysts focus on when they are assessing earnings quality? How do creditors use financial statements to assess the creditworthiness of companies that have requested a loan? We will answer these questions below.

Analyzing a Statement of Financial Position

The statement of financial position (SFP) provides information about a company's liquidity and solvency in order to help users assess the risk of investing (or increasing the investment) in the company. In addition, the SFP provides details about the company's financial structure, such as whether it is financed primarily by debt or equity. If a company is heavily indebted, it may not be able to make the most of opportunities that occur as the economy improves. On the other hand, as discussed later in this chapter, companies with more financial flexibility are typically better able to survive economic downturns and to take advantage of opportunities to invest and expand. Investors can use the SFP and related notes to the financial statements to assess companies' financial flexibility and the risk of business failure.

Assessing Earnings Quality

Ethics It is important to understand how financial analysts and other users of the statement of cash flows use it to assess earnings quality. One concern of financial statement users is that company insiders might manipulate information to make earnings look better or worse than they are, for strategic reasons. For example, if managers are trying to increase their bonuses or prevent the company from violating the terms of a loan, they may be tempted to artificially increase earnings. They could do this by reducing the allowance for doubtful accounts or reducing the provision for inventory obsolescence. Likewise, managers might try to lower earnings in a year when they have missed their bonuses, so that they can more easily increase earnings and their bonuses the next year. Analyzing the statement of cash flows is often done to assess earnings quality. For example, if net income is significantly higher than cash flow from operations, this is a sign of poor earnings quality that may require further analysis. Similarly, if a company relies on the issuance of shares or other financing activities to offset repeated negative cash flow from operations, then financial statement users should be concerned.

Assessing the Creditworthiness of Companies

Creditors often rely on the SFP to assess a company's liquidity and its ability to service debt. Similarly, a review of a company's long-term debt and shareholders' equity section helps to evaluate its solvency level. For example, when a company has a high debt to total assets ratio, it is at higher risk of bankruptcy. Companies that use a higher proportion of debt are typically at higher risk and require higher cash flow from operations to ensure that they are able to make interest and principal payments as they come due. We discuss the preparation and use of the SFP and statement of cash flows in more detail below.

PART 1	Statement of Financial Position

Usefulness and Limitations of the Statement of Financial Position

LEARNING OBJECTIVE 2

Identify the uses and limitations of a statement of financial position.

The **statement of financial position**, called the balance sheet under ASPE, reports a business enterprise's assets, liabilities, and shareholders' equity at a specific date. This financial statement provides information about the nature and amounts of investment in enterprise resources, obligations to creditors, and owners' equity (net resources). It therefore helps in predicting the amounts, timing, and uncertainty of future cash flows.

Usefulness

Finance 5.1.1 By providing information about assets, liabilities, and shareholders' equity, the SFP becomes a basis for calculating rates of return on invested assets and for evaluating the enterprise's capital structure. Information in the SFP is also used to assess business risk and future cash flows.[1] In this regard, the **SFP is useful for analyzing a company's liquidity, solvency, and financial flexibility**, as described below. It also helps in analyzing profitability (even though this is not the statement's main focus).

Liquidity **depends on the amount of time that is expected to pass until an asset is realized** (converted into cash) or until a liability has to be paid. Does the company have enough cash on hand and cash coming in to cover its short-term liabilities? Certain ratios help assess overall liquidity, including the **current ratio**, **quick or acid-test ratio**, and **current cash debt coverage ratio**. The liquidity of certain assets, such as receivables and inventory, is assessed through **activity** or **turnover ratios**.[2] These ratios look at how fast the receivables or inventories are being collected or sold. Creditors are interested in **short-term** liquidity ratios, because these ratios indicate whether the enterprise will have the resources to pay its current and maturing obligations. Similarly, shareholders assess liquidity to evaluate the possibility of future cash dividends or the buyback of shares. In general, the greater the liquidity, the lower the risk of enterprise or business failure.[3]

Solvency reflects an **enterprise's ability to pay its debts and related interest**. For example, when a company carries a high level of long-term debt compared with its assets, it is at higher risk for insolvency than a similar company with less long-term debt. Companies with higher debt are riskier because more of their assets will be required to meet these fixed obligations (such as interest and principal payments). Certain ratios help assess solvency. These are often called **coverage ratios** because they indicate a company's ability to cover its interest and long-term debt payments.

Liquidity and solvency affect an entity's financial flexibility, which measures the **"ability of an enterprise to take effective actions to alter the amounts and timing of cash flows so it can respond to unexpected needs and opportunities."**[4] For example, a company may become so loaded with debt—so financially inflexible—that its cash sources to finance expansion or to pay off maturing debt are limited or non-existent. An enterprise with a high degree of financial flexibility is better able to survive bad times, to recover from unexpected setbacks, and to take advantage of profitable and unexpected investment opportunities. Generally, the greater the financial flexibility, the lower the risk of enterprise or business failure. **What Do the Numbers Mean? 5.1** shows a case of a company facing liquidity and other business risks.

What Do the Numbers Mean? 5.1

Eastman Kodak Company is a technology company that focuses on digital imaging and commercial printing for businesses. Kodak reported assets of U.S. $5.1 billion and debt of U.S. $6.8 billion in its Chapter 11 (bankruptcy) documents filed in New York in 2012. The company had failed to adapt from its strengths in areas such as traditional film and the Instamatic camera. At the time it entered into bankruptcy protection, Kodak had made a push into inkjet printers and commercial digital printers, but the new products did not generate enough demand to make up for a business model based on traditional film. The company had developed the first digital camera in 1975 but shelved it due to worries that it would threaten the more profitable film business.[5]

In September 2013, Kodak emerged from bankruptcy protection, with a plan to focus more on printing equipment and related

---

[1]Risk means the unpredictability of the enterprise's future events, transactions, circumstances, and results.

[2]The formulas for these and other ratios are summarized in Appendix 5A.

[3]Liquidity measures are important inputs to bankruptcy prediction models, such as those developed by Altman and others. These models range from very simple, to quite complex "new age statistical learning models." For an in-depth discussion, see S. Jones, D. Johnstone, and R. Wilson, "Predicting Corporate Bankruptcy: An Evaluation of Alternative Statistical Frameworks," *Journal of Business, Finance and Accounting*, 44(1–2), 2017: 3–34.

[4]"Reporting Income, Cash Flows, and Financial Position of Business Enterprises," Proposed Statement of Financial Accounting Concepts (Stamford, Conn.: FASB, 1981), par. 25.

[5]D. McCarty and B. Jinks, "Kodak Files for Bankruptcy as Digital Era Spells End to Film," Bloomberg News, January 2, 2012.

services for businesses. While it had some encouraging results in the first few years after bankruptcy protection, by the first two quarters of 2017 Kodak had earnings per share from continuing operations of only $0.09 (partially offset by a loss on discontinued operations of $0.07). It also had negative net assets of U.S. $59 million. Indeed, the company still faces significant business risks. For example, it was still generating negative cash flow from operations in the first half of 2017 (U.S. $74 million) and acknowledged in its U.S. Securities and Exchange Commission filings at the end of 2016 that "The ability to generate positive operating cash flows will be necessary for Kodak to continue to operate its business." The company also noted that it would need to introduce successful innovative products at competitive prices and at an appropriate scale in order to grow its businesses, improve margins, and achieve its financial objectives.[6] Liquidity and solvency risks are ongoing concerns for the company given the nature of the industry. These risks are examined further below as part of our discussion of the SFP and the calculation of free cash flow.

Limitations

Because the income statement and the SFP are interrelated, it is not surprising that the SFP has many of the same limitations as the income statement. Here are some of the major limitations of the SFP:

1. Many assets and liabilities are stated at their historical cost. As a result, the information reported in the SFP has higher reliability but it can be criticized as being less relevant than the current fair value would be. We discussed the use of historical cost and other valuation methods in Chapters 2 and 3. As noted there, the trend is toward greater use of fair value, especially for things like investments and biological assets.

> **Underlying Concept 5.1**
>
> "Soft" numbers are less reliable than "hard" numbers and have less predictive value because they are likely to change.

2. Judgements and estimates are used in determining many of the items reported in the SFP. Recall the issues we identified in Chapter 4 when discussing income statement limitations. As we stated there, the financial statements include many "soft" numbers; that is, numbers that are significantly uncertain. See **Underlying Concept 5.1**. In addition, entities often need to make materiality judgements when preparing financial statements. IFRS Practice Statement 2 (PS2) was issued in September 2017 and provides non-mandatory guidance for reporting entities to consider. Remember from Chapter 2 that information is material if its omission or misstatement could influence financial information users' decisions. PS2 suggests a **four-step process for assessing materiality** when preparing financial statements:

   a. Identify information that is potentially material.

   b. Assess whether the identified information is material.

   c. Organize the information to communicate it clearly and concisely to key users.

   d. Review the draft financial statements to determine if all material information has been properly identified and materiality considered based on the complete set of financial statements.

3. The SFP necessarily **leaves out many items** that are relevant to the business but cannot be recorded objectively.[7] These may be either assets or liabilities. Because liquidity and solvency ratios worsen when liabilities are recognized, a company may be biased against including liabilities in the financial statements. Knowing this, analysts habitually look for and capitalize many liabilities that may be "off–balance sheet" before they calculate key liquidity and solvency ratios.[8] For example, when reviewing a company, analysts consider off–balance sheet liabilities such as certain types of leases for companies following ASPE. The information that is disclosed in the notes to the financial statements and the analyst's knowledge of the business and industry become critical in this context, because they make it possible to identify and measure off–balance sheet items that often represent additional risk to the company.

---

[6]See Eastman Kodak Co. Form 10K, annual report filed March 7, 2017, for the period ended December 31, 2016.

[7]We discuss several of these omitted items (such as internally generated goodwill and certain commitments) in later chapters.

[8]While the term "capitalize" is often used in the context of recording costs as assets, it is sometimes used differently: in the context here, it means including the liabilities on the SFP for the purpose of performing financial statement analysis.

Classification in the Statement of Financial Position

> **LEARNING OBJECTIVE 3**
> Identify the major classifications of a statement of financial position.

SFP accounts are **classified** (like the income statement) so that **similar items are grouped together** to arrive at significant subtotals. The material is also arranged so that important relationships are shown.

As is true of the income statement, the SFP's parts and subsections can be more informative than the whole. Individual items should be separately reported and classified in enough detail so that users can assess the amounts, timing, and uncertainty of future cash flows, and evaluate the company's liquidity and financial flexibility, profitability, and risk.

Classification in financial statements helps analysts and other financial statement users by **grouping items with similar characteristics** and **separating items with different characteristics**. In this regard, the SFP provides additional information. Many users use the information in financial statements to assess risk, including the company's financial flexibility, as noted earlier. Consider how the following groupings of assets and liabilities provide additional insight:

1. Assets that are of a different type or that have a different **function** in the company's activities should be reported as separate items. For example, merchandise inventory should be reported separately from property, plant, and equipment. Inventory will be sold and property, plant, and equipment will be used. In this way, investors can see how fast inventory is turning over or being sold.

2. Liabilities and equity items with **different implications for the enterprise's financial flexibility** should be reported separately. For example, long-term liabilities should be reported separately from current liabilities, and debt should be separate from equity.

3. Assets and liabilities with different **general liquidity characteristics** should be reported as separate items. For example, property being used by a company is reported separately from property held for sale.

4. Certain assets, liabilities, and equity instruments have **attributes that allow them to be measured or valued more easily**. Reporting these separately takes advantage of this characteristic. Monetary assets and liabilities, and financial instruments are two examples of groupings. We will discuss each separately below.

Monetary versus Nonmonetary Assets and Liabilities

Monetary assets are either money itself **or claims to future cash flows that are fixed or determinable in amount and timing**.[9] Because of these characteristics, they are said to be easier to measure, and they generally are. In addition, their carrying values (which approximate net realizable value) are more representative of economic reality because they normally are close to the amount of cash that the company will receive in the future. Examples are accounts and notes receivable. Likewise, liabilities that require **future cash outflows that are fixed or determinable in amount and timing** are also considered to be monetary and are easier to measure.[10] Accounts and notes payable and long-term debt are examples. In contrast, other assets—such as inventory; property, plant, and equipment; certain investments; and

---

[9]Reprinted/adapted with permission from the *CPA Canada Handbook—Accounting* © 2018, Part II, Section 3831.05, by Chartered Professional Accountants of Canada. All rights reserved by the copyright owner.

[10]Reprinted/adapted with permission from the *CPA Canada Handbook—Accounting* © 2018, Part II, Section 3831.05, by Chartered Professional Accountants of Canada. All rights reserved by the copyright owner.

Underlying Concept 5.2
With nonmonetary assets, historical cost is often a more reliable measure where market values are not available.

intangibles—are **nonmonetary assets** because their value in terms of a monetary unit such as dollars is not fixed. There is therefore additional measurement uncertainty. These assets are frequently recorded at their historical cost (or amortized cost), which often does not reflect the economic value to the firm. See **Underlying Concept 5.2.**

Financial Instruments

Law **Financial instruments** are contracts between two or more parties that create a financial asset for one party and a financial liability or equity instrument for the other.[11] They are often marketable or tradable, and therefore easy to measure. Many financial instruments are also monetary assets or liabilities. Financial assets include the following:

- **Cash**
- **Contractual rights to receive cash or another financial instrument**
- **Equity instruments of other companies**[12]

Contractual rights to **receive** cash or other financial instruments are assets, whereas contractual obligations to **pay** are liabilities. Cash, accounts receivable, and all payables are examples of financial instruments. These instruments are all monetary. Investments in shares of other companies are also financial instruments. Current accounting standards on financial instruments require fair value accounting for certain types of financial instruments, including certain types of investments, especially where market values are readily available. This is due to the fact that fair value (often based on market prices for financial instruments) is often relatively easy to obtain and represents an objective view of the measurement of the instrument. In addition, IFRS and ASPE generally allow an entity to choose to value financial instruments at fair value as an accounting policy choice (with gains and losses booked through net income). This is called the **fair value** option. Financial instruments should not be offset against each other on the SFP except under limited circumstances. We discuss the accounting and reporting of financial instruments more extensively in Chapters 7, 9, 13, 14, 15, and 16. Derivatives, a more complex type of financial instrument, will be covered in Chapter 16.

Elements of the Statement of Financial Position

The three general classes of items that are included in the SFP are assets, liabilities, and equity.

1. **Assets: Present economic resources** controlled by an entity as a result of past transactions or events with the potential to produce economic benefits.
2. **Liabilities: Present duty or responsibility that obligates the entity, arising from past transactions or events** (that is, an obligation that an entity would have no practical ability to avoid).
3. **Equity/Net assets:** The **residual interest** in an entity's assets that remains after deducting its liabilities. In a business enterprise, equity is the ownership interest.

Significant Change These definitions of elements are based on the discussion of the conceptual framework summarized in Chapter 2. **Illustration 5.1** shows a standard format for presenting the SFP for many companies.

Although the SFP can be classified or presented in other ways, in actual practice the major subdivisions in Illustration 5.1 are closely followed, with exceptions in certain industries. When

---

[11]See *CPA Canada Handbook—Accounting*, Part II, Section 3856.05 for the definition of a financial instrument. Markets often exist or can be created for these instruments because of their nature and measurability. Liabilities are included because they represent the other side of an asset contract; for example, accounts payable to one company represent accounts receivable to another. This excerpt is reprinted with permission from the *CPA Canada Handbook—Accounting* © 2018, by Chartered Professional Accountants of Canada. All rights reserved by the copyright owner.

[12]See *CPA Canada Handbook—Accounting*, Part II, Section 3856.05 and IAS 32.11 for more complete definitions. Reprinted/adapted with permission from the *CPA Canada Handbook—Accounting* © 2018, by Chartered Professional Accountants of Canada. All rights reserved by the copyright owner.

Assets	Liabilities and Shareholders' Equity
Current assets	Current liabilities
Long-term investments	Long-term debt
Property, plant, and equipment	Shareholders' equity
Intangible assets	Capital shares
Other assets	Contributed surplus
	Retained earnings
	Accumulated other comprehensive income/ other surplus

ILLUSTRATION 5.1

Statement of Financial Position Classifications

the SFP is for a proprietorship or partnership, the classifications in the owners' equity section are presented a little differently, as we will show later in the chapter. In addition, some companies following IFRS, such as British Airways plc, choose to reverse the order of items in their SFP. It lists non-current assets first and current assets last. Similarly, it lists shareholders' equity first, followed by non-current liabilities, and then current liabilities.

These standard classifications followed by most companies make it easier to calculate important ratios, such as the current ratio for assessing liquidity and debt to equity ratios for assessing solvency. Because total assets are broken down into categories, users can easily calculate which assets are more significant than others and how these relationships change over time.[13] This gives insight into management's strategy and stewardship. Illustration 5.2 shows a classified SFP for Air Canada.

CONSOLIDATED STATEMENT OF FINANCIAL POSITION

CANADIAN DOLLARS IN MILLIONS		DECEMBER 31, 2017	DECEMBER 31, 2016
ASSETS			
CURRENT			
Cash and cash equivalents		$ 642	$ 787
Short-term investments		3,162	2,192
Total cash, cash equivalents and short-term investments		3,804	2,979
Restricted cash	Note 2P	148	126
Accounts receivable		814	707
Aircraft fuel inventory		91	79
Spare parts and supplies inventory	Note 2Q	115	107
Prepaid expenses and other current assets		325	349
Total current assets		5,297	4,347
Deposits and other assets		465	468
Property and equipment	Note 4	9,252	8,520
Pension assets	Note 8	1,583	1,153
Deferred income tax	Note 10	472	–
Intangible assets	Note 5	318	315
Goodwill	Note 6	311	311
Total Assets		**$17,698**	**$15,114**

(continued)

---

[13]This type of comparison is done by performing a **vertical analysis**, which calculates the percentage that a specific asset represents when divided by total assets. This number may then be compared with the same percentage from past years. The latter comparison is generally called **horizontal** or **trend analysis**. Horizontal and vertical analyses are discussed further in Chapter 23.

ILLUSTRATION 5.2
(*continued*)

CANADIAN DOLLARS IN MILLIONS		DECEMBER 31, 2017	DECEMBER 31, 2016
LIABILITIES			
CURRENT			
Accounts payable and accrued liabilities		$ 1,961	$ 1,644
Advance ticket sales		2,428	2,073
Current portion of long-term debt and finance leases	Note 7	671	707
Total current liabilities		5,060	4,424
Long-term debt and finance leases	Note 7	5,448	5,911
Pension and other benefit liabilities	Note 8	2,592	2,436
Maintenance provisions	Note 9	1,003	922
Other long-term liabilities		216	202
Total liabilities		**14,319**	**13,895**
SHAREHOLDERS' EQUITY			
Share capital	Note 11	799	797
Contributed surplus		69	83
Hedging reserve		–	3
Retained earnings		2,511	336
Total shareholders' equity		3,379	1,219
Total liabilities and shareholders' equity		**$17,698**	**$15,114**

The accompanying notes are an integral part of the consolidated financial statements.

Note that the total shareholders' equity position improved in 2017, with total shareholders' equity (in millions) ending the year at $3,379 versus $1,219 at the end of 2016. Not too long ago, Air Canada was in a significantly worse equity position, with shareholders' equity of $(1,133) at the end of 2014.

Air Canada's improved equity position is partly due to passenger revenue increasing by over 10% to a record level of $14.5 billion. Although passenger load (or capacity utilization) was down slightly to 82.3%, it still resulted in a record of approximately 48 million customers for the company. The improvement in equity of almost $2.2 billion was also due in part to improvement in the Canadian dollar relative to the U.S. dollar that resulted in a foreign exchange gain of $120 million compared to a loss in 2016 of $38 million, and a $412-million improvement in equity as the result of a recovery of income taxes relating to previously unrecognized income tax assets. We examine income tax assets in Chapter 18.

Preparation of the Classified Statement of Financial Position (Balance Sheet)

LEARNING OBJECTIVE 4
Prepare a classified statement of financial position.

Current Assets

Current assets **include cash and other assets that will ordinarily be realized within one year** from the date of the SFP or within the normal operating cycle if the cycle is longer than a year.[14] The operating cycle is the average time between the acquisition of assets for processing and the realization of cash or cash equivalents. Cash is realized through sales of the product that is created from the materials and supplies. The cycle begins with cash and then moves through inventory, production, and receivables, and back to cash. When there are several operating cycles within one year, the one-year period is used. If the operating cycle is more than one year, the longer period is used. **Illustration 5.3** shows the operating cycle for manufacturing companies.

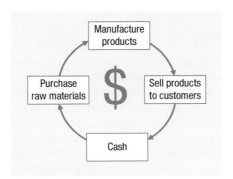

ILLUSTRATION 5.3

The Business Operating Cycle for Manufacturing Companies

For most industries, current assets are segregated and presented in the SFP in order according to their liquidity.[15] The five major items that are found in the current assets section are cash, short-term investments (including derivatives), receivables, inventories, and prepayments. These items are valued as follows:

1. Cash: at its stated value
2. Short-term investments: at cost/amortized cost or fair value
3. Accounts receivable: at the estimated amount that is collectible
4. Inventories: generally at the lower of cost and net realizable value
5. Prepaid items: at cost

Cash

Cash is often grouped with other cash-like liquid assets and reported as **cash and cash equivalents**. See **Underlying Concept 5.3**. Cash and cash equivalents are defined as **cash, demand deposits, and short-term, highly liquid investments that are readily convertible into known amounts of cash and have an insignificant risk of changing in value**.[16] **Illustration 5.4** details the cash and cash equivalents for retailer **Canadian Tire**.

Cash and Cash Equivalents

Cash and cash equivalents are defined as cash plus highly liquid and rated certificates of deposit or commercial paper with an original term to maturity of three months or less.

Underlying Concept 5.3

Grouping similar items together reduces the amount of redundant information on the SFP and therefore makes the information easier to understand.

ILLUSTRATION 5.4

Consolidated Balance Sheet Presentation of Cash and Cash Equivalents—Excerpt from Canadian Tire Corporation's December 31, 2017 Financial Statements

---

[14]IAS 1.66. Copyright © IFRS Foundation. All rights reserved. Reproduced with permission. Reprinted/adapted with permission from the *CPA Canada Handbook—Accounting* © 2018, Part II, Section 1510.03, by Chartered Professional Accountants of Canada. All rights reserved by the copyright owner.

[15]The real estate industry does not follow this approach. The industry feels that the presentation is more meaningful when the most important assets are presented first. In most real estate development companies, the most important and largest asset is investment properties. This asset includes hotels, shopping centres, leased buildings, and so on that generate revenue or profits for the company. As an example, **Brookfield Property Partners, L.P.** recorded this asset first on its consolidated balance sheet. On the liabilities side, the corresponding debt related to the properties is recorded. For Brookfield, this asset represented over 60% of total assets in 2017. Many real estate companies follow specialized industry accounting principles (REALpac *IFRS Handbook* and REALpac *ASPE Handbook*) as published by the Real Property Association of Canada or REALpac (www.realpac.ca).

[16]IAS 7.6. Copyright © IFRS Foundation. All rights reserved. Reproduced with permission. Reprinted/adapted with permission from the *CPA Canada Handbook—Accounting* © 2018, Part II, Section 1540.06, by Chartered Professional Accountants of Canada. All rights reserved by the copyright owner.

Any restrictions on the general availability of cash or any commitments regarding how it is likely to be used must be disclosed and may affect whether the items are presented as current.

How much cash should a company hold? In general, a company needs enough liquid assets, including cash, to be able to settle its current liabilities in a timely manner; however, it must also ensure that its assets do not sit idle. Cash itself is generally non–interest-bearing and so does not contribute to net income. Too much cash can make a company a more likely target for a takeover bid if it is publicly traded.

Short-Term Investments

Investments in debt and equity securities are presented separately and valued at cost/amortized cost or fair value. Those measured at cost are written down when impaired. Companies that have excess cash often have significant amounts of short-term investments. While deciding what to do with the money, they will temporarily invest it to generate some profits (instead of letting the funds sit idle as non–interest-bearing cash). In addition, the way a company does business can result in higher levels of investments. For instance, the business models of insurance companies, pension funds, and banks result in significant amounts of temporary as well as long-term investments. Insurance companies collect premiums up front and invest the money so that they have funds available to pay out future claims that arise under the insurance policies. Pension plans likewise collect money up front (through pension contributions from individuals and companies) and invest it for future payout when the contributors retire. Most investments are considered short-term if they are expected to be sold or realized within 12 months of the SFP date or if held for trading purposes. So FV-NI investments could be short or long-term, while FV-OCI investments are typically long-term.

Receivables

Accounts receivable should be segregated to show **ordinary trade accounts**, amounts owing by **related parties**, and other **unusual items** of a substantial amount. Anticipated losses due to uncollectibles should be accrued. The amount and nature of any nontrade receivables and any receivables that have been designated or pledged as collateral should be disclosed. Accounts receivable are valued at their net realizable value. **Illustration 5.5** shows how **IBI Group Inc.**, a Canadian architecture, engineering, and technology company, reported its financial instruments, including receivables and Fair Value Through Profit and Loss (FVTPL) financial assets and liabilities, in Note 6 to its financial statements. (See **What Do the Numbers Mean? 5.2**.)

ILLUSTRATION 5.5

Statement of Financial Position Presentation of Financial Assets—Excerpt from IBI Group Inc.'s December 31, 2017 Financial Statements (from Note 6(c)) (in thousands of Canadian dollars)

(c) FINANCIAL ASSETS AND LIABILITIES

The fair values of cash, restricted cash, accounts receivable, accounts payable and accrued liabilities, vendor notes payable, consent fee notes payable and finance lease obligation approximate their carrying amounts due to their short-term maturity.

The carrying amount of the Company's financial instruments as at December 31, 2017 are as follows:

	Financial assets and liabilities at FVTPL	Loans and receivables	Other financial liabilities	Total
FINANCIAL ASSETS				
Cash	$ 9,833	$ –	$ –	$ 9,833
Restricted cash	2,936	–	–	2,936
Accounts receivable	–	111,219	–	111,219
TOTAL	$12,769	$111,219	$ –	$123,988

(continued)

ILLUSTRATION 5.5

(continued)

FINANCIAL LIABILITIES				
Accounts payable and accrued liabilities	$ –	$ –	$ 45,934	$ 45,934
Deferred share plan liability[1]	2,848	–	–	2,848
Finance lease obligation	–	–	67	67
Credit facilities	–	–	63,842	63,842
Convertible debentures	–	–	47,157	47,157
Other financial liabilities	13,011	–	–	13,011
TOTAL	$15,859	$ –	$157,000	$172,859

[1]The deferred share plan liability is grouped with accounts payable and accrued liabilities on the consolidated statement of financial position. See Note 16 – Deferred Share Plan, for further discussion.

What Do the Numbers Mean? 5.2

IBI Group Inc. (Intelligence Buildings Infrastructure) is a planning, architecture, engineering, and technology firm that is based in Canada and operates globally. It focuses its consulting services on areas such as intelligent systems, building design, and infrastructure development. For the year ended December 31, 2017, the company had revenues of $361 million, and recorded net income of $11.4 million due largely to operating income of approximately $31.0 million, offset by interest and finance costs of $11.8 million, prior to taxes. The company continues to show signs of recovery from many of the significant challenges it faced a few years ago. For example, during 2013, it recorded a net loss of $223 million after it incurred significant impairment of goodwill and intangible assets ($174 million), and a major writedown of accounts receivable ($13 million) due to uncertainty about collection of older amounts receivable. It also had a major writedown ($35 million) of work-in-process inventory (which, for this type of firm, relates mainly to time and materials charged to projects in excess of the amounts that can be billed to customers). The company took steps since then to improve its financial performance by eliminating dividends in and distributions to its management partnership (from 2013 through 2017). It implemented cost management initiatives in 2015 and continued to focus on these into 2017, together with efforts to strengthen its quality management program.[17]

Inventories

"Inventories are assets:

1. **held for sale in the ordinary course of business,**
2. **in the process of production for such sale, or**
3. **in the form of materials or supplies to be consumed in the production process or in the rendering of services.**"[18]

Inventories are valued at the lower of cost and net realizable value, with cost being determined using a **cost formula**, such as first-in, first-out (FIFO), weighted average cost, or specific identification (where items are not ordinarily interchangeable). It is important to disclose these details because this information helps users understand the amount of judgement that was used in measuring this asset. For a manufacturer, the stage of the inventories' completion is also indicated (raw materials, work in process, and finished goods). **Illustration 5.6** shows the breakdown of **Linamar Corporation's** inventory.

---

[17]IBI Group 2017 annual report (www.ibigroup.com).

[18]IAS 2.6. Copyright © IFRS Foundation. All rights reserved. Reproduced with permission. This excerpt is reprinted with permission from the *CPA Canada Handbook—Accounting* © 2018, Part II, Section 3031.07, by Chartered Professional Accountants of Canada. All rights reserved by the copyright owner.

ILLUSTRATION 5.6

Balance Sheet Presentation of Inventories—Excerpt from Linamar Corporation's December 31, 2017 Financial Statements (in thousands of Canadian dollars)

8. INVENTORIES

	December 31 2017 $	December 31 2016 $
General stores	129,257	121,886
Raw materials	193,255	172,912
Work-in-process	240,255	182,753
Finished goods	228,903	213,834
	791,670	691,385

The cost of inventories recognized as an expense during the year ended December 31, 2017 was $4,920,466 (2016 - $4,423,974).

A provision for obsolescence for slow moving inventory items is estimated by management based on historical and expected future sales and is included in cost of sales. In the year ended December 31, 2017 the Company recognized a charge to cost of sales for the write-down of slow moving and obsolete inventory, and adjustments to net realizable value aggregating $26,300 (2016 - $41,172). In the year ended December 31, 2017 the Company recognized a gain to cost of sales for reversal of inventory provisions with a value of $260 (2016 - $283). The inventory balance has been reduced by a provision of $73,880 as at December 31, 2017 (2016 - $68,633).

As one of Canada's largest manufacturers, Linamar Corporation has a significant investment in inventories, including General Stores Inventory, which is not often separately disclosed by manufacturers, as discussed in **What Do the Numbers Mean? 5.3**.

What Do the Numbers Mean? 5.3

In addition to the regular inventory categories seen at most manufacturers, Linamar also separately discloses its General Stores inventory. This includes many of the consumable items that are required in the manufacturing process for its goods, other than the raw materials. It would include small consumable tooling (like drills and boring bars), and other items like lubricants, fluids to assist in cutting, and maintenance supplies used in the manufacturing process. In its annual report, Linamar discloses the following relating to inventory in its significant accounting policy note:

Inventories

Inventories are valued at the lower of cost and net realizable value. The cost of finished goods and work-in-process is comprised of material costs, direct labour costs and other direct costs and related production overheads (based on normal operating capacity). Costs are allocated to inventory on the basis of weighted average costs. Net realizable value for finished goods and work-in-process is the estimated selling price in the ordinary course of business, less estimated costs of completion and applicable variable selling expenses. For raw materials and general stores inventories the replacement cost is considered to be the best available measure of net realizable value.

The amount of inventories recognized as an expense during the period is shown in costs of sales. Write-downs for inventories are recorded when the net realizable value is lower than cost. The write-downs may be reversed if the circumstances which caused them no longer exist.

Strategy & Governance **2.3.1** Which types of companies are likely to have significant inventory? Companies that sell and manufacture goods will normally carry inventory (as compared with companies that offer services only). How much inventory is enough or, conversely, how much inventory is too much? Companies must have at least enough inventory to meet customer demands. On the other hand, inventory ties up significant amounts of cash flows, creates storage costs, and subjects the company to risk of theft, obsolescence, and so on. Many companies operate with a just-in-time philosophy, meaning that they streamline their production and supply channels so that they can order the raw materials and produce the product in a very short time. Car manufacturers often follow this philosophy, thus freeing up working capital and reducing the need for storing inventory.

Prepaid Expenses

Prepaid expenses included in current assets are **expenditures already made for benefits (usually services) that will be received within one year or the operating cycle**, whichever is longer. These items are current assets because cash does not need to be used for them again in the current year or operating cycle because they have already been paid for. A common example is the payment in advance for an insurance policy. It is classified as a prepaid expense at the time of the expenditure because the payment occurs before the coverage benefit is received. Prepaid expenses are reported at the amount of the unexpired or unconsumed cost. Other common prepaid expenses include rent, advertising, property taxes, and office or operating supplies.

Companies sometimes include insurance and other prepayments for two or three years in current assets even though part of the advance payment applies to periods beyond one year or the current operating cycle. This is done by convention even though it is inconsistent with the definition of current assets.

Non-current Investments

Non-current investments normally consist of one of the types shown in Illustration 5.7.

ILLUSTRATION 5.7

Types of Non-current Investments

TYPES OF NON-CURRENT INVESTMENTS	MEASUREMENT
Debt Securities	
Debt instruments held to collect cash flows (such as bonds, long-term notes, and loans receivable)	Amortized cost or (under IFRS) FV-OCI
Equity Securities	
Investments in associates (significant influence investments)	Equity method
Subsidiaries	Consolidated
Non-consolidated subsidiaries	Fair value or at cost
Where no influence or control	Fair value or at cost
Other	
Sinking funds, tangible assets held as investments, other	Generally at cost

Long-term investments are usually presented on the SFP just below current assets in a separate section called "Investments." Many securities that are properly shown among long-term investments are, in fact, readily marketable. They are not included as current assets unless management intends to convert them to cash in the short term; that is, within a year or the operating cycle, whichever is longer. So, FV-OCI investments are typically considered non-current.

Management may be holding some of these investments for strategic reasons (such as for significant influence investments or non-consolidated subsidiaries). Investments that are held for strategic reasons are generally held for longer periods of time and are consolidated (subsidiaries) or accounted for using the equity method (significant influence investments in associates). We will examine the classification and accounting for investments in greater detail in Chapter 9.

Long-term investments carried at other than fair value must be written down when impaired.

Property, Plant, and Equipment

IFRS Property, plant, and equipment are tangible capital assets—that is, properties of a durable nature—that are **used in ongoing business operations to generate income**. These assets consist of physical or tangible property, such as land, buildings, machinery, furniture, tools, and wasting resources (for example, timberland and minerals). They are generally carried at their cost or amortized cost. With the exception of land, most assets are either depreciable (such as buildings) or depletable (such as timberland or oil reserves). IFRS allows an option to carry them at fair value using a revaluation or fair value method. Like all other assets, property, plant, and equipment are written down when impaired.

TWC Enterprises Limited (owners of ClubLink golf clubs) has significant capital assets. (See **What Do the Numbers Mean? 5.4**.) In fact, in 2017, property, plant, and equipment and intangible assets represented 91.7% of the corporation's total assets. This is not surprising as the company is one of Canada's largest golf club developers and operators. The bulk of these assets are in land (golf courses) and buildings and land improvements. **Illustration 5.8** shows the detailed breakdown of these assets, as presented in Note 6 to TWC's financial statements.

What Do the Numbers Mean? 5.4

In the investing activities section of its statement of cash flows, TWC further segregates its spending into **operating** and **expansion** expenditures, with $12.7 million and $5.1 million of each type, respectively, in 2017. This helps users understand which expenditures are made to maintain existing operations and which ones will be to expand operations, and are therefore enhancing the company's growth potential. The basis of measuring the property, plant, and equipment; any liens (creditor claims) against the properties; and accumulated depreciation should be disclosed, usually in notes to the statements.

Under IFRS, a reconciliation is provided, reconciling the capital assets from the beginning to the end of the period, showing items such as additions, disposals, impairment, and depreciation.

Aside from companies in the golf club business, those based in real estate, manufacturing, resources, or pharmaceuticals also have large amounts of capital assets on their statements of financial position. These types of companies are often called **capital-intensive** since they require large amounts of capital to invest in their long-term revenue-generating assets.

ILLUSTRATION 5.8 SFP Presentation of Property, Plant, and Equipment—Excerpt from TWC Enterprises Limited's December 31, 2017 Financial Statements

PROPERTY, PLANT AND EQUIPMENT

Property, plant and equipment consist of the following:

(thousands of Canadian dollars)	Land	Buildings and Land Improvements	Docks	Bunkers, Cart Paths and Irrigation	Rolling Stock and Equipment	Total
Cost						
At January 1, 2016	$309,489	$210,914	$86,303	$105,591	$169,250	**$881,547**
Additions	2,883	4,608	1,406	2,209	8,594	**19,700**
Disposals	–	–	–	–	(1,622)	**(1,622)**
Foreign exchange difference	(1,030)	(1,711)	(2,519)	(320)	(2,617)	**(8,197)**
At December 31, 2016	311,342	213,811	85,190	107,480	173,605	**891,428**
Additions	1,967	4,955	806	1,529	8,537	**17,794**
Disposals	(1,887)	(3,762)	–	(130)	(7,790)	**(13,569)**
Foreign exchange difference	(2,106)	(4,026)	(5,637)	(753)	(6,155)	**(18,677)**
At December 31, 2017	$309,316	$210,978	$80,359	$108,126	$168,197	**$876,976**
Accumulated Depreciation						
At January 1, 2016	$ –	$ 77,954	$27,856	$ 63,320	$ 98,834	**$267,964**
Depreciation	–	6,805	4,382	5,429	8,598	**25,214**
Disposals	–	–	–	–	(1,622)	**(1,622)**
Foreign exchange difference	–	(421)	(773)	(81)	(1,033)	**(2,308)**
At December 31, 2016	$ –	$ 84,338	$31,465	$ 68,668	$104,777	**$289,248**
Depreciation	–	6,425	4,452	5,383	8,576	**24,836**
Disposals	–	(2,135)	–	(112)	(6,350)	**(8,597)**
Foreign exchange difference	–	(1,169)	(2,215)	(260)	(2,708)	**(6,352)**
At December 31, 2017	–	87,459	33,702	73,679	104,295	**299,135**
Net book value at December 31, 2016	$311,342	$129,473	$53,725	$ 38,812	$ 68,828	**$602,180**
Net book value at December 31, 2017	$309,316	$123,519	$46,657	$ 34,447	$ 63,902	**$577,841**

Certain property, plant and equipment have been assigned as collateral for borrowings (Note 10). As at December 31, 2017, ClubLink had equipment under finance lease with a net book value of $3,555,000 (2016 – $6,690,000).

Intangible Assets and Goodwill

Intangible assets **are capital assets that have no physical substance** and usually have a higher degree of uncertainty about their future benefits. They include patents, copyrights, franchises, trademarks, trade names, and secret processes. These intangibles are initially recorded at cost and are divided into two groups for accounting purposes:

- those with finite lives, and
- those with indefinite lives.

Those with finite lives are amortized to expense over their useful lives. Those with indefinite lives are not amortized. Both are tested for impairment. Similarly, goodwill is not amortized—it is tested for impairment. Goodwill is an asset that arises in a business combination, based on the difference between the fair value of consideration given up and the fair value amounts assigned to identifiable net assets acquired.

Intangibles can amount to significant economic resources, yet financial analysts often ignore them. This is because their **valuation and measurement are difficult**. Many intangible assets, especially those that are **internally generated** (such as internally generated goodwill), are not recognized at all on the SFP.

As **Illustration 5.9** shows, a significant portion of **Valeant Pharmaceuticals International's** total assets is composed of goodwill and intangibles. (See **What Do the Numbers Mean? 5.5**.)

ILLUSTRATION 5.9

Balance Sheet Presentation of Goodwill and Intangible Assets—Excerpt from Valeant Pharmaceuticals International Inc.'s Financial Statements (amounts in U.S. $ millions)

	At December 31	
	2017	2016
ASSETS		
Current assets		
Cash and cash equivalents	$ 720	$ 542
Restricted cash	77	–
Trade receivables, net	2,130	2,517
Inventories, net	1,048	1,061
Current assets held for sale	–	261
Prepaid expenses and other current assets	771	696
Total current assets	4,746	5,077
Property, plant and equipment, net	1,403	1,312
Intangible assets, net	15,211	18,884
Goodwill	15,593	15,794
Deferred tax assets, net	433	146
Non-current assets held for sale	12	2,132
Other non-current assets	99	184
Total assets	$37,497	$43,529

What Do the Numbers Mean? 5.5

A further look at the detail behind the amount for intangibles shows that **Valeant's** intangibles include product brands, product rights, and patents for several pharmaceutical products. It makes sense that the company would have a large amount of money invested in intangibles because Valeant is in the business of developing pharmaceutical products. The drugs are patented by the company and become main revenue generators. However, the true value of **internally generated** patents is generally not reflected in the SFP. Instead, it is most often the **purchased** rights to drugs that show up as intangible assets because the value of these rights is measured through their acquisition.

Other Assets

The items included in the **other assets** section vary widely in practice. Some of the items that are commonly included (if they are not included anywhere else) are non-current receivables, intangible assets, assets in special funds, deferred income tax assets, land held for speculation, and advances to subsidiaries. The company should be careful to disclose these assets in enough detail for users to get a good idea of their nature.

Deferred income tax assets (called future income tax assets under ASPE; see Alternative Terminology 5.1) represent the taxes that may be avoided or saved due to deductions that a company may take when it prepares its **future** tax returns. These accounts are mainly a result of timing differences between what has been recognized in the accounts as revenues and expenses under GAAP and what has been recognized on the tax return under the provisions of the Income Tax Act. We will discuss deferred (or future) income taxes in greater detail in Chapter 18.

Current Liabilities

Current liabilities are the **obligations that are due within one year from the date of the SFP or within the operating cycle, where this is longer**.[19] This concept includes:

1. Payables resulting from the acquisition of goods and services, such as trade accounts payable, wages payable, or taxes payable
2. Collections received in advance for the delivery of goods or the performance of services, such as unearned rent revenue or unearned subscriptions revenue
3. Other liabilities whose liquidation will take place within the operating cycle, such as the portion of long-term bonds to be paid in the current period, or short-term obligations arising from a purchase of equipment
4. Short-term financing that is payable on demand (such as a bank overdraft)
5. Derivative financial instruments

At times, a liability that is payable within the year may not be included in the current liabilities section. This may occur either when the debt will be refinanced through another long-term issue, or when the debt is retired out of non-current assets.[20] This approach is justified because the liquidation of the liability does not result from the use of current assets or the creation of other current liabilities.

Current liabilities are not reported in any consistent order. The items that are most commonly listed first are bank indebtedness, accounts payable, or accrued liabilities. Those that are most commonly listed last are income taxes payable, current maturities of long-term debt, or other current liabilities. Any secured liability—for example, notes payable that have shares held as collateral for them—is fully described in the notes so that the assets providing the security can be identified.

The excess of total current assets over total current liabilities is called working capital (sometimes called "net working capital"). Working capital is the net amount of a company's relatively liquid resources. That is, it is the liquidity buffer (or cushion) that is available to meet the operating cycle's financial demands. Working capital, as an amount, is rarely disclosed on the SFP, but it is calculated by bankers and other creditors as an indicator of a company's short-term liquidity. To determine the availability of working capital to meet current obligations, however, one must analyze the current assets' composition and their nearness to cash.

Long-Term Debt and Liabilities

Long-term liabilities are **obligations that are not reasonably expected to be liquidated within the normal operating cycle but instead are payable at some later date.** Bonds payable, notes payable, some deferred (future) income tax liabilities, lease obligations, and pension obligations are the most common examples. The terms of long-term liability agreements (including the maturity date or dates, interest rates, nature of the obligation, and any security

---

[19]IAS 1.69. Copyright © IFRS Foundation. All rights reserved. Reproduced with permission. Reprinted/adapted with permission from the *CPA Canada Handbook—Accounting* © 2018, Part II, Section 1510.08, by Chartered Professional Accountants of Canada. All rights reserved by the copyright owner.

[20]In Chapter 13, there is a more detailed discussion of debt refinancing.

pledged to support the debt) are frequently described in notes to the financial statements. Long-term liabilities that mature within the current operating cycle are generally classified as current.

Generally, long-term liabilities are of three types:

1. Obligations arising from **specific financing situations**, such as the issuance of bonds, long-term lease obligations, and long-term notes payable

2. Obligations arising from **ordinary enterprise operations**, such as pension obligations, deferred income tax liabilities, and deferred or unearned revenues

3. Obligations that **depend on the occurrence or non-occurrence of one or more future events to confirm the amount payable, the payee, or the date payable**, such as service or product warranties (and other contingencies (ASPE) or provisions (IFRS) that are not due within one year or operating cycle; we will discuss these further in Chapter 13)

Long-term liabilities such as bonds often include debt covenants to help protect lenders. For example, companies may be required to limit their debt to total assets ratio or they may be restricted in the amount of dividends that they can pay to their common shareholders. Covents can reduce companies' financial flexibility as we discuss in Underlying Concept 5.4.

It is desirable to report any premium or discount as an addition to, or subtraction from, bonds payable. Generally, extensive supplementary disclosure is also needed for bonds and notes payable, because most long-term debt is subject to various covenants and restrictions in order to protect lenders.[21] **Deferred income tax liabilities** (or **future income tax liabilities** under ASPE) are future amounts that the company expects to owe to the government for income taxes. Deferred or unearned revenues are often treated as liabilities because a service or product is owed to the customer (performance obligation). They may be classified as long-term or current.

The excerpt from **Empire Company Limited** in **Illustration 5.10** is an example of the liabilities section of the balance sheet. It also shows the treatment of shareholders' equity by

> **Underlying Concept 5.4**
>
> Information about covenants and restrictions gives insight into the entity's financial flexibility and is therefore disclosed based on the full disclosure principle.

ILLUSTRATION 5.10

Balance Sheet Presentation of Liabilities and Shareholders' Equity—Excerpt from Empire Company Limited's 2017 Balance Sheet (in $ millions)

Liabilities		
Current	**May 6, 2017**	May 7, 2016
Accounts payable and accrued liabilities	**$2,230.2**	$2,173.1
Income taxes payable	**38.4**	21.2
Provisions (Note 14)	**88.1**	174.9
Long-term debt due within one year (Note 15)	**134.0**	350.4
	2,490.7	2,719.6
Provisions (Note 14)	**105.8**	131.7
Long-term debt (Note 15)	**1,736.8**	2,017.0
Other long-term liabilities (Note 16)	**141.7**	108.7
Employee future benefits (Note 17)	**374.0**	336.8
Deferred tax liabilities (Note 13)	**143.8**	141.7
	4,992.8	5,455.5
Shareholders' Equity		
Capital stock (Note 18)	**2,034.4**	2,045.1
Contributed surplus	**25.3**	22.5
Retained earnings	**1,572.8**	1,546.4
Accumulated other comprehensive income	**11.7**	9.9
	3,644.2	3,623.9
Non-controlling interest	**58.5**	59.1
	3,702.7	3,683.0
	$8,695.5	$9,138.5

See accompanying notes to the consolidated financial statements.

[21]The rights and privileges of the various securities that are outstanding (both debt and equity) are usually explained in the notes to the financial statements. Examples of information that should be disclosed are dividend and liquidation preferences, participation rights, call prices and dates, conversion or exercise prices and dates, sinking fund requirements, and unusual voting rights.

Empire, which is discussed next in the Owners' Equity section of this chapter. The company owns Sobeys Inc. food stores.

Note that the company's long-term debt mainly consists of notes payable and credit facilities. Details of the long-term debt are provided in Note 15 of Empire's financial statements. For example, the notes have interest rates that range between 3.5% and 7.2%, with maturity dates that extend as far as 2040!

Owners' Equity

Law The **owners' equity** (shareholders' equity) section is one of the most difficult sections to prepare and understand. This is due to the complexity of capital share agreements and the various restrictions on residual equity that are imposed by corporation laws, liability agreements, and boards of directors. As shown for Empire Company Limited in Illustration 5.10, the section is usually divided into four parts:

1. **Capital shares**, which represents the exchange value of shares that have been issued

2. **Contributed surplus**, which may include items such as amounts related to the repurchase of shares at an amount lower than the original purchase price

3. **Retained earnings**, which includes undistributed earnings, and is sometimes called "earned surplus"

4. **IFRS** **Accumulated other comprehensive income**, which may include unrealized gains and losses on certain investments; certain gains or losses from hedging activities; gains or losses on revalued property, plant, and equipment; and other items. This is not required to always be called "accumulated other comprehensive income" under IFRS, so you may see different terminology used by some companies.

The major disclosure requirements for capital shares (or stock) are their authorized, issued, and outstanding amounts. Contributed surplus is usually presented as one amount. Retained earnings, also presented as one amount, is positive if the company has undistributed accumulated profits. Otherwise, it will be a negative number and labelled "deficit." Any capital shares that have been reacquired by the company (treasury stock) are shown as a reduction of shareholders' equity.[22] The decrease in Capital Stock in 2017 relates to shares repurchased by a trust fund set up by the company to facilitate the future settlement of units under Empire's stock-based compensation plan.

A corporation's ownership or shareholders' equity accounts are quite different from the equivalent accounts in a partnership or proprietorship. Partners' permanent capital accounts and the balances in their temporary accounts (drawings accounts) are shown separately. Proprietorships ordinarily use a single capital account that handles all of the owner's equity transactions.

Illustration 5.11 presents the shareholders' equity section from **Shopify Inc.**, a leading cloud-based platform designed for small and medium-sized businesses to coordinate their business across multiple sales channels, including web- and mobile-based storefronts, physical (bricks and mortar) retail locations, and social media–based selling. The company was incorporated in Canada, but now follows U.S. GAAP and reports in U.S. dollars.

Note that Shopify has chosen to show the details on the number of shares issued and authorized on the face of its balance sheet, whereas many companies prefer to show this information in the notes to their financial statements. Common stock is sometimes called "common shares" on company balance sheets, and is also called "ordinary shares" under IFRS. Shopify also had preferred shares outstanding until the completion of its initial public offering (IPO), when they were converted into Class B multiple voting shares.[23]

---

[22]In Canada, under the Canada Business Corporations Act, shares that are reacquired must be cancelled. However, some provincial jurisdictions and other countries (such as the United States) still allow treasury shares to exist.

[23]Shopify Inc., 2017 Annual Report, accessed at www.sedar.com.

	Note	2017	2016
Common stock, unlimited Class A subordinate voting shares authorized, 87,067,604 and 77,030,952 issued and outstanding; unlimited Class B multiple voting shares authorized, 12,810,084 and 12,374,528 issued and outstanding	16	1,077,477	468,494
Additional paid-in capital		43,392	27,009
Accumulated other comprehensive income (loss)	17	3,435	(1,818)
Accumulated deficit		(123,204)	(83,209)
Total shareholders' equity		1,001,100	410,476
Total liabilities and shareholders' equity		1,113,564	490,558

ILLUSTRATION 5.11

Balance Sheet Presentation of Shareholders' Equity—Excerpt from Shopify Inc.'s December 31, 2017 Balance Sheet (in U.S. $ thousands)

Statement of Financial Position Format

One method of presenting a classified SFP is to list assets, by section, on the left side and liabilities and shareholders' equity, by section, on the right side. The main disadvantage of this format is that it requires two facing pages. To avoid the use of facing pages, another format, shown in Illustration 5.12, lists liabilities and shareholders' equity directly below assets.

ILLUSTRATION 5.12

Classified SFP

SCIENTIFIC INNOVATION PRODUCTS, INC.
Statement of Financial Position
December 31, 2020

Assets

Current assets
Cash		$ 42,485	
Investments—trading		28,250	
Accounts receivable	$165,824		
Less: Allowance for doubtful accounts	1,850	163,974	
Notes receivable		23,000	
Inventory (at lower of average cost and net realizable value)		489,713	
Supplies on hand		9,780	
Prepaid expenses		16,252	
Total current assets			$ 773,454
Long-term investments			87,500
Property, plant, and equipment			
Land (at cost)		125,000	
Buildings (at cost)	975,800		
Less: Accumulated depreciation	341,200	634,600	
Total property, plant, and equipment			759,600
Intangible assets, net of accumulated amortization			80,000
Goodwill			20,000
Total assets			$1,720,554

(continued)

ILLUSTRATION 5.12
(*continued*)

Liabilities and Shareholders' Equity
Current liabilities

Accounts payable	$247,532	
Accrued interest	500	
Income taxes payable	62,520	
Accrued salaries, wages, and other liabilities	9,500	
Deposits received from customers	420	
Total current liabilities		$ 320,472

Long-term debt
(Twenty-year 12% debentures, due January 1, 2023)

		500,000
Total liabilities		820,472

Shareholders' equity
Paid in on capital shares

Preferred (7%, cumulative—authorized, issued, and outstanding, 30,000 shares)	$300,000	
Common (authorized, 500,000 shares; issued and outstanding, 400,000 shares)	400,000	
Contributed surplus	37,500	737,500
Retained earnings	102,333	
Accumulated other comprehensive income	60,249	162,582
Total shareholders' equity		900,082
Total liabilities and shareholders' equity		$1,720,554

Other Required Disclosures

LEARNING OBJECTIVE 5

Identify statement of financial position information that requires supplemental disclosure.

The following is information often reported by companies as part of their supplemental disclosure.

1. **Contingencies and provisions.** Material events that have an uncertain outcome.
2. **Accounting policies.** Explanations of the valuation methods that are used or the basic assumptions that are made for inventory valuations, amortization methods, investments in subsidiaries, and so on.
3. **Contractual situations.** Explanations of certain restrictions or covenants that are attached to specific assets or, more likely, to liabilities.
4. **Additional detail.** Expanded details on specific SFP line items.
5. **Subsequent events.** Events that happened after the SFP data were compiled.

Contingencies and Provisions

A **contingency** is an **existing situation in which there is uncertainty about whether a gain or loss will occur and that will finally be resolved when one or more future events occur or fail to occur** under ASPE. In short, contingencies are material (or potentially material) events that have an uncertain future. An example of a gain contingency is unsettled company litigation against another party. Typical loss contingencies relate to litigation against the company, environmental issues, or possible tax assessments. IFRS uses different terminology. For example, if a company is sued and it is more likely than not that it will lose the lawsuit, the estimated loss would be set up as a "provision" under IFRS (rather than as a contingent liability). A **provision** is a **liability that has an uncertain timing or amount** under IFRS.[24]

IFRS **ASPE** In general terms, a liability is recognized when it is probable or likely and measurable under ASPE and when it meets the definition of a liability under IFRS. Under IFRS, for provisions, probable is defined as more likely than not whereas under ASPE the threshold for recognition of a loss contingency is higher, requiring a high chance of occurrence. **Contingent gains** are not recognized under IFRS or ASPE, but are **disclosed** where an inflow of economic benefits is seen as probable.[25] The accounting and reporting requirements for provisions and contingencies are examined fully in Chapter 13.

Accounting Policies

Accounting standards recommend disclosure for all significant accounting principles and methods that management has chosen from among alternatives or that are peculiar to a particular industry. See Underlying Concept 5.5. For instance, inventories can be calculated under different cost formulas (such as weighted average and FIFO); plant and equipment can be amortized under several accepted methods of cost allocation (such as diminishing balance and straight-line); and investments can be carried at different amounts (such as cost or fair value). Users of financial statements who are more informed know of these possibilities and examine the statements closely to determine the methods that are used and their impact on net income and key ratios.

The disclosure of significant accounting principles is particularly useful when this information is given as one of the first notes or when it is presented in a separate summary that precedes the notes to the financial statements. Companies are also required to disclose information about their use of estimates in preparing the financial statements when the related measurement uncertainty is material.[26]

> **Underlying Concept 5.5**
>
> The basis for including additional information is the full disclosure principle; that is, the information needs to be important enough to influence the decisions of an informed user.

Contractual Situations

In addition to contingencies and different valuation methods, contractual obligations should also be disclosed in the notes to the financial statements when they are significant.[27] It is mandatory, for example, that the essential provisions of guarantees, lease contracts, pension obligations, and stock option plans be clearly stated in the notes. The analyst who examines a set of financial statements wants to know not only the liability amounts but also how the different contractual provisions (that is, the terms and conditions) are affecting the company now, and will affect it in the future.

Commitments that oblige a company to maintain a certain amount of working capital, limit its payment of dividends, restrict its use of assets, or require it to maintain certain financial ratios must all be disclosed if they are material. Considerable judgement is needed to determine whether leaving out such information is misleading. The principle in this situation is, "When in doubt, disclose." It is better to disclose a little too much information than not enough.

Ethics The accountant's judgement should include ethical considerations, because the way of disclosing the accounting principles, methods, and other items that have important effects on the enterprise may reflect the interests of a particular stakeholder in subtle ways that are at the

---

[24]Reprinted/adapted with permission from the *CPA Canada Handbook—Accounting* © 2018, Part II, Section 3290.05, by Chartered Professional Accountants of Canada. All rights reserved by the copyright owner. The IFRS definition differs somewhat (see IAS 37.10). Under IFRS, provisions are required for situations such as lawsuits where it is more likely than not that a present obligation exists. (Under IFRS, these are considered liabilities, not contingencies.) However, provisions are not required for loss contingencies for items like lawsuits where it is more likely than not that no obligation exists at the date of the financial statements. These are "possible obligations" whose existence will only be confirmed by uncertain future events. We examine the differences in the definitions in more detail in Chapter 13. Copyright © IFRS Foundation. All rights reserved. Reproduced with permission.

[25]IAS 37.27 to IAS 37.35 and *CPA Canada Handbook—Accounting*, Part II, Section 3290.08 to 3290.24. IFRS uses the term "contingent assets" (IAS 37.31), rather than "contingent gains." Copyright © IFRS Foundation. All rights reserved. Reproduced with permission.

[26]*CPA Canada Handbook—Accounting*, Part II, Section 1508 discusses measurement uncertainty, as do various other sections.

[27]Reprinted/adapted with permission from the *CPA Canada Handbook—Accounting* © 2018, Part II, Section 3280.02, by Chartered Professional Accountants of Canada. All rights reserved by the copyright owner.

expense of other stakeholders. A reader, for example, may benefit from having certain information highlighted in comprehensive notes, whereas the company—not wanting to emphasize that information—may prefer to provide limited (rather than comprehensive) information in its notes.

Additional Detail

For many SFP items, further detail is disclosed to make them clearer. This has already been discussed under the various headings of the SFP: assets, liabilities, and equity. We will discuss disclosure requirements for SFP items in more detail in upcoming chapters.

Subsequent Events

> **Underlying Concept 5.6**
>
> There is a trade-off here. Timely information is more relevant but may not be as reliable because it takes time to verify the information to ensure that it is complete and accurate.

Several weeks or months may pass after the end of the year before the financial statements are issued. See Underlying Concept 5.6. This time is used to count and price inventory, reconcile subsidiary ledgers with controlling accounts, prepare necessary adjusting entries, ensure that all transactions for the period have been entered, and obtain an audit of the financial statements.

During this period, important transactions and events may occur that materially affect the company's financial position or operating situation. These events are known as **events after the reporting period** or **subsequent events**.[28] Notes to the financial statements should explain any significant financial events that occur after (subsequent to) the formal date of the SFP but before the financial statements have been issued.

These events fall into two types:

1. Events that provide further evidence of **conditions that existed** at the date of the SFP
2. Events that indicate **conditions that occurred after** the financial statement date

In the first type, the financial statements must be adjusted for the events reflecting conditions that existed at the date of the SFP. In the second type, the events reflecting conditions that occurred after the financial statements date must be disclosed in notes if the condition causes a significant change to assets or liabilities, and/or it will have a significant impact on future operations. We will cover these issues in further detail in Chapter 23.

Techniques of Disclosure

> **LEARNING OBJECTIVE 6**
>
> Identify major disclosure techniques for the statement of financial position.

The additional information that is reported should be disclosed as completely and as understandably as possible. The following methods of disclosing pertinent information are available: explanations in parentheses, notes, cross-references and contra items, and supporting schedules, as we will explain next.

Parenthetical Explanations

Additional information is often provided by explanations in parentheses that follow the item. For example, shareholders' equity may be shown as it is in Illustration 5.12 in the financial statements of the hypothetical company Scientific Innovation Products.

Using parentheses makes it possible to disclose relevant additional SFP information that adds clarity and completeness. It has an advantage over a note because it brings the additional

---

[28]IAS 10. Copyright © IFRS Foundation. All rights reserved. Reproduced with permission. Reprinted/adapted with permission from the *CPA Canada Handbook—Accounting* © 2018, Part II, Section 3820, by Chartered Professional Accountants of Canada. All rights reserved by the copyright owner.

information into the body of the statement where it is less likely to be missed. Of course, lengthy parenthetical explanations that might distract the reader from the SFP information must be used carefully.

Notes

Notes are used if additional explanations cannot be shown conveniently as parenthetical explanations or to reduce the amount of detail on the face of the statement. For example, the details for the book values of the property, plant, and equipment of Air Canada are shown in Note 4 to its financial statements rather than on the face of the statement. As Illustration 5.13 shows, including this level of detail on the face of the SFP would make it more difficult to read and to focus on the main groupings of assets.

ILLUSTRATION 5.13

Note Disclosure—Excerpt from Note 4 to Air Canada's 2017 Financial Statements (in $ millions)

4. PROPERTY AND EQUIPMENT

	AIRCRAFT AND FLIGHT EQUIPMENT	BUILDINGS AND LEASEHOLD IMPROVEMENTS	GROUND AND OTHER EQUIPMENT	PURCHASE DEPOSITS AND ASSETS UNDER DEVELOPMENT	TOTAL
Year ended December 31, 2017					
At January 1, 2017	$ 7,030	$ 409	$ 184	$ 897	$ 8,520
Additions	1,769	8	29	573	2,379
Reclassifications	309	62	36	(407)	–
Disposals	(713)	–	–	–	(713)
Depreciation	(852)	(41)	(41)	–	(934)
At December 31, 2017	$ 7,543	$ 438	$ 208	$ 1,063	$ 9,252
At December 31, 2017					
Cost	$11,320	$ 899	$ 545	$ 1,063	$13,827
Accumulated depreciation	(3,777)	(461)	(337)	–	(4,575)
	$ 7,543	**$ 438**	**$ 208**	**$1,063**	**$ 9,252**

As at December 31, 2017, property and equipment included finance leased assets including nine aircraft (2016 – 9) with a net book value of $104 (2016 – $130) and facilities with a net book value of $34 (2016 – $37).

Included in aircraft and flight equipment are 21 aircraft and 14 spare engines (2016 – 21 aircraft and five spare engines) which are leased to CPA [Capacity Purchase Agreement] carriers with a cost of $387 (2016 – $349) less accumulated depreciation of $142 (2016 – $115) for a net book value of $245 (2016 – $234). Depreciation expense for 2017 for these aircraft and flight equipment amounted to $21 (2016 – $18).

Certain property and equipment are pledged as collateral as further described under the applicable debt instrument in Note 7. There are no impairment values recorded as at December 31, 2017.

The notes should present all essential facts as completely and concisely as possible. Loose wording can mislead readers instead of helping them. Notes should add to the total information that is made available in the financial statements, not raise unanswered questions or contradict other parts of the statements. For example, the property and equipment note for Air Canada provides users with additional information about changes in the major classifications of property and equipment items during the year. The full Air Canada Note 4 also provides further details of flight equipment, leased equipment, and other items of property and equipment that are not reproduced here.

Cross-References and Contra Items

When there is a direct relationship between an asset and a liability, this can be cross-referenced on the SFP. For example, a company with a sinking fund, used to set aside funds to redeem a bond payable, might deposit cash with a trust company for eventual redemption of the bond issue. This might be shown as follows among the current assets section of an SFP dated as at December 31, 2020:

> Cash on deposit with sinking fund trustee for redemption $800,000
> of bonds payable—see Current liabilities

In the same SFP, in the current liabilities section, would be the amount of bonds payable to be redeemed within one year:

> Bonds payable to be redeemed in 2021—see Current assets $2,300,000

This cross-reference points out that $2.3 million of bonds payable are to be redeemed currently, and thus far only $800,000 in cash has been set aside for the redemption. This means, therefore, that the additional cash will need to come from unrestricted cash, from sales of investments, from profits, or from some other source. The same information can be shown in parentheses if this technique is preferred.

Another common procedure is to establish contra or adjunct accounts. A **contra account** on an SFP is an item that reduces an asset, liability, or owners' equity account. Examples include Accumulated Depreciation and Allowance for Doubtful Accounts. Contra accounts provide some flexibility in presenting the financial information. Use of the Accumulated Depreciation account, for example, allows a statement reader to see the asset's original cost and its amortization to date.

An **adjunct account**, on the other hand, increases an asset, liability, or owners' equity account. An example is Premium on Bonds Payable, which, when added to the Bonds Payable account, describes the enterprise's total bond liability.

Supporting Schedules

Often a separate schedule is needed to present more detailed information about certain assets or liabilities because the SFP provides only a single summary item.

Terminology

Account titles in the general ledger often use terms that are not the most helpful ones for an SFP. Account titles are often brief and may include technical terms that are understood only by accountants. Statements of financial position, meanwhile, are examined by many people who are not familiar with the technical vocabulary of accounting. Thus, statements of financial position should contain descriptions that will be generally understood and are less likely to be misinterpreted.

PART **2**	**Statement of Cash Flows**

Purpose, Content, and Format of a Statement of Cash Flows

LEARNING OBJECTIVE 7
Indicate the purpose and identify the content of the statement of cash flows.

The SFP, the income statement, and the statement of changes in shareholders' equity each present information about an enterprise's cash flows during a period, but they do this to a limited extent and in a fragmented manner. For instance, comparative statements of financial position might provide an indication of what new assets have been acquired or disposed of and what liabilities have been incurred or liquidated. The income statement presents information about the resources provided by operations, but not the details of the cash that has been provided. The statement of changes in shareholders' equity shows the amount of dividends declared. None of these statements presents a detailed summary of all the cash inflows and outflows, or the sources and uses of cash during the period. To satisfy this need, the statement of cash flows (also called the cash flow statement; see Alternative Terminology 5.2) is required.[29]

The statement's value is that it helps users evaluate liquidity, solvency, and financial flexibility, as previously defined. The material in Chapter 5 is introductory as it reviews the statement of cash flows' existence and usefulness, the mechanics of calculating cash flow from operations, and the basics of preparing the statement using both the indirect and the direct methods. Chapter 22 deals with the preparation and content of the statement of cash flows in greater detail.

The main purpose of a statement of cash flows is to allow users to **assess the enterprise's capacity to generate cash and cash equivalents and to enable users to compare the operating performance and cash flows of different entities**.[30]

Reporting the sources, uses, and net increase or decrease in cash helps investors, creditors, and others know what is happening to a company's most liquid resource. Because many people use online banking, which presents receipts and disbursements on a cash basis, they can relate to and understand the statement of cash flows because it shows the causes and effects of cash inflows and outflows and the net increase or decrease in cash. The statement of cash flows helps answer the following simple but important questions:

1. Where did cash come from during the period?
2. What was cash used for during the period?
3. What was the change in the cash balance during the period?

Cash receipts and cash payments during a period are classified in the statement of cash flows into three different activities: **operating**, **investing**, and **financing** activities. These are the main types of activities that companies engage in. These classifications are defined as follows:

1. Operating activities are the enterprise's main revenue-producing activities and all other activities that are not related to investing or financing.
2. Investing activities are the acquisitions and disposals of long-term assets and other investments that are not included in cash equivalents.
3. Financing activities are activities that result in changes in the size and composition of the enterprise's borrowings and equity capital.[31]

With cash flows classified into each of these categories, the statement of cash flows has assumed the basic format shown in Illustration 5.14.

> **Alternative Terminology 5.2**
>
> In 2007, the IASB changed the name of the cash flow statement to the statement of cash flows (see IAS 7). It is still known as the cash flow statement under ASPE (see *CPA Canada— Accounting*, Part II, Section 1540).

ILLUSTRATION 5.14

Basic Format of Statement of Cash Flows

Statement of Cash Flows	
Cash flows from operating activities	$XXX
Cash flows from investing activities	XXX
Cash flows from financing activities	XXX
Net increase (decrease) in cash	XXX
Cash at beginning of period	XXX
Cash at end of period	$XXX

---

[29]According to the *CPA Canada Handbook—Accounting*, Part II, Section 1540.03 (and IAS 7.1), the cash flow statement (statement of cash flows) should be presented as an integral part of the financial statements.

[30]IAS 7.4. Copyright © IFRS Foundation. All rights reserved. Reproduced with permission. Reprinted/adapted with permission from the *CPA Canada Handbook—Accounting* © 2018, Part II, Section 1540.01, by Chartered Professional Accountants of Canada. All rights reserved by the copyright owner.

[31]IAS 7.6 Copyright © IFRS Foundation. All rights reserved. Reproduced with permission. Reprinted/adapted with permission from the *CPA Canada Handbook—Accounting* © 2018, Part II, Section 1540.06, by Chartered Professional Accountants of Canada. All rights reserved by the copyright owner.

ILLUSTRATION 5.15

Cash Inflows and Outflows

Illustration 5.15 shows examples of cash inflows and outflows by activity when using the indirect method.

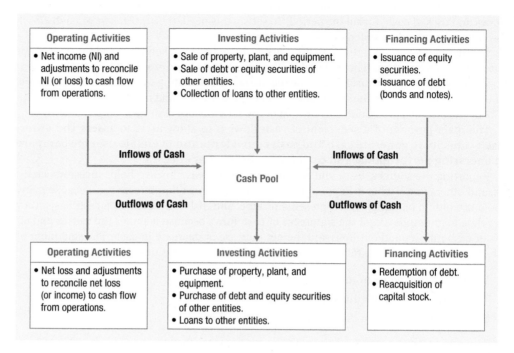

The statement of cash flows of the 2017 fiscal year for Loblaw Companies Limited in Illustration 5.16 starts with the operating activities section. This provides a summary of typical adjustments found in the reconciliation of net earnings to cash flows from operating activities. The statement also shows the investing and financing activities.

ILLUSTRATION 5.16

Consolidated Statements of Cash Flow—Loblaw Companies Limited

Consolidated Statements of Cash Flow
For the years ended December 30, 2017 and December 31, 2016

(millions of Canadian dollars)	2017	2016
Operating Activities		
Net earnings	$ 1,526	$ 990
Add (Deduct):		
Income taxes (note 7)	443	449
Net interest expense and other financing charges (note 6)	525	653
Depreciation and amortization	1,568	1,543
Asset impairments, net of recoveries	97	139
Gain on disposition of gas bar operations, (note 13)	(501)	—
Change in provisions (note 20)	233	(39)
PC Optimum program (note 19)	189	—
	$ 4,080	$ 3,735
Change in non-cash working capital	132	173
Change in credit card receivables (note 11)	(174)	(136)
Income taxes paid	(866)	(329)
Interest received	17	9
Other	20	67
Cash Flows from Operating Activities	$ 3,209	$ 3,519
Investing Activities		
Fixed asset purchases	$ (979)	$ (896)
Intangible asset additions (note 16)	(280)	(328)
Acquisition of QHR, net of cash acquired	—	(153)
Cash assumed on initial consolidation of franchises (note 5)	26	42
Change in short term investments (note 9)	(305)	(177)

(continued)

ILLUSTRATION 5.16

(*continued*)

Proceeds from disposal of assets	**17**	62
Proceeds from disposition of gas bar operations, (note 13)	**540**	—
Other	**(53)**	13
Cash Flows used in Investing Activities	**$(1,034)**	$(1,437)
Financing Activities		
Change in bank indebtedness	**$ (5)**	$ (28)
Change in short term debt (note 11)	**(25)**	115
Long Term Debt (note 21)		
Issued	**686**	815
Retired	**(450)**	(1,049)
Interest Paid	**(471)**	(474)
Dividends paid on common and preferred shares	**(327)**	(425)
Common Share Capital		
Issued (note 26)	**41**	42
Purchased and held in trust (note 23)	**(48)**	(90)
Purchased and cancelled (note 23)	**(1,091)**	(708)
Other	**5**	20
Cash Flows used in Financing Activities	**$(1,685)**	$(1,782)
Effect of foreign currency exchange rate changes on cash and cash equivalents	**$ (6)**	$ (4)
Change in cash and cash equivalents	**$ 484**	$ 296
Cash and cash equivalents, beginning of period	**1,314**	1,018
Cash and Cash Equivalents, End of Period	**$ 1,798**	$ 1,314

Preparation of the Statement of Cash Flows

LEARNING OBJECTIVE 8

Prepare a statement of cash flows using the indirect and direct methods.

Companies can prepare their statements of cash flows by using either the direct or indirect method. Only the operating activities section of the statement differs between the two methods. In this chapter, we introduce the statement and concentrate on preparing a basic statement using both methods. We will cover more complex aspects of the statement in Volume 2.

Companies obtain the information to prepare a statement of cash flows from a variety of sources. These include the SFP, income statement, and selected transaction data—normally data in the general ledger Cash account. Because the statement is intended to include all cash transactions, the Cash account is an important source of information. Preparation of the statement requires the following steps:

1. Determine the cash provided by or used in operating, investing, and financing activities by analyzing changes in SFP balances, related income statement balances, and other selected transaction information.

2. Determine the change (increase or decrease) in cash and cash equivalents during the period.

3. Reconcile the change in cash and cash equivalents with the beginning and ending cash and cash equivalents balances.

In this chapter, we use the following simple example to first prepare a statement of cash flows using the indirect method. We first look briefly at how to calculate the cash provided by or used in operating activities. Assume that on January 1, 2020, in its second year of operations, Telemarketing Inc. expanded its business. First it issued 30,000 shares for $30,000 cash. The company then rented additional office space, purchased additional furniture and telecommunications equipment, and performed marketing services throughout the year. On December 31, 2020, the company also purchased land with a fair value of $150,000, which was financed partially by the issuance of bonds. Finally, it paid cash dividends of $15,000 during the year. **Illustration 5.17** shows the company's comparative statements of financial position at the beginning and end of 2020.

ILLUSTRATION 5.17

Comparative Statements of Financial Position for Telemarketing Inc.

TELEMARKETING INC.
Statements of Financial Position

Assets	Dec. 31, 2020	Dec. 31, 2019	Increase/Decrease
Cash	$ 61,000	$ 30,000	$ 31,000 increase
Accounts receivable	86,000	45,000	41,000 increase
Inventory	100,000	120,000	20,000 decrease
Land	150,000	–0–	150,000 increase
Property, plant, and equipment, net	300,000	200,000	100,000 increase
Total	$697,000	$395,000	
Liabilities and Shareholders' Equity			
Accounts payable	$ 62,000	$ 50,000	12,000 increase
Bonds payable	200,000	–0–	200,000 increase
Common shares	280,000	250,000	30,000 increase
Retained earnings	155,000	95,000	60,000 increase
Total	$697,000	$395,000	

Illustration 5.18 shows the company's income statement.

ILLUSTRATION 5.18

Income Statement Data for Telemarketing Inc.

TELEMARKETING INC.
Income Statement
For the Year Ended December 31, 2020

Sales revenue	$580,000
Cost of goods sold	300,000
Gross profit	280,000
Salaries and wages expense	150,000
Depreciation expense	30,000
Income before income tax	100,000
Income tax	25,000
Net income	$ 75,000

Additional information:
Dividends of $15,000 were paid during the year. The bonds were issued on December 31, 2020, to help finance the acquisition of the land. Specifically, $100,000 worth of the land was acquired in exchange for $100,000 of bonds, with the remainder of the bonds being issued for cash.

Finance 5.2.1 Cash provided by operating activities is the excess of cash receipts over cash payments for operating activities. Companies determine this amount by converting net income on an accrual basis to a cash basis. To do this, they add to or deduct from net income those items in the income statement that do not affect cash, such as depreciation expense and non-cash gains or losses. They then adjust net income for the items that are affected by changes in current asset or liability account balances. For example, increases in accounts receivable between years would reflect the fact that more sales remain uncollected at the end of the current year compared with the prior year. Similarly, a decrease in accounts payable would suggest that the current year's purchases have been paid off more quickly than similar purchases in the prior year. Determination of cash provided by (or used for) operating activities requires that a company analyze not only the current year's income statement but also the comparative SFP and selected transaction data (especially items affecting the Cash account). This analysis is important since, for instance, credit sales from last year that are collected this year (and were previously recorded as accounts receivable) will increase cash. **Example 5.1** analyzes Telemarketing Inc.'s operating, investing, and financing activities.

Example 5.1 | Analysis of Operating, Investing, and Financing Activities

Facts Illustrations 5.17 and 5.18 provide the comparative statements of financial position (SFP) for 2020 and 2019, and the income statement for the year ended 2020, of Telemarketing Inc. used in Examples 5.1, 5.2, and 5.3.

Instructions Prepare an analysis of Telemarketing Inc.'s operating activities, investing activities, and financial activities based on the company's increases and decreases in SFP balances and its income statement. (Note: This analysis is used in Example 5.2 to prepare a statement of cash flows using the indirect method.)

Solution A review of the SFP reveals items that will affect the calculation of net cash provided by operating activities:

a. The increase in accounts receivable is a non-cash increase of $41,000 in revenues from uncollected credit sales. This amount would have been included in net income as sales revenue and so must be deducted in arriving at cash from operations. In short, the company has to reduce cash flow from operations by $41,000, because it has fewer cash resources available to it due to a higher accounts receivable balance in 2020.

b. The decrease in inventory is a non-cash decrease of $20,000 relating to inventory, as the company has fewer cash resources used for operations with inventory being monitored more effectively in 2020 than in 2019.

c. The increase in accounts payable is a non-cash increase of $12,000 in expenses accrued but not yet paid relating to inventory acquired. This amount would have been deducted in arriving at net income but, since these expenses did not require a cash outlay, they will be added back in arriving at cash from operations. The company has conserved some of its cash resources by not paying off its accounts as quickly in 2020 as in 2019.

A review of the income statement indicates that depreciation expense totalling $30,000 was deducted in arriving at net income. Because depreciation is a non-cash item that has been deducted as an expense, it must be added back to net income to arrive at cash from operations. In addition, to obtain cash from operations, Telemarketing Inc. deducts from net income the increase in accounts receivable ($41,000) and it adds back to net income the decrease in inventory ($20,000) and the increase in accounts payable ($12,000), as discussed above. Note that, since there were no sales of property, plant, and equipment during the year, there is no need to adjust for non-cash gains or losses. As a result of these adjustments, the company determines that cash provided by operations amounted to $96,000, as calculated below:

Net income		$75,000
Adjustments to reconcile net income to net cash provided by operating activities:		
Depreciation expense	$30,000	
Increase in accounts receivable	(41,000)	
Decrease in inventory	20,000	
Increase in accounts payable	12,000	21,000
Net cash provided by operating activities		$96,000

Telemarketing Inc.'s only investing activities were the land and property, plant, and equipment purchases. From the analysis of changes in SFP balances, we can see that land increased by $150,000. However, other available information states that $100,000 of the land purchased was paid for via an exchange for bonds. Since this is a non-cash exchange, $100,000 of the increase in land (and the related $100,000 non-cash increase in bonds payable) is not included on the statement of cash flows. Details of the exchange would be disclosed via a note to the financial statements. The remaining increase to land ($50,000) was cash-based and must be disclosed on the statement of cash flows.

There is also an increase to (net) property, plant, and equipment (PPE) of $100,000 on the SFP that requires further analysis. Since PPE is shown on a net basis on the SFP, it is net of related accumulated depreciation. From our analysis of operating activities and the income statement, we know that depreciation expense was $30,000 for the year. So the increase in PPE must have been $130,000 prior to the recording of depreciation expense ($130,000 − $30,000 = $100,000 [net] increase to PPE). The purchase of PPE of $130,000 is shown as part of investing activities.

Telemarketing Inc. has three financing activities:

1. the increase of $30,000 in common shares resulting from the issuance of these shares,

2. the cash portion of the increase in bonds payable as discussed above, and

3. the payment of $15,000 in cash dividends. (Dividends charged to retained earnings are a financing activity under ASPE, but could be shown as financing or operating under IFRS. Illustration 5.23 provides further discussion.)

Note that, in addition to the exchange of bonds payable for land illustrated above for Telemarketing Inc., other examples of a company's activities not involving cash would include the conversion of bonds to shares, an issuance of debt in exchange for assets, and other nonmonetary exchanges. These activities should not be included in the body of the statement of cash flows but should be disclosed elsewhere in the financial statements.

Example 5.2 shows the preparation of Telemarketing Inc.'s statement of cash flows using the indirect method.

Example 5.2 | Preparation of Statement of Cash Flows— Indirect Method

Facts Example 5.1 provides the analysis of Telemarketing Inc.'s financial statement information and sorts the information into operating, investing, and financing activities.

Instructions Prepare a statement of cash flows for Telemarketing Inc. using the indirect method.

Solution The increase in cash of $31,000 that will be reported on Telemarketing Inc.'s statement of cash flows agrees with the increase in cash that was calculated from the comparative statements of financial position in Illustration 5.17. For the statement of cash flows to be in balance, the total of the operating, investing, and financing activities also need to equal $31,000.

Based on the increase in cash of $31,000, and using the details of the operating, investing, and financing activities from Example 5.1, we can now prepare a statement of cash flows for Telemarketing Inc. Note that the net cash provided by operating activities section begins with net income and reconciles to cash. This presentation is the indirect method of presenting cash flows from operating activities.

Cash flows from operating activities		
Net income		$ 75,000
Adjustments to reconcile net income to net cash provided		
by operating activities:		
Depreciation expense	$ 30,000	
Increase in accounts receivable	(41,000)	
Decrease in inventory	20,000	
Increase in accounts payable	12,000	21,000
Net cash provided by operating activities		96,000
Cash flows from investing activities		
Purchase of land	(50,000)	
Purchase of property, plant, and equipment	(130,000)	
Net cash used by investing activities		(180,000)

Cash flows from financing activities		
Issuance of common shares	30,000	
Issuance of bonds payable	100,000	
Payment of cash dividends	(15,000)	
Net cash provided by financing activities		115,000
Net increase in cash		31,000
Cash at beginning of year		30,000
Cash at end of year		$ 61,000

Another option for presentation of the statement of cash flows is the direct method. The direct method normally presents the following information in the operating activities portion of the statement:

- Cash received from customers
- Cash paid to suppliers and employees
- Interest paid or received
- Taxes paid
- Other

The investing and financing activities sections of the statement are the same for both the direct and indirect methods. Under IFRS and ASPE, either method is acceptable, although standard setters prefer the direct method. See Chapter 22 for a more detailed discussion.

Example 5.3 shows the preparation of Telemarketing Inc.'s statement of cash flows using the direct method.

Example 5.3 | Preparation of Statement of Cash Flows— Direct Method

Facts Illustrations 5.17 and 5.18 provide the comparative statements of financial position (SFP) for 2020 and 2019, and the income statement for the year ended 2020, of Telemarketing Inc. Example 5.1 provides the analysis of Telemarketing Inc.'s financial statement information and sorts the information into operating, investing, and financing activities.

Instructions Prepare the operating activities section of the statement of cash flows for Telemarketing Inc. using the direct method.

Solution The direct method adjusts income statement amounts for the same types of changes in balances that we saw for the indirect method. So, cash received from customers represents revenues from the income statement adjusted by the increase in accounts receivable (that is, the change in revenues not yet collected). Similarly, cash paid to suppliers and employees represents cost of goods sold ($300,000) adjusted for the decrease in inventory ($20,000) and increase in accounts payable ($12,000), plus the cash paid for salaries and wages ($150,000). So in summary, the operating activities for Telemarketing Inc. under the direct method are as follows:

- Cash received from customers ($580,000 – $41,000 = $539,000)
- Cash paid to suppliers and employees ($300,000 – $20,000 – $12,000 + $150,000 = $418,000)
- Taxes paid ($25,000)

The operating activities section of the statement of cash flows for Telemarketing Inc. follows:

Cash flows from operating activities		
Cash received from customers		$539,000
Cash paid to suppliers and employees	$418,000	
Taxes paid	25,000	443,000
Net cash provided by operating activities		96,000

Usefulness of the Statement of Cash Flows

LEARNING OBJECTIVE 9

Understand the usefulness of the statement of cash flows.

Although net income provides a long-term measure of a company's success or failure, cash is a company's **lifeblood**. Without cash, a company will not survive. For small and newly developing companies, cash flow is often the single most important element of survival. Even medium and large companies indicate that controlling cash flow is a major concern.

Creditors examine the statement of cash flows carefully because they are concerned about being paid. They will usually start by assessing **net cash provided by operating activities**. What if there is a high amount of net cash provided by operating activities? This indicates that a company was able to generate enough cash internally from operations in the most recent period to pay its bills without further borrowing. Conversely, a low or negative amount of net cash provided by operating activities indicates that a company did not generate enough cash internally from its operations and, therefore, may have had to borrow or issue equity securities to acquire additional cash.

Just because a company was able to generate cash flows from operating activities in the most recent period, however, does not mean that it will be able to do so again in future periods. Consequently, creditors look for answers to the following questions in the company's statement of cash flows:

- How successful is the company in generating net cash provided by operating activities?
- What are the trends in net cash flow provided by operating activities over time?
- What are the major reasons for the positive or negative net cash provided by operating activities?
- Are the cash flows sustainable or renewable? In other words, are they expected to be repeated over time?

You should recognize that companies can fail even though they are profitable. The difference between net income and net cash provided by operating activities can be substantial. Why? One of the main reasons for the difference between a positive net income and negative net cash provided by operating activities is major increases in receivables and/or inventory. To illustrate, assume that in its first year of operations, Hinchcliff Inc. reported net income of $80,000. Its net cash provided by operating activities, however, was a negative $95,000, as shown in **Illustration 5.19**.

 Video

ILLUSTRATION 5.19

Negative Net Cash Provided by Operating Activities

Net income		$ 80,000
Adjustments to reconcile net income to net cash provided by operating activities:		
Increase in receivables	$ (75,000)	
Increase in inventory	(100,000)	(175,000)
Net cash provided by operating activities		$ (95,000)

Note that the negative net cash provided by operating activities occurred for Hinchcliff even though it reported a positive net income. The company could easily experience a "cash crunch" because it has tied up its cash in receivables and inventory. If problems in collecting receivables occur or inventory is slow-moving or becomes obsolete, the company's creditors may have difficulty collecting on their loans.

Companies that are expanding often experience this type of "cash crunch" because they must buy increasing inventory amounts to meet increasing sales demands. This means that the cash outflow to purchase the inventory occurs before the cash inflow from the customer for sale of that product. This is often referred to as a "lead-lag" factor. The cash outflow leads (occurs first) and the cash inflow from sales lags (occurs later). The lead-lag factor requires the company to use up any excess cash that it has on hand or to borrow more funds. Refer back to Illustration 5.3 on the business operating cycle.

As mentioned earlier in the chapter, you can assess a company's financial flexibility by using information from the financial statements. The statement of cash flows is especially good for providing this type of information.

Financial Liquidity

Finance 5.2.1 One ratio that is used to assess liquidity is the **current cash debt coverage ratio**. It indicates whether the company can pay off its current liabilities for the year from its operations. The formula for this ratio is shown in **Illustration 5.20**.

ILLUSTRATION 5.20

Formula for Current Cash Debt Coverage Ratio

The higher this ratio, the less likely it is that a company will have liquidity problems. For example, a ratio of at least 1:1 is good because it indicates that the company can meet all of its current obligations from internally generated cash flow. To compare this ratio with a benchmark number, it can be compared with the ratios for similar companies in the industry (or with the ratios of prior years for the company itself).

Financial Flexibility

A more long-term measure that provides information on financial flexibility is the **cash debt coverage ratio**. This ratio indicates a company's ability to repay its liabilities from net cash provided by operating activities without having to liquidate the assets that it uses in its operations. **Illustration 5.21** presents the formula for this ratio.

ILLUSTRATION 5.21

Formula for Cash Debt Coverage Ratio

The higher this ratio, the less likely it is that a company will experience difficulty in meeting its obligations as they come due. As a result, this ratio signals whether the company can pay its debts and survive if external sources of funds become limited or too expensive.

Perspectives

Cash Flow Patterns

Finance 5.1.1 Refer to Example 5.2 showing a full statement of cash flows for Telemarketing Inc. The statement of cash flows can yield some interesting results when users look at the various patterns between cash inflows and outflows for the following subtotals on the statement: operating, investing, and financing cash flows. For instance, Telemarketing Inc. has positive cash flows (cash inflows; "+") from operating activities of $96,000, negative cash flows (cash outflows; "−") from investing activities of $180,000, and positive cash flows (cash inflows; "+") from financing activities of $115,000. Together these numbers thus yield a "+" "−" "+" pattern.

Interpreting this, the company is getting its cash from operations (which is a very good sign) and also from the issuance of common shares and long-term debt. It is investing this cash to expand the business. The fact that the company is able to raise funds in the capital markets by issuing shares indicates that the capital markets have faith in the company's ability to prosper. As the company expands, it may be able to move to having the bulk of the money used to finance purchases of capital assets being generated from operations. This would mean that the company would not have to increase its solvency risk by issuing debt or further dilute its shareholders' equity by issuing more shares. Telemarketing Inc. appears to be a successful company that's expanding.

Companies that generate cash from investing activities may be selling off long-term assets. This pattern generally goes with a company that is downsizing or restructuring. If the assets that are being disposed of are not needed, then it makes sense to free up the capital that is tied up. Similarly, if the assets being disposed of relate to operations that are not profitable, disposal reflects a good management decision. However, if the company **must** sell off core income-producing assets to generate cash, then it may be sacrificing future profitability and revenue-producing potential. This is obviously undesirable. So, cash flow patterns can reveal significant information.

Free Cash Flow

Finance 5.1.1 A more sophisticated way to examine a company's financial flexibility is to develop a **free cash flow** analysis. This analysis starts with net cash provided by operating activities and ends with free cash flow, which is calculated as follows:

$$\text{Net cash provided by operating activities} - \text{Capital expenditures} - \text{dividends} = \text{Free cash flow}^{32}$$

Free cash flow is the amount of discretionary cash flow that a company has for purchasing additional investments, retiring its debt, purchasing treasury stock, or simply adding to its liquidity. This measure indicates a company's level of financial flexibility. A free cash flow analysis can answer questions such as these:

- Is the company able to pay its dividends without the help of external financing?
- If business operations decline, will the company be able to maintain its needed capital investment?
- What is the free cash flow that can be used for additional investments, retirement of debt, purchases of treasury stock, or additions to liquidity?

Illustration 5.22 shows a free cash flow analysis for Nestor Corporation.

ILLUSTRATION 5.22

Free Cash Flow Analysis

NESTOR CORPORATION
Free Cash Flow Analysis

Net cash provided by operating activities	$411,750
Less: Capital expenditures	(252,500)
Dividends	(19,800)
Free cash flow	$139,450

This analysis shows that Nestor has positive, and substantial, net cash provided by operating activities of $411,750. Nestor reports on its statement of cash flows that it purchased equipment of $182,500 and land of $70,000 for total capital spending of $252,500. This amount

---

[32]In determining free cash flow, some companies do not subtract dividends, because they believe these expenditures are discretionary.

is subtracted from net cash provided by operating activities because, without continued efforts to maintain and expand its facilities, it is unlikely that Nestor can continue to maintain its competitive position. Capital spending is deducted first on the analysis above to indicate it is generally the least discretionary expenditure that a company makes. Dividends are then deducted to arrive at free cash flow.

Nestor has more than enough cash flow to meet its dividend payment and therefore has satisfactory financial flexibility. Nestor used its free cash flow to redeem bonds and add to its liquidity. If it finds additional investments that are profitable, it can increase its spending without putting its dividend or basic capital spending in jeopardy. Companies that have strong financial flexibility can take advantage of profitable investments even in tough times. In addition, strong financial flexibility frees companies from worry about survival in poor economic times. In fact, those with strong financial flexibility often do better in poor economic times because they can take advantage of opportunities that other companies cannot.

Cash flow problems can be very serious for companies, and can sometimes lead companies to the brink of bankruptcy, as we discuss in What Do the Numbers Mean? 5.6.

What Do the Numbers Mean? 5.6

In 2015, Performance Sports Group (PSG), a leading maker of hockey, lacrosse, and baseball equipment and apparel and owner of various subsidiaries including Bauer Hockey Corporation, found itself under pressure with respect to its free cash flow. This was due in part to its acquisition of the Easton baseball and softball business in 2014. Although PSG had cash of almost $3 million at the end of its 2015 fiscal year, its free cash flow was negative, with net cash flow from operations of $11.6 million being exceeded by the purchase of property, plant, and equipment and intangible assets of $17.6 million (PSG reports in U.S. dollars). PSG's investing activities from the prior fiscal year may have been too much for the company to handle, as its net cash used in investing activities was $358.4 million in its 2014 fiscal year. After entering into creditor protection proceedings in Ontario under the Companies' Creditors Arrangement Act (and U.S. Bankruptcy Court under Chapter 11) in late 2016, substantially all of its assets were sold to affiliates of Sagard Holdings Inc. and Fairfax Financial Holdings Limited in 2017. The new company is privately held.[33]

Caution

As more and more complex financial instruments are created, more presentation issues arise for financial statement preparers. Many instruments have attributes of both debt and equity. This is significant for analysts because a misclassification will affect key ratios. Note disclosure of the details of the instruments helps analysts and other users in assessing a company's liquidity and solvency. We will discuss this issue further in subsequent chapters on liabilities and equity.

IFRS/ASPE Comparison

LEARNING OBJECTIVE 10
Identify differences in accounting between IFRS and ASPE and identify the significant changes planned by the IASB for financial statement presentation.

A Comparison of IFRS and ASPE

Illustration 5.23 shows the differences between the IFRS and ASPE sets of standards in how assets, liabilities, and shareholders' equity are accounted for and presented on the SFP and how cash activity is reported on the statement of cash flows.

---

[33]"Performance Sports Group Completes Sale of Substantially All of Its Assets to Investor Group Led by Sagard and Fairfax Financial," PSG news release, February 28, 2017.

ILLUSTRATION 5.23   **IFRS and ASPE Comparison Chart**

	IFRS—IAS 1, 7, and 40	Accounting Standards for Private Enterprises (ASPE)—*CPA Canada Handbook—Accounting*, Part II, Sections 1400, 1510, 1521, 1540, and 3251	References to related illustrations and select brief exercises
Specific items to be presented in the balance sheet/SFP	For the most part, IFRS and ASPE require the same items to be presented. The following additional items are also required to be presented under IFRS: • investment property • biological assets • provisions	The following additional items are also required to be presented under ASPE: • government assistance receivable • investments in non-consolidated subsidiaries and joint arrangements accounted for using the cost or equity method	Illustration 10.5 Illustration 8.14 Illustration 8.15
Current versus non-current liabilities	If no unconditional right to defer payment of financial liability beyond one year as at the SFP date, must show as current (including situations where the company has refinanced the debt after the SFP date but before issue).	If company has refinanced debt by the issue date of the financial statements, may present as non-current.	BE5.8 and BE5.9
Statement of cash flows (cash flow statement)	Certain preferred shares acquired within a short period of the maturity date may be classified as cash and cash equivalents. IFRS allows flexibility in how to treat interest and dividends (may be classified as operating, investing, or financing activities).	Equity investments are excluded from cash and cash equivalents. Interest and dividends included in net income are treated as operating activities and those booked through retained earnings are treated as financing activities.	BE5.19
Cash flow per share information	No prohibition on disclosure of this number.	Prohibited—may not be disclosed.	BE5.21
Disclosure of date financial statements authorized for issue	Must disclose date that the financial statements were authorized for issue.	No requirement to disclose.	

Looking Ahead

The IASB has been working on a Primary Financial Statements project with a goal of targeted improvements to the structure and content of primary financial statements such as the statement of financial position and statement of cash flows. The idea is to highlight major business and financing activities within the main financial statements.

The IASB issued a new "Conceptual Framework for Financial Reporting" (CF) in March 2018 that included changes to the definitions of assets and liabilities. The new CF defines an asset as "a present economic resource controlled by the entity as a result of past events" where "an economic resource is a right that has the potential to produce economic benefits." The new CF then provides additional details regarding the definition as it relates to "rights," "economic benefits," and "control." Similarly, the new CF defines a liability as "a present obligation of the entity to transfer an economic resource as a result of past events" and goes on to clarify aspects of the proposed definition. For most assets and liabilities, applying the new definition will yield the same accounting results as the previous definitions (CF 4.3 and 4.4).

In January 2016, the IASB issued its "Disclosure Initiative—Amendments to IAS 7." Rather than making major changes to IAS 7 *Statement of Cash Flows*, the amendments require entities to provide additional information to financial statement users about financing activities (other than those that relate to equity items). Companies are encouraged, but not required, to provide a reconciliation of items such as changes in long-term borrowings and lease liabilities. The disclosure initiative is ongoing. For example, in March 2018, the IASB added a project to perform a targeted "Standards-Level" review of its disclosure requirements.[34]

| Appendix 5A | # Ratio Analysis: A Reference |

LEARNING OBJECTIVE 11

Identify the major types of financial ratios and what they measure.

Business Risks

Companies expose themselves to many risks in doing business. Strategically, the goal is to identify these risks and then manage them in order to take advantage of opportunities and maximize shareholder value. How do users know whether a company is managing its risks in a way that will create the most shareholder value? **Illustration 5A.1** shows the business model that we originally introduced in Chapter 4. Now risks have been added to the model, along with the key management personnel responsible for managing the risks.[35]

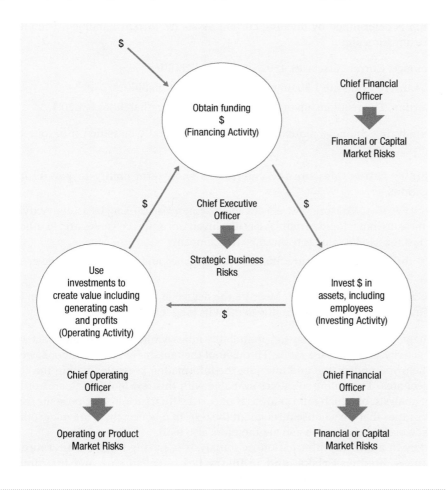

ILLUSTRATION 5A.1

The Business Model and Various Related Risks That a Company Must Manage

---

[34]For further details on the "disclosure initiative" on financial statement presentation, see the related page on the IASB website www.ifrs.org.

[35]This is a brief overview only. It is meant to link risk with the business model and with the use of financial statements in communicating information about risk management. A thorough review of risk models and risk management is beyond the scope of this text.

Financial or capital market risks are related to financing and investing activities. For example, when a company borrows funds, it might increase its solvency and liquidity risk. **Operating or product market risks** are related to operating activities. For instance, when it manufactures a drug, there is a risk that a company might not be able to produce quality products on time or successfully target the appropriate market for sale of the drug.

Information about risks is useful and much of this information is included in the annual report, both within the financial statements and in other parts. The financial statements give **information** about financing, investing, and operating activities and therefore provide indirect feedback on how related risks are being managed and how this in turn affects performance. A solvent company that constantly generates cash from operations has a solid business model where risks and opportunities are well managed to create value. Companies usually disclose explicit information about risks and risk management policies in the Management Discussion and Analysis section of the annual report.

Financial Ratios

Finance 5.1.1 **Ratio analysis** helps in assessing operating and financial risks by **expressing the relationship between selected financial statement data**. Qualitative information from financial statements is gathered by **examining relationships** between items on the statements and **identifying trends** in these relationships. Relationships are often expressed in terms of a percentage, a rate, or a simple proportion.

To illustrate, in its December 30, 2017 financial statements, **Loblaw Companies Limited** had current assets of $11,327 million and current liabilities of $8,694 million. The following relationship is determined by dividing current assets by current liabilities. The alternative means of expression are:

Percentage: Current assets are 130% of current liabilities.

Rate: Current assets are 1.30 times as great as current liabilities.

Proportion: The relationship of current assets to current liabilities is 1.30:1.

For analyzing financial statements, ratios are generally classified into four types, as follows:

1. **Liquidity ratios.** Measure the enterprise's short-term ability to pay its maturing obligations.
2. **Activity ratios.** Measure how effectively the enterprise is using its assets. Activity ratios also measure how liquid certain assets like inventory and receivables are; in other words, how fast the asset's value is realized by the company.
3. **Profitability ratios.** Measure financial performance and shareholder value creation for a specific time period.
4. **Coverage** or **solvency ratios.** Measure the degree of protection for long-term creditors and investors or a company's ability to meet its long-term obligations.

In Chapter 4, we briefly discussed profitability ratios, while in this chapter, we touched on liquidity, activity, and coverage ratios. Throughout the remainder of the textbook, we provide ratios to help you understand and interpret the information presented within the context of each subject area. The online resources available with this text look at the area of financial statement analysis, of which ratio analysis is one part. **Illustration 5A.2** presents some common, basic ratios that we will use throughout the text. In practice, there are many other ratios that provide useful information and are therefore also used.

The key to a refined, information-rich analysis is having a good **understanding of the business, business risks, and industry** before calculating and interpreting any ratios. Specialized industries focus on different ratios depending on the critical success factors in their business. As discussed throughout the chapter, different companies and businesses would be expected to have different types of assets and capital structures. Furthermore, they would be expected to have different types of costs, revenue streams, and business models.

ILLUSTRATION 5A.2   **A Summary of Financial Ratios**

Ratio	Formula	What It Measures
I. Liquidity		
1. Current ratio	$\dfrac{\text{Current assets}}{\text{Current liabilities}}$	Short-term debt-paying ability
2. Quick or acid-test ratio	$\dfrac{\text{Cash, marketable securities, and receivables}}{\text{Current liabilities}}$	Immediate short-term liquidity
3. Current cash debt coverage ratio	$\dfrac{\text{Net cash provided by operating activities}}{\text{Average current liabilities}}$	Company's ability to pay off its current liabilities in a specific year from its operations
II. Activity		
4. Receivables turnover	$\dfrac{\text{Net sales*}}{\text{Average trade receivables}}$	Liquidity of receivables
5. Inventory turnover	$\dfrac{\text{Cost of goods sold}}{\text{Average inventory}}$	Liquidity of inventory
6. Asset turnover	$\dfrac{\text{Net sales*}}{\text{Average total assets}}$	How efficiently assets are used to generate sales
III. Profitability		
7. Gross profit margin	$\dfrac{\text{Gross profit}}{\text{Net sales*}}$	Gross profit generated by each dollar of sales
8. Profit margin on sales	$\dfrac{\text{Net income}}{\text{Net sales*}}$	Net income generated by each dollar of sales
9. Rate of return on assets	$\dfrac{\text{Net income}}{\text{Average total assets}}$	Overall profitability of assets
10. Rate of return on common share equity	$\dfrac{\text{Net income minus preferred dividends}}{\text{Average common shareholders' equity}}$	Profitability of owners' investment
11. Earnings per share	$\dfrac{\text{Net income minus preferred dividends}}{\text{Weighted average shares outstanding}}$	Net income earned on each common share
12. Price earnings ratio	$\dfrac{\text{Market price of shares}}{\text{Earnings per share}}$	Ratio of the market price per share to earnings per share
13. Payout ratio	$\dfrac{\text{Cash dividends}}{\text{Net income}}$	Percentage of earnings distributed as cash dividends
IV. Coverage		
14. Debt to total assets	$\dfrac{\text{Total debt}}{\text{Total assets}}$	Percentage of total assets provided by creditors
15. Times interest earned	$\dfrac{\text{Income before interest charges and taxes}}{\text{Interest charges}}$	Ability to meet interest payments as they come due
16. Cash debt coverage ratio	$\dfrac{\text{Net cash provided by operating activities}}{\text{Average total liabilities}}$	Company's ability to repay its total liabilities in a specific year from its operations
17. Free cash flow to operating cash flow	$\dfrac{\text{(Net cash provided by operating activities} - \text{capital expenditures} - \text{dividends)}}{\text{Cash flow from operations}}$	Amount of free cash flow available for every dollar of operating cash flow generated. (Note: In determining free cash flow, some companies do not subtract dividends.)
18. Book value per share	$\dfrac{\text{Common shareholders' equity}}{\text{Number of common shares outstanding at SFP date}}$	Amount each share would receive if the company were liquidated at the amounts reported on the statement of financial position

*As discussed in Chapter 6, under IFRS 15, companies would typically report one amount for sales, Sales Revenue. Under ASPE, companies would tend to show Sales Revenues and Net Sales separately. Use Sales Revenue in ratios if Net Sales is not provided.

Success in the retail industry, for instance, may reflect the ability to set prices and target customers in a way that gets maximum market penetration. Also critical is the ability to minimize inventory shrinkage (because there is a high risk of theft) and keep inventory moving so that it does not become obsolete or out of fashion. A company's ability to achieve this, or its failure to do so, is reflected in the gross profit margin (a ratio). This is calculated by dividing gross profit (where gross profit = net sales – cost of goods sold) by revenues. Companies must achieve a gross profit that is high enough to cover other costs. A high and stable gross profit margin is a positive sign that management is dealing with all of the above issues.

Once ratios are calculated, they must then be examined and the information interpreted. Examining ratios by themselves provides very little insight. Instead, the **ratios must be compared with** or benchmarked against similar ratios, perhaps for **the same company from prior periods or, alternatively, for similar companies in the same industry**.

When benchmarking is done against industry numbers, it may be necessary to create industry benchmarks if they are not available. To do this, select several companies that have a similar business model and are in the same industry. Companies that are the same size are better comparators.

Note that average amounts may be approximated by taking opening and closing balances and dividing by 2.

Review and Practice

Summary of Learning Objectives

1. Understand the statement of financial position and statement of cash flows from a business perspective.

It is important to understand how users of financial statements use the SFP and the statement of cash flows. For example, potential investors in a company may use the SFP to analyze a company's liquidity and solvency in order to assess the risk of investing. In addition, the SFP provides details about the company's financial structure. Users may use a company's statement of cash flows to assess its earnings quality and obtain information about its operating, investing, and financing activities.

2. Identify the uses and limitations of a statement of financial position.

The SFP provides information about the nature and amounts of investments in enterprise resources, obligations to creditors, and the owners' equity in net resources. The SFP contributes to financial reporting by providing a basis for (1) calculating rates of return, (2) evaluating the enterprise's capital structure, and (3) assessing the enterprise's liquidity, solvency, and financial flexibility. The limitations of an SFP are as follows: (1) The SFP often does not reflect current value, because accountants have adopted a historical cost basis in valuing and reporting many assets and liabilities. (2) Judgements and estimates must be used in preparing an SFP. In addition, entities often need to make materiality judgements when preparing financial statements. IFRS Practice Statement 2 suggests a four-step process for assessing materiality when preparing financial statements. (3) The SFP leaves out many items that are of financial value to the business but cannot be recorded objectively, such as its human resources, customer base, and reputation.

3. Identify the major classifications of a statement of financial position.

The SFP's general elements are assets, liabilities, and equity. The major classifications within the SFP on the asset side are current assets; investments; property, plant, and equipment; intangible assets; and other assets. The major classifications of liabilities are current and long-term liabilities. In a corporation, owners' equity is generally classified as shares, contributed surplus, retained earnings, and accumulated other comprehensive income.

4. Prepare a classified statement of financial position.

The most common format lists liabilities and shareholders' equity directly below assets on the same page.

5. Identify statement of financial position information that requires supplemental disclosure.

Five types of information are normally supplemental to account titles and amounts presented in the SFP. (1) Contingencies: Material events that have an uncertain outcome. (2) Accounting policies: Explanations of the valuation methods that are used or the basic assumptions that are made for inventory valuation, amortization methods, investments in subsidiaries, and so on. (3) Contractual situations: Explanations of certain restrictions or covenants that are attached to specific assets or, more likely, to liabilities. (4) Additional information: Clarification by giving more detail about the composition of SFP items. (5) Subsequent events: Events that happen after the reporting period.

6. Identify major disclosure techniques for the statement of financial position.

There are four methods of disclosing pertinent information for the SFP: (1) Parenthetical explanations: Additional information or description is often provided by giving explanations in parentheses that follow the item. (2) Notes: Notes are used if additional explanations or descriptions cannot be shown conveniently as parenthetical explanations. (3) Cross-reference and contra items: A direct relationship between an asset and a liability is cross-referenced on the SFP. (4) Supporting schedules: Often a separate schedule is needed to present more detailed information about certain assets or liabilities because the SFP provides just a single summary item.

7. Indicate the purpose and identify the content of the statement of cash flows.

The main purpose of a statement of cash flows is to provide relevant information about an enterprise's cash receipts and cash payments during a period. Reporting the sources, uses, and net increase or decrease in cash lets investors, creditors, and others know what is happening to a company's most liquid resource. Cash receipts and cash payments during a period are classified in the statement of cash flows into three different activities: (1) Operating activities: Involve the cash effects of transactions that enter into the determination of net income. (2) Investing activities: Include making and collecting loans and acquiring and disposing of investments (both debt and equity) and property, plant, and equipment. (3) Financing activities: Involve liability and owners' equity items and include (a) obtaining capital from owners and providing them with a return on their investment and (b) borrowing money from creditors and repaying the amounts borrowed.

8. Prepare a statement of cash flows using the indirect and direct methods.

This involves determining cash flow from operations by starting with net income and adjusting it for non-cash activities, such as changes in accounts receivable (and other current asset/liability) balances, depreciation, and gains/losses for the indirect method. It is important to look carefully at prior year operating activities that might affect cash this year, such as cash collected this year from last year's credit sales and cash spent this year for last year's accrued expenses. The same types of adjustments are required to determine cash flow from operations under the direct method, but the groupings on the statement are different. The cash flows from investing and financing activities can then be determined by analyzing changes in SFP accounts and the cash account.

9. Understand the usefulness of the statement of cash flows.

Creditors examine the statement of cash flows carefully when they are concerned about being repaid. The amount of net cash flow provided by operating activities in relation to the company's liabilities is helpful in making this assessment. In addition, measures such as a free cash flow analysis provide creditors and shareholders with a better picture of the company's financial flexibility.

10. Identify differences in accounting between IFRS and ASPE and identify the significant changes planned by the IASB for financial statement presentation.

Illustration 5.23 details the major differences in how both sets of standards account for and present items on the SFP and statement of cash flows. Both sets of standards largely require that the same SFP elements be presented. In addition, IFRS requires presentation of biological assets, investment properties, and provisions. The statement of cash flow presentation requirements are similar. The IASB issued the new "Conceptual Framework for Financial Reporting" in March 2018 that included changes to the definitions of assets and liabilities. The IASB was also working on a Primary Financial Statements project with a goal of targeted improvements to the structure and content of primary financial statements such as the statement of financial position and statement of cash flows.

11. Identify the major types of financial ratios and what they measure.

Ratios express the mathematical relationship between one quantity and another, in terms of a percentage, a rate, or a proportion. Liquidity ratios measure the short-term ability to pay maturing obligations. Activity ratios measure how effectively assets are being used. Profitability ratios measure an enterprise's success or failure. Coverage ratios measure the degree of protection for long-term creditors and investors.

Practice Problem

Cassy Corporation's statement of financial position at the end of 2019 included the following items.

Land	$ 36,000
Buildings	144,000
Equipment	108,000
Accumulated depreciation—buildings	(36,000)
Accumulated depreciation—equipment	(13,200)
Patents	48,000
Current assets	282,000
Total	$568,800

Share capital—ordinary	$216,000
Retained earnings	52,800
Bonds payable	120,000
Current liabilities	180,000
Total	$568,800

The following information is available for 2020.

1. Cassy repurchased some of its ordinary shares at a cost of $13,200.
2. Cash dividends of $36,000 were declared and paid.
3. A FV-OCI investment in shares was purchased for $19,200 on December 31, 2020.
4. Current assets other than cash increased by $34,800. Current liabilities increased by $15,600.
5. Depreciation expense was $4,800 on the building and $10,800 on the equipment.
6. Net income was $66,000.
7. Bonds payable of $60,000 were issued.
8. An addition to buildings was completed at a cost of $32,400.
9. Patent amortization was $3,000.
10. Equipment (cost $24,000 and accumulated depreciation $9,600) was sold for $12,000.

Instructions

a. Prepare a statement of financial position at December 31, 2020. Assume Cassy has decided to use the more common order of assets and liabilities items in its SFP in 2020 (for example, current items listed first). (*Hint:* The amount to be determined for current assets in 2020 is calculated last and is a "plug" figure.)

b. Prepare a statement of cash flows for 2020. (*Hint:* Complete the statement only to the line "net increase in cash.")

Solution

a.

Cassy Corporation
Statement of Financial Position
December 31, 2020

Assets

Current assets ($282,000 + $34,800 + $39,000)			$355,800
FV-OCI investments			19,200
Property, plant, and equipment			
Land		$ 36,000	
Buildings ($144,000 + $32,400)	$176,400		
Less: Accumulated depreciation—buildings			
($36,000 + $4,800)	40,800	135,600	
Equipment ($108,000 − $24,000)	84,000		
Less: Accumulated depreciation—equipment			
($13,200 − $9,600 + $10,800)	14,400	69,600	
Total			241,200
Intangible assets—patents ($48,000 − $3,000)			45,000
Total assets			$661,200

Liabilities and Shareholders' Equity

Current liabilities ($180,000 + $15,600)	$195,600
Non-current liabilities	
Bonds payable ($120,000 + $60,000)	180,000
Total liabilities	375,600
Shareholders' equity	
Share capital—ordinary ($216,000 − $13,200)	202,800
Retained earnings ($52,800 + $66,000 − $36,000)	82,800
Total shareholders' equity	285,600
Total equity and liabilities	$661,200

Notes: The amount determined for current assets is calculated last and is a "plug" figure. That is, total equity and liabilities is calculated because information is available to determine this amount. Because the total assets amount is the same as the total equity and liabilities amount, the amount of total assets can be determined. Information is available to calculate all the asset amounts except current assets. Therefore, current assets of $355,800 can be determined by deducting the total of all the other asset balances from the total asset balance ($661,200 − $45,000 − $241,200 − $19,200).

b.

Cassy Corporation
Statement of Cash Flows
For the Year Ended December 31, 2020

Cash flows from operating activities		
Net income	$66,000	
Adjustments to reconcile net income to net cash provided by operating activities:		
Loss on sale of equipment	2,400	
Depreciation expense	15,600	
Patent amortization	3,000	
Increase in current liabilities	15,600	
Increase in current assets (other than cash)	(34,800)	
Net cash provided by operating activities		$ 67,800
Cash flows from investing activities		
Proceeds on sale of equipment	12,000	
Addition to buildings	(32,400)	
Purchase of FV-OCI investment	(19,200)	
Net cash used by investing activities		(39,600)
Cash flows from financing activities		
Issuance of bonds	60,000	
Payment of dividends	(36,000)	
Repurchase of shares	(13,200)	
Net cash provided by financing activities		10,800
Net increase in cash		$ 39,000

Key Terms

activity ratios, p. 5-40
adjunct account, p. 5-26
cash and cash equivalents, p. 5-11
cash debt coverage ratio, p. 5-35
contingency, p. 5-22
contra account, p. 5-26
coverage ratios, p. 5-40
current assets, p. 5-10
current cash debt coverage ratio, p. 5-35
current liabilities, p. 5-18
deferred income tax assets, p. 5-18
deferred income tax liabilities, p. 5-19
financial flexibility, p. 5-5
financial instruments, p. 5-8

financing activities, p. 5-27
free cash flow, p. 5-36
future income tax assets, p. 5-18
future income tax liabilities, p. 5-19
intangible assets, p. 5-17
investing activities, p. 5-27
liquidity, p. 5-5
liquidity ratios, p. 5-40
long-term liabilities, p. 5-18
monetary assets, p. 5-7
non-current investments, p. 5-15
nonmonetary assets, p. 5-8
operating activities, p. 5-27
other assets, p. 5-17

owners' equity, p. 5-20
prepaid expenses, p. 5-15
profitability ratios, p. 5-40
property, plant, and equipment, p. 5-15
provision, p. 5-23
ratio analysis, p. 5-40
solvency, p. 5-5
solvency ratios, p. 5-40
statement of cash flows, p. 5-27
statement of financial position, p. 5-4
subsequent events, p. 5-24
working capital, p. 5-18

Assignment Material

Note: All assignment material with an asterisk (*) relates to the appendix to the chapter.

Enabling Competencies Completion of this end-of-chapter material will help develop CPA-enabling competencies (such as ethics and professionalism, problem-solving and decision-making, and communication) and technical competencies. We have highlighted selected items with a specific integration word mark and material in *WileyPLUS* has been linked to the competencies. All cases emphasize integration, especially of the enabling competencies. The brief exercises, exercises, and problems generally emphasize problem-solving and decision-making.

All questions relating to the statement of cash flows assume usage of the indirect method, unless the question states otherwise. The direct method is covered in Volume 2, Chapter 22.

Brief Exercises

BE5.1 (LO 1) Wong Corporation is a popular clothing retailer with 15 stores across Canada. After five consecutive years of increasing sales, Wong would like to expand operations by adding 10 stores within the next three years. To help fund the expansion, Wong is seeking a loan from its bank. As Wong's bank manager, discuss the usefulness of (a) the statement of financial position and (b) the statement of cash flows, in evaluating Wong's operations.

BE5.2 (LO 1) Gator Printers Inc. is an online retailer of printing services, reaching thousands of customers across North America every year. The company was founded 15 years ago as a university campus copy shop and has reported consistent year-over-year sales growth every year since, with a fast-growing base of individual customers, as well as large corporate accounts. Two years ago, the company issued shares to the general public through a highly publicized and successful initial public offering. Gator is currently considering expanding to South America, and issuing bonds to fund the expansion. Identify the users of Gator Printers' statement of cash flows and how they are likely to use the statement.

BE5.3 (LO 2) One of the weaknesses or limitations of the statement of financial position is that it leaves out financial statement elements if they cannot be objectively recorded. Name three examples of items that are omitted because of this limitation.

BE5.4 (LO 3) Kahnert Corporation's adjusted trial balance contained the following asset accounts at December 31, 2020: Cash $3,000; Treasury Bills (with original maturity of three months) $4,000; Land $60,000; Intangible Assets—Patents $12,500; Accounts Receivable $90,000; Prepaid Insurance $5,200; Inventory $40,000; Allowance for Doubtful Accounts $4,000; and FV-NI (Fair Value—Net Income) Investments $11,000. Prepare the current assets section of the statement of financial position, listing the accounts in proper sequence. Identify which items are monetary.

BE5.5 (LO 3) The following accounts are in Tan Limited's December 31, 2020 trial balance: Prepaid Rent $1,600; FV-OCI (Fair Value—Other Comprehensive Income) Investments $62,000; Unearned Revenue $7,000; Land Held for Speculation $119,000; and Goodwill $45,000. Prepare the long-term investments section of the statement of financial position. Identify which items are financial instruments.

BE5.6 (LO 3) Lowell Corp.'s December 31, 2020 trial balance includes the following accounts: Inventory $120,000; Buildings $207,000; Accumulated Depreciation—Equipment $19,000; Equipment $190,000; Land Held for Speculation $46,000; Accumulated Depreciation—Buildings $45,000; Land $71,000; Equipment Under Lease $229,000; and Accumulated Depreciation—Leased Equipment $103,000. Prepare the property, plant, and equipment section of the statement of financial position.

BE5.7 (LO 3) Pine Corporation's adjusted trial balance contained the following asset accounts at December 31, 2020: Prepaid Rent $22,000; Goodwill $50,000; Franchise Fees Receivable $2,000; Intangible Assets—Franchises $47,000; Intangible Assets—Patents $33,000; and Intangible Assets—Trademarks $10,000. Prepare the intangible assets section of the statement of financial position.

BE5.8 (LO 3, 10) Included in Cellin Limited's December 31, 2020 trial balance are the following accounts: Accounts Payable $251,000; Obligations under Lease $175,000; Unearned Revenue $141,000; Bonds Payable $480,000 (due October 31, 2032); Salaries and Wages Payable $127,000; Interest Payable $42,000; Income Tax Payable $9,000; and Notes Payable $97,000 (due on March 31, 2021). On January 31, 2021, Cellin finalized refinancing of the notes payable with a new note payable due on March 31, 2022. The financial statements were issued on February 28, 2021.

a. Prepare the current liabilities section of the statement of financial position if Cellin prepares financial statements in accordance with IFRS, and identify which items are monetary.

b. Explain how your answer to part (a) would be different if Cellin prepares financial statements in accordance with ASPE.

BE5.9 (LO 3, 10) Use the information presented in BE5.8 for Cellin Limited to prepare the non-current liabilities section of the statement of financial position in accordance with (a) IFRS and (b) ASPE.

BE5.10 (LO 3) Southern Corporation's adjusted trial balance contained the following accounts at December 31, 2020: Retained Earnings $120,000; Common Shares $700,000; Bonds Payable $100,000; Contributed Surplus $200,000; Preferred Shares $50,000; Goodwill $55,000; and Accumulated Other Comprehensive Income (Loss) ($150,000). Prepare the shareholders' equity section of the statement of financial position.

BE5.11 (LO 7) What is the purpose of the statement of cash flows? How does it differ from a statement of financial position and an income statement?

BE5.12 (LO 8) How does a statement of cash flows prepared using the indirect method differ from one prepared using the direct method?

BE5.13 (LO 8) Agnu Inc. shows on its statement of financial position its investments accounted for as FV-OCI investments. At its year end of May 31, 2018, the balance in the FV-OCI Investments account was $96,000 and at its year end of May 31, 2019, the balance was $120,000. Agnu's statement of comprehensive income for the year ended May 31, 2019, shows an unrealized loss from fair value adjustment on FV-OCI investments of $23,000. There were no sales of FV-OCI investments during the year, only purchases. Determine the necessary caption(s) and amount(s) that should appear on Agnu's statement of cash flows prepared using the indirect method and determine if the entry(ies) appear under the operating, investing, or financing section(s) of the statement.

BE5.14 (LO 8) Newvo Ltd. shows on its statement of financial position a patent. At its year end of October 31, 2018, the caption read Patent (net) $66,000 and at its year end of October 31, 2019, the caption read Patent (net) $40,000. Newvo's recorded amortization on the patent in the amount of $6,000 for the 2019 fiscal year and the remaining change in the account resulted from recording a loss on impairment for the year ended October 31, 2019. There were no purchases or sales of patents during the year. Determine the necessary caption(s) and amount(s) that should appear on Newvo's statement of cash flows, using the indirect method. Be clear regarding where the item(s) would appear on the statement (the operating, investing, or financing section(s)).

BE5.15 (LO 8) Healey Corporation's statement of financial position as at December 31, 2020, showed the following amounts: Cash $100; Accounts Receivable $600; Land $1,000; Accounts Payable $300; Bonds Payable $500; Common Shares $400; and Retained Earnings $500. Healey's statement of financial position as at December 31, 2019, showed the following amounts: Cash $150; Accounts Receivable $450; Land $800; Accounts Payable $700; Common Shares $400; and Retained Earnings $300. Assume that no dividends were declared or paid in 2020. Calculate the net cash provided (used) by operating activities for the year ended December 31, 2020, using the indirect method.

BE5.16 (LO 8) Ames Company reported 2020 net income of $151,000. During 2020, accounts receivable increased by $15,000 and accounts payable increased by $9,000. Depreciation expense was $44,000. Prepare the cash flows from operating activities section of the statement of cash flows using the indirect method.

 ▶ Video

BE5.17 (LO 8) Assume that Ames Company's net income of $151,000 in BE5.16 was based on sales of $600,000, cost of goods sold of $200,000, salaries and wages of $157,000, depreciation expense of $44,000, and income tax expense of $48,000. Prepare the cash flows from operating activities section of the statement of cash flows using the direct method.

BE5.18 (LO 8) Miller Ltd. engaged in the following cash transactions during 2020:

Proceeds from sale of land and building	$176,000
Repurchase of company's own shares	25,000
Purchase of land	44,000
Payment of cash dividends	58,000
Purchase of equipment	35,000
Issuance of common shares	140,000
Retirement of bonds payable	200,000

Miller prepares financial statements in accordance with ASPE. Calculate the net cash provided (used) by investing activities.

BE5.19 (LO 8, 10) Use the information from BE5.18 for Miller Ltd. (a) Calculate the net cash provided (used) by financing activities, under ASPE. (b) Explain how your answer to part (a) would be different if Miller prepares financial statements in accordance with IFRS, if Miller's policy is to treat dividends paid as operating activities.

*BE5.20 (LO 11) Finance Use the information from BE5.18 for Miller Ltd. Determine Miller's free cash flow, assuming that it reported net cash provided by operating activities of $400,000. The purchase of land was for use.

▶ **Video**   *BE5.21 (LO 8, 10, 11) Finance Midwest Co. reported the following items in the most recent year:

Net income	$40,000
Dividends paid	5,000
Increase in accounts receivable	10,000
Increase in accounts payable	7,000
Purchase of equipment	8,000
Depreciation expense	4,000
Issue of notes payable for cash	20,000

a. Calculate net cash provided (used) by operating activities, the net change in cash during the year, and free cash flow. Dividends paid related to the company's common shares and are treated as financing activities. Midwest uses the indirect method for its statement of cash flows.

b. Assuming Midwest had 100,000 common shares outstanding for the entire year, calculate cash flow per share to be included in the financial statements if Midwest follows IFRS and chooses to disclose the ratio. Assume Midwest uses cash flow from operations for this ratio.

c. How would your answer to part (b) change if Midwest follows ASPE?

*BE5.22 (LO 11) Finance Melbourne Inc. reported a current ratio of 1.5:1 in the current year, which is higher than last year's current ratio of 1.3:1. It also reported an acid-test ratio of 1:1, which is higher than last year's acid-test ratio of 0.6:1. Is Melbourne's liquidity improving or deteriorating? Explain.

Exercises

E5.1 (LO 3)   (Statement of Financial Position Classifications)   Several statement of financial position accounts of Greenspoon Inc. follow:

1. FV-OCI Investments
2. Common Shares
3. Dividends Payable
4. Accumulated Depreciation—Equipment
5. Construction in Process (warehouse for own use)
6. Petty Cash
7. Interest Payable
8. Deficit

9. FV-NI Investments
10. Income Tax Payable
11. Land Improvements
12. Work-in-Process Inventory—Direct Materials
13. Salaries and Wages Payable
14. Unearned Revenue
15. Litigation Liability

Instructions

For each account, indicate the proper statement of financial position classification. In the case of items that could be classified in more than one category, indicate the additional information that would be required to determine the proper classification. (Refer to Illustration 5.1 as a guideline.) Also identify which items are monetary and which are financial instruments (or both).

E5.2 (LO 3)   (Classification of Statement of Financial Position Accounts)   The classifications on Chesapeake Limited's statement of financial position are as follows:

1. Current assets
2. Long-term investments
3. Property, plant, and equipment
4. Intangible assets
5. Other assets
6. Current liabilities

7. Long-term debt
8. Capital shares
9. Contributed surplus
10. Retained earnings
11. Accumulated other comprehensive income

Instructions

Indicate by number where each of the following accounts would be classified:

a. Preferred Shares
b. Franchises
c. Salaries and Wages Payable
d. Accounts Payable
e. Leasehold Improvements
f. FV-NI Investments
g. Current Portion of Long-Term Debt

h. Obligations under Lease (portion due next year)
i. Allowance for Doubtful Accounts
j. Accounts Receivable
k. Bonds Payable (maturing in two years)
l. Notes Payable (due next year)
m. Supplies

n. Mortgage Payable (principal portion due beyond next year)

o. Land (for use)

p. Bond Sinking Fund Investment

q. Inventory

r. Prepaid Insurance

s. Bonds Payable (maturing next year)

t. Income Tax Payable

u. Unrealized Gain or Loss—OCI

v. Deficit

E5.3 (LO 3) (Classification of Statement of Financial Position Accounts) Plato Inc. prepares financial statements in accordance with IFRS and uses the following headings on its statement of financial position:

1. Current assets
2. Long-term investments
3. Property, plant, and equipment
4. Intangible assets
5. Other assets
6. Current liabilities
7. Long-term debt
8. Capital shares
9. Contributed surplus
10. Retained earnings
11. Accumulated other comprehensive income

Instructions

Indicate by number how each of the following should usually be classified. If an item need not be reported at all on the statement of financial position, use the letter X. Also indicate whether an item is monetary and/or represents a financial instrument.

a. Prepaid insurance

b. Investment in associate

c. Unearned revenue (portion earned next year)

d. Advances to employees

e. Unearned rent revenue (portion to be earned in two years)

f. Intangible assets—copyrights

g. Petty cash

h. HST payable

i. Accrued interest on notes receivable

j. Twenty-year issue of bonds payable that will mature within the next year (no sinking funds exist, and refinancing is not planned)

k. Machinery retired from use and reclassified as held for sale

l. Fully depreciated machine still in use

m. Investment in bonds that will be held until their maturity in two years

n. Accrued interest on bonds payable

o. Salaries that the company budget shows will be paid to employees within the next year

p. Accumulated depreciation related to equipment

q. Accumulated unrealized gains on securities accounted for under the FV-OCI model

r. Bank demand loan

s. Land held for speculation

E5.4 (LO 3, 4, 11) (Preparation of Corrected Statement of Financial Position) Bruno Corp. has decided to expand its operations. The bookkeeper recently completed the following statement of financial position in order to obtain additional funds for expansion:

Bruno Corp.
Statement of Financial Position
For the Year Ended December 31, 2020

Current assets	
Cash (net of bank overdraft of $30,000)	$260,000
Accounts receivable (net)	340,000
Inventory at the lower of cost and net realizable value	401,000
FV-NI investments (at cost—fair value $120,000)	140,000
Property, plant, and equipment	
Buildings (net)	570,000
Equipment (net)	160,000
Land held for future use	175,000

(continued)

Bruno Corp.
Statement of Financial Position
For the Year Ended December 31, 2020

Intangible assets	
Goodwill	$ 80,000
Investment in bonds to collect cash flows, at amortized cost	90,000
Prepaid expenses	12,000
Current liabilities	
Accounts payable	195,000
Notes payable (due next year)	125,000
Pension obligation	82,000
Rent payable	49,000
Long-term liabilities	
Bonds payable	553,000
Shareholders' equity	
Common shares, unlimited authorized, 290,000 issued	290,000
Contributed surplus	180,000
Retained earnings	?

Instructions

a. Prepare a revised statement of financial position using the available information. Assume that the bank overdraft relates to a bank account held at a different bank from the account with the cash balance. Assume that the accumulated depreciation balance for the buildings is $160,000 and that the accumulated depreciation balance for the equipment is $105,000. The allowance for doubtful accounts has a balance of $17,000. The pension obligation is considered a long-term liability.

*b. **Digging Deeper** **Finance** What effect, if any, does the classification of the bank overdraft have on the working capital and current ratio of Bruno Corp.? What is the likely reason why the bank overdraft was given that particular classification?

E5.5 (LO 3, 4, 11) **(Correction of Statement of Financial Position)** The bookkeeper for Garfield Corp. has prepared the following statement of financial position as at July 31, 2020:

Garfield Corp.
Statement of Financial Position
As at July 31, 2020

Cash	$ 69,000	Notes and accounts payable	$ 44,000
Accounts receivable (net)	40,500	Long-term liabilities	75,000
Inventory	60,000	Shareholders' equity	155,500
Equipment (net)	84,000		$274,500
Patents (net)	21,000		
	$274,500		

The following additional information is provided:

1. Cash includes $1,200 in a petty cash fund and $12,000 in a bond sinking fund.

2. The net accounts receivable balance is composed of the following three items: (a) accounts receivable debit balances $52,000; (b) accounts receivable credit balances $8,000; and (c) allowance for doubtful accounts $3,500.

3. Inventory costing $5,300 was shipped out on consignment on July 31, 2020. The ending inventory balance does not include the consigned goods. Receivables of $5,300 were recognized on these consigned goods.

4. Equipment had a cost of $112,000 and an accumulated depreciation balance of $28,000.

5. Income tax payable of $9,000 was accrued on July 31. Garfield Corp., however, had set up a cash fund to meet this obligation. This cash fund was not included in the cash balance, but was offset against the income tax payable account.

6. Long-term liabilities are bonds payable issued at par, due in 2025.

7. Shareholders' equity is made up of two account balances: Common Shares of $105,000 and Retained Earnings of $50,500.

Instructions

a. Use the information available to prepare a corrected classified statement of financial position as at July 31, 2020. (Adjust the account balances based on the additional information.)

*b. **Digging Deeper** **Finance** What effect, if any, does the treatment of the credit balances in accounts receivable of $8,000 have on the working capital and current ratio of Garfield Corp.? What is likely the reason that the credit balances in accounts receivable were given that particular classification? What is likely the cause of the credit balances in accounts receivable?

E5.6 (LO 3, 4) **(Preparation of Classified Statement of Financial Position)** Assume that Lee Inc. has the following accounts at the end of the current year:

1. Common Shares
2. Raw Materials Inventory
3. FV-OCI Investments
4. Unearned Rent Revenue
5. Work-in-Process Inventory
6. Intangible Assets—Copyrights
7. Buildings
8. Notes Receivable (due in three months)
9. Cash (includes Restricted Cash—see item 12)
10. Salaries and Wages Payable
11. Accumulated Depreciation—Buildings
12. Restricted Cash (for plant expansion)
13. Land Held for Future Plant Site
14. Allowance for Doubtful Accounts
15. Retained Earnings
16. Unearned Revenue (earned in the next year)
17. Accounts Receivable—Officers (due in one year)
18. Finished Goods Inventory
19. Accounts Receivable
20. Bonds Payable (due in four years)
21. Accounts Payable
22. Goodwill

Instructions

Prepare a classified statement of financial position in good form (no monetary amounts are necessary).

E5.7 (LO 4) **(Current versus Long-Term Liabilities)** Samson Corporation is preparing its December 31, 2020 statement of financial position. The following items may be reported as either current or long-term liabilities:

1. On December 15, 2020, Samson declared a cash dividend of $1.50 per common share to shareholders of record on December 31. The dividend is payable on January 15, 2021. Samson has issued 1 million common shares.

2. Also, on December 31, Samson declared a 10% stock dividend to shareholders of record on January 15, 2021. The dividend will be distributed on January 31, 2021. Samson's common shares have a market value of $54 per share.

3. At December 31, bonds payable of $100 million is outstanding. The bonds pay 7% interest every September 30 and mature in instalments of $25 million every September 30, beginning on September 30, 2021.

4. At December 31, 2019, customer advances were $12 million. During 2020, Samson collected $40 million in customer advances, and advances of $25 million were earned.

5. At December 31, 2020, Samson has an operating line of credit with a balance of $3.5 million outstanding. For several years now, Samson has successfully met all the conditions of this bank loan. If Samson defaults on any of the loan conditions in any way, the bank has the right to demand payment of the loan.

6. Samson is contingently liable for a bank loan in the amount of $10 million of its associated company, DD Ross Ltd. Samson has guaranteed the bank that, should DD Ross default on the loan or any outstanding interest payable, Samson will have to pay any and all outstanding balances. DD Ross is in an excellent financial position and shows no signs of defaulting on the terms of the bank loan.

Instructions

a. For each item above, indicate the dollar amounts to be reported as a current liability and as a long-term liability, if any.

b. Referring to the definition of a liability (discussed in Chapter 2), explain the accounting treatment of item 4 above.

c. **Digging Deeper** Can you think of a reason why Samson would be willing to guarantee the bank loan of its associate, DD Ross Ltd.? What possible benefit could this burden bring Samson?

E5.8 (LO 4) **(Preparation of Statement of Financial Position)** The trial balance of Zhang Ltd. at December 31, 2020, follows:

	Debits	Credits
Cash	$ 205,000	
Sales revenue		$ 8,010,000
FV-NI investments (at fair value)	153,000	
Cost of goods sold	4,800,000	
Bond investment at amortized cost	299,000	
FV-OCI investments (fair value $345,000)	277,000	
Notes payable (due in six months)		98,000
Accounts payable		645,000
Selling expenses	1,860,000	
Investment income or loss*		13,000
Land	260,000	
Buildings	1,040,000	
Dividends payable		36,000
Income tax payable		96,000
Accounts receivable	515,000	
Accumulated depreciation—buildings		152,000
Allowance for doubtful accounts		25,000
Administrative expenses	900,000	
Interest expense	211,000	
Inventory	687,000	
Gain on disposal of land		60,000
Dividends	40,000	
Notes payable (due in five years)		900,000
Equipment	600,000	
Bonds payable (due in three years)		1,000,000
Accumulated depreciation—equipment		60,000
Intangible assets—franchises (net)	160,000	
Common shares		809,000
Intangible assets—patents (net)	195,000	
Retained earnings		218,000
Accumulated other comprehensive income		80,000
Totals	$12,202,000	$12,202,000

* The investment income or loss relates to the FV-NI investments.

Instructions

a. Prepare a classified statement of financial position as at December 31, 2020. Ignore income taxes.

b. **Digging Deeper** Is there any situation where it would make more sense to have a statement of financial position that is not classified? If so, explain what it is and why.

E5.9 (LO 4, 5) (Current Liabilities) Lujie Xie is the controller of Lincoln Corporation and is responsible for the preparation of the year-end financial statements on December 31, 2020. Lincoln prepares financial statements in accordance with ASPE. The following transactions occurred during the year:

1. On December 20, 2020, an employee filed a legal action against Lincoln for $100,000 for wrongful dismissal. Management believes the action to be frivolous and without merit. This opinion is shared by the corporate lawyer involved in the matter. The likelihood of payment to the employee is remote.

2. Bonuses to key employees based on net income for 2020 are estimated to be $150,000.

3. On December 1, 2020, the company borrowed $900,000 at 5% per year. Interest is paid quarterly.

4. Credit sales for the year amounted to $10 million. Lincoln's expense provision for doubtful accounts is estimated to be 2% of credit sales.

5. On December 15, 2020, the company declared a $2.00 per common share dividend on the 40,000 common shares outstanding, to be paid on January 5, 2021.

6. During the year, customer advances of $160,000 were received; $50,000 of this amount was earned by December 31, 2020.

7. Late in December 2020, Lincoln received a notice of assessment for its 2019 income tax filing. The Canada Revenue Agency disallowed a deduction claimed by Lincoln and an additional $6,000 of income taxes are owing and will be paid in early January 2021.

Instructions

For each item above, indicate the dollar amount to be reported as a current liability. If a liability is not reported, explain why.

E5.10 (LO 4, 5, 6) `Excel` **(Current Assets Section of Statement of Financial Position)** Selected accounts follow of Aramis Limited at December 31, 2020:

Finished Goods Inventory	$152,000	Cost of Goods Sold	$2,100,000
Unearned Revenue	90,000	Notes Receivable	40,000
Bank Overdraft	8,000	Accounts Receivable	161,000
Equipment	253,000	Raw Materials Inventory	187,000
Work-in-Process Inventory	34,000	Supplies Expense	60,000
Cash	50,000	Allowance for Doubtful Accounts	12,000
FV-NI Investments	31,000	Intangible Assets—Trade Names	18,000
Interest Payable	36,000	Contributed Surplus	16,000
Restricted Cash (for Plant Expansion)	50,000	Common Shares	272,000

The following additional information is available:

1. Inventory is valued at the lower of cost and net realizable value using FIFO.

2. Equipment is recorded at cost. Accumulated depreciation, calculated on a straight-line basis, is $50,600.

3. The FV-NI investments have a fair value of $29,000.

4. The notes receivable are due April 30, 2021, with interest receivable every April 30. The notes bear interest at 6%. (*Hint:* Accrue interest due on December 31, 2020.)

5. The allowance for doubtful accounts applies to the accounts receivable. Accounts receivable of $50,000 are pledged as collateral on a bank loan.

6. Intangible Assets—Trade Names are reported net of accumulated amortization of $14,000.

7. The bank overdraft is at the same bank as the amount reported above under Cash.

Instructions

a. Prepare the current assets section of Aramis Limited's statement of financial position as at December 31, 2020, with appropriate disclosures.

b. Outline the other ways or methods that can be used to disclose the details that are required for the financial statement elements in part (a).

E5.11 (LO 4, 8) **(Preparation of Statement of Financial Position)** Uddin Corp.'s statement of financial position at the end of 2019 included the following items:

Current assets	$1,105,000	Current liabilities	$1,020,000
Land	30,000	Bonds payable	1,100,000
Buildings	1,120,000	Common shares	180,000
Equipment	320,000	Retained earnings	174,000
Accumulated depreciation—buildings	(130,000)	Total	$2,474,000
Accumulated depreciation—equipment	(11,000)		
Intangible assets—patents	40,000		
Total	$2,474,000		

The following information is available for the 2020 fiscal year:

1. Net income was $391,000.

2. Equipment (cost of $20,000 and accumulated depreciation of $8,000) was sold for $10,000.

3. Depreciation expense was $4,000 on the building and $9,000 on equipment.

4. Amortization expense on a patent was $3,000.

5. Current assets other than cash increased by $29,000. Current liabilities increased by $13,000.

6. An addition to a building was completed at a cost of $31,000.

7. An FV-OCI investment in shares was purchased for $20,500 on the last day of the year. This was the first such investment made by Uddin in its history.

8. Bonds payable of $75,000 were issued at par.

9. Cash dividends of $180,000 were declared and paid. Dividends paid are treated as financing activities.

Uddin prepares financial statements in accordance with IFRS.

Instructions

a. Prepare a statement of financial position (SFP) as at December 31, 2020. (*Hint:* You will need to adjust ("plug") the December 31, 2020 amount of current assets to ensure the SFP balances.)

b. Prepare a statement of cash flows for the year ended December 31, 2020, using the indirect method.

E5.12 (LO 4, 11) **(Current Assets and Current Liabilities)** The current assets and current liabilities sections of the statement of financial position of Agincourt Corp. are as follows:

Agincourt Corp. Statement of Financial Position (partial) December 31, 2020				
Cash		$ 40,000	Accounts payable	$ 61,000
Accounts receivable	$89,000		Notes payable	67,000
Allowance for doubtful accounts	7,000	82,000		$128,000
Inventory		171,000		
Prepaid expenses		9,000		
		$302,000		

The following errors have been discovered in the corporation's accounting:

1. January 2021 cash disbursements that were entered as at December 2020 included payments of accounts payable in the amount of $34,300.

2. The inventory balance is based on an inventory count that included $27,000 of merchandise that was received at December 31 but with no purchase invoices received or entered. Of this amount, $10,000 was received on consignment; the remainder was purchased f.o.b. destination.

3. Sales for the first four days of January 2021 in the amount of $30,000 were entered in the sales book as at December 31, 2020. Of these, $21,500 were sales on account and the remainder were cash sales.

4. Cash, not including cash sales, collected in January 2021 and entered as at December 31, 2020, totalled $35,324. Of this amount, $23,800 was received on account; the remainder was proceeds on a bank loan. (The amount owed to the bank for January 2021 was included as part of the Notes Payable account.)

Instructions

a. Adjust (correct) the statement of financial position's current assets and current liabilities sections.

*b. **Finance** Calculate the current ratio before and after the corrections prepared in part (a). Did the changes improve or worsen this ratio?

c. Calculate the net effect of your adjustments on Agincourt Corp.'s retained earnings balance.

d. Assume that in February 2021, Agincourt approaches its bank for another bank loan, based on its corrected statement of financial position as at December 31, 2020. Also assume that the terms of the new bank loan would require that Agincourt maintain a current ratio of 1.5. As Agincourt's bank manager, discuss the importance of recording the adjustments above and correcting the statement of financial position as at December 31, 2020.

e. **Digging Deeper** If the adjustments had not been reflected in the statement of financial position provided to the bank manager, do you think the bank manager would have suspected that the financial statements were incorrect? If so, how would the manager have suspected this misstatement to be the case?

E5.13 (LO 5) **(Supplemental Disclosures)** It is February 2021 and Janix Corporation is preparing to issue financial statements for the year ended December 31, 2020. To prepare financial statements and related disclosures that are faithfully representative, Janix is reviewing the following events in 2020 and 2021:

1. In August 2020, Maddux Incorporated filed a lawsuit against Janix for alleged patent infringement, claiming $1.8 million in damages. In the opinion of Janix's management and legal counsel, it is not likely that damages will be awarded to Maddux.

2. In January 2021, there was a significant decline in the fair value of Janix's FV-NI investments, resulting in an unrealized holding loss of $720,000.

3. In January 2021, a customer filed a lawsuit against Janix for alleged breach of contract related to services provided in 2020. The customer is seeking damages of $950,000. Janix's legal counsel believes that Janix will likely lose the lawsuit and have to pay between $850,000 and $950,000.

4. In August 2020, Janix signed a contract to purchase 200,000 inventory units in August 2021 for a price of $12 per unit. According to the supplier's price list at December 31, 2020, the price per inventory unit had decreased to $10 per unit.

5. At December 31, 2020, Janix had a $1.1-million demand loan outstanding. The terms of the demand loan restrict Janix's payment of dividends to $2 per common share.

6. On January 31, 2021, Janix issued 100,000 new common shares, raising $2 million in new capital.

7. On January 28, 2021, management settled a dispute with the union of its factory workers. A strike had started on November 14, 2020. A portion of the settlement involved a lump sum payment to each worker in lieu of a retroactive adjustment in pay rate dating back to the beginning of the strike.

Janix prepares financial statements in accordance with IFRS.

Instructions

For each item above, indicate whether the event relates to a provision, contingency, commitment, or subsequent event, and explain the appropriate accounting treatment. If no adjustment or disclosure is required, explain why.

E5.14 (LO 8, 9)   (Preparation of Statement of Cash Flows)   A comparative statement of financial position for Carmichael Industries Inc. follows:

Carmichael Industries Inc.
Statement of Financial Position
December 31, 2020

	December 31	
Assets	**2020**	**2019**
Cash	$ 21,000	$ 34,000
Accounts receivable	104,000	54,000
Inventory	220,000	189,000
Land	71,000	110,000
Equipment	260,000	200,000
Accumulated depreciation—equipment	(69,000)	(42,000)
Total	$607,000	$545,000
Liabilities and Shareholders' Equity		
Accounts payable	$ 52,000	$ 59,000
Bonds payable	150,000	200,000
Common shares	214,000	164,000
Retained earnings	191,000	122,000
Total	$607,000	$545,000

Additional information:

1. Net income for the fiscal year ending December 31, 2020, was $129,000.

2. Cash dividends of $60,000 were declared and paid. Dividends paid are treated as financing activities.

3. Bonds payable amounting to $50,000 were retired through issuance of common shares.

4. Land was sold at a gain of $5,000.

5. No equipment was sold during the year.

Instructions

a. Prepare a statement of cash flows using the indirect method along with any necessary note disclosure.

b. Comment in general on the results reported in the statement of cash flows.

E5.15 (LO 7)   (Statement of Cash Flows—Classifications)   The major classifications of activities reported in the statement of cash flows are operating, investing, and financing. For this question, assume the following:

Instructions

Assume that the statement of cash flows is being prepared in accordance with ASPE using the indirect method. Classify each of the transactions in the lettered list that follows as:

1. Operating activity   3. Financing activity

2. Investing activity   4. Not reported as a cash flow

Transactions

a. Issuance of common shares   e. Depreciation of machinery

b. Purchase of land and building   f. Amortization of patent

c. Redemption of bonds   g. Issuance of bonds in exchange for land

d. Proceeds on sale of equipment   h. Payment of cash dividends

i. Exchange of furniture for equipment

j. Loss on disposal of equipment

k. Increase in accounts receivable during year

l. Decrease in accounts payable during year

m. Payment of interest

n. Receipt of dividend revenue

E5.16 (LO 8, 9) **(Preparation of Partial Statement of Cash Flows—Operating Activities)** The statement of income of Kneale Transport Inc. for the year ended December 31, 2020, reported the following condensed information:

<table>
<tr><td colspan="3" align="center">**Kneale Transport Inc.**
Year Ended December 31, 2020
Statement of Income</td></tr>
<tr><td>Service revenue</td><td></td><td>$545,000</td></tr>
<tr><td>Operating expenses</td><td></td><td>370,000</td></tr>
<tr><td>Income from operations</td><td></td><td>175,000</td></tr>
<tr><td>Other revenues and expenses</td><td></td><td></td></tr>
<tr><td>   Gain on disposal of equipment</td><td>$25,000</td><td></td></tr>
<tr><td>   Interest expense</td><td>10,000</td><td>15,000</td></tr>
<tr><td>Income before income tax</td><td></td><td>190,000</td></tr>
<tr><td>Income tax</td><td></td><td>42,000</td></tr>
<tr><td>Net income</td><td></td><td>$148,000</td></tr>
</table>

Kneale's statement of financial position included the following comparative data at December 31:

	2020	2019
Accounts receivable	$50,000	$60,000
Prepaid insurance	8,000	5,000
Accounts payable	30,000	41,000
Interest payable	2,000	750
Income tax payable	8,000	4,500
Unearned revenue	10,000	14,000

Additional information:

Operating expenses include $70,000 in depreciation expense. The company follows IFRS. Assume that interest is treated as an operating activity for purposes of the statement of cash flows.

Instructions

a. Prepare the operating activities section of the statement of cash flows for the year ended December 31, 2020, using the

1. indirect method and

2. direct method.

b. **Digging Deeper** From the perspective of an external user of Kneale Transport's financial statements, discuss the usefulness of the statement of cash flows prepared using either the indirect or the direct method.

E5.17 (LO 8, 9) **(Preparation of Statement of Cash Flows)** The comparative statement of financial position of Dropafix Inc. as at June 30, 2020, and a statement of comprehensive income for the 2020 fiscal year follow:

<table>
<tr><td colspan="3" align="center">**Dropafix Inc.**
Statement of Financial Position
June 30, 2020</td></tr>
<tr><td></td><td colspan="2" align="center">June 30</td></tr>
<tr><td>**Assets**</td><td>**2020**</td><td>**2019**</td></tr>
<tr><td>Cash</td><td>$ 20,000</td><td>$ 38,000</td></tr>
<tr><td>Accounts receivable</td><td>86,000</td><td>74,000</td></tr>
<tr><td>Inventory</td><td>103,000</td><td>102,000</td></tr>
<tr><td>Prepaid expenses</td><td>2,000</td><td>6,000</td></tr>
<tr><td>FV-OCI investments</td><td>47,000</td><td>45,000</td></tr>
<tr><td>Equipment</td><td>173,000</td><td>159,000</td></tr>
<tr><td>Accumulated depreciation—equipment</td><td>(35,000)</td><td>(25,000)</td></tr>
<tr><td>Total</td><td>$396,000</td><td>$399,000</td></tr>
</table>

(continued)

Liabilities and Shareholders' Equity

Accounts payable	$115,000	$100,000
Income tax payable	2,000	3,000
Dividends payable	5,000	-0-
Long-term notes payable	84,000	119,000
Common shares	31,000	24,000
Retained earnings	148,000	144,000
Accumulated other comprehensive income	11,000	9,000
Total	$396,000	$399,000

Dropafix Inc.
Statement of Comprehensive Income
For the Year Ended June 30, 2020

Net sales	$323,000
Cost of goods sold	175,000
Gross profit	148,000
Operating expenses	120,000
Income from operations	28,000
Interest expense	9,000
Income before income tax	19,000
Income tax	6,000
Net income	13,000
Other comprehensive income	
Unrealized gain or loss—OCI	2,000
Comprehensive income	$ 15,000

Additional information:

1. Dropafix follows IFRS. Assume that interest is treated as an operating activity for purposes of the statement of cash flows.
2. Operating expenses include $10,000 in depreciation expense.
3. There were no disposals of equipment during the year.
4. Common shares were issued for cash.
5. During the year, Dropafix acquired $8,000 of equipment in exchange for long-term notes payable.

Instructions

a. Prepare the statement of cash flows for Dropafix for the year ended June 30, 2020, using the indirect method along with any necessary note disclosure.

b. Prepare the operating activities section of the statement of cash flows for Dropafix using the direct method.

c. **Digging Deeper** From the perspective of a creditor holding several of the long-term notes in substantial amounts owed by Dropafix, how do you view the cash management demonstrated by Dropafix?

E5.18 (LO 8, 9) (Preparation of Statement of Cash Flows) The comparative statement of financial position of Sensify Corporation as at December 31, 2020, follows:

Sensify Corporation
Statement of Financial Position
December 31

Assets	2020	2019
Cash	$ 53,000	$ 13,000
Accounts receivable	91,000	88,000
Equipment	27,000	22,000
Less: Accumulated depreciation	(10,000)	(11,000)
Total	$161,000	$112,000

(continued)

	December 31	
Liabilities and Shareholders' Equity	**2020**	**2019**
Accounts payable	$ 20,000	$ 15,000
Common shares	100,000	80,000
Retained earnings	41,000	17,000
Total	$161,000	$112,000

Net income of $37,000 was reported and dividends of $13,000 were declared and paid in 2020. New equipment was purchased, and equipment with a carrying value of $5,000 (cost of $12,000 and accumulated depreciation of $7,000) was sold for $8,000.

Instructions

Prepare a statement of cash flows using the indirect method for cash flows from operating activities. Assume that Sensify prepares financial statements in accordance with ASPE.

*E5.19 (LO 11) **Finance** **(Analysis)** Use the information in E5.18 for Sensify Corporation.

Instructions

a. Calculate the current ratio and debt to total assets ratio as at December 31, 2019 and 2020. Calculate the free cash flow for December 31, 2020.

b. Based on the analysis in part (a), comment on the company's liquidity and financial flexibility.

*E5.20 (LO 11) **Finance** **(Analysis)** Use the information in E5.14 for Carmichael Industries.

Instructions

a. Calculate the current and acid-test ratios for 2019 and 2020.

b. Calculate Carmichael's current cash debt coverage ratio for 2020.

c. Based on the analyses in parts (a) and (b), comment on Carmichael's liquidity and financial flexibility.

d. Calculate Carmichael's payout ratio. From the company's perspective, is the ratio too high? What would be a reasonable payout ratio?

*E5.21 (LO 11) **Finance** **(Analysis)** Use the information in E5.17 for Dropafix Inc.

Instructions

a. Calculate the current and acid-test ratios for 2019 and 2020.

b. Calculate Dropafix's current cash debt coverage ratio for 2020.

c. Calculate Dropafix's cash debt coverage ratio for 2020.

d. Calculate Dropafix's times interest earned ratio for 2020.

e. Based on the analyses in parts (a) through (d), comment on Dropafix's liquidity, financial flexibility, and ability to repay current and all liabilities from its operations and ability to meet interest payments as they come due.

f. **Digging Deeper** Looking at the statement of income, the statement of financial position, and the statement of cash flows, provide one recommendation that could improve Dropafix's liquidity, financial flexibility, and ability to repay current and all liabilities from its operations.

Problems

P5.1 A list of accounts follows:

Accounts Receivable
Land
Salaries and Wages Payable
Land Held for Future Plant Site
Accumulated Depreciation—Buildings
Loss on Impairment
Accumulated Depreciation—Equipment
Notes Payable (due in six months)
Accumulated Other Comprehensive Income

Intangible Assets—Patents (net of accumulated amortization)
Advances to Employees
Advertising Expense
Petty Cash
Allowance for Doubtful Accounts
Preferred Shares
FV-OCI Investments
Equipment

Income Tax Payable
Gain on Disposal of Equipment
FV-NI Investments
Interest Receivable
Pension Obligation (non-current)
Bonds Payable (due in four years)
Prepaid Rent
Buildings
Dividends
Cash
Cost of Goods Sold
Restricted Cash

Notes Receivable (due in five years)
Commission Expense
Retained Earnings
Common Shares
Sales Revenue
Intangible Assets—Copyrights (net of
    accumulated amortization)
Dividends Payable
Selling Expenses
Inventory
Unearned Revenue
Unrealized Gain or Loss—OCI

Instructions

Prepare a classified statement of financial position in good form, without specific amounts.

P5.2 **Excel** Statement of financial position items for Montoya Inc. follow for the current year, 2020:

Goodwill	$ 125,000	Accumulated depreciation—equipment	$ 292,000
Bank loan	177,591	Inventory	239,800
Bonds payable due 2024	270,000	Rent payable	45,000
Cash	360,000	Income tax payable	98,362
Land	480,000	Rent payable (long-term)	480,000
Notes receivable	445,700	Common shares (20,000 shares issued)	200,000
Notes payable	265,000	Preferred shares (15,000 shares issued)	150,000
Accounts payable	490,000	Prepaid expenses	87,920
Retained earnings	?	Equipment	1,470,000
Income tax receivable	97,630	FV-NI investments	121,000
Notes payable (due in five		Accumulated depreciation—buildings	270,200
years)	1,600,000	Buildings	1,640,000

Instructions

a. Prepare a classified statement of financial position in good form. The numbers of authorized shares are as follows: unlimited common and 20,000 preferred. Assume that income tax accounts, notes receivable, bank loan, and notes payable are short-term, unless stated otherwise, and that the FV-NI investments are stated at fair value.

b. What additional disclosures would you expect to provide for the rental obligation?

P5.3 The trial balance of Eastwood Inc. and other related information for the year 2020 follows:

Eastwood Inc.
Trial Balance
December 31, 2020

	Debits	Credits
Cash	$ 41,000	
Accounts receivable	163,500	
Allowance for doubtful accounts		$ 8,700
Prepaid insurance	5,900	
Inventory	208,500	
FV-OCI investments	339,000	
Land	85,000	
Construction in process	124,000	
Intangible assets—patents	36,000	
Equipment	400,000	
Accumulated depreciation—equipment		240,000
Accounts payable		148,000
Income tax payable		49,200
Notes payable		94,000
Bonds payable		180,000
Common shares		500,000
Accumulated other comprehensive income		45,000
Retained earnings		138,000
	$1,402,900	$1,402,900

Additional information:

1. The inventory has a net realizable value of $212,000. The FIFO method of inventory valuation is used.

2. The FV-OCI investments' fair value is $378,000.

3. The amount of the Construction in Process account represents the costs to date on a building in the process of construction. (The company is renting factory space while waiting for the new building to be completed.) The land that the building is being constructed on cost $85,000, as shown in the trial balance.

4. The company purchased the patents at a cost of $40,000 and the patents are being amortized on a straight-line basis.

5. The bonds payable have a face value of $200,000, bear interest at 7% payable every December 31, and are due January 1, 2032.

6. Of the remaining $20,000 unamortized discount on bonds payable (face value $200,000 less carrying amount $180,000), $2,000 will be amortized in 2021.

7. The notes payable represent bank loans that are secured by FV-OCI investments carried at $120,000. These loans are due in 2021.

8. For common shares, an unlimited number are authorized and 500,000 are issued and outstanding.

Instructions

a. Prepare a statement of financial position as at December 31, 2020, ensuring that all important information is fully disclosed.

b. **Digging Deeper** From the perspective of a potential creditor, discuss the importance of proper classification of Eastwood's Construction in Process account.

P5.4 The statement of financial position of Delacosta Corporation as at December 31, 2020, is as follows:

Delacosta Corporation
Statement of Financial Position
December 31, 2020

Assets	
Goodwill (Note 1)	$ 70,000
Buildings (Note 2)	1,640,000
Inventory	312,100
Investments—trading (Note 3)	100,000
Land	950,000
Accounts receivable	170,000
Investments in shares (FV-OCI) (Note 4)	87,000
Cash	175,900
Assets allocated to trustee for plant expansion	
Cash	120,000
Treasury notes, at cost and fair value	138,000
	$3,763,000
Equities	
Notes payable (Note 4)	$ 600,000
Common shares, unlimited authorized, 500,000 issued	730,000
Retained earnings	958,000
Accounts payable	420,000
Appreciation capital (Note 2)	570,000
Income tax payable	75,000
Reserve for depreciation of building	410,000
	$3,763,000

Note 1: Goodwill in the amount of $70,000 was recognized because the company believed that the carrying amount of assets was not an accurate representation of the company's fair value. The gain of $70,000 was credited to Retained Earnings.

Note 2: Buildings are stated at cost, except for one building that was recorded at its appraised value as management determined the building to be worth more than originally paid at acquisition. The excess of the appraisal value over cost was $570,000. Depreciation has been recorded based on cost.

Note 3: Investments—trading are FV-NI (fair value through net income) investments and have a fair value of $75,000. Investments in shares (FV-OCI) have a fair value of $200,000. Both investments are currently recorded at cost.

Note 4: Notes payable are long-term except for the current principal instalment due of $100,000.

Instructions

a. Prepare a corrected classified statement of financial position in good form. The notes above are for information only. Assume that you have decided not to use the revaluation model for property, plant, and equipment.

b. **Digging Deeper** From the perspective of a user of Delacosta's statement of financial position, discuss the importance of proper accounting for goodwill.

P5.5 Lydia Trottier has prepared baked goods for sale since 1998. She started a baking business in her home and has been operating in a rented building with a storefront since 2003. Trottier incorporated the business as MLT Inc. on January 1, 2020, with an initial share issue of 1,000 common shares for $2,500. Lydia Trottier is the principal shareholder of MLT Inc.

Sales have increased by 30% annually since operations began at the present location, and additional equipment is needed for the continued growth that is expected. Trottier wants to purchase some additional baking equipment and to finance the equipment through a long-term note from a commercial bank. Fidelity Bank & Trust has asked Trottier to submit a statement of income for MLT Inc. for the first five months of 2020 and a statement of financial position as at May 31, 2020.

Trottier assembled the following information from the corporation's cash basis records to use in preparing the financial statements that the bank wants to see:

1. The bank statement showed the following 2020 deposits through May 31:

Issuance of common shares	$ 2,500
Cash sales	22,770
Rebates from purchases of raw materials	130
Collections on credit sales	5,320
Bank loan proceeds	2,880
	$33,600

2. The following amounts were disbursed through May 31, 2020:

Raw materials	$14,400
Rent	1,800
Salaries and wages	5,500
Repairs and maintenance	110
Utilities	4,000
Insurance premium	1,920
Equipment	3,600
Principal and interest payment on bank loan	298
Advertising	424
	$32,052

3. Unpaid invoices at May 31, 2020, were as follows:

Raw materials	$256
Utilities	270
	$526

4. Accounts receivable records showed uncollected sales of $4,336 at May 31, 2020.

5. Raw materials inventory costing $2,075 was on hand at May 31, 2020. There were no materials in process or finished goods on hand at that date. No raw materials were on hand or in process and no finished goods were on hand at January 1, 2020.

6. The note for the three-year bank loan is dated January 1, 2020, and states a simple interest rate of 8%. The loan requires quarterly payments on April 1, July 1, October 1, and January 1. Each payment is to consist of equal principal payments [$2,880 ÷ (3 × 4) = $240] plus accrued interest since the last payment.

7. Employees have been paid through May 25, 2020, and are due an additional $270 on May 31, 2020.

8. Equipment costing $3,600 was purchased on January 2, 2020, and has an estimated useful life of five years with no residual value. Straight-line depreciation is used.

9. Rent was paid for six months in advance on January 2, 2020.

10. A one-year insurance policy was purchased on January 2, 2020.

11. MLT Inc. is subject to an income tax rate of 20%. No tax instalments have been paid.

12. Payments and collections from the unincorporated business through December 31, 2019, were not included in the corporation's records, and no cash was transferred from the unincorporated business to the corporation.

Instructions

a. Using the accrual basis of accounting, prepare a statement of income for the five months ended May 31, 2020.

b. Using the accrual basis, prepare a statement of financial position as at May 31, 2020.

*c. **Digging Deeper** **Finance** Assume the role of a bank manager at Fidelity Bank & Trust. Based only on MLT's current ratio as a measure of liquidity, and times interest earned ratio as a measure of MLT's ability to pay interest, would you recommend extending a long-term note for financing of MLT's purchase of additional baking equipment?

P5.6 In an examination of Garganta Limited as at December 31, 2020, you have learned about the following situations. No entries have been made in the accounting records for these items.

1. The corporation erected its present factory building in 2004. Depreciation was calculated using the straight-line method, based on an estimated life of 35 years. Early in 2020, the board of directors conducted a careful survey and estimated that the factory building had a remaining useful life of 25 years as at January 1, 2020.

2. An additional assessment of 2019 corporate income tax was levied and paid in 2020.

3. When calculating the accrual for officers' salaries at December 31, 2020, it was discovered that the accrual for officers' salaries for December 31, 2019, had been overstated.

4. On December 15, 2020, Garganta Limited declared a common shares dividend of $1 per share on its issued common shares outstanding, payable February 1, 2021, to the common shareholders of record on December 31, 2020.

5. Garganta Limited, which is on a calendar-year basis, changed its inventory cost formula as at January 1, 2020. The inventory for December 31, 2019, was costed by the weighted average method, and the inventory for December 31, 2020, was costed by the FIFO method.

6. On January 15, 2021, Garganta's warehouse containing raw materials was damaged by a flash flood.

7. During December 2020, the former president retired and a new president was appointed.

8. Garganta suffered a loss from a former employee stealing cash from a deposit of cash sales in the first quarter of the year. The amount has been a reconciling item on the bank reconciliation ever since the theft. Garganta has not yet made any journal entry.

Instructions

Describe fully how each item above should be reported in the financial statements of Garganta Limited for the year 2020.

P5.7 **Excel** Aero Inc. had the following statement of financial position at the end of operations for 2019:

Aero Inc.			
Statement of Financial Position			
December 31, 2019			
Cash	$ 20,000	Accounts payable	$ 30,000
Accounts receivable	21,200	Bonds payable	41,000
FV-NI investments	32,000	Common shares	100,000
Equipment (net)	81,000	Retained earnings	23,200
Land	40,000		
	$194,200		$194,200

During 2020, the following occurred:

1. Aero liquidated its FV-NI investments portfolio at a loss of $5,000.

2. A parcel of land was purchased for $38,000.

3. An additional $30,000 worth of common shares was issued.

4. Dividends totalling $10,000 were declared and paid to shareholders.

5. Net income for 2020 was $35,000, including $12,000 in depreciation expense.

6. Land was purchased through the issuance of $30,000 in additional bonds.

7. At December 31, 2020, Cash was $70,200; Accounts Receivable was $42,000; and Accounts Payable was $40,000.

Instructions

a. Prepare the statement of financial position as it would appear at December 31, 2020.

b. Prepare a statement of cash flows for the year ended December 31, 2020, using the indirect method along with any necessary note disclosure. Assume dividends paid are treated as financing activities.

*c. `Finance` Calculate the current and acid-test ratios for 2019 and 2020.

*d. `Finance` Calculate Aero's free cash flow and the current cash debt coverage ratio for 2020.

e. What is the cash flow pattern? Discuss the sources and uses of cash.

f. `Digging Deeper` Use the analysis of Aero to illustrate how information in the statement of financial position and statement of cash flows helps the user of the financial statements.

P5.8 Jia Inc. applies ASPE and had the following statement of financial position at the end of operations for 2019:

Jia Inc.
Statement of Financial Position
December 31, 2019

Cash	$ 50,500	Accounts payable	$ 93,000
Accounts receivable	90,000	Long-term debt	85,000
Inventory	82,000	Common shares	100,000
Machinery (net)	125,000	Retained earnings	89,500
Trademarks	20,000		
	$367,500		$367,500

During 2020, the following occurred:

1. Jia Inc. sold some of its trademarks. The trademarks had an unlimited useful life and a cost of $10,000. They were sold for proceeds of $20,000.
2. Machinery was purchased in exchange for long-term debt of $40,000.
3. Long-term debt in the amount of $15,000 was retired before maturity by paying $15,000 cash.
4. An additional $12,000 in common shares was issued.
5. Dividends totalling $14,000 were declared and paid to shareholders.
6. Net income for 2020 was $44,000 after allowing for depreciation of $19,000.
7. Machinery with a carrying value of $18,000 was sold at a gain of $7,000.
8. At December 31, 2020, Cash was $68,500; Accounts Receivable was $111,000; Accounts Payable was $83,000; and Inventory increased to $107,000.

Instructions

a. Prepare a statement of cash flows for the year ended December 31, 2020, using the indirect method along with any necessary note disclosure.

b. Prepare the statement of financial position as it would appear at December 31, 2020.

c. How might the statement of cash flows help the user of the financial statements?

*d. `Finance` Calculate the following ratios:

1. Free cash flow
2. Current cash debt coverage ratio
3. Cash debt coverage ratio

e. `Digging Deeper` What is Jia's cash flow pattern? Discuss any areas of concern.

P5.9 The statement of financial position of Sargent Corporation follows for the current year, 2020:

Sargent Corporation
Statement of Financial Position
December 31, 2020

Current assets	$ 485,000	Current liabilities	$ 380,000
Investments	640,000	Long-term liabilities	960,000
Property, plant, and equipment	1,720,000	Shareholders' equity	1,770,000
Intangible assets	265,000		$3,110,000
	$3,110,000		

The following additional information is available:

1. The Current Assets section includes the following: cash $150,000; accounts receivable $170,000, less $10,000 allowance for doubtful accounts; inventory $180,000; and unearned revenue $5,000.

The cash balance is composed of $190,000, less a bank overdraft of $40,000 (at a separate financial institution). Inventory is stated at the lower of FIFO cost and net realizable value.

2. The Investments section includes the following: note receivable from a related company, due in 2026, $40,000; FV-NI investments in shares $80,000 (fair value $80,000); FV-OCI investments in shares $125,000 (fair value $155,000); bond sinking fund $250,000; and patents $115,000, net of accumulated amortization.

3. Property, Plant, and Equipment include buildings $1,040,000, less accumulated depreciation $360,000; equipment $450,000, less accumulated depreciation $180,000; land $500,000; and land held for future use $270,000.

4. Intangible Assets include franchise, net of accumulated amortization, $265,000.

5. Current Liabilities include the following: accounts payable $140,000; notes payable, short-term $80,000, long-term $120,000; and income tax payable $40,000.

6. Long-term Liabilities are composed solely of 7% bonds payable issued at a discount, due in 2028.

7. Shareholders' Equity has 70,000 preferred shares (200,000 authorized), which were issued for $450,000, and 100,000 common shares (unlimited number authorized), which were issued at an average price of $10 per share. In addition, the corporation has retained earnings of $290,000 and accumulated other comprehensive income of $30,000.

Instructions

a. Prepare a statement of financial position in good form. (Adjust the amounts in each SFP classification based on the additional information.)

b. **Digging Deeper** What makes the condensed format of the original SFP inadequate in terms of the amount of detail that needs to be disclosed under IFRS and ASPE?

P5.10 The statement of financial position of Manion Corporation follows (in thousands):

Manion Corporation
Statement of Financial Position
December 31, 2020

Assets		
Current assets		
Cash	$26,000	
Accounts receivable	25,000	
Inventory	20,000	
Supplies	4,000	
Investment in subsidiary company	38,000	$113,000
Investments		
Investments in shares		25,000
Property, plant, and equipment		
Buildings and land	91,000	
Less: Reserve for depreciation	31,000	60,000
Other assets		
Investment in bonds to be held to maturity (at cost)		19,000
		$217,000
Liabilities and shareholders' equity		
Current liabilities		
Accounts payable	$22,000	
Reserve for income taxes	15,000	
Customer accounts with credit balances	1	$ 37,001
Long-term liabilities		
Bonds payable		62,000
Total liabilities		99,001
Shareholders' equity		
Common shares issued	85,000	
Earned surplus and other accumulated surplus	24,999	
Cash dividends declared	8,000	117,999
		$217,000

Instructions

Evaluate the statement of financial position. Briefly describe the proper treatment of any item that you find incorrect. Assume the company follows IFRS.

P5.11 A comparative statement of financial position for Spencer Corporation follows:

Spencer Corporation
Statement of Financial Position

	December 31	
Assets	**2020**	**2019**
Cash	$ 65,000	$ 29,000
Accounts receivable	87,000	59,000
Inventory	133,000	81,000
FV-OCI investments in shares	63,000	84,000
Land	65,000	103,000
Equipment	390,000	430,000
Accumulated depreciation—equipment	(117,000)	(86,000)
Goodwill	124,000	173,000
Total	$810,000	$873,000
Liabilities and Shareholders' Equity		
Accounts payable	$ 12,000	$ 51,000
Dividends payable	15,000	32,000
Notes payable	220,000	335,000
Common shares	265,000	125,000
Retained earnings	288,000	284,000
Accumulated other comprehensive income	10,000	46,000
Total	$810,000	$873,000

Additional information:

1. Net income for the fiscal year ending December 31, 2020, was $19,000.

2. In March 2020, a plot of land was purchased for future construction of a plant site. In November 2020, a different plot of land with original cost of $86,000 was sold for proceeds of $95,000.

3. In April 2020, notes payable amounting to $140,000 were retired through the issuance of common shares. In December 2020, notes payable amounting to $25,000 were issued for cash.

4. FV-OCI investments were purchased in July 2020 for a cost of $15,000. By December 31, 2020, the fair value of Spencer's portfolio of FV-OCI investments decreased to $63,000. No FV-OCI investments were sold in the year.

5. On December 31, 2020, equipment with an original cost of $40,000 and accumulated depreciation to date of $12,000 was sold for proceeds of $21,000. No equipment was purchased in the year.

6. Dividends on common shares of $32,000 and $15,000 were declared in December 2019 and December 2020, respectively. The 2019 dividend was paid in January 2020 and the 2020 dividend was paid in January 2021. Dividends paid are treated as financing activities.

7. A loss on impairment was recorded in the year to reflect a decrease in the recoverable amount of goodwill. No goodwill was purchased or sold in the year.

Instructions

a. Prepare a statement of cash flows using the indirect method for cash flows from operating activities along with any necessary note disclosure.

b. **Digging Deeper** From the perspective of a shareholder, comment in general on the results reported in the statement of cash flows.

P5.12 L&G Inc., a retailer of garden tools that follows ASPE, had the following statements prepared as of December 31, 2020:

L&G Inc.
Comparative Statement of Financial Position
December 31

	2020	2019
Cash	$ 57,600	$ 53,850
Accounts receivable	58,000	51,000
Inventory	40,000	60,000
Prepaid rent	5,000	4,000
Equipment	154,000	130,000
Accumulated depreciation—equipment	(35,000)	(25,000)
Total assets	$279,600	$273,850

(continued)

	2020	2019
Accounts payable	$ 46,000	$ 40,000
Income tax payable	4,000	6,000
Long-term loans payable	60,000	69,000
Common shares	130,000	130,000
Retained earnings	39,600	28,850
Total liabilities and shareholders' equity	$279,600	$273,850

L&G Inc.
Income Statement
Year Ending December 31, 2020

Sales revenue		$368,150
Cost of goods sold		195,000
Gross margin		173,150
Operating expenses		120,000
Operating income		53,150
Interest expense	$11,400	
Gain on disposal of equipment	(2,000)	9,400
Income before income tax		43,750
Income tax expense		21,000
Net income		$ 22,750

Additional information:

1. Dividends on common shares in the amount of $12,000 were declared and paid during 2020.
2. Depreciation expense of $24,000 is included in operating expenses.
3. Equipment with a cost of $20,000 that was 70% depreciated was sold during 2020.

Instructions

a. Prepare a statement of cash flows using the direct method.
b. Prepare a statement of cash flows using the indirect method.

P5-13 Martineau Inc., a major retailer of high-end office furniture, operates several stores and is a publicly traded company. The company is currently preparing its statement of cash flows. The comparative statement of financial position and income statement for Martineau as at May 31, 2020, are as follows:

Martineau Inc.
Statement of Financial Position
May 31, 2020, and May 31, 2019

	2020	2019
Assets		
Cash	$ 33,250	$ 20,000
Accounts receivable	74,800	55,600
Inventory	188,700	199,000
Prepaid insurance	8,800	7,000
Total current assets	305,550	281,600
Plant assets	596,500	501,500
Less: Accumulated depreciation	148,000	122,000
Net plant assets	448,500	379,500
Total assets	$754,050	$661,100
Liabilities and Shareholders' Equity		
Accounts payable	$123,000	$115,000
Salaries and wages payable	11,000	12,000
Interest payable	4,700	2,600
Total current liabilities	138,700	129,600
Mortgage payable	75,000	100,000
Total liabilities	213,700	229,600
Shareholders' equity		
Common shares	405,750	360,000
Retained earnings	134,600	71,500
Total shareholders' equity	540,350	431,500
Total liabilities and shareholders' equity	$754,050	$661,100

Martineau Inc.
Income Statement
For the Year Ended May 31, 2020

Sales	$945,000
Cost of goods sold	414,000
Gross margin	531,000
Expenses	
Salaries and wages expense	207,800
Other operating expenses	120,000
Depreciation expense	26,000
Total operating expenses	353,800
Operating income	177,200
Interest expense	26,700
Income before income tax	150,500
Income tax expense	55,400
Net earnings	$ 95,100

The following is additional information about transactions during the year ended May 31, 2020 for Martineau Inc., which follows IFRS.

1. Plant assets costing $95,000 were purchased by paying $64,000 in cash and issuing 5,000 common shares.

2. In order to supplement its cash, Martineau issued 4,000 additional common shares.

3. Cash dividends of $48,000 were declared and paid at the end of the fiscal year.

Instructions

a. Prepare a statement of cash flows for Martineau Inc. for the year ended May 31, 2020 using the direct method. Support the statement with appropriate calculations, and provide all required disclosures.

b. Using the indirect method, calculate only the net cash flow from operating activities for Martineau Inc. for the year ended May 31, 2020.

Cases

Refer to the Case Primer on the Student Website and in WileyPLUS *to help you answer these cases.*

CA5.1 Real World Emphasis In the late 1990s, **CIBC** helped **Enron Corporation** structure 34 "loans" that appeared in the financial statements as cash proceeds from sales of assets. Enron subsequently went bankrupt in 2001 and left many unhappy investors and creditors with billions of dollars lost. In December 2003, CIBC settled four regulatory investigations with the U.S. Securities and Exchange Commission, U.S. Federal Reserve, U.S. Justice Department, and Canadian Office of the Superintendent of Financial Institutions. The settlement, which amounted to U.S. $80 million, was then one of the largest regulatory penalties against a Canadian bank. The regulatory authorities felt that CIBC had aided Enron in boosting its earnings and hiding debt. CIBC set aside a $109-million reserve in early 2003 in preparation for this settlement. No additional reserves were set aside.

As part of the settlement, CIBC agreed to get rid of its structured financing line of business (where all of these "loans" were created). Bank management noted that the decision to get rid of the structured financing business would reduce annual earnings by 10 cents a share. The bank had previously reported annual earnings of $5.21 per share. In addition, the bank had to accept the appointment of an outside monitor whose role, among other things, would be to review the bank's compliance with the settlement. Strategically, the bank had already reduced its emphasis on corporate lending (having suffered heavy losses in 2002) in favour of an increased focus on earnings from branch banking operations.

At the end of 2003, CIBC was still owed $213 million by Enron. There were many additional Enron-related lawsuits pending against the bank, but the bank announced that the lawsuits were without merit. The bank had insurance against many of these claims and noted that it planned to vigorously defend itself.

In 2005, the bank settled a lawsuit with institutional investors, paying $2.4 billion, again setting a standard for the size of the settlement. Then in 2009, the Canada Revenue Agency (CRA) challenged the bank regarding the tax deductibility of the payment.

In Note 20 to CIBC's annual financial statements for the year ending October 31, 2017, relating to the subject of income taxes, the bank updated the outstanding issue. CIBC stated that the Tax Court of Canada trial on the deductibility of the Enron payments was scheduled to begin in 2018. As well, CIBC stated that, should it successfully defend its tax filing position in its entirety, the bank would recognize an additional accounting tax benefit of $231 million and taxable refund interest of approximately $198 million. Should CIBC fail to defend its position in its entirety, the bank would incur an additional tax expense of approximately $820 million and non-deductible interest of approximately $157 million.

Instructions

Discuss any financial reporting issues relating to CIBC's 2003 and 2017 financial statements. Use the conceptual framework noted in Chapter 2 for the analysis.

CA5.2 **Ethics** Hastings Inc. is a manufacturer that produces stainless steel car parts. It began as a family business several years ago and all shares are owned by the Hastings family. The company's main assets are its manufacturing facility and surrounding land. The property was purchased many years ago and the carrying value reflects only a fraction of the asset's current fair value.

The company currently follows ASPE and is wondering what the impact would be of switching to IFRS. Several of the Hastings family members would like to take the company public in the next five to 10 years.

Because of the recent dip in the economy, the company has suffered losses over the past three years. However, as the economy has recently begun picking up, management is confident that this year will be a profitable one.

Instructions

Adopt the role of the company's auditors and discuss any financial reporting issues. Use the conceptual framework noted in Chapter 2 for the analysis.

Integrated Cases

(*Hint:* If there are issues here that are new, use the conceptual framework to help you support your analysis with solid reasoning.)

IC5.1 **Ethics** **Audit & Assurance** Franklin Drug Ltd. (FDL) is a global public company that researches, develops, markets, and sells prescription drugs. Revenues and net income are down this year, partly because one of the company's competitors, Balogun Drug Inc. (BDI), has created and is selling generic versions of two of FDL's best-selling drugs. The drugs, known as FD1 and FD2, are still protected by patents that will not expire for another three years. Normally, when a drug is patented, other drug companies are not legally allowed to sell generic versions of the drug. This practice of patenting new drugs allows the companies that develop the drugs enough time to recover their large investment in research and development.

In recent years, however, generic drug companies have become more aggressive in producing and selling generic copies of drugs before patents expire. FDL refers to this practice as "launching the generic products at risk" because, legally, the competitors are not allowed to sell them while the patent is still in force. Currently, FDL has about $2 million in development costs capitalized on the statement of financial position. It has launched a lawsuit against BDI, ordering it to cease and desist selling the generic drugs. These types of lawsuits are usually long and very expensive. By the time the lawsuit is settled one way or the other, the patents will have expired. So far, legal costs incurred for the lawsuit are $300,000.

During the year, the patent on a third drug, FD3, expired and several competitor drug companies began actively marketing generic replacements. FDL still has $500,000 worth of FD3 development costs on the statement of financial position. Although the increased competition may result in this asset being impaired, FDL feels that it can hold its market share based on FD3's past success in treating patients. So far, sales of FD3 have declined only 3%, but there remains considerable price pressure on the drug. On the other hand, the company's share price has declined significantly because of the uncertainty surrounding future sales. Company management is not happy with the drop in share price, because a significant portion of their remuneration is based on stock options.

The company gives volume rebates to some of its larger customers. Under the terms of the sales agreements, the more purchases that a customer makes in a certain time frame, the larger the rebate percentage is on these purchases. The length of the time frame varies. Three large contracts are currently outstanding at year end with new customers. The time frames on these contracts extend beyond year end. FDL must estimate the volume rebates by considering what the total sales will be under these contracts. The company always bases this estimate on past experience.

FDL had a distribution centre in South America. Late in the year, FDL was approached by a competitor to buy the distribution centre. FDL accepted the offer and is confident the price obtained is generous. FDL has not yet arrived at an analysis of what the corresponding effect of the sale will be on its global operations, along with the impairment of remaining assets whose values are affected by the sale and will require impairment writedowns.

It is now early January and the auditors are coming in for an audit planning meeting.

Instructions

In preparation for the meeting, you, as audit senior on the job, have done some preliminary research on the company. Write a memo that outlines the potential financial reporting issues.

Research and Analysis

RA5.1 `Real World Emphasis` **Hudson's Bay Company**

The financial statements of Hudson's Bay Company for its year ended February 3, 2018 (fiscal 2017) appear at the end of this book.

Instructions

a. What alternative formats could the company have used for its balance sheet? Which format did it adopt?

b. Identify the various techniques of disclosure that the company could have used to present additional financial information that is pertinent. Which techniques does it use in its financial statements?

c. Why does Hudson's Bay Company not have the same year-end date in 2017 as it did in 2016? (Hudson's Bay considers the year ended February 3, 2018, to be fiscal 2017 and the year ended January 28, 2017, to be fiscal 2016.) What is the length of the reporting period in 2017, as opposed to 2016? Why does the company have a reporting period that is not the same length for each of the two years? Is there any impact on the difference in length of reporting period in terms of comparability?

d. Which presentation method does the company use for its statement of cash flows (direct or indirect method)? What were the company's cash flows from its operating, investing, and financing activities for the year ended February 3, 2018? What was the change in net cash provided by operating activities over the year ended February 3, 2018? Is the cash generated from operating activities significantly different from net losses in both fiscal 2016 and 2017? Suggest why this might happen.

e. Calculate the company's (1) current cash debt coverage ratio, (2) cash debt coverage ratio, and (3) free cash flow for fiscal 2016 and 2017. What do these ratios indicate about the company's financial condition?

RA5.2 `Real World Emphasis` **Bombardier Inc.**

The financial statements for Bombardier Inc. for the year ended December 31, 2017, can be found on the company's website or from SEDAR (www.sedar.com).

Instructions

a. What form of presentation does the company use in preparing its balance sheet?

b. Calculate the ratios identified in Appendix 5A for both years that are presented in the financial statements. Make note of any ratios that cannot be reported and provide the reason why.

c. Comment on the company's liquidity, solvency, activity, and profitability.

d. Review the cash flow patterns on the statements of cash flows. Comment on the basic sources of the company's cash and where it is spent.

e. Perform a "vertical analysis" of the assets. (Calculate each asset as a percentage of total assets.) Comment on the results of your analysis. How have the assets changed from year to year?

RA5.3 `Real World Emphasis` **Maple Leaf Foods Inc.**

The audited annual financial statements of Maple Leaf Foods Inc. for the year ended December 31, 2017, can be found on the company's website or from SEDAR (www.sedar.com).

Instructions

a. Calculate the liquidity and coverage (solvency) ratios identified in Appendix 5A for both years that are presented in the financial statements.

b. Comment on the company's financial flexibility.

c. Review the cash flow patterns on the statements of cash flows and comment on the basic sources of the company's cash and where it is spent.

d. Perform a "horizontal analysis" for the components of working capital. (Calculate each financial statement item for the current year as a percentage of the amount reported for a specific prior year.) Comment on any change in the company's liquidity.

RA5.4 Real World Emphasis **Goldcorp Inc.**

Obtain the 2001 and 2017 annual reports of Goldcorp Inc. from SEDAR (www.sedar.com).

Instructions

Read the annual report material leading up to the financial statement section and answer the following questions:

a. Explain how the company's business changed in the 16 years from 2001 to 2017. Did any significant events occur in 2017?

b. Prepare a horizontal analysis of key elements of the financial statements from 2001 to 2017. (Calculate each financial statement item for the current year as a percentage of the amount reported for a specific prior year.) Include revenue, operating earnings (loss), current assets, current liabilities, working capital, net earnings (loss), and shareholders' equity. Include also the ratios of operating income (loss) to revenue, the current ratio, and the return on shareholders' equity.

c. What was the effect of the changes to the company's business since 2001 on Goldcorp's operations? Include in your answer as well the total cost to produce an ounce of gold and the average selling price of gold. (This information can be found in the Management Discussion and Analysis part of the annual report.)

RA5.5 Real World Emphasis **Quebecor Inc. and Thomson Reuters Corporation**

The financial statements of Quebecor Inc. and Thomson Reuters Corporation for their fiscal years ended December 31, 2017, can be found on SEDAR (www.sedar.com) or the companies' websites.

Instructions

a. What business is Quebecor Inc. in? Is Thomson Reuters Corporation a good benchmark for comparing against? Explain.

b. Identify three other companies that might be used for comparisons.

c. Calculate industry averages for these five companies for their current ratio and debt to total assets ratio.

d. Based on this very brief analysis, which company, Quebecor or Thomson Reuters, is in a better position in terms of liquidity and solvency? How do these companies compare with the other three companies you identified in part (b)?

e. Review the statements of cash flows for Quebecor and Thomson Reuters for 2016 and 2017. Summarize the cash flow patterns for each company.

f. Comment on these cash flow patterns, noting changes over the two-year period.

RA5.6 Auditor's Letter

The partner in charge of the James Spencer Corporation audit comes by your desk and leaves a letter he has started to the CEO and a copy of the statement of cash flows for the year ended December 31, 2020. Because he must leave on an emergency, he asks you to finish the letter by explaining (1) the difference between the net income and cash flow amounts, (2) the importance of operating cash flow, (3) the sustainable source(s) of cash flow, and (4) possible suggestions to improve the cash position. Spencer is a small corporation that relies on its auditor for financial statement preparation.

Cash flows from operating activities

Net income		$ 100,000
Adjustments to reconcile net income to net cash provided by operating activities:		
Depreciation expense	$ 11,000	
Loss on sale of fixed assets	5,000	
Increase in accounts receivable (net)	(40,000)	
Increase in inventory	(35,000)	
Decrease in accounts payable	(41,000)	(100,000)
Net cash provided by operating activities		–0–

Cash flows from investing activities		
Sale of plant assets	25,000	
Purchase of equipment	(100,000)	
Purchase of land	(200,000)	
Net cash used by investing activities		(275,000)
Cash flows from financing activities		
Payment of dividends	(10,000)	
Redemption of bonds	(100,000)	
Net cash used by financing activities		(110,000)
Net decrease in cash		(385,000)
Cash balance, January 1, 2020		400,000
Cash balance, December 31, 2020		$ 15,000

Date

James Spencer III, CEO
James Spencer Corporation
125 Bay Street
Toronto, ON

Dear Mr. Spencer:

I have good news and bad news about the financial statements for the year ended December 31, 2020. The good news is that net income of $100,000 is close to what we predicted in the strategic plan last year, indicating strong performance this year. The bad news is that the cash balance is seriously low. Enclosed is the Statement of Cash Flows, which best illustrates how both of these situations occurred at the same time . . .

Instructions

Complete the letter to the CEO, including the four elements that the partner asked for.

RA5.7 Ethics **A Moral Dilemma**

The ethical accountant for Khouri Industries is trying to decide how to present property, plant, and equipment in the notes to the balance sheet. She realizes that the statement of cash flows will show that the company made a significant investment in purchasing new equipment this year, but overall she knows the company's plant assets are rather old. She feels that she can disclose one amount for the title "Property, plant, and equipment, net of depreciation," and the result will be a low figure. However, it will not disclose the assets' age. If she chooses to show the cost less accumulated depreciation, the assets' age will be visible. She proposes the following:

Property, plant, and equipment, net of depreciation	$10,000,000
rather than	
Property, plant, and equipment	$50,000,000
Less: Accumulated depreciation	(40,000,000)
Net book value	$10,000,000

Instructions

Discuss the financial reporting issues, including any ethical issues.

Cumulative Coverage and Task-Based Simulation: Chapters 3 to 5 and Appendix C

Templates to complete this task-based simulation are available in WileyPLUS *and on the instructor website.*

Erskine Consulting Ltd. has been in business for several years, providing software consulting to its customers on an annual contract or special assignment basis. All work is done over the Internet, although some travel is occasionally required for meeting with customers to negotiate contracts and renewals of contracts, as well as resolving possible disputes in invoicing for their services. Erskine operates out of rented premises and has a modest investment in equipment that is used by the consulting team. Erskine is a private company that follows ASPE and that has a calendar year end.

At the end of each year, Erskine obtains the services of an accountant to complete the annual accounting cycle of the business and prepare any year-end adjusting of journal entries, financial statements, and corporate tax returns.

Upon arrival in early 2020, the accountant was given an unadjusted trial balance and obtained the following additional information to complete his work.

Erskine Consulting Ltd.
Unadjusted Trial Balance
December 31, 2020

Account	Debit	Credit
Petty cash	$ 600	
Cash	18,500	
Accounts receivable	44,700	
Allowance for doubtful accounts		$ 1,800
Interest receivable	–0–	
Prepaid insurance	4,000	
Supplies	2,000	
FV-NI investments	20,000	
Notes receivable	25,000	
Equipment	94,000	
Accumulated depreciation—equipment		36,000
Goodwill	22,000	
Bank loans		18,000
Accounts payable		7,950
Salaries and wages payable		–0–
Interest payable		–0–
Unearned revenue		4,200
Litigation liability		–0–
Income tax payable	30,000	
Common shares		36,000
Retained earnings		59,800
Dividends	26,000	
Service revenue		242,768
Interest income		1,042
Unrealized gain or loss		–0–
Gain on disposal of equipment		300
Depreciation expense	–0–	
Office expense	4,100	
Travel expense	6,700	
Insurance expense	900	
Interest expense	1,300	
Utilities expense	750	
Rent expense	54,000	
Salaries and wages expense	49,510	
Supplies expense	–0–	
Bad debt expense	–0–	
Telephone and Internet expense	3,200	
Repairs and maintenance expense	600	
Litigation expense	–0–	
Income tax expense	–0–	
	$407,860	$407,860

Additional information:

1. Management has been going over the list of accounts receivable for possible accounts that are not collectible. One account for $700 must be written off. In the past, 5% of the balance of all accounts receivable has been the basis of an estimate for the required balance in the allowance for doubtful accounts. Management feels that this estimate should be followed for 2020.

2. After doing a count of supplies on hand, management determined that $400 of supplies remained unused at December 31, 2020.

3. The account balance in Prepaid Insurance of $4,000 represents the annual cost of the renewal of all of Erskine's insurance policies that expire in one year. The policies' coverage started April 1, 2020.

4. FV-NI Investments are long-term investments. The fair value of the portfolio of investments was $22,500 at December 31, 2020, based on quoted market values on the TSX.

5. In January 2020, some old equipment was sold for proceeds of $300 cash. The entry made when depositing the cash was debit Cash, credit Gain on Disposal of Equipment. The original cost of the equipment was $4,300 and the accumulated depreciation was $4,200.

6. The depreciation expense for the remaining equipment was calculated to be $7,200 for the 2020 fiscal year.

7. The notes receivable from customers are due October 31, 2023, and bear interest at 5%, with interest paid semi-annually. The last interest collected related to the notes was for the six months ended October 31, 2020.

8. Bank loans are demand bank loans for working capital needs and vary in amount as the needs arise. The bank advised that the interest charge for December 2020 that will go through on the January 2021 bank statement is in the amount of $200.

9. Unpaid salaries and wages at December 31, 2020, totalled $790. These will be paid as part of the first payroll of 2021.

10. After some analysis, management informs the accountant that the Unearned Revenue account should have a balance of $1,000.

11. Erskine was sued by one of its former clients for $50,000 for giving bad advice and instructions. Upon discussion with legal counsel, it has been agreed that it will likely take $5,000 to settle this dispute out of court, in the next fiscal year. No entry has yet been recorded.

12. The accountant is told that a sublet lease arrangement for some excess office space has been negotiated and signed. It will provide Erskine with rent revenue starting on February 1, 2021, at a rate of $400 per month.

13. Erskine has been making income tax instalments as required by the Canada Revenue Agency. All instalment payments have been debited to the Income Taxes Payable account.

14. After recording all of the necessary adjustments and posting to the general ledger, management drafted a new trial balance to arrive at the income before income taxes. Using this result, the accountant prepared the tax returns, and determined that a tax rate of 28% needed to be applied to the income before income tax amount. The necessary adjusting entry for taxes has not yet been recorded.

Instructions

a. Prepare all necessary adjusting and correcting entries required based on the information given, up to item 13.

b. Post the journal entries in adjustment columns and arrive at an adjusted trial balance. Enter the journal entries in the following worksheet format:

Account	Unadjusted Trial Balance		Adjustments		Adjusted Trial Balance	
	Debit	Credit	Debit	Credit	Debit	Credit

c. Using the adjusted trial balance columns of your worksheet, calculate the amount of income before income taxes. Use the information provided in item 14 to record income tax expense for the year.

d. Prepare a single-step statement of income, a statement of retained earnings, and a statement of financial position for 2020.

e. Explain the various levels of input in the fair value hierarchy. Based on the IFRS 13 guidance, indicate at which level in the fair value hierarchy the FV-NI investments will fall (level 1, 2, or 3). Explain your choice. How would your analysis change under ASPE? Is the amount reported in the unadjusted trial balance of $20,000 equal to the cost of the investments in the portfolio? Explain.

f. Calculate the current ratio and the payout ratio.

CHAPTER 6

Revenue Recognition

Justin Sullivan/Getty Images

The Actual Accounting for Virtual Gaming

Today's digital economy presents some interesting accounting challenges. For example, how does a company that produces online games recognize revenue—when the gamer pays for access or when they actually play? When to recognize revenue has been a challenge for California-based Zynga Inc., maker of such popular online games as FarmVille, Zynga Poker, and Words With Friends.

Zynga's business model is to sell "virtual" services—access to its games through online social media or mobile apps. While basic access to its online games through social media such as Facebook is free, players who want to add features, such as moving up to the next level of play, need to pay for them. Facebook collects these fees and then remits to Zynga 70% of the amount Zynga requests that Facebook charge players. Another way Zynga earns revenues is from advertisers whose ads and products appear in the games. (Some product placements can cost up to $750,000 per game.) It also licenses its software and other intellectual property to other companies.

How does Zynga recognize revenue from players? Within its games, players can buy virtual goods with Facebook local currency payments or other means, such as a credit card, PayPal, or Google Wallet. "We recognize revenue when all of the following conditions are satisfied: there is persuasive evidence of an arrangement; the service has been provided to the player; the collection of our fees is reasonably assured; and the amount of fees to be paid by the player is fixed or determinable," the company said in its 2017 annual report.

How does Zynga recognize revenue from advertisers? That practice changed recently, when the U.S. Financial Accounting Standards Board (FASB) updated its standard on recognizing revenue from contracts. Under the old standard, for advertising contracts for which Zynga assessed that collectibility was "not reasonably assured due to unfavorable payment terms or a history of slow collections," it deferred revenue recognition until it received payment. "However, under the new standard, we will be required to make an assessment of collectability at the inception of the contract and if deemed probable for collection, recognize revenue at the amount we expect to be entitled to as advertisements are delivered, which will result in an acceleration in revenue recognition compared to the current method," Zynga said in its 2017 annual report. The U.S. standard on revenue recognition is largely harmonized with the new IFRS standard.

The new standard also changed how Zynga recognizes revenue from licensing its intellectual property. It used to recognize revenue at a point in time, when it delivered a licence. The new standard requires Zynga to distinguish between licences issued for "symbolic intellectual property," such as trademarks, brands, and character images, and for "functional intellectual property," such as software. Under the new standard, Zynga will continue to recognize functional intellectual property at a point in time, but it must recognize symbolic intellectual property over time, which the company says will result in a deceleration of revenue recognition compared with its previous method.

The FASB required companies to adopt the new standard for reporting periods after December 31, 2017. "As a result of adoption, we expect to record a transition adjustment in the range of [U.S.]$3.0 to $5.0 million," the company said in its 2017 annual report.

Sources: Brandon Gaille, "Zynga Business Model and Growth Strategy," The Blog Millionaire, www.brandongaille.com, February 23, 2015; Zynga Inc. 2017 annual report; Zynga Inc. corporate website, https://zynga.com.

LEARNING OBJECTIVES	CHAPTER OUTLINE	CPA COMPETENCIES
After studying this chapter, you should be able to:	The chapter headings related to the learning objective are:	Competencies addressed by each learning objective are as follows:
1. Understand the economics and legalities of selling transactions from a business perspective.	**Understanding the Nature of Sales Transactions from a Business Perspective** • Economics of sales transactions • Legalities of sales transactions • Information for decision-making	**1.1.1, 1.2.1, 1.2.2, 1.2.3, 1.4.5**
2. Identify the five steps in the revenue recognition process.	**The Asset-Liability Approach to Revenue Recognition: An Overview of the Five-Step Process**	**1.2.1, 1.2.2**
3. Identify the contract with customers.	**Identifying the Contract With Customers—Step 1** • Basic accounting • Contract modifications	**1.2.1, 1.2.2**
4. Identify the separate performance obligations in the contract.	**Identifying Separate Performance Obligations—Step 2** • Material rights • Warranties • Upfront fees • Series of goods and services that are substantially the same	**1.2.1, 1.2.2**
5. Determine the transaction price.	**Determining the Transaction Price—Step 3** • Variable consideration • Time value of money • Non-cash consideration • Consideration paid or payable to customers	**1.1.2, 1.2.1, 1.2.2, 1.2.3**
6. Allocate the transaction price to the separate performance obligations.	**Allocating the Transaction Price to Separate Performance Obligations—Step 4**	**1.1.2, 1.2.1, 1.2.2**
7. Understand how to recognize revenue when the company satisfies its performance obligation.	**Recognizing Revenue When (or As) Each Performance Obligation Is Satisfied—Step 5**	**1.2.1, 1.2.2**
8. Analyze and determine whether a company has earned revenues under the earnings approach.	**Earnings Approach to Revenue Recognition** • Selling goods • Selling services • Measurability and collectibility	**1.2.1, 1.2.2**

9.	Identify other revenue recognition issues.	**Other Revenue Recognition Issues** • Repurchase agreements • Bill-and-hold arrangements • Principal-agent relationships • Consignments • Summary of other revenue recognition issues	**1.2.1, 1.2.2, 1.2.3**
10.	Describe presentation and disclosure regarding revenue.	**Presentation and Disclosure** • Presentation • Disclosure	**1.2.1, 1.2.2, 1.3.1, 1.3.2**
11.	Identify differences in accounting between IFRS and ASPE and potential changes.	**IFRS/ASPE Comparison** • A comparison of IFRS and ASPE • Looking ahead	**1.1.4**

After studying Appendix 6A, you should be able to:

12.	Apply the percentage-of-completion method for long-term contracts.	**Percentage-of-Completion Method** • Measuring the Progress Toward Completion	**1.2.1, 1.2.2, 1.3.1**
13.	Apply the zero-profit method for long-term contracts.	**Zero-Profit Method**	**1.2.1, 1.2.2**
14.	Apply the completed-contract method for long-term contracts.	**Completed-Contract Method**	**1.2.1, 1.2.2**
15.	Account for losses on long-term contracts.	**Losses on Long-Term Contracts** • Loss in Current Period on a Profitable Contract • Loss on an Unprofitable Contract	**1.2.1, 1.2.2**

Preview of Chapter 6

As indicated in the opening story, the issue of when revenue should be recognized is complex. The many methods of marketing products and services make it difficult to develop guidelines that will apply to all situations. This chapter provides you with general guidelines used in most business transactions.

The new standard, IFRS 15 *Revenue from Contracts with Customers*, became effective for years beginning on or after January 1, 2018. Thus there were many companies applying the standard for the first time in 2018. It was expected that there would be some significant differences in revenue recognition decisions, especially in industries such as telecommunications, franchising, aerospace, and others.

Understanding the Nature of Sales Transactions from a Business Perspective

> **LEARNING OBJECTIVE 1**
> Understand the economics and legalities of selling transactions from a business perspective.

<table>
<tr><td>

Underlying Concept 6.1

Users of financial statements must be able to see the economics and legalities underlying the business and business transactions when looking at the financial statements.

</td></tr>
</table>

Much of the complexity of accounting for revenues comes from the way sales transactions are structured. It is critical to understand from a **business perspective** what is being given up in the transaction and what is being received. See Underlying Concept 6.1. Business people are not necessarily accountants, yet they generally understand how to price their products and services in order to make a profit and what they need to do to make a sale. In most selling transactions, an entity gives up one asset (for instance, inventory) in exchange for another (for instance, cash). The process of capturing this information for financial reporting purposes involves deciding when to recognize the transaction (on both the statement of financial position and income statement) and how to measure and present it. Accountants must therefore understand the business an entity is engaged in, in order to account for transactions properly.[1]

Let's go a little deeper and examine the economics and the legalities of sales transactions. We will return to many of these basics later in the chapter when we examine the specific accounting requirements.

Economics of Sales Transactions

Economics Certain economic attributes underlie most sales transactions. We will discuss some of these below and explain why these attributes matter for accounting purposes.

Fundamentals of Understanding Sales Transactions

Before we can account for a sales transaction, we need to ask some basic questions. Are we selling goods, services, or both? What is the physical nature of the transaction?

Selling transactions involve an entity transferring goods or services to its customers. The goods or services are often called deliverables. It is important to focus on whether goods or services (or both) are being transferred.

Why Does This Matter for Accounting Purposes? Sales of goods and of services are different.

Goods are tangible assets. As a result, there is a definite point in time when control over the goods or the item being sold passes to the buyer. Control of an asset means that the entity has access to the benefits provided by the asset where others do not. This normally coincides with the transfer of risks and rewards as indicated by **possession** and **legal title**. Normally this would be a point in time but it may span several periods, such as in a construction contract.

Services are not tangible assets and therefore the concepts of possession and legal title are irrelevant. Service contracts may be completed in one period but often span more than one period. Therefore, there is the added complexity of how much, if any, revenue is earned in any given period. Many contracts involve both goods and services (referred to as **multiple deliverables** or **bundled sales**), and this complicates the accounting when the goods and services are sold together as a bundle for one price. This is because possession and legal title to goods might pass before, after, or during the time when the services are rendered. Example 6.1 looks at a bundled sale.

---

[1]Recall that we presented a view of the business model in Chapters 4 and 5.

Example 6.1 | Bundled Sales

Facts A manufacturing company sells cameras and provides a warranty for a total of $100. Under the terms of the warranty, the company promises to fix the camera if it breaks over the next year. The value of the camera is estimated at $80 and the warranty at $20.

Instructions What has the company agreed to provide? Is it goods, services, or both?

Solution The company has contracted to provide not only the camera (goods) but also a service (under the warranty).

Understanding what the company is selling will help to determine when to recognize revenues. Care should be taken to identify the terms of the transaction, whether it is documented in one or more agreements or not at all. When products and services are sold and priced together as one package, as in Example 6.1, this creates complexities when determining how much revenue to recognize and when. How much should be attributed to the sale of the camera and how much to the warranty service? Obligations to deliver something in the future can increase measurement uncertainty because we do not always know what will happen in the future. We will revisit this issue later in the chapter.

Reciprocal Nature

Next, we need to ask regarding a sales transaction: What is being received?

Most business transactions are **reciprocal**; that is, the entity gives something up and receives something in return. In addition to assessing what we are giving up, we should determine what we are getting back. **Consideration** is what the entity receives in return for the provision of goods or services. Is the consideration cash or cash-like or is it another good or service?

Why Does This Matter for Accounting Purposes? If we assume that the transactions are at **arm's length**—that is, they are between unrelated parties—then we may assume that the value of what is given up usually approximates the value of what is received in the transaction. Unless otherwise noted, we will generally assume that transactions are at arm's length and reciprocal. **Example 6.2** illustrates this.

Example 6.2 | Arm's-Length Transactions

Facts A retail company sells books for $100 cash.

Instructions Does it matter if both parties are related? Why or why not?

Solution If the company and customer are unrelated, both of them will want to give up and receive things that have the same value. Therefore, it is reasonable to assume that the books have a fair value equal to the cash consideration. If the parties are related, there might be other reasons (such as tax or legal purposes) to transfer something that has a different value from the consideration received.

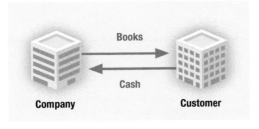

Sales agreements normally specify what is being given up and what is being acquired as follows:

- **Acquired:** Consideration or rights to the consideration. The amount, nature, and timing of what the customer agrees to pay are normally agreed upon.
- **Given up:** Goods/services (now or in the future). Details regarding delivery (quantities, nature of goods/services, timing, shipping terms) are agreed upon.

Recognizing and focusing on the reciprocal and arm's-length nature of transactions, as well as the detailed agreement between the customer and vendor, allows us to better capture and measure the economics of transactions in the financial statements. Just as obligations to deliver in the future create measurement uncertainty, so do rights to receive consideration in the future. For instance, if the entity sells on credit, there is a risk that the customer will not pay. (This is known as **credit risk**.)

Consideration that is nonmonetary (as with **barter** transactions) presents greater challenges for accounting purposes.[2] **Barter** or **nonmonetary transactions** are transactions where few or no monetary assets are received as consideration when goods or services are sold. For instance, a computer manufacturing company might sell a computer, but instead of receiving cash as consideration, the company might receive another type of asset, such as office furniture. From a business perspective, is this still a sale? How should it be measured?

Generally, a barter transaction is seen as a sale if the transaction has **commercial substance**. What does "commercial substance" mean? It means that the transaction is a **bona fide**—or legitimate—purchase and sale and that the entity has entered into the transaction for business purposes, exchanging one type of asset or service for a different type of asset or service. After the transaction, the entity will be in a different position and its future cash flows are expected to change significantly as a result of the transaction in terms of timing, amount, and/or riskiness.

When a reciprocal transaction occurs, the entity's risk profile changes. See **Underlying Concept 6.2**. For instance, in **Example 6.3**, before the sale, the company did not know how

> **Underlying Concept 6.2**
>
> The representational faithfulness concept supports full disclosure of risks and changes in risk, because they affect the entity's ability to generate future cash flows.

Example 6.3 | Commercial Substance

Facts A resource company sells gold bars (which it has mined and refined) to its customers in exchange for electricity. It uses the electricity immediately in its production operations.

Instructions Does the transaction have commercial substance? Explain.

Solution The transaction does have commercial substance, because the company no longer has the price risk associated with the gold. It also has the use of the electricity.

---

[2]Monetary consideration includes anything that is cash or measured in terms of cash, such as a receivable. Nonmonetary consideration includes other types of assets such as other inventory or fixed assets.

much it would eventually sell the gold for or how much it would realize on the sale.[3] The risk that the price of an asset will change is called a price risk. Once the sale occurs, the company gets rid of the price risk of the gold.

Sometimes, it is common in an industry for companies to swap inventory in order to facilitate a sale. For instance, oil Company A may ask oil Company B to ship oil to A's customer, who might be geographically located close to B. In this way, A's customer receives the oil faster. A would then repay B with the oil at a later date. B would not treat this as a sale as it is not a bona fide sale to B. After the transaction is complete, it is in exactly the same situation as before; that is, it has oil. We will discuss nonmonetary transactions further in Chapter 10.

Concessionary Terms

Another question to ask regarding a sales transaction is: Are the terms of sale normal or is this a special deal?

In some cases, one party is in a better bargaining position than the other. This might occur, for instance, where supply exceeds demand. In this case, the buyer in the transaction may be able to negotiate a better deal than normal because there are many sellers who want to sell their products but there are few buyers. **Concessionary terms** are terms negotiated by a party to the contract that are more favourable than normal.

Examples of concessionary terms are as follows:

- The selling price is deeply discounted.
- The seller agrees to a more **lenient return or payment policy** (including paying in instalments over an extended term or using consignment sales).
- The seller loosens its **credit policy**.
- The seller transfers legal title but allows the customer to take delivery at a later date (sometimes called "**bill and hold**").
- The goods are shipped subject to **customer acceptance conditions**. Extended trial periods are an example.
- The seller agrees to provide **ongoing or additional services** beyond the main goods/services agreed to in order to make the sale. This might include, for example, installation of an asset, ongoing servicing, or continuing fees, such as in a franchise agreement.
- The **seller continues to have some involvement**, including a guarantee of resale (or permission to return) or guarantee of profit.

Why Does This Matter for Accounting Purposes? Care must be taken to identify concessionary (or abnormal) terms in any deal because they may complicate the accounting. Concessionary terms are terms that are more lenient than usual and are meant to induce sales.

Concessionary or abnormal terms may create additional obligations or may reflect the fact that the risks and rewards or control has not yet passed to the customer. These situations must be carefully analyzed because they create additional recognition and measurement uncertainty. They may even indicate that no sale has taken place at all.

The question we should ask is whether the selling terms are normal business practices for the company or are special or unusual in some way. There is a fine line between what is normal and what is abnormal. In order to do this analysis properly, we must obtain an understanding of normal business practices. (We can do this by looking at standard documentation of selling transactions, such as contracts and/or a history of past transactions.)

Illustration 6.1 helps differentiate between normal selling terms and abnormal concessionary terms. The normal selling terms are examples of the standard terms that many companies use.

---

[3]Where the asset being sold is a commodity, prices fluctuate because they are based on supply and demand.

ILLUSTRATION 6.1

Normal versus Concessionary Terms

	Examples of Normal Selling Terms	Examples of Concessionary Selling Terms
Selling price	Selling price reflects a normal profit margin for the company for that product.	Selling price is deeply discounted.
Payment terms	Sell for cash or on credit. If credit, payment is usually expected within 30 to 60 days.	Any terms that are more lenient than this; for example, • selling on credit where the buyer does not have to pay for 90 days or more, or • instalment sales where these are not normal industry practice.
Extension of credit	Sell to customers that are creditworthy.	Sell to customers that are riskier than the existing customer base.
Shipping terms	Ship when ordered and ready to ship.	Ship at a later date; for example, the entity may hold the inventory in its warehouse for an extended period.
Other terms	Once shipped and legal title passes, no continuing involvement except for normal rights of return and/or standard warranties.	Extended right of return/warranty period, cash flow guarantee on future rental of building sold, profit guarantees on future resale, or buy-back provisions.

Example 6.4 illustrates a contract with concessionary terms and also highlights the fact that accounting is more complex when concessionary terms are present.

Example 6.4 | Concessionary Terms

Facts A merchandising company sells inventory to a customer for $100 cash. Legal title passes when the cash is paid (a few days before year end). The merchandise is stored in the warehouse for a few days until after year end.

Instructions Is this a sale at year end or not? Explain.

Solution It is not clear. Normally, delivery to the customer would accompany the sales order and payment. However, the merchandising company is agreeing to a non-standard selling term (that is, to store the goods) in order to make the sale more attractive. This might mean revenue cannot be recognized until the goods are delivered to the customer or that the company is selling both the inventory and a storage service. This is sometimes called a bill-and-hold arrangement. We will revisit this later in the chapter.

One last thought on the topic of normal business practices. Note that many companies continue to change their product mix and selling terms in an effort to provide maximum value to customers and shareholders. This is a completely normal part of evolving the business and dealing with changes that may be happening in the industry. For instance, a company that usually sells a product to ensure a certain profit margin may sell the product at a deep discount in order to achieve market penetration and get customers using the product.

Legalities of Sales Transactions

Companies operate within environments governed by law, including contract law, common law, and securities law. Laws exist to protect the rights of individuals and legal entities. It is important to understand the legal environment because rights and obligations often arise from the operation of the law. In this section, we explore the legalities of sales transactions and what each item means for accounting purposes.

Contract Law

Law When an entity sells something, both the entity and the customer enter into a contract. A contract with customers is an agreement that creates enforceable obligations and establishes the terms of the deal. See **Underlying Concept 6.3**. The contract may be written or verbal or may be evidenced by, for instance, a cash register receipt. The important thing is that two parties have promised to exchange assets and this creates a contract. There is a promissor (the seller), a promissee (the customer), and an agreement. Thus, the act of entering into a sales agreement creates legal rights and obligations.

> **Underlying Concept 6.3**
>
> Any promise that is enforceable under law and any obligation that is imposed by law should be included in the statements under the full disclosure principle, assuming that they are material.

In addition, the contract establishes the point in time when **legal title** (entitlement and ownership under law) passes. When the customer takes physical **possession** of the goods straight away, legal title would normally pass at this point. If the goods are shipped, the point at which legal title passes is often indicated by the shipping terms as follows:

    f.o.b. shipping point: title passes at the point of shipment.

    f.o.b. destination: title passes when the asset is delivered to the customer.

Why Does This Matter for Accounting Purposes? As noted above, if the entity has promised to provide goods and/or services now or in the future, the contract binds it and can be enforced. It creates contractual rights and obligations that may meet the definition of assets and liabilities. The contract also establishes the substantive terms of the deal, which need to be analyzed when determining if revenue has been earned (including when legal title has passed). If, for instance, the contract stipulates that customers must sign invoices as evidence that they are satisfied with the goods, it may mean that no revenue may be recognized until this is done.

Constructive Obligation

Performance obligations may arise even if not stated in a contract. In many cases, an entity may have an implicit obligation even if it is not explicitly noted in a selling contract. This is called a **constructive obligation**. A constructive obligation is an obligation that is created through past practice or by signalling something to potential customers. Constructive obligations are often enforceable under common or other law. **Example 6.5** illustrates the concept of a constructive obligation.

Example 6.5 | Constructive Obligations

Facts A clothing company sells goods worth $100 with a standard return policy. The policy states that the customer may return the goods within 30 days of purchase if defective. This policy is stated on the bill of sale and creates a contractual obligation. In practice, the company advertises that it stands behind its products 100%. Furthermore, it has a history and a customary business practice of accepting all returns for any reason and even after the 30-day period.

Instructions Does the company also have a constructive obligation? Explain.

Solution The company may have a constructive obligation regarding these returns. In other words, it effectively has an obligation to accept customer returns for any reason beyond the 30-day contractual obligation because it has created an expectation.

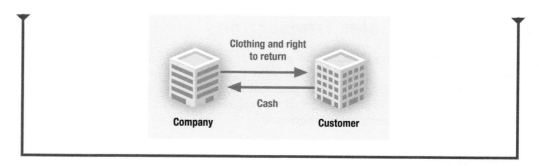

Why Does This Matter for Accounting Purposes?   Any enforceable promise that results from the sale (whether implicit or explicit) may create a performance obligation that needs to be recognized in the statement of financial position. This includes both contractual and other promises.

Information for Decision-Making

A trend analysis showing changes in revenues from year to year is a very common form of analysis. Due to the sensitivity and high profile of the revenues number on the income statement, there is a lot of pressure to report biased revenue numbers. Biased reporting is possible under both a principles-based accounting standards system (because there is less specific guidance) and a rules-based accounting standards system (by finding loopholes in the rules). Revenue is a key number used to judge management's job performance and it is a signal in the marketplace of sustainable growth potential. The value of firms in certain industries, such as Internet companies, is often based on revenues, since many of these firms do not generate profits in their early years.

Ethics   Revenue recognition is one of the main areas of misrepresentation in financial statements. It is often difficult to spot such misrepresentations, because the note disclosures may be very general. It is therefore important to carefully understand the company's underlying business and business model and to ensure that changes in the business model are reflected appropriately in the statements. Care should also be taken to ensure that large and unusual transactions are entered into for bona fide business reasons (for example, to add value for the shareholders) rather than to make the company's performance look better than it really is.

The Asset-Liability Approach to Revenue Recognition: An Overview of the Five-Step Process

LEARNING OBJECTIVE 2

Identify the five steps in the revenue recognition process.

There are two approaches to recognizing revenues: (1) the asset-liability approach (sometimes called the contract-based approach) and (2) the earnings approach.

IFRS   **Significant Change**   The new IFRS standard, IFRS 15 *Revenue from Contracts with Customers*, adopts an **asset-liability approach** as the basis for revenue recognition. The asset-liability approach recognizes and measures revenue based on changes in assets and liabilities. The earnings approach recognizes and measures revenue based on whether it has been earned. We will discuss this approach in greater detail later in this section. The IASB decided that focusing on (a) the recognition and measurement of assets and liabilities and

(b) changes in those assets or liabilities over the life of the contract brings more discipline to the measurement of revenue than the "earned and realized" criteria in prior IFRS standards. Note that ASPE still follows the **earnings approach**.

Under the IFRS 15 asset-liability approach, companies account for revenue based on the asset or liability arising from contracts with customers. Companies analyze contracts with customers because contracts are the lifeblood of most businesses. Contracts indicate the terms of the transaction, provide measurement of the consideration, and specify the promises that must be met by each party.

Illustration 6.2 shows the key concepts related to this new standard on revenue recognition. The new standard first identifies the key objective of revenue recognition, followed by a five-step process that companies should use to ensure that revenue is measured and reported correctly. Revenue should be recognized when the performance obligation is satisfied. We examine all steps in more detail in the following section.

ILLUSTRATION 6.2

Key Concepts of Revenue Recognition[4]

KEY OBJECTIVE

Recognize revenue to depict the transfer of goods or services to customers in an amount that reflects the consideration that the company receives, or expects to receive, in exchange for these goods or services.

FIVE-STEP PROCESS FOR REVENUE RECOGNITION

1. Identify the contract with customers.
2. Identify the separate performance obligations in the contract.
3. Determine the transaction price.
4. Allocate the transaction price to the separate performance obligations.
5. Recognize revenue when each performance obligation is satisfied.

REVENUE RECOGNITION PRINCIPLE

Recognize revenue in the accounting period when the performance obligation is satisfied.

The hypothetical example in **Example 6.6** gives a high-level overview of the five-step revenue recognition process.

Example 6.6 | Example of Five-Step Process—Sale of Airplane

Facts Assume that Bombardier Inc. signs a contract to sell airplanes to Air Canada for $100 million.[5]

Instructions When should Bombardier recognize the revenues? Explain.

Solution The analysis is done using the five-step process.

---

[4]Illustration based on IFRS 15.IN7 of the introduction that accompanied the issue of IFRS 15 in May 2014. Copyright © IFRS Foundation. All rights reserved. Reproduced with permission.

[5]Although a new class of aircraft (such as the Bombardier A220 Series) could take several years to design, develop, test, and receive regulatory clearances, once this is all completed, the actual production of one aircraft may only take several months. According to its annual financial statements, historically, Bombardier has recognized revenues on new aircraft when delivered (assuming other revenue recognition criteria have been met). The company notes that under IFRS 15, it will continue to recognize revenues of new aircraft upon delivery.

Step 1: Identify the contract with customers.

A contract is an agreement between two parties that creates enforceable rights or obligations. In this case, Bombardier has signed a contract to deliver airplanes to Air Canada.

Step 2: Identify the separate performance obligations in the contract.

Bombardier has only one performance obligation: to deliver airplanes to Air Canada. If Bombardier also agreed to maintain the planes, a separate performance obligation would be recorded for this promise.

Step 3: Determine the transaction price.

Transaction price is the amount of consideration that a company expects to receive from a customer in exchange for transferring a good or service. In this case, the transaction price is straightforward—it is $100 million.

Step 4: Allocate the transaction price to the separate performance obligations.

In this case, Bombardier has only one performance obligation: to deliver airplanes to Air Canada.

Step 5: Recognize revenue when each performance obligation is satisfied.

Bombardier recognizes revenue of $100 million for the sale of airplanes to Air Canada when it satisfies its performance obligation: the delivery of the airplanes to Air Canada.

Step 5 is when Bombardier recognizes revenue from the sale of the airplanes to Air Canada. At this point, Bombardier delivers the airplanes to Air Canada and satisfies its performance obligation.

In general, the performance obligation is satisfied when there is a change in **control** from the seller to the customer. In our example above, upon delivery, Air Canada now controls the assets because it has the "ability to direct the use of, and obtain substantially all of the remaining benefits from" the airplanes. Control also includes Air Canada's ability to prevent other companies from directing the use of, or receiving the benefits from, the airplanes.[6]

How will this affect the way we account for these contracts? (See **What Do the Numbers Mean? 6.1.**) In the following sections, we provide an expanded discussion of this five-step process.

What Do the Numbers Mean? 6.1

IFRS 15 introduces a new approach to revenue recognition, providing a significant amount of guidance and accompanying examples. How will this affect practice, if at all? Companies are required to signal (in the notes to their financial statements) the changes that they think will happen when a new standard is issued. Many companies have been doing just that in their most recent financial statements.

In addition, many public accounting firms are doing their own analysis of industries that might be affected. KPMG performed such an analysis and looked at not only which industries

---

[6]IFRS 15.33. We will discuss control later in the chapter. Copyright © IFRS Foundation. All rights reserved. Reproduced with permission.

would be affected but also at which step in the five-step process.[7] Their findings are noted in the chart below. Some industries, such as aerospace and defence, will be affected at almost every step. Note that steps 2 and 3 dealing with measurement will cause significant change, as will step 5 dealing with recognition.

Industry	Step 1	Step 2	Step 3	Step 4	Step 5
Aerospace and defense	✔	✔	✔		✔
Asset managers			✔		
Building and construction			✔		✔
Contract manufacturers					✔
Health care (US)	✔		✔		
Licensors (media, life sciences, franchisors)	✔*	✔	✔		✔
Real estate	✔	✔			✔
Software		✔	✔	✔	✔
Telecommunications (mobile networks, cable)		✔		✔	

*In particular, life sciences.

After IFRS 15 came into effect on January 1, 2018, many companies began applying IFRS 15 for the first time. Thus, the real impact would be evident starting in the 2018 financial reporting year.

As we can see in the excerpt below from the 2017 third-quarter interim financial statements of **Rogers Communications**, many companies were still trying to determine the impact.

> **Recent Accounting Pronouncements Not Yet Adopted**
>
> The IASB has issued new standards and amendments to existing standards. These changes are not yet adopted by us and will have an impact on future periods.
>
> - IFRS 9, *Financial Instruments* (effective January 1, 2018)
> - IFRS 15, *Revenue from Contracts with Customers* (effective January 1, 2018)
> - IFRS 16, *Leases* (effective January 1, 2019)
>
> These changes are described in our 2016 financial statements. We continue to assess the impact of each of these standards on our consolidated financial statements and we are progressing with the implementation of each of these standards. As at the date of these interim financial statements, there have been no significant changes to the disclosure related to the implementation of these standards that was included in our 2016 financial statements. With respect to IFRS 15, we have a team dedicated to ensuring our compliance with this standard. We are implementing a new system to enable us to comply with the requirements of the standard on a contract-by-contract basis and expect to begin a parallel run under both IAS 18 and IFRS 15 using this system in 2017. We have completed the system configurations and commenced the data validation process, which we expect will continue throughout the course of 2017. As a result, we continue to assess the impact of this standard on our consolidated financial statements and it is not yet possible to make a reliable estimate of its impact. We will disclose the estimated financial effects of the adoption of IFRS 15 in our 2017 annual consolidated financial statements.

Identifying the Contract with Customers—Step 1

LEARNING OBJECTIVE 3

Identify the contract with customers.

Law **Economics** A **contract** is an agreement between two or more parties that creates enforceable rights or obligations. Contracts can be written, oral, or implied from customary business practice. A company following IFRS applies the revenue guidance to a contract according to the criteria summarized in **Illustration 6.3**.

---

[7]KPMG, *Revenue Issues In-Depth*, Second Edition. IFRS and US GAAP. May 2016, page 3. Copyright © 2016 KPMG LLP, a Delaware limited liability partnership and the US member firm of KPMG network of independent member firms affiliated with KPMG International Cooperative, a Swiss entity. All rights reserved.

Contract Criteria for Revenue Guidance

Apply IFRS 15 to Contract If:	Disregard IFRS 15 If:
• The contract has commercial substance. • The parties to the contract have approved the contract and are committed to perform their respective obligations. • The company can identify each party's rights regarding the goods or services to be transferred. • The company can identify the payment terms for the goods and services to be transferred. • It is probable that the company will collect the consideration to which it will be entitled.[8]	• The contract is wholly unperformed, and • Each party can unilaterally terminate the contract without compensation.

In some cases, there are multiple contracts related to the transaction, and accounting for each contract may or may not occur, depending on the circumstances. These situations often develop when not only is a product provided but some type of service is performed as well. In other cases, a company should combine contracts and account for them as one contract.

If a contract does not meet the criteria specified above, revenue is recognized only when the performance obligation is satisfied and substantially all consideration has been received.[9] This added revenue recognition criterion (related to receipt of the consideration) is more conservative than under the five-step method.

ASPE Note that ASPE has similar criteria for determining whether there is persuasive evidence of a contract. Under ASPE, collectibility is considered as part of the general recognition criteria.

Basic Accounting

On entering into a contract with a customer, a company obtains rights to receive consideration from the customer and assumes obligations to transfer goods or services to the customer (performance obligations). The combination of those rights and performance obligations gives rise to a (net) asset or (net) liability. If the measure of the remaining rights exceeds the measure of the remaining performance obligations, the contract is an asset (a contract asset). Conversely, if the measure of the remaining performance obligations exceeds the measure of the remaining rights, the contract is a liability (a contract liability) under IFRS.

However, **a company does not recognize contract assets or liabilities until one or both parties to the contract perform** (that is, when the customer makes an advance payment or the company delivers a product or provides a service). Therefore, the signing of the contract by the two parties is not recorded (does not result in a journal entry) until one or both of the parties **perform under the contract**. We will revisit accounting for contract assets and liabilities in more detail later in the chapter.

The basic accounting for a contract in which both parties perform is shown in **Example 6.7.**

---

[8]The IASB introduced this criterion (which acts like a collectibility threshold) because the board concluded that the assessment of a customer's credit risk was an important part of determining whether a contract is valid. Under step 5 of the five-step revenue recognition guidance, collectibility is not a consideration for determining whether revenue is recognized. However, collectibility may be a consideration in assessing whether parties to the contract are committed to perform. In determining whether it is probable that a company will collect the amount of consideration to which it is entitled, the company assesses both the customer's ability and intent to pay as amounts become due (IFRS 15.9). Copyright © IFRS Foundation. All rights reserved. Reproduced with permission.

[9]IFRS 15.15. Copyright © IFRS Foundation. All rights reserved. Reproduced with permission.

Example 6.7 | Accounting for a Basic Revenue Transaction

Facts   On March 1, 2020, Margo Company enters into a contract to sell a product to Soon Yoon on July 31, 2020. The contract is structured such that Soon Yoon is required to pay the full contract price of $5,000 on August 31, 2020. The cost of goods transferred is $3,000. Margo delivers the product to Soon Yoon on July 31, 2020.

Instructions   What journal entries should Margo Company make regarding this contract in 2020?

Solution   No entry is required on March 1, 2020, because neither party has performed on the contract. On July 31, 2020, Margo delivers the product and therefore should recognize revenue on that date because it satisfies its performance obligation by delivering the product to Soon Yoon. There is now an unconditional right to receive the payment (and therefore an Account Receivable).

The journal entries to record the sale and related cost of goods sold are as follows.

July 31, 2020

Accounts Receivable	5,000	
Sales Revenue		5,000
Costs of Goods Sold	3,000	
Inventory		3,000

August 31, 2020

Cash	5,000	
Accounts Receivable		5,000

A	=	L	+	SE
+2,000				+2,000

Cash flows: No effect

A	=	L	+	SE
0				

Cash flows: ↑ 5,000 inflow

Contract Modifications

Companies sometimes change the contract terms while the contract is ongoing. This is called a **contract modification**. When a contract modification occurs, companies determine whether a new contract (and performance obligations) results or whether it is a modification of the existing contract.

A company accounts for a contract modification as a new contract if **both** of the following conditions are satisfied:

1. The promised **goods or services are distinct**. (We will look at this in more detail in the next section.)

2. The price increases by an amount of consideration that reflects the stand-alone selling price of the promised goods or services (that is, the price for which the entity could sell the goods or services).[10]

ASPE   ASPE has no guidance on contract modifications.
Example 6.8 looks at contract modifications.

Example 6.8 | Contract Modifications

Facts   Crandall Co. has a contract to sell 100 products to a customer for $10,000 ($100 per product) at various times over a six-month period. After 60 products have been delivered, Crandall modifies the contract by promising to deliver 20 extra products for an additional $1,900, or $95 per product (which is the stand-alone selling price of the products at the time of the contract modification). Crandall regularly sells the products separately and they are considered to be distinct.

Instructions   Is this accounted for as a new contract? Explain, calculating the total amount of revenue yet to be recognized.

Solution   In this situation, the contract modification for the additional 20 products is, in effect, a **new and separate contract** because it meets both of the conditions above. The additional

> products are separate (distinct) and the contract price reflects the stand-alone selling price of those products. It does not affect the accounting for the original contract.
>
> Given a new contract, Crandall recognizes an additional $4,000 [(100 units − 60 units) × $100] related to the original contract terms and $1,900 (20 units × $95) related to the new products. Total revenue after the modification is therefore $5,900 ($4,000 + $1,900).

Accounting for modifications of existing contracts that are not treated as if they are new contracts is beyond the scope of this book.[11]

Identifying Separate Performance Obligations—Step 2

LEARNING OBJECTIVE 4

Identify the separate performance obligations in the contract.

A **performance obligation** is a promise in a contract to provide a product or service to a customer. This promise may be explicit, implicit, or possibly based on customary business practice. To determine whether a performance obligation exists, **the company must assess whether it provides a distinct product or service**.[12] Let's look at the concept of a performance obligation more deeply.

A good or service is distinct if the customer can separately benefit from it.[13] **Illustration 6.4** summarizes some classic situations when revenue is recognized as a result of providing a distinct product or service, therefore satisfying a performance obligation.

ILLUSTRATION 6.4 **Revenue Recognition Situations**

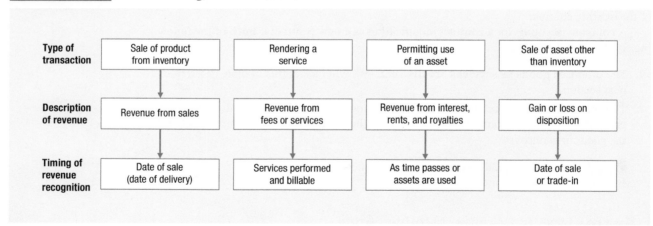

The accounting for the transactions in Illustration 6.4 is straightforward because only one performance obligation exists. However, many revenue arrangements may have more than one performance obligation. To determine whether a company has to account for multiple performance obligations, it evaluates a second condition. That is, it assesses **whether the product is distinct within the contract**.[14] In other words, if the performance obligation

---

[11]Essentially, the company must decide which of the following treatments is acceptable: (1) termination of the existing contract and creation of a new contract (prospective basis), (2) revision of the existing contract and adjustment of revenue on a cumulative catch-up basis, or (3) a combination of the first two options.

[12]IFRS 15.22.

[13]IFRS 15.27. Copyright © IFRS Foundation. All rights reserved. Reproduced with permission.

[14]IFRS 15.27. Copyright © IFRS Foundation. All rights reserved. Reproduced with permission.

is not highly dependent on, or interrelated with, other promises in the contract, then each performance obligation should be accounted for separately. Conversely, if these services are **interdependent** or **interrelated**, these services are combined and reported as one performance obligation.

Examples **6.9** and **6.10** illustrate this concept.

Example 6.9 | Multiple Goods and Services—Multiple Performance Obligations

Facts   Assume that Genus Motors sells an automobile to Marquart Auto Dealers at a price that includes six months of telematics services such as navigation and remote diagnostics. These telematics services are regularly sold on a stand-alone basis by Genus Motors for a monthly fee. After the six-month period, the consumer can renew these services on a fee basis with Genus Motors.

Instructions   Are the automobile and the telematics services distinct within the contract? Explain.

Solution   In this case, **two performance obligations exist**: one related to providing the automobile and the other related to the telematics services. The two are distinct and are **not** interdependent because the customer can benefit from the use of both the car and the service on their own (they are both sold separately).

Example 6.10 | Multiple Goods and Services—One Performance Obligation

Facts   Soft Tech Inc. sells customer-relationship software to Lopez Company. In addition to providing the software itself, Soft Tech promises to perform consulting services, extensively customizing the software to Lopez's information technology environment, for a total consideration of $600,000.

Instructions   Are the software and consulting services distinct within the contract? Explain.

Solution   In this case, Soft Tech is providing a significant service by **integrating** the goods and services (the licence and the consulting service) into one combined item for which Lopez has contracted. In addition, the software is significantly **customized** by Soft Tech in accordance with specifications negotiated by Lopez. As a result, the licence and the consulting services are **distinct but interdependent**, and therefore should be accounted for as **one performance obligation**.

Material Rights

When a customer purchases goods or services, sometimes, a company will grant the customer an option to acquire future items (for free or at a discount). Examples include loyalty points and coupons. These rights are treated as separate performance obligations as long as the option gives the customer what is known as a material right. A material right is a right that the customer would not otherwise have been entitled to. In these cases, the customer is in effect paying in advance for future goods or services and the transaction price must be allocated between the goods or services currently purchased and the goods or services to be purchased in the future under the option. These are two distinct performance obligations. The revenue relating to the option is deferred.

For instance, many airline companies offer points to their customers based on the amount paid and distance travelled on purchased flight tickets. These points transfer to the customer a right to travel for free or at a discount in future (that is, less than the fair value of the flight).

The revenue would generally be recognized when the future goods or services are transferred to the customer. Note that where loyalty points or gift certificates are awarded by a company, they are often not all redeemed or used by the customer. Often only a percentage of the total value will be redeemed by the customer. The unredeemed amount is known as **breakage**.

Example 6.11 illustrates an example of breakage under IFRS 15 in the form of loyalty points issued as part of a sale of an airline ticket.

Example 6.11 | Multiple Goods and Services—Customer Loyalty Programs

Facts   Assume Air Orillia offers its customers points every time they fly with the airline. During the year, the airline offered 1,000 points on a flight that was paid for in advance by the customer for $1,000 cash. Air Orillia estimates that based on history, only 90% of the points will be redeemed. The stand-alone value of the points expected to be redeemed is $50 (taking into account the breakage factor) and the value for the flight is $980.

Instructions   Do the loyalty points offer a material right to the customer? Explain.

Solution   Air Orillia is offering two services: the current flight and a discount on a future flight. The discount on the future flight has a stand-alone value of $50. This is a material right since the customer can use it to reduce the cost of future flights. Without it, the customer would have to pay full fare. Thus the flight and points represent separate performance obligations. The $1,000 payment would be allocated proportionately between the two performance obligations, as we shall see under step 4 of the five-step model.

Warranties

Companies often provide one of two types of **warranties** to customers. **Illustration 6.5** identifies and explains the two types.

ILLUSTRATION 6.5

Two Types of Warranties

Warranty Type	Description	Accounting Treatment
Assurance	Provides assurance that the product meets agreed-upon specifications in the contract at the time the product is sold.	Represents a cost of selling the product (and a warranty liability).
Service	Provides an additional service beyond the assurance-type warranty.	Represents a performance obligation.

An **assurance-type warranty** is nothing more than a quality guarantee that the good or service is free from defects at the point of sale. These types of obligations should be expensed in the period when the goods are provided or services performed (in other words, at the point of sale). In addition, the company should record a warranty liability. The estimated amount of the liability includes all the costs that the company will incur after sale due to the correction of defects or deficiencies required under the warranty provisions.

In addition, companies sometimes provide customers with an option to purchase a warranty separately. In most cases, these extended warranties provide the customer with a service beyond fixing defects that existed at the time of sale. For example, when you purchase a TV, you are entitled to the company's warranty. You will also undoubtedly be offered an extended warranty on the product at an additional cost. These **service-type warranties** represent a **separate service and are an additional performance obligation**. As a result, companies should allocate a portion of the transaction price to this performance obligation. The company recognizes revenue in the period that the service-type warranty is in effect.

Example 6.12 presents an example of both an assurance-type and a service-type warranty.

Example 6.12 | Multiple Goods and Services—Warranties

Facts   Chen Computer Inc. manufactures and sells computers that include a warranty to make good on any defect in its computers for 120 days. In addition, Chen sells separately an extended warranty, which provides protection from defects for three years beyond the 120 days.

Instructions   Are the computer and warranties distinct within the contract? Explain.

Solution   In this case, two performance obligations exist: one related to the sale of the computer and the assurance warranty, and the other to the extended warranty (service warranty). The sale of the computer and related assurance warranty are one performance obligation because they are **interdependent and interrelated** with each other. However, the extended warranty is separately sold and is **not interdependent**.

Example 6.13 looks at the journal entries relating to the two types of warranties.

Example 6.13 | Multiple Goods and Services—Warranties

Facts   Maverick Company sold 1,000 Rollomatics on December 31, 2020, at a total price of $6 million, with a warranty guarantee that the product was free from any defects. The cost of Rollomatics sold is $4 million. The term of the assurance warranty is two years, with an estimated cost of $30,000. In addition, Maverick sold extended warranties on 400 Rollomatics for three years beyond the two-year period for $12,000.

Instructions   What are the journal entries that Maverick Company should make in 2020 for the sale and the related warranties?

Solution   To record the revenue and liabilities related to the warranties:

Cash ($6,000,000 + $12,000)	6,012,000	
Warranty Expense	30,000	
Warranty Liability		30,000
Unearned Revenue		12,000
Sales Revenue		6,000,000

To reduce inventory and recognize cost of goods sold:

Cost of Goods Sold	4,000,000	
Inventory		4,000,000

A	=	L	+	SE
+2,012,000		+42,000		+1,970,000

Cash flows: ↑ 6,012,000 inflow

Maverick Company reduces the Warranty Liability account over the first two years as the actual warranty costs are incurred. The company also recognizes revenue related to the service-type warranty over the three-year period that extends beyond the assurance warranty period (two years). In most cases, the unearned warranty revenue is recognized on a straight-line basis. The costs associated with the service-type warranty are expensed as incurred.

ASPE does not provide detailed guidance regarding accounting for warranties but in principle, the economic substance of the transaction should prevail so the accounting should be similar.[15] Accounting for warranties is revisited in Chapter 13.

Upfront Fees

Companies sometimes receive payments (**upfront fees**) from customers before they deliver a product or perform a service. Upfront payments generally relate to the initiation, activation, or set-up of a good or service to be provided or performed in the future. In most cases, these

---

[15]In the past, these warranties may have been accounted for inconsistently due to the limited guidance. IFRS 15 provides a structured way to think about the economic substance of the warranty.

upfront payments are non-refundable. Examples include fees paid for membership in a health club or buying club, and activation fees for phone, Internet, or cable. These upfront fees may also include gift cards.

Are these non-refundable advance payments for products or services in the current period or are they for future delivery of products and services? Do they provide the customer with a **material right**? Recall that we discussed the concept of material right earlier using loyalty points as an example. Let's look at another example involving a health club initiation and annual fee. Often these contracts are structured such that, once the initiation fee is paid, the customer has the right of renewal at a lower annual price than would be charged if the initiation fee had not been paid. The right to renew at a lower price is a material right if the discount is significant compared with the price charged to customers who have not paid the initiation fee.

Normally this would be recognized as a separate performance obligation (similar to the loyalty points). However, **instead of recording the option to renew as a separate performance obligation, IFRS 15 allows the entity to treat the whole thing as one performance obligation**. This is because it would be difficult to determine a stand-alone value for renewal options. Therefore, as long as similar services are provided in each period, including the renewal period, and the customer uses the services as provided, then we can treat this as one performance obligation.[16]

Example 6.14 illustrates this.

Example 6.14 | Multiple Goods and Services—Initiation Fees as One Performance Obligation

Facts   Erica Felise signs a one-year contract with Bigelow Health Club. The terms of the contract are that Erica is required to pay a non-refundable initiation fee of $200 and an annual membership fee of $50 per month. Bigelow determines that its customers, on average, renew their annual membership twice before terminating their membership.

Instructions   What is the amount of revenue Bigelow Health Club should recognize in the first year?

Solution   In this case, the membership fee arrangement may be viewed as a **single performance obligation**. (Similar services are provided in all periods and the customers use the services as they are provided.) Bigelow determines the total transaction price to be $2,000—the upfront fee of $200 and the three years of monthly fees of $1,800 ($50 × 36)—and allocates it over the three years. In this case, Bigelow would report revenue of $55.56 ($50 + $200/36) each month for three years.

Series of Goods and Services That Are Substantially the Same

Some longer-term contracts provide a series of goods or services that are substantially the same over the life of a contract. An example is a two-year contract to provide monthly payroll processing services. Is this one performance obligation or multiple monthly obligations?

Under IFRS, as long as the services are substantially the same, and the customer receives the benefits each month, this is treated as one performance obligation.[17] Even though the monthly services are distinct (in that the customer benefits from them each month), the monthly services are combined into one larger performance obligation because they are the same each month. We will revisit this under step 5.

ASPE   Step 2 is a very important one in the five-step process because it affects when revenues will be recognized (step 5). ASPE has very little guidance in terms of multiple element arrangements; however, it may be necessary to look at separately identifiable components in a bundled sale.[18]

----

[16]IFRS 15.B43.

[17]IFRS 15.22.

[18]Reprinted/adapted with permission from the *CPA Canada Handbook—Accounting* © 2018, Part II, Section 3400.11, by Chartered Professional Accountants of Canada. All rights reserved by the copyright owner.

Determining the Transaction Price—Step 3

LEARNING OBJECTIVE 5
Determine the transaction price.

The **transaction price** is the amount of consideration that a company **expects to receive from a customer in exchange for transferring goods and services**. The transaction price in a contract is often easily determined because the customer agrees to pay a fixed amount of cash to the company over a short period of time. In other contracts, companies should also consider the following factors:

- Variable consideration
- Time value of money
- Non-cash consideration
- Consideration paid or payable to customers.

ASPE Note that the requirements below are largely IFRS requirements. ASPE has very little, if any, guidance on measurement, leaving the decisions to professional judgement.

Variable Consideration

In some cases, the price of a good or service is dependent on future events. These future events might include volume discounts, rebates, credits, returns, performance bonuses, and price concessions, to name a few. In these cases, the company estimates the amount of variable consideration it expects to receive from the contract to determine the amount of revenue to recognize. Companies use either the **expected value**, which is a probability-weighted amount, or the **most likely amount** in a range of possible amounts to estimate variable consideration. Companies choose between these two methods based on which approach better predicts the amount of consideration to which a company is entitled. **Illustration 6.6** highlights the issues to be considered in selecting the appropriate method.

ILLUSTRATION 6.6

Estimating Variable Consideration[19]

Expected value: Probability-weighted amount in a range of possible consideration amounts.	**Most likely amount**: The single most likely amount in a range of possible consideration outcomes.
• May be appropriate if a company has a large number of contracts with similar characteristics. (See Example 6.13.) • Can be based on a limited number of discrete outcomes and probabilities.	• May be appropriate if the contract has only two possible outcomes. (For instance, a bonus will be paid if the goods are delivered early but it will not be paid if the goods are not delivered early.)

Example **6.15** provides an application of the two estimation methods.

Example 6.15 | Transaction Price—Variable Consideration

Facts Peabody Construction Company enters into a contract with a customer to build a warehouse for $100,000, with a performance bonus of $50,000 that will be paid based on the timing of completion. The amount of the performance bonus decreases by 10% per week for every week

---

[19]Although not required under ASPE, the estimation methods noted above could be used.

beyond the agreed-upon completion date. The contract requirements are similar to contracts that Peabody has performed previously, and management believes that such experience is predictive for this contract. Management estimates that there is a 60% probability that the contract will be completed by the agreed-upon completion date, a 30% probability that it will be completed one week late, and a 10% probability that it will be completed two weeks late.

Instructions

a. How should Peabody measure the transaction price?

b. What is the transaction price?

Solution

a. The transaction price should include management's estimate of the amount of consideration to which Peabody will be entitled. Management has concluded that the **probability-weighted method** is the most predictive approach for estimating the variable consideration in this situation.

b.
60% chance of $150,000 [$100,000 + ($50,000 × 1.0)]	=	$ 90,000
30% chance of $145,000 [$100,000 + ($50,000 × .90)]	=	43,500
10% chance of $140,000 [$100,000 + ($50,000 × .80)]	=	14,000
		$147,500

Thus, the total transaction price is $147,500, based on the probability-weighted estimate. Management should update its estimate at each reporting date. Using a most likely outcome approach may be more predictive if a performance bonus is binary (Peabody either will or will not earn the performance bonus), such that Peabody earns either $50,000 for completion on the agreed-upon date or nothing for completion after the agreed-upon date. In this scenario, if management believes that Peabody will meet the deadline and estimates the consideration using the **most likely outcome**, the total transaction price would be $150,000 (the outcome with 60% probability).

Sales with **right of return** have long been a challenge in the area of revenue recognition. A sales contract that allows customers the right to return goods obligates the seller to honour that promise and to provide a refund. For example, assume that Hogland Glass Works transfers control of hurricane glass to Henlo Builders. Hogland grants Henlo the **right of return** for the product for various reasons (for example, dissatisfaction with the product) and the right to receive any combination of the following.

1. A refund.

2. A credit.

3. An alternative product in exchange.

   Hogland should recognize all of the following.

a. Revenue (considering the products expected to be returned).

b. A refund liability.

c. An asset (and corresponding adjustment to cost of sales) for its right to recover glass from Henlo on settling the refund liability.

   An example of a return situation is presented in **Example 6.16**.[20]

Example 6.16 | Transaction Price—Right of Return

Facts Venden Company sells 100 products for $100 each to Amaya Inc. payable in 30 days. Venden allows Amaya to return any unused product within 60 days and receive a full refund. The cost of each product is $60. To determine the transaction price, Venden decides that the approach that is most predictive of the amount of consideration to which it will be entitled is the most likely amount. Using the **most likely amount**, Venden estimates that:

1. Three products will be returned.

2. The costs of recovering the products will be immaterial.

3. The returned products are expected to be resold at a profit.

---

[20]Adapted from IFRS 15 Illustrative Example 22 and taking into account guidance in IFRS 15.B20 and B21. Copyright © IFRS Foundation. All rights reserved. Reproduced with permission.

Instructions **IFRS** **ASPE** How should Venden record this sale? Show journal entries under both IFRS and ASPE including the entries to reflect cost of sales.

Solution Upon transfer of control of the products, Venden recognizes (a) revenue of $9,700 ($100 × 97 products expected not to be returned), (b) a refund liability for $300 ($100 refund × 3 products expected to be returned), and (c) an asset of $180 ($60 × 3 products) for its right to recover products from customers on settling the refund liability. Hence, the amount recognized in cost of sales for 97 products is $5,820 ($60 × 97). The journal entries are slightly different under IFRS and ASPE. Having said this, the amount recorded as sales is the same ($9,700) although, under ASPE a Sales Return and Allowances account has historically been used.

Venden records the sale as follows.

IFRS

A	=	L	+	SE
+4,180		+300		+3,880

Cash flows: No effect

ASPE

A	=	L	+	SE
+3,880				+3,880

Cash flows: No effect

IFRS			ASPE		
Accounts Receivable	10,000		Accounts Receivable	10,000	
Sales Revenue		9,700[21]	Sales Revenue		10,000
Refund Liability		300[22]	Sales Returns and Allowances	300	
			Allowance for Sales		
			Returns and Allowances		300

Venden also records the related cost of goods sold with the following entry.

IFRS			ASPE[23]		
Cost of Goods Sold	5,820		Cost of Goods Sold	5,820	
Estimated Inventory Returns	180		Estimated Inventory Returns	180	
Inventory		6,000	Inventory		6,000

When a return occurs, Venden should reduce the Refund Liability/Allowance and Estimated Inventory Returns accounts. In addition, Venden recognizes the returned inventory in a Returned Inventory account as shown in the following entries for the return of two products (2 × $100). If material, companies record the returned asset in a separate account from inventory to provide transparency. The carrying value of the returned asset is subject to impairment testing, separate from the other inventory.

IFRS

A	=	L	+	SE
0		0		

Cash flows: No effect

ASPE

A	=	L	+	SE
+200		+200		

Cash flows: No effect

IFRS			ASPE		
Refund Liability	200		Allowance for Sales Returns		
Accounts Payable		200	and Allowances	200	
Returned Inventory	120		Accounts Payable		200
Estimated Inventory			Returned Inventory	120	
Returns		120	Estimated Inventory		
			Returns		120

Volume discounts are another feature of sales contracts that are considered variable consideration. Generally, if a customer buys a certain amount, they will receive a discount in the price since they are buying a lot of inventory. Often these arrangements span the year. If a customer buys more than a set volume by the end of the year, then the discounted price is applied to the annual sales.

---

[21]IFRS 15 caps the amount of revenue recognized at the amount the entity expects to receive. This is the amount that would be presented in the financial statements ($9,700 in our example). For bookkeeping purposes (in order to keep track of the amount that the company is legally entitled to), the entity could instead record the full amount of sales ($10,000 in our example) **and** a debit to Sales Returns and Allowances ($300 in our example) as we have shown under the ASPE column. **As long as the net amount is presented on the financial statements ($9,700), the company is in accordance with IFRS 15.** We have chosen to record the **expected amount** in the Sales Revenue to emphasize the IFRS requirement. Recall that bookkeeping is a system of collecting and sorting the data whereas preparation of financial statements is governed by IFRS and ASPE and generally requires grouping or aggregation of accounts.

[22]IFRS 15 Illustrative Example 22 notes that a "Refund Liability" would be recorded and so we have chosen to use this terminology.

[23]Historically, many companies have recorded the decrease in sales revenue only and not the inventory side of things. This may be overly conservative. We have done both sides in this example in order to simplify things. If there is a concern that the returned inventory would not have value or that costs to refurbish or fix the inventory are too high, the full amount of the inventory would be recorded as cost of sales when initially sold (in this case $6,000).

Example 6.17 provides an example of volume discounts.[24]

Example 6.17 | Transaction Price—Volume Discount

Facts Sung Inc. offers its customers a 3% volume discount if they purchase at least $2 million of its products during the calendar year. On March 31, 2020, Sung has made sales of $700,000 to Arctic Inc. In the previous two years, Sung sold over $3 million to Arctic in the period from April 1 to December 31.

Instructions **IFRS** **ASPE** How much revenue should Sung recognize for the first three months of 2020? Show journal entries under IFRS and ASPE.

Solution In this case, Sung should reduce its revenue by $21,000 ($700,000 × 3%) because it is **probable** that it will provide this rebate. Revenue is therefore $679,000 ($700,000 − $21,000). To not recognize this volume discount overstates Sung's revenue for the first three months of 2020. In other words, the appropriate revenue is $679,000, not $700,000. As noted earlier, under ASPE a Sales Returns and Allowances account (contra Sales Revenue account) is generally used.

Given these facts, Sung makes the following entry on March 31, 2020, to recognize revenue. The second journal entry below may be recorded at the end of the quarter or year so that revenues are not recorded at greater than the **expected amount**. IFRS would support recording no more than the expected amount as revenues whereas ASPE would allow the full revenues to be recognized with a Sales Return and Allowances Account such that net sales are also recorded at expected value. Historically, Sales Revenues have been presented on a net basis in the financial statements.

IFRS			ASPE		
Accounts Receivable	700,000		Accounts Receivable	700,000	
Sales Revenue		700,000	Sales Revenue		700,000
Sales Revenue	21,000		Sales Returns and		
Contract Liability		21,000[25]	Allowances	21,000	
			Allowance for Sales		
			Returns and Allowances		21,000

Assuming that Arctic meets the discount threshold, Sung makes the following entry.

IFRS			ASPE		
Contract Liability	21,000		Allowance for Sales Returns		
Accounts Receivable		21,000	and Allowances	21,000	
			Accounts Receivable		21,000

IFRS

A	=	L	+	SE
+700,000		+21,000		+679,000

Cash flows: No effect

ASPE

A	=	L	+	SE
+679,000				+679,000

Cash flows: No effect

IFRS

A	=	L	+	SE
−21,000		−21,000		

Cash flows: No effect

ASPE

A	=	L	+	SE
0				

Cash flows: No effect

Alternative Terminology 6.1

A contract liability may be referred to as Unearned Revenue or another appropriate account title.

See **Alternative Terminology 6.1**.

In many cases, companies provide cash discounts to customers for timely payment. (This is often referred to as a prompt settlement discount.) For example, assume that terms are payment due in 60 days, but if payment is made within five days, a 2% discount is given (referred to as 2/5, net 60). **These prompt settlement discounts should reduce revenues, if material.**[26]

---

[24]IFRS 15 Illustrative Example 24 provides an additional example involving volume discounts.

[25]In its meeting of January 10, 2018, the IFRS Discussion Group discussed how to account for volume discounts. Members generally felt that discounts would be set up as a liability to the customer similar to IFRS 15 Illustrative Example 22, which deals with right of return. Note that different terminology could be used for a contract liability, such as "discount liability." We have used contract liability for simplicity since it estimates the amount payable to customers if a discount threshold is reached. In the IFRS journal entry, the entry could be collapsed to credit Sales Revenues only for the $679,000.

[26]Since you would have learned about sales/cash discounts in your introductory accounting course, we will not cover them here. Historically, for discounts, many texts have illustrated what are called the "gross method" (where the Accounts Receivable and Sales are recorded at full value and discounts are recognized when the customer pays) and the "net method" (Accounts Receivable and Sales are initially recorded net of discounts and adjusted later if need be). In reality, most companies would use a hybrid of the two "methods." In other words, the full value of the Accounts Receivable is recorded in order to keep track of the full amount legally owed by the customer. In addition, an adjusting entry is booked to reflect estimated discounts where material. This is the method we have illustrated for returns and volume discounts in Examples 6.16 and 6.17.

A word of caution—a company **allocates variable consideration only if it is reasonably assured that it will be entitled to that amount**. Companies therefore may recognize variable consideration only if (1) they have experience with similar contracts and are able to estimate the cumulative amount of revenue, and (2) based on experience, it is **highly probable** that there will not be a **significant reversal** of revenue previously recognized.[27] If these criteria are not met, revenue recognition is constrained, meaning that the uncertain amounts are not included as part of the consideration until a later point when the uncertainty is resolved. Although ASPE does not explicitly deal with this issue, basic accounting concepts would preclude companies following ASPE from recognizing revenues where there is significant uncertainty.

Example 6.18 provides an example of how the revenue constraint works.

Example 6.18 | Transaction Price—Revenue Constraint

Facts   On January 1, Shera Company enters into a contract with Hornung Inc. to perform asset-management services for one year. Shera receives a quarterly management fee based on a percentage of Hornung's assets under management at the end of each quarter. In addition, Shera receives a performance-based incentive fee of 20% of the fund's return in excess of an observable index at the end of the year.

Shera accounts for the contract as a single performance obligation to perform investment-management services for one year because the services are interdependent and interrelated. To recognize revenue for satisfying the performance obligation over time, Shera selects an output method of measuring progress toward complete satisfaction of the performance obligation. Shera has had a number of these types of contracts with customers in the past.

Instructions   At what point should Shera recognize the management fee and the performance-based incentive fee related to Hornung?

Solution   Shera should record the management fee each quarter as it manages the fund over the year. However, Shera should not record the incentive fee until the end of the year. Although Shera has experience with similar contracts, that experience is not predictive of the outcome of the current contract because the amount of consideration is highly susceptible to volatility in the market. In addition, the incentive fee has a large number and high variability of possible consideration amounts. Thus, revenue related to the incentive fee is constrained (not recognized) until the incentive fee is known at the end of the year.

Royalties and similar payments are a form of variable consideration. The amount to be paid is often dependent upon future sales or usage, which are uncertain. Are these types of payments included in the measurement of the transaction price? IFRS specifically notes that payments based on sales or usage are not recognized until the sale or usage occurs and the performance obligation has been satisfied (or partly satisfied).[28]

Time Value of Money

The timing of payment to the company sometimes does not match the transfer of the goods or services to the customer. In most situations, companies receive consideration after the product is provided or the service performed. In essence, the company provides financing for the customer.

---

[27]According to IFRS 15.57, conditions such as any of the following would indicate that the revenue is constrained (or not recognized):

  1. The amount of consideration varies based on factors such as volatility in a market or weather conditions, which are outside the control of the company.
  2. The uncertainty will not be resolved for a long period of time.
  3. The company's experience with similar contracts is limited.
  4. There are a large number and broad range of possible amounts.

[28]IFRS 15.B63.

Underlying Concept 6.4

Refer back to Chapters 2 and 3 for a discussion on measurement and the time value of money.

Companies account for the time value of money if the contract **involves a significant financing component**. See Underlying Concept 6.4. When a sales transaction involves a significant financing component (that is, interest is accrued on consideration to be paid over time), the amount of revenue is determined by discounting the payments. The discount rate reflects the credit risk associated with the sales contract and the customer. For instance, the discount rate would be higher for a customer who has a higher credit risk.[29] Alternatively, you would calculate the interest rate needed to equate the discounted amount of payments to the cash consideration that a customer would pay for the item at the time of sale.

The company will report the effects of the financing as either interest expense or interest revenue. A customer may also pay upfront. In this case, care should be taken to consider whether there is a significant financing component. Under ASPE, there is no explicit requirement to account for the time value of money, although it is implied since receivables must be originally recognized at fair value (which would presumably reflect the time value of money if significant).[30]

Example 6.19 provides an example of a financing transaction.

Example 6.19 | Transaction Price—Extended Payment Terms

Facts On July 1, 2020, SEK Company sold goods to Grant Company for $900,000 in exchange for a four-year, zero-interest-bearing note with a face amount of $1,416,163. The goods have an inventory cost on SEK's books of $590,000 and their fair value is $900,000.

Instructions

a. How much revenue should SEK Company record on July 1, 2020?

b. How much revenue should it report related to this transaction on December 31, 2020? Show journal entries.

Solution

a. SEK should record revenue on July 1, 2020 of $900,000, which is the fair value of the inventory in this case.

b. SEK is also financing this purchase and records interest income on the note over the four-year period. Since no other information is available, the interest rate is imputed and is determined to be 12%. The 12% is the rate that discounts the final payment of $1,416,163 to the fair value of the goods ($900,000). SEK records interest revenue of $54,000 (12% × ½ × $900,000) at December 31, 2020.

The entry to record SEK's sale to Grant Company is as follows.

July 1, 2020

Notes Receivable	900,000	
Sales Revenue		900,000

The related entry to record the cost of goods sold is as follows.

July 1, 2020

Cost of Goods Sold	590,000	
Inventory		590,000

SEK makes the following entry to record interest revenue at the end of the year.

December 31, 2020

Notes Receivable	54,000	
Interest Income (12% × ½ × $900,000)		54,000

A	=	L	+	SE
+310,000				+310,000

Cash flows: No effect

A	=	L	+	SE
+54,000				+54,000

Cash flows: No effect

As a practical expedient, companies are not required to reflect the time value of money to determine the transaction price if the time period for payment is less than a year.[31]

[29]IFRS 15.64.

[30]Reprinted/adapted with permission from the *CPA Canada Handbook—Accounting* © 2018, Part II, Section 3856.07, by Chartered Professional Accountants of Canada. All rights reserved by the copyright owner.

[31]IFRS 15.63.

Non-cash Consideration

Companies sometimes receive consideration in the form of goods, services, or other non-cash consideration. When these situations occur, **companies generally recognize revenue on the basis of the fair value of what is received**.[32] Example 6.20 looks at a simple example.

Example 6.20 | Transaction Price—Non-cash Consideration

Facts   Assume that Raelin Limited receives common stock of Monroe Limited in payment for consulting services. The company follows IFRS.

Instructions   How should the transaction price be measured?

Solution   Raelin Limited recognizes revenue in the amount of the fair value of the common stock received. If Raelin cannot determine this amount, then it should estimate the selling price of the services performed and recognize this amount as revenue.

Customers sometimes contribute goods or services, such as equipment or labour, to help fulfill the contract. This consideration should be treated as non-cash consideration and included in the transaction price as long as control of the goods or services passes to the company.[33]

Consideration Paid or Payable to Customers

Companies often make payments to their customers as part of a revenue arrangement. Consideration paid or payable may include coupons, vouchers, or other items. In general, these elements reduce the consideration received and the revenue to be recognized (or are treated as separate performance obligations) as noted earlier under steps 2 and 3. In certain situations, these amounts may be treated as assets or expenses. For instance, where the company is reimbursing the customer for shared advertising costs, the amounts paid would be treated as an expense.[34]

Where gift cards are sold, they may not all be redeemed by the customer (or redeemed for less than the full value). As noted earlier in this chapter when we discussed loyalty points, this is called **breakage**. How is breakage accounted for when gift cards are sold separately and not part of a bundled sale?

Example 6.21 provides an example of an upfront fee payment in the form of a gift card.

Example 6.21 | Transaction Price—Gift Cards[35]

Facts   Ocean Limited sells a $500 gift card to a customer on January 1, with no expiry date. Based on past gift card sales, 85% of gift cards are redeemed and 15% are unexercised. Ocean feels that this information has good predictive value and estimates that 15% of the gift card will remain unredeemed. On December 31, the customer makes one purchase of $50 using the gift card.

Instructions   How should the company account for this sale? Show journal entries.

---

[32]IFRS 15.66.

[33]IFRS 15.69.

[34]IFRS 15.70/.71.

[35]Based on an example in the publication *IFRS 15 Revenue from Contracts with Customers—Your Questions Answered* (CPA Canada, March 1, 2015); page 38. See also IFRS 15.B46.

A	=	L	+	SE
+500		+500		

Cash flows: ↑ $500

A	=	L	+	SE
		−59		+59

Cash flows: No effect

Solution Upon sale of the card, the company records a Contract Liability or Unearned Revenue for $500.

January 1

Cash	500	
Contract Liability		500

The breakage is recognized proportionately as the customer uses the card to purchase goods. Therefore, when the $50 purchase is made, rather than recognizing $50 of revenue, $59 of revenue will be recognized to incorporate expected breakage (that is, $50 * (500/425)).

December 31

Contract Liability	59	
Sales Revenue		59

Allocating the Transaction Price to Separate Performance Obligations—Step 4

LEARNING OBJECTIVE 6

Allocate the transaction price to the separate performance obligations.

Companies often have to allocate the transaction price to more than one performance obligation in a contract. If an allocation is needed, the transaction price allocated to the various performance obligations is based on their **relative values**. The best measure of the value is the amount that the company could sell the good or service for on a stand-alone basis, called the stand-alone selling price. If this information is not available, companies should use their **best estimate** of what the good or service might sell for as a stand-alone unit. **Illustration 6.7** provides a brief overview of how to calculate stand-alone selling price.

ILLUSTRATION 6.7
How to Determine Stand-Alone Selling Price

Illustration 6.8 summarizes the approaches that companies may follow (in preferred order of use).[36] All information that is reasonably available should be used (such as market conditions and type of customer) and maximum use should be made of **observable** information.

---

[36]IFRS 15.79. Copyright © IFRS Foundation. All rights reserved. Reproduced with permission.

Allocation Approach	Implementation
Adjusted market assessment approach	Estimate the price that customers purchasing the goods or services will pay. The company might also look at competitor prices for similar goods or services.
Expected cost plus a margin	Forecast expected costs and add a reasonable profit margin.
Residual approach	Use where the selling price is highly variable or uncertain. Estimate the stand-alone selling price by starting with the total price for the contract and deducting the observable selling prices of other items being sold.[37]

ILLUSTRATION 6.8

Estimating Stand-Alone Selling Price—Allocation of Transaction Price to Performance Obligations

Examples 6.22 and 6.23 involve multiple performance obligations where the transaction price must be allocated.

Example 6.22 | Allocation of Transaction Price—Build, Run, and Maintain Equipment

Facts   Lonnie Company enters into a contract to build, run, and maintain a highly complex piece of electronic equipment for five years, starting upon delivery of the equipment. There is a fixed fee for each of the build, run, and maintenance deliverables. Any progress payments made are non-refundable. There is **verifiable evidence of the selling price** for the building and maintenance but not for running the equipment. It is determined that the transaction price must be allocated to the three performance obligations: building, running, and maintaining the equipment.

Instructions   What allocation approach should Lonnie Company use to allocate the transaction price to the three performance obligations?

Solution   The performance obligations relate to building the equipment, running the equipment, and maintaining the equipment. As indicated, Lonnie can determine the stand-alone values for the equipment and the maintenance agreements. The company can then make a best **estimate of the selling price** for running the equipment, using the **adjusted market assessment approach or expected cost plus a margin approach**. Lonnie next identifies the relative value of each deliverable at the inception of the transaction to determine the proper allocation to each performance obligation. Once the allocation is performed, Lonnie recognizes revenue independently for each performance obligation using regular revenue recognition criteria (step 5).

   If Lonnie is unable to estimate the stand-alone selling price for running the equipment because such an estimate is highly variable or uncertain, Lonnie may use a **residual approach**. In this case, Lonnie starts with the value from the total transaction price and then deducts the stand-alone selling price of the other two deliverables to arrive at a residual value for running the equipment.

In many cases, the sum of the value of each good and/or service in a bundled sale is often greater than the transaction price. Generally, the discount is allocated proportionately to each good and/or service. Example 6.23 looks at specific calculations relating to allocating the transaction price where this is the case.

---

[37]A selling price is highly variable when a company sells the same good or service for different amounts. A selling price may be uncertain when a company has not yet established a selling price (IFRS 15.79).

Example 6.23 | Allocation of Transaction Price—Equipment, Installation, and Training

Facts Handler Company is an experienced manufacturer of construction equipment. Handler's products range from small to large pieces of automated equipment, to complex systems containing numerous components. Unit selling prices range from $600,000 to $4 million and are quoted inclusive of installation and training. The installation process does not involve changes to the equipment's features and does not require proprietary information about the equipment in order for the installed equipment to perform to specifications. Handler has the following arrangement with Chai Company.

- Chai purchases equipment from Handler for $2 million and chooses Handler to do the installation. Handler charges $2 million for the equipment whether it does the installation or not. (Some companies do the installation themselves because they prefer their own employees to do the work or because of relationships with other customers.) The installation service if sold separately is estimated to have a fair value of $20,000.

- The fair value of the training sessions is estimated at $50,000. Other companies could also perform these training services but Chai chooses to use Handler for its training so it does not have to pay extra to another company.

- Chai is obligated to pay Handler the $2 million upon the delivery and installation of the equipment.

- Handler delivers the equipment and completes the installation on November 1, 2020. (In other words, transfer of **control** is complete.) Training related to the equipment starts once the installation is completed and lasts for one year.

Instructions

a. What are the performance obligations for purposes of accounting for the sale of the equipment?

b. If there is more than one performance obligation, how should the payment of $2 million be allocated to various components? Show journal entries.

Solution

a. The equipment, installation, and training are **distinct and not interdependent** because the equipment, installation, and training are three separate products or services. Each of these items has a **stand-alone selling price**.

b. The total revenue of $2 million should be allocated to the three components based on their relative values. In this case, the equipment's **stand-alone selling price** should be considered to be $2 million, the installation fee is $20,000, and the training is $50,000. The total value to consider is $2,070,000 ($2,000,000 + $20,000 + $50,000).

The allocation is as follows.

Equipment	$1,932,367 [($2,000,000 ÷ $2,070,000) × $2,000,000]
Installation	$19,324 [($20,000 ÷ $2,070,000) × $2,000,000]
Training	$48,309 [($50,000 ÷ $2,070,000) × $2,000,000]

Handler makes the following entry on November 1, 2020, to record both sales revenue and service revenue on the installation, as well as the unearned service revenue.

November 1, 2020

Cash	2,000,000	
Service Revenue—Installation		19,324
Unearned Revenue		48,309
Sales Revenue		1,932,367

Assuming the cost of the equipment is $1.5 million, the entry to record cost of goods sold is as follows.

November 1, 2020

Cost of Goods Sold	1,500,000	
Inventory		1,500,000

As indicated by these entries, Handler recognizes revenue from the sale of the equipment once the installation is completed on November 1, 2020. In addition, it recognizes revenue for the installation fee because these services have been performed.

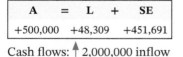

A	=	L	+	SE
+500,000		+48,309		+451,691

Cash flows: ↑ 2,000,000 inflow

Handler recognizes the training revenues on a straight-line basis starting on November 1, 2020, or $4,026 ($48,309 ÷ 12) per month for one year (unless a more appropriate method such as the percentage-of-completion method is warranted). The journal entry to recognize the training revenue for two months in 2020 is as follows.

December 31, 2020

Unearned Revenue	8,052	
Service Revenue—Training ($4,026 × 2)		8,052

A	=	L	+	SE
		−8,052		+8,052

Cash flows: No effect

Therefore, Handler recognizes revenue for the year ended December 31, 2020, in the amount of $1,959,743 ($1,932,367 + $19,324 + $8,052). Handler makes the following journal entry to recognize the training revenue in 2021, assuming adjusting entries are made at year end.

December 31, 2021

Unearned Revenue	40,257	
Service Revenue—Training ($48,309 − $8,052)		40,257

A	=	L	+	SE
		−40,257		+40,257

Cash flows: No effect

When a company sells a bundle of goods or services, the selling price of the bundle may be less than the sum of the individual stand-alone prices and this may be due to a specific service or product. In this case, the company should allocate the discount to the service or product that is causing the discount and not to the entire bundle. **Example 6.24** indicates this.

Example 6.24 | Allocating Transaction Price—Discount Allocated to Specific Performance Obligations

Facts Manitoba Joe's Golf Shop provides the following information about three items that are often sold as a package. The company often sells the putter and irons as a separate bundle for $550.

Item	Stand-Alone Selling Price	Price When Bundled
a. Lessons (per session)	$100	(b) + (c) $550
b. Custom irons	$525	
c. Putter	$125	
Total	$750	(a) + (b) + (c) $650

Instructions How should the discount be allocated to the elements of the revenue arrangement?

Solution As indicated, the stand-alone prices for the lesson, custom irons, and putter total $750, but the bundled price for all three is $650. In this case, the discount applies to the performance obligations related to providing the custom irons and putter. As a result, Manitoba Joe's allocates the discount solely to the custom irons and putter, and not to the lessons, as follows.

	Allocated Amounts
Lessons	$100
Custom irons and putter	550
Total	$650

As a final note, ASPE does not provide much guidance on allocating the transaction price and it is left up to professional judgement.

Recognizing Revenue When (or As) Each Performance Obligation Is Satisfied—Step 5

LEARNING OBJECTIVE 7

Understand how to recognize revenue when the company satisfies its performance obligation.

A company satisfies its performance obligation when the customer obtains control of the good or service. As indicated earlier, the concept of change in control is the deciding factor in determining when a performance obligation is satisfied. The customer controls the product or service when it has the ability to direct the use of and obtain substantially all the remaining benefits from the asset or service. Control also includes the customer's ability to prevent other companies from directing the use of, or receiving the benefits from, the asset or service.[38] **Illustration 6.9** summarizes some indicators that the customer has obtained control.[39]

ILLUSTRATION 6.9

Change in Control Indicators

1. The company has a right to payment for the asset.
2. The company has transferred legal title to the asset.
3. The company has transferred physical possession of the asset.
4. The customer has significant risks and rewards of ownership.
5. The customer has accepted the asset.

Companies satisfy performance obligations either at a point in time or over a period of time. **Illustration 6.10** provides an overview of this decision.

ILLUSTRATION 6.10

When to Recognize Revenue?

According to IFRS 15.35, companies recognize revenue over a period of time only if one or more of the following **three criteria** are met:

1. The customer **receives and consumes the benefits** as the seller performs. (An example of this is a one-year contract to water the plants in an office building bi-weekly.)
2. The **customer controls the asset** as it is created or enhanced. (For example, a builder constructs a building on a customer's property.)
3. The company does **not have an alternative use for the asset** created or enhanced and the amount is collectible. (For example, an aircraft manufacturer builds specialty jets to a customer's specifications **and** the company has an enforceable right to payment.)

Example 6.25 provides an example of a contract that meets one of the three criteria for recognition over time.

---

[38]IFRS 15.33.

[39]IFRS 15.38. Copyright © IFRS Foundation. All rights reserved. Reproduced with permission.

Example 6.25 | Recognition—Satisfying a Performance Obligation over Time

Facts   Gomez Software Company enters into a contract with Hurly Company to develop and install customer relationship management (CRM) software. Progress payments are required to be made upon completion of each stage of the contract. If the contract is terminated, then the partly completed CRM software passes to Hurly Company. Gomez Software is prohibited from redirecting the software to another customer.

Instructions   On what basis should Gomez Software Company recognize revenue related to its contract with Hurly Company?

Solution   Gomez Software creates an asset with **no alternative use** because it is prohibited from redirecting the software to another customer. In addition, Gomez Software is **entitled to payments** for performance to date and expects to complete the project. Therefore, Gomez Software concludes that the contract meets the criteria for recognizing revenue **over time**.

A company recognizes revenue from a performance obligation over time by measuring the progress toward completion. The method selected for measuring progress should depict the transfer of control from the company to the customer. Companies use various methods to determine the extent of progress toward completion. The most common are the cost-to-cost and units-of-delivery methods. The objective of all these methods is to measure the extent of progress in terms of costs, units, or value added. Companies identify the various measures (such as costs incurred, labour hours worked, tonnes produced, or floors completed) and classify them as input or output measures.

Input measures (such as costs incurred and labour hours worked) are efforts devoted to a contract. Output measures (with units of delivery measured as tonnes produced, floors of a building completed, kilometres of a highway completed, and so on) track results. Neither is universally applicable to all long-term projects. Their use requires the exercise of judgement and careful tailoring to the circumstances.

Recall our earlier discussion about a series of goods or services that were substantially the same. Under IFRS, as discussed, this may be treated as one performance obligation. When is revenue recognized in this case? **Example 6.26** looks at a long-term contract for cleaning.

Example 6.26 | Recognition—Satisfying a Performance Obligation over Time

Facts   Dandy Limited provides cleaning services to large corporations. Most contracts are two-year contracts under which the company cleans the offices on a monthly basis. On January 1, Dandy signed a two-year contract for $30,000 with $6,000 being paid January 31 and the rest monthly at $1,000 per month (end of month). Historically, Dandy finds that it spends more time cleaning in the winter and spring and less time in the summer.

Instructions   When should revenue be recognized? Show journal entries.

Solution   Since the contract involves a series of services that are delivered monthly and are substantially the same, this is considered as **one performance obligation**. Even though the company spends more time cleaning in winter and spring, the cleaning services are essentially the same each month. By treating it as one performance obligation, the entity does not have to determine a separate stand-alone price for each month's service (step 4).

The customer receives and benefits from the cleaning services each month, and therefore revenue is recognized **over time**. This allows the entity to allocate the total contract amount evenly over the period of the contract (24 months). At the end of January, Dandy would record the following, assuming the upfront and first payments have been made:

Cash	7,000	
Unearned Revenue		5,750
Service Revenue		1,250
($6,000 + $24,000)/24 months		

A	=	L	+	SE
+7,000		+5,750		+1,250

Cash flows: ↑ $7,000 inflow

The most popular input measure used to determine the progress toward completion is the cost-to-cost basis. Under this basis, a company measures the percentage of completion by comparing costs incurred to date with the most recent estimate of the total contract costs. We discuss the percentage-of-completion method more fully in Appendix 6A, which revisits the accounting for long-term contracts.

Many companies enter into licensing type arrangements with customers. The arrangements allow the customer to use the company's intellectual property. These can be highly complex arrangements like franchises. Other examples include rights to use software, patents, movies, pharmaceuticals, team logos, and songs. Should the company recognize revenue up-front or over time?

Under IFRS, if the intellectual property is static (it doesn't change), then revenue may be recognized at a point in time. An example is an agreement that gives the customer a right to reproduce a historical work of art on T-shirts. If the intellectual property is constantly changing, then revenue is recognized over time. An example of this is a contract that gives the customer the right to use a team logo on clothing. For instance, if your favourite hockey team all of a sudden advances to the next round of the playoffs, then the value of the right to use the team logo increases.[40] **Illustration 6.11** shows a decision tree for deciding whether to recognize licensing revenue at a point in time or over time.

ILLUSTRATION 6.11

Licensing and Similar Agreements to Use Intellectual Property

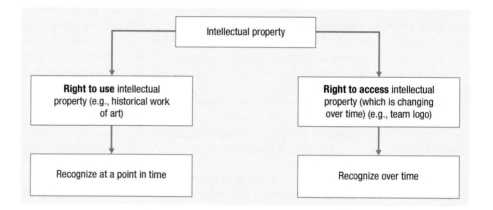

Example 6.27 looks at an example of recognizing licensing type arrangements.

Example 6.27 | Recognition—Licensing Type Arrangements

Facts Tech Limited sells accounting software to customers. It recently signed a contract with a customer, allowing the customer to use the software (which is downloadable). The accounting software is self-installing and this particular version will not be updated. The company has plans to develop a newer version of the software using different technology. The customer may use the software for as long as it wishes.

Instructions When should Tech recognize revenue?

Solution The contract allows the customer to use the software (intellectual property owned by Tech). For this, Tech is charging a fee. Because the software will not be updated, Tech may recognize revenue at a point in time.

Illustration 6.12 provides a summary of the five-step revenue recognition process.

[40]This is obviously an area of significant complexity. As we move more toward online access to things such as software, music, and other forms of changing and interactive platforms and content, we are moving toward recognition over time.

ILLUSTRATION 6.12

Summary of the Five-Step Revenue Recognition Process[41]

Step in Process	Description	Implementation
1. Identify the contract with customers.	A contract is an **agreement that creates enforceable rights and obligations**.	A company applies the revenue guidance to contracts with customers and must determine if new performance obligations are created by a contract modification.
2. Identify the separate performance obligations in the contract.	A **performance obligation** is a promise in a contract to provide a product or service to a customer. A performance obligation exists if the customer can benefit from the good or service on its own or together with other readily available resources.	A contract may be composed of **multiple performance obligations**. The accounting for multiple performance obligations is based on evaluation of whether the product or service is **distinct** within the contract. If the goods or services are distinct, but are **interdependent and interrelated**, these goods and services are combined and reported as one performance obligation.
3. Determine the transaction price.	The transaction price is the amount of consideration that a company **expects to receive** from a customer in exchange for transferring goods and services.	In determining the transaction price, companies must consider the following factors: (1) variable consideration, (2) time value of money, (3) non-cash consideration, and (4) consideration paid or payable to the customer.
4. Allocate the transaction price to the separate performance obligations.	If more than one performance obligation exists, allocate the transaction price based on relative fair values.	The best measure of value is what the good or service could be sold for on a stand-alone basis (the stand-alone selling price). Estimates of stand-alone selling price can be based on (1) adjusted market assessment, (2) expected cost plus a margin approach, or (3) a residual approach.
5. Recognize revenue when each performance obligation is satisfied.	A company satisfies its performance obligation when the customer obtains control of the good or service.	Companies satisfy performance obligations either at a point in time or over a period of time. Companies recognize revenue over a period of time if (1) the customer controls the asset as it is created or (2) the company does not have an alternative use for the asset.

Earnings Approach to Revenue Recognition

LEARNING OBJECTIVE 8

Analyze and determine whether a company has earned revenues under the earnings approach.

IFRS **ASPE** Under IFRS, as noted earlier, revenue is recognized under the **asset-liability approach** when the performance obligation is settled (when control passes). ASPE uses the

earnings approach. Under the earnings approach, revenues for **sale of goods** and related costs are recognized when all the following conditions are met:[42]

1. The **risks and rewards** of ownership are transferred to the customer or revenues are earned.
2. The vendor has no continuing involvement in, nor effective control over, the goods sold.
3. Costs and revenues can be **measured reliably**.
4. **Collectibility** is probable.[43]

If the company cannot measure the transaction, then either there is too much uncertainty surrounding the transaction (for instance, where there are abnormal concessionary terms), or the company has not completed all that it has to do to earn the revenues.

What does the company do to create valuable products or services that customers will pay for? How does it add value? The **earnings process** consists of the actions that a company takes to add value. It is an important part of the business model because it focuses on operating activities. The earnings process is unique to each company and each industry. Different industries add value in different ways. For example, companies that sell goods that they manufacture have vastly differing earnings processes than those that sell goods that they buy wholesale and sell retail. In addition, companies that are in the biotechnology business have models that are different from real estate companies. For this reason, it is important to begin with an understanding of the earnings process.

Selling Goods

When an entity sells goods, there is often one main act or **critical event** in the earnings process that signals **substantial completion or performance**. At this point, although some uncertainty remains, its level is acceptable and revenues can be recognized under accrual accounting. In businesses that sell goods, substantial completion normally occurs at the **point of delivery**. This is generally when the **risks and rewards (benefits) of ownership** (including legal title and possession) pass. If the earnings process has a critical event, it is often called a **discrete earnings process**.

The concept of risks and rewards (benefits) of ownership is a core concept in the earnings approach to revenue recognition. It helps to establish ownership and to indicate when ownership passes from one party to another. As a general rule, the entity that has the risks and rewards treats the goods as an asset.[44]

Example 6.28 presents some of the risks and rewards associated with the sale of wine.

Example 6.28 | Recognition—Risks and Rewards of Producing Wine

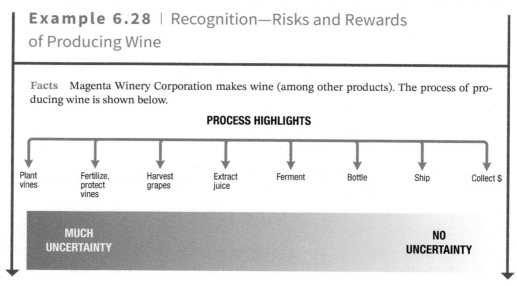

Facts Magenta Winery Corporation makes wine (among other products). The process of producing wine is shown below.

PROCESS HIGHLIGHTS

Plant vines | Fertilize, protect vines | Harvest grapes | Extract juice | Ferment | Bottle | Ship | Collect $

MUCH UNCERTAINTY — **NO UNCERTAINTY**

---

[42]Recognition is the process of including an item in the financial statements. Recognition is not the same as realization, although the terms are sometimes used interchangeably in accounting literature and practice.

[43]*CPA Canada Handbook*, Part II, Section 3400.04. Note that the predecessor standards to IFRS 15 (IAS 11 and 18) generally followed the earnings approach.

[44]In order to recognize an asset on the balance sheet, a company must prove that it has control over substantially all of the risks and rewards of ownership. If these have been passed on to another party, a disposition has occurred.

Magenta must perform all of the acts in order to make a profit from the sale of its wine. The entity starts with cash, invests it in producing inventory, sells the inventory at a price that is higher than its cost, and collects cash. At the early points of the earnings process, there is significant uncertainty about how much product will be produced and its quality. What if the vines get diseased? What if temperatures are too low or it rains too much? What if there is no market for the product? Moving along the earnings process timeline (from left to right), the conditions creating the uncertainty resolve themselves. At the far right-hand side of the earnings process, once the product is shipped and paid for, all uncertainty is eliminated about the creation of the product itself, the measurability of both its costs and revenues, and the collectibility of those revenues.

Instructions   What are the risks and rewards of ownership?

Solution   The risks and rewards are shown in the following chart.

Risks	**Rewards**
— Wine will age poorly and therefore decline in value	— Wine will age well and appreciate in value
— Wine will be stolen/vandalized	— Wine can be consumed by owner or buyer
— Wine will be stored improperly	— Wine inventory may be used as collateral for bank loan
	— Wine may be sold for cash

In determining who has the risks and rewards of ownership and, therefore, whether a sale has occurred at the point of delivery, it is important to look at who has **possession** of the goods and who has **legal title**. The risks and rewards usually stem from these two factors. For example, Magenta is not entitled to sell inventory or pledge it as collateral (that is, to reap the rewards) unless it has legal title to it. Legal title and possession expose Magenta to risk of loss.

The principle is quite general and, therefore, there are a wide range of practical applications. Different companies interpret these principles in different ways.[45] We will discuss inventory more fully in Chapter 8.

What about recognizing income before possession and legal title to goods pass to a customer? Is there ever a situation whereby revenue might be recognized before this critical event? In some cases, revenue may be recognized even before there is a specific customer. Examples of such situations can be found in the forestry and agricultural industries when some products have assured prices and ready markets. Revenue is recognized over time as the assets mature. The critical event is the appreciation in value of the asset.[46]

Selling Services

The focus is different when determining the earnings process for services. When services are provided, the focus is on **performance of the service**. An example of an earnings process for a service that is a discrete earnings process is a maintenance inspection on a car. The service is offered on the spot and is completed in a very short time. The critical event is when the mechanic hands over the inspected car and the bill. As mentioned earlier, long-term contracts are more challenging to account for and will be covered in further detail in Appendix 6A.

---

[45]Because of this, and in part also because of the increased profile of revenue recognition issues with securities commissions, companies are required to disclose the revenue recognition method in the notes to their financial statements.

[46]IAS 41 deals with biological assets such as beef cattle. It requires that these assets be measured at fair value less estimated point-of-sale costs. We will discuss this topic in greater detail in Chapter 8.

Measurability and Collectibility

ASPE does not provide much guidance on how to measure transactions or how to assess collectibility at contract inception.

Other Revenue Recognition Issues

There are several other situations where revenue recognition issues arise. In this section, we illustrate the **revenue recognition principle** and the concept of control for the following situations. This section is based on IFRS 15. ASPE has little specific guidance in these areas, but is otherwise generally consistent with the following material in terms of basic principles.

- Repurchase agreements
- Bill and hold
- Principal-agent relationships
- Consignments

Repurchase Agreements

In some cases, companies enter into **repurchase agreements**, which allow them to transfer an asset to a customer but result in an obligation or right to repurchase the asset at a later date. In these situations, the question is whether the company sold the asset. Generally, companies report these transactions as a financing (borrowing). That is, if the company has an obligation or right to repurchase the asset for an amount **greater than or equal to its selling price**, then the transaction is a financing transaction by the company. **Example 6.29** examines the issues related to a repurchase agreement.

Example 6.29 | Recognition—Repurchase Agreement

Facts   Morgan Inc., an equipment dealer, sells equipment on January 1, 2020, to Lane Company for $100,000. It agrees to repurchase this equipment from Lane Company on December 31, 2021, for a price of $121,000. Assume that Morgan continues to have control over the asset during the period.

Instructions   Should Morgan Inc. record a sale for this transaction? Show journal entries.

Solution   For a sale and repurchase agreement, the terms of the agreement need to be analyzed to determine whether Morgan Inc. has transferred control to the customer, Lane Company. As indicated earlier, control of an asset refers to the ability to direct the use of and obtain substantially all the benefits from the asset. Control also includes the ability to prevent other companies from directing the use of and receiving the benefit from a good or service. Therefore, this agreement is a financing transaction and not a sale. Thus, the asset is not removed from the books of Morgan Inc.

Assuming that an interest rate of 10% is imputed from the agreement, Morgan Inc. makes the following entries to record this agreement. Morgan Inc. records the financing on January 1, 2020, as follows.

	January 1, 2020	
Cash	100,000	
Contract Liability		100,000

A	=	L	+	SE
+100,000		+100,000		

Cash flows: ↑ 100,000 inflow

Morgan Inc. records interest on December 31, 2020, as follows.

December 31, 2020

Interest Expense	10,000	
Contract Liability ($100,000 × 10%)		10,000

A	=	L	+	SE
		+10,000		−10,000

Cash flows: No effect

Morgan Inc. records interest and retirement of its liability to Lane Company as follows.

December 31, 2021

Interest Expense	11,000	
Contract Liability ($110,000 × 10%)		11,000
Contract Liability	121,000	
Cash ($100,000 + $10,000 + $11,000)		121,000

A	=	L	+	SE
−121,000		−110,000		−11,000

Cash flows: ▼ 121,000 outflow

Bill-and-Hold Arrangements

A **bill-and-hold arrangement** is a contract under which an entity bills a customer for a product but the entity retains physical possession of the product until it is transferred to the customer at a point in the future. Bill-and-hold sales result when the buyer is not yet ready to take delivery but does take title and accepts billing. For example, a customer may request that a company enter into such an arrangement because of (1) lack of available space for the product, (2) delays in its production schedule, or (3) more than sufficient inventory in its distribution channel. **Example 6.30** provides an example of a bill-and-hold arrangement.

Example 6.30 | Recognition—Bill and Hold

Facts Butler Company sells $450,000 (cost $280,000) of fireplaces on March 1, 2020, to a local coffee shop, Baristo, which is planning to expand its locations around the city. Under the agreement, Baristo asks Butler to retain these fireplaces in its warehouses until the new coffee shops that will house the fireplaces are ready. Title passes to Baristo at the time the agreement is signed.

Instructions When should Butler recognize the revenue from this bill-and-hold arrangement? Show journal entries.

Solution When to recognize revenue in a bill-and-hold arrangement depends on the circumstances. Butler determines when it has satisfied its performance obligation to transfer a product by evaluating when Baristo obtains control of that product. For Baristo to have obtained control of a product in a bill-and-hold arrangement, all of the following criteria should be met (IFRS 15.B81):

a. The reason to hold the inventory must be substantive.

b. The product must be identified separately and belong to Baristo.

c. The product must be ready to ship.

d. Butler cannot use the product nor sell it to another customer.

In this case, it appears that the above criteria were met, and therefore revenue recognition should be permitted at the time the contract is signed. Butler has transferred control to Baristo; that is, Butler has a right to payment for the fireplaces and legal title has transferred.

    Butler makes the following entry to record the bill-and-hold sale and related cost of goods sold.

March 1, 2020

Accounts Receivable	450,000	
Sales Revenue		450,000
Cost of Goods Sold	280,000	
Inventory		280,000

A	=	L	+	SE
+170,000				+170,000

Cash flows: No effect

Principal-Agent Relationships

In a **principal-agent relationship**, the principal's performance obligation is to provide goods or perform services for a customer. The agent's performance obligation is to arrange for the principal to provide these goods or services to a customer. Examples of principal-agent relationships are as follows.

- Preferred Travel Company (agent) facilitates the booking of cruise excursions by finding customers for Regency Cruise Company (principal).
- Pricey Limited (agent) facilitates the sale of various services such as car rentals at Hero Limited (principal).

In these types of situations, amounts collected on behalf of the principal are not revenue of the agent. Instead, revenue for the agent is the amount of the commission it receives (usually a percentage of the total sale price).

Example 6.31 provides an example of the issues related to principal-agent relationships.

Example 6.31 | Recognition—Principal-Agent Relationship

Facts   Fly-Away Travel sells airplane tickets for British Airways (BA) to various customers.

Instructions

a. What are the performance obligations in this situation?

b. How should revenue be recognized for both the principal and agent?

Solution

a. The principal in this case is BA and the agent is Fly-Away Travel. Because BA has the performance obligation to provide air transportation to the customer, it is the principal. Fly-Away Travel facilitates the sale of the airline ticket to the customer in exchange for a fee or commission. Its performance obligation is to arrange for BA to provide air transportation to the customer.

b. Although Fly-Away collects the full airfare from the customer, it then remits this amount to BA less the commission. Fly-Away therefore should not record the full amount of the fare as revenue on its books; to do so overstates revenue. Its revenue is the commission, not the full price. Control of performing the air transportation is with BA, not Fly-Away Travel.

Some might argue that there is no harm in letting Fly-Away record revenue for the full price of the ticket and then charging the cost of the ticket against the revenue. (This is often referred to as recognizing revenue on a gross basis.) Others note that this approach overstates the agent's revenue and is misleading. The revenue received is the commission for providing the travel services, not the full fare price. (This is often referred to as recognizing revenue on a net basis.)

There are specific criteria to determine when a principal-agent relationship exists.[47]

Consignments

A common principal-agent relationship involves consignments. In these cases, manufacturers (or wholesalers) deliver goods but retain title to the goods until they are sold. This specialized method of marketing certain types of products makes use of an agreement known as a **consignment**. Under this arrangement, the **consignor** (manufacturer or wholesaler) ships merchandise to the **consignee** (dealer), who is to act as an agent for the consignor in selling the merchandise. Both consignor and consignee are interested in selling—the consignor to make a profit or develop a market, the consignee to make a commission on the sale.

The consignee accepts the merchandise and agrees to exercise due diligence in caring for and selling it. The consignee remits to the consignor cash received from customers, after deducting a sales commission and any chargeable expenses. In consignment sales, the consignor

---

[47]Indicators that the company is an agent (and should recognize revenue in the net amount) include the following: (a) the other party is primarily responsible for fulfilling the contract, (b) the company does not have risks associated with the inventory, (c) the company does not have the ability to set selling prices, (d) the company receives commission, and (e) the company does not have customer credit risk for the amount receivable (IFRS 15.B37).

uses a modified version of the point-of-sale basis of revenue recognition. That is, the consignor recognizes revenue only after receiving notification of the sale and the cash remittance from the consignee.

The consignor carries the merchandise as inventory throughout the consignment, separately classified as Inventory (consignments). **The consignee does not record the merchandise as an asset on its books.** Upon sale of the merchandise, the consignee has **a liability for the net amount due to the consignor.** The consignor periodically receives from the consignee a report called **account sales** that shows the merchandise received, merchandise sold, expenses chargeable to the consignment, and cash remitted. Revenue is then recognized by the consignor. Analysis of a consignment arrangement is provided in **Example 6.32**.

Example 6.32 | Recognition—Sales on Consignment

Facts   Nelba Manufacturing Co. ships merchandise costing $36,000 on consignment to Best Value Stores. Nelba pays $3,750 of freight costs, and Best Value pays $2,250 for local advertising costs that are reimbursable from Nelba. By the end of the period, Best Value has sold two thirds of the consigned merchandise for $40,000 cash. Best Value notifies Nelba of the sales, retains a 10% commission, and remits the cash due to Nelba.

Instructions   What are the journal entries that the consignor (Nelba) and the consignee (Best Value) make to record this transaction?

Solution

NELBA MFG. CO. (Consignor)			BEST VALUE STORES (Consignee)		
Shipment of consigned merchandise					
Inventory on Consignment	36,000		No entry (record memo of merchandise received).		
Finished Goods Inventory		36,000			
Payment of freight costs by consignor					
Inventory on Consignment	3,750		No entry.		
Cash		3,750			
Payment of advertising by consignee					
No entry until notified.			Accounts Receivable	2,250	
			Cash		2,250
Sales of consigned merchandise					
No entry until notified.			Cash	40,000	
			Accounts Payable		40,000
Notification of sales and expenses and remittance of amount due					
Cash	33,750		Accounts Payable	40,000	
Advertising Expense	2,250		Accounts Receivable		2,250
Commission Expense	4,000		Revenue from		
Revenue from			Consignment Sales		4,000
Consignment Sales		40,000	Cash		33,750
Adjustment of inventory on consignment for cost of sales					
Cost of Goods Sold	26,500		No entry.		
Inventory on Consignment		26,500			
[2/3 ($36,000 + $3,750) = $26,500]					

Under the consignment arrangement, the consignor accepts the risk that the merchandise might not sell and relieves the consignee of the need to commit part of its working capital to inventory. Consignors use a variety of systems and account titles to record consignments, but they all share the common goal of postponing the recognition of revenue until it is known that a sale to a third party has occurred. **Consignees only recognize revenue from commissions.**

Summary of Other Revenue Recognition Issues

Illustration 6.13 provides a summary of the additional issues related to transfer of control and revenue recognition.

ILLUSTRATION 6.13

Summary—Other Revenue Recognition Issues

Issue	Description	Implementation
Repurchase agreements	Seller has an obligation or right to repurchase the asset at a later date.	Generally, if the company has an obligation to repurchase the asset for an amount greater than its selling price, then the transaction is a financing transaction.
Bill and hold	Results when the buyer is not yet ready to take delivery but takes title and accepts billing.	Revenue is recognized depending on when the customer obtains control of that product.
Principal-agent	Arrangement in which the principal's performance obligation is to provide goods or perform services for a customer. The agent's performance obligation is to arrange for the principal to provide these goods or services to a customer.	Amounts collected on behalf of the principal are not revenue of the agent. Instead, revenue for the agent is the amount of the commission it receives. The principal recognizes revenue when the goods or services are sold or provided to a third-party customer.
Consignments	A principal-agent relationship in which the consignor (manufacturer or wholesaler) ships merchandise to the consignee (dealer), who is to act as an agent for the consignor in selling the merchandise.	The consignor recognizes revenue only after receiving notification of the sale and the cash remittance from the consignee. (Consignor carries the merchandise as inventory throughout the consignment.) The consignee records commission revenue (usually some percentage of the selling price).

Presentation and Disclosure

LEARNING OBJECTIVE 10

Describe presentation and disclosure regarding revenue.

Presentation

When General Mills delivers cereal to a Loblaw Companies Limited warehouse (satisfying its performance obligation), it has a right to consideration from Loblaw and if this is a conditional right it would record a contract asset. If, on the other hand, Loblaw performs first, by prepaying for this cereal, General Mills has a contract liability. Companies must present these contract assets and contract liabilities on their balance sheets.

Contract Assets and Liabilities

Contracts with customers create contractual rights and obligations. Contractual rights are of two types:

1. **unconditional rights to receive consideration;** for instance, where the company has satisfied its performance obligation with a customer or the amounts due to the company are non-refundable; or

2. **conditional rights to receive consideration;** for instance, where the company has not satisfied the performance obligation or has satisfied one performance obligation but must satisfy another performance obligation in the contract before it is entitled to the consideration.

Companies should report unconditional rights to receive consideration as a receivable on the SFP. Conditional rights on the SFP should be reported separately as **contract assets**. **Example 6.33** provides an example of the accounting and reporting for a contract asset.[48]

Example 6.33 | Contract Asset Recognition and Presentation

Facts On January 1, 2020, Finn Company enters into a contract to transfer Product A and Product B to Obermine Co. for $100,000. The contract specifies that payment for Product A will not occur until Product B is also delivered. In other words, payment will not occur until both Product A and Product B are transferred to Obermine. Finn determines that stand-alone prices are $30,000 for Product A and $70,000 for Product B. Finn delivers Product A to Obermine on February 1, 2020. On March 1, 2020, Finn delivers Product B to Obermine.

Instructions What journal entries should Finn Company make in regard to this contract in 2020?

Solution No entry is required on January 1, 2020, because neither party has performed on the contract. On February 1, 2020, Finn records the following entry.

February 1, 2020

Contract Asset	30,000	
Sales Revenue		30,000

A	= L +	SE
+30,000		+30,000

Cash flows: No effect

On February 1, Finn has satisfied its performance obligation and therefore reports revenue of $30,000. However, it does not record an account receivable at this point because it does not have an unconditional right to receive the $100,000 unless it also transfers Product B to Obermine. In other words, a contract asset occurs generally when a company must satisfy another performance obligation before it is entitled to bill the customer. When Finn transfers Product B on March 1, 2020, it makes the following entry.

March 1, 2020

Accounts Receivable	100,000	
Contract Asset		30,000
Sales Revenue		70,000

A	= L +	SE
+70,000		+70,000

Cash flows: No effect

A **contract liability** is a company's obligation to transfer goods or services to a customer for which the company has received (or will receive) consideration from the customer. **Example 6.34** provides an example of the recognition and presentation of a contract liability.

Example 6.34 | Contract Liability Recognition and Presentation

Facts On March 1, 2020, Henly Company enters into a contract to transfer a product to Propel Inc. on July 31, 2020. Propel agrees to pay the full price of $10,000 in advance on April 15, 2020. Henly delivers the product on July 31, 2020. The cost of the product is $7,500.

Instructions What journal entries are required in 2020?

Solution No entry is required on March 1, 2020, because neither party has performed on the contract. On receiving the cash on April 15, 2020, Henly records the following entry.

April 15, 2020

Cash	10,000	
Unearned Revenue		10,000

A	=	L	+ SE
+10,000		+10,000	

Cash flows: ↑ 10,000 inflow

[48]Adapted from IFRS 15 Illustrative Example 39.

A	=	L	+	SE
−7,500		−10,000		+2,500

Cash flows: No effect

July 31, 2020

Unearned Revenue	10,000	
Sales Revenue		10,000

In addition, Henly records cost of goods sold as follows.

Cost of Goods Sold	7,500	
Inventory		7,500

Companies are not required to use the terms "contract assets" and "contract liabilities" on the Statement of Financial Position. For example, contract liabilities are performance obligations and therefore more descriptive titles (as noted earlier)—such as unearned revenue, repurchase liability, and return liability—may be used where appropriate. For contract assets, it is important that financial statement users can differentiate between unconditional and conditional rights through appropriate account presentation.

Costs to Obtain and/or Fulfill a Contract

Significant Change In the process of obtaining a contract, a company may incur costs such as commissions, legal fees, and proposal costs. These are treated as assets as long as they are incremental (that is, they would not be incurred unless the contract had been obtained) and recoverable.[49]

In completing the contract, the company also incurs costs known as **fulfillment costs**. These are the costs that the company must incur to fulfill the contract, once obtained. Examples of these include inventory costs; costs of constructing property, plant, or equipment; costs chargeable to the customer under the contract; payments to subcontractors; and others. If these costs are not covered by another standard (such as inventory costs or costs to create property, plant, or equipment/intangible assets), they may still be treated as assets as long as they **relate directly** to the contract, **enhance or create economic resources** that can be used in **future**, and are **recoverable**.[50]

Other costs that are expensed as incurred include **general and administrative** costs (unless those costs are explicitly chargeable to the customer under the contract) as well as costs of **wasted materials and labour**.

Illustration 6.14 summarizes these types of costs and their treatment.

ILLUSTRATION 6.14

Costs to Obtain and Fulfill a Contract

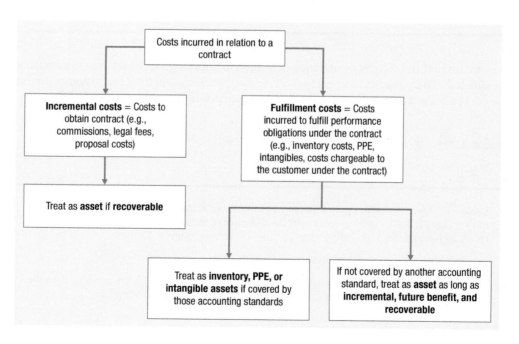

[49]IFRS 15.91.

[50]IFRS 15.95.

Example 6.35 provides an example of costs to obtain and to fulfill a contract.[51]

Example 6.35 | Contract Costs

Facts   Rock Integrators enters into a contract to operate Dello Company's information technology data centre for five years. Rock Integrators incurs selling commission costs of $10,000 to obtain the contract. Before performing the services, Rock Integrators designs and builds a technology platform that interfaces with Dello's systems. That platform is not transferred to Dello. Dello promises to pay a fixed fee of $20,000 per month. Rock Integrators incurs the following costs: design services for the platform $40,000, hardware for the platform $120,000, software $90,000, and migration and testing of data centre $100,000.

Instructions   What are Rock Integrators' costs for fulfilling the contract to Dello Company?

Solution   The $10,000 selling commission costs related to obtaining the contract are recognized as an asset. These are considered **incremental costs**. The design services, the hardware, and the software are also capitalized. These are considered **fulfillment costs** but are accounted for as property, plant, and equipment and intangible assets. The migration and testing costs may also be capitalized since they are direct, generate a future resource, and are recoverable. If these are not covered under IAS 16 or 38, they are capitalized as **fulfillment costs** under IFRS 15.

As a practical expedient, a company recognizes the incremental costs of obtaining a contract as an expense when incurred if the amortization period of the asset that the company otherwise would have recognized is one year or less. See **What do the Numbers Mean? 6.2**.

What Do the Numbers Mean? 6.2

Will the change in accounting for contract costs affect companies? This appears to be an area of concern for many companies in different industries. Interestingly, many companies report that, while they currently expense these costs, the new standard will require them to treat the costs as assets. Thus, income and assets will increase.

Below is an excerpt from the 2016 annual report for **Air Canada** (notes to financial statements).

> **IFRS 15 – Revenue from contracts with customers**
> IFRS 15 replaces IAS 18 Revenue and related interpretations. The core principle of the new standard is to recognize revenue to depict the transfer of goods of services to customers in amounts that reflect the consideration to which the company expects to be entitled in exchange for those goods or services. The new standard is intended to enhance disclosures about revenue, provide more comprehensive guidance for transactions that were not previously addressed and improve guidance for multiple-element arrangements. IFRS 15 is effective for annual periods beginning on January 1, 2018, with early adoption permitted.
> Air Canada will apply the standard effective January 1, 2018. The standard will be applied retrospectively with adjustment to the opening consolidated statement of financial position as at January 1, 2017. Under IFRS 15, incremental costs of obtaining passenger revenues, such as credit card fees and global distribution system charges, will be capitalized at time of sale and expensed at the time of passenger revenue recognition. Currently, these costs are expensed as incurred at the time the flight ticket is sold. With this change in accounting policy for contract costs, the timing of expense recognition will be impacted. Air Canada continues to evaluate the financial impact of this expected change to capitalize contract costs along with other possible impacts of this standard on its consolidated financial statements.

Depending on the time between sale of the airline tickets and the point in time when the passenger takes the flight, this could result in a change in the calculation of net income for the company.

Disclosure

IFRS   The disclosure requirements for revenue recognition are designed to help financial statement users understand the nature, amount, timing, and uncertainty of revenue and cash

---

[51]Adapted from IFRS 15 Illustrative Example 37.

flows arising from contracts with customers. To achieve that objective, companies disclose qualitative and quantitative information about all of the following:

- *Contracts with customers.* These disclosures include the disaggregation of revenue, presentation of opening and closing balances in contract assets and contract liabilities, and significant information related to their performance obligations.
- *Significant judgements.* These disclosures include judgements and changes in these judgements that affect the determination of the transaction price, the allocation of the transaction price, and the determination of the timing of revenue.
- *Assets recognized from costs incurred to fulfill a contract.* These disclosures include the closing balances of assets recognized to obtain or fulfill a contract, the amount of amortization recognized, and the method used for amortization.

To implement these requirements and meet the disclosure objectives, companies provide a range of disclosures, as summarized in **Illustration 6.15**.[52]

ILLUSTRATION 6.15

Revenue Disclosures

Disclosure Type	Requirements
Disaggregation of revenue	Disclose disaggregated revenue information in categories that depict how the nature, amount, timing, and uncertainty of revenue and cash flows are affected by economic factors. Reconcile disaggregated revenue to revenue for reportable segments.
Reconciliation of contract balances	Disclose opening and closing balances of contract assets (such as unbilled receivables) and liabilities (such as deferred revenue) and provide a qualitative description of significant changes in these amounts. Disclose the amount of revenue recognized in the current period relating to performance obligations satisfied in a prior period (such as from contracts with variable consideration). Disclose the opening and closing balances of trade receivables if not presented elsewhere.
Remaining performance obligations	Disclose the amount of the transaction price allocated to performance obligations of any remaining performance obligations not subject to significant revenue reversal. Provide a narrative discussion of potential additional revenue in constrained arrangements.
Costs to obtain or fulfill contracts	Disclose the closing balances of capitalized costs to obtain and fulfill a contract and the amount of amortization in the period. Disclose the method used to determine amortization for each reporting period.
Other qualitative disclosures	Disclose significant judgements and changes in judgements that affect the amount and timing of revenue from contracts with customers. Disclose how management determines the minimum amount of revenue not subject to the variable consideration constraint.

ASPE disclosure requirements include accounting policy and major revenue categories (only).

---

[52]See *PricewaterhouseCoopers Dataline* 2013–2014.

IFRS/ASPE Comparison

LEARNING OBJECTIVE 11
Identify differences in accounting between IFRS and ASPE and potential changes.

A Comparison of IFRS and ASPE

This was a very challenging chart for this particular chapter. The main reason is that ASPE has extremely little guidance and that IFRS 15 and supporting material has a significant amount of guidance. So in essence, almost everything appears to be different. Since IFRS 15 is new, it is difficult to assess the impact that it may have on practice and on the evolution of how ASPE is interpreted going forward. Therefore, in this chart, we have attempted to point out only a handful of differences that we think stand out at this point in time. Where ASPE is vague, this may not represent a difference in practice.

Illustration 6.16 presents a comparison of IFRS and ASPE related to revenue recognition.

ILLUSTRATION 6.16 **IFRS and ASPE Comparison Chart**

	IFRS 15	**Accounting Standards for Private Enterprises (ASPE)—*CPA Canada Handbook*, Part II, Section 3400**	**References related to examples, illustrations, and select brief exercises**
Recognition	Contract-based approach consists of five steps: **1.** Identify contract. **2.** Identify separate performance obligations (must be distinct and separately identifiable from other obligations in the contract). **3.** Determine transaction price (expected consideration). **4.** Allocate transaction price to each performance obligation on the basis of stand-alone value. **5.** Recognize revenue when performance obligation is satisfied (when control passes).	Earnings approach requires recognition when performance is achieved (risks and rewards have passed and services are rendered and measurable) and collectible.	Illustrations 6.2 and 6.12 Examples 6.6 and 6.28
	Recognize revenue for each distinct performance obligation at a point in time or over time. Recognize revenue over time only if one of the following is met: (1) the customer receives and consumes the benefit over time, (2) the customer controls the asset being created, or (3) the asset does not have any alternate use and the company has an enforceable right to payment.	Recognize over time for long-term contracts.	Illustration 6.10 and 6A.1 Examples 6.25, 6.26, and 6.27 BE 6.5, 6.7, and 6.20

(continued)

ILLUSTRATION 6.16 *(continued)*

	IFRS 15	Accounting Standards for Private Enterprises (ASPE)—*CPA Canada Handbook*, Part II, Section 3400	References related to examples, illustrations, and select brief exercises
Recognition *(continued)*	If providing goods and services together, must consider if performance obligations are interrelated. (If they are, treat as one performance obligation.)		
	Percentage-of-completion method is acceptable. See Appendix 6A.	Percentage-of-completion method is acceptable.	Illustrations 6A.1 and 6A.5
	May recognize revenue equal to cost if outcome is not determinable (zero-profit method). See Appendix 6A.	Use completed-contract method where percentage complete is not estimable. See Appendix 6A	Examples 6A.4 and 6A.5
	Assurance-type warranties are accrued as costs/liabilities and service-type warranties are treated as separate performance obligations (if sold separately).	Warranty costs have historically been accrued as costs/obligations when revenues recognized. More recently, these may have been accounted for as bundled sales (unearned revenues).	Illustration 6.5 In practice, the two standards are very similar. Example 6.12 and 6.13 BE 6.6, 6.23, and 6.24
Measurement	Transaction price is the amount that the entity expects to receive.	At transaction or consideration price, which is generally assumed to be fair value.	Illustrations 6.6 and 6.8 Example 6.17 BE 6.9, 6.10, 6.12
	Greater emphasis is placed on using measurement models to quantify risk/uncertainty.	Where payment is received over time, ASPE notes that the amount should be discounted using a prevailing market rate.	
	Guidance is provided as to how to calculate discount rate where the sale is financed. If the term is less than one year, there is no need to separate out the financing component.		
	Where variable consideration exists, revenue is recognized only if it is highly probable that a future reversal will not occur.		
	IAS 41 deals with biological assets. It still stands because the proposed standard does not cover these areas.	Accounting for biological assets is not explicitly discussed.	Illustration 8.18 (Chapter 8)
	The transaction price for transactions with multiple elements is allocated using relative value (although may estimate where not available and may use residual method to estimate). Specific guidance is given.	The transaction price for transactions with multiple elements is allocated using relative value or residual value method (choice).	In most cases relative value would be used so in practice, this would be similar.
	Where a right of return exists, a refund liability is recognized.	Where a right of return exists, sales returns and allowances are recognized as contra accounts to Revenues and Accounts Receivable.	Example 6.16

Looking Ahead

Given that ASPE guidance is general and high level, and IFRS 15 provides a fair bit of insight as to the nature of different revenue contracts, these insights may find their way into ASPE informally, even if the wording of the standard is not changed. The AcSB has issued a Discussion Paper dealing with the accounting issues in the agricultural industry in Canada (April 2017). Discussions were still in early stages in 2018.

Long-Term Contracts

Percentage-of-Completion Method

> **LEARNING OBJECTIVE 12**
> Apply the percentage-of-completion method for long-term contracts.

For the most part, companies recognize revenue at a point in time because that is when the control over the goods and services passes and the performance obligation is satisfied. Accounting for long-term contracts poses some challenges, however, because they have some unique features. Not only are they longer term (often spanning several reporting periods) but they often include unique contract terms, such as granting the ability to send progress billings. This right to bill helps the company finance the project. Examples of long-term contracts are construction-type contracts, development of military and commercial aircraft, weapons delivery systems, service contracts, and space exploration hardware.

We view some long-term contracts as a **series of distinct performance obligations** and therefore revenue is recognized over time as each performance obligation is satisfied (at various points in time throughout the life of the contract). For instance, when the project consists of separable units, such as a group of buildings, the contract may provide for delivery over time as each unit is complete. Revenue is recognized as each building is completed.

Significant Change As noted earlier in the chapter, under IFRS 15.35, a company satisfies a performance obligation and recognizes revenue over time **if** at least one of these criteria is met and the company is able to estimate progress toward completion:

1. The customer receives and consumes the benefit as the seller performs.
2. The customer controls the asset.
3. The company does not have an alternate use for the asset and has a right to payment for its performance.[53]

ASPE If at least one of these criteria is not met, then revenue is recognized at a point in time. ASPE criteria are more general, requiring that revenue reflect the work accomplished. This is not necessarily different but could result in differences in accounting in practice. **Illustration 6A.1** looks at some of the different outcomes in accounting for long-term contracts.

ILLUSTRATION 6A.1 Some Examples of Long-Term Contracts and Their Treatment under IFRS 15

Long-Term Contracts	Example	Accounting under IFRS	When to Recognize Revenue under IFRS 15
Many distinct performance obligations within a long-term contract	Three-year contract to build 50 planes	Treat as many performance obligations	As each performance obligation is completed
One performance obligation within a long-term contract and IFRS 15.35 criteria not met	Construction of hotel in downtown area	Treat as one performance obligation	Recognize revenue at the end when performance obligation satisfied

(continued)

---

[53]According to IFRS 15.37, the company must be entitled to an amount that would compensate the company for performance completed to date (even if the customer can terminate the contract for reasons other than the company's failure to perform as promised).

Long-Term Contracts	Example	Accounting under IFRS	When to Recognize Revenue under IFRS 15
One performance obligation within a long-term contract and IFRS 15.35 criteria met	Construction of satellite where company cannot sell to anyone else and has right to payment or construction of luxury cottage on customer-owned property	Treat as one performance obligation	Recognize revenue over time using **percentage-of-completion method** (or **zero-profit method**)
Many distinct performance obligations within a long-term contract but each is substantially the same and has the same pattern of transfer to the customer	Two-year contract to provide cleaning services on a monthly basis	Treat as one performance obligation	Recognize revenue over time using **percentage-of-completion method** or other method (such as **time-based method**, which recognizes revenue as time passes)

Alternative Terminology 6A.1

For construction contracts, Contract Assets may be referred to as "Construction in Process" and Contract Liabilities as "Billings." We will use the terms Contract Asset/Liability, since the amount is reported on a net basis and is more transparent in that it shows the net contract position.

IFRS If one of the criteria is met, **and if the company can reasonably estimate its progress toward satisfaction of the performance obligations, then the company recognizes revenue over time**. That is, it recognizes revenues and gross profits each period based upon the progress of the construction—referred to as the percentage-of-completion method. The company accumulates construction costs and progress billings in separate accounts that represent contractual rights and obligations (Contract Asset/Liability and Accounts Receivable; see Alternative Terminology 6A.1). If the company deferred recognition of these items until it completed the entire contract, it would misrepresent the efforts (costs) and accomplishments (revenues) of the accounting periods during the contract.

The rationale for using percentage-of-completion accounting is that, under most of these contracts, the buyer and seller have enforceable rights. The buyer has the legal right to require specific performance on the contract. The seller has the right to require progress payments that provide evidence of the buyer's ownership interest. As a result, a continuous sale occurs as the work progresses. Companies should recognize revenue according to that progression.

IFRS **ASPE** Under IFRS, if one of the IFRS 15.35 criteria is met but an estimate cannot be made, then the company records recoverable revenues equal to costs until the uncertainty is resolved. This is known as the zero-profit method. Under ASPE, the entity would use the completed-contract method in these circumstances and recognize revenues only at the end of the contract. We will discuss this further later in this appendix.

In order to apply the percentage-of-completion method, a company must have some basis or standard for measuring the progress toward completion at particular interim dates.

Measuring the Progress Toward Completion

Companies use various methods to determine the **extent of progress toward completion**. The most common are the cost-to-cost and units-of-delivery methods.

As indicated in the chapter, the objective of all these methods is to measure the extent of progress in terms of costs, units, or value added. Companies identify the various measures (costs incurred, labour hours worked, tonnes produced, floors completed, and so on) and classify them as input or output measures. Input measures (costs incurred, labour hours worked) are efforts devoted to a contract. Output measures (with units of delivery measured as such things as tonnes produced, floors of a building completed, and kilometres of a highway completed) track results. Neither measure is universally applicable to all long-term projects. Their use requires the exercise of judgement and careful tailoring to the circumstances.

Both input and output measures have certain disadvantages. The input measure is based on an established relationship between a unit of input and productivity. If inefficiencies cause the productivity relationship to change, inaccurate measurements result. Another potential problem is front-end loading, in which significant upfront costs result in higher estimates of completion. To avoid this problem, companies should disregard some early-stage construction costs—for example, costs of uninstalled materials or costs of subcontracts not yet performed—if they do not relate to contract performance.

Similarly, output measures can produce inaccurate results if the units used are not comparable in time, effort, or cost to complete. For example, using floors (storeys) completed can be deceiving. Completing the first floor of an eight-storey building may require more than one eighth of the total cost because of the substructure and foundation construction.

The most popular input measure used to determine the progress toward completion is the **cost-to-cost basis**. Under this basis, a company like CGI, the Montreal-based information technology consulting company, could measure the percentage of completion by comparing costs incurred to date with the most recent estimate of the total costs of the contract. **Illustration 6A.2** shows the formula for the cost-to-cost basis.

$$\frac{\text{Costs incurred to date}}{\text{Most recent estimate of total costs}} = \text{Percent complete}$$

ILLUSTRATION 6A.2

Formula for Percentage-of-Completion, Cost-to-Cost Basis

Once CGI knows the percentage that costs incurred represent of total estimated costs, it would apply that percentage to the total revenue and the estimated total gross profit on the contract. The resulting amount is the revenue or the gross profit to be recognized to date. **Illustration 6A.3** shows this calculation.

$$\begin{array}{c}\text{Percent}\\\text{complete}\end{array} \times \begin{array}{c}\text{Estimated total revenue}\\\text{(or gross profit)}\end{array} = \begin{array}{c}\text{Revenue (or gross}\\\text{profit) to be}\\\text{recognized to date}\end{array}$$

ILLUSTRATION 6A.3

Formula for Total Revenue (or Gross Profit) to Be Recognized to Date

To find the amounts of revenue and gross profit recognized each period, CGI would subtract total revenue or gross profit recognized in prior periods, as shown in **Illustration 6A.4**.

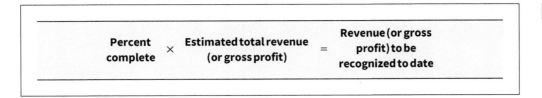

$$\begin{array}{c}\text{Revenue (or gross}\\\text{profit) to be}\\\text{recognized to date}\end{array} - \begin{array}{c}\text{Revenue (or gross}\\\text{profit) recognized}\\\text{in prior periods}\end{array} = \begin{array}{c}\text{Current-period}\\\text{revenue (or}\\\text{gross profit)}\end{array}$$

ILLUSTRATION 6A.4

Formula for Amount of Current-Period Revenue (or Gross Profit), Cost-to-Cost Basis

Because **the cost-to-cost method is widely used** (without excluding other bases for measuring progress toward completion), we have adopted it in our examples.

Examples 6A.1, **6A.2**, and **6A.3** illustrate the percentage-of-completion method.

Example 6A.1 | Application of Percentage-of-Completion Method, Cost-to-Cost Basis

Facts Assume that Hardhat Construction Company has a non-cancellable contract to construct a $4.5-million bridge at an estimated cost of $4 million. The contract is to start in July 2020, and the bridge is to be completed in October 2022. The following data pertain to the construction period. (Note that, by the end of 2021, Hardhat has revised the estimated total cost from $4,000,000 to $4,050,000.) Assume that progress billings are non-refundable.

	2020	2021	2022
Costs to date (12/31)	$1,000,000	$2,916,000	$4,050,000
Estimated costs to complete (12/31)	3,000,000	1,134,000	-0-
Progress billings during the year	900,000	2,400,000	1,200,000
Cash collected during the year	750,000	1,750,000	2,000,000

Instructions How would Hardhat calculate the percentage complete?

Solution

	2020	2021	2022
Contract price	$4,500,000	$4,500,000	$4,500,000
Less estimated cost:			
Costs to date	1,000,000	2,916,000	4,050,000
Estimated costs to complete	3,000,000	1,134,000	-0-
Estimated total costs	4,000,000	4,050,000	4,050,000
Estimated total gross profit	$ 500,000	$ 450,000	$ 450,000
Percent complete	25%	72%	100%
	$\left(\dfrac{\$1,000,000}{\$4,000,000}\right)$	$\left(\dfrac{\$2,916,000}{\$4,050,000}\right)$	$\left(\dfrac{\$4,050,000}{\$4,050,000}\right)$

Having calculated the percent complete, the next step is preparing the journal entry. Example 6A.2 looks at the journal entries for Hardhat.

Example 6A.2 | Application of Percentage-of-Completion Method, Cost-to-Cost Basis—Journal Entries

Facts Assume the same information as in Example 6A.1.

Instructions Prepare all journal entries required for Hardhat Construction to account for this contract.

Solution On the basis of the data above, Hardhat would make the following entries to record (1) the costs of construction, (2) progress billings, (3) collections, and (4) revenues and costs. These entries appear as summaries of the many transactions that would be entered individually as they occur during the year. Note that the amount of billings represents consideration that is unconditional because the contract is non-cancellable and the billings non-refundable. It is therefore recorded as Accounts Receivable. The entries are shown below.

	2020	2021	2022
Contract Asset/Liability	1,000,000	1,916,000	1,134,000
Materials, Cash,			
Payables	1,000,000	1,916,000	1,134,000
(To record cost of			
construction)			

	2020	2021	2022
Accounts Receivable	900,000	2,400,000	1,200,000
Contract Asset/Liability	900,000	2,400,000	1,200,000
(To record progress billings)			
The debit represents an unconditional right to receive consideration because the billings are non-refundable and the contract non-cancellable. The credit represents unearned revenue.			
Cash	750,000	1,750,000	2,000,000
Accounts Receivable	750,000	1,750,000	2,000,000
(To record collections)			
Contract Asset/Liability	1,125,000	2,115,000	1,260,000
Revenue from Long-Term Contracts	1,125,000	2,115,000	1,260,000
(To record revenues)			
Construction Expense	1,000,000	1,916,000	1,134,000
Contract Asset/Liability	1,000,000	1,916,000	1,134,000
(To record construction expense)			

In this example, the costs incurred to date are a measure of the extent of progress toward completion. To determine this, Hardhat evaluates the costs incurred to date as a proportion of the estimated total costs to be incurred on the project. The estimated revenues that Hardhat will recognize for each year are calculated as shown below.

	To Date	Recognized in Prior Years	Recognized in Current Year
2020			
Revenues ($4,500,000 × 25%)	$1,125,000		$1,125,000
Costs	1,000,000		1,000,000
Gross profit	$ 125,000		$ 125,000
2021			
Revenues ($4,500,000 × 72%)	$3,240,000	$1,125,000	$2,115,000
Costs	2,916,000	1,000,000	1,916,000
Gross profit	$ 324,000	$ 125,000	$ 199,000
2022			
Revenues ($4,500,000 × 100%)	$4,500,000	$3,240,000	$1,260,000
Costs	4,050,000	2,916,000	1,134,000
Gross profit	$ 450,000	$ 324,000	$ 126,000

Recall that the Hardhat Construction Company example contained a **change in estimated costs**: In the second year, 2021, it increased the estimated total costs from $4,000,000 to $4,050,000. The change in estimate is accounted for in a **cumulative catch-up manner**. This is done by first adjusting the percent completed to the new estimate of total costs. Next, Hardhat deducts the amount of revenues recognized in prior periods from revenues calculated for progress to date. That is, it accounts for the change in estimate in the period of change. That way, the statement of financial position at the end of the period of change and the accounting in subsequent periods are as they would have been if the revised estimate had been the original estimate.

Financial Statement Presentation—Percentage-of-Completion

During the life of the contract, Hardhat reports the contract asset/liability **as current** (assuming the related revenues will be earned in the following year). Accounts receivable are reported as current assuming they will be received within the following year. In general, the Contract Asset/ Liability position is shown net on the statement of financial position. A debit balance represents the excess of the amounts earned to date minus amounts billed. A credit balance represents the excess of amounts billed over amounts earned.

Example 6A.3 shows the financial statement presentation.

Example 6A.3 | Application of Percentage-of-Completion Method, Cost-to-Cost Basis—Presentation

Facts Assume the information from Examples 6A.1 and 6A.2.

Instructions How would Hardhat Construction Company present the information each year in the financial statements?

Solution Hardhat Construction Company would report the status and results of its long-term construction activities under the percentage-of-completion method as shown below for 2020, 2021, and 2022.

Hardhat Construction Company	
Income Statement	**2020**
Revenue from long-term contracts	$1,125,000
Construction expenses	1,000,000
Gross profit	$ 125,000
Balance Sheet (12/31)	**2020**
Current assets	
Accounts receivable ($900,000 – $750,000)	$ 150,000
Contract asset (net)	$ 225,000*
*($1,000,000 – $900,000 + $1,125,000 – $1,000,000)	

Hardhat Construction Company	
Income Statement	**2021**
Revenue from long-term contracts	$2,115,000
Construction expenses	1,916,000
Gross profit	$ 199,000
Balance Sheet (12/31)	**2021**
Current assets	
Accounts receivable ($150,000 + $2,400,000 – $1,750,000)	$ 800,000
Current liabilities	
Contract liability (net)	$ 60,000
($225,000 + $1,916,000 – $2,400,000 + $2,115,000 – $1,916,000)	

In 2022, presentation in Hardhat's financial statements affects only the income statement because the bridge project was completed and settled.

Hardhat Construction Company	
Income Statement	**2022**
Revenue from long-term contracts	$1,260,000
Construction expenses	1,134,000
Gross profit	$ 126,000

Zero-Profit Method

During the early stages of a contract, a company like Bombardier may not be able to estimate the outcome of the contract. As long as the company is confident that it will be able to recover costs incurred from the customer, it may use the zero-profit method. This method recognizes revenue equal to costs incurred as long as the costs are recoverable from the customer.

Example 6A.4 illustrates this method for the bridge project for Hardhat Construction Company.

IFRS Example 6A.4 | Zero-Profit Method, Revenue, Costs, and Profit by Year

Facts Assume the information given in Example 6A.1 for Hardhat Construction Company except assume that the company uses the zero-profit method.

Instructions

a. How much revenue and expense would Hardhat recognize each year over the life of the contract?

b. What would the journal entries be?

Solution

a. The company would report the following revenues over the life of the contract.

	To Date	Recognized in Prior Years	Recognized in Current Year
2020			
Revenues (= costs incurred)	$1,000,000		$1,000,000
Costs	1,000,000		1,000,000
Gross profit	$ 0		$ 0
2021			
Revenues (= costs incurred)	$2,916,000	$1,000,000	$1,916,000
Costs	2,916,000	1,000,000	1,916,000
Gross profit	$ 0	$ 0	$ 0
2022			
Revenues (= costs incurred)	$4,500,000	$2,916,000	$1,584,000
Costs	4,050,000	2,916,000	1,134,000
Gross profit	$ 450,000	$ 0	$ 450,000

b. The journal entries are shown below. These would replace the ones shown earlier in Example 6A.2 under the percentage-of-completion method for the recognition of construction revenue and expense. The first three entries in Example 6A.2 remain the same.

	2020		2021		2022	
Construction Expense	1,000,000		1,916,000		1,134,000	
Contract Asset/Liability		1,000,000		1,916,000		1,134,000
(To record construction expense)						
Contract Asset/Liability	1,000,000		1,916,000		1,584,000	
Revenue from Long-Term Contracts		1,000,000		1,916,000		1,584,000
(To record revenues)						

Completed-Contract Method

LEARNING OBJECTIVE 14

Apply the completed-contract method for long-term contracts.

ASPE Under ASPE and the completed-contract method, companies recognize revenue and gross profit when the contract is completed. Companies accumulate costs of long-term contracts in process, but they make no interim charges or credits to income statement accounts for revenues, costs, or gross profit. The completed-contract method is used where performance consists of a single act or the company is unable to estimate progress toward completion.

The main advantage of the completed-contract method is that reported revenue reflects final results rather than **estimates** of unperformed work. Its major disadvantage is that it does not reflect current performance when the period of a contract extends into more than one accounting period. Although operations may be fairly uniform during the period of the contract, the company will not report revenue until the year of completion, which distorts earnings.

Under the completed-contract method, the company would make the same **annual entries** to record costs of construction, progress billings, and collections from customers as those illustrated under the percentage-of-completion method. The significant difference is that the company **would not make entries to recognize revenue and construction expenses until the final year**.

Example 6A.5 shows the completed-contract method.

Example 6A.5 | Completed-Contract Method

Facts Assume the information given in Example 6A.1 for Hardhat Construction Company except assume that the company uses the completed-contract method.

Instructions What would the journal entries be?

Solution Hardhat Construction Company would make the same first three entries in Example 6A.2 each year, and the following entry in 2022 to recognize revenue and costs and to close out the inventory and billing accounts. As noted earlier, sometimes the Construction in Process account is used instead of Contract Asset/Liability.

Contract Asset/Liability	450,000	
Construction Expense	4,050,000	
Revenue from Long-Term Contracts		4,500,000

A	= L	+	SE
+450,000			+450,000

Cash flows: No effect

Illustration 6A.5 compares the amount of gross profit that Hardhat Construction Company would recognize for the bridge project under the three revenue recognition methods assuming that, under the zero-profit method, the outcome of the contract is finally determinable at the end of the contract. Note that, under the completed-contract and zero-profit methods, even though the profit recognized is the same, there is a difference in that, under the completed-contract method, no revenue is recognized at all until the final year, whereas under the zero-profit method, recoverable revenue equal to costs is recognized each year.

ILLUSTRATION 6A.5

ASPE IFRS Comparison of Gross Profit Recognized under Different Methods

	Percentage-of-Completion	Zero-Profit	Completed-Contract
2020	$125,000	$ –0–	$ –0–
2021	199,000	–0–	–0–
2022	126,000	450,000	450,000

Losses on Long-Term Contracts

LEARNING OBJECTIVE 15
Account for losses on long-term contracts.

Two types of losses can occur under long-term contracts:

1. **Loss in current period on a profitable contract:** This condition occurs when there is a significant increase in the estimated total contract costs during construction but the increase does not eliminate all profit on the contract. Under the percentage-of-completion method only, the increase in the estimated cost requires an adjustment in the current period for the excess gross profit that was recognized on the project in prior periods. This adjustment is recorded as a loss in the current period because it is a change in accounting estimate (discussed in Chapter 21). Under the other two methods, no profit has been recorded yet so there is no adjustment needed.

2. **Loss on an unprofitable contract:** Cost estimates at the end of the current period may indicate that a loss will result once the contract is completed. Under the percentage-of-completion, zero-profit, and completed-contract methods, the entire loss that is expected on the contract must be recognized in the current period.[54]

Loss in Current Period on a Profitable Contract

Example 6A.6 illustrates a loss in a current period on a profitable contract.

> ### Example 6A.6 | Loss in a Current Period on a Profitable Contract—Percentage-of-Completion Method, Cost-to-Cost
>
> **Facts** Assume the facts given in Example 6A.1 except assume that on December 31, 2021, Hardhat estimates the costs to complete the bridge contract at $1,468,962 instead of $1,134,000.
>
> **Instructions**
> **a.** How much loss would the company recognize in 2021?
> **b.** What would the journal entries be?
>
> **Solution** Hardhat would calculate the percent complete and recognize the loss as shown below. Compare these calculations with those for 2021 in Example 6A.1 and 6A.2. The percent complete has dropped from 72% to 66½% due to the increase in estimated future costs to complete the contract.
>
> | | |
> |---|---:|
> | Cost to date (12/31/21) | $2,916,000 |
> | Estimated costs to complete (revised) | 1,468,962 |
> | Estimated total costs | $4,384,962 |
> | Percent complete ($2,916,000 ÷ $4,384,962) | 66½% |
> | Revenue recognized in 2021 | |
> | ($4,500,000 × 66½%) − $1,125,000 | $1,867,500 |
> | Costs incurred in 2021 | 1,916,000 |
> | Loss recognized in 2021 | $ (48,500) |
>
> The loss of $48,500 in 2021 is a cumulative adjustment of the gross profit that was recognized on the contract in 2020. Instead of restating the prior period, the new estimation is absorbed entirely in the current period. In this illustration, the adjustment was large enough to result in recognition of a loss.

---

[54]The accounting for these contracts follows accounting for onerous contracts.

A	=	L	+	SE
−48,500				−48,500

Cash flows: No effect

Hardhat would record the loss in 2021 as follows:

Construction Expense	1,916,000	
Contract Asset/Liability		48,500
Revenue from Long-Term Contracts		1,867,500

The loss of $48,500 will be reported on the 2021 income statement as the difference between the reported revenues of $1,867,500 and the costs of $1,916,000.[55]

Under the **completed-contract** and **zero-profit methods**, no loss is recognized in 2021, because the contract is still expected to result in a profit that will be recognized in the year of completion.

Loss on an Unprofitable Contract

Where a contract becomes **onerous** (that is, the total estimated costs associated with the contract exceed the total revenues), the entity would recognize an overall loss. Any prior profits would be reversed and additional losses recognized. **Example 6A.7** illustrates a loss on an unprofitable contract.

Example 6A.7 | Loss in a Current Period on an Unprofitable Contract

Facts Assume the facts given in Example 6A.1 except assume that at December 31, 2021, Hardhat Construction Company estimates the costs to complete the bridge contract at $1,640,250 instead of $1,134,000. Revised estimates for the bridge contract are as follows.

	2020 Original Estimates	2021 Revised Estimates
Contract price	$4,500,000	$4,500,000
Estimated total cost	4,000,000	4,556,250*
Estimated gross profit	$ 500,000	
Estimated loss		$ (56,250)

*$2,916,000 + $1,640,250

Instructions How would Hardhat record the losses?

Solution Under the **percentage-of-completion method**, Hardhat recognized $125,000 of gross profit in 2020 (see Example 6A.2). This amount must be offset in 2021 because it is no longer expected to be realized. In addition, since losses must be recognized as soon as estimable, the company must recognize the total estimated loss of $56,250 in 2021. Therefore, Hardhat must recognize a total loss of $181,250 ($125,000 + $56,250) in 2021.

Revenue recognized in 2021:	
Contract price	$4,500,000
Percent complete (based on costs to date/total estimated costs)	× 64%*
Revenue recognizable to date	2,880,000
Less: Revenue recognized prior to 2021	1,125,000
Revenue recognized in 2021	$1,755,000

*$2,916,000/$4,556,250 = 64%

To calculate the construction costs to be expensed in 2021, Hardhat adds the total loss to be recognized in 2021 ($125,000 + $56,250) to the revenue to be recognized in 2021.

---

[55]In 2022, Hardhat will recognize the remaining $33\frac{1}{2}$% of the revenue ($1,507,500), with costs of $1,468,962 as expected, and report a gross profit of $38,538. The total gross profit over the three years of the contract would be $115,038 [$125,000 (2020) − $48,500 (2021) + $38,538 (2022)], which is the difference between the total contract revenue of $4,500,000 and the total contract costs of $4,384,962.

Revenue recognized in 2021			$1,755,000
Total loss recognized in 2021:			
Reversal of profit from 2020		$125,000	
Total estimated loss on contract		56,250	181,250
Construction cost expensed in 2021			$1,936,250

Hardhat Construction would record the long-term contract revenues, expenses, and loss in 2021 as follows.

Construction Expense	1,936,250	
Contract Asset/Liability		181,250
Revenue from Long-Term Contracts		1,755,000

A	= L +	SE
−181,250		−181,250

Cash flows: No effect

At the end of 2021, Contract Asset/Liability has a balance of $2,859,750, as shown below.

Contract Asset/Liability Account

Dr.		Cr.	
2020 Construction costs	1,000,000	2020 Billings	900,000
2020 Recognized gross profit	125,000	2021 Billings	2,400,000
2021 Construction costs	1,916,000	2021 Recognized loss	181,250
		Account Balance	**440,250**

Under the **zero-profit and completed-contract methods**, Hardhat would also recognize the contract loss of $56,250 through the following entry in 2021 (the year in which the loss first became evident):

Loss on Long-Term Contract	56,250	
Contract Asset/Liability		56,250

A	= L +	SE
−56,250		−56,250

Cash flows: No effect

Review and Practice

Summary of Learning Objectives

1. Understand the economics and legalities of selling transactions from a business perspective.

It is critical to understand a transaction from a business perspective before attempting to account for it. The analysis should begin with what is being sold to the customer (goods or services) and also the nature and amount of the consideration. When one party is in a better bargaining position than the other, it may be able to negotiate concessions such as more lenient payment terms. These concessions complicate the accounting because they introduce measurement uncertainty in many cases.

Selling transactions are based on contractual arrangements between a buyer and a seller. Contracts create rights and obligations under law that must be considered when accounting for the transactions. In addition to contract law, rights and obligations may exist under other forms of the law, such as common law or contract law. These should also be considered.

2. Identify the five steps in the revenue recognition process.

The five steps in the revenue recognition process are (1) identify the contract with customers, (2) identify the separate performance obligations in the contract, (3) determine the transaction price, (4) allocate the transaction price to the separate performance obligations, and (5) recognize revenue when each performance obligation is satisfied.

3. Identify the contract with customers.

A contract is an agreement that creates enforceable rights or obligations. A company applies the revenue guidance to contracts with customers and must determine if new performance obligations are created by a contract modification.

4. Identify the separate performance obligations in the contract.

A performance obligation is a promise in a contract to provide a product or service to a customer. A contract may be composed of multiple performance obligations. The accounting for multiple performance obligations is based on evaluation of whether the product or service is distinct within the contract. If each of the goods or services is distinct, but they are interdependent and interrelated, these goods and services are combined and reported as one performance obligation.

5. Determine the transaction price.

The transaction price is the amount of consideration that a company expects to receive from a customer in exchange for transferring goods and services. In determining the transaction price, companies must consider the following factors: (1) variable consideration, (2) time value of money, (3) non-cash consideration, and (4) consideration paid or payable to a customer.

---

6. Allocate the transaction price to the separate performance obligations.

If more than one performance obligation exists in a contract, allocate the transaction price based on relative values. The best measure of value is what the good or service could be sold for on a stand-alone basis (the stand-alone selling price). Estimates of stand-alone selling price can be based on (1) adjusted market assessment, (2) expected cost plus a margin approach, or (3) a residual approach.

---

7. Understand how to recognize revenue when the company satisfies its performance obligation.

A company satisfies its performance obligation when the customer obtains control of the good or service. Companies satisfy performance obligations either at a point in time or over a period of time. Companies recognize revenue over a period of time if (1) the customer controls the asset as it is created or the company does not have an alternative use for the asset, and (2) the company has a right to payment.

---

8. Analyze and determine whether a company has earned revenues under the earnings approach.

Under ASPE, the revenues are earned when the risks and rewards of ownership are passed or when the company has done what it said it would do to be entitled to the revenues. Where sales of goods are involved, legal title and possession provide evidence of this. The accounting is more complex when the contract is a long-term contract and when it involves both goods and services.

---

9. Identify other revenue recognition issues.

Refer to Illustration 6.13 for a summary of the accounting for (1) repurchase agreements, (2) bill-and-hold sales, (3) principal-agent relationships, and (4) consignments.

---

10. Describe presentation and disclosure regarding revenue.

Under the asset-liability approach, to recognize revenue, companies present contract assets and contract liabilities on their balance sheets (net). Contract assets are rights to receive consideration. A contract liability is a company's obligation to transfer goods or services to a customer for which the company has received consideration from the customer. Companies may also report assets associated with fulfillment costs and contract acquisition costs related to a revenue arrangement. Companies disclose qualitative and quantitative information about (1) contracts with customers with disaggregation of revenue, presentation of opening and closing

balances in contract assets and contract liabilities, and significant information related to their performance obligations; (2) significant judgements that affect the determination of the transaction price, the allocation of the transaction price, and the determination of the timing of revenue; and (3) assets recognized from costs incurred to fulfill a contract.

---

11. Identify differences in accounting between IFRS and ASPE and potential changes.

The main differences are identified in the chart in Illustration 6.16.

---

12. Apply the percentage-of-completion method for long-term contracts.

To apply the percentage-of-completion method to long-term contracts, a company must have some basis for measuring the progress toward completion at particular interim dates. One of the most popular input measures used to determine the progress toward completion is the cost-to-cost basis. Using this basis, a company measures the percentage of completion by comparing costs incurred to date with the most recent estimate of the total costs to complete the contract. The company applies that percentage to the total revenue or the estimated total gross profit on the contract, to arrive at the amount of revenue or gross profit to be recognized to date.

---

13. Apply the zero-profit method for long-term contracts.

Under this IFRS method, revenue equal to costs is recognized when the outcome is not determinable. This results in no profits being recognized. Otherwise the journal entries are the same as under the percentage-of-completion method.

---

14. Apply the completed-contract method for long-term contracts.

Under this ASPE method, companies recognize revenue and gross profit only when the company completes the contract. Therefore, unlike the zero-profit method, no revenue is recognized until the contract is completed. The company accumulates costs of long-term contracts in process and current billings. It makes no interim charges or credits to income statement accounts for revenues, costs, and gross profit. The annual journal entries to record costs of construction, progress billings, and collections from customers would be identical to those for the percentage-of-completion method—with the significant exclusion of the recognition of revenue and gross profit.

---

15. Account for losses on long-term contracts.

There are two types of situations: losses in the period on a profitable contract and losses on an unprofitable contract (onerous contracts). For all three methods of accounting for long-term contracts, the second type must be accrued for. The first type must only be adjusted for when using the percentage-of-completion method.

Practice Problem

Outback Industries manufactures emergency power equipment. Its most popular generator is a model called the E-Booster, which has a retail price of $1,500 and costs Outback $740 to manufacture. It sells the E-Booster on a stand-alone basis directly to businesses, and also provides installation services. Outback also distributes the E-Booster through a consignment agreement with Lenz Home Store. Income data for Outback's first quarter of 2020 from operations other than the E-Booster generator are as follows.

Revenues	$6,500,000
Expenses	4,350,000

Outback has the following information on four E-Booster revenue arrangements during the first quarter of 2020.

1. Outback entered into an arrangement with the Grocers Co-op to deliver E-Boosters for the meat lockers in the grocers' stores in Ottawa. Outback provides a 5% volume discount for E-Boosters purchased by Grocers Co-op if at least $450,000 of E-Boosters are purchased during 2020. By March 31, 2020, Outback has made sales of $360,000 ($1,500 × 240 generators) to Grocers Co-op. Based on prior experience with this promotion in two other cities, the discount threshold is met for the year if more than one half of the target had been met by mid-year.

2. On January 1, 2020, Outback sells 20 E-Boosters to Nick's Wholesale. Nick's signs a six-month note at an annual interest rate of 12%. Outback allows Nick's to return any E-Boosters that it cannot use within 120 days and receive a full refund. Based on experience, Outback estimates that three units will be returned (using the most likely outcome approach). Outback's costs to recover the products will be immaterial, and the returned generators are expected to be resold at a profit. No E-Boosters have been returned as at March 31, 2020, and Outback still estimates that three units will be returned in the future.

3. Outback sells 30 E-Boosters to First Bank, to provide uninterrupted power for bank branches with ATMs, for a total contract price of $50,000 including installation. In addition to the E-Boosters, Outback also provides installation at a stand-alone selling price of $200 per E-Booster; the cost to Outback to install is $150 per E-Booster. The E-Boosters are delivered and installed on March 1, 2020, and full payment is made to Outback.

4. Outback ships 300 E-Boosters to Lenz Home Store on consignment. By March 31, 2020, Lenz Home Store has sold three quarters of the consigned merchandise at the listed price of $1,500 per unit. Lenz Home Store notifies Outback of the sales, retains an 8% commission, and remits the cash due to Outback.

Instructions

a. Determine net income for Outback Industries for the first quarter of 2020. (Ignore taxes.)

b. In reviewing the credit history of Nick's Wholesale, Outback has some concerns about the collectibility of the full amount due on the note. Briefly discuss how collectibility of the note affects revenue recognition and income measurement for Outback assuming IFRS.

Solution

a. The amount of revenue and expense recognized on each of the arrangements is as follows.

1.	Sales revenue [95% × ($1,500 × 240)]	$342,000	
	Cost of goods sold ($740 × 240)	177,600	
	Gross profit		$164,400
2.	Sales revenue (20 × $1,500)	30,000	
	Less: Estimated returns (3 × $1,500)	4,500	
	Net sales	25,500	
	Cost of goods sold (17 × $740)	12,580	
	Gross profit	12,920	
	Interest revenue ($30,000 × 12% × 3/12)	900	
	Net income on this arrangement		13,820

3. The total transaction price of $50,000 is allocated between the equipment and installation. The transaction price for the equipment and installationis allocated based on relative stand-alone selling prices:

Equipment: $44,118 = ($45,000 ÷ $51,000*) × $50,000
Installation: $5,882 = ($6,000 ÷ $51,000) × $50,000

....

*$45,000 + $6,000

Sales revenue	$44,118		
Cost of goods sold (30 × $740)	22,200		
Gross profit		21,918	
Installation revenue	5,882		
Installation expense (30 × $150)	4,500		
Net profit		1,382	
Net income on this arrangement			23,300
4. Sales revenue (225* × $1,500)		337,500	
Cost of goods sold (225 × $740)		166,500	
Gross profit		171,000	
Commission expense ($337,500 × 8%)		27,000	
Net income on this arrangement			144,000
Net income on E-Booster			$345,520

....

*300 × 75%

Outback Industries' net income for the quarter: $6,500,000 − $4,350,000 + $345,520 = $2,495,520.

b. Whether a company will get paid for satisfying a performance obligation is not a consideration in determining revenue recognition. That is, the amount recognized is not adjusted for customer credit risk. If significant doubt exists at contract inception about collectibility, Outback reports the revenue gross and then presents an allowance for any impairment due to bad debts, which will reduce net income and which is reported as an operating expense in the income statement.

Key Terms

arm's length, p. 6-5
asset-liability approach, p. 6-10
assurance-type warranty, p. 6-18
barter transactions, p. 6-6
bill-and-hold arrangement, p. 6-39
breakage, p. 6-18
bundled sales, p. 6-4
commercial substance, p. 6-6
completed-contract method, p. 6-51
consignee, p. 6-40
consignment, p. 6-40
consignor, p. 6-40
constructive obligation, p. 6-9
contract, p. 6-13
contract assets, p. 6-43
contract liability, p. 6-43

contract modification, p. 6-15
control, p. 6-12
cost-to-cost basis, p. 6-51
credit risk, p. 6-6
earnings approach, p. 6-11
expected value, p. 6-21
f.o.b. destination, p. 6-9
f.o.b. shipping point, p. 6-9
fulfillment costs, p. 6-44
input measures, p. 6-51
legal title, p. 6-9
material right, p. 6-17
most likely amount, p. 6-21
multiple deliverables, p. 6-4
nonmonetary transactions, p. 6-6
output measures, p. 6-51

percentage-of-completion method, p. 6-50
performance obligation, p. 6-16
possession, p. 6-9
price risk, p. 6-7
principal-agent relationship, p. 6-39
repurchase agreements, p. 6-38
revenue recognition principle, p. 6-38
right of return, p. 6-22
service-type warranty, p. 6-18
stand-alone selling price, p. 6-28
transaction price, p. 6-21
upfront fees, p. 6-19
volume discount, p. 6-23
warranties, p. 6-18
zero-profit method, p. 6-51

Assignment Material

Note: All assignment material with an asterisk (*) relates to the appendix to the chapter.

Enabling Competencies Completion of this end-of-chapter material will help develop CPA-enabling competencies (such as ethics and professionalism, problem-solving and decision-making, and communication) and technical competencies. We have highlighted selected items with a specific integration word mark and material in *Wiley PLUS* has been linked to the competencies. All cases emphasize integration, especially of the enabling competencies. The brief exercises, exercises, and problems generally emphasize problem-solving and decision-making.

Brief Exercises

BE6.1 (LO 1) Explain the basic economics of what is being received and what is being given up in each of the following business transactions.

a. A company sells packaging material to another company. The terms of sale require full payment upon delivery.

b. A company sells packaging material to another company. The terms of sale require payment over one year with interest.

c. A law firm provides legal services to an accounting firm. In lieu of payment, the accounting firm provides accounting services to the law firm.

d. A company sells telecommunications equipment for a set fee that includes delivery, installation, a 60-day trial period, a three-year maintenance package (often sold separately), and a one-year warranty (often sold separately). Payment will be received over one year without interest.

BE6.2 (LO 1) `Law` Explain the rights and obligations created in the following transactions.

a. A manufacturer sells goods with terms f.o.b. shipping point.

b. A manufacturer sells goods with terms f.o.b. destination.

c. A manufacturer sells goods with terms f.o.b. shipping point, but routinely replaces products lost or damaged during shipping.

BE6.3 (LO 1, 8) XYZ Company has manufactured a new product that will be marketed and sold during the current year. To encourage distributors to carry the product, XYZ will not require payment until the distributor receives the final payment from its customers. This is not a normal business practice for XYZ Company. Should XYZ record revenue from the new product upon delivery to its distributors under the earnings approach? Why or why not?

BE6.4 (LO 3) On May 10, 2020, Cosmo Co. enters into a contract to deliver a product to Greig Inc. on June 15, 2020. Greig agrees to pay the full price of $2,000 on July 15, 2020. The cost of goods is $1,300. Cosmo delivers the product to Greig on June 15, 2020, and receives payment on July 15, 2020. Prepare the journal entries for Cosmo related to this contract.

BE6.5 (LO 4) Ellicott Construction enters into a contract to design and build a hospital. Ellicott is responsible for the overall management of the project and identifies various goods and services to be provided, including engineering, site clearance, foundation, procurement, construction of the structure, piping and wiring, installation of equipment, and finishing. Under IFRS, does Ellicott have a single performance obligation to the customer in this revenue arrangement? Explain.

BE6.6 (LO 4) Talarczyk Company sold 10,000 Super Spreaders on July 1, 2020, at a total price of $1 million, with a warranty guarantee that the product was free of any defects. The cost of the spreaders sold is $550,000. The assurance warranties extend for a two-year period and are estimated to cost $40,000. Talarczyk also sold extended warranties (service-type warranties) related to 2,000 spreaders for two years beyond the two-year period for $12,000. Prepare the journal entries that Talarczyk should make in 2020 related to the sale and the related warranties.

BE6.7 (LO 4) Nate Beggs signs a one-year contract with BlueBox Video. The terms of the contract are that Nate is required to pay a non-refundable initiation fee of $100. After the first year, Nate can renew his membership by paying an annual membership fee of $5 per month. BlueBox determines that its customers, on average, renew their annual membership three times after the first year before terminating their membership. What amount of revenue should BlueBox recognize in its first year given that the membership renewal is a material right? The company follows IFRS.

BE6.8 (LO 5) Massey Ltd., an equipment manufacturer, sold and delivered a piece of equipment to a buyer for $100,000, with 50% payable in one year and the remaining 50% payable in two years from the date of sale. Massey estimates that the interest rate for a similar financing arrangement would be 12%. Calculate the amount of revenue that Massey should recognize on the date of sale using Excel or a financial calculator.

BE6.9 (LO 5) Nair Corp. enters into a contract with a customer to build an apartment building for $1 million. The customer hopes to rent apartments at the beginning of the school year and offers a performance bonus of $150,000 to be paid if the building is ready for rental beginning August 1, 2020. The bonus is reduced by $50,000 each week that completion is delayed. Nair commonly includes these completion bonuses in its contracts and, based on prior experience, estimates the following completion outcomes:

Completed by	Probability
August 1, 2020	70%
August 8, 2020	20
August 15, 2020	5
After August 15, 2020	5

Determine the transaction price for this contract under IFRS.

BE6.10 (LO 5) Referring to the revenue arrangement in BE6.9, determine the transaction price for this contract, assuming (a) Nair is only able to estimate whether the building can be completed by August 1, 2020, or not (Nair estimates that there is a 70% chance that the building will be completed by August 1, 2020); and (b) Nair has limited information with which to develop a reliable estimate of completion by the August 1, 2020 deadline.

BE6.11 (LO 5) **Excel** On January 2, 2020, Adani Inc. sells goods to Geo Company in exchange for a zero-interest-bearing note with a face value of $11,000, with payment due in 12 months. The fair value of the goods at the date of sale is $10,000 (cost $6,000). Assume that the company chooses to reflect the interest component. (a) Prepare the journal entries to record this transaction on January 2, 2020. (b) How much total revenue should be recognized in 2020? (c) Using Excel or a financial calculator, determine the interest rate that will be earned by Adani.

BE6.12 (LO 5) **Excel** On March 1, 2020, Parnevik Company sold goods to Goosen Inc. for $660,000 in exchange for a five-year, zero-interest-bearing note in the face amount of $1,062,937. The goods have an inventory cost on Parnevik's books of $400,000. (a) Determine the effective interest rate imputed in the note using Excel or a financial calculator. Prepare the journal entries for Parnevik on (b) March 1, 2020, and (c) December 31, 2020.

BE6.13 (LO 5) On July 10, 2020, Amodt Ltd. sold GPS systems to retailers on account for a selling price of $700,000 (cost $560,000). Amodt grants the right to return systems that do not sell in three months following delivery. Past experience indicates that the normal return rate is 15%. By October 11, 2020, retailers returned systems to Amodt and were granted credits of $78,000. Prepare Amodt's journal entries to record (a) the sale on July 10, 2020, including any expected returns, and (b) the $78,000 of actual returns on October 10, 2020. The company follows IFRS.

BE6.14 (LO 5, 11) Use the information for Amodt Ltd. in BE6.13 and assume instead that the company follows ASPE. Follow the same instructions as in parts (a) and (b) in BE6.13.

BE6.15 (LO 5) Kristin Company sells 300 units of its products for $20 each to Logan Inc. for cash. Kristin allows Logan to return any unused product within 30 days and receive a full refund. The cost of each product is $12. To determine the transaction price, Kristin decides that the approach that is most predictive of the amount of consideration to which it will be entitled is the probability-weighted amount. Using the probability-weighted amount, Kristin estimates that (1) 10 products will be returned, and (2) the returned products are expected to be resold at a profit. Prepare the journal entries for Kristin at the time of the sale to Logan including any expected returns. The company follows IFRS.

BE6.16 (LO 5, 11) Manual Company sells goods to Nolan Company during 2020. It offers Nolan the following rebates based on total sales to Nolan. If total sales to Nolan are 10,000 units, it will grant a rebate of 2%. If it sells up to 20,000 units, it will grant a rebate of 4%. It if sells up to 30,000 units, it will grant a rebate of 6%. In the first quarter of the year, Manual sells 11,000 units to Nolan at a sales price of $110,000. Based on past experience, Manual has sold over 40,000 units to Nolan, and these sales normally take place in the third quarter of the year. Prepare the journal entries including any rebates that Manual should make to record the sale of the 11,000 units in the first quarter of the year assuming (a) Manual follows IFRS and (b) Manual follows ASPE. Ignore any cost of goods sold entry.

BE6.17 (LO 5) During February 2020, Master Massage Ltd. sells $10,000 of gift cards for Valentine's Day gifts. From reliable past experience, management estimates that 10% of the gift cards sold will not be redeemed. By the end of February, $4,000 was redeemed by customers. Prepare the journal entries for Master Massage for February 2020. Round to the nearest dollar.

BE6.18 (LO 6) Telephone Sellers Inc. sells prepaid telephone cards to customers. Telephone Sellers then pays the telecommunications company, TeleExpress, for the actual use of its telephone lines related to the prepaid telephone cards. Assume that Telephone Sellers sells $4,000 of prepaid cards in January 2020. It then pays TeleExpress based on usage, which turns out to be 50% in February, 30% in March, and 20% in April. The total payment by Telephone Sellers for TeleExpress lines over the three months is $3,000. Indicate how much income Telephone Sellers should recognize in January, February, March, and April under IFRS.

BE6.19 (LO 7) Mauer Company follows IFRS and sells consumer-relationship software to Hedges Inc. to be used for three years. In addition to providing the software, Mauer promises to provide consulting services over the life of the contract to maintain operability within Hedges' computer system. The total transaction price is $200,000. Based on stand-alone values, Mauer estimates the consulting services have a value of $75,000 and the software has a value of $125,000. Upon installation of the software on July 1, 2020, Hedges pays $100,000; the contract balance is due on December 31, 2020. Identify the performance obligations and the revenue in 2020, assuming (a) the performance obligations are interdependent, and (b) the performance obligations are not interdependent.

BE6.20 (LO 2, 6, 7) Geraths Windows manufactures and sells custom storm windows for three-season porches. Geraths also provides installation service for the windows. The installation process does not involve changes in the windows, so this service can be performed by other vendors. Geraths enters into the following non-cancellable contract on July 1, 2020, with a local homeowner. The customer purchases windows for a price of $2,400 and chooses Geraths to do the installation. Geraths charges the same price for the windows regardless of whether it does the installation or not. The price of the installation service is estimated to have a fair value of $600. The customer pays Geraths $2,000 (which equals the fair value of the windows, which have a cost of $1,100) upon delivery and the remaining balance upon installation of the windows. The windows are delivered on September 1, 2020, Geraths completes installation on October 15, 2020, and the customer pays the balance due. Using the five-step process for revenue recognition, determine when and how much revenue would be recognized by Geraths. Round percentage allocations to two decimal places and final amounts to the nearest dollar. Assume Geraths follows IFRS.

BE6.21 (LO 6, 7) Refer to the revenue arrangement in BE6.20. Prepare the journal entries for Geraths on July 1, September 1, and October 15, 2020.

BE6.22 (LO 6, 7) Refer to the revenue arrangement in BE6.20 and BE6.21. Perform step 4 of the five-step process for revenue recognition. Round percentage allocations to two decimal places and final amounts to the nearest dollar and prepare the journal entries for Geraths assuming (a) Geraths estimates the stand-alone value of the installation based on an estimated cost of $400 plus a margin of 20% on cost, and (b) given the uncertainty of finding skilled labour, Geraths is unable to develop a reliable estimate for the fair value of the installation.

BE6.23 (LO 2, 8) What is the earnings process under ASPE for each of the following scenarios?

a. A manufacturer makes and sells farm equipment. The customer picks up the equipment upon purchase. In addition, there is a one-year warranty that will be honoured by another company.

b. A company sells books online and ships to the customer. Payment is made via credit cards and the company does not accept any product returns.

c. A company provides cable television services for residential customers. The customer signs a three-year contract. The wiring was already in place from the prior homeowner.

BE6.24 (LO 8) For each of the scenarios noted in BE6.23, when would revenue be recognized under the earnings approach?

BE6.25 (LO 9) On August 15, 2020, Japan Ideas consigned 500 electronic play systems, costing $100 each, to YoYo Toys Company. The cost of shipping the play systems amounted to $1,250 and was paid by Japan Ideas. On December 31, 2020, an account sales summary was received from the consignee, reporting that 420 play systems had been sold for $160 each. Remittance was made by the consignee for the amount due, after deducting a 20% commission. Calculate the following at December 31, 2020.

a. The inventory value of the units unsold in the hands of the consignee.

b. The profit for the consignor for the units sold.

c. The amount of cash that will be remitted by the consignee.

BE6.26 (LO 9) On June 1, 2020, Mills Company sells $200,000 of shelving units to a local retailer, Shop-Barb, which is planning to expand its stores in the area. Under the agreement, ShopBarb asks Mills to retain the shelving units at its factory until the new stores are ready for installation. Title passes to Shop-Barb at the time the agreement is signed. The shelving units are delivered to the stores on September 1, 2020, and ShopBarb pays in full. Prepare the journal entries for this bill-and-hold arrangement (assuming that conditions for recognizing the sale have been met) for Mills on June 1 and September 1, 2020. The cost of the shelving units to Mills is $110,000.

BE6.27 (LO 9) Travel Inc. sells tickets for a Caribbean cruise on ShipAway Cruise Lines to Carmel Company employees. The total cruise package price to Carmel Company employees is $70,000. Travel Inc. receives a commission of 6% of the total price. Travel Inc. therefore remits $65,800 to ShipAway. Prepare the journal entry to record the remittance and revenue recognized by Travel Inc. on this transaction.

BE6.28 (LO 9) Jansen Corporation shipped $20,000 of merchandise on consignment to Gooch Company. Jansen paid freight costs of $2,000. Gooch Company paid $500 for local advertising, which is reimbursable from Jansen. By year end, 60% of the merchandise had been sold for $21,500. Gooch notified Jansen, retained a 10% commission, and remitted the cash due to Jansen. Prepare Jansen's journal entry when cash is received.

BE6.29 (LO 9, 10) On May 1, 2020, Mount Company enters into a contract to transfer a product to Eric Company on September 30, 2020. It is agreed that Eric will pay the full price of $25,000 in advance on June 15, 2020. Eric pays on June 15, 2020, and Mount delivers the product on September 30, 2020, which cost $18,000. Prepare the journal entries required for Mount in 2020.

BE6.30 (LO 10) Icon Construction Ltd. paid the following costs. For each item listed, determine if the costs are: (a) incremental costs to obtain a contract or (b) fulfillment costs incurred to perform the obligations under a contract.

1. Consulting fee for drafting a bid to submit a sealed tender.
2. Engineering fees to obtain building permits.
3. Legal fees for reviewing the bid.
4. Project staff costs for drafting documents for the bid submission.
5. Project management staff salaries for developing construction work schedules.
6. Performance bond secured to permit submission of the bid.
7. Engineering fees for environmental impact of waste disposal on construction, incurred during the bidding process.
8. Project management staff salaries for coordinating subcontract bids integrated into the tender during the bidding process.
9. Drawings for tender submission.
10. Cost of project mock-ups required in bid submission.

BE6.31 (LO 12) Turner Inc. began work on a $7-million non-cancellable contract in 2020 to construct an office building. During 2020, Turner Inc. incurred costs of $1.7 million, billed its customers for $1.2 million (non-refundable), and collected $960,000. At December 31, 2020, the estimated future costs to complete the project totalled $3.3 million. Prepare Turner's 2020 journal entries using the percentage-of-completion method.

BE6.32 (LO 10, 14) Guillen Inc. began work on a $7-million non-cancellable contract in 2020 to construct an office building. Guillen uses the completed-contract method under ASPE. At December 31, 2020, the balances in certain accounts were Contract Asset/Liability $715,000 (debit balance) and Accounts Receivable $240,000.

a. Indicate how these accounts would be reported in Guillen's December 31, 2020 statement of financial position (SFP).

b. Repeat part (a) assuming instead that the Contract Asset/Liability account had a credit balance of $215,000.

BE6.33 (LO 10, 12, 14) During 2020, Darwin Corporation started a construction job with a contract price of $4.2 million. Darwin ran into severe technical difficulties during construction but managed to complete the job in 2022. The contract is non-cancellable. Under the terms of the contract, Darwin sends billings as revenues are earned. Billings are non-refundable. The following information is available:

	2020	2021	2022
Costs incurred to date	$ 600,000	$2,100,000	$4,100,000
Estimated costs to complete	3,150,000	2,100,000	–0–

a. Calculate the amount of gross profit that should be recognized each year under the percentage-of-completion method.

b. Prepare the year-end journal entries for 2021 to record revenues and expenses from the contract, assuming the percentage-of-completion method is used. Explain the treatment of the reduction in overall gross profit under the percentage-of-completion method.

c. Calculate the amount of gross profit or loss that should be recognized each year under the completed-contract method. Explain the treatment of losses under the completed-contract method.

BE6.34 (LO 13) Assume the facts given in BE6.33 for Darwin Corporation. Calculate the amount of gross profit or loss that should be recognized each year under the zero-profit method.

BE6.35 (LO 12, 13, 14) Assume the facts given in BE6.33 for Darwin Corporation. Assume billings for the construction contract were as follows: 2020, $500,000; 2021, $2 million; and 2022, $1.7 million. Calculate the balance of the Contract Asset/Liability account at the end of each year using (a) the percentage-of-completion method and (b) the zero-profit and completed-contract methods.

*BE6.36 **(LO 15)** Inexperienced construction company Martin Corp. signed a risky non-cancellable contract to build a research facility at a fixed contract amount of $2 million. The work began in early 2020 and Martin incurred costs of $900,000. At December 31, 2020, the estimated future costs to complete the project totalled $900,000. During 2021, Martin ran into trouble with weather conditions and incurred the expected costs of $900,000 and estimated that it would need to spend an additional $300,000 to complete the project. During 2022, Martin reluctantly completed the project, incurring further costs of $350,000. Calculate the amount of gross profit or loss that should be recognized each year under the percentage-of-completion method and prepare the December 31, 2021 year-end journal entry to record costs, revenues, expenses, and losses from the contract. Round the percent complete to four decimal places.

*BE6.37 **(LO 15)** Assume the facts given in BE6.36 for Martin Corp. Prepare the December 31, 2021 year-end journal entry to record any loss from the contract assuming Martin uses the completed-contract method.

Exercises

E6.1 **(LO 1)** **(Economics of the Transaction—Various Consumer Industries)** The following are independent situations that require professional judgement for determining when to recognize revenue from the transactions.

1. Costco sells you a one-year membership with a single, one-time upfront payment. This non-refundable fee is paid at the time of signing the contract, and entitles you to shop at Costco for one year.

2. DOT Home and Patio sells you patio furniture on a "no money down, no interest, and no payments for one year" promotional deal. The furniture is delivered to your home the same day.

3. The Toronto Blue Jays sell season tickets online to games in the Rogers Centre. Fans can purchase the tickets at any time, although the season does not officially begin until April 1. The season runs from April 1 through September each year. Payment is due in full at the time of purchase.

4. CIBC lends you money in August. The loan and interest are repayable in full in two years.

5. Students pre-register for fall classes at Seneca College in August. The fall term runs from September to December.

6. Hudson's Bay Company (HBC) sells you a sweater. In August, you place an online order. The sweater is shipped and arrives in September and you charge it to your HBC credit card. In October, you receive the HBC credit card statement and pay the amount due.

7. In March, Hometown Appliances sells a washing machine with an extended warranty plan for five years. The washing machine will not be delivered to the customer until June. Payment is due upon delivery. The extended warranty plans are normally sold separately.

8. Premier Health Clubs sells you a membership with an initiation fee (which covers a medical assessment) and an ongoing monthly fee. The initiation fee is payable at the time of the medical assessment and approximates the cost of the medical assessment.

Instructions

For each scenario, identify what is being "sold": goods, services, or a combination.

E6.2 **(LO 4, 10)** **(Service Contracts)** Best Lawn Care Inc. (BLC) offers its customers two lawn maintenance services. One service is for a one-year maintenance plan at a cost of $200. Customers can earn a 5% discount from this price if they pay before BLC's calendar fiscal year for maintenance services to be performed in the following year. The second service offered by BLC is a three-year maintenance plan that sells for $500. The first year's maintenance service for this three-year plan will be delivered before BLC's fiscal year end. No discount for early payment is offered for the second plan.

Instructions

a. Prepare the summary journal entry for the cash sale of 200 one-time plans for the current year, 100 discounted one-time plans for the following year, and 300 three-year maintenance plans.

b. Determine the statement of financial position (SFP) classification of the unearned portion of the revenue collected.

E6.3 **(LO 4, 11)** **(Loyalty Programs)** To increase sales, Letourneau Inc., a public company following IFRS, implemented a customer loyalty program that rewards a customer with one loyalty point for every $30 of merchandise purchased. Each point is redeemable for a $2.50 discount on any purchases of Letourneau merchandise in the next three years. After the program launched, during 2020, customers bought merchandise for $300,000 (all products are sold to provide a 35% gross profit) and earned 10,000 points redeemable for future purchases. The stand-alone selling price of the merchandise sold is $300,000. Based on prior experience with incentive programs like this, Letourneau expects 7,500 points to be redeemed related to these sales.

Instructions

a. Identify the separate performance obligation in the Letourneau bonus point program, and briefly explain the point in time when the performance obligations are satisfied. Round percentage allocations to two decimal places and final amounts to the nearest dollar.

b. Prepare the journal entries for cash sales including the issuance of loyalty points for Letourneau in 2020.

c. Would the accounting of the customer loyalty program be different if Letourneau had been following ASPE?

E6.4 (LO 4) (Warranty Arrangement) On December 31, 2020, Grando Company sells production equipment to Fargo Inc. for $50,000. Grando includes a one-year assurance warranty service with the sale of all its equipment. The customer receives and pays for the equipment on December 31, 2020. Grando estimates the prices to be $48,800 for the equipment and $1,200 for the cost of warranty.

Instructions

a. Are the sale of the equipment and the warranty separate performance obligations within the contract? Explain.

b. Prepare the journal entry to record this transaction on December 31, 2020. Ignore any related cost of goods sold entry.

c. Repeat the requirements for part (a), assuming that, in addition to the assurance warranty, Grando sold an extended warranty (service-type warranty) for an additional two years (2022–2023) for $800.

E6.5 (LO 4) (Warranties) Celic Inc. manufactures and sells computers that include an assurance-type warranty for 90 days. Celic offers an optional extended coverage plan under which it will repair or replace any defective part for three years from the expiration of the assurance-type warranty. Because the optional extended coverage plan is sold separately, Celic determines that the three years of the extended coverage represent a separate performance obligation. The total transaction price for the sale of a computer and the extended warranty is $3,600 on October 1, 2020. Celic determines that the stand-alone selling price of each is $3,200 and $400, respectively. Further, Celic estimates, based on historical experience, that it will incur $200 in costs to repair defects that arise within the 90-day coverage period for the assurance-type warranty. The cost of the equipment is $1,440.

Instructions

a. Are the computer and warranties distinct within the contract? Explain.

b. Prepare the journal entry (or entries) to record the cash sale of the computer, cost of goods sold, and liabilities related to the warranties.

c. Briefly describe the accounting for the service-type warranty after the 90-day assurance-type warranty period.

E6.6 (LO 5) (Transaction Price) Presented below are four revenue recognition situations.

1. Grupo sells goods to MTN for $1 million, payment due at delivery.

2. Grupo sells goods on account to Grifols for $800,000, payment due in 30 days. The terms are f.o.b. destination.

3. Grupo sells goods to Magnus for $500,000, payment due in two instalments: the first instalment payable in 18 months, and the second payment due 6 months later. The present value of the future payments is $464,000.

4. Grupo sells merchandise with a retail price of $45,000 in exchange for common shares of its customer. The customer is a private company and issuance of common shares is rare.

Instructions

Indicate the transaction price for each of these transactions and when revenue will be recognized.

E6.7 (LO 5) (Variable Consideration) Blair Biotech enters into a licensing agreement with Pang Pharmaceutical for a drug under development. Blair will receive a payment of $10,000 if the drug receives regulatory approval. Based on prior experience with the drug-approval process, Blair determines it is 90% likely that the drug will gain approval, with a 10% chance of denial.

Instructions

a. Determine the transaction price of the arrangement for Blair Biotech.

b. Assuming that regulatory approval was granted on December 20, 2020, and that Blair received the payment from Pang on January 15, 2021, prepare the journal entries for Blair.

E6.8 (LO 5) `Excel` **(Trailing Commission)** Aaron's Agency sells an insurance policy offered by Capital Insurance Company for a commission of $100. In addition, Aaron will receive a further commission of $10 each year for as long as the policyholder does not cancel the policy. After selling the policy, Aaron does not have any remaining performance obligations. Based on its significant experience with these types of policies, Aaron estimates that policyholders on average renew the policy for 4.5 years. It has no evidence to suggest that previous policyholder behaviour will change.

Instructions

a. Determine the transaction price of the arrangement for Aaron, assuming 100 policies are sold.

b. Prepare the journal entries, assuming that the 100 policies are sold in January 2020 and that Aaron receives commissions from Capital.

E6.9 (LO 5) `Excel` **(Time Value of Money)** Gardi Inc. sold a unit of inventory to a buyer for $1,000 payable in one year. Gardi estimates that the interest rate for a similar financing arrangement would be 8%. The unit of inventory normally sells for $900. Assuming that the company recognizes an interest component, calculate the discount rate to be applied in calculating the cash selling price of the unit of inventory. Use Excel or a financial calculator. Gardi prepares financial statements in accordance with IFRS.

E6.10 (LO 5, 7, 11) **(Sales with Returns)** Organic Growth Company is testing a number of new agricultural seeds that it has recently harvested. To stimulate interest, it has decided to grant five of its largest customers the unconditional right to return these products if not fully satisfied. The right of return extends for four months. Organic Growth sells these seeds on account for $1.5 million (cost $800,000) on April 2, 2020. Customers are required to pay the full amount due by June 15, 2020. The company follows IFRS.

 Video

Instructions

a. Prepare the journal entry for Organic Growth at April 2, 2020, assuming Organic Growth estimates returns of 20% based on prior experience.

b. Assume that one customer returns the seeds on July 1, 2020. Prepare the journal entry to record this transaction, assuming this customer purchased $100,000 of seeds from Organic Growth.

c. Briefly describe the accounting for these sales if Organic Growth is unable to reliably estimate returns.

d. Repeat parts (a) and (b) under the assumption that Organic follows ASPE.

E6.11 (LO 5, 7, 11) **(Sales with Returns)** Uddin Publishing Co. publishes college textbooks that are sold to bookstores on the following terms. Each title has a fixed wholesale price, terms f.o.b. shipping point, and payment is due 60 days after shipment. The retailer may return a maximum of 30% of an order at the retailer's expense. Sales are made only to retailers who have good credit ratings. Past experience indicates that the normal return rate is 12% and the average collection period is 72 days. The company follows IFRS.

Instructions

a. Identify the revenue recognition criteria that Uddin could use concerning textbook sales.

b. Briefly discuss the reasoning for your answers in part (a).

c. On August 8, 2020, Uddin shipped books invoiced at $15 million (cost $12 million). Prepare the journal entry to record this transaction, including the expected returns.

d. On October 3, 2020, $1.5 million of the invoiced July sales were returned according to the return policy, and the remaining $13.5 million was paid. Prepare the journal entries for the return and payment.

e. Repeat parts (c) and (d) under the assumption that Uddin follows ASPE.

E6.12 (LO 5) `Finance` **(Advance Rentals)** Taylor Marina has 300 available slips that rent for $800 per season. Payments must be made in full by the start of the boating season, April 1, 2021. The boating season ends October 31, and the marina has a December 31 year end. Slips for future seasons may be reserved if paid for by December 31, 2021. Under a new policy, if payment for 2022 season slips is made by December 31, 2021, a 5% discount is allowed. If payment for 2023 season slips is made by December 31, 2021, renters get a 20% discount. (Taylor hopes this promotion will provide cash flow for major dock repairs.)

On December 31, 2020, all 300 slips for the 2021 season were rented at full price. On December 31, 2021, 200 slips were reserved and paid for the 2022 boating season, and 60 slips were reserved and paid for the 2023 boating season.

Instructions

a. Prepare the appropriate journal entries for December 31, 2020, and December 31, 2021.

b. **Digging Deeper** Assume the marina operator is unsophisticated in business. Explain the managerial significance of the above accounting to this person.

E6.13 (LO 5) **(Gift Card Sales and Redemptions)** During December 2020, Soft Skin Ltd. sells $20,000 of gift cards to customers. From reliable past experience, management estimates that 8% of the gift cards sold will not be redeemed by customers. In January 2021, $2,000 of these cards is redeemed for merchandise with a cost of $1,500. In February 2021, a further $10,000 of these cards is redeemed for merchandise with a cost of $8,000. The company uses a perpetual inventory system and has a February 28 year end.

Instructions

a. Prepare the journal entry needed for December 2020.

b. Prepare the journal entry needed for the January 2021 redemptions. Round to the nearest dollar.

c. Prepare the journal entry needed for the February 2021 redemptions. Round to the nearest dollar.

d. What amount, if any, will appear on the SFP concerning gift cards at February 28, 2021?

E6.14 (LO 6) **(Allocation of Transaction Price)** Sanchez Co. enters into a contract to sell Product A and Product B on January 2, 2020, for an upfront cash payment of $150,000. Product A will be delivered in two years (January 2, 2022) and Product B will be delivered in five years (January 2, 2025). Sanchez Co. allocates the $150,000 to Products A and B on a relative stand-alone selling price basis as follows.

	Stand-Alone Selling Prices	Percent Allocated	Allocated Amounts
Product A	$ 40,000	25%	$ 37,500
Product B	120,000	75%	112,500
	$160,000		$150,000

Sanchez Co. uses an interest rate of 6%, which is its incremental borrowing rate.

Instructions

a. Prepare the journal entries needed on January 2, 2020, and December 31, 2020.

b. Prepare the journal entry needed on December 31, 2021.

c. Prepare the journal entry needed on January 2, 2022.

d. Using Excel or a financial calculator, calculate the amount of revenue to be recognized for Product B and prepare the journal entry needed on January 2, 2025.

E6.15 (LO 2, 6, 7) **Excel** **(Allocation of Transaction Price)** Shaw Company sells goods that cost $300,000 to Ricard Company for $400,000 on January 2, 2020. The sales price includes an installation fee, which is valued at $40,000. The fair value of the goods is $370,000. The goods were delivered on March 1, 2020. Installation is considered a separate performance obligation and was completed on June 18, 2020. Under the terms of the contract, Ricard Company pays Shaw $270,000 upon delivery of the goods and the balance at the completion of the installation.

Instructions

a. Using the five-step process for revenue recognition, determine when and how much revenue would be recognized by Shaw. Round percentage allocations to two decimal places and final amounts to the nearest dollar. Assume IFRS is followed.

b. Prepare the journal entries for Shaw on January 2, March 1, and June 18, 2020.

E6.16 (LO 6, 7) **(Allocation of Transaction Price)** Crankshaft Company manufactures equipment. Crankshaft's products range from simple automated machinery to complex systems containing numerous components. Unit selling prices range from $200,000 to $1.5 million, and are quoted inclusive of installation. The installation process does not involve changes to the features of the equipment to perform to specifications. Crankshaft has the following arrangement with Winkerbean Inc.

- Winkerbean purchases equipment from Crankshaft on May 2, 2020, for a price of $1 million and contracts with Crankshaft to install the equipment. Crankshaft charges the same price for the equipment irrespective of whether it does the installation or not. Using market data, Crankshaft determines that the installation service is estimated to have a fair value of $50,000. The cost of the equipment is $600,000.

- Winkerbean is obligated to pay Crankshaft the $950,000 upon delivery of the equipment and the balance on the completion of the installation.

Crankshaft delivers the equipment on June 1, 2020, and completes the installation of the equipment on September 30, 2020. Assume that the equipment and the installation are two distinct performance obligations that should be accounted for separately.

Instructions

a. Allocate the transaction price of $1 million among the performance obligations of the contract. Round percentage allocations to two decimal places and final amounts to the nearest dollar. Assume Crankshaft follows IFRS.

b. Prepare any journal entries for Crankshaft on May 2, June 1, and September 30, 2020.

E6.17 (LO 6, 7) (Allocation of Transaction Price) Refer to the revenue arrangement in E6.16.

Instructions

Repeat requirements (a) and (b), assuming Crankshaft does not have market data with which to determine the stand-alone selling price of the installation services. As a result, an expected cost plus margin approach is used. The cost of installation is $36,000; Crankshaft prices these services with a 25% margin relative to cost.

E6.18 (LO 6) (Allocation of Transaction Price) Appliance Centre is an experienced home appliance dealer. Appliance Centre also offers a number of services together with the home appliances that it sells. Assume that Appliance Centre sells ovens on a stand-alone basis. Appliance Centre also sells installation services and maintenance services for ovens. However, Appliance Centre does not offer installation or maintenance services to customers who buy ovens from other vendors. Pricing for ovens is as follows.

Oven only	$ 800
Oven with installation service	850
Oven with maintenance services	975
Oven with installation and maintenance services	1,000

In each instance in which maintenance services are provided, service is separately priced within the arrangement at $175. Additionally, the incremental amount charged by Appliance Centre for installation approximates the amount charged by independent third parties.

Instructions

a. Assume that a customer purchases an oven with both installation and maintenance services for $1,000. Based on its experience, Appliance Centre believes that it is probable that the installation of the equipment will be performed satisfactorily to the consumer. Assume that the maintenance services are priced separately. Identify the separate performance obligations related to the Appliance Centre revenue arrangement.

b. Allocate the transaction price of $1,000 among the performance obligations of the contract. Round percentage allocations to two decimal places and final amounts to the nearest dollar. Assume IFRS is followed.

E6.19 (LO 6) (Existence of a Contract) On January 1, 2020, Gordon Co. enters into a contract to sell a customer a wiring base and a shelving unit that sits on the base in exchange for $3,000. The contract requires delivery of the base first but states that payment for the base will not be made until the shelving unit is delivered. Gordon identifies two performance obligations and allocates $1,200 of the transaction price to the wiring base and the remainder to the shelving unit. The cost of the wiring base is $700; the shelves have a cost of $320.

Instructions

a. Prepare the journal entry on January 1, 2020, for Gordon.

b. Prepare the journal entries on February 5, 2020, for Gordon when the wiring base is delivered to the customer.

c. Prepare the journal entries on February 25, 2020, for Gordon when the shelving unit is delivered to the customer and Gordon receives full payment.

E6.20 (LO 7, 11) (Existence of a Contract) On May 1, 2020, Richardson Inc. entered into a contract to deliver one of its specialty mowers to Kickapoo Landscaping Co. The contract requires Kickapoo to pay the contract price of $900 in advance on May 15, 2020. Kickapoo pays Richardson on May 15, 2020, and Richardson delivers the mower (with a cost of $565) on May 31, 2020. Richardson follows IFRS.

Instructions

a. Prepare the journal entry on May 1, 2020, for Richardson.

b. Prepare the journal entry on May 15, 2020, for Richardson.

c. Prepare the journal entry on May 31, 2020, for Richardson.

d. Would the journal entries above change had Richardson followed ASPE?

E6.21 (LO 7) (Licensing Agreement) Omega Pharmaceuticals Inc. licenses its patent rights for North America to an approved drug compound for five years to Crane Distributing Ltd. Omega determines that the patented drug formula has significant stand-alone value. Under the terms of the licensing agreement, Omega has no obligations to support the drug formula over the five years of the agreement.

Instructions

When should Omega recognize revenue from the licensing agreement: at one point in time or over the five-year term of the agreement? Explain.

E6.22 (LO 8) (Revenue Recognition under Earnings Approach—Various Consumer Industries)

Instructions

a. Explain the principles and criteria for revenue recognition under the earnings approach.

b. For each scenario noted in E6.1, discuss when revenue should be recognized under the earnings approach. Provide the journal entries that would be recorded to recognize the revenue under the earnings approach.

E6.23 (LO 8) (Transactions with Customer Acceptance Provisions under Earnings Approach) Consider the following unrelated situations:

1. Book of the Week Limited sends books out to potential customers on a trial basis. If the customers do not like the books, they can return them at no cost.

2. Sea Clothing Company Inc. has a return policy that allows customers to return merchandise in good order for a full refund within 30 days of purchase.

3. Shivani Inc. sells machinery to manufacturers. Customers have the right to inspect the equipment upon delivery and may return it if certain customer-specific requirements for size and weight are not met.

Instructions

a. Explain the implications of customer acceptance provisions for revenue transactions.

b. Indicate the point at which these transactions may be recognized as sales under the earnings approach.

c. **Digging Deeper** Using the information provided in scenario 2, assume Sea Clothing Company Inc. advertises that "customer satisfaction is guaranteed," and assume the role of a customer of Sea Clothing Company. Has the company's advertised statement created an expectation that returns will be accepted at any time, perhaps even beyond the 30-day refund period? Discuss the implications of this expectation for Sea Clothing Company's books, if any.

E6.24 (LO 9) (Sales with Repurchase) Cramer Corp. sells idle machinery to Enyart Company on July 1, 2020, for $40,000. Cramer agrees to repurchase this equipment from Enyart on June 30, 2021, for a price of $42,400 (an imputed interest rate of 6%).

Instructions

a. Prepare the journal entry for Cramer for the receipt of cash from Enyart on July 1, 2020.

b. Prepare any other necessary journal entries for Cramer in 2020.

c. Prepare the journal entries for Cramer when the machinery is repurchased on June 30, 2021.

E6.25 (LO 9) (Repurchase Agreement) Zagat Inc. enters into an agreement on March 1, 2020, to sell aluminum ingots for $200,000 cash to Werner Metal Company. As part of this agreement, Zagat also agrees to repurchase from Werner the ingots in 60 days at the original sales price of $200,000 plus 2%.

Instructions

a. Prepare the journal entry necessary on March 1, 2020.

b. Prepare the journal entry for the repurchase of the ingots on May 1, 2020.

E6.26 (LO 9) (Bill-and-Hold) Wood-Mode Company is involved in the design, manufacture, and installation of various types of wood products for large construction projects. Wood-Mode recently completed a large contract for Stadium Inc., which consisted of building 35 different types of concession counters for a new soccer arena under construction. The terms of the contract are that, upon completion of the counters, Stadium would pay $2 million. Unfortunately, due to the depressed economy, the completion of the new soccer arena is now delayed. Stadium has therefore asked Wood-Mode to hold the counters for two months at its manufacturing plant until the arena is completed. Stadium acknowledges in writing that it ordered the counters and that it now has ownership. The time that Wood-Mode Company must hold the counters is totally dependent on when the arena is completed. Because Wood-Mode has not received additional progress payments for the arena due to the delay, Stadium has provided a deposit of $300,000.

Instructions

a. Explain this type of revenue recognition transaction.

b. What factors should be considered in determining when to recognize revenue in this transaction?

c. Prepare the journal entry(ies) that Wood-Mode should make, assuming it signed a valid sales contract to sell the counters and received the $300,000 deposit at the time.

E6.27 (LO 9) (Principal and Agent) Sider Inc., a registered broker, enters into a finder's fee agreement with HOM Homes Ltd. on June 15, 2020. Sider will find leads in the form of buyers potentially interested in purchasing HOM's real estate holdings. Along with finding potential buyers, Sider helps negotiate the selling price and provides advice on contract details. If and when HOM closes a sale, Sider will be paid within 30 days of the closing date, based on the following formula: 5% of any transaction value up to and including $1 million, plus 4% of any transaction value greater than $1 million and less than and including $2 million, plus 3% of any transaction value greater than $2 million and less than and including $3 million, plus 2% of any transaction value greater than $3 million and less than and including $4 million, plus 1% of any transaction value in excess of $4 million. If Sider is represented by another broker and this information is not shared with HOM, the fee is reduced by 50%. On September 1, 2020, HOM paid Sider $50,000 to provide some needed cash flow for seeking out buyers. On October 15, 2020, an offer was made and accepted for a parcel of real estate at a price of $3.5 million. The transaction closed on November 1, 2020, and Sider was paid the finder's fee net of $50,000 on November 30, 2020.

Instructions

Explain the accounting treatment of the above events for Sider Inc. and prepare any journal entries needed on:

a. June 15, 2020

b. September 1, 2020

c. October 15, 2020

d. November 1, 2020

e. November 30, 2020

E6.28 (LO 9) (Consignment Sales) On May 31, 2020, Eisler Company consigned 80 freezers, costing $500 each, to Remmers Company. The cost of shipping the freezers amounted to $740 and was paid by Eisler Company. On December 30, 2020, a report was received from the consignee, indicating that 40 freezers had been sold for $750 each. Remittance was made by the consignee for the amount due after deducting a commission of 6%, advertising of $200, and total installation costs of $320 on the freezers sold.

Instructions

a. Calculate the inventory value of the units unsold in the hands of the consignee.

b. Calculate the profit for the consignor for the units sold.

c. Calculate the amount of cash that will be remitted by the consignee.

E6.29 (LO 9) (Consignment Sales) The following are transactions between Wang Corp., the consignor, and Ren Stores Ltd., the consignee, for the month of June 2020. Wang uses a perpetual inventory system and has a separate perpetual record for inventory sent out on consignment. At the end of each month, sales are reported by Ren to Wang and a net payment is made. The agreement stipulates that Ren is to receive a 15% (of sales) commission and a 6% (of sales) rebate to offset its advertising expenses.

June	1	Wang Corp. ships merchandise costing $455,000 on consignment to Ren Stores Ltd.
June	5	Wang pays the freight of $5,000 for the above shipment of June 1.
June	30	Summary entry for the month of June: Ren sells half of the merchandise for $600,000 cash.
June	30	Ren notifies Wang that 50% of the merchandise has been sold for $600,000 and remits a cheque for the amount due under the consignment agreement. Wang records the receipt of the cheque from Ren.

Instructions

a. Prepare the journal entries necessary on the books of Wang Corp.

b. Prepare the journal entries necessary on the books of Ren Stores Ltd.

E6.30 (LO 10) **(Contract Costs)** Rex's Reclaimers entered into a contract with Dan's Demolition to manage the processing of recycled materials on Dan's various demolition projects. Services for the three-year contract include collecting, sorting, and transporting reclaimed materials to recycling centres or contractors who will reuse them. Rex's incurs selling commission costs of $2,000 to obtain the contract. Before performing the services, Rex's also designs and builds specialty receptacles and loading equipment that interface with Dan's demolition equipment, at a cost of $27,000. These receptacles and equipment are retained by Rex's. Dan's promises to pay a fixed fee of $12,000 per year, payable every six months, for the services under the contract. Rex's incurs the following costs: design services for the receptacles to interface with Dan's equipment $3,000, loading equipment controllers $6,000, and special testing and health and safety inspection fees $2,000 (some of Dan's projects are on government property).

Instructions

a. Determine the costs that should be capitalized as part of Rex's revenue arrangement with Dan's Demolition.

b. Rex's also expects to incur general and administrative costs related to this contract, as well as costs of wasted materials and labour that likely cannot be factored into the contract price. Can these costs be capitalized? Explain.

E6.31 (LO 10) **(Contract Costs, Collectibility)** Refer to the information in E6.30.

Instructions

a. Does the accounting for capitalized costs change if the contract is for one year rather than three years? Explain.

b. **Digging Deeper** Dan's Demolition is a start-up company; as a result, there is more than insignificant uncertainty about Dan's ability to make the six-month payments on time. Does this uncertainty affect the amount of revenue to be recognized under the contract? Explain.

*E6.32 (LO 12, 14) **Excel** **(Recognition of a Profit on Long-Term Contracts)** During 2020, Nilsen Company started a construction job with a contract price of $1.6 million. The job was completed in 2022. The following information is available. The contract is non-cancellable.

	2020	2021	2022
Costs incurred to date	$400,000	$825,000	$1,070,000
Estimated costs to complete	600,000	275,000	–0–
Billings to date (non-refundable)	300,000	900,000	1,600,000
Collections to date	270,000	810,000	1,425,000

Instructions

a. Calculate the amount of gross profit to be recognized each year, assuming the percentage-of-completion method is used.

b. Prepare all necessary journal entries for 2021.

c. Calculate the amount of gross profit to be recognized each year, assuming the completed-contract method is used.

*E6.33 (LO 10, 12) **(Gross Profit on Uncompleted Contract)** On April 1, 2020, Dougherty Inc. entered into a cost plus fixed fee non-cancellable contract to construct an electric generator for Altom Corporation. At the contract date, Dougherty estimated that it would take two years to complete the project at a cost of $2 million. The fixed fee stipulated in the contract was $450,000. Dougherty appropriately accounts for this contract under the percentage-of-completion method. During 2020, Dougherty incurred costs of $800,000 related to this project. The estimated cost at December 31, 2020, to complete the contract is $1.2 million. Altom was billed $600,000 under the contract. The billings are non-refundable.

Instructions

a. Prepare a schedule to calculate the amount of gross profit to be recognized by Dougherty under the contract for the year ended December 31, 2020. Show supporting calculations in good form.

b. Show how the contract will be reported on the income statement for the year ended December 31, 2020.

(Adapted from AICPA)

*E6.34 **(LO 12, 14)** **(Recognition of Revenue on Long-Term Contract and Entries)** Hamilton Construction Company uses the percentage-of-completion method of accounting. In 2020, Hamilton began work under a non-cancellable contract #E2-D2, which provided for a contract price of $2.2 million. Other details follow:

	2020	2021
Costs incurred during the year	$640,000	$1,425,000
Estimated costs to complete, as at December 31	960,000	–0–
Billings during the year (non-refundable)	420,000	1,680,000
Collections during the year	350,000	1,500,000

Instructions

a. How much revenue should be recognized in 2020? In 2021?

b. Assuming the same facts as those above except that Hamilton uses the completed-contract method of accounting, how much revenue should be recognized in 2021?

c. Prepare a complete set of journal entries for 2020 (using the percentage-of-completion method).

*E6.35 **(LO 12, 14)** **(Recognition of Profit and SFP Amounts for Long-Term Contracts)** Yanmei Construction Company began operations on January 1, 2020. During the year, Yanmei entered into a non-cancellable contract with Lundquist Corp. to construct a manufacturing facility. At that time, Yanmei estimated that it would take five years to complete the facility at a total cost of $4,500,000. The total contract price for construction of the facility is $6,000,000. During the year, Yanmei incurred $1,185,800 in construction costs related to the project. The estimated cost to complete the contract is $4,204,200. Lundquist Corp. was billed and paid 25% of the contract price. The billings are non-refundable.

Instructions

Prepare schedules to calculate the amount of gross profit to be recognized for the year ended December 31, 2020, and the amount to be shown as contract assets or liabilities at December 31, 2020, under each of the following methods. Show supporting calculations in good form.

a. Completed-contract method.

b. Percentage-of-completion method.

(Adapted from AICPA)

*E6.36 **(LO 12, 14)** **Excel** **(Recognition of Profit on Long-Term Contract)** Shanahan Construction Company has entered into a non-cancellable contract beginning January 1, 2020, to build a parking complex. It has been estimated that the complex will cost $600,000 and will take three years to construct. The complex will be billed to the purchasing company at $900,000. The following data pertain to the construction period.

	2020	2021	2022
Costs to date	$270,000	$450,000	$610,000
Estimated costs to complete	330,000	150,000	–0–
Progress billings to date (non-refundable)	270,000	550,000	900,000
Cash collected to date	240,000	500,000	900,000

Instructions

a. Using the percentage-of-completion method, calculate the estimated gross profit that would be recognized during each year of the construction period.

b. Using the completed-contract method, calculate the estimated gross profit that would be recognized during each year of the construction period.

*E6.37 **(LO 12)** **(Recognition of Profit on Long-Term Contract)** Vaughn Enterprises Ltd. has entered into a contract beginning in February 2020 to build two warehouses for Atlantis Structures Ltd. The contract is a non-cancellable fixed price contract for $10 million. The following data pertain to the construction period (all figures in thousands).

	2020	2021	2022
Costs for the year	$3,825	$4,675	$1,200
Estimated costs to complete	4,675	1,270	–0–
Progress billings for the year (non-refundable)	3,500	4,100	2,400
Cash collected for the year	3,100	4,150	2,750

Instructions

a. Using the percentage-of-completion method, calculate the percent complete for each year of the contract. Round the percentage completion to the nearest whole percentage point.

b. Calculate the amount of the gross profit to be recognized each year of the contract.

c. Prepare the journal entries for 2020 and 2021.

d. What is the balance in the Contract Asset/Liability account at December 31, 2020 and 2021?

e. Show how the construction contract would be reported on the SFP and the income statement for the year ended December 31, 2021.

*E6.38 (LO 13)   (**Recognition of Profit on Long-Term Contract**)   Assume the facts given in E6.37 except now assume that the construction industry has experienced significant expansion, making construction materials and labour more costly than originally estimated. Vaughn finds it extremely difficult to estimate the costs to complete construction and therefore difficult to estimate the percent complete.It must account for the construction project using the zero-profit method.

Instructions

a. Calculate the amount of the gross profit to be recognized each year of the contract.

b. Prepare the journal entries for 2020 and 2021.

c. What is the balance in the Contract Asset/Liability account at December 31, 2020 and 2021?

d. Show how the construction contract would be reported on the SFP and the income statement for the year ended December 31, 2021.

*E6.39 (LO 15)   (**Recognition of Profit on Long-Term Contract—Overall Loss**)   Assume the facts given in E6.37 except that Vaughn's non-cancellable fixed price contract with Atlantis is for $9.5 million. Billings and collections are lower in 2022 by $500,000 each.

	2020	2021	2022
Costs for the year	$3,825	$4,675	$1,200
Estimated costs to complete	4,675	1,270	–0–
Progress billings for the year (non-refundable)	3,500	4,100	1,900
Cash collected for the year	3,100	4,150	2,250

Instructions

a. Using the percentage-of-completion method, calculate the percent complete for 2020 and 2021. Round the percent complete to the nearest whole percentage point.

b. Calculate the amount of revenue to be recognized in 2020 and 2021.

c. Calculate the construction costs to be expensed in 2021.

d. Prepare the journal entry at December 31, 2021, to record long-term contract revenues, expenses, and losses for 2021.

e. What is the balance in the Contract Asset/Liability account at December 31, 2020 and 2021?

f. Show how the construction contract would be reported on the SFP and the income statement for the year ended December 31, 2021.

g. Assume that Vaughn uses the zero-profit or completed-contract method. What would be the journal entry recorded on December 31, 2021?

Problems

P6.1 BBQ Master Company sells total outdoor barbecue solutions, providing gas and charcoal barbecues, accessories, and installation services for custom patio barbecue stations.

Instructions

Respond to the requirements related to the following independent revenue arrangements for BBQ Master products and services. Assume that BBQ Master follows IFRS.

a. BBQ Master offers contract BM205, which consists of a free-standing gas barbecue for small patio use plus installation to a customer's gas line for a total price of $800. On a stand-alone basis, the barbecue sells for $700 (cost $425), and BBQ Master estimates that the fair value of the installation service (based on cost-plus estimation) is $150. BBQ Master signed 10 BM205 contracts on April 20, 2020, and customers paid the contract price in cash. The barbecues were delivered and installed on May 15, 2020. Prepare journal entries for BBQ Master for BM205 in April and May 2020.

b. The province of Ontario is planning major renovations in its parks during 2020 and enters into a contract with BBQ Master to purchase 400 durable, easy-maintenance, standard charcoal barbecues during 2020. The barbecues are priced at $200 each (with a cost of $160 each), and BBQ Master provides a 6% volume discount if Ontario purchases at least 300 grills during 2020. BBQ Master delivers and receives payment for 280 barbecues on April 17, 2020. Based on prior experience with province of Ontario renovation projects, the delivery of this many barbecues makes it certain that Ontario will meet the volume discount threshold. Prepare the journal entries for BBQ Master for barbecues sold on April 17, 2020, including any volume discounts.

c. On October 1, 2020, BBQ Master sold one of its super deluxe combination gas/charcoal barbecues to a local builder. The builder plans to install it in one of its "Parade of Homes" houses. BBQ Master accepted a three-year, zero-interest-bearing note with a face amount of $5,324. The barbecue has an inventory cost of $2,700. An interest rate of 10% is an appropriate market rate of interest for this customer. Prepare the journal entries on October 1, 2020, and December 31, 2020.

P6.2 Economy Appliance Co. manufactures low-price, no-frills appliances that are in great demand for rental units. Pricing and cost information on Economy's main products are as follows.

Item	Stand-Alone Selling Price (Cost)
Refrigerator	$500 ($260)
Range	$560 ($275)
Stackable washer/dryer unit	$700 ($400)

Customers can contract a purchase either individually at the stated prices or for a three-item bundle with a price of $1,800. The bundle price includes delivery and installation. Economy provides delivery and installation as a stand-alone service for any of its products for $100. The company follows IFRS.

Instructions

Respond to the requirements related to the following independent revenue arrangements for Economy Appliance Co.

a. On June 1, 2020, Economy sold 100 washer/dryer units without installation to Laplante Rentals for $70,000 (on credit). Laplante is a newer customer and is unsure of how this product will work in its older rental units. Economy offers a 60-day return privilege and estimates, based on prior experience with sales of this product, that 4% of the units will be returned. Prepare the journal entries for the sale and related cost of goods sold on June 1, 2020.

b. YellowCard Property Managers operates upscale student apartment buildings. On May 1, 2020, Economy signs a contract with YellowCard for 300 appliance bundles to be delivered and installed in one of its new buildings. YellowCard pays 20% cash at contract signing and will pay the balance upon delivery and installation no later than August 1, 2020. Prepare journal entries for Economy on (1) May 1, 2020, and (2) August 1, 2020, when all appliances are delivered and installed.

c. Digging Deeper Refer to the arrangement in part (b). It would help YellowCard secure lease agreements with students if the delivery and installation of the appliance bundles can be completed by July 1, 2020. YellowCard offers a 10% bonus payment if Economy can complete delivery and installation by July 1, 2020. Economy estimates its chances of meeting the bonus deadline to be 60%, based on a number of prior contracts of similar scale. Repeat the requirement for part (b), given this bonus provision. Assume installation is completed by July 1, 2020.

d. Epic Rentals would like to take advantage of the bundle price for its 400-unit project. On February 1, 2020, Economy signs a contract with Epic for delivery and installation of 400 bundles. Under the agreement, Economy will hold the appliance bundles in its warehouses until the new rental units are ready for installation. Epic pays 10% cash at contract signing. On April 1, 2020, Economy completes manufacture of the appliances in the Epic bundle order and places them in the warehouse. Economy and Epic have documented the warehouse arrangement and identified the units designated for Epic. The units are ready to ship, and Economy may not sell these units to other customers. Prepare journal entries for Economy on (1) February 1, 2020, and (2) April 1, 2020.

P6.3 Van Hatten Consolidated has three operating divisions: DeMent Publishing Division, Ankiel Security Division, and Depp Advisory Division. Each division maintains its own accounting system but follows IFRS.

DeMent Publishing Division

The DeMent Publishing Division sells large volumes of novels to a few book distributors, which in turn sell to several national chains of bookstores. DeMent allows distributors to return up to 30% of sales, and the distributors give the same terms to bookstores. While returns from individual titles fluctuate greatly, the returns from distributors have averaged 20% in each of the past five years. A total of $7 million of paperback novel sales were made to distributors during fiscal 2020. On November 30, 2020 (the end of the fiscal year), $1.5 million of fiscal 2020 sales were still subject to return privileges over the next six months. The remaining $5.5 million of fiscal 2020 sales had actual returns of 21%.

Sales from fiscal 2019 totalling $2 million were collected in fiscal 2020 less 18% returns. This division records revenue according to the revenue recognition method when the right of return exists.

Ankiel Security Division

The Ankiel Security Division works through manufacturers' agents in various cities. Orders for alarm systems and down payments are forwarded from agents, and the division ships the goods f.o.b. factory directly to the customers (usually police departments and security guard companies). Customers are billed directly for the balance due plus actual shipping costs. The company received orders for $6 million of goods during the fiscal year ended November 30, 2020. Down payments of $600,000 were received, and $5.2 million of goods were billed and shipped. Actual freight costs of $100,000 were also billed. Commissions of 10% on product price are paid to manufacturing agents after goods are shipped to customers. Such goods are covered by the warranty for 90 days after shipment, and warranty claims have been about 1% of sales. Revenue is recognized at the point of sale by this division.

Depp Advisory Division

The Depp Advisory Division provides asset management services. This division grew out of Van Hatten's own treasury and asset management operations, which several of its customers asked to have access to. On January 1, 2020, Depp entered into a contract with Scutaro Co. to perform asset management services for one year. Depp receives a quarterly management fee of 0.25% on Scutaro's assets under management at the end of each quarter. In addition, Depp receives a performance-based incentive fee of 20% of the fund's annual return in excess of the return on the S&P 500 index at the end of the year. At the end of the first quarter of 2020, Depp was managing $2.4 million of Scutaro assets. The annualized return on the portfolio was 6.2%. (The S&P 500 index had an annualized return of 5.7%.)

Instructions

a. For each division's revenue arrangements, identify the separate performance obligations, briefly explain the allocation of the transaction process to each performance obligation, and indicate when the performance obligations are satisfied.

b. Calculate the revenue to be recognized in fiscal year 2020 for each of the three operating divisions of Van Hatten in accordance with generally accepted accounting principles.

P6.4 Presented below are three independent revenue arrangements for Colbert Company. The company follows IFRS.

Instructions

Respond to the requirements related to each revenue arrangement.

a. Colbert sells 3-D printer systems. Recently, Colbert provided a special promotion of zero-interest financing for two years on any new 3-D printer system. Assume that Colbert sells Lyle Cartright a 3-D system, receiving a $5,000 zero-interest-bearing note on January 1, 2020. The cost of the 3-D printer system is $4,000. Colbert imputes a 6% interest rate on this zero-interest note transaction. Prepare the journal entry to record the sale on January 1, 2020, and calculate the total amount of revenue to be recognized in 2020.

b. Colbert sells 20 non-refundable $100 gift cards for 3-D printer plastic on March 1, 2020. The plastic has a stand-alone selling price of $100 (cost $80). The gift card expiration date is June 30, 2020. Colbert estimates that customers will not redeem 10% of these gift cards. The pattern of redemption is as follows.

	Cumulative Redemption Rate to Date
March 31	50%
April 30	80%
June 30	85%

Prepare the 2020 journal entries related to the gift cards at March 1, March 31, April 30, and June 30. Round amounts to the nearest dollar.

c. Colbert sells 3-D printers along with a number of retail items. The package price and stand-alone selling prices of each item are as follows. The printer and stand are often sold as a bundle with the bundling discount noted below.

Item	Stand-Alone Selling Price	Price When Bundled	Bundling Discount
3-D printer (cost $4,000)	$5,000	$4,500	$500
Custom stand (cost $200)	450	450	–0–
Special 3-D plastic (cost $135)	175	175	–0–
Total for bundle	$5,625	$5,125	$500

Due to the timing of the delivery—the plastic is delivered six months after the printer is delivered to the customer—Colbert chooses to account for two performance obligations: (1) the printer and stand, and (2) the plastic. Prepare the journal entries for Colbert on (a) March 1, 2020, when Colbert receives $51,250 for the sale of 10 printer bundles, and (b) September 1, 2020, when the plastic is delivered to customers.

P6.5 Ritt Ranch & Farm is a distributor of ranch and farm equipment. Its products include small tools, power equipment for trench-digging and fencing, grain dryers, and barn winches. Most products are sold direct via its company Internet site. However, given some of its specialty products, select farm implement stores carry Ritt's products. Pricing and cost information on three of Ritt's most popular products are as follows.

Item	Stand-Alone Selling Price (Cost)
Mini-trencher	$ 3,600 ($2,000)
Power fence hole auger	1,200 ($800)
Grain/hay dryer	14,000 ($11,000)

Instructions

Respond to the requirements related to the following independent revenue arrangements for Ritt Ranch & Farm. IFRS is a constraint.

a. On January 1, 2020, Ritt sells augers to Mills Farm & Fleet for $48,000. Mills signs a six-month note at an annual interest rate of 12%. Ritt allows Mills to return any auger that it cannot use within 60 days and receive a full refund. Based on prior experience, Ritt estimates that 5% of units sold to customers like Mills will be returned (using the most likely outcome approach). Ritt's costs to recover the products will be immaterial, and the returned augers are expected to be resold at a profit. Prepare the journal entry for Ritt on January 1, 2020.

b. On August 10, 2020, Ritt sells 16 mini-trenchers to a farm co-op in western Canada. Ritt provides a 4% volume discount on the mini-trenchers if the co-op has a 15% increase in purchases from Ritt compared with the prior year. Given the slowdown in the farm economy, sales to the co-op have been flat, and it is highly uncertain that the benchmark will be met. Prepare the journal entry for Ritt on August 10, 2020.

c. Ritt sells three grain/hay dryers to a local farmer at a total contract price of $45,200. In addition to the dryers, Ritt provides installation, which has a stand-alone sales value of $1,000 per unit installed. The contract payment also includes a $1,200 maintenance plan for the dryers for three years after installation. Ritt signs the contract on June 20, 2020, and receives a 20% down payment from the farmer. The dryers are delivered and installed on October 1, 2020, and full payment is made to Ritt. Round percentage allocations to two decimal places and final amounts to the nearest dollar. Prepare the journal entries for Ritt in 2020 related to this arrangement as well as any adjusting journal entries at its December year end.

d. On April 25, 2020, Ritt ships 100 augers to Farm Depot, a farm supply dealer in Alberta, on consignment. By June 30, 2020, Farm Depot has sold 60 of the consigned augers at the listed price of $1,200 per unit. Farm Depot notifies Ritt of the sales, retains a 10% commission, and remits the cash due to Ritt. Prepare the journal entries for Ritt and Farm Depot for the consignment arrangement.

P6.6 Martz Inc. has a customer loyalty program that rewards a customer with one customer loyalty point for every $100 of purchases. Each point is redeemable for a $3 discount on any future purchases. On July 2, 2020, customers purchase products for $300,000 (with a cost of $171,000) and earn 3,000 points redeemable for future purchases. Martz expects 2,500 points to be redeemed (based on its past experience, which is predictive of the amount of consideration to which it will be entitled). Martz estimates a stand-alone selling price of $2.50 per point (or $7,500 total) on the basis of the likelihood of redemption. The points provide a material right to customers that they would not receive without entering into a contract. As a result, Martz concludes that the points are a separate performance obligation.

Instructions

a. Determine the transaction price for the product and the customer loyalty points. Round percentage allocations to two decimal places and final amounts to the nearest dollar.

b. Prepare the journal entries to record the sale of the product and related points on July 2, 2020.

c. At the end of the first reporting period (July 31, 2020), 1,000 loyalty points are redeemed. Martz continues to expect 2,500 loyalty points to be redeemed in total. Determine the amount of loyalty point revenue to be recognized at July 31, 2020. Prepare the journal entry for cash sales on July 31, 2020, assuming the points were applied to cash sales of $75,000 with a cost of $39,000. Round the calculation of revenue per point to three decimal places.

P6.7 Tablet Tailors sells tablet PCs combined with Internet service (Tablet Bundle A) that permits the tablet to connect to the Internet anywhere (that is, set up a WiFi hot spot). The price for the tablet and a four-year Internet connection service contract is $500. The stand-alone selling price of the tablet is $250 (cost to Tablet Tailors $175). Tablet Tailors sells the Internet access service independently for an upfront payment of $100, plus $72 payments due January 2, 2021, 2022, and 2023. With an imputed interest rate of 8%, the stand-alone value of the service is $286. On January 2, 2020, Tablet Tailors signed 100 contracts, receiving a total of $31,445 in cash (full payment of $500 each in cash, less the present value of the note for the future service plan payments due January 2 each year), delivered the tablets, and started service for 100 tablet packages. Tablet Tailors has a calendar year end and records adjusting entries at the end of the year.

Instructions

a. **Excel** Allocate the transaction price among the performance obligations of the contract. Round percentage allocations to two decimal places and final amounts to the nearest dollar. Assume IFRS is followed. Use Excel to calculate the present value of the note receivable and prepare an instalment note receivable schedule for the term of the note. Round amounts to the nearest dollar.

b. Prepare any journal entries on January 2, 2020, and at year end on December 31, 2020.

c. Prepare any journal entries on January 2, 2021, and on December 31, 2021.

d. Prepare any journal entries on January 2, 2022, and on December 31, 2022.

e. Prepare the requirements for part (b), assuming that Tablet Tailors has no reliable data with which to estimate the stand-alone selling price for the Internet service.

P6.8 Hale Hardware takes pride in being the "shop around the corner" that can compete with the big-box home improvement stores by providing good service from knowledgeable sales associates (many of whom are retired local handymen). Hale has developed the following two revenue arrangements to enhance its relationships with customers and increase its bottom line.

1. Hale sells a specialty portable winch that is popular with many of the local customers for use at their lake homes (putting docks in and out, launching boats, and so on). The Hale winch is a standard-manufacture winch that Hale modifies so it can be used for a variety of tasks. Hale sold 70 of these winches during 2020 at a total price of $21,000, with a warranty guarantee that the product was free of any defects. The cost of winches sold is $16,000. The assurance warranties extend for a three-year period with an estimated cost of $2,100. In addition, Hale sold extended warranties related to 29 Hale winches for two years beyond the three-year period for $400 each.

2. To bolster its already strong customer base, Hale implemented a customer loyalty program that rewards a customer with one loyalty point for every $10 of purchases on a select group of Hale products. Each point is redeemable for a $1 discount on any purchases of Hale merchandise in the following two years. During 2020, customers purchased select group products for $100,000 (all products are sold to provide a 45% gross profit) and earned 10,000 points redeemable for future purchases. The stand-alone selling price of the purchased products is $100,000. Based on prior experience with incentive programs like this, Hale expects 9,500 points to be redeemed related to these sales. (Hale appropriately uses this experience to estimate the value of future consideration related to loyalty points.)

Instructions

a. Identify the separate performance obligations in the Hale warranty and loyalty point programs, and briefly explain the point in time when the performance obligations are satisfied.

b. Prepare the journal entries for Hale related to the cash sales of Hale winches with warranties.

c. Prepare the journal entries for the loyalty point sales for Hale in 2020. Round percentage allocations to two decimal places and final amounts to the nearest dollar.

*P6.9 **Excel** Essan Construction Inc., which has a calendar year end, has entered into a non-cancellable fixed price contract for $2.8 million beginning September 1, 2020, to build a road for a municipality. It has been estimated that the road construction will be complete by June 2022. The following data pertain to the construction period.

	2020	2021	2022
Costs to date	$ 800,000	$1,800,000	$2,350,000
Estimated costs to complete	1,700,000	600,000	–0–
Progress billings to date (non-refundable)	850,000	2,300,000	2,800,000
Cash collected to date	700,000	2,200,000	2,800,000

Instructions

a. Using the percentage-of-completion method, calculate the estimated gross profit that would be recognized during each year of the construction period. Round the percent complete to the nearest whole percentage point.

b. Prepare the journal entries for 2020 and 2021.

c. What is the balance in the Contract Asset/Liability account at December 31, 2020 and 2021?

d. Show how the construction contract would be reported on the statement of financial position (SFP) and the income statement for the year ended December 31, 2021.

e. Using the zero-profit method, repeat part (a).

f. Using the zero-profit method, repeat part (b).

g. Using the zero-profit method, repeat part (c).

h. Using the zero-profit method, repeat part (d).

i. Prepare a table comparing the gross profit recognized in each of the three years under (1) the percentage-of-completion method, (2) the zero-profit method, and (3) the completed-contract method.

*P6.10 Assume the facts given in P6.9 for Essan Construction Inc. except assume that at December 31, 2021, Essan estimates the costs to complete the road contract at $1,050,000 instead of $600,000.

Instructions

a. Using the percentage-of-completion method, calculate the percent complete for 2020 and 2021. Round the percent complete to four decimal places.

b. Calculate the amount of revenue to be recognized in 2020 and 2021.

c. Calculate the construction costs to be expensed in 2021.

d. Prepare the journal entry at December 31, 2021, to record long-term contract revenues, expenses, and losses for 2021.

e. What is the balance in the Contract Asset/Liability account at December 31, 2020 and 2021?

f. Show how the construction contract would be reported on the SFP and the income statement for the year ended December 31, 2021.

g. Assume that Essan uses the zero-profit or completed-contract method. What would be the journal entry recorded on December 31, 2021?

Cases

Refer to the Case Primer on the Student Website and in WileyPLUS *to help you answer this case.*

CA6.1 *BudgetVacations* is a monthly magazine that has been on the market for 18 months. It is owned by a private company and has a circulation of 1.4 million copies. The company is thinking of going public to raise funds for expansion. However, currently, negotiations are under way to obtain a bank loan in order to update its facilities. It expects its capacity to grow at an average of 20% per year over the next three years.

After reviewing the financial statements of *BudgetVacations*, Grace Hall, the bank loan officer, said that a loan could only be offered to *BudgetVacations* if it could increase its current ratio and decrease its debt to equity ratio to a specified level. Thomas Zang, the marketing manager of *BudgetVacations*, has devised a plan to meet these requirements. Zang indicates that an advertising campaign can be used to immediately increase circulation. The potential customers would be contacted after *BudgetVacations* purchases another magazine's mailing list. The campaign would include:

1. An offer to subscribe to *BudgetVacations* at three quarters of the normal price.

2. A special offer to all new customers to receive the most current world atlas whenever requested at a guaranteed price of $2.00.

3. An unconditional guarantee of a full refund for any subscriber who is dissatisfied with the magazine.

Although the offer of a full refund is risky, Zang claims that few people will ask for a refund after receiving half of their subscription issues. Zang notes that other magazine companies have tried this sales promotion technique and had great success. Their average cancellation rate was 25%. On average, each company increased its initial circulation threefold and in the long run increased circulation to twice the level that it was before the promotion. In addition, 60% of the new subscribers are expected to take advantage of the atlas premium. Zang feels confident that the increased subscriptions from the advertising campaign will increase the current ratio and decrease the debt to equity ratio.

In addition to the above, Zang has just signed a large deal with a newly opened store to take delivery of the current edition of the magazine. The new customer has asked that the magazines be held by *BudgetVacations* for a couple of weeks.

Instructions

Assume the role of the controller and discuss the financial reporting issues that *BudgetVacations* faces.

CA6.2 Rouge Valley Golf and Health Club (RVGH) is a public company that operates eight clubs in a large city and offers one-year memberships. Membership gives members access to golf and the fitness centre including fitness classes. The members may use any of the eight facilities but must reserve golf time and pay a separate fee before using one of the golf courses. As an incentive, RVGH advertised that any customers who are not satisfied for any reason can receive a refund of the remaining portion of their unused membership fees. Membership fees are due at the beginning of the individual membership period; however, customers have the option of financing the membership fee over the membership period at an interest rate of 8%.

In the past, some customers have said they would like to take only the regularly scheduled aerobic classes and not pay for the full membership. During the current fiscal year, RVGH began selling coupon books for only aerobic classes to accommodate these customers. Each book is dated and contains 50 coupons that may be redeemed for any regularly scheduled aerobics class over a one-year period. After the one-year period, unused coupons are no longer valid.

During 2020, RVGH expanded into the health equipment market by purchasing a local company that manufactures elliptical machines. These machines are used in RVGH's facilities and are sold through the clubs and catalogues. Customers must make a 20% down payment when placing an equipment order. Delivery is in 60 to 90 days after an order is placed. The machines are sold with a one-year unconditional guarantee against defaults. Based on experience, RVGH expects the costs of repairing machines under guarantee to be 4% of sales.

RVGH is preparing financial statements as at May 1, 2020, the end of its fiscal year. Jaymie Hogan, corporate controller, expressed concern over the company's performance for the year and decided to review the preliminary financial statements prepared by Zahra Browning, RVGH's assistant controller, for the company's bankers. After reviewing the statements, Hogan proposed that the following changes be reflected in the May 31, 2020 published financial statements.

1. Membership revenue should be recognized when the membership fee is collected.
2. Revenue from the coupon books should be recognized when the books are sold.
3. Down payments on equipment purchases and expenses associated with the guarantee on the elliptical machines should be recognized when they are paid.

Browning told Hogan that the proposed changes are not in accordance with IFRS, but Hogan insisted that the changes be made. Browning believes Hogan wants to manipulate income to delay any potential financial problems and increase her year-end bonus. At this point, Browning is unsure what action to take.

Instructions

Ethics Discuss the financial reporting issues and how any ethical issues should be handled. If RVGH decided that it wanted to become a private company, describe how the financial reporting issues should be handled.

Integrated Cases

(*Hint:* If there are issues that are new, use the conceptual framework to help support your analysis with solid reasoning.)

IC6.1 Standford Pharmaceuticals Inc. (SP) researches, develops, and produces over-the-counter drugs. During the year, it acquired 100% of the net assets of Jenstar Drugs Limited (JDL) for $200 million. The fair value of the identifiable assets at the time of the purchase was $150 million (which included $120 million for patents). The plan is to sell the patents to a third party at the end of seven years, even though the remaining legal life of the patents at that time will be five years. SP already has a commitment from a specific third party that has agreed to pay $50 million for the patents (in seven years).

In January, in an unrelated deal, the company acquired a trademark that has a remaining legal life of three years. The trademark is renewable every 10 years at little cost. SP is unsure if it will renew the trademark or not.

Because of the two acquisitions, SP was short of cash and entered into an arrangement with Dev Drugs Corporation (DDC) whereby DDC paid $30 million to SP upfront when the contract was signed. Under the terms, the money is to be used to develop drugs and new distribution channels, and SP has already spent a considerable portion of this money. SP agreed that it will pay DDC 2% of the revenues from the subsequent sale of the drugs (which are now close to the point of commercial production).

Because of the cash shortage, the company entered into negotiations with its bank to increase its line of credit. The bank is concerned about the company's liquidity. SP's top management has graciously agreed to take stock options instead of any bonuses or pay raises for the next two years in order to reduce cash flow constraints.

It is now year end and SP is preparing its financial statements. It is concerned because one of its major competitors has just come out with several new drugs that will compete directly with the drugs that JDL sells. Management is worried that this may erode the market for JDL's products. In fact, SP is considering selling JDL and has contacted a consultant to find a buyer.

Joe Song, the controller, is preparing for a planning meeting with SP's auditors. The auditors are analyzing SP's draft financial statements to identify critical and high-risk areas. The draft financial statements show the company is barely breaking even. The CFO has commented that the company's share price is likely to "take a tumble," since the company has always been profitable in past years and its competitors seem to be doing well. Song is also considering the latest news from SP's lawyers—apparently, the company is being sued in a class-action lawsuit (by a significant number of people) for an illness that was allegedly caused by one of SP's main pharmaceutical products. The claim is for an amount equal to revenues from last year. At this point, the lawyers are concerned that the case against SP may be successful and they are trying to estimate the potential loss to the company.

Instructions

Audit & Assurance Adopt the role of the auditor and prepare an analysis of all financial reporting issues that SP is facing.

IC6.2 Shannonrock Racing Inc. (SR) is a promoter and sponsor of motorsport activities. It is privately owned. The owner is looking to expand and has approached the local bank, which has agreed to accept financial statements prepared in accordance with ASPE. The company owns two racetracks where it hosts races (including those sponsored by NASCAR—the National Association for Stock Car Auto Racing) and operates a driving school. In between races, it rents the facilities out.

SR operates like a club. An upfront fee is charged, which gives the individual the right to belong to the club for his or her lifetime. SR owns a fleet of high-performance stock cars that members may "adopt." All members adopt a car, as this is a main reason for joining the club. Under the adoption agreement, individuals pay a monthly fee for access to the stock car and the rights to race the car on the racetracks for a certain number of hours a week (including unlimited gas). Individuals must get insurance in order to adopt a car, but this is provided by SR, which has a master insurance plan. Race-car driving is risky and insurance premiums are very high (as is the injury and mortality rate). The master insurance plan is negotiated by SR with an outside insurance company and covers all club members. The monthly fee covers the insurance. Adoptions are annual and individuals often switch cars each year. The company just completed a membership drive and has signed 100 new members at $20,000 each. This amount has been paid upfront and received prior to year end. It is non-refundable. In order to become a member, individuals have to prove that they are capable of driving race cars safely. To this end, all members must take a two-week racing course and qualify for the company's stringent insurance program. All new members had completed the requirements by year end.

Last year, oil and gas prices began to skyrocket. Given that the company uses a lot of oil and gas in its business, Ted Rocket (the president and CEO of the company) decided to strategically diversify the company's operations into the oil and gas sector. Ted hired two additional traders to deal with this part of the business. At first, they were entering into advance gas purchase commitments to secure a steady supply of gas at a fixed price. However, the traders soon found that they were able to create profits by trading in the gas contracts. As a matter of fact, half of the company's net income for the current year came from trading gains. As part of their activities, the traders have purchased shares in three oil and gas companies. They have not decided whether they will keep these shares for the longer term. It really depends on the markets. Ted is currently in discussions with the traders as to what their job is supposed to be. Even though he likes the profits, he is not convinced that he likes the additional risk that this activity is exposing the company to. The company has a major shareholder who has declared that SR should only be in the business of racing cars and nothing else.

The company is being sued by the surrounding community for alleged pollution from the racing activities. Apparently, the racing cars produce a fair amount of airborne toxins, which settle in the surrounding area. Unknown to SR, the nearby city had passed a bylaw stating that companies must clean up any pollution that they are responsible for. SR's lawyers have argued on a preliminary basis that the alleged pollution in the surrounding area is due to the nearby superhighway and airport and that it is not possible to prove that SR is the cause of the pollution. Even if it were found to be responsible for a small fraction of it, it would be very difficult to determine just what that fraction is. The lawyers are therefore denying that SR has any responsibility with respect to cleanup. The lawyers for the surrounding community have asked for SR's financial statements to determine whether the company is profiting at their expense.

Instructions

Assume the role of the controller and discuss the financial reporting issues.

IC6.3 Towers Inc. (TI) is a leader in delivering communications technology that powers global commerce and secures the world's most critical information. Its shares trade on the Canadian and U.S. national stock exchanges. The company had been experiencing unprecedented growth, but then, in 2018, industry demand for the company's services and products declined dramatically due to an industry realignment, an economic downturn, and a tightening in global capital and product markets. By the end of 2020, the industry stabilized and the company began to enter a turnaround period after significant downsizing.

In 2020, employee morale was very low because of all the downsizing. Many employees were being actively recruited away from TI. Management decided to set up bonus programs for employees who stayed to see the company through the difficult times and back to profitability. Under one plan, every employee would receive a bonus in the first quarter that the company achieved enough profit to cover the bonus costs. In order to help achieve profitability, the CFO met with the managers of his divisions and established profitability targets and what he called "roadmaps" that showed how these targets could be achieved. The roadmaps included statements that the profits could be achieved only through the release from the statement of financial position of excess provisions (that is, provisions for obsolete inventory and bad debts). The provisions had been overprovided for in earlier years in an effort to "manage" profits.

In 2021, the company came under scrutiny from the securities regulators. The government notified it of a criminal investigation into alleged accounting irregularities. In addition, there were several class-action lawsuits outstanding against the company by shareholders alleging that TI had provided misleading information to them in the financial statements for 2019 and 2020. Once news of this was released, credit-rating agencies significantly downgraded their ratings of TI's securities. As a result of this negative activity, the company had not released its financial statements for 2021 and was now in breach of stock exchange requirements to file financial statements. Although the stock exchanges had not done so, they now had the power to delist TI's shares.

The controller of TI must now finalize the financial statements and has come across the following information.

1. During the year, the company signed contracts to sell optical software products. Before year end, the company shipped out what it called an "interim product solution"—in other words, the optical software product ordered by the company was not yet ready in its final form so the company shipped a beta or draft version of it. This interim product would be followed shortly by the final version. Revenues were recognized upon shipment of the interim product solution, as it was felt that the final version just needed minor refinements. The customers generally paid more than half of what was owed under the contract when they received the interim product solution. It was rare for customers to back out of this type of contract for any reason.

2. In 2020, TI had purchased a subsidiary of DEF Inc. and agreed to pay additional future consideration for the purchase (the consideration would take the form of additional TI shares). The additional consideration was a function of the profitability of the subsidiary. The more profitable the subsidiary, the more shares that TI would issue as consideration. Given that TI's shares are highly volatile, TI and DEF agreed that the number of shares to be issued should be based on the average price per share in the three months prior to the future issuance date of the shares. So far, the subsidiary has been performing above expectations.

3. By the end of 2021, TI was still restructuring to streamline its core operations and activities. Part of the restructuring included abandoning its voice-over-fibre operations. The operations would be closed down in early 2022, and this would involve workforce reductions and abandonment of plant and equipment.

Instructions

Adopt the role of controller and analyze the financial reporting issues.

Research and Analysis

RA6.1 `Real World Emphasis` Hudson's Bay Company

Hudson's Bay Company's financial statements for its year ended February 3, 2018 (fiscal 2017) can be found at the end of this book.

Instructions

Refer to the company's financial statements and accompanying notes to answer these questions.

a. What business is Hudson's Bay Company in?

b. What were the company's gross revenues for the fiscal years 2017 and 2016? What is the percentage change? Why has the company seen this result?

c. Based on your findings in part (b), comment on the company's net income/loss over the period.

d. Review the notes to the financial statements to determine the company's revenue recognition policies. Identify the major policies, considering the nature of the business and the industry.

RA6.2 `Real World Emphasis` BCE Inc. and TELUS Corporation

Access the financial statements of both BCE Inc. and TELUS Corporation for their years ended December 31, 2017, from either the companies' websites or SEDAR (www.sedar.com).

Instructions

Using the financial statements for BCE and TELUS, answer the following.

a. What types of revenue does BCE have and when are they recognized?

b. What types of revenue does TELUS have and when are they recognized?

c. Are there any examples of when either company would report revenue on a net basis? What factors does the company consider?

d. Explain the types of contracts where the companies have multiple deliverables. How does each company allocate the revenues on these types of contracts?

e. TELUS has a unique accounting policy for dealing with revenues in non-high-cost serving areas. Review the accounting policy note as well as Note 7 for details. Explain the business reason for the transaction and comment on the appropriateness of the accounting.

f. Do you find one company's disclosure on revenue recognition better than the other's? Comment.

g. Does either company address IFRS 15 *Revenue from Contracts with Customers*, issued in 2014 but with a 2018 effective date? Comment.

RA6.3 `Real World Emphasis` Airbus SE

Airbus SE, previously known as European Aeronautic Defence and Space Company or EADS NV, is incorporated in the Netherlands and its shares are traded in France, Germany, and Spain. Access the financial statements of Airbus SE for its year ended December 31, 2017, from the company's website (www.airbus.com/investors/financial-results-and-annual-reports.html).

Instructions

Answer the following questions with respect to Airbus SE.

a. What business is Airbus in?

b. Explain how the revenue related to construction contracts is recorded. How does the company determine when revenue should be recognized on these contracts?

c. What are the balance sheet amounts related to this revenue recognition? What was the aggregated amount of costs and profits recognized to December 31, 2017? What was the gross amount due from customers and due to customers at December 31, 2017? What do these amounts represent? (*Hint*: See Note 21.)

RA6.4 `Real World Emphasis` The Procter & Gamble Company

Access the financial statements of The Procter & Gamble Company (P&G) for its year ended June 30, 2017, from the company's website (www.pginvestor.com).

Instructions

Refer to P&G's financial statements and the accompanying notes to answer the following questions.

a. What business is P&G in?

    b. What were P&G's net sales for its year ended June 30, 2017?

    c. What was the percentage of increase or decrease in P&G's net sales from 2016 to 2017? From 2015 to 2016? From 2015 to 2017?

    d. What is the source of P&G's revenues? How does P&G decide on the timing of revenue recognition, and how does the company define its net sales?

    e. What are trade promotions and how does P&G account for them? Does the accounting conform to accrual accounting concepts? Explain.

RA6.5   `Real World Emphasis`   **The Coca-Cola Company and PepsiCo**

Coca-Cola Company and **PepsiCo** are two of the best-known companies worldwide. Their 2017 financial statements can be found in the investor information sections of their company websites: www.coca-colacompany.com/investors/archives-annual-other-reports and www.pepsico.com/Investors/Annual-Reports-and-Proxy-Information.

Instructions

Go to the company websites and use information found there as part of their annual reports to answer the following questions about Coca-Cola Company and PepsiCo.

    a. What were Coca-Cola's and PepsiCo's net revenues (sales) for the year 2017? Which company increased its revenue more (dollars and percentage) from 2016 to 2017?

    b. Are the revenue recognition policies of Coca-Cola and PepsiCo similar? Explain.

    c. In which foreign countries (geographical areas) did Coca-Cola and PepsiCo earn significant revenues in 2017? Compare the amounts of foreign revenues with U.S. revenues for both Coca-Cola and PepsiCo.

Analytics in Action

AIA6.1 Clothing Manufacturers Limited (CML) is a public company that sells clothing on a wholesale basis to retail stores. During the past year, the company has adopted IFRS 15 and is looking to estimate sales revenues and refunds. The company has a fair bit of data, including monthly sales and returns for the past five years.

    As the controller, you have asked your assistant to do the following:

a. Create pivot tables (using Excel) showing the following:

    a. Year, number of items sold in the year and number of items returned in the year. Calculate average returns for each year.

    b. Percentage returns by year and month.

b. Create a bar chart showing percentage returns each January for the past five years.

c. What information does this visualization tell you about returns in January over the past five years?

d. Create a line chart showing percentage returns by month and by year.

e. What information does this visualization tell you about year over year and month over month returns?

Instructions   Go to *WileyPLUS* for additional instructions and material to complete this question.

CHAPTER 7

Cash and Receivables

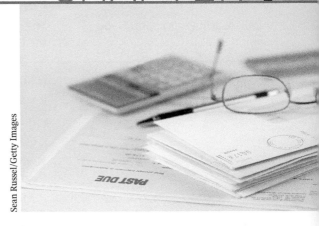

Sean Russel/Getty Images

Last Call for Customer Payments

Internet and phone bills are ones that most Canadians pay in full every month. But what happens when customers fall behind in their accounts?

One of Canada's top communications companies, TELUS Corporation, has accounts receivable in the hundreds of millions every month, from both residential and business customers. Its revenues, which were $13.3 billion in 2017, include fees for home and business telephone, cellular, high-speed Internet, television, and information technology services.

Some of TELUS's billing terms are regulated by the federal Canadian Radio-television and Telecommunications Commission (CRTC). The company bills monthly for services in advance, and payments are due within about three weeks of the billing date. Late payment charges begin to accrue at 30 days from the billing date. Most companies intend late payment charges to be punitive, to encourage customers to pay on time. TELUS charges 2% per month for overdue accounts. "We follow a program of credit evaluations of customers and limit the amount of credit extended when deemed necessary," TELUS says in its annual report. For example, if a customer does not have a satisfactory credit history, TELUS may require a security deposit from them.

If a customer's bill does not get paid on time, companies such as TELUS will start making calls, sending reminder notices, and perhaps negotiating new payment terms. If there is still no payment, a telecom company will typically suspend the account for 21 days, then reconnect for one day, and contact the client again. If there is still no payment, it will permanently disconnect the customer. The company then would send final notices to the client, and finally the bill goes to a collection agency.

As at December 31, 2017, TELUS reported accounts receivable of $1.6 billion, up 10% from the year before. The company attributed this partly to "an increase in roaming revenue accruals, as well as an increase in wireless receivables."

While having significant accounts receivable can be a credit risk, many companies, including TELUS, capitalize on their accounts receivable. TELUS has an ongoing agreement to sell part of its accounts receivable to an unnamed financial institution, borrowing against the expected revenue to raise money, a strategy known as securitization. In 2017, TELUS had sold $119 million in trade receivables under its accounts receivable securitization program.

Sources: Richard Bloom, "Telus Unit to Raise $500-Million," *The Globe and Mail*, March 29, 2017; TELUS Corporation 2017 annual report; TELUS service term documents for various services.

LEARNING OBJECTIVES	CHAPTER OUTLINE	CPA COMPETENCIES
After studying this chapter, you should be able to:	The chapter headings related to the learning objective are:	Competencies addressed by each learning objective are as follows:
1. Understand cash and accounts receivable from a business perspective.	**Understanding Cash and Accounts Receivable** • How do companies manage and control cash? • What types of companies have extensive accounts receivable? • What are the types of accounts receivable? • How do companies manage accounts receivable?	**1.1.1, 1.4.5, 2.4.1, 5.2.1**
2. Define financial assets, and identify items that are considered cash and cash equivalents and how they are reported.	**Cash** • What is cash? • Reporting cash • Summary of cash-related items	**1.2.1, 1.2.2**
3. Define receivables, and identify the different types of receivables from an accounting perspective.	**Receivables**	**1.2.1, 1.2.2**
4. Account for and explain the accounting issues related to the recognition and measurement of accounts receivable.	**Recognition and Measurement of Accounts Receivable** • Trade discounts • Cash discounts (sales discounts) • Sales returns and allowances • Nonrecognition of interest element • Measurement of accounts receivable after acquisition	**1.1.2, 1.2.1, 1.2.2, 1.2.3, 5.2.1**
5. Account for and explain the accounting issues related to the impairment in value of accounts receivable.	**Impairment of Accounts Receivable** • Estimating uncollectible trade accounts receivable • Allowance method • Effects on accounts • Direct write off method	**1.2.1, 1.2.2, 1.2.3**
6. Account for and explain the accounting issues related to the recognition and measurement of notes and loans receivable.	**Notes and Loans Receivable** • Recognition and measurement of short-term notes and loans receivable • Recognition and measurement of long-term notes and loans receivable	**1.2.1, 1.2.2, 1.2.3**

7.	Account for and explain the basic accounting issues related to the derecognition of receivables.	**Derecognition of Receivables** • Secured borrowings • Sales of receivables • Securitized receivables-transparency	**1.2.1, 1.2.2, 1.2.3, 1.2.4, 5.2.3**
8.	Explain how receivables and loans are reported and analyzed.	**Presentation, Disclosure, and Analysis of Receivables** • Presentation and disclosure • Analysis	**1.2.1, 1.2.2, 1.2.3, 1.2.4, 1.3.2, 1.4.1, 1.4.2, 1.4.4, 5.1.1, 5.2.1**
9.	Identify differences in accounting between IFRS and accounting standards for private enterprises (ASPE), and what changes are expected in the near future.	**IFRS/ASPE Comparison** • A comparison of IFRS and ASPE • Looking ahead	**1.1.4**

After studying Appendix 7A, you should be able to:

10.	Explain common techniques for controlling cash.	**Appendix 7A—Methods for Controlling Cash** • Management and control of cash • Using bank accounts • The imprest petty cash system • Physical protection of cash balances • Reconciliation of bank balances	**1.2.1, 1.2.2, 1.2.3, 1.2.4, 3.1.1, 3.1.2, 4.1.1, 4.1.2**

Preview of Chapter 7

As our opening story implies, estimating the collectibility of accounts receivable has important implications for accurate reporting of operating profits, net income, and assets. In this chapter, we discuss cash and receivables—two assets that are important to companies as diverse as giant TELUS and small owner-operated private operations.

Understanding Cash and Accounts Receivable

LEARNING OBJECTIVE 1

Understand cash and accounts receivable from a business perspective.

It is important to understand the business of the company when considering issues relating to cash and accounts receivable. We need to ask ourselves questions such as the following.

- How do companies manage and control cash?
- What types of companies are more likely to have significant accounts receivable balances?

- What are the different types of accounts receivable?
- What aspects of accounts receivable must be managed and how do companies do this?

We will address these questions below.

How Do Companies Manage and Control Cash?

Finance 5.2.1 Cash management and control is a key issue for many companies, including retailers that have significant cash sales. Businesses rely on cash flow budgets to help anticipate cash needs and minimize borrowing requirements. Generally, companies with surplus cash try to minimize "idle" cash by putting the surplus into short-term deposits. Banks and other financial institutions take this to the extreme with very short-term borrowing and lending in the overnight money market, where borrowed funds plus interest must be repaid at the start of the next business day. For companies without surplus cash, management must still carefully manage its cash resources to minimize any bank loans and other borrowings. The control of cash includes implementing internal control over physical custody of cash on hand and preparing regular bank reconciliations. Control of cash is so important that we devote an entire appendix to it at the end of this chapter, where we discuss it in much more detail.

What Types of Companies Have Extensive Accounts Receivable?

As a general rule, manufacturers and wholesalers often have a significant amount of accounts receivable. For instance, **Magna International Inc.**, a large Canadian automobile supplier, reported accounts receivable of U.S. $6,878 million (or over 60% of current assets) at the end of 2017. This was Magna's largest current asset and it reflected an increase of 11.6% from 2016 to 2017. An increase in accounts receivable might be cause for concern for some companies, if it indicates an inability to collect receivables on a timely basis. However, Magna also showed a significant 6.9% increase in sales in 2017. In addition, Magna noted that sales to its six largest customers represented 81% of the company's total sales, which should make monitoring of its accounts receivable easier than for most companies. Magna adopted U.S. generally accepted accounting principles in 2011, and uses the U.S. dollar as its functional currency. Therefore, its Canadian accounts receivable are translated into U.S. dollars on its balance sheet.

On the other hand, retailers such as **Hudson's Bay Company (HBC)** often have relatively low accounts receivable. This is due to customers' use of major credit cards (like Visa) and debit cards for payments. For example, at the end of the 2017 fiscal year, HBC had trade and other receivables of only $391 million (or approximately 9.6% of current assets). The company reported that its trade and other receivables consisted of credit card issuer, vendor, and other receivables and that there was no concentration of accounts receivable balances. HBC's types of receivables and its lack of concentration with any individual parties make monitoring of collection issues less difficult.

What Are the Types of Accounts Receivable?

Manufacturers and wholesalers have accounts receivable relating to their sales transactions, as discussed in Chapter 6. Let's look for instance at **Suncor Energy**, a major Canadian integrated energy company with operations including oil sands development, retail operations (such as products marketed under the PetroCanada brand), and wholesale operations. Suncor had accounts receivable of $3,281 million at the end of 2017 (or 10.2% of revenues, down from 11.9% at the end of 2016). These receivables represent one of Suncor's largest current assets each year. Large accounts receivable balances are typical in the oil and gas industry, in part due to extended payment terms, which can stretch from 30 to 60 days. The company noted that, at the end of 2017, substantially all of its trade receivables were current.

For most companies, typical accounts receivable–related categories include trade receivables, loans receivable, and nontrade receivables (including items like interest receivable, amounts due from officers, and advances to employees). However, there are more complicated items sometimes included in accounts receivable. For example, Suncor enters into arrangements that allow the off-setting of derivative financial instruments and accounts receivable as part of its accounts receivable balance. Suncor's derivatives include swaps related to its fixed rate debt. The fair value of derivative contracts recorded as part of accounts receivable totalled $74 million at the end of 2017 ($155 million at the end of 2016). Interest rate swaps generally involve one party that was making payments based on a fixed interest rate, and another that was making payments based on a floating rate, agreeing to swap or exchange their payment streams. Swaps are discussed in more detail in Chapter 16, as part of Complex Financial Instruments.

How Do Companies Manage Accounts Receivable?

For many reasons, it is important for management to carefully consider how to manage and control its accounts receivable balances. Of course, accounts receivable are directly related to sales. If the sales department is overly aggressive with its credit policy, it could result in significant increases in bad debts and uncollectible accounts. Companies will typically assess the creditworthiness of new customers and grant them a credit limit accordingly. Established customers' track records and payment history will also affect how credit limits change over time.

Strategy & Governance 2.4.1 Receivables management can be a delicate balancing act. If credit policies are too "tight," or restrictive, potential sales could be lost to competitors. On the other hand, if the credit policy is too "loose," or flexible, an aggressive sales team might enter into contracts with higher-risk customers, resulting in collectibility difficulties. Some companies offer discounts to encourage faster payment of outstanding balances. These discounts are popular with customers, because the savings from early payment are much better than the interest that could be earned on short-term investments. However, the costs to the company offering the discount must also be considered.

Finance 5.2.1 Companies also need to monitor outstanding accounts receivable balances. An important tool is an aged accounts receivable analysis, discussed in the section "Impairment of Accounts Receivable" later in this chapter. Companies that do not regularly assess and follow up on overdue accounts receivable may find that some of their customers take advantage of the situation. In particular, customers that are facing cash flow problems may be influenced regarding which companies they pay first by the number of phone calls and follow-up letters they receive from collection departments. (After all, it is easier to "oil the squeaky wheel" than to listen to it!) Discussions with tardy customers may result in a schedule of payments that benefits both the seller and customer.

Companies should therefore monitor accounts receivable levels carefully to:

- minimize the stress on working capital and related bank debt, and also
- encourage prompt payment by their customers.

See **What Do the Numbers Mean? 7.1**.

What Do the Numbers Mean? 7.1

Companies typically do not limit themselves to one technique in order to speed up collections. For example, **Bell Aliant**, one of North America's largest land-line communications and Internet service providers, uses a collection agency only as a last resort in the collection process! It uses late payment charges and follow-up letters to help encourage prompt payment. Late payment fees can be substantial; Bell indicates that, for payments not received within 30 days of the bill date, it will charge a 3% monthly (42.6% per annum) fee.[1] The opening story to this chapter provides details of how companies encourage payment of their overdue accounts.

Companies may sell accounts receivable to factors to convert their receivables into cash more quickly, rather than waiting for customers to pay. These services tend to be used more by small and medium-sized businesses that may not have the cash resources to wait for payment (or the credit history to allow them to obtain a bank loan at a better interest rate). Alternatively, larger companies may rely on securitization of pools of accounts receivable, where the receivables are grouped together and turned into securities for sale to investors. We discuss the use of factors and asset-backed securities by large companies to raise funds and improve cash flow in more detail as part of the subsection "Derecognition of Receivables" later in this chapter.

---

[1] "Late payment fees and overdue payments," Bell Canada, http://support.bell.ca/Billing-and-Accounts/Billing/What_happens_if_I_don_t_pay_my_bill_on_time#displayStep.

Cash

LEARNING OBJECTIVE 2
Define financial assets, and identify items that are considered cash and cash equivalents and how they are reported.

We now begin our detailed study of statement of financial position (SFP) accounts and the recognition and measurement concepts that apply to the different categories of assets, liabilities, and shareholders' equity. The first assets we cover are highly liquid, and they are considered financial assets. A **financial asset** is any asset that is:

   i. cash;

  ii. a contractual right to receive cash or another financial asset from another party;

 iii. a contractual right to exchange financial instruments with another party under conditions that are potentially favourable; or

  iv. an equity instrument of another entity.[2]

Financial assets are covered in several chapters of this text. Chapter 7 deals with cash and cash equivalents, and with accounts, notes, and loans receivable. Chapter 9 covers other major categories of financial assets—mainly investments in the debt and equity instruments of other companies. The financial assets in these two chapters fit parts (i), (ii), and (iv) of the definition above. Chapter 3 highlights the profession's recent move away from the long-standing transactions-based historical cost model toward one that relies more on fair values. Chapter 3 also includes a discussion of what fair value is and how it is measured. We will cover the more complex instruments that fit part (iii) of the definition above, such as derivatives, along with financial liabilities and equity, in Chapter 16 of Volume 2.

What Is Cash?

Cash is the most liquid asset and is the standard medium of exchange and the basis for measuring and accounting for all other items. It meets the definition of a financial asset, and is generally classified as a current asset.

Cash consists of coins, currency, and other available funds that are on deposit at a bank. Negotiable instruments such as money orders, certified cheques, cashier's cheques, and bank drafts are also viewed as cash. Although a company's bank may have a legal right to demand advance notice before it allows a withdrawal from a savings account, banks rarely ask for this notice. Therefore, savings accounts are also usually classified as cash.

It is more appropriate to classify money-market funds, certificates of deposit, and similar types of deposits and "short-term paper" that allow investors to earn interest as **cash equivalents** (defined in the subsection "Reporting Cash" below) or **short-term investments** than as cash. The reason is that there are usually restrictions, or penalties, on these securities if they are converted to cash before maturity. Money-market funds that give chequing account privileges, however, are usually classified as cash.

Certain items may present classification problems: for example, postdated cheques from customers and IOUs are treated as receivables. It is proper to treat travel advances granted to employees as receivables if the advances are to be collected from the employees or deducted from their salaries. Otherwise, it is more appropriate to classify the travel advance as a prepaid

---

[2]This excerpt is reprinted with permission from the *CPA Canada Handbook—Accounting* © 2018, Part II, Section 3856, *Financial Instruments*, by Chartered Professional Accountants of Canada. All rights reserved by the copyright owner. The IFRS definition in IAS 32.11 introduces additional complexity beyond the scope of this text related to when the entity enters into a contract that will be settled with its own shares. Copyright © IFRS Foundation. All rights reserved. Reproduced with permission.

expense. Petty cash funds and change funds are included in current assets as cash because these funds are used to meet current operating expenses and to liquidate current liabilities.

Reporting Cash

Although the reporting of cash is fairly straightforward, there are some issues that need special attention. They concern the reporting of:

- Restricted cash
- Cash in foreign currencies
- Bank overdrafts
- Cash equivalents

Restricted Cash

Petty cash (see Appendix 7A) and special payroll and dividend bank accounts are examples of cash that has been set aside for a particular purpose. In most situations, these balances are not material and therefore are not segregated from cash when it is reported in the financial statements. When an amount is material, restricted cash is segregated from regular cash for reporting purposes. The **restricted cash** is separately disclosed and reported in the current assets section or is classified separately in the long-term assets section, depending on the date of availability or of the expected disbursement.[3] In general, cash should not be classified in current assets if there are restrictions that prevent it from being used for current purposes, unless the restricted cash offsets a current liability. Cash that is classified in the long-term section has often been set aside for investment or financing purposes, such as for a plant expansion, long-term debt retirement, or as collateral for a long-term loan.

Some lending institutions require customers who borrow money from them to keep minimum cash balances in their chequing or savings accounts. These minimum cash balances are more common in the United States and are called **compensating balances**. By requiring a compensating balance, the bank gets an effective interest rate on its loan that is higher than the stated rate because it can use the restricted amount that must remain on deposit. Some banks, like CIBC, offer borrowers a choice of compensating balances, direct fees, or a combination of both.

Law To ensure that investors are not misled about the amount of cash that is available to meet recurring obligations, legally restricted balances have to be reported separately in current assets or non-current assets, as appropriate. In practice, many companies report this through note disclosure.

Cash in Foreign Currencies

Many companies have bank accounts in other countries, especially if they have recurring transactions in that country's currency. The foreign currency is translated into Canadian dollars at the exchange rate on the date of the SFP. See **Underlying Concept 7.1**. In situations where there is no restriction on the transfer of those funds to the Canadian company, they are included as cash in current assets. If there are restrictions on the flow of capital out of a country, the cash is reported as restricted. The classification of the cash as current or non-current is based on the circumstances. In extreme cases, restrictions may be so severe that the foreign balances do not even qualify for recognition as assets.

Bank Overdrafts

Bank overdrafts occur when cheques are written for more than the amount in the bank account. Overdrafts are reported in the current liabilities section, and companies sometimes do this by adding the amount to what is reported as accounts payable. If the overdraft amount is material, it should be disclosed separately, either on the face of the SFP or in the related notes.

> **Underlying Concept 7.1**
>
> When entities have cash accounts in more than one currency, they are remeasured into a common monetary unit, typically Canadian dollars, using the rate at the date of the SFP. Some Canadian companies, however, identify the U.S. dollar as their functional currency and present their statements in this unit instead.

---

[3]Under IFRS, if current and non-current asset classifications are not used on the SFP, separate disclosure is required of amounts to be recovered within 12 months and more than 12 months after the SFP date.

In general, bank overdrafts should not be offset against the Cash account. A major exception is when there is available cash in another account at the same bank as the overdraft. Offsetting in this case is appropriate.

Cash Equivalents

IFRS **ASPE** Cash is often reported with the asset category called cash equivalents. **Cash equivalents** are defined as "short-term, highly liquid investments that are readily convertible to known amounts of cash and which are subject to an insignificant risk of changes in value."[4] Companies usually hold cash equivalents to meet upcoming cash requirements. Generally, only investments with **maturities of three months or less** when acquired qualify under the definition of cash equivalents. Equity investments are excluded from the ASPE definition of cash equivalents. However, IFRS allows preferred shares that are acquired close to their maturity date to qualify. Examples of cash equivalents are investments in treasury bills, commercial paper, and money-market funds.

In some circumstances, bank overdrafts may be deducted when the amount of cash and cash equivalents is being determined. Overdrafts may be considered part of cash and cash equivalents if:

- they are part of the firm's cash management activities,
- they are repayable on demand, and
- the bank balance fluctuates often between a positive and negative balance.

Because some companies report investments that qualify as cash equivalents in other categories of current assets, such as short-term or trading investments, it is important for entities to disclose their reporting policy in a note to the financial statements. Investments that are classified as cash equivalents are held to be sold in the very short term. These are generally reported at fair value. Their fair values at acquisition plus accrued interest to the date of the SFP often approximate fair value at the date of the SFP.

Illustration 7.1 shows the information that Centerra Gold Inc. reported in its consolidated financial statements for the year ended December 31, 2017 (in thousands of U.S. dollars). Centerra is a Canadian gold mining and exploration company listed on the Toronto Stock Exchange with gold properties in North America, Asia, and other markets around the world. At the end of 2016, Centerra had U.S. $247.8 million of restricted cash relating to a Kyrgyz Republic court order requiring that cash generated from its Kumtor Project continue to be held

ILLUSTRATION 7.1

Reporting of Cash and Cash Equivalents—Centerra Gold Inc. (in thousands of U.S. dollars)

	Notes	2017	2016
ASSETS			
Current assets:			
Cash and cash equivalents		$ 415,891	$160,017
Restricted cash and restricted short-term investments	7	–	247,844
Restricted cash	7	687	824

3. Summary of significant accounting policies

d. Cash and cash equivalents
Cash and cash equivalents comprise cash balances and short-term investments with original maturities of 90 days or less. Cash and cash equivalents are classified as financial instruments carried at amortized cost.

f. Restricted cash and restricted short-term investments
Cash and short-term investments which are subject to legal or contractual restrictions on their use are classified separately as restricted cash and restricted short-term investments.

---

[4]*CPA Canada Handbook*, Part II, Section 1540.06(b) and IAS 7.6. Copyright © IFRS Foundation. All rights reserved. Reproduced with permission.

in one of its subsidiaries. Among other things, it restricted the distribution of the subsidiaries' cash to any Centerra group entity as a loan, advance, or dividend. However, the court order restricting the cash was terminated during 2017, and the cash was classified as part of cash and cash equivalents at the end of 2017.

Summary of Cash-Related Items

Cash and cash equivalents include currency and most negotiable instruments. If the item cannot be converted to coin or currency on short notice, it is classified separately as an investment, receivable, or prepaid expense. Cash that is not available for paying liabilities that are currently maturing is classified in the long-term assets section. **Illustration 7.2** summarizes the classification of cash-related items. Appendix 7A provides further details on the control of cash.

ILLUSTRATION 7.2 **Classification of Cash, Cash Equivalents, and Non-Cash Items**

Item	Classification	Comment
Cash	Cash	Report as cash. If restricted, identify and report separately as a current or non-current asset.
Petty cash	Cash	Report as cash.
Short-term paper	Cash equivalents	Classify as cash equivalents if investments have a maturity of three months or less when acquired.
Short-term paper	Short-term investments	Classify as short-term investments if maturity is over 3 months, and up to 12 months, when acquired.
Postdated cheques and IOUs	Receivables	Classify as receivables if they are considered to be collectible.
Travel advances	Receivables or prepaid expenses	Classify as receivables or prepaid expenses if they are collectible from employees or will be spent on travel in the future, respectively.
Postage on hand (for example, within postage meters)	Prepaid expenses	Alternatively, these may be classified as office supplies inventory.
Bank overdrafts	Current liability	If there is a right of offset, report as a reduction of cash.
Compensating balances	Classified separately as a deposit that is maintained as a compensating balance	Classify as current asset in the SFP. Disclose details of the arrangement.

Receivables

LEARNING OBJECTIVE 3

Define receivables, and identify the different types of receivables from an accounting perspective.

We now turn to a second type of asset that is important to companies: receivables. In general, receivables are claims that a company has against customers and others, usually for specific cash receipts in the future. As we saw in the introduction to this chapter, when the claim is a **contractual** right to receive cash or other financial assets from another party, the receivable is a financial asset. On a classified SFP, receivables are either current (short-term) or non-current (long-term). Current receivables are expected to be realized (converted to cash) within a year or during the current operating cycle, whichever is longer. All other receivables are classified as non-current.

These financial assets are generally referred to in a more specific way as loans or receivables, with loans being a type of receivable.[5] **Loans and receivables** result from one party delivering cash (or other assets or services) to a borrower in exchange for a promise to repay the amount on a specified date or dates, or on demand, along with interest to compensate for the time value of money and the risk of non-payment. They are not usually acquired to be held as a cash equivalent or temporary investment of excess cash. Investments in government debt, corporate bonds, convertible debt, commercial paper, and other securities, while similar, are not loans and receivables. They are traded in an active market, while loans and receivables are not.

Trade receivables are amounts owed by customers to whom the company has sold goods or services as part of its normal business operations; that is, they are amounts that result from operating transactions. They can be either open accounts receivable or notes receivable. Open accounts receivable are short-term extensions of credit that are based on a purchaser's **verbal promise** to pay for goods and services that have been sold. They are normally collectible within 30 to 60 days, but credit terms may be longer—or shorter—depending on the industry. **Notes receivable** are **written promises** to pay a certain amount of money on a specified future date. They may arise from sales of goods and services, or from other transactions.

As the term "loan" suggests, **loans receivable** are created when one party advances cash or other assets to a borrower and receives a promise to be repaid later. Loans tend to result from financing transactions by borrowers and investing transactions by lenders. When there is a written document that gives the terms and conditions of the loan receivable, the loan is then also called a note receivable.

Nontrade receivables are created by a variety of transactions and can be written promises either to pay cash or to deliver other assets. Examples of nontrade receivables include the following:

- Advances to officers and employees, or to subsidiaries or other companies
- Amounts owing from a purchaser on the sale of capital assets or investments where delayed payment terms have been agreed on
- Amounts receivable from the government for income taxes paid in excess of the amount owed, GST/HST payments recoverable, investment tax credits, or other tax rebates receivable
- Dividends and interest receivable
- Claims against insurance companies for losses the company has suffered; against trucking companies or railways for damaged or lost goods; against creditors for returned, damaged, or lost goods; or against customers for returnable items (crates, containers, etc.)

Because of their special nature, nontrade receivables are generally classified and reported as separate items in the SFP or in a note that is cross-referenced to the statement. **Illustration 7.3** shows the assets on the balance sheet and extracts from separate reporting of loans and other receivables in the notes to the financial statements of Nova Scotia–based **Empire Company Limited** for its year ended May 6, 2017 (in millions of dollars).

Loans receivable represent long-term financing by Empire to certain retail associates. These loans are primarily secured by inventory, fixtures, and equipment; bear various interest rates; and have repayment terms of up to 10 years. The carrying amount of the loans receivable approximates fair value based on the variable interest rates charged on the loans.

Included in notes receivable and other as at May 6, 2017, is $13.2 (2016 – $14.5) due from a third party related to equipment sales.

Note that in the following discussion of **accounts and notes receivable**, we assume that they are short-term trade receivables, and that the discussion of **loans receivable** is based on long-term nontrade loans or notes. In addition, we assume that they all are financial assets. The basic accounting issues are discussed in the following sections: **recognition and measurement**, **impairment**, and **derecognition**.

---

[5]Some receivables are not financial assets. They are excluded when the claim does not result from a contractual right (such as income taxes receivable because they result from government legislation and are not contractual), and prepaid expenses because the claim is not for cash or another financial asset. (See IAS32.AG3 to AG12 for further details.)

ILLUSTRATION 7.3

**Receivables Reporting—
Empire Company Limited**

**CONSOLIDATED BALANCE SHEETS
(in millions)**

	May 6, 2017	May 7, 2016
Assets		
Current		
Cash and cash equivalents	$ 207.3	$ 264.7
Receivables	413.6	489.4
Inventories (Note 4)	1,322.2	1,287.3
Prepaid expenses	117.5	117.3
Loans and other receivables (Note 5)	25.5	26.4
Income taxes receivable	31.9	11.9
Assets held for sale (Note 6)	48.5	407.1
	2,166.5	2,604.1
Loans and other receivables (Note 5)	82.1	93.5
Investments	25.1	24.7
Investments, at equity (Note 7)	648.4	574.9
Other assets (Note 8)	43.3	57.3
Property and equipment (Note 9)	3,033.3	3,144.7
Investment property (Note 10)	103.0	82.9
Intangibles (Note 11)	880.5	911.5
Goodwill (Note 12)	1,003.4	998.7
Deferred tax assets (Note 13)	709.9	646.2
	$8,695.5	$9,138.5

5. Loans and Other Receivables

	May 6, 2017	May 7, 2016
Loans receivable	$ 64.8	$ 76.6
Notes receivable and other	42.8	43.3
	107.6	119.9
Less amount due within one year	25.5	26.4
	$ 82.1	$ 93.5

Recognition and Measurement of Accounts Receivable

LEARNING OBJECTIVE 4

Account for and explain the accounting issues related to the recognition and measurement of accounts receivable.

The general accounting standards for the recognition and initial measurement of accounts receivable are as follows:

- Recognize an account receivable when the entity becomes a party to the contractual provisions of the financial instrument.
- Measure the receivable initially at its fair value.[6]
- After initial recognition, measure receivables at amortized cost.

The entity becomes a party to the contractual provisions of the financial instrument only when it has a legal claim to receive cash or other financial assets. While a commitment to sell

---

[6]Receivables that are created by related party transactions may be an exception. Chapter 23 discusses the issues underlying related party transactions.

goods or services to a customer might be made when a customer's order is received, there is usually no legal claim until one of the parties to the contract has performed under the agreement. Therefore, the timing of recognition of accounts receivable is intertwined with the recognition of revenue, which we discussed in Chapter 6. Typically, when the sale is recognized, either cash is received (realized) or an account receivable is recognized.

Recognizing receivables initially at their fair value is not as straightforward as it might seem. This is because fair value may not be the same as the exchange price that the parties agree on. The **exchange price**, the **amount due** from the customer or borrower, is generally indicated on a business document, usually an invoice. Two factors can make measuring the fair value of short-term receivables more complicated: (1) the availability of discounts (trade and cash discounts) and (2) the length of time between the sale and the payment due date (the interest element).

Trade Discounts

Customers are often quoted prices based on list or catalogue prices that may have trade or quantity discounts. Trade discounts are used to avoid frequent changes in catalogues, to quote different prices for different quantities purchased, or to hide the true invoice price from competitors.

Trade discounts are commonly quoted in percentages. For example, if your textbook has a list price of $120 and the publisher sells it to college and university bookstores for list less a 30% trade discount, the receivable recorded by the publisher is $84 per textbook. The normal practice is simply to deduct the trade discount from the list price and recognize the net amount as the receivable and revenue.

Cash Discounts (Sales Discounts)

Finance 5.2.1 Cash discounts or sales discounts are offered to encourage fast payment. They are expressed in specific terms. For example, 2/10, n/30 means that there is a 2% discount if the invoice is paid within 10 days and that the gross amount is due in 30 days. Meanwhile, 2/10 E.O.M., n/30 E.O.M. means there is a 2% discount if the invoice is paid before the 10th day of the following month, with full payment due by the 30th of the following month. (E.O.M. stands for "end of month.")

Companies that buy goods or services but fail to take sales discounts are usually not using their money as effectively as they could. For example, let's say a company would receive a 1% reduction in the sales price for paying within 10 days, when the amount is due within 30 days. If it does pay within 10 days, it is basically earning 18.25% interest (1.0% divided by 20/365) because of the discount—or, more technically, it is at least avoiding being charged at the rate of interest implicit in the undiscounted price. For this reason, companies usually take such a discount unless their cash is severely limited. As discussed in Chapter 6, these cash discounts (also known as prompt settlement discounts) should reduce revenues if material.

Sales Returns and Allowances

IFRS **ASPE** To properly measure **sales revenues** and **receivables**, allowance accounts are normally used under ASPE (and refund liability accounts under IFRS). Probable sales returns and price reductions are estimated and deducted as contra accounts against sales on the income statement and accounts receivable on the SFP. This results in net sales and the net estimated amount of accounts receivable being properly reported.

This procedure is followed so that the sales returns or price allowances (called sales returns and allowances) are reported in the same period as the related sales. If this adjustment is not made, however, the amount of mismatched returns and allowances is usually not material as long as the items are handled consistently from year to year. The situation may change if a company completes a few special orders for large amounts near the end of its accounting period. In this case, sales returns and allowances should be anticipated and recognized in the period of the sale to avoid distorting the current period's income statement. There are some companies that by their nature have significant returns and therefore usually have an allowance for sales returns. **Example 7.1** illustrates the year-end adjustment to be made for estimated sales returns.

Example 7.1 | Sales Returns

Facts Astro Corporation estimates that approximately 5% of its $1 million of trade receivables outstanding will be returned or a similar adjustment will be made to the sales price.

Instructions What journal entry should Astro make to show expected sales returns and allowances under IFRS vs. ASPE?

Solution As noted in Chapter 6 (Example 6.16), at the time of sale, assuming that coincides with the transfer of goods to its customer, the company would recognize Sales Revenue and a related Refund Liability under IFRS. Leaving out a $50,000 charge could have a material effect on net income for the period. Typically, under ASPE, companies would record a related allowance rather than a refund liability. Rather than recording the Refund Liability or Allowance at the time of each sale, companies may also choose to record these amounts at the end of the period to ease financial statement preparation. If Astro chooses this alternative, it would record the following:

IFRS		ASPE	
Sales Revenue	50,000	Sales Returns and	
Refund Liability	50,000	Allowances	50,000
		Allowance for Sales	
		Returns and Allowances	50,000

ASPE

A	=	L	+	SE
−50,000				−50,000

Cash flows: No effect

The account Sales Returns and Allowances is reported as a deduction from Sales Revenue in the income statement. Allowance for Sales Returns and Allowances is an asset valuation account (contra asset) that is deducted from total accounts receivable. It is similar to the Allowance for Doubtful Accounts discussed below.

Nonrecognition of Interest Element

Ideally, receivables should be measured initially at their fair value, represented by their present value; that is, the amount of cash that would be required at the date of the sale to satisfy the outstanding claim. As mentioned in the previous section, this is equivalent to the discounted value of the cash that will be received in the future. When a company has to wait for the cash receipts, the receivable's face amount is not a precise measure of its fair value. **Example 7.2** illustrates the concept of sale with delayed payment of the related account receivable.
  See also **Underlying Concept 7.2**.

> **Underlying Concept 7.2**
>
> Materiality means that an amount in question would make a difference to a decision-maker. Standard setters believe that interest and present value concepts do not need to be strictly applied if omitting them results in financial statements that are not materially different.

Example 7.2 | Sale with Delayed Payment Date by Customer

Facts The Furniture Company makes a sale on account for $1,000. The market rate of interest is 12%, and the terms of the sale indicate that $1,000 cash is to be received at the end of four months.

Instructions What amount should The Furniture Company record regarding this sale and the related account receivable?

Solution The receivable's present value is not $1,000 but $961.56 ($1,000 × 0.96156; Table A.2, $n = 1$, $i = 4\%$).[7] In other words, $1,000 to be received in four months is equivalent to $961.56 received today. In theory, the discounted amount of $961.56 is the fair value of the receivable and sales revenue, and any additional amount received after the sale is interest revenue. **In practice, accountants generally ignore this for accounts receivable because the discount amount is not usually material when compared with the net income for the period.**

---

[7]Present and future value tables are provided after the specimen financial statements.

ASPE and IFRS both support measuring financial assets at the **present value of the cash that is expected to be received**. However, both allow net realizable value (the net amount expected to be received in cash) to approximate the present value for short-term trade receivables because the effect of the time value of money is immaterial.

Measurement of Accounts Receivable after Acquisition

Accounts receivable are measured in subsequent accounting periods at amortized cost. Where there is no interest element recognized, as discussed above, there is nothing to amortize, so amortized cost and cost are the same thing. For notes and loans receivable that have an interest component, the asset's carrying amount is amortized as described later in this chapter.

Impairment of Accounts Receivable

LEARNING OBJECTIVE 5

Account for and explain the accounting issues related to the impairment in value of accounts receivable.

IFRS **ASPE** The goal in valuing accounts receivable on the statement of financial position is to report them at no more than the benefits they will ultimately provide to the entity. Because of this, in addition to reductions for expected returns, allowances, or cash discounts that will be granted, all receivables have to be assessed for indications of uncollectibility or impairment. Loans and receivables are impaired if there has been a "significant adverse change" in either the expected timing of the future cash flows or in the amount expected to be repaid. Impaired trade receivables are usually referred to as bad debts or **uncollectible accounts**. **Significant Change** Under IFRS 9, for accounts receivable without a significant financing component, the loss allowance is to be based on "lifetime expected credit losses." This is defined as expected credit losses resulting from all possible default events over the life of the accounts receivable, consistent with the expected loss impairment model discussed in Chapter 9.

Estimating Uncollectible Trade Accounts Receivable

As one accountant so aptly noted, the credit manager's idea of heaven would probably be a place where everyone (eventually) paid his or her debts.[8] With the exception of some segments in the retail sector, the usual method of conducting business is through extending credit to customers. This means that most companies are exposed to varying levels of credit risk: the likelihood of loss because of the other party's failure to fully pay the amount owed. Except for cash sales, it is possible that the full amount of any sale will never be collected. Many companies set their credit policies to allow for a certain percentage of uncollectible accounts. In fact, some companies feel that if the control over sales is too "tight," it may indicate that sales are being lost because credit policies are too strict.

The **accounting issue**, therefore, is ensuring that a reasonable estimate is made of the amount of the accounts receivable that is unlikely to be collected. An allowance for this

---

[8]William J. Vatter, *Managerial Accounting* (Englewood Cliffs, N.J.: Prentice-Hall, 1950), p. 60.

amount is then deducted from the receivables reported on the SFP. If there are only a few relatively large accounts, an analysis of each separate account can be made, but most companies have large numbers of similar accounts with smaller balances in each. How does management estimate how much may be uncollectible?

The most important indicator used to identify impaired accounts receivable is the age of the accounts; that is, how long the amounts owed have been outstanding, especially for those beyond their due dates. Other factors that are considered include the company's past loss experience and current economic conditions. Accounts are also analyzed by grouping those with similar credit risk characteristics—perhaps by geographic location or type of industry. If one area of the country is experiencing high unemployment and depressed economic conditions, this may affect the ability of debtors in that area to pay their accounts. Or a particular industry, such as forestry or real estate, may be going through a low in the business cycle with a higher than usual incidence of tight cash, or receivership or bankruptcy.

One common method most companies use to estimate how much of their total accounts receivable is probably uncollectible is the aging method. Under this approach, a company uses its past experience to estimate the percentage of its outstanding receivables that will become uncollectible, without identifying specific accounts. This is called the percentage-of-receivables approach. Its objective is to report receivables on the SFP at their net realizable value—the net amount expected to be received in cash. The percentage that is used in this approach may be a combined rate that reflects an overall estimate of the uncollectible receivables. A better approach is to set up an aging schedule, which is more sensitive to the actual status of the accounts receivable. This approach determines the age of each account receivable and uses a provision matrix to apply a different percentage estimated to be uncollectible to each of the various age categories, based on historical observed default rates. At each reporting date, these default rates in the provision matrix are updated to take into account matters such as changes in economic conditions. Aging schedules are often used because they show which accounts need special attention by highlighting how long various accounts receivable have been outstanding. Example 7.3 illustrates an aging schedule for accounts receivable and the related journal entries.

Example 7.3 | Accounts Receivable Aging Schedule

Facts Assume that Wilson & Co. has prepared the following aging of its accounts receivable. The company's collection history suggests that the probability of collection for its accounts receivable is 96% for balances under 61 days, 85% for balances 61–90 days old, 80% for balances 91–120 days old, and 75% for balances over 120 days.

	Wilson & Co. Aging Schedule				
		Age (number of days accounts are outstanding)			
Customer Name	Balance Dec. 31	Under 61 days	61–90 days	91–120 days	Over 120 days
Atlantic Stainless Steel Corp	$ 9,800	$ 7,000	$ 2,800		
Brockville Steel Company	34,000	34,000			
Cambridge Sheet & Tube Co.	4,500				$ 4,500
Eastern Iron Works Ltd.	7,200	6,000		$ 1,200	
Other individual customers	491,500	413,000	15,200	12,800	50,500
	$547,000	$460,000	$18,000	$14,000	$55,000

Instructions Prepare an analysis to estimate uncollectible amounts for Wilson.

Solution The following is a summary of Wilson's estimated uncollectible accounts receivable.

Age	Amount	Percentage Estimated to Be Uncollectible	Estimate of Uncollectible Accounts
Under 61 days old	$460,000	4%	$18,400
61–90 days old	18,000	15%	2,700
91–120 days old	14,000	20%	2,800
Over 120 days	55,000	25%	13,750
Year-end balance of Allowance for Doubtful Accounts should equal this amount.			$37,650

Allowance Method

The analysis in Example 7.3 shows that Wilson & Co. expects to receive $547,000 less $37,650, or $509,350 net cash receipts from the December 31 amounts owed. That is, $509,350 is the accounts receivable's estimated net realizable value. The **allowance method** is used to account for this estimate of impairment. This method is illustrated in **Example 7.4**.

> **Example 7.4** | Allowance Method, Financial Statement Presentation and Adjusting Journal Entry
>
> **Facts** Assume the same facts for Wilson & Co. as in Example 7.3.
>
> **Instructions**
>
> **a.** Show how Wilson would reflect the estimated uncollectible amounts on its statement of financial position (SFP) using the allowance method.
>
> **b.** Assume that **the allowance account already has a credit balance of $18,800** before adjustment. What journal entry would Wilson prepare?
>
> **Solution**
>
> **a.** On Wilson & Co.'s December 31 SFP, a contra account, Allowance for Doubtful Accounts (or Allowance for Uncollectible Accounts) of $37,650, is reported, as shown below. A contra account is used because the Accounts Receivable account is supported by a subsidiary ledger of each customer's balance owing and management does not know yet which specific accounts will result in non-collection and bad debt losses.
>
> | Wilson & Co. Statement of Financial Position December 31 | |
> |---|---|
> | Current assets | |
> | Accounts receivable | $547,000 |
> | Less: Allowance for doubtful accounts | 37,650 |
> | | $509,350 |
>
> **b.** The ending balance in the allowance account should be $37,650. The appropriate entry, therefore, depends on what the balance is in the account before making the adjusting entry. If we assume that **the allowance account already has a credit balance of $18,800 before adjustment**, then the amount to be added to the account is $18,850 ($37,650 − $18,800). This will bring the balance in the allowance account to $37,650. The following entry is made:
>
> | Bad Debt Expense | 18,850 | |
> | Allowance for Doubtful Accounts | | 18,850 |

A	=	L	+	SE
−18,850				−18,850

Cash flows: No effect

If instead in Example 7.4 the **balance in the allowance account before adjustment was a debit balance of $200**, then the amount to bring the allowance account to the correct credit balance of $37,650 is $37,850 ($37,650 desired credit balance + elimination of the $200 debit balance). When using the allowance method, the balance that is already in the allowance account before the adjusting entry is made **cannot be ignored**; it has to be considered to calculate the amount needed for the adjustment.

Bad Debt Expense and the Allowance Account

So far, we have focused on the balance in the Allowance for Doubtful Accounts. This is because our current accounting model emphasizes ensuring good measurements of assets and liabilities. The model assumes that, if assets and liabilities are measured properly, the related revenues and expenses will be as well. Let's turn now to bad debt expense.

The allowance method reports receivables at their estimated realizable value and recognizes bad debt losses as an expense in the same accounting period as when the sales on account are made. The allowance method accomplishes two things: a proper carrying amount for receivables on the SFP, and the resulting matching of expenses and revenues in the same period. Using the allowance method, companies typically follow one of two accounting procedures. Both of them result in the same ending balances in the Allowance and Bad Debt Expense accounts.

1. **Allowance method only:** At the end of every month, management carries out an analysis of the Accounts Receivable balances and assesses the estimated uncollectible accounts. An accounting entry is prepared, as illustrated above for Wilson & Co., adjusting the Allowance for Doubtful Accounts to its correct balance. The Bad Debt Expense account is debited or credited as necessary and at the end of the fiscal year, the total of all the entries to the expense account during the year is the bad debt expense for the year. The balance in the allowance account is an appropriate amount because all entries are based on an analysis of the receivables.

2. **Mix of procedures:** At the end of every month, management estimates the company's **bad debt expense** for that month. This estimate is based on a percentage of the sales reported, and is therefore called the **percentage-of-sales approach**. If there is a fairly stable relationship between previous years' credit sales and bad debts, then that relationship can be turned into a percentage and used to estimate any period's bad debt expense. Because the amount of sales is known, this is a **fast and simple way** to estimate the expense each period. Each month, Bad Debt Expense is debited and Allowance for Doubtful Accounts is credited. See **Underlying Concept 7.3**.

Data Analytics At the end of the fiscal year, however, when financial statements are issued, management still has to assess the year-end receivables to ensure that the balance in the allowance account is appropriate. Management can estimate the collectibility of its accounts receivable using an aged method as described above, or a more sophisticated **data analytics** approach as data availability and data analysis tools improve. For example, using **predictive analytics**, a type of data analytics, companies can develop models to calculate a credit score for each customer by considering not just aged accounts receivable, but multiple indicators such as input from customer relationship management systems and resource planning systems, third-party credit ratings, and the rates of responsiveness of customers to email vs. telephone reminders.[9]

If necessary, an adjustment is then made to the allowance account to bring it to the needed balance, with the offsetting debit or credit made to Bad Debt Expense.

Examples 7.5 and **7.6** describe the percentage-of-sales approach.

 Video

Underlying Concept 7.3

The percentage-of-sales approach is a good illustration of the matching concept, which relates expenses to revenues earned. However, the year-end adjustment based on the net realizable value of the receivables illustrates the importance of the fair value principle.

Example 7.5 | The Percentage-of-Sales Approach

Facts   Assume that every month, Dockrill Corp. estimates from experience that about 2% of net credit sales will become uncollectible.

Instructions   If Dockrill Corp. has net credit sales of $400,000 in 2020, what journal entries would it make during the year to record bad debt expense?

Solution   The bad debt expense adjustment for Dockrill in 2020 can be summarized in one entry as follows:

Bad Debt Expense (2% × $400,000)	8,000	
Allowance for Doubtful Accounts		8,000

A	=	L	+	SE
−8,000				−8,000

Cash flows: No effect

Data Analytics   For further details, and a summary of data analytics skills, see Norbert Tschakert, Julia Kokina, Stephen Kozlowski, and Miklos Vasarhelyi, "The Next Frontier in Data Analytics: Why CPAs and Organizations Need to Learn to Use Advanced Technology to Predict and Achieve Outcomes," *Journal of Accountancy*, August 1, 2016.

Example 7.6 | The Year-End Adjustment for Bad Debts

Facts At year end, management of Dockrill prepares an analysis of receivables and estimates that $9,900 will not be collectible. Therefore, the balance in the allowance account **after adjustment** must be a credit of $9,900.

Instructions What journal entry should Dockrill make at year end assuming that the balance in Allowance for Doubtful Accounts before adjustment is a $7,500 credit?

Solution The correct adjusting entry depends on the balance in the Allowance for Doubtful Accounts before the adjustment is made. The allowance is an SFP account and therefore would have had an opening balance. Entries to record increases and accounts written off (as we will explain below) would also have been made to the account during the current year.

Assuming the balance in Allowance for Doubtful Accounts before adjustment is a $7,500 credit, then the following adjusting entry is needed:

Bad Debt Expense	2,400	
Allowance for Doubtful Accounts ($9,900 − $7,500 = $2,400)		2,400

A	=	L	+	SE
−2,400				−2,400

Cash flows: No effect

Either approach can be used. Many companies use the percentage-of-sales method for internal reporting through the year because of its ease of use. For their external financial statements, they make an adjustment at year end based on the collectibility of receivable balances at the date of the SFP.

Accounts Written Off and the Allowance Account

Accounts Receivable Written Off Under the allowance method, after all efforts have been made to collect a **specific account** and it is determined to be uncollectible, its balance is removed from Accounts Receivable and Allowance for Doubtful Accounts is reduced. For example, assuming the account of Brown Ltd. of $550 is considered uncollectible, the write off entry is as follows:

Allowance for Doubtful Accounts	550	
Accounts Receivable		550

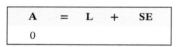

A	=	L	+	SE
0				

Cash flows: No effect

Note that there is no effect on the income statement **from writing off an account**, nor should there be. This is because the associated bad debt expense was **previously** recognized as an estimate **in the period of the sale**. There is also no effect on the net amount of the receivables because Accounts Receivable and its contra account are **both** reduced by equal amounts.

Collection of an Account Previously Written Off If a collection is made on a receivable that was previously written off, the procedure is to first re-establish the receivable by reversing the write off entry, and then recognize the cash inflow as a regular receipt on account. To illustrate, assume that Brown Ltd. eventually remits $300, and states that it will not pay more. The entries to record this transaction are as follows:

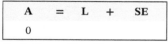

A	=	L	+	SE
0				

Cash flows: No effect

A	=	L	+	SE
0				

Cash flows: ↑ 300 inflow

Accounts Receivable	300	
Allowance for Doubtful Accounts		300
(To reinstate the account written off and now determined to be collectible)		
Cash	300	
Accounts Receivable		300
(To record the receipt of cash on account from Brown Ltd.)		

Effects on Accounts

Illustration 7.4 summarizes the transactions and events that affect the accounts related to accounts receivable.

ILLUSTRATION 7.4

Effects on Related Accounts

Accounts Receivable		Allowance for Doubtful Accounts	
Opening balance 1. Credit sales 5. Reinstatement of accounts previously written off	2. Cash received on account 4. Accounts written off	4. Accounts written off 6. Year-end adjustment to reduce balance in allowance account	Opening balance 3. Bad debt expense recognized 5. Reinstatement of accounts previously written off 7. Year-end adjustment to increase balance in allowance account

Bad Debt Expense		Sales	
3. Bad debt expense recognized 7. Year-end adjustment to increase balance in allowance account	6. Year-end adjustment to reduce balance in allowance account		1. Credit sales

The ending balance of the Accounts Receivable account represents the total of all amounts owed to the company at the date of the SFP, except those accounts written off, of course. This amount is backed up by a subsidiary ledger of the individual customers and the amount owed by each. The ending balance of the allowance account represents management's estimate of the total accounts receivable that will not be collected. When reported together, the net amount is the estimated net realizable value of the total amount owed.

The allowance for doubtful accounts as a percentage of receivables varies considerably, depending on the industry and recent economic conditions. **Stantec Inc.**, a professional engineering services firm, for example, reported an allowance for doubtful accounts of $29.1 million (3.6% of its trade receivables at December 31, 2017, up slightly from the 3.5% reported in 2016). Consider also **Nutrien Ltd.**, which on January 1, 2018, acquired all the issued and outstanding shares of **Agrium Inc.** and **Potash Corporation of Saskatchewan Inc.** The new entity became the world's largest provider of crop inputs and services, including the production of potash, nitrogen, and phosphate products. Nutrien had $2.9 billion (U.S.) of receivables on its January 1, 2018 Pro Forma Consolidated Balance Sheet.[10] Nutrien had a combined allowance for doubtful accounts and provision for impairment of U.S. $84 million on its receivables at that date (approximately 3% of its trade receivables). It will be interesting to see how the new company's collection efforts impact its allowance for doubtful accounts requirements in coming years! See **What Do the Numbers Mean? 7.2** for another real world example.

What Do the Numbers Mean? 7.2

In its 2017 management discussion and analysis (MD&A) that accompanies its consolidated financial statements, **Canadian Tire Corporation** notes that the results for its Financial Services subsidiaries are influenced in large part by growth in "gross average accounts receivable," which drives interest revenue. The key indicators of performance in the Financial Services segment are the size, profitability, and quality of the total managed portfolio of receivables. Growth in the total managed portfolio of receivables is measured by growth in the average number of accounts and growth in the average account balance. A key profitability

---

[10]Pro forma financial statements are typically unaudited and are based on assumptions made (and disclosed) by management. So, for example, Nutrien's pro forma balance sheet was derived from the December 31, 2017 balance sheets of Agrium and Potash Corp. It combines the two companies' balance sheets to give users an indication of the effect of the merger on the new company's financial position.

measure the company tracks is the return on the average total managed portfolio (also referred to as "return on receivables"), which the company reported as being 7.4% for 2017. This is calculated by dividing income before tax and gains/losses on disposal of property and equipment by its average total managed portfolio over a 12-month period (including loans receivable, and credit card and line of credit loans). The quality of the portfolio is reflected in the allowance for credit losses, the aging of the portfolio, and the allowance rate (which was 1.97% based on the total managed portfolio of loans receivable in the fourth quarter of 2017).

A continuity schedule from Canadian Tire's 2017 MD&A shows changes in its **allowances for loans receivable** (below). As the continuity schedule shows, the change in the allowance relates primarily to an increase in the impairments for credit losses of $5.2 million. The overall increase in the amount set aside for "Impairments for credit losses, net of recoveries" reflects the fact that the aged "loans receivable that are past due, but not impaired" discussed in the notes to the financial statements increased by $1.7 million (from $366.9 million to $368.6 million). Similarly, increases in the amounts in loans receivable past due over 90 days totalled $63.6 million for the year, versus $58.3 million for the prior year (see below). Canadian Tire notes that its credit risk relates primarily to its credit card customers, Dealer network, and financial instruments held with bank and non-bank counterparties. The following is an extract from Note 9 of Canadian Tire's 2017 financial statements:

A continuity schedule of the Company's allowances for loans receivable[1] is as follows:

(C$ in millions)	2017	2016
Balance, beginning of year	$ 106.9	$ 111.5
Impairments for credit losses, net of recoveries	298.9	293.7
Recoveries	70.8	69.4
Write-offs	(365.6)	(367.7)
Balance, end of year	$ 111.0	$ 106.9

[1]Loans include credit card loans and line of credit loans. No allowances for credit losses have been made with respect to Franchise Trust and FGL loans receivable.

The Company's aging of the loans receivable that are past due, but not impaired is as follows:

	2017			2016		
	1–90	>90		0–90	>90	
(C$ in millions)	days	days	Total	days	days	Total
Loans receivable	$305.0	$63.6	$368.6	$308.6	$58.3	$366.9

Credit card loans are considered impaired and written off when a payment is 180 days in arrears. Line of credit loans are considered impaired when a payment is over 90 days in arrears and are written off when a payment is 180 days in arrears. No collateral is held against loans receivable, except for loans to Dealers, as discussed above.

Direct Write Off Method

Some cash-based businesses, such as corner grocery stores, do not extend credit often and therefore have very few credit transactions and have small accounts receivable balances. Such businesses, **where the effect of not applying the allowance method is highly immaterial**, sometimes use the simpler direct write off method. No estimates are made in advance and no allowance account is used. Instead, when an account is determined to be uncollectible, the specific account receivable is written off, with the debit recognized as bad debt expense:

A	=	L	+	SE
−$$		0		−$$

Cash flows: No effect

Bad Debt Expense $$
     Accounts Receivable $$

If amounts are later collected on an account that was previously written off, a notation is made in the customer's record. The amount collected is recognized through entries to Cash and a revenue account entitled Uncollectible Amounts Recovered.

A	=	L	+	SE
+$$		0		+$$

Cash flows: ↑ $$ inflow

Cash $$
     Uncollectible Amounts Recovered $$

Notes and Loans Receivable

LEARNING OBJECTIVE 6

Account for and explain the accounting issues related to the recognition and measurement of notes and loans receivable.

A note receivable is similar to an account receivable, with one difference: the note is supported by a formal **promissory note**, which is a **written** promise to pay a specific sum of money at a specific future date. This makes a note receivable a negotiable instrument.

The note is signed by a **maker** in favour of a designated **payee** who can then legally and readily sell or transfer the note to others. **Notes always contain an interest element** because of the time value of money, but they may be classified as interest-bearing or non–interest-bearing. **Interest-bearing notes** have a stated rate of interest that is payable in addition to the face value of the note. **Zero-interest-bearing notes** (or **non–interest-bearing notes**) also include interest, but the rate is equal to the difference between the amount that was borrowed (the proceeds) and the higher face amount that will be paid back. The rate may not be stated explicitly.

Companies sometimes accept notes receivable from customers who need to extend the payment period of an outstanding account receivable. Notes are also sometimes required from high-risk or new customers. In addition, they are often used in loans to employees and subsidiaries and in sales of property, plant, and equipment. In some industries (such as the pleasure and sport boat industry), almost all credit sales are supported by notes. Most notes, however, are created by lending transactions. The basic issues in accounting for notes receivable are the same as those for accounts receivable: recognition, measurement, impairment, and disposition.

Recognition and Measurement of Short-Term Notes and Loans Receivable

This section discusses the recognition and measurement of only **short-term** notes or loans. Longer-term instruments are covered in the next section. **Example 7.7** illustrates the accounting for notes or loans receivable.

Example 7.7 | Accounting for Notes Receivable

Facts   On March 14, 2020, Prime Corporation agreed to allow its customer, Gouneau Ltd., to substitute a six-month note for the account receivable of $1,000 that Gouneau was unable to pay when it came due for payment. This means that Gouneau is basically borrowing $1,000 from Prime for six months. It was agreed that the note would bear interest at a rate of 6%.

Instructions   What journal entries would Prime make to record the substitution and payment of the note?

Solution

March 14, 2020

Notes Receivable	1,000	
Accounts Receivable		1,000

September 14, 2020

Cash	1,030	
Notes Receivable		1,000
Interest Income		30*

*$1,000 × .06 × 6/12

A	=	L	+	SE
0				

Cash flows: No effect

A	=	L	+	SE
+30				+30

Cash flows: ↑ 1,030 inflow

Alternatively, a note could be accepted in exchange for lending money to an employee or subsidiary company; for example, in a **non–interest-bearing note** situation. In this case, the interest is the difference between the amount of cash that is borrowed and the face or maturity value of the note receivable, as shown in **Example 7.8**.

> ### Example 7.8 | Accounting for Non–Interest-Bearing Note Receivable
>
> **Facts**   Assume that the president of Ajar Ltd. borrowed money from the company on February 23, 2020, and signed a promissory note for $5,000 repayable in nine months' time. Assume an interest rate of 8% is appropriate for this type of loan. Instead of borrowing $5,000 and repaying this amount with 8% interest added at the maturity date, the president receives only $4,717 on February 23.
>
> **Instructions**   How should Ajar account for the difference between the $4,717 borrowed and the $5,000 repaid?
>
> **Solution**   The $283 difference represents interest for the nine-month period that the note is outstanding: $4,717 \times 8\% \times \%_{12} = \$283$. Ajar's entries are as follows:[11]
>
> **February 23, 2020**
>
> | | | |
> |---|---|---|
> | Notes Receivable | 4,717 | |
> | Cash | | 4,717 |
>
> **November 23, 2020**
>
> | | | |
> |---|---|---|
> | Cash | 5,000 | |
> | Notes Receivable | | 4,717 |
> | Interest Income | | 283* |
>
> *$4,717 \times .08 \times \%_{12}$

A = L + SE

0

Cash flows: ▼4,717 outflow

A = L + SE

+283 +283

Cash flows: ▲5,000 inflow

In both examples provided, if financial statements are prepared while the note receivable is still outstanding, interest is accrued to the date of the SFP.

Recognition and Measurement of Long-Term Notes and Loans Receivable

Because some form of **promissory note** is often the proof that a loan exists, the above explanation of notes receivable applies equally well to loans receivable. The examples of loans receivable that are illustrated below assume that a note is the basis for each transaction. What changes as we move from short-term to long-term notes and loans is the length of time to maturity and the importance of interest in measuring and accounting for the financial asset.

The accounting standards for the recognition and measurement of loans receivable are the same as those identified above for accounts receivable.

- Recognize a loan receivable when the entity becomes a party to the contractual provisions of the financial instrument.
- When recognized initially, measure the loan receivable at its fair value.
- After initial recognition, measure loans receivable at amortized cost.
- Recognize bad debt losses on the loans receivable when they are deemed to be impaired.[12]

[11]Alternatively, the entries could initially recognize the note's maturity value in Notes Receivable and the discount in Discount on Notes Receivable, a contra account to Notes Receivable:

Feb. 23	Notes Receivable	5,000	
	Cash		4,717
	Discount on Notes Receivable		283
Nov. 23	Cash	5,000	
	Notes Receivable		5,000
	Discount on Notes Receivable	283	
	Interest Income		283

[12]Because impairment of long-term loans is discussed in Chapter 9, along with the impairment of other financial asset investments, it is not repeated in Chapter 7.

The fair value of a note or loan receivable is measured as **the present value of the cash amounts that are expected to be collected in the future, with the amounts discounted at the market rate of interest that is appropriate for a loan with similar credit risk and other characteristics**. When the interest stated on an interest-bearing note is the same as the effective (market) rate of interest, the note's fair value is equal to its face value. (The stated interest rate, also referred to as the face rate or the coupon rate, is the rate that is included as part of the note contract. The effective interest rate, also referred to as the market rate or the yield rate, is the rate that is used in the market to determine the note's value; that is, the discount rate that is used to determine its present value.) When the stated rate is not the same as the market rate, the note's **fair value** (its **present value**) is different from the note's **face value**. The difference between the price for the note now and its maturity value—resulting in either a discount or a premium—is then amortized over the note's life, affecting the amount of interest income that is reported.

IFRS ASPE   Under **IFRS**, the effective interest method of amortization is required, while under **ASPE**, the **amortization method is not specified**. The effective interest method is illustrated further below in the subsection "Notes Issued at Other than Face Value."

Transaction costs that are incurred in acquiring a loan or note receivable, such as commissions, could be treated in one of two ways:

1. They can be recognized as an expense when they are incurred.
2. They can be added to the fair value of the instrument, which then increases the original amount that is recognized as its "cost" at acquisition. In this case, the transaction costs are recorded as an adjustment to the discount or premium that will be amortized over the life of the loan, requiring the effective rate of interest to be recalculated under IFRS (and ASPE for companies that choose to use the effective interest method of amortization).

Both ASPE and IFRS agree that transaction costs associated with financial assets that are carried at amortized cost should be accounted for as explained in the second treatment above.[13]

Under ASPE, loans and receivables are accounted for at amortized cost. Amortized cost is the amount that is recognized when the instrument is acquired, reduced by any principal payments received, and adjusted for the amortization of any discount or premium, if appropriate, and writedowns for impairment. Under IFRS, the same accounting applies provided the note or loan has basic loan features and is managed on a contractual yield basis.[14] Basic loan features means that the instrument has contractual terms that result in cash flows that are payments of principal and interest. Management on a contractual yield basis is a company's business model of holding the instruments for their principal and interest flows. Let's see how this works.

Notes Issued at Face Value

The calculations and journal entries for an interest-bearing note issued at face value are illustrated in **Example 7.9**.

Example 7.9 | An Interest-Bearing Note Issued at Face Value

Facts   Assume that Bigelow Corp. lends Scandinavian Imports $10,000 in exchange for a $10,000, three-year note bearing interest at 10% payable annually. The market rate of interest for a note of similar risk is also 10%. An important step in understanding the facts is to identify the amounts and timing of the cash flows. For our example, the following diagram shows both the interest and principal cash flows:

---

[13]For most examples in this textbook, we assume that transaction costs for the acquisition of financial assets held at amortized cost are zero.

[14]IFRS also allows a "fair value option" for loans and receivables in restricted circumstances and ASPE provides the same option for any financial instrument. These are explained in more detail in Chapter 9.

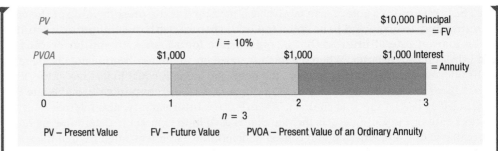

Instructions Calculate the note's present value and exchange price and provide the journal entries at the date of issue of the note and for the related interest income.

Solution In this situation, stated and market rates of interest are the same and the present value of the note is calculated as follows:

Face value of the note		$10,000
Present value of the lump sum principal:		
$10,000 (PV*$_{3, 10\%}$) = $10,000 (0.75132) (Table A.2)	$7,513	
Present value of the ordinary interest annuity:		
$1,000 (PVOA$_{3, 10\%}$) = $1,000 (2.48685) (Table A.4)	2,487	
Present value of the note		10,000
Difference		$ –0–

*Present value (PV) factors found in Tables A.1 to A.5

The note's fair value, present value, and face value are the same ($10,000) **because the effective and stated interest rates are the same**. Bigelow Corp. records its acquisition of the note as follows:

Notes Receivable	10,000	
Cash		10,000

Bigelow Corp. later recognizes the interest earned each year ($10,000 × 0.10) as follows:

Cash	1,000	
Interest Income		1,000

A	=	L	+	SE
0				

Cash flows: ↓ 10,000 outflow

A	=	L	+	SE
+1,000				+1,000

Cash flows: ↑ 1,000 inflow

Notes Issued at Other than Face Value

Not all long-term notes are issued at market rates of interest. Sometimes companies issue non–interest-bearing notes or notes with interest rates below market rates to encourage sales or to facilitate intercompany transactions.

Zero-Interest-Bearing Notes If a zero-interest-bearing note is received in exchange for cash, its present value is usually the cash paid to the issuer. Because both the note's future amount and present value are known, the interest rate can be calculated; in other words, it is implied. The **implicit interest rate** is the rate that equates the cash paid with the amounts receivable in the future. The difference between the future (face) amount and the present value (cash paid) is a discount and this amount is amortized to interest income over the life of the note. In most cases, the implicit interest rate is the market rate. This is because the transaction is usually carried out between two parties who are at arm's length and acting in their own best interests.[15] **Example 7.10** shows sample calculations and journal entries.

---

[15]There may be situations when the implicit interest rate is not the market rate; that is, when the fair value of the loan differs from the cash consideration. This circumstance is dealt with later in this chapter.

Example 7.10 | Issuance of a Zero-Interest-Bearing Note

Facts Jeremiah Company receives a three-year, $10,000, zero-interest-bearing note, and the present value is known to be $7,721.80. The time diagram for the single cash flow of Jeremiah's note is as follows:

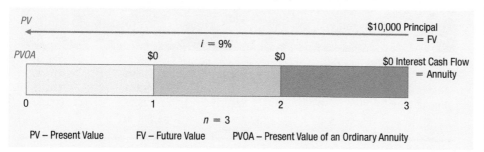

Instructions Calculate and explain the implicit rate of interest (assumed to approximate the market rate) for the note and provide the related journal entry at the date of issuance.

Solution Determination of implicit interest rate:

$$\text{PV of note} = \text{PV of future cash flows}$$
$$\text{PV of note} = \text{Maturity value of note} \times \text{PVF}_{3,\,?\%} \text{ (Table A.2)}$$
$$\$7{,}721.80 = \$10{,}000 \times \text{PVF}_{3,\,?\%}$$
$$\text{PVF}_{3,\,?\%} = \frac{\$7{,}721.80}{\$10{,}000}$$
$$\text{PVF}_{3,\,?\%} = 0.77218$$

From Table A.2: Where $n = 3$ and PVF $= 0.77218$, $i = 9\%$

[Note: PVF = present value factor.]

Thus, the implicit rate that makes the total cash to be received at maturity ($10,000) equal to the present value of the future cash flows ($7,721.80) is 9%. Note that if any two of the three variables of the equation on the second line in the formula above are known, the third variable can be determined. For example, if the note's maturity value **(face value)** and the **present value factor (i and n)** are known, the note's **present value** can be calculated.

The entry to record the transaction is:

Notes Receivable	7,721.80	
Cash		7,721.80

A	=	L	+	SE
0				

Cash flows: ↓ 7,721.80 outflow

Effective Interest Method of Amortization Under IFRS, and as applied by many private enterprises, the discount is amortized each year using the **effective interest method** to recognize the interest income. (In the case of Example 7.10, the discount is the $2,278.20 difference between the $7,721.80 provided as a loan and the $10,000 that will be repaid.) Under this method, the effective interest or yield rate is calculated when the investment is made. This rate is then later used to calculate interest income by applying it to the investment's carrying amount (book value) for each interest period. The note's carrying amount changes as it is increased by the amount of discount amortized. **Thus, the net carrying amount is always equal to the present value of the note's remaining cash flows (principal and interest payments) discounted at the market rate at acquisition.** Example 7.11 shows sample calculations and journal entries.

Example 7.11 | Discount Amortization Schedule— Effective Interest Method

Facts Jeremiah Company receives a three-year, $10,000, zero-interest-bearing note, and the related present value with a market interest rate of 9% is $7,721.80.

Instructions Prepare a three-year discount amortization and interest income schedule for Jeremiah's three-year note receivable and the related journal entries to record (a) interest income at the end of Year 1 and (b) receipt of payment of the note at maturity.

Solution

				Carrying
Schedule of Note Discount Amortization				
Effective Interest Method				
0% Note Discounted at 9%				
	Cash Received	Interest Income	Discount Amortized	Carrying Amount of Note
Date of issue				$ 7,721.80
End of Year 1	$–0–	$ 694.96ᵃ	$ 694.96ᵇ	8,416.76ᶜ
End of Year 2	–0–	757.51	757.51	9,174.27
End of Year 3	–0–	825.73ᵈ	825.73	10,000.00
	$–0–	$2,278.20	$2,278.20	

ᵃ$7,721.80 × 0.09 = $694.96
ᵇ$694.96 − 0 = $694.96
ᶜ$7,721.80 + $694.96 = $8,416.76 or $10,000 − ($2,278.20 − $694.96) = $8,416.76
ᵈIncludes $0.05 adjustment for rounding

a. Interest income at the end of the first year using the effective interest method is recorded as follows:

Notes Receivable	694.96	
Interest Income ($7,721.80 × 9%)		694.96

Note that the amount of the total discount, $2,278.20 in this case, represents the interest income on the note over the three years. Rather than recognize it as interest income on a straight-line basis over this period, Jeremiah Company recognizes it in increasing amounts based on the balance of the loan and previous interest earned that is still outstanding. This can be seen in the schedule above.

b. When the note comes due at the end of Year 3, the Notes Receivable account will have a balance of $10,000.00. Therefore, Jeremiah Company makes the following entry:

Cash	10,000	
Notes Receivable		10,000

A	=	L	+	SE
+694.96				+694.96

Cash flows: No effect

A	=	L	+	SE
0				

Cash flows: ↑ 10,000 inflow

Underlying Concept 7.4

Using a simpler method that gives similar results to the effective interest method is an application of the materiality concept.

Straight-Line Method of Amortization   Some private entities that follow ASPE prefer to use the **straight-line method** of amortizing discounts and premiums because of its simplicity. See **Underlying Concept 7.4**. **Example 7.12** shows sample calculations, and journal entries under the straight-line and effective interest methods.

Example 7.12 | Journal Entries under Straight-line and Effective Interest Methods

Facts   In the Jeremiah Company example (7.11), the total discount of $2,278.20 under the straight-line method is amortized over the three-year period in equal amounts each year. Therefore, the annual amortization is $2,278.20 ÷ 3 or $759.40.

Instructions   **IFRS**   **ASPE**   Prepare the entry to record the annual interest for years 1 and 2 under the straight-line method compared with the effective interest method.

Solution

Straight-line

A	=	L	+	SE
+759.40				+759.40

Cash flows: No effect

	Effective interest		Straight-line	
Notes Receivable (Year 1)	694.96		759.40	
Interest Income		694.96		759.40
Notes Receivable (Year 2)	757.51		759.40	
Interest Income		757.51		759.40

At the end of Year 3, the Notes Receivable balance is $10,000 and the same $10,000 entry shown above is made to record the receipt of the cash.

While straight-line amortization is easier to apply, its results do not reflect the economic reality of a loan. That is, in Year 3 Jeremiah should be reporting more interest income than in Year 1 because compound interest accrues on the accumulating and unpaid interest for years 1 and 2. Under the straight-line method, equal amounts of income are reported each period.

Interest-Bearing Notes   A note's stated rate and its effective rate are often different, as they were in the zero-interest-bearing case above. **Example 7.13** shows the accounting for an interest-bearing note issued with a nominal interest rate that is lower than the market rate.

Example 7.13 | An Interest-Bearing Note Issued at a Discount

Facts   Assume that Morgan Corp. makes a loan to Marie Co. and receives in exchange a $10,000, three-year note bearing interest at 10% annually. The market rate of interest for a note of similar risk is 12%. The time diagram for all cash flows is as follows:

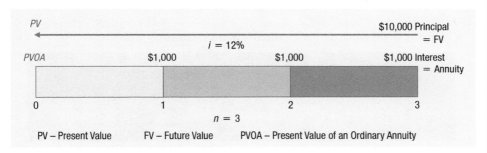

Instructions   Calculate the present value of the note and prepare the journal entry to record the receipt of the note in exchange for cash equal to the fair value.

Solution   Note that the **interest cash flows are dictated by the stated rate** (10%) but that **all cash flows are discounted at the market rate** (12%) in determining the note's present value. The present value ($9,520) of the two streams of cash is calculated as follows:[16]

Face value of the note		$10,000
Present value of the principal:		
$10,000 (PVF*$_{3, 12\%}$) = $10,000 (0.71178)	$7,118	
Present value of the interest:		
$1,000 (PVFOA**$_{3, 12\%}$) = $1,000 (2.40183)	2,402	
Present value of the note		9,520
Difference		$ 480

*Present value factor (Table A.2)

**Present value factor of an ordinary annuity (Table A.4)

Morgan would record the receipt of the note in exchange for cash equal to its fair value as follows:

Notes Receivable	9,520	
Cash		9,520

A	=	L	+	SE
0				

Cash flows: ▼ 9,520 outflow

[16]Note that "*n*" equals the number of interest periods, **not one year**, and that "*i*" is the interest rate **for the period defined by** *n*. If interest were paid semi-annually in this example, *n* would be 6, not 3, and *i* would be 6%, not 12%, and these would be used to discount both the maturity amount **and** the interest cash flows. The interest cash flow used in the present value calculation would be $500, not $1,000.

Because the effective interest rate or market interest rate (12%) is higher than the rate that the note actually pays (10%), the note's present value (also its fair value) is less than its face value. That is, the note would be exchanged at a **discount**. This makes intuitive sense. If you were to invest in a note that promises 10% when you could get 12% elsewhere in the market at the same level of risk, you would not be willing to pay face value for the 10% note. **Example 7.14** looks at how to account for the discount.

Example 7.14 | Discount Amortization Schedule—
Effective Interest Method

Facts   Assume the same facts as in Example 7.13. Over the term of the note, Morgan Corp. will receive $1,000 interest each year (a rate of 10%) and at maturity will get $480 more than the cash originally loaned. This $480 (the discount) effectively increases the return on the investment from 10% to 12%. It is amortized each period and the amount of interest income that is recognized is greater than the $1,000 received each year.

Instructions

a. Prepare a three-year discount amortization and interest income schedule for Morgan using the effective interest method.

b. Describe how Morgan would account for the discount of $480 under the effective interest vs. the straight-line methods, including the journal entry at the end of year 1.

Solution

a. Discount amortization schedule—effective interest method:

Schedule of Note Discount Amortization Effective Interest Method 10% Note Discounted at 12%				
	Cash Received	Interest Income	Discount Amortized	Carrying Amount of Note
Date of issue				$ 9,520
End of Year 1	$1,000[a]	$1,142[b]	$142[c]	9,662[d]
End of Year 2	1,000	1,159	159	9,821
End of Year 3	1,000	1,179	179	10,000
	$3,000	$3,480	$480	

[a]$10,000 \times 10\% = \$1,000$
[b]$9,520 \times 12\% = \$1,142$
[c]$1,142 - \$1,000 = \$142$
[d]$9,520 + \$142 = \$9,662$ or $10,000 - (\$480 - \$142) = \$9,662$

b. On the date of issue, the note has a present value of $9,520. Its unamortized discount—the interest income that will be spread over the three-year life of the note—is $480. At the end of Year 1, Morgan receives $1,000 in cash, but the interest income under the effective interest method is based on the note's carrying amount and effective interest rate: $1,142 ($9,520 × 12%). The difference between $1,000 and $1,142 is the discount to be amortized, $142, and it is amortized directly to the Notes Receivable account.

The note's carrying amount has now been increased to $9,662 ($9,520 + $142). This process is repeated until the end of Year 3.

ASPE   Under the **straight-line method**, allowed only under ASPE, the initial discount of $480 is amortized at a rate of $480 ÷ 3 = $160 each year with the following entry. The same entry is made each year. Morgan records the annual interest received at the end of the first year as follows:

	Effective interest		Straight-line	
Cash	1,000		1,000	
Notes Receivable	142		160	
Interest Income		1,142		1,160

Effective interest

A	=	L	+	SE
+1,142				+1,142

Cash flows: ↑ 1,000 inflow

When the stated rate is higher than the effective interest rate, the note's fair value (its present value) is more than its face value and the note is exchanged at a **premium**. The premium on a note receivable is recognized by recording the note receivable at its higher initial present value. The excess is amortized over the life of the note by crediting Notes Receivable and reducing (debiting) the amount of interest income that is recognized.

Notes Received for Property, Goods, or Services

When property, goods, or services are sold and a long-term note is received as the consideration instead of cash or a short-term receivable, there may be an issue in determining the selling price. If an appropriate market rate of interest is known for the note, or for a note of similar risk, there would be no problem. The sale amount is the present value of the cash flows promised by the note, discounted at the market rate of interest. Remember that, **if the stated rate and market rate are the same, the note's face value and fair value are also the same**. It is when the two rates are different that the note's fair value has to be calculated by discounting the cash flows at the market rate. What if we don't know what the market rate is? In this case, we can use one of two approaches.

1. We can use the fair value of the property, goods, or services that are given up as an estimate of the fair value of the note received. In this case, because we would have an estimate of the note's present value, the actual cash flow amounts, and the timing of the cash flows, we can calculate the market or yield interest rate. We need this in order to apply the effective interest method.

2. An appropriate interest rate can be imputed. **Imputation** is the process of estimating an appropriate interest rate. The resulting rate is called an **imputed interest rate**. The objective is to approximate the rate that would have been agreed on if an independent borrower and lender had negotiated a similar transaction. The choice of a rate is affected by the prevailing rates for similar instruments of issuers with similar credit ratings. It is also affected by such factors as restrictive covenants, collateral, the payment schedule, and the prime interest rate.

To illustrate, assume that Oasis Corp. sold land in exchange for a five-year note that has a maturity value of $35,247 and no stated interest rate. The property originally cost Oasis $14,000. What are the proceeds on disposal of the land? In other words, what selling price should be recognized in this transaction?

Situation 1: Assume that the market rate of interest of 12% is known. In this case, the proceeds from the sale are equal to the present value of the note, which we calculate (below) to be $20,000. This is a non–interest-bearing note, so the only cash flow is the $35,247 received in five periods' time: $35,247 × .56743 (Table A.2) = $20,000. The entry to record the sale is:

Notes Receivable	20,000	
Land		14,000
Gain on Disposal of Land ($20,000 − $14,000)		6,000

A	=	L	+	SE
+6,000				+6,000

Cash flows: No effect

Situation 2: Assume that the market rate of interest is unknown, but the land has been appraised recently for $20,000 and the future cash flow amount is known to be $35,247. In this case, the property's fair value determines the amount of the proceeds and the note's fair value. The entry is the same as in Situation 1. To amortize the discount using the effective interest method, however, we must determine the implicit interest rate. We do this by finding the interest rate that makes the present value of the future cash flow amount of $35,247 equal to its present value of $20,000. The procedure is as follows. First we calculate the present value factor: $20,000 ÷ $35,247 = .567424. Table A.2 then identifies the interest rate for five periods and a factor of .56743 as 12%.

Situation 3: Assume that neither the market rate nor the land's fair value is known. In this case, a market rate must be imputed and then used to determine the note's present value. It will also be used to recognize the effective interest income over the five years and amortize the discount. If a 12% rate is estimated based on prevailing interest rates for companies similar to the one purchasing the land, and the future cash flow amount is $35,247, then the entry will be the same as in Situation 1. If a different rate results, the note receivable and the gain on disposal will both be different as well.

Fair Value Not Equal to Cash Consideration

Accountants need to be alert when recognizing and measuring loans receivable. Sometimes, the cash that is exchanged when the loan is made may not be the same as the fair value of the loan. In this situation, the substance of the transaction has to be determined and accounted for. **Example 7.15** looks at such a scenario.

Example 7.15 | Non–Interest-Bearing Loan to a Company Officer

---

Facts   Generous Company advances $20,000 to an officer of the company, charges no interest on the advance, and makes it repayable in four years. Assuming a market rate of 6%, the fair value of the loan receivable is $15,842 ($20,000 × .79209, the PV factor for $n = 4$ and $i = 6$). Although the loan's fair value is $15,842, the company officer actually received $20,000.

Instructions   How is the $4,158 difference recognized and accounted for to reflect its substance? Provide the related journal entry required at the date of the advance.

Solution   In this case, the difference between the fair value and the actual amount received is likely a form of additional compensation. It must be recognized immediately as an expense unless it qualifies to be reported as an asset.[17] The entry to record this transaction is as follows:

Notes Receivable	15,842	
Salaries and Wages Expense	4,158	
Cash		20,000

A	=	L	+	SE
−4,158				−4,158

Cash flows: ▼ 20,000 outflow

Derecognition of Receivables

LEARNING OBJECTIVE 7

Account for and explain the basic accounting issues related to the derecognition of receivables.

Normally, accounts and notes receivable are collected when they are due and then removed from the books, or **derecognized**. However, as credit sales and receivables have grown in size and significance, this process has evolved. **In order to receive cash more quickly from receivables, owners now often transfer accounts or loans receivable to another company for cash.**

There are various reasons for this early transfer. First, for competitive reasons, providing sales financing for customers is almost mandatory in many industries. In the sale of durable goods, such as automobiles, trucks, industrial and farm equipment, computers, and appliances, most sales are on an instalment contract basis. This means that the seller is financing the purchase by allowing the buyer to pay for it over time, usually in equal periodic payments or instalments. Many major companies in these and other industries have created wholly owned subsidiaries that specialize in receivables financing. For example, Canadian Tire Corporation, Limited's financial services segment incorporated a federally regulated bank, **Canadian Tire Bank**. This wholly owned subsidiary manages and finances Canadian Tire's MasterCard and retail credit card and personal loan portfolios, as well as other finance-related products.

---

[17]For example, if the loan required that the officer pay 6% interest per annum unless the officer remains employed by the company for the full four-year period, then it could be argued that a Prepaid Salaries and Wages asset totalling $4,158 should be recognized and amortized to expense over the four-year period.

Second, the **holder** may sell receivables because money is tight and access to normal credit is not available or is far too expensive, or because the holder wants to accelerate its cash inflows. A firm may have to sell its receivables, instead of borrowing, to avoid violating the terms of its current borrowing agreements. In addition, the billing and collecting of receivables is often time-consuming and costly. Credit card companies, such as MasterCard and Visa, and other finance companies take over the collection process. They provide merchants with immediate cash in exchange for a fee to cover their collection and bad debt costs. There are also **purchasers** of receivables who buy the receivables to obtain the legal protection of ownership rights that are given to a purchaser of assets, instead of the lesser rights that an unsecured creditor like Visa or MasterCard has. In addition, banks and other lending institutions may be forced to purchase receivables because of legal lending limits. That is, they may not be allowed to make any additional loans but still are able to buy receivables and charge a fee for this service.

Finance   5.2.3 Receivables can be used to generate immediate cash for a company in two ways. Often referred to as asset-backed financing, these ways are:

1. secured borrowings and
2. sales of receivables.

Secured Borrowings

Like many other assets, receivables are often used as collateral in borrowing transactions. A creditor may require that the debtor assign or pledge receivables as security for a loan, but leave the receivables under the control of the borrowing company. The note or loan payable, a liability, is reported on the SFP. If it is not paid when it is due, the creditor has the right to convert the collateral to cash; that is, to collect the receivables. Canadian banks commonly use receivables as collateral under lending agreements.

A company accounts for the collateralized assets in a **secured borrowing in the same way as it did before the borrowing**, and it accounts for the liability according to accounting policies for similar liabilities. The debtor thus recognizes interest expense on the borrowed amount, and may have to pay an additional finance charge, which is expensed. Each month, the proceeds from collecting accounts receivable are used to retire the loan obligation. In addition, details of the secured borrowing are disclosed in the company's financial statements.

Sales of Receivables

The selling of receivables has increased significantly in recent years. One common type is a sale to a factor. **Factors** are financial intermediaries, such as finance companies, that buy receivables from businesses for a fee and then collect the amounts owed directly from the customers. Factoring receivables was traditionally associated with the garment trade in Montreal, but it is now common in other industries as well, such as furniture, consumer electronics, and automotive aftermarkets. Illustration 7.5 shows a factoring arrangement.

ILLUSTRATION 7.5

Basic Procedures in Factoring

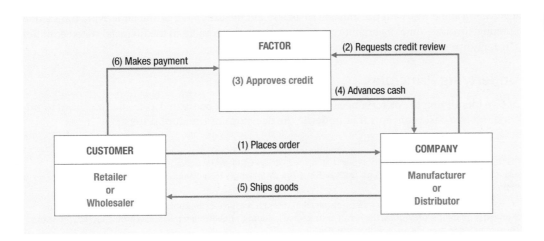

It is common today for larger companies to **transfer receivables** through a process known as **securitization**, where interests in financial assets are sold to a third party. It is the transformation of financial assets such as loans and receivables into securities, which are then called **asset-backed securities**. The process takes a pool of assets producing interest and principal payments, such as credit card receivables, mortgage receivables, or car loan receivables, and issues debt and equity interests in these pools. The resulting securities are backed by pools of assets. Almost every asset that has a payment stream (that is, it produces payments) and a long-term payment history is a candidate for securitization.

For example, Canadian Tire Corporation, Limited's 2017 MD&A states that, instead of owning all of its receivables throughout the collection period, it sells interests in its customer credit card loans receivable to **Glacier Credit Card Trust**. Glacier was created by **Canadian Tire** to handle receivables portfolios and is financed by the issue of debt securities to third-party investors. By this process, the receivables are transformed into securities being held by a **structured entity**, the trust.[18]

The arrangements that are made in a securitization transaction differ from company to company. Canadian Tire, for example, transfers co-ownership in pools of credit card loans receivable and retains substantially all of the credit risk associated with the transferred assets. Canadian Tire had transferred $1,915.1 million of credit card loans receivable through Glacier at the end of 2017, but this was offset by an almost equal amount of associated liabilities, resulting in a net position of only $4.6 million. Canadian Tire continues to recognize the assets within loans receivable, and separately recognizes the associated liabilities. Overall, the transfers are accounted for as "secured financing transactions" (that is, secured borrowings). See **What Do the Numbers Mean? 7.3** for background on why companies like Canadian Tire use securitization transactions.

What Do the Numbers Mean? 7.3

What is the motivation for a securitization transaction? Basically, it is a financing transaction that gives companies a more attractive way to raise funds than by issuing a corporate bond or note. The credit risk for a bond or note issued by a company is higher than the credit risk of a special purpose entity that holds the company's receivables. For example, Canadian Tire's 2017 MD&A stated a credit rating of AAA and R-1 (High) **for its Glacier asset-backed senior notes and asset-backed commercial paper**, respectively, which are the highest possible ratings for these debt classifications. Compare these with the BBB (High) ratings at the same time for Canadian Tire's **medium-term notes and issuer rating debt**. The higher credit ratings for entities like Glacier typically relate to two things: (1) receivables transferred to a structured entity (SE) are often credit enhanced[19] and (2) the cash flows to the SE are much more predictable than the cash flows to the operating company because there are no operating risks for an SE. When the risk is less, the cost of financing is also less. The net result is that the company that transfers its receivables gets access to lower-cost financing that it can then use to pay off debt that has a higher interest rate.

The differences between factoring and securitization are as follows. **Factoring** usually involves a sale to only one company, fees are relatively high, the quality of the receivables may be lower, and the seller does not usually service the receivables afterward. In a **securitization**, many investors are involved, margins are tight, the receivables are generally of higher quality, and the seller usually continues to service the receivables. When the company making the transfer continues to be involved in some way with the transferred assets, and measurement of the underlying transaction amounts involves some uncertainty, many disclosures are required in the financial statements. See **Underlying Concept 7.5**.

Underlying Principles

Before identifying the criteria needed for a transaction to be treated as a sale, you need to understand two basic concepts that underlie the decisions of standard setters.

---

[18]IFRS 12 defines a structured entity as one that has been designed so voting rights are not the dominant factor regarding who controls the entity (see IFRS 12.B21-B24). Copyright © IFRS Foundation. All rights reserved. Reproduced with permission.

[19]Credit enhancements include guaranteeing payment through recourse to the company selling the receivables or third-party guarantee provisions, the use of cash reserve accounts, or overcollateralization (providing security with a greater fair value than the amount that is at risk).

1. The first concept, which is the focus under IFRS, is that an entity (the transferor) should derecognize the financial asset from its financial statements only when it transfers substantially all of the risks and rewards of ownership of that financial asset. (However, the transferor would recognize separately as assets or liabilities any rights and obligations created or retained in the transfer.)

2. Where it cannot be determined whether the risks and rewards have been transferred, then IFRS considers the second concept: control. When assessing control, if the transferee can sell the entire asset to an unrelated party, and can make that decision on its own and without imposing further restrictions on the transfer, then the transferor has not retained control. If the transferor has not retained control, it would derecognize the financial asset (and recognize separately as assets or liabilities any rights and obligations created or retained in the transfer). If the transferee cannot sell the entire asset to an unrelated party or cannot make the decision to sell an asset on its own without any further restrictions, then the transferor has retained control. If the transferor has retained control, it will continue to recognize the financial asset.

IFRS ASPE Accounting standards governing the derecognition of financial assets continue to differ somewhat between ASPE and IFRS. For example, as discussed above, the initial focus under IFRS is the first concept of whether the risks and rewards have been transferred. The focus under ASPE is the second concept of whether the entity retains control of the financial assets. In many cases, change in control and transfer of the risks and rewards occur at the same time. (See, for example, BCE Inc. in Illustration 7.7 later in this chapter.) However, the treatment under IFRS and ASPE often differs. For example, under IFRS, Canadian Tire Corporation, Limited noted in its 2011 annual report that "Since 1995, the Company has securitized credit card receivables . . . Under previous GAAP, the Company recorded a gain/loss on sale and derecognized the credit card receivables. Under IFRS, an entity may not derecognize an asset when it maintains the majority of the risks and rewards associated with the asset. Therefore, the securitization transactions no longer qualify for derecognition under IFRS and the Company must recognize the receivables in the Consolidated Balance Sheets. Accordingly, the gain/loss on the sale of the receivables was reversed."

The following discussion illustrates the key concepts involved, with some illustrative examples that would apply under ASPE and IFRS.

Criteria for Treatment as a Sale

Not long ago, companies tended to account for many transactions as sales of receivables, even when they had a major continuing interest in and control over the transferred receivables. Doing this resulted in derecognizing accounts receivable (that is, removing them from the SFP), reporting no additional debt but often recording a gain on disposal. The major challenge for accounting standards is to identify when a transfer of receivables qualifies for **being treated as a sale** (derecognition), and when it is merely a secured borrowing. Most managers would prefer to have the transaction treated as a sale for accounting purposes because this results in not having to record additional debt on the SFP.

In general, standard setters have concluded that the receivable or component parts of the receivable should be derecognized when the risks and rewards have been transferred (IFRS) or when control over the accounts receivable has been surrendered (ASPE). This is problematic in situations when the company "selling" the receivables has a continuing involvement in the asset. Currently there are disagreements as to how to interpret and apply the control criteria and the retention of partial interests. The accounting issues are important because of a company's ability to remove significant assets from the SFP, and not report liabilities when substantial risks have been retained.

IFRS The discussion below illustrates standards set out in IFRS 9. The following conditions are used to indicate whether the receivables have actually been transferred by an entity, supporting treatment as a sale. The entity transfers a financial asset, such as accounts receivable, if the entity:

1. transfers the contractual rights to receive cash flows from the accounts receivable; or

2. retains the contractual rights to receive cash flows from the accounts receivable, but has a contractual obligation to pay the cash flows to one or more recipients. Three additional conditions must be met:

a. The entity has no obligation to pay amounts to the eventual recipient unless it collects equivalent amounts from the original receivable.

b. The entity is prohibited by the terms of the transfer contract from selling or pledging the original asset other than as security to the eventual recipients for the obligation to pay them cash flows.

c. The entity has an obligation to remit any cash flows it collects on behalf of the eventual recipients without material delay.

ASPE Accounting for transfers of receivables under ASPE also focuses on whether a company has retained or given up control of the receivables. Under ASPE, if all three conditions set out in **Illustration 7.6** do not apply, the transferring company records the transfer as a secured borrowing. **Only when all three conditions are satisfied** is control over the assets assumed to be given up, and the transaction accounted for as a sale. If accounting for the transaction as a sale is appropriate but there is continuing involvement, the specific asset components retained need to be identified, as well as any liability components that were assumed. This approach is shown in a decision tree format in Illustration 7.6.

ILLUSTRATION 7.6

Accounting for Transfers of Receivables—ASPE

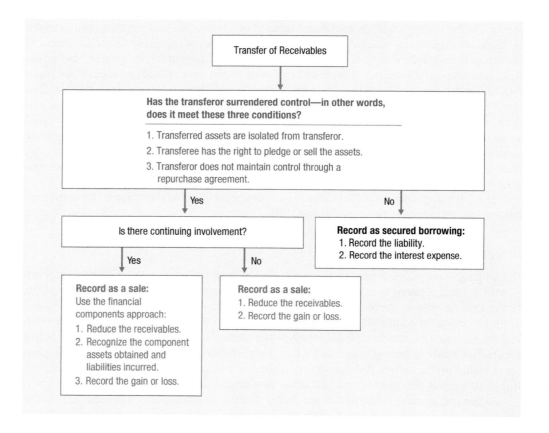

These transactions become more complex because of specialized contracts with different terms and conditions between companies, the securitization of receivables, and special purpose entities. The examples that follow are somewhat simplified to make the basic process of accounting for such transactions easier to follow.

Sale with No Continuing Involvement by Transferor

The most straightforward transaction is when the receivables are sold outright to another unrelated party, such as a factor, and they are sold without recourse. In this situation, it is apparent that the risks and rewards have been transferred to the other party (the factor). This is because the company is no longer exposed to risk associated with variability in the amounts and timing of cash flows from the factored accounts receivable.

When receivables are sold **without recourse**, the purchaser assumes the risk of collection and absorbs any credit losses.[20] Such a transfer is an outright sale of the receivables, both in form (the title is transferred) and substance (control is transferred). In nonrecourse transactions, as in any sale of assets, Cash is debited for the proceeds. Accounts Receivable is credited for the receivables' face value. The difference, reduced by any provision for probable adjustments (such as discounts, returns, and allowances), is recognized in the account Loss on Disposal of Receivables (if it is a loss). When appropriate, the seller uses a Due from Factor account (reported as a receivable) to account for the proceeds that are retained by a factor in order to cover probable sales discounts, sales returns, and sales allowances. **Example 7.16** looks at factoring without recourse.

Example 7.16 | Factoring on a Without Recourse Basis

Facts Crest Textiles Ltd. factors $500,000 of accounts receivable with Commercial Factors, Inc. on a **without recourse** basis. The receivables records are transferred to Commercial Factors, which takes over full responsibility for the collections. Commercial Factors assesses a finance charge of 3% of the amount of accounts receivable and withholds an initial amount equal to 5% of the accounts receivable for returns and allowances.

Instructions Provide the journal entries for both Crest Textiles and Commercial Factors for this receivables transfer without recourse.

Solution Entries for sale of receivables without recourse:

Crest Textiles Ltd.			Commercial Factors, Inc.		
Cash	460,000		Accounts Receivable	500,000	
Due from Factor	25,000[a]		Due to Crest Textiles		25,000
Loss on Disposal			Finance Revenue		15,000
of Receivables	15,000[b]		Cash		460,000
Accounts Receivable		500,000			

[a](5% × $500,000)
[b](3% × $500,000)

To recognize the outright sale of the receivables, Crest Textiles records a loss of $15,000. The factor's net income will be the difference between the financing revenue of $15,000 and the amount of any uncollectible receivables. The accounting treatment for a transfer of receivables without recourse would be the same under IFRS and ASPE, assuming that the risks and rewards have been transferred and that control has also been transferred.

Sale with Continuing Involvement by Transferor— Recourse Component Retained

If receivables are sold **with recourse**, the seller or transferor guarantees payment to the purchaser if the customer fails to pay. In this situation, under IFRS, if the risks and rewards have not been transferred to the factor company, then the transaction would not be treated as a sale (and the secured borrowing treatment discussed earlier could be applied). However, under ASPE, the accounting treatment would be based on the decision tree set out in Illustration 7.6. Specifically, a **financial components approach** is used to record this type of transaction because the seller has a continuing involvement with the receivable. Each party to the sale recognizes the components (assets and liabilities) that it controls after the sale and derecognizes the assets and liabilities that were sold or extinguished. **Example 7.17** looks at factoring with recourse.

[20]Recourse is defined as "the right of a transferee of receivables to receive payment from the transferor of those receivables for failure of debtors to pay when due, the effects of prepayments, or adjustments resulting from defects in the eligibility of the transferred receivables." This excerpt is reprinted with permission from the *CPA Canada Handbook—Accounting* © 2018, Part II, Section 3856 *Financial Instruments*, Appendix B, Transfer of Receivables by Chartered Professional Accountants of Canada. All rights reserved by the copyright owner.

Example 7.17 | Factoring on a With Recourse Basis

Facts ASPE Assume the same information as in Example 7.16 for Crest Textiles and Commercial Factors except that the receivables are sold **with recourse**. Crest Textiles estimates that the recourse obligation (a liability) has a fair value of $6,000. This is the company's estimate of the cost of its agreement in the contract to pay the amount of any receivables that debtors fail to pay.

Instructions Determine the loss on the sale of Crest Textiles' receivables. Provide and discuss the journal entries for both companies on the date of sale of the receivables.

Solution To determine the loss, the net proceeds from the sale are calculated and compared with the carrying amount of the assets that were sold, as shown below. Net proceeds are cash or other assets received in a sale less any liabilities incurred.

Calculation of net proceeds:		
Cash received (an asset)	$460,000	
Due from factor (an asset)	25,000	$485,000
Less: Recourse obligation (a liability)		6,000
Net proceeds		$479,000
Calculation of loss on disposal:		
Carrying amount of receivables		$500,000
Net proceeds		479,000
Loss on disposal of receivables		$ 21,000

The journal entries for both Crest Textiles and Commercial Factors for the receivables sold with a recourse component being retained are as follows:

Crest Textiles Ltd.		
Cash	460,000	
Due from Factor	25,000	
Loss on Disposal of Receivables	21,000	
Accounts Receivable		500,000
Recourse Liability		6,000

Commercial Factors, Inc.		
Accounts Receivable	500,000	
Due to Crest Textiles		25,000
Finance Revenue		15,000
Cash		460,000

In this case, Crest Textiles recognizes a loss of $21,000. In addition, it records a liability of $6,000 to indicate the probable payment to Commercial Factors for uncollectible receivables. If all the receivables are collected, Crest Textiles would eliminate its recourse liability and increase income. Commercial Factors' net income is the financing revenue of $15,000 because it will have no bad debts related to these receivables.

What about servicing? Often, the transferor in a securitization will retain the responsibility for servicing the receivables. This usually includes collecting the principal and interest, monitoring slow-paying accounts, and remitting cash to those who hold beneficial interests in the receivables. It may also include other specified services. If the transferor receives no reimbursement for these activities or receives less than the estimated cost of carrying them out, a servicing liability component is recorded. This decreases the net proceeds on disposal. Alternatively, a servicing asset component is recognized if the benefits of servicing (such as servicing fees under contract or late charges recovered from customers) are greater than the estimated cost.

Most of the complications of accounting for the disposition of accounts receivable arise in situations when the transferor continues to have some involvement with those assets.

Securitized Receivables-Transparency

Transparency requires significant disclosures for securitized receivables that are accounted for as sales. The goal is to inform readers about the fair value measurements and key assumptions that were used, the characteristics of the securitizations, cash flows between the special purpose entity and the transferor, and the balances and risk of servicing the assets and liabilities. Illustration 7.7 in the next section of the chapter gives an example of the main securitization disclosures made by BCE Inc. for its year ended December 31, 2017.

Presentation, Disclosure, and Analysis of Receivables

LEARNING OBJECTIVE 8
Explain how receivables and loans are reported and analyzed.

Presentation and Disclosure

When financial statements are prepared, the presentation of and disclosures related to receivables have to be addressed. The objective is to allow users to evaluate.

- the significance of these financial assets to the entity's financial position and performance and
- the nature and extent of the associated risks.

Aside from providing information about the accounting policies applied, entities are required to present the following data about loans and receivables, with more information required under IFRS than ASPE:

1. The segregation and separate reporting of ordinary trade accounts, amounts owing by related parties, prepayments, and other significant amounts

2. An indication of the amounts and, where practicable, the maturity dates of accounts with a maturity of more than one year

3. Separate reporting of receivables that are current assets from those that are non-current

4. Separate reporting of any impaired balances, and the amount of any allowance for credit losses with, under IFRS, a reconciliation of the changes in the allowance account during the accounting period

5. Disclosure on the income statement of the amounts of interest income, impairment losses, and any reversals associated with such losses

Major disclosures are also required about the securitization or transfers of receivables, whether derecognized or not. Users are particularly interested in the risks to which the entity is exposed in general, and as a result of such transactions. Credit risk is the major concern with loans and receivables. Therefore, under IFRS, extensive qualitative and quantitative information is required about the entity's situation, as is fair value information about loans and receivables, except for short-term trade accounts. Far less information about risk exposures and fair values is required under ASPE.

Real World Emphasis Extensive excerpts from the December 31, 2017 SFP of the well-known Canadian communications company BCE Inc., along with the notes cross-referenced to its statement of financial position, are in **Illustration 7.7**. These disclosures are based on IFRS. Where BCE uses the abbreviation "AFS" in Note 16 below, it refers to "Available for Sale" investments, similar to Fair Value Through Other Comprehensive Income Investments under IFRS 9, as discussed in Chapter 9.

Disclosures of Trade and Other Receivables—BCE Inc.

Consolidated Statements of Financial Position

AT DECEMBER 31 (in millions of Canadian dollars)	NOTE	2017	2016
ASSETS			
Current assets			
Cash		**442**	603
Cash equivalents		**183**	250
Trade and other receivables	11	**3,135**	2,979
Inventory	12	**380**	403
Prepaid expenses		**375**	420
Other current assets		**124**	200
Total current assets		**4,639**	4,855
Other non-current assets	16	**900**	1,010

Note 2: Significant Accounting Policies (Extracts)

Cash Equivalents

Cash equivalents are comprised of highly liquid investments with original maturities of three months or less from the date of purchase.

Securitization of Trade Receivables

Proceeds on the securitization of trade receivables are recognized as collateralized borrowing as we do not transfer control and substantially all of the risks and rewards of ownership to another entity.

Note 11: Trade and Other Receivables

FOR THE YEAR ENDED DECEMBER 31	NOTE	2017	2016
Trade receivables		**3,138**	2,967
Allowance for doubtful accounts	24	**(55)**	(60)
Allowance for revenue adjustments		**(80)**	(85)
Current tax receivable		**31**	35
Other accounts receivable		**101**	122
Total trade and other receivables		**3,135**	2,979

Note 16: Other Non-Current Assets

FOR THE YEAR ENDED DECEMBER 31	NOTE	2017	2016
Net assets of post-employment benefit plans	22	**262**	403
Investments[1]		**106**	88
AFS publicly-traded and privately-held investments	24	**103**	103
Long-term notes and other receivables		**101**	63
Derivative assets	24	**51**	126
Other		**277**	227
Total other non-current assets		**900**	1,010

(1) *These amounts have been pledged as security related to obligations for certain employee benefits and are not available for general use*

Note 24: Financial and Capital Management (Extracts)

Financial Management

Management's objectives are to protect BCE and its subsidiaries on a consolidated basis against material economic exposures and variability of results from various financial risks that include credit risk, liquidity risk, foreign currency risk, interest rate risk and equity price risk.

Credit Risk

We are exposed to credit risk from operating activities and certain financing activities, the maximum exposure of which is represented by the carrying amounts reported on the statements of financial position.

We are exposed to credit risk if counterparties to our trade receivables and derivative instruments are unable to meet their obligations. The concentration of credit risk from our customers is minimized because we have a large and diverse customer base. There was minimal credit risk relating to derivative instruments at December 31, 2017 and 2016. We deal with institutions that have investment-grade credit ratings and as such we expect that they will be able to meet their obligations. We regularly monitor our credit risk and credit exposure.

The following table provides the change in allowance for doubtful accounts for trade receivables.

	NOTE	2017	2016
Balance, January 1		**(60)**	(64)
Additions		**(99)**	(102)
Usage		**104**	106
Balance, December 31	11	**(55)**	(60)

In many instances, trade receivables are written off directly to bad debt expense if the account has not been collected after a predetermined period of time.

The following table provides further details on trade receivables not impaired.

AT DECEMBER 31	2017	2016
Trade receivables not past due	**2,257**	2,187
Trade receivables past due and not impaired		
Under 60 days	**491**	286
60 to 120 days	**279**	359
Over 120 days	**56**	75
Trade receivables, net of allowance for doubtful accounts	**3,083**	2,907

Analysis

Analysts often calculate financial ratios to evaluate the liquidity of a company's accounts receivable. See **Underlying Concept 7.6**. To assess the receivables' liquidity, the **receivables turnover ratio** is used. This ratio measures the number of times, on average, that receivables are collected during the period. The ratio is calculated by dividing net sales by average receivables (net) outstanding during the year. Theoretically, the numerator should include only credit sales, but this information is often not available. As long as the relative amounts of credit and cash sales stay fairly constant, the trend shown by the ratio will still be valid. Average receivables outstanding can be calculated from the beginning and ending balances of net trade receivables unless seasonal factors are significant. If significant, as they often are for many retailers, using an average of the year's opening balance and the amounts at the end of each quarter will be more representative. The calculation of the accounts receivable turnover for a utility company is in **Example 7.18**.

> **Underlying Concept 7.6**
>
> Providing information that will help users assess an enterprise's current liquidity and potential future cash flows is one of the main objectives of accounting.

Example 7.18 | Calculation of Accounts Receivable Turnover

Facts **Finance** 5.2.1 **Canadian Utilities Limited**, a Canadian-based company in the power generation, transmission, and distribution business, reported 2017 revenue of $4,027 million and accounts receivable balances at December 31, 2016 and 2017, of $518 million and $619 million, respectively.

Instructions Calculate Canadian Utilities' accounts receivable turnover ratio for 2017 and discuss how the ratio can be used to assess the quality of accounts receivable.

Solution

$$\text{Accounts Receivable Turnover} = \frac{\text{Net Sales/Revenue}}{\text{Average Trade Receivables (net)}}$$

$$= \frac{\$4,027}{(\$518 + \$619)/2}$$

$$= 7.1 \text{ times, or every } 51.4 \text{ days } (365/7.1 = 51.4)$$

The results give information about the quality of the receivables. They also give an idea of how successfully the firm collects its outstanding receivables, particularly when compared with prior periods, industry standards, the company's credit terms, or internal targets. Management

> would also prepare an aging schedule to determine how long specific receivables have been outstanding. It is possible that a satisfactory receivables turnover may have resulted because certain receivables were collected quickly, although others have been outstanding for a relatively long time. An aging schedule would reveal such patterns.

Theory Because the estimated expense for uncollectible accounts is subject to judgement, there is always some concern that companies can use this judgement to manage earnings. By overestimating the amount of uncollectible loans in a good earnings year, a bank, for example, can "save for a rainy day." In future less profitable periods, the bank will then be able to reduce its overly conservative allowance for its loan loss account and increase earnings as a result. Remember, though, that reversals of such impairment losses should be based on specific events and circumstances occurring after the original bad debt loss was recognized.

Finance 5.1.1 Further analysis is often carried out on changes in the basic related accounts. Ordinarily, sales, accounts receivable, and the allowance for doubtful accounts should all move in the same direction. Higher sales should generate more receivables and an increased allowance. If sales have increased as well as receivables, but the allowance has not increased proportionately, the reader should be alert to the possibility of earnings management. If the allowance grows faster than receivables, particularly when sales have not increased, this could mean that credit quality has deteriorated. Alternatively, perhaps the company has built up its allowance account so that there is a cushion for poorer-performing years ahead. The answers are not always obvious, but this type of analysis can identify concerns.

With the increased practice of selling receivables through securitization transactions, especially where a company retains servicing (such as collection) responsibilities, the financial ratios have to be calculated and interpreted carefully. Consider the following:

- It is not appropriate to directly compare the turnover ratio of a company that securitizes or factors its receivables with the ratio of another company that does not. This financing comes at a cost, but should provide cash flow for other value-adding purposes. Therefore, each company's situation has to be analyzed separately.

- Growth in a company's sales and growth in its receivables generally go hand in hand, but will not for a company involved in selling its receivables. Any company that begins such a program in the year should notice a significant change in the key accounts receivable ratios due to the lower receivable balances.

- Securitization is "off–balance sheet" because the receivables sold are removed from the current assets and because the amount "borrowed" is not reported in a company's liabilities. This affects liquidity ratios such as the current and quick ratios. Even though the same dollar amount is missing from the assets and liabilities, the ratios can be significantly affected.

Securitization transactions can be complex, so you need to be very cautious when interpreting financial statement ratios. Companies are increasingly required by regulators to provide a full discussion in the management discussion and analysis of critical issues like liquidity, especially if the company depends on such off–balance sheet financing arrangements.

IFRS/ASPE Comparison

LEARNING OBJECTIVE 9
Identify differences in accounting between IFRS and accounting standards for private enterprises (ASPE), and what changes are expected in the near future.

A Comparison of IFRS and ASPE

From an intermediate accounting perspective, the general approaches explained in the chapter are expected to continue, although the standards may evolve to have more specific application guidance. ASPE is designed to eliminate much of the complexity in pre-2011 financial instrument standards, and IFRS has a similar goal.

Illustration 7.8 presents the more important differences that are expected to continue.

ILLUSTRATION 7.8 **IFRS and ASPE Comparison Chart**

	International Financial Reporting Standards (IFRS)— IAS 1, 7, 32 and IFRS 7, 9	**Accounting Standards for Private Enterprises (ASPE)— *CPA Canada Handbook*, Part II, Sections 1510 and 3856**	**References to Related Examples, Illustrations, and Select Brief Exercises**
Cash and cash equivalents	IFRS allows preferred shares that are acquired close to their maturity date to qualify as a cash equivalent.	Cash equivalents are non-equity, short-term, highly liquid investments that are readily convertible to known amounts of cash with a negligible risk of change in value.	BE7.3
Receivables: Recognition and measurement	The effective interest method is required for recognizing interest income and amortizing discounts and premiums.	The standard does not require use of the effective interest method of recognizing interest income and amortizing any discounts or premiums; therefore, either the straight-line method or the effective interest method may be used.	Examples 7.11 to 7.14 BE7.12 and BE7.13
Derecognition	To determine whether a financial asset should be derecognized, IFRS first considers whether the risks and rewards of ownership have been transferred.	To determine whether a financial asset should be derecognized, ASPE considers whether control of receivables has been retained or given up.	Illustration 7.6 and Examples 7.16 and 7.17. More detailed analysis is beyond the scope of this text. BE7.15 and BE7.16
Disclosures	Detailed quantitative and qualitative disclosures are required about the receivables, interest income, related risks, and sensitivity analysis linked to the measurements made. IFRS has detailed disclosure requirements for transferred financial assets that are either partly or entirely derecognized.	Basic disclosures are required regarding the significance of receivables to the entity's financial position and financial performance, and the financial risks to which it is exposed.	Not applicable

Looking Ahead

IFRS

In March 2018, the IFRS Interpretations Committee issued a Staff Paper (SP) on proper classification of short-term loans and credit facilities within cash and cash equivalents. They noted that if banking arrangements are always or almost always negative they should be considered a form of financing, and not a key part of the cash management system. While IAS 7 was considered adequate in terms of what should be part of cash and cash equivalents, the SP recommended that the IASB publish a clarification (an "Agenda Decision") regarding disclosure requirements for companies with short-term loans and credit facilities.

ASPE

While most requirements set out under ASPE are not likely to change in the short term, one area that is open to change is that of the derecognition (transfer) of receivables. The

Accounting Standards Board (AcSB) had indicated that changes may be made to ASPE after the International Accounting Standards Board (IASB) and Financial Accounting Standards Board (FASB) develop final standards on derecognition of financial assets, and these are now complete. The AcSB issued a "Post-implementation Review: Section 3856, Financial Instruments" in September 2015. It focused on the usefulness and challenges of applying the financial instruments section of the *CPA Canada Handbook*, including challenges in the initial measurement of some financial instruments, some confusion regarding measurement of financial instruments issued between related parties, and some questions regarding the usefulness of risk and uncertainty disclosures for financial statement users. Changes in ASPE are unlikely in the near term, and any amendments would follow AcSB due process.

Appendix 7A	# Methods for Controlling Cash

LEARNING OBJECTIVE 10
Explain common techniques for controlling cash.

Management and Control of Cash

Of all assets, cash is at the greatest risk of being used or diverted improperly. Management must overcome two problems in accounting for cash transactions:

1. It must establish proper controls to ensure that no unauthorized transactions are entered into by officers, employees, or others.
2. It must ensure that the information that is needed in order to properly manage cash on hand and cash transactions is made available.

Yet even with sophisticated control devices, errors can and do happen. *The Wall Street Journal* once ran a story entitled "A $7.8 Million Error Has a Happy Ending for a Horrified Bank," which described how **Manufacturers Hanover Trust Co.** mailed about $7.8 million too much in cash dividends to its shareholders. As the headline suggests, most of the money was eventually returned.

Management Accounting 3.1.1, 3.1.2 To safeguard cash and ensure the accuracy of the accounting records for this asset, companies need effective **internal control** over cash. There are new challenges to maintaining control over liquid assets as more and more transactions are done with the swipe of a debit or credit card or through unregulated electronic payment services like PayPal. Canadians are among the highest users of debit and credit cards in the world. The shift from hard cash to digital cash brings new challenges for the internal control systems that are designed to control this asset. The purpose of this appendix is to identify some of the basic controls related to cash.

Using Bank Accounts

Even with the increased use of electronic banking, a company may use different banks in different locations and different types of bank accounts. For large companies that operate in multiple locations, the location of bank accounts can be important. Having collection accounts in strategic locations can speed up the flow of cash into the company by shortening the time between a customer's payment mailing and the company's use of the cash. Multiple collection centres are generally used to reduce the size of a company's **collection float**. The collection float is the difference between the amount on deposit according to the company's records and the amount of collected cash according to the bank record.

The **general chequing account** is the main bank account in most companies and is often the only bank account in small businesses. Cash is deposited in and disbursed from this account as all transactions are cycled through it. Deposits from and disbursements to all other bank accounts are made through the general chequing account. Traditionally companies also used **imprest bank accounts** for some disbursements such as payroll or dividend payments. Direct deposit is now much more common for these types of payments.[21]

Lockbox accounts are often used by large companies with multiple locations to make collections in cities where most of their customer billing occurs. The company rents a local post office box and authorizes a local bank to pick up the remittances mailed to that box number. The bank empties the box each day and immediately credits the company's account for collections. The greatest advantage of a lockbox is that it accelerates the availability of collected cash. Generally, in a lockbox arrangement, the bank makes a copy of each cheque for record-keeping purposes and provides the company with a deposit slip, a list of collections, and any customer correspondence. If the control over cash is improved, savings are made by outsourcing remittance processing, and if the related cost savings (and income generated from accelerating the receipt of funds) is more than what the lockbox system costs, it is considered worthwhile to use it.

Companies continue to increase their use of systems that electronically transfer funds from customers and to suppliers. While these advances will make many of the controls in a paper cheque-based system obsolete, companies will still always need to improve the effectiveness of the controls that are part of their information and processing systems.

The Imprest Petty Cash System

Almost every company needs to pay small amounts for a great many things, such as Uber rides and taxi fares, minor office supplies, and other miscellaneous expenses. It is usually impractical to require that such disbursements be made by cheque, but some control over them is important. A simple method of obtaining reasonable control, while following the rule of disbursement by cheque, is the **petty cash** system, particularly an imprest system.

This is how the system works.

1. Someone is designated as the petty cash custodian and given a small amount of currency from which to make small payments. The transfer of funds from the bank account to petty cash is recorded as follows, assuming a $300 transfer:

Petty Cash	300	
Cash		300

A	=	L	+	SE
0				

   Cash flows: No effect

2. As payments are made out of this fund, the petty cash custodian gets signed receipts from each individual who receives cash from the fund. If possible, evidence of the disbursement should be attached to the petty cash receipt. Petty cash transactions are not recorded in the accounts until the fund is reimbursed, and they should be recorded by someone other than the petty cash custodian.

3. When the cash in the fund runs low, the custodian presents to the controller or accounts payable cashier a request for reimbursement that is supported by the petty cash receipts and other disbursement evidence. In exchange for these, the custodian receives a company cheque to replenish the fund. At this point, transactions are recorded in the accounting system based on the petty cash receipts. For example:

---

[21]Imprest bank accounts are used to make a specific amount of cash available for a limited purpose. The account acts as a clearing account for a large volume of cheques or for a specific type of cheque. The specific and intended amount to be cleared through the imprest account, such as for dividends, is deposited by transferring that amount from the general chequing account or other source. In addition to payroll and dividend cheques, imprest bank accounts are sometimes used for disbursing commissions, bonuses, and officers' salaries, although increasingly these payments are being made in electronic form.

A	=	L	+	SE
−173				−173

Cash flows: ↓ 173 outflow

A	=	L	+	SE
0				

Cash flows: No effect

Office Expense	42	
Postage Expense	53	
Entertainment Expense	76	
Cash Over and Short	2	
Cash		173

4. If it is decided that the fund's balance is too high, an adjustment may be made and the surplus amount is then deposited back into the bank account. The following adjustment is made to record the reduction in the fund balance from $300 to $250:

Cash	50	
Petty Cash		50

Note that **only** entries to increase or decrease the size of the fund are made **to the Petty Cash account**.

A **Cash Over and Short** account is used when the cash in the petty cash fund plus the dollar amount of the receipts does not add up to the imprest petty cash amount. When this occurs, it is usually due to an error, such as a failure to provide correct change, overpayment of an expense, or a lost receipt. If cash is short (in other words, the sum of the receipts and cash in the fund is less than the imprest amount), the shortage is debited to the Cash Over and Short account. If there is more cash than there should be, the overage is credited to Cash Over and Short. Cash over and short is typically left open until the end of the year, when it is closed and generally shown on the income statement as part of "other expense or revenue."

Unless a reimbursement has just been made, there are usually expense items in the fund. This means that, if accurate financial statements are wanted, the fund needs to be reimbursed at the end of each accounting period in addition to when it is nearly empty.

Under an imprest system, the petty cash custodian is responsible at all times for the amount of the fund on hand, whether the amount is in cash or signed receipts. These receipts are the evidence that the disbursing officer needs in order to issue a reimbursement cheque. Two additional procedures are followed to obtain more complete control over the petty cash fund.

1. Surprise counts of the fund are made from time to time by a superior of the petty cash custodian to determine that the fund is being accounted for satisfactorily.

2. Petty cash receipts are cancelled or mutilated after they have been submitted for reimbursement so that they cannot be used again.

Physical Protection of Cash Balances

It is not only cash receipts and cash disbursements that need to be safeguarded through internal control measures. Cash on hand and in banks must also be protected. Because receipts become cash on hand and disbursements are made from the cash in banks, adequate control of receipts and disbursements is part of protecting cash balances. Certain other procedures, therefore, are also carried out.

The physical protection of cash is such an elementary necessity that it requires little discussion. Every effort should be made to minimize the cash on hand in the office. A petty cash fund, the current day's receipts, and perhaps funds for making change should be the only funds on hand at any time. As much as possible, these funds should be kept in a vault, safe, or locked cash drawer. Each day's receipts should be transmitted intact to the bank as soon as is practical. Intact means that the total receipts are accounted for together and no part of the amount is used for other purposes. This leaves a clear trail from the receipts activity to the bank.

Every company needs a record of cash received and disbursed, and the cash balance. Because of the many cash transactions, however, errors or omissions can occur in keeping this record. It is therefore necessary to periodically prove the balance shown in the general ledger. Cash that is actually present in the office—petty cash, funds kept for making change, and undeposited receipts—can be counted and compared with the company records. Cash on deposit is not available for count so it is proved by preparing a bank reconciliation, which is a reconciliation of the company's record and the bank's record of the company's cash.

Reconciliation of Bank Balances

At the end of each calendar month, the bank sends each customer a bank statement (a copy of the bank's account with the customer), together with the customer's cheques that were paid by the bank during the month or a list of the company's payments that have been presented to and cleared by the bank during the month.[22] Less and less hard copy is being returned as banks provide companies with electronic access to this information. The balance of cash reported by the bank to the customer will be the same as the balance in the customer's own records if:

- no errors were made by the bank or the customer,
- all deposits made and all cheques drawn by the customer reached the bank within the same month, and
- no unusual transactions occurred that affected either the company's or the bank's record of cash.

This rarely occurs, because of one or more of the following:

Reconciling Items

1. **Deposits in transit**: End-of-month deposits of cash that are recorded on the depositor's books in one month are received and recorded by the bank in the following month.

2. **Outstanding cheques**: Cheques written by the depositor are recorded when they are written but may not be recorded by (or "clear") the bank until the next month.

3. **Bank charges**: Charges are recorded by the bank against the depositor's balance for such items as bank services, printing cheques, **not-sufficient-funds (NSF) cheques**, and safe-deposit box rentals. The depositor may not be aware of these charges until the bank statement is received.

4. **Bank credits**: Collections or deposits by the bank for the depositor's benefit may not be known to the depositor until the bank statement is received. These are reconciling items as long as they have not yet been recorded on the company's records. Examples are note collections for the depositor, interest earned on interest-bearing accounts, and direct deposits by customers and others.

5. **Bank or depositor errors**: Errors by either the bank or the depositor cause the bank balance to disagree with the depositor's book balance.

For these reasons, differences between the depositor's record of cash and the bank's record are usual and expected. The two records therefore need to be reconciled to determine the reasons for the differences between the two amounts.

Audit & Assurance 4.1.1, 4.1.2 A **bank reconciliation** is a schedule that explains any differences between the bank's and the company's records of cash. If the difference results only from transactions not yet recorded by the bank, the company's record of cash is considered correct. But if some part of the difference is due to other items, the bank's records or the company's records must be adjusted. The bank reconciliation helps to safeguard cash by ensuring the accuracy of the accounting records. Timely bank reconciliations are needed to provide effective internal control, and to detect errors and possible misappropriations of cash. Bank reconciliations are typically reviewed by senior accounting personnel and company auditors to ensure that the control is operating effectively.

Two forms of bank reconciliation can be prepared. One form reconciles from the bank statement balance to the book balance or vice versa. The other form reconciles both the bank

---

[22]Use of paper cheques continues to be a popular means of payment in Canada. However, easy access to desktop publishing software and hardware has created new opportunities for cheque fraud in the form of duplicate, altered, or forged cheques. At the same time, new fraud-fighting technologies, such as ultraviolet imaging, high-capacity bar codes, and biometrics, are being developed. These technologies convert paper documents into document files that are processed electronically, thereby reducing the risk of fraud.

balance and the book balance to a correct cash balance. This latter form is more popular. A sample of this form and its common reconciling items is shown in **Illustration 7A.1**.

Bank Reconciliation Form and Content

Balance per bank statement (end of period)		$$$
Add: Deposits in transit	$$	
Undeposited receipts (cash on hand)	$$	
Bank errors that understate the bank statement balance	$$	$$
		$$$
Deduct: Outstanding cheques	$$	
Bank errors that overstate the bank statement balance	$$	$$
Correct cash balance		$$$
Balance per company's books (end of period)		$$$
Add: Bank credits and collections not yet recorded in the books	$$	
Book errors that understate the book balance	$$	$$
		$$$
Deduct: Bank charges not yet recorded in the books	$$	
Book errors that overstate the book balance	$$	$$
Correct cash balance		$$$

This form of reconciliation has two sections: (1) the "Balance per bank statement" and (2) the "Balance per company's books." Both sections end with the same correct cash balance. The correct cash balance is the amount that the books must be adjusted to and is the amount reported on the SFP. **Adjusting journal entries are prepared for all the addition and deduction items that appear in the "Balance per company's books" section**, and the bank should be notified immediately about any errors that it has made. **Example 7A.1** provides a sample bank reconciliation.

Example 7A.1 | Sample Bank Reconciliation

Facts Nugget Mining Company's books show a cash balance at the Ottawa National Bank on November 30, 2020, of $20,502. The bank statement covering the month of November shows an ending balance of $22,190. An examination of Nugget's accounting records and the November bank statement identified the following reconciling items.

1. A deposit of $3,680 was taken to the bank late on November 30 but does not appear on the November bank statement.

2. Cheques written in November but not charged to (deducted from) the November bank statement are:

Cheque	#7327	$ 150
	#7348	4,820
	#7349	31

3. Nugget has not yet recorded the $600 of interest collected by the bank on November 20 on Sequoia Co. bonds held by the bank for Nugget.

4. Bank service charges of $18 are not yet recorded on Nugget's books.

5. A $220 cheque for Nugget from a customer was returned with the bank statement and marked "NSF." The bank, having originally recognized this as part of one of Nugget's deposits, now deducted this bad cheque as a disbursement from Nugget's account.

6. Nugget discovered that cheque #7322, written in November for $131 in payment of an account payable, had been incorrectly recorded in its books as $311.

7. A cheque written on Nugent Oil Co.'s account for $175 had been incorrectly charged to Nugget Mining and was included with the bank statement.

Instructions   Prepare a reconciliation of the bank and book balances to the correct cash balance and provide the journal entries to adjust and correct Nugget's books.

Solution

Nugget Mining Company Bank Reconciliation Ottawa National Bank, November 30, 2020			
Balance per bank statement, November 30/20			$22,190
Add: Deposit in transit	(1)	$3,680	
Bank error—bank incorrectly charged cheque to account	(7)	175	3,855
			26,045
Deduct: Outstanding cheques	(2)		5,001
Correct cash balance, November 30/20			$21,044
Balance per books, November 30/20			$20,502
Add: Interest collected by the bank	(3)	$ 600	
Error in recording cheque #7322	(6)	180	780
			21,282
Deduct: Bank service charges	(4)	18	
NSF cheque returned	(5)	220	238
Correct cash balance, November 30/20			$21,044

The journal entries to adjust and correct Nugget Mining's books in early December 2020 are taken from the items in the "Balance per books" section and are as follows:

Cash	600	
Interest Income		600
(To record interest on Sequoia Co. bonds, collected by bank)		
Cash	180	
Accounts Payable		180
(To correct error in recording amount of cheque #7322)		
Bank Charges Expense	18	
Cash		18
(To record bank service charges for November)		
Accounts Receivable	220	
Cash		220
(To record customer's cheque returned NSF)		

A	=	L	+	SE
+762		+180		+582

Cash flows: ↑ 542 inflow

Alternatively, one summary entry could be made with a net $542 debit to Cash, which is the difference between the balance before adjustment of $20,502 and the correct balance of $21,044. When the entries are posted, Nugget's cash account will have a balance of $21,044. Nugget should return the Nugent Oil Co. cheque to Ottawa National Bank, informing the bank of the error.

Review and Practice

Summary of Learning Objectives

1. Understand cash and accounts receivable from a business perspective.

Companies often have a significant amount of accounts receivable, which require time and effort to manage and control. Companies strive to ensure that their collection policy is restrictive enough to minimize large losses in the form of uncollectible accounts receivable, while not being so restrictive that it interferes with the ability to attract new customers. Typical accounts receivable-related categories include trade receivables, loans receivable, and nontrade receivables

(including items like interest receivable, amounts due from officers, and advances to employees).

2. Define financial assets, and identify items that are considered cash and cash equivalents and how they are reported.

Financial assets are a major type of asset, defined as cash, a contractual right to receive cash or another financial asset, an equity holding in another company, or a contractual right to exchange financial instruments under potentially favourable conditions. To be reported as cash, an asset must be readily available to pay current obligations and not have any contractual restrictions that would limit how it can be used in satisfying debts. Cash consists of coins, currency, and available funds on deposit at a bank. Negotiable instruments such as money orders, certified cheques, cashier's cheques, personal cheques, and bank drafts are also viewed as cash. Savings accounts are usually classified as cash. Cash equivalents include highly liquid short-term investments (that is, those maturing three months or less from the date of purchase) that can be exchanged for known amounts of cash and have an insignificant chance of changing in value. Examples include treasury bills, commercial paper, and money-market funds. In certain circumstances, temporary bank overdrafts may be deducted in determining the balance of cash and cash equivalents.

Cash is reported as a current asset in the SFP, with foreign currency balances reported at their Canadian dollar equivalent at the date of the SFP. The reporting of other related items is as follows: (1) Restricted cash: Legally restricted deposits that are held as compensating balances against short-term borrowing are stated separately in current assets. Restricted deposits held against long-term borrowing arrangements are separately classified in non-current assets either in investments or other assets. (2) Bank overdrafts: These are reported in the current liabilities section and may be added to the amount reported as accounts payable. (3) Cash equivalents: This item is often reported together with cash as "cash and cash equivalents."

3. Define receivables, and identify the different types of receivables from an accounting perspective.

Receivables are claims held against customers and others for money, goods, or services. Most receivables are financial assets. The receivables are described in the following ways: (1) current or non-current; (2) trade or nontrade; and (3) accounts receivable or notes or loans receivable.

4. Account for and explain the accounting issues related to the recognition and measurement of accounts receivable.

The entity becomes a party to the contractual provisions of the accounts receivable financial instrument only when it has a legal claim to receive cash or other financial assets. Therefore the timing of recognition of accounts receivable is intertwined with the timing of recognition of revenue, as we discussed in Chapter 6. For most companies, when the sale is recognized, either cash is received (realized) or an account receivable is recognized.

Two issues that may complicate the measurement of accounts receivable are (1) the availability of discounts (trade and cash discounts) and (2) the length of time between the sale and the payment due dates (the interest element). Ideally, receivables should be measured initially at their fair value, which is their present value (discounted value of the cash to be received in the future). Receivables that are created by normal business transactions and are due in the short term are excluded from present value requirements.

5. Account for and explain the accounting issues related to the impairment in value of accounts receivable.

Short-term receivables are reported at their net realizable value—the net amount that is expected to be received in cash, which is not necessarily the amount that is legally receivable. Determining net realizable value requires estimating uncollectible receivables and any future

returns or allowances and discounts that are expected to be taken. The adjustments to the asset account also affect the income statement amounts of bad debt expense, sales returns and allowances, and sales discounts. The assessment of impairment is usually based on an aged accounts receivable report, with higher percentages of uncollectible accounts shown for older amounts outstanding. Even if a company estimates bad debt expense each period as a percentage of sales, the accounts receivable at the date of the SFP are analyzed to ensure the balance in the allowance account is appropriate.

6. Account for and explain the accounting issues related to the recognition and measurement of notes and loans receivable.

The accounting issues for short-term notes receivable are similar to those of accounts receivable. However, because notes always contain an interest element, interest income must be properly recognized. Notes receivable either bear interest on the face amount (interest-bearing) or have an interest element that is the difference between the amount lent and the maturity value (non–interest-bearing). Long-term notes and loans receivable are recognized initially at their fair value (the present value of the future cash flows) and subsequently at their amortized cost. Transaction costs are capitalized. This requires amortizing any discount if the item was issued at less than its face value, or any premium if it was issued for an amount greater than its face value, using the effective interest method. The straight-line method may be used under ASPE. Amortization of the premium (or discount) results in a reduction of (or increase in) interest income below (or above) the cash amount received.

7. Account for and explain the basic accounting issues related to the derecognition of receivables.

To accelerate the receipt of cash from receivables, the owner may transfer the receivables to another entity for cash. The transfer of receivables to a third party for cash may be done in one of two ways: (1) Secured borrowing: The creditor requires the debtor to designate or pledge receivables as security for the loan. (2) Sale (factoring or securitization) of receivables: Factors are finance companies or banks that buy receivables from businesses and then collect the remittances directly from the customers. Securitization is the transfer of receivables to a special purpose entity that is mainly financed by highly rated debt instruments. In many cases, transferors have some continuing involvement with the receivables they sell. For the transfer to be recorded as a sale, IFRS focuses on whether the risks and rewards of ownership have been transferred to the transferee. ASPE focuses on whether the transferor has surrendered control and has continued involvement with the receivables.

8. Explain how receivables and loans are reported and analyzed.

Disclosure of receivables requires that (1) valuation accounts be appropriately offset against receivables, (2) the receivables be appropriately classified as current or non-current, and (3) pledged or designated receivables be identified. As financial instruments, specific disclosures are required for receivables so that users can determine their significance to the company's financial position and performance and can assess the nature and extent of associated risks and how these risks are managed and measured. Private entities require less disclosure than those reporting under IFRS. Receivables are analyzed in terms of their turnover and age (number of days outstanding), and in terms of relative changes in the related sales, receivables, and allowance accounts.

---

9.   Identify differences in accounting between IFRS and accounting standards for private enterprises (ASPE), and what changes are expected in the near future.

The two sets of standards are very similar, with minor differences relating to what is included in cash equivalents. ASPE does not require use of the effective interest method, whereas IFRS does require it for financial asset investments that are not held for trading purposes. Impairment provisions were recently addressed under IFRS 9, and the changes under IFRS 9 have led to additional differences between IFRS and ASPE.

---

10.   Explain common techniques for controlling cash.

The common techniques that are used to control cash are as follows: (1) Using a variety of bank accounts: A company can vary the number and location of banks and the types of accounts to meet its control objectives. (2) The imprest petty cash system: It may be impractical to require small amounts of various expenses to be paid by cheque, yet some control over them is important. (3) Physical protection of cash balances: Adequate control of receipts and disbursements is part of protecting cash balances. Every effort should be made to minimize the cash on hand in the office. (4) Reconciliation of bank balances: Cash on deposit is not available for counting and is proved by preparing a bank reconciliation.

Practice Problem

The trial balance before adjustment for Slamar Company shows the following balances.

	Debit	Credit
Net sales		$860,000
Accounts receivable	$338,000	
Allowance for doubtful accounts		4,240

Consider the following independent situations:

1. To obtain additional cash, Slamar factors without recourse $50,000 of accounts receivable with Pierce Finance. The finance charge is 11% of the amount factored.

2. To obtain a 1-year loan of $75,000, Slamar assigns $80,000 of specific receivable accounts to Milo Financial. Interest expense of 9% is charged on the loan; the cash of $80,000 is received and the accounts are assigned to Milo Financial.

3. Based on a review of the company's aged accounts receivable, the company determines that it requires an Allowance for Doubtful Accounts of 6% of gross accounts receivable.

Instructions

a. Using the data above, give the journal entries required to record situations 1 to 3 at the date of the initial transaction. For situation 2, also discuss how interest expense would be recognized.

b. Discuss how analysis based on the current ratio and the accounts receivable turnover would be affected if Slamar had transferred the receivables in situation 1 using a secured borrowing.

Solution

a. 1. Cash   44,500
      Loss on Disposal of Receivables ($50,000 × 11%)   5,500
          Accounts Receivable   50,000

2. Cash   75,000
      Notes Payable   75,000

Interest expense will be recognized on an accrual basis each time financial statements are prepared (for example, monthly or quarterly).

3. Bad Debt Expense   16,040
      Allowance for Doubtful Accounts   16,040
      [($338,000 × 6%) − $4,240]

b. With a secured borrowing, the receivables would stay on Slamar's books, and Slamar would record a note payable. This would typically reduce the current ratio and accounts receivable turnover.

Key Terms

aging method, p. 7-15
aging schedule, p. 7-15
allowance method, p. 7-16
amortized cost, p. 7-23
asset-backed financing, p. 7-31
asset-backed securities, p. 7-32
bad debts, p. 7-14
bank overdrafts, p. 7-7
bank reconciliation, p. 7-45
basic loan features, p. 7-23
beneficial interest, p. 7-36
cash, p. 7-6
cash discounts, p. 7-12
cash equivalents, p. 7-8
compensating balances, p. 7-7
contra, p. 7-12
contractual yield basis, p. 7-23
coupon rate, p. 7-23
credit risk, p. 7-14
data analytics, p. 7-17
deposits in transit, p. 7-45
derecognized, p. 7-30
direct write off method, p. 7-20

discount, p. 7-28
effective interest method, p. 7-23
effective interest rate, p. 7-23
face rate, p. 7-23
face value, p. 7-23
factoring receivables, p. 7-31
fair value, p. 7-23
financial asset, p. 7-6
financial components approach, p. 7-35
implicit interest rate, p. 7-24
imprest system, p. 7-44
imputed interest rate, p. 7-29
interest-bearing notes, p. 7-21
loans and receivables, p. 7-10
loans receivable, p. 7-10
market rate, p. 7-23
net realizable value, p. 7-15
non–interest-bearing notes, p. 7-21
nontrade receivables, p. 7-10
not-sufficient-funds (NSF) cheques, p. 7-45
notes receivable, p. 7-10
outstanding cheques, p. 7-45
percentage-of-receivables approach, p. 7-15

percentage-of-sales approach, p. 7-17
petty cash, p. 7-43
predictive analytics, p. 7-17
premium, p. 7-29
promissory note, p. 7-20
provision matrix, p. 7-15
receivables turnover ratio, p. 7-39
restricted cash, p. 7-7
sales discounts, p. 7-12
sales returns and allowances, p. 7-12
secured borrowing, p. 7-33
securitization, p. 7-32
servicing asset component, p. 7-36
servicing liability component, p. 7-36
stated interest rate, p. 7-23
straight-line method, p. 7-26
trade discounts, p. 7-12
trade receivables, p. 7-10
with recourse, p. 7-35
without recourse, p. 7-35
yield rate, p. 7-23
zero-interest-bearing notes, p. 7-21

Assignment Material

Note: All assignment material with an asterisk (*) relates to the appendix to the chapter.

Enabling Competencies Completion of this end-of-chapter material will help develop CPA enabling competencies (such as ethics and professionalism, problem-solving, and decision-making and communication) and technical competencies. We have highlighted selected items with a specific integration word mark and material in *WileyPLUS* has been linked to the competencies. All cases emphasize integration, especially of the enabling competencies. The brief exercises, exercises, and problems generally emphasize problem-solving and decision-making.

Brief Exercises

BE7.1 (LO1) **Finance** Creative Corporation manufactures children's toys. Creative has significant debt outstanding that has been used to buy equipment and inventory used in its manufacturing process. Creative has positive cash from operating activities during the holiday season (November and December), but negative cash from operating activities during the months preceding the holiday season. Meanwhile, Technology Inc. is a mature, successful software development company with no debt outstanding and very few non-current assets. Which company requires a higher amount of cash on hand? Discuss, in general terms, how much cash each firm should have on hand for effective cash management.

BE7.2 (LO 1) **Finance** Topaz Inc. has accounts receivable terms of 2/10, n/30. In the past, 50% of Topaz's customers have taken advantage of the discount and paid within 10 days of the invoice date, and the remaining 50% of customers have paid in full within 30 days of the invoice date. However, due to an economic recession this year, 30% of customers have paid within 10 days, 60% of customers have paid within 30 days, and the remaining 10% of customers have paid within 40 days. What steps might Topaz consider to speed up collection of its accounts receivable?

BE7.3 (LO 2) Stowe Enterprises owns the following assets at December 31, 2020:

Cash in bank savings account	$56,200	Chequing account balance	$46,300
Cash on hand	14,800	Postdated cheque from Yu Co.	450
Cash refund due (overpayment		Cash in a foreign bank (CAD	
of income taxes)	21,400	equivalent)	90,000
Preferred shares acquired shortly		Debt instrument with a maturity	
before their fixed maturity date	15,500	date of three months from the	
		date acquired	12,000

If Stowe follows ASPE, what amount should be reported as cash and cash equivalents? Explain how your answer would differ if Stowe followed IFRS.

BE7.4 (LO 3) Staj Co., a clothing manufacturer, is preparing its statement of financial position at December 31, 2020. For each of the following amounts as at December 31, 2020, state whether the amount is (a) current or non-current; and (b) a trade receivable, a nontrade receivable, or not a receivable. If the amount is not a receivable, state its correct SFP classification.

1. Cheque received from a customer for $1,200, dated January 1, 2021
2. Bank overdraft balance of $50,000
3. Income taxes recoverable of $14,000
4. $10,300 owing from a customer (now 10 days overdue), exchanged for a two-year note bearing interest at 8% payable annually
5. Staj sold a piece of machinery to Marus Company this past year. As part of the sale transaction, $20,000 is owing from Marus, due to be received on January 31, 2022

BE7.5 (LO 4) To promote the sale of some specialty goods, Ropers Ltd. began a generous return policy to its customers. Customers can return merchandise for up to three months following the date of the invoice, no questions asked. For the current period, sales of these specialty goods totalled $40,000. Ropers chooses to estimate any expected sales returns at the end of each reporting period, rather than recording the Refund Liability at the point of sale. At the end of the reporting period, Ropers estimates that outstanding returns will be $3,500. Assuming Ropers follows IFRS, prepare the required adjusting journal entry at the end of the reporting period.

BE7.6 (LO 4) Use the information for Ropers Ltd. in BE7.5, but assume instead that Ropers follows ASPE and records expected outstanding returns to Allowance for Sales Returns and Allowances. Prepare the required adjusting journal entry at the end of the reporting period.

BE7.7 (LO 5) Battle Tank Limited had net sales in 2020 of $2.3 million. At December 31, 2020, before adjusting entries, the balances in selected accounts were as follows: Accounts Receivable $350,000 debit; Allowance for Doubtful Accounts $4,600 credit. Assuming Battle Tank has examined the aging of the accounts receivable and has determined the Allowance for Doubtful Accounts should have a balance of $42,000, prepare the December 31, 2020 journal entry to record the adjustment to Allowance for Doubtful Accounts.

BE7.8 (LO 5) Use the information for Battle Tank Limited in BE7.7 and assume instead that the unadjusted balance in Allowance for Doubtful Accounts is a debit balance of $3,000. Based on this, prepare the December 31, 2020 journal entry to record the adjustment to Allowance for Doubtful Accounts.

BE7.9 (LO 6) Emil Family Importers sold goods to Acme Decorators for $20,000 on November 1, 2020, accepting Acme's $20,000, six-month, 6% note. (a) Prepare Emil's November 1 entry, December 31 annual adjusting entry, and May 1 entry for the collection of the note and interest. (b) Assume instead that Emil uses reversing entries. Prepare any appropriate reversing entry at January 1, 2021, and the May 1, 2021 entry for the collection of the note and interest.

BE7.10 (LO 6) Aero Acrobats lent $47,573 to Afterburner Limited, accepting Afterburner's $49,000, three-month, zero-interest-bearing note. The implied interest is approximately 12%. Prepare Aero's journal entries for the initial transaction and the collection of $49,000 at maturity.

BE7.11 (LO 6) On January 1, Lin Du Corp. lent $30,053 to Prefax Ltd., accepting Prefax's $40,000, three-year, zero-interest-bearing note. The implied interest is 10%. (a) Prepare Lin Du's journal entries for the initial transaction, recognition of interest each year assuming use of the effective interest method, and collection of $40,000 at maturity. (b) Use time value of money tables, a financial calculator, or Excel functions to prove that the note will yield 10%.

BE7.12 (LO 6) On January 1, Aitocs Inc. sold used equipment with a cost of $15,000 and a carrying amount of $2,500 to Disc Corp. in exchange for a $5,000, three-year non–interest-bearing note receivable.

Although no interest was specified, the market rate for a loan of that risk would be 9%. Assume that Aitocs follows IFRS. Prepare the entries to record (a) the sale of Aitocs' equipment and receipt of the note, (b) the recognition of interest each year, and (c) the collection of the note at maturity.

BE7.13 (LO 6) Use the information for Aitocs Inc. in BE7.12 and assume instead that Aitocs follows ASPE. Prepare the entries to record (a) the sale of Aitocs' equipment and receipt of the note, (b) the recognition of interest each year if Aitocs uses the straight-line method, and (c) the collection of the note at maturity.

BE7.14 (LO 7) On October 1, 2020, Alpha Inc. assigns $3 million of its accounts receivable to Alberta Provincial Bank as collateral for a $2.6-million loan evidenced by a note. The bank's charges are as follows: a finance charge of 4% of the assigned receivables and an interest charge of 10% on the loan. Prepare the October 1 journal entries for both Alpha Inc. and Alberta Provincial Bank.

BE7.15 (LO 7) Landstalker Enterprises sold $750,000 of accounts receivable to Leander Factors, Inc. on a without recourse basis under IFRS, as the risks and rewards have been transferred to Leander. The transaction meets the criteria for a sale, and no asset or liability components of the receivables are retained by Landstalker. Leander Factors assesses a finance charge of 4% of the amount of accounts receivable and retains an amount equal to 5% of accounts receivable. Prepare journal entries for both Landstalker and Leander.

BE7.16 (LO 7) Use the information for Landstalker Enterprises in BE7.15 and assume instead that the receivables are sold with recourse. Prepare the journal entry for Landstalker to record the sale, assuming that the recourse obligation has a fair value of $9,000 and that Landstalker follows ASPE.

BE7.17 (LO 7) Keyser Woodcrafters sells $600,000 of receivables with a fair value of $620,000 to Keyser Trust in a securitization transaction that meets the criteria for a sale. Keyser Woodcrafters receives full fair value for the receivables and agrees to continue to service them, estimating that the fair value of this service liability component is $26,000. Prepare the journal entry for Keyser Woodcrafters to record the sale.

BE7.18 (LO 8) **Finance** The financial statements of winery **Andrew Peller Limited** reported net sales of $342,606 thousand for its year ended March 31, 2017. Accounts receivable were $26,973 thousand at March 31, 2017, and $28,223 thousand at March 31, 2016. Calculate the company's accounts receivable turnover ratio and the average collection period for accounts receivable in days.

BE7.19 (LO 8) **Finance** The financial statements of **BCE Inc.** reported net sales of $21,719 million for its year ended December 31, 2016, and $21,514 million for its year ended December 31, 2015. Accounts receivable (net) were $2,979 million at December 31, 2016, $3,009 million at December 31, 2015, and $3,069 million at December 31, 2014. Calculate the company's accounts receivable turnover ratio for 2015 and 2016. Did it improve in 2016?

*BE7.20 **(LO 10)** Genesis Ltd. designated Alexa Kidd as petty cash custodian and established a petty cash fund of $400. The fund is reimbursed when the cash in the fund is at $57. Petty cash receipts show that funds were disbursed for $174 of supplies and $167 of freight charges on inventory purchases. Genesis uses a perpetual inventory system. Prepare journal entries for the establishment of the fund and the reimbursement.

*BE7.21 **(LO 10)** Use the information in BE7.20. Assume that Genesis decides (a) to increase the size of the petty cash fund to $600 immediately after the reimbursement, and (b) to reduce the size of the petty cash to $250 immediately after the reimbursement. Prepare the entries needed to record the (a) and (b) transactions.

*BE7.22 **(LO 10)** Jaguar Corporation is preparing a bank reconciliation and has identified the following potential reconciling items. For each item, state if it is (a) added to the balance per bank statement, (b) deducted from the balance per bank statement, (c) added to the balance per books, (d) deducted from the balance per books, or (e) not needed for the reconciliation.

1. Deposit in transit of $5,500
2. Previous month's outstanding cheque for $298 clearing the bank in the current month
3. Interest credited by the bank to Jaguar's account of $31
4. Bank service charges of $20
5. A deposit in transit from previous month of $876 shown by bank as deposit of current month
6. Outstanding cheques of $7,422
7. NSF cheque returned of $260, and related service charge of $20

*BE7.23 **(LO 10)** Use the information for Jaguar Corporation in BE7.22. Prepare any entries needed to make Jaguar's accounting records correct and complete.

Exercises

E7.1 (LO 2) **Excel**   **(Determining Cash Balance)**   The controller for Fashion Co. is trying to determine the amount of cash to report on the December 31, 2020 statement of financial position. The following information is provided:

1. A commercial savings account with $600,000 and a commercial chequing account balance of $900,000 are held at First National Bank. There is also a bank overdraft of $35,000 in a chequing account at the Royal Scotia Bank. No other accounts are held at the Royal Scotia Bank.

2. Fashion has agreed to maintain a cash balance of $100,000 at all times in its chequing account at First National Bank to ensure that credit is available in the future.

3. Fashion has a $5-million investment in a Commercial Bank of Montreal money-market mutual fund. This fund has chequing account privileges.

4. There are travel advances of $18,000 for executive travel for the first quarter of next year. (Employees will complete expense reports after they travel.)

5. A separate cash fund in the amount of $1.5 million is restricted for the retirement of long-term debt.

6. There is a petty cash fund of $3,000.

7. A $1,900 IOU from Marianne Koch, a company officer, will be withheld from her salary in January 2021.

8. There are 20 cash floats for retail operation cash registers: 8 at $475, and 12 at $600.

9. The company has two certificates of deposit, each for $500,000. These certificates of deposit each had a maturity of 120 days when they were acquired. One was purchased on October 15 and the other on December 27.

10. Fashion has received a cheque dated January 12, 2021, in the amount of $25,000 from a customer owing funds at December 31. It has also received a cheque dated January 8, 2021, in the amount of $11,500 from a customer as an advance on an order that was placed on December 29 and will be delivered February 1, 2021.

11. Fashion holds $2.1 million of commercial paper of Rocco Leone Co., which is due in 60 days.

12. Currency and coin on hand amounted to $7,700.

13. Fashion acquired 1,000 shares of Sortel for $3.90 per share in late November and is holding them for trading. The shares are still on hand at year end and have a fair value of $4.10 per share on December 31, 2020.

Instructions

a. Calculate the amount of cash to be reported on Fashion's SFP at December 31, 2020.

b. Show the proper way to report items that are not reported as cash on the December 31, 2020 SFP.

c. Referring to item 2 above, why would First National Bank require Fashion to maintain a cash balance of $100,000 at all times in its chequing account?

d. **Digging Deeper**   From the perspective of a potential lender to Fashion, discuss the importance of proper reporting of item 5.

E7.2 (LO 2)   **(Determining Cash Balance)**   Several independent situations follow.

1. Chequing account balance $625,000; certificate of deposit $1.1 million; cash advance to subsidiary $980,000; utility deposit paid to gas company $180.

2. Chequing account balance $500,000; overdraft in special chequing account at same bank as normal chequing account $17,000; cash held in bond sinking fund $200,000; petty cash fund $300; cash on hand $1,350.

3. Chequing account balance $540,000; postdated cheque from customer $11,000; cash restricted to maintain compensating balance requirement $100,000; certified cheque from customer $9,800; postage stamps on hand $620.

4. Chequing account balance at bank $57,000; money-market balance at mutual fund (has chequing privileges) $38,000; NSF cheque received from customer $800.

5. Chequing account balance $700,000; cash restricted for future plant expansion $500,000; short-term (60-day) treasury bills $180,000; cash advance received from customer $900 (not included in chequing account balance); cash advance of $7,000 to company executive, payable on demand; refundable deposit of $26,000 paid to federal government to guarantee performance on construction contract.

Instructions

For each situation above, determine the amount that should be reported as cash. If items are not reported as cash, explain why.

E7.3 (LO 3, 8) (Financial Statement Presentation of Receivables) LeBlanc Inc. shows a balance of $519,289 in the Accounts Receivable account on December 31, 2020. The balance consists of the following:

Instalment accounts due in 2021	$ 91,000
Instalment accounts due after 2021	80,000
Overpayments to creditors	12,640
Due from regular customers, of which $40,000 represents accounts pledged as security for a bank loan	165,000
Advances to employees	69,649
Advance to subsidiary company (made in 2015)	101,000
	$519,289

Instructions

Show how the information above should be presented on the SFP of LeBlanc Inc. at December 31, 2020.

*E7.4 (LO 4, 10) Audit (Determining Ending Accounts Receivable) Your accounts receivable clerk, Mitra Adams, to whom you pay a salary of $1,500 per month, has just purchased a new Cadillac. You have decided to test the accuracy of the accounts receivable balance of $86,500 shown in the general ledger. The following information is available for your first year in business:

1. Collections from customers are $198,000.

2. Merchandise purchased totalled $320,000.

3. Ending merchandise inventory is $99,000.

4. Goods are marked to sell at 40% above cost.

Instructions

a. Estimate the ending balance of accounts receivable from customers that should appear in the ledger and any apparent shortages. Assume that all sales are made on account.

b. Discuss cash controls that can be implemented to prevent theft in this situation. Also discuss a cash control that can be implemented to detect any differences between the company's records of cash collected and cash actually received by the company.

E7.5 (LO 4, 5, 7) (Journalizing Various Receivable Transactions) Information on Janut Corp., which reports under ASPE, follows:

July	1	Janut Corp. sold to Harding Ltd. merchandise having a sales price of $9,000, terms 2/10, n/60. Ignore cost of goods sold entry.
	3	Harding Ltd. returned defective merchandise having a sales price of $700. The merchandise was not saleable and was scrapped.
	5	Accounts receivable of $19,000 are factored with Jackson Credit Corp. without recourse at a financing charge of 9%. Cash is received for the proceeds and collections are handled by the finance company.
	9	Specific accounts receivable of $15,000 are pledged to Landon Credit Corp. as security for a loan of $11,000 at a finance charge of 3% of the loan amount plus 9% interest on the outstanding balance. Janut will continue to make the collections. All the accounts receivable pledged are past the discount period and were originally subject to a 2% discount.
Dec.	29	Harding Ltd. notifies Janut that it is bankrupt and will be able to pay only 10% of its account. Give the entry to write off the uncollectible balance using the allowance method.

Instructions

a. Prepare all necessary journal entries on Janut Corp.'s books.

b. Would your treatment of the July 5 transaction change if Janut reported under IFRS? If yes, how?

c. What if the receivables factored on July 5 were with recourse? Would your answer change if Janut reported under IFRS or ASPE?

E7.6 (LO 5) (Recording Bad Debts)   At the end of 2020, Perez Corporation has accounts receivable of $2.5 million and an allowance for doubtful accounts of $120,000. On January 16, 2021, Perez determined that its $20,000 receivable from Morganfield Ltd. will not be collected, and management has authorized its write off. On January 31, 2021, Perez received notification that the company will be receiving $0.10 for every $1.00 of accounts receivable relating to McKinley Ltd. The company had previously written off 100% of the amount due from McKinley ($60,000).

Instructions

a. Prepare the journal entry for Perez Corporation to write off the Morganfield receivable and any journal entry needed to reflect the notice regarding McKinley Ltd.

b. What is the estimated net realizable value of Perez's accounts receivable before and after the entries in part (a)? What is the book value of Perez's accounts receivable before and after the entries in part (a)?

E7.7 (LO 5) (Calculating Bad Debts)   At January 1, 2020, the credit balance of Andy Corp.'s Allowance for Doubtful Accounts was $400,000. During 2020, the bad debt expense entry was based on a percentage of net credit sales. Net sales for 2020 were $80 million, of which 90% were on account. Based on the information available at the time, the 2020 bad debt expense was estimated to be 0.8% of net credit sales. During 2020, uncollectible receivables amounting to $500,000 were written off against the allowance for doubtful accounts. The company has estimated that at December 31, 2020, based on a review of the aged accounts receivable, the allowance for doubtful accounts would be properly measured at $525,000.

Instructions

Prepare a schedule calculating the balance in Andy Corp.'s Allowance for Doubtful Accounts at December 31, 2020. Prepare any journal entry needed at year end to adjust the allowance for doubtful accounts to the required balance.

E7.8 (LO 5) (Reporting Bad Debts)   The chief accountant for Dickinson Corporation provides you with the following list of accounts receivable that were written off in the current year:

Date	Customer	Amount
Mar. 31	Eli Masters Ltd.	$ 7,700
June 30	Crane Associates	6,800
Sept. 30	Annie Lowell's Dress Shop	12,000
Dec. 31	Vahik Uzerian	6,830

Dickinson Corporation follows the policy of debiting Bad Debt Expense as accounts are written off. The chief accountant maintains that this procedure is appropriate for financial statement purposes.

All of Dickinson Corporation's sales are on a 30-day credit basis, and the accounts written off all related to current year sales. Sales for the year total $3.2 million, and your research suggests that bad debt losses approximate 2% of sales.

Instructions

a. Do you agree with Dickinson Corporation's policy on recognizing bad debt expense? Why or why not?

b. By what amount would net income differ if bad debt expense was calculated using the allowance method and percentage-of-sales approach?

c. Under what conditions is using the direct write off method justified?

E7.9 (LO 5) (Calculating Bad Debts and Preparing Journal Entries)   The trial balance before adjustment of Chloe Inc. shows the following balances:

	Dr.	Cr.
Accounts receivable	$105,000	
Allowance for doubtful accounts	1,950	
Sales revenue (all on credit)		$684,000
Sales returns and allowances	30,000	

Instructions

a. Give the entry for bad debt expense for the current year assuming:

   1. The allowance should be 4% of gross accounts receivable.

   2. Historical records show that, based on accounts receivable aging, the following percentages will not be collected:

	Balance	Percentage Estimated to Be Uncollectible
0–30 days outstanding	$36,000	1%
31–60 days outstanding	48,000	5%
61–90 days outstanding	12,200	12%
Over 90 days outstanding	8,800	18%

   3. Allowance for Doubtful Accounts is $1,950 but it is a credit balance and the allowance should be 4% of gross accounts receivable.

   4. Allowance for Doubtful Accounts is $1,950 but it is a credit balance and historical records show that the same percentages in part 2 are to be used to determine the Allowance for Doubtful Accounts.

b. From the perspective of an independent reviewer of Chloe's trial balance, comment on the unadjusted debit balance in Chloe's allowance for doubtful accounts at year end.

c. **Digging Deeper** Assume Chloe reports under IFRS and has adopted IFRS 9. Should Chloe's approach to determining its Allowance for Doubtful Accounts consider "lifetime expected credit losses"? What is meant by this concept? Would a percentage-of-sales approach be appropriate for determining the Allowance for Doubtful Accounts under IFRS 9? Why or why not?

E7.10 (LO 5) (Bad Debts—Aging) Lenai Co. has the following account among its trade receivables:

Hopkins Co.

1/1	Balance forward	$ 850	1/28	Cash (#1710)	1,100
1/20	Invoice #1710	1,100	4/2	Cash (#2116)	1,350
3/14	Invoice #2116	1,350	4/10	Cash (1/1 Balance)	155
4/12	Invoice #2412	2,110	4/30	Cash (#2412)	1,000
9/5	Invoice #3614	490	9/20	Cash (#3614 and part of #2412)	790
10/17	Invoice #4912	860	10/31	Cash (#4912)	860
11/18	Invoice #5681	2,000	12/1	Cash (#5681)	1,250
12/20	Invoice #6347	800	12/29	Cash (#6347)	800

Instructions

Age the Hopkins Co. account at December 31 and specify any items that may need particular attention at year end.

E7.11 (LO 6) (Interest-Bearing and Non–Interest-Bearing Notes) Little Corp. was experiencing cash flow problems and was unable to pay its $105,000 account payable to Big Corp. when it fell due on September 30, 2020. Big agreed to substitute a one-year note for the open account. The following two options were presented to Little by Big Corp.:

Option 1: A one-year note for $105,000 due September 30, 2021. Interest at a rate of 8% would be payable at maturity.

Option 2: A one-year non–interest-bearing note for $113,400. The implied rate of interest is 8%.

Assume that Big Corp. has a December 31 year end.

Instructions

a. Assuming Little Corp. chooses Option 1, prepare the entries required on Big Corp.'s books on September 30, 2020, December 31, 2020, and September 30, 2021.

b. Assuming Little Corp. chooses Option 2, prepare the entries required on Big Corp.'s books on September 30, 2020, December 31, 2020, and September 30, 2021.

c. Compare the amount of interest income earned by Big Corp. in 2020 and 2021 under both options. Comment briefly.

d. **Digging Deeper** From management's perspective, does one option provide better liquidity for Big at December 31, 2020? Does one option provide better cash flows than the other?

E7.12 (LO 6) Finance   (Non–Interest-Bearing Note) On September 1, 2020, Myo Inc. sold goods to Khin Corporation, a new customer. Before shipping the goods, Myo's credit and collections department conducted a procedural credit check and determined that Khin is a high credit-risk customer. As a result, Myo did not provide Khin with open credit by recording the sale as an account receivable. Instead, Myo required Khin to provide a non–interest-bearing promissory note for $35,000 face value, to be repaid in one year. Khin has a credit rating that requires it to pay 12% interest on borrowed funds. Myo pays 10% interest on a loan recently obtained from its local bank. Myo has a December 31 year end.

Instructions

a. Prepare the entries required on Myo's books to record the sale, annual adjusting entry, and collection of the note's full face value.

b. Assume that on the note's maturity date, Khin informs Myo that it is having cash flow problems and can pay Myo only 80% of the note's face value. After extensive discussions with Khin's management, Myo's credit and collections department considers the remaining balance of the note uncollectible. Prepare the entry required on Myo's books on the note's maturity date.

c. What else could Myo have done to decrease collection risk related to the sale to Khin?

E7.13 (LO 6)   (Notes Receivable with Zero and Unrealistic Interest Rates)   On July 1, 2020, Agincourt Inc. made two sales:

1. It sold excess land in exchange for a four-year, non–interest-bearing promissory note in the face amount of $1,101,460. The land's carrying value is $590,000.

2. It rendered services in exchange for an eight-year promissory note having a face value of $400,000. Interest at a rate of 3% is payable annually.

   The customers in the above transactions have credit ratings that require them to borrow money at 12% interest. Agincourt recently had to pay 8% interest for money it borrowed from British Bank.

3. On July 1, 2020, Agincourt also agreed to accept an instalment note from one of its customers in partial settlement of accounts receivable that were overdue. The note calls for four equal payments of $20,000, including the principal and interest due, on the anniversary of the note. The implied interest rate on this note is 10%.

Instructions

a. Prepare the journal entries to record the three notes receivable transactions of Agincourt Inc. on July 1, 2020.

b. **Digging Deeper** Prepare an instalment note receivable schedule. From Agincourt's perspective, what are the advantages of an instalment note compared with a non–interest-bearing note?

E7.14 (LO 6, 8)   (Notes Receivable with Zero Interest Rate)   By December 31, 2020, Clearing Corp. had performed a significant amount of environmental consulting services for Rank Ltd. Rank was short of cash, and Clearing agreed to accept a $200,000, non–interest-bearing note due December 31, 2022, as payment in full. Rank is a bit of a credit risk and typically borrows funds at a rate of 12%. Clearing is much more creditworthy and has various lines of credit at 9%. Clearing Corp. reports under IFRS.

Instructions

a. Prepare the journal entry to record the transaction on December 31, 2020, for Clearing Corp.

b. Assuming Clearing's fiscal year end is December 31, prepare the journal entry required at December 31, 2021.

c. Assuming Clearing's fiscal year end is December 31, prepare the journal entry required at December 31, 2022.

d. What are the amount and classification of the note on Clearing Corp.'s SFP as at December 31, 2021?

e. Assume instead that Clearing reports under ASPE and uses the straight-line method to amortize the discount on the note. What would the interest income be relating to the note for 2021 and 2022?

f. If an appropriate market rate of interest for the note receivable is not known, how should the transaction be valued and recorded on December 31, 2020?

E7.15 (LO 7)   (Assigning Accounts Receivable)   On April 1, 2020, Ibrahim Corporation assigns $400,000 of its accounts receivable to First National Bank as collateral for a $200,000 loan that is due July 1, 2020. The assignment agreement calls for Ibrahim to continue to collect the receivables. First National Bank assesses a finance charge of 3% of the accounts receivable, and interest on the loan is 10%, a realistic rate for a note of this type.

Instructions

a. Prepare the April 1, 2020 journal entry for Ibrahim Corporation.

b. Prepare the journal entry for Ibrahim's collection of $350,000 of the accounts receivable during the period April 1 to June 30, 2020.

c. On July 1, 2020, Ibrahim paid First National Bank the entire amount that was due on the loan.

E7.16 (LO 7) (Journalizing Various Receivables Transactions) The trial balance before adjustment for Bassel Company shows the following balances.

	Dr.	Cr.
Accounts receivable	$82,000	
Allowance for doubtful accounts	1,750	
Sales revenue		$430,000

The following cases are independent:

1. To obtain cash, Bassel factors without recourse $20,000 of receivables with Anila Finance. The finance charge is 10% of the amount factored.

2. To obtain a one-year loan of $55,000, Bassel assigns $65,000 of specific accounts receivable to Ruddin Financial. The finance charge is 8% of the loan; the cash is received.

3. The company wants to maintain the Allowance for Doubtful Accounts at 5% of gross accounts receivable.

4. The company wishes to increase the allowance account by 1.5% of sales.

Instructions

Using the data above, prepare the journal entries to record each of the above cases.

E7.17 (LO 7, 8) (Transfer of Receivables with Recourse) Chessman Corporation factors $600,000 of accounts receivable with Liquidity Financing, Inc. on a with recourse basis. Liquidity Financing will collect the receivables. The receivable records are transferred to Liquidity Financing on August 15, 2020. Liquidity Financing assesses a finance charge of 2.5% of the amount of accounts receivable and also reserves an amount equal to 5.25% of accounts receivable to cover probable adjustments. Chessman prepares financial statements under ASPE.

Instructions

a. According to ASPE, what conditions must be met for a transfer of receivables to be accounted for as a sale?

b. Assume the conditions from part (a) are met. Prepare the journal entry on August 15, 2020, for Chessman to record the sale of receivables, assuming the recourse obligation has a fair value of $6,000.

c. **Finance** What effect will the factoring of receivables have on calculating the accounts receivable turnover for Chessman? Comment briefly.

d. Assume that Chessman is a private enterprise and prepares financial statements under IFRS. What conditions must be met for the transfer of receivables to be accounted for as a sale?

E7.18 (LO 7, 8) (Transfer of Receivables with Servicing Retained) Lute Retail Ltd. follows ASPE. It transfers $355,000 of its accounts receivable to an independent trust in a securitization transaction on July 11, 2020, receiving 96% of the receivables balance as proceeds. Lute will continue to manage the customer accounts, including their collection. Lute estimates this obligation has a liability value of $12,500. In addition, the agreement includes a recourse provision with an estimated value of $9,900. The transaction is to be recorded as a sale.

Instructions

a. Prepare the journal entry on July 11, 2020, for Lute Retail Ltd. to record the securitization of the receivables.

b. **Finance** What effect will the securitization of receivables have on Lute Retail Ltd.'s accounts receivable turnover? Comment briefly.

c. Would the treatment of the transaction change if Lute Retail followed IFRS? Compare how ASPE and IFRS differ in how you determine if the receivables should be derecognized.

E7.19 (LO 8) (Analysis of Receivables) Information follows for Patuanak Company:

1. The beginning-of-the-year Accounts Receivable balance was $25,000.

2. Net sales for the year were $410,000. (Credit sales were $200,000 of the total sales.) Patuanak does not offer cash discounts.

3. Collections on accounts receivable during the year were $140,000.

Instructions

a. Prepare summary journal entries to record the items noted above.

b. **Finance** Calculate Patuanak Company's accounts receivable turnover ratio for the year. How old is the average receivable?

c. **Finance** Use the turnover ratio calculated in part (b) to analyze Patuanak Company's liquidity. The turnover ratio last year was 4.85.

E7.20 (LO 8) [Real World Emphasis] **(Receivables Turnover)** The Becker Milk Company Limited, a real estate and investment management company, reports the following information in its financial statements for the years ended April 30, 2017, 2016, and 2015:

Accounts receivable, net of allowance for	April 30, 2017	$ 357,896
doubtful accounts	April 30, 2016	152,403
	April 30, 2015	614,255
Revenue, year ended	April 30, 2017	3,656,548
	April 30, 2016	3,766,437
	April 30, 2015	3,952,076

Note 12: Revenue and Economic Dependence

For the year ended April 30, 2017, the Company's largest single tenant, Alimentation Couche-Tard Inc., accounted for 85% (2016–81%) of rental revenue.

Instructions

a. [Finance] Calculate the accounts receivable turnover and days sales outstanding (or average collection period of accounts receivable in days) for the two most recent years provided.

b. Comment on your results.

c. [Digging Deeper] Why do you think the company provided the information in Note 12?

*E7.21 (LO 10) (Petty Cash) Kali Corp. established a petty cash fund early in 2020 to increase the efficiency of accounting for small cash transactions and to improve control over many of the small expenditures it makes. The company decided to set up the imprest fund at $500 and a cheque was issued for this amount and given to the petty cash custodian.

During January, the petty cash custodian made the following disbursements and placed a receipt for each in the cash box provided.

Tim Hortons coffee order for a management meeting	$ 28.62
Supplies purchased	49.50
Freight charge to ship goods to a customer	25.00
Travel advance to employee	150.00
Card, wrapping paper for gift for employee in hospital	19.40

The petty cash was replenished on January 22 when the amount of cash in the fund was $225.15. In June, after six months' experience with the fund, management decided to increase the imprest fund to $700.

Instructions

a. Prepare the journal entries to establish the petty cash fund, to reimburse it on January 22, and to increase the fund in June.

b. Describe where the petty cash will be reported on Kali Corp.'s financial statements.

c. Explain briefly why many companies have a policy of reimbursing the petty cash fund on each balance sheet date.

*E7.22 (LO 10) (Bank Reconciliation and Adjusting Entries) Ling Corp. deposits all receipts intact and makes all payments by cheque. The following information is available from the cash records:

April 30 Bank Reconciliation

Balance per bank	$ 7,120
Add: Deposits in transit	1,540
Deduct: Outstanding cheques	(2,000)
Balance per books	$ 6,660

Month of May Results

	Per Bank	Per Books
Balance on May 31	$8,760	$9,370
May deposits	5,000	5,810
May cheques	4,000	3,100
May note collected (not included in May deposits)	1,000	—
May bank service charge	25	—
May NSF cheque from a customer, returned by the bank (recorded by the bank as a charge)	335	—

Instructions

a. Determine the amount of deposits in transit and outstanding cheques at May 31. Keep in mind the time lag between deposits and cheques being recorded in the books and when they are recorded by the bank.

b. Prepare a May 31 bank reconciliation showing balance per bank statement and balance per books and correct cash balance.

c. Prepare the journal entry or entries to correct the Cash account at May 31.

*E7.23 (LO 10) **Audit & Assurance** (Bank Reconciliation and Adjusting Entries) Eli Corp. has just received its August 31, 2020 bank statement, which is summarized as follows:

Provincial Bank of Manitoba	Disbursements	Receipts	Balance
Balance, August 1			$ 9,369
Deposits during August		$32,200	41,569
Note collected for depositor, including $40 interest		1,040	42,609
Cheques cleared during August	$34,500		8,109
Bank service charges	20		8,089
Balance, August 31			8,089

The general ledger Cash account contained the following entries for the month of August:

Cash			
Balance, August 1	10,050	Disbursements in August	34,903
Receipts during August	35,000		

Deposits in transit at August 31 are $3,800, and cheques outstanding at August 31 total $1,050. Cash currently on hand at August 31 is $310 and there were postdated cheques from customers (for September 1) in the amount of $540. The bookkeeper improperly entered one cheque in the books at $146.50. The cheque was actually written for $164.50 for supplies (expense) and cleared the bank during the month of August.

Instructions

a. Prepare a bank reconciliation dated August 31, 2020, proceeding to a correct balance.

b. Prepare any entries that are needed to make the books correct and complete.

c. What amount of cash should be reported on the August 31 SFP?

Problems

P7.1 **Excel** Dev Equipment Corp. usually closes its books on December 31, but at the end of 2020 it held its cash book open so that a more favourable statement of financial position could be prepared for credit purposes. Cash receipts and disbursements for the first 10 days of January were recorded as December transactions. The company uses a periodic inventory system.

The following information is given:

1. January cash receipts recorded in the December cash book totalled $38,900. Of that amount, $25,300 was for cash sales and $13,600 was for collections on 2020 accounts receivable.

2. January cash disbursements that were recorded in the December cheque register were for payments relating to $24,850 of accounts payable.

3. The general ledger has not been closed for 2020.

4. The amount shown as inventory was determined by a physical count on December 31, 2020.

Instructions

a. Prepare any entries that you consider necessary to correct Dev Equipment Corp.'s accounts at December 31.

b. To what extent was Dev Equipment Corp. able to show a more favourable SFP at December 31 by holding its cash book open? (*Hint:* calculate working capital and relevant liquidity ratios.) Assume that the SFP that the company prepared showed the following amounts before any required adjustments:

	Debit	Credit
Cash	$39,000	
Accounts receivable	42,000	
Inventory	67,000	
Accounts payable		$45,000
Interest payable		14,200

c. **Ethics** Discuss the ethical implications of holding the cash book open and showing a more favourable SFP.

P7.2 A series of unrelated situations follow for several companies that use ASPE:

1. Atlantic Inc.'s unadjusted trial balance at December 31, 2020, included the following accounts:

	Debit	Credit
Allowance for doubtful accounts	$ 8,000	
Sales revenue		$1,980,000
Sales returns and allowances	60,000	
Sales discounts	4,400	

2. An analysis and aging of Central Corp.'s accounts receivable at December 31, 2020, disclosed the following:

Amounts estimated to be uncollectible	$ 160,000
Accounts receivable	1,790,000
Allowance for doubtful accounts (per books)	125,000

3. Western Co. provides for doubtful accounts based on 4.5% of credit sales. The following data are available for 2020:

Credit sales during 2020	$3,200,000
Allowance for doubtful accounts 1/1/20	37,000
Collection of accounts written off in prior years	
(customer credit was re-established)	18,000
Customer accounts written off as uncollectible during 2020	36,000

4. At the end of its first year of operations, on December 31, 2020, Pacific Inc. reported the following information:

Accounts receivable, net of allowance for doubtful accounts	$950,000
Customer accounts written off as uncollectible during 2020	24,000
Bad debt expense for 2020	92,000

5. The following accounts were taken from Northern Inc.'s unadjusted trial balance at December 31, 2020:

	Debit	Credit
Sales revenue (all on credit)		$950,000
Sales discounts	$ 21,400	
Allowance for doubtful accounts	34,000	
Accounts receivable	610,000	

Instructions

a. For situation 1, Atlantic estimates its bad debt expense to be 1.5% of net sales. Determine its bad debt expense for 2020.

b. For situation 2, what is the net realizable value of Central Corp.'s receivables at December 31, 2020?

c. For situation 3, what is the balance in Allowance for Doubtful Accounts at December 31, 2020?

d. For situation 4, what is the balance in Accounts Receivable at December 31, 2020, before subtracting the allowance for doubtful accounts?

e. For situation 5, if doubtful accounts are 7% of accounts receivable, what is the bad debt expense amount to be reported for 2020?

P7.3 **Excel** Fortini Corporation had record sales in 2020. It began 2020 with an Accounts Receivable balance of $475,000 and an Allowance for Doubtful Accounts of $33,000. Fortini recognized credit sales during the year of $6,675,000 and made monthly adjusting entries equal to 0.5% of each month's credit sales to recognize bad debt expense. Also during the year, the company wrote off $35,500 of accounts that were deemed to be uncollectible, although one customer whose $4,000 account had been written off surprised management by paying the amount in full in late September. Including this surprise receipt, $6,568,500 in cash was collected on account in 2020.

To assess the reasonableness of the allowance for doubtful accounts, the controller prepared the following aged listing of the receivables at December 31, 2020:

Days Account Outstanding	Amount	Probability of Collection
Less than 16 days	$270,000	97%
Between 16 and 30 days	117,000	92%
Between 31 and 45 days	80,000	80%
Between 46 and 60 days	38,000	70%
Between 61 and 75 days	20,000	50%
Over 75 days	25,000	0%
	$550,000	

Instructions

a. Reconcile the 2020 opening balance in Accounts Receivable to the $550,000 ending balance on the controller's aged listing.

b. Prepare the adjusting entry to bring the Allowance for Doubtful Accounts to its proper balance at year end.

c. Show how Fortini would present accounts receivable on the December 31, 2020 SFP.

d. What is the dollar effect of the year-end bad debt adjustment on the before-tax income?

P7.4 From its first day of operations to December 31, 2020, Campbell Corporation provided for uncollectible accounts receivable under the allowance method:

1. Entries for bad debt expense were made monthly based on 2.5% of credit sales.

2. Bad debts that were written off were charged to the Allowance for Doubtful Accounts.

3. Recoveries of bad debts previously written off were credited to the allowance account.

4. No year-end adjustments were made to the allowance account.

The balance in Allowance for Doubtful Accounts was $184,000 at January 1, 2020. During 2020, credit sales totalled $9.4 million, interim entries for bad debt expense were based on 2.5% of credit sales, $95,000 of bad debts were written off, and recoveries of accounts previously written off amounted to $15,000. Campbell upgraded its computer facility in November 2020, and an aging of accounts receivable was prepared for the first time as at December 31, 2020. Campbell's usual credit terms were net 30 days, and remain unchanged. A summary of the aging analysis follows:

Classification by Month of Sale	Balance in Each Category	Estimated % Uncollectible
November–December 2020	$1,080,000	8.0%
July–October 2020	650,000	12.5%
January–June 2020	420,000	20.0%
Before January 1, 2020	150,000	60.0%
	$2,300,000	

Based on a review of how collectible the accounts really are in the "Before January 1, 2020" aging category, additional receivables totalling $69,000 were written off as at December 31, 2020. The 60% uncollectible estimate therefore only applies to the remaining $81,000 in the category. Finally, beginning with the year ended December 31, 2020, Campbell adopted a new accounting method for estimating the allowance for doubtful accounts: it now uses the amount in the year-end aging analysis of accounts receivable.

Instructions

a. Prepare a schedule that analyzes the changes in Allowance for Doubtful Accounts for the year ended December 31, 2020. Show supporting calculations in good form. (*Hint*: In calculating the allowance amount at December 31, 2020, subtract the $69,000 write off of receivables.)

b. Prepare the journal entry for the year-end adjustment to the Allowance for Doubtful Accounts balance as at December 31, 2020.

(AICPA adapted)

P7.5 The following information relates to Shea Inc.'s accounts receivable for the 2020 fiscal year:

1. An aging schedule of the accounts receivable as at December 31, 2020, is as follows:

Age	Net Debit Balance	% to Be Applied after Write Off Is Made
Under 60 days	$172,342	1%
61–90 days	136,490	3%
91–120 days	39,924*	7%
Over 120 days	23,644	$4,200 definitely uncollectible; 20% of remainder is estimated uncollectible
	$372,400	

> *The $2,740 write off of receivables (see item 4 below) is related to the 91–120-day category.

2. The Accounts Receivable control account has a debit balance of $372,400 on December 31, 2020.

3. Two entries were made in the Bad Debt Expense account during the year: (1) a debit on December 31 for the amount credited to Allowance for Doubtful Accounts, and (2) a credit for $2,740 on November 3, 2020 and a debit to Allowance for Doubtful Accounts because of a bankruptcy.

4. Allowance for Doubtful Accounts is as follows for 2020:

Allowance for Doubtful Accounts

11/3 Uncollectible accounts written off	2,740	1/1	Beginning balance	8,750
		12/31	5% of $372,400	18,620

5. There is a credit balance in Accounts Receivable (61–90 days) of $4,840, which represents an advance on a sales contract.

Instructions

Assuming that the books have not been closed for 2020, make the necessary correcting entries.

P7.6 The SFP of Alice Inc. at December 31, 2019, includes the following:

Notes receivable	$300,000	
Accounts receivable	282,100	
Less: Allowance for doubtful accounts	(47,300)	$534,800

Transactions in 2020 include the following:

1. Accounts receivable of $146,000 were collected.

2. Customer accounts of $39,500 were written off during the year.

3. An additional $16,700 was received in payment of an account that was written off in 2020.

4. At year end, Allowance for Doubtful Accounts was estimated to need a balance of $52,000. This estimate is based on an analysis of aged accounts receivable.

Instructions

Prepare all necessary journal entries for Alice Inc. to reflect the information above.

(AICPA adapted)

P7.7 On October 1, 2020, Healy Farm Equipment Corp. sold a harvesting machine to Homestead Industries. Instead of a cash payment, Homestead Industries gave Healy Farm Equipment a $150,000, two-year, 10% note; 10% is a realistic rate for a note of this type. The note required interest to be paid annually on October 1, beginning October 1, 2021. Healy Farm Equipment's financial statements are prepared on a calendar-year basis.

Instructions

a. Assuming that no reversing entries are used and that Homestead Industries fulfills all the terms of the note, prepare the necessary journal entries for Healy Farm Equipment Corp. for the entire term of the note.

b. Repeat the journal entries under the assumption that Healy Farm Equipment Corp. uses reversing entries.

P7.8 On December 31, 2020, Zhang Ltd. rendered services to Beggy Corp. at an agreed price of $91,844.10. In payment, Zhang accepted $36,000 cash and agreed to receive the balance in four equal instalments of $18,000 that are due each December 31. An interest rate of 11% is applicable.

Instructions

a. Calculate the value of the note receivable at December 31, 2020, and prepare an instalment note receivable schedule.

b. Prepare the entries recorded by Zhang Ltd. for the sale and for the receipts including interest on the following dates:

1. December 31, 2020

2. December 31, 2021

3. December 31, 2022

4. December 31, 2023

5. December 31, 2024

c. **Digging Deeper** From Zhang Ltd.'s perspective, what are the advantages of an instalment note compared with a non–interest-bearing note?

P7.9 Desrosiers Ltd. had the following long-term receivable account balances at December 31, 2019:

Notes receivable	$1,800,000
Notes receivable—Employees	400,000

Transactions during 2020 and other information relating to Desrosiers' long-term receivables were as follows:

1. The $1.8-million note receivable is dated May 1, 2019, bears interest at 9%, and represents the balance of the consideration received from the sale of Desrosiers's electronics division to New York Company. Principal payments of $600,000 plus appropriate interest are due on May 1, 2020, 2021, and 2022. The first principal and interest payment was made on May 1, 2020. Collection of the note instalments is reasonably assured.

2. The $400,000 note receivable is dated December 31, 2019, bears interest at 8%, and is due on December 31, 2022. The note is due from Marcia Cumby, president of Desrosiers Ltd., and is secured by 10,000 Desrosiers common shares. Interest is payable annually on December 31, and the interest payment was made on December 31, 2020. The quoted market price of Desrosiers's common shares was $45 per share on December 31, 2020.

3. On April 1, 2020, Desrosiers sold a patent to Pinot Company in exchange for a $200,000 non–interest-bearing note due on April 1, 2022. There was no established exchange price for the patent, and the note had no ready market. The prevailing rate of interest for a note of this type at April 1, 2020, was 12%. The present value of $1 for two periods at 12% is 0.79719 (use this factor). The patent had a carrying amount of $40,000 at January 1, 2020, and the amortization for the year ended December 31, 2020 would have been $8,000. The collection of the note receivable from Pinot is reasonably assured.

4. On July 1, 2020, Desrosiers sold a parcel of land to Four Winds Inc. for $200,000 under an instalment sale contract. Four Winds made a $60,000 cash down payment on July 1, 2020, and signed a four-year, 11% note for the $140,000 balance. The equal annual payments of principal and interest on the note will be $45,125, payable on July 1, 2021, through July 1, 2024. The land could have been sold at an established cash price of $200,000. Desrosiers had paid $150,000 for the land when it purchased it. Collection of the instalments on the note is reasonably assured.

5. On August 1, 2020, Desrosiers agreed to allow its customer, Saini Inc., to substitute a six-month note for accounts receivable of $200,000 it owed. The note bears interest at 6% and principal and interest are due on the note's maturity date.

Instructions

a. For each note:

1. Describe the relevant cash flows in terms of amount and timing.

2. Determine the amount of interest income that should be reported in 2020.

3. Determine the portion of the note and any interest that should be reported in current assets at December 31, 2020.

4. Determine the portion of the note that should be reported as a long-term investment at December 31, 2020.

b. Prepare the long-term receivables section of Desrosiers's SFP at December 31, 2020.

c. Prepare a schedule showing the current portion of the long-term receivables and accrued interest receivable that would appear in Desrosiers's SFP at December 31, 2020.

d. Determine the total interest income from the long-term receivables that would appear on Desrosiers's income statement for the year ended December 31, 2020.

P7.10 Logo Limited follows ASPE. It manufactures sweatshirts for sale to athletic-wear retailers. The following summary information was available for Logo for the year ended December 31, 2019:

Cash	$20,000
Accounts receivable	40,000
Inventory	85,000
Accounts payable	65,000
Accrued liabilities	15,000

Part 1

During 2020, Logo had the following transactions:

1. Total sales were $465,000. Of the total sales amount, $215,000 was on a credit basis.
2. On June 30, a $50,000 account receivable of a major customer was settled, with Logo accepting a $50,000, one-year, 11% note, with the interest payable at maturity.
3. Logo collected $160,000 on accounts receivable during the year.
4. At December 31, 2020, Cash had a balance of $15,000, Inventory had a balance of $80,000, Accounts Payable was $70,000, and Accrued Liabilities was $16,000.

Instructions

a. Prepare summary journal entries to record the items noted above.
b. **Finance** Calculate the current ratio and the receivables turnover ratio for Logo at December 31, 2020. Use these measures to assess Logo's liquidity. The receivables turnover ratio last year was 4.75.

Part 2

Now assume that at year end 2020, Logo enters into the following transactions related to the company's receivables:

1. Logo sells the note receivable to Prairie Bank for $50,000 cash plus accrued interest. Given the creditworthiness of Logo's customer, the bank accepts the note without recourse and assesses a finance charge of 3.5%. Prairie Bank will collect the note directly from the customer.
2. Logo factors some accounts receivable at the end of the year. Accounts totalling $40,000 are transferred to Primary Factors, Inc., with recourse. Primary Factors retains 6% of the balances and assesses a finance charge of 4% on the transfer. Primary Factors will collect the receivables from Logo's customers. The fair value of the recourse obligation is $4,000.

Instructions

c. Prepare the journal entry to record the transfer of the note receivable to Prairie Bank.
d. Prepare the journal entry to record the sale of receivables to Primary Factors.
e. Calculate the current ratio and the receivables turnover ratio for Logo at December 31, 2020. Use these measures to assess Logo's liquidity. The receivables turnover ratio last year was 4.75.
f. Discuss how the ratio analysis in part (e) would be affected if Logo had transferred the receivables in secured borrowing transactions.
g. From Prairie Bank's perspective, what is the total effect on its net income as a result of purchasing the note receivable without recourse?
h. **Digging Deeper** From Primary Factors' perspective, what is the total effect on its net income as a result of purchasing the accounts receivable with recourse?

P7.11 In 2020, Ibran Corp. required additional cash for its business. Management decided to use accounts receivable to raise the additional cash and has asked you to determine the income statement effects of the following transactions:

1. On July 1, 2020, Ibran assigned $600,000 of accounts receivable to Provincial Finance Corporation as security for a loan. Ibran received an advance from Provincial Finance of 90% of the assigned accounts receivable less a commission of 3% on the advance. Before December 31, 2020, Ibran collected $220,000 on the assigned accounts receivable, and remitted $232,720 to Provincial Finance. Of the latter amount, $12,720 was interest on the advance from Provincial Finance.
2. On December 1, 2020, Ibran sold $300,000 of accounts receivable to Wunsch Corp. for $275,000. The receivables were sold outright on a without recourse basis and Ibran has no continuing interest in the receivables.

3. On December 31, 2020, an advance of $120,000 was received from First Bank by pledging $160,000 of Ibran's accounts receivable. Ibran's first payment to First Bank is due on January 30, 2021.

Instructions

a. Prepare a schedule showing the income statement effects of these transactions for the year ended December 31, 2020.

b. **Finance** Considering the three different methods Ibran used to obtain financing above, why might a company choose one method over the other?

P7.12 Finance The Cormier Corporation sells office equipment and supplies to many organizations in the city and surrounding area on contract terms of 2/10, n/30. In the past, over 75% of the credit customers have taken advantage of the discount by paying within 10 days of the invoice date. However, the number of customers taking the full 30 days to pay has increased within the last year. It now appears that fewer than 60% of the customers are taking the discount. Bad debts as a percentage of gross credit sales have risen from the 1.5% of past years to about 4% in the current year.

The controller responded to a request for more information on the deterioration in collections of accounts receivable by preparing the following report:

The Cormier Corporation
Finance Committee Report: Accounts Receivable Collections
May 31, 2020

The fact that some credit accounts will prove uncollectible is normal. Annual bad debt write offs have been 1.5% of credit sales over the past five years. During the last fiscal year, this percentage increased to slightly less than 4%. The current Accounts Receivable balance is $1.6 million. The condition of this balance in terms of age and probability of collection is as follows:

Proportion of Total (%)	Age Categories	Probability of Collection (%)
68	not yet due	99
15	less than 30 days past due	96.5
8	30 to 60 days past due	95
5	61 to 120 days past due	91
2.5	121 to 180 days past due	70
1.5	more than 180 days past due	20

Allowance for Doubtful Accounts had a credit balance of $43,300 on June 1, 2019. The Cormier Corporation has provided for a monthly bad debt expense accrual during the current fiscal year based on the assumption that 4% of gross credit sales will be uncollectible. Total gross credit sales for the 2019–20 fiscal year amounted to $4 million. Write offs of bad accounts during the year totalled $145,000.

Instructions

a. Prepare an accounts receivable aging schedule for the Cormier Corporation using the age categories identified in the controller's report to the finance committee. Show (1) the amount of accounts receivable outstanding for each age category and in total, and (2) the estimated amount that is uncollectible for each category and in total.

b. Calculate the amount of the year-end adjustment that is needed to bring Allowance for Doubtful Accounts to the balance in the aging analysis. Then prepare the journal entry needed to adjust the accounting records.

c. Assuming that the economy is currently in recession, with tight credit and high interest rates:

1. Identify steps that the Cormier Corporation might consider to improve the accounts receivable situation.

2. Evaluate each step you identify in terms of the risks and costs that it involves.

(CMA adapted)

P7.13 The Patchwork Corporation manufactures sweaters for sale to athletic-wear retailers. The following information was available on Patchwork for the years ended December 31, 2019 and 2020:

	12/31/19	12/31/20
Cash	$ 20,000	$ 15,000
Accounts receivable	90,000	?
Allowance for doubtful accounts	8,500	?
Inventory	85,000	80,000
Current liabilities	80,000	86,000
Total credit sales	600,000	550,000
Collections on accounts receivable	440,000	500,000

During 2020, Patchwork had the following transactions:

1. On June 1, 2020, sales of $80,000 to a major customer were settled, with Patchwork accepting an $80,000, one-year note bearing 7% interest that is payable at maturity. The $80,000 is not included in the total credit sales amount above.

2. Patchwork factors some accounts receivable at the end of the year. Accounts totalling $60,000 are transferred to Primary Factors Inc., with recourse. Primary Factors retains 5% of the balances, and will receive the collections directly from Patchwork's customers. Patchwork is assessed a finance charge of 6% on this transfer. The fair value of the recourse obligation is $7,000.

3. Patchwork wrote off $3,200 of accounts receivable during 2020.

4. Based on the latest available information, the 2020 allowance for doubtful accounts should have a balance of $12,000 at December 31, 2020.

Additional information:

Included in the cash balance at December 31, 2020, are the following: a chequing account with a balance of $9,600, postage stamps of $100, petty cash of $300, coins and currency on hand of $3,000, and post-dated cheques from customers of $2,000. Patchwork is a private company that follows ASPE.

Instructions

a. Prepare the journal entry for the sale to the customer from June 1.

b. Prepare the journal entry for the factoring of the accounts receivable to Primary Factors Inc.

c. Based on the above transactions and additional information, determine the balances of Accounts Receivable and Bad Debt Expense at December 31, 2020.

d. Prepare the current assets section of Patchwork's SFP at December 31, 2020.

e. **Finance** Calculate the current ratios for Patchwork for 2019 and 2020.

f. **Finance** Calculate the receivables turnover ratio for Patchwork for 2020. Patchwork's receivables turnover ratio for 2019 was 3.8 times.

g. **Finance** Comment on Patchwork's liquidity and ability to collect accounts receivable. Comment also on the improvement or deterioration of the current and accounts receivable turnover ratios.

h. **Digging Deeper** Discuss the effect on the current and accounts receivable turnover ratios if Patchwork had decided to assign $40,000 of accounts receivable instead of factoring them to Primary Factors Inc. Recalculate the ratios to support your conclusions.

*P7.14 Joseph Kiuvik is reviewing the cash accounting for Connolly Corporation, a local mailing service. Joseph's review will focus on the petty cash account and the bank reconciliation for the month ended May 31, 2020.

Petty cash

Joseph has collected the following information from Connolly's bookkeeper:

1. The petty cash fund was established on May 10, 2020, in the amount of $400.

2. Expenditures from the fund as at May 31, 2020 were supported by approved receipts for the following:

Postage expense	$63.00
Envelopes and other supplies	25.00
In-house business lunch provided to customers	99.50
Donation to local charity	35.00
Shipping charges, for goods to customers	48.50
Newspaper advertising	22.80
Taxi for sales manager to attend meeting downtown	18.75
Freight paid on incoming purchases	37.70

3. On May 31, 2020, the petty cash fund was replenished and increased to $500; currency and coin in the fund at that time totalled $47.10.

Connolly's bookkeeper also provided the following summary bank statement and general ledger information:

Scotia Imperial Bank
Bank Statement

	Disbursements	Receipts	Balance
Balance, May 1, 2020			$9,019
Deposits		$28,000	
Note payment, received from customer plus interest of $30		930	
Cheques cleared during May	$31,100		
Bank service charges	37		
Balance, May 31, 2020			6,812

Connolly's general ledger Cash account had a balance of $9,300 on May 1. During the month, the company deposited $31,000 in the bank and wrote cheques in payment of accounts payable and the payroll for $31,685. Deposits in transit at the end of the month are determined to be $3,000, cash (from cash sales) still on hand with the company cashier is $246 (besides petty cash), and cheques outstanding at May 31 total $550. Connolly uses a periodic inventory system.

Instructions

a. Prepare the journal entries to record the transactions related to the petty cash fund for May. Connolly uses a periodic inventory system.

b. Prepare a bank reconciliation dated May 31, 2020, proceeding to a correct balance, and prepare the journal entries to make the books correct and complete.

c. What amount of cash should be reported in the May 31, 2020 SFP?

*P7.15 The cash account of Villa Corp. shows a ledger balance of $3,969.85 on June 30, 2020. The bank statement as at that date shows a balance of $4,150. When the statement was compared with the cash records, the following facts were determined:

1. There were bank service charges for June of $25.00.

2. A bank memo stated that a note from Bao Dai for $900 and interest of $36 had been collected on June 29, and the bank had made a charge of $5.50 on the collection. (No entry had been made on Villa's books when Bao Dai's note was sent to the bank for collection.)

3. Receipts for June 30 of $2,890 were not deposited until July 2.

4. Cheques outstanding on June 30 totalled $2,136.05.

5. On June 29, the bank had charged Villa Corp.'s account for a customer's NSF cheque amounting to $453.20.

6. A customer's cheque for $90 had been entered as $60 in the cash receipts journal by Villa Corp. on June 15 as a collection on account.

7. Cheque no. 742 in the amount of $491 had been entered in the cash book as $419, and cheque no. 747 in the amount of $58.20 had been entered as $582. Both cheques were issued to pay for cash purchases of equipment.

8. In May 2020, the bank had charged a $27.50 Wella Corp. cheque against the Villa Corp. account. The June bank statement showed that the bank had reversed this charge and corrected its error.

Instructions

a. Prepare a bank reconciliation dated June 30, 2020, proceeding to a correct cash balance.

b. Prepare any entries that are needed to make the books correct and complete.

*P7.16 Information for Bonzai Books Ltd. is as follows: balance per books at October 31, $41,847.85; November receipts, $173,528.91; November disbursements, $166,193.54; balance per bank statement at November 30, $56,270.20. The following cheques were outstanding at November 30:

#1224	$1,635.29	#1232	$3,625.15
#1230	2,468.30	#1233	482.17

Included with the November bank statement and not recorded by the company were a bank debit memo for $31.40 covering bank charges for the month, a debit memo for $572.13 for a customer's cheque returned and marked NSF, and a credit memo for $1,400 representing bond interest collected by the bank in the name of Bonzai Books Ltd. None of the interest collected had been previously recorded. Cash on hand at November 30 that had been recorded and was not yet deposited amounted to $1,920.40.

Instructions

a. Prepare a bank reconciliation proceeding to the correct balance at November 30 for Bonzai Books Ltd.

b. Prepare any journal entries that are needed to adjust the Cash account at November 30.

*P7.17 Information follows for Quartz Industries Ltd.:

Quartz Industries Ltd.
Bank Reconciliation
May 31, 2020

Balance per bank statement		$30,928.46
Less: Outstanding cheques		
No. 6124	$2,125.00	
No. 6138	932.65	
No. 6139	960.57	
No. 6140	1,420.00	5,438.22
		25,490.24
Add deposit in transit		4,710.56
Balance per books (correct balance)		$30,200.80

Cheque Register—June

Date	Payee	No.	Invoice Amount	Discount	Cash
June 1	Bren Mfg.	6141	$ 237.50		$ 237.50
1	Stempy Mfg.	6142	915.00	$ 9.15	905.85
8	Regent Co., Inc.	6143	122.90	2.45	120.45
9	Bren Mfg.	6144	306.40		306.40
10	Petty Cash	6145	89.93		89.93
17	Pretty Babies Photo	6146	706.00	14.12	691.88
22	Hey Dude Publishing	6147	447.50		447.50
23	Payroll Account	6148	4,130.00		4,130.00
25	Dragon Tools, Inc.	6149	390.75	3.91	386.84
28	Be Smart Construction	6150	2,250.00		2,250.00
29	M M T, Inc.	6151	750.00		750.00
30	Lasso Co.	6152	400.00	8.00	392.00
			$10,745.98	$37.63	$10,708.35

Provincial Bank
Bank Statement
General Chequing Account of Quartz Industries—June 2020

Date	Debits			Credits	Balance
					$30,928.46
June 1	$2,125.00	$ 237.50	$ 905.85	$4,710.56	32,370.67
12	932.65	120.45		1,507.06	32,824.63
23	1,420.00	447.50	306.40	1,458.55	32,109.28
26	4,130.00	11.05			27,968.23
30	89.93	2,250.00	1,050.00	4,157.48	28,735.78

Additional information:

1. One June 26 transaction was for bank service charges.

2. One June 30 transaction was a bank debit memo for $1,050.00 for a customer's cheque returned and marked NSF (included with the June bank statement).

3. Cash received on June 30 and put in the bank's night deposit box on the evening of June 30 was recorded by the bank in the general chequing account on July 3 for the amount of $4,607.96.

Instructions

a. **Audit & Assurance** Prepare a bank reconciliation to the correct balance as at June 30, 2020, for Quartz Industries.

b. **Enabling Competencies** Discuss the importance of the bank reconciliation to control cash.

Cases

Refer to the Case Primer on the Student Website and in WileyPLUS *to help you answer these cases.*

CA7.1 **Finance** **Ethics** Hanley Limited manufactures products that capture solar energy. The company plans to list its shares on the Venture Exchange. To do so, it must meet all of the following initial listing requirements (among others):

1. Net tangible assets must be at least $500,000.
2. Pre-tax earnings must be $50,000.
3. The company must have adequate working capital.

Hanley has experienced significant growth in sales and is having difficulty estimating its bad debt expense. During the year, the sales team has been extending credit more aggressively in order to increase their commission compensation. Under the percentage-of-receivables approach using past percentages, the estimate is $50,000. Hanley has performed an aging and estimates the bad debts at $57,000. Finally, using a percentage of sales, the expense is estimated at $67,000. Before booking the allowance, net tangible assets are approximately $550,000. The controller decides to accrue $50,000, which results in pre-tax earnings of $60,000.

Instructions

Adopt the role of the Venture Exchange staff and decide whether the company meets the financial aspects of the initial requirements for listing on the Venture Exchange.

CA7.2 **Real World Emphasis** TELUS Corporation is one of Canada's largest telecommunications companies and provides both products and services. Its shares are traded on the Toronto and New York stock exchanges, and its credit facilities contain certain covenants relating to the amount of debt the company is allowed to hold.

The following are selected excerpts from the 2017 audited financial statements:

Note 1(o) – Sales of trade receivables – SUMMARY OF SIGNIFICANT ACCOUNTING POLICIES

Sales of trade receivables in securitization transactions are recognized as collateralized short-term borrowings and thus do not result in our de-recognition of the trade receivables sold.

Note 22 - SHORT-TERM BORROWINGS

On July 26, 2002, one of our subsidiaries, TELUS Communications Inc., entered into an agreement with an arm's-length securitization trust associated with a major Schedule I bank under which it is able to sell an interest in certain of its trade receivables up to a maximum of $500 million (2016 – $500 million). This revolving-period securitization term ends December 31, 2018, and it requires minimum cash proceeds of $100 million from monthly sales of interests in certain trade receivables. TELUS Communications Inc. is required to maintain a credit rating of at least BB (2016 – BB) from Dominion Bond Rating Service or the securitization trust may require the sale program to be wound down prior to the end of the term.

When we sell our trade receivables, we retain reserve accounts, which are retained interests in the securitized trade receivables, and servicing rights. As at December 31, 2017, we had sold to the trust (but continued to recognize) trade receivables of $119 million (2016 – $116 million). Short-term borrowings of $100 million (2016 – $100 million) are comprised of amounts advanced to us by the arm's-length securitization trust pursuant to the sale of trade receivables.

The balance of short-term borrowings (if any) comprised amounts drawn on our bilateral bank facilities.

Instructions

Assume the role of a private company in the same business as TELUS that is considering going public. Discuss the differing accounting treatment regarding the securitization transactions under IFRS and ASPE.

Integrated Cases

(*Hint:* If there are issues here that are new, use the conceptual framework to help you support your analysis with solid reasoning.)

IC7.1 Fritz's Furniture (FF) is a mid-sized owner-operated business that was started 25 years ago by Fred Fritz. The retail furniture business is cyclical, with business dropping off in times of economic downturn, as is the case currently. In order to encourage sales, the store offers its own credit cards to good customers. FF has run into a bit of a cash crunch and is planning to go to the bank to obtain an increase in its line of credit in order to replenish and expand the furniture stock. At present, the line of credit is limited to 70% of the credit card receivables and inventory. The receivables and inventory have been pledged as security for the loan.

Fred has identified two possible sources of the cash shortage: outstanding credit card receivables and a buildup in old inventory. He has come up with two strategies to deal with the problem:

1. **Credit card receivables:** For the existing receivables, Fred has found the company Factors Inc., which will buy the receivables for 93% of their face value. The two companies are currently negotiating the terms of the deal. So far, FF has agreed to transfer legal title to the receivables to Factors Inc., and FF will maintain and collect the receivables. The one term that is still being discussed is whether Factors Inc. will have any recourse to FF if the amounts become uncollectible.

2. **Excess inventory:** A new sales promotion has been advertised in the newspaper for the past two months. Under the terms of the promotion, customers do not pay anything up front and will be able to take the furniture home and begin payments the following year. Response to the advertisement has been very good and a significant amount of inventory has been moved to date, leaving room for new inventory once the bank financing comes through.

Instructions

Assume the role of FF's bookkeeper and advise Fred about the impact of the strategies on the company's financial reporting. The company follows ASPE.

IC7.2 Bowearth Limited (BL) is in the lumber business. The company sells pulp and paper products as well as timber and lumber. It has over 500,000 hectares of timberland that it either owns or leases. The company's shares trade on the public stock exchange. Net income for the past few years has been positive and increasing, and it has averaged approximately $1 million over the past five years. This year, however, due to various factors, the company is expecting to just break even.

During the year, BL announced an exclusive licensing agreement with Lindor Inc. (LI), an unrelated company. Under the terms of the agreement, BL will have exclusive sales and distribution rights for LI's technology and products. In return, it will pay LI royalties. The technology and products target the pulp and paper industry. During the first five years of the agreement, royalty payments that BL must pay to LI are 3% of sales in the first year, 2% in the second, and 1% thereafter. A minimum royalty of $500,000 must be paid regardless of the level of sales. LI has been in business many years and the technology is proven and in great demand. It is therefore very likely that BL will have to pay.

The U.S. government has recently levied anti-dumping fees of 8% on all softwood lumber shipped to the United States. Anti-dumping fees are levied on foreign imports that a government thinks are being sold below fair market value. The U.S. government has also imposed countervailing duties of 20% on Canadian lumber. Countervailing duties are meant to counteract imported goods that are subsidized by their home countries. The amounts must be paid by the company to the U.S. government in order to continue to sell in the United States. The Canadian government has challenged the right of the U.S. government to charge these duties and has appealed to the World Trade Organization (WTO). Canada feels that, under both WTO rules and the North American Free Trade Agreement (NAFTA), such charges cannot be legally levied. In the meantime, BL has been accruing and setting the amounts aside in cash deposits with the bank just in case the appeal is unsuccessful. The amounts accrued and set aside to date are approximately $3 million. The U.S. government is allowing the company to ship lumber as long as the cash is set aside. To date, the appeal process is going well and the Canadian government feels that the duties will at least be reduced significantly, if not completely eliminated. There are rumours that the duties may be cancelled next year.

In addition, BL is currently being sued by a former major shareholder, who alleges BL provided misleading financial statements. The lawsuit alleges that net income was materially misstated. The case has not yet gone to court. BL feels that the case is not very strong but has nonetheless fired the president, William Chesiuk, to be on the safe side. As a result, Chesiuk is suing BL for wrongful dismissal, seeking a lost bonus of $300,000 as well as lost future income of $10 million. BL is investigating the claim of overstated net income and, to date, has not found anything that indicates a material misstatement.

BL's controller, Youssef Haddad, is unsure of how to book all of the above in the financial statements (or if he even should). He has a meeting with the bank next week to discuss increasing the company's line of credit. He is hopeful that once the ruling comes down from the World Trade Organization, the increased line of credit will not be needed. In the meantime, the bank has signalled that it will be looking at the company's liquidity very closely. The auditors will also be coming in to review the statements in the next month.

Instructions

Adopt the role of Youssef Haddad and discuss the financial reporting issues.

IC7.3 Creative Choice Corporation (CC) is a publicly traded company that has been providing traditional mortgage loans for the past 10 years. In an effort to grow its business, it has decided to build another five banking service locations across the country. The expected cost of construction is around $10 million. The company contracted to build the new banks requires a $2-million retainer upfront before it begins construction.

To accelerate cash flow, CC pooled outstanding mortgage loans for a value of $2 million and transferred them to a newly created special purpose entity (the trust). The trust in turn has sold mortgage-backed securities to third-party investors for cash. CC will continue to service and manage the mortgage receivables sold, including collecting the principal and interest payments from customers and remitting cash to the trust for payment to investors. CC will earn an annual fee of $25,000 for servicing and collecting the mortgage receivables. The fee will be paid as a reduction of the returns earned on the securities.

As part of the agreement, CC is still responsible to pay the full payment to investors even when a customer defaults on a mortgage payment. This recourse obligation, or the liability that CC may be at risk of incurring as a result of any mortgage payments not collected, has an estimated fair value of 2% of the mortgage receivables at year end, based on CC's historical payment defaults. The majority of pooled mortgage receivables sold have adjustable rates after five years, meaning the interest rate charged on the mortgage may increase if there is an overall increase in interest rates.

At the beginning of the year, CC loaned $133,500 to a smaller independent bank in exchange for a two-year, $150,000 non–interest-bearing note. The note's present value is $133,500. CC has recorded the note receivable at $150,000. No interest has been recorded in relation to the note receivable.

In the last quarter, customer mortgage defaults have increased by 1 percentage point over the 2% historical rate. With a 1-percentage-point increase in market interest rates chargeable on the mortgage expected over the next quarter, CC expects another increase of 1 percentage point in the default rate next quarter.

An excerpt of the note for the mortgage receivables is provided below.

Mortgage loans (pooled and sold)	$ 2,000,000
Mortgage loans, net of allowance	45,700,000
Mortgage servicing asset	0
Accrued interest receivable	15,000

CC uses credit lines from a larger independent bank to finance the majority of its mortgage lending practice. Given the recent changes in economic conditions, the bank has been monitoring CC's liquidity. As such, CC is subject to certain covenants, including a debt to equity ratio of no more than 2 to 1. Before pooling the mortgage receivables, CC's debt to equity ratio was 1.8 to 1. The majority of mortgage loans that remain on the balance sheet have also been pledged as collateral to the bank.

Instructions

It is now the week after month end and you are reviewing the current-year results. Assume the role of the controller and discuss the financial reporting issues. Provide journal entries when appropriate.

Research and Analysis

RA7.1 ⬛ Real World Emphasis ⬛ Maple Leaf Foods Inc.

Access the annual financial statements for Maple Leaf Foods Inc. for the year ended December 31, 2017. These statements are available from the company's website or from SEDAR (www.sedar.com).

Instructions

a. Explain the securitization that the company is involved in (see Notes 5 and 23). What are the amounts involved and how does the company account for the securitized receivables?

b. Calculate the accounts receivable turnover for 2017 and 2016 and the average age of the accounts receivable at December 31, 2017 and 2016. Comment on your results. For the calculation of turnover and average age, use the closing balance of accounts receivable rather than an average in the formula.

c. Calculate the percentage growth in sales and accounts receivable in 2017 and 2016. Comment on your results.

d. Recalculate your ratios and percentages taking into account the amounts of accounts receivable securitized as indicated in Note 23. Did the securitizations have an effect on your assessment of the company? Explain. Should securitizations be taken into account in the calculations in parts (b) and (c) above, or not taken into account at all?

RA7.2 Impairment Testing

IFRS provides guidance on impairment testing—in particular, what is supportable evidence of impairment of loans and receivables.

Instructions

Read IFRS 9, 5.5 "Impairment" and reference as appropriate IFRS 9's Appendix A "Defined Terms" to answer the following questions.

a. When is a financial asset tested for impairment?

b. How does IFRS 9 define "lifetime expected credit losses"?

c. What are the requirements regarding reviewing forward-looking information to assess credit risk?

RA7.3 `Real World Emphasis` Canadian Tire Corporation, Limited

Canadian Tire Corporation, Limited is one of Canada's best-known retailers. The company operates 501 "hard-goods" retail stores through associate dealers, 386 corporate and franchise stores under its subsidiary Mark's Work Wearhouse, 298 independently operated gasoline sites, and 427 FGL Sports retail stores (operating under banners including Sport Chek, Sports Experts, and Atmosphere). It offers financial services through its branded credit cards and now provides personal loans and a variety of insurance and warranty products.

Instructions

Access the financial statements of Canadian Tire Corporation, Limited for its year ended December 30, 2017, either on the company's website or the SEDAR website (www.sedar.com). Refer to these financial statements and their accompanying notes to answer the following questions.

a. How does Canadian Tire define cash and cash equivalents on its SFP? What is included in the cash and cash equivalents balance at December 30, 2017?

b. What criteria does the company use to determine what short-term investments to include in this category?

c. Review the financial statements and notes and identify the assets reported by Canadian Tire that qualify as loans and receivables. Does the company disclose the amount of its allowance for doubtful accounts? What was the amount of impairment for credit losses for the year? How does the company determine the allowance for impairment? Be specific. What were the amounts for the write offs, recoveries, and impairment for credit losses for the year?

d. When is a loan impaired? How does Canadian Tire value an impaired loan? Be specific.

e. Accounting standards require companies to disclose information about their exposure to credit risk. What is credit risk? What does Canadian Tire report? What is your assessment of its exposure to credit risk?

f. Canadian Tire uses its accounts receivable to generate cash before the receivables are due via securitization. Briefly describe the forms of "securitization" activities that the company uses. Does Canadian Tire have a continuing relationship with the accounts?

RA7.4 `Audit` Auditor's Report

Soon after beginning the year-end audit work on March 10 for the 2020 year end at Arkin Corp., the auditor has the following conversation with the controller:

Controller: The year ending March 31, 2020, should be our most profitable in history and, because of this, the board of directors has just awarded the officers generous bonuses.

Auditor: I thought profits were down this year in the industry, at least according to your latest interim report.

Controller: Well, they were down, but 10 days ago we closed a deal that will give us a substantial increase for the year.

Auditor: Oh, what was it?

Controller: Well, you remember a few years ago our former president bought shares of Hi-Tek Enterprises Ltd. because he had those grandiose ideas about becoming a conglomerate? They cost us $3 million, which is the current carrying amount. On March 1, 2020, we sold the shares to Campbell Inc., an unrelated party, for $4 million. So, we'll have a gain of $686,000, which results from $1 million pre-tax minus a commission of $20,000 for legal fees and taxes at 30%. This should increase our net income for the year to $5.2 million, compared with last year's $4.8 million. The transaction fees were higher than normal due to the setting up of the note receivable. As far as I know, we'll be the only company in the industry to register an increase in net income this year. That should help the market value of our shares!

Auditor: Do you expect to receive the $4 million in cash by March 31, your fiscal year end?

Controller: No. Although Campbell Inc. is an excellent company, they're a little tight for cash because of their rapid growth. We have a $4-million non–interest-bearing note with $400,000 due each year for the next 10 years, which Campbell signed. The first payment is due March 1 of next year and future payments are due on the same date every year thereafter.

Auditor: Why is the note non–interest-bearing? I thought the market rate of interest was closer to 8%.

Controller: Because that's what everybody agreed to. Since we don't have any interest-bearing debt, the funds invested in the note don't cost us anything, and we weren't getting any dividends on the Hi-Tek shares.

Instructions

a. Prepare the auditor's written report to the controller on (1) how this transaction should be accounted for, and (2) how any corrections that are necessary will affect the reported results for the current year ending March 31. Assume that the company reports under IFRS. Make assumptions where required.

b. Make the appropriate journal entries at March 1 and March 31, 2020, relating to the transaction and corrections in part (a).

c. What is the company's revised net income for the year ending March 31?

d. What changes would be needed if the company reported under ASPE? (Assume that Arkin records the investment in Hi-Tek as a fair value through net income investment under both IFRS and ASPE, and that in all prior years, fair value equalled cost.)

RA7.5 Real World Emphasis   **Loblaw Companies Limited and Empire Company Limited**

Instructions

From SEDAR (www.sedar.com) or the company websites, access the financial statements of Loblaw Companies Limited for its year ended December 30, 2017, and of Empire Company Limited for its year ended May 6, 2017. Review the financial statements and answer the following questions.

a. What businesses are the companies in?

b. Compare how the two companies report cash and cash equivalents on the SFP. What is included in the cash and cash equivalents of each and what are the amounts of these? Is any restricted cash reported by either company?

c. What types of receivables do Loblaw and Empire have and what was the reported amount for each? How does each type of receivable arise? Which types are similar or different between the companies? How are the loans and receivables reported?

d. Explain the type of credit risk that the companies have and how this risk is managed. What was the allowance for doubtful accounts at the end of the year? What percentages of the accounts receivable were past due? How was the allowance for doubtful accounts determined for each company? How does the company test for impairment? What was the bad debt expense for the year? Is the allowance adequate?

e. Does either company dispose of receivables before their due date to generate cash? Comment on how this is done and what the company has retained.

f. Can an accounts receivable turnover ratio be determined for either company? Why or why not?

RA7.6 Ethics   **An Ethical Dilemma**

Rudolph Corp. is a subsidiary of Huntley Corp. The ethical accountant, working as Rudolph's controller, believes that the yearly charge for doubtful accounts for Rudolph should be 2% of net credit sales. The president, nervous that the parent company might expect the subsidiary to sustain its 10% growth rate in earnings, suggests that the controller increase the charge for doubtful accounts to 3% yearly. The president thinks that the lower net income, reflecting a 6% earnings growth rate, will be more sustainable for Rudolph.

Instructions

a. Should the controller be concerned with Rudolph Corp.'s growth rate in estimating the allowance? Explain.

b. Does the president's request pose an ethical dilemma for the controller? Why or why not?

Analytics in Action

AIA7.1 As an intern hired by Filip Industries Limited (FIL), you have been asked to use predictive analytics to estimate FIL's allowance for doubtful accounts (AFDA). FIL recently hired a consultant who provided inputs for a credit score model that can be used to refine its AFDA estimate. Your role is to analyse FIL's raw data to estimate its required AFDA using various estimation techniques.

Specifically, you have been provided with detailed information for 100 of FIL's customers, including (i) customer region (ii) a schedule of aged accounts receivable (iii) the impact of a third-party credit rating on default risk (iv) a customer response score (CRS) of customer responsiveness to email and telephone reminders, and (v) the percentage of accounts receivable written off in prior years for each customer.

Your task is to do the following: 1. Briefly describe predictive analytics. 2. Using the information provided in *WileyPLUS* compute FIL's AFDA requirements based on (a) a percentage of overall accounts receivable (b) default risk percentages that depend on the aging of the receivables, and (c) a credit score model using predictive analytics that takes into account: aged receivables and credit rating; CRS; and prior write-off history and region. 3. Discuss the pros and cons of your AFDA estimates.

Instructions   Go to *WileyPLUS* for additional instructions and material to complete this question.

CHAPTER 8

Inventory

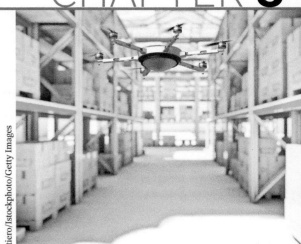

tiero/Istockphoto/Getty Images

Data Analytics **From Science Fiction to Accounting Fact**

In just a few years, drones went from being science fiction to a common presence on beaches, parks, and tourist attractions. But their applications go far beyond a novel hobby. Drones can be used to capture all sorts of data that can later be analyzed. Drones are also being put to work to help companies perform what used to be a labour-intensive, slow, and costly job: counting inventory.

Traditionally, retailers had to count their merchandise by hand, so they did it just once or twice a year for accounting purposes, to value and report on what they had on hand at the end of the fiscal year. Over time, technology such as bar code scanners, and more recently, radio-frequency identification (RFID) tags, have allowed retailers to count inventory almost in real time. This helps not just with valuation for accounting purposes, but with avoiding merchandise stockouts (running out of an item). But this technology has its limitations. Bar code and RFID scanners still need humans to get close to the merchandise to count it, which requires employees to move through warehouses, pointing their scanners at the inventory. It can still take up to three months for a large store to get a complete inventory count using RFID tags. Some companies, both retailers and manufacturers, have started using drones to count their inventory. Drones can operate around the clock. Some are so tiny they can fly between tightly packed pallets in warehouses. They can fly over remote agricultural properties to assess the state of crops. Drones can survey inventory in dangerous situations, such as reaching boxes stacked high on shelves. Their onboard sensors and cameras can count inventory from tens of metres away, penetrating stacks of boxes and pallets. They can locate missing boxes or pallets, or identify ones that might be empty when employees thought they were full. Auto giant Daimler uses drones to count its finished vehicles, which sit bumper to bumper in yards, where employees cannot physically move to read the RFID tags of vehicles in the middle of the yards.

Drones are being used not just to count inventory but to ship it out. Walmart and Amazon have tested using drones for order fulfillment, picking up items from warehouse shelves and packing them for shipment. The French logistics company Geodis planned to use drones in its warehouses by the end of 2018.

There are some down sides to using drones for inventory management. Though their costs continue to decrease, they are still beyond the reach of many smaller companies. Their use outdoors is tightly controlled by aviation regulations. Some unions are protesting the loss of warehouse jobs to drones. And drones need to be safely operated by trained employees to avoid colliding with people and causing injuries.

Sources: Nicholas Shields, "This French Logistics Giant Is Going to Start Using Drones in Warehouses," Business Insider, April 16, 2018; Larry Hardesty, "Drones Relay RFID Signals for Inventory Control," MIT News, August 25, 2017; Bloomberg, "Walmart Wants to Take on Amazon with Flying Warehouses," *Fortune*, August 20, 2017; Deniz Appelbaum and Robert Nehmer, "The Coming Disruption of Drones, Robots, and Bots: How Will It Affect CPAs and Accounting Practice?," *CPA Journal*, June 2017; Erin Myers, "Drones and Robots in the Warehouse Are Assistants, For Now," SystemID.com blog, January 17, 2017.

LEARNING OBJECTIVES	CHAPTER OUTLINE	CPA COMPETENCIES
After studying this chapter, you should be able to:	The chapter headings related to the learning objective are:	Competencies addressed by each learning objective are as follows:
1. Understand inventory from a business perspective.	**Understanding Inventory** • What types of companies have inventory? • Inventory categories • Inventory planning and control • Information for decision-making	**1.1.1, 1.1.2, 1.2.1, 1.2.2, 1.4.5, 3.3.1**
2. Identify which inventory items should be included in ending inventory.	**Recognition of Physical Goods Included in Inventory** • Accounting definition of inventory • Goods included in inventory	**1.2.1, 1.2.2, 3.3.1, 3.3.2, 4.3.6**
3. Identify the effects of inventory errors on the financial statements and adjust for them.	**Inventory Errors** • Ending inventory misstated • Purchases and inventory misstated	**1.2.1, 1.2.2, 5.1.1**
4. Determine the components of inventory cost.	**Measurement of Inventory—Costs Included** • Volume rebates • Product costs	**1.2.1, 1.2.2, 3.3.1**
5. Distinguish between perpetual and periodic inventory systems and account for them.	**Measurement and Inventory Accounting Systems** • Perpetual system • Periodic system • Comparing perpetual and periodic systems • Supplementary system—quantities only	**1.1.3, 1.2.1, 1.2.2**
6. Identify and apply GAAP cost formula options and indicate when each cost formula is appropriate.	**Measurement and Cost Formulas** • Specific identification • Weighted average cost • First-in, first-out (FIFO) • Choice of cost formula • Last-in, first-out (LIFO)	**1.2.1, 1.2.2**

7.	Explain why inventory is measured at the lower of cost and net realizable value, and apply the lower of cost and net realizable value principle.	**Measurement and the Lower of Cost and Net Realizable Value (LC&NRV) Principle** • What is net realizable value? • Application of the LC&NRV principle • Evaluation of the LC&NRV principle	1.2.1, 1.2.2
8.	Identify inventories that are or may be valued at amounts other than the lower of cost and net realizable value.	**Exceptions to Lower of Cost and Net Realizable Value** • Inventories measured at net realizable value • Inventories measured at fair value less costs to sell	1.2.1, 1.2.2, 1.2.3
9.	Apply the gross profit method of estimating inventory.	**Measuring Inventory Using Estimates** • The need for estimates • Gross profit method	1.2.1, 1.2.2
10.	Identify how inventory should be presented, disclosed, and analyzed.	**Presentation, Disclosure, and Analysis** • Presentation and disclosure of inventories • Analysis	1.2.1, 1.2.2, 1.3.2, 1.4.1, 1.4.2, 1.4.4, 5.1.1
11.	Identify differences in accounting between IFRS and ASPE, and what changes are expected in the near future.	**IFRS/ASPE Comparison** • A comparison of IFRS and ASPE • Looking ahead	1.1.4

After studying Appendix 8A, you should be able to:

12.	Apply the retail method of estimating inventory.	**Appendix 8A: The Retail Inventory Method of Estimating Inventory Cost** • Retail method terminology • Special items • Evaluation of retail inventory method	1.2.1, 1.2.2

After studying Appendix 8B, you should be able to:

13.	Identify other primary sources of GAAP for inventory.	**Appendix 8B: Accounting Guidance for Specific Inventory**	1.2.1, 1.2.2, 1.2.3, 1.2.4

Preview of Chapter 8

This chapter introduces the issues related to the recognition, measurement, and reporting of inventory on the statement of financial position and income statement. Appendix 8A explains how to determine inventory cost using the retail inventory method. We examined accounting for long-term construction and other contracts, a closely related topic, in Chapter 6.

Understanding Inventory

LEARNING OBJECTIVE 1
Understand inventory from a business perspective.

> **Underlying Concept 8.1**
>
> The statements must be transparent. In other words, they must represent the underlying business. Therefore, accountants need to understand a company's underlying business model.

It is important to understand the business of the company before thinking about issues relating to inventory. (See Underlying Concept 8.1.) What types of companies carry significant amounts of inventory? What are the different types of inventory? What aspects of inventory must be managed and how is this done? Finally, what information do financial statement users need? We will answer these questions below.

What Types of Companies Have Inventory?

As a general rule, companies in industries such as manufacturing, retail, and wholesale often have a significant amount of inventories. For instance, Airbus Group S.E. manufactures commercial aircraft, civil and military helicopters, commercial space launch vehicles, missiles, military aircraft, satellites, defence systems, and defence electronics. Inventories make up approximately 28% of its total assets. As another example, The Jean Coutu Group (PJC) Inc. is one of the leading pharmacy chains in Canada. The company operates primarily through its franchised outlets and inventories make up approximately 20.7% of its total assets.

Some companies, such as Toyota Motor Corporation, follow a strategy of producing inventories on a "just-in-time" basis. This means they wait until a customer orders a product and then they arrange with other companies to actually manufacture the product. Thus their inventories are only about 4.3% of total assets.

Inventory Categories

Retailers and wholesalers have inventory that is ready for sale. For instance, Hudson's Bay Company (HBC), a major Canadian retailer of consumer products, reported just over $3.3 billion of inventory at the end of 2017. This accounted for 27.6% of total assets. Like other **merchandising concerns**, HBC purchases most of its merchandise in a form that is ready for sale, and unsold units left on hand at each reporting date are usually called merchandise inventory.

Manufacturing companies, on the other hand, have inventories in various states of completion. Potash Corporation of Saskatchewan Inc. was an integrated fertilizer and related industrial and feed products company. It produced potash, nitrogen, and phosphate. At December 31, 2017, its last fiscal year, Potash Corporation reported inventories amounting to 23.7% of its current assets. If you subtract the assets held for sale (classified as current assets), this number increased to 54% of current assets (excluding assets held for sale). Potash merged with competitor Agrium Inc. to become Nutrien Ltd., the world's largest provider of crop inputs and services. Shares in Nutrien began trading on January 2, 2018. Before the merger, Agrium's inventories accounted for 44.6% of its current assets as at the end of 2017.

Although the products that manufacturers produce can be quite different, they normally have three types of inventory accounts: Raw Materials, Work in Process, and Finished Goods. Amounts for goods and materials that are on hand but have not yet gone into production are reported as **raw materials inventory**. Raw materials include the wood to make a baseball bat, for example, or the steel to make a car. These materials can be traced directly to the end product. At any point in a continuous production process, some units are not completely processed. The cost of the raw material on which production has started but is not yet complete, plus the direct labour cost applied specifically to this material and its applicable share of manufacturing overhead costs, make up the **work-in-process inventory**. The costs associated with the completed but still unsold units on hand are reported as **finished goods inventory**.

Inventory Planning and Control

How much and what types of inventories should be on hand? How does a company control inventories so that it can maximize profits? For many reasons, management is vitally interested in inventory planning and control.

Management Accounting 3.3.1 Inventory management is a double-edged sword. On the one hand, management wants to have a wide variety and sufficient quantities on hand so that customers have the greatest selection and always find what they want in stock. On the other hand, such a policy may result in excessive carrying costs (for example, in investment, storage, insurance, taxes, obsolescence, risk of theft, and damage). The higher the levels of inventories held, the higher the costs of looking after them. For instance, most retailers have a significant risk of theft and so must incur costs to reduce this risk, such as insurance and theft deterrent equipment. Low inventory levels generally have lower carrying costs, but this may lead to running out of specific products, lost sales, and unhappy customers.

Inefficient purchasing procedures, faulty manufacturing techniques, or inadequate sales efforts may leave management with excessive and unusable inventories. All of this reduces profits.

Companies must therefore monitor inventory levels carefully to:

- minimize carrying costs, and
- meet customer demands. (See **What Do the Numbers Mean? 8.1**.)

Whether a company manufactures or merchandises goods, it needs an accurate accounting system with up-to-date records.

What Do the Numbers Mean? 8.1

Data Analytics As just noted, companies must monitor the quantity and quality of inventories on hand. **Eli Lilly and Company** actually goes one step further and also monitors inventory levels of its wholesale customers for significant products that it supplies. The company develops, manufactures, and distributes pharmaceuticals, primarily through wholesalers or major retail chains. According to the company's annual report, Eli Lilly's management tries to keep wholesaler inventory levels at an average of one month's supply. They monitor unusual wholesaler buying patterns to determine the impact on future sales and demand for product. The company notes that the production processes are complex and highly regulated, varying from product to product. Unusual demand could result in an interruption of supply, which is undesirable. It could also signal potential problems with a drug (if there is a significant decrease in demand, for instance).

Information for Decision-Making

Just as management is interested in monitoring and controlling inventory, users of financial statements such as creditors and investors are also interested in this information. While management has access to all types of inventory-related information that is generated by internal management information systems, external users of financial statements often look to the statements as a significant source of information. Therefore, they also want to know how management is controlling and managing its inventory in order to maximize profits. Information about inventory must therefore be presented so that it is transparent regarding the nature of the business. The company must clearly represent the **existence** of various types of inventory that it owns and must also disclose information as to **how this inventory has been measured**. The rest of the chapter will look at how inventory is accounted for, including how it is recognized, measured, presented, and disclosed in the statements.

Because the goods that are sold or used during an accounting period almost never correspond exactly with the goods that were bought or produced during that period, the physical inventory of items either increases or decreases. In addition, the cost of the number of items could be higher or lower at the end of the period than at the beginning. The cost of all the goods that are available for sale or use has to be allocated between the goods that were sold or used and those that are still on hand. The **cost of goods available for sale or use** is calculated as follows:

Cost of goods on hand at the beginning of the period + Cost of goods acquired or produced during the period = Cost of goods available for sale or use

The **cost of goods sold** is calculated as follows:

Cost of goods available for sale during the period − Cost of goods on hand at the end of the period = Cost of goods sold

The calculation of cost of goods sold is shown in **Illustration 8.1**.

ILLUSTRATION 8.1

Calculation of Cost of Goods Sold

Beginning inventory, Jan. 1	$100,000
Cost of goods acquired or produced during the year	800,000
Total cost of goods available for sale	**900,000**
Ending inventory, Dec. 31	200,000
Cost of goods sold during the year	**$700,000**

Calculating the cost of ending inventory takes several steps. It can be a complex process that requires answers to each of the following questions:

1. **Which physical goods should be included as part of inventory?** Who owns inventory still in transit at the statement of financial position date, or inventory on consignment? What about inventory under special sales agreements?

2. **What costs should be included as part of inventory cost?** Consider purchase discounts and vendor rebates, product versus period costs, capacity considerations in allocating overhead, and standard costs.

3. **What cost formula should be used?** Consider specific identification, average cost, or first-in, first-out (FIFO).

Determining the final value that should be reported on the statement of financial position requires answering one additional question:

4. **Has there been an impairment in value of any of the inventory items?** Inventory cannot be reported on the statement of financial position at more than the net cash amount that is expected to be recovered from its sale or use.

We will now explore these and other basic issues one at a time.

Recognition of Physical Goods Included in Inventory

Which items should be recognized as inventory in the financial statements and at what point should they be recognized? In order to make this decision, we need a common understanding of what inventory is.

Inventory comes in many forms. Here are just a few examples of items of inventory:

- securities held by an investment dealer
- land and other property held by developers for resale
- unbilled employee and partner time spent on client files in a law office or professional accounting practice
- grain in silos
- salmon in a fish farming operation

Some of these are not covered by the basic accounting standards for inventories: *CPA Canada Handbook—Accounting*, Part II, Section 3031 under ASPE or IAS 2 under IFRS. These standards exclude some inventories entirely, and exclude others from only the measurement requirements of the standards.

In general, inventories of financial instruments, biological assets and agricultural products, mineral products, and inventories held by producers of agricultural and forest products and by commodity broker-traders may have special requirements. Appendix 8B summarizes the accounting guidance for these forms of inventory.

Accounting Definition of Inventory

For accounting purposes, inventories are defined as:

"assets

a. held for sale in the ordinary course of business;

b. in the process of production for such sale; or

c. in the form of materials or supplies to be consumed in the production process or in the rendering of services."[1]

Recall the definition of an asset as previously discussed in Chapter 2. As assets, inventories represent a present resource, which the entity has **control over or access to**. The inventory purchase is the **transaction** that gives rise to the recognition of an inventory asset.

An inventory purchase is the opposite side of a sales transaction. The diagram here was taken from Chapter 6 and was used there to illustrate a basic sale transaction.

Just as accountants recognize a sale when the risks and rewards of ownership are passed to the purchaser (when control passes), the purchaser can use the same "risks and rewards" test to determine when the inventory should be recognized. Once the risks and rewards pass, the inventory meets the definition of an asset for the purchaser. (That is, it is no longer an asset for the vendor.) Recall Example 6.28 from Chapter 6, which lists the risk and rewards of ownership for wine. We have reproduced this in **Illustration 8.2**.

ILLUSTRATION 8.2

Risks and Rewards of Wine Inventory

Risks	Rewards
— Wine will age poorly and therefore decline in value	— Wine will age well and appreciate in value
— Wine will be stolen/vandalized	— Wine can be consumed by owner or buyer
— Wine will be stored improperly	— Wine inventory may be used as collateral for bank loan
	— Wine may be sold for cash

Goods Included in Inventory

Underlying Concept 8.2

It is important to look at the terms of the transaction to identify when legal title passes. If there is some doubt about whether or not title has passed, in coming to a conclusion, the accountant considers other evidence, such as the sales agreement's intent, past transactions, the policies of the parties involved, and industry practices.

When substantially all risks and rewards of ownership and therefore control have passed to the purchaser, inventory is recognized. Legal title and possession help make this determination. (See **Underlying Concept 8.2**.) Usually purchased goods would be included as inventory when legal title passes. In practice, however, acquisitions are often recorded when the goods are received (possession) because it may be difficult for the buyer to identify the exact time when the legal title passes to the buyer for every purchase. At the point when the goods are received, the entity has control over and access to the future benefits. As a general rule, legal title has often passed by then as well.

Both legal title and possession are important factors because they give rise to risks and rewards and signal the passing of control. For instance, possession allows the owner to use the inventory and legal title allows the owner to sell the inventory or pledge it to obtain a loan. It is important to use professional judgement to decide when the inventory should be recognized as an asset, because legal title and possession do not always pass to the purchaser at the same time. Let's analyze some specific transactions in a little more detail.

Goods in Transit

Law Sometimes purchased goods are in transit—that is, not yet received—at the end of a fiscal period. Although the company does not yet have possession, we may look to the legal title to determine whether the goods should be recognized as inventory. The legal title is determined by the shipping terms that have been agreed upon between the buyer and the seller. If the goods are shipped **f.o.b. shipping point**, the legal title passes to the buyer when the seller delivers the goods to the common carrier (transporter), who then acts as an agent for the buyer. (The abbreviation "f.o.b." stands for "free on board.") If the goods are shipped **f.o.b. destination**, legal title passes when the goods reach the destination. "Shipping point" and "destination" are often indicated by naming a specific location; for example, f.o.b. Regina.[2]

---

[2]Terms other than "f.o.b. shipping point" or "f.o.b. destination" (for example, "CIF" for "cost, insurance, freight") are often used to identify when legal title passes. The f.o.b. terms are used in this text to reflect that an agreement on when title passes must be reached between the buyer and seller in the purchase–sale contract. In a particular situation, the terms of the sales contract are examined to determine when the risks and rewards of ownership pass from the seller to the buyer.

Once legal title passes, it is argued that the purchaser has the risks of ownership. For instance, if something happened to the inventory while in transit for goods shipped f.o.b. shipping point, it would be the purchaser's loss.

Goods in transit at the end of a fiscal period that were sent f.o.b. shipping point are recorded by the buyer as purchases of the period and should be included in ending inventory. If these purchases are not recognized, the result is **understated** inventories and accounts payable in the statement of financial position and **understated** purchases and ending inventories when calculating the cost of goods sold for the income statement.

The accountant normally prepares a purchase cut-off schedule for the end of each period to ensure that goods received from suppliers around the end of the year are recorded in the appropriate period. Cut-off procedures can be extensive and include the following controls:

- Curtailing and controlling the receipt and shipment of goods around the time of the count
- Marking freight and shipping documents as "before" or "after" the inventory count
- Ensuring that receiving reports on goods received before the count are linked to invoices that are also recorded in the same period

Audit & Assurance 4.3.6 Because goods that are bought f.o.b. shipping point may still be in transit when a period ends, the cut-off schedule is not completed until a few days after the period's end. This gives time for goods in transit at year end to be received. Auditors often verify the cut-off procedures during their audit to ensure the existence and completeness of the inventory reported in the financial statements.

Consigned Goods

Accounting for the sale of consigned goods was covered in Chapter 6. In terms of accounting for inventory, it is important to recognize that goods out on consignment remain the consignor's property. (See **Underlying Concept 8.3**.) They are included in the consignor's inventory at their purchase price or production cost plus the cost of handling and shipping the goods to the consignee. In this case, even though possession rests with the consignee, legal title is held by the consignor. The consignor essentially has the risks and rewards of ownership. For instance, if the inventory becomes obsolete while held by the consignee, it is the consignor that suffers the loss. When the consignee sells the consigned goods, the revenue, less a selling commission and expenses incurred in accomplishing the sale, is remitted to the consignor.

Occasionally, the inventory out on consignment is shown as a separate item or there are additional disclosures in the notes, but unless the amount is large, there is little need for this. For the consignee, no entry is made to adjust its Inventory account for the goods it received, because the goods remain the consignor's property. In addition, the consignee should be extremely careful not to include any consigned goods in its inventory count.

Repurchase Agreements

Sometimes an enterprise uses its inventory to obtain financing without reporting either the liability or the inventory on its statement of financial position. This type of transaction—often called a product financing arrangement—usually involves a transfer of the inventory with either a real or implied "buyback" agreement. Under the terms of these types of arrangements, the purchaser agrees to buy the inventory and then sell it back later to the same supplier. These are sometimes called "parking transactions" because the seller simply "parks" the inventory on another company's statement of financial position for a short period of time, agreeing to repurchase it in the future. (See **Underlying Concept 8.4**.) **If the risks and rewards of ownership and therefore control have not been transferred, the inventory should remain on the seller's books. Example 8.1** looks at a repurchase arrangement.

Underlying Concept 8.3

Even though some transactions are not called consignment sales, they may be consignment sales in substance. Therefore, the terms of the agreement should be examined carefully because consignment accounting may have to be used.

Underlying Concept 8.4

Recognizing revenue when inventory is "parked" violates the revenue recognition principle. This principle requires that the earnings process be substantially completed, with the risks and rewards of ownership transferred to the purchaser. In addition, the economic substance of this transaction is that it is a financing transaction.

Example 8.1 | Repurchase Agreements

Facts Company A needs $1,000 of financing but is unable to borrow funds from traditional sources (such as the bank) because the bank believes the loan would be too risky. The company therefore enters into an agreement with Company B to obtain the funds. A's inventory is used to support the value of the loan and legal title is transferred to B. At the same time, both parties agree to transfer the same inventory back to A at the end of 30 days for $1,010.

Instructions Would the inventory be derecognized on the financial statements of A? Explain.

Solution The risks and rewards (and therefore control) have not transferred to B in this example when you look at the two transactions as one (even though the legal title and possession are transferred in the first part of the transaction). To illustrate, if the value of the inventory declines over the 30-day period, Company A still has to pay $1,010 to buy it back. Company A therefore retains the risk that the inventory will decline in value. This is sometimes called **price risk**. The inventory therefore remains on the financial statements of A.

We looked at this issue in Chapter 6 from the perspective of revenue recognition. (See the section "Repurchase Agreements" in Chapter 6.)

Purchase Commitments

In many lines of business, it is common for a company to agree to buy inventory weeks, months, or even years in advance. Such arrangements may be made based on either estimated or firm sales commitments from the company's customers. Generally, title to the merchandise or materials described in these **purchase commitments** does not pass to the buyer until delivery. Indeed, when the commitment is made, the goods may exist only as natural resources or, in the case of commodities, as unplanted seed, or in the case of a product, as work in process.

Ordinary orders, where the prices are determined at the time of shipment and **the buyer or seller can still cancel the order**, do not represent either an asset or a liability to the buyer. They are therefore not recorded in the books or reported in the financial statements.

Even with formal, **non-cancellable purchase contracts**, no asset or liability is recognized on the date when the contract takes effect, because it is an **executory contract**. In other words, neither party has performed (or fulfilled) its part of the contract. However, if the amounts are abnormal in relation to the entity's normal business operations or financial position, the contract details should be disclosed in the notes to the buyer's financial statements.

If the unavoidable costs of completing the contract are higher than the benefits expected from receiving contracted goods or services, a loss provision is recognized according to IAS 37 *Provisions, Contingent Liabilities, and Contingent Assets*. This is known as an **onerous contract**. Although ASPE has no similar requirement, Canadian practice has historically been to recognize the loss and liability as well. Under ASPE, if the loss is likely and measurable, the loss would be recognized. (See **Underlying Concept 8.5**.)

Example 8.2 looks at accounting for a purchase commitment where the contract becomes onerous.

Example 8.2 | Purchase Commitments That Are Onerous

Facts   Company A signs several purchase contracts in 2019. Under the terms of one contract, Company A will take delivery of the inventory in 2020 and pay a price of $640,000 to Company B. The fair value of the inventory at the company's December 31, 2019 year end declines to $500,000. Company A does not expect to be able to recover its additional costs. Assume that the fair value remains at $500,000 until the goods are delivered.

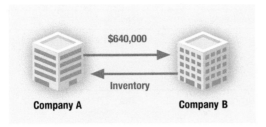

Instructions   Is this an onerous contract in 2019? If so, why? Show journal entries for 2019 and 2020.

Solution   No journal entry is recorded when the contract is signed. The contract is onerous since Company A must pay $640,000 for inventory worth $500,000. The following entry is made on December 31, 2019, given that the contract is now considered onerous:

Loss on Purchase Contracts	140,000	
Liability for Onerous Contracts		140,000

A	=	L	+	SE
		+140,000		−140,000

Cash flows: No effect

When the goods are received in 2020, the entry is:

Inventory	500,000	
Liability for Onerous Contracts	140,000	
Accounts Payable		640,000

A	=	L	+	SE
+500,000		+500,000		

Cash flows: No effect

If the price has partially or fully recovered before the inventory is received, the Liability for Onerous Contracts amount is reduced. A resulting gain (Recovery of Loss) is then reported in the period of the price increase for the amount of the partial or full recovery. This accounting treatment is very similar to recognizing an impairment in inventory value by recording inventories at the lower of cost and net realizable value.

Accounting for purchase commitments (indeed, for all commitments) is unsettled and controversial. Some argue that these contracts should be reported as assets and liabilities when the contract is signed; others believe that recognition at the delivery date is more appropriate.[3]

Summary of When to Recognize Inventory Based on Change in Control and Risks and Rewards

Illustration 8.3 summarizes various purchase transactions in terms of the risks and rewards/ change in control test and inventory recognition. Note that, in cases where the legal title is held by one party and the other party has possession, increased judgement is required to determine whether risks and rewards of ownership have passed. Even where the same party has legal title and possession, care should be taken to analyze the underlying substance of the transaction.

---

[3]Purchase commitments sometimes have the characteristics of derivatives. Derivatives are generally recognized and valued at fair value on an ongoing basis. Should purchase commitments be accounted for as derivatives? We will revisit this topic in Chapter 16.

ILLUSTRATION 8.3 Determining When to Recognize Inventory Based on Change in Control and Risks and Rewards

Transaction	Who has legal title?	Who has possession?	Have control/ substantially all risks and rewards passed?	Who recognizes inventory?
Goods in transit shipped f.o.b. shipping point	Purchaser	Shipping company	Yes	Purchaser
Consignment sale	Consignor	Consignee	No	Consignor
Sale with buyback (same goods, fixed buyback price that includes a charge for carrying costs)	Purchaser	Purchaser	No (where it is essentially a financing transaction)	Vendor
Sales with high rates of return where returns estimable	Purchaser	Purchaser	Yes	Purchaser
Sales with delayed payment terms where vendor retains title until consideration collected (bad debts are estimable)	Vendor	Purchaser	Yes	Purchaser
Purchase commitments (non-cancellable)	Vendor (assuming the inventory has been produced)	Vendor (assuming the inventory exists)	No, but purchaser may have to accrue losses if onerous contract	Vendor (assuming the inventory exists)

Flow of Costs

Management Accounting 3.3.1, 3.3.2 As **Illustration 8.4** shows, the flow of costs for merchandising and manufacturing companies is different. The **cost of goods manufactured** referred to in Illustration 8.4 represents the product costs of goods that are completed and transferred to Finished Goods Inventory. You are probably familiar with a statement of cost of goods manufactured that summarizes all the product costs incurred during the period that resulted in finished

ILLUSTRATION 8.4

Flow of Costs through Manufacturing and Merchandising Companies

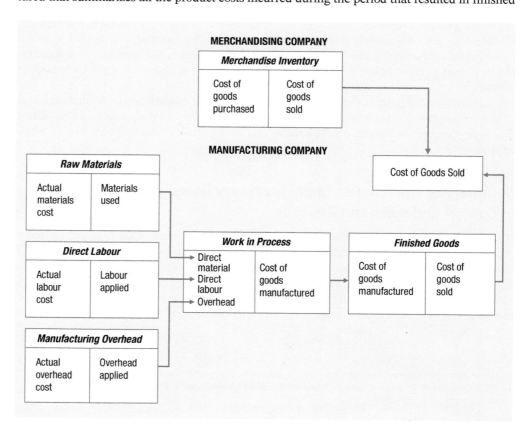

goods. (You may want to refer to a managerial accounting text for an example.) A cost of goods manufactured statement is far more detailed than information found in published financial statements. Note that **the cost of goods manufactured during the year is similar to the cost of goods purchased in a merchandising company**. Each is the source of the cost of goods available for sale in the period. Business models continue to change and therefore, the amount of inventory recognized may chage as well, as noted in **What Do the Numbers Mean? 8.2**.

What Do the Numbers Mean? 8.2

Before we move on to the next section, it is important to look at changing business models and how they might affect which assets are included in inventory on the statement of financial position. Consider **Indigo Books & Music Inc.** Indigo is the largest book retailer in Canada and operates under the names of Chapters, Indigo, Coles, SmithBooks, and others. In 2009, the company launched a new business called Shortcovers. Shortcovers provided online access to books and other print materials. In December 2009, Indigo transferred the net assets of Shortcovers to a newly created company called Kobo Inc. Indigo described 2010 as a "tipping point," a year when reading digitally went mainstream. Indigo now had two quite differing business segments: one selling hard copy books and one selling online access to books.

While we would generally agree that the hard copy books are inventory to Indigo, what about the e-books? In essence, Indigo is in the business of selling books, whether hard copies or e-books, so shouldn't they both appear as inventory on the balance sheet? Not necessarily. Selling access to an e-book represents a very different business model than selling an actual hard copy of a book. With paper books, the company has to purchase the books, merchandise them, and hopefully sell them. One might argue that it has control of the inventory. In other words, if a book sells, the company profits, but if it does not sell, unless it can be returned to the publisher, the company suffers a loss. With an e-book, all the company needs is an agreement that allows it to sell or distribute access to the e-books. For this, the company likely earns some sort of percentage of the revenues. This relationship is more of an agency relationship: the company is acting as a selling agent and essentially earning a commission.

In November 2011, Indigo announced that it had entered a deal to sell Kobo to Rakuten Inc., a large Japanese e-commerce company. Indigo still sells Kobo e-reader devices as well as e-books. The following excerpt from the 2017 financial statements shows that revenues from e-reading made up less than 2% of total revenues. Revenues from printed material continued to be the most significant. This can be a bit misleading, however, since the revenues on sale of e-books are only a share of the revenues (like a commission) since Indigo is acting as an agent in selling e-books.

17. Supplementary Operating Information

Supplemental product line revenue information:

(thousands of Canadian dollars)	52-week period ended April 1, 2017	53-week Period ended April 2, 2016
Print[1]	598,107	615,410
General merchandise[2]	384,097	343,488
eReading[3]	12,510	14,452
Other[4]	25,131	20,831
Total	1,019,845	994,181

1 Includes books, magazines, newspapers, and shipping revenue.
2 Includes lifestyle, paper, toys, calendars, music, DVDs, electronics, and shipping revenue.
3 Includes eReaders, eReader accessories, Kobo revenue share, and shipping revenue.
4 Includes cafés, irewards, gift card breakage, plum breakage, and corporate sales.

Inventory Errors

LEARNING OBJECTIVE 3
Identify the effects of inventory errors on the financial statements and adjust for them.

Items that have been incorrectly included or excluded in determining the ending inventory amount create errors in both the income statement and the statement of financial position. Decisions that are based on financial statement amounts affected by such errors (such as bonuses paid to management based on net income) would therefore be in error and comparability would also be impaired. Let's look at two cases and the effects on the financial statements.

Ending Inventory Misstated

What would happen if the beginning inventory and purchases were recorded correctly, but some items were omitted from ending inventory by mistake? For example, what if items were in the warehouse but were missed in the physical count, or they were out on consignment? The effects of this error on the financial statements at the end of the period are shown in **Illustration 8.5**.

Statement of Financial Position		Income Statement	
Inventory	Understated	Cost of goods sold	Overstated
Retained earnings	Understated	Net income	Understated
Working capital	Understated		
(current assets less current liabilities)			
Current ratio	Understated		
(current assets divided by current liabilities)			

Finance 5.1.1 Working capital and the current ratio are understated because a portion of the ending inventory is omitted. Net income is understated because cost of goods sold is overstated. This could affect decisions made by investors and lenders. **Example 8.3** illustrates the effect of a misstatement on net income.

Example 8.3 | Impact of Ending Inventory Misstatement

Facts   Assume that the 2020 ending inventory of Wei Ltd. is understated by $10,000 and that all other items are stated correctly.

Instructions   How does this misstatement affect net income over a two-year period?

Solution   The effect of this error is an understatement of net income in the current year and an overstatement of net income in the following year. The error affects the following year because the beginning inventory of that year is understated, which causes net income to be overstated. Both net income figures are misstated, but the total for the two years is correct because the two errors will be counterbalanced (or offset), as shown below.

Wei Ltd.				
	Incorrect Recording		**Correct Recording**	
	2020	**2021**	**2020**	**2021**
Revenues	$100,000	$100,000	$100,000	$100,000
Cost of goods sold				
Beginning inventory	25,000	20,000	25,000	30,000
Purchased or produced	45,000	60,000	45,000	60,000
Goods available for sale	70,000	80,000	70,000	90,000
Less: Ending inventory*	20,000	40,000	30,000	40,000
Cost of goods sold	50,000	40,000	40,000	50,000
Gross profit	50,000	60,000	60,000	50,000
Administrative and selling expenses	40,000	40,000	40,000	40,000
Net income	$ 10,000	$ 20,000	$ 20,000	$ 10,000

Total income for two years = $30,000   Total income for two years = $30,000

*Ending inventory understated by $10,000 in 2020; correct amount is $30,000.

If the error is discovered in 2020 just before the books are closed, the correcting entry in 2020 would be:

Inventory	10,000	
Cost of Goods Sold		10,000

A	=	L	+	SE
+10,000				+10,000

Cash flows: No effect

If the error is not discovered until 2021, after the books are closed for 2020, the correcting entry in 2021 would be:

Inventory	10,000	
Retained Earnings		10,000

A	=	L	+	SE
+10,000				+10,000

Cash flows: No effect

If the error is discovered after the books for 2021 are closed, **no entry is required because the error is self-correcting over the two-year period**. The inventory on the statement of financial position at the end of 2021 would be correct, as is the total amount of retained earnings. **However, whenever comparative financial statements are prepared that include 2020 or 2021, the inventory and net income for those years are restated and reported at the correct figures.**

If ending inventory is **overstated** at the end of 2020, the reverse effect occurs. Inventory, working capital, current ratio, and net income are overstated and cost of goods sold is understated in 2020. The error's effect on net income will be counterbalanced in the next year, but both years' net income figures are incorrect, which distorts any analysis of trends in earnings and ratios.

Purchases and Inventory Misstated

Suppose that certain goods that the company owns are **not recorded as a purchase** and are **not counted in ending inventory**. Illustration 8.6 shows the effect on the financial statements, assuming this is a purchase on account.

Statement of Financial Position		Income Statement	
Inventory	Understated	Purchases	Understated
Retained earnings	No effect	Ending inventory	Understated
Accounts payable	Understated	Cost of goods sold	No effect
Working capital	No effect	Net income	No effect
Current ratio	Overstated		

ILLUSTRATION 8.6

Financial Statement Effects of Understated Purchases and Inventory

Omitting both the purchase of goods and the inventory results in understated inventory and accounts payable on the statement of financial position, and understated purchases and ending inventory on the income statement. **Net income for the period is not affected by omitting such goods, because purchases and ending inventory are both understated by the same amount. That is, the error offsets itself in cost of goods sold.**[4] Total working capital is unchanged, but the current ratio is overstated (assuming it was greater than 1 to 1) because equal amounts were omitted from inventory and accounts payable. Example 8.4 looks at the impact of the misstatement on the current ratio.

---

[4]To correct the error in the same year before the books are closed, and assuming inventories are adjusted before the closing entries, the following entries are needed, depending on whether the periodic or perpetual method is used. We will come back to these two methods later in the chapter.

Periodic Method			Perpetual Method		
Purchases	$x		Inventory	$x	
Accounts Payable		$x	Accounts Payable		$x
Inventory	$x				
Cost of Goods Sold		$x			

> ### Example 8.4 | Purchases and Inventory Misstated—Impact on Current Ratio
>
> **Facts** Assume that a company understates its accounts payable and ending inventory by $40,000. The understated and correct data are shown below.
>
> | Purchases and Ending Inventory Understated | | Purchases and Ending Inventory Correct | |
> | --- | --- | --- | --- |
> | Current assets | $120,000 | Current assets | $160,000 |
> | Current liabilities | $ 40,000 | Current liabilities | $ 80,000 |
>
> **Instructions** What is the current ratio for both scenarios (incorrect balances and correct balances)?
>
> **Solution** The correct current ratio is 2 to 1 ($160,000/$80,000) rather than 3 to 1 ($120,000/$40,000). Thus, understating accounts payable and ending inventory can lead to a "window dressing" of the current ratio. In other words, it can appear better than it really is.

If purchases (on account) and ending inventory are both overstated, then the effects on the statement of financial position are exactly the reverse. That is, inventory and accounts payable are overstated, and the current ratio is understated, even though the dollar amount of working capital is not affected. Cost of goods sold and net income are also unaffected because the errors offset each other. The preceding examples show some of the errors that can occur and their consequences, but there are many other types of possible errors. These include:

- not recording a purchase but counting the new inventory,
- not recording a sale in the current period although the items have been delivered,
- omitting the adjusting entry to update the account Allowance for Sales Returns and Allowances in situations where the sales are known to have a high rate of return, and
- failing to adjust inventory to the lower of cost and net realizable value.

Ethics **Determining correct amounts for purchases, sales, and inventory in the correct accounting period is a critical step in preparing reliable financial statements.** We only have to read the financial press to learn how misstating inventory can generate high income numbers. For example, in the past some Canadian farm equipment manufacturers treated deliveries to dealers as company sales (which reduced their inventory), even though sales to the ultimate consumer did not occur as quickly as the deliveries to the dealers. The result was significantly inflated reported income for the manufacturers.

When an error from a prior period is corrected, it is accounted for retrospectively as an adjustment to retained earnings. Full disclosure requires a description of the error and a statement of the effect on the current and prior-period financial statements.

Measurement of Inventory—Costs Included

LEARNING OBJECTIVE 4

Determine the components of inventory cost.

Management Accounting 3.3.1 After deciding what items are to be included in the ending inventory, the next step in accounting for inventory is to determine its cost. As mentioned previously, inventories—like other non-financial assets—are generally recognized initially on the basis of cost. How is cost determined, and what should be included in "cost"?

Both IFRS and ASPE indicate that inventory cost is made up of "all costs of purchase, costs of conversion and other costs incurred in bringing the inventories to their present location and condition."[5] This includes transportation and handling costs and other direct costs of acquisition, such as non-recoverable taxes and duties.

Volume Rebates

We looked at the issue of volume rebates (or discounts) in Chapter 6. Now let's look at it from the purchaser's perspective. **Volume rebates** are recorded as a reduction of the purchase cost of inventory. If the "rebate receivable" meets both the definition of an asset and its recognition criteria, the rebate is recognized before it is received. (See **Underlying Concept 8.6**.)

In general:

- If the rebate is discretionary on the part of the supplier, no rebate is recognized until it is paid or the supplier becomes obligated to make a payment.
- If the rebate is **probable** and the amount can be **reasonably estimated**, the asset recognition criteria are met and the receivable can be recorded. In this case, it is recognized as a reduction in the cost of purchases for the period. The amount receivable is allocated between the goods remaining in inventory, and the goods sold.
- The amount of the receivable recognized is based on the proportion of the total rebate that is expected relative to the transactions to date.

Example 8.5 looks at an example of a volume rebate.

> **Underlying Concept 8.6**
>
> Revenues and expenses are defined in terms of changes in assets and liabilities. Therefore, if an asset does not exist or cannot be recognized in this situation, an expense recovery cannot be recognized either.

Example 8.5 | Volume Rebates—Purchaser Perspective

Facts   Assume that Johnston Corp., with a June 30 year end, has been purchasing more and more inventory from Roster Limited in recent years. Roster offers its customers a special **volume rebate** of $0.10 per unit on each unit purchased, if the customer buys more than 100,000 units in the calendar year (from January 1 to December 31). This year, for the first time, Johnston management expects to exceed the 100,000-unit volume. It has purchased 60,000 units in the first six months of the current year (up to June 30) and its forecast purchases for the next six months are well over 50,000 units. Assume that 55,000 of the purchased units have been sold by Johnson by year end (June 30).

Instructions   Should Johnston recognize the anticipated rebate in its current year ended June 30? If so, how much should be recognized, and how does this affect the financial statements? Prepare the journal entries.

Solution   Johnston will recognize the rebate in the entry that follows for its current year ended June 30 if:

- the rebate offered by Roster Limited is not discretionary,
- it is probable that Johnston will purchase 110,000 units by December 31, and
- management is able to make a reasonable estimate of the total rebate for the calendar year.

The terms of the contract with Roster are clear that a rebate will occur if the set volume level is reached. Given that Johnston forecasts additional purchases that will exceed the threshold, the rebate is recognized in the June 30 financial statements.

The following journal entry is recorded.

Rebate Receivable	6,000	
Inventory (5,000 units)		500
Cost of Goods Sold (55,000 units)		5,500

110,000 units × $0.10 = $11,000; 60,000/110,000 × $11,000 = $6,000
or 60,000 units × $0.10 = $6,000

A	=	L	+	SE
+5,500				+5,500

Cash flows: No effect

Rebates may be given for purchasing large volumes of inventory, for reimbursement of selling costs, and for other reasons. Illustration 8.7 provides an excerpt from the financial statement notes for Canadian Tire Corporation, Limited. In the note, the company states that a rebate may be recorded as a reduction of selling, general, and administrative costs where, for instance, they represent a reimbursement of selling costs.

ILLUSTRATION 8.7

Note on Vendor Rebates—Excerpt from Canadian Tire Financial Statements

Vendor rebates

The Company records cash consideration received from vendors as a reduction in the price of vendors' products and recognizes it as a reduction to the cost of related inventory or, if the related inventory has been sold, to the cost of producing revenue. Certain exceptions apply where the cash consideration received is either a reimbursement of incremental selling costs incurred by the Company or a payment for assets or services delivered to the vendor, in which case the cost is reflected as a reduction in selling, general and administrative expenses.

The Company recognizes rebates that are at the vendor's discretion when the vendor either pays the rebates or agrees to pay them and payment is considered probable and can be reasonably estimated.

Product Costs

Product costs are costs that "attach" to inventory and are recorded in the inventory account. That is, they are capitalized. These costs are directly connected with bringing goods to the buyer's place of business and converting them to a saleable condition. They include freight charges on goods purchased, other direct costs of acquisition, and labour and other production costs that are incurred in processing the goods up to the time they are ready for sale.

IFRS **ASPE** Under IFRS, product costs also include any eventual decommissioning or restoration costs incurred as a result of production, even though the related expenditures may not be incurred until far into the future. Under ASPE, such costs are generally added to the cost of the related property, plant, and equipment. Asset retirement costs are discussed more fully in Chapters 10 and 13.

How should taxes be accounted for? Taxes that cannot be recovered from the government by the purchaser, such as some provincial sales taxes that are paid on goods that are purchased for resale or manufacturing purposes, are a cost of inventory. Taxes that can be recovered from the government, such as the federal Goods and Services Tax and the Harmonized Sales Tax charged in many provinces, are not included as part of the inventory's cost. Chapter 13 discusses these types of taxes in more detail.

Conversion costs include direct labour and an allocation of the fixed and variable production overhead costs that are incurred in processing direct materials into finished goods. The allocation of fixed production costs is based on the company's normal production capacity.[6] In this way, costs of idle capacity or low production levels do not end up in inventory, but instead are charged to expense as they are incurred. However, if production levels are abnormally high, the fixed costs are spread out over the larger number of units that are produced so that inventory is not measured at an amount higher than its cost. Actual production levels can be used if they are close to normal levels. Actual levels are also used to charge variable costs to production.

It is theoretically correct to allocate a share of any buying costs to inventory, or expenses of a purchasing department, insurance costs in transit, or other costs that are incurred in handling the goods before they are ready for sale. This is because such costs are incurred to bring the inventories "to their present location and condition." However, on a cost/benefit basis, these items are not ordinarily included in inventory cost.

---

[6]Normal capacity is "the production expected to be achieved on average over a number of periods or seasons under normal circumstances, taking into account the loss of capacity resulting from planned maintenance" (*CPA Canada Handbook*, Part II, Section 3031.14 and IAS 2.13). Copyright © IFRS Foundation. All rights reserved. Reproduced with permission.

Borrowing Costs

IFRS **ASPE** If interest costs are incurred to finance activities that help bring inventories to a condition and place ready for sale, they are considered by many to be as much a cost of the asset as materials, labour, and overhead.[7] Under IFRS, interest costs incurred for an inventory item that takes an extended period of time to produce or manufacture are considered **product costs**. However, if the financing relates to inventories that are manufactured or produced in large quantities and on a repetitive basis, companies can choose whether to capitalize them or not.[8] Under ASPE, the only requirement is that, **if interest is capitalized**, this policy and the amount that is capitalized in the current period must be **disclosed**.

Standard Costs

A company that uses a standard cost system predetermines the unit costs for material, labour, and manufacturing overhead. Usually the standard costs are based on the costs that should be incurred per unit of finished goods when the plant is operating at normal levels of efficiency and capacity. When actual costs are not the same as the standard costs, the differences are recorded in variance accounts that management can examine and follow up on by taking appropriate action to achieve greater control over costs. For financial statement purposes, **reporting inventories at standard cost is acceptable only as long as the results approximate actual cost**. Unallocated overheads are **expensed** as they are incurred.

Cost of Service Providers' Work in Process

Companies that provide services rather than manufacture products may accumulate significant costs of work-in-process inventories. These, too, are measured at their production costs. For service providers, the major "production" costs are for service personnel and overhead costs associated with this "direct labour." Supervisory costs and other overheads are allocated using the same principles as for manufactured products.

Costs Excluded from Inventory

Some costs are closely related to acquiring and converting a product, but they are not considered to be product costs. An example is storage costs, unless they are necessary because the product must be held before the next stage of production, such as in wine production. Other examples are abnormal spoilage or wastage of materials, labour, or other production costs; and interest costs when inventories that are ready for use or sale are purchased on delayed payment terms.

Selling expenses and, under ordinary circumstances, **general and administrative expenses** are not considered directly related to the acquisition or conversion of goods and, therefore, are not considered a part of inventory. Such costs are period costs. Why are these costs not considered part of inventory? Selling expenses are generally more directly related to the cost of goods sold than to the unsold inventory. In most cases, these costs are so unrelated or indirectly related to the actual production process that any allocation would be completely arbitrary.

"Basket" Purchases and Joint Product Costs

A special problem occurs when a group of units with different characteristics is purchased at a single lump-sum price, in what is called a basket purchase. When this kind of situation occurs—and it is not at all unusual—the most reasonable practice is to allocate the total cost among the various units **based on their relative sales value**.

---

[7]The reporting rules on interest capitalization have their greatest impact in accounting for property, plant, and equipment and, therefore, are discussed in detail in Chapter 10.

[8]IAS 23.7 and 8 as well as IAS 23.4. This option also exists for qualifying inventory items measured at fair value, such as biological assets.

Example 8.6 looks at basket purchases.

Example 8.6 | Basket Purchases

Facts Assume that Woodland Developers purchases land for $1 million. The land can be subdivided into 400 lots. These lots are of different sizes and shapes but can be roughly sorted into three groups, graded A (100 lots), B (100 lots), and C (200 lots). The lots will be sold for the following selling prices: A, $10,000; B, $6,000; and C, $4,500.

Instructions How should the purchase price be allocated to each lot?

Solution The purchase cost of $1 million must be allocated among the lots so that the cost of the lots that are later sold (cost of goods sold) and those remaining on hand (ending inventory) can be calculated. It is inappropriate to use the average lot cost of $2,500 (the total cost of $1 million divided by the 400 lots) because the lots vary in size, shape, and attractiveness. Instead, the purchase price is allocated based on the relative sales value as follows.

Lots	Number of Lots	Sales Price per Lot	Total Sales Value	Relative Sales Value	Total Cost	Cost Allocated to Lots	Cost per Lot
A	100	$10,000	$1,000,000	100/250	$1,000,000	$ 400,000	$4,000
B	100	6,000	600,000	60/250	1,000,000	240,000	2,400
C	200	4,500	900,000	90/250	1,000,000	360,000	1,800
			$2,500,000			$1,000,000	

This method, the **relative sales value method**, is rational, can be applied consistently, and is commonly used whenever there is a **joint cost** that needs to be allocated. In Chapter 6, this was referred to as the relative value method. Other examples where amounts are allocated using sales or market values include when two or more products are produced at the same time and the costs for each product cannot be distinguished. The petroleum industry uses this technique to value (at cost) the many products and by-products obtained from a barrel of crude oil, as does the food processing industry, where different cuts of meat of varying value are "split off" from one animal carcass. When the value of a by-product is relatively minor, it is often measured at its net realizable value and deducted from the cost of the major product.

Measurement and Inventory Accounting Systems

LEARNING OBJECTIVE 5

Distinguish between perpetual and periodic inventory systems and account for them.

Technology has played an important role in the development of inventory systems. For example, radio-frequency identification data communications systems for warehouses have helped companies increase the accuracy of their inventory information and the efficiency of their inventory management.

Management is well aware that the level of inventory can materially affect the amount of current assets, total assets, net income, and, therefore, retained earnings. These amounts, or totals that include them, are used to calculate ratios that allow users to evaluate management's performance (for use in calculation of bonuses) and adherence to debt restrictions (for calculation of the debt to total assets ratio or dividend payout ratio).

For these and other reasons, companies are very interested in having an inventory accounting system that gives accurate, up-to-date information. One of two systems is commonly used for maintaining accurate inventory records: a perpetual system or a periodic system.

Perpetual System

A **perpetual inventory system** continuously tracks changes in the Inventory account. This means that the cost of all purchases and the cost of the items sold (or issued out of inventory) are recorded directly in the Inventory account as the purchases and sales occur. The accounting features of a perpetual inventory system are as follows.

1. Purchases of merchandise for resale or raw materials for production are debited to Inventory rather than to Purchases.
2. Freight in is debited and purchase returns and allowances and purchase discounts are credited to Inventory instead of being accounted for in separate accounts.
3. The cost of the items sold is recognized at the time of each sale by debiting Cost of Goods Sold and crediting Inventory.
4. Inventory is a control account that is supported by a subsidiary ledger of individual inventory records. The subsidiary records show the quantity and cost of each type of inventory on hand.

The perpetual inventory system provides a continuous record of the balances in both the Inventory account and the Cost of Goods Sold account. In a computerized record-keeping system, changes in these accounts can be recorded almost instantaneously. The popularity and affordability of computerized accounting software have made the perpetual system cost-effective for many kinds of businesses. (See **What Do the Numbers Mean? 8.3**.) It is now common for most retail stores, big or small, to use optical scanners at the cash register that record reductions in inventory as it is sold as part of the store's perpetual inventory system.

What Do the Numbers Mean? 8.3

In 2014, **Loblaw Companies Limited** completed the conversion of its information technology system to a perpetual inventory system, which allowed it to better estimate the value of the inventory. An excerpt from the notes to the company's financial statements is presented below.

As at the end of 2014, with the upgrade of its information technology ("IT") infrastructure, the Company had completed the conversion of substantially all of its corporate grocery stores to the new systems. The implementation of a perpetual inventory system, combined with visibility to integrated costing information provided by the new IT systems,

enabled the Company to estimate the cost of inventory using a more precise system-generated average cost. As a result of the conversion, the Company recognized a $190 million charge to cost of merchandise inventories sold and a corresponding reduction in inventory, representing the estimate of the difference between the measurement of the cost of corporate grocery store inventory using a system generated weighted average cost compared to the retail inventory method and other conversion differences associated with the implementation of a perpetual inventory system.

According to the 2017 financial statements, software costs are capitalized as intangible assets and represent 10% of the total recorded as intangible assets.

Periodic System

In a **periodic inventory system**, the quantity of inventory on hand is determined, as the name implies, only **periodically**. Each acquisition of inventory during the accounting period is recorded by a debit to the Purchases account. The total in the Purchases account at the end of the accounting period is added to the cost of the inventory on hand at the beginning of the period to determine the total cost of the goods available for sale during the period. The cost of ending inventory is subtracted from the cost of goods available for sale to calculate the cost of goods sold.

Note that, under a periodic inventory system, the **cost of goods sold** is a **residual amount that depends on first calculating the cost of the ending inventory**. The cost of the ending inventory can be determined by physically counting and costing it. This process is called "taking a physical inventory." Companies that use the periodic system take a physical inventory at least once a year.

Comparing Perpetual and Periodic Systems

Example 8.7 compares the perpetual and periodic inventory systems.

Example 8.7 | A Comparison of Perpetual and Periodic Inventory Systems

Facts   Fesmire Limited had the following balances and transactions during the current year as shown below.

Beginning inventory	100 units at $6 = $600
Purchases	900 units at $6 = $5,400
Defective units returned to the supplier	50 units at $6 = $300
Sales	600 units at $12 = $7,200
Ending inventory	350 units at $6 = $2,100

Instructions   How would the journal entries be recorded under each system?

Solution   The entries to record these transactions during the current year are shown below.

Perpetual Inventory System			Periodic Inventory System		
1. Beginning inventory, 100 units at $6:					
The Inventory account shows the inventory on hand at $600.			The Inventory account shows the inventory on hand at $600.		
2. Purchase 900 units at $6:					
Inventory	5,400		Purchases	5,400	
Accounts Payable		5,400	Accounts Payable		5,400
3. Return 50 defective units:					
Accounts Payable	300		Accounts Payable	300	
Inventory		300	Purchase Returns and		
			Allowances		300
4. Sale of 600 units at $12:					
Accounts Receivable	7,200		Accounts Receivable	7,200	
Sales Revenue		7,200	Sales Revenue		7,200
Cost of Goods Sold					
(600 at $6)	3,600				
Inventory		3,600	(No entry)		
5. End-of-period entries for inventory accounts, 350 units at $6 = $2,100:					
No entry necessary.			Purchase Returns		
The account, Inventory, shows the ending			and Allowances	300	
balance of $2,100			Inventory ($2,100 − $600)	1,500	
($600 + $5,400 − $300 − $3,600)			Cost of Goods Sold	3,600	
			Purchases		5,400

When a **perpetual inventory system** is used and there is a difference between the perpetual inventory record and the physical inventory count, a separate entry is needed to adjust the perpetual Inventory account. The overage or shortage may be due to normal and expected shrinkage, breakage, shoplifting, or record-keeping errors, and is usually recognized as an adjustment of Cost of Goods Sold (Inventory Over and Short account).

In a **periodic inventory system**, there is no separate account to track these inventory losses. This is because there is no up-to-date inventory account that can be compared with the physical count. The amount of any inventory overage or shortage is therefore included in cost of goods sold.

To illustrate, let's look at Example 8.8.

Example 8.8 | Inventory Counts and Perpetual Inventory Systems

Facts   Assume that at the end of the reporting period, the perpetual Inventory account reported a balance of $4,000, but a physical count indicated that $3,800 was actually on hand.

Instructions   What is the adjusting journal entry that must be recorded to reflect the inventory count?

Solution   The adjusting entry is:

Inventory Over and Short	200	
Inventory		200

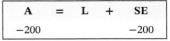

A	=	L	+	SE
−200				−200

Cash flows: No effect

Supplementary System—Quantities Only

In a perfect world, companies would like a continuous record of inventory levels, their cost, and the cost of goods sold. However, even with advances in technology, it may not be cost-effective to have a complete perpetual inventory system that keeps track of both inventory quantities and their cost. Because management needs current information about inventory levels to avoid stockouts and overpurchasing, to respond to customer queries, and to help prepare monthly or quarterly financial data, many companies use a **quantities only system**. This system provides detailed inventory records of increases and decreases **in quantities only**—not dollar amounts. This memorandum record is not part of the double-entry accounting system; therefore, the company would need to use a periodic system in its main accounts.

Whether a company maintains a perpetual inventory in quantities and dollars, in quantities only, or no perpetual inventory record at all, it usually takes a physical inventory once a year. No matter what type of inventory records is used or how well controlled the procedures for recording purchases and requisitions are, the dangers of loss and error are always present. Waste, breakage, theft, improper data entry, failure to prepare or record requisitions, and similar possibilities may cause the inventory records to be different from the actual inventory on hand. Therefore, all companies need periodic verification of the inventory records by actual count, weight, or measurement, with the **counts compared with the detailed records**. The **records are then corrected** so that they agree with the quantities actually on hand.

As far as possible, the physical inventory should be taken near the end of a company's fiscal year so that correct inventory quantities are used in preparing annual accounting reports and statements. Because this is not always possible, physical inventories that are taken within two or three months of the year end are considered satisfactory as long as the **internal controls** indicate that the detailed inventory records are maintained with a fair degree of accuracy.

Measurement and Cost Formulas

LEARNING OBJECTIVE 6

Identify and apply GAAP cost formula options and indicate when each cost formula is appropriate.

Two main issues have now been addressed in determining inventory cost: which inventory items to include, and which costs to include in, or exclude from, the product's cost. The next issue is this: if many purchases have been made at different unit costs, which of the various cost prices should be assigned to **Inventory** on the statement of financial position and which costs should be charged to **Cost of Goods Sold** on the income statement?

Conceptually, **identifying the specific costs** of the actual items sold and those unsold seems ideal, but doing this is often too expensive or simply impossible to achieve. Consequently, companies must choose another acceptable inventory cost formula. A **cost formula** is a method of assigning inventory costs incurred during the accounting period to inventory that is still on hand at the end of the period (ending inventory) and to inventory that was sold during the period (cost of goods sold).

Illustration 8.8 provides data to use in the discussion of the cost formula choice. The data summarize the inventory-related activities of Call-Mart Inc. for the month of March. Note that the company experienced increasing unit costs for its purchases throughout the month.

ILLUSTRATION 8.8

Data Used to Illustrate Inventory Calculation—Cost Formula Choice

	Call-Mart Inc.		
Date	**Purchases**	**Sold or Issued**	**Balance**
Mar. 1	(beginning inventory)		
	500 @ $3.80		500 units
Mar. 2	1,500 @ $4.00		2,000 units
Mar. 15	6,000 @ $4.40		8,000 units
Mar. 19		4,000	4,000 units
Mar. 30	2,000 @ $4.75		6,000 units
	10,000	4,000	

From this information, we see that there were 10,000 units available for sale, made up of 500 units in opening inventory and 9,500 units purchased during the month. Of the 10,000 available, 4,000 were sold, leaving 6,000 units in ending inventory.

The **cost of goods available for sale** is calculated and shown in **Illustration 8.9.**

ILLUSTRATION 8.9

Data Used to Illustrate Inventory Calculation—Cost of Goods Available for Sale

500 units @ $3.80 =	$ 1,900
1,500 units @ $4.00 =	6,000
6,000 units @ $4.40 =	26,400
2,000 units @ $4.75 =	9,500
10,000 units	$43,800

Having this information, the question now is: which price or prices should be assigned to the 6,000 units still in inventory and which to the 4,000 units sold? The answer depends on which cost formula is chosen.

Both IFRS and ASPE recognize three acceptable cost methods:

1. Specific identification
2. Weighted average cost
3. First-in, first-out (FIFO)

Specific Identification

When using the **specific identification** cost formula, each item that is sold and each item in inventory needs to be identified. The costs of the specific items that are sold are included in the cost of goods sold, and the costs of the specific items on hand are included in the ending inventory. This method is appropriate and required for goods that are not ordinarily interchangeable, and for goods and services that are produced and segregated for specific projects. It is used most often in situations involving a relatively small number of items that are costly and easily distinguishable by such things as their physical characteristics, serial numbers, or special markings. In the retail trade, this includes some types of jewellery, fur coats, automobiles, and furniture. In manufacturing, it includes special orders and many products manufactured under a job cost system.

Example 8.9 calculates ending inventory and cost of goods sold using the specific identification cost formula.

Example 8.9 | Specific Identification Cost Formula

Facts Use the data from Illustrations 8.8 and 8.9. In addition, assume that Call-Mart Inc.'s inventory items are distinguishable and that the 6,000 units of ending inventory consist of 100 units from the opening inventory, 900 from the March 2 purchase, 3,000 from the March 15 purchase, and 2,000 from the March 30 purchase.

Instructions How are ending inventory and cost of goods sold calculated using the specific identification cost formula?

Solution Ending inventory and cost of goods sold are calculated as follows.

Units from	No. of Units	Unit Cost	Total Cost
Beginning inventory	100	$3.80	$ 380
March 2 purchase	900	4.00	3,600
March 15 purchase	3,000	4.40	13,200
March 30 purchase	2,000	4.75	9,500
Ending inventory	**6,000**		**$26,680**
Cost of goods available for sale			
(beginning inventory + purchases)	$43,800		
Deduct: Ending inventory	26,680		
Cost of goods sold	**$17,120**		

Conceptually, this method appears ideal because actual costs are matched against actual revenue, and ending inventory items are reported at their specific cost. In fact, the requirement that this method only be used for goods that are not ordinarily interchangeable is an attempt to make sure this benefit is achieved and to prevent management from manipulating the amount of net income.

Consider what might happen if businesses were allowed to use this method more generally. Assume, for instance, that a wholesaler purchases identical plywood early in the year at three different prices. When the plywood is sold, the wholesaler can choose either the lowest or the highest price to charge to expense simply by choosing which plywood is delivered to the customer. This means that a manager can manipulate net income simply by delivering to the customer the higher- or lower-priced item, depending on whether lower or higher reported income is wanted for the period.

Another problem with the broader use of the specific identification cost formula is that allocating certain costs can become arbitrary when the inventory items are interchangeable. In many circumstances, it is difficult to directly relate shipping charges, storage costs, discounts, and other blanket charges to a specific inventory item. The only option, then, is to allocate these costs somewhat arbitrarily, which eliminates some of the benefits offered by the specific identification method.

Weighted Average Cost

As its name implies, an average cost method prices inventory items based on the average cost of the goods that are available for sale during the period. The **weighted average cost formula** takes into account that the volume of goods acquired at each price is different. **Example 8.10** looks at the weighted average cost formula for periodic inventory.

Example 8.10 | Weighted Average Cost Formula—Periodic Inventory

Facts Use the data from Illustrations 8.8 and 8.9 and assume that Call-Mart Inc. uses a periodic inventory method.

Instructions How are ending inventory and cost of goods sold calculated using the weighted average cost formula?

Solution Note that the beginning inventory units and cost are both included in calculating the average cost per unit. Ending inventory and cost of goods sold are calculated as follows.

	Date	No. of Units	Unit Cost	Total Cost
Inventory	Mar. 1	500	$3.80	$ 1,900
Purchases	Mar. 2	1,500	4.00	6,000
Purchases	Mar. 15	6,000	4.40	26,400
Purchases	Mar. 30	2,000	4.75	9,500
Total goods available		10,000		$43,800

Weighted average cost per unit	$\dfrac{\$43,800}{10,000} = \$4.38$
Ending inventory in units	6,000
Cost of ending inventory	**6,000 × $4.38 = $26,280**
Cost of goods available for sale	$43,800
Deduct ending inventory	26,280
Cost of goods sold	$17,520 (= 4,000 × $4.38)

Another weighted average cost method uses the **moving-average cost formula**. This method is used with **perpetual** inventory records that are **kept in both units and dollars**. In this method, a new average unit cost is calculated each time a purchase is made. This is because the cost of goods sold at the updated average cost has to be recognized at the time of the next sale. Use of the moving-average cost formula for full perpetual records is shown in **Example 8.11**.

Example 8.11 | Moving-Average Cost Formula—Full Perpetual Inventory

Facts Use the data from Illustrations 8.8 and 8.9 and assume that Call-Mart Inc. uses a full perpetual inventory method (both units and dollars).

Instructions How are ending inventory and cost of goods sold calculated using the moving-average cost formula?

Solution Note that the beginning inventory units and cost are both included in calculating the average cost per unit. Ending inventory and cost of goods sold are calculated as follows.

Date	Purchased	Sold or Issued	Balance*	
Mar. 1	Beginning inventory		(500 @ $3.80)	$ 1,900
Mar. 2	(1,500 @ $4.00) $ 6,000		(2,000 @ $3.95)	7,900
Mar. 15	(6,000 @ $4.40) 26,400		(8,000 @ $4.2875)	34,300
Mar. 19		(4,000 @ $4.2875)		
		$17,150	(4,000 @ $4.2875)	17,150
Mar. 30	(2,000 @ $4.75) 9,500		(6,000 @ $4.4417)	26,650

*Calculation of moving-average cost per unit:

After March 2 purchase
  = Cost of units available / Units available
  = [$1,900 + (1,500 × $4.00)] / (500 + 1,500)
  = ($1,900 + $6,000) / 2,000
  = $7,900 / 2,000
  = $3.95

After March 15 purchase
  = [$7,900 + (6,000 × $4.40)] / (2,000 + 6,000)
  = ($7,900 + $26,400) / 8,000
  = $34,300 / 8,000
  = $4.2875

After March 30 purchase
  = [$17,150 + (2,000 × $4.75)] / (4,000 + 2,000)
  = ($17,150 + $9,500) / 6,000
  = $26,650 / 6,000
  = $4.4417

On March 15, after 6,000 units are purchased for $26,400, 8,000 units with a total cost of $34,300 ($7,900 plus $26,400) are on hand. The average unit cost is $34,300 divided by 8,000, or $4.2875. This unit cost is used in costing withdrawals of inventory until another purchase is made, when a new average unit cost is calculated. Accordingly, the cost of each of the 4,000 units withdrawn on March 19 is shown at $4.2875, which makes a total cost of goods sold of $17,150. On March 30, following the purchase of 2,000 units for $9,500, the total inventory cost of the 6,000 units is $26,650. The new unit cost is now $4.4417.

Justification for using an average cost method is that the costs it assigns to inventory and cost of goods sold closely follow the actual physical flow of many inventories that are interchangeable. While it may be impossible to measure the specific physical flow of inventory, it is reasonable to cost items based on an average price. There are also practical reasons that support this method. It is simple to apply, objective, and not very open to income manipulation. This argument is particularly persuasive when the inventory involved is relatively homogeneous in nature. In terms of achieving financial statement objectives, an average cost method results in an average of costs being used to determine both the cost of goods sold in the income statement and ending inventory in the statement of financial position.

First-In, First-Out (FIFO)

The **first-in, first-out (FIFO) cost formula** assigns costs based on the assumption that goods are used in the order in which they are purchased. In other words, it assumes that **the first items purchased are the first ones used** (in a manufacturing concern) **or sold** (in a merchandising concern). The inventory remaining, therefore, must come from the most recent purchases. **Example 8.12** uses the FIFO cost formula to calculate ending inventory and cost of goods sold.

Example 8.12 | FIFO Cost Formula—Periodic Inventory

Facts Use the data from Illustrations 8.8 and 8.9 and assume that Call-Mart Inc. uses a periodic inventory system, where the inventory cost is calculated only at the end of the month.

Instructions How are ending inventory and cost of goods sold calculated using the FIFO cost formula?

Solution The ending inventory's cost for the 6,000 units remaining is calculated by taking the cost of the most recent purchase and working back until all units in the ending inventory are accounted for. The ending inventory and cost of goods sold are calculated as shown below.

Date	No. of Units	Unit Cost	Total Cost
Mar. 30	2,000	$4.75	$ 9,500
Mar. 15	4,000	4.40	17,600
Ending inventory	6,000		$27,100
Cost of goods available for sale	$43,800		
Deduct: Ending inventory	27,100		
Cost of goods sold	$16,700		

If a full perpetual inventory system **in quantities and dollars** is used, a cost figure is attached to each withdrawal from inventory when the units are withdrawn and sold. Example 8.13 shows the calculations where a full perpetual inventory and FIFO are used.

Example 8.13 | FIFO Cost Formula—Perpetual Inventory

Facts Use the data from Illustrations 8.8 and 8.9 and assume that Call-Mart Inc. uses a full perpetual inventory system.

Instructions How are ending inventory and cost of goods sold calculated using the FIFO cost formula?

Solution The cost of the 4,000 units removed on March 19 is made up first from the items in the beginning inventory, then the items purchased on March 2, and finally some from the March 15 purchases. The inventory recorded under FIFO and a perpetual system for Call-Mart Inc., shown below, results in an ending inventory of $27,100 and a cost of goods sold of $16,700.

Date	Purchased	Sold or Issued	Balance	
Mar. 1	Beginning inventory		500 @ $3.80	$ 1,900
Mar. 2	(1,500 @ $4.00) $ 6,000		500 @ $3.80 ⎱ 1,500 @ $4.00 ⎰	7,900
Mar. 15	(6,000 @ $4.40) 26,400		500 @ $3.80 ⎱ 1,500 @ $4.00 ⎬ 6,000 @ $4.40 ⎰	34,300
Mar. 19		500 @ $3.80 ⎱ 1,500 @ $4.00 ⎬ 2,000 @ $4.40 ⎰ **$16,700**	4,000 @ 4.40	17,600
Mar. 30	(2,000 @ $4.75) 9,500		4,000 @ $4.40 ⎱ 2,000 @ $4.75 ⎰	**27,100**

Notice that in these two FIFO examples, the cost of goods sold and ending inventory are the same. In all cases where FIFO is used, the inventory and cost of goods sold are the same at the end of the period whether a perpetual or periodic system is used. This is true because the same costs will always be first in and, therefore, first out, whether cost of goods sold is calculated as goods are sold throughout the accounting period (the perpetual system) or based on what remains at the end of the accounting period (the periodic system).

One objective of FIFO is to roughly follow the actual physical flow of goods. When the physical flow of goods really is first-in, first-out, the FIFO method approximates the use of specific identification. At the same time, it does not permit manipulation of income because the enterprise is not free to choose a certain cost to be charged to expense.

Another advantage of the FIFO method is that the ending inventory is close to its current cost. Because the costs of the first goods in are transferred to cost of goods sold, the ending inventory is made up of the cost of the most recent purchases. This approach generally provides a cost that is close to the replacement cost for inventory on the statement of financial position, particularly when the inventory turnover is rapid or price changes have not occurred since the most recent purchases.

The FIFO method's basic disadvantage is that current costs are not matched against current revenues on the income statement. The oldest costs are charged against current revenue, which can lead to distortions in gross profit and net income when prices are changing rapidly.

Choice of Cost Formula

Accounting standards limit the ability of preparers to choose a cost formula. Specific identification is required when inventory is made up of goods that are not ordinarily interchangeable, and when goods and services are produced and segregated for specific projects. Otherwise, the choice is between an average cost method and FIFO. The choice is further restricted by the requirement that companies apply the same inventory cost formula to all inventories of a similar nature and use.

The overriding objectives that underlie the inventory standards and guide management are as follows.

1. Choose an approach that corresponds as closely as possible to the physical flow of goods.
2. Report an inventory cost on the statement of financial position that is representative of the inventory's recent cost.
3. Use the same method for all inventory assets that have similar economic characteristics for the entity.

These requirements are consistent with standard setters' emphasis on an asset and liability approach to the accounting model, as we explained in Chapter 2. That is, assets and liabilities are the fundamental building blocks whose definition and measurement underlie the amounts and timing of revenues and expenses.

Income taxes are also a consideration. Methods that permit a lower ending inventory valuation result in lower income and reduced cash outflows for taxes. Compared with the FIFO cost formula, an average cost formula results in recent costs being reflected more in the cost of goods sold and older costs in ending inventory. In a period of rising prices, there may be tax advantages to an average cost formula.

If companies were permitted to switch from one inventory costing method to another, this would adversely affect the comparability of financial statements. Therefore, companies choose the costing formula that is most suitable to their particular circumstances and, once selected, apply it consistently from then on. (See Underlying Concept 8.7.) If conditions indicate that another accounting policy would result in a reliable and more relevant presentation in the financial statements, a change may be made. Such a change is unusual but is accounted for retroactively, and its effect should be clearly disclosed in the financial statements.

> **Underlying Concept 8.7**
>
> Applying the standards results in statement of financial position and income statement amounts that faithfully represent the asset's cost and the cost of the inventory that was sold, respectively. Consistently applying the same formula also improves the comparability of the financial statements.

Last-In, First-Out (LIFO)

The last-in, first-out (LIFO) cost formula is no longer permitted under IFRS and ASPE. LIFO assigns costs based on the assumption that the cost of the most recent purchase is the first cost to be charged to cost of goods sold. The cost assigned to the inventory remaining therefore comes from the earliest acquisitions (those that are "first-in, still-here") and is made up of the oldest costs.

This method is no longer permitted under IFRS and ASPE for the following reasons.

1. In almost all situations, LIFO does not represent the actual flow of costs.
2. The statement of financial position cost of ending inventory is not a fair representation of the recent cost of inventories on hand. (See Underlying Concept 8.8.)
3. Use of LIFO can result in serious distortions of reported income, especially when old inventory costs are expensed in the period. This happens when old, low-cost inventory gets charged to cost of goods sold due to a reduction in base inventory levels.

Because the Canada Revenue Agency has never allowed companies to use LIFO to calculate their income for tax purposes, this method was not widely used in Canada. However, it is permitted under U.S. GAAP, and allowed for tax purposes there if a company also uses the method for financial reporting purposes.

Measurement and the Lower of Cost and Net Realizable Value (LC&NRV) Principle

LEARNING OBJECTIVE 7

Explain why inventory is measured at the lower of cost and net realizable value, and apply the lower of cost and net realizable value principle.

So far in the chapter, we have learned how to calculate the cost of ending inventory at the statement of financial position date, determining:

1. the goods to include in ending inventory,
2. the costs to capitalize in inventory cost, and
3. the cost formulas available to allocate costs to ending inventory.

The last step in applying this cost-based model is to decide whether cost is appropriate for reporting inventory on the statement of financial position.

A departure from reporting inventory at cost makes sense if the value of inventory to the entity falls below its cost. This reduction in value may be due to the inventory itself (if, for example, the goods are obsolete or damaged), a reduction in selling prices, or an increase in the costs to complete and dispose of the inventory. Cost is not appropriate if the asset's value (its ability to generate net cash flows) is now less than its carrying amount. Inventories therefore are valued at the lower of cost and net realizable value. (See Underlying Concept 8.9.)

This departure from cost is justified for two main reasons. First, readers presume that current assets can be converted into at least as much cash as the amount reported on the statement of financial position. Second, a loss of utility should be deducted from (matched with) revenues in the period in which the loss occurs, not in the period when the inventory is sold.

For many years, inventory was valued in the cost-based system at the lower of cost and market (LCM), and there were a variety of alternative definitions of "market." The term **market** in LCM valuation could mean replacement cost, net realizable value, or net realizable value less a normal profit margin. Under U.S. GAAP, all these terms are still incorporated in a rule that is applied to calculate market and therefore to measure inventory on the statement of financial position.

The option of choosing a meaning of "market" has been eliminated under IFRS and ASPE. The phrase **lower of cost and market** is no longer part of GAAP in Canada, and "market" is now strictly defined as net realizable value (NRV): the estimated selling price less the estimated costs to complete and sell the goods. Why has there been such support for this concept of market?

The use of a "replacement cost" definition of market is based on the assumption that a decline in an item's replacement cost results in a decline in its selling price. While replacement cost may be appropriate in a few specific circumstances, it is not reasonable to assume that prices will fall in the same proportion as input costs fall, or that they will fall below inventory cost, or that such market conditions exist for all products. Also, the use of a "net realizable value less a normal profit margin" definition of market value has the effect of arbitrarily shifting profits from one period to another. In effect, a very large writedown may be taken in the year the inventory's value drops, so that a normal profit can be reported in the period in which it is later sold.

If inventory is written down only to its net realizable value, a lower loss is recognized in the current period and, if the estimates are correct, the company breaks even on the sale of the item. Although the net result is the same when you add the two periods together, there is little justification for the arbitrary shifting of profit into a future period as happens when the NRV is further reduced by the profit margin. Therefore, ASPE and IFRS both require the use of NRV as "market."

What Is Net Realizable Value?

Net realizable value is an estimate. Unlike inventory cost, which usually remains at a determined value, net realizable value changes over time for a variety of reasons, including the following.

- Inventory may deteriorate or become obsolete with time.
- Selling prices fluctuate with changes in supply and demand.
- Substitute products become available.
- Input costs to complete and sell, liquidate, or otherwise dispose of the product vary with conditions and the specific markets that the inventory is sold into.

Estimates of NRV are based on the best evidence available at and shortly after the statement of financial position date. The objective is to determine the most likely (net) realizable value of the product on hand at the end of the accounting period given the specific circumstances of the particular entity. A new assessment is required at each statement of financial position date. If economic circumstances change and the estimate of the net realizable value changes from the previous estimate, the revised amount is used in determining the lower of cost and NRV at the end of the next period.

Application of the LC&NRV Principle

The **lower of cost and net realizable value (LC&NRV)** principle requires that inventory be valued at cost unless NRV is lower than cost, in which case the inventory is valued at NRV. To apply this:

1. Determine the cost.
2. Calculate the net realizable value.
3. Compare the two.
4. Use the lower value to measure inventory for the statement of financial position.

To demonstrate, consider the information in **Illustration 8.10** for the inventory of Regner Foods Limited.

Assume the following details regarding various types of inventory for Regner Foods Limited.

Food	Cost	Net Realizable Value	LC&NRV
Spinach	$ 80,000	$120,000	$ 80,000
Carrots	100,000	100,000	100,000
Cut beans	50,000	40,000	40,000
Peas	90,000	72,000	72,000
Mixed vegetables	95,000	92,000	92,000
Final inventory value at LC&NRV			$384,000

ILLUSTRATION 8.10

Applying the Lower of Cost and NRV

Examples 8.14 and 8.15 calculate the value of inventory using LC&NRV.

Example 8.14 | Applying the Lower of Cost and NRV to Individual Inventory Items

Facts   Assume the data in Illustration 8.10 for Regner Limited. Assume further that Regner applies the LC&NRV principle to individual inventory items.

Instructions   What is the inventory amount that should be recorded on the statement of financial position for Regner Limited (applying LC&NRV)?

Solution   To establish the LC&NRV of each item of inventory, compare the net realizable value in the NRV column with cost. The lower of the two values is then chosen. Cost is the lower amount for spinach; net realizable value is lower for cut beans, peas, and mixed vegetables; and cost and NRV are identical for carrots. The inventory amount reported on Regner Foods' statement of financial position is therefore $384,000.

This analysis is usually applied only to losses in value that occur in the normal course of business from such causes as style changes, a shift in demand, or regular shop wear. Damaged or deteriorated goods are reduced directly to net realizable value. If the amount is significant, such goods may be carried in separate inventory accounts.

In Example 8.14 for Regner Foods, we assumed that the lower of cost and net realizable value rule is applied to each separate item of food. Indeed, the accounting standards specify that the comparison is usually applied on an item-by-item basis. However, the standards recognize that it may be appropriate in some circumstances to group similar or related items and then compare their cost and NRV as a group. Grouping inventory for this purpose may be appropriate, for example, for inventory items relating to the same product line in the following situations:

1. They are closely related in terms of their end use.
2. They are produced and marketed in the same geographical area.
3. They cannot be evaluated separately from other items in the product line in a practical or reasonable way.[9]

Grouping all finished goods inventory, all products within a geographic area, or all inventory that is specific to an industry, is **not** considered appropriate.

The extent to which inventory items are grouped and their subtotals of cost and net realizable value are compared can affect the amount of inventory that is reported on the statement of financial position.

To illustrate, assume that Regner Foods separates its food products into "frozen" and "canned" categories. Example 8.15 revisits the value of inventory for Regner.

Example 8.15 | Grouping Inventory Categories When Applying LC&NRV

Facts   Assume the data in Illustration 8.10 for Regner Limited. Assume further that Regner applies the LC&NRV principle to the following groups of inventory items: Frozen: spinach, carrots and cut beans; and Canned: peas and mixed vegetables.

Instructions   What is the inventory amount that should be recorded on the statement of financial position for Regner Limited (applying LC&NRV) when inventory is grouped together in categories?

---

[9]The Canada Revenue Agency requires that, in determining the lower of cost and NRV, the comparison should be made separately and individually in respect of each item in the inventory (or each usual class of items if specific items are not readily distinguishable). Comparing total cost and total market is only permitted when the cost of the specific items (using specific identification, FIFO, or average cost) is not known and only an average cost is available (*CRA Interpretation Bulletin*—473R, December 21, 1998, on "Inventory Valuation," par. 3).

Solution   If the lower of cost and NRV rule is applied to the **subtotals** of these groups, the valuation of inventory is $394,000. Recall that, if it is applied to individual items as noted in Example 8.14, it is $384,000. The reason for the difference is that individual realizable values lower than cost are offset against realizable values higher than cost when categories are used. For example, the lower NRVs for cut beans, peas, and mixed vegetables are partially offset by the higher NRV for spinach.

			Lower of Cost and NRV by:	
	Cost	**NRV**	**Individual Items**	**Related Products**
Frozen				
Spinach	$ 80,000	$120,000	$ 80,000	
Carrots	100,000	100,000	100,000	
Cut beans	50,000	40,000	40,000	
Total frozen	230,000	260,000		$230,000
Canned				
Peas	90,000	72,000	72,000	
Mixed vegetables	95,000	92,000	92,000	
Total canned	185,000	164,000		164,000
Total			$384,000	$394,000

The **item-by-item approach** is always the more conservative method (that is, lower asset cost) because net realizable values above cost are never included in the calculations.[10]

Two different methods are used for **recording** inventory at the lower market amount. The **direct method** records the NRV of the inventory directly in the Inventory account at the reporting date if the amount is lower than cost. No loss is reported separately in the income statement because the loss is buried in cost of goods sold. The other method does not change the Inventory account itself. Instead it keeps the Inventory account at cost and establishes a separate contra asset account to Inventory on the statement of financial position. (This is very similar to Accounts Receivable and the Allowance for Doubtful Accounts.) A loss account is recognized in the income statement to record the write off. This second approach is called the **indirect method** or **allowance method**.

The data in **Illustration 8.11** are the basis for **Examples 8.16** and **8.17**, which show the entries under both methods using periodic and perpetual systems.

Inventory	At Cost	At NRV
Beginning of the period	$65,000	$65,000
End of the period	82,000	70,000

ILLUSTRATION 8.11

Application of LC&NRV Using the Direct and Indirect Methods

The entries in Example 8.16 assume the use of a **periodic** inventory system. Those in Example 8.17 assume a **perpetual** inventory system.

Example 8.16 | Accounting for the Reduction of Inventory to NRV—Periodic Inventory System

Facts   Assume the information in Illustration 8.11. Assume further that the company uses a periodic inventory system.

Instructions   What are the journal entries using the direct method and the allowance method?

---

[10]While fair value less costs to sell appears to be the same as net realizable value (selling price less costs to sell), it is different. NRV is an entity-specific value, whereas fair values reflect a market-based valuation.

Solution

Ending Inventory Recorded at Lower of Cost and NRV (Direct Method)			Ending Inventory Recorded at Cost and Reduced to Lower of Cost and NRV Using an Allowance		
To transfer out beginning inventory balance:					
Cost of Goods Sold	65,000		Cost of Goods Sold	65,000	
Inventory		65,000	Inventory		65,000
To record ending inventory:					
Inventory	70,000		Inventory	82,000	
Cost of Goods Sold		70,000	Cost of Goods Sold		82,000
To write down inventory to lower NRV:					
No entry			Loss on Inventory Due to Decline in NRV*	12,000	
			Allowance to Reduce Inventory to NRV		12,000

*A debit to Cost of Goods Sold is also acceptable. In either case, the debit would be presented as part of cost of goods sold.

Example 8.17 | Accounting for the Reduction of Inventory to NRV—Perpetual Inventory System

Facts Assume the information in Illustration 8.11. Assume further that the company uses a perpetual inventory system.

Instructions What are the journal entries using the direct method and the allowance method?

Solution

Direct Method			Indirect or Allowance Method		
To reduce inventory from cost to NRV:					
Cost of Goods Sold	12,000		Loss on Inventory Due to Decline in NRV*	12,000	
Inventory		12,000	Allowance to Reduce Inventory to NRV		12,000

*A debit to Cost of Goods Sold is also acceptable. In either case, the debit would be presented as part of cost of goods sold.

The advantage of identifying the loss due to the decline in net realizable value separately is that it may be reported separately. It thus clearly discloses the loss resulting from the market decline in inventory prices instead of burying it in the cost of goods sold. The advantage of using an allowance account is that inventory cost numbers are retained in both the Inventory control and subsidiary ledger accounts.

Although using an allowance account makes it possible to disclose the inventory at cost and at the lower of cost and NRV on the statement of financial position, it raises the problem of how to dispose of the new account balance in the following period. If the particular merchandise is still on hand, the allowance account should be retained. Otherwise, beginning inventory and cost of goods available for sale will be overstated. But if the goods have been sold, then the account should be closed. A new allowance account balance is then established for any decline in inventory value that exists at the end of the next accounting period.

Many accountants leave the allowance account on the books and merely adjust its balance at the next reporting date to agree with the difference between cost and the lower of cost and NRV at that time. If NRV is falling, a loss is recorded. If NRV is rising, a loss recorded in prior years is recovered and a gain (which is not really a gain, but a recovery of a previously recognized loss) is recorded, as shown in Illustration 8.12. The recovery amount is ordinarily recognized as a reduction in the cost of goods sold.

ILLUSTRATION 8.12   **Effect on Net Income of Adjustments to the Allowance Account**

Date	Inventory at Cost	Inventory at NRV	Amount Required in Allowance Account	Allowance Account before Adjustment	Adjustment of Allowance Account Balance	Effect on Net Income
Dec. 31/19	$188,000	$176,000	$12,000 cr.	$ –0–	$12,000 increase	Loss
Dec. 31/20	194,000	187,000	7,000 cr.	12,000 cr.	5,000 decrease	Gain
Dec. 31/21	173,000	174,000	–0–	7,000 cr.	7,000 decrease	Gain
Dec. 31/22	182,000	180,000	2,000 cr.	–0–	2,000 increase	Loss

Any net "gain" can be thought of as the excess of the credit effect of closing the beginning allowance balance over the debit effect of setting up the current year-end allowance account. Recovering the loss up to the original cost is permitted, **but it may not exceed the original cost**. That is, the Allowance account cannot have a debit balance.

Evaluation of the LC&NRV Principle

Measuring inventories at the LC&NRV has some conceptual and practical deficiencies. Recognizing net realizable values only when they are lower than cost is an inconsistent treatment that can lead to distortions in reported income. The accounting values that are reported are not neutral and unbiased measures of income and net assets. Also, because NRV is an estimate, company management has the opportunity to over- or underestimate realizable values, depending on the results it would like to report for the period. Others feel that any accounting method that arbitrarily transfers income from one period to another reduces the quality of earnings.

On the other hand, many financial statement users appreciate the lower of cost and net realizable value requirement because they know that inventory and income are not overstated. The real question is why we do not move to a full fair value method. If we can measure net realizable value, then clearly we should be able to measure fair value, whether it is above or below cost. We will look at the limited use of fair values in the next section.

Exceptions to Lower of Cost and Net Realizable Value

LEARNING OBJECTIVE 8

Identify inventories that are or may be valued at amounts other than the lower of cost and net realizable value.

Inventories Measured at Net Realizable Value

For most companies and in most situations, inventory is reported at the lower of cost and net realizable value. Some critics believe that inventory should always be valued at its **net realizable value** because that is the net amount that will be collected in cash from the inventory in the future. In certain restricted circumstances, it is possible to record inventory at its net realizable value even if that amount is above cost. The following criteria have to be met to value inventory above cost and for revenue to be recognized before the point of sale:

1. The sale is assured or there is an active market for the product and minimal risk of failure to sell.
2. The costs of disposal can be estimated.

In certain industries, items such as agricultural produce, forest products, and mineral products inventories may be accounted for at net realizable value in accordance with well-established industry practices.

Measurement at net realizable value may also be used when cost figures are too difficult to obtain. In some cases, minor marketable by-products are produced where the costs are indistinguishable. Instead of the company attempting a costly exercise of arbitrary cost allocation, the by-products are measured at the selling price of the by-products less any costs to bring them to market.

Inventories Measured at Fair Value Less Costs to Sell

Inventories of Commodity Broker-Traders and Similar Entities

Another exception to the lower of cost and net realizable value measurement standard is the inventory of commodity broker-traders and entities with similar business models that measure their inventories at **fair value less costs to sell**.[11] This inventory consists of such items as grain and livestock futures contracts. Changes in the fair value less costs to sell the inventory items are recognized in net income in the period of the change.

Glencore PLC, with operations in grain handling, agri-products, and agri-food processing, among others, reports such a policy in the notes to its 2017 financial statements. The note is shown in **Illustration 8.13**. Recall from Chapter 3 that, when measuring fair value, the inputs to the measurement are classified as levels 1, 2, or 3, with level 1 being the highest quality input and level 3 being the lowest quality input. The asset is then classified as a level 1, 2, or 3 asset based on the level of inputs used to measure fair value. You will note that the bulk of Glencore's inventory is measured at fair value less costs of disposal. In addition, these inventories are categorized as a level 2 fair value measurement.

Inventory Valued at Net Realizable Value—Glencore PLC

11. Inventories
Current inventory

Inventories of $24,084 million (2016: $18,347 million) comprise $15,344 million (2016: $11,323 million) of inventories carried at fair value less costs of disposal and $8,740 million (2016: $7,024 million) valued at the lower of cost or net realisable value. The amount of inventories and related ancillary costs recognised as an expense during the year was $185,371 million (2016: $137,903 million).

Fair value of inventories is a Level 2 fair value measurement (see note 27) using observable market prices obtained from exchanges, traded reference indices or market survey services adjusted for relevant location and quality differentials. There are no significant unobservable inputs in the fair value measurement of such inventories.

(continued)

---

[11]The entries to account for inventories carried at net realizable value are similar to those for assets carried at fair value less costs to sell. The changes in NRV are recognized in the Inventory account and in income in the period the NRV changes.

ILLUSTRATION 8.13

(continued)

Glencore has a number of dedicated financing facilities, which finance a portion of its inventories. In each case, the inventory has not been derecognised as the Group retains the principal risks and rewards of ownership. The proceeds received are recognised as current borrowings (see note 19). As at 31 December 2017, the total amount of inventory secured under such facilities was $435 million (2016: $1,632 million). The proceeds received and recognised as current borrowings were $221 million (2016: $1,320 million) and $80 million (2016: $61 million) as non-current borrowings.

Non-current inventory

$369 million (2016: $564 million) of inventories valued at lower of cost or net realisable value are not expected to be utilised or sold within 12 months and are therefore classified as non-current inventory.

Biological Assets and Agricultural Produce at Point of Harvest

There is often confusion about what is a biological asset, agricultural produce, and a product that results from processing after harvest.

Illustration 8.14 contains excerpts of examples from IAS 41 *Agriculture to* help clarify what is included as each type of asset.

ILLUSTRATION 8.14

Examples of Agricultural Activity Assets

Biological assets	Agricultural produce	Products that are the result of processing after harvest
Sheep	Wool	Yarn, carpet
Trees in a timber plantation	Felled trees	Logs, lumber
Dairy cattle	Milk	Cheese
Pigs	Carcass	Sausage, cured hams
Cotton plants	Harvested cotton	Thread, clothing
Sugarcane	Harvested cane	Sugar
Tobacco plants	Picked leaves	Cured tobacco
Tea bushes	Picked leaves	Tea
Grapevines	Picked grapes	Wine
Fruit trees	Picked fruit	Processed fruit
Oil palms	Picked fruit	Palm oil
Rubber trees	Harvested latex	Rubber products

Some plants—for example, tea bushes, grapevines, oil palms, and rubber trees—usually meet the definition of a bearer plant and are within the scope of IAS 16. However, the produce growing on bearer plants—for example, tea leaves, grapes, oil palm fruit, and latex—is within the scope of IAS 41.

ASPE Inventories of **biological assets** (living plants and animals) and products of the entity's biological assets (**agricultural produce**) at the point of harvest are excluded from the measurement requirements of ASPE for inventories if they are accounted for at NRV in accordance with well-established industry practices, as noted earlier. However, these inventories must follow the accounting requirements relating to expense recognition and disclosure. Otherwise, Section 3031 applies in full.

A review of the financial statements of many Canadian companies with such assets indicates that, historically, they tend to follow a lower of cost and net realizable value approach for the inventory. This is reasonable considering that this valuation corresponds closely to the primary source of GAAP for similar assets.

There is no guidance for biological assets such as the grapevines or olive trees themselves (that is, those assets that produce the inventory over a long period of time). They may be treated as property, plant, and equipment for accounting purposes.

IFRS Under IFRS, accounting for biological assets and agricultural produce at the point of harvest is covered in a separate standard: IAS 41 *Agriculture*. Similar to ASPE, those inventories that are measured at NRV in accordance with well-established industry practices do not fall under IAS 2 for measurement purposes.

Biological assets are measured at fair value less costs to sell under IAS 41. (See Underlying Concept 8.10.) Note that plants used to grow produce, including tea bushes, grapevines, and rubber trees, are called **bearer plants**. Because they produce saleable products such as tea or grapes each season, they are treated like property, plant, and equipment under IFRS. As such, they are accounted for using the cost or the revaluation method. We will cover these two methods in Chapters 10 and 11.

Otherwise, for all other agricultural produce at the point of harvest, such as grapes or picked fruit, the "fair value less costs to sell" measure is deemed to be the inventory's "cost" for purposes of subsequent accounting (and further processing, if applicable) under IAS 2 *Inventories*.[12]

Costs to raise or produce animals, such as livestock, may be capitalized to the Biological Assets account.[13] This is an accounting policy choice. If these costs are capitalized as the accounting policy choice, direct costs would be included, whereas more general costs would be expensed. In this manner, when revalued to fair value less costs to sell, the unrealized gain for instance will be net of the direct costs. The account Biological Assets, representing the fair value less selling costs of the livestock seems to have some of the characteristics of both inventory and plant and equipment assets. However, biological assets are classified as neither. They require separate disclosure on the statement of financial position under IFRS.

Example 8.18 looks at an example dealing with biological assets.

> **Underlying Concept 8.10**
>
> While revaluing the assets, unrealized gains/losses are generated. Once sold, the gains/losses become realized. This is an important distinction and should be disclosed under the full disclosure principle.

Example 8.18 | Accounting for Inventories at Fair Value Less Costs to Sell

Facts Assume that the enterprise is a farm that raises sheep for their wool (Woolright Limited). During the year, the following occurred:

1. A lamb was born (fair value less costs to sell: $500).
2. General farm expenses incurred were $200.
3. The value of lambs and other sheep increased by $700.
4. Wool valued at $100 was produced from the sheep.
5. Wool was sold for $100.

Instructions **IFRS** **ASPE**

a. Are the sheep biological assets? Is the wool?

b. What would the journal entries be for the transactions noted above? Assume that all amounts are paid in cash.

Solution

a. The sheep are biological assets. Lambs born into the existing flock are also biological assets. This is because they all meet the definition of biological assets, being living plants or animals (they are not bearer plants). Wool is an agricultural product since it is a by-product of the sheep.

---

[12]The IASB issued an amendment to IAS 41 in June 2014 effective for years beginning on or after January 1, 2016. Essentially, the amendment treats bearer plants like property, plant, and equipment; however, animals are still accounted for under IAS 41.

[13]IAS 41.B61 notes that the standard does not deal with how to account for expenditures related to biological assets. As previously discussed, ASPE provides no specific guidance at all. Therefore, there is a choice to capitalize or expense. In addition, there is judgement involved in determining which costs should be capitalized if this option is used. Inventory accounting would generally support direct costs and a reasonable allocation of overhead.

b. The journal entries follow.

	IFRS		ASPE*	
To record the birth of a lamb (fair value $500):				
Biological Assets	500		NA	
Unrealized Gain or Loss		500		
To record general farm expenses of $200:				
Supplies Expense	200		200	
Cash		200		200
To record an increase in value of lambs and other sheep of $700:				
Biological Assets	700		NA	
Unrealized Gain or Loss		700		
To record the wool inventory produced from the sheep (valued at $100):				
Inventory	100		NA	
Biological Assets		100		
To record the immediate sale of wool produced for $100:				
Cash	100		100	
Inventory		100		
Unrealized Gain or Loss	100			
Realized Gain or Loss		100		100

*ASPE does not offer any guidance. Therefore, as long as the accounting policy choice is supportable under the conceptual framework, companies following ASPE might use the same accounting as IFRS or perhaps use historical cost as a default. The above-noted accounting uses historical cost and recognizes gains/profits when realized (that is, when the wool is sold). The flock would have to be tested for impairment. In other words, how long will the sheep produce wool? Older sheep might not have the same value as younger sheep. Some interesting questions arise. If one animal dies, should we write off part of the flock? Alternatively, given that the flock is likely replenishing itself because new lambs are born as old animals die, is there a need to write anything down? There are no easy answers here and first principles must be applied as well as professional judgement. Care would also be taken to determine how significant the amounts are. If animals die, the company would have to write the balance down to recoverable or net realizable value if this was below cost. New sheep would not necessarily be recorded since they were not purchased; however, all costs directly attributable to getting the sheep ready to produce could be capitalized. Finally, it may be argued that direct costs of maintaining the sheep could also be capitalized. If this were done, we would have to be careful to set a limit on the total carrying value. In addition, if this were the case, we would likely have to recognize some costs when sold. The sale of the wool could also be recorded as Sales Revenue.

Let's see how a real-world company accounts for biological assets. **Canopy Growth Corporation** is a multi-brand cannabis company, which currently grows and sells medical marijuana and other related products. **Illustration 8.15** is taken from the notes to the 2017 financial statements, notes 4 (part) and 7.

ILLUSTRATION 8.15

Disclosures from Notes to the 2017 Financial Statements—Canopy Growth Corporation

FOR THE YEARS ENDED MARCH 31, 2017 AND 2016

(Expressed in CDN $000's except share amounts)

4(b) Biological assets

The Company measures biological assets consisting of medical cannabis plants at fair value less cost to sell up to the point of harvest, which becomes the basis for the cost of finished goods inventories after harvest. Seeds are measured at fair market value. Unrealized gains or losses arising from changes in fair value less cost to sell during the year are included in the results of operations of the related year.

7. BIOLOGICAL ASSETS AND INVENTORY

The Company's biological assets consists of seeds and medical cannabis plants. The continuity of biological assets for the years ended March 31, 2017 and 2016 was as follows:

	March 31, 2017	March 31, 2016
Balance, beginning of year	$ 5,321	$ 2,028
Purchase (use) of seeds	70	(92)
Acquired biological assets	1,691	1,799
Changes in fair value less costs to sell due to biological transformation	61,073	38,897
Transferred to inventory upon harvest	(53,430)	(37,311)
Balance, end of year	$ 14,725	$ 5,321

(*continued*)

ILLUSTRATION 8.15

(*continued*)

As at March 31, 2017, included in the carrying amount of biological assets was $377 in seeds and $14,348 in live plants ($275 in seeds and $5,046 in live plants as at March 31, 2016).

The significant assumptions used in determining the fair value of medical cannabis plants are as follows:

- wastage of plants based on their various stages;
- yield by strain of plant;
- percentage of costs incurred to date compared to the total costs to be incurred are used to estimate the fair value of an in-process plant; and
- percentage of costs incurred for each stage of plant growth was estimated.

On average, the grow cycle is 12 weeks. All of the plants are to be harvested as agricultural produce (i.e., medical cannabis) and as at March 31, 2017, on average, were 43% complete, compared to 45% average stage of completion as at March 31, 2016.

The Company estimates the harvest yields for the plants at various stages of growth. As of March 31, 2017, it is expected that the Company's biological assets will yield approximately 5,858 kg compared to 2,121 kg at March 31, 2016. The Company's estimates are, by their nature, subject to change. Changes in the anticipated yield will be reflected in future changes in the gain or loss on biological assets.

As at March 31, 2017, the Company held 8,360 kg of dry cannabis (377 kg of which was finished goods, 3,173 kg awaiting release for sale, and 4,810 kg held for future extract production) and 3,049 L of cannabis oils, compared to 4,447 kg of dry cannabis (1,198 kg of which was finished goods, 787 kg awaiting release for sale, and 2,462 held for future extract production) and 570 L of cannabis oils held at March 31, 2016.

Inventory was comprised of the following items:

	March 31, 2017	March 31, 2016
Dry Cannabis		
Finished goods	$ 2,980	$ 7,346
Work-in-process	33,418	12,669
	36,398	20,015
Cannabis Oils		
Finished goods	2,085	433
Work-in-process	5,492	1,331
	7,577	1,764
Seeds – Finished goods	74	-
	44,049	21,779
Product for resale (vaporizers and other)	515	172
Supplies and consumables	1,417	202
	$45,981	$22,153

The company notes the significant assumptions that must be made in order to value the biological assets as fair value less cost to sell, including growth stage, yield, and wastage. Since the plants have a 12-week growth cycle and are completely harvested, they are not considered bearer plants.

Measuring Inventory Using Estimates

LEARNING OBJECTIVE 9

Apply the gross profit method of estimating inventory.

The Need for Estimates

Recall that the basic purpose of taking a physical inventory is to verify the accuracy of the perpetual inventory records or, if there are no perpetual records, to arrive at an inventory amount. Sometimes, taking a physical inventory is impractical or impossible. In such cases, estimation methods are used to approximate inventory on hand. One such method is called the gross profit, or gross margin, method. This method is used in situations where (1) only an estimate of inventory is needed (for example, preparing interim reports or testing the reasonableness of the cost calculated by some other method), or where (2) inventory has been destroyed by fire or some other catastrophe. It may also be used to provide a rough check on the accuracy of a physical inventory count. For example, the estimated amount is compared with the physical count amount to see if they are reasonably close; if they are not, the reason for the difference is investigated.

Another method that is widely used with retail inventories is the retail inventory method. Like the gross profit method, it depends on establishing a relationship between selling (retail) prices and cost. Appendix 8A discusses the retail inventory method in detail.

Gross Profit Method

The **gross profit method** is based on three premises:

1. The beginning inventory plus purchases equals the **cost of goods available for sale**.
2. Goods not included in cost of goods sold must be on hand **in ending inventory**.
3. When an estimate of cost of goods sold is deducted from the cost of goods available for sale, the result is an estimate of ending inventory.

Example 8.19 provides an illustration of this method.

Example 8.19 | Application of Gross Profit Method

Facts   Assume that a company has a beginning inventory of $60,000 and purchases of $200,000, both at cost. Sales at selling price amount to $280,000. The gross profit on the selling price is 30%.

Instructions   What is the estimated inventory?

Solution   The calculation below walks you through the gross profit method of estimating ending inventory.[14]

Beginning inventory (at cost)		$ 60,000
Purchases (at cost)		200,000
Goods available for sale (at cost)		260,000
Sales (at selling price)	$280,000	
Less: Gross profit (30% of $280,000)	84,000	
Sales at cost = Estimated cost of goods sold		196,000
Estimated inventory (at cost)		$ 64,000

---

[14]An alternative approach to estimating inventory using the gross profit percentage, considered by some to be less complicated than the method in Example 8.19, uses the standard income statement format as follows (assume the same data as in Example 8.19):

	Step 1			Step 2	
Sales		$280,000			$280,000
Cost of goods sold					
Beginning inventory	$ 60,000			$ 60,000	
Purchases	200,000			200,000	
Goods available for sale	260,000			260,000	
Ending inventory	(3) ?			(3) 64,000 Est.	
Cost of goods sold (2) ?		(2) ?			(2) 196,000 Est.
Gross profit on sales (30%)		(1) ?			(1) $84,000 Est.

Calculate the unknowns as follows: first the gross profit amount, then cost of goods sold, and then the ending inventory.

1. $280,000 × 30% = $84,000 (gross profit on sales)
2. $280,000 − $84,000 = $196,000 (cost of goods sold)
3. $260,000 − $196,000 = $64,000 (ending inventory)

Note that the estimated cost of goods sold could also have been calculated directly as 70% of sales; that is, 100% less 30%. The cost of goods sold percentage is always the complement of the gross profit percentage. That is, the cost of goods sold percentage plus the gross profit percentage add up to 100%.

All the information needed to estimate the inventory at cost, except for the gross profit percentage, is available in the current period's accounting records. The gross profit percentage is determined by reviewing company policies and the records of prior periods. The percentage is adjusted if the prior periods are not considered representative of the current period.

Gross Profit Percentage Versus Markup on Cost

In most situations, the **gross profit percentage** is used and it is the gross profit as a percentage of the selling price. (See **Alternative Terminology 8.1**.) Example 8.19, for example, used a 30% gross profit on sales. Gross profit on selling price is the common method for quoting the profit for several reasons.

1. Most goods are stated on a retail basis, not a cost basis.
2. A profit quoted on the selling price is lower than one based on cost, and this lower rate gives a favourable impression to the consumer.
3. The gross profit based on selling price can never exceed 100%.

In Example 8.19, the percentage was given to you. But how was that figure derived? **Example 8.20** looks at this issue.

> **Alternative Terminology 8.1**
>
> The terms "gross profit percentage," "gross margin percentage," "rate of gross profit," and "rate of gross margin" mean the same thing: they all reflect the relationship of gross profit to the selling price. The terms "percentage markup" or "rate of markup" are used to describe the relationship of gross profit to cost. It is important to understand the difference.

 Video

Example 8.20 | Gross Profit Percentage Versus Percentage of Markup on Cost

Facts   Assume that an article cost $15.00 and sells for $20.00, a gross profit of $5.00.

Instructions   What is the gross profit percentage? What is the markup? *Hint:* Do two calculations, one based on selling price and one based on cost.

Solution

$$\frac{\text{Gross profit}}{\text{Selling price}} = \frac{\$5.00}{\$20.00} = 25\% \text{ of selling price} \qquad \frac{\text{Gross profit}}{\text{Cost}} = \frac{\$5.00}{\$15.00} = 33\frac{1}{3}\% \text{ of cost}$$

This markup of $5.00 is one quarter or 25% of the selling (or retail) price but is one third or 33⅓% of cost.

Although gross profit is based on sales, you should understand the relationship between this ratio and the percentage of **markup on cost**. **Example 8.21** examines this in more detail.

Example 8.21 | Markup on Cost

Facts   Assume that you were told that the **markup on cost** for a specific item is 25% and that the item's selling price is $1.00.

Instructions
   a. What is the gross profit on selling price?
   b. What is the dollar amount of the markup?

Solution
   a. The following formula applies:

$$\text{Cost} + \text{Gross profit} = \text{Selling price}$$
$$C + .25C = \$1.00$$
$$1.25C = \$1.00$$
$$C = \$0.80$$

The amount of gross profit is $0.20 ($1.00 − $0.80), and the rate of gross profit on selling price is 20% ($0.20/$1.00).

b. The dollar amount of the markup is also $0.20.

Assume that we do not know the markup on cost, but we know, instead, the gross profit percentage (20%). To find the dollar amount of the markup, the same formula can be used.

$$\text{Cost} + \text{Gross profit} = \text{Selling price}$$
$$C + .20\,(\$1.00) = \$1.00$$
$$C + \$0.20 = \$1.00$$
$$C = \$0.80$$

The amount of the markup or gross profit is $0.20 ($1.00 − $0.80), and the percentage markup on cost is 25% ($0.20/$0.80).

Retailers use the formulas in **Illustration 8.16** to express these relationships.

ILLUSTRATION 8.16

Formulas Relating to Gross Profit

1. Percent gross profit on selling price $= \dfrac{\text{Percent markup on cost}}{100\% + \text{Percent markup on cost}}$

2. Percent markup on cost $= \dfrac{\text{Percent gross profit on selling price}}{100\% - \text{Percent gross profit on selling price}}$

Evaluation of the Gross Profit Method

What are the disadvantages of using the gross profit method? There are several.

1. The gross profit method **provides an estimate** only.
2. The gross profit method uses **past percentages** in determining the markup. Although the future may repeat the past, a current rate is usually more appropriate. Whenever fluctuations in the rate of profit occur, the percentage must be adjusted appropriately.
3. **It may be inappropriate to apply a single gross profit rate.** Often, a store or department handles merchandise with very different rates of gross profit. In these situations, the gross profit method may have to be applied by type of merchandise, or by combining merchandise with similar profit margins.

Because the result is only an estimate, the gross profit method is **not normally acceptable for financial reporting purposes**. A physical inventory is needed as an additional verification that the inventory indicated in the records is actually on hand. Nevertheless, the gross profit method is used to estimate ending inventory for **interim** (monthly and quarterly) **reporting** and for **insurance purposes** (such as fire losses). Note that the results of applying the gross profit method will reflect the inventory method that is used (specific identification, FIFO, or an average cost method) because this method is based on historical records.

Presentation, Disclosure, and Analysis

LEARNING OBJECTIVE 10

Identify how inventory should be presented, disclosed, and analyzed.

Presentation and Disclosure of Inventories

Sometimes there is a fine line between what is considered to be inventory and what is better classified as property, plant, and equipment. Minor spare parts and servicing equipment, for example, are usually classified as inventory. Major spare parts and standby equipment, on the other hand, are recognized as capital assets if they are expected to provide benefits beyond the current accounting period. The classification issue often requires the exercise of professional judgement. In addition, as previously mentioned in this chapter, certain biological assets referred to as bearer plants are classified as property, plant, and equipment.

Inventories are one of the most significant assets of manufacturing and merchandising companies, and of many service enterprises. For this reason, companies are required to disclose additional information about these resources.

Some disclosures are similar to the ones required for other statement of financial position items:

- the choice of accounting policies adopted to measure the inventory;
- the carrying amount of the inventory in total and by classification (such as supplies, material, work in process, and finished goods);
- the amount of inventories recognized as an expense in the period, including unabsorbed and abnormal amounts of production overheads; and
- the carrying amount of inventory pledged as collateral for liabilities.

The amount of inventory recognized as an expense is usually reported according to its function—as cost of goods sold. However, a company that chooses to present its expenses according to the nature of its costs instead of by function would present expenses for raw materials and consumables used, labour costs, and other expenses along with the change in inventories for the period.

IFRS **Additional disclosures** are required for inventories **under IFRS**. These include the carrying amount of inventory carried at fair value less costs to sell, and details about inventory writedowns and reversals of writedowns, such as information about what led to the reversal of any writedowns. Considerable information is required in addition for biological assets and agricultural produce at the point of harvest, such as a reconciliation of opening to ending account balances.

Note also that IAS 1 requires the disclosure of any judgements used in applying accounting policies as well as sources of estimation uncertainty in measuring financial statement elements.

The excerpt in **Illustration 8.17** is taken from note 4(q) of the 2017 financial statements of **Canopy Growth Corporation**. The partial excerpt illustrates the company's disclosure of its critical accounting estimates and judgements relating to determining the value of biological assets and related inventory (once harvested).

ILLUSTRATION 8.17

Disclosures from Notes to the 2017 Financial Statements— Canopy Growth Corporation— Critical Accounting Estimates and Judgements

Biological assets and inventory

In calculating the value of the biological assets and inventory, management is required to make a number of estimates, including estimating the stage of growth of the cannabis up to the point of harvest, harvesting costs, selling costs, sales price, wastage and expected yields for the cannabis plant. In calculating final inventory values, management is required to determine an estimate of spoiled or expired inventory and compares the inventory cost to estimated net realizable value.

Analysis

Finance 5.1.1 Financial ratios can be used to help management make decisions about how much and what types of inventory to carry and to help investors assess management's performance in terms of controlling inventory to maximize profits. Common ratios that are used to evaluate inventory levels are the inventory turnover and a related measure: average days to sell (or average age of) the inventory.

The **inventory turnover ratio** measures the number of times on average that the inventory was sold during the period. This ratio helps to measure the liquidity of the investment in inventory because the faster the turnover, the sooner the company generates cash inflows from this asset. A manager may use past turnover experience to determine how long the inventory now in stock will take to be sold. This ratio is calculated by dividing the cost of goods sold by the average inventory on hand during the period. Average inventory can be calculated from the beginning and ending inventory balances.[16] A closely related ratio is the **average days to sell inventory**, which represents the average age of the inventory on hand or the number of days it takes to sell inventory after it is acquired. **Example 8.22** looks at calculating inventory turnover ratios.

Example 8.22 | Inventory Turnover Ratio

Facts   **Hudson's Bay Company** reported beginning inventory of $3,404 million, ending inventory of $3,376 million, and cost of goods sold of $8,481 million for its 2017 fiscal year.

Instructions   What is the inventory turnover for 2017?

Solution   The calculation of HBC's 2017 inventory turnover is shown below.

$$\text{Inventory turnover} = \text{Cost of goods sold/Average inventory}$$
$$= \$8,481/[(\$3,376 + \$3,404)/2]$$
$$= 2.5 \text{ times}$$

For example, if HBC's inventory turns over 2.5 times per year, that means it takes, on average, 365 days divided by 2.5 or approximately 146 days to sell its investment in inventory.

Is this a good turnover ratio? If the company sells fresh fruit and vegetables, you would know that this is not a good number. However, for other products, it is not as easy to come to a firm conclusion. For example, HBC sells a wide range of household goods and fashion items so you might expect that it would move its inventory out faster than only every four to five months. Each industry has its norms, however, so the industry average is one standard that the company's ratio can be compared against. Because the choice of inventory cost formula may affect the inventory reported on the statement of financial position and the cost of goods sold, these differences make adjustments necessary in any intercompany comparisons. This is true not only for turnover ratios but for any analysis that includes inventory: the amount of working capital, the working capital ratio, and the gross profit percentage, for example. Internally, company management compares these numbers with its goals and objectives for the year.

There is no absolute standard of comparison for most ratios, but generally speaking, companies that are able to keep their inventory at lower levels with higher turnovers than those of their competitors, and still satisfy customer needs, are the most successful.

IFRS/ASPE Comparison

LEARNING OBJECTIVE 11

Identify differences in accounting between IFRS and ASPE, and what changes are expected in the near future.

A Comparison of IFRS and ASPE

The *CPA Canada Handbook*, Part II, Section 3031 *Inventories* is converged with IAS 2 *Inventories*. Therefore, there are few differences in the recognition and measurement standards for most inventories. The most significant difference is that there is a separate international

---

[16]Some seasonal variation is common in most companies. Fiscal year ends are usually chosen at a low activity point in the year's operations, which means that inventories in the annual financial statements are at their lowest levels in the year. Management can make adjustments to use the average monthly inventory level. External users, however, are limited to using the average between the opening and closing annual inventory balances. Public companies are required to issue quarterly reports, so external users can base the average on four inventory amounts through the year.

standard (IAS 41) covering biological assets and agricultural produce at the point of harvest, and these assets are not specifically covered by ASPE. **Illustration 8.18** identifies the differences between IFRS and ASPE.

ILLUSTRATION 8.18 **IFRS and ASPE Comparison Chart**

	IFRS—IAS 2, 11, 23, and 41	Accounting Standards for Private Enterprises (ASPE)—*CPA Canada Handbook*, Part II, Sections 3031 and 3850	References Related to Examples, Illustrations, and Select Brief Exercises
Scope	IAS 41 provides standards for biological assets and agricultural produce at the point of harvest.	There is no primary source of GAAP covering biological assets and agricultural produce at the point of harvest.	Illustrations 8.14, 8.15, and 8.17 Example 8.18
Measurement	Asset retirement and decommissioning costs arising from production activities are added to the cost of the inventory.	Asset retirement and decommissioning costs arising from production activities are added to the carrying amount of the property, plant, and equipment asset.	Discussed in further detail in Chapter 10.
	Interest costs directly attributable to the acquisition, construction, or production of qualifying inventory are capitalized. Such costs may be expensed for inventory measured at fair value and for qualifying inventory produced in large quantities on a repetitive basis.	Companies may choose a policy of capitalizing interest or a policy of expensing the costs. No guidance is provided on what is a qualifying asset.	BE8.13
	A liability and loss are required to be recognized for onerous contracts if the unavoidable costs exceed the benefits from receiving the contracted goods or services.	No guidance is provided for onerous contractual obligations such as may occur with purchase commitments.	Example 8.2 BE 8.10
	Biological assets and agricultural produce at the point of harvest are measured at fair value less costs to sell. At harvest, this becomes the inventory's deemed cost, and subsequently it is accounted for at the lower of cost and NRV unless it is accounted for at NRV in accordance with well-established practices in industry (and is therefore not covered by IAS 2). Bearer plants are accounted for under IAS 16. Once the biological assets are harvested from the bearer plants, the harvest becomes inventory and is accounted for as noted above (either under IAS 2 or at NRV).	No guidance is provided for measuring biological assets and agricultural produce prior to and at the point of harvest. After harvest, its carrying amount becomes the inventory's deemed cost, and subsequently it is accounted for at the lower of (the deemed) cost and net realizable value (NRV) unless it is accounted for at NRV in accordance with well-established practices in industry (and it is therefore not covered by Section 3031).	Illustrations 8.14, 8.15, and 8.17 Example 8.18 BE 8.19 and 8.20
Presentation and disclosure	Additional disclosures are required, particularly about writedowns and any reversals as well as critical judgements and sources of estimation uncertainty. In addition, significant information is required about biological assets and agricultural produce.	Limited disclosures are required.	Illustrations 8.15 and 8.17 BE 8.23

Looking Ahead

No major changes were expected in the general inventory standards in the near future.

Appendix 8A | # The Retail Inventory Method of Estimating Inventory Cost

LEARNING OBJECTIVE 12
Apply the retail method of estimating inventory.

Accounting for inventory in a retail operation presents several challenges. Some retailers can use the specific identification method to value their inventories. As explained in the chapter, this approach makes sense when individual inventory unit costs are significant, such as for automobiles, pianos, or fur coats. However, imagine attempting to use such an approach at Hudson's Bay or Walmart—high-volume retailers that have many different types of merchandise at relatively low unit costs! It would be difficult to determine the cost of each sale, to enter cost codes on the tickets, to change the codes to reflect declines in value of the merchandise, to allocate costs such as transportation, and so on. An alternative is to estimate inventory cost when necessary by taking a physical inventory at retail prices. Also, to avoid misstating the inventory, especially in retail operations where losses due to shoplifting and breakage are common, periodic inventory counts are made at retail prices and are then converted to cost. Differences between the records and the physical count require an adjustment to make the records agree with the count.

In most retail businesses, there is an observable pattern between cost and selling prices. Retail prices can be converted to cost simply by multiplying them by the cost-to-retail ratio. This method, called the **retail inventory method**, requires that the following information be available:

1. the total cost and retail value of the goods purchased,
2. the total cost and retail value of the goods available for sale, and
3. the sales for the period.

Here is how it works. The sales for the period are deducted from the retail value of the goods available for sale. The result is an estimate of the ending inventory at retail (selling prices). The ratio of cost to retail for all goods is calculated by dividing the total goods available for sale at cost by the total goods available for sale at retail. The ending inventory valued at selling prices is then converted to the ending inventory at cost by applying the **cost-to-retail ratio**.

Use of the retail inventory method historically was very common in preparing financial statements. For example, **Empire Company Limited**, a retailer with its roots in Eastern Canada, reports using the retail inventory method in determining inventory cost. Empire Company Limited's note disclosure of its policy for the year ended May 6, 2017, is shown in **Illustration 8A.1**.

ILLUSTRATION 8A.1

Example of Retail Inventory Method Note—Empire Company Limited—Note 3(e) (in part)

(e) Inventories

Warehouse inventories are valued at the lower of cost and net realizable value with cost being determined on a weighted average cost basis. Retail inventories are valued at the lower of cost and net realizable value. Cost is determined using a weighted average cost using either the standard cost method or retail method. The retail method uses the anticipated selling price less normal profit margins, on a weighted average cost basis. The cost of inventories is comprised of directly attributable costs and includes the purchase price plus other costs incurred

(continued)

in bringing the inventories to their present location and condition, such as freight. The cost is reduced by the value of rebates and allowances received from vendors. The Company estimates net realizable value as the amount that inventories are expected to be sold taking into consideration fluctuations of retail price due to seasonality less estimated costs necessary to make the sale. Inventories are written down to net realizable value when the cost of inventories is not estimated to be recoverable due to obsolescence, damage or permanent declines in selling prices. When circumstances that previously caused inventories to be written down below cost no longer exist or when there is clear evidence of an increase in retail selling price, the amount of the write-down previously recorded is reversed. Costs that do not contribute to bringing inventories to their present location and condition, such as storage and administrative overheads, are specifically excluded from the cost of inventories and are expensed in the period incurred.

An example of how the retail inventory method works is shown in **Illustration 8A.2**.

	Cost	Retail
Beginning inventory	$14,000	$ 20,000
Purchases	63,000	90,000
Goods available for sale	$77,000	110,000
Deduct: Sales		85,000
Ending inventory, at retail		$ 25,000
Ratio of cost to retail ($77,000 ÷ $110,000)		70%
Ending inventory at cost (70% of $25,000)		$ 17,500

The retail method is approved by various retail associations and the accounting profession under both ASPE and IFRS. It is also allowed by the Canada Revenue Agency. One advantage of the retail inventory method is that the inventory balance can be approximated without a physical count. This makes the method particularly useful when preparing interim reports. Insurance adjusters use this approach to estimate losses from fire, flood, or other types of casualty.

This method also **acts as a control device** because any deviations from a physical count at year end have to be explained. In addition, the retail method speeds up the physical inventory count at year end. The crew taking the inventory needs to record only the retail price of each item, which is often done using a scanner. There is no need to determine each item's invoice cost, thus saving time and expense.

Retail Method Terminology

The amounts shown in the Retail column of Illustration 8A.2 represent the original retail or selling prices (cost plus an original markup or mark-on), assuming no price changes.

Sales prices, however, are often marked up or down from the original sales price. For retailers, the term **markup** means an increase in the price above the original sales price. **Markup cancellations** are decreases in merchandise prices that had been marked up above the original retail price. Markup cancellations cannot be greater than markups. **Net markups** are markups less markup cancellations.

Markdowns are reductions in price below the original selling price. They are a common phenomenon and occur because of a decline in general price levels, special sales, soiled or damaged goods, overstocking, and competition. **Markdown cancellations** occur when the markdowns are later offset by increases in the prices of goods that had been marked down, such as after a one-day sale. A markdown cancellation cannot exceed the original markdown. Markdowns less markdown cancellations are known as **net markdowns**.

Example 8A.1 illustrates the concepts.

Example 8A.1 | Retail Inventory Method

Facts   Assume that Designer Clothing Store recently purchased 100 dress shirts from a supplier. The cost for these shirts was $1,500, or $15 a shirt. Designer Clothing established the selling price on these shirts at $30 each. The manager noted that the shirts were selling quickly, so she added $5 to the price of each shirt. This made the price too high for customers and sales lagged. The manager then responded by reducing the price to $32. When the major marketing season ended, the manager set the price of the remaining shirts at $23.

Instructions   What are the markups, markdowns, markup cancellations, and markdown cancellations?

Solution   The first increase in selling price is a **markup** of $5. The reduction in price to $32 is a **markup cancellation** of $3. The next change in price to $23 constitutes a **markup cancellation** of $2 and a $7 **markdown**. If the shirts are later priced at $24, a **markdown cancellation** of $1 occurs.

To illustrate the retail method, consider the data for In-Fashion Stores Inc., shown in Example 8A.2.

Example 8A.2 | Retail Inventory Method with Markups and Markdowns

Facts   Assume the following for In-Fashion Stores Inc.

Information in Records		
	Cost	**Retail**
Beginning inventory	$ 500	$ 1,000
Purchases (net)	20,000	35,000
Markups		3,000
Markup cancellations		1,000
Markdowns		2,500
Markdown cancellations		2,000
Sales (net)		25,000

Instructions
  a. What is the cost-to-retail ratio?
  b. What is the ending inventory?

Solution

Retail Inventory Method			
	Cost		**Retail**
a. Beginning inventory	$ 500		$ 1,000
Purchases (net)	20,000		35,000
Merchandise available for sale	20,500		36,000
Add: Markups		$ 3,000	
Less: Markup cancellations		(1,000)	
Net markups			2,000
	20,500		38,000
Deduct:			
Markdowns		2,500	
Less: Markdown cancellations		(2,000)	
Net markdowns			(500)
	$20,500		37,500

Cost-to-retail ratio $\dfrac{\$20,500}{\$37,500} = 54.7\%$

b. Deduct: Sales (net)		25,000
Ending inventory at retail		$12,500

The cost of ending inventory for In-Fashion Stores is therefore $12,500 × 54.7% = $6,837.50.

In calculating cost-to-retail ratios, the inventory cost formula should be considered. **Illustration 8A.3** summarizes how including or excluding various items in the cost-to-retail ratio relates to specific inventory valuation methods. Note that net purchases are always included in the ratio.

ILLUSTRATION 8A.3

What to Include in Inventory Cost Formula Under the Retail Method

Beginning Inventory	Net Markups	Net Markdowns	Inventory Cost Formula
Include	Include	Include	Average cost
Exclude	Include	Include	FIFO cost

Using the FIFO cost formula, the estimated ending inventory (and its cost) will, by definition, come from the purchases of the current period. Therefore, the opening inventory, at cost and retail, is excluded in determining the cost ratio. The retail price of the opening inventory is then added to determine the total selling price of goods available for the period.

CPA Canada Handbook, Part II, Section 3031 and IAS 2 are clear that, for purposes of determining inventory **cost**, markdowns below the original sales price are included in calculating the ratio. This means that a separate adjustment has to be made to get a lower of cost and **NRV** valuation.

Special Items

The retail inventory method becomes more complicated when such items as freight in, purchase returns and allowances, and purchase discounts are involved. In the retail method, we treat such items as follows:

- **Freight costs** are treated as a part of the purchase cost.
- **Purchase returns** are ordinarily considered a reduction of the cost price and retail price.
- **Purchase allowances** are considered a reduction of the purchase cost only unless normal selling prices are adjusted because of the allowance.
- **Purchase discounts** are usually considered a reduction of the purchase cost only.

In short, the treatment for the items affecting the cost column of the retail inventory approach follows the calculation of cost of goods available for sale.

Note also that it is considered proper to treat **sales returns and allowances** as adjustments to gross sales.

In addition, a number of special items require careful analysis.

- **Transfers in** from another department are reported in the same way as purchases from an outside enterprise.
- **Normal shortages** (breakage, damage, theft, shrinkage) are deducted in the retail column because these goods are no longer available for sale. These costs are reflected in the selling price because a certain amount of shortage is considered normal in a retail enterprise. As a result, this amount is not considered in calculating the cost-to-retail percentage. Rather, it is shown as a deduction, similar to sales, to arrive at ending inventory at retail.
- **Abnormal shortages** are deducted from both the cost and retail columns before calculating the cost-to-retail ratio and are reported as a special inventory amount or as a loss. To do otherwise distorts the cost-to-retail ratio and overstates ending inventory.
- **Employee discounts** (given to employees to encourage loyalty, better performance, and so on) are deducted from the retail column in the same way as sales. These discounts should not be considered in the cost-to-retail percentage because they do not reflect an overall change in the selling price.

Illustration 8A.4 shows some of these concepts in more detail.

	Cost	Retail
Beginning inventory	$ 1,000	$ 1,800
Purchases	30,000	60,000
Freight in	600	-0-
Purchase returns	(1,500)	(3,000)
Totals	30,100	58,800
Net markups		9,000
Abnormal shrinkage	(1,200)	(2,000)
		65,800
Deduct:		
Net markdowns		(1,400)
Totals	$28,900	64,400
Sales	$36,000	
Sales returns	(900)	35,100
Employee discounts		800
Normal shrinkage		1,300
Ending inventory at retail		$ 27,200
Cost-to-retail ratio $28,900/$64,400 = 44.9%		
Ending inventory, LC&NRV (44.9% × $27,200)		$12,212.80

Evaluation of Retail Inventory Method

The retail inventory method of calculating inventory is used for these reasons:

1. To permit the calculation of net income without a physical count of inventory
2. As a control measure in determining inventory shortages
3. To control quantities of merchandise on hand
4. As a source of information for insurance and tax purposes
5. As a technique for estimating cost in financial statements (as long as the results estimate actual cost)

One characteristic of the retail inventory method is that it **has an averaging effect for varying rates of gross profit**. When it is used in a business where rates of gross profit vary among departments, the method should be refined by calculating inventory separately by departments or by classes of merchandise with similar rates of gross profit. This method's reliability rests on the assumption that the mix of inventory items is similar to the mix in the total goods available for sale.

A final note: as more sophisticated accounting systems (including technology to track physical inventory) are increasingly used, the need for estimation techniques such as the retail method should decrease over time. Many systems today can easily track costs, physical inventory, and selling prices (which include markups and markdowns).

Appendix 8B | Accounting Guidance for Specific Inventory

LEARNING OBJECTIVE 13

Identify other primary sources of GAAP for inventory.

Illustration 8B.1 summarizes the primary sources of GAAP for most types of inventory.

**Inventory—Primary Sources
of GAAP**

Form of Inventory	ASPE Source of Guidance	IFRS Source of Guidance
Most inventories apply a lower of cost and net realizable value model	*CPA Canada Handbook—Accounting*, Part II, Section 3031 *Inventories*	IAS 2 *Inventories*
Excluded from Section 3031 and IAS 2 but Covered by Other Primary Sources of GAAP		
Financial instruments	*CPA Canada Handbook—Accounting*, Part II, Section 3856 *Financial Instruments*	IAS 32 *Financial Instruments: Presentation* and IFRS 9 *Financial Instruments*
Biological assets related to agricultural activity, and agricultural produce at the point of harvest	See below.	IAS 41 *Agriculture*
Industry-Specific Exclusions, from Only the Measurement Provisions of Section 3031 and IAS 2 (disclosure requirements still apply)		
Inventory held by producers of agricultural and forest products, agricultural produce after harvest, and minerals and mineral products	Excluded from the measurement provisions of Section 3031 if measured at net realizable value in accordance with established industry practice; otherwise, apply Section 3031.	Excluded from the measurement provisions of IAS 2 if measured at net realizable value in accordance with established industry practice; otherwise, apply IAS 2.
Inventory held by commodity broker-traders	Excluded from the measurement provisions of Section 3031 if measured at fair value less costs to sell; otherwise, apply Section 3031.	Excluded from the measurement provisions of IAS 2 if measured at fair value less costs to sell; otherwise, apply IAS 2.
Biological assets and harvested agricultural produce	Excluded from the measurement provisions of Section 3031. Not covered by any specific primary source of GAAP.	See above.

Review and Practice

Summary of Learning Objectives

1. Understand inventory from a business perspective.

It is important to understand the nature of the various types of businesses that have significant inventory as well as the different types of inventory. Retailers, manufacturers, and wholesalers generally carry significant amounts of inventory. However, different companies have different business models. For example, some manufacturers follow a just-in-time strategy and carry very little inventory on hand. Only one inventory account, Merchandise Inventory, appears in the financial statements of a merchandising concern. A manufacturer normally has three inventory accounts: Raw Materials, Work in Process, and Finished Goods. There may also be an inventory account for factory or manufacturing supplies. Management must manage inventory levels in order to ensure sufficient choice and quantities to meet customer needs yet keep costs to a minimum. The financial statements need to provide information about all of this.

2. Identify which inventory items should be included in ending inventory.

Differing companies have different types of inventories including such things as securities, land for development, work in progress, and grain. For accounting purposes, inventory is defined as an asset that is held for sale in the ordinary course of business or for the production of such inventory (including raw materials, work in process, and supplies). Special guidance and/or industry practice exists for inventories of financial instruments, biological assets, agricultural products, mineral products, inventories held by producers of agricultural and forest products, and inventories held by commodity broker-traders.

Inventory is included on the statement of financial position of the entity that has substantially all of the risks and rewards of ownership, which is generally the company that has possession and legal title to the goods. Professional judgement must be used to determine whether substantially all of the risks and rewards have passed. For instance, consigned goods remain the property of the consignor. Purchase commitments are generally not recognized unless onerous.

3. Identify the effects of inventory errors on the financial statements and adjust for them.

If the ending inventory is misstated, (1) inventory, retained earnings, working capital, and current ratio in the statement of financial position will be incorrect; and (2) cost of goods sold and net income in the income statement will be incorrect. If both purchases and inventory are misstated, (1) inventory, accounts payable, and current ratio will be incorrect; and (2) purchases and ending inventory will be incorrect.

4. Determine the components of inventory cost.

Inventory costs include all costs of purchase, conversion, and other costs incurred in bringing the inventories to the present location and condition necessary for sale. Such charges include freight charges on goods purchased, other direct costs of acquisition, and labour and other direct production costs incurred in processing the goods up to the time of sale. Manufacturing overhead costs are allocated to inventory based on the normal capacity of the production facilities. Interest and asset retirement costs may be included as part of the cost of inventory in some circumstances.

5. Distinguish between perpetual and periodic inventory systems and account for them.

Under a perpetual inventory system, a continuous record of changes in inventory is maintained in the Inventory account. That is, all purchases into and transfers of goods out of the account are recorded directly in the Inventory account as they occur. No such record is kept under a periodic inventory system. Under the periodic system, year-end inventory is determined by a physical count, and the amount of ending inventory and cost of goods sold is based on this count. Even under the perpetual system, an annual count is needed to test the accuracy of the records.

6. Identify and apply GAAP cost formula options and indicate when each cost formula is appropriate.

The specific identification method is used to assign costs for items of inventory that are not ordinarily interchangeable or that are produced for specific projects. The weighted average or first-in, first-out cost formula is used to assign costs to other types of inventory. All inventory items that have a similar nature and use to the entity apply the same cost formula.

7. Explain why inventory is measured at the lower of cost and net realizable value, and apply the lower of cost and net realizable value principle.

Current assets should not be reported on the statement of financial position at a higher amount than the net cash that is expected to be generated from their use or sale. When this amount is less than "cost," inventory is written down and the loss in value is recognized in the same period as the decline. Net realizable value is the estimated selling price in the ordinary course of business reduced by the expected costs to complete and sell the goods. Ordinarily, each item's cost and NRV are compared and the lower value is chosen. However, items that are related to each other and have similar purposes, that are produced and marketed in the same geographical area, and that cannot be evaluated separately from other items may be grouped and the lower of the group's cost and net realizable value is chosen.

8. Identify inventories that are or may be valued at amounts other than the lower of cost and net realizable value.

Inventories of financial instruments, biological assets related to agricultural activity, agricultural produce at the point of harvest and after harvest, inventories held by producers of agricultural and forest products, mineral products, and inventories of commodity broker-traders all may be accounted for at other than the lower of cost and net realizable value.

9. Apply the gross profit method of estimating inventory.

Ending inventory is determined by deducting an estimate of cost of goods sold from the actual cost of goods available for sale. Cost of goods sold is estimated by multiplying net sales by the percentage of cost of goods sold to sales. This percentage is derived from the gross profit percent: 100% – gross profit percentage = cost of goods sold percentage.

10. Identify how inventory should be presented, disclosed, and analyzed.

ASPE requires disclosure of how cost is determined, inventory that is pledged as security, the amount charged to the income statement as expense in the period, and the inventories' carrying value by category. Additional information is required by IFRS, including details about inventory impairment writedowns and any recoveries, the circumstances responsible for these, and the carrying amounts and reconciliations of items measured at NRV or fair value. Biological assets must be presented separately on the statement of financial position under IFRS. In general, cost of sales is presented on the income statement under both IFRS and ASPE unless expenses are grouped by nature.

Common ratios that are used in the management and evaluation of inventory levels are the inventory turnover and a related measure, average days to sell the inventory, often called the average age of inventory. This is useful information because excessive investment in inventory is expensive to carry, yet too little inventory results in lost sales and dissatisfied customers.

11. Identify differences in accounting between IFRS and ASPE, and what changes are expected in the near future.

IFRS and ASPE are substantially harmonized. IFRS has specific guidance on the measurement of biological assets, the capitalization of borrowing costs on qualifying assets, and onerous contracts. Asset retirement obligations may be treated differently under IFRS. No major changes are expected in the near future.

<table>
<tr><td>

12. Apply the retail method of estimating inventory.

</td><td>

costs and retail prices for beginning inventory, net purchases, and abnormal spoilage, as well as the retail amount of net markups, net markdowns, and net sales.

</td></tr>
</table>

The retail inventory method is based on converting the retail price of ending inventory to an estimate of cost by a cost-to-retail percentage, which is derived from information in the accounting and supplementary records. To use this method, records must be kept of the

13. Identify other primary sources of GAAP for inventory.

The primary sources of GAAP for inventory are listed in Illustration 8B.1.

Practice Problem 8.1

Mayhew Limited has the following inventory, purchases, and sales data for the month of March. The physical inventory count on March 31 shows 500 units on hand.

Inventory:	March 1	200 units @ $4.00	$ 800
Purchases:	March 10	500 units @ $4.50	2,250
	March 20	400 units @ $4.75	1,900
	March 30	300 units @ $5.00	1,500
Sales:	March 15	500 units	
	March 25	400 units	

Instructions

a. Under a **periodic inventory system**, determine the cost of inventory on hand at March 31 and the cost of goods sold for March under (1) FIFO and (2) weighted average cost.

b. Under a **perpetual inventory system**, determine the cost of inventory on hand at March 31 and the cost of goods sold for March under (1) FIFO and (2) moving-average cost.

Solution

a. The cost of goods available for sale is $6,450 as follows:

Inventory:	March 1	200 units @ $4.00	$ 800
Purchases:	March 10	500 units @ $4.50	2,250
	March 20	400 units @ $4.75	1,900
	March 30	300 units @ $5.00	1,500
Total		1,400	$6,450

Under a **periodic inventory system**, the cost of goods sold under each cost flow method is as follows.

1. FIFO method

Ending inventory: $1,400 - (500 + 400) = 500$ units

Date	Units	Unit Cost	Total Cost	
March 30	300	$5.00	$1,500	
March 20	200	4.75	950	$2,450

Cost of goods sold: $6,450 - $2,450 = $4,000

2. Weighted average cost method

Average unit cost: $6,450 \div 1,400 = 4.607
Ending inventory: $500 \times $4.607 = $2,303.50$
Cost of goods sold: $6,450 - $2,303.50 = $4,146.50$

b. The cost of goods available for sale is $6,450, as follows:

Inventory:	March 1	200 units @ $4.00	$ 800
Purchases:	March 10	500 units @ $4.50	2,250
	March 20	400 units @ $4.75	1,900
	March 30	300 units @ $5.00	1,500
Total		1,400	$6,450

Under a **perpetual inventory system**, the cost of goods sold under each cost flow method is as follows:

1. FIFO method

Date	Purchases	Cost of Goods Sold	Balance
March 1			(200 @ $4.00) $ 800
March 10	(500 @ $4.50) $2,250		(200 @ $4.00)
			(500 @ $4.50) $3,050
March 15		(200 @ $4.00)	
		(300 @ $4.50)	(200 @ $4.50) $ 900
		$2,150	
March 20	(400 @ $4.75) $1,900		(200 @ $4.50)
			(400 @ $4.75) $2,800
March 25		(200 @ $4.50)	
		(200 @ $4.75)	(200 @ $4.75) $ 950
		$1,850	
March 30	(300 @ $5.00) $1,500		(200 @ $4.75)
			(300 @ $5.00) $2,450
	Ending inventory $2,450	Cost of goods sold: $2,150 + $1,850 = $4,000	

2. Moving-average cost method

Date	Purchases	Cost of Goods Sold	Balance
March 1			(200 @ $4.00) $ 800
March 10	(500 @ $4.50) $2,250		(700 @ $4.357) $3,050
March 15		(500 @ $4.357) $2,179	(200 @ $4.357) $ 871
March 20	(400 @ $4.75) $1,900		(600 @ $4.618) $2,771
March 25		(400 @ $4.618) $1,847	(200 @ $4.618) $ 924
March 30	(300 @ $5.00) $1,500		(500 @ $4.848) $2,424
	Ending inventory $2,424	Cost of goods sold: $2,179 + $1,847 = $4,026	

Practice Problem 8.2

Norwood Company makes miniature circuit boards that are components of wireless phones and personal organizers. The company has experienced strong growth, and you are especially interested in how well Norwood is managing its inventory balances. You have collected the following information for the current year.

Inventory at the beginning of year	$ 1,026,000
Inventory at the end of year, before any adjustments	1,007,000
Total cost of goods sold, before any adjustments	11,776,000

The company values inventory at lower of cost (using the FIFO cost flow assumption) and net realizable value.

Instructions

a. Calculate Norwood's inventory turnover before any adjustment.

b. Recalculate the inventory turnover after adjusting Norwood's inventory information for the following items.

1. During the year, Norwood recorded sales and costs of goods sold on $22,000 of units shipped to various wholesalers on consignment. At year end, none of these units have been sold by wholesalers.

2. Shipping contracts changed two months ago from f.o.b. shipping point to f.o.b. destination. At the end of the year, $25,000 of products are en route to China and will not arrive until after financial statements are released. Current inventory balances do not reflect this change in procedure.

3. At the end of the year, Norwood determined that a certain section of inventory with a historical cost of $112,000 has a net realizable value of $100,800. There is no need to make a lower of cost or net realizable value adjustment to other inventory.

Solution

a. $\dfrac{\$11,776,000}{(\$1,026,000 + \$1,007,000)/2} = 11.6$ times

b. Adjustments to ending inventory

Item	Adjustment to Ending Inventory	Explanation
1. Consigned goods	$22,000	Norwood should count the goods it has consigned to other stores.
2. Goods in transit	$25,000	Goods officially change hands at the point of destination. Norwood should still show these goods in inventory (not cost of goods sold), until they reach the destination.
3. Lower of cost or net realizable value	$(11,200)	($112,000 – $100,800). The correct valuation is $100,800 since the net realizable value of $100,800 is less than the original cost.

Adjusted inventory turnover $= \dfrac{\$11,740,200^{a}}{(\$1,026,000 + \$1,042,800^{b})/2} = 11.3$ times

^{a}Cost of goods sold: $11,776,000 − $22,000 − $25,000 + $11,200 = $11,740,200
^{b}Ending inventory: $1,007,000 + $22,000 + $25,000 − $11,200 = $1,042,800

Key Terms

agricultural produce, p. 8-37
asset retirement costs, p. 8-18
average days to sell inventory, p. 8-45
basket purchase, p. 8-19
bearer plants, p. 8-38
biological assets, p. 8-37
consigned goods, p. 8-9
conversion costs, p. 8-18
cost formula, p. 8-24
cost of goods available for sale or use, p. 8-6
cost of goods manufactured, p. 8-12
cost of goods sold, p. 8-6
cost-to-retail ratio, p. 8-47
current ratio, p. 8-15
cut-off schedule, p. 8-9
finished goods inventory, p. 8-5
first-in, first-out (FIFO) cost formula, p. 8-27
f.o.b. (free on board) destination, p. 8-8

f.o.b. (free on board) shipping point, p. 8-8
gross profit method, p. 8-41
gross profit percentage, p. 8-42
inventories, p. 8-7
inventory turnover ratio, p. 8-44
joint cost, p. 8-20
last-in, first-out (LIFO) cost formula, p. 8-29
lower of cost and net realizable value (LC&NRV), p. 8-31
markdown, p. 8-48
markdown cancellations, p. 8-48
markup, p. 8-48
markup cancellations, p. 8-48
markup on cost, p. 8-42
merchandise inventory, p. 8-4
moving-average cost formula, p. 8-26
net markdowns, p. 8-48
net markups, p. 8-48

net realizable value (NRV), p. 8-30
normal production capacity, p. 8-18
onerous contract, p. 8-10
period costs, p. 8-19
periodic inventory system, p. 8-21
perpetual inventory system, p. 8-21
price risk, p. 8-10
product costs, p. 8-18
purchase commitments, p. 8-10
raw materials inventory, p. 8-5
relative sales value method, p. 8-20
retail inventory method, p. 8-47
specific identification, p. 8-24
standard cost system, p. 8-19
volume rebate, p. 8-17
weighted average cost formula, p. 8-26
work-in-process inventory, p. 8-5

Assignment Material

Note: All assignment material with an asterisk (*) relates to the appendices to the chapter.

Enabling Competencies Completion of this end-of-chapter material will help develop CPA-enabling competencies (such as ethics and professionalism, problem-solving and decision-making, and communication) and technical competencies. We have highlighted selected items with a specific integration word mark and material in *WileyPLUS* has been linked to the competencies. All cases emphasize integration, especially of the enabling competencies. The brief exercises, exercises, and problems generally emphasize problem-solving and decision-making.

Brief Exercises

BE8.1 (LO 1) `Management Accounting` Walmart uses a just-in-time inventory system to reduce its costs, allowing it to sell goods to its customers at lower prices. What are the benefits of a good inventory management system? What are the risks associated with a very tight inventory control system? How does a good just-in-time inventory system affect key ratios?

BE8.2 (LO 1, 11) Show whether the following would be considered inventory for a public company like Ford Motor Corporation. If so, show the inventory category to which that item would belong.

a. Engines purchased to make the Ford F-150

b. Nuts and bolts purchased to attach the engine to the car body

c. Spare parts purchased for the manufacturing equipment

d. Standby equipment in case a machine breaks down

e. Wages paid to assembly-line employees

f. Rent for a manufacturing facility

g. Wages paid to a supervisor

h. Ford F-150 ready to be shipped to the dealer

i. Manufacturing plant

How would your responses change if the manufacturer followed ASPE?

BE8.3 (LO 2, 10) Betadyne Corp. is a public company that manufactures and sells medical equipment. What kind of information would be useful for users of the company's financial statements?

BE8.4 (LO 2) Highfliers Inc. is a public company that purchases airplanes for sale to others (including individuals and corporations). However, until the airplanes are sold, the company charters and services them. What is the proper way to report these airplanes in the company's financial statements?

BE8.5 (LO 2) Which of the following would be included in inventory? For any amount not included in inventory, explain where the amount would be recorded.

a. Raw materials costs of leather to a manufacturer of leather furniture

b. The cost of cans of corn held on the shelves of a grocery store

c. The cost of a truck in the process of being manufactured by an automobile manufacturer

d. The cost of land being held for development to a property developer

e. The cost of a van being used as a courtesy vehicle to an automobile service centre

f. The costs of construction for a home being built for a specific customer to a builder

g. The cost of soap and paper towels for the washrooms of a restaurant

BE8.6 (LO 2) Saving Energy Inc. is a company that wants to buy coal deposits but does not want the financing for the purchase to be reported on its financial statements. The company therefore establishes a trust to acquire the coal deposits. The company agrees to buy the coal over a certain period of time at specified prices. The trust is able to finance the coal purchase and then pay off the loan when it is paid by the company for the minerals. How should this transaction be reported?

BE8.7 (LO 2) Able Limited is a company that is involved in the wholesaling and retailing of automobile tires for foreign cars. Most of the inventory is imported, and it is valued on the company's records at the actual inventory cost plus freight in.

a. At year end, the warehousing costs are pro-rated over cost of goods sold and ending inventory. Are warehousing costs considered a product cost or a period cost?

b. A certain portion of Able Limited's inventory consists of obsolete items. Should obsolete items that are not currently consumed in the production of goods or services to be available for sale be classified as part of inventory?

BE8.8 (LO 2) Tansley Ltd. took a physical inventory count on December 31 and determined that goods costing $4,000 were on hand. This amount included $1,000 of goods held on consignment for Woods Corporation. Not included in the physical count were $800 of goods purchased from Timmons Corporation, f.o.b. shipping point, and $400 of goods sold to Myers Ltd. for $600, f.o.b. destination. Both the

Timmons purchase and the Myers sale were in transit at year end. What amount should Tansley report as its December 31 inventory?

BE8.9 (LO 2, 5) Global Ltd. had beginning inventory of 50 units that cost $100 each. During September, the company purchased 200 units on account at $100 each, returned 6 units for credit, and sold 150 units at $200 each.

a. Journalize the September transactions, assuming that Global Ltd. uses a perpetual inventory system.

b. Journalize the September transactions, assuming that Global Ltd. uses a periodic inventory system.

c. Assume that Global Ltd. uses a periodic system and prepares financial statements at the end of each month. An inventory count determines that there are 94 units of inventory remaining at September 30. Prepare the adjusting entry that is needed at September 30 to report cost of goods sold.

BE8.10 (LO 4, 11) Best Corp., a public company using IFRS, signed a long-term non-cancellable purchase commitment with a major supplier to purchase raw materials at an annual cost of $1 million. At December 31, 2019, the raw materials to be purchased in 2020 have a market price of $950,000.

a. Prepare any December 31, 2019 entry that is needed.

b. In 2020, Best receives the raw materials and pays the required $1 million. The raw materials now have a market value of $920,000. Prepare the entry to record the purchase.

c. Explain how the accounting treatment under part (a) compares with the accounting treatment for private companies under ASPE.

BE8.11 (LO 3) Angus Enterprises Ltd. reported cost of goods sold for 2020 of $2.5 million and retained earnings of $4.0 million at December 31, 2020. Angus later discovered that its ending inventories at December 31, 2019 and 2020, were overstated by $150,000 and $50,000, respectively. Determine the correct amounts for 2020 cost of goods sold and December 31, 2020 retained earnings.

BE8.12 (LO 4) Gamers' World buys 1,000 computer game CDs from a distributor that is discontinuing those games. The purchase price for the lot is $7,500. Gamers' World will group the CDs into three price categories for resale, as follows:

Group	Number of CDs	Price per CD
1	100	$ 5
2	800	10
3	100	15

Determine the cost per CD for each group, using the relative sales value method. Round per-unit cost to two decimal places.

BE8.13 (LO 4, 11) Sunny Valley Limited produces wine. Certain vintage wines take more than one year to age. The company has borrowed funds to cover the costs of this aging process. The company meets the interest capitalization criteria under IFRS. Capitalizable interest under IFRS is $1,000.

a. Prepare the journal entry to record the $1,000 interest under IFRS.

b. Show the possible journal entries under ASPE.

c. Discuss the accounting treatment under IFRS for the grapevines used to grow grapes that are eventually used for wine production.

d. Discuss the accounting treatment under ASPE for the grapevines used to grow grapes that are eventually used for wine production.

BE8.14 (LO 4) Doors Unlimited Ltd. purchases units of wood frames that have manufacturer's volume rebates from Traders Inc. The rebate requires Doors Unlimited to purchase a minimum number of units in a calendar year. The initial unit cost of each wood frame is $2.50 before any rebate. If more than 3,500 units are purchased, the rebate is $0.25 per unit for all units purchased beyond the base amount of 3,500 units. Doors Unlimited Ltd. has a June 30 fiscal year end. By June 30, 2020, Doors Unlimited had purchased 3,000 wood frames for the six-month period from January 1, 2020, to June 30, 2020. Doors Unlimited estimates that an additional 3,000 wood frames will be purchased from July 1, 2020, to December 31, 2020. Doors Unlimited's management is very confident that this estimate will be confirmed by future purchases from Traders.

a. Explain the conceptual principles involved in determining if an accrual should be made for the volume rebate from Traders. Under what circumstances would an accrual not be permissible?

b. Calculate the amount of any rebate that Doors Unlimited should accrue at June 30, 2020, assuming the rebate cannot be cancelled by Traders.

c. Calculate the unit cost that Doors Unlimited should use in the costing of wood frames, using the perpetual inventory system. (Round to four decimal places.)

BE8.15 (LO 5, 6) Canali Corporation uses a perpetual inventory system. On November 19, the company sold 600 units. The following additional information is available:

	Units	Unit Cost	Total Cost
Nov. 1 inventory	250	$12	$ 3,000
Nov. 15 purchase	400	14	5,600
Nov. 23 purchase	350	15	5,250
	1,000		$13,850

Calculate the November 30 inventory and the November cost of goods sold, using

a. the moving-average cost formula (round per-unit cost to two decimal places) and

b. the FIFO cost formula.

BE8.16 (LO 7) Bluebell Enterprises Ltd.'s records reported an inventory cost of $55,600 and a net realizable value of $54,000 at December 31, 2018. At December 31, 2019, the records indicated a cost of $68,700 and a net realizable value of $61,625. All opening inventory had been sold during the year.

a. Assuming that Bluebell Enterprises uses a perpetual inventory system, prepare the December 31, 2019 entry that is needed under (1) the direct method and (2) the indirect method.

b. Assume that at December 31, 2020, the records indicate inventory with a cost of $60,000 and a net realizable value of $60,900. Prepare the December 31, 2020 entry that is needed under (1) the direct method and (2) the indirect method. Explain why a "gain" is reported under the indirect method of accounting.

BE8.17 (LO 6) More & More Limited uses a periodic inventory system. On June 24, the company sold 600 units. The following additional information is available:

	Units	Unit Cost	Total Cost
June 1 inventory	200	$12	$ 2,400
June 15 purchase	400	14	5,600
June 23 purchase	400	15	6,000
	1,000		$14,000

a. Calculate the June 30 inventory and the June cost of goods sold, using the weighted average cost formula. Round per-unit cost to two decimal places.

b. Calculate the June 30 inventory and the June cost of goods sold, using the FIFO formula.

c. Assume that 200 units sold on June 24 had a unit cost of $12; 300 had a unit cost of $14; and the remaining 100 units had a unit cost of $15. Calculate the June 30 inventory and the June cost of goods sold, using the specific identification method.

BE8.18 (LO 7, 11) Antimatter Corporation has the following four items in its ending inventory:

Item	Cost	Estimated Selling Price	Estimated Disposal Costs
Neutrinos	$1,820	$2,100	$100
Ocillinos	5,000	4,900	100
Electrons	4,290	4,625	200
Protons	3,200	4,210	100

a. Assume that Antimatter is a public company using IFRS. Determine the total value of ending inventory using the lower of cost and net realizable value model applied on an individual item basis.

b. Would there be any difference in accounting if Antimatter were a private entity using ASPE? If so, what?

BE8.19 (LO 8, 11) Consider a large dairy farming company that reports under IFRS. Beyond manufacturing, farm property, and equipment, the farm's main assets are the dairy cows and the milk that they produce. (a) Describe how these assets may be presented on the financial statements. (b) Discuss the accounting treatments of the following events: (1) a new dairy cow is bought by the farm and (2) a cow owned by the farm loses its ability to produce milk. (c) How would these events differ if the farm reported under ASPE? (d) Comment on which standard you believe provides better presentation of the assets, and why.

BE8.20 (LO 8, 11) Farmer Brown Industries Inc. is in the business of producing organic foods for sale to restaurants and in local markets. The company uses IFRS and has a June 30 fiscal year end.

As an experiment, the company has decided to try raising organic free-range chickens. On May 1, 2020, Farmer Brown purchased 100 new hatchlings for cash at a total cost of $1,000. The company paid cash for feed and labour costs of $150 per month to look after the chicks. Their (acceptable) accounting policy is to capitalize these costs.

On June 30, the company estimated that the chickens would mature in mid-October. At year end they had a fair value of $1,800 and the company would have to transport the chickens to their customers at an average cost of $3 per chicken.

On October 30, all 100 chickens had matured and the company sold and shipped 50 of the chickens to one of its key customers for $30 per chicken. Transportation costs were $3 per chicken, as expected.

a. Prepare the journal entries to record the inventory activity relating to the chickens for the month of May.

b. Prepare the journal entries to record the inventory activity relating to the chickens for the month of June, including any year-end adjustments required under IAS 41.

c. How would the result be different if the company used ASPE?

BE8.21 (LO 8, 11)

a. Briefly explain the criteria that have to be met for inventory to be recorded at an amount greater than cost.

b. Briefly explain the accounting for the following inventory items under ASPE:

1. Sheep

2. Wool

3. Carpet

c. Briefly explain the accounting for the items in part (b) under IFRS.

d. Briefly explain the treatment of a bearer plant under IFRS.

BE8.22 (LO 9) Oil Tankers Inc.'s April 30 inventory was destroyed by the explosion of an underground oil tank. January 1 inventory was $250,000 and purchases for January through April totalled $620,000. Sales for the same period were $1 million. Oil Tankers' normal gross profit percentage is 30%. Using the gross profit method, estimate the amount of Oil Tankers' April 30 inventory that was destroyed.

BE8.23 (LO 10) IFRS requires greater disclosure for inventory than ASPE. List the additional requirements and explain what benefit each one might provide for the users of the financial statements. List some items that would specifically contribute to estimation uncertainty as it relates to inventory and how this would impact disclosure requirements.

 BE8.24 (LO 10) Delicious Foods Inc. reported inventory of $5,706 million at the end of its 2020 fiscal year and $5,310 million at the end of its 2019 fiscal year. It reported cost of goods sold of $35,350 million for the fiscal year 2020 and net sales of $54,365 million for fiscal year 2020. Calculate the company's inventory turnover and the average days to sell inventory for the fiscal year 2020. Round to two decimal places. If the turnover ratio was 6 times in 2019, was there an improvement or a deterioration in the company's ability to turn over inventory in 2020?

*****BE8.25 (LO 12)** Furniture Madness Inc. recently purchased 1,000 mattresses from a supplier for its big box stores. The cost for these mattresses was $140,000, or $140 per mattress. Furniture Madness established the selling price on these mattresses at $230 each. The store manager noted that the mattresses were selling quickly and changed the selling price to $250 per unit. This made the price too high for customers and sales lagged. The manager then responded by reducing the selling price to $235. At the end of the summer, the manager set the price of the remaining mattresses at $200. Not all mattresses were sold and all remaining units went to storage until the next season. When the next season started, the remaining mattresses were put on sale for $220 each. Calculate the per-unit (a) markup, (b) markup cancellation, (c) markdown, and (d) markdown cancellation.

*****BE8.26 (LO 12)** Lang Inc. had beginning inventory of $22,000 at cost and $30,000 at retail. Net purchases were $157,500 at cost and $215,000 at retail. Net markups were $10,000, net markdowns were $7,000, and sales were $184,500. Calculate the ending inventory at cost using the retail method. Round the cost-to-retail percentage to two decimal places.

*****BE8.27 (LO 13)** What are the primary sources of GAAP relating to inventory

a. under IFRS?

b. under ASPE?

*****BE8.28 (LO 13)** There are many forms of inventory that are not covered under the basic accounting standards for inventory: *CPA Handbook*, Part II, Section 3031 (ASPE) and IAS 2 for IFRS. For each of the following forms of inventory, briefly explain how the inventory would be reported and where guidance would be found under ASPE and IFRS. Explain the impact on the statement of financial position (SFP) and the income statements that would result.

a. Unbilled work in progress for a legal firm (that is, employee and partner time spent on client work not yet billed)

b. Milk from dairy cattle

c. Sheep that are kept for wool production

d. Construction contracts in progress

e. Nickel resources not yet mined

Exercises

E8.1 (LO 2, 3) `Management Accounting` **(Inventoriable Costs—Perpetual)** The Ogale Equipment Corporation maintains a general ledger account for each class of inventory, debiting the individual accounts for increases during the period and crediting them for decreases. The transactions that follow are for the Raw Materials inventory account, which is debited for materials purchased and credited for materials requisitioned for use.

1. An invoice for $8,100, terms f.o.b. destination, was received and entered on January 2, 2021. The receiving report shows that the materials were received on December 28, 2020.

2. Materials costing $7,300 were returned to the supplier on December 29, 2020, on f.o.b. shipping point terms. The returns were entered into Ogale's general ledger on December 28, even though the returned items did not arrive at the vendor's office until January 6, 2021.

3. Materials costing $28,000, shipped f.o.b. destination, were not entered by December 31, 2020, because they were in a railroad car on the company's siding on that date and had not been unloaded.

4. An invoice for $7,500, terms f.o.b. shipping point, was received and entered on December 30, 2020. The receiving report shows that the materials were received on January 4, 2021, and the bill of lading shows that they were shipped on January 2, 2021.

5. Materials costing $19,800 were received on December 30, 2020. No entry was made for them as at that date, because they were ordered with a specified delivery date of no earlier than January 10, 2021.

6. Materials costing $20,000 were received on December 29, 2020. The supplier's warehouse was full and the supplier asked Ogale to hold these items on its behalf and has also insured these items for the period that Ogale will be holding them. The purchase terms indicate that the supplier will buy these items back from Ogale in early January 2021 at $20,000 plus storage fees.

7. Materials costing $5,500 were received on December 20, 2020, on consignment from P. Perry Company.

Instructions

a. Prepare any correcting journal entries that are required at December 31, 2020, assuming that the books have not been closed. Also show which entries must be reversed after closing so that the next period's accounts will be correct.

b. `Ethics` Are there any ethical concerns raised by any of these transactions? How should Ogale deal with this situation?

E8.2 (LO 2, 3, 5, 11) (Inventoriable Costs—Error Adjustments) Jaeco Corporation asks you to review its December 31, 2020 inventory values and prepare the adjustments that are needed to the books. The following information is given to you:

1. Jaeco uses the periodic method of recording inventory. A physical count reveals $234,890 of inventory on hand at December 31, 2020, although the books have not yet been adjusted to reflect the ending inventory.

2. Not included in the physical count of inventory is $10,420 of merchandise purchased on December 15 from Shamsi. This merchandise was shipped f.o.b. shipping point on December 29 and arrived in January. The invoice arrived and was recorded on December 31.

3. Included in inventory is merchandise sold to Sage on December 30, f.o.b. destination. This merchandise was shipped after it was counted. The invoice was prepared and recorded as a sale on account for $12,800 on December 31. The merchandise cost $7,350, and Sage received it on January 3.

4. Included in the count of inventory was merchandise received from Dutton on December 31 with an invoice price of $15,630. The merchandise was shipped f.o.b. destination. The invoice, which has not yet arrived, has not been recorded.

5. Not included in inventory is $8,540 of merchandise purchased from Growler Industries. This merchandise was received on December 31, after the inventory had been counted. The invoice was received and recorded on December 30.

6. Included in inventory was $10,438 of inventory held by Jaeco on consignment from Jackel Industries.

7. Included in inventory was merchandise sold to Kemp, f.o.b. shipping point. This merchandise was shipped after it was counted, on December 31. The invoice was prepared and recorded as a sale for $18,900 on December 31. The cost of this merchandise was $11,520, and Kemp received the merchandise on January 5.

8. Excluded from inventory was a carton labelled "Please accept for credit." This carton contained merchandise costing $1,500, which had been sold to a customer for $2,600. No entry had been made to the books to record the return, but none of the returned merchandise seemed damaged.

9. Jaeco sold $12,500 of inventory to Simply Corp. for $21,000 on account on December 15, 2020. These items were shipped f.o.b. shipping point. The terms of sale indicate that Simply Corp. will be permitted to return an unlimited amount until May 15, 2021. Jaeco has never provided unlimited returns in the past and is not able to estimate the amount of any potential returns that Simply may make.

Instructions

a. Determine the proper inventory balance for Jaeco Corporation at December 31, 2020.

b. Prepare any adjusting/correcting entries that are needed at December 31, 2020. Assume the books have not been closed and that Jaeco follows IFRS.

c. Assume instead that Jaeco follows ASPE. Prepare any adjusting/correcting entries at December 31, 2020, that are needed.

E8.3 **(LO 2, 3, 4, 11)** **(Inventoriable Costs)** The following is a list of items that may or may not be reported as inventory in a SFP:

1. Goods out on consignment at another company's store

2. Goods sold on an instalment basis

3. Goods purchased f.o.b. shipping point that are in transit at December 31

4. Goods purchased f.o.b. destination that are in transit at December 31

5. Goods sold to another company, with Soukas having signed an agreement to repurchase the goods at a set price that covers all costs related to the inventory

6. Goods sold where large returns are predictable

7. Goods sold f.o.b. shipping point that are in transit at December 31

8. Freight charges on goods purchased

9. Freight charges on goods sold

10. Factory labour costs incurred on goods that are still unsold

11. Interest costs incurred for inventories that are routinely manufactured in large quantities

12. Costs incurred to advertise goods held for resale

13. Materials on hand and not yet placed into production by a manufacturing firm

14. Supplies used in the office

15. Raw materials on which a manufacturing firm has started production, but which are not completely processed

16. Manufacturing supplies

17. Goods held on consignment from another company

18. Goods held on consignment by another company

19. Costs identified with units completed by a manufacturing firm, but not yet sold

20. Goods sold f.o.b. destination that are in transit at December 31

21. Temporary investments in shares and bonds that will be resold in the near future

22. Costs of uncleared land to be developed by a property development company

23. Cost of normal waste or spoilage of raw materials during production

24. Cost of waste and spoilage experienced above normal levels—that is, abnormal levels of waste of raw materials

25. Costs to store excess materials inventory for a manufacturer

26. Costs to store wine as it ages for a wine producer

27. Decommissioning costs incurred as a part of the extraction of minerals

Instructions

a. Assuming that ASPE is followed, show which of these items would typically be reported as inventory in the financial statements. If an item should not be reported as inventory, show how it should be reported in the financial statements.

b. How would your response to part (a) change under IFRS?

E8.4 (LO 2, 4, 11) Excel   **(Inventoriable Costs)**   In an annual audit of Solaro Company Limited, you find that a physical inventory count on December 31, 2020, showed merchandise of $441,000. You also discover that the following items were excluded from the $441,000:

1. Merchandise of $61,000 is held by Solaro on consignment from BonBon Corporation.

2. Merchandise costing $33,000 was shipped by Solaro f.o.b. destination to XYZ Ltd. on December 31, 2020. This merchandise was accepted by XYZ on January 6, 2021.

3. Merchandise costing $46,000 was shipped f.o.b. shipping point to ABC Company on December 29, 2020. This merchandise was received by ABC on January 10, 2021.

4. Merchandise costing $73,000 was shipped f.o.b. destination from Wholesaler Inc. to Solaro on December 30, 2020. Solaro received the items on January 3, 2021.

5. Merchandise costing $51,000 was shipped by Distributor Ltd. f.o.b. shipping point on December 30, 2020, and received at Solaro's office on January 2, 2021.

6. Solaro had excess inventory and incurred an additional $1,500 in storage costs due to delayed shipment in transaction (3) above.

7. Solaro incurred $2,000 for interest expense on inventory it purchased through delayed payment plans in fiscal 2020.

Instructions

a. Based on the information provided above, calculate the amount of inventory that should appear on Solaro's December 31, 2020 SFP.

b. Under what circumstances can a private company reporting under ASPE capitalize interest costs incurred to finance inventory?

c. Under what circumstances can a public company reporting under IFRS capitalize interest costs incurred to finance inventory?

d. Audit   Explain some audit procedures that the auditor would perform to satisfy the financial statement assertion for cut-off for inventory transactions and events.

E8.5 (LO 2, 7)   (Cost Allocation and Lower of Cost and NRV)   During 2020, Buildit Furniture Limited purchased a railway carload of wicker chairs. The manufacturer of the chairs sold them to Buildit for a lump sum of $59,850, because it was discontinuing manufacturing operations and wanted to dispose of its entire stock. Three types of chairs are included in the carload. The three types and the estimated selling price for each are as follows:

Type	Number of Chairs	Estimated Selling Price per Chair
Lounge chairs	400	$95
Straight chairs	700	55
Armchairs	300	85

Buildit estimates that the costs to sell this inventory would be $2 per chair. During 2020, Buildit sells 350 lounge chairs, 210 armchairs, and 120 straight chairs, all at the same prices as estimated. At December 31, 2020, the remaining chairs were put on sale: the lounge chairs at 25% off the regular price, the armchairs at 30% off, and the straight chairs at 40% off. All were expected to be sold at these prices.

Instructions

a. Rounding percentages to one decimal place and all other amounts to two decimal places, what is the total cost of the chairs remaining in inventory at the end of 2020, using the relative sales value method?

b. What is the net realizable value of the chairs remaining in inventory?

c. What is the appropriate inventory value to be reported on the December 31, 2020 statement of financial position, assuming the lower of cost and NRV is applied on an individual item basis?

E8.6 (LO 2, 11) **(Purchase Commitments)** At December 31, 2020, Igor Ltd. has outstanding non-cancellable purchase commitments for 32,500 litres of raw material at $2.00 per litre. The material will be used in Igor's manufacturing process, and the company prices its raw materials inventory at cost or NRV, whichever is lower.

Instructions

a. Explain the accounting treatment for purchase commitments under ASPE and IFRS.

b. Assuming that the market price as at December 31, 2020, is $2.25 per litre, how would this commitment be treated in the accounts and statements? Explain.

c. Assuming that the market price as at December 31, 2020, is $1.80 per litre instead of $2.25, how would you treat this commitment in the accounts and statements?

d. Prepare the entry for January 15, 2021, when the entire shipment is received, assuming that the situation in part (c) existed at December 31, 2020, and that the market price in January 2021 is $1.80 per litre. Explain your treatment.

e. **Ethics** Why would users of the financial statements want to see disclosure about purchase commitments? Is it ever ethical for a company to decide not to disclose this information?

E8.7 (LO 3) **(Inventory Errors—Periodic)** Salamander Limited makes the following errors during the current year. Each error is an independent case.

1. Ending inventory is overstated by $1,020, but purchases are recorded correctly.

2. Both ending inventory and a purchase on account are understated by the same amount. (Assume this purchase of $1,500 was recorded in the following year.)

3. Ending inventory is correct, but a purchase on account was not recorded. (Assume this purchase of $850 was recorded in the following year.)

Instructions

Finance Show the effect of each error on working capital, current ratio (assume that the current ratio is greater than 1), retained earnings, and net income for the current year and the following year.

E8.8 (LO 3) **(Inventory Errors)** Eureka Limited has a calendar-year accounting period. The following errors were discovered in 2020.

1. The December 31, 2018 merchandise inventory had been understated by $51,000.

2. Merchandise purchased on account in 2019 was recorded on the books for the first time in February 2020, when the original invoice for the correct amount of $2,400 arrived. The merchandise had arrived on December 28, 2019, and was included in the December 31, 2019 merchandise inventory. The invoice arrived late because of a mix-up by the wholesaler.

3. Inventory, valued at $1,000, held on consignment by Eureka was included in the December 31, 2019 count.

Instructions

a. Calculate the effect of each error on the 2019 net income.

b. Calculate the effect, if any, that each error had on the related December 31, 2019 statement of financial position items.

E8.9 (LO 3) **(Inventory Errors)** The net income per books of Russell Industries Limited was determined without any knowledge of the following errors. The 2015 year was Russell's first year in business. No dividends have been declared or paid.

Year	Net Income per Books	Error in Ending Inventory	
2015	$50,000	Overstated	$ 5,000
2016	52,000	Overstated	9,000
2017	54,000	Understated	11,000
2018	56,000	No error	
2019	58,000	Understated	2,000
2020	60,000	Overstated	10,000

Instructions

a. Prepare a work sheet to show the adjusted net income figure for each of the six years after taking the inventory corrections into account.

b. Prepare a schedule that shows both the original retained earnings balance reported at the end of each year and the corrected amount.

c. Consider the trends in the increase in income from 2019 to 2020 as originally reported and as revised after the corrections. Would you suspect that the income is being manipulated by adjusting the ending balance in the inventory account?

E8.10 (LO 3, 7, 10, 11) **(Lower of Cost and Net Realizable Value—Effect of Error)** Iqbal Corporation uses the lower of FIFO cost and net realizable value method on an individual item basis, applying the direct method. The inventory at December 31, 2019, included product AG. Relevant per-unit data for product AG follow:

Estimated selling price	$50
Cost	45
Replacement cost	51
Estimated selling expense	19
Normal profit	14

There were 1,000 units of product AG on hand at December 31, 2019. Product AG was incorrectly valued at $35 per unit for reporting purposes. All 1,000 units were sold in 2020.

Instructions

Assume that Iqbal follows ASPE, and answer the following questions.

a. Was net income for 2019 overstated or understated? By how much? (Ignore income tax aspects.)

b. Was net income for 2020 overstated or understated? By how much?

c. **Finance** Show whether the current ratio, inventory turnover ratio, and debt to total assets ratio would be overstated, understated, or not affected for the years ended December 31, 2019, and December 31, 2020. Explain briefly.

d. Assume that management did not discover the error in inventory until after the end of the fiscal year but before the closing entries were made and the financial statements were released. Should the adjustment be recorded? How would the error be treated if it were discovered after the financial statements were released?

e. How would your responses above change if Iqbal followed IFRS?

E8.11 (LO 3, 9) **(Gross Profit Method)** Linsang Corporation's retail store and warehouse closed for an entire weekend while the year-end inventory was counted. When the count was finished, the controller gathered all the count books and information from the clerical staff, completed the ending inventory calculations, and prepared the following partial income statement for the general manager for Monday morning:

Sales		$2,750,000
Beginning inventory	$ 650,000	
Purchases	1,550,000	
Total goods available for sale	2,200,000	
Less ending inventory	650,000	
Cost of goods sold		1,550,000
Gross profit		$1,200,000

The general manager called the controller into her office after quickly reviewing the preliminary statements. "You've made an error in the inventory," she stated. "My pricing all year has been carefully controlled to provide a gross profit of 35%, and I know the sales are correct."

Instructions

a. How much should the ending inventory have been?

b. If the controller's ending inventory amount was due to an error, suggest where the error might have occurred.

E8.12 (LO 4) **(Relative Sales Value Method)** In fiscal 2020, Ivanjoh Realty Corporation purchased unimproved land for $55,000. The land was improved and subdivided into building lots at an additional cost of $34,460. These building lots were all the same size but, because of differences in location, were offered for sale at different prices, as follows:

Group	Number of Lots	Price per Lot
1	9	$3,500
2	15	4,500
3	17	2,400

Operating expenses that were allocated to this project totalled $18,200 for the year. At year end, there were also unsold lots remaining, as follows:

Group 1	5 lots
Group 2	7 lots
Group 3	2 lots

Instructions

Determine the year-end inventory and net income of Ivanjoh Realty Corporation. Round all amounts to the nearest dollar. Ignore income taxes.

E8.13 (LO 5) **(Determining Merchandise Amounts—Periodic)** Two or more items are omitted in each of the following tabulations of income statement data for a business following ASPE.

Instructions

Fill in the amounts that are missing.

	2018	2019	2020
Sales	$290,000	$_____	$410,000
Sales returns	6,000	13,000	
Net sales	_____	347,000	_____
Beginning inventory	20,000	32,000	_____
Ending inventory	_____		
Purchases	_____	260,000	298,000
Purchase returns and allowances	5,000	8,000	10,000
Transportation in	8,000	9,000	12,000
Cost of goods sold	238,000		303,000
Gross profit on sales	46,000	91,000	97,000

E8.14 (LO 5, 6) [Excel] **(Periodic Versus Perpetual Entries)** Ruggers Corporation sells one product, with information for July as follows:

July 1	Inventory	100 units at $15.00 each
4	Sale	80 units at $18.00 each
11	Purchase	150 units at $16.50 each
13	Sale	120 units at $18.75 each
20	Purchase	160 units at $17.00 each
27	Sale	100 units at $20.00 each

Ruggers uses the FIFO cost formula. All purchases and sales are on account. Ignore any estimated returns on purchases and sales.

Instructions

a. Assume Ruggers uses a periodic system. Prepare all journal entries needed, including the end-of-month adjusting entry to record cost of goods sold. A physical count indicates that the ending inventory for July is 110 units.

b. Calculate gross profit using the periodic system.

c. Assume Ruggers uses the periodic system, and a count on July 31 reports only 102 units in ending inventory. How would your entries in part (a) change, if at all? Explain briefly.

d. Assume Ruggers uses a perpetual system. Prepare all July journal entries.

e. Calculate gross profit using the perpetual system.

f. Assume Ruggers uses the perpetual system, and a count on July 31 reports only 102 units in ending inventory. Prepare any entries needed. Explain briefly.

E8.15 (LO 5, 6) **(FIFO and Weighted Average)** Aquino Corporation is a multi-product firm. The following information concerns one of its products, the Trinton:

Date	Transaction	Quantity	Price/Cost
Jan. 1	Beginning inventory	1,000	$12
Feb. 4	Purchase	2,000	18
Feb. 20	Sale	2,500	30
Apr. 2	Purchase	3,000	23
Nov. 4	Sale	2,000	33

Instructions

Calculate cost of goods sold, assuming Aquino uses:

a. A periodic inventory system and FIFO cost formula

b. A periodic inventory system and weighted average cost formula. Round cost per unit to two decimal places.

c. A perpetual inventory system and moving-average cost formula. Round cost per unit to two decimal places.

E8.16 (LO 5, 6) **(Alternative Inventory Methods)** Schonfeld Corporation began operations on December 1, 2019. The only inventory transaction in 2019 was the purchase of inventory on December 10, 2019, at a cost of $20 per unit. None of this inventory was sold in 2019. Relevant information for fiscal 2020 is as follows:

Ending inventory units:		
Dec. 31, 2019		100
Dec. 31, 2020, by purchase date		
Dec. 2, 2020	100	
July 20, 2020	30	130

During 2020, the following purchases and sales were made:

Purchases		Sales	
Mar. 15	300 units at $24	Apr. 10	200
July 20	300 units at $25	Aug. 20	300
Sept. 4	200 units at $28	Nov. 18	170
Dec. 2	100 units at $30	Dec. 12	200

The company uses the periodic inventory method.

Instructions

Determine ending inventory under (a) specific identification, (b) FIFO, and (c) weighted average cost. Round weighted average cost per unit to two decimal places.

E8.17 (LO 5, 6, 10) **(Calculating FIFO, Weighted Average Cost—Periodic)** The following information is for the inventory of mini-kettles at Funnell Company Limited for the month of May:

▶ Video

Date	Transaction	Units In	Unit Cost	Total	Units Sold	Unit Price	Total
May 1	Balance	100	$4.10	$ 410			
6	Purchase	800	4.20	3,360			
7	Sale				300	$7.00	$ 2,100
10	Sale				300	7.30	2,190
12	Purchase	400	4.50	1,800			
15	Sale				200	7.40	1,480
18	Purchase	300	4.60	1,380			
22	Sale				400	7.40	2,960
25	Purchase	500	4.58	2,290			
30	Sale				200	7.50	1,500
Totals		2,100		$9,240	1,400		$10,230

Instructions

a. Assuming that the periodic inventory method is used, calculate the inventory cost at May 31 under each of the following cost flow formulas:

1. FIFO

2. Weighted average (round the weighted average unit cost to the nearest one tenth of one cent)

b. Finance Which method will yield the higher current ratio or gross profit?

E8.18 (LO 5, 6) (Calculating FIFO, Moving-Average Cost—Perpetual) Information is presented in E8.17 on the inventory of mini-kettles at Funnell Company Limited for the month of May.

Instructions

a. Assuming that the perpetual inventory method is used, calculate the inventory cost at May 31 under each of the following cost flow formulas:

1. FIFO

2. Moving-average (round all unit costs to the nearest one tenth of one cent)

b. Show where the inventory costs that were calculated in this exercise are different from the ones in E8.17 and explain the possible reasons why.

E8.19 (LO 5, 7, 10) (Lower of Cost and Net Realizable Value, Periodic Method—Journal Entries) As a result of its annual inventory count, Tarweed Corp. determined its ending inventory at cost and at lower of cost and net realizable value at December 31, 2019, and December 31, 2020. December 31, 2019, was Tarweed's first year end. This information is as follows:

	Cost	Lower of Cost and NRV
Dec. 31, 2019	$321,000	$283,250
Dec. 31, 2020	385,000	351,250

Instructions

a. Prepare the journal entries required at December 31, 2019 and 2020, assuming that the inventory is recorded directly at the lower of cost and net realizable value and a periodic inventory system is used.

b. Prepare the journal entries required at December 31, 2019 and 2020, assuming that the inventory is recorded at cost and an allowance account is adjusted at each year end under a periodic system.

c. Which of the two methods above provides the higher net income in each year?

E8.20 (LO 7) (Lower of Cost and Net Realizable Value) The inventory of 3T Company on December 31, 2020, consists of the following items.

Part No.	Quantity	Cost per Unit	NRV
110	600	$ 90	$100
111	1,000	60	52
112	500	80	76
113	200	170	180
120	400	205	208
121*	1,600	16	.20
122	300	240	235

*Part No. 121 is obsolete and has a realizable value of $0.20 each as scrap.

Instructions

a. Determine the inventory as at December 31, 2020, by the lower of cost and net realizable value method, applying this method directly to each item.

b. Determine the inventory as at December 31, 2020, by the lower of cost and net realizable value method, applying the method to the total of the inventory.

E8.21 (LO 7) (Lower of Cost and NRV Valuation Account) The following information is for Takin Enterprises Ltd.:

	Jan. 31	Feb. 28	Mar. 31	Apr. 30
Inventory at cost	$25,000	$25,100	$29,000	$23,000
Inventory at the lower of cost and net realizable value	24,500	17,600	22,600	17,300
Purchases for the month		20,000	24,000	26,500
Sales for the month		29,000	35,000	40,000

Instructions

a. Using the above information, prepare monthly income statements (as far as the data permit) in columnar form for February, March, and April. Show the inventory in the statement at cost; show the gain or loss due to fluctuations in NRV separately. Takin uses the indirect or allowance method.

b. Prepare the journal entry that is needed to establish the valuation account at January 31 and the entries to adjust it at the end of each month after that.

E8.22 (LO 8, 11) **(Biological Inventory Assets)** Nicholas's Christmas Tree Farm Ltd. grows pine, fir, and spruce trees. The farm cuts and sells trees during the Christmas season and exports most of the trees to the United States. The remaining trees are sold to local tree-lot operators.

It normally takes 12 years for a tree to grow to a suitable size, and the average selling price of a tree is $24. The biggest costs to the business are pest control, fertilizer, and pruning trees over the 12-year period. These costs average $12 per tree (assume these are incurred evenly over the 12-year growing cycle).

Instructions

a. How should this inventory be recorded under ASPE?

b. How should the costs of pest control, fertilizer, and pruning be recognized under IFRS?

c. Assume that the fair value of each tree at the end of 2020 is $8 and the opening value was $5. Prepare the journal entries if the costs are capitalized each year.

d. Assume that the fair value of each tree at the end of 2020 is $8 and the opening value was $5. Prepare the journal entries if the operating costs are expensed each year.

E8.23 (LO 9) **(Gross Profit Method)** Milan Company Limited, which follows ASPE, uses the gross profit method to estimate inventory for monthly reports. Information follows for the month of May:

Video

Inventory, May 1	$360,000	Sales	$1,200,000
Purchases	700,000	Sales returns	70,000
Freight in	50,000	Purchase discounts	12,000

Instructions

a. Calculate the estimated inventory at May 31, assuming that the gross profit is 25% of sales.

b. Calculate the estimated inventory at May 31, assuming that the markup on cost is 25%. Round the gross profit percentage to two decimal places.

E8.24 (LO 10) **(Analysis of Inventories)** The financial statements of Trifolium Corporation for fiscal 2018 to fiscal 2020 are as follows (in thousands):

	Fiscal 2020	**Fiscal 2019**	**Fiscal 2018**
Inventory	$ 291,497	$ 319,445	$ 302,207
Sales	1,346,758	1,331,009	1,263,955
Gross margin	483,519	478,401	451,592
Net income	29,325	47,451	35,217

Instructions

a. **Finance** Calculate Trifolium's (1) inventory turnover and (2) average days to sell inventory for each of the two years ended in 2020 and 2019. Round inventory turnover to two decimal places and average days to the nearest day.

b. Calculate Trifolium's gross profit percentage and percentage markup on cost for each fiscal year. Round your answers to two decimal places (for example, 52.75%).

c. Is the growth in inventory levels over the last year consistent with the increase in sales? Explain your answer.

E8.25 (LO 10) **(Ratios)** Partial information follows for a Canadian manufacturing company:

	Year 10	**Year 9**	**Year 8**	**Year 7**
Sales	$401,244	$_____	$344,759	
Cost of goods sold	_____	286,350	263,979	
Gross margin	95,086	87,957	_____	
Ending inventory	34,511	_____	34,750	36,750
Gross profit percentage	_____	23.5%	_____	
Inventory turnover	_____	8.19 times	_____	
Days sales in inventory	_____	44.57 days	_____	

Instructions

a. Enter the missing amounts where indicated for years 8, 9, and 10 in the above schedule.

b. **Management Accounting** Comment on the profitability and inventory management trends, and suggest possible reasons for these results.

*E8.26 **(LO 12)** **(Retail Inventory Method)** The records of Sudbury Menswear report the following data for the month of September:

Sales	$118,500	Purchases (at cost)	$ 59,500
Sales returns	2,500	Purchases (at sales price)	112,600
Additional markups	10,500	Purchase returns (at cost)	2,500
Markup cancellations	1,500	Purchase returns (at sales price)	3,500
Markdowns	9,300	Beginning inventory (at cost)	32,000
Markdown cancellations	2,800	Beginning inventory (at sales price)	48,500
Freight on purchases	3,600		

Instructions

a. Estimate the ending inventory using the retail inventory method. Round the cost-to-retail ratio to two decimal places.

b. Assuming that a physical count of the inventory determined that the actual ending inventory at retail prices at the end of September was $42,000, estimate the loss due to shrinkage and theft.

c. Identify four reasons why the estimate of inventory may be different from the actual inventory at cost.

*E8.27 **(LO 13)** **(Primary Sources of GAAP)** There are a few primary sources of GAAP for inventory under both ASPE and IFRS.

Instructions

List the sources of guidance in the table below.

Type of Inventory	Primary Guidance under ASPE	Primary Guidance under IFRS
Equipment manufactured		
Financial derivatives held by a financial institution		
Biological assets at the point of harvest		
Harvested agricultural produce		

Problems

P8.1 The following independent situations relate to inventory accounting:

1. Sanderson Company's inventory of $1.1 million at December 31, 2020, was based on a physical count of goods priced at cost and before any year-end adjustments relating to the following items:

a. Goods shipped f.o.b. shipping point on December 24, 2020, from a vendor at an invoice cost of $69,000 to Sanderson Company, received on January 4, 2021.

b. Goods worth $29,000 and included in the physical count, billed to Makee Corp., f.o.b. shipping point, on December 31, 2020. The carrier picked up these goods on January 3, 2021.

c. Goods shipped f.o.b. destination received by Sanderson on January 5, 2021. The invoiced amount was $77,000.

d. Goods shipped f.o.b. destination and received by Sanderson on December 25, 2020, that are on consignment. The value of the goods is $83,500 and they have not been included in the physical inventory count.

2. Howe Corp. had 1,500 units on hand of part 54169 on May 1, 2020, with a cost of $21 per unit. Howe uses a periodic inventory system. Purchases of part 54169 during May were as follows:

	Units	Unit Cost
May 9	2,000	$22.00
17	3,500	23.00
26	1,000	24.00

A physical count on May 31, 2020, shows 2,000 units of part 54169 on hand.

3. Grossman Ltd., a retail store chain, had the following information in its general ledger for the year 2020:

Merchandise purchased for resale	$909,400
Interest on notes payable to vendors for the purchase of inventory	8,700
Purchase returns	16,500
Freight in	22,000
Freight out	17,100
Cash discounts on purchases	6,800
Storage costs incurred when warehouse became full	8,300

Instructions

Answer the following questions for the situations above and explain your answer in each case:

a. For situation 1, what should Sanderson Company report as its inventory amount on its 2020 SFP?

b. For situation 2, using the FIFO method, what is the inventory cost of part 54169 at May 31, 2020? Using the weighted average cost formula, what is the inventory cost?

c. For situation 3, assume that Grossman Ltd. is a private company reporting under ASPE. What is Grossman's inventoriable cost for 2020? Explain any items that are excluded.

d. How would your answer to part (c) differ if Grossman used IFRS? Which of these standards provides the most useful information to users: ASPE or IFRS? Why?

P8.2 On February 1, 2020, Akeson Ltd. began selling electric scooters that it purchased exclusively from Ionone Motors Inc. Ionone Motors offers volume rebates based on the volume of annual sales to its customers and calculates and pays the rebates at its fiscal year end, December 31. Akeson has a September fiscal year end and uses a perpetual inventory system. The rebate offer that Akeson received is for a $75 rebate on each scooter that is purchased in excess of 150 units in the calendar year, ending December 31. An additional rebate of $30 is given for all units purchased in excess of 175 units in the same year. By September 30, 2020, Akeson had purchased 190 units from Ionone Motors and had sold all but 35. Although it only made its first purchase on February 1, 2020, Akeson expects to purchase a total of 250 electric scooters from Ionone Motors by December 31, 2020. Before arriving at the estimate of 250 electric scooters, Akeson's management looked carefully at trends in purchases by its competitors and the strong market for sales of electric scooters in the coming months; sales are especially strong among environmentally conscious customers in suburban areas. Management is very confident the 250 electric scooters will be purchased by December 31, 2020.

Instructions

Assuming that Akeson follows the reporting requirements under ASPE, answer the following questions.

a. Based on the conceptual framework, discuss the reasoning that Akeson should use in how it treats the rebate that it expects to receive from Ionone Motors.

b. Would your opinion change if the rebate that is expected from Ionone Motors had been discretionary?

c. Discuss some of the factors that management should consider in arriving at a reasonable estimate of its amount of purchases to December 31, 2020.

d. Calculate the amount of any accrued rebate to be recorded by Akeson at September 30, 2020, assuming that the rebate is not discretionary and that management has a high degree of confidence in its estimate of the amount of purchases that will occur by December 31, 2020.

e. Record the accruals that are needed at Akeson's fiscal year end of September 30, 2020.

f. How would your response change if Akeson followed the reporting requirements of IFRS?

P8.3 Ianthe Limited, a manufacturer of small tools, provided the following information from its accounting records for the year ended December 31, 2020:

Inventory at December 31, 2020 (based on physical count of goods in Ianthe's plant, at cost, on December 31, 2020)	$1,720,000
Accounts payable at December 31, 2020	1,300,000
Total current assets	2,680,000
Total current liabilities	1,550,000
Net sales (sales less sales returns)	8,550,000

Additional information:

1. Included in the physical count were tools billed to a customer f.o.b. shipping point on December 31, 2020. These tools had a cost of $37,000 and were billed at $57,000. The shipment was on Ianthe's loading dock waiting to be picked up by the common carrier.

2. Goods were in transit from a vendor to Ianthe on December 31, 2020. The invoice was for $51,000, and the goods were shipped f.o.b. shipping point on December 29, 2020. Ianthe will sell these items in 2021 for $87,500. These were excluded from the inventory count.

3. Work-in-process inventory costing $38,000 was sent to an outside processor for plating on December 30, 2020. This was excluded from the inventory count.

4. Tools that were returned by customers and awaiting inspection in the returned goods area on December 31, 2020, were not included in the physical count. On January 8, 2021, these tools, costing $38,000, were inspected and returned to inventory. Credit memos totalling $48,000 were issued to the customers on the same date.

5. Tools shipped to a customer f.o.b. destination on December 26, 2020, were in transit at December 31, 2020, and had a cost of $21,000. When it was notified that the customer received the goods on January 2, 2021, Ianthe issued a sales invoice for $42,000. These were excluded from the inventory count.

6. Goods with an invoice cost of $27,000 that were received from a vendor at 5:00 p.m. on December 31, 2020, were recorded on a receiving report dated January 2, 2021. The goods were not included in the physical count, but the invoice was included in accounts payable at December 31, 2020.

7. Goods that were received from a vendor on December 26, 2020, were included in the physical count. However, the vendor invoice of $56,000 for these goods was not included in accounts payable at December 31, 2020, because the accounts payable copy of the receiving report was lost.

8. On January 3, 2021, a monthly freight bill in the amount of $7,000 was received. The bill specifically related to merchandise purchased in December 2020, and half of this merchandise was still in the inventory at December 31, 2020. The freight charges were not included in either the inventory account or accounts payable at December 31, 2020.

Instructions

a. Using the format shown below, prepare a schedule of adjustments to the initial amounts in Ianthe's accounting records as at December 31, 2020. Show separately the effect, if any, of each of the eight transactions on the December 31, 2020 amounts. If the transaction has no effect on the initial amount that is shown, write "NONE."

	Inventory	Accounts Payable	Net Sales
Initial amounts	$1,720,000	$1,300,000	$8,550,000
Adjustments—increase (decrease)			
Total adjustments			
Adjusted amounts	$	$	$

b. **Digging Deeper** After you arrive at the adjusted balances for part (a) above, determine if the following have improved or if they have deteriorated:

1. Working capital
2. Current ratio
3. Gross profit
4. Profit margin

(Adapted from AICPA)

P8.4 Halm Skidoos Limited, a private company that began operations in 2017, always values its inventories at their current net realizable value. The company uses ASPE. Its annual inventory figure is arrived at by taking a physical count and then pricing each item in the physical inventory at current resale prices. The condensed income statements for the company's past four years are as follows:

	2017	2018	2019	2020
Sales	$850,000	$880,000	$950,000	$990,000
Cost of goods sold	560,000	590,000	630,000	650,000
Gross profit	290,000	290,000	320,000	340,000
Operating expenses	190,000	180,000	200,000	210,000
Income before taxes	$100,000	$110,000	$120,000	$130,000

Instructions

a. Comment on the procedures that Halm uses for valuing inventories.

b. Prepare corrected condensed income statements using an acceptable method of inventory valuation, assuming that the inventory at cost and as determined by the corporation (using net realizable value) at the end of each of the four years is as follows:

Year	At Cost	Net Realizable Value
2017	$150,000	$160,000
2018	147,000	160,000
2019	178,000	170,000
2020	175,000	189,000

c. Finance Compare the trend in income for the four years using the corporation's approach to valuing ending inventory and using a method that is acceptable under GAAP.

d. Calculate the cumulative effect of the difference in the valuation of inventory on the ending balance of retained earnings from 2017 through 2020.

e. Comment on the differences that you observe after making the corrections to the inventory valuation over the four years.

P8.5 Lupulin Limited stocks a variety of sports equipment for sale to institutions. The following stock record card for basketballs was taken from the records at the December 31, 2020 year end:

Date	Invoice Number	Terms	Units Received	Unit Invoice Cost	Gross Invoice Amount
Jan. 1	balance	Net 30	100	$20.00	$2,000
15	10624	Net 30	60	20.00	1,200
Mar. 15	11437	1/5, net 30	65	16.00	1,040
June 20	21332	1/10, net 30	90	15.00	1,350
Sept. 12	27644	1/10, net 30	84	12.00	1,008
Nov. 24	31269	1/10, net 30	76	11.00	836
	Totals		475		$7,434

A physical inventory on December 31, 2020, reveals that 100 basketballs are in stock. The bookkeeper informs you that all the discounts were taken. Assume that Lupulin Limited uses a periodic inventory system and records purchases at their invoice price less discounts. During 2020, the average sales price per basketball was $22.25.

Instructions

a. Calculate the December 31, 2020 inventory using the FIFO formula.

b. Calculate the December 31, 2020 inventory using the weighted average cost formula. (Round unit costs to the nearest cent.)

c. Prepare income statements for the year ended December 31, 2020, as far as the "gross profit" line under each of the FIFO and weighted average methods, and calculate the gross profit rate for each. Explain the difference in the gross profit under the two methods.

d. Digging Deeper If the selling prices for the basketballs that were sold follow the same pattern as their wholesale prices from the supplier, might this have an effect on the inventory cost that is reported on the December 31, 2020 SFP? (*Hint:* Review your answers to parts [a] to [c].)

P8.6 The summary financial statements of Langford Landscaping Ltd. on December 31, 2020, are as follows:

Langford Landscaping Ltd.
Statement of Financial Position
December 31, 2020

Assets

Cash	$ 5,000
Accounts and notes receivable	39,000
Inventory	79,000
Property, plant, and equipment (net)	125,000
	$248,000

Liabilities and Shareholders' Equity

Accounts and notes payable	$ 75,000
Long-term debt	62,000
Common shares	60,000
Retained earnings	51,000
	$248,000

The following errors were made by the inexperienced accountant on December 31, 2019, and were not corrected.

1. The inventory was overstated by $13,000.

2. A prepaid expense of $2,400 was omitted. (It was fully expensed in 2019.)

3. Accrued revenue of $2,500 was omitted. (It was recognized when cash was received in 2020.)

4. A supplier's invoice for $1,700 for purchases made in 2019 was not recorded until 2020.

On December 31, 2020, there were further errors:

5. The inventory was understated by $17,000.

6. A prepaid expense of $750 was omitted.

7. Accrued December 2020 salaries of $1,800 were not recognized.

8. Unearned income of $2,300 was recorded in the 2020 revenue.

9. In addition, it was determined that $20,000 of the accounts payable were long-term, and that a $500 dividend was reported as dividend expense and deducted in calculating net income.

The net income reported on the books for 2020 was $53,000.

Instructions

a. **Finance** Calculate the working capital, current ratio, and debt to equity ratio for Langford Landscaping Ltd. based on the original SFP information provided above. Round ratios to two decimal places.

b. Calculate the corrected net income for 2020.

c. Prepare a corrected SFP at December 31, 2020.

d. **Finance** Using the corrected data, recalculate the working capital and the ratios in part (a). Explain the resulting differences in the ratios as a result of the use of the corrected data.

P8.7 Astro Languet established Languet Products Co. as a sole proprietorship on January 5, 2020. At the company's year end of December 31, 2020, the accounts had the following balances (in thousands):

Current assets, excluding inventory	$ 10
Other assets	107
Current liabilities	30
Long-term bank loan	50
Owner's investment (excluding income)	40
Purchases during year	
Jan. 2: 5,000 @ $11	55
June 30: 8,000 @ $12	96
Dec. 10: 6,000 @ $16	96
	247
Sales	284
Other expenses	40

A count of ending inventory on December 31, 2020, showed there were 4,000 units on hand.

Astro is now preparing financial statements for the year. He is aware that inventory may be costed using the FIFO or weighted average cost formula. He is unsure of which one to use and asks for your assistance. In discussions with Astro, you learn the following.

1. Suppliers to Languet Products provide goods at regular prices as long as Languet Products' current ratio is at least 2 to 1. If this ratio is lower, the suppliers increase their price by 10% in order to compensate for what they consider to be a substantial credit risk.

2. The terms of the long-term bank loan include the bank's ability to demand immediate repayment of the loan if the debt to total assets ratio is greater than 45%.

3. Astro thinks that, for the company to be a success, the rate of return on total assets should be at least 30%.

4. Astro has an agreement with the company's only employee that, for each full percentage point above a 25% rate of return on total assets, she will be given an additional one day off with pay in the following year.

Instructions

a. Prepare an income statement and a year-end SFP, assuming the company applies:

1. The FIFO cost formula

2. The weighted average cost formula

b. Finance Recalculate the key ratios given each formula in part (a). Round the current ratio to two decimal places and the remaining ratios to one decimal place.

c. Ethics Discuss the impact of using each formula on the key ratios.

d. Which method do you recommend? Explain briefly.

e. Digging Deeper Considering the choice of inventory cost formulas that are available, do the ratios noted above adequately measure the financial performance of Languet Products from the perspective of the users?

P8.8 Milford Company determined its ending inventory at cost and at lower of cost and net realizable value at December 31, 2018, 2019, and 2020, as follows:

	Cost	Lower of Cost and Net Realizable Value
Dec. 31, 2018	$60,000	$60,000
Dec. 31, 2019	79,000	74,500
Dec. 31, 2020	78,800	69,000

Instructions

a. Prepare the journal entries that are required at December 31, 2019 and 2020, assuming that a periodic inventory system and the direct method of adjusting to NRV are used.

b. Prepare the journal entries that are required at December 31, 2019 and 2020, assuming that a periodic inventory system is used, with inventory recorded at cost and reduced to NRV through the use of an allowance account.

P8.9 Riverdale Farms Ltd. operates dairy farms. The following are selected transactions that occurred during the fiscal years ended December 31, 2020 and 2021, for one dairy cow and its calf.

1. A calf was born in March 2020. Its fair value less costs to sell at date of birth was $100.

2. Milk produced by the dairy cow for the year sold for $1,000, all for cash. No milk is kept on the farm.

3. General farm expenses of $200 were incurred in 2020, all paid in cash.

4. Cost to feed the calf was $150 for 2020 and $60 for 2021, all paid in cash.

5. The calf was sent to pasture. When it returned to the herd on December 31, 2020, it had increased in value to $500 net of any selling costs.

6. The calf was sold for $850 cash on April 1, 2021, net of auction fees and delivery costs of $75.

Instructions

a. Is the calf a biological asset? Is the milk a biological asset?

b. Prepare the entries for Riverdale Farms Ltd. for the transactions listed assuming the company follows IFRS.

c. Prepare the entries for Riverdale Farms Ltd. for the transactions listed assuming the company follows ASPE and chooses to expense all costs related to the upkeep of the calf.

P8.10 Reena Corp. lost most of its inventory in a fire in December, just before the year-end physical inventory was taken. The corporation's books disclosed the following:

Beginning inventory	$440,000	Sales	$1,350,000
Purchases for the year	850,000	Sales returns	50,000
Purchase returns	55,000	Gross margin on sales	40%

Merchandise with a selling price of $42,000 remained undamaged after the fire. Damaged merchandise with an original selling price of $30,000 had a net realizable value of $10,600.

Instructions

a. Calculate the amount lost because of the fire, assuming that the corporation had no insurance coverage.

b. Prepare the journal entry to record the loss and account for the damaged inventory in a separate Damaged Inventory account. In the same entry, record cost of goods sold for the year ended December 31.

c. How would the loss be classified on the income statement of Reena Corp.?

d. Digging Deeper While the gross profit percentage has averaged 40% over the past five years, it has been as high as 42% and as low as 37.5%. Given this information, should a range of possible loss amounts be provided instead of a single figure? Explain.

P8.11 Sier Specialty Corp., a division of FH Inc., manufactures three models of bicycle gearshift components that are sold to bicycle manufacturers, retailers, and catalogue outlets. Since beginning operations in 1969, Sier has used normal absorption costing and has assumed a first-in, first-out cost flow in its perpetual inventory system. Except for overhead, manufacturing costs are accumulated using actual costs. Overhead is applied to production using predetermined overhead rates. The balances of the inventory accounts at the end of Sier's fiscal year, September 30, 2020, follow. The inventories are stated at cost before any year-end adjustments.

Finished goods	$757,000
Work in process	192,500
Raw materials	300,000
Factory supplies	69,000

The following information relates to Sier's inventory and operations:

1. The finished goods inventory consists of these items:

	Cost	Net realizable value
Down tube shifter		
Standard model	$ 97,500	$ 67,000
Click adjustment model	94,500	87,000
Deluxe model	108,000	110,000
Total down tube shifters	300,000	264,000
Bar end shifter		
Standard model	133,000	120,050
Click adjustment model	79,000	108,150
Total bar end shifters	212,000	228,200
Head tube shifter		
Standard model	128,000	103,650
Click adjustment model	117,000	145,300
Total head tube shifters	245,000	248,950
Total finished goods	$757,000	$741,150

2. Half of the finished goods inventory of head tube shifters is at catalogue outlets on consignment.

3. Three quarters of the finished goods inventory of bar end shifters has been pledged as collateral for a bank loan.

4. Half of the raw materials balance is for derailleurs acquired at a contracted price that is 20% above the current market price. The net realizable value of the rest of the raw materials is $135,500.

5. The total net realizable value of the work-in-process inventory is $105,500.

6. Included in the cost of factory supplies are obsolete items with a historical cost of $4,200. The net realizable value of the remaining factory supplies is $65,900.

7. Sier applies the lower of cost and net realizable value method to each of the three types of shifters in finished goods inventory. For each of the other three inventory accounts, Sier applies the lower of cost and net realizable value method to the total of each inventory account.

8. Consider all of the amounts presented above as being material amounts in relation to Sier's financial statements as a whole.

Instructions

a. Assuming that ASPE is followed, prepare the inventory section of Sier's statement of financial position as at September 30, 2020, including any required note(s).

b. Regardless of your answer to part (a), assume that the net realizable value of Sier's inventories is less than cost. Explain how this decline would be presented in Sier's income statement for the fiscal year ended September 30, 2020, under ASPE.

c. Assume that Sier has a firm purchase commitment for the same type of derailleur that is included in the raw materials inventory as at September 30, 2020, and that the purchase commitment is at a contracted price that is 15% higher than the current market price. These derailleurs are to be delivered to Sier after September 30, 2020. Discuss the impact, if any, that this purchase commitment would have on Sier's financial statements prepared for the fiscal year ended September 30, 2020, under ASPE.

d. How would your response to part (c) change under IFRS?

e. Explain and compare the disclosure requirements under ASPE and IFRS.

P8.12 The Eserine Wood Corporation manufactures desks. Most of the company's desks are standard models that are sold at catalogue prices. At December 31, 2020, the following finished desks appear in the company's inventory:

Finished Desks	Type A	Type B	Type C	Type D
2020 catalogue selling price	$460	$490	$890	$1,040
FIFO cost per inventory list, Dec. 31, 2020	410	450	830	960
Estimated current cost to manufacture				
(at Dec. 31, 2020, and early 2021)	460	440	790	1,000
Sales commissions and estimated other costs				
of disposal	40	65	95	130
2021 catalogue selling price	575	650	780	1,420
Quantity on hand	15	117	113	110

The 2020 catalogue was in effect through November 2020, and the 2021 catalogue is effective as of December 1, 2020. All catalogue prices are net of the usual discounts. Generally, the company tries to obtain a 20% gross margin on the selling price and it has usually been successful in achieving this.

Instructions

a. Assume that the company has adopted a lower of FIFO cost and net realizable value approach for the valuation of inventories and applies it on an individual inventory item basis. At what total inventory value will the desks appear on the company's December 31, 2020 SFP?

b. Explain the rationale for using the lower of cost and net realizable rule for inventories.

c. Explain the impact if inventory was valued at lower of cost and net realizable value on a total basis.

*P8.13 The records for the Clothing Department of Danny's Discount Store are summarized below for the month of January.

Inventory, January 1: at retail $25,000; at cost $17,000
Purchases in January: at retail $137,000; at cost $82,500
Freight in: $7,000
Purchase returns: at retail $3,000; at cost $2,300
Transfers in from suburban branch: at retail $13,000; at cost $9,200
Net markups: $8,000
Net markdowns: $4,000
Inventory losses due to normal breakage and so on: at retail $400
Sales revenue at retail: $95,000
Sales returns: $2,400

Instructions

a. Calculate the inventory for this department as at January 31, at retail prices.

b. Calculate the ending inventory at cost using the retail method. Round the cost-to-retail ratio to two decimal places.

*P8.14 The records for the Clothing Department of Ji-Woon's Department Store are summarized as follows for the month of January:

1. Inventory, January 1: at retail, $28,000; at cost, $18,000
2. Purchases in January: at retail, $147,000; at cost, $110,000
3. Freight in: $6,000
4. Purchase returns: at retail, $3,500; at cost, $2,700
5. Purchase allowances: $2,200
6. Transfers in from suburban branch: at retail, $13,000; at cost, $9,200
7. Net markups: $8,000
8. Net markdowns: $4,000
9. Inventory losses due to normal breakage and so on: at retail, $400
10. Sales at retail: $121,000
11. Sales returns: $2,400

Instructions

a. Estimate the inventory for this department as at January 31 at (1) retail and (2) cost using the retail method. Round the cost-to-retail ratio to two decimal places.

b. Assume that a physical inventory count taken at retail prices after the close of business on January 31 indicated an inventory amount that is $450 less than what was estimated in part (a), item (1). What could have caused this discrepancy?

P8.15 Some of the information found on a detailed inventory card for Soave Stationery Ltd. for May is as follows:

Date	Received No. of Units	Received Unit Cost	Issued No. of Units	Balance No. of Units
May 1 (opening balance)	1,150	$2.90		1,150
2	1,050	3.00		2,200
7			700	1,500
10	600	3.20		2,100
13			500	1,600
18	1,000	3.30	300	2,300
20			1,100	1,200
23	1,300	3.40		2,500
26			800	1,700
28	1,500	3.60		3,200
31			1,300	1,900

Instructions

a. From the above data, calculate the ending inventory based on each of the following cost formulas. Assume that perpetual inventory records are kept in units only and average cost is calculated monthly at each month end. Calculate unit costs to the nearest cent and ending inventory to the nearest dollar.

  1. First-in, first-out (FIFO)

  2. Weighted average cost

b. Based on your results in part (a), and assuming that the average selling price per unit during May was $7.25, prepare partial income statements up to the "gross profit on sales" line. Calculate the gross profit percentage under each inventory cost formula. Round your answers to one decimal place. Comment on your results.

c. Digging Deeper Assume the perpetual inventory record is kept in dollars, and costs are calculated at the time of each withdrawal. Recalculate the amounts under this revised assumption, rounding average unit costs to four decimal places. Would the ending inventory amounts under each of the two cost formulas above be the same? Explain.

P8.16 Excel Hull Company's record of transactions concerning part X for the month of April was as follows.

Purchases		Sales	
April 1 (balance on hand)	100 @ $5.00	April 5	300
4	400 @ 5.10	12	200
11	300 @ 5.30	27	800
18	200 @ 5.35	28	150
26	600 @ 5.60		
30	200 @ 5.80		

a. Calculate the inventory at April 30 on each of the following bases. Assume that perpetual inventory records are kept in units only. Calculate unit costs to the nearest cent.

  1. First-in, first-out (FIFO)

  2. Average cost

b. If the perpetual inventory record is kept in dollars, and costs are calculated at the time of each withdrawal, what amount would be shown as ending inventory in (1) and (2) above? (Calculate average unit costs to four decimal places.)

Cases

Refer to the Case Primer on the Student Website and in WileyPLUS *to help you answer these cases.*

CA8.1 Tobacco Group Inc. (TGI) is in the consumer packaged goods industry. Its shares are widely held and key shareholders include several very large pension funds.

In the current year, 59% of the net revenues and 61% of operating income came from tobacco product sales. Because of the health risks related to the use of tobacco products, the industry is increasingly regulated by government and the company is implicated in substantial tobacco-related litigation.

During the past three years, the company entered into agreements with the government to settle asserted and unasserted health-care recovery costs and other claims. The agreements, known as the Government Settlement Agreements, call for payments by the domestic tobacco industry into a fund in the following amounts:

Current year	$10.9 billion
Following four years	$8 billion each year
Thereafter	$9 billion each year

The fund will be used to settle claims and aid tobacco growers. Each company's share of these payments is based on its market share, and TGI records its portion of the settlement costs as cost of goods sold upon shipment. These amounts may increase based on several factors, including inflation and industry volume. In the past three years, the company has accrued costs of more than $5 billion each year.

Another significant lawsuit, the class action, is still in process. Last year, the jury returned a verdict assessing punitive damages against various defendants, and TGI was responsible for $74 billion. The company is contesting this and the lawsuit continues. As a result of preliminary judicial stipulations, the company has placed $500 million in a separate interest-bearing escrow account. This money will be kept by the court and distributed to the plaintiffs regardless of the outcome of the trial. The company also placed $1.2 billion in another escrow account, and this amount will be returned to the company if it wins the case.

Instructions

Assume the role of a financial analyst and discuss the related financial reporting issues. Specifically, note alternative accounting treatments for each issue and recommend how each issue should be treated in the financial statements.

CA8.2 Findit Gold Inc. (FGI) was created in 2012 and is 25% owned by Findit Mining Corporation (FMC). FGI's shares trade on the local exchange and its objective is to become a substantial low-cost mineral producer in developing countries. FMC provided substantial financial support to FGI when FGI was in the exploration stage.

Over the most recent five-year period, FGI carried its gold bullion inventory at net realizable value and recognized revenues on the gold produced (net of refining and selling costs) at net realizable value, when the minerals were produced. Gold is a commodity that trades actively and whose price fluctuates according to supply and demand.

Instructions

Assume the role of the controller of FMC and assess the financial reporting policies relating to inventory valuation and revenue recognition.

CA8.3 Finance Lots Lumber Limited is a private company that operates in the forestry sector and owns timber lots. The company produces specialty lumber and sells to distributors and retailers. Currently, Lots uses ASPE when preparing its financial statements. It has an October 31 year end. The company has a management bonus plan, which is based on net earnings and gross profits.

In the past, the company estimated decommissioning costs related to its sawmill facility and recorded them as a liability, with an offsetting increase to the cost of the plant. Since the production period can be fairly long, including the curing and special treatments applied to the lumber, the company has had to borrow to finance the production process. Lots' borrowings are primarily from a private investor, who has set two key requirements in the loan agreement. The agreement requires Lots to maintain a certain debt to equity ratio and to submit audited financial statements prepared using GAAP. The audited financial statements are due within 60 days of the year-end date. Historically, the company has expensed this interest for borrowings from the private investor.

The company has a purchase commitment to buy a minimum amount of specialty resins used to treat the lumber. This is a five-year contract at a fixed price. At the time the contract was signed, Lots was very excited about it, but now, early in the fourth year of the contract, the company has realized that it will not need the volumes that it committed to buy, because it has developed a new technique that is cheaper and that uses a different solution to treat the wood. In fact, it looks as though the company will have to pay for items that will not be required. Lots is trying to decide whether to break the contract or remain with the contract and just pay for the items but not take delivery. There are two years remaining on the contract.

Instructions

Lots Lumber Limited has just hired you as its new controller. It is trying to decide whether to adopt IFRS or continue to report under ASPE. Provide the president with a report that details the impact of reporting under IFRS on the company's financial results, management bonus plan, and debt covenant, giving consideration to the issues indicated above.

Integrated Case

(*Hint:* If there are issues here that are new, use the conceptual framework to help you support your analysis with solid reasoning.)

IC8.1 Grappa Grapes Inc. (GGI) grows grapes and produces sparkling wines. The company is located in a very old area of town with easy access to fertile farmland that is excellent for growing grapes. It is owned by the Grappa family. The company has been in operation for 100 years and a large part of its success lies in the excellent vineyards and unique process for producing vintage wines. About every three years, new farmland is purchased from landowners adjacent to the original farm. New vines are planted on the newly purchased land. Generally, it takes about another three years for the vines to produce quality grapes for wine-making.

The winery sits at the edge of a range of hills that are composed of chalk. GGI has dug "caves" into the side of the hills at a significant cost and the chalk caves provide the perfect temperature and humidity for the maturing wines. All of the vintage wines are produced, aged, and stored in these chalk caves. People come from all over the country to visit the "caves." As a matter of fact, 25% of the company's revenues are from winery tours.

The company has had three years where it has managed to produce vintage wines. Vintage wines are of higher quality and sell for a higher price. In addition, they contribute to the prestige of the winery. Because of this success, GGI has started to sell wine "futures." Under the terms of the contract, large wholesalers pay GGI up front and agree to take delivery of a certain number of bottles in two years at 20% off the predetermined future price. A market for trading these contracts now exists for the buyers of the futures.

During the year, in anticipation of increasing costs, the company placed a purchase order for a significant number of oak barrels from France. The barrels are used to age the wines. Because of the declining value of the dollar during a current economic recession and the demand for wines in general over the past year, the value of the barrels has actually declined to below the price locked into under the purchase commitments. The supplier is confident that this is only a temporary decline in value and that the price of the barrels will increase within the next couple of months. GGI may get out of the purchase commitment either by taking delivery of the barrels at the agreed-upon price or by settling net in cash for the difference between the agreed-upon price and the market price (times the number of barrels ordered).

The year has been a very rainy one and some of the very old chalk caves have begun to leak and deteriorate. One of the caves holding a large number of vintage wines collapsed. It is unclear whether the wine is salvageable. The company's insurance will not cover the expected loss, although GGI has hired its lawyers to challenge this, as it feels that the insurance company should cover the loss.

GGI has decided to follow GAAP for the current year's financial statements, as it is planning to go to the bank for a loan. The company's bookkeeper has prepared the draft comparative financial statements for the years ended March 2020 and 2019, but has not dealt with the special issues identified above. GGI's comparative draft financial statements are presented below.

Grappa Grapes Inc.
Balance Sheet
March 31, 2020
(in thousands of Canadian dollars)

Assets

	March 31, 2020	March 31, 2019
Cash	$ 87	$ 44
Accounts and notes receivable	3,900	3,256
Inventory	17,453	16,112
Prepaid expense	137	124
Property, plant, and equipment (net)	15,890	14,389
	$37,467	$33,925

Liabilities and Shareholders' Equity

Accounts payable and accrued liabilities	$ 5,009	$ 4,678
Unearned revenue	3,208	3,320
Income taxes payable	3	2
Current portion of long-term debt	490	490
Long-term debt	4,520	5,010
Common shares	100	100
Retained earnings	24,137	20,325
	$37,467	$33,925

Grappa Grapes Inc.
Income Statement
For the Years Ended March 31
(in thousands of Canadian dollars)

	2020	2019
Sales	$43,303	$41,039
Cost of goods sold	26,329	24,956
Depreciation of plant and equipment used in production	754	686
Gross profit	16,220	15,397
Selling and administration	10,143	9,461
Depreciation of plant and equipment used in selling and administration	441	410
Interest	352	385
Operating earnings	5,284	5,141
Other expenses	21	15
Earnings before income taxes	5,263	5,126
Income taxes	1,412	1,314
Net earnings for the year	$ 3,851	$ 3,812

Instructions

Assume the role of the controller and analyze the financial reporting issues.

Research and Analysis

RA8.1 `Real World Emphasis` Hudson's Bay Company

Hudson's Bay Company (HBC), as described in Note 1 to its financial statements, is a Canadian corporation that "owns and operates department stores in Canada, United States and . . . Europe." HBC's financial statements for its annual period ended February 3, 2018, are at the end of this book.

Instructions

a. How much inventory does HBC have at February 3, 2018, and at January 28, 2017, and what percentage of total assets does the inventory represent? Identify the type of inventory that the company reports on its February 3, 2018 balance sheet. What else does the note on inventory, Note 9, disclose?

b. What is the company's accounting policy for inventory? How is net realizable value determined (see Note 3 on accounting estimates)? What additional items does the company include as part of the cost of its inventory?

c. How much inventory was recognized as an expense in the year? What additional items are included in cost of sales?

d. Describe the accounting policies for revenue recognition of retail merchandise sales. Does the company expect its adoption of IFRS 15 on revenue recognition will change the amount recognized as revenue?

RA8.2 `Real World Emphasis` Stora Enso Oyj

Stora Enso Oyj described itself in its annual report as the "leading provider of renewable solutions in packaging, biomaterials, wooden constructions, and paper globally."

Instructions

Access the financial statements in the financial report of Stora Enso Oyj for its year ended December 31, 2017, from the company's website. With reference to the financial statements, answer the following questions.

a. Describe the accounting policies that the company uses for reporting inventories. What types of expenses are included in costs? Is interest included in inventory costs?

b. What different components make up Stora Enso's inventory and what is the percentage of each of the total for December 31, 2017 and 2016? Which items represent a high percentage of the inventory?

How has this changed over the years? Is there any cause for concern? What was the amount reported on the income statement related to inventory items? Is it possible to calculate the days in inventory ratio?

c. Does the company use the allowance method or the direct method to record writedowns to the inventory? What was the writedown amount during 2017? Were there any amounts reversed during the year?

d. How are the inventories of standing trees measured and reported? What types of assumptions are needed to determine the reported amount of these assets? Where are these assets located? How much was harvested in 2017? What other changes occurred in 2017 in the company's biological assets? What are the effects on earnings for the current year and previous year?

e. Is this inventory-related disclosure useful to the reader? Is there any other information you would like to have?

RA8.3 **Real World Emphasis** **Canadian Tire Corporation, Limited**

Refer to the 2016 and 2017 annual reports of Canadian Tire Corporation, Limited, available at SEDAR (www.sedar.com) or the company's website (www.canadiantire.ca). Note that the company provides a 10-year financial review at the end of its 2016 annual report, but not in 2017. This summary gives relevant comparative information that is useful for determining trends and predicting the company's future results and position.

Instructions

Prepare three graphs covering the 2012–2016 period. (Express all amounts for the first two graphs in millions of dollars.) The first graph is for net income over this five-year period, the second for working capital, and the third for the current ratio. Based on the graphs, predict the values you might expect for the next fiscal period. Compare your predictions with actual results achieved in 2017 and comment on the usefulness of the graphs as a predictive tool.

RA8.4 **Real World Emphasis** **Andrew Peller Limited**

Access the annual financial statements of Andrew Peller Limited for the year ended March 31, 2017, on SEDAR (www.sedar.com) or the company's website (www.andrewpeller.com).

Instructions

Refer to these financial statements and the accompanying notes to answer the following questions.

a. How significant are the inventories relative to total current assets? What categories of inventory does Andrew Peller Limited report?

b. Identify all the accounting policies that are the basis for the inventory values reported on the March 31, 2017 balance sheet.

c. Which category of inventory represents the highest percentage? Is this what you would expect?

d. What was the amount recognized in expense related to inventory for the years ended March 31, 2017 and 2016? Were there any writedowns of inventory or reversals of writedowns for these two years?

e. What was Andrew Peller's inventory turnover ratio for the year ended March 31, 2017? What is the average age of the inventory? Comment briefly.

f. Compare the gross profit ratios for the two most recent years that are reported. Comment briefly on why there might be changes from year to year.

g. If Andrew Peller Limited was a private enterprise that followed ASPE, how would the company have accounted for its vineyard and grape assets? What would be the likely impact on the balance sheet? On the income statement?

RA8.5 **Real World Emphasis** **Loblaw Companies Limited and Empire Company Limited**

Instructions

From SEDAR (www.sedar.com) or the company websites, access the financial statements of Loblaw Companies Limited for its year ended December 30, 2017, and Empire Company Limited for its year ended May 6, 2017. Review the financial statements and answer the following questions.

a. Describe the businesses that Loblaw and Empire operate in.

b. What is the amount of inventory reported by Loblaw at December 30, 2017, and by Empire at May 6, 2017? What percent of total assets is invested in inventory by each company? How does this compare with the previous year?

c. Identify the inventory policies for each company that support the inventory values reported on their respective balance sheets. Comment on whether any aspects of inventory valuation might be open to significant estimation.

d. How much did each company report for inventory expenses in the current and previous year? What was the writedown (and reversal of writedowns) related to inventories for the current and previous year for each company?

e. What are vendor rebates and allowances? How do the companies account for these? Is this the appropriate treatment?

f. Calculate and compare the inventory turnover ratios and days to sell inventory for the two companies for the most current year.

g. Comment on the results of your calculations in part (f) above. Would any differences identified in any of the earlier analyses above help explain differences in the ratios between the two companies? What might be some reasons for the differences between the two companies?

RA8.6 **Research: Manufacturing Inventory**

Identify a company in your local community that develops a product through some form of manufacturing process. Consider a farming operation, bakery, cement supplier, or other company that converts or assembles inputs to develop a different product.

Instructions

Write a report on the company's inventory and its conversion process. (Suggestions: Visit the manufacturing site, view a video of the operation, or speak to company management.) Identify what types of costs are incurred in the manufacturing process. Determine which costs are included in inventory cost in the accounting records, and explain why some may be treated as period costs. Does the company use a periodic or a perpetual system? What cost formula does the company use? How does the company determine NRV, or does it?

Analytics in Action

AIA8.1 Wheels and Skis Inc. is a seasonal business that sells bikes and skis. Offering products for both summer and winter outdoor activities allows sales to be more evenly spread over the year. The key period for selling skis is from October to December and for selling bikes from April to August.

The company is looking to gather some historical data regarding inventory turnover and has collected monthly sales and inventory data for both the bikes and skis categories. The company is hoping to use this data to manage inventories a bit better.

You are the newly hired data analyst for the company and have been asked to do the following:

a. Create a pivot table (using Excel) showing the following:
(1) Year, (2) average value of inventory for each year, and (3) cost of goods sold for the year.

b. Calculate average turnover for each year and add to the pivot table.

c. Create a bar chart showing turnover for the past 5 years.

d. What information does this visualization tell you about turnover over the past 5 years?

e. Create a line chart showing cost of goods sold versus inventory for the past year.

f. What information does this visualization tell you about monthly sales and inventory levels?

Instructions Go to *WileyPLUS* for additional instructions and material to complete this question.

CHAPTER 9

Investments

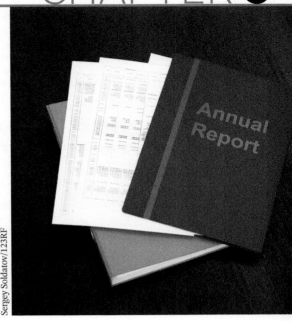

Institutional Investors Rely on Financial Reporting

Some of the biggest investors in the world aren't billionaires or even corporations. They're institutional investors—pension funds, insurance companies, and investment funds—which invest money on behalf of large groups of people. The stakes are high, as these funds often need billions of dollars to pay benefits to retirees, settle insurance claims, or pay returns to individual investors. In 2016, Canadian institutional investors managed nearly $4.8 trillion in assets, according to the Organisation for Economic Co-operation and Development. Their investment strategies have to pay off in the long term.

Most of these Canadian institutional investors' assets consist of equities—shares in corporations. So managers with these institutional funds pay close attention to corporate financial information when deciding whether to buy, keep, or sell their shares. And the most important source of financial information for these money managers is corporate financial statements.

Institutional investors need financial information to estimate companies' future cash flows or earnings, and to assess the associated risk. Research shows that, among the financial statements, institutional investors rely most heavily on the income statement. Among other things, financial statements provide the numbers that institutional investors use to calculate analytical ratios such as the price earnings ratio. Institutional investors report that they also find the management discussion and analysis and the notes to the financial statements to be useful.

But institutional investors get financial information from other sources, including by meeting with company managers, which they say is sometimes more influential on their decision-making than the financial statements. These investors use meetings with managers to help interpret the audited accounting information in financial statements.

Institutional investors also use information produced by professional analysts, such as those working for large investment banks who make recommendations to their clients for buying or selling shares. These analysts also closely analyze corporate financial statements, but they, too, meet regularly with company managers to get non-financial information or further interpretation of the financial statements. These analysts produce regular earnings forecasts, predicting how the companies will fare when they publish their next financial statements. And institutional investors in turn use these analysts' earnings forecasts as part of their investment strategy decision-making.

With so much corporate information available from multiple sources, including the Internet, we may wonder how relevant financial statements are to users such as institutional investors and analysts. Studies have considered this very question. "Why then are financial statements considered useful when they are published infrequently and are less timely and less future-orientated than other sources, such as analysts' forecasts and information from company personnel?" asked a team of European researchers who reviewed the literature on who uses financial reports and why. "Analysts appear to recognise these limitations of accounting data and emphasize the importance of the annual report as a reference document, both as the basis for forecasts of future earnings, and for resolving uncertainty about the present and recent past," they found.

Sources: "OECD Institutional Investors Statistics 2009–2016," Organisation for Economic Co-operation and Development, 2017; Stefano Cascino, Mark Clatworthy, Beatriz García Osma, Joachim Gassen, Shahed Imam, and Thomas Jeanjean, "Who Uses Financial Reports and for What Purpose? Evidence from Capital Providers," *Accounting in Europe*, 11(2), 2014, pp. 185–209; Anja Hjelström, Tomas Hjelström, and Ebba Sjögren, "Decision Usefulness Explored: An Investigation of Capital Market Actors' Use of Financial Reports," Confederation of Swedish Enterprise, April 2014.

LEARNING OBJECTIVES	CHAPTER OUTLINE	CPA COMPETENCIES
After studying this chapter, you should be able to:	The chapter headings related to the learning objective are:	Competencies addressed by each learning objective are as follows:
1. Understand the nature of and basic accounting for investments, including which types of companies have significant investments.	**Understanding Investments** • Types of investments • Types of companies that have investments • Information for decision-making • Measurement: Overview	**1.1.1, 1.1.2, 1.2.1, 1.4.5, 5.2.2**
2. Explain and apply the cost/amortized cost model of accounting for investments.	**Measurement—Cost/Amortized Cost Model** • Investments in shares of other entities • Investments in debt instruments of other entities	**1.2.1, 1.2.2, 5.2.2**
3. Explain and apply the fair value through net income model of accounting for investments.	**Measurement—Fair Value Through Net Income (FV-NI) Model**	**1.2.1, 1.2.2, 1.2.3**
4. Explain and apply the fair value through other comprehensive income model of accounting for investments.	**Measurement—Fair Value Through Other Comprehensive Income (FV-OCI) Model** • Investments in shares of other entities • Investments in debt instruments of other entities	**1.1.2, 1.2.1, 1.2.2, 1.2.3**
5. Explain and apply the incurred loss, expected loss, and fair value loss impairment models.	**Measurement—Impairment Models** • Incurred loss impairment model • Expected loss impairment model • Fair value loss impairment model • Summary of impairment models	**1.2.1, 1.2.2, 1.2.3**
6. Explain the concept of significant influence and apply the equity method.	**Strategic Investments—Investments in Associates** • Significant influence • Equity method • Summary of accounting standards for associates	**1.2.1, 1.2.2, 1.2.3, 2.3.1**

7. Explain the concept of control and when consolidation is appropriate.	**Strategic Investments—Investments in Subsidiaries**	**1.2.1, 1.2.2, 1.2.3**
8. Explain how investments are presented and disclosed in the financial statements, noting how this facilitates analysis.	**Presentation, Disclosure, and Analysis** • Presentation and disclosure • Analysis	**1.2.1, 1.2.2, 1.2.3, 1.3.2, 1.4.1, 1.4.2, 1.4.4, 1.4.5, 5.1.1, 5.2.2**
9. Identify differences in accounting between IFRS and ASPE, and what changes are expected in the near future.	**IFRS/ASPE Comparison** • A comparison of IFRS and ASPE • Looking ahead	**1.1.4**

Preview of Chapter 9

This chapter focuses on the different types of financial asset investments in equity and debt instruments, and the various models used to account for them under IFRS and ASPE. The nature of the investments and the company's business model help determine how the investments are accounted for and reported. This chapter covers a variety of investments, from those held for short-term profit-taking to those held for longer-term strategic purposes. We covered accounting for investments in loans and receivables, which are also financial assets, in Chapter 7. We will cover accounting for investments in nonmonetary assets such as land and investment properties in Chapter 10.

The problems with the historical cost model have been recognized for a long time, especially in accounting for financial instruments. Because of this, accounting for such instruments has been on the agendas of standard-setting bodies around the world for many years. Standard setters have put accounting standards in place that require many of these assets to be accounted for at fair value. However, financial reporting under these standards has its problems. Because only some of the instruments are recognized at fair value, the standards are unnecessarily complicated. While many of the problems are related to more complex issues, accounting for ordinary debt and equity instruments continues to be controversial, from the perspective of both the issuer and the investor. Chapter 9 looks at accounting from the investor perspective while Chapters 14, 15, and 16 will look at the issues from the issuer perspective.

The IASB has issued comprehensive guidance on how to measure fair values, as we discussed in Chapters 2 and 3, as well as a new standard dealing with investments (IFRS 9), which became effective in 2018.

Understanding Investments

LEARNING OBJECTIVE 1
Understand the nature of and basic accounting for investments, including which types of companies have significant investments.

Types of Investments

Companies may hold investments for many reasons, including the following:

1. to have the capital appreciate, or
2. to earn dividends, interest, and/or income.

Various types of investments can provide a return for either or both of these reasons. There are two basic types of investments in terms of contractual rights and obligations: debt instruments and equity instruments. They are both considered to be financial assets to the investor. We introduced financial assets in Chapter 5.

Companies that invest in **debt instruments** of another entity are creditors of the issuing company. Debt instruments include **debt securities**, whose prices are normally quoted in an active market, such as investments in government and corporate bonds, convertible debt, and commercial paper. Debt instruments generally have contractual requirements regarding repayment of principal and payment of interest. The rights depend on the specific debt instrument. As shown in **Example 9.1**, when a company invests in debt instruments, it usually pays cash upfront and obtains the rights to receive interest and the return of principal at a later date.

Example 9.1 | A Simple Debt Instrument Investment

Facts   Company A buys bonds from Company B. The bonds carry with them contractual rights to annual interest and repayment of principal in 10 years. Bonds may also be purchased through intermediaries.

Instructions   Is this a debt instrument? Why?

Solution   This is a debt instrument because it gives the holder the contractual rights to receive interest and principal payments.

Law **Finance** 5.2.2 **Equity instruments**, on the other hand, generally represent ownership interests. Typical examples are common, preferred, or other capital stock or shares. They also include rights to acquire or dispose of ownership interests at an agreed-upon or determinable price, such as warrants, rights, and call or put options. An equity instrument is any contract that represents a residual interest in the net assets of an entity.[1] Equity instruments generally do not have a maturity date and pay dividends (instead of interest). The holder of shares is entitled to certain rights depending on the nature of the instrument. As shown in **Example 9.2**, when a company purchases equity instruments, it pays cash upfront and receives various rights, which may include rights to dividends, voting rights, and rights to residual assets upon liquidation.

Example 9.2 | A Simple Equity Instrument Investment

Facts   Company A invests in common shares of Company B. The shares carry with them contractual rights to declared dividends, voting rights, and rights to residual assets upon windup of the company.

[1]IAS 32.11 and CPA Canada Handbook, Part II, Section 3856.05(e). We will examine equity instruments in greater detail from an issuer perspective in Chapters 15 and 16. Copyright © IFRS Foundation. All rights reserved. Reproduced with permission.

Instructions   Is this an equity instrument? Why?

Solution   This is an investment in an equity instrument because the shares carry contractual rights to the residual assets of the entity upon windup, rights to dividends, and voting rights.

This chapter will look at investments in equity and debt instruments, both temporary and long-term. Chapter 16 will discuss the more complex financial instruments such as stock options and other derivatives.

Types of Companies That Have Investments

Before looking at how to account for investments, we will discuss the **different motivations that companies have for investing** in debt and equity instruments issued by other companies. One motivation is **the returns provided by investments** through interest, dividends, or capital appreciation (an increase in the underlying value of the investment). Note that some types of investments provide guaranteed returns (such as term deposits), while others are riskier (such as investments in shares of other companies). Managers may invest for **short-term returns** or **longer-term returns**, depending on their business and whether, and when, they need the cash for other purposes.

Another reason for investing in equity instruments such as common shares has more to do with **corporate strategy** than returns. Companies may invest in common shares of other companies because they want to have a special relationship with a supplier or customer, such as being able to access certain distribution channels or a supply of raw materials. Other investments are made so that the **investor** can exercise its rights to influence or control the operations of the other company, the **investee**. The intent with these strategic investments is usually to establish a long-term operating relationship between the two entities.

Not all companies invest in other companies. It depends on the nature of the business model and the industry that they operate in. Examples of companies that carry significant amounts of investments in financial instruments include financial institutions such as banks, pension funds, and insurance companies. Banks add value by investing other people's money and earning a return that is higher than their cost of capital. Their expertise lies in understanding how and when to buy and sell shares and debt instruments in order to maximize profits. They often buy and sell investments over the short term for profit (referred to as **trading**). Pension plans, one type of institutional investor mentioned in our feature story, collect money from employers and employees and pay out funds as pensions when the employees retire. In order to maximize the payout on retirement, pension plans invest the money in the interim and try to maximize the value of the investments. **Illustration 9.1** shows the significance of investments in securities for the **Royal Bank of Canada**. Investments in securities represent approximately 18% of total assets, with the trading portfolio accounting for most of the investments.

ILLUSTRATION 9.1

Excerpt from the Financial Statements of the Royal Bank of Canada

Consolidated Balance Sheets

	As at	
	October 31	October 31
(Millions of Canadian dollars)	**2017**	2016
Assets		
Cash and due from banks	**$ 28,407**	$ 14,929
Interest-bearing deposits with banks	**32,662**	27,851
Securities (Note 4)		
Trading	**127,657**	151,292
Available-for-sale	**90,722**	84,801
	218,379	236,093

(continued)

ILLUSTRATION 9.1

(*continued*)

Assets purchased under reverse repurchase agreements and securities borrowed	220,977	186,302
Loans (Note 5)		
Retail	385,170	369,470
Wholesale	159,606	154,369
	544,776	523,839
Allowance for loan losses (Note 5)	(2,159)	(2,235)
	542,617	521,604
Segregated fund net assets (Note 16)	1,216	981
Other		
Customers' liability under acceptances	16,459	12,843
Derivatives (Note 8)	95,023	118,944
Premises and equipment, net (Note 9)	2,670	2,836
Goodwill (Note 10)	10,977	11,156
Other intangibles (Note 10)	4,507	4,648
Other assets (Note 13)	38,959	42,071
	168,595	192,498
Total assets	**$1,212,853**	**$1,180,258**

Illustration 9.2 is an excerpt from the financial statements of Canada Life Financial Corporation, an insurance company. Note that insurance companies sell coverage against risk of loss. They charge their customers insurance premiums upfront in return for assuming the risk of loss. If an insured loss occurs in future, they have to pay out a settlement to the insured party. In the meantime, they invest the premiums in order to maximize their value.

ILLUSTRATION 9.2

Excerpt from the Financial Statements of Canada Life Financial Corporation

CONSOLIDATED BALANCE SHEETS
(in Canadian $ millions)

	December 31	
	2017	2016
		(note 33)
Assets		
Cash and cash equivalents (note 4)	$ **2,043**	$ 1,939
Bonds (note 5)	**63,432**	59,958
Mortgage loans (note 5)	**6,799**	6,610
Stocks (note 5)	**2,791**	2,774
Investment properties (note 5)	**3,222**	3,033
Loans to policyholders	**933**	973
	79,220	75,287
Funds held by ceding insurers (note 6)	**9,499**	10,186
Goodwill (note 9)	**794**	756
Intangible assets (note 9)	**362**	335
Derivative financial instruments (note 29)	**206**	206
Owner occupied properties (note 10)	**281**	221
Fixed assets (note 10)	**65**	60
Other assets (note 11)	**1,104**	994
Premiums in course of collection, accounts and interest receivable	**2,511**	2,322
Reinsurance assets (note 12)	**8,503**	9,309
Current income taxes	**7**	18
Deferred tax assets (note 26)	**97**	125
Investments on account of segregated fund policyholders (note 13)	**110,035**	97,173
Total assets	**$212,684**	**$196,992**

Investments in bonds and stocks represent 31.1% of the total assets of Canada Life. In addition, the segregated funds are primarily investments in stocks and bonds, so when we adjust for this, the percentage is actually approximately 82.8%.

Note the diversity in presentation in these two illustrations. Sometimes the investments are labelled for the nature of the instruments, such as bonds or stocks, and sometimes they are labelled with accounting labels, such as **available for sale** or trading.[2] Many companies use different labels, so it is important to recognize which items represent investments.

A quick look at the level of investments in other industries, such as the airline, resort, and retail industries, shows that very few, if any, investments are generally reported on the statement of financial position unless they are short-term (excess cash). Examples include Air Canada, TWC Enterprises (ClubLink), Empire Company Limited (Sobeys), and Indigo Books & Music. Why don't they have significant amounts of investments? The answer lies in the fact that these companies' business models do not require investments to be held. Excess cash is normally used to reinvest in the business, pay down loans, or pay dividends. These companies make their income in other ways, such as selling airline tickets, golf club memberships, groceries, and books.

Information for Decision-Making

Because the nature and risk of various investments are different, it is useful to provide this information in the financial statements. It is also important to show how significant the investments are, including how much income is being earned (both realized and unrealized). In order to be transparent, financial reporting should therefore present this information, either in the notes or on the face of the statement of financial position. For this reason, disclosure and presentation requirements for investments are significant. See Underlying Concept 9.1.

How investments are accounted for can depend on **the type of instrument, management's intent**, company **strategy**, and the **ability to reliably measure the investment's fair value**.

The next section of this chapter explains the accounting models generally applied in accounting for straightforward investments in other companies' debt and equity instruments—situations where the investment does not result in the investor having significant influence or control over the other company. After these models are explained, the chapter turns to investments where the investor can exercise significant influence over or control the strategic decisions of the investee company. For these investments, the investor's ownership interest is usually large enough to give the investor a substantial voice at the investee's boardroom table in decisions about the entity's operations, investments, and financing. This, in turn, affects how these investments are accounted for and reported.

> **Underlying Concept 9.1**
>
> Any information that helps users with decision-making is important. As we will see later, ASPE and IFRS mandate numerous specific disclosures regarding investments. Care must be taken to ensure that all material relevant information is disclosed under the full disclosure principle.

Measurement: Overview

Accounting for investments usually requires them to be recognized and measured initially at their fair value at acquisition. Recall that Chapters 2 and 3 discuss what is meant by fair value under IFRS 13 and identify various ways that fair value can be measured. Chapters 2 and 3 also indicate that some methods of measuring fair value are preferred over others, with prices in an active market being the best evidence of the value we are trying to capture. We saw in previous chapters that, unless there is evidence to the contrary, the price paid to acquire an asset is usually considered to be its fair value. Example 9.3 revisits the concept of fair value in the context of measuring the value of a debt instrument. The price of a **debt** instrument is quoted as a percentage of its par or face value.

---

[2]IAS 39 introduced the labels "held to maturity," "available for sale," and "held for trading." These are defined terms for investments under this legacy standard. Although the standard notes that the labels do not need to be used, many companies do indeed use these labels, even though the standard has been superseded by IFRS 9. Note that IFRS 9 does not use these labels. It will be interesting to see if these labels eventually stop being used.

Example 9.3 | The Price of a Debt Instrument

Facts   Assume that a $25,000 face value bond is priced at 99.

Instructions   What is the bond's fair value?

Solution   The fair value is 99% of $25,000, or $24,750. If it is priced at 103.5, it will sell for 103.5% of $25,000, or $25,875.

Shares that are traded on a stock exchange are usually quoted at the market price per share in dollars and cents.

Finance 5.2.2 Investments in shares may be acquired **on margin**. This means that the investor pays only part of the purchase price to acquire the shares. The rest is financed by the broker. Since the shares legally belong to the investor, the asset is recorded at the full share price and a liability to the broker for the amount that was financed is also recognized.

If financial assets are measured initially at their fair value, how should **transaction costs** that are directly related to the acquisition—such as fees, commissions, or transfer taxes—be accounted for?[3] The obvious choices are either (1) to expense these amounts immediately or (2) to add them to the cost of the assets acquired. The answer is—it depends.[4] It is logical to capitalize the transaction costs associated with any investment that is accounted for using a cost-based model because transaction costs are a necessary cost of acquiring the asset. Alternatively, for assets accounted for using a fair value model, it makes more sense to expense the transaction costs because the fair value of an asset is its market price. Regardless of how transaction costs are accounted for at acquisition, they are **not included** in the fair value amount at later statement of financial position dates.

When a financial instrument is measured at fair value, after acquisition changes in its fair value carrying amount are called **unrealized holding gains or losses**. The change in value is unrealized because it has not been converted to cash or a claim to cash—the asset is still held by the entity. Such gains and losses are only **realized** when the asset is disposed of. Unrealized holding gains and losses may be separately identified from realized gains and losses on the financial statements.[5]

With this brief introduction to the basics, let's turn to the specific accounting models for a variety of investments in debt and equity securities. This next section of the chapter identifies and explains three major models of accounting for investments:

IFRS **ASPE**

1. Cost/amortized cost model
2. Fair value through net income (FV-NI) model
3. Fair value through other comprehensive income (FV-OCI) model

---

[3]Brokerage commissions are usually incurred when buying and selling most securities. Commissions vary with the share value and the number of shares/units or may be a flat fee instead of a percentage. Discount brokerages offer significant discounts even on smaller trades. Transactions involving mutual funds may have no commission attached to them (no-load funds) but a commission may be charged when the funds are redeemed (back-end commission).

[4]Companies also have a choice of when to recognize (and derecognize) the financial asset. This could be on the trade date, when the commitment is made to buy or sell, or on the settlement date, when the asset is delivered and title is transferred—usually a short time thereafter. When the period between these dates is the standard term for the instrument and the market—termed a **regular-way purchase or sale**—either trade-date or settlement-date accounting may be used. Canadian equities settle in three business days. The same policy is applied consistently to all purchases and sales that belong to the same category of financial asset and the policy that is chosen is disclosed. This chapter's illustrations and examples assume that trade and settlement dates are the same.

[5]It is interesting to note how accounting for investments at fair value may have influenced the new revenue and lease standards. Accounting for financial instruments such as investments and derivatives reflects a contract-based approach, which is the approach adopted for revenues and leases. In addition, the accounting standards for financial instruments have helped move our thinking forward regarding embracing fair value as opposed to historical cost for measurement purposes.

These models are summarized in Illustration 9.3.

ILLUSTRATION 9.3

Application of Accounting Models

	Cost/Amortized Cost Model	Fair Value through Net Income (FV-NI) Model	Fair Value through OCI (FV-OCI) Model
At acquisition, measure at:	Cost (equal to fair value + transaction costs)	Fair value	Fair value (transaction costs tend to be added at acquisition)
At each reporting date, measure at:	Cost or amortized cost	Fair value	Fair value
Report unrealized holding gains and losses (changes in fair value):	N/A	In net income	In OCI
Report realized holding gains and losses:	In net income	In net income	**Significant Change** Transfer total realized gains/losses to net income (recycling) (debt instruments) or directly to retained earnings (no recycling) (equity instruments)

Note that there are only two choices when it comes to measuring these types of investments: (1) cost/amortized cost and (2) fair value. Note further that, where fair value is used, the unrealized gains and losses are booked either to net income or to OCI. It is easier to think about how to account for investments using this simple framework rather than focusing on the labels and various definitions that the different standard setters use for investments. The equity method is another method that we will look at later in the chapter.

Measurement—Cost/Amortized Cost Model

LEARNING OBJECTIVE 2

Explain and apply the cost/amortized cost model of accounting for investments.

The accounting standards do not always differentiate between the cost and the amortized cost models, referring to them both as amortized cost. The amortized cost model applies only to investments in debt instruments and long-term notes and loans receivable, while the cost model may be applied to investments in equity instruments (shares) of other companies. Regardless, they are both cost-based methods.

Investments in Shares of Other Entities

ASPE Application of the cost model to the investment one company makes in another entity's shares is summarized below:[6]

1. Recognize the cost of the investment at the fair value of the shares acquired (or the fair value of what was given up to acquire them, if more reliable). Add to this any direct transaction costs (such as commissions) incurred to acquire the shares.

---

[6]Under IFRS, all equity instruments are measured at fair value except in very limited situations where fair value may not be determined (IFRS 9.B5.2.3). In general, there is a rebuttable presumption that fair value is determinable under IFRS 9.

2. Unless impaired, report the investment at its cost at each statement of financial position date.

3. Recognize dividend income when the entity has established its right to receive the dividend.

4. When the shares are disposed of, derecognize them and report a gain or loss on disposal in net income. The gain or loss is the difference between the investment's carrying amount and the net proceeds on disposal.

Example 9.4 illustrates the cost model.

Example 9.4 | Cost Model—Investment in Shares of Other Entities

Facts Assume that Kiwan Corp. (KC) purchases 1,000 shares of Hirj Co. at $4.25 per share on March 8, 2020. A 1.5% commission is charged on the transaction. On December 15, 2020, Hirj Co. directors declare a dividend of $0.10 per share to shareholders of record on December 31, 2020, payable on January 15, 2021. On July 11, 2021, KC sells 800 of the Hirj Co. shares for $5.08 per share and pays a 1.5% commission on the sale. KC has a December 31 year end.

Instructions How would these transactions be recorded?

Solution KC's entries to record these transactions and events are as follows:

A = L + SE		
0		

Cash flows: ▼ 4,314 outflow

March 8, 2020

Other Investments	4,314	
Cash		4,314
(1,000 × $4.25) + (1,000 × $4.25 × .015)		

A = L + SE		
+100	+100	

Cash flows: No effect

December 15, 2020

Dividend Receivable	100	
Dividend Revenue		100
(1,000 × $0.10)		

A = L + SE		
0		

Cash flows: ▲ 100 inflow

January 15, 2021

Cash	100	
Dividend Receivable		100

A = L + SE		
+552	+552	

Cash flows: ▲ 4,003 inflow

July 11, 2021

Cash	4,003	
Other Investments		3,451
Gain on Disposal of Investments—Cost/Amortized Cost		552
(800 × $5.08) – (800 × $5.08 × .015) = $4,003		
$4,314 × 800/1,000 = $3,451		
$4,003 – $3,451 = $552		

When shares of a company have been purchased at various times and at various costs and only a portion of the holdings is sold, it is logical to use an average carrying value for the disposal. This is specifically required under ASPE and by the CRA.[7]

---

[7]Canada Revenue Agency Capital Gains 2017 T4037(E).

Investments in Debt Instruments of Other Entities

When the cost model is applied to an investment in debt instruments (and long-term notes and loans receivable), it is called the amortized cost model. See **Alternative Terminology 9.1.**

This is because any difference between the acquisition cost recognized and the face value of the security is amortized over the period to maturity.[8] Amortized cost is the amount recognized at acquisition minus principal repayments, where applicable, plus or minus the cumulative amortization of any discount or premium; that is, amortization of the difference between the initial amount recognized and the maturity value. Impairment charges, discussed later in the chapter, also reduce the amortized cost. The following statements describe this method.

> **Alternative Terminology 9.1**
>
> Investments in debt securities accounted for under the amortized cost model are sometimes called **held to maturity investments**.

1. Recognize the cost of the investment at the fair value of the debt instrument acquired (or the fair value of what was given up to acquire it, if a more reliable measure). Add to this any direct transaction costs, such as commissions, incurred to acquire the investment.

2. Unless impaired, report the investment at its amortized cost as well as any outstanding interest receivable at each statement of financial position date.

3. Recognize interest income as it is earned, amortizing any discount or premium at the same time by adjusting the carrying amount of the investment.

4. When the investment is disposed of, first record the accrued interest and discount or premium amortization up to date. Derecognize the investment, reporting any gain or loss on disposal in net income. The gain or loss is the difference between the proceeds received for the security and the investment's amortized cost at the date of disposal.

Finance 5.2.2 Accounting for investments in debt securities using the amortized cost method should be familiar to you. The procedures are the same as accounting for long-term notes and loans receivable, and you may find it useful to review this section of Chapter 7 before continuing. One complication is added in this chapter: the acquisition and disposal of investments between interest payment dates.

Income under the Amortized Cost Model

Income from debt investments is usually in the form of interest. It can be received in one of two ways, depending on whether the investment is interest-bearing or non–interest-bearing. If it is **interest-bearing**, the party holding the investment on the interest payment date receives all the interest accrued since the last interest payment date. Because debt securities can be bought and sold throughout the year, practice has developed for the purchaser to pay the seller an amount equal to the accrued interest since the last interest payment date. This interest is paid to the seller over and above the agreed-upon exchange price for the investment. If the instrument is **non–interest-bearing**, the price of the bond or other instrument is equal to its present value at the date of the transaction.

The total income from this type of investment is the net cash flow over the time that the investment is held. In the case of investments that are held until they mature, the total income is the difference between the principal amount that is received at maturity plus all periodic interest that is received, and the amount paid to acquire the investment including the accrued interest. Because the decision to acquire and hold the investment is usually based on its yield on the date when it is purchased, the yield rate is also the most appropriate rate to measure periodic income over the term that the investment is held.

---

[8]If the instrument's "cost" and face value are the same, the method is applied in the same way as for an investment in shares except that interest income is recognized instead of dividend income/revenue.

Example 9.5 illustrates the amortized cost model for debt instruments.

Example 9.5 | Amortized Cost Model—Investment in Debt Instruments of Other Entities

Facts Assume that on January 1, 2020, Robinson Limited pays $92,278 to purchase $100,000 of Chan Corporation 8% bonds.[9] The market rate of interest at the time was 10%. Robinson accounts for this investment at amortized cost using the effective interest method. The bonds mature on January 1, 2025, and interest is payable each July 1 and January 1. Note that the bond is acquired on an interest payment date and there is therefore no accrued interest for Robinson to pay on January 1. Assume Robinson Limited has an August 31 year end.

Instructions How was the price determined? Prepare an amortization table, and the entry to record the purchase of the bond.

Solution

Maturity of bonds		$100,000
Present value of $100,000 due in 5 years at 10%, interest payable semi-annually - see Table A.2 ($100,000 × 0.61391)	$61,391	
Present value of $4,000 interest payable semi-annually for 5 years at 10% annually - see Table A.4 ($4,000 × 7.72173)	30,887	
Proceeds from sale of bonds		92,278
Discount on investment in bonds		$ 7,722

The lower-than-face-value purchase price of $92,278 provides an effective interest rate of 10%. This is a combination of the 8% interest received in cash each year and the benefit of the $7,722 discount on the bond ($100,000 – $92,278).

8% Bonds Purchased to Yield 10%				
Date	Cash Received	Interest Income	Bond Discount Amortized	Amortization Cost of Bonds
1/1/20				$ 92,278
7/1/20	$ 4,000[a]	$ 4,614[b]	$ 614[c]	92,892[d]
1/1/21	4,000	4,645	645	93,537
7/1/21	4,000	4,677	677	94,214
1/1/22	4,000	4,711	711	94,925
7/1/22	4,000	4,746	746	95,671
1/1/23	4,000	4,783	783	96,454
7/1/23	4,000	4,823	823	97,277
1/1/24	4,000	4,864	864	98,141
7/1/24	4,000	4,907	907	99,048
1/1/25	4,000	4,952	952	100,000
	$40,000	$47,722	$7,722	

[a]$4,000 = 100,000 × 0.08 × 6/12

[b]$4,614 = $92,278 × 0.10 × 6/12

[c]$614 = $4,614 – $4,000

[d]$92,892 = $92,278 + $614

---

[9]As previously indicated, the value is determined by the investment community and is equal to the present value (PV) of the cash inflows of principal and interest payments on the bond, discounted at the market rate. This is relatively straightforward if the bond is bought or sold on its issue date or on an interest payment due date. At other times, a bond's purchase price can be estimated as follows:

PV of cash flows on the immediately preceding interest payment date	= $x
Add the increase in PV to date of sale or purchase at yield rate:	
$x × annual yield rate × portion of year since interest payment date	= y
Deduct the cash interest earned since last interest payment date:	
Face value × annual stated rate × portion of year since last interest date	= z
Purchase price of a bond bought or sold between interest payment dates:	x + y − z

The entry to record the purchase of the investment is:

Jan. 1/20	Bond Investment at Amortized Cost		92,278	
	Cash			92,278

A	=	L	+	SE
0				

Cash flows: ↓ 92,278 outflow

Because Robinson decided to purchase the bond based on its yield, the amount of income that is recognized each period should ideally reflect the yield rate.

The **effective interest method**, required under IFRS unless the investment is held for trading purposes, results in recognizing interest income at a constant yield rate on the investment each period. In addition to the effective interest method, ASPE also permits the use of the **straight-line method**. We explained both methods in Chapter 7. ASPE allows the use of the straight-line method as a simplification. Example 9.6 looks at the journal entries under both the effective interest and straight-line methods. Note that under either method, the original discount is fully amortized by the date the bond matures.

Example 9.6 | Amortized Cost Model—Effective Interest and Straight-Line Methods of Amortizing Discounts and Premiums on Bonds

Facts   Assume the same information as in Example 9.5.

Instructions   **IFRS**   **ASPE**   Calculate the amortization of the discount using the straight-line method. Prepare the journal entries for the first two interest payments using both the effective interest and straight-line methods.

Solution   Under the straight-line method, the original discount of $7,722 ($100,000 − $92,278) is amortized to interest income in equal amounts from the date of acquisition to maturity, a period of 60 months. For each month of interest income recognized, 1/60 of $7,722 or $128.70 of discount is amortized. Under this approach, a constant **amount** of interest income is recognized each period instead of a constant **rate** of interest. All the other entries that involve interest income and the carrying amount of the investment will be affected in the same way when the straight-line method is used.

The journal entry to record the receipt of the first semi-annual interest payment on July 1, 2020, is:

IFRS: effective interest method (allowed under ASPE as well)			**ASPE: may use straight-line method since no specific method is mandated**		
July 1/20			July 1/20		
Cash	4,000		Cash	4,000	
Bond Investment at			Bond Investment at Amortized		
Amortized Cost	614		Cost (6 × $128.70)	772	
Interest Income		4,614	Interest Income		4,772

IFRS

A	=	L	+	SE
+4,614				+4,614

Cash flows: ↑ 4,000 inflow

ASPE

A	=	L	+	SE
+4,772				+4,772

Cash flows: ↑ 4,000 inflow

At its year end on August 31, 2020, Robinson recognizes the interest income that has accrued since July 1 and amortizes the discount for the two-month period:

IFRS: effective interest method (allowed under ASPE as well)			**ASPE: may use straight-line method since no specific method is mandated**		
August 31/20			August 31/20		
Interest Receivable	1,333		Interest Receivable	1,333	
($4,000 × 2/6)			($4,000 × 2/6)		
Bond Investment at			Bond Investment at		
Amortized Cost	215		Amortized Cost	257	
($645 × 2/6)			(2 × $128.70)		
Interest Income		1,548	Interest Income		1,590
($4,645 × 2/6)					

IFRS

A	=	L	+	SE
+1,548				+1,548

Cash flows: No effect

ASPE

A	=	L	+	SE
+1,590				+1,590

Cash flows: No effect

IFRS

A	=	L	+	SE
+3,097				+3,097

Cash flows: ↑ 4,000 inflow

ASPE

A	=	L	+	SE
+3,182				+3,182

Cash flows: ↑ 4,000 inflow

When the interest payment is received on January 1, 2021, the following entry is made, assuming that Robinson does not use reversing entries:

IFRS: effective interest method (allowed under ASPE as well)			ASPE: may use straight-line method since no specific method is mandated		
January 1/21			January 1/21		
Cash	4,000		Cash	4,000	
Bond Investment at			Bond Investment at		
Amortized Cost	430		Amortized Cost	515	
($645 × 4/6)			(4 × $128.70)		
Interest Receivable		1,333	Interest Receivable		1,333
Interest Income		3,097	Interest Income		3,182
($4,645 × 4/6)					

In practice, and as illustrated, **the discount or premium on a bond investment is not usually reported separately**.

Sale of Investments

When the investment is sold, the carrying value is generally updated for any additional discount or premium amortization as well as any accrued interest. **Example 9.7** looks at the sale of a bond.

Example 9.7 | Amortized Cost Model—Sale of a Bond

Facts   Building on Examples 9.5 and 9.6, assume that Robinson Limited sells its investment in the Chan Corporation bonds on November 1, 2024, at 99.75% plus accrued interest. Remember that interest receivable of $1,333 (2/6 × $4,000) and discount amortization of $317 (2/6 × $952) would have been recognized at the company's August 31, 2024 year end.

Instructions   Prepare the journal entries to update the carrying value of the bond and to then record the sale. Use the effective interest method.

Solution   The following entry is made on November 1, 2024, to accrue an additional two months' interest (September and October), to amortize the discount from September 1 to November 1, and to bring the investment to its correct carrying amount at the date of disposal. The discount amortization for this two-month period is $317 (2/6 × $952). Assume the effective interest method is used.

A	=	L	+	SE
+1,650				+1,650

Cash flows: No effect

Nov. 1/24	Interest Receivable (2/6 × $4,000)	1,333	
	Bond Investment at Amortized Cost	317	
	Interest Income (2/6 × $4,952)		1,650

The calculation of the realized gain on the sale is explained below.

Selling price of bonds ($100,000 × .9975)			$99,750
Less: Carrying amount of bonds on November 1, 2024:			
Amortized cost, July 1, 2024 (see amortization schedule)		$99,048	
Add: Discount amortized for the period July 1, 2024, to			
November 1, 2024 ($317 to August 31 + $317 from			
September 1 to November 1)		634	99,682
Gain on sale of bonds			$ 68

The entry to record the sale of the bonds is:

A	=	L	+	SE
+68				+68

Cash flows: ↑ 102,416 inflow

Nov. 1/24	Cash	102,416	
	Interest Receivable		2,666
	Bond Investment at Amortized Cost		99,682
	Gain on Disposal of Investments—		
	Cost/Amortized Cost		68

> The credit to Interest Receivable is for the four months of accrued interest from July 1 to November 1, all of which the purchaser pays in cash to Robinson. The debit to Cash is made up of the selling price of the bonds, $99,750, plus the four months of accrued interest, $2,666. The credit to the Bond Investment at Amortized Cost account is the bonds' carrying amount on the sale date, and the credit to Gain on Sale of Investments is the excess of the selling price over the bonds' carrying amount.

Measurement—Fair Value Through Net Income (FV-NI) Model

LEARNING OBJECTIVE 3

Explain and apply the fair value through net income model of accounting for investments.

The **fair value through net income (FV-NI)** model is required for many financial assets and liabilities, including many investments in other entities' debt and equity securities. (See **Alternative Terminology 9.2**.) When investments to be accounted for at FV-NI are acquired, they are recognized at their fair value. Consistent with measurement at fair value, transaction costs incurred in acquiring such assets are expensed as incurred. The name of the method—fair value through net income—is very descriptive of how the accounting works! The carrying amount of each FV-NI investment is adjusted to its current fair value at each reporting date. All resulting holding gains and losses are reported in net income along with any dividends or interest income earned.

For FV-NI investments, periodic income is a combination of the change in an investment's carrying amount plus the interest or dividend income that has been received or is receivable for the period. For FV-NI investments in general, and especially those that are held for trading purposes—that is, they are held to sell in the near term or to generate a profit from short-term fluctuations in price—it may not be important to report interest and dividend income separately from the holding gains or losses.

Under IFRS, both types of income may be accounted for and reported together because this tends to mirror how such investments are managed.[10] ASPE requires separate reporting of interest income and net gains or losses recognized on financial instruments. Note that many companies may wish to report dividends and interest separately for tax purposes and, because the financial statements provide the basis for the tax returns, it may be worthwhile to show these items separately in the financial statements as well. For this reason, we have not treated this as an IFRS/ASPE difference.

The reporting entity may need or want to keep track of holding gains and losses separately from interest and dividend income, whether it is required or for additional transparency and decision-making. Accounting for dividend income separately from holding gains and losses is straightforward.

- When a dividend is received (or receivable), it is recognized as Dividend Revenue.

- When the investment is adjusted to its fair value at each reporting date, the change in value is recognized in a separate account, such as Unrealized Gain or Loss.

It is now easier for the entity to report the dividend income separately from the fair value changes because the information has been captured in two different accounts.

> **Alternative Terminology 9.2**
>
> FV-NI is sometimes called *fair value through profit or loss*.

---

[10]IFRS 7 *Financial Instruments: Disclosures* indicates in paragraph B5(e) that entities may disclose whether the net gains or losses on financial assets measured at fair value through profit or loss (FV-NI) and reported on the income statement include interest and dividend income. ASPE, on the other hand, requires separate reporting (*CPA Canada Handbook*, Part II, Section 3856.52).

Recognizing interest income under the effective interest method (or even the straight-line method) separately requires more complex entries than described above. This is because **any discount or premium must be amortized before the change in fair value is recognized**. Amortizing the discount or premium changes the investment's carrying amount. Therefore, the subsequent adjustment to bring the investment to its new fair value has to take this interest adjustment into account. Two sets of information have to be kept to make this work: (1) a schedule of the investment's amortized cost, for purposes of interest income calculations; and (2) information on its fair value, in order to report the asset at the appropriate amount.

The bookkeeping can be handled in at least two different ways.

1. One method keeps the investment in the accounts at its amortized cost and uses a separate valuation allowance account to bring it to its fair value at each statement of financial position date.

2. Alternatively, the investment account itself is maintained at fair value and the necessary amortized cost information is kept in records that are supplementary to the accounts.

In this chapter, for purposes of explanation, we use the second approach. We prefer this method because it emphasizes the use of fair value measurement rather than an adjusted cost-based measure. In short, the entries are as follows.

- Recognize interest income in an account such as Interest Income as it is earned, adjusting the investment's book value by the amount of any discount or premium amortization.

- When the investment is adjusted to its current fair value at each reporting date, the change in value is recognized in a separate account such as Investment Income or Loss.

Example 9.8 illustrates the accounting for an investment in a **debt instrument** at FV-NI using the effective interest method.

Example 9.8 | FV-NI Model—Investment in a Bond

Facts Assume that a company purchases $100,000, 10%, five-year bonds of Graff Corporation on January 1, 2020, with interest payable on July 1 and January 1. The bond sells for $108,111, resulting in a bond premium of $8,111 and an effective interest rate of 8%. Assume IFRS.

Instructions Prepare the journal entries for 2020. In addition, prepare an amortization table.

Solution The entry to record the purchase of the bonds is:

Jan. 1/20	FV-NI Investments	108,111	
	Cash		108,111

The amortization table below shows the effect that the premium amortization has on the interest income that is reported each period. The process is identical to the amortization of debt investments explained earlier in this chapter, except this situation involves a premium instead of a discount.

A	=	L	+	SE
0				

Cash flows: ▼ 108,111 outflow

	10% Bonds Purchased To Yield 8%			
Date	Cash Received	Interest Income	Bond Premium Amortization	Amortized Cost of Bonds
1/1/20				$108,111
7/1/20	$ 5,000[a]	$ 4,324[b]	$ 676[c]	107,435[d]
1/1/21	5,000	4,297	703	106,732
7/1/21	5,000	4,269	731	106,001
1/1/22	5,000	4,240	760	105,241
7/1/22	5,000	4,210	790	104,451
1/1/23	5,000	4,178	822	103,629
7/1/23	5,000	4,145	855	102,774
1/1/24	5,000	4,111	889	101,885
7/1/24	5,000	4,075	925	100,960
1/1/25	5,000	4,040	960	100,000
	$50,000	$41,889	$8,111	

[a]$5,000 = $100,000 \times 0.10 \times 6/12$

[b]$4,324 = $108,111 \times 0.08 \times 6/12$

[c]$676 = $5,000 - $4,324$

[d]$107,435 = $108,111 - 676

The entries to record interest income on the first interest date and at the December 31 year end are:

July 1/20

Cash	5,000	
FV-NI Investments		676
Interest Income		4,324

A	=	L	+	SE
+4,324				+4,324

Cash flows: ↑ 5,000 inflow

December 31/20

Interest Receivable	5,000	
FV-NI Investments		703
Interest Income		4,297

A	=	L	+	SE
+4,297				+4,297

Cash flows: No effect

Assume that at December 31, 2020, the fair value of the Graff Corporation bonds is $105,000. Their carrying amount at this time is $106,732 (assuming that we have amortized the premium) and the adjustment needed to bring the Investment account to fair value is $1,732:

Original cost and carrying amount of bonds		$108,111
Entries made to Investment in Graff Corp.		
Bonds account during year when recognizing		
interest income:		
July 1, 2020	$676 credit	
Dec. 31, 2020	703 credit	(1,379)
Carrying amount before fair value adjustment		106,732
Fair value, December 31, 2020		105,000
Fair value adjustment needed		$ 1,732 credit

If we had not amortized the premium, the carrying amount would still be $108,111 and the adjustment amount would be $108,111 − $105,000 = $3,111.

The entry to adjust the investment to its fair value at December 31, 2020 (assuming that we have amortized the premium as shown in the earlier journal entries), is:

December 31/20

Investment Income or Loss	1,732	
FV-NI Investments		1,732

A	=	L	+	SE
−1,732				−1,732

Cash flows: No effect

For a **non–interest-bearing debt investment** that is held for short-term trading, the investment income that is earned is the difference between the instrument's purchase price and its maturity value (or the proceeds on its disposal if sold prior to maturity). Treasury bills, for example, are usually traded in non–interest–bearing form. **Example 9.9** looks at an investment in a treasury bill.

Example 9.9 | FV-NI Model—Investment in Treasury Bill (Non–Interest-Bearing Instrument)

Facts Assume that Investor Inc. pays $19,231 on March 15 for a $20,000 six-month treasury bill that matures on September 15. The investment, purchased to yield an 8% return, is designated as an FV-NI investment.

Instructions How would the treasury bill be accounted for? Prepare the journal entries.

Solution

Mar. 15	FV-NI Investments	19,231	
	Cash		19,231
	(To record purchase of a $20,000, six-month treasury bill)		

A	=	L	+	SE
0				

Cash flows: ↓ 19,231 outflow

Sept. 15	Cash	20,000	
	FV-NI Investments		19,231
	Gain on Disposal of Investments—FV-NI		769
	(To record the proceeds on maturity of a $20,000 treasury bill)		

A	=	L	+	SE
+769				+769

Cash flows: ↑ 20,000 inflow

Note that the investment income, which consists entirely of interest in this case, is equal to an 8% yield on the amount paid for the investment: $19,231 × 8% × 6/12 = $769. If Investor Inc. needed cash before September 15 and sold the investment before maturity, the investment income reported is the difference between its carrying amount and the proceeds on disposal.

Investments in **equity securities (shares)** that are held for short-term trading profits (temporary investments) may pay dividends. See **Alternative Terminology 9.3**. Because the holder of the shares on the date of record is entitled to the dividend and this date is generally a few weeks before the dividend is paid, a dividend receivable and the related income may be recognized before the cash is received. As an FV-NI investment, the shares are remeasured to their fair value at each statement of financial position date with the change in fair value also recognized in the Investment Income or Loss account. When the investment is sold, its carrying amount is removed from the investment account and investment income is recognized.

Example 9.10 illustrates the accounting for a portfolio of investments accounted for under the FV-NI model. The portfolio includes both debt and equity securities (bonds and shares).

Alternative Terminology 9.3

The terms "temporary investments" and "held-for-trading" investments are often used interchangeably.

Example 9.10 | FV-NI Model—Investment in a Portfolio of Securities, December 31, 2020

Facts   Assume that on December 31, 2020, Western Publishing Corporation provides the following information about its investment portfolio. Assume that all investments were acquired in 2020. The investments were recorded at their fair value at acquisition in an account entitled FV-NI Investments, and this value is their **carrying amount** on the books before any adjustment. For simplicity, assume the bonds were purchased at par.

FV-NI Investment Portfolio December 31, 2020		
Investments	**Carrying Amount**	**Fair Value**
Burlington Corp. shares	$ 43,860	$ 51,500
Genesta Corp. 8% bonds	184,230	175,200
Warner Ltd. shares	86,360	91,500
Total portfolio	$314,450	$318,200

Adjustment needed to the portfolio to bring it to fair value at December 31, 2020:
$318,200 − $314,450 = $3,750 debit

At December 31, an adjusting entry is made to bring the investment portfolio to its year-end fair value and to record the holding gain. This entry assumes that Western Publishing has one control account in its general ledger for the entire portfolio. It would be equally correct to make a separate entry for each of the three different investments.

Dec. 31/20	FV-NI Investments	3,750	
	Investment Income or Loss		3,750

The Investment Income or Loss account is included in net income on the income statement, and the fair values of the investments at December 31, 2020, now become the carrying amounts on the books. With a fair value measurement approach, the original cost or fair value at acquisition is not relevant.[11]

A	=	L	+	SE
+3,750				+3,750

Cash flows: No effect

Example 9.11 carries the example further, looking at a sale of one of the securities as well as an additional purchase.

---

[11]Management's ability to earn a return and realize gains on the investments is relevant. However, in addition, the entity has to keep track in its files of the securities' original cost because only realized gains and losses are taxable or deductible for tax purposes.

Example 9.11 | FV-NI Model—Changes in an Investment Portfolio of Securities

Facts Assume the information from Example 9.10 and assume further that the Genesta Corp. bonds are sold for $174,000 on February 4, 2021—their interest payment date—and that 1,000 shares of Next Ltd. are acquired for their fair value of $49,990 on September 21, 2021. Note that the bonds' carrying amount before the sale is $175,200, their fair value at the last statement of financial position date.

Instructions Prepare the journal entries to record the sale and purchase.

Solution The entries to record the February 4 and September 21 transactions follow.

Feb. 4/21	Cash	174,000	
	Loss on Disposal of Investments—FV-NI	1,200	
	FV-NI Investments		175,200
Sept. 21/21	FV-NI Investments	49,990	
	Cash		49,990

A	=	L	+	SE
−1,200				−1,200

Cash flows: ↑ 174,000 inflow

A	=	L	+	SE
0				

Cash flows: ↓ 49,990 outflow

Because the gains and losses on FV-NI investments are reported in net income, the distinction between the portions that are realized and unrealized is blurred. This is not usually an issue, however, particularly for trading securities that are acquired for short-term profit-taking.

Let's take the example one step further and look at the carrying values at December 31, 2021, as shown in **Example 9.12**.

Example 9.12 | FV-NI Model—Investment in a Portfolio of Securities, December 31, 2021

Facts Carrying on the example from Examples 9.10 and 9.11, assume that the carrying amounts and fair values of the investment portfolio at December 31, 2021, are as follows. As Western Publishing prepares financial statements only once a year, the carrying amounts of the Burlington Corp. and Warner Ltd. shares that are still on hand are the fair values reported at December 31, 2021. The carrying amount of the Next Ltd. shares acquired during the year is their fair value at acquisition.

FV-NI Investment Portfolio December 31, 2021		
Investments	**Carrying Amount**	**Fair Value**
Burlington Corp. shares	$ 51,500	$ 50,500
Warner Ltd. shares	91,500	90,100
Next Ltd. shares	49,990	50,600
Total portfolio	$192,990	$191,200

Adjustment needed to bring the portfolio to fair value at December 31, 2021:
$192,990 − $191,200 = $1,790 credit

Instructions Prepare the journal entries to revalue the investments at year end.

Solution At December 31, an adjusting entry is made to bring the investments to their year-end fair values.

Dec. 31/21	Investment Income or Loss	1,790	
	FV-NI Investments		1,790

A	=	L	+	SE
−1,790				−1,790

Cash flows: No effect

The investment loss is included in the 2021 income statement, added to the loss recognized on February 4.

Measurement—Fair Value Through Other Comprehensive Income (FV-OCI) Model

---

LEARNING OBJECTIVE 4

Explain and apply the fair value through other comprehensive income model of accounting for investments.

IFRS We explained the concept of other comprehensive income in Chapter 4. It is an income statement account and is closed out to an account called Accumulated Other Comprehensive Income.[12]

See **Alternative Terminology 9.4**.

Illustration 9.4 shows how these financial statement categories are related.

Income Statement	Statement of Comprehensive Income	Statement of Changes in Shareholders' Equity	Shareholders' Equity End of Period
			Share capital
Revenue, gains – Expenses, losses		Opening balance, Retained earnings	
Net income ⟶	Net income ⟶	+ Net income	
		– Dividends	
		Ending balance, Retained earnings ⟶	Retained earnings
		Opening balance, AOCI	
	± Other comprehensive income for period ⟶	± Other comprehensive income for period	
			Accumulated other comprehensive income
	Comprehensive income	Ending balance, AOCI ⟶	Shareholders' equity

Investments accounted for at **fair value through other comprehensive income (FV-OCI)** are recognized at acquisition at their fair value. However, unlike the FV-NI model, the transaction costs tend to be added to the carrying amount of the investment. When the investment is adjusted to its fair value at the first reporting date, the transaction costs automatically end up as part of the holding gain or loss recognized in OCI at that time.

At each reporting date, the carrying amount of each FV-OCI investment is remeasured and adjusted to its current fair value. As the name of the model implies, the changes in fair value—the holding gains and losses—are recognized in other comprehensive income net of income tax.[13]

There are two different versions of the FV-OCI model. The difference between them relates to how they treat the holding gains and losses once they are realized. The two methods are as follows:

1. FV-OCI with recycling, and
2. FV-OCI without recycling.

---

[12]ASPE does not make use of OCI.

[13]Intraperiod tax allocation requires that the unrealized holding gains and losses be recognized in other comprehensive income, net of tax. This is explained more fully in Chapter 18. The illustrations that follow do not include the related taxes to simplify the examples.

Under the **FV-OCI model with recycling**, when the investments are disposed of and converted to cash or a claim to cash, the previously unrealized holding gains or losses to the date of disposal are transferred or "recycled" into net income. Under the **FV-OCI model without recycling**, the realized gains and losses do not get recycled through net income but are transferred directly into retained earnings. See Underlying Concept 9.2. Aside from this, both versions of the FV-OCI model are essentially the same except one is used for equity investments (FV-OCI without recycling) and one is used for debt investments (FV-OCI with recycling).

> **Underlying Concept 9.2**
>
> Recycling supports the continued use of net income as the main performance measure, while not recycling supports the concept that comprehensive income is the appropriate measure of performance.

Investments in Shares of Other Entities

Income from FV-OCI Investments (Shares)

Dividend income from these investments is reported directly in net income. Remeasurement gains and losses are recorded in OCI. Let's look at an example of FV-OCI accounting for investments in shares of another entity in Example 9.13.

Example 9.13 | FV-OCI Model—Investment in a Portfolio of Shares

Facts   Assume that on November 3, 2019, Manitoba Corporation purchases common shares of three companies, with the investments to be accounted for at FV-OCI. The purchases are as follows:

	Fair value and cost at acquisition
Nova Industries Ltd.	$259,700
Columbia Soup Corp.	317,500
St. Boniface Pulp Ltd.	141,350
Total cost	$718,550

On December 6, 2019, the company receives a cash dividend of $4,200 on its investment in the common shares of Columbia Soup.

Instructions   How should the purchase be recorded? Prepare the journal entries to record the purchase and the dividends.

Solution   The purchase of the investments is recorded as follows:

| Nov. 3/19 | FV-OCI Investments | 718,550 | |
| | Cash | | 718,550 |

Above we have used one control account for all three investments. Alternatively, Manitoba Corporation could use separate investment accounts to track each investment separately. The cash dividend is recorded through net income as follows:

| Dec. 6/19 | Cash | 4,200 | |
| | Dividend Revenue | | 4,200 |

A	=	L	+	SE
0				

Cash flows: ▼ 718,550 outflow

A	=	L	+	SE
+4,200				+4,200

Cash flows: ▲ 4,200 inflow

Let's follow up with additional information in Example 9.14.

Example 9.14 | FV-OCI Model—Investment in a Portfolio of Shares, December 31, 2019

Facts   Assume the same information as in Example 9.13. In addition, the carrying amounts (and cost), fair values, and unrealized gains and losses at December 31, 2019, for Manitoba's FV-OCI investments are noted below.

FV-OCI Investment Portfolio
December 31, 2019

Investments in Shares	Carrying Amount	Fair Value	Holding Gain (Loss) for Period
Nova Industries Ltd.	$259,700	$275,000	$ 15,300
Columbia Soup Corp.	317,500	304,000	(13,500)
St. Boniface Pulp Ltd.	141,350	104,000	(37,350)
Total of portfolio	$718,550	$683,000	$(35,550)

Instructions How would the company record the change in fair value?

Solution For Manitoba's portfolio, the gross holding gains are $15,300, and the gross holding losses are $50,850 ($13,500 + $37,350), resulting in a net unrealized loss of $35,550. The portfolio's fair value is $35,550 less than its carrying amount (and cost, in this first accounting period). The unrealized gains and losses are recorded in a Holding Gain or Loss account and are reported as part of OCI. The carrying amount of the investments is adjusted in the following entry to their fair value at the statement of financial position date. Note that, even though there is a loss (and perhaps an impairment), the loss is booked through OCI.

A	=	L	+	SE
−35,550				−35,550

Cash flows: No effect

Dec. 31/19
Unrealized Gain or Loss—OCI   35,550
    FV-OCI Investments   35,550

Sale of FV-OCI Investments (Shares)

Significant Change We carry on our example to show how to account for the sale of FV-OCI investments in shares. While it is possible to record a sale using different combinations of entries, the following series of three entries clearly accomplishes what is needed:

1. The **first entry** adjusts the investment's carrying amount to its fair value at the date of disposal and captures the holding gain or loss up to that date in OCI.

2. The **second entry** removes the investment's carrying amount from the asset account and records the proceeds on disposal.

3. The **third entry** is a **reclassification adjustment** that transfers the holding gain or loss that is now realized out of OCI and into retained earnings (**FV-OCI without recycling under IFRS 9**). This is an optional entry under IFRS 9. Example 9.15 illustrates the reclassification adjustment.

Example 9.15 | FV-OCI Model—Portfolio of Shares; Sale of Shares

Facts Now assume that Manitoba sells all of its Nova Industries Ltd. common shares on January 23, 2020, receiving proceeds of $287,220. This is $12,220 more than the current carrying amount of the Investment in Nova Industries in the accounts.

Instructions Prepare the journal entries to record the revaluation and sale of the shares.

Solution

A	=	L	+	SE
+12,220				+12,220

Cash flows: No effect

A	=	L	+	SE
0				

Cash flows: ↑ 287,220 inflow

A	=	L	+	SE
				0

Cash flows: No effect

Jan. 23/20   (a) FV-OCI Investments   12,220
      Unrealized Gain or Loss—OCI   12,220
    ($287,220 – $275,000)
   (b) Cash   287,220
      FV-OCI Investments   287,220
    ($275,000 + $12,220)
   (c) Accumulated Other Comprehensive Income[14]   27,520
      Retained Earnings   27,520
    ($287,220 – $259,700) or ($15,300 + $12,220)

---

[14]IFRS 9.B5.7.1 notes that an entity *may* transfer the cumulative amount to retained earnings. We have chosen to interpret this as a debit to Accumulated OCI (rather than OCI), although the outcome on the balance sheet would be the same. Note further that the entity does not have to prepare this last journal entry. If the last journal entry is not booked, then the accumulated gains would remain in AOCI.

The amount transferred to Retained Earnings is the difference between the investment's original cost and the proceeds on disposal ($287,220 – $259,700). It is also the sum of all prior entries to OCI for the Nova Industries shares: a $15,300 gain on December 31, 2019, and a $12,220 gain on January 23, 2020, for a total of $27,520. All that remains in Accumulated Other Comprehensive Income now is the unrealized net holding gains/losses on the remaining investments.

Example 9.16 looks at the portfolio at the end of 2020.

Example 9.16 | FV-OCI Model—Investment in a Portfolio of Shares, December 31, 2020

Facts Assume the same information as noted in Examples 9.13 to 9.15. In addition, assume that the information noted below is provided for Manitoba's FV-OCI portfolio at December 31, 2020.

FV-OCI Investment Portfolio December 31, 2020				
Investments in Shares	Cost	Carrying Amount	Fair Value	Holding Gain (Loss)
Columbia Soup Corp.	$317,500	$304,000	$362,550	$58,550
St. Boniface Pulp Ltd.	141,350	104,000	139,050	35,050
Total of portfolio	$458,850	$408,000	$501,600	$93,600

Instructions Prepare the journal entry to adjust the portfolio to fair value at year end.

Solution The entry to bring the investments to their fair value at December 31, 2020, is:

Dec. 31/20
FV-OCI Investments	93,600	
Unrealized Gain or Loss—OCI		93,600

A	=	L	+	SE
+93,600				+93,600

Cash flows: No effect

Investments in Debt Instruments of Other Entities

Now let's look at debt instruments.

Income from FV-OCI Investments (Debt Instruments)

Under IFRS 9, interest income is recognized in net income (similar to dividends for shares). Also, amortization of premiums/discounts, and impairment losses are recognized directly in net income. Finally, remeasurement gains and losses recognized through OCI are subsequently recycled through net income when the investment is disposed of. Therefore, the **FV-OCI (with recycling) approach is followed under IFRS 9 for debt instruments**.

Example 9.17 illustrates the basic accounting under FV-OCI. It builds on the Graff Corporation example from Example 9.8.

Example 9.17 | FV-OCI Model—Investment in Bonds

Facts Recall the following facts from Example 9.8. Assume that a company purchases $100,000, 10%, five-year bonds of Graff Corporation on January 1, 2020, with interest payable on July 1 and January 1. The bond sells for $108,111, resulting in a bond premium of $8,111 and an effective interest rate of 8%. In addition, assume that the company accounts for the investment at FV-OCI (with recycling).

Instructions Prepare the journal entries to record the purchase and interest income for 2020. *Hint:* Revisit the amortization table for this bond as shown in the solution to Example 9.8.

A	=	L	+	SE
0				

Cash flows: ↓ 108,111 outflow

A	=	L	+	SE
4,324				4,324

Cash flows: ↑ 5,000 inflow

A	=	L	+	SE
4,297				4,297

Cash flows: No effect

Solution The buyer records the purchase of the bond in the FV-OCI Investments account as follows:

Jan. 1/20	FV-OCI Investments	108,111	
	Cash		108,111

The entry to record the interest income on July 1, 2020, is as follows:

July 1/20	Cash	5,000	
	FV-OCI Investments		676
	Interest Income		4,324

The entry to record interest receivable at December 31, 2020, is as follows:

Dec. 31/20	Interest Receivable	5,000	
	FV-OCI Investments		703
	Interest Income		4,297

So far, the accounting is straightforward. It generally follows the same accounting as for the amortized cost method. Now we will look at how to account for the remeasurement to fair value in **Example 9.18**.

Example 9.18 | FV-OCI Model—Investment in Bonds, December 31, 2020

Facts Following along with Example 9.17, assume that at year end (December 31, 2020), the fair value of the Graff bonds is $105,000 and the carrying value is $106,732 ($108,111 − $676 − $703). Assume there is no impairment.

Instructions Prepare the journal entry to revalue the bonds.

Solution The carrying value is $106,732, so a writedown is required. The company reports this loss through OCI and makes the following entry:

Unrealized Gain or Loss—OCI	1,732	
FV-OCI Investments		1,732

A	=	L	+	SE
−1,732				−1,732

Cash flows: No effect

At each reporting date, the company remeasures the bonds at fair value and records the gain or loss through OCI as noted above. **Example 9.19** looks at the accounting for a portfolio of investments.

Example 9.19 | FV-OCI Model—Investment in a Portfolio of Bonds, December 31, 2020

Facts Assume that Robinson Limited has two debt securities classified as FV-OCI. For the Chan bonds, assume the amortization table noted in Example 9.5. Assume further that the Anacomp bonds were purchased at par value (therefore there is no premium or discount) and that no impairment exists.

FV-OCI Investment Portfolio December 31, 2020			
Investments in Bonds	**Amortized Cost**	**Fair Value**	**Unrealized Gain (Loss)**
Chan Corporation 8% bonds	$ 93,537	$103,600	$ 10,063
Anacomp Corporation 10% bonds	200,000	180,400	(19,600)
Total portfolio	$293,537	$284,000	(9,537)
Previous fair value adjustment balance			–0–
Fair value adjustment—Cr.			$ (9,537)

Instructions Prepare the journal entry to revalue the portfolio.

Solution The fair value of Robinson's portfolio totals $284,000. The gross unrealized gains are $10,063, and the gross unrealized losses are $19,600. The fair value of the portfolio is lower than the amortized cost. Therefore, an adjusting entry is needed to record the remeasurement to fair value. The entry is shown below.

Unrealized Gain or Loss—OCI	9,537	
FV-OCI Investments		9,537

A	=	L	+	SE
−9,537				−9,537

Cash flows: No effect

Sale of FV-OCI Investments (Debt Instruments)

If a company sells its FV-OCI debt securities before maturity, it must derecognize the investments. To illustrate, let's look at **Example 9.20**.

Example 9.20 | FV-OCI Model—Portfolio of Bonds; Sale of Bonds

Facts Following along with Example 9.19, assume that Robinson Limited sold the Chan bonds on July 1, 2021, for $90,000, at which time they had an amortized cost of $94,214 (after adjusting for discount amortization of $677). Assume further that the fair value of the Anacomp bonds at December 31, 2021, is $195,000. There was no other activity in the investment portfolio between July 1 and December 31, 2021. Recall the carrying value of the Chan bonds ($103,600) from the prior example.

Instructions Prepare the journal entry to record the sale. In addition, prepare the journal entry to revalue the remaining bonds at year end.

Solution The three journal entries approach that we used to record the sale of the FV-OCI Investments in shares will be used (with slight modifications since we are dealing with a bond).

1. First we revalue the investment to fair value.
2. Then we recognize the sale.
3. Then we reclassify (recycle) the accumulated unrealized loss (in this case, from OCI to net income because we are dealing with a bond). Under IFRS 9, this entry must be booked.

Robinson records the following entries:

July 1/21	(a) Unrealized Gain or Loss—OCI		14,277	
	FV-OCI Investments			14,277
	[$103,600 + $677 (amortization of discount to July 1) − $90,000]			
	(b) Cash		90,000	
	FV-OCI Investments			90,000
	(c) Loss on Disposal of Investments FV-OCI		4,214	
	Unrealized Gain or Loss—OCI			4,214
	($10,063 gain − $14,277 loss or $94,214 − $90,000)			

A	=	L	+	SE
−14,277				−14,277

Cash flows: No effect

A	=	L	+	SE
0				

Cash flows: ↑ 90,000 inflow

A	=	L	+	SE
				0

Cash flows: No effect

After adjusting for the sale of the Chan bonds, the balance in the Unrealized Gain or Loss—OCI account is $9,537 + $14,277 − $4,214 = $19,600. This needs to be adjusted for the Anacomp bonds.

Robinson prepares the following schedule on December 31, 2021, when the fair value of the remaining bonds is $195,000.

FV-OCI Investment Portfolio December 31, 2021			
Investments in Bonds	**Amortized Cost**	**Fair Value**	**Unrealized Gain (Loss)**
Anacomp Corporation 10% bonds	$200,000	$195,000	($5,000)
Total portfolio	$200,000	$195,000	($5,000)

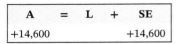

A	=	L	+	SE
+14,600				+14,600

Cash flows: No effect

We need one more entry to adjust the carrying value of the remaining bonds to fair value. The entry is as follows:

FV-OCI Investments	14,600	
Unrealized Gain or Loss—OCI		14,600
($19,600 − $5,000 or $195,000 − $180,400)		

Now that the three common methods of accounting for financial instruments have been explained and illustrated, how does a company decide which method is accepted under accounting standards for a particular investment? We have summarized the models used under both IFRS and ASPE for debt and equity instruments at the end of the chapter. See Illustration 9.12.

Measurement—Impairment Models

> ### LEARNING OBJECTIVE 5
> Explain and apply the incurred loss, expected loss, and fair value loss impairment models.

In the previous section, we generally ignored impairment. Let's take a closer look at this now. Financial asset investments are reviewed for possible impairment for the same reasons that non-financial assets are: the statement of financial position (SFP) carrying value for any asset cannot be more than the expected benefits the asset can bring to the organization. Since financial assets measured at fair value are already measured at their current fair value amount, it is usually only those measured at cost or amortized cost that need a method of accounting for impairment (unless impairment losses are required to be recycled).

Both IFRS and ASPE require that entities review for impairment at least at each reporting date. To the extent possible, this review is carried out on individual assets. However, sometimes the information is not available on a timely basis to do this for each specific asset, so investments with similar characteristics are grouped. Even if assets are assessed for impairment on an individual basis, they should also be assessed for impairment as a group where they share similar risk characteristics. For instance, a portfolio of loans to a certain industry that is experiencing an economic downturn should be assessed as a group as well as individually. If an instrument, or portfolio of instruments, is determined to be impaired, the amount of the impairment loss is calculated and recognized. There are differences of opinion, however, on how such a loss should be determined and reported. Three different impairment measurement models are explained next: an **incurred loss model**, an **expected loss model**, and a full **fair value model**. We will then summarize which models are used under IFRS and ASPE.

Incurred Loss Impairment Model

ASPE Under the incurred loss impairment model, investments are recognized as impaired when there is no longer reasonable assurance that the future cash flows associated with them will be collected either in their entirety or when due. Entities look for *objective evidence that there has been a significant adverse change in the period in the expected amount of future cash flows, or in the timing of those cash flows.*[15] These events are called **trigger events or loss events**. Examples of situations that might indicate impairment include the fact that the entity that issued the debt or equity instrument:

- is experiencing significant financial difficulties;
- has defaulted on, or is late making, interest or principal payments;

---

[15]ASPE 3856.17.

- is likely to undergo a major financial reorganization or enter bankruptcy; or
- is in a market that is experiencing significant negative economic change.[16]

If such evidence exists, the next step is to measure the investment's estimated realizable amounts. According to Section 3856.17, this is calculated as the highest of the following:

1. present value of the revised amounts and timing of the future cash flows, discounted at the current market rate, or
2. the amount that would be realized if the asset were sold, or
3. the amount that would be realized if the entity called the financial asset (for instance a loan) and took any collateral that it had rights to.

The **impairment loss** is the difference between this amount and the instrument's carrying amount.

After the impairment is recorded, interest income is recognized based on the revised cash flow estimates and the **discount rate that was used to determine the present value of those flows**. Any further change in the investment's realizable value related to an event occurring after the original impairment is recognized as an adjustment of the impairment loss. The change could result from a further decline in value (an increased loss) or a recovery of the previous estimated impairment loss.

This impairment method is described as an incurred loss impairment model because it captures only credit losses that were triggered by events that occurred by the SFP date. Let's look at this further in **Example 9.21**.

Example 9.21 | Incurred Loss Impairment Model

Facts   Assume a company purchased an investment in AB Ltd. bonds for $100,000 at par value at the beginning of the year. The bonds pay interest on December 31 each year. The bond is carried at amortized cost. AB Ltd. is experiencing financial difficulties and is not able to make the payment of principal and interest on the bond. The present value of the discounted revised cash flows is $70,000 using the current market interest rate. The company follows ASPE.

Instructions   Is the investment impaired? If so, prepare the journal entry to reflect the impairment.

Solution   The existence of financial difficulties provides objective evidence of impairment and represents a triggering or loss event, as does the company's inability to make the payments.
The journal entry to record the impairment is as follows:

Loss on Impairment	30,000	
Bond Investment at Amortized Cost		30,000
($100,000 − $70,000)		

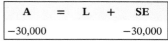

A	=	L	+	SE
−30,000				−30,000

Cash flows: No effect

Expected Loss Impairment Model

IFRS **Significant Change**   Under an **expected loss impairment model**, estimates of future cash flows used to determine the present value of the investment are made on a **continuous basis** and do not rely on a triggering event to occur. See **Underlying Concept 9.3**. These revised expected cash flows are generally discounted at the same effective interest rate used when the instrument was **first acquired**, therefore retaining a cost-based measurement.[17] Estimates of impairment losses are based on reasonably available information that is obtainable without undue cost or effort. Under this approach, almost all financial assets will need to be assessed to determine if there might be expected losses.

> **Underlying Concept 9.3**
>
> The expected loss model provides more objective information because the assessment of a trigger or loss event can be very subjective. This may be offset by the fact that it is not easy to measure the expected loss.

---

[16]ASPE 3856.A15.

[17]IFRS 9.B5.5.44.

The company must record any impairment loss by the first reporting date and must assess whether the credit risk on an investment has increased significantly since the investment was first recognized. As a general rule, there is a significant increase in credit risk when principal or interest payments are more than 30 days past due (unless the entity has evidence to the contrary).[18] Credit risk may also have increased significantly even before the debtor defaults on payments. Factors to consider include decreased sales, profit, or cash flows, worsening economy, breach of covenants, and risk of default.[19]

If the company determines that the credit risk has **not significantly increased**, then it considers the 12-month expected credit losses. This approach looks at the possibility of defaults within the 12-month period (and the present value of any losses due to defaults over the 12-month period, probability weighted).

If the company decides that the default risk on the investment has **increased significantly**, then the company must assess lifetime expected credit losses.[20] This means that it would consider all possible default events over the life of the instrument. So if the instrument was a 10-year bond, then the company would consider possible default events over the 10-year life of the bond (and the present value of these cash shortfalls over the life, probability weighted).

Illustration 9.5 contains a decision tree summarizing this approach.

ILLUSTRATION 9.5 **IFRS** Decision Tree of the Expected Loss Model for Impairment

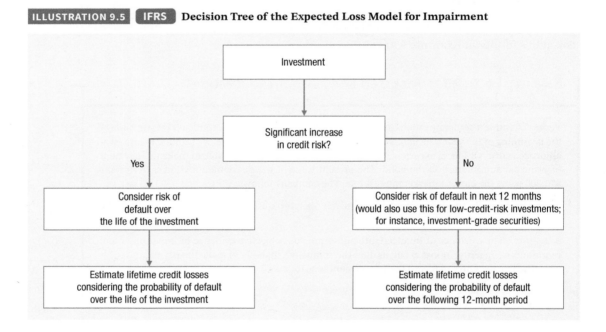

For instance, in a situation where there is no significant increase in the risk of default (such as if the credit risk is low), an entity might feel that the probability of default within the next 12 months is zero and therefore no impairment loss would be recognized. Conversely, if there is a significant increase in the risk of default, the entity would have to consider the probability of default over the life of the investment, which would generally be higher.[21]

IFRS notes that there are three stages of impairment, as shown in **Illustration 9.6**.[22]

---

[18]IFRS 9.5.5.11.

[19]IFRS 9 does not define the word "default." Instead, the standard allows companies to apply their own definition. The standard does note, however, that financial assets that are 90 days past due are in default unless the company can make a case to argue otherwise.

[20]Both 12-month and lifetime expected credit losses are defined in IFRS 9 – Appendix A.

[21]These calculations are fairly complex and generally beyond the scope of this text.

[22]Based on information from IFRS 9 Project Summary, July 2014.

ILLUSTRATION 9.6

IFRS   **Stages of Impairment**

Stage 1	Stage 2	Stage 3
– There is no significant increase in expected credit losses.	– There is a significant increase in expected credit losses.	– The asset is a credit-impaired investment (for instance, the company is in financial difficulty, a default in payment has occurred, or bankruptcy is probable).*
– Use a 12-month time frame to assess the probability of default.	– Use the investment lifetime to assess the probability of default.	– Use the investment lifetime to assess the probability of default.
– Calculate interest income on the investment's gross carrying amount.	– Calculate interest income on the investment's gross carrying amount.	– Calculate interest income on the investment's net carrying amount.

*This would generally be when an impairment loss is first recognized under the incurred loss model.

As a practical expedient, IFRS 9 allows the use of lifetime expected credit losses for trade receivables, contract assets, and lease receivables.[23]

When measuring the amount of the impairment under either scenario (that is, lifetime or 12-month expected credit losses), the company must consider the following:

1. an unbiased and probability-weighted amount,
2. the time value of money (as mentioned earlier, this is usually the effective rate of interest as determined when the company first made the investment), and
3. information that is reasonable and supportable (that is, it is available without undue effort or cost).[24]

The impairment loss is measured as the difference between the asset's gross carrying amount and the present value of the expected cash flows discounted at the original effective interest rate.[25]

Let's look at this further, in **Example 9.22.**

Example 9.22 | Expected Loss Model—Bond

Facts Jay Corporation purchases a 5% bond at par value for $100,000. Interest is paid annually. The bond is carried at amortized cost. Because the bond is issued at par, there is no amortization of discount or premium. Jay determines that there has not been a significant increase in the credit risk. Upon detailed analysis, Jay estimates that there is a slight chance that it might not collect 25% of the face value of the bond. In addition, Jay estimates that there is a 0.5% probability of default within the next 12 months.

Instructions How should the impairment loss be estimated? Calculate the impairment loss that should be recognized and prepare the journal entry.

Solution The loss is calculated based on the 12-month expected credit losses because there has not been a significant increase in the credit risk.

The loss is calculated as follows:

$$.005 \times .25 \times \$100,000 = \$125$$

---

[23]IFRS 9.5.5.15.

[24]IFRS 9.5.5.17. Copyright © IFRS Foundation. All rights reserved. Reproduced with permission.

[25]IFRS 9.B5.5.33.

A	=	L	+	SE
−125				−125

Cash flows: No effect

The journal entry is as follows:

Loss on Impairment	125	
Bond Investment at Amortized Cost		125

Recall that the face value of the bond ($100,000) represents the present value of the principal and interest payments. Therefore, the impairment loss is calculated as a percentage of that present value number and the time value is already considered.[26]

We could also do this calculation as follows:

$$.005 \times .25 \times [(\$100,000 + \$5,000)/1.05]$$

When the market interest rate changes, the fair value of a bond will also change. For instance, if the market interest rate increases, the fair value will decrease. This is not considered to be an impairment and should not be treated as such. Let's look at another example relating to impairment of a debt instrument accounted for using FV-OCI where the market interest rate changes, in **Example 9.23**.[27]

Example 9.23 | Expected Loss Model—Investment Accounted for Using FV-OCI

Facts   Assume Sandal Inc. purchases a debt instrument for $10,000 (fair value). At the following reporting date, the fair value of the instrument is $9,000. Half of this is due to changes in market interest rates. There has not been a significant increase in credit risk and therefore the entity will measure the expected losses using a 12-month time frame (estimated at $500). The instrument is accounted for using FV-OCI.

Instructions   How will this be recorded in the books of Sandal?

Solution   The journal entry follows.

Loss on Impairment	500	
Unrealized Gain or Loss—OCI	500	
FV-OCI Investments		1,000

The part of the loss relating to changes in market interest rates is booked through OCI. It is not considered to be an impairment. It arises solely due to changes in the market and has nothing to do with whether the debt instrument is potentially in default. The other half, however, is considered to be an impairment and must be booked through net income, as discussed earlier. In this case, because the investment is measured at fair value, the time value of money is already considered.

A	=	L	+	SE
−1,000				−1,000

Cash flows: No effect

Because the impairment loss under the expected loss model reflects both incurred losses to date and future expected credit losses, it results in earlier recognition of such losses in net income. This model is more difficult to apply, especially in continually estimating the amounts of the expected future cash flows. In addition, this model is only relevant for investments at cost/amortized cost and FV-OCI debt investments. There is no need to worry about FV-NI investments because they are continually revalued to fair value with all gains and losses booked to net income. There is no need to worry about FV-OCI equity investments either, because they are also continually revalued to fair value. In addition, all gains and losses are booked

[26]IFRS 9 IE 8 (footnote 68).

[27]Based on IFRS 9 IE – Example 13.

to OCI with no recycling. This means that impairment losses are not separately assessed or recycled through net income.

Fair Value Loss Impairment Model

Under the fair value loss impairment model, the impairment loss is the difference between the asset's fair value and its current carrying amount, assuming the fair value is less than the carrying amount. Fair value is calculated using all current information, including revised cash flows, current interest rates, and market values. Refer back to Chapters 2 and 3 for a discussion regarding calculating fair values. For investments valued using FV-NI, there is no need to do a separate impairment test. This is because the FV-NI model requires that all changes in fair value be recognized in net income, whether they are gains or losses.

Summary of Impairment Models

Illustration 9.7 summarizes the various impairment models under ASPE and IFRS.

ILLUSTRATION 9.7 **IFRS** **ASPE**   **Summary of Impairment Models**

Impairment Models	ASPE	IFRS 9
Incurred loss	Used for all investments measured at cost/amortized cost.	N/A
	Reduce carrying value to the higher of the discounted cash flow (discounted using the current market interest rate) and net realizable value (either through sale or by exercising the entity's rights to collateral).	
	May use an allowance account or reduce carrying value directly.	
	Impairment losses may be reversed.	
Expected loss	N/A	Used for all investments carried at cost/amortized cost as well as debt investments carried at FV-OCI.
		Must determine whether the credit risk has significantly increased. If not, use a 12-month time frame for assessing defaults. Otherwise, consider defaults over the lifetime of the investment.
		Must consider a probability-weighted range of outcomes and the time value of money using the historical rate. Based on information that is reasonable, supportable and available without undue cost.
Fair value	Used for all investments accounted for as FV-NI.	Used for all investments that are accounted for as FV-NI and equity investments accounted for at FV-OCI.
	No need to do a separate impairment test because the assets are continually revalued to fair value with gains and losses booked to net income.	No need to do a separate impairment test because the assets are continually revalued to fair value under the FV-NI model with gains and losses booked to net income.
		Impairment losses on equity investments accounted for at FV-OCI are not recycled to net income so impairment testing is not done.

Strategic Investments—Investments in Associates

LEARNING OBJECTIVE 6

Explain the concept of significant influence and apply the equity method.

Alternative Terminology 9.5

Under ASPE, investments in associates are often called *significant influence investments*. We will use the term "investment in associates" in the end-of-chapter material.

Strategy & Governance 2.3.1 Accounting for investments in the common shares of another corporation (or associate) after acquisition depends mostly on the relationship that exists between the investor and the investee. These are called investments in associates; see **Alternative Terminology 9.5**. Relationships are classified by the level of influence that is exercised by the investor and this, in turn, is generally related to the degree of share ownership. In other words, more shares usually mean more influence. When the investment is made for strategic purposes, management usually wants to influence or control the investee's policies. Therefore, the investor is more likely to acquire a higher percentage of the outstanding voting shares.

The levels of influence and types of investment are summarized in **Illustration 9.8** with reference to the percentage of ownership. Note that the percentages given are guidelines only.

ILLUSTRATION 9.8

Levels of Influence and Types of Investment

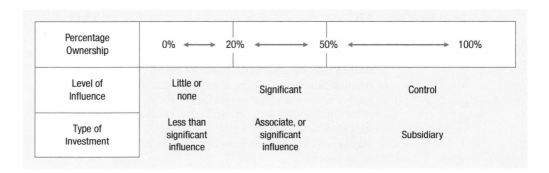

The accounting standards and reporting for equity investments depend on the level of influence that dictates what type of investment a particular holding is.[28] The first part of this chapter covered how to account for investments where the investor is not able to exercise significant influence, let alone control of the investee company. Although some of those investments could have been made for strategic purposes, it was assumed earlier in the chapter that the required level of **significant influence** was not reached.

Significant Influence

When an investor has an interest of less than 20%, **it is presumed that the investor has little or no influence over the investee**. This may not be the case, however. For example, a 16% interest may allow an investor to significantly influence decisions if the remaining shares are widely held. Alternatively, ownership of 30% of a company's shares may not give an investor company any influence at all if a 70% majority shareholder does not permit any.

Although an equity interest of less than 50% of an investee corporation does not give an investor **legal control**, it might give an investor significant influence over the investee's strategic policies. To provide guidance, the IASB defines significant influence as "the power to participate in the financial and operating policy decisions" of an entity, but not control over

---

[28]Joint ventures are another type of equity investment. Since they can be incorporated companies, they can issue shares. Joint ventures are characterized by joint control (versus unilateral control). This is usually shown through a contractual agreement that states that the venturers (investors) must share key decision-making.

those policies.[29] This is similar to the ASPE concept, and both indicate that an ability to exercise influence at a significant level over another company's operating, investing, and financing activities may be indicated in several ways. Examples include the following: representation on the board of directors, participation in policy-making processes, material inter-company transactions, interchange of managerial personnel, or provision of technical information.[30] Under IFRS, the term associate refers to the entity that the investor has significant influence over, provided it is neither a subsidiary nor a joint venture.

To ensure that the significant influence criterion is applied in a reasonably consistent manner, the standard setters concluded that an investment (direct or indirect) of 20% or more of the voting shares of another company should lead to a presumption that, unless there is evidence to the contrary, an investor can exercise significant influence over an investee. With less than a 20% voting interest, the assumption is that the investor cannot exercise the required degree of influence, unless the ability to influence is clearly shown. If the investor holds potential voting rights that can be exercised or converted currently, these should also be considered in deciding whether or not it has the power to exercise significant influence.

IFRS **ASPE** As indicated above, the extent of influence dictates the type of investment, and this, in turn, dictates the appropriate method of accounting. For investments in associates, **IFRS** requires the investor to use the equity method of accounting.[31] **ASPE** allows investors to choose the equity method or the cost method in accounting for this type of investment, but the investor must choose one method for all "significant influence" investments. However, if the associate's shares are quoted in an active market, the cost method cannot be used. Instead, the fair value approach, with gains and losses being recognized in income, can be chosen under ASPE. We explained both the cost and FV-NI models earlier in this chapter, so we turn next to how the equity method works.

Equity Method

Under the equity method, the investment is initially recorded at the cost of the acquired shares. After this, its carrying amount is adjusted each period for the investor's proportionate share of the changes in the investee's net assets. The equity method sounds complex at first, but it is basically **the accrual basis of accounting applied to investment income**.

The investor recognizes its share of investment income as the investee earns income by debiting the Investment account and crediting Investment Income. When cash is received from the investment (that is, the investee pays a dividend on the shares), this converts part of an asset that has already been recognized—the Investment—to cash. Therefore, Cash is debited and the Investment account is credited.

As indicated, the Investment account under the equity method changes to mirror the increases and decreases in the investee's book value:

- **When the associate's net assets increase** because it earns income, **the investor increases the carrying amount of its investment** for its proportionate share of the associate's increase in net assets and also **reports its share of the associate's income as investment income**.

- **When the associate's net assets decrease** because the company pays a dividend, **the investor recognizes the cash received and decreases the carrying amount of the investment** by its share of the decrease in the associate's net assets.

To illustrate the basics of the equity method, we will look at Example 9.24.

---

[29]IAS 28 *Investments in Associates*, para. 3. Copyright © IFRS Foundation. All rights reserved. Reproduced with permission.

[30]*CPA Canada Handbook*, Part II, Section 3051.05.

[31]IAS 28 identifies some exceptions. These include investments in associates that are held for sale and those reported by a parent that is not required to prepare consolidated financial statements.

Example 9.24 | Equity Method

Facts Maxi Corp. purchases a 20% interest in Mini Corp. and has the ability to exercise significant influence over Mini's financial and operating policies. On January 2, 2019, Maxi Corp. acquires 48,000 shares (20% of Mini Corp. common shares) at a cost of $10 a share. For the year 2019, Mini Corp. reports net income of $200,000; Maxi Corp.'s share is 20%, or $40,000. At December 31, 2019, the 48,000 shares of Mini Corp. have a fair value of $12 a share, or $576,000. On January 28, 2020, Mini Corp. announces and pays a cash dividend of $100,000; Maxi Corp. receives 20%, or $20,000. For the year 2020, Mini Corp. reports a net loss of $50,000; Maxi Corp.'s share is 20%, or $10,000. At December 31, 2020, the 48,000 Mini Corp. shares have a fair value of $11 a share, or $528,000. The investment value is not considered impaired.

Instructions **IFRS** **ASPE** Which methods are allowed under IFRS and ASPE? Prepare the journal entries for 2019 and 2020 under IFRS as well as ASPE (for all methods allowed).

Solution IFRS requires the use of the equity method. ASPE allows a choice, including equity method, FV-NI (where shares are traded in an active market), and cost method. The entries are shown below. Note the effects on the Investment account and on the income statement.

	IFRS/ASPE Equity Method ($000)		ASPE FV-NI (may use where traded in an active market) ($000)		ASPE Cost Model (may use except where shares are traded in an active market) ($000)	

On January 2, 2019, Maxi Corp. acquires 48,000 shares (20% of Mini Corp. common shares) at a cost of $10 a share.	Investment in Associate
	  Cash
		480
		  480
			FV-NI Investments
			  Cash
				480
				  480
					Other Investments
					  Cash
						480
						  480

For the year 2019, Mini Corp. reports net income of $200,000; Maxi Corp.'s share is 20%, or $40,000.	Investment in Associate
	  Investment
	    Income or Loss*
		40
		  40
			N/A		N/A	

At December 31, 2019, the 48,000 shares of Mini Corp. have a fair value of $12 a share, or $576,000.	N/A		FV-NI Investments
			  Investment
			    Income or Loss
				96
				  96
					N/A	

On January 28, 2020, Mini Corp. announces and pays a cash dividend of $100,000; Maxi Corp. receives 20%, or $20,000.	Cash
	  Investment in
	    Associate
		20
		  20
			Cash
			  Investment
			    Income or Loss
				20
				  20
					Cash
					  Dividend Revenue
						20
						  20

For the year 2020, Mini Corp. reports a net loss of $50,000; Maxi Corp.'s share is 20%, or $10,000.	Investment
	  Income or Loss*
	  Investment in
	    Associate
		10
		  10
			N/A		N/A	

At December 31, 2020, the 48,000 Mini Corp. shares have a fair value of $11 a share, or $528,000. The investment value is not considered impaired.	N/A		Investment Income
			  or Loss
			  FV-NI
			    Investments
				48
				  48
					N/A	

*This entry is sometimes called the **equity pickup**, because the investor is picking up its share of income or loss under the equity method. Another commonly used account title is Equity in Earnings of Associate Company.

Under the equity method, **the accrual basis of accounting** is applied. Maxi Corp. therefore reports investment income as Mini Corp. earns income. Revenue recognition is permitted before receiving a dividend, because of the degree of influence that the investor has over the investee's decisions, including dividend decisions. If the investee company suffers a loss, as Mini Corp. did in 2020, the investor accrues its share of the loss and reduces the carrying amount of its investment.

One of the benefits of this method is that the investor's income statement reports the economics of the situation: if the associate performs well, the investor's income statement reflects positive investment income. If the associate incurs losses, the investor's income statement reflects its share of the loss. See **Underlying Concept 9.4.** In addition, when the equity method is used, the investor cannot manipulate its own income by influencing the timing of a dividend from the associate.

There are two more complexities in applying the equity method:[32]

<table>
<tr><td>**1.**</td><td>Differences between what was originally paid for the investment and the investor's share of the associate's book value need to be identified and accounted for according to the reason for the extra payment.</td></tr>
<tr><td>**2.**</td><td>The major classifications of the income reported by the associate are retained and reported in the same way on the investor's income statement.</td></tr>
</table>

The first item requires an understanding of what the cost of the investment represents. It is unusual for the investor to pay an amount for the investment that is exactly equal to its share of the other company's book value. The excess payment (usually it is extra) could be due to several reasons, such as the following:

- There may be unrecorded assets.
- There may be assets whose fair value is greater than the carrying amount on the associate's books, or liabilities whose fair value is less than book value.
- There may be intangibles, such as goodwill, that the associate has but that are not recognized in its books.

Any payment in excess of (or less than) the investor's share of book value is part of the cost of the investment, and after acquisition, it has to be accounted for appropriately. If the difference is caused by long-lived assets with fair values that are greater than book value, the amount above the asset's book value must be amortized. If it relates to inventory with a fair value in excess of its carrying amount on the associate's books, it will be recognized as an increased expense as the inventory is sold. There may also be assets with fair values that are lower than book value or liabilities with present values higher than book value. **None of these differences are recorded on the associate's books, but they are captured as part of the purchase cost of the investment,** so it is the investment account itself and the investment income or loss that need to be adjusted over time.

Because the equity method recognizes and reports the investor's share of the associate's income, **the type of income that is reported should remain the same.** That is, the portion that is the investor's share of the associate's discontinued operations is reported separately from the investor's share of income before discontinued operations. The same principle applies to the investor's portion of the associate's other comprehensive income, changes in accounting policy reported in retained earnings, and capital charges. The investor reports its share of all of these in the appropriate place in its financial statements. Let's look at **Example 9.25.**

> **Underlying Concept 9.4**
>
> The equity method of accounting results in income statement amounts that more faithfully represent the underlying economic results of the investor company's management decisions.

Example 9.25 | Equity Method—Expanded Example

Facts   On January 1, 2020, Investor Company purchases 250,000 of Investee Company's 1 million outstanding common shares for $8.5 million. Investor has therefore acquired a 25% interest in Investee. The book value (net assets) of Investee Company on this date is $30 million and Investor's proportionate share is 25% of this, or $7.5 million. Investor Company has therefore paid

---

[32]A third aspect involves eliminating the effects of unrealized inter-company gains and losses. This issue and situations where investors pay less for the shares than their proportionate interest in the identifiable net assets of the associate (that is, "negative goodwill") are topics for an advanced accounting course.

$1 million in excess of its share of the book value ($8,500,000 − $7,500,000). Investee's depreciable assets **are undervalued on its books** by $2.4 million. Investor Company estimates the remaining life of the depreciable assets to be eight years.

Instructions Prepare an analysis of why Investor paid $1 million more than its share of Investee's book value?

Solution The depreciable assets acquired are undervalued by $2.4 million. This explains $600,000 ($2,400,000 × 25%) of the excess, because Investor would only pay more in proportion to its ownership interest. The $600,000 excess payment included in the Investment account will have to be amortized over eight years. The remaining $400,000 is unexplained and therefore is determined to be unrecorded goodwill. Investor will have to assess the carrying amount of the balance of the Investment account each year to determine whether there has been any impairment in its value. This purchase is analyzed below.

Cost of 25% investment in Investee Co. shares	$8,500,000
25% of book value of Investee Co. represented by investment	
25% × $30,000,000	7,500,000
Payment in excess of share of book value	1,000,000
Fair value allocation to depreciable assets	
25% × $2,400,000	600,000
Unexplained excess assumed to be goodwill	$ 400,000
Annual amortization of excess payment for capital assets	
$600,000/8-year life	$ 75,000

Let's look at what happens following the purchase, in **Example 9.26**.

Example 9.26 | Equity Method—After the Purchase

Facts Building on the facts in Example 9.25, Investee Company later reports net income of $2.8 million for its 2020 fiscal year, including a loss on discontinued operations of $400,000. **Income before discontinued operations**, therefore, is $3.2 million. Dividends of $1.4 million are declared and paid by Investee Company on December 31, 2020.

Instructions Prepare the journal entries to record the events in 2020 including the acquisition.

Solution To record these transactions and events, Investor Company makes the following entries.

Jan. 1/20	Investment in Associate	8,500,000	
	Cash		8,500,000
	(To record the acquisition of 25% of Investee Co.)		

Dec. 31/20	Cash	350,000	
	Investment in Associate		350,000
	(To record the dividend from Investee Co.		
	[$1,400,000 × 0.25])		

On December 31, Investor Company recognizes its 25% share of Investee Company's net income. Because its associate's income includes both continuing and discontinued operation components, 25% of each amount is reported separately by Investor Company. The account Investment in Associate is increased by 25% of the increase in Investee's net assets from earning net income (25% × $2,800,000). Furthermore, Investor Company paid more than book value for Investee Company's net assets and a portion of the excess amount relates to assets that are depreciable. The "extra cost" of the depreciable assets to Investor has not been recognized on the associate's books, nor has the additional depreciation. As a result, the investment income needs to be adjusted for this additional amount.

Dec. 31/20	Investment in Associate	700,000	
	Loss on Discontinued Operations	100,000	
	Investment Income or Loss		800,000
	(To record the investment income from Investee		
	Co. [Investee Co. income × 0.25])		

A = L + SE
0

Cash flows: ▼8,500,000 outflow

A = L + SE
0

Cash flows: ▲350,000 inflow

A = L + SE
+700,000 +700,000

Cash flows: No effect

Dec. 31/20	Investment Income or Loss	75,000	
	Investment in Associate		75,000
	(Amortization of fair value difference, depreciable assets)		

A	=	L	+	SE
−75,000				−75,000

Cash flows: No effect

The following shows the calculation of the investment in Investee Company that is presented on Investor Company's December 31, 2020 SFP.

Acquisition cost, January 1, 2020	$8,500,000
Add: 25% of increase in Investee's net assets from earning net income	700,000
Less: 25% of decrease in Investee's net assets from declaration/ payment of dividend	(350,000)
Less: Amortization of fair value difference related to capital assets	(75,000)
Investment in Investee Co., December 31, 2020, at equity	$8,775,000

Under both **IFRS** and **ASPE**, an investment that results in significant influence is assessed at each statement of financial position date to determine if there are any indications that the investment may be impaired (**objective evidence of a loss event**). If there are, and it is determined that it is impaired (that is, **there is a significant adverse change**), its carrying amount is compared with the investment's **recoverable amount**: the higher of its value in use and fair value less costs to sell, both of which are discounted cash flow concepts. If the carrying amount is more than the investment's recoverable amount, an impairment loss equal to the difference is recognized in net income and the investment is written down directly. This loss may be reversed if future events indicate that the recoverable amount has improved.

When the investment in the associate is sold, the statement of financial position Investment in Associate account and the Investment Income or Loss account are first brought up to date as at the date of sale. This involves adjusting these accounts for the investor's share of the associate's earnings and changes in book value since the last reporting date. Then the investment's carrying value is removed from the accounts and the difference between this and the proceeds on disposal is recognized in income as a gain or loss. **Example 9.27** illustrates a sale.

Example 9.27 | Equity Method—Sale

Facts   Continuing with Examples 9.25 and 9.26, assume that Investor Company sells its investment in Investee Company on January 2, 2021, for $9 million.

Instructions   What would the journal entry be to record the sale?

Solution: Because the accounts are already up to date in this case, the entry to record the sale is:

Cash	9,000,000	
Investment in Associate		8,775,000
Gain on Disposal of Investments in Associate		225,000

A	=	L	+	SE
+225,000				+225,000

Cash flows: ↑ 9,000,000 inflow

Summary of Accounting Standards for Associates

The equity method is also known as "one-line consolidation" and is applied in ways that are related to how consolidation principles are applied. In fact, the equity method "investment income" is the same amount that would be needed to increase or decrease the investor's income to the amount that would be reported if the investor had consolidated the results of the investee with those of the investor, with possible exceptions related to goodwill and investment impairment. Given this similarity, other complexities that result from such investments are left for an advanced accounting course that covers inter-corporate investments.

IFRS **ASPE** **Illustration 9.9** summarizes the accounting for investments in the equity instruments of companies in which the investor has significant influence.

ILLUSTRATION 9.9 **Accounting for Associates**

	IFRS	ASPE		
Measurement after recognition	Equity method	Equity method is used for all or the cost method/model is used for all. However, if shares are quoted in an active market, cannot use cost method (may use equity method or FV-NI).		
		Equity method	**Cost method/model**	**FV-NI model**
Unrealized holding gains/losses	Not recognized	Not recognized	Not recognized	Recognized in net income
Investment income	Percentage of associate's income, adjusted for differences between cost and share of book value and for inter-company profits	Percentage of associate's income, adjusted for differences between cost and share of book value and inter-company profits	Dividends received or receivable	Dividends received or receivable
Impairment, when assessment so indicates	Loss = carrying amount less recoverable amount (higher of value in use and fair value less costs to sell)	Loss = carrying amount less recoverable amount (higher of value in use and fair value less costs to sell)	Loss = carrying amount less recoverable amount (higher of value in use and fair value less costs to sell)	N/A
Impairment reversal	Permitted	Permitted	Permitted	N/A

Strategic Investments—Investments in Subsidiaries

LEARNING OBJECTIVE 7

Explain the concept of control and when consolidation is appropriate.

When one corporation acquires control of another entity, the investor corporation is called the **parent** and the investee corporation is called the subsidiary. Control is assumed when the investor owns more than 50% of the voting shares of another company. This is because it holds a majority of the votes at the board of directors' meetings of the investee company, and therefore, the investor's management controls all the subsidiary's net assets and operations.

IFRS ASPE Standard setters have wrestled for many years with the best way to explain what control really is. They acknowledge that sometimes an entity with less than 50% of the voting shares can have control, while an entity with more than 50% sometimes may not have control. According to **ASPE**, control is the continuing power to determine the strategic operating, financing, and investing policies of another entity without the co-operation of others. Under **IFRS**, an investor controls another if it has the power to direct the activities of the other entity to generate returns, either positive or negative, for the investor. The "power to direct the activities of another" means that an investor can determine the other entity's strategic operating and financing policies. The differences in the definitions are subtle but real, and they will become more apparent in an advanced accounting course that deals with inter-corporate investments.

IFRS ASPE An investment in the common shares of a subsidiary is presented as a long-term investment on the separate financial statements of the parent, usually accounted for by either the equity or cost method. When preparing **IFRS** statements, however, an investor with subsidiaries is required to present consolidated financial statements for the group of companies under its control. In other words, the investor **eliminates the investment account** and instead **reports all the assets and liabilities of the subsidiary on a**

line-by-line basis. Under **ASPE**, this is a **permitted**, but **not required**, option. A parent company following ASPE can choose to:

1. consolidate all its subsidiaries, or
2. present all of its subsidiaries under either the equity method or cost model.

The same choice is applied to all subsidiaries, although investments in shares that are quoted in an active market are not permitted to be accounted for using the cost model. They may instead be measured and reported at FV-NI. You can see here the similarities between ASPE for associates and subsidiary companies. Separate reporting on the balance sheet is required for subsidiaries accounted for using the equity method and for those using the cost method. The income statement also reports the income from each group of subsidiaries accounted for on a different basis.

Because we have already covered the cost, equity, and FV-NI methods and models, the emphasis now is on understanding consolidation. In place of the one-line long-term investment in subsidiary, the parent reports 100% of each of the assets and liabilities over which it has control. Instead of reporting investment income on the income statement, 100% of each of the revenues and expenses reported by the subsidiary is reported on a line-by-line basis with those of the parent company. That is, the parent presents **consolidated financial statements**. This method of reporting an investment in a controlled company is much more informative to the parent company's shareholders than a single-line statement of financial position and a single-line income statement account.

The requirement to include 100% of the assets and liabilities and 100% of the revenues, expenses, gains, and losses under the parent's control even when the ownership is less than 100% leads to the recognition of unique statement of financial position and income statement accounts. These noncontrolling interest accounts (sometimes referred to as minority interest) represent the portion of the net assets **not** owned and the portion of the entity's consolidated net income that does **not** accrue to the parent company's shareholders. These claims to net assets and net income are **equity claims** because they represent the interests of the noncontrolling **shareholders** of the subsidiary companies.

Consolidated financial statements disregard the distinction between separate legal entities and treat the parent and subsidiary corporations as an economic unit—an **economic entity**. See Underlying Concept 9.5. After acquisition, this means that all inter-company balances and unrealized inter-company gains and losses are eliminated for reporting purposes. An entity cannot report sales or make a profit selling to itself. The preparation of consolidated financial statements is discussed in detail in advanced financial accounting.

The rules for consolidation seem very straightforward: If a company owns more than 50% of another company, it generally should be consolidated. If it owns less than 50%, it generally is not consolidated. However, with complex modern business relationships, standard setters realize that this test is too artificial, and that determining who really has control is often based on factors other than share ownership. This topic is covered in advanced accounting courses.

> **Underlying Concept 9.5**
>
> The consolidation of the financial results of different companies follows the economic entity assumption. It disregards the legal boundaries between entities. The key objective is to provide useful information to financial statement users about all the resources under the control of parent company management.

Presentation, Disclosure, and Analysis

LEARNING OBJECTIVE 8
Explain how investments are presented and disclosed in the financial statements, noting how this facilitates analysis.

Where should a company report investments on its statement of financial position? What types of disclosures are needed for transparency? Finally, what information is important for users when analyzing financial statements? We will answer these questions in this section of the chapter.

Presentation and Disclosure

First, let's take a look at presentation and disclosure issues. For purposes of this discussion, investments are subdivided into two groups: those where the investor has no significant influence or control and those where the investor has significant influence.

IFRS ASPE Investments without Significant Influence or Control

Should investments that the investor cannot exercise significant influence over or control be reported as current or long-term assets? The requirements for presentation of an investment as a current asset are the same as for other assets. In general, those classified as current are continuously turning over or affecting working capital. As indicated in Chapter 5, **IFRS** specifies that, if an investment has any one of the following characteristics, it is classified as current:

- It is expected to be sold or otherwise realized within the entity's normal operating cycle or within 12 months from the statement of financial position date.
- It is held primarily for trading purposes.
- It is a cash equivalent.

Under **ASPE**, the conditions are similar: an investment is classified as a current asset only if it is usually realizable within 12 months from the balance sheet date (or normal operating cycle, if longer) and it can be converted to cash relatively quickly.

This means that debt and equity investments measured at cost or amortized cost and those at FV-NI could be either current or long-term assets, depending on the specific situation. Debt instruments are likely to be classified as current only if they are held to be traded, or expected to mature or be sold, within the following year. Equity instruments will be current only if they are marketable and are expected to be converted to cash that can be used for current purposes. Under the revised IFRS 9, investments carried at FV-OCI are most likely non-current assets: they are held for longer-term strategic purposes, and not for current trading.

Finance 5.2.2 The **objective of the disclosures** required for financial assets that are investments in debt and equity instruments is generally the same under both ASPE and IFRS: to provide information that allows users to assess the following:

- how significant these financial assets are to an entity's financial position and performance,
- the nature and extent of risks that the entity faces as a result of these assets, and
- how the entity manages these risks.

The specific standards are the best source of the many required disclosures for financial asset investments. The following section is meant to provide you with an understanding of the **types of information** that are required to be made available to users of the financial statements. Understanding the goal of the disclosures is helpful in determining and even predicting what information is reported.

- To help readers understand the significance of these investments to the statement of financial position, companies disclose the following:
  - the **carrying amount of investments** in instruments carried at amortized cost, cost, FV-NI (noting those where the fair value option was taken), and FV-OCI (noting those that were designated as such as an accounting policy choice and why this choice was made); and
  - the carrying amount of any impaired investments (including defaults and breaches) and related allowances for impairment, by type (method of accounting for the assets), which is also separately reported, as well as any reclassifications and collateral underlying the investments.
- To enable readers to relate the **income statement effects** to the investments on the statement of financial position, companies disclose the following:

- net gains or losses recognized (by method of accounting),
- total interest income (under IFRS, include only interest income calculated using the effective interest method for financial assets except for those at FV-NI), and
- gains/losses on derecognition including reasons for derecognizing.

- **IFRS** requires significant amounts of fair value information including valuation techniques and inputs for those investments measured using fair value and those measured using level 3 inputs.

- For each type of **financial risk** that results from the investments, disclose what the risk exposures are, how they arise, any changes over the accounting period, and information about any concentrations of risk such as those that arise from significant investments in particular industries or foreign currency. IFRS requires additional information, such as how risks are managed, credit risk by classification of instrument, past due and impaired investments, and sensitivity analyses for each type of market risk to which the entity is exposed.[33]

- For impaired assets, IFRS requires disclosures of the following:
  - impairment losses and reversals,
  - interest on impaired investments,
  - the basis for expected credit loss calculations,
  - how these losses are measured, and
  - how the company assesses changes in credit risks.

IFRS also requires reconciliation between opening balances in the impairment allowance and closing balances.

Refer back to Illustration 9.2, which shows the balance sheet of Canada Life. Illustration 9.10 provides additional excerpts from the financial statements. Note the discussion regarding how fair value is measured. Recall our discussions from Chapters 2 and 3 on fair value measurement. The actual disclosures are significantly greater than we have presented here and it would be worthwhile for you to read through the full set of disclosures in the financial statements by accessing the annual report on the company's website.

ILLUSTRATION 9.10

Excerpts from Selected Notes to the Financial Statements— Canada Life Financial Corporation

(a) Portfolio Investments

Portfolio investments include bonds, mortgage loans, stocks and investment properties. Portfolio investments are classified as fair value through profit or loss, available-for-sale, held-to-maturity, loans and receivables, equity-method investments or as non-financial instruments based on management's intention relating to the purpose and nature of the instrument or characteristics of the investment. The Company has not classified any investments as held-to-maturity.

Investments in bonds and stocks normally actively traded on a public market or where fair value can be reliably measured are either designated or classified as fair value through profit or loss or classified as available-for-sale on a trade date basis. A financial asset is designated as fair value through profit or loss on initial recognition if it eliminates or significantly reduces an accounting mismatch. Changes in the fair value of financial assets designated as fair value through profit or loss are generally offset by changes in insurance contract liabilities, since the measurement of insurance contract liabilities is determined with reference to the assets supporting the liabilities. A financial asset is classified as fair value through profit or loss on initial recognition if it is part of a portfolio that is actively traded for the purpose of earning investment income. Fair value through profit or loss investments are recognized at fair value on the Consolidated Balance Sheets with realized and unrealized gains and losses reported in the Consolidated Statements of Earnings. Available-for-sale investments are recognized at fair value on the Consolidated Balance Sheets with unrealized gains and losses recorded in other comprehensive income. Realized gains and losses on available-for-sale investments are

(continued)

---

[33]The types of risk that are associated with financial assets in general—credit, liquidity, and market risk—are discussed more fully in Chapter 16.

ILLUSTRATION 9.10
(*continued*)

reclassified from other comprehensive income and recorded in the Consolidated Statements of Earnings when the investment is sold. Interest income earned on both fair value through profit or loss and available-for-sale bonds is recorded as net investment income in the Consolidated Statements of Earnings.

Investments in stocks where a fair value cannot be measured reliably are classified as available-for-sale and carried at cost. Investments in stocks for which the Company exerts significant influence over but does not control are accounted for using the equity method of accounting.

Investments in mortgages and bonds not normally actively traded on a public market are classified as loans and receivables and are carried at amortized cost net of any allowance for credit losses. Interest income earned and realized gains and losses on the sale of investments classified as loans and receivables are recorded in the Consolidated Statements of Earnings and included in net investment income.

Investment properties are real estate held to earn rental income or for capital appreciation. Investment properties are initially measured at cost and subsequently carried at fair value on the Consolidated Balance Sheets. All changes in fair value are recorded as net investment income in the Consolidated Statements of Earnings. Properties held to earn rental income or for capital appreciation that have an insignificant portion that is owner occupied or where there is no intent to occupy on a long-term basis are classified as investment properties. Properties that do not meet these criteria are classified as owner occupied properties. Property that is leased that would otherwise be classified as investment property if owned by the Company is also included within investment properties.

Fair Value Measurement

Financial instrument carrying values necessarily reflect the prevailing market liquidity and the liquidity premiums embedded within the market pricing methods the Company relies upon.

Fair value movement on the assets supporting insurance contract liabilities is a major factor in the movement of insurance contract liabilities. Changes in the fair value of bonds designated or classified as fair value through profit or loss that support insurance and investment contract liabilities are largely offset by corresponding changes in the fair value of liabilities except when the bond has been deemed impaired.

The following is a description of the methodologies used to value instruments carried at fair value:

Bonds—Fair Value Through Profit or Loss and Available-for-Sale

Fair values for bonds classified and designated as fair value through profit or loss or available-for-sale are determined with reference to quoted market bid prices primarily provided by third party independent pricing sources. Where prices are not quoted in a normally active market, fair values are determined by valuation models. The Company maximizes the use of observable inputs when measuring fair value. The Company obtains quoted prices in active markets, when available, for identical assets at the balance sheet date to measure bonds at fair value in its fair value through profit or loss and available-for-sale portfolios.

The Company estimates the fair value of bonds not traded in active markets by referring to actively traded securities with similar attributes, dealer quotations, matrix pricing methodology, discounted cash flow analyses and/or internal valuation models. This methodology considers such factors as the issuer's industry, the security's rating, term, coupon rate and position in the capital structure of the issuer, as well as, yield curves, credit curves, prepayment rates and other relevant factors. For bonds that are not traded in active markets, valuations are adjusted to reflect illiquidity, and such adjustments generally are based on available market evidence. In the absence of such evidence, management's best estimate is used.

Bonds and Mortgages—Loans and Receivables

For disclosure purposes only, fair value for bonds and mortgages classified as loans and receivables are determined by discounting expected future cash flows using current market rates for similar instruments. Valuation inputs typically include benchmark yields and risk-adjusted spreads based on current lending activities and market activity.

Stocks—Fair Value Through Profit or Loss and Available-for-Sale

Fair values for stocks traded on an active market are generally determined by the last bid price for the security from the exchange where it is principally traded. Fair values for stocks for which there is no active market is typically based upon alternative valuation techniques such

(*continued*)

as discounted cash flow analysis, review of price movement relative to the market and utilization of information provided by the underlying investment manager. The Company maximizes the use of observable inputs when measuring fair value. The Company obtains quoted prices in active markets, when available, for identical assets at the balance sheet date to measure stocks at fair value in its fair value through profit or loss and available-for-sale portfolios.

Investment Properties

Fair values for investment properties are determined using independent qualified appraisal services and include management adjustments for material changes in property cash flows, capital expenditures or general market conditions in the interim period between appraisals. The determination of the fair value of investment property requires the use of estimates including future cash flows (such as future leasing assumptions, rental rates, capital and operating expenditures) and discount, reversionary and overall capitalization rates applicable to the asset based on current market conditions. Investment property under construction is valued at fair value if such values can be reliably determined; otherwise they are recorded at cost.

Impairment

Investments are reviewed regularly on an individual basis to determine impairment status. The Company considers various factors in the impairment evaluation process, including, but not limited to, the financial condition of the issuer, specific adverse conditions affecting an industry or region, decline in fair value not related to interest rates, bankruptcy or defaults, and delinquency in payments of interest or principal.

Investments are deemed to be impaired when there is objective evidence that timely collection of future cash flows can no longer be reliably estimated. The fair value of an investment is not a definitive indicator of impairment, as it may be significantly influenced by other factors including the remaining term to maturity and liquidity of the asset; however, market price is taken into consideration when evaluating impairment.

For impaired mortgages and bonds classified as loans and receivables, provisions are established or write-offs made to adjust the carrying value to the net realizable amount. Wherever possible the fair value of collateral underlying the loans or observable market price is used to establish net realizable value. For impaired available-for-sale bonds recorded at fair value, the accumulated loss recorded in accumulated other comprehensive income is reclassified to net investment income. Impairments on available-for-sale debt instruments are reversed if there is objective evidence that a permanent recovery has occurred. All gains and losses on bonds classified or designated as fair value through profit or loss are already recorded in net investment income; therefore a reduction due to impairment of these assets will be recorded in net investment income.

ILLUSTRATION 9.10

(continued)

Investments in Associates

As a general rule, the significance of an investment to the investor's financial position and performance generally determines how much disclosure is required. Investments in associates are classified as non-current assets (unless they are held for sale), and income from these significantly influenced companies is reported as income before discontinued operations, discontinued operations, or other comprehensive income, according to its nature in the associate's financial statements. Management reports the following for associates accounted for using the equity method:

1. separate disclosure of the investment category on the statement of financial position or in the notes to the financial statements, and the method of accounting used;

2. the fair value of any of these investments that has a price quoted in an active market;

3. separate disclosure of the income from investments that are accounted for using the equity method; and

4. information about associates' year ends that are different from the investor's year end.

IFRS **ASPE** Under **IFRS**, additional information is required, such as summarized financial information about the associates' assets, liabilities, revenue, and net income, and any relevant contingent liabilities that may affect the investor. Under **ASPE**, the information required to be provided is a list of any significant investments, including a description of the investment, the names, carrying amounts, and percentage ownership held. Because private enterprises are allowed to use methods other than the equity method, they are also required to separately report the carrying amount of investments in companies subject to significant influence accounted for at cost, as well as the amount of investment income reported from these investments.

Analysis

Finance 5.1.1 To effectively analyze a company's performance and position, it is essential to understand the accounting and reporting for the entity's investments. Some of the key aspects that analysts watch for include the following:

1. separation of investment results from operating results (although where the management of investments is a key part of operations, such as for financial institutions, this is not as relevant);
2. the relationship between the investment asset and related returns (income);
3. information that is lost in the process of consolidation; and
4. risks related to the investments and how they are managed.

Because the income statement reports on management's performance in operating the company's assets, it is important to separate the results of active operating income from the investment returns, where management's role is often more passive. As gains or losses on sales of investments or special dividends can obscure a company's operating performance, these must be separately identified and assessed.

Accounting standards require disclosures that make it possible for a reader to relate the investment category on the SFP to the investment income reported on the income statement, and to the holding gains and losses in other comprehensive income.

Understanding the effects of the accounting methods that are used for different categories of investments is a key requirement for the analyst. If an entity has significant investments in companies that are accounted for by the equity method, for example, the analyst needs to be aware that some information is not available because the one-line investment account hides the debt and risk characteristics of the investee company that the entity is exposed to.

Consolidation of subsidiary companies also presents problems. While the financial statements reflect the combined operations of the economic entity, important information is lost through aggregating the parent's results with those of its subsidiaries. This is why segmented information, discussed in Chapter 23, has to be separately reported in the notes. Analysts also watch for major acquisitions during the current or previous year. The statement of financial position contains all the assets of the subsidiary, but the income statement includes only the income earned by the subsidiary after it was acquired by the parent. Any analysis that looks at relationships between income and assets has to adjust for major acquisitions in the period(s) being examined.

IFRS/ASPE Comparison

LEARNING OBJECTIVE 9

Identify differences in accounting between IFRS and ASPE, and what changes are expected in the near future.

As indicated earlier, accounting for financial assets in general has changed significantly in the last few years, with IFRS 9 effective in 2018. This section provides some summaries and decision trees as a recap.

A Comparison of IFRS and ASPE

Illustration 9.11 sets out the major differences between IFRS and ASPE concerning accounting for investments.

ILLUSTRATION 9.11 **IFRS and ASPE Comparison Chart**

	IAS 1, 27, 28, IFRS 3, 7, 9, and 13 (IFRS 9 requires mandatory adoption in 2018)	Accounting Standards for Private Enterprises (ASPE)—*CPA Canada Handbook*, Part II, Sections 1582, 1601, 1602, 3051, and 3856	References to Related Examples, Illustrations, and Select Brief Exercises
Investments—no significant influence or control: Measurement models	Permits three measurement models: 1. amortized cost (for debt instruments where the business model requires holding to maturity), 2. FV-OCI with no recycling (for certain equity instruments only) and FV-OCI for debt securities with recycling where the business model includes both holding to maturity and holding for sale (depending on the security and the circumstances), and 3. FV-NI for everything else.	Permits only two measurement models: 1. FV-NI (for equity investments that trade in an active market, derivatives, and those accounted for under the fair value option), and 2. cost/amortized cost (everything else).	Illustrations 9.3, 9.4, 9.12, and 9.13 Examples 9.4 and 9.13 to 9.20 BE 9.17
Fair value option	FV-NI can be designated on initial recognition if it reduces or eliminates an accounting mismatch.	FV-NI can be designated on initial recognition.	N/A
Interest and dividend income	Use effective interest method when interest income is required to be reported separately; all interest and dividends to net income except for those at FV-OCI where dividends that are a return of investment are recognized in OCI. Where using FV-NI, may show investment income combined (no need to show interest separately).	Use either straight-line or effective interest method when applicable; all interest and dividends to net income. Must show interest separately.	Example 9.6 BE 9.4 and BE9.10
Realized gains and losses	Recognize in net income, except for those equity investments accounted for at FV-OCI (no recycling).	Recognize in net income.	Illustration 9.4 Examples 9.15 and 9.20
Reclassifications	No reclassification is permitted between measurement models unless there is a rare occurrence of a change in the entity's business model.	FV option designation is irrevocable; otherwise this issue is not addressed.	N/A

(continued)

ILLUSTRATION 9.11 *(continued)*

Impairment	Use expected loss model for cost/amortized cost and debt securities accounted for at FV-OCI. May reverse impairment losses.	Use the incurred loss model with a market discount rate to measure revised discounted cash flow; reversals are permitted if due to a specific subsequent event. New carrying value is higher of discounted cash flow and NRV through sale or by exercising right to collateral.	Illustrations 9.5, 9.6, and 9.7 Examples 9.21, 9.22, and 9.23 BE 9.18
Investments—in associates/significant influence: Method of accounting	Requires the equity method.	Allows an accounting policy choice of the equity method or the cost method. If shares are quoted in an active market, cannot use cost model; may use FV-NI.	Illustration 9.9 Example 9.24 BE 9.24 and BE9.25
Investments—in subsidiaries: Control	Definition expands the meaning of control. Emphasis is on the power to direct another entity's activities to generate returns for the investor.	Has a narrower definition of control that relies more strongly on holding more than 50% of the voting interests in another entity.	N/A
Method of reporting	Use consolidation.	Allows an accounting policy choice of consolidation or presenting all subsidiaries using the equity method or the cost method. If shares are quoted in an active market, cannot use cost model; may use FV-NI.	N/A (covered in advanced accounting courses)
Disclosures	Requires more extensive disclosures.	Uses the same financial reporting objectives as IFRS, but more limited disclosures are required.	Illustration 9.10

Reasons for Differences

We have noted throughout the chapter some of the differences in accounting for financial assets between ASPE and IFRS. The question does arise as to why there are differences. Below is a brief recap and some commentary.

1. **Measurement models:** ASPE has fewer measurement models. Presumably this is because ASPE seeks to provide more straightforward accounting where the benefits exceed the costs (cost-benefit). This is also the case with respect to allowing a choice for amortization methods for bond premiums and discounts. While the IFRS approach using effective interest methods for amortization may be conceptually superior, it is nonetheless more difficult to apply.

2. **Other comprehensive income:** IFRS recognizes OCI whereas ASPE does not. We discussed the concept of OCI in Chapter 2. As noted there, it is an interesting concept but the conceptual validity of treating OCI as separate from net income is unclear. The existence of OCI complicates the accounting for investments because not only does it add another measurement option (FV-OCI), but a decision has to be made whether to "recycle" any gains/losses on disposition. Currently, IFRS requires that gains/losses be recycled for debt securities but disallows this for equity securities. The distinction would seem to be slightly arbitrary. Why recycle realized gains/losses on debt securities but not equity securities?

3. **Impairment:** ASPE continues to use the incurred loss model whereas IFRS has moved to the expected loss model. This difference may also be attributed to ASPE requiring a less costly and more straightforward option for accounting since estimating expected losses is a more complex process (even though it provides more relevant information).

4. **Significant influence investments:** While IFRS generally requires the equity method, ASPE allows a choice. ASPE in general allows greater flexibility. In both cases, the equity method, while used extensively and for many years, is a hybrid method—not quite cost and not fair value. Should ASPE require the equity method to ensure more relevant information?

Summary of Models Used under IFRS and ASPE

Illustration 9.12 summarizes how the three measurement models are used by IFRS and ASPE. Recall that we discussed these models earlier in the chapter.

ILLUSTRATION 9.12   **Classification of Investments under IFRS and ASPE (Where No Significant Influence or Control)**

Measurement models	ASPE	IFRS 9 (effective 2018)
Cost/amortized cost	All investments *except* those that are equity instruments quoted in an active market, derivatives, or where the company elects to use FV-NI (see below).	Debt investments that are managed on a contractual yield basis where the business model requires the entity to hold the investments to maturity (and collect principal and interest). Generally *not* equity investments except in limited situations where fair value is not estimable.
FV-NI (sometimes called fair value through profit or loss)	Equity investments that are quoted in an active market and derivatives. Companies may make an accounting policy choice and elect to account for investments using FV-NI (fair value option).	Equity instruments not accounted for under FV-OCI model. Debt instruments that do not meet the criteria for the amortized cost or FV-OCI models. Derivatives. May elect to account for investments under this model (fair value option) as long as certain conditions are met (for example, to avoid an accounting mismatch where an item is hedged and gains and losses on the hedge might not offset).
FV-OCI	N/A	Certain equity investments (where no significant influence or control and not trading investments). The entity must make an election to classify these investments here. For equity investments, no recycling but dividend income recognized in net income unless it is deemed to be a return of capital. Debt investments where the company's business model is to **either** manage on a contractual yield basis **or** sell the securities. For debt instruments, discounts, premiums, interest income, and impairment losses are recognized in net income. Unrealized gains and losses are recycled to net income when the security is sold.[34]
Notes	Interest must be disclosed or presented separately.	Interest must be disclosed or presented separately if FV-NI model not used.
Reclassifications between categories	Not addressed specifically.	Not permitted unless change in business model.

---

[34]Per IFRS 9.5.6.5 and 5.6.7, if an entity reclassifies an FV-OCI debt investment to amortized cost, it is transferred at fair value and any unrealized gain or loss recorded in OCI is removed from OCI and adjusted against the investment account. This means that the investment ends up being measured at the same amount that it would otherwise have been measured at if the investment had always been classified as an amortized cost investment. If the entity reclassifies an FV-OCI investment to FV-NI, any unrealized gain or loss recorded in OCI is reclassified to net income.

Classification of Investments under IFRS 9—Decision Tree

Illustration 9.13 shows a decision tree that helps to determine the classification and measurement of financial assets under IFRS 9. IFRS 9 requires that you look at the company's business model for each type of investment. That is, is the business model such that the investments are held for the longer term to collect principal and interest payments or for sale or both?

ILLUSTRATION 9.13

Classification of Investments under IFRS 9 (Where No Significant Influence or Control)

* Presentation option for equity investments to present fair value changes in OCI

Source: Excerpt from IFRS 9 Project Summary (July 2014). Copyright © International Financial Reporting Standards Foundation. All rights reserved. Reproduced by John Wiley & Sons Canada, Ltd. with the permission of the International Financial Reporting Standards Foundation.® Reproduction and use rights are strictly limited. No permission granted to third parties to reproduce or distribute.

Looking Ahead

At the time of writing, the IASB had recently issued a new standard, IFRS 9, which is effective in 2018. This chapter encompasses the content of this new standard.

Summary of Learning Objectives

1. Understand the nature of and basic accounting for investments, including which types of companies have significant investments.

This chapter deals with investments in basic debt and equity instruments of other companies. Debt instruments such as bonds generally carry contractual rights to receive principal and interest payments. Equity instruments such as shares may carry contractual rights to receive dividends (depending on the type of share)

and may also carry voting rights and/or rights to receive residual assets upon windup of a company. Care must be taken to determine exactly what rights the investments entitle the holder to because this will help determine the accounting. Not all companies carry significant investments. It depends on the business model. Examples of types of companies that generally carry significant investments are financial institutions, insurance companies, and pension funds. There are three basic models for accounting for investments: the cost/amortized cost model, the FV-NI model, and the FV-OCI model.

2. Explain and apply the cost/amortized cost model of accounting for investments.

At acquisition, the cost of the investment is recognized as its fair value plus transaction costs. If the investment is a debt instrument, any premium or discount is amortized to interest income. Holding gains are recognized only when realized, as are holding losses, unless the investment is impaired. The investment is reported at its cost or amortized cost as either a current asset or a long-term investment, depending on its maturity and management's intention to hold it. ASPE uses this model for most investments excluding equity investments where an active market exists for trading the shares and derivatives. IFRS 9 uses this model for debt instruments where the entity's business model is to hold the investments to maturity.

3. Explain and apply the fair value through net income model of accounting for investments.

At acquisition, the investment is recognized at its fair value, with transaction costs being expensed. At each reporting date, the investment is revalued to its current fair value, with holding gains and losses recognized in net income. Dividend and interest income is also recognized in net income. If the investment is not held for trading purposes, any interest income is reported separately and is adjusted for discount or premium amortization. If held for trading or other current purposes, the investment is reported as a current asset. ASPE uses this for equity instruments where there is an active market and for derivatives. IFRS 9 uses this model for all investments not accounted for under the cost/amortized cost model or the FV-OCI model. ASPE and IFRS both allow investments to be accounted for using FV-NI under the fair value option.

4. Explain and apply the fair value through other comprehensive income model of accounting for investments.

At acquisition, the investment is recognized at fair value plus transaction costs. At each reporting date, the investment is revalued to its current fair value, with the holding gains or losses reported in other comprehensive income. On disposal, the accumulated holding gains or losses are either recycled to net income (debt securities) or transferred directly to retained earnings (equity securities). Investments are reported as current or long-term assets, depending on marketability and management intent. ASPE does not allow this method. IFRS 9 allows this method for certain equity investments and debt securities where the business model is achieved by both holding to maturity and selling (depending on the investment and circumstances).

5. Explain and apply the incurred loss, expected loss, and fair value loss impairment models.

The three impairment loss models differ in the timing of the recognition of impairment losses and the discount rate used. Under the incurred loss approach, a triggering event is required before a loss is recognized and measured, and the revised cash flows are discounted using either the historical or a current market rate. Under the expected loss approach, no triggering event is required, and revised cash flows and impairment losses are determined on a continual basis. The discount rate is the historical/original rate. Using the fair value loss model, the asset is written down to fair value taking into account market information (refer back to Chapters 2 and 3). ASPE uses the incurred loss model for all cost/amortized cost investments, although the post-impairment carrying values are measured differently. IFRS 9 uses the expected loss model for all cost/amortized cost investments as well as FV-OCI debt securities. Under IFRS 9, impairment losses on FV-OCI equity investments are not recognized in net income. Where the FV-NI model is used, there is no need to specifically assess impairment because the investment is continually revalued to fair value and any gains or losses are booked to income.

6. Explain the concept of significant influence and apply the equity method.

Significant influence is the ability to have an effect on strategic decisions made by an investee's board of directors, but not enough to control those decisions. The equity method, sometimes called one-line consolidation, is used because income is recognized by the investor as it is earned. The investor's income statement will reflect the performance of the investee company. Under this method, the investment account is adjusted for all changes in the investee's book value and for the amortization of any purchase discrepancy. IFRS requires use of the equity method for its associates (investees a company can significantly influence). ASPE provides a policy choice: either the equity method or the cost method, except that associates with a quoted price in an active market cannot be accounted for at cost. Instead, the FV-NI model can be used.

7. Explain the concept of control and when consolidation is appropriate.

Control relates to the ability to direct the strategic decisions of another entity and to generate returns for your own benefit or loss. When one company controls another, it controls all the net assets of that entity and is responsible for all its revenues and expenses. Therefore, all of the subsidiary's assets and liabilities, and revenues and expenses, are reported by the parent investor on a line-by-line basis in consolidated financial statements. The interests of the noncontrolling shareholders in the subsidiary company are reported separately as noncontrolling interest. Under IFRS, all subsidiaries are consolidated. ASPE, on the other hand, allows consolidation or a choice of the equity or cost method. Investments in companies with shares traded in an active market cannot be reported using the cost method, but may use FV-NI.

8. Explain how investments are presented and disclosed in the financial statements, noting how this facilitates analysis.

The objectives of disclosure are to provide information so users can assess the significance of the financial asset investments to the entity's financial position and performance, the extent of risks to which the company is exposed as a result, and how those risks are managed. As a result, the investments are identified on the statement of financial position according to how they are classified for accounting purposes, with the income statement reporting information on the returns by method of classification. Extensive disclosure is required, particularly under IFRS, on the entity's risk exposures and how it manages those risks.

9. Identify differences in accounting between IFRS and ASPE, and what changes are expected in the near future.

The differences are noted in Illustrations 9.7, 9.9, 9.11, and 9.12. There are significant differences, partly because ASPE has adopted a more simplified approach.

Practice Problem

Mandur Inc. purchases the following investments for cash but incorrectly recorded them in the Other Investments account in the general ledger in error. Mandur Inc. applies IFRS.:

Feb. 1, 2020	Jordy Limited ordinary shares, 200 shares	$ 37,400
April 1	Government bonds, 5%, due April 1, 2029, interest payable April 1 and October 1, 100 bonds at $1,000 each	100,000
July 1	Driver Ltd. 6% bonds, par $50,000, dated March 1, 2015, purchased at par plus accrued interest, interest payable annually on March 1, due March 1, 2039	51,000

Instructions

a. Prepare the entry(ies) to reclassify the amounts in the Other Investments account to the appropriate investment and income accounts at December 31, 2020. The bonds are classified as FV-OCI, and the ordinary shares are trading securities (FV-NI).

b. Prepare the entry to record the accrued interest on December 31, 2020.

c. Prepare any necessary revaluation journal entries. The fair values of the securities on December 31, 2020, were:

Jordy Limited ordinary shares	$ 33,800 (1% of total shares)
Government bonds	124,700
Driver Ltd. bonds	58,600

d. The government bonds were sold on July 1, 2021, for $ 119,200 plus accrued interest. Give the proper entries.

e. Assume instead that Mandur's investment in Jordy represents 30% of Jordy's shares. Prepare the 2020 entries for the investment in Jordy shares. In 2020, Jordy declared and paid dividends of $9,000 (on September 30) and reported net income of $30,000.

Solution

a.   **December 31, 2020**

FV-NI Investments	37,400	
FV-OCI Investments ($100,000 + $50,000)	150,000	
Interest Income (or Interest Receivable)		
($50,000 × .06 × 4/12)	1,000	
Other Investments		188,400

b.   **December 31, 2020***

Interest Receivable	3,750	
Interest Income		3,750**

*If the first journal entry had been booked to Interest Receivable, then this journal entry would have been for $2,750 only since $1,000 had already been recorded.

**($100,000 × .05 × 3/12 = $1,250; $50,000 × .06 × 10/12 = $2,500; $1,250 + $2,500 = $3,750)

c.   **December 31, 2020**

FV-OCI Investments	33,300	
Unrealized Gain or Loss—OCI		33,300

FV-OCI Investment Portfolio, December 31, 2020

Securities	Cost	Fair Value	Unrealized Gain (Loss)
Government bonds	$100,000	$124,700	$24,700
Driver Ltd. bonds	50,000	58,600	8,600
Total	$150,000	$183,000	33,300
Previous fair value adjustment balance			0
Fair value adjustment—Dr.			$33,300

Investment Income or Loss	3,600	
FV-NI Investments ($37,400 – $33,800)		3,600

d.   **July 1, 2021**

Unrealized Gain or Loss—OCI	5,500	
FV-OCI Investments ($124,700 – $119,200)		5,500
Cash ($119,200 + $1,250)	120,450	
FV-OCI Investments		119,200
Interest Income		1,250
Unrealized Gain or Loss—OCI	19,200	
Gain on Disposal of Investments—FV-OCI **		19,200
($119,200 – $100,000)		

e.   **February 1, 2020**

Investment in Associate	37,400	
Cash		37,400

September 30, 2020

Cash	2,700	
Investment in Associate (30% × $9,000)		2,700

December 31, 2020

Investment in Associate	9,000	
Investment Income or Loss (30% × $30,000)		9,000

Key Terms

amortized cost model, p. 9-11	equity pickup, p. 9-34	noncontrolling interest, p. 9-39
associate, p. 9-33	expected loss impairment model, p. 9-27	on margin, p. 9-8
consolidation, p. 9-39	fair value loss impairment model, p. 9-31	realized, p. 9-8
control, p. 9-38	fair value through net income (FV-NI), p. 9-15	significant influence, p. 9-32
cost model, p. 9-9	fair value through other comprehensive	subsidiary, p. 9-38
debt instruments, p. 9-4	income (FV-OCI), p. 9-20	trading, p. 9-7
debt securities, p. 9-4	incurred loss impairment model, p. 9-26	transaction costs, p. 9-8
equity instruments, p. 9-4	joint venture, p. 9-33	unrealized holding gains or losses, p. 9-8
equity method, p. 9-33	minority interest, p. 9-39	

Assignment Material

Note: **Enabling Competencies** Completion of this end-of-chapter material will help develop CPA-enabling competencies (such as ethics and professionalism, problem-solving and decision-making, and communication) and technical competencies. We have highlighted selected items with a specific integration word mark and material in *WileyPLUS* has been linked to the competencies. All cases emphasize integration, especially of the enabling competencies. The brief exercises, exercises, and problems generally emphasize problem-solving and decision-making.

Brief Exercises

BE9.1 (LO 1) **Finance** Bali Corp. has $10,000 in surplus funds to invest and is considering investing in either Company A or Company B. Company A promises to return the $10,000 original amount invested in three years' time and pay a 2% annual return on the principal amount. Company B does not promise to repay the original amount invested, but indicates that it is likely that the $10,000 investment will be worth more than $10,000 if Company B is profitable. Whether Bali will receive an annual return on the investment depends on Company B's cash flows and whether Company B's board of directors votes to distribute the cash.

  a. Identify whether the potential investments are investments in debt or in equity securities.

  b. Explain how you determined your answer.

BE9.2 (LO 1) **Finance** Jax Taylor has the financial statements of an old established university, a manufacturing company, an insurance company, a real estate developer, a major retail enterprise, and a pension plan. (a) Identify the organizations whose statements of financial position are most likely to report a significant proportion of investments. (b) For those identified, what types of investments would you expect to find?

BE9.3 (LO 2) Eastwind Corporation purchased 400 common shares of Ditch Inc. for $13,200 on February 21. Eastwind paid a 1% commission on the share purchase and, because the shares were not publicly traded, decided to account for them following the cost model. On June 30, Ditch declared and paid a cash dividend of $1.50 per share. Prepare Eastwind Corporation's journal entries to record (a) the purchase of the investment, (b) the dividends received, and (c) the sale of the Ditch Inc. shares in early January the following year for $15,100 less a 1% commission paid on the sale.

BE9.4 (LO 2) Beta Corp. invested in a three-year, $100 face value 8% bond, paying $95.03. At this price, the bond will yield a 10% return. Interest is payable annually.

   a. Prepare a bond discount amortization table for Beta Corp., assuming Beta uses the effective interest method required by IFRS. Round amounts to the nearest cent.

   b. Prepare journal entries to record the initial investment, receipt of interest, and recognition of interest income in each of the three years, and the maturity of the bond at the end of the third year.

   c. Assuming Beta Corp. applies ASPE and has chosen to use the straight-line method of amortization, determine the amount of discount that is amortized each year.

   d. Under the assumption in part (c), prepare journal entries to record the initial investment, receipt of interest, and recognition of interest income in each of the three years, and the maturity of the bond at the end of the third year.

   e. Compare the total interest income under the two methods over the three-year period.

BE9.5 (LO 2) Gamma Corp. invested in a three-year, $100 face value 6% bond, paying $105.55. At this price, the bond will yield a 4% return. Interest is payable annually.

   a. Prepare a bond premium amortization table for Gamma Corp., assuming Gamma uses the effective interest method required by IFRS. Round amounts to the nearest cent.

   b. Prepare journal entries to record the initial investment, receipt of interest, and recognition of interest income in each of the three years, and the maturity of the bond at the end of the third year.

   c. Assuming Gamma Corp. applies ASPE and has chosen to use the straight-line method of amortization, determine the amount of premium that is amortized each year.

   d. Under the assumption in part (c), prepare journal entries to record the initial investment, receipt of interest, and recognition of interest income in each of the three years, and the maturity of the bond at the end of the third year.

   e. Compare the total interest income under the two methods over the three-year period.

BE9.6 (LO 2) Carras Corporation purchased $60,000 of five-year, 6% bonds of Hu Inc. for $55,133 to yield an 8% return, and classified the purchase as an amortized cost method investment. The bonds pay interest semi-annually.

   a. Assuming Carras applies IFRS, prepare its journal entries for the purchase of the investment and the receipt of semi-annual interest and discount amortization for the first two interest payments that will be received. Do not round intermediate calculations, but round entry amounts to the nearest dollar and ignore any interest accruals.

   b. Assuming Carras applies ASPE and has chosen the straight-line method of discount amortization, prepare the same three entries requested in part (a), rounding amounts to the nearest dollar and ignoring any interest accruals.

BE9.7 (LO 2) On September 1, Louisa Ltd. purchased $80,000 of five-year, 9% bonds for $74,086, resulting in an effective (yield) rate of 11%. The bonds pay interest each March 1 and September 1. Louisa Ltd. applies ASPE, accounts for the investment under the amortized cost approach using the effective interest accounting policy, and has a December 31 year end. The following March 1, after receiving the semi-annual interest on the bonds, Louisa sells the bonds for $75,100. Do not round intermediate calculations, but round entry amounts to the nearest dollar. Prepare Louisa's journal entries for (a) the purchase of the investment, (b) any adjusting entry(ies) needed at December 31, (c) the receipt of interest on March 1, and (d) the sale of the bond investment on March 1.

BE9.8 (LO 2) Lachapelle Traders Inc. has cyclical cash flows and decided to invest some excess cash on hand by purchasing a 60-day Government of Canada treasury bill. On December 15, 2020, Lachapelle paid $99,509 for a treasury bill that has a maturity amount of $100,000, a maturity date of

February 13, 2021, and a yield of 3%. Lachapelle accounts for this investment using the amortized cost model. Prepare (a) the entry for the purchase, (b) any year-end accrual entry at December 31, 2020, and (c) the entry at the maturity of the treasury bill. Round amounts to the nearest dollar. (*Hint:* Use the account Note Investment at Amortized Cost.)

BE9.9 (LO 3) Abdul Corporation purchased 400 common shares of Sigma Inc. for trading purposes for $13,200 on September 8 and accounted for the investment under ASPE at FV-NI. In December, Sigma declared and paid a cash dividend of $1.75 per share. At year end, December 31, Sigma shares were selling for $35.50 per share. In late January, Abdul sold the Sigma shares for $34.95 per share. Prepare Abdul Corporation's journal entries to record (a) the purchase of the investment, (b) the dividends received, (c) the fair value adjustment at December 31, and (d) the January sale of the investment.

BE9.10 (LO 3) On October 1, Qilan Ltd. purchased 7% bonds with a face value of $1,000 for trading purposes, accounting for the investment at FV-NI. The bonds were priced at 1.044 to yield Qilan 6%, and pay interest annually each October 1. Qilan has a December 31 year end, and at this date, the bonds' fair value was $1,055. Assuming Qilan applies IFRS, prepare Qilan's journal entries for (a) the purchase of the investment, (b) the December 31 interest accrual, and (c) the year-end fair value adjustment. Assuming Qilan applies ASPE, uses the effective interest method, and reports interest income separately, prepare Qilan's journal entries for (d) the December 31 interest accrual, and (e) the year-end fair value adjustment. Round amounts to two decimal places.

BE9.11 (LO 3) On March 31, Ramesh Corp. invests in a $1,000, 6% bond to be held for short-term trading purposes, and accounts for this investment using the FV-NI method. The bond's fair value when acquired was $970, but an additional $10 was paid (and debited to Interest Receivable) representing the interest accrued since the annual interest payment date of February 1. Ramesh applies IFRS, and prepares financial statements each December 31. The fair value of the bond on December 31 is $963 and on February 1, when Ramesh sells the bond, it is $961. Prepare journal entries to record (a) the purchase of the bond, (b) any December 31 adjustments needed, (c) the receipt of interest on February 1, and (d) the sale of the bond on February 1. Ramesh Corp. does not use reversing entries.

BE9.12 (LO 4) Alaska Corporation purchased 300 common shares of Burke Inc. for $23,400 and accounted for them using FV-OCI. During the year, Burke paid a cash dividend of $3.25 per share. At year end, Burke shares had a fair value of $74.50 per share. Prepare Alaska's journal entries to record (a) the purchase of the investment, (b) the dividends received, and (c) the fair value adjustment.

BE9.13 (LO 4) Gauthier Ltd. has a single investment that it accounts for using FV-OCI. The carrying value of the investment at the last reporting period was $72,500. To date, $2,500 of unrealized gains on fair value adjustments have been recorded to other comprehensive income. The original cost of the investment is therefore $70,000. On June 15, when the market value of the investment is $73,000, Gauthier sold the investment. Using the three-step approach, record the sale and reclassification (recycling) entry at June 15, assuming the investment is an equity investment and the company reclassifies gains or losses to Retained Earnings on disposition of the investment.

BE9.14 (LO 4) Trottier Ltd. has a single debt investment that it accounts for using FV-OCI recycled to net income. The carrying value of the debt investment on July 1 after the collection of interest and amortization of premium was $72,500. To date, $1,500 of unrealized losses in fair value adjustments have been recorded to other comprehensive income. On July 1, when the market value of the investment is $72,000, Gauthier sold the debt investment. Using the three-step approach, record the July 1 entries for the sale and reclassification (recycling) entry to net income.

BE9.15 (LO 4) Early in its 2020 fiscal year (December 31 year end), Hayes Company purchased 10,000 Kenyon Corporation common shares for $26.18 per share, plus $1,800 in brokerage commissions. These securities were accounted for at FV-OCI (with no recycling), and transaction costs were capitalized. In September, Kenyon declared and paid a dividend of $1.02 per share, and on December 31, 2020, the fair value of these shares was $271,500. On April 13, 2021, Hayes sold all the Kenyon shares at a price of $28.10 each, incurring $1,925 in brokerage commissions on the sale. Prepare the entries to record (a) the purchase of the Kenyon shares, (b) the receipt of the dividend, (c) the fair value adjustment at December 31, 2020, and (d) all entries associated with the disposal of the investment on April 13, 2021. The company reclassifies any gains or losses to Retained Earnings upon disposition of the securities. (*Hint:* In part [d], first bring the investment to its April 13 fair value net of the brokerage commission.)

BE9.16 (LO 4) The following information relates to Cortez Corp. for 2020: net income of $672,683; unrealized loss of $20,830 related to investments accounted for at FV-OCI during the year; and accumulated other comprehensive income of $37,273 on January 1, 2020. Determine (a) other comprehensive income for 2020, (b) comprehensive income for 2020, and (c) accumulated other comprehensive income at December 31, 2020.

BE9.17 (LO 2, 3, 4, 9) A review of the financial statements of private and publicly accountable enterprises may result in finding the following measurement approaches used for their non-strategic investments: (1) cost/amortized cost, (2) FV-NI (or FVTPL), (3) FV-OCI (with recycling), and (4) FV-OCI (without recycling). Indicate by number (1, 2, 3, or 4) which methods are permitted for enterprises applying (a) ASPE, and (b) IFRS.

BE9.18 (LO 5) The standard setters identify three approaches to accounting for the impairment of financial asset investments: an incurred loss model, an expected loss model, and a fair value model. Identify which models are required to be used by enterprises applying (a) ASPE, and (b) IFRS. If more than one model is used under each of parts (a) and (b), identify when each model would be applied.

BE9.19 (LO 5) Under the expected loss model, the entity must assess whether there has been a significant increase in credit risk. Explain what the impact is if the assessment results in a yes answer or a no answer.

 Video

BE9.20 (LO 5) Assume that Gush Inc. invests in a bond for $55,000. The bond was purchased at par and is accounted for using amortized cost. At year end, management has determined that there is no significant increase in credit risk, but that there is a 1% chance that the company will not collect 20% of the face value of the bond (which also represents the present value of the bond) in the next 12 months. The expected loss model is used. Prepare the required year-end journal entry.

BE9.21 (LO 5) Assume the same information as in BE9.20. Assume also that management feels that there has been a significant increase in the credit risk and that there is a 5% chance that the company will not collect 50% of the face value of the bond over its life. The expected loss model is used. Prepare the required journal entry.

BE9.22 (LO 5) Ramirez Company has an investment in 6%, 10-year bonds of Soto Company. The investment was originally purchased at par for $100 in 2019 and it is accounted for at amortized cost. Early in 2020, Ramirez recorded an impairment on the Soto investment due to Soto's financial distress. At that time, the present value of the cash flows discounted using the original effective interest rate was $90, and the present value of the cash flows using the then current market rate was $91. In 2021, Soto returned to profitability and the Soto investment was no longer considered impaired. Prepare the entries Ramirez would make in 2020 and 2021 under ASPE.

BE9.23 (LO 6) Poot Corporation purchased a 40% interest in Moss Inc. for $100. This investment gave Poot significant influence over Moss. During the year, Moss earned net income of $15 and paid dividends of $5. Assuming the purchase price was equal to 40% of Moss's net carrying amount when it was acquired, prepare Poot's journal entries related to this investment using the equity method. Poot applies IFRS.

BE9.24 (LO 6) Julip Corporation purchased a 25% interest in Krov Corporation on January 2, 2020, for $1,000. At that time, the carrying amount of Krov's net assets was $3,600. Any excess of the cost of the investment over Julip's share of Krov's carrying amount can be attributed to unrecorded intangibles with a useful life of 20 years. Krov declared and paid a dividend of $12 and reported net income of $60 for its year ended December 31, 2020. Prepare Julip's 2020 entries to record all transactions and events related to the investment in its associate. Assume that Julip is a publicly accountable enterprise that applies IFRS.

BE9.25 (LO 6) Use the information from BE9.24, except that Julip Corporation is a private enterprise that applies ASPE. Prepare Julip's 2020 entries to record all transactions and events related to its significant influence investment in Krov Corporation, assuming that (a) Krov's shares are traded in an active market, Julip applies the FV-NI approach, and the fair value of Julip's share of Krov Corp. at December 31, 2020, is $1,020; and (b) Julip applies the cost method to account for its investment in Krov (the shares are not traded in an active market).

BE9.26 (LO 6, 7) Beckett Corp. is facing a decision as to whether to purchase 40% of Kyla Corp.'s shares for $1.6 million cash, giving Beckett significant influence over the investee company, or 60% of Kyla's shares for $2.4 million cash, making Kyla a subsidiary company. The book value of Kyla's net assets is $4 million (assets are $10 million and liabilities are $6 million). How will this investment affect Beckett's statement of financial position if Beckett acquires (a) a 40% interest and (b) a 60% interest, assuming Beckett applies IFRS? That is, for each of parts (a) and (b), indicate the immediate effect on Beckett's total assets, total liabilities, and shareholders' equity.

BE9.27 (LO 8) Both ASPE and IFRS require disclosures about an enterprise's investments that include the carrying amount of each type of investment by the accounting method used and the income, gains, or losses classified in a similar way. Identify the disclosure objective for financial assets that this information is intended to help meet.

Exercises

E9.1 (LO 1, 2, 3, 4)   (Investment Classifications)   Each of the following investments is independent of the others.

1. A bond that will mature in four years was bought one month ago when the price dropped. As soon as the value increases, which is expected next month, it will be sold.

2. Ten percent of the outstanding shares of Farm Corp. were purchased. The company is planning on eventually getting a total of 30% of the outstanding shares.

3. Ten-year bonds were purchased this year. The bonds mature on January 1 of next year.

4. Bonds that will mature in five years are purchased. The company would like to hold them until they mature, but money has been tight recently and the bonds may need to be sold.

5. A bond that matures in 10 years was purchased with money that the company had set aside for an expansion project that is planned for 10 years from now.

6. Preferred shares were purchased for their consistent dividend. The company is planning to hold the preferred shares for a long time.

7. Common shares of a distributor are purchased to meet a regulatory requirement for doing business in the distributor's region. The investment is expected to be held indefinitely.

Instructions

a. Identify the best accounting model classification(s) for each of the investments described above under (1) ASPE, and (2) IFRS. Note where there are choices or options. Assume that the criteria for the fair value option (FV-NI) under IFRS are not met. Assume the investment is not impaired.

b. Assume that the controller of the company would like to use methods that create "less volatility in net income." Identify which methods create less volatility and explain why this is so.

c. **Ethics** Discuss whether it is ethical to make a decision as to which method should be used based on the controller's wishes as explained in part (b).

E9.2 (LO 2) Excel (Entries for Cost/Amortized Cost Investments)   On January 1, 2020, Kenn Corp. purchased at par 10% bonds having a maturity value of $300,000. They are dated January 1, 2020, and mature on January 1, 2025, with interest receivable on December 31 of each year. The bonds are accounted for using the amortized cost model.

Instructions

a. Prepare the journal entry to record the bond purchase.

b. Prepare the journal entry to record the interest received for 2020.

c. Prepare the journal entry to record the interest received for 2021.

d. Prepare the journal entry to record the redemption of the bond at maturity.

E9.3 (LO 2)   (Entries for Cost/Amortized Cost Investments)   On January 1, 2020, Mustafa Limited paid $537,907.40 for 12% bonds with a maturity value of $500,000. The bonds provide the bondholders with a 10% yield. They are dated January 1, 2020, and mature on January 1, 2025, with interest receivable on December 31 of each year. Mustafa accounts for the bonds using the amortized cost approach, applies ASPE using the effective interest method, and has a December 31 year end.

Instructions

a. Prepare the journal entry to record the bond purchase.

b. Prepare a bond amortization schedule, rounding to two decimal places.

c. Prepare the journal entry to record interest received and interest income for 2020.

d. Prepare the journal entry to record interest received and interest income for 2021.

e. Prepare the journal entry to record the redemption of the bond at maturity.

f. If Mustafa used the straight-line method of discount/premium amortization, prepare the journal entry to record interest received and interest income the company would make each year.

g. Compare the total interest income reported over the five-year period under the effective interest method and the straight-line method. What can you conclude?

h. **Digging Deeper** Why might a reader of the financial statements find the effective interest method more relevant than the straight-line method?

E9.4 (LO 2) `Excel` **(Cost/Amortized Cost Investments)** On January 1, 2020, Phantom Corp. acquires $300,000 of Spider Products Inc. 9% bonds at a price of $278,384. The interest is payable each December 31, and the bonds mature on December 31, 2022. The investment will provide Phantom Corp. with a 12% yield. Phantom Corp. applies IFRS and accounts for this investment using the amortized cost model.

Instructions

a. Prepare a three-year bond amortization schedule, rounding to the nearest dollar.

b. Prepare the journal entry to record interest received and interest income on December 31, 2021.

c. Prepare the journal entries to record interest received and interest income on December 31, 2022, and the maturity of the bond.

d. Prepare the entry for the disposal of the investment if Phantom had sold the bond on December 31, 2021 for $285,270 instead of holding it to maturity. Assume that 2021 interest received and interest income have already been recorded.

E9.5 (LO 3) **(FV-NI Investment in Bonds)** Refer to the information in E9.3, except assume that Mustafa hopes to make a gain on the bonds as interest rates are expected to fall. Mustafa accounts for the bonds at fair value with changes in value taken to net income, and separately recognizes and reports interest income. The fair value of the bonds at December 31 of each year end is as follows:

2020	$534,200	2023	$507,000
2021	$515,000	2024	$500,000
2022	$513,000		

Instructions

a. Prepare the journal entry at the date of the bond purchase.

b. Prepare the journal entries to record interest income and interest received and recognition of fair value at December 31, 2020, 2021, and 2022.

c. `Digging Deeper` Did market interest rates fall as expected? Explain briefly.

E9.6 (LO 2, 3) **(Amortized Cost and FV-NI Investments in Bonds Purchased between Interest Payment Dates)** The following information relates to the debt investments of Wildcat Inc. during a recent year:

1. On February 1, the company purchased Gibbons Corp. 10% bonds with a face value of $300,000 at 100 plus accrued interest. Interest is payable on April 1 and October 1.

2. On April 1, semi-annual interest was received on the Gibbons bonds.

3. On June 15, Sampson Inc. 9% bonds were purchased. The $200,000 par-value bonds were purchased at 100 plus accrued interest. Interest dates are June 1 and December 1.

4. On August 31, Gibbons Corp. bonds with a par value of $60,000 purchased on February 1 were sold at 99 plus accrued interest.

5. On October 1, semi-annual interest was received on the remaining Gibbons Corp. bonds.

6. On December 1, semi-annual interest was received on the Sampson Inc. bonds.

7. On December 31, the fair values of the bonds purchased on February 1 and June 15 were 98.5 and 101, respectively.

Assume the investments are accounted for under the recognition and measurement requirements of IFRS 9 *Financial Instruments*. The company does not record interest income separately from other investment income or loss when investments are accounted for at FV-NI.

Instructions

a. `Finance` Prepare all journal entries that you consider necessary, including December 31 year-end entries, assuming these investments are accounted for at FV-NI.

b. Assume instead that Wildcat manages these investments based on their yield to maturity. Prepare all journal entries that you consider necessary, including December 31 adjusting entries.

c. `Digging Deeper` Briefly explain what it means to manage an investment on the basis of yield to maturity, and why the recommended accounting method is reasonable in such a situation.

E9.7 (LO 3) **(FV-NI Equity Investments)** On December 31, 2019, Zurich Corp. provided you with the following pre-adjustment information regarding its portfolio of investments held for short-term profit-taking:

December 31, 2019

Investments	Carrying Amount	Fair Value
Moonstar Corp. shares	$20,000	$19,000
Bilby Corp. shares	10,000	9,000
Radius Ltd. shares	20,000	20,600
Total portfolio	$50,000	$48,600

During 2020, the Bilby Corp. shares were sold for $9,500. The fair values of the securities on December 31, 2020, were as follows: Moonstar Corp. shares $19,300 and Radius Ltd. shares $20,500. Dividends and other investment income and losses are all reported in one investment income account.

Instructions

a. Prepare the adjusting journal entry needed on December 31, 2019.

b. Prepare the journal entry to record the sale of the Bilby Corp. shares during 2020.

c. Prepare the adjusting journal entry needed on December 31, 2020.

E9.8 (LO 3)   (Investment in Debt Instruments Held for Trading Purposes, Accounted for Using FV-NI)   Finance NB Corp. purchased a $100,000 face-value bond of Myers Corp. on August 31, 2019, for $104,490 plus accrued interest. The bond pays interest annually each November 1 at a rate of 9%. On November 1, 2019, NB Corp. received the annual interest. On December 31, 2019, NB's year end, the fair value for these bonds was 103.2. NB sold the bond on January 15, 2020, for $102,900 plus accrued interest. Assume NB Corp. follows IFRS.

Instructions

a. Prepare the journal entries to record the purchase of the bond, the receipt of interest, any adjustments required at year end, and the subsequent sale of the bond. Do not round intermediate calculations but round entry amounts to the nearest dollar.

b. How many months was the bond held for by NB Corp. in 2019? Based on this, how much of the income reported on this bond should be for interest received? Verify that your answer fits with the income that is reported.

c. **Digging Deeper** If this bond had been acquired to earn a return on excess funds, did the company meet its objective? If yes, how much return did NB Corp. earn while the bond was held? If not, why not?

E9.9 (LO 3)   (FV-NI Equity Investment Entries) Activet Corporation, a Canadian-based international company that follows IFRS, has the following securities in its portfolio of investments acquired for trading purposes and accounted for using the FV-NI method on December 31, 2019:

Investments	Carrying Amount (before adjustment)	Fair Value
1,500 shares of David Jones Inc., common	$ 71,500	$ 69,000
5,000 shares of Hearn Corp., common	180,000	175,000
400 shares of Alessandro Inc., preferred	60,000	61,600
	$311,500	$305,600

In 2020, Activet completed the following securities transactions:

Mar. 1   Sold the 1,500 shares of David Jones Inc. common at $45 per share, less fees of $500.

Apr. 1   Bought 700 shares of Oberto Ltd. common at $75 per share, plus fees of $1,300.

Activet Corporation's portfolio of trading securities appeared as follows on December 31, 2020:

Investments	Original Cost	Fair Value
5,000 shares of Hearn Corp., common	$180,000	$175,000
700 shares of Oberto Ltd., common	52,500	50,400
400 shares of Alessandro Inc., preferred	60,000	58,000
	$292,500	$283,400

Instructions

Prepare the Activet Corporation general journal entries for the following, assuming the company does not recognize and report dividends and other components of investment gains and losses separately:

a. The December 31, 2019 adjusting entry

b. The sale of the David Jones Inc. shares

c. The purchase of the Oberto Ltd. shares

d. The December 31, 2020 adjusting entry

 E9.10 (LO 3, 4) (Entries for FV-NI and FV-OCI Equity Investments)   The following information is available about Kao Corp.'s investments at December 31, 2020. This is the first year Kao has purchased securities for investment purposes.

Securities	Cost	Fair Value
3,000 shares of Petra Corporation common shares	$40,000	$46,000
1,000 shares of Dugald Inc. preferred shares	25,000	22,000
	$65,000	$68,000

Assume that Kao Corp. follows IFRS.

Instructions

a. Prepare the adjusting entry(ies), if any, at December 31, 2020, assuming the investments are acquired for trading purposes and accounted for using the FV-NI model with no separate reporting of dividends and other types of FV-NI investment income and losses.

b. Prepare the adjusting entry(ies), if any, at December 31, 2020, assuming the investments are accounted for using the FV-OCI model.

c. Discuss how the amounts reported in the financial statements are affected by the choice of accounting method.

E9.11 (LO 3, 4, 8) (Equity Investment Entries—FV-NI and FV-OCI)   Arantxa Corporation made the following purchases of investments during 2020, the first year in which Arantxa invested in equity securities:

1. On January 15, purchased 9,000 shares of Nirmala Corp.'s common shares at $33.50 per share plus commission of $1,980.

2. On April 1, purchased 5,000 shares of Oxana Corp.'s common shares at $52.00 per share plus commission of $3,370.

3. On September 10, purchased 7,000 shares of WTA Corp.'s preferred shares at $26.50 per share plus commission of $2,910.

On May 20, 2020, Arantxa sold 3,000 of the Nirmala common shares at a market price of $35 per share less brokerage commissions of $2,850. The year-end fair values per share were as follows: Nirmala $30, Oxana $55, and WTA $28. The chief accountant of Arantxa tells you that Arantxa Corporation holds these investments with the intention of selling them in order to earn short-term profits from appreciation in their prices and accounts for them using the FV-NI model.
    Assume that Arantxa Corporation follows IFRS.

Instructions

a. Prepare the journal entries to record the three investments.

b. Prepare the journal entry(ies) for the sale of the 3,000 Nirmala shares on May 20.

c. Prepare the adjusting entries needed on December 31, 2020.

d. Repeat parts (a) to (c), assuming the investments are accounted for using FV-OCI with no recycling. Arantxa's policy is to capitalize transaction costs on the acquisition of FV-OCI investments and reduce the proceeds on disposal. In addition, the company reclassifies any gains or losses on disposition to Retained Earnings.

e. What is the amount that will be reported as other comprehensive income for the year ended December 31, 2020? Show the wording that would appear on the comprehensive income statement.

f. What will be the balance in Accumulated Other Comprehensive Income on December 31, 2020?

E9.12 (LO 2) (Debt Investment Entries—Amortized Cost)   On January 1, 2019, Hi and Lois Company purchased 12% bonds having a maturity value of $300,000 for $322,744.72. The bonds provide the bondholders with a 10% yield. They are dated January 1, 2019, and mature on January 1, 2024, with interest receivable on December 31 of each year. Hi and Lois Company uses the effective interest method to allocate unamortized discount or premium. The bonds are classified as amortized cost investments.

Instructions

a. Prepare the journal entry at the date of the bond purchase.

b. Prepare a bond amortization schedule. Round amounts to the nearest cent.

c. Prepare the journal entry to record the interest received and the amortization for 2019.

d. Prepare the journal entry to record the interest received and the amortization for 2020.

E9.13 (LO 4) **(Debt Investment Entries—FV-OCI)** Assume the same information as in E9.12, except that the bonds are carried at FV-OCI. The fair value of the bonds at December 31 of each year end is as follows:

| | 2019 | $320,500 | | 2020 | $309,000 |

Instructions

a. Prepare the journal entries to record the interest received and recognition of fair value for 2019.

b. Prepare the journal entries to record the recognition of fair value for 2020 and assuming the sale of the investment for $309,000 on December 31, 2020, reclassifying any accumulated holding gains or losses to net income.

E9.14 (LO 4) **(Debt Investment Entries—FV-OCI)** On July 1, 2020, Miron Aggregates Ltd. purchased 6% bonds having a maturity value of $100,000 for $103,585. The bonds provide the bondholders with a 5% yield. The bonds mature four years later, on July 1, 2024, with interest receivable June 30 and December 31 of each year. Miron uses the effective interest method to allocate unamortized discount or premium. The bonds are accounted for using the FV-OCI model with recycling. Miron has a calendar year end. The fair value of the bonds at December 31, 2020 and 2021, was $103,400 and $102,200, respectively. Assume fair value adjustments are recorded at year end only. Immediately after collecting interest on December 31, 2021, the bonds were sold for $102,200.

Instructions

a. Prepare the journal entry at the date of the bond purchase.

b. Prepare a bond amortization schedule to December 31, 2021. Round amounts to the nearest dollar.

c. Prepare the entries and year-end entries from December 31, 2020, through to the collection of interest on December 31, 2021.

d. Following the three-step approach, prepare the journal entries for the sale of the bond on December 31, 2021. Include the reclassification of unrealized gains and losses to net income.

E9.15 (LO 4, 8) **(Debt Investment Entries—FV-OCI Financial Statements)** Assume the same information as in E9.14 and also assume that the bond is the only investment held by Miron Aggregates Ltd.

Instructions

a. Prepare a partial comparative statement of financial position at December 31, 2020 and 2021, showing only the related accounts for the bond investment.

b. Prepare a partial comparative statement of income for the fiscal years ended December 31, 2020 and 2021, showing only the related accounts for the bond investment.

c. Prepare a partial comparative statement of comprehensive income for the fiscal years ended December 31, 2020 and 2021.

d. Prepare a partial statement of changes in equity for the years ended December 31, 2020 and 2021, showing retained earnings and accumulated other comprehensive income. Assume a balance of $200,00 for retained earnings at January 1, 2020, and no declaration of dividends during 2020 or 2021.

e. How much overall income was earned from the investment? Reconcile your answer with the change in retained earnings over the accounting periods reported.

E9.16 (LO 4) **(FV-OCI Investment Entries and Financial Statement Presentation)** At December 31, 2020, the equity investments of Wang Inc. that were accounted for using the FV-OCI model without recycling were as follows:

Investment	Cost and Carrying Amount	Fair Value	Unrealized Gain (Loss)
Ahn Inc.	$175,200	$150,000	$(25,200)
Burnham Corp.	121,500	140,600	19,100
Chi Ltd.	73,000	75,500	2,500
Total	$369,700	$366,100	$ (3,600)

Because of a change in relationship with Ahn Inc., Wang Inc. sold its investment in Ahn for $153,300 on January 20, 2021. No other investments were acquired or sold during 2021; however, a dividend of $1,300 was received from Burnham Corp. in June. At December 31, 2021, the fair values of Burnham and Chi shares were $153,750 and $72,600, respectively.

Instructions

a. Prepare the entry to adjust the portfolio of investments to fair value at December 31, 2020.

b. Prepare the presentation of all investment-related accounts on the statement of financial position at December 31, 2020.

c. Indicate what accounts and amounts would be reported on the statement of comprehensive income for the year ended December 31, 2020, and where each would be reported.

d. Prepare the journal entries for the 2021 sale of the investment in Ahn Inc., including reclassifying holding gains or losses to retained earnings and for the dividend received from Burnham Corp.

e. Prepare the journal entry required at December 31, 2021, to adjust the investments to fair value.

E9.17 (LO 4) (FV-OCI Investments—Entries) Niger Corp. gave you the following information about its investment in Fahad Corp. shares purchased in May 2020 and accounted for using the FV-OCI method:

Cost	$39,900
Fair value, December 31, 2020	41,750
Fair value, December 31, 2021	32,200
Fair value, December 31, 2022	36,400

Instructions

a. Prepare the adjusting journal entries needed on December 31, 2020, 2021, and 2022.

b. Determine the balance in accumulated other comprehensive income on the statement of financial position on each of December 31, 2020, 2021, and 2022.

c. Assume that Niger sold its investment in Fahad Corp. on February 13, 2023, for $38,000. Prepare the journal entry(ies) needed, including reclassifying holding gains or losses to retained earnings on this date, assuming the investments are in shares and no recycling to net income is recorded.

d. What will be the balance in Accumulated Other Comprehensive Income on December 31, 2023?

E9.18 (LO 2, 3, 4, 8, 9) (Entry and Financial Statement Comparison of Cost, FV-NI, and FV-OCI Approaches) In early 2020, for the first time, HTSM Corp. invested in the common shares of another Canadian company. It acquired 5,000 shares of Toronto Stock Exchange–traded Bayscape Ltd. at a cost of $68,750. Bayscape is projected to reach a value of $15.50 per share by the end of 2020 and $17.00 by the end of 2021, and has consistently paid an annual dividend of $0.90 per share. HTSM is also a Canadian public corporation with a December 31 year end.

The controller of HTSM is uncertain about which accounting method to use. The company is interested in establishing a closer relationship with Bayscape, but if that fails, HTSM considers the investment a good opportunity to make a gain on its sale in the future. The controller has been advised that the investment could be accounted for at cost or at fair value. If at fair value, a decision would have to be made about whether to put the changes in fair value through net income or other comprehensive income. As one step in making a decision, the controller would like to know what the effect would be on total assets and net income in each of 2020 and 2021 if the predictions about Bayscape's share prices and dividends are correct. Assume there would be no recycling of realized investment gains and losses.

Instructions

a. Prepare and complete a table with a column for each of the three accounting alternatives indicated and rows for journal entries to recognize each of the following: (1) the 2020 dividend, (2) any December 31, 2020 adjustments, (3) the 2021 dividend, and (4) any December 31, 2021 adjustments.

b. Based on the table in part (a), prepare a summary comparison of each accounting method, indicating the effect of applying each of the three accounting methods on: (1) total assets at December 31, 2020, (2) 2020 net income, (3) total assets at December 31, 2021, and (4) 2021 net income.

c. Determine the effect on net income for the year ended December 31, 2022, under each of the accounting method options, assuming the investment in Bayscape was sold in early 2022 for $17.00 per share.

d. Identify the accounting policy choices that would be available to the controller if HTSM applied ASPE instead of IFRS, and when each would be appropriate.

e. **Ethics** Which method, if any, would result in higher income being reported earlier on? Would it be considered unethical for HTSM to choose that method?

E9.19 (LO 5) **(Impairment of Debt Investment and Subsequent Recovery in Value)** Tsui Corporation owns corporate bonds at December 31, 2020, accounted for using the amortized cost model. These bonds have a par value of $800,000 and an amortized cost of $788,000. After an impairment review was triggered, Tsui determined that the discounted impaired cash flows are $737,500 using the current market rate of interest, but are $734,000 using the market rate when the bonds were first acquired. The company follows a policy of directly reducing the carrying amount of any impaired assets. For simplicity purposes, assume that no impairment loss had been recorded earlier.

Instructions

a. Assuming Tsui Corporation is a private enterprise that applies ASPE, prepare any necessary journal entry(ies) related to (1) the impairment at December 31, 2020, and (2) a December 31, 2021 fair value of $760,000 and an adjusted carrying amount at that date of $741,500.

b. Assuming that Tsui Corporation applies IFRS and that there has been a significant increase in credit risk, prepare any necessary journal entry(ies) related to (1) the impairment at December 31, 2020, and (2) a December 31, 2021 fair value of $760,000 and an adjusted carrying amount at that date of $741,500. Assume that the discounted cash flow numbers provided reflect the lifetime expected risk of default.

c. Assume that Tsui is a private enterprise under the situation described in part (a) and that the company uses a valuation allowance instead of directly reducing the carrying amount of the investment. Prepare the entries required in part (a) for (1) the impairment and (2) the subsequent increase in fair value.

d. **Digging Deeper** In practice, which method would recognize losses earlier—the incurred loss model or the expected loss model? Explain briefly.

E9.20 (LO 2, 3, 5) **(Impairment of FV-NI Investment and Subsequent Recovery in Value)** On January 1, 2018, Mamood Ltd. paid $322,744.44 for 12% bonds of Variation Ltd. with a maturity value of $300,000. The bonds provide the bondholders with a 10% yield. They are dated January 1, 2018, mature on January 1, 2023, and pay interest each December 31. Mamood acquired the bond investment as part of its portfolio of trading securities and it accounts for the bonds at FV-NI, following IFRS. At December 31, 2018, Mamood's year end, the bonds had a fair value of $320,700.

During 2019, the economic outlook related to Variation Ltd.'s primary business took a major downturn, so that Variation's debt was downgraded. By the end of 2019, the bonds were priced at 85.5, and at December 31, 2020, they were selling in the market at 87. Conditions reversed in 2021 and the outlook for Variation Ltd. significantly improved, leaving its bonds with a fair value of 99.5 at December 31, 2021.

Instructions

a. Prepare a bond amortization table for the four-year period ended December 31, 2021. Round amounts to the nearest cent.

b. Prepare the entries to record Mamood's purchase of the bonds on January 1, 2018, the recognition of interest income and interest received on December 31, 2018, and the fair value adjustment required at December 31, 2018.

c. Prepare all entries required for 2019, including recognition of the impairment in value if necessary, and for 2020.

d. Prepare all entries required for 2021, including recognition of the recovery of the impairment in value, if necessary.

e. **Digging Deeper** Identify the impairment loss model applied in this situation. If Mamood had accounted for this investment at amortized cost, identify and briefly describe the impairment model the company would have used if Mamood applied IFRS, or ASPE.

E9.21 (LO 2, 3, 4, 5) **(Investment in Shares, Impairment, and Subsequent Recovery)** Weekly Corp., a December 31 year-end company that applies IFRS, acquired an investment of 1,000 shares of Credence Corp. in mid-2016 for $29,850. Between significant volatility in the markets and in the business prospects of Credence Corp., the accounting for this investment presented a challenge to Weekly. Toward the end of 2020, Credence discontinued the small annual dividend of $0.50 per share that it had been paying and announced that a major patent responsible for 50% of its income had lost most of its value due to a technological improvement by a competitor.

Situation 1: Credence Corp. is a publicly traded company on the Toronto Stock Exchange, and Weekly has opted to account for its investment at FV-NI. By the end of 2019, the price of Credence shares had fallen to $26.50 per share from $29.00 the previous year, and by the end of 2020 they were trading at $11.10.

Situation 2: Credence Corp. is a private enterprise owned by a group of 20 investors and is a supplier of materials to Weekly. Weekly purchased the shares to cement the relationship between the two companies and has opted to account for its investment at FV-OCI. In late 2020, Weekly was beginning to worry about its investment and determined that its value had probably fallen marginally to an estimated fair value of approximately $26,000 from $27,000 the previous year. In 2020, Weekly was more concerned and, at year end, carried out a thorough analysis of the present value of the likely cash flows to be derived from this investment and estimated an amount of $12,400.

Weekly Corp. adjusts the carrying amount of its investments directly when recognizing an impairment loss, and each type of investment income is accounted for and reported separately.

Instructions

a. For each situation, identify the impairment model that Weekly should apply.

b. Prepare the appropriate journal entries at December 31, 2019, and December 31, 2020, under each situation presented.

c. Assuming Weekly is a private company that applies ASPE, prepare the appropriate journal entries at December 31, 2019, and December 31, 2020, under situation 1.

E9.22 (LO 2, 3, 6) (Accounting Methods with and without Significant Influence under ASPE) Finance Holmes Inc. purchased 30% of Nadal Corporation's 30,000 outstanding common shares at a cost of $15 per share on January 3, 2020. The purchase price of $15 per share was based solely on the book value of Nadal's net assets. On September 21, Nadal declared and paid a cash dividend of $39,000. On December 31, Holmes's year end, Nadal reported net income of $85,000 for the year. Nadal shares had a fair value of $14.75 per share at December 31. Holmes Inc., a private Canadian corporation, applies ASPE.

Instructions

a. Under the assumption that the 30% holding of Nadal does not give Holmes significant influence over Nadal, identify the possible accounting methods Holmes could use under ASPE to account for its investment. Prepare all required 2020 journal entries under each acceptable method.

b. Under the assumption that the 30% holding of Nadal gives Holmes significant influence over Nadal, prepare all required 2020 journal entries, assuming Holmes uses the equity method of accounting.

c. Indicate the other possible accounting methods, if any, that Holmes could have chosen under the assumption in part (b).

d. Digging Deeper From the perspective of a financial analyst, why might the equity method be considered a more informative presentation when the investor has significant influence?

E9.23 (LO 6) (Equity Method) Fox Ltd. invested $1 million in Gloven Corp. early in the current year, receiving 25% of its outstanding shares. At the time of the purchase, Gloven Corp. had a carrying amount of $3.2 million. Gloven Corp. pays out 35% of its net income in dividends each year. Assume that Fox Ltd. applies IFRS and that the 25% holding of Gloven shares is enough to enable Fox to significantly influence the operating, investing, and financing decisions of Gloven.

Instructions

Use the information in the following T account for the investment in Gloven to answer the following questions:

Investment in Gloven Corp.

1,000,000	
110,000	
	38,500
	14,000

a. How much was Fox Ltd.'s share of Gloven Corp.'s net income for the year?

b. How much was Fox Ltd.'s share of Gloven Corp.'s dividends for the year?

c. How much was Fox Ltd.'s annual depreciation of the excess payment for capital assets?

d. What was Gloven Corp.'s total net income for the year?

e. What were Gloven Corp.'s total dividends for the year?

f. Assuming that depreciable assets had a remaining useful life of 10 years when Fox acquired its investment in Gloven, how much of the payment in excess of carrying amount was assigned to goodwill?

E9.24 (LO 4, 6, 8) (Fair Value-OCI and Equity Method Compared) Harnish Inc. acquired 25% of the outstanding common shares of Gregson Inc. on December 31, 2019. The purchase price was $1,250,000 for 62,500 shares, and is equal to 25% of Gregson's carrying amount. Gregson declared and paid a $0.75 per share cash dividend on June 15 and again on December 15, 2020. Gregson reported net income of $520,000 for 2020. The fair value of Gregson's shares was $21 per share at December 31, 2020. Harnish is a public company and applies IFRS.

Instructions

a. Prepare the journal entries for Harnish for 2019 and 2020, assuming that Harnish cannot exercise significant influence over Gregson. The investment is accounted for using the FV-OCI model.

b. Prepare the journal entries for Harnish for 2019 and 2020, assuming that Harnish can exercise significant influence over Gregson.

c. What amount is reported for the investment in Gregson shares on the December 31, 2020 statement of financial position under each of these methods in parts (a) and (b), and where is the investment reported on this statement?

d. What amount is reported on Harnish's statement of comprehensive income in 2020 under each of these methods, and where are the amounts reported?

E9.25 (LO 3, 5, 6) (Long-Term Equity Investments, Equity Method, and Impairment) On January 1, 2020, Rae Corporation purchased 30% of the common shares of Martz Limited for $196,000. Martz Limited shares are not traded in an active market. The carrying amount of Martz's net assets was $520,000 on that date. Any excess of the purchase cost over Rae's share of Martz's carrying amount is attributable to unrecorded intangibles with a 20-year life. During the year, Martz earned net income and comprehensive income of $75,000 and paid dividends of $15,000. The investment in Martz had a fair value of $201,000 at December 31, 2020. During 2021, Martz incurred a net loss and comprehensive loss of $80,000 and paid no dividends. At December 31, 2021, the fair value of the investment was $140,000 and the recoverable amount was $149,000. Assume that Rae follows IFRS.

Instructions

a. Prepare all relevant journal entries related to Rae's investment in Martz for 2020 and 2021, assuming this is its only investment and Rae cannot exercise significant influence over Martz's policies. Rae accounts for this investment using the FV-NI model. Illustrate how the statement of comprehensive income is affected in 2020 and 2021.

b. Prepare all relevant journal entries related to Rae's investment in Martz for 2020 and 2021, assuming this is its only investment and Rae exercises significant influence over its associates' policies. Illustrate how the statement of comprehensive income is affected in 2020 and 2021. Briefly explain. Assume that Rae's management assesses the investment as impaired at December 31, 2021.

c. How would your answer to part (b) be different if you were told that Martz's 2020 statement of comprehensive income included a loss from discontinued operations of $20,000 (net of tax)?

E9.26 (LO 4, 6, 8) (Proper Income Reporting) The following are two independent situations.

Situation 1: Lauren Inc. received dividends from its common share investments during the year ended December 31, 2020, as follows:

- A cash dividend of $12,250 is received from Peel Corporation. Lauren owns a 1.2% interest in Peel.

- A cash dividend of $68,000 is received from Vonna Corporation. Lauren owns a 30% interest in Vonna and a majority of Lauren's directors are also directors of Vonna Corporation.

- A cash dividend of $172,000 is received from Express Inc., a subsidiary of Lauren.

Situation 2: On April 11, 2020, Chad Corp. purchased as a long-term investment (accounted for using FV-OCI without recycling) 6,000 common shares of Roddy Ltd. for $76 per share, which represents a 2% interest. On December 31, 2020, the shares' market price was $81 per share. On March 3, 2021, Chad sold all 6,000 shares of Roddy for $94 per share.

Assume that all companies follow IFRS.

Instructions

a. For situation 1, determine how much dividend income Lauren should report on its 2020 consolidated statement of comprehensive income.

b. For situation 2, determine the amount of the gain or loss on disposal that should be included in Chad's net income in 2021 and in its other comprehensive income. The investment in Roddy Ltd. was Chad Corp.'s only investment.

c. Prepare the journal entries for situation 2 for 2021.

E9.27 (LO 5, 6, 8) (Equity Method with Cost in Excess of Share of Carrying Amount, Impairment) On January 3, 2020, Mego Limited purchased 3,000 (30%) of the common shares of Sonja Corp.

for $438,000. The following information is provided about the identifiable assets and liabilities of Sonja at the date of acquisition:

	Carrying Amount	Fair Value
Assets not subject to depreciation	$ 550,000	$ 550,000
Assets subject to depreciation (10 years remaining)	760,000	880,000
Total identifiable assets	1,310,000	1,430,000
Liabilities	110,000	110,000

During 2020, Sonja reported the following information on its statement of comprehensive income:

Income before discontinued operations	$200,000
Discontinued operations (net of tax)	(50,000)
Net income and comprehensive income	150,000
Dividends declared and paid by Sonja on November 15, 2020	110,000

Assume that the 30% interest is enough to make Sonja an associate of Mego, and that Mego is required to apply IFRS for its financial reporting. The fair value of Sonja's shares at December 31, 2020, is $147 per share.

Instructions

a. Prepare the journal entry to record Mego's purchase of the Sonja shares on January 3, 2020. (*Hint:* Any unexplained payment represents unrecognized goodwill of Sonja.)

b. Prepare all necessary journal entries associated with Mego's investment in Sonja for 2020. Depreciable assets are depreciated on a straight-line basis.

c. Would any of your entries in part (b) change if you were told that Mego's long-term business prospects had deteriorated and that the most Mego could expect to recover in the future or to sell its investment in Sonja for at December 31, 2020, is $115 per share? If so, prepare the entry and explain briefly.

d. **Ethics** A member of senior management has approached you, a CPA, informing you that, instead of the shares being worth $115 per share as in part (c), the shares are worth $150 each. Senior management receives a bonus based on net income. He mentions that the assumptions about long-term business prospects are too pessimistic and are not reflective of the economic reality at Sonja. You feel pressure to appease management, given that your boss is a member of senior management. What should you do?

E9.28 (LO 6, 8, 9) (ASPE, Significant Influence, Equity Method with Cost in Excess of Carrying Amount, Alternative Methods) In early January 2020, Chi Inc., a private enterprise that applies ASPE, purchased 40% of the common shares of Washi Corp. for $410,000. Chi was now able to exercise considerable influence in decisions made by Washi's management. Washi Corp.'s statement of financial position reported the following information at the date of acquisition:

Assets not subject to being amortized	$205,000
Assets subject to depreciation (10 years average life remaining)	620,000
Liabilities	115,000

Additional information:

1. Both the carrying amount and fair value are the same for non-depreciable assets and for liabilities.
2. The fair value of the assets subject to depreciation is $750,000.
3. The company depreciates its capital assets on a straight-line basis.
4. Washi reported net income of $163,000 and declared and paid dividends of $112,000 in 2020.

Instructions

a. Prepare the journal entry to record Chi's investment in Washi Corp. Assume that any unexplained payment is goodwill.

b. Assuming Chi applies the equity method to account for its investment in Washi, prepare the journal entries to record Chi's equity in the net income and the receipt of dividends from Washi Corp. in 2020.

c. Assume the same facts as above and in part (b), except that Washi's net income included a loss on discontinued operations of $38,000 (net of tax). Prepare the journal entries necessary to record Chi's equity in the net income of Washi for 2020. Ignore income taxes.

d. Assume that Chi is a publicly accountable enterprise that applies IFRS and therefore also applies the equity method to account for its associate. In addition to the information in parts (a) and (b), you are told that Washi reports an unrealized gain of $45,000 on investments accounted for using FV-OCI. If Chi Inc. reports net income of $172,400 and an unrealized gain in OCI of $10,000 on its own financial statements before including the results of its investment in Washi, determine Chi Inc.'s net income, other comprehensive income, and comprehensive income reported on its 2020 statement of comprehensive income. Neither Chi nor Washi reclassifies realized gains and losses on FV-OCI equity investments to net income. Ignore income taxes.

Problems

P9.1 MacAskill Corp. has the following portfolio of securities acquired for trading purposes and accounted for using the FV-NI model at September 30, 2020, the end of the company's third quarter:

Investment	Cost	Fair Value
50,000 common shares of Yuen Inc.	$215,000	$200,000
3,500 preferred shares of Monty Ltd.	135,000	140,000
2,000 common shares of Oakwood Inc.	180,000	179,000

On October 8, 2020, the Yuen shares were sold for $4.30 per share. On November 16, 2020, 3,000 common shares of Patriot Corp. were purchased at $44.50 per share. MacAskill pays a 1% commission on purchases and sales of all securities. At the end of the fourth quarter, on December 31, 2020, the fair values of the shares held were as follows: Monty $106,000; Patriot $122,000; and Oakwood $203,000. MacAskill prepares financial statements every quarter.

Instructions

a. Prepare the journal entries to record the sale, purchase, and adjusting entries related to the portfolio for the fourth quarter of 2020.

b. Indicate how and where the investments would be reported on the December 31, 2020 statement of financial position.

c. **Digging Deeper** Under what conditions might you recommend that the portfolio accounted for at FV-NI be reported somewhere other than where you indicated in part (b)?

P9.2 The following information relates to the 2020 debt and equity investment transactions of Wildcat Ltd., a publicly accountable Canadian corporation. All of the investments were acquired for trading purposes and accounted for using the FV-NI model, with all transaction costs being expensed. No investments were held at December 31, 2019, and the company prepares financial statements only annually, each December 31, following IFRS.

1. On February 1, the company purchased Williams Corp. 12% bonds, at par value for $500,000, plus accrued interest. Interest is payable April 1 and October 1.

2. On April 1, semi-annual interest was received on the Williams bonds.

3. On July 1, 9% bonds of Saint Inc. were purchased. These bonds, with a par value of $200,000, were purchased at par plus accrued interest. Interest dates are June 1 and December 1.

4. On August 12, 3,000 shares of Scotia Corp. were acquired at a cost of $59 per share. A 1% commission was paid.

5. On September 1, Williams Corp. bonds with a par value of $100,000 were sold at 104 plus accrued interest.

6. On September 28, a dividend of $0.50 per share was received on the Scotia Corp. shares.

7. On October 1, semi-annual interest was received on the remaining Williams Corp. bonds.

8. On December 1, semi-annual interest was received on the Saint Inc. bonds.

9. On December 28, a dividend of $0.52 per share was received on the Scotia Corp. shares.

10. On December 31, the following fair values were determined: Williams Corp. bonds 101.75; Saint Inc. bonds 97; and Scotia Corp. shares $60.50.

Instructions

a. Prepare all 2020 journal entries necessary to properly account for the investment in the Williams Corp. bonds.

b. Prepare all 2020 journal entries necessary to properly account for the investment in the Saint Inc. bonds.

c. Prepare all 2020 journal entries necessary to properly account for the investment in the Scotia Corp. shares.

d. Assume that there were trading investments on hand at December 31, 2019, accounted for using the FV-NI model, and that they consisted of shares with a cost of $400,000 and a fair value of $390,000. These non–dividend-paying shares were sold early in 2020 and their original cost was recovered exactly. What effect would this transaction have on 2020 net income?

P9.3 The following amortization schedule is for Flagg Ltd.'s investment in Spangler Corp.'s $100,000, five-year bonds with a 7% interest rate and a 5% yield, which were purchased on December 31, 2019, for $108,660:

	Cash Received	Interest Income	Bond Premium Amortized	Amortized Cost of Bonds
Dec. 31, 2019				$108,660
Dec. 31, 2020	$7,000	$5,433	$1,567	107,093
Dec. 31, 2021	7,000	5,354	1,646	105,447
Dec. 31, 2022	7,000	5,272	1,728	103,719
Dec. 31, 2023	7,000	5,186	1,814	101,905
Dec. 31, 2024	7,000	5,095	1,905	100,000

The following schedule presents a comparison of the amortized cost and fair value of the bonds at year end:

	Dec. 31, 2020	Dec. 31, 2021	Dec. 31, 2022	Dec. 31, 2023	Dec. 31, 2024
Amortized cost	$107,093	$105,447	$103,719	$101,905	$100,000
Fair value	$106,500	$107,500	$105,650	$103,000	$100,000

Assume that Flagg Ltd. follows IFRS and reports interest income separately from other investment income.

Instructions

a. Prepare the journal entry to record the purchase of these bonds on December 31, 2019, assuming the bonds are accounted for using the amortized cost model.

b. Prepare the journal entry(ies) related to the bonds accounted for using the amortized cost model for 2020.

c. Prepare the journal entry(ies) related to the bonds accounted for using the amortized cost model for 2022.

d. Prepare the journal entry(ies) to record the purchase of these bonds, assuming they are held for trading purposes and accounted for using the FV-NI model.

e. Prepare the journal entry(ies) related to the bonds accounted for using the FV-NI model for 2021.

f. Prepare the journal entry(ies) related to the bonds accounted for using the FV-NI model for 2023.

g. **Digging Deeper** As a member of Flagg's management, suggest a reason why you might have a different policy related to the reporting of interest income separately versus combined with other investment income.

P9.4 **Excel** **Finance** Pascale Corp. has the following securities (all purchased in 2020) in its investment portfolio on December 31, 2020: 2,500 Anderson Corp. common shares, which cost $48,750; 10,000 Munter Ltd. common shares, which cost $580,000; and 6,000 King Corp. preferred shares, which cost $255,000. Their fair values at the end of 2020 were as follows: Anderson Corp. $49,580; Munter Ltd. $569,500; and King Corp. $254,400.

In 2021, Pascale completed the following transactions:

1. On January 15, sold 2,500 Anderson common shares at $21 per share less fees of $2,150.

2. On April 17, purchased 1,000 Castle Ltd. common shares at $33.50 per share plus fees of $1,980.

The company adds transaction costs to the cost of acquired investments and deducts them from cash received on the sale of investments. On December 31, 2021, the fair values per share of the securities were as follows: Munter $61; King $40; and Castle $29. Pascale's accounting supervisor tells you that all these securities have fair values that can be readily determined, but the company is not likely to actively trade them. Management accounts for them using the FV-OCI method without recycling. Any gains or losses are reclassified to Retained Earnings upon disposition of the investment. Ignore income taxes.

Instructions

a. Prepare the entries for the sale of the Anderson Corp. investment on January 15, 2021.

b. Prepare the entry to record the Castle Ltd. share purchase on April 17, 2021.

c. Calculate the unrealized gains or losses and prepare any required adjusting entry(ies) for Pascale Corp. on December 31, 2021.

d. Indicate how all amounts will be reported on Pascale's statement of financial position and statement of comprehensive income, and the changes in the accumulated other comprehensive income portion of the statement of changes in equity for 2021.

P9.5 Castlegar Ltd. had the following investment portfolio at January 1, 2020:

Investment	Quantity	Cost per Share	Fair Value at Dec. 31, 2019
Earl Corp.	1,000	$15.00	$11.50
Josie Corp.	900	20.00	16.50
Asher Corp.	500	9.00	7.20

During 2020, the following transactions took place:

1. On March 1, Josie Corp. paid a $2 per share dividend.

2. On April 30, Castlegar sold 300 shares of Asher Corp. for $10 per share.

3. On May 15, Castlegar purchased 200 more Earl Corp. shares at $16 per share.

4. At December 31, 2020, the shares had the following market prices per share: Earl Corp. $17; Josie Corp. $19; and Asher Corp. $8.

During 2021, the following transactions took place:

5. On February 1, Castlegar sold the remaining Asher Corp. shares for $7 per share.

6. On March 1, Josie Corp. paid a $2 per share dividend.

7. On December 21, Earl Corp. declared a cash dividend of $3 per share to be paid in the next month.

8. At December 31, 2021, the shares had the following market prices per share: Earl Corp. $19 and Josie Corp. $21.

Instructions

a. Assuming that Castlegar Ltd. is a publicly accountable enterprise that accounts for its investment portfolio at FV-OCI (with no recycling to net income), prepare journal entries to record all of the 2020 and 2021 transactions and year-end events.

b. **Finance** Prepare the relevant parts of Castlegar Ltd.'s 2021 and 2020 comparative statements of financial position, statements of comprehensive income, and statements of changes in equity (accumulated other comprehensive income portion), and income statement where applicable, to show how the investments and related accounts are reported.

c. Assume that Castlegar Ltd. is a private enterprise that applies ASPE and accounts for its investment portfolio at cost (that is, the securities do not have actively traded market prices). Determine the amount by which the company's 2020 net income and 2021 net income would differ from the amounts reported under the assumptions in parts (a) and (b). Explain your results.

d. **Digging Deeper** Refer to your answers to parts (b) and (c). From an investor's perspective, what additional relevant information, if any, is provided in the financial statements under part (b) that would not be available in financial statements prepared under the method used in part (c)?

P9.6 On December 31, 2019, Nodd Corp. acquired an investment in GT Ltd. bonds with a nominal interest rate of 10% (received each December 31), and the controller produced the following bond amortization schedule based on an effective rate of approximately 15%. The bonds mature on December 31, 2022. The company prepares financial statements each December 31 following IFRS. Management is in the process of determining whether to hold these bonds for their future cash flows in order to repay debt that is also maturing at the end of 2022, or whether they will hold them for trading purposes.

	Dec. 31, 2019	Dec. 31, 2020	Dec. 31, 2021	Dec. 31, 2022
Amortized cost of GT Ltd. bonds	$487,214	$505,296	$526,090	$550,000
Fair value at each year end	487,214	499,000	523,000	550,000

Instructions

(Round amounts to the nearest dollar.)

a. Assume that management determines these bonds will be held until the end of 2022, with the proceeds being used to retire maturing debt. Prepare all journal entries required at December 31, 2019, 2020, 2021, and 2022, including the recognition of interest income and the bonds' ultimate redemption.

b. Assume that management determines the investment in the bonds is speculative in nature and will be held for trading purposes. Prepare all journal entries required at December 31, 2019, 2020, 2021, and 2022, including the receipt of interest each year and the bonds' ultimate redemption, if Nodd continues to hold the GT Ltd. bonds until maturity. Nodd will not recognize interest separately from other investment income.

P9.7 On January 1, 2020, Novotna Company purchased $400,000 worth of 8% bonds of Aguirre Co. for $369,114. The bonds were purchased to yield 10% interest. Interest is payable semi-annually, on July 1 and January 1. The bonds mature on January 1, 2025. Novotna Company uses the effective interest method to amortize the discount or premium. On January 1, 2022, to meet its liquidity needs, Novotna Company sold the bonds for $370,726, after receiving interest.

Instructions

a. Prepare the journal entry to record the purchase of bonds on January 1. Assume that the bonds are classified as FV-OCI.

b. Prepare the amortization schedule for the bonds. Round all amounts to the nearest dollar.

c. Prepare the journal entries to record the semi-annual interest on July 1, 2020, and December 31, 2020.

d. Assuming the fair value of the Aguirre bonds is $372,726 on December 31, 2021, prepare the necessary adjusting entry. (Assume that the fair value adjustment balance on January 1, 2021, is a debit of $3,375.)

e. Prepare the journal entry to record the sale of the bonds on January 1, 2022, including reclassifying holding gains or losses to net income.

P9.8 Presented below is information taken from a bond investment amortization schedule, with related fair values provided. These bonds are classified as FV-OCI.

	12/31/20	12/31/21	12/31/22
Amortized cost	$491,150	$519,442	$550,000
Fair value	$497,000	$509,000	$550,000

Instructions

a. Were the bonds purchased at a discount or at a premium?

b. Prepare the adjusting entry to record the bonds at fair value at December 31, 2020. The fair value adjustment account has a debit balance of $1,000 prior to adjustment.

c. Prepare the adjusting entry to record the bonds at fair value at December 31, 2021.

P9.9 The following information relates to the debt securities investments of Wild Company:

1. On February 1, the company purchases 10% bonds of Gibbons Co. having a par value of $300,000 at 100 plus accrued interest. Interest is payable April 1 and October 1.

2. On April 1, semi-annual interest is received.

3. On July 1, 9% bonds of Sampson Inc. are purchased. These bonds with a par value of $200,000 are purchased at 100 plus accrued interest. Interest dates are June 1 and December 1.

4. On October 1, semi-annual interest is received.

5. On December 1, semi-annual interest is received.

6. On December 31, the fair values of the bonds purchased on February 1 and July 1 are 95 and 93, respectively.

Instructions

a. Prepare any journal entries you consider necessary, including year-end entries (December 31), assuming these are FV-OCI securities.

b. If Wild Company classified these as cost/amortized cost, explain how the journal entries would differ from those in part (a).

P9.10 On July 1, 2020, Menard Concrete Ltd. purchased 5% bonds having a maturity value of $50,000 for $48,645.70. The bonds provide the bondholders with a 6% yield. The bonds mature July 1, 2023, with interest receivable June 30 and December 31 of each year. Menard uses the effective interest method to allocate unamortized discount or premium. The bonds are accounted for using the FV-OCI model with recycling. Menard has a calendar year end. The fair value of the bonds at December 31, 2020 and 2021, was $49,100 and $49,500, respectively. Assume fair value adjustments are recorded at year end only. Immediately after collecting interest on July 1, 2022, the bonds were sold for $49,850. Assume that the bonds are the only investments held by Menard Concrete Ltd. and ignore all income taxes.

Instructions

a. Prepare the journal entry at the date of the bond purchase.

b. Prepare a bond amortization schedule. Round amounts to the nearest cent.

c. Prepare the entries and year-end entries from December 31, 2020, through to the collection of interest on July 1, 2022.

d. Following the three-step approach, prepare the journal entries for the sale of the bonds on July 1, 2022. Include the reclassification of unrealized gains and losses to net income.

e. Rounding all amounts on financial statements to the nearest dollar, prepare a partial comparative statement of financial position at December 31, 2020, 2021, and 2022, showing only the related accounts for the bond investment.

f. Prepare a partial comparative statement of income for the fiscal years ended December 31, 2020, 2021, and 2022, showing only the related accounts for the bond investment.

g. Prepare a partial comparative statement of comprehensive income for the fiscal years ended December 31, 2020, 2021, and 2022.

h. Prepare a partial statement of changes in shareholders' equity for the years ended December 31, 2020, 2021, and 2022, showing retained earnings and accumulated other comprehensive income. Assume a balance of $800,000 for retained earnings at January 1, 2020, and no declaration of dividends during 2020, 2021, or 2022.

i. **Digging Deeper** How much total income was realized from the investment? Why would Menard sell the bond ahead of the maturity date? What changed in the market rate of interest between the purchase and the resale date?

P9.11 Octavio Corp. prepares financial statements annually on December 31, its fiscal year end. The company follows IFRS. At December 31, 2020, the company has the account Investments in its general ledger, containing the following debits for investment purchases, and no credits:

Feb. 1, 2020	Chiang Corp. common shares, no par value, 200 shares	$ 37,400
Apr. 1	Government of Canada bonds, 6%, due April 1, 2030, interest payable April 1 and October 1, 100 bonds of $1,000 par value each	100,000
July 1	Monet Corp. 12% bonds, par $50,000, dated March 1, 2020, purchased at 108 plus accrued interest to yield 11%, interest payable annually on March 1, due on March 1, 2037	56,000
Nov. 1	$60,000, six-month non–interest-bearing note that matures on May 1, 2021, bought to yield 10%	57,143

The fair values of the individual securities on December 31, 2020, were:

Chiang Corp. common shares (active stock market price)	$ 33,800
Government of Canada bonds	105,900
Monet Corp. bonds	55,600
Note receivable	58,350

Instructions

(Round amounts to the nearest dollar.)

a. Prepare the entries necessary to correct any errors in the Investments account, assuming that the Government of Canada bonds were being managed for their yield to maturity, and that the Monet bonds were acquired with the hope of gaining from falling interest rates. The Chiang Corp. shares were acquired with the hope of ensuring the supply of raw materials from this company in the future. Octavio tracks interest income for all debt investments.

b. Prepare the entries required to record any accrued interest, amortization of any premium or discount, and recognition of fair values on December 31, 2020.

c. During 2021, the following transactions took place:

1. The note was sold on February 1, 2021, for $59,600.

2. The Government of Canada bonds were sold on July 1, 2021, for $109,200 plus accrued interest. Prepare entries to record these transactions.

d. Using the information from parts (a) and (b), assume that the note was not sold on February 1, 2021, but instead was held until it matured. Provide the proper entry to record the disposal of the note at maturity.

e. Assume that Octavio Corp. is a private entity and applies ASPE. Identify which, if any, of your answers to parts (a) to (d) would change under this assumption. Explain briefly.

f. `Digging Deeper` Can Octavio's management choose which standards to follow, or is it restricted by the type of company it is? Explain.

P9.12 Brooks Corp. is a medium-sized corporation that specializes in quarrying stone for building construction. The company has long dominated the market, and at one time had 70% market penetration. During prosperous years, the company's profits and conservative dividend policy resulted in funds becoming available for outside investment. Over the years, Brooks has had a policy of investing idle cash in equity instruments of other companies. In particular, Brooks has made periodic investments in the company's main supplier, Norton Industries Limited. Although Brooks currently owns 18% of the outstanding common shares of Norton, it does not yet have significant influence over the operations of this investee company. Brooks accounts for its investment in Norton using FV-OCI without recycling through net income.

Yasmina Olynyk has recently joined Brooks as assistant controller, and her first assignment is to prepare the 2020 year-end adjusting entries. Olynyk has gathered the following information about Brooks's relevant investment accounts:

1. In 2020, Brooks acquired shares of Delaney Motors Corp. and Isha Electric Ltd. for short-term trading purposes. Brooks purchased 100,000 shares of Delaney Motors for $1.4 million, and the shares currently have a fair value of $1.6 million. Brooks's investment in Isha Electric has not been profitable: the company acquired 50,000 shares of Isha at $20 per share and they currently have a fair value of $720,000.

2. Before 2020, Brooks had invested $22.5 million in Norton Industries and, at December 31, 2019, the investment had a fair value of $21.5 million. While Brooks did not sell or purchase any Norton shares this year, Norton declared and paid a dividend totalling $2.4 million on all of its common shares, and reported 2020 net income of $13.8 million. Brooks's 18% ownership of Norton Industries has a December 31, 2020 fair value of $22,225,000.

Instructions

a. Prepare the appropriate adjusting entries for Brooks as at December 31, 2020.

b. For both categories of investments, describe how the results of the valuation adjustments made in part (a) would appear in the body of and/or notes to Brooks's 2020 financial statements. Ignore income taxes.

c. Prepare the dividend and adjusting entries for the Norton investment, assuming that Brooks's 18% interest results in significant influence over Norton's activities.

d. If Brooks Corp. were a private enterprise and followed ASPE, identify how your answers to parts (a), (b), and (c) would differ.

e. `Digging Deeper` Could an 18% ownership interest actually result in Brooks having significant influence? Could Brooks have a 45% ownership interest and yet not have significant influence? Explain your answers.

P9.13 Harper Corporation had the following portfolio of investments at December 31, 2020, that qualified and were accounted for using the FV-OCI method:

	Quantity	Percent Interest	Cost per Share	Fair Value per Share
Frank Inc.	2,000 shares	8%	$11	$16
Ellis Corp.	5,000 shares	14%	23	19
Mendota Ltd.	4,000 shares	2%	31	24

Early in 2021, Harper sold all the Frank Inc. shares for $17 per share, less a 1% commission on the sale. On December 31, 2021, Harper's portfolio consists of the following common shares:

	Quantity	Percent Interest	Cost	Fair Value per Share
Ellis Corp.	5,000 shares	14%	$23	$28
Mendota Ltd.	4,000 shares	2%	31	23
Kaptein Inc.	2,000 shares	1%	25	22

Assume that Harper reports net income of $158,300 for its year ended December 31, 2021, and that the company follows a policy of capitalizing transaction costs. Realized gains and losses on equity investments are reclassified from accumulated other comprehensive income directly to retained earnings.

Instructions

a. What should be reported on Harper's December 31, 2020 statement of financial position for this long-term portfolio?

b. What should be reported on Harper's December 31, 2021 statement of financial position for these investments?

c. What should be reported on Harper's 2021 statement of comprehensive income for the investments accounted for using the FV-OCI model? Prepare a partial 2021 statement of comprehensive income for Harper and provide an entry for classifying holding gains or losses to Retained Earnings on equity investments sold during 2021.

d. Assuming that comparative financial statements for 2020 and 2021 are presented in 2021, draft the footnote needed to fully disclose Harper's transactions and investments.

e. **Digging Deeper** As a potential investor in Harper Corporation, explain what information the other comprehensive income portion of the statement of comprehensive income provides for you.

P9.14 Fellows Inc., a publicly traded manufacturing company in the technology industry, has a November 30 fiscal year end. The company grew rapidly in its first 10 years and made three public offerings over this period. During its rapid growth period, Fellows acquired common shares in Yukasato Inc. and Admin Importers.

In 2009, Fellows acquired 25% of Yukasato's common shares for $588,000 and accounts for this investment using the equity method. The book value of Yukasato's net assets at the date of purchase was $1.8 million. The excess of the purchase price over the book value of the net assets relates to assets that are subject to amortization. These assets have a remaining life of 20 years. For its fiscal year ended November 30, 2020, Yukasato Inc. reported net income of $250,000 and paid dividends of $100,000.

In 2011, Fellows acquired 10% of Admin Importers' common shares for $204,000 and accounts for this investment using the FV-OCI model.

Fellows also has a policy of investing idle cash in equity securities to generate short-term profits. The following data are for Fellows' trading investment portfolio:

Trading Investments (Using the FV-NI Model)
at November 30, 2019

	Cost	Fair Value
Craxi Electric	$326,000	$314,000
Renoir Inc.	184,000	181,000
Seferis Inc.	95,000	98,500
Total	$605,000	$593,500

Investments (Using the FV-OCI Model)
at November 30, 2019

	Cost	Fair Value
Admin Importers	$204,000	$198,000

Trading Investments (Using the FV-NI Model)
at November 30, 2020

	Cost	Fair Value
Craxi Electric	$326,000	$323,000
Renoir Inc.	184,000	180,000
Mer Limited	105,000	108,000
Total	$615,000	$611,000

Investments (Using the FV-OCI Model)
at November 30, 2020

	Cost	Fair Value
Admin Importers	$204,000	$205,000

On November 14, 2020, Ted Yan was hired by Fellows as assistant controller. His first assignment was to prepare the entries to record the November activity and the November 30, 2020 year-end adjusting entries for the current trading investments and the investment in common shares of Admin Importers. Using Fellows' ledger of investment transactions and the data given above, Yan proposed the following entries and submitted them to Julie O'Brien, controller, for review:

Entry 1 (November 8, 2020)

Cash	99,500	
FV-NI Investments		98,500
Gain on Disposal of Investments—FV-NI		1,000

(To record the sale of Seferis Inc. shares for $99,500) – Assume no change in fair value since November 30, 2019.

Entry 2 (November 26, 2020)

FV-NI Investments	105,000	
Cash		105,000

(To record the purchase of Mer Limited common shares for $102,200 plus brokerage fees of $2,800)

Entry 3 (November 30, 2020)

Investment Income or Loss	3,000	
Allowance for Investment Impairment		3,000

(To recognize a loss equal to the excess of cost over fair value of equity securities)

Entry 4 (November 30, 2020)

Cash	38,500	
Dividend Revenue		38,500

(To record the following dividends received from investments: Yukasato Inc. $25,000; Admin Importers $9,000; and Craxi Electric $4,500)

Entry 5 (November 30, 2020)

Investment in Associate	62,500	
Investment Income or Loss		62,500

(To record share of Yukasato Inc. income under the equity method, $250,000 × 0.25)

Instructions

a. The journal entries proposed by Ted Yan will establish the value of Fellows' equity investments to be reported on the company's external financial statements. Review each journal entry and indicate whether it is in accordance with the applicable accounting standards. If an entry is incorrect, prepare the entry(ies) that should have been made.

b. **Digging Deeper** Because Fellows owns more than 20% of Yukasato Inc., Julie O'Brien has adopted the equity method to account for this investment. Under what circumstances would it be inappropriate to use the equity method to account for a 25% interest in the common shares of Yukasato Inc.? If the equity method is not appropriate in this case, what method would you recommend? Why?

c. **Digging Deeper** Are there any differences between the characteristics of trading investments accounted for using the FV-NI model and investments accounted for using the FV-OCI model in general? Explain. Are there any differences in the specific case of Fellows Inc.'s investments?

P9.15 On January 1, 2020, Melbourne Corporation, a public company following IFRS, acquired 15,000 of the 50,000 outstanding common shares of Noah Corp. for $25 per share. Noah's statement of financial position reported the following information at the date of the acquisition:

Assets not subject to depreciation	$290,000
Assets subject to depreciation	860,000
Liabilities	150,000

Additional information:

1. On the acquisition date, the fair value is the same as the carrying amount for the assets that are not subject to depreciation and for the liabilities.

2. On the acquisition date, the fair value of the assets that are subject to depreciation is $960,000. These assets had a remaining useful life of eight years at that time.

3. Noah reported 2020 net income of $100,000 and paid dividends of $5,000 in December 2020.

4. Noah's shares are not actively traded on the stock exchange, but Melbourne has determined that they have a fair value of $24 per share on December 31, 2020.

Instructions

a. Prepare the journal entries for Melbourne Corporation for 2020, assuming that Melbourne cannot exercise significant influence over Noah and accounts for the investment at FV-OCI.

b. Prepare the journal entries for Melbourne Corporation for 2020, assuming that Melbourne can exercise significant influence over Noah's operations.

c. How would your answers to parts (a) and (b) change if Melbourne had acquired the Noah shares on July 2 instead of January 1?

d. Prepare the 2020 journal entries if Melbourne Corporation were a private company applying ASPE, clearly identifying the methods of accounting you have chosen.

e. `Digging Deeper` For your answers to part (d), prepare a table of the investment amount reported on the statement of financial position and the amount reported on the income statement under each approach identified. As a shareholder of Melbourne Corporation, which method of accounting do you think provides better information? Explain briefly.

P9.16 On December 31, 2019, Acker Ltd. reported the following statement of financial position.

ACKER LTD.
Statement of Financial Position
As at December 31, 2019

Assets		Equity	
FV-OCI investments	$240,000	Contributed capital	$260,000
Cash	50,000	Accumulated other comprehensive income	30,000
Total	$290,000		$290,000

The accumulated other comprehensive income was related only to the company's non-traded equity investments. Some of these were sold in 2020 for cash, resulting in a gain on disposal of $30,000. The fair value of Acker Ltd.'s investments at December 31, 2020, was $185,000 and their cost was $140,000. No FV-OCI investments were purchased during 2020. Although Acker is a private company, it applies IFRS and does not recycle OCI gains and losses for equity investments to net income when realized. The company reclassifies gains and losses to Retained Earnings when the FV-OCI investments are sold.

Acker Ltd. received dividend income of $5,000 (cash) during 2020 and realized a gain of $40,000 on the purchase and sale of FV-NI investments.

Instructions

Ignoring income taxes and assuming that all transactions during the year were for cash:

a. Prepare the journal entry related to the sale of the FV-OCI investments in 2020.

b. Prepare any reclassification entry for the unrealized gains or losses on the FV-OCI investments sold during the year ended December 31, 2020.

c. Prepare the year-end adjusting entry recognizing any adjustment in fair value for the FV-OCI investments.

d. Calculate net income and prepare a statement of comprehensive income for 2020. Ignore income taxes.

e. Prepare a statement of financial position as at December 31, 2020.

f. `Digging Deeper` Assume that Acker Ltd. applies ASPE and management had identified the equity investment as an FV-NI investment when it was first acquired. Identify and explain any differences in the opening SFP at December 31, 2019, the 2020 statement of net income, and the closing SFP at December 31, 2020, when the FV-NI method is used instead of the method used under the original IFRS assumption.

g. Prepare a statement of financial position as at December 31, 2020, based on the assumption in part (f).

P9.17 Minute Corp., a Canadian public corporation that follows IFRS, reported the following on its December 31, 2019 statement of financial position:

	$
Investment in Hysenaj Ltd. shares, at FV-NI: 6,400 shares, original cost of $251,540	316,300
Investment in Growthpen Corp. shares, at FV-OCI, without recycling:	
4,000 shares, original cost of $28,800	26,100
Investment in Metal Corp. bonds, at amortized cost:	
$500,000 face value, 6% bonds, due November 1, 2024, interest paid each May 1	
and November 1 to yield 5% (See Note 1)	521,227
Interest receivable on Metal Corp. bonds	5,000
Shareholders' equity	
Accumulated other comprehensive income: unrealized loss on Growthpen	
Corp. shares	2,700

Additional information:

1. The bond amortization table used by Minute Corp. for this bond indicated the following for the November 1, 2019 interest received and interest income:

Date	Interest Received	Interest Income	Premium Amortization	Balance, Bond Carrying Amount
Nov. 1/19	15,000	13,095	1,905	521,878

Hint: On December 31, 2019, Minute's accountant pencilled in the following numbers below the November 1, 2019 line:

Date	Interest Receivable	Interest Income	Premium Amortization	Balance, Bond Carrying Amount
Dec. 31/19 adjustment	5,000	4,349	651	521,227

2. Minute Corp. uses the FV-NI method for investments acquired for trading purposes, and the FV-OCI method for investments that it intends to hold for their growth potential. For the FV-OCI investments, transaction costs are capitalized, and when gains and losses are realized on equity investments, they are reclassified to Retained Earnings. Interest and dividends are not reported separately from other investment income for investments held for trading and are accounted for at FV-NI.

The following transactions and events took place during the company's year ended December 31, 2020:

Jan. 2   Sold 1,000 Growthpen shares for $8.50 per share less a $300 commission. (*Hint:* Remember that only 25% of the holdings have been sold.)

Jan. 3   Purchased 3,600 of the 12,000 outstanding shares of Lloyd Corp. for $234,000. Minute Corp. and Lloyd Corp. managements have worked together on joint projects in the past and Lloyd often asks Minute management for advice on operational and financing issues that Lloyd faces. A review of Lloyd's financial statements on the date these shares were acquired indicated total assets of $1.4 million and total liabilities of $750,000. In addition, the company has an internally developed patent that has a fair value of $60,000 but is unrecorded in the accounts. The patent is likely to have value to Lloyd for another six years.

Mar. 18   Received a $1 per share dividend on Growthpen shares and a $3 per share dividend on Hysenaj shares.

May 1   Received the semi-annual interest on the Metal Corp. bonds.

June 30   Sold the Metal Corp. bonds for 102 plus accrued interest. (*Hint:* Start by making an entry to accrue the interest income on the bonds to June 30, then make an entry to record the cash received.)

Sept. 17 Sold all the shares of Hysenaj for $58 per share. Paid a 1% commission.

Oct. 15   Received a dividend of $1 per share on the Lloyd Corp. shares.

Dec. 31   Lloyd Corp. management reported that the company earned a net income of $48,000 for its year ended December 31, 2020.

Dec. 31   The fair values of the remaining investments are: Growthpen Corp. $7 per share; Lloyd Corp. $217,800.

Instructions

a. Showing all calculations, prepare all required entries during 2020 and at December 31, 2020, if necessary, for the transactions and adjustments relating to the investments in the Hysenaj Ltd. shares, the

Growthpen Corp. shares, the Metal Corp. bonds, and the Lloyd Corp. shares. Include any required entry for classifying holding gains or losses to retained earnings on equity investments sold during the period.

b. **Digging Deeper** Determine the December 31, 2020 balances in each asset account related to the investments and in accumulated other comprehensive income. Prepare a partial statement of financial position, indicating where and how each of the investments and accumulated other comprehensive income would be reported.

c. Determine the December 31, 2020 balances in each income and OCI account related to the investments. Assuming that Minute Corp. reports net income of $1,422,600, including all revenue, expense, gain, and loss accounts that are correctly included in net income, prepare a statement of comprehensive income for Minute's year ended December 31, 2020.

d. Prepare a partial statement of changes in equity for the year ended December 31, 2020, showing retained earnings and accumulated other comprehensive income. Assume a balance of $1,980,000 for retained earnings at January 1, 2020, and no declaration of dividends during 2020. Reconcile the balance of Accumulated Other Comprehensive Income to the underlying investment.

e. **Digging Deeper** After Minute Corp.'s December 31, 2020 financial statements were released, the members of an investment club met to look at Minute as a possible investment. The club members were not familiar with the term "accumulated other comprehensive income" that they saw on the statement of financial position. Explain what the balance in this account represents, using terms the club members would understand.

Cases

Refer to the Case Primer on the student website and in WileyPLUS *to help you answer these cases.*

CA9.1 Investment Company Limited (ICL) is a private company owned by 10 doctors. The company's objective is to manage the doctors' investment portfolios. It actually began as an investment club 10 years ago. At that time, each doctor invested equal amounts of cash and the group met every other week to determine where the money should be invested. Eventually, they decided to incorporate the company and each doctor now owns one-tenth of the voting shares. The company employs two managers who look after the business full-time and make the investment decisions with input from the owners. Earnings per year after taxes now average $1.5 million. During the year, the following transactions took place:

Investment A (IA): Purchased common shares of IA for $1 million. IA allows researchers to use expensive lab equipment (which is owned by the company) on a pay-per-use basis. These shares represent 15% of the total outstanding common shares of IA. Because of its percentage ownership, ICL is allowed to appoint one member of IA's board of directors. There are three directors on the board. One of the ICL owners has also been hired as a consultant to IA to advise on equipment acquisitions. The company is unsure of how long it will keep the shares. At least two of the ICL owners are interested in holding on to the investment for the longer term, as they use the services of IA. The fair value of the shares of IA is determined annually by a valuations expert.

Investment B (IB): Purchased preferred shares of IB representing 25% of the total outstanding shares. The shares will likely be resold within two months, although no decision has yet been made. The fair value of this investment is known.

Investment C (IC): Purchased a 25% interest in voting common shares of IC for $1 million two years ago. The current carrying amount is $950,000, since the company has been in the drug development stage. IC develops drug delivery technology. In the past week, a major drug on which the company has spent large amounts (approximately $10 million) for research and development was declined by the Food and Drug Administration for sale in the United States. Most of the $10 million had previously been capitalized in the financial statements of IC. This is a significant blow to IC, as it had been projecting that 50% of its future revenues would come from this drug. IC does not produce financial statements until two months after ICL's year end.

Although the investments have been mainly in private companies so far, the doctors are thinking of revising their investment strategy and investing in more public companies. They feel that the stock market is poised for recovery, and are therefore planning to borrow some funds for investment. The accountant is currently reviewing the above transactions in preparation for a meeting with the bank. The company has never prepared GAAP statements before but is considering doing so. The company has not made a decision as to which GAAP to follow (IFRS or ASPE).

Instructions

Adopt the role of the company's accountant and analyze the financial reporting issues.

CA9.2 **Finance** Cando Communications (CC) is a public company that owns and operates 10 broadcast television stations and several specialty cable channels, 10 newspapers (including the *International Post*), and many other non-daily publications. It has a 57.6% economic interest in Australia TV (in Australia), and a 29.9% interest in Ulster TV (in Northern Ireland).

According to the notes to the annual financial statements, the company owns approximately 15% of the shares and all of the convertible and subordinated debentures of Australia TV. The convertible debentures are convertible into shares that would represent 50% of the company's total issued shares at the time of conversion. In total, including the debentures, the investment in Australia TV yields a distribution that is equivalent to 57.5% of all distributions paid by Australia TV. CC has a contractual right to be represented on the board of directors and has appointed three of the board's 12 members.

Although the company has made an attempt to influence the decisions made by Ulster TV management, it has been unsuccessful and does not have any representation on the board of directors.

Investments represent approximately $150 million (about 5% of total assets). Even though revenues were up by 15%, net income was only $8 million for the year, down from $50 million the prior year.

Instructions

Adopt the role of a financial analyst and analyze the financial reporting issues.

CA9.3 Impaired Investments Limited (IIL) is in the real estate industry. Last year, the company divested itself of some major investments in real estate and invested the funds in several instruments, as follows:

1. Investments in 5% bonds: currently carried at amortized cost
2. Investments in common shares (no significant influence or control and not held for trading)—Company A: currently carried at fair value, with gains and losses booked to income
3. Investments in common shares—Company B: currently carried at fair value, with gains and losses booked to income

During the current year, similar bonds available in the marketplace are yielding 6%. Although the company is not certain why this is the case, the controller feels it may be due to greater perceived risk associated with changes in the economy and specifically the real estate industry. The investment in Company A shares is significantly below cost at year end, according to current market prices (Company A's shares trade on a stock exchange). The investment in Company B shares is also below cost, but the controller feels that this is just a temporary decline and not necessarily an impairment. The controller plans to sell these shares as soon as their decline in price reverses and a 10% return on investment is achieved. The shares of Company B also trade on a stock exchange.

IIL is currently a private entity but has recently considered going public, perhaps in the next five years, and plans to adopt IFRS this year.

Instructions

Adopt the role of the controller and discuss the financial reporting issues related to the IIL financial statements.

Integrated Case

IC9.1 **Enabling Competencies** **Finance** EMI Inc. is a public company that operates numerous movie theatres in Canada. Historically, it operated as a trust and its business model consisted of distributing all of its earnings to shareholders through dividends. As a result of tax changes two years ago, it converted to a corporation and adopted a strategy of using its excess cash to invest in short-term and strategic investments. Some of EMI's investment transactions for 2021 are identified below.

In the last quarter of 2020, EMI purchased 40% of the outstanding voting shares of ABC. ABC is a movie distributor and has a contract with EMI whereby it pays management fees to EMI to have two of EMI's executives on its strategic committee. Also, as part of the investment, one member of EMI's board of directors is eligible to serve as a member of ABC's board of 12 executive members. Just before year end, EMI signed as a guarantor for ABC's newly issued debt, which it will use to build new movie theatres. EMI agreed to the arrangement, provided it could use ABC's existing movie theatres as future collateral. ABC is also a public company and, of the remaining 60% of outstanding shares, no individual shareholder holds more than 1%. EMI is unsure of how to treat this strategic investment.

At the beginning of the year, EMI invested some of its excess money in corporate bonds with a face value of $100,000, for $94,758. The bonds pay a 6% semi-annual interest rate and provide an effective interest rate of 8% over three years. The bonds mature on January 1, 2024. Management has purchased similar corporate bonds in the past for short-term profits and continues to do so with its existing bonds. However, at the annual board meeting, management had stated its intention to hold these particular corporate bonds as an investment for earning income. EMI has the ability to hold the investment to maturity. EMI is unsure of how to record the investment upon inception and the initial subsequent semi-annual interest payment.

EMI also invested funds into two stock portfolios, A and B. Management's intention for the investment is unclear; however, in the past, similar stock portfolios were purchased with the intention of holding only to generate a short-term gain. Portfolio A consists of a 5% ownership of shares in a publicly traded company, Masrani Corp., for a total investment of $25,000. Portfolio B consists of a 3% ownership in another private movie theatre, for a total investment of $15,000. Transaction costs for both portfolios were 2% of the purchase price. At year end, the fair value of portfolio A had dropped to $19,222. EMI is unsure of the method of measurement for each portfolio investment.

As EMI's shares are trading on the capital market, its financial information and filings are tracked by an equity analyst who produces quarterly analyst reports. These reports are used by shareholders and future investors as an independent review of EMI's results. It is now year end and management is preparing for a meeting with its equity analyst to review its accounting policies. The board of directors is expected to approve the financial statements after the meeting with the analyst.

An excerpt from EMI's 2021 financial statements is shown below.

Consolidated Statement of Financial Position
As at December 31, 2021
Assets
Current assets

Cash and cash equivalents	$ 1,890,877
Accounts receivable	567,321
Inventory	36,455
Securities	
Bonds—FV-NI and held to maturity	756,210
Portfolio investments (FV-NI and cost)	899,321
Total current assets	4,150,184
Property, plant, and equipment	
Equipment	12,321,888
Accumulated depreciation	(3,490,211)
Net property, plant, and equipment	8,831,677
Long-term investments	21,999
Deferred tax assets	563,422
Total assets	**$13,567,282**

Instructions

Assume the role of EMI's equity analyst and complete an analysis of EMI's required application of accounting policies for investments. Discuss any choices and differences between IFRS and ASPE for information purposes only.

Research and Analysis

RA9.1 [Real World Emphasis]   **Hudson's Bay Company**

Refer to the annual financial statements of Hudson's Bay Company for its fiscal year ended February 3, 2018 (fiscal 2017), found at the end of the book.

Instructions

a. Review Hudson's Bay's balance sheet. Identify all financial investments that are reported, along with their carrying amounts and the method of accounting for each. You may need to read the notes to the financial statements to get the necessary details. Do you think these financial asset investments are significant to an assessment of the company? Comment.

b. Does Hudson's Bay have any investments in subsidiary companies? Does it own 100% of all its subsidiaries? Can you tell this by looking at the balance sheet? At the income statement? The statement of cash flows? What information is disclosed about these subsidiaries?

c. Did Hudson's Bay Company acquire any companies during the current or prior year? If so, what type of information is provided about these acquisitions? Comment briefly on how such transactions might affect any analysis of the parent company for the year.

RA9.2 **Real World Emphasis** **Royal Bank of Canada**

Refer to the 2017 financial statements and accompanying notes of Royal Bank of Canada (RBC) that are found on the company's website (www.royalbank.ca) or at www.sedar.com.

Instructions

a. What percentage of RBC's total assets is held in investments (at October 31, 2017 and 2016)? Note that RBC also holds a significant loan portfolio. What is the business reason for holding loans versus securities? Comment on how the investments are classified and presented on the balance sheet.

b. What percentage of total interest income comes from securities (2017 and 2016)? Are there any other lines on the income statement or in other comprehensive income (OCI) relating to the securities? What percentage of net income (include any relevant OCI items) relates to securities (2017 versus 2016)? Calculate an approximate return on the investments in securities. Comment on the return, while looking at the nature of the securities that are being invested in.

c. Read the notes to the financial statements that relate to the securities. Indicate and briefly explain the valuation method(s) applied.

RA9.3 **Research Issue—Structured or Variable Interest Entities**

Structured entities or variable interest entities (VIEs) have long been on the agendas of the financial accounting standard-setting communities. Recently, however, standards have been updated to deal with the issues presented by such entities.

Instructions

Write a one- to two-page report on structured entities or VIEs. Your report should indicate what the major accounting issue was that needed resolution, how the IASB has dealt with it, and what the FASB and ASPE positions are on similar situations. Also, identify at least one company that has a structured entity and discuss how the investment is reported.

RA9.4 **Real World Emphasis** **Potash Corporation of Saskatchewan**

Gain access to the 2017 financial statements of Potash Corporation of Saskatchewan from the company's website or www.sedar.com. On January 1, 2018, PotashCorp and Agrium completed a merger and formed a new company called Nutrien Ltd. You can still access the Potash Corporation financial statements using either www.potashcorp.com or www.nutrien.com.

Instructions

a. Note 31 provides information on the principles of consolidation that PotashCorp applies. What does the company mean by "control"? Does any judgement have to be applied in determining whether control over another entity exists? Explain briefly.

b. Does PotashCorp apply IAS 39 or IFRS 9 in accounting and reporting its financial asset investment assets?

c. Refer to Note 19 Investments. Identify, by name, the investee companies of PotashCorp. For each, identify the classification of investment, the percentage of voting rights held by PotashCorp, the method of accounting for the investee, its carrying amount, and its fair value.

d. What additional information is provided in Note 19 about the investments accounted for using the equity method? Explain, in general terms only, why the income reported on the statement of income from associates and joint ventures differs from the $172 million of dividends received from them as reported in this note.

e. Explain the impairment assessment policy for PotashCorp's available-for-sale investments discussed in Note 19. Include information about the event that triggered the impairment assessment in 2017.

RA9.5 **Real World Emphasis** **Impairment Models**

Write a short essay (one or two pages) describing the incurred loss model and the expected loss model of impairment. Summarize each model and compare the two models, indicating the potential benefits and drawbacks of each. Which model do you think provides the more transparent information for users?

RA9.6 Specific Disclosure Requirements

Discuss the three objectives of disclosure of financial instruments under ASPE and IFRS. In your discussion, explain how specific disclosure requirements meet these objectives.

Cumulative Coverage and Task-Based Simulation: Chapters 6 to 9

Templates to complete this task-based simulation are available in WileyPLUS *and on the instructor website.*

Posh Hotels Ltd. (PHL) is a small boutique hotel that provides 38 suites that can be rented by the day, week, or month. Food service is available through room service as well. In addition, there are two suites that have been rented on a long-term basis to corporate tenants, who have access to their suites anytime throughout the year without making a reservation. The company has a December 31 year end, and you are preparing the year-end financial statements using IFRS.

The following issues require your consideration:

1. Cash

   - The hotel keeps a significant amount of euro currency on hand to meet the needs of its guests. At year end, there was €12,000 on hand. The year-end exchange rate was $1.35, and the average rate for the year was $1.42.

   - The bank statement balance at December 31 was $158,293. There were outstanding cheques of $52,375 and an outstanding deposit of $15,487. Bank charges per the bank statement were $65 for the month of December and have been recorded.

2. Accounts receivable and allowance for doubtful accounts

   - The hotel charges $150 per night for accommodation in one of the rental suites, and guests pay at the end of their stay, with daily revenue being accrued as it is earned. At December 31, the amount outstanding from short-term guests was $10,500. At year end, management expects to be unable to collect an amount equal to 5% of the outstanding receivables for this type of suite. During the year, Service Revenue amounted to $1,750,000, and the balance in Allowance for Doubtful Accounts at the end of the previous year was $15,000. During the year, $32,000 in accounts was written off.

   - The two corporate suites are rented for $45,000 apiece per year. The payment for these longer-term rentals is due in advance each July 1 for the following 12 months. One of these corporate suites has been in use for part of the year, but the corporate tenant went bankrupt and was unable to pay the $45,000 fee. Hotel management had hoped the tenant would eventually be able to pay, and it allowed the company to use the suite until the end of October. Since then, the hotel has been in negotiations with the bankruptcy accountant and expects to eventually receive a settlement of $10,000. The balance will become uncollectible; no allowance for doubtful accounts has been recorded with respect to these suites as there have never been collection problems in the past.

3. Inventory

   - PHL follows a policy of FIFO costing, and values items at the lower of cost and net realizable value based on an individual item basis.

   - The hotel has a standing weekly order at set prices with a local catering firm. If the food is not eaten before the next delivery is received, it is donated to the local women's shelter. This ensures that all meals are of appropriate quality for the hotel guests.

   - On December 31, the following items were delivered:

Item	Unit Cost	Net Realizable Value
40 chicken dinners	$5	$12
35 beef dinners	$6	$15
75 frozen vegetable servings	$1	$2
75 units of fresh fruit	$1	$2
100 desserts	$3	$5

   - The invoice for the food delivery on December 31 included an additional delivery charge of $0.10 per item, totalling $32.50.

   - On December 31, an ice storm resulted in a loss of electricity to the hotel building. As a result, 20 chicken and 10 beef dinners thawed and were unusable.

- The hotel also maintains an inventory of white terry cloth bathrobes and towels that are available for sale to its clients. At December 31, the following information is available:

Product	Quantity	Cost/Unit	Selling Price/Unit
Bathrobes, assorted sizes	40	$49.50	$85.00
Towels, extra-large	25	$19.30	$18.00*
Towels, large	20	$15.00	$28.00

*The extra-large towels are no longer popular and management has decided to discontinue them. It offers the hotel staff a 20% commission for all extra-large towels they sell at the sale price of $18.00.

4. Investments

- On December 1, PHL purchased a $100,000, 90-day Canadian government treasury bill for $98,039 to yield 8%.

- During the year, PHL purchased 30% of the shares in Western Hotel Company, a company that owns a similar hotel property in a nearby city, for $5 million, a price corresponding to 30% of its book value. Subsequently, Western Hotel Company paid a dividend totalling $100,000 and earned income of $250,000. The fair value of the common shares as at December 31 was $5.1 million.

- PHL also purchased common shares of Dufort Corp. as a temporary investment for $48,000. At the end of the year, these shares had a fair value of $47,000, according to the December 31 closing price on the Toronto Stock Exchange. A dividend of $500 was received during the year.

Instructions

Part A: Cash and investments presentation

Determine whether each financial instrument should be presented in the cash and cash equivalents or in the investments section of the statement of financial position. Place an X in the appropriate column in the table below.

Financial Instrument	Cash and Cash Equivalents	Investments
Euro currency		
Bank account		
90-day Canadian government treasury bill		
Western Hotel Company common shares		
Dufort Corp. common shares		

Part B: Bank reconciliation

Prepare a bank reconciliation for PHL as at December 31 to determine the adjusted cash balance per the general ledger. Enter the description and amount of any adjustment in the table below.

	(Description)	($)
Cash per bank account:		
Add:		
Deduct:		
Adjusted cash per general ledger:		

Part C: Investment income

Calculate the carrying amount as at December 31 and investment income for the year ended December 31 for each of the financial instruments listed below. Enter the total investment income in the appropriate space in the table below. Round to the nearest dollar.

Financial instrument	Carrying Amount ($)	Investment Income ($)
90-day Canadian government treasury bill Using: amortized cost		
Western Hotel Company common shares Using: equity method		
Western Hotel Company common shares Using: FV-OCI		
Dufort Corp. common shares Using: FV-NI		

Part D: Inventory carrying values

Calculate the carrying amount of each inventory item as at December 31. Identify any inventory that requires a writedown. Enter the carrying amount in the appropriate space in the table below. Place an X in the space for any inventory that requires a writedown.

	Carrying Amount ($)	Writedown Required
Food:		
Chicken dinners		
Beef dinners		
Vegetable servings		
Fruit servings		
Desserts		
Bathrobes and towels:		
Bathrobes		
Towels, extra-large		
Towels, large		

Part E: Accounts receivable

Calculate the accounts receivable, allowance for doubtful accounts, and bad debt balances as at December 31. Enter the dollar amount for each item in the appropriate space in the table below.

	Amount as at December 31
Accounts receivable	
Allowance for doubtful accounts	
Bad debt expense	

CHAPTER 10

Property, Plant, and Equipment: Accounting Model Basics

Pawel Gaul/Getty Images

Moving to Fair Value

Toronto-based Brookfield Asset Management Inc. is a global alternative asset manager with over $285 billion in assets under management, including some of the priciest office real estate in London, New York City, and Los Angeles. The company has an over 115-year history of owning and operating assets, with a focus on property, renewable power, infrastructure, and private equity in Canada and around the world.

With so much property, plant, and equipment (PP&E) under management, asset valuations are a critical component of Brookfield's business model. The company has always internally measured the fair value of its PP&E, so management would know how much Brookfield's assets were actually worth. But it reported these balances under its previous accounting framework, Canadian GAAP, using the historical cost method, which depreciated PP&E based on their actual cost, over a number of years. For example, Brookfield has owned some of its power plants for more than five decades. It had fully depreciated some of them under Canadian GAAP but, because the amount of financing placed on them increased to reflect their current value, this resulted in a negative net asset value.

IFRS, however, allows public companies to utilize the fair value method for certain assets. Partly because of this, Brookfield adopted IFRS in 2010, one year earlier than required. The company chose the fair value method because it felt it provided shareholders with better information regarding its asset value.

The move to IFRS and fair value for reporting for the company's PP&E had a material impact on Brookfield's financial statements. For example, when it accounted for its power assets at fair value, it recognized an approximately $5-billion fair value adjustment to record these assets at their current values. This reflected increases in the assets' value since acquisition and the fact that it had depreciated them. All told, the move to fair value under IFRS from Canadian GAAP doubled the common equity reported on Brookfield's consolidated balance sheet the first year to $11.3 billion. Common equity, which includes Accumulated Other Comprehensive Income, has continued to increase since then to a total of $24.1 billion as at December 31, 2017.

While the company feels the move to IFRS was overall very positive, the international standards do present some challenges. For example, Brookfield's different asset classes are treated differently for valuation and recognition purposes. Its commercial (office and retail) properties are considered investment properties, and its timber assets are considered biological assets. Both of these asset classes are fair valued through net income; they are not depreciated. On the other hand, its power plants and infrastructure are considered to be PP&E. These assets are recorded at fair value (because the company elects to do so) annually via other comprehensive income but depreciated quarterly through net income. Furthermore, other asset classes are carried at historical cost. Net income includes only some of Brookfield's asset revaluations, while others are recorded through other comprehensive income or not at all.

Sources: Eric Reguly, "CEOs of the Year: How Bruce Flatt and the Brookfield Four Built Canada's Most Successful International Player," *Report on Business* magazine, November 23, 2017; Brookfield Asset Management corporate website, www.brookfield.com; Brookfield Asset Management 2017 annual report.

LEARNING OBJECTIVES	CHAPTER OUTLINE	CPA COMPETENCIES
After studying this chapter, you should be able to:	The chapter headings related to the learning objective are:	Competencies addressed by each learning objective are as follows:
1. Identify the business importance and characteristics of property, plant, and equipment assets and explain the recognition criteria.	**Definition and Recognition of Property, Plant, and Equipment** • Property, plant, and equipment—business perspective • Property, plant, and equipment—characteristics	**1.1.1, 1.1.5, 1.2.1, 1.2.2, 1.2.3, 2.3.3**
2. Identify the costs to include in the measurement of property, plant, and equipment at acquisition.	**Cost Elements** • Self-constructed assets • Borrowing costs • Dismantling and restoration costs	**1.2.1, 1.2.2, 1.2.3**
3. Determine asset cost when the transaction has delayed payment terms or is a lump-sum purchase, a nonmonetary exchange, or a contributed asset.	**Measurement of Cost for Nonmonetary Exchange** • Cash discounts not taken • Deferred payment terms • Lump-sum purchases • Nonmonetary exchanges • Contributed assets and government grants	**1.2.1, 1.2.2, 1.2.3**
4. Identify the costs included in specific types of property, plant, and equipment.	**Measurement of Costs Associated with Specific Assets** • Land • Buildings • Leasehold improvements • Equipment • Investment property • Natural resource properties • Biological assets	**1.2.1, 1.2.2, 1.2.3**

5. Understand and apply the cost model, the revaluation model using the asset adjustment method, and the fair value model.	**Measurement after Acquisition** • Cost and revaluation models • Fair value model	**1.1.2, 1.2.1, 1.2.2, 1.2.3, 1.2.4**
6. Explain and apply the accounting treatment for costs incurred after acquisition.	**Costs Incurred after Acquisition** • Additions • Replacements, major overhauls, and inspections • Rearrangement and reinstallation • Repairs	**1.1.2, 1.2.1, 1.2.2, 1.3.2**
7. Identify differences in accounting between IFRS and ASPE, and what changes are expected in the near future.	**IFRS/ASPE Comparison** • A comparison of IFRS and ASPE • Looking ahead	**1.1.4**

After studying Appendix 10A, you should be able to:

8. Calculate the amount of borrowing costs to capitalize for qualifying assets.	**Appendix 10A: Capitalization of Borrowing Costs** • Qualifying assets • Capitalization period • Avoidable borrowing costs • Disclosures	**1.1.1, 1.1.2, 1.2.1, 1.2.3**

After studying Appendix 10B, you should be able to:

9. Understand and apply the revaluation model using the proportionate method.	**Appendix 10B: Revaluation: The Proportionate Method**	**1.1.2, 1.2.1, 1.2.3, 1.2.4**

Preview of Chapter 10

This chapter is the first of three chapters that explain the accounting, reporting, and disclosure requirements for an entity's investment in long-lived non-financial assets. Chapter 10 introduces investments in property, plant, and equipment assets and how they are accounted for at acquisition. It then sets out and explains three accounting models that are used to measure such assets, and the accounting treatment for costs incurred after acquisition. This chapter, like those preceding it, finishes by summarizing significant differences between IFRS and ASPE requirements.

Chapter 11 continues the coverage of tangible long-lived assets by explaining how these assets are accounted for after acquisition (depreciation), when their capacity to generate future cash flows is reduced (impairment), and when they are disposed of (derecognition). That chapter also addresses significant presentation and disclosure requirements. Chapter 12 zeroes in on recognition and measurement issues related to long-lived intangible assets pland goodwill.

Definition and Recognition of Property, Plant, and Equipment

> **LEARNING OBJECTIVE 1**
>
> Identify the business importance and characteristics of property, plant, and equipment assets and explain the recognition criteria.

Property, Plant, and Equipment—Business Perspective

Almost every enterprise, whatever its size or activity, invests in long-lived assets. Such long-lived assets include both those that are physical assets—property, plant, and equipment—and those that are not physical, such as patents. Long-lived assets are particularly important for manufacturers because these assets allow them to produce goods and/or provide services. Too much investment in long-lived assets may result in costly overcapacity, and too little investment means lost opportunities for profits and future cash flows. Both situations lower the company's rate of return. To properly assess an enterprise's potential for future cash flows, users need:

1. a solid understanding of the enterprise's investment in long-term productive assets,

2. information regarding the extent to which this investment has changed in the period, and

3. an assessment of the accounting policies applied to these assets.

Strategy & Governance 2.3.3 It is not just companies, however, that need to focus on investment in long-lived assets. Local and municipal governments often have a significant stock of long-lived assets. These can include buildings, roads, public transit vehicles, fleets of trucks and other vehicles used for servicing parks and open spaces, and water and sewage infrastructure. The Public Sector Accounting Board of the Chartered Professional Accountants of Canada (CPA Canada) has provided some guidance for municipalities and local governments as they struggle to maintain and revitalize their long-lived assets. They draw on the accounting requirements set out in the CPA Canada *Public Sector Accounting Handbook* and research reports on infrastructure in the public sector.[1] The federal government's Infrastructure Canada is helping to develop a long-term infrastructure plan for the federal government, provinces, territories, and municipalities.[2] The plan includes an investment of over $180 billion over 12 years in five main infrastructure priorities: public transit, green, social, trade and transportation, and rural and northern communities infrastructure. While in this chapter, and the next two, we concentrate on accounting for long-lived assets by companies and the requirements of IFRS and ASPE, keep in mind that many of the issues faced by businesses also need to be considered by governments as they renew infrastructure over the next decade and beyond.

Property, Plant, and Equipment—Characteristics

Property, plant, and equipment (PP&E) include long-term resources such as office, factory, and warehouse buildings; investment property; equipment (machinery, furniture, and tools); and mineral resource properties. PP&E is also commonly referred to as **tangible capital assets**, **plant assets**, or **fixed assets**.

---

[1]For details, see "Guide to Accounting for and Reporting Tangible Capital Assets: Guidance for Local Governments and Local Government Entities that Apply the Public Sector Handbook" (available online at www.frascanada.ca/standards-for-public-sector-entities/resources/reference-materials/item14603.pdf).

[2]See www.infrastructure.gc.ca/plan/plan-eng.html for details.

Consistent with the terminology in IFRS, the term "depreciation" is used in this and other chapters to refer specifically to the amortization of property, plant, and equipment. We use "depletion" for the amortization of mineral resource properties, and "amortization" for intangibles. In addition, the term **amortization** may be used in a general sense to refer to the allocation of the cost of any long-lived asset to different accounting periods.

Types of Assets Classified as Property, Plant and Equipment

Let's begin by defining the types of assets discussed in this chapter. Property, plant, and equipment are defined both in IAS 16 *Property, Plant, and Equipment* and in the standards that apply to private enterprises, *CPA Canada Handbook*, Part II, Section 3061, as assets that have the following characteristics:

1. **They are held for use in the production of goods and services, for rental to others, or for administrative purposes.** They are not intended for sale in the ordinary course of business.
2. **They are used over more than one accounting period** and are usually depreciated. Property, plant, and equipment provide services over many years. Through periodic depreciation charges, the cost of the investment in these assets, with the usual exception of land, is assigned to the periods that benefit from using them.
3. **They are tangible.** These assets have a physical existence or substance, which makes them different from goodwill and intangible assets such as patents.

At times there is a fine line between what is categorized as a capital asset and what is categorized as a supply inventory. Assume, for example, that a company has a substantial fleet of trucks (capital assets) and a variety of assets related to the trucks: spare tires, major motor parts, oil and grease, and truck cleaning equipment. What type of asset is each of these? The general approach is to include any items that have multiple uses and are regularly used and replaced within the accounting period as **inventory**. Major spare parts and standby or servicing equipment used only with a specific capital asset and useful for more than one period are classified as items of **property, plant, and equipment**.

IFRS **ASPE** What about agricultural assets, such as trees in an apple orchard, grapevines in a vineyard, or livestock held to produce milk, wool, or additional livestock? These biological assets—living plants and animals—have many of the characteristics necessary to be items of PP&E. Entities with such assets apply the same accounting principles used for other items of property, plant, and equipment if they report under ASPE. However, companies applying IFRS must follow specific standards for biological assets and agricultural produce that are set out in IAS 41 *Agriculture*, and standards for bearer plants set out in IAS 16. We briefly describe these later in this chapter. We also discussed biological assets in Chapters 6 and 8.

Recognition Principle

Entities incur many costs, but how do they know which ones should be recognized as an item of PP&E? IFRS focuses on the item meeting the definition of an asset, while APSE requires that the following two recognition criteria be satisfied:

1. It is probable that the item's associated future economic benefits will flow to the entity.
2. Its cost can be measured reliably (see *CPA Canada Handbook*, Section 1000.39).

If both are met, the item is capitalized (included in the asset's cost) and recognized as a PP&E asset. See Underlying Concept 10.1. Some costs, such as those for government-imposed pollution reduction equipment, may not appear to generate any net future cash inflows (future economic benefits), but are still recognized as property, plant, and equipment. This is because these expenditures are necessary to obtain the economic benefits from the related assets.

If costs are incurred but these recognition criteria are **not met**, the costs are recognized as an expense, such as when repair and ongoing maintenance expenditures are made.

While the recognition principle is clear, the standards do not specify what level of asset should be recognized. This is referred to as a unit of measure (or unit of account) issue. For

> **Underlying Concept 10.1**
>
> This recognition principle applies to costs incurred when an asset is first acquired and later when incurring costs to upgrade, replace, or service the asset.

example, if you buy or construct a building, what items should be recognized? Should it be one asset—"building"—or should each component be recognized as a separate asset, such as the foundation and frame, roof, windows, and elevators? Alternatively, can a number of smaller items, such as individual tools, be aggregated and recognized as a single asset?

The degree of **componentization** is left up to professional judgement. A primary consideration is the **significance of the individual parts** to the "whole" asset. On a cost-benefit basis, an entity would only separate out components that make up a relatively significant portion of the asset's total cost. As we will explain in the depreciation discussion in Chapter 11, other factors include whether items have **differing useful lives** and/or **different patterns of delivering economic benefits** to the company, making alternative depreciation methods appropriate. The significance of the items and the similarity of their life and use are also considerations in deciding whether to aggregate smaller items into a single larger asset component. While both IFRS and ASPE speak to the need to recognize components, the discussion and application under IFRS are more fully developed.

Once an item of property, plant, and equipment meets the definition and recognition criteria, it is recognized at its cost. This raises two issues that need to be addressed:

1. What elements of cost are capitalized?
2. How is cost measured?

We answer these questions in the next two sections.

Cost Elements

LEARNING OBJECTIVE 2
Identify the costs to include in the measurement of property, plant, and equipment at acquisition.

In general, the cost of an item of property, plant, and equipment includes all expenditures needed to **acquire** the asset and bring it to its **location** and **ready it for use**. Once the item reaches this stage, no further costs are included in the asset's acquisition cost, and capitalization stops. More specifically, costs capitalized include the following:

- The item's purchase price net of trade discounts and rebates, plus any non-refundable purchase taxes (such as many provincial sales taxes) and duties.
- The expenditures needed to bring the asset to its required location and condition to operate as management intended. These include directly attributable employee costs needed to acquire or construct the asset (such as salaries, wages, and benefits); delivery and handling costs; site preparation, installation, and assembly costs; net material and labour costs incurred to ensure it is working properly; and professional fees.
- An estimate of the costs of obligations associated with the asset's eventual disposal. For example, the estimated decommissioning and site restoration costs for the asset.

Costs that are not capitalized as part of the PP&E asset include initial operating losses, the costs of training employees to use the asset, and costs associated with a reorganization of operations. Also excluded are administration and general overhead costs and the costs of opening a new facility, introducing a new product or service, and operating in a new location.

Although this general principle is the same under both IFRS and ASPE, it is applied somewhat differently under each and this may result in different outcomes. Consider a situation where a company, after clearing land and while waiting for construction to be completed, either incurs net costs or generates net income from using the property as a parking lot. Should these net costs or revenue be added to or deducted from the cost of the building, or should they be recognized immediately in net income? The answer depends on whether the company follows IFRS or ASPE, as shown in **Illustration 10.1**.

ILLUSTRATION 10.1

Accounting for Temporary Use of Land during Construction

IFRS	ASPE
Capitalization of costs stops when the asset is in place and ready to be used as management intended, even if it has not begun to be used or is used at less than a desirable capacity level.	Capitalization of costs stops when an asset is substantially complete and ready for productive use. This is normally determined in advance by management in relation to factors such as the passage of time, reaching a given level of productive capacity, occupancy level, or industry-specific considerations.
The principle of being a necessary cost to acquire and get in place, and to be ready for use, is strictly applied. The temporary use of land as a parking lot and its net cost or revenue is not necessary to develop the asset being constructed; therefore, it cannot be included in the asset cost. The net cost or net revenue is recognized in income when incurred or earned.	Any net revenue or expenses generated prior to substantial completion and readiness for use are included in determining the asset's cost. Therefore, the net parking lot cost or net revenue while the asset is being readied for use would be debited or credited to the asset account.
If the rent from parking lot spaces in the basement of the building was $1,000 while the rest of the building was being finished, the following journal entry would be recorded:	If the rent from parking lot spaces in the basement of the building was $1,000 while the rest of the building was being finished, the following journal entry would be recorded:

Cash	1,000			Cash	1,000	
Rent Revenue		1,000		Building		1,000

Three specific cost issues are more fully discussed in this chapter. They are (1) costs incurred when assets are constructed internally rather than purchased outright, (2) associated borrowing costs, and (3) site restoration or asset retirement costs.

Self-Constructed Assets

Often, companies construct their own assets. Even after deciding what components will be separately recognized, determining the cost of self-constructed assets such as machinery or buildings can be a challenge. See Underlying Concept 10.2. Without a firm purchase or contract price, the company has to review numerous expenditures that were incurred to arrive at its cost.

The costs of materials and direct labour used in construction are not difficult to identify and measure; they can be traced directly to actual work orders and materials used in the constructed assets. However, allocating the indirect costs of manufacturing may create special problems. These indirect costs, called **overhead** or **burden**, include power, heat, light, insurance, property taxes on factory buildings and equipment, factory supervisory labour, depreciation of fixed assets, and supplies. Which of the following accounting choices is appropriate?

1. Assign a portion of all overhead to the construction project.
2. Assign no fixed overhead to the cost of the constructed asset.

Although the standards for manufactured inventories (see Chapter 8) require that a portion of all production overhead costs be applied to an inventory asset, the principle for PP&E assets is different. For these assets, only **directly attributable costs**—costs directly related

> **Underlying Concept 10.2**
>
> A company determines the cost of a self-constructed asset by applying the same general principles as for an acquired asset.

to the specific activities involved in the construction process—are capitalized. Therefore, no fixed overhead is usually charged to the PP&E asset account.[3] Whether or not the entity also makes similar assets for resale or uniquely for its own purposes, care has to be taken to ensure that no abnormal amounts of wasted inputs and related excess costs are experienced. If so, these are expensed in the period.

Borrowing Costs

Entities often acquire or construct capital assets that take substantial time to get ready for their intended use. To finance any interim expenditures that have to be made, a company may have to increase its bank loans, otherwise borrow money, or use existing company funds that could be used for other purposes. Do the financing or borrowing costs that are incurred for this purpose meet the criteria to be capitalized as part of the asset's cost, or should they be expensed in the period incurred?

IFRS **ASPE** Not surprisingly, IAS 23 *Borrowing Costs* requires capitalization of costs that would otherwise be **avoidable:** borrowing costs that are directly attributable to the cost of acquiring, constructing, or producing qualifying assets that take a substantial period of time to get ready for use, such as manufacturing plants. These costs are therefore added to the cost of the PP&E asset. See **Underlying Concept 10.3.** ASPE permits management to choose between a policy of capitalizing interest and expensing interest costs.

Appendix 10A explains how **borrowing costs** are defined, how to determine which are **avoidable**, and how to determine the **amount to capitalize**. **What Do the Numbers Mean? 10.1** provides an example of the impact of capitalizing interest by a large Canadian electricity provider.

> **Underlying Concept 10.3**
>
> The accounting treatment for borrowing costs under IFRS is consistent with the general asset recognition principle.

What Do the Numbers Mean? 10.1

Until Canadian publicly accountable entities adopted IFRS in 2011, they had a choice of whether to capitalize interest for qualifying assets or to report all interest as an expense in the income statement as incurred. Interest capitalization can have a substantial effect on the financial statements. For example, **TransAlta Corporation** capitalized $9.0 million of interest to property, plant, and equipment in 2017 under IFRS (and $16.0 million in 2016). Because it previously capitalized interest under prior Canadian GAAP, it did not have to change this accounting policy when it adopted IFRS. But what if TransAlta had expensed all interest? Earnings per share would have been $0.35 in 2016 if TransAlta had expensed its interest as allowed under prior Canadian GAAP, instead of $0.41 per share (a decrease of $0.06 per share). Similarly Transalta's loss per share in 2017 would have increased.*

How can statement users determine the effect of interest capitalization on a company's bottom line? The amount of interest capitalized in the period has to be disclosed in the notes to the financial statements. For example, **Imperial Metals Corporation**, a British Columbia exploration, development, and mining company, reported $24.4 million of capitalized interest in 2015. The following year no interest was capitalized, and interest expense increased from $27.7 million to $70.2 million in 2016. Capitalized interest can have a huge effect on the bottom line for a company like Imperial Metals, as its net loss of $54.1 million in 2016 would have been cut in half* if it had capitalized the same amount in 2016 as the prior year!

*These calculations are just for illustrative purposes. For example, the comparisons ignore the impact of depreciation of previously capitalized interest costs on EPS.

Regardless, the policy chosen and amount capitalized must be disclosed. In 2017, **Canadian Utilities Limited** (a large diversified company that is engaged in electricity, pipelines and liquids, retail energy, and logistics) capitalized $17.0 million of its interest costs under IFRS (versus $18.0 million in 2016 and $97.0 million in 2015; see **Illustration 10.2**).

---

[3]If a company is involved in a significant amount of self-construction activity, some of its fixed overhead costs may be considered "directly attributable."

NOTES TO CONSOLIDATED FINANCIAL STATEMENTS

7. INTEREST EXPENSE

(Tabular amounts in millions of Canadian Dollars, except as otherwise noted).

Interest expense primarily arises from interest on long-term debentures. The components of interest expense are summarized below.

	2017	2016
Long-term debt	**396**	384
Non-recourse long-term debt	**21**	8
Retirement benefits net interest expense	**5**	5
Amortization of deferred financing charges	**3**	3
Accretion of asset retirement obligations	**2**	4
Short-term debt	**11**	4
Other	**10**	5
	448	413
Less: interest capitalized *(Note 12)*	**(17)**	(18)
	431	395

Borrowing costs capitalized to property, plant and equipment during 2017 were calculated by applying a weighted average interest rate of 4.82 per cent to expenditures on qualifying assets (2016 - 4.89 per cent).

ILLUSTRATION 10.2

Excerpt from Canadian Utilities Limited Annual Report 2017

Dismantling and Restoration Costs

In some industries, when a company acquires and uses its long-lived assets, it takes on obligations that need to be met when the assets are eventually retired. For example, a nuclear facility must be decommissioned at the end of its useful life, mine sites must be closed and dismantled and the property restored, and landfill sites have significant closure and post-closure costs associated with the end of their operations.

In order to be able to use the long-lived asset, companies typically assume responsibility for the costs associated with dismantling the item, removing it, and restoring the site at the end of its useful life. These asset retirement costs meet the recognition criteria for capitalization and are added to the PP&E asset cost.

Once again, while this general principle underlies both IFRS and ASPE, it is applied differently under each, as shown in Illustration 10.3. The differences relate to the types of obligations and activities undertaken.

ILLUSTRATION 10.3

Law **Asset Retirement Costs: IFRS versus ASPE**

	IFRS	ASPE
Category of obligations	Recognizes costs of both legal and constructive obligations, such as when an entity creates an expectation in others through its own actions that it will meet this obligation.	Recognizes costs associated with legal obligations only.
Category of activities	Costs include only those related to the acquisition of the asset, not those related to the use of the asset in the production of goods or services (product costs).	Costs include both retirement obligations resulting from the acquisition of the asset and its subsequent use in producing inventory, such as the mining of coal.

Under both IFRS and ASPE, the original cost estimates and any changes in them are capitalized in the asset account and a credit is made to an asset retirement or restoration liability. Because the actual expenditures will often not be incurred for a number of years, the obligation provision and the asset are both measured using the present value of the future costs. There is a fuller discussion of provisions and liability recognition and measurement issues in Chapters 2 and 13. For now, you should be aware that the cost of property, plant, and equipment in the mining and oil and gas industries will often include such a charge when the asset is acquired.

Measurement of Cost for Nonmonetary Exchange

LEARNING OBJECTIVE 3

Determine asset cost when the transaction has delayed payment terms or is a lump-sum purchase, a nonmonetary exchange, or a contributed asset.

Now that you have a better idea of what is included in "cost," the second step is to determine how it is measured. In general, **cost** is measured by the amount of cash or cash equivalents paid or the fair value of the other consideration given to acquire an asset.[4]

Cost is the **cash cost** when an asset is recognized. This amount may not always be obvious. This section discusses how several common issues are resolved when cash is not exchanged at the date of acquisition:

1. Cash discounts not taken
2. Deferred payment terms
3. Lump-sum purchases
4. Nonmonetary exchanges—share-based payments
5. Nonmonetary exchanges—asset exchanges
6. Contributed assets and government grants

Cash Discounts Not Taken

When cash discounts for prompt payment are offered on purchases of plant assets, how should the discount be handled? If the discount is taken, it is definitely a reduction in the asset's purchase price. It is not recognized in a purchase discount account (see Chapter 8), because purchase discounts relate only to inventory purchases that are included in the cost of goods sold. What is not clear, however, is whether the asset's cost should be reduced even if the discount is not taken. There are two points of view on this matter.

Under one approach, the net-of-discount amount is considered the asset's cost, **regardless of whether the discount is taken or not**. The rationale for this view is that an asset's cost is its cash or cash equivalent price. The discount, if it is lost, is the cost of not paying at an earlier date and should be recognized according to its nature as a Finance Expense. Supporters of the **other approach** argue that the discount should not always be deducted from the asset's cost, because the terms may be unfavourable or because it might not be prudent for the company to take the discount. Recognition of the asset at its lower "cash cost" is preferred, at least on conceptual grounds. However, most companies prefer the simpler approach, and do not deduct discounts unless they are taken.

---

[4]Sometimes a standard will specify that another amount will be the asset's **deemed cost**. The deemed cost is the amount recognized under the specific requirements of a particular standard, such as IFRS 1 *First Time Adoption of International Financial Reporting Standards*, where fair value can be used in the opening statement of financial position when a company first adopts IFRS (IFRS 1.30). Copyright © IFRS Foundation. All rights reserved. Reproduced with permission.

Deferred Payment Terms

Plant assets are often purchased on long-term credit arrangements through the use of notes, mortgages, bonds, or equipment obligations. The cost of an asset whose payment is deferred beyond normal credit terms is its **cash price equivalent**. Any difference between this fair value and the total payments made is recognized as **interest**. That is, the asset's cost is the **present value of the consideration** that is exchanged at the transaction date. See Underlying Concept 10.4.

For example, equipment purchased today in exchange for a $10,000, non–interest-bearing note that is payable four years from now is not recorded at $10,000 because waiting four years without charging interest before payment far exceeds normal credit terms. Assuming the cash price is not known, the **present value of the note is the transaction's exchange price** and the asset's "cash cost." If 8% is an appropriate interest rate, the equipment is recognized at a cost of $7,350.30 [$10,000 × 0.73503; see Table A.2 for the present value of a single sum, $PV = \$10,000\ (PV_{4,8\%})$].

When no interest rate is stated, or if the specified rate is unreasonable, an appropriate interest rate is imputed. The objective is to approximate the interest rate that the buyer and seller would negotiate in a similar arm's-length borrowing transaction. Factors to consider in determining an appropriate interest rate are the borrower's credit rating, the note's amount and maturity date, and prevailing interest rates. If the acquired asset's cash exchange price can be determined, it is used as the basis for measuring the asset's cost and identifying the interest element, as shown in Example 10.1.

> **Underlying Concept 10.4**
>
> Use of present value is consistent with the IAS 16 definition of cost, which includes the fair value of other consideration given to acquire an asset at the time of its acquisition or construction.

Example 10.1 | Purchase of Equipment Using a Non–Interest-Bearing Note

Facts   Sutter Corporation purchases a specially built robot spray painter for its production line. The company issues a $100,000, five-year, non–interest-bearing note to Wrigley Robotics Ltd. for the new equipment when the prevailing market interest rate for obligations of this nature is 10%. Sutter is to pay off the note in five $20,000 instalments made at the end of each year. Assume that the fair value of this specially built robot cannot readily be determined. Therefore, it has to be approximated by establishing the note's fair value (the present value of an ordinary annuity [PVOA]).

Instructions   At what amount should Sutter record the equipment purchased? Provide the calculation and the journal entries at the purchase and payment dates.

Solution

At date of purchase		
Equipment	75,816	
Notes Payable		75,816

Present value of note $= \$20,000\ (PVOA_{5,\ 10\%})$
$= \$20,000\ (3.79079)$ (Table A.4)
$= \$75,816$

The $24,184 difference between the asset's cash cost of $75,816 and the $100,000 cash that is eventually payable ($20,000 × 5) is the discount or interest on the $75,816 amount borrowed.

At end of first year		
Interest Expense	7,582	
Notes Payable		7,582
Notes Payable	20,000	
Cash		20,000

Interest expense for the first year under the effective interest method (as required by IFRS and allowed by ASPE) is $7,582 [($75,816) × 10%]. The entries at the end of the second year to record interest and to pay off a portion of the note are as follows:

At end of second year		
Interest Expense	6,340	
Notes Payable		6,340
Notes Payable	20,000	
Cash		20,000

A	=	L	+	SE
+75,816		+75,816		

Cash flows: No effect

A	=	L	+	SE
		+7,582		−7,582

Cash flows: No effect

A	=	L	+	SE
−20,000		−20,000		

Cash flows: ↓ 20,000 outflow

A	=	L	+	SE
		+6,340		−6,340

Cash flows: No effect

A	=	L	+	SE
−20,000		−20,000		

Cash flows: ↓ 20,000 outflow

> Interest expense in the second year is calculated by applying the 10% interest rate to the net book value of the outstanding Notes Payable. At the end of the first year, the Notes Payable account was reduced to $63,398 ($75,816 + $7,582 − $20,000) and this was the note's carrying amount throughout the second year. The second year's interest expense is $63,398 × 10%, or $6,340.

If interest is not taken into account in such deferred payment contracts, the asset would be recorded at an amount that is higher than its fair value. In addition, no interest expense would be reported in any of the periods involved.

Lump-Sum Purchases

Underlying Concept 10.5

Allocating total cost among the various assets based on relative fair values for property, plant and equipment is the same approach that is applied to a basket purchase of inventory.

There is a special problem in determining the cost of specific capital assets when they are purchased together for a single **lump-sum price**. When this occurs, and it is not at all unusual, the practice is to allocate the total cost among the various assets based on their relative fair values. The assumption is that costs will vary in direct proportion to those values. See **Underlying Concept 10.5**.

To determine the individual fair value of the parts making up the total purchase, any of the following might be used: an appraisal for insurance purposes, the assessed valuation for property taxes, estimates of replacement costs, or simply an independent appraisal by an engineer or other appraiser. Which approach is most appropriate will depend on the information available in the specific situation. When a property is acquired consisting of a building and the land it sits on, the relative property tax value of each is often used. Estimates of replacement cost or independent appraisal might be used to determine the relative values of the components making up the building acquired.

Example 10.2 shows how estimates and appraisals might be used to arrive at values of the components of the acquired building.

Example 10.2 | Allocation of Purchase Price Based on Relative Fair Values

Facts Assume that a company decides to purchase several assets of a smaller company in the same business for a total price of $80,000. The assets purchased are as follows:

	Seller's Book Value	Asset Fair Value
Inventory	$30,000	$ 25,000
Land	20,000	25,000
Building	35,000	50,000
	$85,000	$100,000

Instructions

a. Provide a calculation to allocate the $80,000 purchase price based on the relative fair values.

b. Discuss the impact of carrying amounts of the assets on your calculation.

Solution

a.

	Asset Cost
Inventory	$\dfrac{\$25,000}{\$100,000} \times \$80,000 = \$20,000$
Land	$\dfrac{\$25,000}{\$100,000} \times \$80,000 = \$20,000$
Building	$\dfrac{\$50,000}{\$100,000} \times \$80,000 = \$40,000$
	$80,000

b. The assets' carrying amounts on the seller's books are not representative of their fair values. **They are irrelevant and do not affect the calculation.** Depending on the situation and the company's accounting policies, the $40,000 cost allocated to the building may have to be further broken down and allocated to more specific components of the building, such as the basic structure, the roof, and the windows. If so, once the relative fair value of each is determined, the process of allocation is carried out using the same approach that is explained above.

Nonmonetary Exchanges

Share-Based Payments

When property, plant, and equipment assets are acquired and the company issues its own shares in payment, the cost of the asset is based on either the fair value of the shares given up or the fair value of the assets acquired. But which should be used?

IFRS **ASPE** IFRS 2 *Share-based Payment* indicates that the fair value of the asset acquired should be used to measure its acquisition cost, and it presumes that this value can be determined except in rare cases.[5] If the asset's fair value cannot be determined reliably, then its fair value and cost are determined by using the fair value of the shares given in exchange. If the company shares are widely traded, their fair value should be a good indication of the current cash-equivalent price of the PP&E asset acquired.[6] ASPE is more flexible, indicating only that the more reliable of the fair value of the goods received or the equity instruments given up is the asset cost. Because private company shares are not widely traded, the acquired asset's fair value is more likely to be used for share-based payments from private companies. **Example 10.3** would apply to companies following either IFRS or ASPE that use shares to pay for a land purchase.

Example 10.3 | Share-Based Purchase of Property, Plant, and Equipment

Facts   Assume that a hardware company decides to purchase land next to its current property in order to expand its carpeting and cabinet operation. Instead of paying cash for the land, it issues 5,000 no par value common shares to the seller.

Instructions

a. Assuming that a recent appraisal valued the land at $62,000, and that the hardware company's shares are not publicly traded, what journal entry would be made?

b. If no fair value can be reliably determined for the land, and the company's shares have been recently traded with a fair value of $12 per share, how would your solution to part (a) change?

Solution

a. Land   62,000
          Common Shares   62,000

b. If we assume instead that no fair value can be reliably determined for the land, and the company's shares have been recently traded with a fair value of $12 per share, the land is assigned a cost equal to the estimated fair value of the shares, or 5,000 × $12 = $60,000.

A	=	L	+	SE
+62,000				+62,000

Cash flows: No effect

---

[5]IFRS 2 *Share-based Payment* is considerably more complex than is illustrated here. The recognition and measurement guidance depends on what is being acquired as well as whether the payment is in shares directly or in cash with the amount based on the share price, or whether there is a choice of cash-based settlement or settlement in shares.

[6]Keep in mind that IFRS 2 *Share-based Payment* "uses the term 'fair value' in a way that differs in some respects from the definition of fair value in IFRS 13 Fair Value Measurement. Therefore, when applying IFRS 2, an entity measures fair value in accordance with IFRS 2, not IFRS 13" (see IFRS 2.6A). Copyright © IFRS Foundation. All rights reserved. Reproduced with permission.

Underlying Concept 10.6

The FASB recommends that a nonmonetary exchange be considered monetary if 25% or more of the fair value of the consideration is monetary. There is no such threshold under ASPE or IFRS, so the transaction's economic substance has to be assessed.

Asset Exchanges

When nonmonetary assets such as property, plant, and equipment are acquired for cash or other monetary assets, the cost of the acquired asset is measured by the fair value (present value) of the cash or other monetary assets that are given up. As discussed in Chapter 5, monetary assets are money or claims to future cash receipts that are fixed or determinable in amount and timing. Cash and accounts receivable are the most common types of monetary assets. Nonmonetary assets, on the other hand, are assets that are not claims to fixed or determinable cash flows. Examples include inventory, long-lived plant assets, and equity investments in other companies. See Underlying Concept 10.6.

When nonmonetary assets such as property, plant, and equipment **are disposed of and the company receives monetary assets in exchange**, a gain or loss on disposal is recognized in income. The gain is recognized in income because it is realized—that is, it has been converted to cash or a claim to cash—and the entity's economic situation has clearly changed in terms of its future cash flows.

However, when an existing **nonmonetary asset is exchanged for a new nonmonetary asset, such as an item of property, plant, and equipment**, the proper accounting is not necessarily obvious. There are two underlying issues:

1. What should be the cost of the nonmonetary asset acquired?
2. Should a gain or loss on disposal be recognized on the nonmonetary asset that was given up?

Some argue that the new asset's cost should be determined by its **fair value**, or by the fair value of the assets given up, and that a **gain or loss should be recognized** on the disposal of the old asset. Others believe that the cost of the new asset should be determined by the **carrying amount** of the assets given up, with **no gain or loss recognized**. Still others favour an approach that would **recognize losses** in all cases, but **defer gains** in special situations.

General Principle—The Fair Value Standard

International and Canadian standard setters have been in agreement for a number of years on the preferred answer to these choices. The general principle is that **nonmonetary transactions are accounted for on the same basis as monetary transactions**. Therefore, the cost of the PP&E asset acquired—by giving up a nonmonetary asset or a combination of monetary and nonmonetary assets—is determined by the fair value of the assets given up unless the fair value of the asset received can be more reliably measured (IAS 16.26). Any gains or losses that result are recognized in income.

Why is the accounting like this? Although cash or a claim to cash is not received or is relatively minor in nonmonetary exchanges, the earnings process related to the "old" asset is usually substantially complete. The specific values to the entity of the assets that are received generally are different from those of the assets that are given up. That is, the company's economic circumstances change as a result of the exchange.

The general standard that **nonmonetary exchanges are measured at fair value** is applied, therefore, **unless one of the following conditions is true**:

1. The transaction lacks commercial substance.
2. Fair values are not reliably measurable. See Underlying Concept 10.7.

In these situations, as explained below, the exchange is recorded **at the carrying amount of the asset(s) given up, which is adjusted for the inclusion of any cash or other monetary assets.**

1. **Commercial substance.** When following the general standard, the entity:
   - derecognizes (removes from the accounts) the carrying value of the asset(s) given up,
   - recognizes the fair value of the asset(s) received in exchange, and then
   - reports the difference as a gain (or loss) in net income.

Because the company's underlying economic situation has changed as a result of the transaction—in other words, the transaction has commercial or economic substance—

Underlying Concept 10.7

Under ASPE, another condition is an exchange of products or property to be sold in the same line of business to facilitate sales, but this could also be seen as an example of a transaction that lacks commercial substance.

income is permitted to be reported. However, if the company is in the same economic position after the exchange as it was before, then no gain or loss would be reported. This is because there is little or no justification for reporting increased asset values or income.[7]

What does **commercial substance** really mean? Simply, it means that there is a **significant change** in the company's expected future cash flows and therefore its value. The exchange transaction has commercial substance if the:

- amount, timing, or risk of future cash flows associated with the asset(s) received is different from the configuration of cash flows for the asset(s) given up, or
- entity-specific value of the asset received differs significantly from the entity-specific value of the asset given up. For example, a company may benefit from significant cost savings from economies of scale made possible by acquiring and using the asset.

In either case, the change must be **significant relative to the fair values of the exchanged assets**. This often requires using professional judgement.

2. **Ethics** **Ability to measure fair values.** As might be expected, the exchange cannot be recorded at fair value if the fair value of neither the asset given up nor the asset received can be reliably measured. Also, this exception helps reduce the risk that entities can assign arbitrarily high values to assets exchanged as a way of engineering and reporting gains.

In an exchange lacking commercial substance, the cost of the new asset is based on the carrying amount of the asset(s) given up. **An overriding caution:** When an asset is acquired, **it cannot be recognized at more than its fair value**. If the carrying amount of the asset(s) given up in the exchange is more than the fair value of the asset(s) received, the new asset has to be recorded at the lower amount (the fair value of the asset received) and a loss would be recognized.

Accounting for asset exchanges is summarized in **Illustration 10.4**. We follow this with **Examples 10.4, 10.5**, and **10.6** to illustrate the appropriate entries.

ILLUSTRATION 10.4

Accounting for Asset Exchanges

Does the exchange meet both criteria? In other words, does it have commercial substance, and can fair values can be reliably determined?	
Yes	No
Apply the fair value standard:	Exception to the fair value standard:
Cost of asset(s) received = fair value of what is given up, or what is acquired, if more reliably measurable.	Cost of asset(s) received = carrying amount of asset(s) given up.
Difference between carrying amount and fair value of asset(s) given up is recognized in income as a gain or loss.	No gain is recognized. Loss is recognized if fair value of asset(s) acquired is less than the carrying amount of the asset(s) given up.

When assets are exchanged or traded in, the transaction often requires a payment or receipt of cash or some other monetary asset. When the transaction's monetary component— or **boot**, as it is sometimes called—is significant, there is less need to question whether the transaction has commercial substance. As the percentage gets smaller, the transaction becomes primarily a nonmonetary exchange and the need to evaluate whether or not the transaction has commercial substance increases.

Note that the amount agreed on as a **trade-in allowance is not necessarily the used asset's fair value**. In many cases, such as with automobiles, the trade-in allowance is essentially used to change the new asset's selling price without reducing its list price.

---

[7]For example, if a company exchanges inventory held for sale for other similar merchandise for sale in order to facilitate a sale, it would be difficult to justify the claim that the company's economic position has changed significantly. (See *CPA Canada Handbook*, Part II, Section 3831.06 and 3831.11 and IAS 16.25.) There is an exception that we discuss after Example 10.6, which requires a loss to be reported if the fair value of the asset acquired is less than the cost assigned to it.

Example 10.4 | Nonmonetary Exchange of Machines—Commercial Substance

Facts Information Processing Inc. (IPI) trades in its used machine for a new model. The machine given up has a book value of $8,000 (original cost of $12,000 less $4,000 accumulated depreciation) and a fair value of $6,000. It is traded for a new model that has a list price of $16,000. In negotiations with the seller, a trade-in allowance of $9,000 is finally agreed on for the used machine.

Instructions

    a. Discuss whether this exchange has commercial substance, and why.

    b. Calculate the cash payment that is needed for the exchange and the cost of the new machine to be recorded by IPI, and provide the related journal entry to be recorded by IPI.

Solution

    a. Because the cash paid is significant relative to the fair value of the total consideration, the change in the configuration of the company's future cash flows justifies a conclusion that this transaction has commercial substance.

    b. Calculation of cost of new machine:

Fair value of assets given up	
Amount of cash given up =	
list price less trade-in allowance	$16,000 – $9,000 = $ 7,000
Fair value of machine given up	6,000
Cost of new machine = fair value of assets given up	$13,000

The journal entry to record this transaction is:

Machinery (new)	13,000	
Accumulated Depreciation—Machinery (old)	4,000	
Loss on Disposal of Machinery	2,000	
Machinery (old)		12,000
Cash		7,000

The loss on the disposal of the used machine is verified below.

Calculation of loss on disposal of used machine:

Fair value of used machine	$6,000
Carrying amount of used machine	8,000
Loss on disposal of used machine	$2,000

A	=	L	+	SE
−2,000				−2,000

Cash flows: ▼ 7,000 outflow

Example 10.5 | Nonmonetary Exchange of Trucks for Land—Commercial Substance

Facts Cathay Corporation exchanges several used trucks plus cash for vacant land that might be used for a future plant site. The trucks have a combined carrying amount of $42,000 (cost of $64,000 less $22,000 of accumulated depreciation). Cathay's purchasing agent, who has had previous dealings in the second-hand market, indicates that the trucks have a fair value of $49,000. In addition to the trucks, Cathay pays $4,000 cash for the land.

Instructions

    a. Discuss whether this exchange has commercial substance, and why.

    b. Calculate the acquisition cost of the land to be recorded by Cathay, and provide the related journal entry to be recorded by Cathay.

    c. Discuss how your answer would change if the trucks' fair value was $39,000, instead of $49,000.

Solution

    a. This exchange has commercial substance because the pattern and timing of cash flows from the investment in land are very different from those of the trucks. In addition, fair values can be determined.

    b. Assuming that the land's fair value is not known, or its fair value is not as reliable as that of the trucks, the acquisition cost of the land is calculated as follows:

Calculation of land's acquisition cost:

Cost of land = fair value of assets given up:

Fair value of trucks exchanged	$49,000
Fair value of cash given up	4,000
Acquisition cost of the land	$53,000

The journal entry to record the exchange is:

Land	53,000	
Accumulated Depreciation—Vehicles	22,000	
Vehicles		64,000
Cash		4,000
Gain on Disposal of Vehicles		7,000

A	=	L	+	SE
+7,000				+7,000

Cash flows: ▼ 4,000 outflow

The gain is the difference between the trucks' fair value of $49,000 and their carrying amount of $42,000.

c. If the trucks' fair value was $39,000 instead of $49,000, the land's cost would be $43,000 ($39,000 + $4,000) and a loss on the exchange of $3,000 ($42,000 − $39,000) would be reported.

Example 10.6 | Nonmonetary Exchange of Commercial Properties—No Commercial Substance

Facts   Westco Limited owns a number of rental properties in Western Canada as well as a single property in Ontario. Management has decided to concentrate its business in the west and to dispose of its one property outside this area. Westco agrees to exchange its Ontario property for a similar commercial property outside Lethbridge, Alberta, owned by Eastco Limited, a company with most of its properties east of Manitoba. The two properties are almost identical in size, rentals, and operating costs. Eastco agrees to the exchange but requires a cash payment of $30,000 from Westco to equalize and complete the transaction. Further information about these two properties is provided below:

	Westco Ltd. Property	Eastco Ltd. Property
Carrying amounts:		
Building	$520,000	$540,000
Accumulated depreciation	100,000	145,000
	$420,000	$395,000
Fair value	$615,000	$645,000
Cash paid	$ 30,000	
Cash received		$ 30,000

Instructions   Assume an evaluation by both Westco and Eastco management shows that there is an insignificant difference in the configuration of future cash flows and that commercial substance is not indicated. What entry would be made by each company to record this asset exchange?

Solution   Fair values are not recorded in this situation and the cost of the assets acquired by each company is recognized at the carrying amount of the assets given up by each. Because the companies are recognizing amounts equal to the book value of what is given up, no gain or loss is recorded by either.

Westco Ltd. Entry		
Building (new)	450,000	
Accumulated Depreciation—Building (old)	100,000	
Building (old)		520,000
Cash		30,000

A	=	L	+	SE
0		0		0

Cash flows: ▼ 30,000 outflow

Eastco Ltd. Entry		
Building (new)	365,000	
Accumulated Depreciation (old)	145,000	
Cash	30,000	
Building (old)		540,000

A	=	L	+	SE
0		0		0

Cash flows: ▲ 30,000 inflow

> Westco recognizes its new asset (the Lethbridge building) at the carrying amount of the assets given up. It gave up cash with a book value of $30,000 and a building with a book value of $420,000, for a total of $450,000. Eastco recognizes its new asset at the carrying amount of what it gave up, which is $395,000. Of this, $30,000 was cash received, leaving $365,000 to be recognized as the new building's cost. Because both companies remain in the same economic position after the exchange as before, there is no reason to recognize any change in asset values and a related gain or loss on the exchange.

For exchanges without commercial substance, remember to check whether the fair value of the asset acquired is less than the cost assigned to it. Assets cannot be recognized at more than their fair value, so if the fair value of the asset acquired is less than the cost assigned to it, the asset would have to be recorded at the lower fair value amount and a loss equal to the difference recognized.

Contributed Assets and Government Grants

Companies sometimes receive contributions of assets as donations, gifts, or government grants. Such contributions are called **non-reciprocal transfers** because they are transfers of assets in one direction only—nothing is given in exchange. The grants may be in the form of assets such as land, buildings, or equipment, or cash to acquire such assets, or even the forgiveness of a debt. There are two important accounting issues for non-reciprocal transfers:

1. How should the asset be measured at acquisition?
2. What account should be credited?

When assets are acquired as a donation, a strict cost concept would dictate that the asset's acquisition cost is zero. A departure from the cost principle is justified, however. This is because, if we record only the costs that are incurred (legal fees and other relatively minor expenditures), it would not form a reasonable basis of accounting for the assets received. To record nothing would ignore the economic reality of an increase in the entity's resources. Therefore, accounting standards generally require that **the asset's fair value be used to establish its "cost" on the books**.[8]

Having established that fair value should be used to determine the contributed asset's acquisition cost, a further question remains about the credit entry in the transaction. Is it income, or is it contributed capital? Two general approaches have been used to record the credit in this type of transaction.

The **capital approach** considers donated assets as contributed capital financing and they are therefore accounted for with a credit directly to Contributed Surplus—Donated Capital. This approach is only appropriate, however, for a donation from an owner, and such donations are rare. The **income approach** reflects contributions in **net income** because the contribution is a non-owner source of the change in net assets.[9]

Accounting standards generally take the position that government assistance should be recognized in income, either as revenue or as a reduction of expense. If the contributed assets are expected to be used over several future periods, as in the case of a grant for a building or equipment, then the effect on income is spread out over the future periods that benefit from having received the grant. When assets or funds to acquire assets are received from federal, provincial, territorial, or municipal governments, GAAP requires that recipients defer and

---

[8]IAS 20 *Accounting for Government Grants and Disclosure of Government Assistance* indicates that, while government grants in the form of nonmonetary assets are usually measured at their fair value, an entity may record both the asset and the grant at a nominal amount (see IAS 20.23). Copyright © IFRS Foundation. All rights reserved. Reproduced with permission.

[9]While a credit to Other Comprehensive Income (OCI) may seem like a valid option, accounting standards tend to be prescriptive about what can bypass net income and be recognized directly in OCI. This option is not provided in either IFRS or ASPE for government grants.

recognize the amount received over the periods when the related assets are used. This is accomplished in one of two ways:

1. by reducing the asset cost and therefore future depreciation by the amount of government assistance received (the **cost reduction method**); or
2. by recording the amount of assistance received as a deferred credit and amortizing it to revenue over the life of the related asset (the **deferral method**).

To illustrate the **cost reduction method**, assume that a company receives a grant of $225,000 from the federal government to upgrade its sewage treatment equipment. The entry to record the receipt of the grant under this method is as follows:

Cash	225,000	
Equipment		225,000

A	=	L	+	SE
0				

Cash flows: ↑225,000 inflow

This results in the equipment being carried on the books **at cost less the related government assistance**. Assuming a 10-year life and straight-line depreciation, the annual depreciation expense for the equipment is reduced by $22,500 and net income therefore is higher by this amount each year.

Alternatively, the **deferral method** credits a deferred revenue account with the grant amount. This amount is then recognized in income each year **on the same basis that is used to amortize the underlying asset**. The entries to record the receipt of the grant and its amortization for the first year under the **deferral method** are as follows:

Cash	225,000	
Deferred Revenue—Government Grants		225,000
Deferred Revenue—Government Grants	22,500	
Revenue—Government Grants		22,500

A	=	L	+	SE
+225,000		+225,000		

Cash flows: ↑225,000 inflow

A	=	L	+	SE
0		−22,500		+22,500

Cash flows: No effect

A weakness of the cost reduction method is that it reports assets at less than their fair value to the entity. This issue is resolved if the deferral method is used, but this method also has a weakness. The deferral method is not consistent with the conceptual framework because the Deferred Revenue account does not usually meet the definition of a liability.

Note that a donation **of land** by a government would be deferred and taken into income over future periods if the grant requires the company to fulfill certain obligations or conditions. If the requirement is to build and operate a manufacturing plant on the land over a specific period of time, then the grant is taken into income over the same period. Only when there is no way to associate the grant with future period costs is it taken directly into income when received.

Government grants that are awarded to a company **for incurring certain current expenditures**, such as those related to payroll, are recognized in income in the same period as the related expenses. If grants or donations that have been received have a condition attached to them that requires a future event to occur—such as being required to maintain a specified number of employees on the payroll—the contingency is reported in the notes to the financial statements.

Entities are required to provide extensive disclosure about the amounts, terms and conditions, and accounting treatment they use for government assistance they have received. Readers can then evaluate the effect of such assistance on the entity's financial position and performance.

Measurement of Costs Associated with Specific Assets

LEARNING OBJECTIVE 4
Identify the costs included in specific types of property, plant, and equipment.

This section discusses the measurement of costs for specific types of property, plant, and equipment. See Underlying Concept 10.8.

Underlying Concept 10.8

The acquisition cost of each specific property, plant and equipment asset is determined by applying the recognition and cost principles explained earlier in the chapter.

Land

Land costs typically include (1) the purchase price; (2) closing costs, such as title to the land, legal fees, and recording fees; (3) costs incurred to condition the land for its intended use, such as grading, filling, draining, and clearing; (4) the costs of assuming any liens, such as taxes in arrears or mortgages or encumbrances on the property; and (5) any additional land improvements that have an indefinite life.

When land has been purchased to construct a building, all costs that are incurred up to the excavation for the new building are considered land costs. **Removal of old buildings, clearing, grading, and filling are considered land costs because these costs are necessary to get the land in condition and ready for its intended purpose.** Any proceeds that are obtained in the process of getting the land ready for its intended use—such as amounts received for salvaged materials from the demolition of an old building or the sale of timber that has been cleared—are treated as reductions in the land cost.

Special amounts assessed for local improvements—such as for roads, street lights, and sewers and drainage systems—are usually charged to the Land account because they are relatively permanent and are maintained and replaced by the local government. In addition, it is also proper to charge permanent improvements that are made by the owner, such as landscaping, to the Land account. Improvements with limited lives—such as private driveways, walks, fences, and parking lots—are recorded separately as Land Improvements so they can be amortized over their estimated useful lives.

Generally, land is considered part of property, plant, and equipment. If the major purpose of acquiring and holding land is for capital appreciation or rentals or an undetermined future use, it is classified as investment property, a special category of PP&E we discuss below. If the land is held by a real estate company for resale, or is held by land developers or subdivided, it is classified as inventory.

Buildings

One accounting issue relates to the cost of an old building that is on the site of a planned new building. Is the cost to remove the old building a cost of the land or of the new building? The standards indicate that, if land is purchased with an old building on it that will not be used, then the demolition cost less its salvage value is a cost of getting the land ready for its intended use. The costs relate to the land rather than to the new building.

On the other hand, if a company razes (tears down) an old building that it owns and previously used in order to construct a new building on the same land, the costs of the demolition net of any cost recoveries are expensed as disposal costs of the old building. This increases any loss on disposal of the old asset. The remaining book value of the old building is included in depreciation expense in its final year of use.

ASPE Under ASPE, an exception is made when a building is torn down to redevelop rental real estate. In this case, the remaining carrying amount of the building and the net costs of removing it would be capitalized as part of the redeveloped property, but only to the extent the costs can be recovered from the project in the future (*CPA Canada Handbook*, Part II, Section 3061.15).

Leasehold Improvements

What is the proper accounting by lessees for capital expenditures that are made on property that is being leased or rented? Long-term leases ordinarily specify that any leasehold improvements revert to the lessor at the end of the lease. If the lessee constructs new buildings on leased land or renovates and improves existing buildings, the lessee has the right to use those facilities during the life of the lease, but they become the property of the lessor when the lease expires. The lessee charges the facilities' cost to a separate capital asset account, Leasehold Improvements, and the cost is amortized as an operating expense over the remaining life of the lease or the useful life of the improvements, whichever is shorter.

Equipment

The term "equipment" in accounting includes delivery equipment, office equipment, machinery, furniture and fixtures, furnishings, factory equipment, and similar tangible capital assets. The cost of such assets includes the purchase price, freight and handling charges that are incurred, insurance on the equipment while it is in transit, the cost of special foundations if they are required, assembling and installation costs, testing (less net proceeds of items, such as samples produced and sold during testing), and costs of making any adjustments to the equipment to make it operate as intended.[10] The asset's acquisition cost does not include Goods and Services Tax (GST), Harmonized Sales Tax (HST), or Quebec Sales Tax (QST) that is paid on the acquired assets as a recoverable tax eligible for an input tax credit.

Investment Property

Investment property, or rental real estate, is a separate category of PP&E that may be accounted for after acquisition in a special way by entities using IFRS. It is defined as property held to generate rentals and/or appreciate in value rather than to sell in the ordinary course of business or to use in production, administration, or supplying goods and services.[11] It includes property that is currently under construction for investment purposes as well.

IFRS Investment property is covered in international standards by IAS 40. This is different from owner-occupied property, which is covered by IAS 16 *Property, Plant, and Equipment*. Complexities arise when one property is used partly as an investment property and is partly owner-occupied. In general, if the two parts could be sold separately (or leased under a finance lease separately), then the two parts should be accounted for separately. Another problem arises when an owner provides a variety of services in connection with an investment property. If providing the services exposes the owner to the normal risks of running a business (as distinct from investment risk), the classification as an investment property may not be appropriate. Consider a situation where a company rents out office space to tenants and provides furnished units and secretarial support in addition to the space. Judgement is often needed to determine whether the services provided are such a significant component of the arrangement that the property is actually "owner-occupied" space and not investment property.[12]

The cost of investment property under IFRS and ASPE is determined following the same principles as used for PP&E. Also, if the property continues to be accounted for at cost, the components of the property are accounted for separately for purposes of depreciation.

Natural Resource Properties

Mineral resources, sometimes called "wasting assets," generally are minerals and oil and gas resources that do not regenerate. Mineral resource properties are capitalized costs associated with the acquired rights, and the exploration, evaluation, and development of these minerals. Unlike buildings and machinery, natural resource properties are consumed physically over the period of use and do not retain their original physical characteristics. Regardless, many of the accounting problems with these assets are similar to those for other capital assets.

How is the acquisition cost of a mineral resource property determined? For example, a company like Petro-Canada needs to spend large amounts to find oil and gas reserves, and projects often end in failure. Furthermore, there are long delays between the time it incurs

---

[10]In a 2017 Exposure Draft that would amend IAS 16, the IASB proposed that proceeds from selling items produced during the testing phase, while a PP&E item is being made available for use, should not be netted off the cost of the PP&E item. Instead, the sale proceeds would be included in profit or loss. See the Looking Ahead section at the end of this chapter for details.

[11]Investment property includes land or buildings, or part of a building, or both, under IAS 40.5, and could be property held under a finance lease or directly owned. Copyright © IFRS Foundation. All rights reserved. Reproduced with permission.

[12]See IAS 40.11 to 40.14 for further details.

costs and the time it obtains benefits from any extracted resources. The acquisition cost of natural resource property normally includes some costs from each of four stages: (1) acquisition of the property, (2) exploration for and evaluation of reserves, (3) development, and (4) decommissioning and site restoration. In general, the capitalized costs of acquisition, exploration, development, and restoration make up the depletion base of the natural resource. As its name implies, the depletion base is the amount that will later be amortized (through a depletion charge) and will form a significant portion of the cost of the mined or extracted inventory. Through depletion, the costs of the long-term mineral resource capital asset become part of the cost of the inventory that is produced—very similar to the direct materials cost of a manufactured product.

Two main methods of accounting for oil and gas properties are the full cost method and the successful efforts method. While IFRS 6 does not currently discuss these, the full cost method is covered under ASPE by Accounting Guideline 16 (AcG-16 *Oil and Gas Accounting—Full Cost*). Under the full cost method, companies capitalize all of their exploration costs, even those representing "dry holes" that do not contain oil and gas reserves. Each time a company prepares its annual financial statements, it assesses the net capitalized costs to determine whether it is likely that the costs will be recovered in the future. Companies must determine the proper level of analysis when assessing the cost centres for possible impairment. This assessment is based on an estimate of the recoverable amount of oil and gas reserves (and, for example, the level of analysis of the amount of recoverable reserves could be based on a comparison of the costs capitalized and the total reserves in a province, a country, or an entire continent). AcG-16 recommends that recoverability be assessed by country, with only one cost centre for each country. An impairment loss is recognized if the carrying amount of the cost centre exceeds the sum of the undiscounted cash flows expected to arise from its use and eventual disposition (AcG-16.40). In contrast, under the successful efforts method, companies initially capitalize exploration costs until the drilling activities for each oil field are complete. If the drilling activities are not successful and no proven reserves are found, the costs are written off to expense as a "dry hole." Alternatively, for successful efforts exploration activities that are likely to be commercially developed, the costs remain capitalized as an asset until production (and related amortization) begins. Later in this chapter, we provide an example of the accounting policy of a company that follows the successful efforts method (BP plc, in Illustration 10.7).

Accounting for natural resources is a specialized area, and it is only introduced here. Because of the complex nature of this industry, additional coverage is beyond the scope of an intermediate text. You should note, however, that many of the issues that need to be resolved are familiar ones: they involve bringing accounting practice into greater consistency with general standards for asset recognition and measurement, cost allocation, and impairment testing. Not surprisingly, these issues are complicated by the uncertainties caused by estimating the volume and fair values of reserves and resources. Differences between IFRS and ASPE exist.

Biological Assets

Significant Change Under ASPE, the general principles established for PP&E assets are also followed for biological assets. Under IFRS, however, separate standards are set out in IAS 16 *Property, Plant and Equipment* for bearer plants and IAS 41 *Agriculture* for other assets related to agricultural activity. Bearer plants include fruit trees, grapevines, and rubber trees. However, as discussed in Chapter 8, livestock such as sheep are considered biological assets (and the wool is an agricultural product). Biological assets are measured initially, and at every statement of financial position date, at **fair value less costs to sell**, with changes in value recognized in the income statement as gains or losses as the values change. The accounting is similar to the fair value model we explain later in this chapter. In the rare situation that no reliable fair value measure can be determined, the asset is measured at cost less accumulated depreciation and accumulated impairment losses. However, bearer plants are accounted for using the cost or revaluation methods, which we describe later in this chapter.

Measurement after Acquisition

> **LEARNING OBJECTIVE 5**
> Understand and apply the cost model, the revaluation model using the asset adjustment method, and the fair value model.

After recognizing the cost of property, plant, or equipment assets at acquisition, companies may have a choice of how to account for them after this point. Three different models have been identified and are currently used: a cost model (CM), a revaluation model (RM), and a fair value model (FVM). However, the GAAP choice of model depends on the type of asset and whether international or private enterprise standards are being applied. The features of the three models are summarized in **Illustration 10.5**.

ILLUSTRATION 10.5
Accounting Model Choices

	ASPE			IFRS		
	CM	**RM**	**FVM**	**CM**	**RM**	**FVM**
Investment property	✓			✓		✓
Other property, plant, and equipment assets	✓			✓	✓	

For example, under IFRS, a company must choose whether to measure all of its **investment property** under the cost model or under the fair value model, with few exceptions. All **other items defined as PP&E** are separated into classes and a decision is made whether to apply the cost model or the revaluation model to each class. The same method must be used for **all assets in each class**. Common classes of assets include:

- Land
- Land and buildings
- Office equipment
- Motor vehicles
- Machinery
- Ships
- Aircraft
- Furniture and fixtures

> **Underlying Concept 10.9**
> IAS 29 sets out how companies reporting in the currency of a hyper-inflationary economy should restate their financial statements.

Not surprisingly, the revaluation model can be applied only to assets whose fair value can be reliably measured. This method is used by relatively few companies but is included as an IFRS alternative. It tends to be used by some companies for real estate holdings, and others that operate in countries with relatively high rates of inflation—see Underlying Concept 10.9 (or by making the revaluation measure more relevant than historical cost—see Underlying Concept 10.10). **IFRS** **ASPE** This leaves the cost model as the most commonly used method under IFRS and the only one acceptable under ASPE. Let's now review how each of these models works.

> **Underlying Concept 10.10**
> Historical costs are verifiable and therefore are considered more reliable. On the other hand, they often do not faithfully represent the value of the asset to the business and therefore are considered a less relevant measure. This is an example of a qualitative characteristic trade-off.

Cost and Revaluation Models

Cost Model

The **cost model (CM)** is by far the most widely used model to account for PP&E, and you are probably familiar with the basics of how it works from introductory accounting. This model measures property, plant, and equipment assets after acquisition **at their cost less accumulated depreciation and any accumulated impairment losses**. We provide details about depreciation and impairment in Chapter 11.

Revaluation Model

The **revaluation model (RM)** alternative is not used by most Canadian companies. Under this approach, property, plant, and equipment assets **whose fair value can be measured reliably** are carried after acquisition **at their fair value at the date of the revaluation less any subsequent accumulated depreciation and any subsequent impairment losses**. We discuss depreciation and impairment under this model in detail in Chapter 11.

A revaluation is not required at each reporting date but must be carried out often enough that the carrying amount reported is not materially different from the assets' fair value. Some assets need to be remeasured only every three to five years, but for assets whose values change rapidly, an annual revaluation may be needed. Between revaluation dates, **depreciation is taken** on the revalued amount.

IFRS What is fair value, and how do companies determine this value for their PP&E assets? **Fair value** is "the price that would be received to sell an asset or paid to transfer a liability in an orderly transaction between market participants at the measurement date."[13] Professional valuators use active market or market-related evidence where possible, but may have to revert to other methods if equipment, for example, is very specialized.[14]

Before walking through an example of how the RM works, we need to resolve one issue. If you regularly revalue or change the asset's carrying amount, what do you do with the increases and decreases in the carrying amount? The changes are accounted for as shown in **Illustration 10.6**.

ILLUSTRATION 10.6

Revaluation Surplus, OCI

If the asset's carrying amount is **increased (debited)**	If the asset's carrying amount is **decreased (credited)**
The amount is recorded as a credit to Revaluation Surplus (OCI), and accumulated in an equity account Revaluation Surplus (AOCI). However, it would be recognized as an increase in profit or loss to the extent it reverses a revaluation decrease for the same asset that was previously recognized in profit or loss.	The amount is recorded as a debit to Revaluation Surplus (OCI), reducing the equity account Revaluation Surplus (AOCI), to the extent of any credit balance associated with that asset. This account cannot have a debit (that is, a negative) balance. Any remaining amount is recognized in profit or loss.

IFRS The amounts debited or credited to the Revaluation Surplus account are reported in the statement of comprehensive income as other comprehensive income (OCI) items. Over the life of the asset, the effect of the treatment described is that there is no **net increase** in net income from revaluing the asset.

When revaluing an asset, two methods of accounting for the balance in the Accumulated Depreciation account are permitted. The account (1) **may be adjusted proportionately**, or (2) under the **asset adjustment (or elimination) method**, its balance may be eliminated. The proportionate approach adjusts both the asset's carrying amount and its accumulated

---

[13]IFRS 13 *Fair Value Measurement*, Paragraph 9. Copyright © IFRS Foundation. All rights reserved. Reproduced with permission.

[14]Chapter 3 includes a discussion of the meaning of fair value and ways in which fair values are determined, and Appendix B of IFRS 13 provides detailed guidance relating to the fair value measurement approach.

depreciation, so that the net balance is the fair value of the asset at the revaluation date.[15] The second method eliminates the balance in the Accumulated Depreciation account, writing it off against the asset itself. The asset is then adjusted to its new revalued amount. The second, and simpler, method is illustrated in **Examples 10.7** and **10.8**. For a similar example using the proportionate method, see Appendix 10B.

Example 10.7 | Revaluation Asset Adjustment Method 2017–2019

Facts   Convo Corp. (CC) purchases a building in early January 2017 and the cost of the basic structure of $100,000 is classified in an account called Buildings. CC accounts for this class of asset using the revaluation model, revalues the class every three years, and uses straight-line depreciation. The building structure is expected to have a useful life of 25 years with no residual value. CC has a December 31 fiscal year end. The asset's fair value at December 31, 2019, is $90,000.

Instructions `IFRS`

a. Calculate CC's depreciation for the first three years and the revaluation entries needed at December 31, 2019, assuming the balance in the Accumulated Depreciation account is eliminated.

b. Provide the SFP presentation at December 31, 2019.

Solution

a. Annual depreciation in each of 2017, 2018, and 2019 for CC would be $4,000 and would be recorded as shown below:

Depreciation Expense	4,000	
Accumulated Depreciation—Buildings		4,000

$$\frac{\$100,000 - \$0}{25 \text{ years}} = \$4,000$$

December 31, 2019

	Before Revaluation	Adjustments	After Revaluation
Buildings	$100,000	$(12,000)	$90,000
		2,000	
Accumulated depreciation ($4,000 × 3)	(12,000)	12,000	–0–
Carrying amount	$ 88,000	$ 2,000	$90,000

The revaluation-related journal entries at December 31, 2019, follow:

Accumulated Depreciation—Buildings	12,000	
Buildings		12,000
(To eliminate the accumulated depreciation.)		

Buildings (90,000 – 88,000)	2,000	
Revaluation Surplus (OCI)		2,000
(To adjust the Buildings account to fair value.)		

b. Statement of financial position presentation, December 31, 2019:

Long-term assets:

Buildings	$90,000
Less accumulated depreciation	–0–
	$90,000
Shareholders' equity	
Revaluation surplus (AOCI)	$ 2,000

A	=	L	+	SE
0				

Cash flows: No effect

A	=	L	+	SE
+2,000				+2,000

Cash flows: No effect

---

[15]This method is easy to apply when fair values are based on an index of specific prices, such as a construction price index. It also has the benefit of providing additional information to users about the relative age of the assets because the accumulated depreciation continues.

Example 10.8 | Revaluation Asset Adjustment Method 2020–2022

Facts Convo Corp. (CC) continues to own the building that it purchased in early January 2017 and continues to account for this class of asset using the revaluation model (revaluing the class every three years, and using straight-line depreciation over 25 years). The building structure is expected to have a useful life of 25 years with no residual value. The asset's fair value at December 31, 2022, is $75,000.

Instructions `IFRS`

a. Calculate a new depreciation rate for 2020 to 2022 to take into account the change in the asset's carrying amount. Show the related journal entries.

b. Provide a calculation to illustrate CC's accumulated depreciation account before and after the related revaluation adjustment for the change in fair value at December 31, 2022. Include all related journal entries and provide the SFP presentation at December 31, 2022.

Solution

a. CC's depreciation for 2020 to 2022 and its December 31, 2022 adjustment for revaluation would be calculated and recorded as follows:

Annual depreciation in each of 2020, 2021, and 2022:

Depreciation Expense	4,091	
Accumulated Depreciation—Buildings		4,091

$$\frac{\$90,000 - \$0}{22 \text{ years}} = \$4,091$$

b.

December 31, 2022

	Before Revaluation	Adjustments	After Revaluation
Buildings	$90,000	$(12,273) (2,727)	$75,000
Accumulated depreciation ($4,091 × 3)	(12,273)	12,273	–0–
Carrying amount	$77,727	$ (2,727)	$75,000

The revaluation-related journal entries at December 31, 2022, follow:

Accumulated Depreciation—Buildings	12,273	
Buildings		12,273
(To eliminate the accumulated depreciation.)		

Revaluation Surplus (OCI)	2,000	
Revaluation Gain or Loss	727	
Buildings		2,727
(To adjust the Buildings account to fair value.)		

Statement of financial position presentation, December 31, 2022:

Long-term assets:	
Building	$75,000
Less accumulated depreciation	–0–
	$75,000

A	=	L	+	SE
0				

Cash flows: No effect

A	=	L	+	SE
−2,727				−2,727

Cash flows: No effect

Note that the SFP Revaluation Surplus (AOCI) account can only be reduced to zero. The remaining loss in value is recognized in the income statement. Once again, the depreciation rate going forward has to be recalculated. So, for the Convo Corp. example, the $75,000 carrying amount would now be allocated over the remaining 19 years of useful life, so the new rate would be $75,000/19 = $3,947 each year.

What happens to the Revaluation Surplus (AOCI) account? A company has two choices. One option is to transfer some of the surplus directly into Retained Earnings every period. The amount transferred is the difference between the depreciation expense based on the revalued carrying amount and the expense based on the original cost. Alternatively, the balance in the Revaluation Surplus (AOCI) could remain there until the asset is retired or disposed of. At that point, the balance would be transferred directly to Retained Earnings, without going through the income statement, as shown in **Example 10.9**.[16]

Example 10.9 | Revaluation Surplus Adjustment at Disposal

Facts   Assume that in the Convo Corp. example, the company chose the alternative of not transferring any amounts to retained earnings until the building is sold.[17]

Instructions **IFRS** Provide the journal entries to be made by CC assuming that it sells the building (from Example 10.7) on **January 2, 2020**, for $93,000.

Solution   After the revaluation adjustment on December 31, 2019, the carrying value of the building would be $90,000. So a Gain on Disposal of Buildings of $3,000 would be recorded on January 3, 2020, as follows:

Cash	93,000	
Buildings		90,000
Gain on Disposal of Buildings		3,000
(To record the proceeds on sale of the building)		
Revaluation Surplus (AOCI)	2,000	
Retained Earnings		2,000
(To transfer the Revaluation Surplus in Accumulated OCI related to the building sold to Retained Earnings)		

A	=	L	+	SE
+3,000				+3,000

Cash flows: ↑ 93,000 inflow

A	=	L	+	SE
0				0

Cash flows: No effect

Fair Value Model

IFRS As discussed above, investment property is the only tangible capital asset that may be accounted for under the **fair value model (FVM)**. Under this approach, the investment property is recognized on the statement of financial position after acquisition at its fair value. Changes in its value are reported in net income in the period of the change, and no depreciation is recognized over the life of the asset. Once this method is chosen instead of the cost model, the property continues to be measured at fair value until it is disposed of, becomes owner-occupied, or is developed for sale in the ordinary course of business. **What Do the Numbers Mean? 10.2** and **Example 10.10** illustrate how the FV model is applied. Note that, although biological assets are measured at **fair value less costs to sell** instead of **fair value**, the example provided for investment property is similar to the accounting for changes in value of biological assets.

What Do the Numbers Mean? 10.2

As discussed in the feature story at the start of this chapter, **Brookfield Asset Management** adopted the fair value model to account for its commercial properties when it moved from former Canadian GAAP to IFRS in 2010. This resulted in an increase of $2,640 million in equity for its opening consolidated balance sheet, relating to its commercial properties, when it adopted IFRS. Brookfield continues to use the fair value model for its investment properties. For the year ended December 31, 2017, its investment properties (including office, retail, multifamily, and industrial properties) had a fair value of $56,870 million (including fair value gains during the year of $421 million, compared with 2016, where losses of $130 million were recorded). For 2017, Brookfield recorded total fair value increases of $1,021 million relating to its investment properties, but had offsetting decreases relating to its core office portfolio and other items such as financial contracts. The changes in fair value were recorded in its consolidated statement of operations.

---

[16]Notice that the amounts in the Revaluation Surplus (AOCI) account are not "recycled" through net income. The revaluation model treats holding gains and losses as equity adjustments, which differs from a true fair value model, which can be used for investment property, as discussed in the next section.

[17]IAS 16 discusses the revaluation model in more detail, including the two alternatives for transferring the revaluation surplus to retained earnings (see IAS 16.41).

Example 10.10 | Fair Value Model for Investment Property

Facts Erican Corp. (EC) acquired a small 10-store shopping mall in eastern Canada for $1 million on February 2, 2020. The mall qualifies as investment property under IAS 40 *Investment Property*. At this time, nine of the stores were leased, with remaining lease terms of two to four years. In addition to the purchase price, EC had to pay a $40,000 property transfer fee and legal fees of $3,000, and the company decided to paint the empty store at a cost of $2,000 before advertising it for rent. The acquisition was financed by assuming a $730,000 mortgage from the previous owner, who also turned over $37,000 of tenant damage deposits. The remainder of the transaction was settled in cash. On December 31, 2020, the fair value of the shopping centre property was determined to be $1,040,000; on December 31, 2021, it was $1,028,000; and on December 31, 2022, it had risen to $1,100,000. EC has a December 31 year end and applies the fair value method to all its investment property.

Instructions `IFRS`

a. Provide a summary journal entry to record the acquisition of the property on February 2, 2020, and discuss how the related costs would be treated for accounting purposes.

b. Provide the entries to adjust to fair value at the end of 2020, 2021, and 2022.

Solution

a. The entry to record the acquisition of the property on February 2, 2020, follows:

A	=	L	+	SE
+765,000		+767,000		−2,000

Cash flows: ↓ 278,000 outflow

February 2, 2020		
Investment Property (1,000,000 + 40,000 + 3,000)	1,043,000	
Repairs and Maintenance Expense	2,000	
Mortgage Payable		730,000
Tenant Deposits Liability		37,000
Cash		278,000

The acquisition cost includes the transfer and legal fees, while the incidental painting is a period expense. The mortgage and the tenant deposits are both liabilities and they reduce the amount of cash EC has to pay on the date of acquisition. Because the building is not being amortized, the land and the building may be reported together, as illustrated in the entry.

b. On each December 31, the investment property is remeasured to its new fair value, with the following entries being made.

A	=	L	+	SE
−3,000				−3,000
−12,000				−12,000
+72,000				+72,000

Cash flows: No effect

December 31, 2020		
Gain or Loss in Value of Investment Property	3,000	
Investment Property		3,000
($1,043,000 − $1,040,000)		

December 31, 2021		
Gain or Loss in Value of Investment Property	12,000	
Investment Property		12,000
($1,040,000 − $1,028,000)		

December 31, 2022		
Investment Property	72,000	
Gain or Loss in Value of Investment Property		72,000
($1,100,000 − $1,028,000)		

As shown in the Erican Corp. example in Example 10.10, gains and losses for changes in fair value are recognized directly in income. They are not reported in other comprehensive income.

It is important to realize that the fair value of investment property must be **disclosed in the financial statements, even if the cost model is used**. Therefore, all companies with such properties need to develop appropriate methods to measure fair value.

Costs Incurred after Acquisition

> **LEARNING OBJECTIVE 6**
> Explain and apply the accounting treatment for costs incurred after acquisition.

After plant assets are installed and ready for use, additional costs are incurred for anything from ordinary servicing and repairs to periodic overhauls, significant additions, or replacement of components. The major problem is allocating these costs to the proper time periods. Is the cost expensed in the current period, or capitalized and recognized over the future periods benefiting?

Accounting standards take the position that the recognition criteria for these costs should be the same when an asset is initially acquired. See **Underlying Concept 10.11**. If future economic benefits are expected to result from an expenditure, then the cost is capitalized, assuming it can be measured reliably. For a cost after acquisition to be included as part of an asset's cost, the assumption is that there has been a betterment in the form of enhanced service potential, **not merely a restoration** of the asset to normal operating efficiency.

Day-to-day servicing costs and other maintenance-type expenditures do not meet the asset recognition criteria and are expensed in the period incurred. These costs tend to keep an asset in its proper working condition; they do not add significantly to the asset's future cash-generating ability.

It is not uncommon, however, for companies to expense costs below an arbitrary minimum amount even if they meet the capitalization criteria. For example, an entity may adopt a rule that expenditures below, say, $300 or $500 or even higher (depending on the size of the company) are always expensed. Although this treatment may not be correct conceptually, a cost-benefit assessment and materiality may justify it. See **Underlying Concept 10.12**.

The distinction between a **capital expenditure** (an asset) and a **revenue expenditure** (an expense) is not always clear-cut, and **this accounting choice can have a significant effect on reported income** as discussed in **What Do the Numbers Mean? 10.3**. If costs are capitalized as assets on the statement of financial position, the income statement is freed from immediate expense charges that would otherwise reduce the bottom line and earnings per share in that period.

> **Underlying Concept 10.11**
>
> Applying the same principle both at acquisition and at a point after acquisition makes for more consistent accounting for similar events.

> **Underlying Concept 10.12**
>
> Expensing long-lived staplers, pencil sharpeners, and wastebaskets is an application of the materiality constraint.

What Do the Numbers Mean? 10.3

The "managing" of earnings has been behind many of the well-publicized accounting scandals. **WorldCom** executives accounted for billions of dollars of current operating costs as capital additions. **Adelphia Communications Corp.** aggressively deferred operating items as assets on its statement of financial position. Closer to home, **Livent** carried out similar actions in Canada. There is also the case of Toronto-based **Atlas Cold Storage Income Trust**, the second-largest cold storage firm in North America, which announced that expenditures of approximately $3.6 million were inappropriately recorded as additions to capital assets during the previous year. Atlas also adjusted the financial statements of another prior year for an additional $1.6 million of expenditures that had been recognized as assets. While management may not set out intentionally to exaggerate profits and mislead investors, decisions are made daily where the distinction between whether an expenditure should be capitalized or expensed is not always obvious.

Generally, companies incur four major types of expenditures related to existing assets.

1. **Additions:** Increase or extension of existing assets.
2. **Replacements, major overhauls, and inspections:** Substitution of a new part or component for an existing asset, and performing significant overhauls or inspections of assets, whether or not physical parts are replaced.
3. **Rearrangement and reinstallation:** Movement of assets from one location to another.
4. **Repairs:** Servicing expenditures that maintain assets in good operating condition.

We will now look at the accounting treatment for each of these major types of expenditures incurred after acquisition.

Additions

Additions present no major accounting problems. By definition, any **addition to plant assets is capitalized** because a new asset has been acquired. Adding a wing to a hospital or an air conditioning system to an office, for example, increases the service potential of that facility. These costs are capitalized and then recognized as expenses in the future periods that benefit from the asset's use.

One problem that arises in this area is the accounting for any changes related to an existing structure as a result of the addition. Is the cost incurred to tear down an old wall to make room for an addition a cost of the addition or a disposal cost of the portion of the existing asset that is being eliminated? In theory, it is a disposal cost of a part of the existing asset. From a practical standpoint, however, if the wall is a minor portion of the cost of the original asset, most companies would keep the carrying amount of the old wall in the accounts and include the cost to tear down the wall in the cost of the addition.

Replacements, Major Overhauls, and Inspections

Replacements are substitutions of one asset or asset component for another, often resulting from a general policy to modernize or rehabilitate a building, piece of equipment, or interior of an aircraft, for example. Costs of **major overhauls**, reconditioning, or **inspections** are similar to replacements in that they recur and are often needed in order to permit continued use of an asset.

Costs such as those for the replacement of significant parts, or the periodic inspection, overhaul, or reconditioning of major assets, often meet the capitalization criteria. If so, they are, in effect, asset acquisitions and the costs are capitalized and added to the asset's carrying amount. Because it is a replacement of something already incorporated in the asset's cost or of an item recognized as a separate component, the depreciated carrying amount of the original part or inspection is removed. If the original cost of the replaced part or previous overhaul is not known, it has to be estimated. The current cost of the part or overhaul can be used to help estimate the original cost of what is being replaced. Once the original cost is determined, it and the associated accumulated depreciation are both removed from the accounts.

Let's work through **Examples 10.11** and **10.12** for asset replacements and overhauls.

Example 10.11 | Asset Replacement

Facts Ace Manufacturing Ltd. (AML) incurred $27,000 in costs for roofing work on its factory: $26,000 to replace the previous roof installed when the building was first built, and $1,000 to repair and replace a few shingles on the garage extension as a result of a recent storm. The factory building was constructed 15 years ago. The following are two independent situations.

Situation 1(a): The original roof was identified as a separate component of the building (Building—Roof) when it was constructed. It cost $16,000 and had been depreciated on a straight-line basis over its (estimated) 20-year life.

Situation 1(b): The original roof was not recognized as a separate component of the building and its original cost is not known. The building had been depreciated on a straight-line basis assuming a 40-year useful life. Construction costs in the area have doubled since the factory was completed 15 years ago.

Instructions Discuss situations 1(a) and 1(b) and provide the related journal entries for each.

Solution In **Situation 1(a)**, $26,000 of the roofing costs meets the capitalization criteria and $1,000 does not. The first journal entry below accounts for the $27,000 expenditure; the second removes the original roof's carrying amount and recognizes the associated loss.

A	=	L	+	SE
−1,000				−1,000

Cash flows: ↓ 27,000 outflow

Repairs and Maintenance Expense	1,000	
Buildings—Roof (new)	26,000	
Cash		27,000

Accumulated Depreciation—Buildings (Roof) (old)	12,000	
Loss on Disposal of Roof	4,000	
Buildings—Roof (old)		16,000
($16,000/20 years × 15 years = $12,000)		

A	=	L	+	SE
−4,000				−4,000

Cash flows: No effect

Under **Situation 1(b)**, the exact cost and accumulated depreciation are not known, but can be estimated. If construction costs have doubled in the area since the building was acquired, a reasonable estimate of the roof's original cost might be 50% of $26,000, or $13,000. The first entry below records the $27,000 expenditure assuming the roof is not accounted for after replacement as a separate component. This is a reasonable decision if AML estimates that the new roof will not have to be replaced before the building's useful life is over. If the new roof has a useful life of only 15 years, however, then it should be recognized as a separate asset. The numbers in the second entry below are different than in Situation 1(a) because the old roof was being depreciated over a 40-year life as part of the building.

Repairs and Maintenance Expense	1,000	
Buildings	26,000	
Cash		27,000
Accumulated Depreciation-Buildings	4,875	
Loss on Disposal of Roof	8,125	
Buildings		13,000
($13,000/40 years × 15 years = $4,875)		

A	=	L	+	SE
−1,000				−1,000

Cash flows: ▼ 27,000 outflow

A	=	L	+	SE
−8,125				−8,125

Cash flows: No effect

Example 10.12 | Asset Overhaul Costs

Facts   Beta Corp. (BC) maintains a fleet of specialized trucks. BC has an operating policy of taking its trucks out of service and giving them a significant overhaul after every 50,000 km of use. The overhaul is a requirement for maintaining the company's insurance coverage. When Truck #B14, acquired two years ago for $63,000, completed its first 50,000 km of service, it was taken off the road and given its first major overhaul. The overhaul cost BC $9,000. When Truck #B14's odometer reading was 92,100 km, the truck was experiencing difficulties and BC management decided to take it in for an early overhaul. This time, the servicing costs totalled $11,000. The useful life of a truck is assumed to be 300,000 km. The following are two independent situations.

Situation 1(a): When the truck was acquired, the cost of the benefits to be restored by the overhaul after 50,000 km was estimated to be $8,000, based on current overhaul costs. Therefore the truck was recognized in Vehicles at its cost of $63,000 − $8,000 = $55,000, and the overhaul service component was recognized separately as Vehicle Overhaul at a cost of $8,000.

Situation 1(b): No separate asset components were recognized initially for the truck, but one will be recognized separately when the first full overhaul is carried out.

Instructions   Discuss Situations 1(a) and 1(b) and provide the related journal entries for each.

Solution   In **Situation 1(a)**, the same approach is used for the overhaul as for the replacement of the roof in Situation 1(a) in Example 10.11. The first entry below records the $9,000 overhaul expenditure, and the second one removes the original overhaul component's cost and accumulated depreciation from the accounts. The third entry recognizes the asset cost of the second overhaul at 92,100 km, and the fourth entry removes the cost of the first overhaul and its accumulated depreciation to the date of the second one. The first actual overhaul costs of $9,000 were being depreciated at a rate of $9,000 ÷ 50,000 = $0.18 per km. When the truck reached 92,100 km, it had travelled an additional 92,100 − 50,000 = 42,100 km.

First overhaul

Vehicle Overhaul	9,000	
Cash		9,000
Accumulated Depreciation-Vehicle Overhaul	8,000	
Vehicle Overhaul		8,000
($8,000/50,000 km × 50,000 km = $8,000)		

A	=	L	+	SE
0				

Cash flows: ▼ 9,000 outflow

A	=	L	+	SE
0				

Cash flows: No effect

Cash flows: ▼ 11,000 outflow

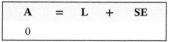

Cash flows: No effect

Second overhaul		
Vehicle Overhaul	11,000	
Cash		11,000
Accumulated Depreciation-Vehicle Overhaul	7,578	
Loss on Vehicle Overhaul	1,422	
Vehicle Overhaul		9,000
(42,100 km × $0.18/km = $7,578)		

Under **Situation 1(b)**, because no "overhaul" component was recognized separately when the truck was acquired, a representative cost and the carrying amount have to be determined for it at the time of the 50,000 km servicing. If truck service bay costs have increased 10% over the two-year period since the truck was acquired, this might imply an original cost of $9,000/1.10, or $8,182. The first entry below records the overhaul cost as a separate asset component and the second entry removes the appropriate amount from the truck's book value. We assumed that the cost of the truck, and therefore any unrecognized overhaul component, was being depreciated over the full useful life of the truck in this situation.

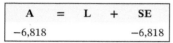

Cash flows: ▼ 9,000 outflow

Cash flows: No effect

First overhaul		
Vehicle Overhaul	9,000	
Cash		9,000
Accumulated Depreciation-Vehicle Overhaul	1,364	
Loss on Vehicle Overhaul	6,818	
Vehicles		8,182
($8,182/300,000 km ÷ 50,000 km = $1,364)		

Now recognized separately, the Vehicle Overhaul asset is depreciated over the next 50,000 km at a rate of $9,000/50,000 km, or $0.18 per km. When Truck #B14's odometer reads 92,100 km and it is taken out of service again, the depreciation accumulated on the Vehicle Overhaul asset is $0.18 × 42,100 km, or $7,578. The two entries required for the second overhaul are exactly the same as under Situation 1(a) above. The first entry below recognizes the cost of the second overhaul and the second entry removes the old overhaul's carrying amount and recognizes a loss.

Second overhaul		
Vehicle Overhaul	11,000	
Cash		11,000
Accumulated Depreciation-Vehicle Overhaul	7,578	
Loss on Vehicle Overhaul	1,422	
Vehicle Overhaul		9,000
(42,100 km × $0.18/km = $7,578)		

When an entity uses the revaluation model or the fair value model, the basic principle for replacements and overhauls continues to apply. If the **revaluation model** is used, the cost of the "new" asset component, part, or overhaul is added to the asset's carrying amount, and the carrying amount of the replaced asset component or part is removed, with a gain or loss recognized on disposal. When the **fair value model** is applied to investment property, the property's fair value may already reflect the reduced value of the part to be replaced. This fact may not be known or it may be difficult to reasonably determine the carrying amount of the part being replaced. A practical solution, therefore, is to add the cost of the replacement part or overhaul to the asset and then reassess and adjust the asset to its fair value after the replacement.

IFRS **ASPE** Accounting for replacements and major overhauls or inspections, as illustrated in Examples 10.11 and 10.12 above, is required by IFRS, with the entries being a direct application of general PP&E principles. ASPE has not required such a strict application of general principles, although this may change.

For now, ASPE removes the net book value of a part and capitalizes the replacement only if the cost and accumulated depreciation of the old part are known. When the carrying amount cannot be determined, and when major overhauls or renovations are carried out, practice differs depending on the circumstances. If the asset's useful life is extended, the Accumulated Depreciation account is often debited, on the basis that the renewal is "recovering" part of the past depreciation. If the quantity or quality of the asset's service potential or productivity is increased, the cost of the improvement is usually capitalized as part of the asset's cost.

Rearrangement and Reinstallation

Rearrangement and reinstallation costs that are intended to benefit future periods are different from additions, replacements, and major overhauls. An example is the rearrangement and reinstallation of a group of machines to facilitate future production. If the original installation cost and the accumulated depreciation to date can be determined, the rearrangement and reinstallation cost could be handled as a replacement. These amounts, however, are rarely known and may be difficult to estimate. In this case, because the asset's cost at acquisition already includes installation costs, any additional costs incurred to rearrange or reinstall it are recognized as an expense of the current period.

ASPE If the amounts are material, ASPE may allow capitalization of such costs on the basis that the original cost of installation is not known, and is likely to have been depreciated to a significant extent.

Repairs

Ordinary repairs are expenditures that are made to maintain plant assets in good operating condition. They are charged to an expense account in the period in which they are incurred, based on the argument that there is no increase in a PP&E asset. See **Underlying Concept 10.13**. Replacing minor parts, the ongoing lubricating and adjusting of equipment, repainting, and cleaning are examples of maintenance charges that occur regularly and are treated as ordinary operating expenses.[18]

BP plc, an international integrated oil and gas giant, reported net property, plant, and equipment including Oil and Gas properties, of U.S. $129,471 million on its December 31, 2017 "group balance sheet." **Illustration 10.7** includes excerpts from Note 1 to BP's financial statements that explain the acquisition costs of these assets. BP engages in oil and gas exploration and production activities, operates refineries and service stations, and provides a variety of petrochemical products. The company's financial statements are prepared under IFRS.

> **Underlying Concept 10.13**
>
> This accounting treatment for ordinary repairs and maintenance is an example of how the asset-liability approach to our accounting model works. If the cost is not an asset, it is an expense.

ILLUSTRATION 10.7

Property, Plant, and Equipment Accounting Policies—BP plc

BP Annual Report and Accounts 2017

Notes on financial statements [excerpt]
1. Significant accounting policies, judgements, estimates and assumptions

Oil and natural gas exploration, appraisal and development expenditure
Oil and natural gas exploration, appraisal and development expenditure is accounted for using the principles of the successful efforts method of accounting as described below.

Exploration and appraisal expenditure
Geological and geophysical exploration costs are recognized as an expense as incurred. Costs directly associated with an exploration well are initially capitalized as an intangible asset until the drilling of the well is complete and the results have been evaluated. These costs include employee remuneration, materials and fuel used, rig costs and payments made to contractors. If potentially commercial quantities of hydrocarbons are not found, the exploration well is written off. If hydrocarbons are found and, subject to further appraisal activity, are likely to be capable of commercial development, the costs continue to be carried as an asset. If it is determined that development will not occur then the costs are expensed.

Costs directly associated with appraisal activity, undertaken to determine the size, characteristics and commercial potential of a reservoir following the initial discovery of hydrocarbons, including the costs of appraisal wells where hydrocarbons were not found, are initially capitalized as an intangible asset. When proved reserves of oil and natural gas

(continued)

---

[18]Note that, to the extent these ordinary expenditures are classified as factory overhead, the costs are included as an inventory (product) cost before being charged to the income statement as an expense—cost of goods sold.

ILLUSTRATION 10.7
(*continued*)

are determined and development is approved by management, the relevant expenditure is transferred to property, plant and equipment.

The determination of whether potentially economic oil and natural gas reserves have been discovered by an exploration well is usually made within one year of well completion, but can take longer, depending on the complexity of the geological structure. Exploration wells that discover potentially economic quantities of oil and natural gas and are in areas where major capital expenditure (e.g. an offshore platform or a pipeline) would be required before production could begin, and where the economic viability of that major capital expenditure depends on the successful completion of further exploration or appraisal work in the area, remain capitalized on the balance sheet as long as such work is under way or firmly planned.

Development expenditure

Expenditure on the construction, installation and completion of infrastructure facilities such as platforms, pipelines and the drilling of development wells, including service and unsuccessful development or delineation wells, is capitalized within property, plant and equipment and is depreciated from the commencement of production as described below in the accounting policy for property, plant and equipment.

Property, plant and equipment

Property, plant and equipment is stated at cost, less accumulated depreciation and accumulated impairment losses. The initial cost of an asset comprises its purchase price or construction cost, any costs directly attributable to bringing the asset into the location and condition necessary for it to be capable of operating in the manner intended by management, the initial estimate of any decommissioning obligation, if any, and, for assets that necessarily take a substantial period of time to get ready for their intended use, directly attributable finance costs. The purchase price or construction cost is the aggregate amount paid and the fair value of any other consideration given to acquire the asset. The capitalized value of a finance lease is also included within property, plant and equipment.

Expenditure on major maintenance refits or repairs comprises the cost of replacement assets or parts of assets, inspection costs and overhaul costs. Where an asset or part of an asset that was separately depreciated is replaced and it is probable that future economic benefits associated with the item will flow to the group, the expenditure is capitalized and the carrying amount of the replaced asset is derecognized. Inspection costs associated with major maintenance programmes are capitalized and amortized over the period to the next inspection. Overhaul costs for major maintenance programmes, and all other maintenance costs are expensed as incurred.

IFRS/ASPE Comparison

LEARNING OBJECTIVE 7

Identify differences in accounting between IFRS and ASPE, and what changes are expected in the near future.

A Comparison of IFRS and ASPE

Illustration 10.8 sets out the major differences between international accounting standards for publicly accountable enterprises and ASPE.

ILLUSTRATION 10.8   **IFRS versus ASPE Comparison**

	IFRS—IAS 16, 20, 23, 37, 40, and 41; IFRS 6	Accounting Standards for Private Enterprises (ASPE)—CPA *Canada Handbook*, Part II, Sections 3061, 3110, 3800, 3831, 3850, and AcG-16	References to related examples, illustrations, and select brief exercises
Scope	The costs of mineral rights and reserves, including oil, natural gas, and similar non-regenerative resources, are not covered specifically as PP&E in IAS 16. Only the costs of the exploration for and evaluation of mineral resources are addressed in IFRS 6.	The costs of mining and oil and gas properties are considered items of PP&E, with specific application guidance for the full cost method of accounting in the oil and gas industry covered in AcG-16.	N/A
	Investment property is considered an item of PP&E, but a separate IFRS—IAS 40—applies to it. Biological assets are accounted for by standards IAS 41 for agricultural assets and IAS 16 for bearer plants.	Investment property is considered an item of PP&E and Section 3061 applies.	BE10.20 Illustration 10.5 Example 8.18 (Chapter 8)
Recognition	Recognition criteria are incorporated in IAS 16 and used for costs both at and after initial recognition—same criteria, based on measurement reliability and probability that associated future economic benefits will flow to the entity.	Uses general recognition principle in Section 1000 based on measurability and probability of future economic benefits to be received. Less guidance is provided.	N/A
Components	Requires the parts of PP&E with relatively significant costs to be depreciated separately. There is no mention made of practicability. Practice under IAS 16 results in more componentization than under Section 3061.	Indicates that the costs of significant separable component parts are allocated to those parts when practicable, but practice has not been to carry this out to the same extent as required internationally.	BE10.2
Measurement at recognition	Initial measurement is at cost, but more detail is provided on how cost is measured.	Initial measurement is at cost.	BE10.9
	Net revenue or expense derived from an item of PP&E prior to its being in place and ready for use as intended is taken into income, on the basis that it was not needed to acquire the asset and bring it to its location and use.	Any net revenue or expense from using an item of PP&E prior to substantial completion and readiness for use is included in the asset's cost.	Illustration 10.1 BE10.3
	Capitalization of costs in the initial carrying amount stops when the item is in the location and condition necessary for it to be used as management intended, even if it has not begun to be used or is used at less than desired capacity. No initial operating losses or costs of relocation or reorganization of the asset(s) are capitalized.	Capitalization of costs at acquisition stops when the asset is substantially complete and ready for productive use, as predetermined by management with reference to productive capacity, occupancy level, passage of time, or other industry considerations. This is a more flexible approach than under IFRS.	BE10.4
	Borrowing costs directly attributable to the acquisition, construction, or development of qualifying assets are capitalized under IAS 23.	Interest costs directly attributable to the acquisition, construction, or development of items of PP&E may be capitalized or expensed depending on the accounting policy used by the entity.	Example 10A.3 BE10.25

(continued)

ILLUSTRATION 10.8 (*continued*)

	IFRS—IAS 16, 20, 23, 37, 40, and 41; IFRS 6	Accounting Standards for Private Enterprises (ASPE)—CPA *Canada Handbook*, Part II, Sections 3061, 3110, 3800, 3831, 3850, and AcG-16	References to related examples, illustrations, and select brief exercises
	The cost of legal and constructive obligations related to asset retirement is capitalized, measured under IAS 37 *Provisions, Contingent Liabilities and Contingent Assets*. Increases in the cost of the obligation related to the production of inventory are specifically excluded.	Only the cost of legal obligations related to asset retirement is capitalized. Changes in the estimate of the cost are also capitalized in the asset.	Illustration 10.3 BE10.17
Measurement after recognition	All investment property is accounted for under either the cost model or fair value model. Each class of items of other PP&E is accounted for under the cost model or the revaluation model. Companies using the revaluation model have the choice of using the asset adjustment method or the proportionate method. Changes in fair value above carrying amount under the cost model are recorded via Revaluation Surplus (OCI). The cost model continues to be used to the greatest extent.	Only one model—the cost model—applies to all items of PP&E.	Examples 10.7, 10.8, 10.9, 10.10, 10B.1, and 10B.2 BE10.18, BE10.19, and BE10.20
Costs incurred after acquisition	All expenditures that meet the recognition criteria for an item of PP&E are capitalized. Does not specifically refer to betterments, but does refer to replacement parts that meet the recognition criteria. These are capitalized and the replaced part's carrying amount is removed, whether originally recognized as a separate component or not.	Betterments are capitalized and costs that are incurred to maintain service potential are expensed. Increased service potential means increased physical output or service capacity, lower operating costs, an increase in useful life, or an increase in quality of output. For betterments and major replacements, if the cost of the previous part is known, its carrying amount is removed. If not, and depending on the circumstances, the asset account, its accumulated depreciation, or an expense could be charged with the cost.	Examples 10.11 and 10.12 BE10.22
	The carrying amount of the building being redeveloped would not be carried forward as part of the cost of the new asset.	The redevelopment of rental real estate qualifies as a betterment, with the book value of the existing building included in the cost of the redeveloped property, if recoverable.	
	Major inspections or overhauls that allow the continued use of an asset are treated similarly to replacements.	Overhauls are not specifically addressed and are usually expensed when incurred.	

When Canadian publicly accountable entities applied IFRS for the first time, they were permitted to revalue items of PP&E to fair value at the transition date. This amount became the assets' deemed cost at that point. Many Canadian companies took advantage of this transition exemption, even though they were likely to apply the cost model going forward.

Looking Ahead

A project included in the IASB's research pipeline may turn out to be particularly important to many companies in Canada. The project's objective is to eventually issue a replacement standard for IFRS 6 *Exploration and Evaluation of Mineral Resources*, which was intended to be only a temporary standard when it was first issued. Therefore, IFRS 6 includes a number of exemptions from other standards that would otherwise apply. The project expects to cover all financial reporting issues regarding extractive activities, including exploration, evaluation, development and production of minerals, and oil and gas. No work had been done on this project as of December 2017, but work was expected to start before the next Agenda Consultation in 2021.

An Exposure Draft proposing "narrow-scope" amendments to IAS 16 was issued in June 2017 to prohibit companies from deducting sales proceeds of inventory items produced in the testing phase of an asset from the cost of the PP&E item. That is, proceeds from selling items produced during the testing of technical or physical performance of a PP&E item to determine if it is functioning properly should not be netted off the cost of the PP&E item. Instead, the net proceeds from selling such items would be included in profit or loss.

| Appendix 10A | # Capitalization of Borrowing Costs |

LEARNING OBJECTIVE 8
Calculate the amount of borrowing costs to capitalize for qualifying assets.

Chapter 10 introduces the issues for the capitalization of borrowing costs, underscoring the principle that borrowing costs that are directly attributable to acquiring, producing, or constructing a qualifying asset are included as part of the cost of the asset under IFRS. Other borrowing costs are expensed. This appendix continues the discussion in more detail and illustrates the recognition guidance in IAS 23 *Borrowing Costs*. Private enterprises that choose a policy of capitalizing interest costs for relevant PP&E assets are also likely to apply this guidance.

Borrowing costs are made up of interest and related costs that a company incurs related to the borrowing of funds. The cost of equity financing is specifically excluded. Interest and other costs include interest expense that results from applying the effective interest method, finance charges on finance leases, and exchange adjustments on foreign currency borrowings if they are viewed as adjustments to interest costs.

Four issues need to be considered in determining the amount of borrowing costs to be capitalized and how to report them:

1. Which assets qualify?
2. What is the capitalization period?
3. What are the avoidable borrowing costs—the amount eligible to capitalize?
4. What disclosures are needed?

Qualifying Assets

To qualify for inclusion in the cost of an asset, the borrowing costs must:

1. be directly attributable to acquiring, constructing, or producing a qualifying asset and
2. meet both recognition criteria—it is probable that associated future economic benefits will flow to the entity, and the cost can be measured reliably.

Qualifying assets must require **substantial time to get ready** for their intended use or sale. This may include inventories; items of property, plant, and equipment; investment properties; bearer plants; or intangible assets.

Borrowing costs for qualifying assets measured at fair value and inventories that are produced in large quantities on a repetitive basis **may be capitalized**, but it is not required.

Examples of assets that **do not qualify**, aside from financial assets, include (1) assets that are already in use or ready for their intended use when acquired; (2) those produced over a short period of time; and (3) assets not undergoing activities necessary to get them ready for use, such as land that is not being developed and assets that are not being used because of obsolescence, excess capacity, or needed repairs.

Capitalization Period

The **capitalization period** is the time over which interest must be capitalized. It **begins** on the **commencement date**, which is when **all three** of the following conditions are met:

1. Expenditures for the asset have been made.
2. Activities that are necessary to get the asset ready for its intended use or sale are in progress, including necessary pre-construction administrative and technical work.
3. Borrowing costs are being incurred.

Capitalization **ends** when substantially all the activities needed to prepare the asset for its intended use or sale are complete. This is usually when the physical activities associated with construction are finished, even if minor matters are still outstanding. If a project is finished in stages so that the parts completed can be used while activities continue on the remainder, capitalization stops on the parts that are substantially complete. If active development of a project is on hold, capitalization of the borrowing costs is **suspended**. Note that this does not refer to temporary delays needed as part of the development process.

Let's apply capitalization of borrowing costs to different situations associated with land. What if land was purchased with the intention of developing it for a particular use? If the land is purchased as a site for a structure (such as a plant site), the borrowing costs that are capitalized **during the construction period** are part of the cost of the plant, not of the land. Borrowing costs on the land while held and awaiting the start of construction are expensed. If land is being developed for sale as lots, the borrowing cost is part of the developed land's acquisition cost. However, borrowing costs involved in purchasing land that is held for speculation are not capitalized, because the asset is ready for its intended use.

Avoidable Borrowing Costs

To qualify for capitalization, the costs must be **directly attributable** to a project; in other words, they must be **avoidable borrowing costs**. When an entity borrows funds to finance a specific qualifying asset, the avoidable costs are the actual borrowing costs that would not have been incurred if the expenditures for the qualifying asset had not been made. These costs are reduced by the investment income earned on any temporary investment of these monies.

Avoidable costs are more difficult to calculate when a company's borrowings are not directly related to specific assets or projects. Some companies borrow funds using a variety of debt instruments to support their general financing requirements. In this case, the calculation is not as straightforward and professional judgement is often needed to determine which costs were avoidable.

In general, the following steps are taken to calculate the borrowing costs to capitalize:

1. Determine the expenditures on the qualifying asset.
2. Determine the avoidable borrowing costs on the asset-specific debt.
3. Determine the avoidable borrowing costs on the non–asset-specific debt.
4. Determine the borrowing costs to capitalize.

Step 1: Determine the Expenditures on the Qualifying Asset

The **expenditures on the qualifying asset** mean the **weighted-average accumulated expenditures**—the construction expenditures weighted by the amount of time (fraction of a year or accounting period) in which borrowing costs could be incurred. The expenditures include amounts paid for by cash or other assets or an interest-bearing liability, including previously capitalized borrowing costs. The expenditures are reduced by any progress payments received from a customer (in the case of construction of an inventory item) and by any grants received, such as from one or more levels of government. The following two examples, **Example 10A.1** and **10A.2**, are related, and provide sample calculations for a 17-month bridge construction project.

Example 10A.1 | Calculation of Weighted-Average Accumulated Expenditures

Facts Assume a 17-month bridge construction project with current-year payments to the contractor of $240,000 on March 1, $480,000 on July 1, and $360,000 on November 1.

Instructions Calculate and discuss the weighted-average accumulated expenditures for the year ended December 31.

Solution Calculation of weighted-average accumulated expenditures:

Expenditures			Capitalization		Weighted-Average Accumulated
Date	Amount	×	Period*	=	Expenditures
Mar. 1	$ 240,000		10/12		$200,000
July 1	480,000		6/12		240,000
Nov. 1	360,000		2/12		60,000
	$1,080,000				$500,000

*Months between the date of expenditure and the date when interest capitalization stops or year end arrives, whichever comes first (in this case, December 31)

The costs incurred are weighted by the amount of time that borrowing costs could have been incurred on each expenditure in the year. For the March 1 expenditure, 10 months of borrowing costs could be associated with the expenditure. For the expenditure on July 1, only six months of interest could have been incurred. For the November 1 expenditure, there would only be two months.

Step 2: Determine the Avoidable Borrowing Costs on the Asset-Specific Debt

In this example, there is no asset-specific borrowing and therefore, no asset-specific borrowing costs. If there were, remember that the borrowing costs on this debt would have to be reduced by the investment income on any temporary investment of the funds.

Step 3: Determine the Avoidable Borrowing Costs on the Non–Asset-Specific Debt

The next step entails (a) calculating an appropriate **capitalization rate** and (b) applying it to the weighted-average expenditures financed by general debt. The rate is a weighted-average borrowing rate on the general borrowings.

Example 10A.2 | Calculation of Capitalization Interest Rate

Facts Assume that the borrowings identified below are all outstanding for the full year.

	Principal	Borrowing costs[19]
12%, 2-year note	$ 600,000	$ 72,000
9%, 10-year bonds	2,000,000	180,000
7.5%, 20-year bonds	5,000,000	375,000
	$7,600,000	$627,000

Instructions Calculate the weighted-average capitalization rate for the company's general-purpose debt.

---

[19]Unlike investment income earned on the temporary investment of asset-specific borrowings, IAS 23 *Borrowing Costs* does not discuss whether investment income earned on general-purpose debt should reduce the borrowing costs eligible to be capitalized or not. The principles set out in this IFRS and the company-specific circumstances would have to be assessed to determine the best approach in each case.

Solution Because each debt instrument was outstanding for the full year, each principal amount is already weighted by $^{12}/_{12}$. The interest also represents a full 12 months of borrowing costs. The weighted-average capitalization rate on the general-purpose debt is calculated as follows:

$$\frac{\text{Total borrowing costs}}{\text{Weighted-average principal outstanding}} = \frac{\$627,000}{\$7,600,000} = 8.25\%$$

The avoidable borrowing cost on non–asset-specific debt is the total weighted-average amount of accumulated expenditures (from Example 10A.1) reduced by the weighted-average expenditures financed by asset-specific debt ($0 per step 2), multiplied by the capitalization rate (from Example 10A.2): ($500,000 – $0) × 8.25% = $41,250.

Step 4: Determine the Borrowing Costs to Capitalize

This step adds the eligible borrowing costs on asset-specific borrowings of $0 (step 2) and those on general borrowings of $41,250 (step 3) for a total of $41,250. This is the amount of cost to capitalize for Examples 10A.1 and 10A.2 above, unless the actual borrowing costs incurred in the year are less than this. The lower amount is used.

Illustration 10A.1 provides information relating to both asset-specific and general borrowings that is used for **Example 10A.3** below.

ILLUSTRATION 10A.1

Asset-Specific and General Borrowings—Shalla Corporation

Assume that on November 1, 2020, Shalla Corporation contracted with Pfeifer Construction Co. Ltd. to have a building constructed for its own use for $1.4 million, on land costing $100,000. The land is acquired from the contractor and its purchase price is included in the first payment. Shalla made the following payments to the construction company during 2021:

January 1	March 1	May 1	December 31	Total
$210,000	$300,000	$540,000	$450,000	$1,500,000

Construction of the building began very early in January and it was completed and ready for occupancy on December 31, 2021. Shalla had the following debt outstanding at December 31, 2021:

Specific Construction Debt	
15%, 3-year note to finance construction of the building, dated December 31, 2020, with interest payable annually on December 31	$750,000
Other Debt	
10%, 5-year note payable, dated December 31, 2018, with interest payable annually on December 31	$550,000
12%, 10-year bonds issued December 31, 2014, with interest payable annually on December 31	$600,000

Example 10A.3 | Calculation of Weighted-Average Accumulated Expenditures

Facts See Illustration 10A.1 for details of expenditures made by Shalla Company.

Instructions

a. Calculate and discuss the weighted-average accumulated expenditures for Shalla for the year ended December 31, 2021.

b. Determine the avoidable borrowing costs on the asset-specific debt.

c. Determine the avoidable borrowing costs on the non–asset-specific debt.

d. Determine the borrowing costs to capitalize.

e. Provide the land and building related journal entries made by Shalla during 2021.

Solution

Step 1

a. Calculation of weighted-average accumulated expenditures:

Expenditures			Current Year Capitalization		Weighted-Average Accumulated
Date	Amount	×	Period	=	Expenditures
Jan. 1	$ 210,000		12/12		$210,000
Mar 1	300,000		10/12		250,000
May 1	540,000		8/12		360,000
Dec. 31	450,000		–0–		–0–
	$1,500,000				$820,000

Note that the expenditure made on December 31, the last day of the year, gets a zero weighting in the calculation. It will have no borrowing cost assigned to it.

Step 2

b. To determine the avoidable borrowing costs on the asset-specific debt, keep in mind that the asset-specific construction debt of $750,000 was outstanding for the full year and is therefore weighted for a full 12 months. Therefore, the avoidable borrowing cost on this debt is $750,000 × 15% = $112,500.

Step 3

c. The avoidable borrowing costs on the non–asset-specific debt are shown below. They are the weighted-average accumulated expenditures financed by general borrowings multiplied by the capitalization rate.

Total weighted-average accumulated expenditures	$820,000
Less financed by specific construction loan	750,000
Weighted-average accumulated expenditures financed by general borrowings	$ 70,000

Capitalization rate calculation:	Principal	Borrowing Cost
10%, 5-year note: $550,000 × 12/12	$ 550,000	$ 55,000
12%, 10-year bonds: $600,000 × 12/12	600,000	72,000
	$1,150,000	$127,000

$$\text{Capitalization rate} = \frac{\text{Borrowing cost on general debt}}{\text{Weighted principal outstanding}} = \frac{\$127,000}{\$1,150,000} = 11.04\%$$

Avoidable borrowing cost on general debt: $70,000 × 11.04% = $7,728

Step 4

d. To determine the borrowing costs to capitalize, use the lower of the total avoidable borrowing costs eligible for capitalization (result of steps 2 and 3 above) and the actual borrowing costs incurred. The calculations are as follows:

Calculation of total avoidable and actual borrowing costs:

Avoidable costs on asset-specific debt		$112,500
Avoidable costs on general debt		7,728
Total avoidable borrowing costs		$120,228
Total actual borrowing costs for the period:		
Construction note	$750,000 × 0.15 =	$112,500
5-year note	$550,000 × 0.10 =	55,000
10-year bonds	$600,000 × 0.12 =	72,000
Actual borrowing costs		$239,500

The amount of borrowing costs capitalized, therefore, is $120,228.

e. The journal entries made by Shalla Company during 2021 are:

Jan. 1	Land	100,000	
	Buildings (or Construction in Process)	110,000	
	Cash		210,000
Mar. 1	Buildings	300,000	
	Cash		300,000
May 1	Buildings	540,000	
	Cash		540,000
Dec. 31	Buildings	450,000	
	Cash		450,000
Dec. 31	Buildings	120,228	
	Interest Expense		120,228

IFRS **ASPE** The capitalized borrowing costs of $120,228 in Example 10A.3 would be added to the building's acquisition cost and are amortized as part of its depreciation charge. In other words, under IFRS and ASPE, where it is the company's policy to capitalize interest costs, they will be recognized in expense over the useful life of the asset and not over the term of the debt. However, if under ASPE the company's policy is to expense all interest costs, the final journal entry in Example 10A.3 would not be recorded.

Disclosures

Only two disclosures are required for capitalized borrowing costs: the amount capitalized and the capitalization rate.

Illustration 10A.2 provides an example of BCE Inc.'s disclosures in its 2017 financial statements.

Disclosures Related to Borrowing Costs Capitalized—BCE Inc.

NOTE 7 INTEREST EXPENSE
(in millions of Canadian dollars, except where noted)

FOR THE YEAR ENDED DECEMBER 31	2017	2016
Interest expense on long-term debt	(898)	(852)
Interest expense on other debt	(101)	(86)
Capitalized interest	44	50
Total interest expense	(955)	(888)

Interest expense on long-term debt includes interest on finance leases of $145 million and $153 million for 2017 and 2016, respectively.

Capitalized interest was calculated using an average rate of 3.81% and 3.95% for 2017 and 2016, respectively, which represents the weighted average interest rate on our outstanding long-term debt.

Appendix 10B # Revaluation: The Proportionate Method

LEARNING OBJECTIVE 9

Understand and apply the revaluation model using the proportionate method.

IFRS Like the asset adjustment method, when using the proportionate method, a revaluation should be carried out often enough to ensure the carrying amount reported does not become materially different from fair value. For Example 10B.1, we will assume that the asset needs to be remeasured only every three years. Between revaluation dates, **depreciation is taken** on the revalued amount that has been adjusted proportionately.

Similar to the asset adjustment method, the amounts debited or credited to the Revaluation Surplus account are reported in the statement of comprehensive income as other comprehensive income (OCI) items. Also, over the life of the asset, the effect of the treatment described is that there is no **net increase** in net income from revaluing the asset. However, when revaluing an asset, the account is adjusted proportionately. Specifically, both the asset's carrying amount and its accumulated depreciation are adjusted (upward if there has been an increase in fair value, or downward for a decrease in fair value), so that the net balance is the fair value of the asset at the revaluation date. Examples 10B.1 and 10B.2 demonstrate the proportionate method.

Example 10B.1 | Proportionate Method—2017–2019

Facts   On January 1, 2017, Convo Corporation acquires a building at a cost of $100,000. The building is expected to have a 25-year life and no residual value, resulting in depreciation of $4,000 per year for the first three years ($100,000/25 years = $4,000). The asset is accounted for using the proportionate revaluation method and revaluation is carried out every three years. On December 31, 2019, the fair value of the building is appraised at $90,000.

Instructions   **IFRS**   Calculate the amounts to be adjusted under the proportionate method, and provide the related journal entry for the building on December 31, 2019, when fair value was $90,000.

Solution   The following journal entry records the differences for the building and accumulated depreciation between the amounts before (and after) revaluation, with the overall net increase being credited to revaluation surplus.

Proportionate method: Calculation and journal entry

	Before revaluation (A)		Proportionate amount after revaluation (B)	(B) – (A)
Buildings	$100,000	× 90/88	$102,273	$2,273
Accumulated depreciation	12,000	× 90/88	12,273	273
Carrying amount	$ 88,000	× 90/88	$ 90,000	$2,000

Buildings	2,273	
Accumulated Depreciation—Buildings		273
Revaluation Surplus (OCI)		2,000

A	=	L	+	SE
+2,000				+2,000

Cash flows: No effect

Example 10B.2 | Proportionate Method—2020–2022

Facts   We continue with the Convo Corporation example with the building at a cost of $100,000, with a 25-year life and no residual value. As detailed in Example 10B.1, on December 31, 2019, the fair value of the building was appraised at $90,000.

Instructions   **IFRS**
a. Calculate the amount of depreciation to be charged for each year from 2020 to 2022 and the amounts to be adjusted under the proportionate method in 2022.

b. Calculate the revaluation adjustment and provide the related journal entry on December 31, 2022, when it is determined that fair value of the building is appraised at $75,000.

Solution
a. The calculations and journal entries for the 2020–2022 depreciation entries and the revaluation adjustment are provided below using the proportionate method. The accumulated depreciation before revaluation in 2022 is calculated as $12,273 + ($4,091 × 3) = $24,546. The second journal entry records the differences for Buildings and Accumulated Depreciation—Buildings similar to the entry in 2019 in Example 10B.1. However, in 2022, because the adjustment results in the Revaluation Surplus (AOCI) account being reduced to zero, the remaining loss is recognized in the income statement.

Annual depreciation in each of 2020, 2021, and 2022 (journal entry and calculation):

Depreciation Expense	4,091	
Accumulated Depreciation—Buildings		4,091

$$\frac{(\$102,273 - \$12,273)}{22 \text{ years}} = \$4,091$$

A	=	L	+	SE
–4,091				–4,091

Cash flows: No effect

b. Revaluation model using the proportionate method (calculations and journal entry):

	Before revaluation (A)		Proportionate amount after revaluation (B)	(B) – (A)
Buildings	$102,273	× 75,000/77,727	$98,685	$(3,588)
Accumulated depreciation	24,546	× 75,000/77,727	23,685	(861)
Carrying amount	$ 77,727	× 75,000/77,727	$75,000	$(2,727)

A	=	L	+	SE
–2,727				–2,727

Cash flows: No effect

Accumulated Depreciation—Buildings	861	
Revaluation Surplus (OCI)	2,000	
Revaluation Gain or Loss	727	
Buildings		3,588

Review and Practice

Summary of Learning Objectives

1. Identify the business importance and characteristics of property, plant, and equipment assets and explain the recognition criteria.

Almost every enterprise invests in long-lived assets. These long-term items include both those that are physical assets—property, plant, and equipment—and those that are intangible. Long-lived assets are particularly important for manufacturing companies because they provide the capacity or infrastructure to produce goods and/or provide services.

Property, plant, and equipment assets are tangible assets held for use in the production of goods and services, for rental to others, or for administrative purposes, and have a useful life of more than one accounting period. This type of asset provides an entity with its operating capacity and infrastructure, but also adds to fixed costs. For this reason, it is important that a company invest enough in PP&E to meet its potential, but not so much that it has to bear the related costs of overcapacity.

PP&E costs that provide probable future economic benefits to the entity and that can be measured reliably are recognized as assets. Asset components should be recognized separately under IFRS to the extent their costs are significant and/or the related assets have different useful lives or patterns of depreciation.

2. Identify the costs to include in the measurement of property, plant, and equipment at acquisition.

Asset costs used when measuring PP&E include all necessary costs directly attributed to acquiring the asset, bringing it to its location, and making it ready for use. These include direct material, direct labour, and variable overhead costs for self-constructed PP&E assets, borrowing costs for those taking substantial time to get ready for use, and dismantling and restoration costs required as a result of the asset's acquisition. Once the asset is in place and ready for use, costs are no longer capitalized.

3. Determine asset cost when the transaction has delayed payment terms or is a lump-sum purchase, a nonmonetary exchange, or a contributed asset.

Cost means the asset's cash equivalent cost. When payment is deferred beyond normal credit terms, the excess paid over cash cost is interest. When a number of assets are acquired in a basket purchase, the cost is allocated based on the relative fair value of each. When PP&E assets are acquired and paid for by issuing the entity's shares, cost is usually determined as the fair value of the asset acquired. When acquired in an exchange of assets, cost is the fair value of the assets given up, unless the fair value of the assets received can be more reliably measured. However, if the transaction lacks commercial substance or fair values cannot be reliably determined, the assets acquired are measured at the book value of the assets given up. This amount cannot exceed the fair value of the assets acquired. Assets contributed to a company are measured at fair value and credited to Contributed Surplus if donated by a shareholder. This is rare. If contributed by government, the contribution is accounted for under the income approach: the amount credited flows through the income statement, usually as the asset is used by the entity.

4. Identify the costs included in specific types of property, plant, and equipment.

Land: Includes all expenditures made to acquire land and to make it ready for use. Land costs typically include the purchase price; closing costs, such as title to the land, legal fees, and registration fees; costs incurred to condition the land for its intended use, such as grading, filling, draining, and clearing; the assumption of any liens, mortgages, or encumbrances on the property; and any additional land improvements that have an indefinite life. **Buildings, including investment property:** Includes all expenditures related directly to their acquisition or construction. These costs include materials, labour, and direct overhead costs that are incurred during construction and professional fees and building permits. **Equipment:** Includes the purchase price, freight, and handling charges that are incurred; insurance on the equipment while it is in transit; the cost of special foundations if they are required; assembling and installation costs; and the costs incurred in calibrating the equipment so that it can be used as intended. **Mineral resource properties:** Four types of costs may be included in establishing the cost of mineral resource assets: (1) acquisition, (2) exploration and evaluation, (3) development, and (4) site restoration and asset retirement costs. Two main methods of accounting for oil and gas properties are the full cost method and the successful efforts method. **Biological Assets:** separate standards are set out in IAS 16 for bearer plants and IAS 41 for other assets related to agricultural activity.

---

5. Understand and apply the cost model, the revaluation model using the asset adjustment method, and the fair value model.

The cost model is appropriate for all classes of PP&E, including investment property. Under this model, the assets are carried at cost less accumulated depreciation and any accumulated impairment losses.

Under IFRS, the revaluation model may be applied to any class of PP&E except investment property, provided fair value can be measured reliably. Under this model, the assets are carried at their fair value at the revaluation date less any subsequent accumulated depreciation and any subsequent accumulated impairment losses. While held, net increases in fair value are not reported in income, but are accumulated in a Revaluation Surplus (OCI) account in equity. Net losses are reported in income once the revaluation surplus has been eliminated. At the time of revaluation, under the asset adjustment method, the accumulated depreciation account is eliminated (written off against the asset itself). The asset is then adjusted to its new revalued amount.

The fair value model can be applied only to investment property under IFRS, and the choice between cost and fair value must be made for all investment property reported. Under this model, all changes in fair value are recognized in net income. No depreciation is recognized.

---

6. Explain and apply the accounting treatment for costs incurred after acquisition.

Day-to-day servicing, repair, and maintenance costs, and costs of rearrangement and relocation, are expensed as incurred. PP&E expenditures that provide future economic benefits and whose costs can be reliably measured are capitalized. The cost of additions, replacements, and major overhauls and inspections are capitalized and the carrying amount of the replaced asset or the previous overhaul or inspection is removed.

---

7. Identify differences in accounting between IFRS and ASPE, and what changes are expected in the near future.

In general, the accounting for PP&E assets is very similar under both IFRS and ASPE because the principles underlying both are very similar. However, under IFRS, rules are more strict regarding accounting for components and major overhauls and inspections, incidental revenues and expenses before asset use, and borrowing costs. IFRS permits application of a revaluation model and a fair value model, neither of which is acceptable under ASPE. The IASB is researching extractive industry activities with the objective of developing accounting standards to cover the exploration for, and the development and extraction of, minerals and oil and gas resources and assets.

---

8. Calculate the amount of borrowing costs to capitalize for qualifying assets.

The avoidable borrowing costs related to the financing of eligible expenditures on qualifying assets are capitalized under IFRS to the extent they are less than the total borrowing costs incurred in the period.

---

9. Understand and apply the revaluation model using the proportionate method.

The revaluation model may be applied using the proportionate method, provided fair value can be measured reliably. Similar to the asset adjustment method, the amounts debited or credited to the Revaluation Surplus (OCI) account are reported in the statement of comprehensive income as other comprehensive income (OCI) items. However, when revaluing an asset, the account is adjusted proportionately so that both the carrying amount of the asset and the accumulated depreciation are adjusted (upward if there has been an increase in fair value, or downward for a decrease in fair value). After adjustment, the net balance is the fair value of the asset at the revaluation date.

Practice Problem

Columbia Ltd., which manufactures machine tools, had the following transactions related to plant assets in 2020.

Asset A: On June 2, 2020, Columbia purchased a stamping machine at a retail price of $12,000. Columbia paid 6% provincial sales tax on this purchase. Columbia paid a contractor $2,800 to install the machine. Columbia estimates the machine will have a four-year useful life, with a residual value of $2,000 at the end of four years. The machine was put into use on July 1, 2020.

Asset B: On January 1, 2020, Columbia signed a fixed-price contract for construction of a warehouse facility at a cost of $1 million. It was estimated that the project will be completed by December 31, 2020. On March 1, 2020, to finance the construction cost, Columbia borrowed $1 million payable on April 1, 2021, at an interest rate of 10%. During 2020, Columbia made deposit and progress payments totalling $750,000 under the contract; the weighted-average amount of accumulated expenditures was $400,000 for the year. The excess borrowed funds were invested in short-term securities, from which Columbia realized investment revenue of $13,000. The warehouse was completed on December 31, 2020, at which time Columbia made the final payment to the contractor. Columbia estimates the warehouse will have a 25-year useful life, with a residual value of $20,000.

Columbia uses straight-line depreciation and calculates depreciation to the nearest full month for its partial-year depreciation. Columbia's fiscal year ends on December 31.

Instructions

a. At what amount should Columbia record the acquisition cost of the machine?

b. What amount of capitalized interest should Columbia include in the cost of the warehouse?

c. On July 1, 2022, Columbia decides to outsource its stamping operation to Medek Group. As part of this plan, Columbia sells the machinery to Medek for $7,000. What is the impact of this disposal on Columbia's 2022 income before taxes?

Solution

a. Historical cost is measured by the cash or cash equivalent price of obtaining the asset and bringing it to the location and condition for its intended use. For Columbia, this is:

Price	$12,000
Sales tax ($12,000 × .06)	720
Installation	2,800
Total	$15,520

b. $40,000 ($400,000 × .10)—Weighted-Average Accumulated Expenditures × Interest Rate = Avoidable Interest

Since Columbia has outstanding debt incurred specifically for the construction project, in an amount greater than the weighted-average accumulated expenditures of $400,000, the interest rate of 10% is used for capitalization purposes. Capitalization stops upon completion of the project at December 31, 2020. Therefore, the avoidable interest is $40,000, which is less than the actual interest. The investment income earned of $13,000 reduces the interest capitalized. Thus, total interest capitalization is $27,000 ($40,000 − $13,000).

c. The income effect is a gain or loss, determined by comparing the book value of the asset with the disposal value. In this situation, it would be a loss of $1,760 as detailed below:

Cost	$15,520
Less: Accumulated depreciation ($1,690 + $3,380 + $1,690)	6,760*
Book value of machine and platform	8,760
Less: Cash received for machine and platform	7,000
Loss before income taxes	$ 1,760

Depreciable base: $15,520 − $2,000 = $13,520. Depreciation expense: $13,520 ÷ 4 = $3,380 per year.

2020: 6/12 months ($3,380 × .50)	$1,690
2021: full year	3,380
2022: 6/12 months	1,690
Total	$6,760

Key Terms

additions, p. 10-29
asset retirement costs, p. 10-9
avoidable borrowing costs, p. 10-38
biological assets, p. 10-5
boot, p. 10-15
borrowing costs, p. 10-37
capital approach, p. 10-18
capital expenditure, p. 10-29
capitalization period, p. 10-38
capitalization rate, p. 10-39
capitalized, p. 10-5
commercial substance, p. 10-15
cost, p. 10-6
cost model (CM), p. 10-23
cost reduction method, p. 10-19
deferral method, p. 10-19

depletion base, p. 10-22
fair value, p. 10-24
fair value model (FVM), p. 10-27
fixed assets, p. 10-4
full cost method, p. 10-22
income approach, p. 10-18
inspections, p. 10-30
investment property, p. 10-21
leasehold improvements, p. 10-20
lump-sum price, p. 10-12
major overhauls, p. 10-30
mineral resource properties, p. 10-21
mineral resources, p. 10-21
monetary assets, p. 10-14
nonmonetary assets, p. 10-14
non-reciprocal transfers, p. 10-18

ordinary repairs, p. 10-33
plant assets, p. 10-4
property, plant, and equipment, p. 10-5
qualifying assets, p. 10-37
rearrangement and reinstallation costs,
   p. 10-33
replacements, p. 10-30
revaluation model (RM), p. 10-24
revenue expenditure, p. 10-29
self-constructed assets, p. 10-7
successful efforts method, p. 10-22
tangible capital assets, p. 10-4
unit of measure, p. 10-5
weighted-average accumulated expenditures,
   p. 10-38

Assignment Material

All assignment material with an asterisk (*) relates to the appendices to the chapter.

Note: **Enabling Competencies** Completion of this end-of-chapter material will help develop CPA-enabling competencies (such as ethics and professionalism, problem-solving and decision-making, and communication) and technical competencies. We have highlighted selected items with a specific integration word mark and material in *WileyPLUS* has been linked to the competencies. All cases emphasize integration, especially of the enabling competencies. The brief exercises, exercises, and problems generally emphasize problem-solving and decision-making.

Brief Exercises

BE10.1 (LO 1) Caruso Airlines Incorporated is a privately owned commercial airline servicing short-haul routes in Western Canada. Caruso has operated successfully and profitably for five years. It is now considering expanding its fleet of 10 aircraft by adding 15 new aircraft, in order to service its existing routes more efficiently. Caruso would pay for the expansion with a combination of internally generated funds and a new bank loan. Discuss the effects of Caruso's expansion on the company's (a) business and operations, (b) financial statements, and (c) rate of return on assets and asset turnover.

BE10.2 (LO 1, 7) Playtime Corporation purchased a new piece of equipment for production of a new children's toy. According to market research tests, the toy is expected to be very popular among preschool-aged children. The equipment consists of the following significant and separable parts: injection unit (useful life of six years), clamping unit (useful life of six years), and electrical equipment (useful life of three years). The equipment also includes other parts (useful life of five years). Discuss (a) the recognition criteria for recording the purchase of the equipment, (b) how the equipment purchase should be recorded if Playtime prepares financial statements in accordance with IFRS, and (c) how the equipment purchase should be recorded if Playtime prepares financial statements in accordance with ASPE.

BE10.3 (LO 2, 4, 7) Barnet Brothers Inc. purchased land and an old building with the intention of removing the old building and then constructing the company's new corporate headquarters on the land. The land and old building were purchased for $570,000. Closing costs were $6,000. The old building was removed at a cost of $48,000. After readying the land for its intended use, and while waiting for construction to begin, Barnet generated net revenue of $4,000 from using the land as a parking lot. Determine the amount to be recorded as the land cost, and the treatment of the net revenue of $4,000, if Barnet prepares financial statements in accordance with (a) IFRS and (b) ASPE.

BE10.4 (LO 2, 4, 7) Northern Utilities Corporation incurred the following costs in constructing a new maintenance building during the fiscal period:

  Video

a. Direct labour costs incurred up to the point when the building is in a condition necessary for use as management intended, but before Northern begins operating in the building, $73,000

b. Additional direct labour costs incurred before Northern begins operating in the building, $6,000

c. Material purchased for the building, $82,500

d. Interest on the loan to finance construction until completion, $2,300

e. Allocation of variable plant overhead based on labour hours worked on the building, $29,000

f. Architectural drawings for the building, $7,500

g. Allocation of the president's salary, $54,000

What costs should be included in the cost of the new building if Northern prepares financial statements in accordance with IFRS? With ASPE? (Assume that, if there is no specific guidance from GAAP, Northern's management would consider a building ready for productive use when Northern begins operating in the building and would prefer not to capitalize interest costs directly attributable to the acquisition, construction, or development of property, plant, and equipment.)

BE10.5 (LO 3) Parolin Limited purchased equipment for an invoice price of $40,000, terms 2/10, n/30. (a) Record the purchase of the equipment and the subsequent payment, assuming the payment was made within the discount period. (b) Repeat part (a), but assume the company's payment missed the discount period. (c) What would be a good policy or procedure to adopt for purchases of property, plant, and equipment where a discount is offered, and how would it work?

BE10.6 (LO 3) Chavez Corporation purchased a truck by issuing an $80,000, four-year, non–interest-bearing note to Equinox Inc. The market interest rate for obligations of this nature is 8%. Calculate the purchase price using any of the three methods (tables, financial calculator, or Excel). Prepare the journal entry to record the truck purchase.

BE10.7 (LO 3) Martin Corporation purchased a truck by issuing an $80,000, 8% note to Equinox Inc. Interest is payable annually and the note is payable in four years. Prepare the journal entry to record the truck purchase.

BE10.8 (LO 3) Hamm Inc. purchased land, a building, and equipment from Spamela Corporation for a cash payment of $406,000. The assets' estimated fair values are land $95,000, building $250,000, and equipment $110,000. At what amounts should each of the three assets be recorded? Do not round intermediate calculations for the percentage allocation between the assets.

BE10.9 (LO 3, 7) Wizard Corp., a private company, obtained land by issuing 2,000 of its common shares. The land was appraised at $85,000 by a reliable, independent valuator on the date of acquisition. Last year, Wizard sold 1,000 common shares at $41 per share. Prepare the journal entry to record the land acquisition (a) if Wizard elects to prepare financial statements in accordance with IFRS and (b) if Wizard prepares financial statements in accordance with ASPE.

BE10.10 (LO 3) Kongus Inc. traded a used vehicle (cost $23,000, accumulated depreciation $20,700) for another used vehicle with a fair value of $3,700. Kongus also paid $300 cash in the transaction. Prepare the journal entry to record the exchange, assuming the transaction lacks commercial substance.

BE10.11 (LO 3) Seymour Ltd. traded a used welding machine (cost $9,000, accumulated depreciation $2,000, fair value $3,000) for equipment with an estimated fair value of $8,000. Seymour also paid $4,000 cash in the transaction. Prepare the journal entry to record the exchange. The equipment results in different cash flows for Seymour, compared with those the welding machine produced.

BE10.12 (LO 3) Spencer Ltd. traded a used truck (cost $30,000, accumulated depreciation $27,000, fair value $2,000) for a new truck with a fair value of $33,000. Spencer also made a cash payment of $31,000. Prepare Spencer's entry to record the exchange, and state any assumptions that you have made.

BE10.13 (LO 3) Use the information for Spencer Ltd. from BE10.12. The same used truck is being traded, but Spencer does not know the fair value of the new truck. Spencer did look up the value of its used truck and determined its fair value at the date of the trade is $2,000. The list price of the new truck is $36,000 and the trade-in allowance given on the trade was $5,000. If Spencer paid $31,000, what should be the amount used as the cost of the new truck? Prepare Spencer's entry to record the exchange.

BE10.14 (LO 3) In early January, Swanton Corp. purchased land as a building site to house its manufacturing operations in Moose Jaw for $470,000. The municipality donated $140,000 to Swanton as an incentive to locate in the area and acquire the land. Prepare entries to record the cash that was exchanged in each of the transactions, assuming the cost reduction method is used.

BE10.15 (LO 3) Use the information for Swanton Corp. in BE10.14. Prepare the entries to record the cash transactions, assuming the deferral method is used.

BE10.16 (LO 3) Dubois Inc. received equipment as a donation. The equipment has a fair value of $55,000. Prepare the journal entry to record the receipt of the equipment under each of the following assumptions:

a. The equipment was donated by a shareholder.

b. The equipment was donated by a retired employee.

BE10.17 (LO 4, 7) Lowell Corporation acquires a gold mine at a cost of $400,000. Development costs that were incurred total $100,000, including $12,300 of depreciation on movable equipment to construct mine shafts. Based on construction to date, the legal obligation to restore the property after the mine is exhausted has a present value of $75,000. Lowell has publicly pledged an additional $20,000 (present value) for improved reclamation of the area surrounding the mine. Prepare the journal entries to record the cost of the natural resource if Lowell prepares financial statements in accordance with (a) IFRS and (b) ASPE. (*Hint:* Use a Mineral Resources account.)

*BE10.18 (LO 5, 9)** Valued Assets Inc., a publicly listed company, has a building with an initial cost of $400,000. At December 31, 2020, the date of revaluation, accumulated depreciation amounted to $110,000. The fair value of the building, by comparing it with transactions involving similar assets, is assessed to be $330,000. Prepare the journal entries to revalue the plant under the revaluation model using (a) the asset adjustment method and (b) the proportionate method. Do not round intermediate calculations but round final amounts to the nearest dollar.

*BE10.19 **(LO 5, 9)** Use the information for Valued Assets Inc. from BE10.18. On January 5, 2021, Valued sold the building for $325,000 cash. Prepare the journal entries to record the sale of the building after having used (a) the cost model, (b) the revaluation model using the asset adjustment method, and (c) the revaluation model using the proportionate method. Do not round intermediate calculations for the percentage allocation when using the proportionate method.

BE10.20 **(LO 5, 7)** TrueNorth Investment Properties Inc. and its subsidiaries have provided you with a list of the properties they own:

a. Land held by TrueNorth for undetermined future use

b. A vacant building owned by TrueNorth and to be leased out under an operating lease

c. Property held by a subsidiary of TrueNorth, a real estate firm, in the ordinary course of its business

d. Property held by TrueNorth for use in the manufacturing of products

Advise TrueNorth and its subsidiaries as to the proper presentation and measurement options for the above properties under both IFRS and ASPE.

BE10.21 **(LO 8)** Identify whether the following costs should be treated as a capital expenditure or a revenue expenditure when they are incurred.

a. $13,000 paid to rearrange and reinstall machinery

b. $400 paid for a tune-up and oil change on a delivery truck

c. $200,000 paid for an addition to a building

d. $7,000 paid to replace a wooden floor with a concrete floor

e. $4,000 paid for a major overhaul that extends the useful life of a truck

f. $700,000 paid for relocating company headquarters

g. $6,000 to replace 18 tires on a trailer

BE10.22 **(LO 6, 7)** Shipper Inc. has acquired a large transport truck at a cost of $90,000 (with no breakdown of the component parts). The truck's estimated useful life is 10 years. At the end of the seventh year, the powertrain requires replacement. It is determined that it is not economical to put any more money or time into maintaining the old powertrain. The rest of the transport truck is in good working condition and is expected to last for the next three years. The cost of a new powertrain is $40,000. (a) Should the cost of the new powertrain be recognized as an asset or as an expense? (b) How should the transaction be measured and recorded if Shipper prepares financial statements in accordance with IFRS? (c) How should the transaction be measured and recorded if Shipper prepares financial statements in accordance with ASPE?

*BE10.23 **(LO 2, 8)** Brent Hill Company is constructing a building. Construction began on February 1 and was completed on December 31. Expenditures were $1.5 million on March 1, $1.2 million on June 1, and $3 million on December 31. Calculate Brent Hill's weighted-average accumulated expenditures that would be used for capitalization of borrowing costs.

*BE10.24 **(LO 2, 8)** Brent Hill Company (see BE10.23) borrowed $1 million on March 1 on a five-year, 12% note to help finance the building construction. In addition, the company had outstanding all year a $2-million, five-year, 13% note payable and a $3.5-million, four-year, 15% note payable. Calculate the appropriate capitalization rate on general borrowings that would be used for capitalization of borrowing costs. Round to two decimal places.

*BE10.25 **(LO 2, 7, 8)** Use the information for Brent Hill Company from BE10.23 and BE10.24. Calculate the company's avoidable borrowing costs assuming Brent Hill Company follows IFRS. How would your answer change if the company followed ASPE?

Exercises

E10.1 **(LO 1)** **(Cost Elements and Asset Componentization)** The following assets have been recognized as items of property, plant, and equipment:

1. Head office boardroom table and executive chairs

2. Landfill site

3. Escalator in shopping mall

4. Forklift vehicles in a manufacturing plant

5. Stand-alone training facility for pilot training, including a flight simulator and classrooms equipped with desks, whiteboards, and electronic instructional aids

6. Large passenger aircraft used in commercial flights

7. Medical office building

8. Computer equipment

Instructions

For each of the items listed:

a. Identify what specific costs are likely to be included in the acquisition cost.

b. Explain whether any components of this asset should be given separate recognition, and why.

E10.2 (LO 2, 3) **(Purchase and Cost of Self-Constructed Assets)** Wen Corp., a public company located in Manitoba, both purchases and constructs various pieces of machinery and equipment that it uses in its operations. The following items are for machinery that was purchased and a piece of equipment that was constructed during the 2020 fiscal year:

Machinery

Cash paid for machinery, including sales tax of $7,000 and recoverable GST of $5,000	$112,000
Freight and insurance cost while in transit	2,000
Cost of moving machinery into place at factory	3,100
Wage cost for technicians to test machinery	4,000
Materials cost for testing	500
Insurance premium paid on the machinery for its first year of operation	1,500
Special plumbing fixtures required for new machinery	8,000
Repair cost on machinery incurred in first year of operations	1,300
Cash received from provincial government as incentive to purchase machinery	25,000

Equipment (Self-Constructed)

Material and purchased parts (gross cost $200,000; failed to take 2% cash discount; the company uses the net method of recording purchases of material and parts)	$200,000
Imputed interest on funds used during construction (*Note:* The company has no borrowing costs but it has calculated imputed interest on its equity/ share financing)	14,000
Labour costs for manufacturing the equipment	190,000
Overhead costs (fixed $20,000; variable $30,000)	50,000
Profit on self-construction	30,000
Cost of installing equipment	4,400

Instructions

Prepare a schedule to (a) calculate the cost of the machinery and (b) calculate the cost of the equipment (show details of each item separately). (*Note:* If an item is not capitalized as a machinery or equipment cost, indicate how it should be reported.)

E10.3 (LO 2, 3, 7) **(Entries for Asset Acquisition, Including Self-Construction)** The following are transactions related to Producers Limited:

1. The City of Piedmont gives the company five hectares of land as a plant site. This land's fair value is determined to be $92,000.

2. Producers issues 13,000 common shares in exchange for land and buildings. The property has been appraised at a fair value of $1,630,000, of which $407,000 has been allocated to land, $887,000 to the structure of the buildings, $220,000 to the building HVAC (heating, ventilation, air conditioning), and $116,000 to the interior coverings in the buildings (such as flooring). Producers' shares are not listed on any exchange, but a block of 100 shares was sold by a shareholder 12 months ago at $57 per share, and a block of 200 shares was sold by another shareholder 18 months ago at $33 per share.

3. No entry has been made to remove amounts for machinery constructed during the year that were charged to the accounts Inventory, Supplies, and Salaries and Wages Expense and should have been

charged to plant asset accounts. The following information relates to the costs of the machinery that was constructed:

Construction materials on hand in opening inventory used	$ 23,000
Direct materials used in calibrating the equipment	625
Supplies used	980
Direct labour incurred	56,000
Additional variable overhead (over regular) caused by construction of machinery, excluding supplies used (charged to Inventory)	8,700
Fixed overhead rate applied to regular manufacturing operations	70% of direct labour cost
Lost revenue due to downtime during construction	45,000
Cost of similar machinery if it had been purchased from outside suppliers	125,000

Instructions

a. Prepare journal entries on the books of Producers Limited to record these transactions. Assume that Producers Limited prepares financial statements in accordance with IFRS.

b. Determine how your answer in part (a) would change if Producers follows ASPE.

E10.4 (LO 2, 3, 7) **(Treatment of Various Costs)**   Farrey Supply Ltd. is a newly formed public corporation that incurred the following costs related to land, buildings, and machinery:

Legal fees for title search		$ 520
Property tax in arrears at property purchase date		4,500
Architect's fees		2,800
Cash paid for land and dilapidated building on it		112,000
Removal of old building	$20,000	
Less: Salvage	5,500	14,500
Surveying before construction		370
Interest on short-term loans during construction		7,400
Excavation before construction for basement and foundation		19,000
Machinery purchased (subject to 2% cash discount, which was not taken)		65,000
Freight on machinery purchased		1,340
Exchange on foreign currency purchase of machinery		1,200
Storage charges on machinery, made necessary because building was still under construction when machinery was delivered		2,180
New building constructed (building construction took six months from date of purchase of land and old building)		485,000
Assessment by city for drainage project		1,600
Fence surrounding the property for security		15,000
Hauling charges for delivery of machinery from storage to new building		620
Installation of machinery		2,000
Customs duty on importing machinery		5,400
Municipal grant to promote locating building in the municipality		(8,000)

Instructions

a. Determine the amounts that should be included in the cost of land, buildings, and machinery. Indicate how any amounts that are not included in these accounts should be recorded.

b. Assume that Farrey is not a public company, and that it prepares financial statements in accordance with ASPE. Would the solution provided in part (a) be affected? If so, how?

c. From the perspective of a potential investor, what are the financial statement effects of capitalizing borrowing costs related to qualifying assets?

d. **Digging Deeper** What effects, if any, will the recording of purchases to an incorrect account (land, building, machinery, or any other property, plant, and equipment asset) have on the financial statements? Provide an example.

*E10.5 (LO 2, 3, 7, 8)** **(Asset Acquisition)** Hayes Industries Corp. purchased the following assets and also constructed a building. All this was done during the current year using a variety of financing alternatives.

Assets 1 and 2

These assets were purchased together for $100,000 cash. The following information was gathered:

	Initial Cost on Seller's Books	Depreciation to Date on Seller's Books	Book Value on Seller's Books	Appraised Value
Machinery	$100,000	$50,000	$50,000	$90,000
Equipment	60,000	10,000	50,000	30,000

Asset 3

This machine was acquired by making a $10,000 down payment and issuing a $30,000, two-year, zero-interest-bearing note. The note is to be paid off in two $15,000 instalments made at the end of the first and second years. It was determined that the asset could have been purchased outright for $35,000.

Asset 4

A truck was acquired by trading in an older truck that has the same value in use. The newer truck has options that will make it more comfortable for the driver; however, the company remains in the same economic position after the exchange as before. Facts concerning the trade-in are as follows:

Cost of truck traded	$85,000
Accumulated depreciation to date of exchange	35,000
Fair market value of truck traded	60,000
Cash paid by Hayes	10,000
Fair market value of truck acquired	70,000

Asset 5

Equipment was acquired by issuing 100 common shares. The shares are actively traded and had a closing market price a few days before the equipment was acquired of $9.25 per share. Alternatively, the equipment could have been purchased for a cash price of $900.

Construction of Building

A building was constructed on land that was purchased January 1 at a cost of $150,000. Construction began on February 1 and was completed November 1. The payments to the contractor were as follows:

Date	Payment
Feb. 1	$120,000
June 1	360,000
Sept. 1	480,000
Nov. 1	100,000

To finance construction of the building, a $600,000, 12% construction loan was taken out on February 1. At the beginning of the project, Hayes invested the portion of the construction loan that was not yet expended and earned investment income of $4,600. The loan was repaid on November 1 when the construction was completed. The firm had $200,000 of other outstanding debt during the year at a borrowing rate of 8% and a $350,000 loan payable outstanding at a borrowing rate of 6%.

Instructions

a. **Finance** Hayes uses a variety of alternatives to finance its acquisitions. Record the acquisition of each of these assets, assuming that Hayes prepares financial statements in accordance with IFRS.

b. How might your answer to part (a) change regarding the "Construction of Building" item if the company followed ASPE instead of IFRS?

c. What was the effective interest rate used in negotiating the note payable used to acquire the machinery in Asset 3? Use Excel or a financial calculator to arrive at your answer. Round your answer to three decimal places.

E10.6 (LO 2, 4) **(Acquisition Costs of Equipment)** Lavoie Corporation acquired new equipment at a cost of $100,000 plus 7% provincial sales tax and 5% GST. (GST is a recoverable tax.) The company paid $1,700 to transport the equipment to its plant. The site where the equipment was to be placed was not yet ready and Lavoie Corporation spent another $500 for one month's storage costs. When installed, $300 in labour and $200 in materials were used to adjust and calibrate the machine to the company's exact specifications. The units produced in the trial runs were subsequently sold to employees for $400. During the first two months of production, the equipment was used at only 50% of its capacity. Labour costs of $3,000 and material costs of $2,000 were incurred in this production, while the units sold generated $5,500 of sales. Lavoie paid an engineering consulting firm $11,000 for its services in recommending the specific equipment to purchase and for help during the calibration phase. Borrowing costs of $800 were incurred because of the one-month delay in installation.

Instructions

Determine the capitalized cost of the equipment and explain why the remainder of the costs have not been capitalized.

E10.7 (LO 2, 4)   (Directly Attributable Costs)   DAC Manufacturing Inc. is installing a new plant at its production facility. It has incurred these costs:

Cost of the manufacturing plant (cost per supplier's invoice plus non-recoverable taxes)	$2,500,000
Initial delivery and handling costs	200,000
Cost of site preparation	600,000
Consultants used for advice on the acquisition of the plant	100,000
Interest charges paid to supplier of plant (indirect financing charges for amounts borrowed by supplier)	200,000
Estimated dismantling costs to be incurred after seven years	300,000
Operating losses before commercial production	400,000

Instructions

Determine which costs DAC Manufacturing Inc. can capitalize in accordance with IAS 16.

E10.8 (LO 2, 4)   (Acquisition Costs of Realty)   The following expenditures and receipts are related to land, land improvements, and buildings that were acquired for use in a business enterprise. The receipts are in parentheses.

1. Money borrowed to pay a building contractor (signed a note), ($275,000)
2. A payment for building construction from note proceeds, $275,000
3. The cost of landfill and clearing, $8,000
4. Delinquent real estate taxes on property, assumed by the purchaser, $7,000
5. A premium on a six-month insurance policy during construction, $6,000
6. Refund of one month's insurance premium because construction was completed early, ($1,000)
7. An architect's fee on a building, $22,000
8. The cost of real estate purchased as a plant site (land $200,000, building $50,000), $250,000
9. A fee paid to a real estate agency for finding the property, $9,000 relating to the land purchase (see 8)
10. The installation of fences around a property, $4,000
11. The cost of razing (demolishing) and removing the building on the plant site (see item 8), $11,000
12. Proceeds from the salvage of the demolished building, ($5,000)
13. Interest paid during construction on money borrowed for construction, $13,000
14. The cost of parking lots and driveways, $19,000
15. The cost of trees that were planted (non-permanent in nature, to be replaced every 20 years), $14,000
16. Excavation costs for new building, $3,000
17. The recoverable GST on the excavation cost, $150

Instructions

Identify each item by number and list the items in columnar form, as shown below. Using the column headings that follow, write the number for each item in the first column and the amount that would be included in each general ledger account under the column heading where it would be recorded. All receipt amounts should be reported in parentheses. For any amounts that should be entered in the Other Accounts column, also indicate the account title.

Item	Land	Land Improvements	Buildings	Other Accounts

E10.9 (LO 2, 4) Excel **(Acquisition Costs of Realty)**   Glesen Corp. purchased land with two old buildings on it as a factory site for $460,000. The property tax assessment (that is, assessed value) on this property was $350,000: $250,000 for the land and the rest for the buildings. It took six months to tear down the old buildings and construct the factory.

The company paid $50,000 to raze the old buildings and it sold salvaged copper, lumber, and brick for $6,300. Legal fees of $1,850 were paid for title search and drawing up the purchase contract. Payment to an engineering firm was made for a land survey, $2,200, and for drawing the factory plans, $82,000.

The land survey had to be made before final plans could be drawn. The liability insurance premium that was paid during construction was $900. The contractor's charge for construction was $3,640,000. The company paid the contractor in two instalments: $1,200,000 at the end of three months and $2,440,000 upon completion. The architects and engineers estimated the cost of the building to be 55% attributable to the structure, 35% attributable to the HVAC services (heating, ventilation, air conditioning), and the remainder attributable to the roof structure, as each of these elements is expected to have a different useful life. Interest costs of $170,000 were incurred to finance the construction.

Instructions

Determine the land and building costs as they should be recorded on the books of Glesen Corp. Assume that the land survey was for the building.

E10.10 (LO 2, 4, 7) **(Natural Resource—Copper)** Copper Products Limited leases property on which copper has been discovered. The lease provides for an immediate payment of $472,000 to the lessor before drilling has begun and an annual rental of $55,000. In addition, the lessee is responsible for cleaning up the waste and debris from drilling and for the costs of reconditioning the land for farming when the mine is abandoned. It is estimated that the legal obligation related to cleanup and reconditioning has a present value of $46,000. Copper Products has publicly pledged an additional $30,000 (present value) to reclaim the area surrounding the mine. Copper Products prepares financial statements in accordance with IFRS.

Instructions

a. **Finance** Determine the amount that should be capitalized in the Mineral Resources asset account as a result of the lease agreement.

b. Would the amount provided in part (a) differ if Copper Products prepared financial statements in accordance with ASPE?

c. **Digging Deeper** **Finance** Prior to entering into the lease agreement, assume that Copper Products had total debt of $580,000 and total assets of $1 million. Also assume that the immediate payment of $472,000 was paid upfront in cash. From the perspective of a creditor, discuss the effect of the lease agreement on Copper Products' debt to total assets ratio. Assume that Copper Products follows IFRS.

E10.11 (LO 3, 7) **Excel** **(Acquisition Costs of Vehicles)** Wu Inc. operates a retail computer store. To improve its delivery services to customers, the company purchased four new trucks on April 1, 2020. The terms of acquisition for each truck were as follows:

1. Truck #1 had a list price of $27,000 and was acquired for a cash payment of $23,900.

2. Truck #2 had a list price of $28,000 and was acquired for a down payment of $2,000 cash and a non–interest-bearing note with a face amount of $26,000. The note is due April 1, 2021. Wu would normally have to pay interest at a rate of 10% for such a borrowing, and the dealership has an incremental borrowing rate of 8%.

3. Truck #3 had a list price of $25,000. It was acquired in exchange for a computer system that Wu carries in inventory. The computer system cost $16,500 and is normally sold by Wu for $21,000. Wu uses a perpetual inventory system.

4. Truck #4 had a list price of $26,000. It was acquired in exchange for 1,000 common shares of Wu Inc. The common shares trade in an active market valued at $23 per share in the most recent trade.

Instructions

a. Prepare the appropriate journal entries for Wu Inc. for the above transactions, assuming that Wu prepares financial statements in accordance with IFRS. If there is some uncertainty about the amount, give reasons for your choice. For Truck #2, calculate the purchase price using any of the three methods (tables, financial calculator, or Excel).

b. Would the journal entries for transaction 4 prepared in part (a) differ if Wu prepared financial statements in accordance with ASPE?

E10.12 (LO 3) **(Correction of Improper Cost Entries)** Plant acquisitions for selected companies are as follows:

1. Bella Industries Inc. acquired land, buildings, and equipment from a bankrupt company, Torres Co., for a lump-sum price of $700,000. At the time of purchase, Torres's assets had the following book and appraisal values:

	Book Value	Appraisal Value
Land	$200,000	$150,000
Buildings	250,000	350,000
Equipment	300,000	300,000

Bella Industries decided to take the lower of the two values for each asset it acquired. The following entry was made:

Land	150,000	
Buildings	250,000	
Equipment	300,000	
Cash		700,000

Bella Industries expects the building structure to last another 20 years; however, it expects that it will have to replace the roof in the next five years. Torres Co. indicated that, on initial construction of the building, the roof amounted to 20% of the cost of the building. Because of the unique design and materials needed to replace the roof, the contractors stated that the roof structure is currently worth 15% of the value of the building purchase.

2. Hari Enterprises purchased equipment by making a $2,000 cash down payment and signing a $23,000, one-year, 10% note payable. The purchase was recorded as follows:

Equipment	27,300	
Cash		2,000
Notes Payable		23,000
Interest Payable		2,300

3. Kim Company purchased equipment for $20,000, terms 2/10, n/30. Because the company intended to take the discount, it made no entry until it paid for the acquisition. The entry was:

Equipment	20,000	
Cash		19,600
Purchase Discounts		400

4. Kaiser Inc. recently received land at zero cost from the Village of Chester as an inducement to locate its business in the village. The land's appraised value was $27,000. The company made no entry to record the land because it had no cost basis.

5. Zimmerman Company built a warehouse for $600,000. It could have contracted out and purchased the building for $740,000. The controller made the following entry:

Buildings	740,000	
Cash		600,000
Sales Revenue		140,000

Instructions

a. Prepare the entry that should have been made at the date of each acquisition. Do not round intermediate calculations for the percentage allocation between the assets but round final amounts to the nearest dollar.

b. Prepare the correcting entry that is required in each case to correct the accounts. In other words, do not simply reverse the incorrect entry and replace it with the entry in part (a).

c. **Digging Deeper** List the accounting principle, assumption, or constraint from the conceptual framework that has been violated in each case.

E10.13 (LO 3) **(Entries for Equipment Acquisitions)** Geddes Engineering Corporation purchased conveyor equipment with a list price of $50,000. Three independent cases that are related to the equipment follow. Assume that the equipment purchases are recorded gross.

1. Geddes paid cash for the equipment 25 days after the purchase, along with 5% GST (recoverable) and provincial sales tax of $3,500, both based on the purchase price. The vendor's credit terms were 1/10, n/30.

2. Geddes traded in equipment with a book value of $2,000 (initial cost $40,000) and paid $40,500 in cash one month after the purchase. The old equipment could have been sold for $8,000 at the date of trade but was accepted for a trade-in allowance of $9,500 on the new equipment.

3. Geddes gave the vendor a $10,000 cash down payment and a 9% note payable with blended principal and interest payments of $20,000 each, due at the end of each of the next two years.

Instructions

Prepare the general journal entries to record the acquisition and the subsequent payment, including any notes payable, in each of the three independent cases above. Round to the nearest dollar. For item 3, use a table, financial calculator, or Excel.

E10.14 (LO 3, 7) **(Entries for Acquisition of Assets)** Information for Craig Ltd. follows:

1. On July 6, Craig acquired the plant assets of Desbury Company, which had discontinued operations. The property was appraised by a reliable, independent valuator on the date of acquisition as follows:

Land	$ 550,000
Building—structure	1,500,000
Building—HVAC	175,000
Machinery	725,000
Total	$2,950,000

Craig gave 18,000 of its common shares in exchange. The most recent sale of Craig's common shares took place last month, when 5,000 shares were sold for $170 per share.

2. Craig had the following cash expenses between July 6 and December 15, the date when it first occupied the building:

Renovations and refurbishments of building	$ 98,000
Construction of bases for machinery to be installed later	110,000
Driveways and parking lots	131,000
Remodelling of office space in building, including new partitions and walls	59,000
Special assessment by city on land	16,000

On December 20, Craig purchased machinery for $305,000, subject to a 2% cash discount, and paid freight on the machinery of $14,000. The machine was dropped while being placed in position, which resulted in paying the supplier for repairs costing $12,500. The company paid the supplier on the day that the machinery was received, and recorded the purchase of machinery net of any discount.

Instructions

a. Prepare the entries for these transactions on the books of Craig Ltd. Craig prepares financial statements in accordance with IFRS.

b. Would the journal entries for item 1 prepared in part (a) differ if Craig prepared financial statements in accordance with ASPE?

c. Prepare the entry for the purchase and payment of the machinery in item 2, assuming the discount was not taken.

E10.15 (LO 3) **(Purchase of Equipment with Non–Interest-Bearing Debt)** Native Inc. decided to purchase equipment from Central Ontario Industries on January 2, 2020, to expand its production capacity to meet customers' demand for its product. Native issued a $900,000, five-year, non–interest-bearing note to Central Ontario for the new equipment when the prevailing market interest rate for obligations of this nature was 10%. The company will pay off the note in five $180,000 instalments due at the end of each year of the note's life.

Instructions

(Round to nearest dollar in all calculations.)

a. Prepare the journal entry(ies) at the date of purchase. Calculate the purchase price using any of the three methods (tables, financial calculator, or Excel).

b. Prepare the journal entry(ies) at the end of the first year to record the payment of principal and interest, assuming that the company uses the effective interest method.

c. Prepare the journal entry(ies) at the end of the second year to record the payment of principal and interest.

d. Assuming that the equipment has an eight-year life and no residual value, prepare the journal entry that is needed to record depreciation in the first year. (The straight-line method is used.)

[20]**E10.16 (LO 3)** **(Purchase of Equipment with Debt)** On September 1, 2020, Rupert Ltd. purchased equipment for $30,000 by signing a two-year note payable with a face value of $30,000 due on September 1, 2022. The going rate of interest for this level of risk was 8%. The company has a December 31 year end.

---

[20]This item was originally published by Certified General Accountants Association of Canada (CGA Canada), as an examination question. Adapted with permission of the Chartered Professional Accountants of Canada, Toronto, Canada. Any changes to the original material are the sole responsibility of the publisher and have not been reviewed or endorsed by the Chartered Professional Accountants of Canada.

Instructions

a. Calculate the cost of the equipment, where necessary using any of the three methods (tables, financial calculator, or Excel), assuming the note is as follows:

   1. An 8% interest-bearing note, with interest due each September 1.

   2. A 2% interest-bearing note, with interest due each September 1.

   3. A non–interest-bearing note.

b. Record all journal entries from September 1, 2020, to September 1, 2022, for the three notes in part (a). Round all amounts to the nearest dollar. Ignore depreciation of the equipment.

E10.17 (LO 3)   (Asset Exchange, Monetary Transaction)   Cannon Ltd. purchased an electric wax melter on April 30, 2020, by trading in its old gas model and paying the balance in cash. The following data relate to the purchase:

List price of new melter	$15,800
Cash paid	10,000
Cost of old melter (five-year life, $700 residual value)	11,200
Accumulated depreciation on old melter (straight-line)	6,300
Market value of old melter in active secondary market	5,200

Instructions

Assuming that Cannon's fiscal year ends on December 31 and depreciation has been recorded through December 31, 2019, prepare the journal entry(ies) that are necessary to record this exchange. Give reasons for the accounting treatment you used.

E10.18 (LO 3)   (Nonmonetary Exchange)   Stacey Limited exchanged equipment that it uses in its manufacturing operations for similar equipment that is used in the operations of Chokar Limited. Stacey also paid Chokar $3,000 in cash. The following information pertains to the exchange:

	Stacey	Chokar
Equipment (cost)	$50,000	$55,000
Accumulated depreciation	31,250	22,000
Fair value of equipment	25,000	28,000

Instructions

a. Prepare the journal entries to record the exchange on the books of both companies, assuming the exchange is determined to have commercial substance.

b. Repeat part (a), assuming the exchange is determined not to have commercial substance.

c. **Digging Deeper** List some of the factors that the accountant would need to consider in order to determine whether the transaction has commercial substance.

E10.19 (LO 3)   (Nonmonetary Exchange)   Carver Inc. recently replaced a piece of automatic equipment at a net price of $4,000, f.o.b. factory. The replacement was necessary because one of Carver's employees had accidentally backed his truck into Carver's original equipment and made it inoperable. Because of the accident, the equipment had no resale value to anyone and had to be scrapped. Carver's insurance policy provided for a replacement of its equipment and paid the price of the new equipment directly to the new equipment manufacturer, minus the deductible amount paid to the manufacturer by Carver. The $4,000 that Carver paid was the amount of the deductible that it has to pay on any single claim on its insurance policy. The new equipment represents the same value in use to Carver. The used equipment had originally cost $65,000. It had a book value of $45,000 at the time of the accident and a second-hand market value of $50,800 before the accident, based on recent transactions involving similar equipment. Freight and installation charges for the new equipment cost Carver an additional $1,100 cash.

Instructions

a. Prepare the general journal entry to record the transaction to replace the equipment that was destroyed in the accident.

b. Repeat part (a), but assume that the new equipment will result in significant savings to Carver, since the new equipment is more efficient and requires less staff time to operate.

E10.20 (LO 3)   (Nonmonetary Exchange)   Jamil Jonas is an accountant in public practice as a sole propreitor. Not long ago, Jamil struck a deal with his neighbour Ralph to prepare Ralph's business income tax and GST returns for 2020 in exchange for Ralph's services as a landscaper. Ralph provided labour and used his own equipment to perform landscaping services for Jamil's personal residence, for which he would normally charge $500. Jamil would usually charge $650 for the number of hours spent completing Ralph's returns but considers the transaction well worth it since he really dislikes doing his own landscaping.

Instructions

How would each party record this transaction? Prepare the journal entries for both Jamil's and Ralph's companies. Ignore any GST/HST that would apply in each transaction.

E10.21 (LO 3) **(Government Assistance)** Lightstone Equipment Ltd. wanted to expand into New Brunswick and was impressed by the provincial government's grant program for new industry. Once it was sure that it would qualify for the grant program, it purchased property in downtown Saint John on June 15, 2020. The property cost $235,000 and Lightstone spent the next two months gutting the building and reconstructing the two floors to meet the company's needs. The building has a useful life of 20 years and an estimated residual value of $65,000. In late August 2020, the company moved into the building and began operations. Additional information follows:

1. The property was assessed at $195,000, with $145,000 allocated to the land.
2. Architectural drawings and engineering fees related to the construction cost $18,000.
3. The company paid $17,000 to the contractor for gutting the building and $108,400 for construction. Lightstone expects that these improvements will last for the remainder of the life of the building.
4. The provincial government contributed $75,000 toward the building costs.

Instructions

(Round to the nearest dollar in all calculations.)

a. Assuming that the company uses the cost reduction method to account for government assistance, answer the following:

1. What is the cost of the building on Lightstone Equipment's statement of financial position at August 31, 2020, its fiscal year end? Do not round intermediate calculations for the percentage allocation between the assets.

2. What is the effect of this capital asset on the company's income statement for the company's year ended August 31, 2021?

b. Assuming the company uses the deferral method to account for government assistance, answer the following:

1. What is the cost of the building on Lightstone Equipment's statement of financial position at August 31, 2020? Do not round intermediate calculations for the percentage allocation between the assets.

2. What is the effect of this capital asset on the company's income statement for the company's year ended August 31, 2021?

c. **Digging Deeper** Compare the statement of financial position and income statement presentations for the two alternative treatments for government assistance for the fiscal year ended August 31, 2021.

E10.22 (LO 4, 7) **(Biological Assets)** On March 1 2020, Russell Winery Ltd. purchased a five-hectare commercial vineyard for $1,050,000. The total purchase price was based on appraised market values of the building, grapevines, and equipment ($580,000, $260,000, and $210,000, respectively). Russell Winery incurred the following cash expenditures between March 1 and June 30, the date of Russell Winery's first harvest from the grapevines:

Major repairs to sprayer equipment	$28,000
Grapevine fertilizer	7,000
Phase 1 construction of a new grape trellis system for the grapevines	31,000
Construction of a new custom wine cellar	62,000
Harvesting labour	36,000

The fair value of the grapevines was estimated to have increased to $295,000 by December 31, 2020, the company's fiscal year end, and any sale of vineyard assets would attract a 4% realtor commission. Russell Winery prepares financial statements in accordance with IFRS.

Instructions

a. What is the carrying amount of the grapevines on the statement of financial position at December 31, 2020? If there are differing accounting treatments of the items involved, discuss the options.

b. In 2021, Russell Winery incurs $17,000 in costs related to Phase 2 construction of the new grape trellis system for the grapevines, and the fair value of the grapevines increases to $330,000 by December 31, 2021. What is the carrying amount of the grapevines on the statement of financial position at December 31, 2021?

c. Would the carrying amount of the grapevines provided in part (a) differ if Russell Winery prepared financial statements in accordance with ASPE?

E10.23 (LO 5)   (Measurement after Acquisition—Fair Value Model versus Cost Model)   Plaza Holdings Inc., a publicly listed company in Canada, ventured into construction of a mega shopping mall in Edmonton, which is rated as the largest shopping mall in North America. The company's board of directors, after much market research, decided that instead of selling the shopping mall to a local investor who had approached them several times with excellent offers that he steadily increased during the year of construction, the company would hold this property for the purposes of capital appreciation and earning rental income from mall tenants. The construction of the mall ended on December 31, 2019. Plaza Holdings retained the services of a real estate company to find and attract many important retailers to rent space in the shopping mall. The shopping mall was fully occupied soon after construction was completed.

According to the company's accounting department, the total construction cost of the shopping mall was $50 million. The company used an independent appraiser to determine the mall's fair value annually. According to the appraisal, the fair values of the shopping mall at December 31, 2020, and at each subsequent year end were:

2020	$50 million
2021	$60 million
2022	$63 million
2023	$58 million

The independent appraiser felt that the useful life of the shopping mall was 20 years and its residual value was $10 million.

Instructions

Describe the impact on the company's income statement and prepare the necessary journal entries for 2021, 2022, and 2023 if it decides to treat the shopping mall as an investment property under IAS 40:

a. Using the fair value model.

b. Using the cost model.

Note that the mall's rental income and expenses would be the same under both options, and thus can be omitted from the analysis for this exercise.

E10.24 (LO 5)   (Measurement after Acquisition—Fair Value Model)   Nevine Corporation owns and manages a small 10-store shopping centre, which it classifies as an investment property. Nevine has a May 31 year end and initially recognized the property at its acquisition cost of $10.8 million on June 2, 2019. The acquisition cost consisted of the purchase price of $10 million, costs to survey and transfer the property of $500,000, and legal fees to acquire the property of $300,000. Nevine determines that approximately 25% of the shopping centre's value is attributable to the land, with the remainder attributable to the building. The following fair values are determined:

Date	Fair Value
May 31, 2020	$10,500,000
May 31, 2021	$10,300,000
May 31, 2022	$11,000,000

Nevine expects the shopping centre building to have a 35-year useful life and a residual value of $1.1 million. Nevine uses the straight-line method for depreciation.

Instructions

a. Assume that Nevine decides to apply the cost model. What journal entries, if any, are required each year, and how will the investment property be reported on each year-end statement of financial position?

b. Assume that Nevine decides to apply the fair value model. Prepare the journal entries, if any, required at each year end. In addition, explain how the property would be reported if Nevine prepared a statement of financial position shortly after acquisition in 2019.

*E10.25 (LO 5, 9)   (Measurement after Acquisition—Revaluation Model)   A partial statement of financial position of Bluewater Ltd. on December 31, 2019, showed the following property, plant, and equipment assets accounted for under the cost model (accumulated depreciation includes depreciation for 2019):

Buildings	$350,000	
Less: accumulated depreciation	50,000	$300,000
Equipment	120,000	
Less: accumulated depreciation	40,000	80,000

Bluewater uses straight-line depreciation for its building (remaining useful life of 20 years, no residual value) and for its equipment (remaining useful life of 8 years, no residual value). Bluewater applies IFRS and has decided to adopt the revaluation model for its building and equipment, effective December 31, 2019. On this date, an independent appraiser assessed the fair value of the building to be $275,000 and that of the equipment to be $90,000.

Instructions

a. Prepare the necessary general journal entry(ies), if any, to revalue the building and the equipment as at December 31, 2019, using the asset adjustment method.

b. Prepare the entries to record depreciation expense for the year ended December 31, 2020.

c. Repeat parts (a) and (b) using the proportionate method to revalue the building and the equipment. Do not round intermediate calculations but round final amounts to the nearest dollar.

*E10.26 **(LO 5, 9)** **(Measurement after Acquisition—Revaluation Model)** On January 1, 2020, Algo Ltd. acquires a building at a cost of $230,000. The building is expected to have a 20-year life and no residual value. The asset is accounted for under the revaluation model, using the asset adjustment method. Revaluations are carried out every three years. On December 31, 2022, the fair value of the building is appraised at $205,000, and on December 31, 2025, its fair value is $150,000. Algo Ltd. applies IFRS.

Instructions

(Round to the nearest dollar in all calculations.)

a. Prepare the journal entry(ies) required on December 31, 2020.

b. Prepare the journal entry(ies) required on December 31, 2021.

c. Prepare the journal entry(ies) required on December 31, 2022.

d. Prepare the journal entry(ies) required on December 31, 2023.

e. Prepare the journal entry(ies) required on December 31, 2024.

f. Prepare the journal entry(ies) required on December 31, 2025.

g. Prepare the journal entry required on December 31, 2022, and the journal entry required on December 31, 2025, to revalue the building, if Algo uses the proportionate method. Do not round intermediate calculations but round final amounts to the nearest dollar.

h. Prepare a continuity schedule showing the amounts recorded to the Buildings account and to the Accumulated Depreciation account, as well as indicating the carrying amount for each fiscal year from date of purchase to December 31, 2025, using (1) the asset adjustment method and (2) the proportionate method. Show the carrying amount under each method at the end of each fiscal year.

i. **Digging Deeper** From the perspective of an investor in Algo, discuss the financial statement effects of using the revaluation model to determine the carrying amount of Algo's building.

[21]E10.27 **(LO 6)** **(Analysis of Subsequent Expenditures)** On January 1, 2020, the accounting records of Sasseville Ltée included a debit balance of $15 million in the building account and of $12 million in the related accumulated depreciation account. The building was purchased in January 1980 for $15 million, and was estimated to have a 50-year useful life with no residual value. Sasseville uses the straight-line depreciation method for all of its property, plant, and equipment. During 2020, the following expenditures relating to the building were made:

1. The original roof of the building was removed and replaced with a new roof. The old roof cost $1 million. The new roof cost $2.5 million and is expected to have a 15-year useful life.

2. The ongoing frequent repairs on the building during the year cost $57,000.

3. The building's old heating system was replaced with a new one. The new HVAC cost $700,000 and is estimated to have a seven-year useful life and no residual value. The cost of the old HVAC is unknown, but is estimated to be $200,000 and fully depreciated.

4. A natural gas explosion caused $44,000 of uninsured damage to the building. This major repair did not change the estimated useful life of the building or its residual value.

---

[21]This item was originally published by Certified General Accountants Association of Canada (CGA Canada), as an examination question. Adapted with permission of the Chartered Professional Accountants of Canada, Toronto, Canada. Any changes to the original material are the sole responsibility of the publisher and have not been reviewed or endorsed by the Chartered Professional Accountants of Canada.

Instructions

Prepare the journal entries to record the expenditures related to the building during 2020.

E10.28 (LO 6) **(Analysis of Subsequent Expenditures)** The following transactions occurred during 2020. Assume that depreciation of 10% per year is charged on all machinery and 5% per year on buildings, on a straight-line basis, with no estimated residual value. Assume also that depreciation is charged for a full year on all fixed assets that are acquired during the year, and that no depreciation is charged on fixed assets that are disposed of during the year.

Jan. 30	A building that cost $132,000 in 2003 was torn down to make room for a new building structure. The wrecking contractor was paid $5,100 and was permitted to keep all materials salvaged.
Mar. 10	A new part costing $2,900 was purchased and added to a machine that was purchased in 2018 for $16,000. The new part replaces an original machine part, and does not extend the machine's useful life. The old part's cost was not separable from the original machine's cost.
Mar. 20	A gear broke on a machine that cost $9,000 in 2015, and the gear was replaced at a cost of $185. The replacement does not extend the machine's useful life.
May 18	A special base that was installed for a machine in 2014 when the machine was purchased had to be replaced at a cost of $5,500 because of defective workmanship on the original base. The cost of the machinery was $14,200 in 2014. The cost of the base was $3,500, and this amount was charged to the Machinery account in 2014.
June 23	One of the buildings was repainted at a cost of $6,900. It had not been painted since it was constructed in 2016.

Instructions

a. Prepare general journal entries for the transactions. (Round to the nearest dollar.)

b. Assume that the gear replacement purchased on March 20 extends the machine's useful life. How would your journal entry change?

E10.29 (LO 6) **(Analysis of Subsequent Expenditures)** Plant assets often require expenditures subsequent to acquisition. It is important that they be accounted for properly. Any errors will affect both the statements of financial position and income statements for several years.

Instructions

For each of the following items, indicate whether the expenditure should be capitalized ("C") or expensed ("E") in the period when it was incurred:

a. _____ A betterment

b. _____ Replacement of a minor broken part on a machine

c. _____ An expenditure that increases an existing asset's useful life

d. _____ An expenditure that increases the efficiency and effectiveness of a productive asset but does not increase its residual value

e. _____ An expenditure that increases the efficiency and effectiveness of a productive asset and its residual value

f. _____ An expenditure that increases a productive asset's output quality

g. _____ An overhaul to a machine that increases its fair market value and its production capacity by 30% without extending the machine's useful life

h. _____ Ordinary repairs

i. _____ A major overhaul

j. _____ Interest on borrowing that is necessary to finance a major overhaul of machinery that extends its life

k. _____ An expenditure that results in a 10%-per-year production cost saving

l. _____ Costs of a major overhaul that brings the asset's condition back to "new," with no change in the estimated useful life

*E10.30 (LO 2, 8) **(Capitalization of Borrowing Costs)** On December 31, 2020, Omega Inc., a public company, borrowed $3 million at 12% payable annually to finance the construction of a new building. In 2021, the company made the following expenditures related to this building structure (unless otherwise noted): March 1, $510,000; June 1, $600,000; July 1, $1.5 million (of which $400,000 was for the roof); December 1, $1.5 million (of which $700,000 was for the building HVAC).

Additional information follows:

1. Other debt outstanding:

   $4-million, 10-year, 13% bond, dated December 31, 2013, with interest payable annually

   $1.6-million, six-year, 10% note, dated December 31, 2017, with interest payable annually

2. The March 1, 2020 expenditure included land costs of $150,000.

3. Interest revenue earned in 2020 on the unused idle construction loan amounted to $49,000.

Instructions

a. Determine the interest amount that could be capitalized in 2020 in relation to the building construction.

b. Prepare the journal entry to record the capitalization of borrowing costs and the recognition of interest expense, if any, at December 31, 2020. Round percentage allocation to two decimal places and amounts to the nearest dollar.

*E10.31 (LO 2, 8) **(Capitalization of Borrowing Costs)** The following three situations involve the capitalization of borrowing costs for public companies following IFRS.

Situation 1

On January 1, 2020, Oksana Inc. signed a fixed-price contract to have Builder Associates construct a major head office facility at a cost of $4 million. It was estimated that it would take three years to complete the project. Also, on January 1, 2020, to finance the construction cost, Oksana borrowed $4 million that is repayable in 10 annual instalments of $400,000, plus interest at the rate of 10%. During 2020, Oksana made deposit and progress payments totalling $1.5 million under the contract; the weighted-average amount of accumulated expenditures was $800,000 for the year. The excess amount of borrowed funds was invested in short-term securities, from which Oksana realized investment income of $25,000.

Situation 2

During 2020, Midori Ito Corporation constructed and manufactured certain assets and incurred the following borrowing costs in connection with these activities:

Borrowing Costs Incurred	
Warehouse constructed for Midori Ito's own use	$30,000
Special-order machine for sale to unrelated customer, produced according to customer's specifications	9,000
Inventories routinely manufactured, produced on a repetitive basis, that require many months to complete	8,000

Situation 3

Fleming Inc. has a fiscal year ending April 30. On May 1, 2020, Fleming borrowed $10 million at 11% to finance construction of its own building. Repayments of the loan are to begin the month after the building's completion. During the year ended April 30, 2021, expenditures for the partially completed structure totalled $7 million. These expenditures were incurred evenly throughout the year. Interest that was earned on the part of the loan that was not expended amounted to $450,000 for the year.

Instructions

a. For situation 1, what amount should Oksana report as capitalized borrowing costs at December 31, 2020?

b. For situation 2, assuming the effect of capitalization of borrowing costs is material, what is the total amount of borrowing costs to be capitalized?

c. For situation 3, how much should be shown as capitalized borrowing costs on Fleming's financial statements at April 30, 2021?

(Adapted from CPA)

*E10.32 (LO 2, 8) **(Capitalization of Borrowing Costs)** In early February 2020, Huey Corp. began construction of an addition to its head office building that is expected to take 18 months to complete. The following 2020 expenditures relate to the addition:

Feb.	1	Payment #1 to contractor	$120,000
Mar.	1	Payment to architect	24,000
July	1	Payment #2 to contractor	60,000
Dec.	1	Payment #3 to contractor	180,000
Dec.	31	Asset carrying amount	$384,000

On February 1, Huey issued a $100,000, three-year note payable at a rate of 12% to finance most of the initial payment to the contractor. No other asset-specific debt was entered into. Details of other interest-bearing debt during the period are provided in the table below:

Other Debt Instruments Outstanding—2020	Principal Amount
9%, 15-year bonds, issued May 1, 2005, matured May 1, 2020	$300,000
7%, 10-year bonds, issued June 15, 2014	$500,000
6%, 12-year bonds, issued May 1, 2020	$300,000

Instructions

What amount of interest should be capitalized for the fiscal year ended December 31, 2020, according to IAS 23?

Problems

P10.1 Air Canada's December 31, 2017 consolidated statement of financial position lists property and equipment at $9 billion and total assets of $17.7 billion.

Air Canada's Note 4 to the financial statements titled Property and Equipment provides a schedule of the transactions that occurred during the year in four major categories. One category is dedicated to Aircraft and Flight Equipment. Another category is titled Purchase Deposits and Assets under Development (PDAD). Under the latter category, sources of increases are additions and sources of decreases are reclassifications to Aircraft and Flight Equipment. No depreciation is recorded for this category of Property and Equipment. The balance in PDAD at December 31, 2017, was $1,063 million. In Note 4, more details are provided, including a statement that Aircraft and Flight Equipment includes spare engines. The consolidated statement of operations revealed that interest capitalized during 2017 amounted to $36 million. Although not specifically stated, the purchase deposits are likely for the future deliveries of aircraft and related equipment.

Air Canada's significant accounting policies are provided in Note 2 to the financial statements. Note 2Q states that spare parts, other than rotables, are included in inventory. Note 2R states that rotables are components that can be repeatedly and economically restored to a fully serviceable condition. In the case of Air Canada, spare engines are rotables. Strict regulations require that engines be used a limited number of flight hours before they must be removed from the aircraft and completely overhauled regardless of their condition. This explains the need for spare engines that are ready for quick replacement, making the aircraft available at all times.

Instructions

a. For each of the following, provide an argument as to why Air Canada has classified the item under Property and Equipment:
1. Capitalized interest
2. Spare engines
3. Purchase deposits

b. Why does Air Canada not record depreciation on Purchase Deposits and Assets under Development?

c. Discuss the accounting treatment of the costs to overhaul spare engines.

d. **Digging Deeper** If Air Canada were not a public company following IFRS, and instead followed ASPE, would there be any difference in the way it would account for the three items discussed in part (a)? If so, what is the difference?

P10.2 Adamski Corporation manufactures ballet shoes and is in a period of sustained growth. In an effort to expand its production capacity to meet the increased demand for its products, the company recently made several acquisitions of plant and equipment. Tanya Mullinger, newly hired with the title Capital Asset Accountant, requested that Walter Kaster, Adamski's controller, review the following transactions:

Transaction 1

On June 1, 2020, Adamski purchased equipment from Venghaus Corporation. Adamski issued a $20,000, four-year, non–interest-bearing note to Venghaus for the new equipment. Adamski will pay off the note in four equal instalments due at the end of each of the next four years. At the transaction date, the prevailing market interest rate for obligations of this nature was 10%. Freight costs of $425 and installation costs of $500 were incurred in completing this transaction. The new equipment qualifies for a $2,000 government grant.

Transaction 2

On December 1, 2020, Adamski purchased several assets of Haukap Shoes Inc., a small shoe manufacturer whose owner was retiring. The purchase amounted to $210,000 and included the assets in the following list. Adamski engaged Tennyson Appraisal Inc., an independent appraiser, to determine the assets' fair values, which are also provided.

	Haukap Book Value	**Fair Value**
Inventory	$ 60,000	$ 50,000
Land	40,000	80,000
Building	70,000	120,000
	$170,000	$250,000

During its fiscal year ended May 31, 2021, Adamski incurred $8,000 of interest expense to finance these assets.

Transaction 3

On March 1, 2021, Adamski traded in four units of specialized equipment and paid an additional $25,000 cash for a technologically up-to-date machine that should do the same job as the other machines, but much more efficiently and profitably. The equipment that was traded in had a combined carrying amount of $35,000, as Adamski had recorded $45,000 of accumulated depreciation against these assets. Adamski's controller and the sales manager of the supplier company agreed that the new equipment had a fair value of $64,000.

Instructions

a. Tangible capital assets such as land, buildings, and equipment receive special accounting treatment. Describe the major characteristics of these assets that differentiate them from other types of assets.

b. For each of the three transactions described above, determine the value at which Adamski Corporation should record the acquired assets. Support your calculations with an explanation of the underlying rationale. For any measurement involving present value concepts, provide your calculations using any of the following: tables, Excel functions, or a financial calculator. Round results to the nearest dollar.

c. The books of Adamski Corporation show the following additional transactions for the fiscal year ended May 31, 2021:

1. Acquisition of a building for speculative purposes

2. Purchase of a two-year insurance policy covering plant equipment

3. Purchase of the rights for the exclusive use of a process used in the manufacture of ballet shoes

For each of these transactions, indicate whether the asset should be classified as an item of property, plant, and equipment. If it should be, explain why. If it should not be, explain why not, and identify the proper classification.

(Adapted from CMA)

P10.3 Excel At December 31, 2019, certain accounts included in the property, plant, and equipment section of Golden Corporation's statement of financial position had the following balances:

Land	$310,000
Buildings—Structure	883,000
Leasehold Improvements	705,000
Equipment	845,000

During 2020, the following transactions occurred:

1. Land site No. 621 was acquired for $800,000 plus a fee of $7,000 to the real estate agent for finding the property. Costs of $33,500 were incurred to clear the land. In clearing the land, topsoil and gravel were recovered and sold for $11,000.

2. Land site No. 622, which had a building on it, was acquired for $560,000. The closing statement indicated that the land's assessed tax value was $309,000 and the building's value was $102,000. Shortly after acquisition, the building was demolished at a cost of $28,000. A new building was constructed for $340,000 plus the following costs:

Excavation fees	$38,000
Architectural design fees	15,000
Building permit fee	2,500
"Green roof" design and construction (to be retrofitted every seven years)	36,000
Imputed interest on funds used during construction (share financing)	8,500

The building, completed and occupied on September 30, 2020, is expected to have a 30-year useful life.

3. A third tract of land (No. 623) was acquired for $265,000 and was put on the market for resale.

4. During December 2020, costs of $89,000 were incurred to improve leased office space. The related lease will terminate on December 31, 2022, and is not expected to be renewed.

5. Equipment was purchased under a royalty agreement. The terms of the agreement require Golden Corporation to pay royalties based on the units of production for the equipment. The equipment's invoice price was $111,000, freight costs were $3,300, installation costs were $3,600, and royalty payments for 2020 were $15,300.

Instructions

a. Prepare a detailed analysis of the changes in each of the following statement of financial position accounts for 2020: Land, Leasehold Improvements, Buildings—Structure, Buildings—Roof, and Equipment. Ignore the related Accumulated Depreciation accounts.

b. List the items in the transactions above that were not used to determine the answer to part (a), and indicate where, or if, these items should be included in Golden's financial statements.

c. **Digging Deeper** Using the terminology from the conceptual framework in Chapter 2, explain why the items in part (b) were not included in the accounts Land, Leasehold Improvements, Buildings (the Structure and Roof accounts), and Equipment.

(Adapted from AICPA)

P10.4 Webb Corporation prepares financial statements in accordance with IFRS. Selected accounts included in the property, plant, and equipment section of the company's statement of financial position at December 31, 2019, had the following balances:

Land	$ 300,000
Land Improvements	140,000
Buildings	1,100,000
Equipment	960,000

During 2020, the following transactions occurred:

1. A tract of land was acquired for $150,000 as a potential future building site.

2. A plant facility consisting of land and a building was acquired from Knorman Corp. for use in production in exchange for 20,000 of Webb's common shares. The most recent sale of Webb's common shares took place one month earlier, when 4,000 of Webb's common shares sold for $57 per share. The plant facility was carried on Knorman's books at $110,000 for land and $320,000 for the building at the exchange date. At the exchange date, a reliable, independent valuator determined the fair value of the land and building to be $230,000 and $690,000, respectively.

3. Equipment was purchased for a total cost of $400,000. Additional costs incurred were as follows:

Freight and unloading	$13,000
Provincial sales taxes	28,000
GST (recoverable)	20,000
Installation	26,000

4. Expenditures totalling $95,000 were made for new parking lots, streets, and sidewalks at the corporation's various plant locations. These expenditures had an estimated useful life of 15 years.

5. A piece of equipment that cost $80,000 on January 1, 2012, was scrapped on June 30, 2020. Double-declining-balance depreciation had been recorded based on a 10-year life. Round depreciation calculations to the nearest dollar.

6. A piece of equipment was sold for $20,000 on July 1, 2020. Its original cost was $44,000 on January 1, 2017, and it was depreciated on the straight-line basis over an estimated useful life of seven years, assuming a residual value of $2,000.

Instructions

a. Prepare a detailed analysis of the changes in each of the following statement of financial position accounts for 2020: Land, Land Improvements, Buildings, and Equipment. (*Hint:* Ignore the related accumulated depreciation accounts.)

b. List the items in the transactions above that were not used to determine the answer to part (a), and show the relevant amounts and supporting calculations in good form for each item. In addition, indicate where, or if, these items should be included in Webb's financial statements.

c. **Digging Deeper** How will the land in item 1 be accounted for when it is used as a building site?

(Adapted from AICPA)

P10.5 Kiev Corp. was incorporated on January 2, 2020, but was unable to begin manufacturing activities until July 1, 2020, because new factory facilities were not completed until that date. The Land and Building account at December 31, 2020, contained the following entries and balance:

2020			
Jan. 31		Land and building	$166,000
Feb. 28		Cost of removal of building	9,800
May 1		Partial payment of new construction	60,000
	1	Legal fees paid	3,770
June 1		Second payment on new construction	40,000
	1	Insurance premium	2,280
	1	Special tax assessment	4,000
	30	General expenses	36,300
July 1		Final payment on new construction	10,000
	1	Payment for HVAC (furnace, air conditioning system)	30,000
Dec. 31		Asset write-up to market value	43,800
			405,950
	31	Depreciation for 2020 at 1%	4,060
Account balance			$401,890

The following additional information needs to be considered:

1. To acquire land and a building, the company paid $110,400 cash and 600 of its $5 cumulative preferred shares. The fair value of each share was estimated at $98 per share; however, Kiev's shares are not actively traded. The land and building were assessed by an independent, reliable valuator to have a combined fair value of $166,000.

2. The costs for removing the building amounted to $9,800, and the demolition company kept all the salvaged building materials.

3. Legal fees covered the following:

Land title search before purchase	$1,300
Legal work in connection with construction contract	2,470
	$3,770

4. The insurance premium covered the building for a two-year term beginning May 1, 2020.

5. The special tax assessment by the municipality covered street improvements that are permanent in nature.

6. General expenses covered the following for the period from January 2, 2020, to June 30, 2020:

President's salary during construction	$32,100
Plant superintendent's wages covering supervision of new building	4,200
	$36,300

7. Because of a general increase in construction costs after entering into the building contract, the board of directors increased the building's value by $43,800. It believed that such an increase was justified to reflect the current market at the time when the building was completed. Retained Earnings was credited for this amount.

8. The estimated life of the building structure is 50 years. The depreciation for 2020 on the building structure was 1% of the asset value (1% of $405,950, or $4,060). The estimated useful life of the building HVAC (heating system, ventilation, air conditioning) is 20 years. No depreciation has been recorded on the building HVAC. Kiev expects no residual value at the end of the useful life of HVAC assets.

Instructions

Prepare the entries to reallocate the proper balances into the Land, Buildings, and Accumulated Depreciation accounts at December 31, 2020.

(Adapted from AICPA)

P10.6 On June 28, 2020, in relocating to a new town, Kerr Corp. purchased a property consisting of two hectares of land and an unused building for $225,000 plus property taxes in arrears of $4,500. The company paid a real estate broker a fee of $12,000 for finding the property and legal fees on the purchase transaction of $6,000. The closing statement indicated that the assessed values for property tax purposes were $175,000 for the land and $35,000 for the building. Shortly after acquisition, the building was demolished at a cost of $24,000.

Kerr Corp. then entered into a $1.3-million fixed-price contract with Maliseet Builders Inc. on August 1, 2020, for the construction of an office building on this site. The building was completed and occupied on April 29, 2021, as was a separate maintenance building that was constructed by Kerr's employees. Additional costs related to the property included:

Plans, specifications, and blueprints	$25,000
Architects' fees for design and supervision	82,000
Landscaping	42,000
Extras on contract for upgrading of windows	46,000
External signage on the property	23,000
Advertisements in newspaper and on television announcing opening of the building	10,600
Gala opening party for customers, suppliers, and friends of Kerr	18,800
Costs of internal direct labour and materials for maintenance building	67,000
Allocated variable plant overhead based on direct labour hours worked on maintenance building	10,000
Allocated cost of executive time spent on project	54,000
Interest costs on debt incurred to pay contractor's progress billings up to building completion	63,000
Interest costs on short-term loan to finance maintenance building costs	3,200

As an incentive for Kerr to locate and build in the town, the municipality agreed not to charge its normal building permit fees of $36,000. This amount was included in the $1.3-million contract fee. Kerr uses the cost reduction method for any government grants, such as the waiving of these permit fees. The contract amount of $1.3 million was reduced by this grant. The building and the maintenance building are estimated to have a 40-year life from their dates of completion and will be depreciated using the straight-line method with no residual value.

Kerr is a private company with an April 30 year end, and the company accountant is currently analyzing the new Buildings account that was set up to capture all the expenditures and credits explained above that relate to the property.

Instructions

a. Prepare a schedule that identifies the costs that would be capitalized and included in the new Buildings account on the April 30, 2021 statement of financial position, assuming the accountant wants to comply with ASPE but tends to be very conservative in nature; in other words, she does not want to overstate income or assets. Briefly justify your calculations. How would your answer change if Kerr were to comply with IFRS?

b. Prepare a schedule that identifies the costs that would be capitalized and included in the new Buildings account on the April 30, 2021 statement of financial position, assuming the accountant wants to comply with ASPE, but is aware that Kerr needs to report increased income to support a requested increase in its bank loan next month. Briefly justify your calculations.

c. Comment on the difference in results for parts (a) and (b). Calculate the total expenses related to the building under both scenarios. What else should be considered in determining the amount to be capitalized?

P10.7 Vidi Corporation, a private enterprise, made the following purchases related to its property, plant, and equipment during its fiscal year ended December 31, 2020. The company uses the straight-line method of depreciation for all its capital assets.

1. In early January, Vidi issued 140,000 common shares in exchange for property consisting of land and a warehouse. On the date of acquisition, a reliable, independent appraiser estimated that the fair value of the land and warehouse was $600,000 and $300,000, respectively. The seller had advertised a price of $900,000 or best offer for the land and warehouse in a commercial retail magazine. Vidi paid a local real estate broker a finder's fee of $35,000. The most recent sale of Vidi's shares took place a month prior when 15,000 common shares were sold for $9 per share.

2. On March 31, the company acquired equipment on credit. The terms were a $7,000 cash down payment plus payments of $5,000 on March 31 for each of the next two years. The implicit interest rate was 12%. The equipment's list price was $17,000. Additional costs that were incurred to install the equipment included $1,000 to tear down and replace a wall and $1,500 to rearrange existing equipment to make room for the new equipment. An additional $500 was spent to repair the equipment after it was dropped during installation.

During the year, the following events also occurred:

3. A new motor was purchased for $50,000 for a large grinding machine (original cost of the machine, $350,000; accumulated depreciation at the replacement date, $100,000). The motor will not improve

the quality or quantity of production; however, it will extend the grinding machine's useful life from the current 8 years to 10 years. (Ignore the IFRS requirement to estimate and remove the cost of the old motor.)

4. The company purchased a small building in a nearby town for $125,000 to use as a display and sales location. The municipal tax assessment indicated that the property was assessed for $95,000, which consists of $68,000 for the building and $27,000 for the land. The building had been empty for six months and needed considerable maintenance work before it could be used. The following costs were incurred in 2020 before the company moved into the building on September 30: former owner's unpaid property taxes on the property for the previous year, $900; current year's (2020) taxes, $1,000; reshingling of roof, $2,200; cost of hauling refuse out of the basement, $230; cost of spray-cleaning the outside walls and washing windows, $750; cost of painting inside walls, $3,170; and incremental fire and liability insurance for 15 months starting September 30, $940.

5. The company repaired the plumbing system in its factory for $35,000. The original plumbing costs were not known.

6. On June 30, the company replaced a freezer with a new one that cost $20,000 cash (fair value of $21,000 for the new freezer less trade-in value of the old freezer). The cost of the old freezer was $15,000. At the beginning of the year, the company had depreciated 60% of the old freezer; that is, 10% per year of use.

7. The company painted the factory exterior at a cost of $12,000.

Instructions

a. Prepare the journal entries to record the acquisitions and/or costs incurred in the above transactions. In the case of present value calculations, use any of the three methods (PV tables, financial calculator, or Excel functions). Do not round intermediate calculations for the percentage allocation between the assets but round final amounts to the nearest dollar.

b. If there are alternative methods to account for any of the transactions, indicate what the alternatives are and your reason for choosing the method that you used.

P10.8 The production manager of Chesley Corporation wants to acquire a different brand of machine by exchanging the machine that it currently uses in operations for the brand of equipment that others in the industry are using. The brand being used by other companies is more comfortable for the operators because it has different attachments that allow the operators to adjust the controls for a variety of arm and hand positions. The production manager has received the following offers from other companies:

1. Secord Corp. offered to give Chesley a similar machine plus $23,000 in exchange for Chesley's machine.

2. Bateman Corp. offered a straight exchange for a similar machine with essentially the same value in use.

3. Shripad Corp. offered to exchange a similar machine with the same value in use, but wanted $8,000 cash in addition to Chesley's machine. Assume that the exchange is nonmonetary and lacks commercial substance.

4. The production manager has also contacted Ansong Corporation, a dealer in machines. To obtain a new machine from Ansong, Chesley would have to pay $93,000 and also trade in its old machine.

Chesley's equipment has a cost of $160,000, a net book value of $110,000, and a fair value of $92,000. The following table shows the information needed to record the machine exchange between the companies:

	Secord	Bateman	Shripad	Ansong
Machine cost	$120,000	$147,000	$160,000	$130,000
Accumulated depreciation— machinery	45,000	71,000	75,000	–0–
Fair value	69,000	92,000	100,000	185,000

Instructions

a. For each of the four independent situations, assume that Chesley accepts the offer. Prepare the journal entries to record the exchange on the books of each company. (Round to the nearest dollar.) When you need to make assumptions for the entries, state the assumptions so that you can justify the entries.

b. **Digging Deeper** Suggest scenarios or situations where different entries would be appropriate. Prepare the entries for these situations.

P10.9 During the current year, Garrison Construction Ltd. traded in two relatively new small cranes (cranes no. 6RT and S79) for a larger crane that Garrison expects will be more useful for the particular contracts that the company has to fulfill over the next couple of years. The new crane was acquired from Pisani Manufacturing Inc., which has agreed to take the smaller equipment as trade-ins and also pay $17,500 cash to Garrison. The new crane cost Pisani $165,000 to manufacture and is classified as inventory. The following information is available:

	Garrison	Pisani
Cost of crane #6RT	$130,000	
Cost of crane #S79	120,000	
Accumulated depreciation, #6RT	15,000	
Accumulated depreciation, #S79	18,000	
Fair value, #6RT	128,000	
Fair value, #S79	87,500	
Fair value of new crane		$198,000
Cash paid		17,500
Cash received	17,500	

Instructions

a. Assume that this exchange has commercial substance. Prepare the journal entries on the books of (1) Garrison Construction and (2) Pisani Manufacturing. Pisani uses a perpetual inventory system.

b. Assume that this exchange lacks commercial substance. Prepare the journal entries on the books of (1) Garrison Construction and (2) Pisani Manufacturing. Pisani uses a perpetual inventory system.

c. **Digging Deeper** Assume that you have been asked to recommend whether it is more appropriate for the transaction to have commercial substance or not to have commercial substance. Develop arguments that you could present to the controllers of both Garrison Construction and Pisani Manufacturing to justify both alternatives. Which arguments are more persuasive?

P10.10 On July 1, 2020, Lucas Ltd., a publicly listed company, acquired assets from Jared Ltd. On the transaction date, a reliable, independent valuator assessed the fair values of these assets as follows:

Manufacturing plant (building #1)	$400,000
Storage warehouse (building #2)	210,000
Machinery (in building #1)	75,000
Machinery (in building #2)	45,000

The buildings are owned by the company, and the land that the buildings are situated on is owned by the local municipality and is provided free of charge to the owner of the buildings to encourage local employment.

In exchange for the acquisition of these assets, Lucas issued 156,000 common shares. Lucas's shares are thinly traded (that is, traded in relatively low volume leading to more volatile price changes than most public companies). In the most recent sale of Lucas's shares on the Toronto Stock Exchange, 1,000 shares were sold for $5 per share. At the time of acquisition, both buildings were considered to have an expected remaining useful life of 10 years, the machinery in building #1 was expected to have a remaining useful life of 3 years, and the machinery in building #2 was expected to have a useful life of 9 years. Lucas uses straight-line depreciation with no residual values.

At December 31, 2020, Lucas's fiscal year end, Lucas recorded the correct depreciation amounts for the six months that the assets were in use. An independent appraisal concluded that the assets had the following fair values:

Manufacturing plant (building #1)	$387,000
Storage warehouse (building #2)	178,000

At December 31, 2021, Lucas once again retained an independent appraiser and determined that the fair value of the assets was:

Manufacturing plant (building #1)	$340,000
Storage warehouse (building #2)	160,000

Instructions

a. Prepare the journal entries required for 2020 and 2021, assuming that the buildings are accounted for under the revaluation model (using the asset adjustment method), and that the machinery is accounted for under the cost model. Do not combine the buildings in one account nor the machinery in one account. Depreciate assets separately and round all amounts to the nearest dollar.

b. Assume that the asset revaluation surplus for the buildings was prepared based on a class-by-class basis rather than on an individual asset basis as required by IAS 16. Prepare the journal entries for 2020 and 2021 that relate to the buildings. (Ignore the machinery accounts since they are accounted for using the cost model.)

c. Comment on the effects on the 2020 income statement with respect to parts (a) and (b).

*P10.11 Camco Manufacturers Inc., a publicly listed company, has two machines that are accounted for under the revaluation model. Technology in Camco's industry is fast-changing, causing the fair value of each machine to change significantly about every two years. The following information is available:

	Machine #1	Machine #2
Acquisition date	Jan. 2, 2017	June 30, 2016
Original cost	$440,000	$540,000
Original estimate of useful life	8 years	12 years
Original estimate of residual value	–0–	–0–
Pattern of depreciation	Straight-line	Straight-line
Fair value at Dec. 31, 2018	310,000	440,000
Balance in Machinery account after proportionate method revaluation on Dec. 31, 2018	413,333	555,789
Balance in Accumulated Depreciation account after proportionate method revaluation on Dec. 31, 2018	103,333	115,789
Cumulative balance in (Revaluation Gain or Loss)/ Revaluation Surplus (AOCI) at Jan. 1, 2020	(20,000)	12,500
Fair value at Dec. 31, 2020	230,000	328,000

Both machines were last revalued on December 31, 2018. Camco has a December 31 year end.

Instructions

a. Prepare the journal entries required for 2020, using the asset adjustment method.

b. Prepare the journal entries required for 2020, using the proportionate method. Do not round intermediate calculations but round final amounts to the nearest dollar.

c. Prepare a continuity schedule showing for each machine the amounts recorded to the Machine account and to the Accumulated Depreciation account, as well as indicating the carrying amount for each fiscal year from date of purchase to December 31, 2020, using (1) the asset adjustment method and (2) the proportionate method. Show the carrying amount under each method at the end of each fiscal year.

d. Comment on the effects on the 2020 statement of comprehensive income with respect to parts (a) and (b).

e. Comment on the effects on the December 31, 2020 statement of financial position with respect to parts (a) and (b).

f. **Digging Deeper** Would a potential investor prefer Camco to use the asset adjustment method or the proportionate method to apply the revaluation model?

P10.12 On March 1, 2020, Jessi Corp. acquired a 10-unit residential complex for $1,275,000, paid in cash. An independent appraiser determined that 75% of the total purchase price should be allocated to buildings, with the remainder allocated to land. On the date of acquisition, the building's estimated useful life was 25 years, with estimated residual value of $325,000. Jessi estimates that straight-line depreciation would best reflect the pattern of benefits it will receive from the building. Fair value of the complex, as assessed by an independent appraiser on each date, is as follows:

Date	Fair Value
December 31, 2020	$1,322,000
December 31, 2021	$1,255,000
December 31, 2022	$1,223,000

The complex qualifies as an investment property under IAS 40 *Investment Property*. Jessi has a December 31 year end.

Instructions

a. Prepare the journal entries required for 2020, 2021, and 2022, assuming that Jessi applies the fair value model to all of its investment property.

b. Prepare the journal entries required for 2020, 2021, and 2022, assuming that Jessi applies the cost model to all of its investment property.

c. Comment on the effects on the 2020 statement of comprehensive income with respect to parts (a) and (b).

d. Comment on the effects on the December 31, 2020 statement of financial position with respect to parts (a) and (b).

e. **Digging Deeper** From the perspective of an investor in Jessi, discuss the financial statement effects of using the fair value model to determine the property's carrying amount.

P10.13 Donovan Resources Group has been in its plant facility for 15 years. Although the plant is quite functional, numerous repair costs are incurred to keep it in good working order. The book value of the company's plant is currently $800,000, calculated as follows:

Original cost	$1,200,000
Accumulated depreciation	400,000
	$ 800,000

During the current year, the following expenditures were made to the plant:

1. Because of increased demand for its product, the company increased its plant capacity by building a new addition at a cost of $270,000.

2. The entire plant was repainted at a cost of $23,000.

3. The roof was made of asbestos cement slate. For safety purposes, it was removed at a cost of $4,000 and replaced with a wood shingle roof at a cost of $61,000. The original roof's cost had been $40,000 and it was being depreciated over an expected life of 20 years.

4. The electrical system was completely updated at a cost of $22,000. The cost of the old electrical system was not known. It is estimated that the building's useful life will not change as a result of this updating.

5. A series of major repairs was made at a cost of $47,000, because parts of the wood structure were rotting. The cost of the old wood structure was not known. These extensive repairs are estimated to increase the building's useful life.

Instructions

Indicate how each of these transactions would be recorded in the accounting records.

*P10.14 Inglewood Landscaping Corp. began constructing a new plant on December 1, 2020. On this date, the company purchased a parcel of land for $184,000 cash. In addition, it paid $2,000 in surveying costs and $4,000 for title transfer fees. An old dwelling on the premises was immediately demolished at a cost of $3,000, with $1,000 being received from the sale of materials.

Architectural plans were also formalized on December 1, 2020, when the architect was paid $30,000. The necessary building permits costing $3,000 were obtained from the city and paid on December 1, 2020. The excavation work began during the first week in December and payments were made to the contractor as follows:

Date of Payment	Amount of Payment
Mar. 1	$240,000
May 1	360,000
July 1	60,000

The building was completed on July 1, 2021.

To finance the plant construction, Inglewood borrowed $600,000 from a bank on December 1, 2020. Inglewood had no other borrowings. The $600,000 was a 10-year loan bearing interest at 10%.

Instructions

a. Calculate the balance in each of the following accounts at the year ends December 31, 2020, and December 31, 2021. Assume that Inglewood prepares financial statements in accordance with IFRS.

1. Land

2. Buildings

3. Interest Expense

b. Identify what the effects would be on Inglewood's financial statements for the years ended December 31, 2020 and 2021, if its policy were to expense all borrowing costs as they are incurred. Assume that Inglewood prepares financial statements in accordance with ASPE.

c. Prepare a table showing the balance in the Buildings and Interest Expense accounts at the 2020 and 2021 fiscal years under IFRS and ASPE. Indicate the differences in the balances for each year. Do you believe the amounts of the differences are material to the statement of income and statement of financial position?

d. **Digging Deeper** Discuss the financial statement effects of capitalization of borrowing costs. Contrast the financial statement effects of capitalizing borrowing costs against the financial statement effects of paying for the construction with internally generated funds.

*P10.15 Wordcrafters Inc. is a book distributor that had been operating in its original facility since 1991. The increase in certification programs and continuing education requirements in several professions has contributed to an annual growth rate of 15% for Wordcrafters since 2014. Wordcrafters' original facility became obsolete by early 2020 because of the increased sales volume and the fact that Wordcrafters now carries audio books and e-texts in addition to hard-copy books.

On June 1, 2020, Wordcrafters contracted with Favre Construction to have a new building constructed for $5 million on land owned by Wordcrafters. Wordcrafters made the following payments to Favre Construction:

Date	Amount
July 30, 2020	$1,200,000
Jan. 30, 2021	1,500,000
May 31, 2021	1,000,000
June 30, 2021	1,300,000
Total payments	$5,000,000

Construction was completed and the building was ready for occupancy on May 27, 2021. Wordcrafters had no new borrowings directly associated with the new building but had the following debt outstanding at May 31, 2021, the end of its fiscal year:

14½%, five-year note payable of $2 million, dated April 1, 2017, with interest payable annually on April 1

12%, 10-year bond issue of $3 million sold at par on June 30, 2013, with interest payable annually on June 30

The company is an international distributor and prepares financial statements in accordance with IFRS.

Instructions

a. Calculate the weighted-average accumulated expenditures on Wordcrafters' new building during the capitalization period.

b. Calculate the avoidable interest on Wordcrafters' new building.

c. Wordcrafters capitalized some of its interest costs for the year ended May 31, 2021:

  1. Identify the item(s) relating to interest costs that must be disclosed in Wordcrafters' financial statements.

  2. Calculate the amount of the item(s) that must be disclosed.

(Adapted from CMA)

Case

Enabling Competencies *Refer to the Case Primer on the student website and in* WileyPLUS *to help you with your answers for this case.*

CA10.1 Real Estate Investment Trust (RE) was created to hold hotel properties. RE currently holds 15 luxury and first-class hotels in Europe. The entity is structured as an investment trust, which means that the trust does not pay income taxes because it distributes to unitholders taxable income from the assets that it holds directly. Instead, income taxes are paid by the unitholders—those who own units in the trust. The other key feature of the trust is that a certain percentage of the distributable income is required to be paid to unitholders every year. The units of RE trade on a Canadian stock exchange.

Distributable income is calculated as net income (according to GAAP) before special charges, less a replacement reserve (which is an amount set aside to refurbish assets). RE distributed 127% and 112% of its distributable income in 2020 and 2019, respectively. Management calculates distributable income since this calculation is not defined by GAAP. As at the end of 2020, property and equipment was $1.7 billion compared with $1.9 billion in total assets. Net income for the year was $55 million.

According to the notes to the financial statements, RE accounts for its property, plant, and equipment at amortized cost.

Instructions

Assume the role of the entity's auditor, and discuss any financial reporting issues.

Integrated Cases

Enabling Competencies (*Hint:* If there are issues here that are new, use the conceptual framework to help you support your analysis with solid reasoning.)

[22]**IC10.1** Iskra Vremec and Colin McFee are experienced scuba divers who have spent many years in the salvage business. About a year ago, they decided to start their own company to recover damaged and sunken vessels and their cargoes off the east coast of Canada. They incorporated Atlantic Explorations Limited (AEL) on February 1, 2019. Iskra (president) and Colin (vice-president) each own 30% of AEL's shares. The remaining 40% of the shares were purchased by a group of 10 investors who contributed $50,000 each so that AEL could acquire the necessary equipment and cover other start-up costs.

AEL carries on two types of activities. The first is a commercial salvage operation. The second is treasure hunting. To date, commercial salvage operations have generated all of AEL's revenues. The demand for these services is strong, and there are few competitors because of the unpredictable nature of the business and the long hours. Colin manages the commercial salvage operations. Customers pay in three instalments, including an upfront fee, a fee payable approximately midway through the contract, and a fee at the end once the items in question have been salvaged (found and brought to land). If the item is never found or AEL cannot bring the item to the surface and to land, then the final payment is not made.

Iskra spends most of her time locating and recovering underwater artifacts and, where possible, sunken treasure. Her research shows that numerous vessels carrying gold, silver, and other valuables to the "Old World" were wrecked off the shores of Nova Scotia. AEL has permits to investigate three target areas. As compensation for the permits, AEL agrees to remit 1% of the fair value of any treasure found. These funds are to be invested in the local economy by AEL (subject to government approval). The company also pays an upfront fee that allows it to search a given area. AEL recently made a potentially lucrative discovery in the first of these target areas.

It is now September 5, 2019. AEL has engaged your auditing firm to provide advice on the accounting for the ongoing operations and the discovery that AEL has just made. You (as audit manager) and Alex Green, the partner assigned to the engagement, met with Colin and Iskra.

During your meeting, Iskra said that she believes that finding treasure is like winning a lottery, as all revenues would accrue to AEL and thus should be treated accordingly. If this discovery proves to be as substantial as preliminary results suggest, AEL will require additional financing of $1.5 million to acquire equipment and an on-shore laboratory and lease a specially equipped vessel needed to salvage the wreck and its treasures. The bank has said that it is not willing to advance further funds. However, Iskra and Colin know of other individuals who are interested in investing in AEL.

AEL receives grants from the government to help find treasure and salvage sunken vessels. Iskra and Colin have just found out that they are likely to receive a grant in connection with the recent discovery.

Instructions

Audit Draft a memo for the audit partner, Alex Green, analyzing all financial reporting issues and providing recommendations.

IC10.2 OG Limited is in the oil and gas business. It spends quite a bit of money each year exploring for new wells. Currently, it has several wells that are in the production phases. The company's shares trade on the London Stock Exchange. OG is looking to expand its exploration into China and therefore would like to issue more shares next year to fund the exploration. The company's top management is compensated partly with stock options.

One of the company's wells recently exploded, pouring a significant amount of oil into a nearby waterway. It took one month to cap the well, and during that time the company incurred significant costs in capping the well, including costs related to many failed attempts. OG has announced that it will clean up the spilled oil and estimates that it will cost between $5 million and $10 million to do so. It has also announced that it will act in a responsible manner when dealing with any losses and complaints that the local farmers may have in connection with the spill.

OG is now being sued in a class action suit brought about by the farmers. They are suing for $100 million in compensation for their land, which is now unusable because of the oil. The company's lawyers feel they can settle for 10% of that amount.

[22]This item was originally published by the Canadian Institute of Chartered Accountants (CICA) as a question in the Uniform Final Evaluation (UFE). Adapted with permission of the Chartered Professional Accountants of Canada, Toronto, Canada. Any changes to the original material are the sole responsibility of the publisher and have not been reviewed or endorsed by the Chartered Professional Accountants of Canada.

The company capitalizes all costs incurred in connection with searching for new oil and gas wells, even when the exploration does not result in a well that has oil in it. They argue that they must incur those costs in order to find a producing well. In many countries where OG explores and operates, there are no legal requirements to restore the land to its original state once the exploration is complete or a well is depleted. The company does, however, state that it considers this an important activity and will make every effort to restore the site.

When excavating one site, OG came across a significant amount of gold. OG is now mining and selling the gold. Currently, it is trying to decide how to account for the gold inventory and is considering valuing the gold at market price once it has been refined, even though it is not yet sold.

Instructions

Audit Assume the role of the company's auditors and analyze the financial reporting issues.

Research and Analysis

RA10.1 **Real World Emphasis** **Magna International Inc.**

Access the financial statements of **Magna International Inc.** for the company's year ended December 31, 2017. These are available at www.sedar.com or the company's website. Review the information that is provided and answer the following questions about the company.

Instructions

a. What business is Magna International in?

b. Identify the types of tangible capital assets that Magna reports and indicate whether these assets form a significant portion of the company's total assets at December 31, 2017. Also explain why these assets are classified as property, plant, and equipment, and what conditions must exist before Magna reports them on its financial statements.

c. Identify all the accounting policies disclosed in the notes to the financial statements that explain how the company determines the cost of its property, plant, and equipment.

d. How much did Magna spend on new capital asset acquisitions in 2016 and 2017 (excluding business acquisitions)? Identify where the company obtained the funds to invest in these additions.

e. Explain how the company accounts for government assistance.

f. Compare the percentage increase in fixed asset additions from 2016 to 2017 with the percentage increase in sales. Taking the point of view of an investor or a potential investor, comment on the results of your analysis.

RA10.2 **Real World Emphasis** **Stora Enso Oyj**

Access the annual financial statements of **Stora Enso Oyj** for the company's year ended December 31, 2017. These are available at the company's website, www.storaenso.com. Review the information that is provided and answer the following questions about the company.

Instructions

a. What major business(es) is Stora Enso in?

b. What types of biological assets does the company have? Identify the accounting policies disclosed in the notes to the financial statements that explain how the company accounts for these assets.

c. What was the amount in the biological assets account at December 31, 2017 and 2016, owned directly by Stora Enso? What caused this account balance to change from 2016 to 2017? Be specific.

d. How is fair value of the biological assets determined? What kinds of estimates are required to determine fair value?

e. What was the impact on the net earnings for 2017 and 2016 related to the biological assets valuation?

RA10.3 **Data Analytics** **Real World Emphasis** **Empire Company Limited and Loblaw Companies Limited**

Companies in the same line of business usually have similar investments and capital structures, and an opportunity for similar rates of return. One of the key performance indicators to assess company profitability is the return on assets ratio. This ratio results from two key relationships—the profit margin and the total asset turnover—and in general terms can be written as follows:

Return on assets = Total asset turnover (or Sales/Total assets) × Profit margin (or Income/Sales)

This says that profitability depends directly on how many sales dollars are generated for each dollar invested in assets (total asset turnover) and on how costs are controlled for each dollar of sales (profit margin). An increase in either ratio results in an increase in the return on assets. As property, plant, and equipment often represent the largest single asset on the balance sheet, companies need to have strategies to manage their investment in such assets.

Instructions

Access the financial statements of two companies that are in the food distribution and retail business: **Empire Company Limited** for the year ended May 6, 2017, and **Loblaw Companies Limited** for the year ended December 30, 2017. These are available at www.sedar.com or each company's website. Review the financial statements and answer the following questions.

a. At each company's year end, determine the percentage of property, plant, and equipment to total assets.

b. Calculate each company's fixed asset turnover, total asset turnover, and profit margin (using net income) for the most recent year.

c. Determine the return on assets for each company. Which company is more profitable?

d. Which company appears to use its total assets more effectively in generating sales? Its fixed assets?

e. Are there any differences in accounting policies that might explain the differences in the fixed asset turnover ratios?

f. Examine the leasing note for each company. How might the amount of assets that are leased affect the above asset turnover ratios?

g. Which company has better control over its expenses for each dollar of sales? How do you explain the asset turnover ratios and the profit ratio comparisons?

RA10.4 `Real World Emphasis` Brookfield Asset Management Inc.

Access the financial statements of **Brookfield Asset Management Inc.** for the company's year ended December 31, 2017, contained in the company's annual report, available from the company's website (or www.sedar.com). Review the information that is provided and answer the following questions about the company.

Instructions

a. What business is Brookfield Asset Management in? Identify the types of tangible capital assets the company includes on its balance sheet. (*Hint:* See Notes 1 and 2 to the financial statements.)

b. Indicate what accounting model is used to measure and report each type of tangible capital asset identified in part (a).

c. Review the company's statement of operations, statement of comprehensive income, and relevant notes to the financial statements to identify the effect on net income and on other comprehensive income of each accounting model used for its tangible capital assets.

d. For the assets identified in part (b) that were measured using fair values, explain how the company determined their fair values; that is, what methods were used and what types of key assumptions were required.

RA10.5 `Real World Emphasis` Extractive Industry

Access the financial statements of **BHP Billiton plc** (BHP) for the company's year ended June 30, 2017. Also access the financial statements of **Newfield Exploration** for the company's year ended December 31, 2017. These are available at the companies' websites. Review the information that is provided and answer the following questions about the companies.

Instructions

a. What business is BHP in? What business is Newfield Exploration in?

b. How does BHP account for exploration, evaluation, and development expenditures related to its mineral reserves and resources? What specific costs are included?

c. How does Newfield account for exploration, evaluation, and development expenditures related to its mineral reserves and resources? What specific costs are included?

d. Using the two companies as examples, discuss the similarities and differences between the successful efforts method and the full cost method.

e. One method for reporting these assets that is being contemplated by IFRS is the fair value method. What assumptions would be required to determine the fair value of mineral or oil and gas reserves? What are some drawbacks to using the fair value method to value these types of assets?

f. From a user's perspective, which method(s) discussed above would provide the most faithful representation and relevant information?

RA10.6   Ethics   Acquisition and Installation Costs

A machine's invoice price is $40,000. Various other costs relating to the acquisition and installation of the machine—including transportation, electrical wiring, a special base, and so on—amount to $7,500. The machine has an estimated life of 10 years, with no residual value at the end of that period.

The owner-manager of the company that you work for as an accountant suggests that the incidental costs of $7,500 be charged to expense immediately for the following reasons:

- If the machine is ever sold, these costs cannot be recovered in the sale price.

- The inclusion of the $7,500 in the machinery account on the books will not necessarily result in a closer approximation of this asset's market price over the years, because demand and supply levels could change.

- Charging the $7,500 to expense immediately will reduce income taxes.

Instructions

Prepare a memo to the owner-manager that addresses each of the issues assuming that the company follows ASPE.

RA10.7   Government Funding

Hotel Resort Limited is a company that builds world-class resorts in tourist areas around the globe. When the company decided to build a resort in Yellowknife, the federal government agreed to provide a forgivable loan in the amount of $50 million to help fund the construction of the tourist facilities anticipated to cost about $700 million. The loan will be forgiven provided the tourist facility is operated for at least 15 years. If the resort is closed or sold before 15 years have elapsed, the amount of the loan must be repaid in full, along with interest at the prevailing market rate.

In addition, the federal government also agreed to provide annual funding to cover 70% of the related costs of payroll and room and board for 50 summer students, provided the students were hired to work for four full months. The company would receive this annual funding once it proved the costs incurred for these students.

Instructions

Prepare a memo that would be suitable to present to the Hotel Resort Limited board of directors in which you explain how the receipt of the government funding is expected to affect the company's reported total assets and earnings. Also, draft the related note disclosure that would be required.

(Adapted from AICPA)

RA10.8   Capitalizing Costs for Self-Constructed Assets

Gomi Medical Labs Inc. began operations five years ago producing a new type of instrument it hoped to sell to doctors, dentists, and hospitals. The demand for the new instrument was much higher than had been planned for, and the company was unable to produce enough of them to meet demand. The company was manufacturing its product on equipment that had been built at the start of its operations.

To meet demand, more efficient equipment was needed. The company decided to design and build the equipment because the equipment currently on the market was unsuitable for producing this product.

In 2020, a section of the plant was devoted to developing the new equipment and expert employees were hired. Within six months, a machine, developed at a cost of $714,000, increased production dramatically and reduced labour costs substantially. Thrilled by the new machine's success, the company built three more machines of the same type for its own use, at a cost of $441,000 each.

Instructions

a. In general, what costs should be capitalized for self-constructed equipment?

b. Discuss whether the capitalized cost of self-constructed assets should include the following:

1. The increase in overhead that results from the company's own construction of its fixed assets

2. A proportionate share of overhead on the same basis as what is applied to goods that are manufactured for sale

c. Discuss the proper accounting treatment of the $273,000 cost amount ($714,000 – $441,000) that was higher for the first machine than the cost of the subsequent machines.

CHAPTER 11

Depreciation, Impairment, and Disposition

StushD80/iStock/Getty Images

Accounting for Assets That Become Liabilities

There are thousands of mines and oil wells across Canada. Eventually, their resources become depleted or, in some cases, they become contaminated. What happens when they are abandoned by their owners? Usually, the cleanup costs are left to the taxpayer, which is why governments care about asset retirement obligations (AROs). AROs are liabilities recorded by resource companies (among others) as estimates of costs they would incur to retire tangible assets, such as decommissioning an oil well or cleaning up a contaminated mine. Most governments require resource companies to make financial security deposits to help pay for such cleanups. If a company goes bankrupt or its deposits don't cover the cost, the government usually has to step in to pay for these site retirements.

In mid-2017, the non-profit watchdog MiningWatch Canada estimated that governments across Canada had $9.1 billion in liabilities for contaminated mine sites, although official data were only available for Ontario, British Columbia, Quebec, and the territories, which account for two thirds of mining production. In 2017, the province of Alberta offered an up to $235-million loan to the Orphan Well Association to clean up abandoned oil wells. The Pembina Institute, a non-profit energy think tank, estimates that there are 69,000 abandoned wells in Alberta.

Governments themselves have AROs on their books for their obligations to retire their own assets. For example, the federal government had nearly $6.5 billion in AROs in its 2017 fiscal year, mostly to decommission its nuclear facilities.

The federal government's financial statements, called the Public Accounts, describe how it accounts for AROs. "A liability for an asset retirement obligation is recognized when all of the following criteria are satisfied: there is an agreement, contract, legislation, or a constructive or equitable obligation that obligates the Government to incur retirement costs in relation to a tangible capital asset, the past event or transaction giving rise to the retirement liability has occurred, it is expected that future economic benefits will be given up and a reasonable estimate of the amount can be made. These costs are normally capitalized and amortized over the asset's estimated useful life based on the Government's best estimates of the cost to retire the tangible asset. If the related asset is fully amortized, the related cost is expensed."

The federal government also has environmental liabilities to clean up potentially contaminated sites it owns—a bill that taxpayers may also have to foot. The 2017 Public Accounts identified approximately 2,400 federally owned sites across Canada where remediation is possible, recording a liability of $5.7 billion based on estimates from environmental experts.

Sources: Colleen Schmidt, "Province Offers Up to $235M to Remediate Inactive Well Sites in Alberta," CTVNews.ca, May 18, 2017; "Finally! New National Inventory for Orphaned and Abandoned Mine Sites," MiningWatch Canada news release, May 10, 2017; Receiver General for Canada, Public Accounts of Canada 2017.

LEARNING OBJECTIVES	CHAPTER OUTLINE	CPA COMPETENCIES
After studying this chapter, you should be able to:	The chapter headings related to the learning objective are:	Competencies addressed by each learning objective are as follows:
1. Understand the importance of depreciation, impairment, and disposition from a business perspective.	**The Importance of Depreciation, Impairment, and Disposition from a Business Perspective**	**1.1.1, 1.1.2, 1.1.4**
2. Explain the concept of depreciation and identify the factors to consider when determining depreciation charges.	**Depreciation** • Factors considered in the depreciation process	**1.2.1, 1.2.2**
3. Identify how depreciation methods are selected; calculate and recognize depreciation using straight-line, diminishing balance, activity, and other methods.	**Depreciation—Methods of Allocation and Calculation** • Straight-line method • Diminishing balance method • Activity methods • Other methods	**1.2.1, 1.2.2**
4. Explain the accounting issues for depletion of mineral resources.	**Depletion of Mineral Resources** • Pattern of depletion • Estimating recoverable reserves • Liquidating dividends	**1.1.2, 1.2.1, 1.2.2, 1.2.3, 5.4.1, 5.4.2**
5. Explain and apply the accounting procedures for partial periods and a change in depreciation rate.	**Other Depreciation Issues** • Depreciation and partial periods • Revision of depreciation rates	**1.2.1, 1.2.2**
6. Explain the issues and apply the accounting standards for capital asset impairment under both IFRS and ASPE.	**Impairment** • Indicators of impairment • Impairment—recognition and measurement models • Asset groups and cash-generating units	**1.1.2, 1.1.4, 1.2.1, 1.2.3, 5.4.1**
7. Account for derecognition of property, plant, and equipment and explain and apply the accounting standards for long-lived assets that are held for sale.	**Held for Sale and Derecognition** • Long-lived assets to be disposed of by sale • Derecognition	**1.2.1, 1.2.2, 1.2.3**

8. Describe the types of disclosures required for property, plant, and equipment, and provide an analysis of investment in capital assets.	**Presentation, Disclosure, and Analysis** • Presentation and disclosure • Analysis	1.1.2, 1.3.2, 1.4.1, 1.4.2, 1.4.4, 5.1.1
9. Identify differences in accounting between IFRS and ASPE, and what changes are expected in the near future.	**IFRS/ASPE Comparison** • A comparison of IFRS and ASPE • Looking ahead	1.1.4

After studying Appendix 11A, you should be able to:

10. Calculate capital cost allowance in routine and non-routine situations.	**Appendix 11A: Depreciation and Income Tax** • Capital cost allowance method	1.2.1, 1.2.2, 1.2.3, 6.1.2, 6.1.4

Preview of Chapter 11

Capital assets can be a major investment for companies. It is therefore important that you have a firm understanding of this chapter's topics. For example, you should be aware of the alternatives that exist for charging these capital costs to operations and the potential for impairment in their values. Some critics argue that financial statement readers do not need to be concerned with non-cash expenses such as depreciation, so it is important to understand the purpose of charging depreciation and the difference between cost allocation and valuation. It is also important to understand rules governing allocation of capital costs for calculating income taxes. The appendix outlines key aspects of the capital cost allowance system that is required for income tax purposes.

The Importance of Depreciation, Impairment, and Disposition from a Business Perspective

LEARNING OBJECTIVE 1

Understand the importance of depreciation, impairment, and disposition from a business perspective.

The economic benefits of property, plant, and equipment (PP&E) are typically consumed as the items are used by the organization. Because PP&E is used over multiple periods, companies must find an appropriate method for allocating the benefits as the assets' capacity and expected output are used up. Businesses usually cannot determine exactly how long a long-lived asset will be used productively. See **What Do the Numbers Mean? 11.1**. However, they are generally able to make a reasonable estimate of useful life. Several factors may have an impact on the asset's useful life and residual value. These factors include the asset's planned repairs and maintenance, its expected technical or commercial obsolescence, and legal or other limits on its use (such as lease terms).[1]

---

[1]See IAS 16, paragraphs 56–57 for further discussion. Copyright © IFRS Foundation. All rights reserved. Reproduced with permission.

What Do the Numbers Mean? 11.1

Under IFRS, determining a reasonable basis for depreciation has become even more of a challenge for many businesses. For example, Ontario Power Generation (OPG) had planned to adopt IFRS starting in 2012 but it delayed the move. The delay, when most businesses adopted IFRS in 2011, was due partly to the complications for organizations like OPG whose rates are regulated by the government. With its PP&E having a carrying amount of more than $21.0 billion at the end of 2017 (and $20.0 billion at the end of 2016), OPG has to consider matters such as the impact of IFRS's focus on individual components of PP&E. This affects accounting for items such as OPG's nuclear, hydroelectric, and thermal generating stations. The switch to IFRS is still likely to have a significant effect when it does occur, as OPG began a $12.8-billion refurbishment of its Darlington nuclear generating station in 2016, which is expected to extend the life of the four-unit generating station by another 30 years. Instead of IFRS, OPG adopted U.S. GAAP in 2012 to minimize the differences from "old" Canadian GAAP. OPG received an exemption from the Ontario Securities Commission that allowed it to continue to use U.S. GAAP until the earlier of January 1, 2019, and the effective date under IFRS for the mandatory application of an IFRS standard specific to entities with rate-regulated activities.[2]

By allocating the cost of property, plant, and equipment over their useful lives, businesses are better able to match the costs and benefits of the assets to the revenues that they help generate. This also ensures that businesses do not have to record a disproportionate amount of expense in the year the asset is acquired. Similarly, if PP&E is not depreciated, businesses might need to record large losses in the year of disposition

Depreciation helps businesses ensure that assets are carried at an amount no higher than what is expected to be recoverable for the asset. However, over time, the asset could still end up being carried at too high an amount. What if the asset's carrying value exceeds its recoverable amount, due to poor estimates of useful life or residual value, or other factors such as unexpected obsolescence? In that case, the carrying amount should be reduced.[3] Companies therefore need to regularly assess their PP&E for signs of impairment. If there are signs, companies should re-estimate how much will be recoverable. This should help them better understand their business, along with complying with GAAP.

Depreciation

LEARNING OBJECTIVE 2

Explain the concept of depreciation and identify the factors to consider when determining depreciation charges.

Underlying Concept 11.1

Assessing the fair value of long-lived assets at each reporting date may provide more relevant information to users. However, amortized cost is more reliable and verifiable. So, when evaluated on a cost-benefit basis, most preparers continue to support the use of amortized cost.

Many people at one time or another buy and sell a vehicle. The automobile dealer and the buyer typically discuss what the old car's trade-in value is. Also, they may talk about what the new car's trade-in value will be in several years. In both cases, the decline in value is generally referred to as depreciation.

To accountants, however, depreciation is not a matter of valuation (or a method of determining an asset's declining value). **Depreciation**—or amortization, as it is also called—**is a means of cost allocation**. It is the process of allocating the depreciable amount of a PP&E asset to expense in a systematic manner to those periods expected to benefit from its use. As explained in this chapter, the depreciable amount is the asset's cost less its residual amount. (There could, however, sometimes be a different value used instead of cost, such as that used when the revaluation model is applied.) See Underlying Concept 11.1 for further discussion.

---

[2]Ontario Power Generation (OPG) 2017 and 2010 annual reports, and OPG 2017 consolidated financial statements Note 2 ("Basis of Presentation").

[3]See IAS 36.7–23.

It is true that an asset's value changes between the time it is purchased and the time it is sold or scrapped. Most companies use a cost allocation approach rather than a valuation approach, however. This is because objectively measuring the changes in their assets' values every reporting period is often difficult and usually costly.

As mentioned above, the terms **amortization** and **depreciation** are almost interchangeable. Amortization is the general process of allocating the carrying amount of any long-lived asset to the accounting periods that benefit from its use. It can also specifically refer to this process for **intangible assets**. The term depreciation is reserved for property, plant, and equipment, and depletion is used only with natural resource assets.

Factors Considered in the Depreciation Process

Before calculating the dollar amount of depreciation expense, a company has to answer four basic questions:

1. What asset components are depreciated separately?
2. What is the asset's depreciable amount?
3. Over what period is the asset depreciated?
4. What pattern best reflects how the asset's economic benefits are used up?

As you might expect, judgement and estimates are needed to answer these questions. This means that the resulting **depreciation is an estimate**. A perfect measure of items affecting depreciation expense, such as useful life and residual value, is often impossible.

Asset Components

As mentioned in Chapter 10, the degree of componentization is based on professional judgement. So management should consider developing a policy to guide decisions on which fixed asset components to recognize separately. What individual parts of multi-component assets, such as a building, should be pulled out and recorded separately? And when should numerous small PP&E assets, such as small tools, be combined and accounted for together? Determining the unit of account is the first step in the depreciation process.

The following principles guide the componentization decision:

- Identify each part of a PP&E asset whose cost is a significant portion of the total asset cost as a separate component.
- Group together significant components with similar useful lives and patterns of providing economic benefits.
- Add together the costs of the remaining parts of the asset, none of which is individually significant. These may be depreciated as a single component, taking into account the nature of the different parts.
- Group together individual minor assets to depreciate as one component based on the similarity of their useful life and pattern of consumption.

Air Canada indicates that its aircraft and flight equipment are componentized into airframe, engine, and cabin interior equipment and modifications. Cabin interior equipment and modifications are depreciated over a much shorter period of time (eight years) than airframes and engines (no more than 25 years). Similarly, British Airways plc reports that the cabin interior modifications of its aircraft fleet are recognized and depreciated separately from the aircraft themselves (typically five years for cabin interior modifications versus seven to 29 years for its fleet aircraft, depending on aircraft type). It amortizes the cost of major overhaul expenditures, including replacement spares and labour costs, over the average expected life between major overhauls.

Both IFRS and ASPE require entities to recognize separate components for the purpose of depreciation, but the international standards are more fully developed and more strictly applied.

Depreciable Amount

IFRS The amount of an asset that is to be depreciated—its **depreciable amount**—is the difference between the asset's cost (or revalued amount, if the revaluation model is being used) and its residual value.[4] The **residual value** is defined as the estimated amount a company would **receive today** if it disposed of the asset, less any related disposal costs, if the asset were at the **same age and condition expected at the end of its useful life**.[5] It is the amount the company depreciates the asset to over its useful life. For example, as **Example 11.1** shows, if an asset has a cost (or net revalued amount) of $10,000 and a residual value of $3,600, only $6,400 of its cost is depreciated under IFRS.

In some cases, the residual value may be so low as to be immaterial. Some long-lived assets, however, have substantial net realizable values at the end of their useful lives to a specific enterprise. As long as the residual value is less than the asset's carrying amount, depreciation is recognized on the asset. If the residual value increases so it is more than the asset's carrying amount, no depreciation is taken until this situation reverses. It is important that the residual value be reviewed regularly, but particularly whenever changes in the environment occur that might affect its estimate. Under IFRS, this review is required at least at each year end.

ASPE A more technical and conservative policy is required under ASPE where, to ensure that charges to the income statement are adequate, the depreciation charge is based on the higher of two amounts (see *CPA Canada Handbook*, Part II, Section 3061.16):

1. cost less salvage value over the life of the asset, and
2. cost less residual value over the asset's useful life.

The **salvage value** is the estimate of the asset's net realizable value at the end of its life, rather than its value at the end of its useful life to the entity. The salvage value is usually an insignificant amount. In practice, the residual value is most commonly used to calculate depreciation.

Example 11.1 | Accounting for Depreciation

Facts Equipment with a cost (or net revalued amount) of $10,000 and a residual value of $3,600 is acquired. The equipment has an estimated useful life of eight years, and its total expected life is 10 years with no salvage value.

Instructions **IFRS** **ASPE** How much of the cost would be depreciated? Provide the calculation and the journal entries under IFRS, and describe how your answer would change under the requirements of ASPE.

Solution Under IFRS, only $6,400 of its cost is depreciated, as calculated below:

Original cost (or amount substituted for "cost")	$10,000
Less: residual value	3,600
Depreciable amount	$ 6,400

IFRS

A	=	L	+	SE
−800				−800

Cash flows: No effect

ASPE

A	=	L	+	SE
−1,000				−1,000

Cash flows: No effect

Its depreciation under IFRS would be $800 if it uses straight-line depreciation. However, if the total expected life of the asset is 10 years with no salvage value, under ASPE the minimum depreciation charge would be $1,000 per year. Journal entries to record the depreciation under IFRS versus ASPE are provided below.

To record depreciation of the machine:	IFRS[a]	ASPE[b]
Depreciation Expense	800	1,000
Accumulated Depreciation—Machinery	800	1,000

[a]IFRS depreciation ($10,000 − $3,600)/8 = $800
[b]ASPE depreciation is the greater of ($10,000 − $3,600)/8 = $800 or ($10,000 − $0)/10 = $1,000

---

[4]After acquisition, it is the asset's **net carrying amount** and residual value that determine the depreciable amount.

[5]This is the definition in IAS 16 *Property, Plant, and Equipment*. The definition in the *CPA Canada Handbook*, Part II, Section 3061 *Property, Plant, and Equipment* refers only to the asset's net realizable value at the end of its useful life to an entity. These are not necessarily inconsistent.

Depreciation Period

As indicated above, to calculate depreciation, we need an estimate of the asset's **useful life**. An asset's useful life is the period during which the asset is expected to be available for use by the entity based on factors such as the asset's expected capacity. Alternatively, useful life can be stated in terms of the number of units of product or service that the asset is expected to produce or provide over this period.

Depreciation begins when the asset is available for use; that is, when it is in place and in the condition necessary to operate as management intends. The **depreciation process ends** when the asset is derecognized (removed from the accounts), or when it is classified as held for sale, if earlier. **Depreciation continues** even if the asset is idle or has been taken out of service, unless it is fully depreciated, of course.

Useful or service life and physical life are often not the same. A piece of machinery may be physically capable of producing a specific product for many years past its useful life in a particular organization, but the equipment may not be used for all of those years due to **economic factors** such as obsolescence. The useful lives of Air Canada's aircraft components, described earlier, are likely determined through discussions with others in the organization, such as engineering and manufacturing specialists. New processes or techniques or improved machines may provide the same product or service at lower cost or with higher quality. Changes needed in the product or service itself may shorten an asset's useful life. Operational factors and asset management policies also influence asset retirement decisions.

Physical factors set the outside limit for an asset's service life. Physical factors relate to such things as decay or wear and tear that result from use of the asset and the passage of time. Whenever the asset's physical nature is the main factor that determines its useful life, a company's maintenance policies play a vital role—the better the maintenance, the longer the life of the asset.[6] An asset's **legal life** may also limit its useful life to a specific entity. For example, the benefits of leasehold improvements end when the lease term is over.

To illustrate these concepts, consider a new nuclear power plant. Which is most important in determining its useful life: physical factors, economic factors, or its legal life? The limiting factors seem to be (1) ecological considerations, (2) competition from other power sources, and (3) safety concerns. Physical and legal life do not appear to be primary factors affecting the plant's useful life. While the plant's physical life may be far from over, the plant may require refurbishment after 20 or 25 years.

The estimate of useful life is often not easy to determine, but it is an important aspect of accounting theory as discussed in **Underlying Concept 11.2**. In some cases, arbitrary lives are selected; in others, sophisticated statistical methods are used. The main basis for estimating an asset's useful life is often judgement and the company's experience with similar assets. In an industrial economy such as Canada's, where research and innovation are so prominent, economic and technological factors have as much effect on the service lives of tangible assets as do physical factors, if not more. We examine typical patterns of use below.

> **Underlying Concept 11.2**
> Depreciation is a good example of how the matching concept is applied when there is no direct relationship between revenues and costs.

Depreciation—Methods of Allocation and Calculation

> **LEARNING OBJECTIVE 3**
> Identify how depreciation methods are selected; calculate and recognize depreciation using straight-line, diminishing balance, activity, and other methods.

The last major issue in the depreciation process is deciding **which depreciation method is most appropriate**. The underlying principle is that the resulting depreciation should reflect the pattern in which the asset benefits are expected to be used up by the entity. This suggests

---

[6]The airline industry illustrates the type of problem found in estimations. In the past, aircraft were assumed not to wear out; they just became obsolete. However, some jets have been in service for as long as 30 years, and maintenance of these aircraft has become increasingly expensive. As a result, some airlines now replace aircraft, not because of obsolescence, but because of physical deterioration.

that the concern is with the pattern in which the physical capacity, wear and tear, technical obsolescence, or legal life are used up as the asset provides service to the company. Four alternative patterns are identified in **Illustration 11.1**.

ILLUSTRATION 11.1 Possible Benefit Patterns for Assets

Benefits = Use of asset services

Useful life = Time or quantity of input or output

Pattern (1) is a uniform benefit pattern. This applies to an asset that provides roughly the same level of benefits in each year of its life. A warehouse could be an example. For such assets, a straight-line method is rational because it results in a constant depreciation expense each period.

Pattern (2) is a decreasing benefit pattern. An airplane may be an example of an asset with a decreasing benefit pattern. When it is new, it is constantly in service on major routes. As it gets older, its operating efficiency declines—it may be repaired more often and used for less busy routes. Depreciation expense should therefore decline each year.

Pattern (3) is a fluctuating benefit pattern. The use of a truck, in terms of kilometres driven, may fluctuate considerably from period to period, yielding a benefit pattern that varies or fluctuates.

Pattern (4) is an increasing benefit pattern. It is seldom experienced because few assets provide more service potential or generate higher value cash flows as they age. A new hotel might be an example, with lower levels of occupancy in early years and then increasing gradually over time as the hotel's reputation leads to increased use due to "repeat business."

Because of the difficulty in some cases in identifying the pattern in which benefits are received, the **simplicity** of each method may be considered. If so, some argue that a straight-line method should be used. However, others may think that the method used for income tax purposes should be used for book purposes **because it eliminates some record-keeping costs**. Canadian companies are required to use the capital cost allowance approach for tax purposes (explained in Appendix 11A), so some may decide to also use this for financial reporting purposes. While this is more common for smaller companies, a larger company is likely to use one method for tax purposes and a different method for financial reporting. This is more reasonable because the objectives of financial reporting differ from those of calculating income tax. One result of using different methods for financial reporting than for taxes is that the entity's financial statement amounts for property, plant, and equipment will be different from the tax base of capital assets used for calculating taxable income. The financial accounting consequences of such differences are explored in Chapter 18.

[Theory] Management sometimes appears to choose a depreciation method based on the **perceived economic consequences** of the amounts that will be reported. See Underlying Concept 11.3. Companies that want to appear more profitable might be tempted to change from the declining-balance method to a straight-line approach. Because share value tends to be related to reported income, management may feel that such a change favourably affects the firm's market value. In fact, research in this area has found just the opposite: companies that switch to more liberal accounting policies may experience declines in share values. One explanation is that changes like this signal that the company is in trouble and may lead to scepticism about management's attitudes and behaviour.

The choice of a depreciation method affects both the statement of financial position (in terms of the carrying amount of property, plant, and equipment) and the income statement (in terms of the depreciation expense). It follows, therefore, that various ratios are affected by the choice that is made. These ratios include the rate of return on total assets, debt-to-total assets, and total asset turnover. Consequently, contractual commitments based on financial statement ratios, such as agreements related to management compensation plans and bond indentures, are potentially important aspects that tend to be considered when choosing a depreciation method.

Underlying Concept 11.3

The accounting profession is sometimes criticized for failing to consider the economic consequences that accounting principles have for companies. However, the neutrality concept requires that the statements be free from bias in that methods are not chosen to achieve a predetermined result.

Data Analytics Some companies are now using quite advanced methods to manage their property, plant, and equipment, improving cost management and customer satisfaction. For example, at least one consulting firm suggests that firms use a "health index" to track the condition of capital assets, and to help determine if they need maintenance or replacement. Predictive analytics can track baseline measures of performance, machinery failure, and the impact of weather on assets that are exposed to the elements (such as wind turbines), and to develop measures of asset "criticality" to help assess the importance of maintenance and back-up systems for key assets. Using machine learning and other tools, firms can access data on an ongoing basis to assess asset performance and predict capital asset failures. Techniques used for data analysis of capital assets include multivariate analysis, logistic regression, neural networks, and random decision forests (that is, the use of multiple decision trees as a data analysis and prediction device).[7]

How is each of the major depreciation methods applied? Regardless of whether the cost model or the revaluation model is chosen to measure assets after acquisition, the three major types of systematic methods are:

1. Straight-line

2. Diminishing balance

3. Activity

Straight-Line Method

Under the **straight-line method**, depreciation is considered **a function of the passage of time**. This is the most widely used method in practice. Not only is it straightforward to apply, it is often the most conceptually appropriate method as well. See **Underlying Concept 11.4**. When creeping obsolescence is the main reason for a limited service life, the decline in usefulness is likely constant from period to period. The depreciation expense for a crane under the straight-line method is calculated in **Example 11.2**. The same crane is used to illustrate other depreciation methods in **Examples 11.3** and **11.4**.

> **Underlying Concept 11.4**
>
> If the benefits flow evenly over time, there is justification for using the straight-line basis of allocation.

Example 11.2 | Depreciation Calculation, Straight-Line Method—Crane Example

Facts Assume that a company buys a crane for heavy construction purposes. The relevant data on the purchase of the crane follow:

Cost of crane	$500,000
Estimated useful life	5 years
Productive life	30,000 hours
Estimated residual value	$50,000

Instructions Calculate depreciation using the straight-line method.

Solution Depreciation using the straight-line method would be $90,000 per year.

$$\frac{\text{Cost less residual value}}{\text{Estimated useful life}} = \text{Depreciation charge}$$

$$\frac{\$500,000 - \$50,000}{5 \text{ years}} = \$90,000$$

One objection to the straight-line method is that it relies on two assumptions:

1. The asset actually does deliver equal economic benefits each year.

2. Maintenance expense is about the same each period (assuming constant revenue flows).

If these assumptions are not valid, some argue that this method will not give a rational matching of expense with the periods that benefit from the asset. See **Underlying Concept 11.5**.

> **Underlying Concept 11.5**
>
> The matching concept does not justify use of a constant charge to income. If the benefits from the asset decline as it ages, then a decreasing expense better reflects how its benefits are consumed.

---

[7]See Carlos de la Peña, David González Fernández, and Jesús Rodríguez González, "How Analytics Can Improve Asset Management in Electric-Power Networks," McKinsey and Company, October 2016, available at https://www.mckinsey.com/industries/electric-power-and-natural-gas/our-insights/how-analytics-can-improve-asset-management-in-electric-power-networks.

Another issue with this method (and some of the others) is the distortion that develops in a rate of return analysis (income ÷ assets). **Illustration 11.2** indicates how the rate of return increases, assuming one asset and constant income levels, because the asset's book value decreases. The increasing trend in the rate of return can be very misleading as a basis for evaluating the success of operations because the increase is due only to the accounting method used, and not to improvements in underlying economic performance.

Depreciation and Rate of Return Analysis—Crane Example

Year	Depreciation Expense	Undepreciated Asset Balance (net book value)	Income (after depreciation expense)	Rate of Return (income ÷ assets)
0		$500,000		
1	$90,000	410,000	$100,000	24.4%
2	90,000	320,000	100,000	31.2%
3	90,000	230,000	100,000	43.5%
4	90,000	140,000	100,000	71.4%
5	90,000	50,000	100,000	200.0%

Diminishing Balance Method

The **diminishing balance method**, a type of **decreasing charge** or **accelerated amortization method**, creates a higher depreciation expense in the earlier years and lower charges in later periods. The justification for this approach is that many assets offer their greatest benefits in the early years, so that this method best reflects their pattern of use. Another argument is that repair and maintenance costs are often higher in later periods, and an accelerated method therefore provides a fairly constant total expense (for depreciation plus repairs and maintenance). When Canadian companies use a diminishing balance approach, it is usually a version of what is called the declining-balance method. (There is another systematic decreasing charge approach, called the **sum-of-the-years'-digits method**, but it is rarely used in Canada.[8])

The **declining-balance method** uses a depreciation rate that stays constant throughout the asset's life, assuming there is no change in estimate. The depreciation rate is expressed as a percentage and is called the declining-balance rate. This rate is applied each year to the net book value (cost less accumulated depreciation and any accumulated impairment losses) to calculate depreciation expense. For assets accounted for by the revaluation method, the rate is applied to the carrying amount (the revalued asset amount less the total of any accumulated depreciation and accumulated impairment losses).

The rate is usually calculated as a multiple of the straight-line rate.[9] Let's look at some examples.

- For an asset with a 10-year life, the double-declining-balance rate is 20% (the straight-line rate of 100% ÷ 10, or 10%, multiplied by 2).

---

[8]Under the sum-of-the-years' digits method, the depreciable amount is multiplied each year by a decreasing fraction. The **denominator** of the fraction equals the sum of the digits of an asset's useful life. For example, the sum of the digits of the life of an asset with a five-year life is $1 + 2 + 3 + 4 + 5 = 15$. The **numerator** decreases year by year and the denominator stays constant. Because this is a decreasing charge approach, depreciation expense is 5/15 of the depreciable amount in the first year, 4/15 of the depreciable amount in the second year, 3/15 in the third, 2/15 in the fourth, and 1/15 in the fifth year. At the end of the asset's useful life, its net book value is equal to the estimated residual value. Similarly, for an asset with a 10-year life, the sum of the years' digits, 1 through 10, equals 55. Depreciation in the first year is 10/55 of the depreciable amount, in the second year it is 9/55, and so on. (A short-cut calculation of the denominator is $[(n \times (n + 1)]/2 = (10 \times 11)/2 = 55$).

[9]The straight-line rate (%) is equal to 100% divided by the estimated useful life of the asset that is being depreciated. A pure form of the declining-balance method (sometimes called the fixed percentage of book value method) has also been suggested as a possibility, but it is not used very much. This approach finds a rate that depreciates the asset to exactly its residual value at the end of its expected useful life. The formula for determining this rate is as follows:

$$\text{Depreciation rate} = 1 - \sqrt[n]{\frac{\text{Residual value}}{\text{Acquisition cost}}}$$

The life in years is n. Once the rate is calculated, it is applied to the asset's declining book value from period to period.

- For an asset with a 20-year life, the double-declining-balance rate is 10% (100% ÷ 20, or 5%, multiplied by 2).
- For an asset with a 20-year life, the triple-declining-balance rate is 15% (the straight-line rate of 100% ÷ 20, or 5%, multiplied by 3).

Unlike other methods, the declining-balance method does not deduct **the asset's residual value** in calculating depreciation expense. Instead, the declining-balance method applies the appropriate rate to the asset's carrying amount at the beginning of each period. Since the asset's book value is reduced each period by the depreciation charge, the rate is applied to a lower and lower carrying amount each period, resulting in a depreciation charge that gets smaller each year. This process continues until the asset's carrying amount is reduced to its estimated residual value. **When the residual value is reached, the asset is no longer depreciated.**

Example 11.3 shows how to apply the **double-declining-balance method**, based on the crane example.

Example 11.3 | Depreciation Calculation, Double-Declining-Balance Method—Crane Example

Facts Consistent with Example 11.2, assume that a crane has been acquired with a cost of $500,000, estimated useful life of five years, productive life of 30,000 hours, and estimated residual value of $50,000.

Instructions Calculate depreciation, by year, using the double-declining-balance method.

Solution Depreciation by year using the double-declining-balance method would be:

Year	Book Value of Asset, Beginning of Year	Rate on Declining Balance[a]	Depreciation Expense	Balance of Accumulated Depreciation	Net Book Value, End of Year
1	$500,000	40%	$200,000	$200,000	$300,000
2	300,000	40%	120,000	320,000	180,000
3	180,000	40%	72,000	392,000	108,000
4	108,000	40%	43,200	435,200	64,800
5	64,800	40%	14,800[b]	450,000	50,000

[a](100% ÷ 5) × 2
[b]Limited to $14,800 because the book value is not reduced below the residual value.

Activity Methods

The **units of production method**, an example of an **activity method** or a **variable charge approach**, calculates depreciation **according to usage or productivity** instead of the passage of time. The asset's life is defined in terms of either the output it provides (units produced) or the input required (the number of hours it operates). Conceptually, a better cost association results from using output instead of an input measure such as hours used, but both are widely accepted and used.

Example 11.4 | Depreciation Calculation, Activity Method—Crane Example

Facts Consistent with Examples 11.2 and 11.3, assume that a crane has been acquired with a cost of $500,000, estimated useful life of five years, productive life of 30,000 hours, and estimated residual value of $50,000. The crane's usage in hours is relatively easy to measure. Assume it is used for 4,000 hours in the first year.

Instructions Calculate depreciation for the crane in the first year using the activity method.

Solution If the crane is used for 4,000 hours the first year, the depreciation charge is calculated as follows:

$$\frac{\text{Cost less residual value}}{\text{Total estimated hours}} = \text{Depreciation expense per hour}$$

$$\frac{\$500,000 - \$50,000}{30,000 \text{ hours}} = \$15 \text{ per hour}$$

First-year depreciation expense: 4,000 hours × $15 = $60,000

When the asset's economic benefits are consumed by usage, units of production or other activities, activity methods result in the best measure of periodic expense. Companies that adopt this approach have low depreciation during periods of low usage, high charges during high usage, and zero depreciation expense when the asset is available but idle.

The major limitation of an activity method is that it is appropriate in only a few situations. For example, a building usually suffers a great amount of steady deterioration from the weather (a function of time) regardless of how it is used. In addition, when an asset's useful life is affected by economic or functional factors that have nothing to do with its usage, the activity method is not appropriate. If a company is in a rapidly changing industry, production equipment may soon become obsolete for its intended purpose. The level of activity is irrelevant.

One industry where the activity method is particularly relevant is the extractive industry, which includes mining and oil and gas. We discuss accounting for the depletion of natural resources in the next section.

Other Methods

Sometimes, because of cost-benefit considerations or because the assets have unique characteristics, an entity may choose not to use one of the more common depreciation methods. Instead, it may use the method required by the Canada Revenue Agency for tax purposes as explained in Appendix 11A, or develop its own tailor-made amortization method. The IASB clarified IAS 16 to indicate that using depreciation methods based on revenue generated is not appropriate and is not permitted for financial statement periods ending after December 31, 2016. Depreciation is an important cost, as discussed in **What Do the Numbers Mean? 11.2**, and it should be based on the benefits being consumed, not benefits generated by running the business.

What Do the Numbers Mean? 11.2

Some companies try to imply that amortization is not a cost. For example, in their news releases, they often draw more attention to earnings before interest, taxes, depreciation, and amortization (referred to as EBITDA) or pro forma earnings (which may exclude items such as depreciation and restructuring costs) rather than net income as calculated under GAAP.[10] Some companies like the EBITDA figure because it "dresses up" their earnings numbers, and they promote it using the argument that the excluded costs are not operating costs or that amortization and depreciation are non-cash charges. Regardless, when all is said and done, companies must generate enough cash from revenues to cover all their costs, as the amounts they borrow to finance long-term asset acquisitions have to be repaid. Investors need to understand the differences between these various indicators of financial performance.

Consider **Intertape Polymer Group Inc.**'s review of its results for 2017. Adjusted EBITDA was reported at $129.6 million, while net earnings under GAAP amounted to $64.2 million. The company's March 2018 news release relating to its 2017 annual results included a variety of non-GAAP measures, including EBITDA, adjusted EBITDA and free cash flows. At one time, **Hollinger International Inc.** reported EBITDA of U.S. $111.4 million and a GAAP net loss of U.S. $238.8 million! Because of concerns that investors may be confused or misled by non-GAAP earnings measures, the Canadian Securities Administrators, which is the umbrella group for provincial regulators, issued specific guidance for certain disclosures that are associated with non-GAAP earnings measures. These include requiring that entities present a reconciliation of their non-GAAP measure(s) with audited GAAP results.

While reporting EBITDA and other pro forma numbers has not been prohibited, the IASB continues to explore the issue of companies using different performance measures in their financial statements, because companies often do not clarify what is included or excluded from these measures. We discuss this issue further in the Looking Ahead section of the chapter.

---

[10]Some critics suggest that pro forma earnings may confuse or mislead users. Investopedia.com notes that one nickname for pro forma earnings is EEBS (earnings excluding bad stuff!).

Depletion of Mineral Resources

LEARNING OBJECTIVE 4
Explain the accounting issues for depletion of mineral resources.

One industry where the activity method is particularly relevant is the extractive industry. Chapter 10 explains that generally the costs of acquisition, exploration, and development (including asset retirement costs) relating to oil and gas reserves and mineral deposits are capitalized into mineral resource assets using either the full cost or successful efforts method. The amortization of the cost of these reserves, as the wells or ore bodies are put into production, is known as **depletion**. The resulting **depletion expense** is a product cost, and therefore is a part of the direct cost of the minerals or petroleum products (inventory) produced during the period.

The accounting issues associated with the depletion of mineral resources are similar to those encountered with the amortization of other types of property, plant, and equipment. They include:

1. determining the pattern of depletion (amortization) to be used, and
2. the difficulty in estimating the asset's useful life.

Natural resource companies also have to deal with the associated issue of liquidating dividends, as discussed below.

Pattern of Depletion

Once the company establishes the depletion base—the cost of the mineral resource asset to be amortized—the next step is to determine how these capitalized costs will be allocated to accounting periods. Normally, **depletion is calculated using an activity approach, such as the units of production method**. This approach is used because of the close association of the resulting expense with the asset benefits consumed in the period. Under this method, the cost of the resource asset is divided by the estimated recoverable reserves (the number of units that are estimated to be in the resource deposit) to obtain a cost per unit of production. The cost per unit is then multiplied by the number of units extracted during the period to determine the depletion charge. Alacer Gold, a Canadian mining company, uses a units of production method based on a calculation of the average cost per recoverable ounce of gold to be mined from proven and probable reserves. Example 11.5 calculates a depletion rate and provides the related journal entries for a gold mine.

Example 11.5 | Calculating and Recording Depletion

Facts Assume a company acquired the right to use 1,000 hectares of land in the Northwest Territories to mine for gold. The lease cost is $500,000, the related exploration and evaluation costs are $1 million, and development costs incurred in opening the mine are $38.5 million—all of which have been capitalized. Total costs related to the mine before the first ounce of gold is extracted are, therefore, $40 million. The company estimates that the mine will provide approximately 50,000 ounces of gold.

Instructions
  a. Calculate the depletion rate and provide the journal entry to record depletion assuming that 12,500 ounces are extracted in the first year.
  b. Describe how depletion would be presented in the company's financial statements.

Solution
  a.

$$\frac{\text{Total cost} - \text{residual value}}{\text{Total estimated units available}} = \text{Depletion cost per unit}$$

$$\frac{\$40,000,000}{50,000} = \$800 \text{ per ounce}$$

A	=	L	+	SE
0				

Cash flows: No effect

If 12,500 ounces are extracted in the first year, the depletion for the year is $10 million (12,500 ounces at $800). The entry to record the depletion is:

Inventory	10,000,000	
Accumulated Depletion		10,000,000

b. The depletion charge for the extracted resource (in addition to labour and other direct production costs) is initially charged (debited) to inventory. When the resource is sold, the inventory costs are transferred to cost of goods sold and matched with the period's revenue. The remaining mineral resource is reported with property, plant, and equipment as a non-current asset, as follows:

Gold mine (at cost)	$40,000,000	
Less: Accumulated depletion	10,000,000	$30,000,000

The equipment used in extracting a resource such as gold may also be amortized on a units of production basis, especially if the equipment's benefits and useful life are directly related to the quantity of ore extracted from that specific deposit. If the equipment is used on more than one job and at more than one site, other cost allocation methods may be more appropriate.

Estimating Recoverable Reserves

Companies often change the estimate of the resource's useful life; that is, the amount of the recoverable reserves. This may result from new information or from the availability of more sophisticated production processes. Natural resources such as oil and gas deposits and some rare metals are the greatest challenges. Estimates of these reserves are largely "knowledgeable guesses."

Accounting for a change in the estimate of reserves is the same as for a change in the useful life of an item of plant and equipment. The procedure, explained later in this chapter, is to revise the depletion rate by dividing the costs remaining on the books less any residual value by the new estimate of the recoverable reserves. Past depletion is not adjusted. This approach has much merit because the required estimates are so uncertain.

Management makes judgements regarding the application of IFRS for each accounting policy as illustrated in **What Do the Numbers Mean? 11.3**. Critical judgements that have the most significant effect on the amounts recognized in the consolidated financial statements include oil and gas reserves, impairment assessments and the determination of cash-generating units.

What Do the Numbers Mean? 11.3

Husky Energy, a Canadian company in the oil and gas industry, reports in the Critical Accounting Estimates and Key Judgments section of its 2017 annual report that:

. . . amounts recorded for depletion, depreciation, amortization and impairment, asset retirement obligations, assets and liabilities measured at fair value, [and] employee future benefits . . . are based on estimates.

Costs directly associated with an exploration well are initially capitalized as exploration and evaluation assets.

Expenditures related to wells that do not find reserves or where no future activity is planned are expensed as exploration and evaluation expenses. Exploration and evaluation costs are excluded from costs subject to depletion until technical feasibility and commercial viability is assessed or production commences. At that time, costs are either transferred to property, plant, and equipment or their value is impaired. Impairment is charged directly to net earnings.

Illustration 11.3, the Value Pyramid devised by Simmons & Company International, underscores the measurement uncertainty associated with resource quantities, and therefore the depletion expense, recognized by companies in extractive industries such as oil and gas.

Finance 5.4.1, 5.4.2 "OOIP" in the Value Pyramid refers to the original oil in place, and determining this is the starting point in the calculation of reserves. After this, the amount of the OOIP that is technically and economically recoverable is then estimated. The percentages

THE VALUE PYRAMID

ILLUSTRATION 11.3
The Value Pyramid[11]

Probability of being correct

90%	Proved producing: Wells drilled, oil flows
80%	Proved but not yet developed
50%	Probable reserves: Might or might not be producible
20%	Contingent/prospective reserves: High risk

"OOIP"

indicated in each layer of the pyramid give you some idea of the likelihood of these estimates being correct. The bottom line is that estimating oil and gas reserves may be more an art than a science!

Liquidating Dividends

A company may own a property from which it plans to extract mineral resources, and have this as its only major asset. If the company does not expect to buy more properties, it may decide to distribute to shareholders a portion or all of their capital investment by paying a **liquidating dividend**, which is a dividend greater than the amount of accumulated net income. These dividends are typically equal to the accumulated amount of net income (after depletion) **plus the amount of depletion that has been charged**.

The major accounting issue is to distinguish between dividends that are a **return of capital** and those that are not. A company issuing a liquidating dividend reduces the appropriate Share Capital account for the portion of the dividend that is related to the original investment instead of reducing Retained Earnings, because the dividend is a return of part of the investor's original contribution, as shown in **Example 11.6**.

Example 11.6 | Recording Liquidating Dividends

Facts   Assume Callahan Mining Corp. has a retained earnings balance of $1,650,000, accumulated depletion on mineral properties of $2.1 million, and common share capital of $5.4 million. Callahan's board declares and pays a dividend of $3 per share on the 1 million shares outstanding.

Instructions   Provide the journal entry that Callahan would use to record this liquidating dividend and discuss the dividend-related information that Callahan should disclose to shareholders.

Solution   The company records the dividend as follows:

Retained Earnings	1,650,000	
Common Shares	1,350,000*	
Cash		3,000,000

*($3,000,000 − $1,650,000)

Callahan must inform shareholders that the $3 dividend per share represents a $1.65 ($1,650,000/1,000,000) per share **return on investment** and a $1.35 ($1,350,000/1,000,000) per share liquidating dividend, or **return of capital**.

A	=	L	+	SE
−3,000,000				−3,000,000

Cash flows: ▼ 3,000,000 outflow

---

[11]*Source:* Simmons and Company International. From a presentation given by Matthew R. Simmons to the Standing Group on the Oil Market of the International Energy Agency in Paris, France, March 16, 2004.

Other Depreciation Issues

LEARNING OBJECTIVE 5

Explain and apply the accounting procedures for partial periods and a change in depreciation rate.

Two additional depreciation issues remain:

1. How should depreciation be calculated for partial periods?
2. How are revisions to depreciation rates made and reported?

Depreciation and Partial Periods

Plant assets are rarely purchased on the first day of a fiscal period or disposed of on the last day of a fiscal period, except in accounting texts! A practical question therefore is, "How much depreciation should be charged for partial periods?"

Assume, for example, that a piece of equipment with a ten-year life is purchased for $20,000 (no residual value) on October 1, 2020. The company's fiscal year ends December 31, and depreciation is charged for 3 months during the year. The total depreciation for a full year, assuming the straight-line method, is $2,000 ($20,000 ÷ 10). The depreciation for the first, partial, year is therefore:

$$\$2,000 \times \frac{3}{12} = \$500$$

Rather than making a precise allocation of cost for a partial period, many companies set a policy to simplify the process. One variation is to take no depreciation in the year of acquisition and a full year's depreciation in the year of disposal. So, for example, depreciation is calculated for the full period on the opening balance in the asset account, and none for acquisitions in the year. Another variation is to charge a full year's depreciation on assets that are used for a full year and charge a half year of amortization in the years of acquisition and disposal. Alternatively, the company may charge a full year's depreciation in the year of acquisition and none in the year of disposal.

Although not conceptually "correct," companies may adopt one of these fractional-year policies in allocating cost to the first and last years of an asset's life if the method is applied consistently and the resulting effect on the financial statements is not material. For example, for its 2017 fiscal year, **Canadian Pacific Railway Limited** follows a group depreciation policy that applies a single depreciation rate for items within the same class of property. The company accounts for retirements and disposals of items like trains in the normal course of business by charging the cost of the property, less any net salvage, to accumulated depreciation.[12] For the examples and problem material in this text, depreciation is calculated based on the nearest full month, unless something different is stated. **Example 11.7** shows how depreciation would be allocated under five different fractional-year policies using the straight-line method.

Example 11.7 | Fractional-Year Depreciation Policies, Straight-Line Method

---

Facts   Assume a drill machine was purchased for $45,000 on June 10, 2020, with a five-year life and no residual value.

Instructions   Calculate the straight-line depreciation for the drill under the following alternative policies: (a) nearest fraction of a year; (b) nearest full month; (c) half year in period of acquisition

---

[12]CP noted in its 2017 annual report that, for the sale or retirement of larger groups of depreciable assets that are unusual in that they were not predicted by its depreciation studies, the company records a gain or loss for the difference between net proceeds and net book value of the assets sold or retired.

and disposal; (d) full year in period of acquisition, none in period of disposal; and (e) none in period of acquisition, full year in period of disposal.

Solution

Machine cost = $45,000	Depreciation Allocated Each Year over 5-Year Life (rounded to the nearest dollar)					
Fractional-Year Policy	2020	2021	2022	2023	2024	2025
a. Nearest fraction of a year	$5,000[1]	$9,000	$9,000	$9,000	$9,000	$4,000[2]
b. Nearest full month	5,250[3]	9,000	9,000	9,000	9,000	3,750[4]
c. Half year in period of acquisition and disposal	4,500	9,000	9,000	9,000	9,000	4,500
d. Full year in period of acquisition, none in period of disposal	9,000	9,000	9,000	9,000	9,000	0
e. None in period of acquisition, full year in period of disposal	0	9,000	9,000	9,000	9,000	9,000

[1]6.667/12 ($9,000)   [2]5.333/12 ($9,000)   [3]7/12 ($9,000)   [4]5/12 ($9,000)

The partial period calculation is relatively simple when a company uses the straight-line method. But how is partial period depreciation handled when using an accelerated method? Example 11.8 provides the answer.

Example 11.8 | Calculation of Partial Period Depreciation, Double-Declining-Balance Method

Facts   Assume that an asset was purchased for $10,000 on October 1, 2020, with an estimated useful life of five years.

Instructions   Calculate depreciation expense for 2020, 2021, and 2022 using the double-declining-balance method.

Solution   Double-declining-balance method depreciation expense would be calculated as:

Annual calculations
1st full year	$(40\% \times \$10,000) =$ $4,000
2nd full year	$(40\% \times 6,000) =$ 2,400
3rd full year	$(40\% \times 3,600) =$ 1,440

Depreciation October 1, 2020, to December 31, 2020:	$3/12 \times \$4,000 =$ $1,000

Depreciation for 2021:	$9/12 \times \$4,000 =$ $3,000
	$3/12 \times \$2,400 =$ 600
	$3,600

Depreciation for 2022:	$9/12 \times \$2,400 =$ $1,800
	$3/12 \times \$1,440 =$ 360
	$2,160

Alternatively:

Depreciation for 2020: $(40\% \times \$10,000) \times 3/12 =$ $1,000
   Asset carrying amount now = $10,000 − $1,000 = $9,000

Depreciation for 2021: $(40\% \times \$9,000) =$ $3,600
   Asset carrying amount now = $9,000 − $3,600 = $5,400

Depreciation for 2022: $(40\% \times \$5,400) =$ $2,160
   Asset carrying amount now = $5,400 − $2,160 = $3,240

As you can see from Example 11.8, the depreciation amount is identical whether you proceed through yearly "layers" of depreciation or whether you simply apply the rate to the asset's carrying amount at the start of each year.

Revision of Depreciation Rates

IFRS When a plant asset is acquired, depreciation rates are carefully determined based on past experience with similar assets and other pertinent information. Depreciation is only an estimate, however, and the estimates of the expected pattern of consumption of the asset's benefits, useful life, and residual value need to be reviewed regularly and at least at each fiscal year end under IFRS. A change in any one of these variables requires that either the depreciation method or the rate also be changed. Unexpected physical deterioration, unforeseen obsolescence, or changes in the extent or way in which the asset is used may make the asset's useful life less than originally estimated. Improved maintenance procedures, a revision of operating policies, or similar developments may prolong its life beyond what was expected.

When a change in estimate takes place, accounting standards **do not permit companies to go back and "correct" the records, nor to make a "catch-up" adjustment** for any accumulated difference. Instead, a company accounts for a change in estimate **prospectively; that is, in the period of change and in the future, if applicable**. This is because estimates are such an inherent part of the accounting process. As new information becomes available, the changes are incorporated into current and future measurements. So, a new depreciation schedule has to be prepared for the asset. See **Example 11.9**. The new schedule uses the undepreciated costs that remain on the books, along with the most recent estimates of the asset's residual value and remaining useful life. If another depreciation method is more appropriate for the current circumstances, then it will be applied going forward.

Example 11.9 | Calculation of Depreciation after Revision of Estimated Life and Residual Value

Facts Assume that machinery that cost $90,000 was estimated originally to have a 20-year life and a $10,000 residual value. It has already been depreciated for eight years. In year 9, assume that the asset's total life is now expected to be 30 years with a residual value of only $2,000. Depreciation has been recorded on the asset at the rate of 1/20 × ($90,000 – $10,000), or $4,000 each year, by the straight-line method.

Instructions

a. Provide revised calculations of the charges for depreciation in the current and subsequent periods, and the related journal entry to be recorded each year assuming the straight-line method is still appropriate.

b. How would your answer to part (a) change if the double-declining-balance method had been used initially?

Solution

a.

Machinery cost	$90,000
Less: Accumulated depreciation to date: 8 × $4,000/year	32,000
Carrying amount of machinery at end of 8th year	58,000
Less estimated residual value	2,000
Costs to be depreciated	$56,000

Revised depreciation = $56,000 ÷ (30 − 8) years remaining life = $2,545 per year

The entry to record depreciation in each of the remaining 22 years is:

Depreciation Expense	2,545	
Accumulated Depreciation—Machinery		2,545

A	=	L	+	SE
−2,545				−2,545

Cash flows: No effect

b. If the double-declining-balance method had been used initially, the change in estimated life would result in a new depreciation rate to be applied to the book value in the current (ninth) and subsequent years.[13] In this example, a revised remaining life of 22 years results in a revised 100% ÷ 22 or 4.545% straight-line or a 9.09% double-declining rate. As the double-declining-balance method initially ignores residual value in determining depreciation expense, a change in residual value is ignored in the revised calculation and year nine depreciation expense would be $3,522 (i.e., $38,742 × .0909).

TransAlta Corporation is a Canadian power generation and wholesale marketing company operating in Canada, the United States, and Australia. It entered into an "Off-Coal Agreement" (OCA) with the Government of Alberta in November 2016 that will see it receive annual transition payments of approximately $37.4 million in exchange for a total of over $500 million for the cessation of coal-fired emissions at several of its plants by December 31, 2030. It provided information about a change in the estimated useful life of its coal assets in Note 3 of its financial statements. The information, disclosed in Illustration 11.4, also reports the change in its depreciation expense.

ILLUSTRATION 11.4

Change in Estimate of Useful Life and Depreciation Expense—TransAlta Corporation—December 31, 2017

TransAlta Corporation

3. Accounting Changes

A. Current Accounting Changes

Change in Estimates – Useful Lives (extracts)

As a result of the Off-Coal Agreement ("OCA") with the Government of Alberta described in Note 4(H), the Corporation will cease coal-fired emissions by the end of 2030. On Jan. 1, 2017, the useful lives of the PP&E and amortizable intangibles associated with some of the Corporation's Alberta coal assets were reduced to 2030. As a result, depreciation expense and intangibles amortization for the year ended Dec. 31, 2017, increased by approximately $58 million. The useful lives may be revised or extended in compliance with the Corporation's accounting policies, dependent upon future operating decisions and events, such as coal-to-gas conversions.

Due to the Corporation's decision to retire Sundance Unit 1 effective Jan. 1, 2018 (see Note 4(B) for further details), the useful lives of the Sundance Unit 1 PP&E and amortizable intangibles were reduced in the second quarter of 2017 by two years to Dec. 31, 2017. As a result, depreciation expense and intangibles amortization for the year ended Dec. 31, 2017, increased by approximately $26 million.

Impairment

LEARNING OBJECTIVE 6

Explain the issues and apply the accounting standards for capital asset impairment under both IFRS and ASPE.

As indicated in Chapter 10, property, plant, and equipment (PP&E) assets are measured after acquisition by applying the cost model, the revaluation model, or the fair value model. If an **investment property is measured at fair value** and if the asset becomes impaired, the remeasurement of the asset to fair value automatically recognizes this reduction and the associated loss is recognized in income.

---

[13]To determine the undepreciated carrying amount to date when using the double-declining-balance method, the following formula can be used: Book value = $C(1 - r)^n$, where C = cost of asset; r = depreciation rate; and n = number of full years from the asset's acquisition date. For example, if the machinery had been depreciated using the double-declining-balance method instead of the straight-line method, C = $90,000; $r = 2 \times (100\% \div 20) = 10\%$; and $n = 8$. The asset's carrying amount at the end of year 8, therefore, is $90,000(1 - 0.10)^8$, or $38,742.

Assets measured under the **cost or revaluation model**, however, are not automatically adjusted to fair value. Instead, they are reported at cost (or at fair value at the most recent revaluation date) less accumulated depreciation. Is this amount the appropriate value for the statement of financial position? Or should PP&E assets be valued at **the lower of cost and net realizable value** as most inventory assets are?

It is important to report inventory on the statement of financial position at no more than the net cash the entity expects to receive on its disposal because, as a **current asset**, it is expected to be converted into cash within the operating cycle. Property, plant, and equipment assets, however, are **not held to be directly converted into cash**. They are ordinarily **used in operations over the long term**. For this reason, the same "lower of cost and net realizable value" measure is not appropriate for PP&E assets. See **What Do the Numbers Mean? 11.4**. However, it is important that any impairment in value be recognized if the recoverable amount of a PP&E asset is less than its carrying amount.

What Do the Numbers Mean? 11.4

Even when long-lived capital assets become partially obsolete, accountants have been reluctant to reduce their carrying amount. This is because it is often difficult to arrive at a measure for property, plant, and equipment that is not subjective and arbitrary. For example, Falconbridge Ltd. at one time had to decide whether all or a part of its property, plant, and equipment in a nickel-mining operation in the Dominican Republic should be written off. The project had been incurring losses because nickel prices were low and operating costs were high. Only if nickel prices increased by about 33% would the project be reasonably profitable. Whether it was appropriate to recognize an impairment loss depended on the future price of nickel. Even if a decision were made to write

down the asset, the amount to be written off would not be obvious. This same issue faced most Canadian companies in the oil and gas industry in 2014 and 2015 as the price of a barrel of oil dropped by more than 50%. For example, Husky Energy Inc. reported a non-cash impairment charge of $5.0 billion in 2015 on its oil and natural gas assets located in Western Canada, as a result of decreases in forecast short- and long-term crude oil and natural gas prices, and the company's plan to reduce capital investment in those areas. The company recorded an additional pre-tax impairment expense in 2017 (after a pre-tax impairment reversal of $261.0 million in 2016) as the development plans for its PP&E assets continued to evolve.

How do accountants handle this problem? The first step in accounting for **impairments** is for management to be alert to events and circumstances that might indicate that a long-lived asset is **impaired**; in other words, that its carrying amount is higher than its future economic benefits to the company.

Indicators of Impairment

Illustration 11.5 provides examples of indicators of impairment.

External Indicators	Internal Indicators
There are observable indications of a significant reduction in the asset's value.	There is evidence of obsolescence or physical damage related to the asset.
A significant change in the technological, market, economic, or legal environment has affected or is expected to adversely affect the entity.	Significant changes with adverse effects have taken place or are expected to take place in how the asset is used (for example, the asset becoming idle or subject to plans for early disposition).
Market rates of return have increased, with a negative effect on the asset's value in use and recoverable amount.	Internal reports about the asset indicate its performance is or will be worse than expected.
The carrying value of the entity's net assets is more than the company's market capitalization.	Costs incurred for an asset's acquisition or operation significantly exceed the amount originally expected.

There may be other factors that suggest that an asset's carrying amount is overstated. The objective is to be open to the possibility of impairment with changes in the internal and external environment. Even if an impairment loss is not evident, a change may be needed in the estimate of the asset's useful life or residual value, or in the depreciation method applied.

IFRS **ASPE** IFRS requires that assets be assessed for indications of impairment at the end of each reporting period, while ASPE requires this assessment only when events and changes in circumstances indicate that an asset's carrying amount may not be recoverable (at which time the asset is tested for impairment). We describe two different approaches to impairment accounting next.

Impairment—Recognition and Measurement Models

Just as there are different models for measuring capital assets, there are also different models for measuring impairment losses for these assets. One approach, a **cost recovery impairment model**, concludes that a long-lived asset is impaired only if an entity cannot recover the asset's carrying amount from using the asset and eventually disposing of it. Another approach, a **rational entity impairment model**, assumes that an entity makes rational decisions in managing its long-term assets. A company is likely to continue to use an asset if its use and later disposal earn a higher return than if it is currently disposed of (sold). If current disposal generates a higher return, then management is likely to take this action. This model, therefore, incorporates both these values in the impairment decision.

Cost Recovery Impairment Model

ASPE If events or changes in circumstances indicate that an asset's carrying amount may not be recoverable, the cost recovery impairment model (ASPE) uses a **recoverability test** to determine whether an impairment loss needs to be recognized. Two basic assumptions underlie this approach:

1. The asset will continue to be used in operations.
2. As long as the asset's carrying amount is expected to be recovered by future inflows (undiscounted cash flows), this amount is recoverable and no impairment is required to be recorded.

An estimate is made of the future net cash flows that are expected from the use of the asset and its eventual disposal. These cash flows are not discounted. If these **undiscounted** future cash flows are **less than the asset's carrying amount**, the asset is considered impaired. Conversely, if the **undiscounted** future net cash flows are **equal to or greater than the asset's carrying amount**, no impairment has occurred under this impairment model. Essentially, this **recoverability test** acts as a screening device to determine whether an asset is impaired.

If the recoverability test indicates that an asset held for use is impaired, an **impairment loss** is calculated. It is the amount by which the asset's carrying amount exceeds its fair value. See **Example 11.10**. This is **not the same** as the difference between its carrying amount and its recoverable amount in the recoverability test. See **Example 11.11**. **Fair value** under this model is the price that would be agreed upon in an arm's-length transaction between knowledgeable, willing parties that are under no compulsion to act (per *Handbook* 3063.03). By its nature, fair value is a discounted or present value measure. It is best measured by quoted market prices in active markets, but if there is no active market—often the case—other valuation methods are used.

Example 11.10 | Calculation of Impairment Loss—Cost Recovery Impairment Model

Facts Because of changes in the extent to which a piece of equipment is being used, the company decides to review it for possible impairment. The asset's carrying amount is $600,000 ($800,000 cost less $200,000 accumulated depreciation). The expected future undiscounted net cash flows from the use of the equipment and its later disposal are estimated to be $650,000, and its fair value is $525,000.

Instructions [ASPE] Use the **recoverability test** to determine if the asset would be considered impaired under the cost recovery impairment model.

Solution The asset's carrying amount is $600,000 ($800,000 cost less $200,000 accumulated depreciation). The expected future undiscounted net cash flows from the use of the asset and its later disposal are estimated to be $650,000, and the asset's fair value is $525,000. The recoverability test indicates that the $650,000 of expected net cash flows from the asset exceeds its carrying amount of $600,000. As a result, no impairment is evident and no further steps are required.

Example 11.11 | Calculation of Impairment Loss—Cost Recovery Impairment Model

Facts Assume the same facts as in Example 11.10, except that the expected future net cash flows from the equipment are $580,000 instead of $650,000.

Instructions [ASPE] Because of changes in the equipment's usage, review it for possible impairment. If it is impaired, calculate the impairment loss and provide the related journal entry assuming that the asset's fair value is $525,000.

Solution A **recoverability test** for the equipment indicates that the $580,000 of expected net cash flows from the asset is less than its carrying amount of $600,000. Therefore, the asset is considered impaired. If the asset's fair value is $525,000, the impairment loss is calculated as follows:

Carrying amount of the equipment	$600,000
Fair value of equipment	525,000
Impairment loss	$ 75,000

The entry to record the impairment loss is as follows:

Loss on Impairment	75,000	
Accumulated Impairment Losses—Equipment		75,000

A	=	L	+	SE
−75,000				−75,000

Cash flows: No effect

Notice that the entry credits an Accumulated Impairment Losses account rather than Accumulated Depreciation or the capital asset account itself. Any one of these credits may be used in practice. Regardless of which account is credited, the adjusted carrying amount becomes the asset's new "cost" and the writedown is charged to expense. As the asset is considered to have a new cost basis, no reversal of the impairment charge is permitted. After the impairment loss is recorded, the depreciation method chosen for the asset is reviewed, as are the remaining useful life and residual value. Revised depreciation amounts are then calculated.

ASPE uses the cost recovery impairment model.

Rational Entity Impairment Model

[IFRS] Another approach to the recognition and measurement of impairment losses is the **rational entity impairment model**. This approach (used under IFRS) assumes that an entity makes rational decisions in managing its long-term assets and therefore it compares the asset's book value with a recoverable amount **that differs depending on the circumstances**. If management can earn a higher return from using an asset than from selling it, the company will continue to use it. However, if a higher return is possible from selling the asset, then the rational decision is to sell it. This model, therefore, compares the asset's carrying amount with its **recoverable amount**, defined as the **higher of its value in use and its fair value less costs of disposal** (IAS 36.6). If the recoverable amount is less than its carrying amount, the impairment loss is equal to the difference. **Illustration 11.6** indicates how the loss is calculated.

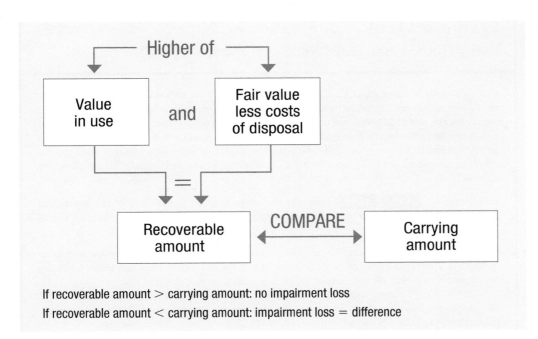

ILLUSTRATION 11.6
IFRS Calculation of Impairment Loss—Rational Entity Model

If recoverable amount > carrying amount: no impairment loss
If recoverable amount < carrying amount: impairment loss = difference

Unlike the cost recovery impairment method, there is **no pre-screening test** to determine whether an asset is impaired. Instead, the carrying amount is compared directly with a fair-value-based recoverable amount that is a discounted present value measure.

Finance 5.4.1 **Value in use** is the present value of the future cash flows expected to be derived from the asset's use and subsequent disposal. **Fair value less costs of disposal** is the amount currently expected to be received from the sale of the asset in an orderly transaction between market participants after subtracting incremental costs directly related to the disposal. Fair value is estimated using the fair value hierarchy set out in IFRS 13. (You may want to review Chapter 3, which discussed IFRS 13 in detail.) The level of the fair value hierarchy used must be disclosed, together with further disclosures if Level 2 or Level 3 measures are used. Disposal costs might include legal costs, transaction taxes, and removal costs, for example, but they would exclude finance costs and income tax expense. IFRS uses this model. See **Example 11.12** for the rational impairment model and **Example 11.13** for a comparison of the IFRS and ASPE approaches to impairment.

Example 11.12 | Calculation of Impairment Loss—Rational Entity Model

Facts   As a result of its annual assessment of property, plant, and equipment for indications of impairment, an entity determines that equipment with a carrying amount of $45,000 (cost of $60,000; accumulated depreciation of $15,000) may be impaired due to technological obsolescence. The asset's value in use is $47,500 and its fair value less costs of disposal (of $2,000) is $40,000.

Instructions   **IFRS**   Calculate the impairment loss, if any, for the asset assuming that the company uses the rational entity model.

Solution   The entity calculates the asset's recoverable amount to be $47,500. This is the higher of its value in use of $47,500 and its fair value less costs of disposal of $40,000. Because the recoverable amount is more than the asset's book value, there is no impairment loss to be recognized.

Example 11.13 | Calculation of Impairment Loss—Rational Entity Model versus Cost Recovery Impairment Model

Facts Similar to Example 11.12, assume that as a result of its annual assessment of property, plant, and equipment for indications of impairment, the entity determines that equipment with a carrying amount of $45,000 (cost of $60,000; accumulated depreciation of $15,000) may be impaired due to technological obsolescence. Assume that the asset's value in use is determined to be $37,500 and its fair value less costs of disposal (of $2,000) is $40,000. In addition, the expected future undiscounted net cash flows from the use of the asset and its later disposal are estimated to be $43,000.

Instructions `IFRS` `ASPE` Compare the accounting for impairment of the equipment under IFRS versus ASPE and prepare the entry to record the impairment loss under both sets of standards.

Solution IFRS—Rational entity model: The entity calculates the asset's recoverable amount to be $40,000. This is the higher of its value in use of $37,500 and its fair value less costs of disposal of $40,000. Now an impairment loss of $5,000 is indicated, as calculated below.

ASPE—Cost recovery impairment model: The recoverability test indicates that the $43,000 of expected net cash flows from the asset is less than the carrying amount of $45,000. As a result, **impairment is evident**, and an impairment loss of $3,000 is calculated as follows:

	Rational Entity Impairment Model	Cost Recovery Impairment Model
Carrying amount of the equipment	$45,000	$45,000
Recoverable amount (IFRS)/Fair value (ASPE)	40,000	42,000
Impairment loss	$ 5,000	$ 3,000

The entry to record the impairment loss under IFRS versus ASPE follows:

IFRS: Rational Entity Impairment Model		ASPE: Cost Recovery Impairment Model	
Loss on Impairment	5,000	Loss on Impairment	3,000
Accumulated Impairment		Accumulated Impairment	
Losses—Equipment	5,000	Losses—Equipment	3,000

IFRS

A	=	L	+	SE
−5,000				−5,000

Cash flows: No effect

ASPE

A	=	L	+	SE
−3,000				−3,000

Cash flows: No effect

The loss from a writedown for impairment is generally recognized in net income. However, if the asset is accounted for under the revaluation model, the loss is accounted for on the same basis as a revaluation decrease, explained in Chapter 10: it is charged first through other comprehensive income to any revaluation surplus that exists for that asset, and only the excess is recognized in income. After the impairment loss is recognized, the depreciation method, remaining useful life, and residual value are reviewed, and revised depreciation amounts are determined.

Under the rational entity method, it is important to keep track separately of any impairment losses recognized because, unlike the cost recovery approach, a portion of **the impairment loss may be reversed in the future**. The recoverable amount is considered to be based on estimates that may change in the future. At each reporting date, companies assess whether there is any indication that an impairment loss recorded in a prior period may no longer exist, or may have decreased. If the estimates used to determine the asset's value in use and fair value less costs of disposal have changed, then a reversal of the impairment can be recognized.

The reversal amount, however, is limited. The specific asset cannot be increased in value to more than what its book value would have been, net of depreciation, if the original impairment loss had never been recognized.

`IFRS` `ASPE` The method described here as the rational entity model is the one applied under IFRS. What is the core difference between this and the cost recovery impairment method? The IFRS approach better reflects the economic circumstances underlying the asset's usefulness to the entity, capturing both the declines and recoveries in value. The cost recovery (ASPE) approach waits until circumstances indicate that conditions are very bad before recognizing impairment. It does not take into account the time value of money in the recoverability test. It is not neutral because, after recognizing impairment, it does not allow for later recognition of any recovery. That is, no reversals of impairment losses are permitted. Overall, the rational entity model used under IFRS provides better information for users because it provides better representational faithfulness as it is more neutral; is more relevant; provides more timely information; and better reflects the time value of money and the fair value of impaired assets.

Asset Groups and Cash-Generating Units

The discussion above assumes that recoverable amounts can be determined for each individual asset. However, many assets do not generate cash flows on their own, but only in combination with other assets. In this case, the cash flows based on a single asset's value in use cannot be independently determined. Instead, the asset has to be identified with an **asset group** or **cash-generating unit (CGU)** and it is the group whose cash flows are tested for impairment. An asset group or CGU is the smallest identifiable group of assets that generates cash inflows that are predominantly independent of the cash flows from other individual assets or other groups of assets.[14] IAS 36 *Impairment of Assets* provides the examples summarized in Illustration 11.7.

ILLUSTRATION 11.7

Examples of Cash-Generating Units

Copyright © IFRS Foundation. All rights reserved. Reproduced with permission.

Situation	Asset Group or CGU
A mining company owns a private railway to support its mining activities. The railway could be sold for scrap value only. It does not generate cash inflows that are independent of those from the mine's other assets. [IAS 36.67]	It is not possible to estimate the recoverable amount of the private railway alone because its value in use cannot be determined and is probably different from its scrap value. So, the entity should estimate the recoverable amount of the CGU that the private railway belongs to. This is the mine as a whole.
A bus company provides services under contract with a municipality that requires minimum service on each of five separate routes. The assets devoted to each route and the cash flows from each are known. One of the routes operates at a significant loss. [IAS 36.68]	Because the company does not have the option to reduce service on any one bus route, the lowest level of identifiable cash flows that are largely independent of the cash inflows from other assets or groups of assets is represented by the cash flows generated by the five routes together. The CGU for each route is the bus company as a whole.

These examples should help provide a basic understanding of what an asset group or CGU is and how each is generally determined. **Both the cost recovery and rational entity impairment models are then applied as explained above to the groups of assets rather than individual assets.** Any resulting impairment loss is then allocated proportionally (based on relative carrying amounts) to the long-lived assets in the asset group. However, no individual asset is reduced below its fair value (cost recovery impairment model), or the highest of its fair value less costs of disposal, its value in use, or zero (under the rational entity model). This is illustrated in Example 11.14 and Example 11.15.

[14]IAS 36.68. This is quite similar to *CPA Canada Handbook*, Part II, Section 3063.03. Both ASPE Section 3063 and IAS 36 include liabilities in the asset group if cash flows from the group are the only source of cash to meet the obligation. Copyright © IFRS Foundation. All rights reserved. Reproduced with permission.

Example 11.14 | Calculation of Impairment Loss—Asset Group

Facts Land-Line Inc. (LLI) is a manufacturer that produces parts for residential telephones. Recent indications are that the market for this product is likely to continue to decline significantly and LLI is testing equipment used in the production process for impairment. The following assets are used only in the manufacture of these parts (in thousands):

	Cost	Accumulated Depreciation	Carrying Amount
Tools and dies	$10,000	$ 6,000	$ 4,000
Specialized equipment	50,000	35,000	15,000
General equipment	30,000	18,000	12,000
	$90,000	$59,000	$31,000

The tools and dies and specialized equipment cannot be used elsewhere and have no resale value, while the general equipment could be sold today for $15,000. LLI plans to continue producing the parts for two more years to fill a commitment to its customer. Net future cash flows from the next two years' production of parts and the disposal of equipment are estimated to be $32,000, with present value of the cash flows of $26,000.

Instructions **ASPE** Calculate the impairment loss assuming that LLI follows ASPE and uses the cost recovery impairment model. If an impairment loss is indicated, how would it be allocated to assets in the group?

Solution Because the tools and dies and specialized equipment cannot generate cash flows on their own, they are combined into an asset group with the general equipment. The carrying amount of the asset group is $31,000. The cost recovery impairment model applies a recoverability test to determine if there is an impairment. The book value of $31,000 is compared with the undiscounted future cash flows expected from the use and later disposal of the asset group of $32,000. Because the book value can be recovered, there is no impairment, and no loss is recognized. If an impairment loss is indicated, it is allocated only to the long-lived assets in the group that are held for use. The allocation is based on the assets' relative carrying amounts, although no asset is written down below its fair value, if readily determinable.

Example 11.15 | Calculation of Impairment Loss—Cash-Generating Unit

Facts Similar to Example 11.14, assume LLI manufactures parts for residential telephones and that indications are that the market for this product is likely to continue to decline significantly. LLI is testing equipment used in the production process for impairment based on a cash-generating unit of tools and dies, specialized equipment, and general equipment with the same carrying amounts as Example 11.14.

Instructions **IFRS** Calculate the impairment loss assuming that LLI follows IFRS and uses the rational entity model. If an impairment loss is indicated, how would it be allocated to assets in the CGU? Provide the related journal entry.

Solution Under this model, the carrying amount of the cash-generating group of $31,000 is compared with the CGU's recoverable amount. The recoverable amount is $26,000—the higher of the CGU's value in use of $26,000 and its fair value less costs of disposal of $14,000.

Carrying amount of CGU	$31,000
Recoverable amount	26,000
Impairment loss	$ 5,000

The impairment loss is then allocated to the individual assets in the group.[15] No individual asset can be reduced below the highest of (1) its value in use, (2) its fair value less costs of disposal,

---

[15]The impairment loss for a cash-generating unit (CGU) is allocated first to reduce the carrying amount of any goodwill allocated to the CGU, and then on a pro rata basis to other individual assets in the CGU. We discuss this further in Chapter 12.

or (3) zero. In this case, the only determinable amount is the general equipment's fair value less costs of disposal of $15,000. Because this asset's book value is already less than this, the $5,000 loss would be allocated only to the tools and dies and specialized equipment pro rata, based on the carrying amount of each (proportion rounded to two decimal places).

Allocation:	Carrying Amount	Proportion	Loss Allocation
Tools and dies	$ 4,000	4/19	$1,050
Specialized equipment	15,000	15/19	3,950
Total	$19,000		$5,000

The entry to record the impairment is:

Loss on impairment	5,000	
Accumulated Impairment Losses—Tools and Dies		1,050
Accumulated Impairment Losses—Equipment		3,950

A	=	L	+	SE
−5,000				−5,000

Cash flows: No effect

Held for Sale and Derecognition

LEARNING OBJECTIVE 7

Account for derecognition of property, plant, and equipment and explain and apply the accounting standards for long-lived assets that are held for sale.

Long-Lived Assets to Be Disposed of by Sale

Held for Sale

What happens if a company intends to dispose of its long-lived assets by sale instead of continuing to use them? Because this is relevant information for financial statement readers, such an asset is classified as **held for sale**, is remeasured at the lower of its carrying amount and fair value less costs of disposal, and is reported separately. A fair value less costs of disposal measurement is used if this is less than its book value because it corresponds better to the amount of cash a company expects to generate from the asset. The usefulness of this measurement is increased by the strict criteria for classifying a long-lived asset as held for sale, including the requirement that the asset be disposed of within a short period of time. These criteria were presented in Chapter 4 in the section on discontinued operations.

Assets that are held for sale **are not depreciated while they are held**. The reason is that it would be inconsistent to amortize assets that are not in use, that are likely to be sold, and that are carried at the equivalent of the lower of (amortized) cost and net realizable value. In many respects, these assets are closer to inventory than capital assets.

After being classified as a held for sale asset, such an asset continues to be carried at the lower of amortized cost and fair value less costs of disposal. Further losses are recognized if the net amount expected from the asset continues to drop. Gains (that is, loss reversals) are recognized for any increases in net realizable value, but these are limited to the amount of the cumulative losses previously recognized.

IFRS ASPE How these assets and gains and losses are reported is governed by the need for users to understand the effects of discontinued operations and disposals of non-current assets. If the long-lived asset is a component of an entity that meets the criteria for being reported as a discontinued operation, the losses and any recoveries are reported as part of discontinued operations on the income statement. Otherwise, they are reported in income from continuing operations. Practice differs on how the PP&E assets held for sale are reported on the statement of financial position. ASPE allows these assets to be reclassified as current assets only if they are sold before the financial statements are completed, and the proceeds to be received qualify as a current asset. Otherwise, they are reported separately as non-current assets. Under IFRS, most non-current assets that meet the stringent requirements for classification as held for sale also meet the criteria for recognition as current assets. In all cases, they are reported separately from other assets on the statement of financial position with note disclosure of the major classes of assets making up the total.

Derecognition

Sale of Property, Plant, and Equipment

Unless an asset has been classified as held for sale, depreciation is taken until the date the asset is **derecognized**; that is, the time when all accounts related to the asset are removed from the accounts. An item of property, plant, and equipment is usually derecognized on the date of disposal, but it could be taken off the books earlier if management thinks it will provide no further economic benefits, from either use or disposal. Ideally, when it is derecognized, the asset's carrying amount would be the same as its disposal value, but this is rarely the case. Therefore, a gain or loss is usually reported.

Under the cost and fair value models, the gain or loss on derecognition is shown on the income statement, but would not be classified as revenue unless the company routinely sells property, plant, and equipment items that it had been renting to others. A gain or loss from the disposal of long-lived assets included in a discontinued business is reported in the discontinued operations section of the statement.

What happens to the gain or loss on disposal if the asset was accounted for under the revaluation model? Theoretically, there would not be a gain or loss on disposal. This is based on the idea that the asset would be revalued to its fair value at the date of disposal, with the change in value accounted for in the same way as all previous revaluations. See **Underlying Concept 11.6**. If so, there would be no difference between the proceeds on disposal and the carrying amount to recognize on the income statement. Any remaining balance in the Revaluation Surplus account would be adjusted directly to Retained Earnings. However, IAS 16 *Property, Plant, and Equipment* does not address this issue, stating only that gains or losses on derecognition are reported in income. A company could, then, recognize the difference between the asset's most recent carrying amount and the proceeds of disposal on the income statement, as shown in **Example 11.16**.

> **Underlying Concept 11.6**
>
> The "ideal" treatment of the change in value suggested here is more consistent with a physical concept of capital maintenance.

Example 11.16 | Disposal of an Asset Held for Use

Facts   Assume that a machine costing $18,000 has been used for nine years and depreciated at a rate of $1,200 per year, and that the machine is sold in the middle of the tenth year for $7,000.

Instructions   Provide all journal entries that would be required at the time of disposal, and calculate the related gain or loss on disposal.

Solution   The entry to record half of a year's depreciation up to the sale date is:

Depreciation Expense	600	
Accumulated Depreciation—Machinery		600

The entry for the asset's sale is:

Cash	7,000	
Accumulated Depreciation—Machinery [($1,200 × 9) + $600]	11,400	
Machinery		18,000
Gain on Disposal of Machinery		400

There is a gain on disposal because the $7,000 proceeds on disposal is $400 more than the machinery's carrying amount of $6,600 ($18,000 − $11,400).

A	=	L	+	SE
−600				−600

Cash flows: No effect

A	=	L	+	SE
+400				+400

Cash flows: 7,000 inflow

If an asset is classified as **held for sale**, it is carried at its fair value less costs of disposal. In this case, the net proceeds from the sale of the asset should be close to the asset's carrying amount and it is likely that only minor gains or losses would be recognized when the actual disposal occurs.

Involuntary Conversion

Sometimes an asset's service ends through an involuntary conversion, such as fire, flood, theft, or expropriation. When this happens, the gains or losses are calculated in the same way as they are for the sale of an item of property, plant, and equipment as shown in **Example 11.17**.

Example 11.17 | Disposal of an Asset—Involuntary Conversion

Facts   Assume that a company is forced to sell its building that stands directly in the path of a planned major highway. For several years, the provincial government has tried to buy the land on which the building stands, but the company has always resisted. The government ultimately exercises its right to expropriate and the courts have upheld its actions. In settlement, the company receives $500,000, which is much higher than the $160,000 book value of the building (cost of $300,000 less accumulated depreciation of $140,000) and the $100,000 book value of the land.

Instructions   Provide the journal entry to record the disposal of the land and buildings.

Solution   The following entry is made:

Cash	500,000	
Accumulated Depreciation—Buildings	140,000	
Buildings		300,000
Land		100,000
Gain on Disposal of Land and Buildings		240,000

A	= L +	SE
+240,000		+240,000

Cash flows: ↑ 500,000 inflow

Similar treatment is given to other types of involuntary conversions. The difference between any amount that is recovered, such as through insurance, and the asset's carrying amount is reported as a gain or loss.

Donation of Capital Assets

When a company donates or contributes an asset, the gift is recorded as an expense and is measured at the asset's fair value as illustrated in **Example 11.18**. The difference between its fair value and its carrying amount is recognized as a gain or loss.

Example 11.18 | Donation of a Capital Asset

Facts   Assume that Kline Industries donates property with a fair value of $120,000 to the City of Saskatoon for a park. The land's book and fair value is $30,000 and a small building on the site is carried at its cost of $95,000 and accumulated depreciation to the contribution date of $45,000.

Instructions   Provide the journal entry to record the donation of property.

Solution   The following entry is made:

Contribution Expense	120,000	
Accumulated Depreciation—Buildings	45,000	
Buildings		95,000
Land		30,000
Gain on Disposal of Buildings		40,000

A	= L +	SE
−80,000		−80,000

Cash flows: No effect

Other Issues

If an asset is scrapped or abandoned without any cash recovery, the entity recognizes a loss that is equal to the asset's book value. If the asset can be sold for scrap, the gain or loss is the difference between its scrap value and its book value. If a fully depreciated asset is still used, both the asset and its accumulated depreciation remain on the books.

Presentation, Disclosure, and Analysis

> **LEARNING OBJECTIVE 8**
> Describe the types of disclosures required for property, plant, and equipment, and provide an analysis of investment in capital assets.

Presentation and Disclosure

A significant amount of information needs to be reported about a company's property, plant, and equipment so that users of financial statements can assess the existence and measurement of, and changes in, such assets. The following is a summary of the types of disclosures that are generally required:[16]

- an entity's gross carrying amount of property, plant, and equipment, investment property, and biological assets;
- changes in the gross carrying amount and in the accumulated depreciation and impairment;
- the nature and circumstances relating to impairment losses (and any reversal, if applicable);
- how net income is affected by the changes related to depreciation, impairment, and impairment reversals;
- the policies, models, and choices made in measuring PP&E, such as depreciation rates and methods and government grants;
- the existence and amounts of restrictions related to the assets;
- the effects related to each of continuing and discontinued operations;
- changes in assets as a result of fair value remeasurements;
- the carrying amount and other details of capital assets that are not being used because they are under construction or held for sale;
- cash inflows and outflows associated with the exploration and evaluation of mineral resources;
- the fair value of investment property assets;
- the level of fair value hierarchy (per IFRS 13) used to measure fair value less costs of disposal for assets or cash-generating units where an impairment loss has been recognized or reversed during the period; and
- any outstanding related contingencies.

The requirement for separate disclosure of both the cost and accumulated depreciation gives financial statement readers more information than if only the net book value is disclosed. As an example, consider two companies, each having capital assets with a carrying amount of $100,000. The first company's assets cost $1 million and have accumulated depreciation of $900,000 charged against them. The second company, on the other hand, has assets with a cost

---

[16]Refer to the specific IFRS and ASPE standards for complete coverage of the specific disclosures. Because the users of private entity financial statements can generally request additional information if needed, there are many fewer required disclosures under ASPE than under IFRS.

of $105,000 and accumulated depreciation of $5,000. With the additional data, information is provided about the size of the original investment in property, plant, and equipment and its relative age. Information about depreciation rates and methods and accounting policy choices represents important disclosures because these result in material charges to the income statement. Depreciation is often the largest non-cash expense recognized by companies.

Illustration 11.8 provides excerpts from the disclosures for The Hershey Company's property, plant, and equipment on its December 31, 2017 balance sheet. The company is based in the United States and reports amounts in thousands of U.S. dollars. These disclosures are quite similar to those that would be required in Canada under ASPE. You are probably familiar with some of Hershey's products!

ILLUSTRATION 11.8

Disclosures for Property, Plant, and Equipment—The Hershey Company

Consolidated Balance Sheets at 31 December 2017

	2017	2016
	000's	000's
Assets		
Property, plant and equipment, net	**2,106,697**	**2,177,248**

1. SUMMARY OF SIGNIFICANT ACCOUNTING POLICIES [excerpts; amounts in thousands]

Property, Plant and Equipment

Property, plant and equipment is stated at cost and depreciated on a straight-line basis over the estimated useful lives of the assets, as follows: 3 to 15 years for machinery and equipment; and 25 to 40 years for buildings and related improvements. At December 31, 2017 and December 31, 2016, property, plant and equipment includes assets under capital lease arrangements with net book values totaling $116,843 and $104,503, respectively. Total depreciation expense for the years ended December 31, 2017, 2016 and 2015 was $211,592, $231,735, and $197,054, respectively, and includes depreciation on assets recorded under capital lease arrangements. Maintenance and repairs are expensed as incurred. We capitalize applicable interest charges incurred during the construction of new facilities and production lines and amortize these costs over the assets' estimated useful lives.

We review long-lived assets for impairment whenever events or changes in circumstances indicate that the carrying amount of such assets may not be recoverable. We measure the recoverability of assets to be held and used by a comparison of the carrying amount of long-lived assets to future undiscounted net cash flows expected to be generated. If these assets are considered to be impaired, we measure impairment as the amount by which the carrying amount of the assets exceeds the fair value of the assets. We report assets held for sale or disposal at the lower of the carrying amount or fair value less cost to sell.

We assess asset retirement obligations on a periodic basis and recognize the fair value of a liability for an asset retirement obligation in the period in which it is incurred if a reasonable estimate of fair value can be made. We capitalize associated asset retirement costs as part of the carrying amount of the long-lived asset.

2. BUSINESS ACQUISITIONS AND DIVESTITURES [excerpts, amounts in thousands]

Acquisitions

Acquisitions of businesses are accounted for as purchases and, accordingly, the results of operations of the businesses acquired have been included in the consolidated financial statements since the respective dates of the acquisitions. The purchase price for each of the acquisitions is allocated to the assets acquired and liabilities assumed.

2016 Activity

Ripple Brand Collective, LLC

On April 26, 2016, we completed the acquisition of all of the outstanding shares of Ripple Brand Collective, LLC, a privately held company that owned the *barkTHINS* mass premium chocolate snacking brand. The *barkTHINS* brand is largely sold in the United States in take-home resealable packages and is available in the club channel, as well as select natural and conventional grocers.

The purchase consideration was allocated to assets acquired and liabilities assumed based on their respective fair values as follows:

(continued)

Goodwill	$128,110
Trademarks	91,200
Other intangible assets	60,900
Other assets, primarily current assets, net of cash acquired totaling $674	12,375
Current liabilities	(7,211)
Net assets acquired	$285,374

Goodwill is calculated as the excess of the purchase price over the fair value of the net assets acquired. The goodwill resulting from the acquisition is attributable primarily to the value of leveraging our brand building expertise, consumer insights, supply chain capabilities and retail relationships to accelerate growth and access to *barkTHINS* products. Acquired trademarks were assigned estimated useful lives of 27 years, while other intangibles, including customer relationships and covenants not to compete, were assigned estimated useful lives ranging from 2 to 14 years. The recorded goodwill, trademarks and other intangibles are expected to be deductible for tax purposes.[17]

16. SUPPLEMENTAL BALANCE SHEET INFORMATION [excerpts, amounts in thousands]

The components of certain Consolidated Balance Sheet accounts are as follows:

December 31 Property, plant and equipment	2017	2016
Land	$ 108,300	$ 103,865
Buildings	1,214,158	1,238,634
Machinery and equipment	2,925,353	3,001,552
Construction in progress	212,912	230,987
Property, plant and equipment, gross	4,460,723	4,575,038
Accumulated depreciation	(2,354,026)	(2,397,790)
Property, plant and equipment, net	$ 2,106,697	$ 2,177,248

Analysis

Because property, plant, and equipment and their related depreciation are so significant on most companies' statements of financial position and income statements, it is important to understand the nature of these long-lived assets, and to ensure that management is generating an acceptable rate of return on its investment in them.

Depreciation and Replacement of Assets

Depreciation is similar to other expenses in that it reduces net income, but is different in that **it does not involve a current cash outflow**. A common misconception about depreciation is that it provides funds to replace capital assets.

To illustrate the fact that depreciation does not provide funds for replacing plant assets, assume that a business starts operating with plant assets of $500,000 with a useful life of five years. The company's statement of financial position at the beginning of the period shows that plant assets are $500,000 and owners' equity is $500,000.

Now if we assume the company earns no revenue over the five years, the income statements are as follows in **Illustration 11.9**.

ILLUSTRATION 11.9

Depreciation—an Expense, not a Funding Method

	Year 1	Year 2	Year 3	Year 4	Year 5
Revenue	$ –0–	$ –0–	$ –0–	$ –0–	$ –0–
Depreciation	(100,000)	(100,000)	(100,000)	(100,000)	(100,000)
Loss	$(100,000)	$(100,000)	$(100,000)	$(100,000)	$(100,000)

[17]This is an extract from the Business Acquisitions and Divestitures note; the full note is available as part of Hershey's annual report available online.

The statement of financial position at the end of the five years reports that plant assets are $0 and owners' equity is $0.

The extreme example in Illustration 11.9 shows that depreciation in no way provides funds to replace assets. Funds to replace assets usually come from new asset inflows represented by revenues. By setting selling prices high enough to recover out-of-pocket costs plus depreciation expense, companies do generate cash flows to help finance replacements. If management wants to accumulate a replacement fund, however, it has to set aside the cash specifically for this purpose.

Efficiency of Asset Use and Return on Investment

Investors are interested in information that tells them how efficiently management uses the long-lived assets it has invested in. Incurring capital costs provides the company with a certain level of operating capacity, and usually creates the need for significant amounts of fixed costs far into the future.

Finance 5.1.1 Which ratios provide information about the usage of the assets? Assets can be analyzed in terms of both activity (turnover) and profitability. How efficiently a company uses its assets to generate revenue is measured by the **asset turnover ratio**. This ratio is calculated by dividing net revenue or sales by average total assets for the period. The resulting number represents the dollars of revenue produced by each dollar invested in assets. **For a given level of investment in assets, a company that generates more revenue per dollar of investment is more efficient and likely to be more profitable.** While this may not be true if the percentage profit on each dollar of revenue is lower than another company's, the asset turnover ratio is one of the key components of return on investment.[18]

To illustrate, the following data are provided from the 2017 financial statements of **Loblaw Companies Limited**. Loblaw is Canada's largest food distributor, with more than 2,400 corporate, franchised, and associate-owned stores across the country. Its asset turnover ratio is calculated in **Illustration 11.10**.

ILLUSTRATION 11.10

Asset Turnover Ratio—Loblaw Companies

LOBLAW COMPANIES LIMITED **(in millions of Canadian dollars)**	
Revenues	$46,702
Total assets, December 31, 2017	35,106
Total assets, December 31, 2016	34,436

$$\text{Asset turnover} = \frac{\text{Net revenue}}{\text{Average total assets}}$$

$$= \frac{\$46,702}{\dfrac{\$35,106 + \$34,436}{2}}$$

$$= 1.34$$

The asset turnover ratio shows that Loblaw generated $1.34 of revenue for each dollar invested in assets during 2017. The ratio is affected by Loblaw's acquisition of Shoppers Drug Mart in the second quarter of 2014. (This led to a dramatic increase in total assets!) The ratio was 1.82 in 2011, 1.57 in 2014, and decreased further by 2017. It will be interesting to see if the ratio returns to the 2014 (or 2011!) level in future years.

Asset turnover ratios vary considerably among industries. For its fiscal year ending in June 2017, **Open Text Corporation**, a software company, had a ratio of 0.36 times, and a

---

[18]The higher the proportion of property, plant, and equipment to total assets, the more information this turnover ratio provides about the efficiency of capital asset use. Analysts often calculate separate turnover ratios for each major type of asset reported on the balance sheet and analyze each.

capital-asset-heavy company like **Canadian Pacific Railway Limited** (CP Railway) had a ratio of only 0.333 times in 2017.

Using the **profit margin ratio** together with the asset turnover ratio allows us to determine another key indicator: the rate of return earned on total assets. By using the CP Railway data for 2017, the profit margin ratio and the rate of return on total assets are calculated as shown in **Illustration 11.11** (in millions of Canadian dollars).

ILLUSTRATION 11.11

Profit Margin—Canadian Pacific Railway Limited

$$\text{Profit margin} = \frac{\text{Net income}}{\text{Net revenue}}$$

$$= \frac{\$2,405}{\$6,554}$$

$$= 36.7\%$$

$$\text{Rate of return on assets} = \text{Profit margin} \times \text{Asset turnover}$$

$$= 36.7\% \times 0.333$$

$$= 12.2\%$$

The profit margin indicates how much is left over from each sales dollar after all expenses are covered. In the CP Railway example, a profit margin of 36.7% indicates that 36.7 cents of profit remained from each $1 of revenue generated. By combining the profit margin with the asset turnover, it is possible to calculate the rate of return on assets for the period. This makes sense. The more revenue that is generated per dollar invested in assets, the better off the company is. Also, the more of each sales dollar that is profit, the better off the company should be. Combined, the ratio provides a measure of the profitability of the company's investment in assets. To the extent that long-lived assets make up a significant portion of total assets, fixed asset management has a definite effect on profitability.

The **rate of return on assets (ROA)** can also be calculated directly by dividing net income by average total assets. Continuing with the same example, **Illustration 11.12** shows the calculation of this ratio.

ILLUSTRATION 11.12

Rate of Return on Assets— Canadian Pacific Railway Limited

$$\text{Rate of return on assets} = \frac{\text{Net income}}{\text{Average total assets}}$$

$$= \frac{\$2,405}{\dfrac{(\$20,135 + \$19,221)}{2}}$$

$$= 12.2\%$$

The 12.2% rate of return calculated in this way is the same as the 12.2% rate calculated by multiplying the profit margin by the asset turnover. The rate of return on assets is a good measure of profitability because it combines the effects of cost control (profit margin) and asset management (asset turnover).

A more sophisticated calculation adds back the after-tax interest expense to net income so that the results are not skewed by how the assets are financed. The ratio can then be used more legitimately for inter-company comparisons. An adjustment should also be made when there are significant assets measured at fair values, with the changes in value bypassing the income statement by being reported directly in Other Comprehensive Income (OCI). To be comparable, either the net income should be compared with the reported assets reduced by the related Accumulated OCI or total comprehensive income should be compared with the total assets as reported.

Care must be taken in interpreting the numbers, however. A manager who is interested in reporting a high return on assets can achieve this in the short run by not investing in new plant and equipment and by cancelling expenditures such as those for research and development and employee training—decisions that may result in lower long-term corporate value. In the short run, the result is a higher return on investment because the net income number (the numerator) will be higher and the average total asset number (the denominator) will be lower.

IFRS/ASPE Comparison

LEARNING OBJECTIVE 9

Identify differences in accounting between IFRS and ASPE, and what changes are expected in the near future.

A Comparison of IFRS and ASPE

In general, the concept of depreciation and how it is applied is quite similar under IFRS and ASPE, and the same is true for non-current assets held for sale. It is also true, however, that there are minor differences not covered in this chapter that require a thorough reading of the specific detailed standards.

The most significant differences between IFRS and ASPE in Chapter 11 relate to the impairment models, as can be seen in **Illustration 11.13**.

ILLUSTRATION 11.13 **IFRS and ASPE Comparison Chart**

	IFRS—IAS 16, 36, 40, and 41; IFRS 5 and 13	Accounting Standards for Private Enterprises (ASPE)—*CPA Canada Handbook*, Part II, Sections 1505, 3061, 3063, and 3475	References to Related Examples, Illustrations and Select Brief Exercises
Depreciation process	Componentization is more common, with parts of assets recognized separately and depreciated over different periods of time.	Practice has been not to recognize asset components to the same extent as under IFRS.	BE11.2
	Depreciation is the allocation of the cost (or other amount) less the residual value over the asset's useful life, including any idle period.	Depreciation is the larger of: **a.** cost less salvage value over asset's life, and **b.** cost less residual value over asset's useful life.	Example 11.1 BE11.3 and BE11.4
Impairment	An assessment of indicators of impairment is required at least at each reporting date.	Evaluation of impairment is required only when events and changes in circumstances indicate that the carrying amount may not be recoverable.	Illustration 11.5 summarizes IFRS examples per IAS 36.12 (see *Handbook* Section 3063.10 for ASPE examples)
	Rational entity approach is applied. Asset or cash-generating unit is impaired only if the carrying amount is more than the higher of the value in use and the fair value less costs of disposal. Fair value is based on IFRS 13 (*Fair Value Measurement*).	Cost recovery approach to impairment is applied. An asset or asset group is impaired only if the entity cannot recover the carrying amount with the net future undiscounted cash flows from use and later disposal.	Examples 11.13, 11.14 and 11.15 BE11.16 and BE11.17

(continued)

ILLUSTRATION 11.13 *(continued)*

	IFRS—IAS 16, 36, 40, and 41; IFRS 5 and 13	Accounting Standards for Private Enterprises (ASPE)—*CPA Canada Handbook*, Part II, Sections 1505, 3061, 3063, and 3475	References to Related Examples, Illustrations and Select Brief Exercises
	"Recoverable amount" is defined as the higher of value in use and the fair value less costs of disposal.	"Recoverability test" is based on a comparison of the undiscounted net future cash flows from use and the carrying amount.	Example 11.13 BE11.14
	An impairment loss is reversed if there is a change in the estimates used to calculate recoverable amount. It is limited in amount.	Once an asset is written down to its impaired value, this becomes the asset's new cost and no reversal of the writedown is allowed.	BE11.12 and BE11.13
Held for sale	Non-current assets may be reclassified as current assets only when they meet the criteria to be classified as held for sale (see IFRS 5.3). This requires that the asset (or disposal group) be available for immediate sale in its present condition and its sale must be highly probable.	Long-lived assets classified as held for sale are classified as current only if sold before the date the financial statements are completed and the proceeds will be received within the period defined for an asset to be a current asset.	BE11.18
Disclosure	A reconciliation of the opening to ending balances of the carrying amounts of each class of PP&E asset is required, along with the same reconciliation for its associated accumulated depreciation and accumulated impairment losses.	A reconciliation of the opening to ending balances of the carrying amounts of each class of PP&E asset is not required. But, for each major category of PP&E, cost; accumulated depreciation, including writedown amounts; and amortization method used must be disclosed.	
	Extensive disclosures are required for investment property measured under the fair value model. Even where the cost model is used for investment property, its fair value must be disclosed.	Because the cost model is the only accepted model, there are no disclosure requirements related to revaluation and fair value measurement models.	

Looking Ahead

Few changes are expected in the near future to standards covering the majority of property, plant, and equipment. There is one possible exception: accounting standards related to the upstream extractive activities undertaken by companies in the mining and oil and gas industries, as discussed in the Looking Ahead section of Chapter 10.

Disclosure requirements under ASPE were clarified, for annual financial statements starting on or after January 1, 2016, regarding amortization of PP&E. While the total amount of amortization charged to income is still required to be disclosed, the amount of amortization for individual items of PP&E does not need to be separately disclosed.

The IASB is exploring the issue of companies using different performance measures in their financial statements, as companies often do not clarify what is included or excluded from these measures. In December 2017, the IASB met and discussed the introduction of management performance measures into the financial statements and where the measures should be located in terms of presentation and disclosure. For example, the IASB was considering presenting a performance measure as a subtotal in the statement of financial performance. Next steps being considered were a discussion paper or exposure draft relating to this issue, together with some possible improvements to the statement of cash flows.

| Appendix 11A | # Depreciation and Income Tax |

LEARNING OBJECTIVE 10
Calculate capital cost allowance in routine and non-routine situations.

Capital Cost Allowance Method

For the most part, issues related to the calculation of income taxes are not discussed in financial accounting courses. However, because the concepts of tax depreciation are similar to those of depreciation for financial reporting purposes, and because the tax method is sometimes adopted for record-keeping purposes, we present an overview of this subject here.

Taxation 6.1.2, 6.1.4 Canadian businesses use the capital cost allowance method to determine depreciation in calculating their taxable income and the tax value of assets, regardless of the method they use for financial reporting purposes. Because companies use this method for tax purposes, some—particularly small businesses—also use it for financial reporting, judging that the benefits of keeping two sets of records are less than the costs of doing this.[19] While keeping only one set of records may be cost-effective, it may not provide a rational measure of expense under GAAP. Therefore, most companies keep a record of capital cost allowance for tax purposes and use another method to determine depreciation for financial reporting purposes.

The **capital cost allowance method** is similar to the declining-balance approach covered in the chapter, except for the following:

1. Instead of being labelled "depreciation expense," it is called **capital cost allowance (CCA)**.

2. The Income Tax Act (Income Tax Regulations, Schedule II) specifies the rate to be used for an asset class. This rate is called the capital cost allowance or CCA rate. The Income Tax Act identifies several classes of assets and the maximum CCA rate for each class. To determine which class a particular asset falls into, it is necessary to examine the definition of each asset class and the examples given in the act. **Illustration 11A.1** provides examples of various CCA classes, the maximum rate for the class, and examples of the types of assets it includes.

ILLUSTRATION 11A.1

Examples of CCA Classes

Class	Rate	Examples of Assets Included in the Class
1	4%	• most buildings acquired after 1987, including component parts such as plumbing, elevators, and sprinkler systems.
8	20%	• property or equipment not included in other specified classes. Also includes furniture, photocopiers, and refrigeration equipment.
10	30%	• computer hardware and automotive equipment, such as motor vehicles and passenger vehicles (unless the vehicles meet class 10.1 conditions below).
10.1	30%	• passenger vehicles purchased during a company's 2011 fiscal year or thereafter having a cost of more than $30,000. (The amount that can be used for capital cost purposes is limited to $30,000 plus PST and GST, or HST.)

Source: Classes of Depreciable Property. Compiled using information available on the Canada.ca website.

3. CCA is calculated separately for each asset class and can be claimed only on fiscal year-end amounts in each class. Assuming there have been no net additions (purchases less proceeds

[19]The widespread availability of accounting software that can maintain detailed records for property, plant, and equipment; the related depreciation expense; and accumulated depreciation under a variety of methods has significantly reduced the cost of record keeping and the likelihood of errors.

of disposals, if any) to a class during a year, the maximum CCA allowed is the undepreciated capital cost (UCC) at year end multiplied by the CCA rate for the class. In a year when there is a net addition (regardless of when it occurs), the maximum CCA on the net addition is one half of the allowed CCA rate multiplied by the amount of the net addition. This is often called the **half-year rule**. The CCA for the net addition plus the CCA on the remaining UCC is the total CCA for the asset class. If there is only one asset in a class, the maximum CCA allowed in the acquisition year is the acquisition cost multiplied by one half of the CCA rate, even if the asset was purchased one week before year end. No CCA would be allowed in the year of disposal for this single asset, even if it is sold just before year end.

4. The government, through the Income Tax Act, requires that any benefits that a company receives from government grants and investment tax credits for the purpose of acquiring a capital asset reduce the cost basis of the capital asset for tax purposes. For investment tax credits deducted or refunded in a tax year, the capital cost of the asset and the UCC of the class of asset are reduced in the next taxation year.

5. CCA can be taken even if it results in a UCC balance that is less than the estimated residual value.

6. Companies are not required to take the maximum rate, or even any CCA, in a particular year, although they normally would as long as they have taxable income. If a company takes less than the maximum CCA in a specific year, it cannot add the remainder to the amount claimed in a subsequent year. In any year, the maximum that can be claimed is limited to the UCC times the specified CCA rate.

Examples 11A.1 and 11A.2 illustrate the usage of the most common aspects of the calculation of CCA and UCC in a relatively simple example.

Example 11A.1 | Basic CCA and UCC Example—Years 1–3

Facts Assume the following for BigQuip (BQ) Company's March 28, 2020 acquisition of manufacturing equipment, its only asset in this CCA class:

Cost of equipment	$500,000	CCA class	Class 8
Estimated useful life	10 years	CCA rate for Class 8	20%
Estimated residual value	$30,000		

Instructions Calculate the CCA for the first three years and the UCC at the end of each of the three years.[20]

Solution The following is the CCA schedule for BQ's equipment.

Class 8–20%	CCA	UCC
January 1, 2020		**0**
Additions during 2020		
Cost of new asset acquisition		$500,000
Disposals during 2020		0
CCA 2020: $500,000 × ½ × 20%	$50,000	(50,000)
December 31, 2020		**$450,000**
Additions less disposals, 2021		0
		$450,000
CCA 2021: $450,000 × 20%	$90,000	(90,000)
December 31, 2021		**$360,000**
Additions less disposals, 2022		0
		$360,000
CCA 2022: $360,000 × 20%	$72,000	(72,000)
December 31, 2022		**$288,000**

---

[20]CCA is subject to rules set by government legislation and can therefore change from time to time. The examples in this chapter are based on the federal income tax regulations for 2017. On November 20, 2018, a Federal Fall Economic Statement was introduced that has the effect of suspending the half-year rule, and allowing a first-year deduction of 1.5 times the standard CCA rate for eligible property. In addition, manufacturing and processing (M&P) and specified clean energy equipment will be allowed a 100% write-off. The new rules apply to property available for use until 2024, and are to be phased out between 2024–28.

The **undepreciated capital cost (UCC)** at any point in time is known as the capital asset's **tax value** or **tax basis**. Note that the asset's carrying amount on the statement of financial position will be different from its tax value whenever the depreciation method for financial reporting is not the tax method. The significance of this difference to financial reporting is explained in Chapter 18.

Example 11A.2 | Basic CCA and UCC Example—Years 4–6

Facts Example 11A.2 builds on the facts from Example 11A.1. Assume that BQ had the following additional transactions in 2023–2025:

1. In 2023, the company bought another Class 8 asset for $700,000.
2. In 2024, the company sold for $300,000 the equipment that it purchased in 2020.
3. In 2025, the company sold the remaining Class 8 asset for $500,000. There are no Class 8 assets remaining after the sale.

Instructions Calculate the CCA for 2023 to 2025 and the UCC at the end of each of the three years.

Solution The following is the CCA schedule for BQ's equipment. (The calculations are discussed further in the paragraphs following this example.)

Class 8–20%	CCA	UCC
December 31, 2022		**$288,000**
Additions less disposals, 2023		
Cost of new asset		700,000
CCA 2023		
$288,000 × 20% =	$57,600	$988,000
$700,000 × ½ × 20% =	70,000	$127,600	(127,600)
December 31, 2023		**$860,400**
Additions less disposals, 2024		
Manufacturing equipment originally purchased in 2020 (lesser of original cost of $500,000 and proceeds of disposal of $300,000)		(300,000)
		$560,400
CCA 2024: $560,400 × 20% =	$112,080	(112,080)
December 31, 2024		**$448,320**
Additions less disposals, 2025		
Asset originally purchased in 2023 (lesser of original cost of $700,000 and proceeds of disposal of $500,000)		(500,000)
		$ (51,680)
Recaptured CCA, 2025	$ (51,680)	51,680
December 31, 2025		$ 0

Additions to an Asset Class

The purchase of another Class 8 asset in 2023 in Example 11A.2 resulted in a **net addition** of $700,000 to the undepreciated capital cost at the end of 2023. Consequently, the balance of the UCC at the end of 2023 prior to calculating CCA is made up of this $700,000 plus the $288,000 UCC of the original equipment. The capital cost allowance for 2023 is therefore 20% of $288,000 ($57,600) plus one half of 20% of the net addition of $700,000 ($70,000) for a total of $127,600.

If a government grant of $35,000 had been received in 2023 to help finance the acquisition of this asset, the addition in 2023 would be reported net of the government grant; that is, at $700,000 – $35,000 = $665,000. If the 2023 acquisition were eligible instead for an investment tax credit (ITC) of $35,000, the tax legislation specifies that the ITC reduces the asset's capital cost and the UCC of the class of assets **in the year following** the year of acquisition.[21] Assuming the Class 8 asset acquired in 2023 in Example 11A.2 was eligible for a $35,000 ITC, the $700,000 addition is recognized in 2023, and the UCC is reduced by the $35,000 ITC in 2024 along with the $300,000 proceeds on the original manufacturing equipment that was sold in 2024. The CCA claimed in 2024 is reduced accordingly.

Retirements from an Asset Class, Continuation of Class

While the CCA class is increased by the cost of additions, it is reduced **by the proceeds on the asset's disposal**, not by the asset's cost. However, if the proceeds on disposal are more than the asset's original capital cost, the class is reduced by the cost only. There is a good reason for this. If the proceeds on disposal are more than the original cost, there is a capital gain on the disposal. Capital gains are taxed differently than ordinary business income; thus, the portion that is a capital gain must be identified as being that. Cost, therefore, is the maximum amount to be deducted from the CCA class. It is not common for depreciable assets to be sold for more than their cost.

In 2024, in Example 11A.2, BQ sells the original manufacturing equipment for $300,000. Because this is less than its $500,000 capital cost, there is no capital gain on disposal. Therefore, Class 8 is reduced by the proceeds on disposal of $300,000, and the CCA for the year is calculated on the remaining balance in the class.

Retirements from an Asset Class, Elimination of Class

When an asset's disposal eliminates the asset class, either because there are no more assets remaining in the class or because the disposal results in the elimination of the UCC balance of the class, one of the following may result:

1. There may be a recapture of capital cost allowance, with or without a capital gain.
2. There may be a terminal loss, with or without a capital gain. This occurs only when the last asset in the class is disposed of and a UCC balance still exists in the class after deducting the appropriate amount on the asset disposal.

A recapture of CCA occurs when, after deducting the appropriate amount from the class on disposal of an asset, a negative amount is left as the UCC balance. The negative balance is the amount of CCA that must be "recaptured" and included in the calculation of taxable income in the year. It is taxed at the normal income tax rates. When this situation occurs, it suggests that too much CCA was deducted throughout the lives of the assets, and the taxing of the recaptured capital cost allowance therefore adjusts for this. This is what occurred in 2025 in Example 11A.2. When the proceeds of disposal were deducted from the UCC, the UCC became negative. The excess of $51,680 is therefore added back and included in taxable income in 2025.

As indicated above, if an asset is sold for more than its cost, a capital gain results. This may occur whether or not the class is eliminated. For tax purposes, a capital gain is treated differently from a recapture of CCA. Essentially, the **taxable** capital gain (that is, the amount subject to tax) is only a portion of the capital gain as defined above.[22] The taxable capital gain is included with other taxable income.

If the Class 8 asset purchased by BQ in 2023 had been sold in 2025 for $750,000, a capital gain and a recapture of CCA would have resulted. The capital gain would be $50,000, but only 50% or $25,000 would be the taxable capital gain. In this case, Class 8 would be reduced by $700,000 and the recapture would be $251,680 ($700,000 less the $448,320 UCC).

A terminal loss occurs when a positive balance remains in the class after the appropriate reduction is made to the CCA class from the disposal of the last asset. This remaining balance is a terminal loss that is deductible in full when calculating taxable income for the period.

---

[21]The rationale is that the ITC is not calculated until after the company's year end, when the tax return is completed and filed.

[22]The percentage of the capital gain that is taxable has varied in recent years. In 2017, the inclusion rate—the taxable portion—was 50%.

If BQ's remaining equipment had been sold in 2025 for $300,000, a terminal loss of $148,320 would have resulted (the UCC of $448,320 less the $300,000 proceeds).

Example 11A.2 illustrating the basic calculations of capital gains, taxable capital gains, recaptured capital cost allowance, and terminal losses has necessarily been simplified. In essence, the tax rate on taxable capital gains is specified by tax law, which may change from time to time and have other implications (such as a refundable dividend tax on hand). Similarly, the tax rate that applies to recaptured CCA is affected by the particular circumstances of the type of taxable income that is being reported, of which the recaptured amount is a component. These and other technical aspects, including definitions, are beyond the scope of this text. Be warned that specialist knowledge of tax law is often required to determine income taxes payable!

Review and Practice

Summary of Learning Objectives

1. Understand the importance of depreciation, impairment, and disposition from a business perspective.

The economic benefits of property, plant, and equipment are typically consumed as the items are used by the organization. Because the benefits are consumed over multiple periods, companies use depreciation to allocate the benefits of the PP&E to each period as the assets' capacity is used up. By allocating the cost of property, plant, and equipment over their useful lives businesses are better able to match the assets' costs and benefits to the revenues that they help generate. Companies also need to assess their PP&E each year under IFRS for indications of impairment, and if these indications are present, they should re-estimate how much will be recoverable. Following GAAP should also help companies better understand their businesses.

2. Explain the concept of depreciation and identify the factors to consider when determining depreciation charges.

Depreciation is the process of allocating the cost of property, plant, and equipment assets in a systematic and rational manner to the periods that are expected to benefit from their use. The allocation of the cost of intangible capital assets is called "amortization" and the allocation of the costs of mineral resource assets is called "depletion." Four factors involved in determining depreciation expense are (1) the recognition of the appropriate asset components, (2) the amount to be depreciated (depreciable amount), (3) the estimated useful life, and (4) the pattern and method of depreciation.

3. Identify how depreciation methods are selected; calculate and recognize depreciation using straight-line, diminishing balance, activity, and other methods.

The depreciation method chosen should amortize an asset in a pattern and at a rate that corresponds to the benefits received from that asset. The choice often involves the use of professional judgement. Tax reporting, simplicity, perceived economic consequences, and

impact on ratios are examples of factors that influence such judgements in practice.

The straight-line method assumes that an asset provides its benefits as a function of time. As such, cost less residual value is divided by the useful life to determine the depreciation expense per period. The decreasing charge method provides for a higher depreciation charge in the early years and lower charges in later periods. For this method, a constant rate (such as double the straight-line rate) is multiplied by the net book value (cost less accumulated depreciation and accumulated impairment losses) at the start of the period to determine each period's expense. The main justification for this approach is that the asset provides more benefits in the earlier periods. The activity method assumes that the benefits provided by the asset are a function of use instead of the passage of time. The asset's life is considered in terms of either the output that it provides or an input measure, such as the number of hours it works. The depreciation charge per unit of activity (depreciable amount divided by estimated total units of output or input) is calculated and multiplied by the units of activity produced or consumed in a period to determine the depreciation.

4. Explain the accounting issues for depletion of mineral resources.

After the depletion base has been established through accounting decisions related to the acquisition, exploration and evaluation, development, and restoration obligations associated with mineral resources, these costs are allocated to the natural resources that are removed from the ground. Depletion is normally calculated using the units of production method. In this approach, the resource's cost less residual value, if any, is divided by the number of units that are estimated to be in the resource deposit, to obtain a cost per unit of product. The cost per unit is then multiplied by the number of units withdrawn in the period to calculate the depletion.

5. Explain and apply the accounting procedures for partial periods and a change in depreciation rate.

Because all the variables in determining depreciation are estimates—with the exception, perhaps, of an asset's original cost—it is common for a change in those estimates to result in a change in the depreciation amount. When this occurs, there is no retroactive change and no catch-up adjustment. The change is accounted for in the current and future periods.

6. Explain the issues and apply the accounting standards for capital asset impairment under both IFRS and ASPE.

A capital asset is impaired when its carrying amount is not fully recoverable. The cost recovery method (ASPE) defines recoverable amount as the undiscounted cash flows from the asset's use and later disposal. If impaired, the asset is written down to its fair value, and this loss cannot be reversed later if the asset's value recovers. The rational entity model (IFRS) defines recoverable amount as the higher of the asset's value in use and fair value less costs of disposal. Both these values are discounted cash flow amounts. If the recoverable amount subsequently improves, the impairment losses recognized are reversed.

7. Account for derecognition of property, plant, and equipment and explain and apply the accounting standards for long-lived assets that are held for sale.

Assets held for sale are no longer depreciated. They are remeasured to their fair value less costs of disposal at each statement of financial position date. Recoveries in value may be recognized to the extent of previous losses. Held for sale items of PP&E are separately reported as non-current assets unless they meet the definition of current assets. Under ASPE, assets held for sale are only permitted to be reported in current assets if sold before the financial statements are completed and the proceeds on sale are expected within 12 months from the date of the statement of financial position (or operating cycle, if longer).

Depreciation continues for PP&E assets until they are classified as held for sale or derecognized. At the date of disposal, all accounts related to the retired asset are removed from the books. Gains and losses from the disposal of PP&E assets are shown on the income statement in income before discontinued operations, unless the conditions for reporting as a discontinued operation are met. For property, plant, and equipment donated to an organization outside the reporting entity, the donation is reported at its fair value with a gain or loss on disposal recognized.

8. Describe the types of disclosures required for property, plant, and equipment, and provide an analysis of investment in capital assets.

The type of information required to be disclosed for PP&E is governed by the information needs of users. Because users of private entities' financial information are often able to seek further specific information from a company, there are fewer required disclosures than for public companies reporting under IFRS. The required disclosures under IFRS include those relating to measurement, changes in account balances and the reasons for the changes, information about how fair values are determined, and many others. The efficiency of use of a company's investment in assets may be evaluated by calculating and interpreting the asset turnover rate, the profit margin, and the rate of return on assets.

9. Identify differences in accounting between IFRS and ASPE, and what changes are expected in the near future.

In most major ways, international and Canadian accounting standards for the depreciation of property, plant, and equipment are similar. Some differences do exist, however, in the extent of componentization for depreciation, the impairment models applied, and the extent of disclosure. The impairment differences relate to how it is determined whether an asset is impaired, how the impairment is measured, and the ability to recognize recoveries in value. No significant changes are expected to these standards in the near future.

10. Calculate capital cost allowance in routine and non-routine situations.

"Capital cost allowance" (CCA) is the term used for depreciation when calculating taxable income in income tax returns. The CCA method is similar to the declining-balance method except that rates are specified for asset classes and the amount claimed is based on year-end balances. The half-year rule is applied to net additions in the year, which means that only 50% of the normal rate is permitted. For an asset class, retirements are accounted for under specific rules that govern the calculation of taxable income. Capital gains occur if the proceeds on disposal are more than the asset's original cost. When an asset class is eliminated, a terminal loss or recapture of CCA can occur.

Practice Problem

Norwel SA manufactures miniature circuit boards used in smart phones. On June 5, 2020, Norwel bought a circuit board stamping machine at a retail price of $24,000. Norwel paid 5% provincial sales tax on this purchase and hired a contractor to build a specially wired platform for the machine for $1,800, to meet safety requirements.

Norwel estimates the machine will have a five-year useful life, with a residual value of $2,000 at the end of five years. Norwel uses straight-line depreciation and uses the "half-year" convention in accounting for partial-year depreciation. Norwel's fiscal year ends on December 31.

Instructions

a. At what amount should Norwel record the acquisition cost of the machine?

b. How much depreciation expense should Norwel record in 2020 and in 2021?

c. At what amount will the machine be reported in Norwel's statement of financial position at December 31, 2021?

d. During 2022, Norwel's circuit board business is experiencing significant competition from companies with more advanced low-heat circuit boards. As a result, at June 30, 2022, Norwel conducts an impairment evaluation of the stamping machine purchased in 2020. Norwel determines that the machine's value in use is estimated to be $15,200 and its fair value less costs to sell, based on prices in the resale market, to be $13,400. Prepare the journal entry to record impairment, if any, on the stamping machine assuming that Norwel follows IFRS.

Solution

a. Historical cost is measured by the cash or cash equivalent price of obtaining the asset and bringing it to the location and condition for its intended use. For Norwel, this is:

Price	$24,000
Provincial sales Tax ($24,000 × .05)	1,200
Platform	1,800
Total	$27,000

b. Depreciable amount: $27,000 − $2,000 = $25,000
Depreciation expense: $25,000 ÷ 5   = $5,000 per year
         2020: 1/2 year = $5,000 × .50 = $2,500
         2021: full year = $5,000

c. The amount reported on the December 31, 2021 statement of financial position is the cost of the asset less accumulated depreciation:

Machinery	$27,000
Less: Accumulated depreciation—Machinery	7,500
Net book value	$19,500

d. Under IFRS, Norwel compares the book value of the machinery of $17,000* with the higher of the value in use ($15,200) and the fair value less costs to sell ($13,400). Thus, Norwel will record impairment, based on a comparison of the value in use of the machinery with the book value. The entry is as follows.

Loss on Impairment ($17,000* − $15,200)	1,800	
Accumulated Impairment Losses—Machinery		1,800

*Cost	$27,000
Less: Accumulated depreciation ($2,500 + $5,000 + $2,500)	(10,000)
Book value of machine and platform	$17,000

Key Terms

accelerated amortization, p. 11-10
activity method, p. 11-11
amortization, p. 11-5
asset group, p. 11-25
asset turnover ratio, p. 11-33
capital cost allowance (CCA), p. 11-37
capital cost allowance method, p. 11-37
capital gain, p. 11-40
cash-generating unit (CGU), p. 11-25
componentization, p. 11-5
cost recovery impairment model, p. 11-21
declining-balance method, p. 11-10
decreasing charge methods, p. 11-10
depletion, p. 11-5

depreciable amount, p. 11-6
depreciation, p. 11-5
derecognized, p. 11-28
diminishing balance method, p. 11-10
double-declining-balance method, p. 11-11
fair value, p. 11-21
half-year rule, p. 11-38
impaired, p. 11-20
impairment loss, p. 11-21
impairments, p. 11-20
liquidating dividend, p. 11-15
profit margin ratio, p. 11-34
rate of return on assets (ROA), p. 11-34
rational entity impairment model, p. 11-22

recapture, p. 11-40
recoverability test, p. 11-21
recoverable amount, p. 11-22
residual value, p. 11-6
salvage value, p. 11-6
straight-line method, p. 11-9
sum-of-the-years'-digits method, p. 11-10
tax basis, p. 11-39
tax value, p. 11-39
terminal loss, p. 11-40
undepreciated capital cost (UCC), p. 11-39
units of production method, p. 11-11
useful life, p. 11-7
value in use, p. 11-23

Assignment Material

Note: All assignment material with an asterisk (*) relates to the appendix to the chapter.

Unless otherwise indicated, depreciation expense should be calculated to the nearest whole month.

Enabling Competencies Completion of this end-of-chapter material will help develop CPA-enabling competencies (such as ethics and professionalism, problem-solving and decision-making, and communication) and technical competencies. We have highlighted selected items with a specific integration word mark and material in *WileyPLUS* has been linked to the competencies. All cases emphasize integration, especially of the enabling competencies. The brief exercises, exercises, and problems generally emphasize problem-solving and decision-making.

Brief Exercises

BE11.1 (LO 1, 8) Cella Corporation's statement of financial position shows property, plant, and equipment of $100,000. The notes to its financial statements state that the amount is represented by a cost of $600,000, accumulated depreciation of $300,000, and accumulated impairment losses of $200,000. Discuss the usefulness of the information provided, referring to the qualitative characteristics identified in the conceptual framework for financial reporting (discussed in Chapter 2).

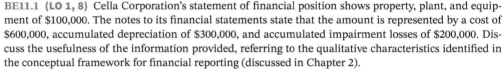

BE11.2 (LO 2) On October 1, 2020, Ocean Airways Ltd. purchased a new commercial aircraft for a total cost of $100 million. Included in the total cost are the aircraft's two engines, at a cost of $10 million each, and the aircraft's body, which costs $80 million. The estimated useful life of each of the aircraft's two engines is 10 years, with a residual value of $1 million. The estimated useful life of the aircraft's body is 10 years, with a residual value of $5 million. The entire aircraft's useful life is limited to the life of the aircraft's body. (a) Prepare the journal entries required on October 1, 2020, and December 31, 2020, if Ocean Airways prepares financial statements in accordance with IFRS and uses straight-line depreciation. (b) Explain any differences in the journal entries if Ocean Airways prepares financial statements in accordance with ASPE.

BE11.3 (LO 2) Chong Corp. purchased a machine on July 1, 2020, for $30,000. Chong paid $200 in title fees and a legal fee of $100 related to the machine. In addition, Chong paid $500 in shipping charges for delivery, and $400 to a local contractor to build and wire a platform for the machine on the plant floor. The machine has an estimated useful life of 10 years, a total expected life of 12 years, a residual value of $6,000, and no salvage value. Chong uses straight-line depreciation. (a) Calculate the 2020 depreciation expense if Chong prepares financial statements in accordance with IFRS. (b) Calculate the 2020 depreciation expense if Chong prepares financial statements in accordance with ASPE.

BE11.4 (LO 3) Gilles Corp. purchased a piece of equipment on February 1, 2020, for $100,000. The equipment has an estimated useful life of eight years, with a residual value of $25,000, and an estimated physical life of 10 years, with no salvage value. The equipment was delivered to Gilles's factory floor, installed, and in working condition, on March 1, 2020. On April 1, 2020, Gilles's staff used the equipment to produce the first saleable units. (a) Calculate the 2020 depreciation expense if Gilles uses straight-line depreciation and prepares financial statements in accordance with IFRS. (b) Calculate the 2020 depreciation expense if Gilles prepares financial statements in accordance with ASPE. Do not round intermediate calculations and round the final answer to the nearest dollar.

BE11.5 (LO 3) Odyssey Ltd. purchased machinery on January 1, 2020, for $60,000. The machinery is estimated to have a residual value of $6,000 after a useful life of eight years. (a) Calculate the 2020 depreciation expense using the straight-line method. (b) Calculate the 2020 depreciation expense using the straight-line method, but assuming the machinery was purchased on September 1, 2020. Do not round intermediate calculations and round the final answer to the nearest dollar.

BE11.6 (LO 3) Use the information for Odyssey Ltd. in BE11.5. (a) Calculate the 2020 depreciation expense using the double-declining-balance method. (b) Calculate the 2021 depreciation expense using the double-declining-balance method, but assuming the machinery was purchased on October 1, 2020. Do not round intermediate calculations and round the final answer to the nearest dollar. (c) Discuss when it might be more appropriate to use the straight-line method of depreciation and when the double-declining-balance method is more appropriate.

BE11.7 (LO 3) Use the information for Odyssey Ltd. in BE11.5. (a) Calculate the 2020 depreciation expense using the sum-of-the-years'-digits method. (b) Calculate the 2020 depreciation expense using the sum-of-the-years'-digits method, but assuming the machinery was purchased on April 1, 2020. Do not round intermediate calculations and round the final answer to the nearest dollar.

*BE11.8 **(LO 3, 10)** `Taxation` Andeo Corporation purchased a truck at the beginning of 2020 for $48,000. The truck is estimated to have a residual value of $3,000 and a useful life of 275,000 km. It was driven for 52,000 km in 2020 and 65,000 km in 2021. (a) Calculate depreciation expense for 2020 and 2021 using the units of production method. Round the per-kilometre charge to four decimal places and the final answer to the nearest dollar. (b) For tax purposes, the asset's capital cost allowance (CCA) rate is 30%. Calculate the CCA for 2020 and 2021. Round the final answer to the nearest dollar.

BE11.9 **(LO 4)** Extract Corporation, a publicly traded mining company, acquires a mine at a cost of $500,000. Capitalized development costs total $125,000. After the mine is depleted, $75,000 will be spent to restore the property, after which it can be sold for $157,500. Extract estimates that 5,000 tonnes of ore can be mined. Assuming that 900 tonnes are extracted in the first year, prepare the journal entry to record depletion. Round the per-tonne charge for depletion to the nearest cent.

BE11.10 **(LO 4)** Wildcat Mining Limited is nearing the end of the useful life of its only remaining natural resource that it is mining in northern Quebec. The balance of its Common Shares account is $2,500,000, Retained Earnings is $3,850,000, and Accumulated Depletion is $2,800,000. The board of directors recently declared and paid a $5.50 dividend to each of the 1 million outstanding common shares. Wildcat records cash dividends directly to Retained Earnings. Prepare the journal entry for the declaration and payment of this liquidating dividend (assume only one journal entry is needed for declaration and payment) and explain how the amount received should be handled by shareholders (that is, what instructions should be communicated by Wildcat's board of directors).

BE11.11 **(LO 5)** Chuckwalla Limited purchased a computer for $7,000 on January 1, 2020. Straight-line depreciation is used for the computer, based on a five-year life and a $1,000 residual value. In 2022, the estimates are revised. Chuckwalla now expects the computer will be used until December 31, 2023, when it can be sold for $500. Calculate the 2022 depreciation expense.

BE11.12 **(LO 6)** Qilin Corp., a small company that follows ASPE, owns machinery that cost $900,000 and has accumulated depreciation of $360,000. The undiscounted future net cash flows from the use of the asset are expected to be $500,000. The equipment's fair value is $400,000. Using the cost recovery impairment model, prepare the journal entry, if any, to record the impairment loss.

 Video

BE11.13 **(LO 6)** Use the information for Qilin Corp. given in BE11.12. By the end of the following year, the machinery's fair value has increased to $490,000. (a) Assuming the machinery continues to be used in production, prepare the journal entry required, if any, to record the increase in its fair value. (b) Explain any differences in your answer to part (a) if Qilin prepares financial statements in accordance with IFRS.

BE11.14 **(LO 6)** Hambrecht Corp. is preparing its financial statements for the fiscal year ending November 30, 2020. Certain specialized equipment was scrapped on January 1, 2021. At November 30, 2020, this equipment was being used in production by Hambrecht and had a carrying amount of $1 million. As at November 30, 2020, it was estimated that the asset had undiscounted net future cash flows of $1.1 million, value in use of $800,000, and fair value less costs of disposal of $50,000 (scrap value). (a) If Hambrecht prepares financial statements in accordance with IFRS, what is the recoverable amount of the equipment at November 30, 2020? (b) If Hambrecht prepares financial statements in accordance with ASPE, what is the recoverable amount of the equipment at November 30, 2020?

BE11.15 **(LO 6)** Greentree Properties Ltd. is a publicly listed company following IFRS. Assume that on December 31, 2020, the carrying amount of land on the statement of financial position (SFP) is $500,000. Management determines that the land's value in use is $425,000 and that the fair value less costs to sell is $400,000. (a) Using the rational entity impairment model, prepare the journal entry required, if any, to record the impairment loss. (b) Due to an economic rebound in the area, by the end of the following year the land has a value in use of $550,000 and fair value less costs of disposal of $480,000. Prepare the journal entry required, if any, to record the increase in its recoverable amount.

BE11.16 **(LO 6)** Riverbed Ltd. is a manufacturer of computer network equipment and has just recently adopted IFRS. The wireless division is a cash-generating unit or asset group that has the following carrying amounts for its net assets: land, $20,000; buildings, $30,000; and equipment, $10,000. The undiscounted net future cash flows from use and eventual disposal of the wireless division are $70,000, and the present value of these cash flows is $45,000. The land can be sold immediately for $35,000; however, the buildings and equipment are specialized and cannot be used elsewhere and thus have no resale value. Allocate the impairment loss to the net assets of the wireless division using (a) the cost recovery model under ASPE and (b) the rational entity model under IFRS.

BE11.17 **(LO 6)** Compare the cost recovery impairment model used under ASPE with the rational entity model used under IFRS. Which model provides better information for financial statement users?

BE11.18 (LO 7) Caley Inc. owns a building with a carrying amount of $1.5 million, as at January 1, 2020. On that date, Caley's management determined that the building's location is no longer suitable for the company's operations and decided to dispose of the building by sale. Caley is preparing financial statements for the fiscal year ending December 31, 2020. As at that date, management had an authorized plan in place to sell the building, the building met all criteria for classification as held for sale, and the building's estimated fair value less costs to sell was $1 million. The building's depreciation expense for 2020 would amount to $200,000. (a) Prepare the journal entry(ies) required on December 31, 2020, if any. (b) Discuss how the building would be classified on the December 31, 2020 SFP if Caley prepared financial statements in accordance with IFRS. (c) Discuss how the building would be classified on the December 31, 2020 SFP if Caley prepared financial statements in accordance with ASPE.

BE11.19 (LO 7) Volumetrics Corporation owns machinery that cost $20,000 when purchased on January 1, 2020. Depreciation has been recorded at a rate of $3,000 per year, resulting in a balance in accumulated depreciation of $6,000 at December 31, 2021. The machinery is sold on September 1, 2022, for $13,500. Prepare journal entries to (a) update depreciation for 2022 and (b) record the disposal.

BE11.20 (LO 7) Use the information presented for Volumetrics Corporation in BE11.19, but assume that the machinery is sold for $5,200 instead of $13,500. Prepare journal entries to (a) update depreciation for 2022 and (b) record the disposal.

BE11.21 (LO 8) In its 2020 annual report, Winkler Limited reports beginning-of-the-year total assets of $1,923 million, end-of-the-year total assets of $2,487 million, total revenue of $2,687 million, and net income of $52 million. (a) Calculate Winkler's asset turnover ratio. (b) Calculate Winkler's profit margin. (c) Calculate Winkler's rate of return on assets (1) using the asset turnover and profit margin, and (2) using net income.

*__BE11.22 (LO 10)__ **Taxation** Fong Limited purchased an asset at a cost of $45,000 on March 1, 2020. The asset has a useful life of seven years and an estimated residual value of $3,000. For tax purposes, the asset belongs in CCA Class 8, with a rate of 20%. Calculate the CCA for each year, 2020 to 2023, assuming this is the only asset in Class 8. How would the calculation change for 2020–2023 based on the new CCA rules implemented in late 2018 (see footnote 20) assuming this is "eligible property"?

Exercises

E11.1 (LO 1, 2, 3) **(Matching the Depreciation Method with Assets)** The following assets have been acquired by various companies over the past year:

1. Boardroom table and chairs for a corporate head office
2. Dental equipment in a new dental clinic
3. Long-haul trucks for a trucking business
4. Weight and aerobic equipment in a new health club facility
5. Classroom computers in a new community college

Instructions

For each long-lived asset listed above:

a. Identify the factors to consider in establishing the useful life of the asset.
b. Recommend the pattern of depreciation that most closely represents the pattern of economic benefits received by the entity that owns the asset.
c. Discuss how good estimates of asset useful life would help a company manage its assets.

E11.2 (LO 2, 3) **(Terminology, Calculations—Straight-Line, Double-Declining-Balance)** Diderot Corp. acquired a property on September 15, 2020, for $220,000, paying $3,000 in transfer taxes and a $1,500 real estate fee. Based on the provincial assessment information, 75% of the property's value was related to the building and 25% to the land. It is estimated that the building, with proper maintenance, will last for 20 years, at which time it will be torn down and have zero salvage value. Diderot, however, expects to use it for 10 years only, as it is not expected to suit the company's purposes after that. The company should be able to sell the property for $155,000 at that time, with $40,000 of this amount being for the land. Diderot prepares financial statements in accordance with IFRS. Depreciation expense should be calculated to the nearest half month.

Instructions

Assuming a December 31 year end, identify all of the following:

a. The building's cost

b. The building's depreciable amount

c. The building's useful life

d. Depreciation expense for 2020, assuming the straight-line method

e. Depreciation expense for 2021, assuming the double-declining-balance method

f. The building's carrying amount at December 31, 2021, assuming the double-declining-balance method

g. Depreciation expense for 2020, assuming the straight-line method and assuming Diderot prepares financial statements in accordance with ASPE

E11.3 (LO 3) (Depreciation Calculations—Straight-Line, Double-Declining-Balance; Partial Periods) Gambit Corporation purchased a new plant asset on April 1, 2020, at a cost of $769,000. It was estimated to have a useful life of 20 years and a residual value of $300,000, a physical life of 30 years, and a salvage value of $0. Gambit's accounting period is the calendar year. Gambit prepares financial statements in accordance with IFRS.

Instructions

a. Calculate the depreciation for this asset for 2020 and 2021 using the straight-line method.

b. Calculate the depreciation for this asset for 2020 and 2021 using the double-declining-balance method.

c. Calculate the depreciation for this asset for 2020 and 2021 using the straight-line method and assuming Gambit prepares financial statements in accordance with ASPE.

d. Discuss when it might be more appropriate to select the straight-line method, and when it might be more appropriate to select the double-declining-balance method.

e. Assume that additional information has been provided relating to the cost ($769,000). There are three components of the plant asset. Components 1, 2, and 3 have costs of $400,000, $254,000, and $115,000, respectively. The useful lives of components 1, 2, and 3 are 25, 20, and 30 years, respectively. Determine straight-line depreciation expense for 2020 and 2021 for each component under IFRS if the residual value is $100,000 for component 1, $154,000 for component 2, and $46,000 for component 3.

f. How would your answer in part (e) differ if the company prepared financial statements in accordance with ASPE?

*E11.4 (LO 3, 5, 10) `Taxation` **(Depreciation Calculations—Six Methods; Partial Periods)** Jupiter Wells Corp. purchased machinery for $315,000 on May 1, 2020. It is estimated that it will have a useful life of 10 years, residual value of $15,000, production of 240,000 units, and 25,000 working hours. The machinery will have a physical life of 15 years and a salvage value of $3,000. During 2021, Jupiter Wells Corp. used the machinery for 2,650 hours and the machinery produced 25,500 units. Jupiter Wells prepares financial statements in accordance with IFRS.

Instructions

From the information given, calculate the depreciation charge for 2021 under each of the following methods, assuming Jupiter Wells has a December 31 year end.

a. Straight-line

b. Units of production. Round the units of production charge to the nearest cent and the final answer to the nearest dollar.

c. Working hours. Round the per-hour charge to the nearest cent and the final answer to the nearest dollar.

d. Declining-balance, using a 20% rate

e. Sum-of-the-years'-digits. Do not round intermediate calculations and round the final answer to the nearest dollar.

f. CCA at 20%

g. Assume that Jupiter Wells is a small privately owned company that follows ASPE and uses straight-line depreciation. How would depreciation expense differ, if at all? Provide calculations to support your answer.

h. **Digging Deeper** Assuming that Jupiter Wells follows ASPE, from the perspective of a potential investor in the company, discuss the advantages and disadvantages of Jupiter Wells using the capital cost allowance approach to calculate and record depreciation expense for financial reporting purposes.

E11.5 (LO 2, 3) **(Different Methods of Depreciation)** Jared Industries Ltd., a public company, presents you with the following information:

Description	Date Purchased	Cost	Residual Value	Life in Years	Depreciation Method	Accumulated Depreciation to Dec. 31, 2023	Depreciation for 2024
Machine A	Dec. 2, 2022	$142,500	$16,000	10	(1)	$39,900	(2)
Machine B	Aug. 15, 2021	(3)	21,000	5	Straight-line	29,000	(4)
Machine C	July 21, 2020	75,400	23,500	8	Double-declining-balance	(5)	(6)

Instructions

a. Complete the table for the year ended December 31, 2024. The company depreciates all assets for a half year in the year of acquisition and the year of disposal. Round all amounts to the nearest dollar.

b. What criteria would you consider in determining whether to select the straight-line or double-declining-balance method?

E11.6 (LO 3) **Excel** **(Depreciation Calculations—Straight-Line, Sum-of-the-Years'-Digits, Double-Declining-Balance)** Deluxe Ezra Company purchases equipment on January 1, 2020, at a cost of $469,000. The asset is expected to have a service life of 12 years and a salvage value of $40,000.

Instructions

a. Calculate the amount of depreciation for each of 2020, 2021, and 2022 using the straight-line depreciation method.

b. Calculate the amount of depreciation for each of 2020, 2021, and 2022 using the sum-of-the-years'-digits method. Do not round intermediate calculations and round the final answer to the nearest dollar.

c. Calculate the amount of depreciation for each of 2020, 2021, and 2022 using the double-declining-balance method. (In performing your calculations, round the constant percentage rate to two decimal places and the final answer to the nearest dollar.)

E11.7 (LO 3) **(Depreciation Calculations—Five Methods)** Jon Seceda Furnace Corp. purchased machinery for $260,000 on July 1, 2020. It is estimated that it will have a useful life of 10 years, residual value of $40,000, production of 110,000 units, and working hours of 44,000. During 2021, Seceda Corp. uses the machinery for 6,000 hours, and the machinery produces 14,500 units.

Instructions

From the information given, calculate the depreciation charge for 2021 under each of the following methods. (Round final answers to the nearest dollar.)

a. Straight-line

b. Units of production. Round the units of production charge to the nearest cent.

c. Working hours. Round the per-hour charge to the nearest cent.

d. Sum-of-the-years'-digits. Do not round intermediate calculations.

e. Declining-balance (use 20% as the annual rate). Do not round intermediate calculations.

E11.8 (LO 3) **(Depreciation Calculations—Straight-Line, Double-Declining-Balance)** Jiang Company Ltd. buys equipment on January 1, 2020, for $387,000 cash. The asset is expected to have a useful life of 12 years and a residual value of $39,000. Jiang prepares financial statements under IFRS.

Instructions

a. Calculate the amount of depreciation for each of 2020, 2021, and 2022 using the straight-line method.

b. Calculate the amount of depreciation for each of 2020, 2021, and 2022 using the double-declining-balance method. (In performing your calculations, round the constant percentage rate to two decimal places and the final answers to the nearest dollar.)

c. Assume that the equipment consists of an input device with a cost of $55,000, residual value of $5,000, and useful life of 5 years; a processor with a cost of $132,000, residual value of $12,000, and useful life of 10 years; and an output device with a cost of $200,000, residual value of $22,000, and useful life of 12 years. Prepare the journal entry to record the purchase on January 1, 2020.

d. Assume the information given in part (c) above. Also assume that the benefits of the input device and processor are expected to flow to Jiang evenly over time, but that the output device is expected to provide the greatest benefits in the early years. Calculate the amount of depreciation for 2020 using the most appropriate methods. Round final answers to the nearest dollar.

e. Assume the information given in part (c) with respect to the cost components. The equipment is expected to provide benefits evenly over time. Also assume that the equipment has a salvage value of $37,000 and a physical life of 14 years. The salvage values of the input device, processor, and output device are $3,000, $10,000, and $19,000, respectively. The physical lives of the input device, processor, and output device are 6 years, 12 years, and 14 years, respectively. Calculate the amount of depreciation for 2020, 2021, and 2022 using the straight-line method. Jiang Company Ltd. prepares financial statements under ASPE.

E11.9 (LO 3) (Depreciation—Conceptual Understanding) Hubbub Company Ltd. acquired equipment at the beginning of Year 1. The asset has an estimated useful life of five years. An employee has prepared depreciation schedules for this asset using two different methods, in order to compare the results of using one method with the results of using the other. Assume that the following schedules have been correctly prepared for this asset using (1) the straight-line method and (2) the double-declining-balance method. Hubbub Company Ltd. prepares its financial statements under IFRS.

Year	Straight-Line	Double-Declining-Balance
1	$12,000	$30,000
2	12,000	18,000
3	12,000	10,800
4	12,000	1,200
5	12,000	–0–
Total	$60,000	$60,000

Instructions

a. What is the cost of the asset that is being depreciated?

b. What amount, if any, was used in the depreciation calculations for the residual value of this asset?

c. Which method will produce the higher net income in Year 1?

d. Which method will produce the higher charge to income in Year 4?

e. Which method will produce the higher carrying amount for the asset at the end of Year 3?

f. Which method will produce the higher cash flow in Year 1? In Year 4?

g. If the asset were sold at the end of Year 3, which method would yield the higher gain (or lower loss) on disposal of the asset?

h. Repeat parts (c) through (g) assuming a salvage value of $0 and a physical life of six years using ASPE.

E11.10 (LO 3) (Depreciation for Fractional Periods) On March 10, 2020, Lucas Limited sold equipment that it bought for $192,000 on August 20, 2013. It was originally estimated that the equipment would have a useful life of 12 years and a residual value of $16,800 at the end of that time, and depreciation has been calculated on that basis. The company uses the straight-line method of depreciation and prepares its financial statements under IFRS.

Instructions

a. Calculate the depreciation charge on this equipment for 2013 and for 2020, and the total charge for the period from 2014 to 2019, inclusive, under each of the following six assumptions for partial periods, rounding all final yearly amounts to the nearest dollar:

1. Depreciation is calculated for the exact period of time during which the asset is owned. (Use 365 days for your base.)

2. Depreciation is calculated for the full year on the January 1 balance in the asset account.

3. Depreciation is calculated for the full year on the December 31 balance in the asset account.

4. Depreciation for a half year is charged on plant assets that are acquired or disposed of during the year.

5. Depreciation is calculated on additions from the beginning of the month following their acquisition and on disposals to the beginning of the month following the disposal.

6. Depreciation is calculated for a full period on all assets in use for over half a year, and no depreciation is charged on assets in use for less than half a year. (Use 365 days for your base.)

b. Briefly evaluate the above methods in terms of basic accounting theory and how simple the methods are to apply.

c. Calculate straight-line depreciation under ASPE only for assumption 1 if the asset has a physical life of 13 years and a salvage value of $1,000. Round to the nearest dollar.

E11.11 (LO 3, 5) (Error Analysis and Depreciation) Gibbs Inc. purchased a machine on January 1, 2020, at a cost of $60,000. The machine is expected to have an estimated residual value of $5,000 at the end of its five-year useful life. The company capitalized the machine and depreciated it in 2020 using the double-declining-balance method of depreciation. The company has a policy of using the straight-line method to depreciate equipment, as this method best reflects the benefits to the company over the life of its machinery. However, the company accountant neglected to follow company policy when he used the double-declining-balance method. Net income for the year ended December 31, 2020, was $53,000 as a result of depreciating the machine incorrectly. Gibbs has not closed its books for 2020 yet. Gibbs uses IFRS to prepare its financial statements.

Instructions

a. Using the method of depreciation that the company normally follows, prepare the correcting entry and determine the corrected net income. Assume the books of account have not yet been closed for 2020, and ignore income taxes.

b. Repeat part (a) assuming Gibbs uses ASPE instead of IFRS, the salvage value is $3,000, and the machinery has a physical life of six years.

c. Digging Deeper Discuss the impact on a potential investor if the error is not detected and corrected by Gibbs.

E11.12 (LO 3, 5) (Error Analysis and Depreciation) Wettlauffer Company Ltd. shows the following entries in its Equipment account for 2020. All amounts are based on historical cost.

Equipment

1/1	Balance	134,750	6/30	Cost of equipment sold		
8/10	Purchases of equipment	32,000		(purchased prior to 2020)		23,000
8/12	Freight on equipment purchased	700				
8/25	Installation costs	2,700				
11/10	Repairs	500				

Instructions

a. Prepare any necessary correcting entries.

b. Assuming that depreciation is to be charged for a full year based on the ending balance in the asset account no matter when acquired, calculate the proper depreciation charge for 2020 under both methods listed below. Round amounts of depreciation to the nearest dollar. Assume an estimated life of 10 years for all equipment at the time of acquisition, with no residual value. The equipment included in the January 1, 2020 Equipment balance was purchased in 2018.

1. Straight-line

2. Declining-balance (assume twice the straight-line rate)

E11.13 (LO 4) (Depletion Calculations—Timber) Rachel Timber Inc., a small private company that follows ASPE, owns 9,000 hectares of timberland purchased in 2007 at a cost of $1,400 per hectare. At the time of purchase, the land without the timber was valued at $420 per hectare. In 2008, Rachel built fire lanes and roads, with a physical life of 30 years, at a cost of $84,000 and separately capitalized these costs. Every year, Rachel sprays to prevent disease at a cost of $3,000 per year and spends $7,000 to maintain the fire lanes and roads. During 2009, Rachel selectively logged and sold 700,000 cubic metres of the estimated 3.5 million cubic metres of timber. In 2010, Rachel planted new seedlings to replace the cut trees at a cost of $100,000.

Instructions

a. Determine the depletion charge and the portion of depletion included in the cost of timber sold in 2010. Round the depletion rate per cubic metre to the nearest cent. Provide the journal entries to record the depletion charged to inventory (and subsequently to cost of goods sold) for the year.

b. Rachel has not logged since 2009. Assume that Rachel logged 900,000 cubic metres of timber in 2020, of which 60% was sold in 2020 and the remainder sold in 2021. The timber cruiser (the appraiser) had estimated a total resource of 5 million cubic metres. Determine the cost of timber sold that relates to the depletion for 2020 and 2021. Provide the journal entries to account for the cost of timber produced in 2020 and subsequently sold in 2020 and 2021.

c. How would Rachel account for the maintenance costs of the fire lanes and roads and the spraying of the timberland?

d. Discuss the depreciation methods that Rachel could use to depreciate the cost of the fire lanes and roads.

e. **Digging Deeper** Explain how your answers for parts (a) to (d) would differ if Rachel were a public company and followed IFRS.

E11.14 (LO 4) **(Depletion Calculations—Oil)** Marmon Drilling Limited leases property on which oil has been discovered. Wells on this property produced 21,000 barrels of oil during the current year, sold at an average of $80 per barrel. The total oil resources of this property are estimated to be 250,000 barrels.

The lease provided for an immediate payment of $5 million to the lessor (owner) before drilling began and an annual rental of $275,000. Development costs of $6,250,000 were incurred before any oil was produced, and Marmon follows a policy of capitalizing these preproduction costs. The lease also specified that each year the lessor would be paid a premium of 5% of the sales price of every barrel of oil that was removed. In addition, the lessee is to clean up all the waste and debris from drilling and to pay the costs of reconditioning the land for farming when the wells are abandoned. It is estimated that the present value of the obligations at the time of the lease for the cleanup and reconditioning for the existing wells is $300,000. All amounts are in Canadian dollars.

Instructions

a. From the information given, provide the journal entry made by Marmon Drilling Limited to record depletion for the current year, assuming that Marmon applies ASPE. Round the depletion rate per barrel to the nearest cent.

b. Assuming that the oil property was acquired at the beginning of the current year, provide the entry to record the acquisition of the asset and the annual rental payment.

E11.15 (LO 4) **(Depletion Calculations—Minerals)** At the beginning of 2020, Kao Company, a small private company, acquired a mine for $850,000. Of this amount, $100,000 was allocated to the land value and the remaining portion to the minerals in the mine. Surveys conducted by geologists found that approximately 12 million units of ore appear to be in the mine. Kao had $170,000 of development costs for this mine before any extraction of minerals. It also determined that the fair value of its obligation to prepare the land for an alternative use when all of the minerals have been removed was $40,000. During 2020, 2.5 million units of ore were extracted and 2.2 million of these units were sold.

Instructions

Calculate the following information for 2020 (rounding your unit cost answers to three decimal places):

a. The depletion cost per unit

b. The total amount of depletion for 2020 (and prepare the required journal entry, if any)

c. The total amount that is charged as an expense for 2020 for the cost of minerals sold during 2020 (and prepare the required journal entry, if any)

E11.16 (LO 5) **(Depreciation—Change in Estimate)** Machinery purchased for $56,000 by Wong Corp. on January 1, 2015, was originally estimated to have an eight-year useful life with a residual value of $4,000. Depreciation has been entered for five years on this basis. In 2020, it is determined that the total estimated useful life (including 2020) should have been 10 years, with a residual value of $4,500 at the end of that time. Assume straight-line depreciation and that Wong Corp. uses IFRS for financial statement purposes.

Instructions

a. Prepare the entry that is required to correct the prior years' depreciation, if any.

b. Prepare the entry to record depreciation for 2020.

c. **Digging Deeper** Repeat part (b) assuming Wong Corp. uses ASPE and the machinery is originally estimated to have a physical life of 8.5 years and a salvage value of $0. In 2020, it is determined that the total estimated physical life (including 2020) should have been 11 years, with a salvage value of $100 at the end of that time. Round annual amounts of depreciation to the nearest dollar.

d. Repeat part (b) assuming Wong Corp. uses the double-declining-balance method of depreciation.

E11.17 (LO 5) (Depreciation Calculation—Addition, Change in Estimate) In 1991, Lincoln Limited completed the construction of a building at a cost of $1.8 million; it occupied the building in January 1992. It was estimated that the building would have a useful life of 40 years and a residual value of $400,000.

Early in 2003, an addition to the building was constructed at a cost of $750,000. At that time, no changes were expected in its useful life, but the residual value with the addition was estimated to increase by $150,000. The addition would not be of economic use to the company beyond the life of the original building.

In 2020, as a result of a thorough review of its depreciation policies, company management determined that the building's original useful life should have been estimated at 30 years. The neighbourhood where the building is has been going through a renewal, with older buildings being torn down and new ones being built. Because of this, it is now expected that the company's building and addition are unlikely to have any residual value at the end of the 30-year period. Lincoln Limited follows IFRS for its financial statements.

Instructions

a. Using the straight-line method, calculate the annual depreciation that was charged from 1992 through 2001.

b. Calculate the annual depreciation that was charged from 2002 through 2019.

c. [Digging Deeper] Prepare the entry, if necessary, to adjust the account balances because the estimated useful life was revised in 2020.

d. Calculate the annual depreciation to be charged beginning with 2020.

e. Comment on the revision of the estimated useful life in 2020, from the perspective of an investor who bought shares in Lincoln in 2019.

f. Repeat parts (a) through (d) assuming Lincoln Limited prepares its financial statements using ASPE. The original estimate of the physical life of the building was 44 years, with a salvage value of $216,000. (Ignore the addition in early 2002.) In 2020, the estimated useful life and physical life were both revised to be 30 years, with no residual value/salvage value for the asset at the end of the 30-year period.

E11.18 (LO 5) (Depreciation Replacement—Change in Estimate) Finlay Limited constructed a building at a cost of $2.8 million and has occupied it since January 2000. It was estimated at that time that its life would be 40 years, with no residual value. In January 2020, a new roof was installed at a cost of $370,000, and it was estimated then that the building would have a useful life of 25 years from that date. The cost of the old roof was $190,000 and was capitalized in the Buildings account at that time. Finlay Limited follows IFRS for its financial statements.

Instructions

a. What amount of depreciation was charged annually for the years 2000 through 2019? (Assume straight-line depreciation.)

b. What entry should be made in 2020 to record the roof replacement? Is there an alternative entry available under ASPE?

c. Prepare the entry in January 2020 to record the revision in the building's estimated life, if necessary.

d. What amount of depreciation should be charged for the year 2020?

E11.19 (LO 6) (Impairment—Cost Recovery Model) The management of Luis Inc., a small private company that uses the cost recovery impairment model, was discussing whether certain equipment should be written down as a charge to current operations because of obsolescence. The assets had a cost of $900,000, and depreciation of $400,000 had been taken to December 31, 2020. On December 31, 2020, management projected the undiscounted future net cash flows from this equipment to be $300,000, and its fair value to be $230,000. The company intends to use this equipment in the future.

Instructions

a. Prepare the journal entry, if any, to record the impairment at December 31, 2020.

b. Where should the gain or loss on the impairment, if any, be reported on the income statement?

c. At December 31, 2021, the equipment's fair value increased to $260,000. Prepare the journal entry, if any, to record this increase in fair value.

d. Assume instead that, as at December 31, 2020, the equipment was expected to have undiscounted future net cash flows of $510,000, and that its fair value was estimated to be $450,000. Prepare the journal entry to record the impairment at December 31, 2020, if any.

e. Assume instead that, as at December 31, 2020, the equipment was expected to have undiscounted future net cash flows of $45,000 per year for each of the next 10 years, and that there is no active market for the equipment. Luis Inc. uses a 10% discount rate in its cash flow estimates. Prepare the journal entry to record impairment at December 31, 2020, if any. Use factor Table A.4, a financial calculator, or Excel function PV in arriving at the discounted fair value.

f. **Digging Deeper** Discuss why impairment is tested using undiscounted future cash flows rather than present value of future cash flows.

E11.20 (LO 6) **(Impairment—Cash-Generating Units)** Perez Corp., a mining company, owns a significant mineral deposit in a northern territory. Perez prepares financial statements in accordance with IFRS. Included in the asset is a road system that was constructed to give company personnel access to the mineral deposit for maintenance and mining activity. The road system cannot be sold separately and separate cash flow information is not available for it. The carrying amounts of two cash-generating units of the mine at June 30, 2020, are as follows:

Machinery	$4,000,000
Mine in the development phase	$9,500,000

The machinery's value in use has been assessed at $4,500,000 while the fair value less costs to sell is $3,800,000. With respect to the mine, the value in use is $9,000,000 while fair value less costs to sell is $9,350,000.

Instructions

a. How should the road system's recoverable amount be determined?

b. Determine if the machinery and the mine are impaired and prepare the journal entries, if any, to record the impairment at June 30, 2020.

E11.21 (LO 6) **(Impairment—Rational Entity Model and Cash-Generating Units, Cost Recovery Model, and Asset Groups)** Green Thumb Landscaping Limited has determined that its lawn maintenance division is a cash-generating unit under IFRS. The carrying amounts of the division's assets at December 31, 2020, are as follows:

Land	$ 25,000
Building	50,000
Equipment	30,000
Vehicles	15,000
	$120,000

The lawn maintenance division has been assessed for impairment and it is determined that the division's value in use is $108,000, fair value less costs to sell is $75,000, and undiscounted future net cash flows are $144,000.

Instructions

a. Determine if the cash-generating unit is impaired and prepare the journal entry, if any, to record the impairment at December 31, 2020, assuming that none of the individual assets in the division has a determinable recoverable amount.

b. Prepare the journal entry, if any, to record the impairment at December 31, 2020, assuming that the division's only individual asset that has a determinable recoverable amount is the building, which has a fair value less costs to sell of $46,000. Do not round intermediate calculations of any loss allocation and round the final answer to the nearest dollar.

c. Assume that Green Thumb prepares financial statements under ASPE instead, and that the lawn maintenance division is an asset group. Determine if the asset group is impaired and prepare the journal entry, if any, to record the impairment at December 31, 2020, assuming that none of the individual assets in the division has a determinable recoverable amount.

E11.22 (LO 6) **(Impairment—Cost Recovery and Rational Entity Models)** The information that follows relates to equipment owned by Gaurav Limited at December 31, 2020:

Cost	$10,000,000
Accumulated depreciation to date	2,000,000
Expected future net cash flows (undiscounted)	7,000,000
Expected future net cash flows (discounted, value in use)	6,350,000
Fair value	6,200,000
Costs to sell (costs of disposal)	50,000

Assume that Gaurav will continue to use this asset in the future. As at December 31, 2020, the equipment has a remaining useful life of four years. Gaurav uses the straight-line method of depreciation.

Instructions

a. Assume that Gaurav is a private company that follows ASPE.

   1. Prepare the journal entry at December 31, 2020, to record asset impairment, if any.

   2. Prepare the journal entry to record depreciation expense for 2021.

   3. The equipment's fair value at December 31, 2021 is $6.5 million. Prepare the journal entry, if any, to record the increase in fair value.

b. Repeat the requirements in part (a) above assuming that Gaurav is a public company that follows IFRS.

c. Referring to the qualitative characteristics identified in the conceptual framework for financial reporting (discussed in Chapter 2), discuss the differences between the cost recovery impairment model and the rational entity impairment model. Which method is preferred?

E11.23 (LO 6, 7, 8) **(Impairment—Cost Recovery and Rational Entity Models)** Assume the same information as in E11.22, except that at December 31, 2020, Gaurav discontinues use of the equipment and intends to dispose of it in the coming year by selling it to a competitor. It is expected that the costs of disposal will total $50,000.

Instructions

a. Assume that Gaurav is a private company that follows ASPE.

   1. Prepare the journal entry at December 31, 2020, to record asset impairment, if any.

   2. Prepare the journal entry to record depreciation expense for 2021.

   3. Assume that the asset was not sold by December 31, 2021. The equipment's fair value (and recoverable amount) on this date is $6.5 million. Prepare the journal entry, if any, to record the increase in fair value. It is expected that the costs of disposal will total $50,000.

   4. Identify where, and at what amount, the asset will be reported on the December 31, 2021 statement of financial position.

b. Repeat the requirements in part (a) above assuming that Gaurav is a public company that follows IFRS, and that the asset meets all criteria for classification as an asset held for sale.

E11.24 (LO 2, 3, 7) **(Depreciation Calculation—Replacement, Trade-in)** Onkar Corporation bought a machine on June 1, 2016, for $31,800, f.o.b. the place of manufacture. Freight costs were $300, and $500 was spent to install it. The machine's useful life was estimated at 10 years, with a residual value of $1,900, while the machine's physical life was estimated at 11 years, with no residual value.

On June 1, 2017, a part that was designed to reduce the machine's operating costs was added to the machine for a cost of $1,980. On June 1, 2020, the company bought a new machine with greater capacity for a cost of $35,000, delivered. A trade-in value was received on the old machine equal to its fair value of $19,000. The cost of removing the old machine from the plant was $75, and the cost of installing the new machine was $1,300. It was estimated that the new machine would have a useful life of 10 years, with a residual value of $4,000.

Instructions

a. Assuming that depreciation is calculated on the straight-line basis, determine (1) the amount of any gain or loss on the disposal of the first machine on June 1, 2020, and (2) the amount of depreciation that should be provided during the company's current fiscal year, which begins on June 1, 2020. The financial statements are prepared under IFRS.

b. How would your answers in part (a) change when assuming the financial statements were prepared under ASPE?

E11.25 (LO 3, 5, 7) **(Depreciation Calculations—Revaluation Model)** Jamoka Corporation is a public company that manufactures farm implements, such as tractors, combines, and wagons. Jamoka uses the revaluation model per IAS 16, and records asset revaluations using the elimination method. (This means the balance in the accumulated depreciation account is eliminated against the asset account just prior to revaluation of the asset to fair value.) A piece of manufacturing equipment included in the property, plant, and equipment section on Jamoka's statement of financial position was purchased on December 31, 2019, for a cost of $100,000. The equipment was expected to have a remaining useful life of five years, with benefits being received evenly over the five years. Residual value of the equipment was estimated to be $10,000.

Consider the following two situations:

Situation 1: At December 31, 2020, no formal revaluation is performed, as management determines that the carrying amount of the property, plant, and equipment is not materially different from its fair value.

Situation 2: At December 31, 2020, a formal revaluation is performed and the independent appraisers assess the equipment's fair value to be $89,000. During the revaluation process, it is determined that the remaining useful life of the equipment is four years, with a residual value of $11,000.

At December 31, 2021, no formal revaluation is performed, as management determines that the carrying amount of the property, plant, and equipment is not materially different from its fair value. The equipment is sold on March 31, 2022, for $62,000.

Instructions

a. Prepare any journal entries required under situation 1 described above for: (1) the fiscal year ended December 31, 2020; (2) the fiscal year ended December 31, 2021; and (3) the disposal of the equipment on March 31, 2022.

b. Prepare any journal entries required under situation 2 described above for: (1) the fiscal year ended December 31, 2020; (2) the fiscal year ended December 31, 2021; and (3) the disposal of the equipment on March 31, 2022.

c. Assume that Jamoka uses the proportional method to record asset revaluations under the revaluation model. Do not round intermediate calculations in the asset revaluations and round final answers to the nearest dollar. Prepare any journal entries required under situation 2 described above for: (1) the fiscal year ended December 31, 2020; (2) the fiscal year ended December 31, 2021; and (3) the disposal of the equipment on March 31, 2022.

d. What is the equivalent standard under ASPE?

E11.26 (LO 7) **(Entries for Disposition of Assets)** Consider the following independent situations for Kwok Corporation. Kwok applies ASPE.

Situation 1: Kwok purchased equipment in 2013 for $120,000 and estimated a $12,000 residual value at the end of the equipment's 10-year useful life. At December 31, 2019, there was $75,600 in the Accumulated Depreciation account for this equipment using the straight-line method of depreciation. On March 31, 2020, the equipment was sold for $28,000.

Situation 2: Kwok sold a piece of machinery for $10,000 on July 31, 2020. The machine originally cost $38,000 on January 1, 2012. It was estimated that the machine would have a useful life of 12 years with a residual value of $2,000, and the straight-line method of depreciation was used.

Situation 3: Kwok sold equipment that had a carrying amount of $3,500 for $5,200. The equipment originally cost $12,000 and it is estimated that it would cost $16,000 to replace the equipment.

Instructions

a. Prepare the appropriate journal entries to record the disposition of the property, plant, and equipment assets, assuming that Kwok's fiscal year end is December 31 and that Kwok only prepares financial statements and adjusts the accounts annually.

b. How would the journal entries in part (a) change if Kwok Corporation applied IFRS?

E11.27 (LO 7) **(Entries for Disposition of Assets)** On December 31, 2019, Grey Inc. owns a machine with a carrying amount of $940,000. The original cost and accumulated depreciation for the machine on this date are as follows:

Machine	$1,300,000
Accumulated depreciation	360,000
	$ 940,000

Depreciation is calculated at $60,000 per year on a straight-line basis.

Instructions

A set of independent situations follows. For each situation, prepare the journal entry for Grey Inc. to record the transaction. Ensure that depreciation entries are recorded to update the machine's carrying amount before its disposal. Do not round intermediate calculations and round final answers to the nearest dollar. Assume that Grey Inc. uses IFRS for financial statement purposes.

a. A fire completely destroyed the machine on August 31, 2020. An insurance settlement of $430,000 was received for this casualty. Assume the settlement was received immediately.

b. On April 1, 2020, Grey sold the machine for $1,040,000 to Dwight Company.

c. On July 31, 2020, the company donated the machine to the Dartmouth City Council. The machine's fair value at the time of the donation was estimated to be $1.1 million.

d. Would the treatment of situations (a) through (c) differ if presented under ASPE instead of IFRS?

E11.28 (LO 7) **(Disposition of Assets)** On April 1, 2020, Lombardi Corp. was awarded $460,000 cash as compensation for the forced sale of its land and building, which were directly in the path of a new highway. The land and building cost $60,000 and $280,000, respectively, when they were acquired. At April 1, 2020, the accumulated depreciation for the building amounted to $165,000. On August 1, 2020, Lombardi purchased a piece of replacement property for cash. The new land cost $160,000 and the new building cost $410,000. The new building is estimated to have a useful life of 20 years, physical life of 30 years, residual value of $230,000, and salvage value of $75,000. Lombardi prepares financial statements in accordance with IFRS.

Instructions

a. Prepare the journal entries to record the transactions on April 1 and August 1, 2020.

b. How would the transactions on April 1 and August 1, 2020, affect the income statement for 2020? Would the effect be different if Lombardi prepared financial statements in accordance with ASPE?

c. Prepare the journal entries required at December 31, 2020, under (1) IFRS and (2) ASPE.

E11.29 (LO 8) **(Ratio Analysis)** The 2020 annual report of Trocchi Inc. contains the following information (in thousands):

	Dec. 31, 2020	Dec. 31, 2019
Total assets	$1,071,348	$ 787,167
Total liabilities	626,178	410,044
Consolidated sales	3,374,463	2,443,592
Net income	66,234	49,062

Instructions

a. **Finance** Calculate the following ratios for Trocchi Inc. for 2020. Round answers to two decimal places.

1. Asset turnover ratio

2. Rate of return on assets

3. Profit margin on sales

b. How can the asset turnover ratio be used to calculate the rate of return on assets?

c. Briefly comment on the results for the ratios calculated in part (a).

*E11.30 (LO 3, 10) **(Depreciation Calculations—Four Methods; Partial Periods)** On August 1, 2020, Iroko Corporation purchased a new machine for its assembly process at a cost of $136,400. The company estimated that the machine would have a trade-in value of $14,200 at the end of its useful life. Its useful life was estimated to be six years and its working hours were estimated to be 18,000 hours. Iroko's year end is December 31. (Round depreciation per unit to three decimal places.) Iroko Corporation prepares its financial statements using IFRS.

Instructions

Calculate the depreciation expense under each of the following:

a. Straight-line method for 2020. Do not round intermediate calculations and round the final answer to the nearest dollar.

b. Activity method for 2020, assuming that machine use was 800 hours. Do not round intermediate calculations and round the per-hour charge to three decimal places.

c. Double-declining-balance method for 2020 and 2021. Round the constant percentage rate to two decimal places and round the final answer to the nearest dollar.

d. **Taxation** Capital cost allowance method for 2020 and 2021 using a CCA rate of 25%. Round the final answer to the nearest dollar.

*E11.31 (LO 10) **(CCA)** During 2020, Laiken Limited sold its only Class 3 asset. At the time of sale, the balance of the undepreciated capital cost for this class was $37,450. The asset originally cost $129,500.

Instructions

a. **Taxation** Calculate recaptured CCA, capital gains, and terminal losses, if any, assuming the asset was sold for proceeds of (1) $132,700, (2) $51,000, and (3) $22,000.

b. **Digging Deeper** Assume the tax rates are scheduled to increase for 2020. What strategy could Laiken use to reduce its taxes payable that are due to the recapture on the disposal of the asset?

*E11.32 **(LO 10)** **(Book versus Tax Depreciation)** Barnett Inc. purchased computer equipment on March 1, 2020, for $31,000. The computer equipment has a useful life of five years and a residual value of $1,000. Barnett uses a double-declining-balance method of depreciation for this type of capital asset. For tax purposes, the computer is assigned to Class 10 with a 30% rate.

Instructions

a. Prepare a schedule of depreciation covering 2020, 2021, and 2022 for financial reporting purposes for the new computer equipment purchased. The company follows a policy of taking a full year's depreciation in the year of purchase and none in the year of disposal. Round all amounts to the nearest dollar.

b. **Taxation** Prepare a schedule of CCA and undepreciated capital cost (UCC) for this asset covering 2020, 2021, and 2022, assuming it is the only Class 10 asset owned by Barnett. Round all amounts to the nearest dollar.

c. How much depreciation is deducted over the three-year period on the financial statements? In determining taxable income? What is the carrying amount of the computer equipment on the December 31, 2022 SFP? What is the tax value of the computer equipment at December 31, 2022?

d. How would the calculation of CCA, in part (b), change for 2020–2022 based on the new CCA rules implemented in late 2018 (see footnote 20) assuming this is "eligible property"?

Problems

P11.1 Phoenix Corp. purchased Machine no. 201 on May 1, 2020. The following information relating to Machine no. 201 was gathered at the end of May:

Price	$85,000
Credit terms	2/10, n/30
Freight costs	$800
Preparation and installation costs	$3,800
Labour costs during regular production operations	$10,500

It was expected that the machine could be used for 10 years, after which the residual value would be zero. However, Phoenix intends to use the machine for only eight years and expects to then be able to sell it for $1,500. The invoice for Machine no. 201 was paid on May 5, 2020. Phoenix has a December 31 year end. Depreciation expense should be calculated to the nearest half month. Phoenix follows IFRS for financial statement purposes.

Instructions

a. Calculate the depreciation expense for the years indicated using the following methods. (Do not round intermediate calculations but round final amounts to the nearest dollar.)

1. Straight-line method for the fiscal years ended December 31, 2020 and 2021

2. Double-declining-balance method for the fiscal years ended December 31, 2020 and 2021

*b. **Taxation** Calculate the capital cost allowance for the 2020 and 2021 tax returns, assuming a CCA class with a rate of 25%. How would the calculation change for 2020 and 2021 based on the new CCA rules implemented in late 2018 (see footnote 20) assuming this is "eligible property"?

c. **Digging Deeper** The president of Phoenix tells you that, because the company is new, she expects it will be several years before production and sales reach optimum levels. She asks you, an accounting policy advisor, to recommend a depreciation method that will allocate less of the company's depreciation expense to the early years and more to later years of the assets' lives. Which method would you recommend? Explain.

d. In your answer to part (c) above, how would cash flows to the new company be affected by the choice of depreciation method? How would current and potential creditors interpret the choice of depreciation method?

e. Assume that Phoenix selects the double-declining-balance method of depreciation. In 2022, demand for the product produced by the machine decreases sharply, due to the launch of a new and better competing product on the market. On August 15, 2022, the management of Phoenix meets and decides to discontinue manufacturing the product. On September 15, 2022, a formal plan to sell the machine is authorized. On this date, the machine meets all criteria for classification as held for sale, and the machine's fair value less costs to sell is $65,500. Calculate the depreciation expense for 2022.

P11.2 Alladin Company purchased a large piece of equipment on October 1, 2020. The following information relating to the equipment was gathered at the end of October:

Price	$60,000
Credit terms	2/10, n/30
Engineering costs	$4,800
Maintenance costs during regular production operations	$8,500

It is expected that the equipment could be used for 12 years, after which the salvage value would be zero. Alladin intends to use the equipment for only 10 years, however, after which it expects to be able to sell it for $3,100. The equipment was delivered on October 1 and the invoice for the equipment was paid on October 9, 2020. Alladin uses the calendar year to prepare financial statements. Alladin follows IFRS for financial statement purposes.

Instructions

a. Calculate the depreciation expense for the years indicated using the following methods. (Do not round intermediate calculations but round final amounts to the nearest dollar.)

1. Straight-line method for 2020

2. Sum-of-the-years'-digits method for 2021

3. Double-declining-balance method for 2020

b. The CEO of Alladin tells you that the company wants a stable level of income, because it plans to expand in the future and does not want to appear overly risky to potential lenders. He asks you, the company's newly hired CPA, to recommend a depreciation method that will best achieve this goal. You know that, because the equipment is new, it should have low repair and maintenance costs for the next few years. However, the repair and maintenance costs are likely to increase steadily during years 3 to 10 of the life of the equipment. Which method would you recommend? Explain.

P11.3 On June 15, 2017, a second-hand machine was purchased for $77,000. Before being put into service, the equipment was overhauled at a cost of $5,200, and additional costs of $400 for direct material and $800 for direct labour were paid in fine-tuning the controls. The machine has an estimated residual value of $5,000 at the end of its five-year useful life. The machine is expected to operate for 100,000 hours before it will be replaced and is expected to produce 1.2 million units in this time. Operating data for the next six fiscal years are provided below. The company has an October 31 fiscal year end.

Year	Hours of Operation	Units Produced
2017	10,000	110,000
2018	20,000	270,000
2019	20,000	264,000
2020	20,000	310,000
2021	18,000	134,000
2022	12,000	112,000

Instructions

a. Calculate the depreciation charges for each fiscal year under each of the following depreciation methods. Where necessary, round depreciation rate per unit to four decimal places. Round final amounts to the nearest dollar.

1. Straight-line method. Pro-rate June 2017 and 2022 to half a month.

2. Activity method: based on output

3. Activity method: based on input

4. Double-declining-balance method. Pro-rate June 2017 to half a month.

*5. **Taxation** CCA, Class 8, 20%

b. What is the machine's carrying amount on the October 31, 2020 statement of financial position under the first four methods above?

c. **Digging Deeper** Compare your answers in part (b) with the asset's tax value at the same date.

d. Which method would the company's management prefer in order to minimize taxes in 2017?

e. What happens if the actual hours of operation or units produced do not correspond to the numbers that were estimated in setting the rate?

P11.4 Comco Tool Corp. records depreciation annually at the end of the year. Its policy is to take a full year's depreciation on all assets that are used throughout the year and depreciation for half a year on all machines that are acquired or disposed of during the year. The depreciation rate for the machinery is 10%, applied on a straight-line basis, with no estimated scrap or residual value.

The balance of the Machinery account at the beginning of 2020 was $172,300; the Accumulated Depreciation on Machinery account had a balance of $72,900. The machinery accounts were affected by the following transactions that occurred in 2020:

Jan. 15	Machine no. 38, which cost $9,600 when it was acquired on June 3, 2013, was retired and sold as scrap metal for $600.
Feb. 27	Machine no. 81 was purchased. The fair value of this machine was $12,500. It replaced two machines, nos. 12 and 27, which were traded in on the new machine. Machine no. 12 was acquired on February 4, 2008, at a cost of $5,500 and was still carried in the accounts, although it was fully depreciated and not in use. Machine no. 27 was acquired on June 11, 2013, at a cost of $8,200. In addition to these two used machines, Comco paid $9,000 in cash.
Apr. 7	Machine no. 54 was equipped with electric controls at a cost of $940. This machine, originally equipped with simple hand controls, was purchased on December 11, 2016, for $1,800. The new electric controls can be attached to any one of several machines in the shop.
12	Machine no. 24 was repaired at a cost of $720 after a fire caused by a short circuit in the wiring burned out the motor and damaged certain essential parts.
July 22	Machines 25, 26, and 41 were sold for $3,100 cash. The purchase dates and cost of these machines were as follows:

No. 25	May 8, 2012	$4,000
No. 26	May 8, 2012	3,200
No. 41	June 1, 2014	2,800

Instructions

a. Record each transaction in general journal form.

b. Calculate and record depreciation for the year. None of the machines currently included in the balance of the account was acquired before January 1, 2012.

c. **Digging Deeper** As an investor of Comco Tool Corp., would you view regular gains on the disposition of equipment favourably? Explain.

P11.5 On January 1, 2018, Dayan Corporation, a small manufacturer of machine tools, acquired new industrial equipment for $1.1 million. The new equipment had a useful life of five years and the residual value was estimated to be $50,000. Dayan estimates that the new equipment can produce 12,000 machine tools in its first year. It estimates that production will decline by 1,000 units per year over the equipment's remaining useful life.

The following depreciation methods may be used: (1) straight-line, (2) double-declining-balance, and (3) units of production. For tax purposes, the CCA class is Class 10, 30%.

Instructions

a. Which of the three depreciation methods would maximize net income for financial statement reporting purposes for the three-year period ending December 31, 2020? Prepare a schedule showing the amount of accumulated depreciation at December 31, 2020, under the method you chose.

*b. **Taxation** Over the same three-year period, how much capital cost allowance would have been claimed for tax purposes?

c. **Digging Deeper** Which pattern of depreciation do you feel best reflects the benefits that are provided by the new equipment? Explain briefly.

P11.6 The following data relate to the Plant Assets account of Keller Inc. at December 31, 2019:

	A	B	C	D
Original cost	$46,000	$58,000	$68,000	$73,000
Year purchased	2014	2015	2016	2017
Useful life	10 years	17,000 hours	15 years	10 years
Residual value	$3,900	$4,450	$8,000	$4,700
Depreciation method	straight-line	activity	straight-line	double-declining
Accumulated depreciation through 2019	$21,050	$31,600	$12,000	$26,280

Note: In the year an asset is purchased, Keller does not record any depreciation expense on the asset. In the year an asset is retired or traded in, Keller takes a full year's depreciation on the asset.

The following transactions occurred during 2020:

1. On May 5, Asset A was sold for $16,500 cash. The company's bookkeeper recorded this retirement as follows:

Cash	16,500	
Asset A		16,500

2. On December 31, it was determined that Asset B had been used 3,200 hours during 2020.

3. On December 31, before calculating depreciation expense on Asset C, Keller management decided that Asset C's remaining useful life should be nine years as of year end.

4. On December 31, it was discovered that a piece of equipment purchased in 2019 had been expensed completely in that year. The asset cost $31,000, had a useful life of 10 years when it was acquired, and had no residual value. Management has decided to use the double-declining-balance method for this asset, which can be referred to as "Asset E." Ignore income taxes.

Instructions

a. Prepare any necessary adjusting journal entries required at December 31, 2020, as well as any entries to record depreciation for 2020. Round all amounts to the nearest dollar.

b. **Digging Deeper** As an owner of Keller Inc., do you have any concerns with respect to the bookkeeper's work?

P11.7 Soon after December 31, 2020, the auditor of Morino Manufacturing Corp. asked the company to prepare a depreciation schedule for semi trucks that showed the additions, retirements, depreciation, and other data that affected the company's income in the four-year period from 2017 to 2020, inclusive. The following data were obtained:

Balance of Trucks account, January 1, 2017:	
Truck no. 1, purchased Jan. 1, 2014, cost	$18,000
Truck no. 2, purchased July 1, 2014, cost	22,000
Truck no. 3, purchased Jan. 1, 2016, cost	30,000
Truck no. 4, purchased July 1, 2016, cost	24,000
Balance, January 1, 2017	$94,000

The account Accumulated Depreciation—Trucks had a correct balance of $30,200 on January 1, 2017. (This includes depreciation on the four trucks from the respective dates of purchase, based on a five-year life, with no residual value.) No charges had been made against the account before January 1, 2017.

Transactions between January 1, 2017, and December 31, 2020, and their records in the ledger were as follows:

July 1, 2017	Truck no. 3 was traded for a larger one (no. 5). The agreed purchase price (fair value) was $34,000. Morino Manufacturing paid the automobile dealer $15,000 cash on the transaction. The entry was a debit to Trucks and a credit to Cash, $15,000.
Jan. 1, 2018	Truck no. 1 was sold for $3,500 cash. The entry was a debit to Cash and a credit to Trucks, $3,500.
July 1, 2019	A new truck (no. 6) was acquired for $36,000 cash and was charged at that amount to the Trucks account. (Assume truck no. 2 was not retired.)
July 1, 2019	Truck no. 4 was so badly damaged in an accident that it was sold as scrap for $700 cash. Morino Manufacturing received $2,500 from the insurance company. The entry made by the bookkeeper was a debit to Cash, $3,200; and credits to Gain on Disposal of Trucks, $700; and Trucks, $2,500.

Entries for depreciation were made at the close of each year as follows: 2017, $20,300; 2018, $21,100; 2019, $24,450; and 2020, $27,800.

Instructions

a. **Auditing** For each of the four years, calculate separately the increase or decrease in net income that is due to the company's errors in determining or entering depreciation or in recording transactions affecting the trucks. Ignore income tax considerations.

b. Prepare one compound journal entry as at December 31, 2020, to adjust the Vehicles account (used for trucks) to reflect the correct balances according to your schedule, and assuming that the books have not been closed for 2020.

c. **Digging Deeper** Based on the errors noted, what recommendations, if any, would the auditors likely make? Are there any implications for the auditors' report in detecting errors several years after they have occurred?

P11.8 Linda Monkland established Monkland Ltd. in mid-2019 as the sole shareholder. The accounts on June 30, 2020, the company's year end, just prior to preparing the required adjusting entries, were as follows:

Current assets		$100,000
Capital assets		
Land	$40,000	
Building	90,000	
Equipment	50,000	180,000
Current liabilities		40,000
Long-term bank loan		120,000
Common shares		90,000
Net income prior to depreciation		30,000

All the capital assets were acquired and put into operation in early July 2019. Estimates and usage information on these assets were as follows:

Building: 25-year life, $15,000 residual value
Equipment: Five-year life, 15,000 hours of use, $5,000 residual value. The equipment was used for 1,000 hours in 2019 and 1,400 hours in 2020 up to June 30.

Linda Monkland is now considering which depreciation method or methods would be appropriate. She has narrowed the choices down for the building to the straight-line or double-declining-balance method, and for the equipment to the straight-line, double-declining-balance, or activity method. She has requested your advice and recommendation. In discussions with her, the following concerns were raised:

1. The company acquires goods from suppliers with terms of 2/10, n/30. The suppliers have indicated that these terms will continue as long as the current ratio does not fall below 2 to 1. If the ratio falls lower, no purchase discounts will be given.

2. The bank will continue the loan from year to year as long as the ratio of long-term debt to total assets does not exceed 46%.

3. **Ethics** Linda Monkland has contracted with the company's manager to pay him a bonus equal to 50% of any net income in excess of $14,000. She prefers to minimize or pay no bonus as long as conditions of agreements with suppliers and the bank can be met.

4. In order to provide a strong signal to attract potential investors to join her in the company, Ms. Monkland believes that a rate of return on total assets of at least 5% must be achieved.

Instructions

a. Prepare a report for Linda Monkland that (1) presents tables, (2) analyzes the situation, (3) provides a recommendation on which method or methods should be used, and (4) justifies your recommendation by considering her concerns and the requirement that the method(s) used be considered generally acceptable accounting principles. Round the ratio and percentage answers to one decimal place.

b. **Digging Deeper** What other factors should you discuss with Ms. Monkland to help her in choosing appropriate depreciation methods for her business?

c. Do any ethical issues arise if a depreciation method is chosen in order to manipulate the financial results in a way that will satisfy the constraints listed above? Explain.

P11.9 On April 30, 2020, Oceanarium Corporation ordered a new passenger ship, which was delivered to the designated cruise port and available for use as of June 30, 2020. Overall, the cost of the ship was $97 million, with an estimated useful life of 12 years and residual value of $30 million. Oceanarium expects that the new ship, as a whole, will provide its greatest economic benefits in its early years of operation. After further research and discussion with management, it is determined that the ship consists of major parts with differing useful lives, residual values, and patterns of providing economic benefits:

Part	Cost	Useful life	Residual value	Pattern of benefits	Total output (nautical miles)
Engines (6)	$975,000 per engine	8 years	$120,000 per engine	Varies with activity	7.0 million
Hull	$3,350,000	10 years	$502,000	Highest in early years	7.8 million
Body	$87.8 million	15 years	$15.5 million	Evenly over life of body	12.6 million

The ship's first voyage took place on August 1, 2020. The ship sailed a total of 328,000 nautical miles in 2020. Oceanarium prepares financial statements in accordance with IFRS.

Instructions

a. Identify the factors to consider in determining how to account for the purchase and depreciation of the ship.

b. Prepare the journal entry to record the purchase of the ship, assuming that Oceanarium paid cash for the purchase.

c. Prepare the journal entry(ies) to record depreciation expense for 2020. Do not round intermediate calculations where the units of production method is used but round final amounts to the nearest dollar in all methods.

d. **Digging Deeper** Explain any differences in part (a) if Oceanarium prepares financial statements in accordance with ASPE instead of IFRS.

e. Oceanarium Corporation's banker has requested financial statements prepared under IFRS to determine Oceanarium's ability to repay a long-term loan granted in 2019. What is the benefit to the banker of having each component of the ship depreciated separately?

P11.10 On January 1, 2019, Locke Company, a small machine-tool manufacturer, acquired a piece of new industrial equipment for $1,260,000. The new equipment had a useful life of five years, and the salvage value was estimated to be $60,000. Locke estimates that the new equipment can produce 12,000 machine tools in its first year. It estimates that production will decline by 1,000 units per year over the remaining useful life of the equipment.

The following depreciation methods may be used: (1) straight-line, (2) double-declining-balance, (3) sum-of-the-years'-digits, and (4) units of output.

Instructions

a. Which depreciation method would maximize net income for financial statement reporting for the three-year period ending December 31, 2021? Prepare a schedule showing the amount of accumulated depreciation at December 31, 2021, under each method to support the method selected. Do not round intermediate calculations but round final amounts to the nearest dollar. Ignore present value, income tax, and deferred income tax considerations.

b. Which depreciation method would minimize net income for the three-year period ending December 31, 2021? Determine the amount of accumulated depreciation at December 31, 2021. Ignore present value considerations.

P11.11 Khamsah Mining Ltd. is a small private company that purchased a tract of land for $720,000. After incurring exploration costs of $83,000, the company estimated that the tract would yield 120,000 tonnes of ore with enough mineral content to make mining and processing profitable. It is further estimated that 6,000 tonnes of ore will be mined in the first and last years and 12,000 tonnes every year in between. The land is expected to have a residual value of $30,000.

The company built necessary bunkhouses and sheds on the site at a cost of $36,000. It estimated that these structures would have a physical life of 15 years but, because they must be dismantled if they are to be moved, they have no residual value. The company does not intend to use the buildings elsewhere. Mining machinery installed at the mine was purchased second-hand at a cost of $60,000. This machinery cost the former owner $150,000 and was 50% depreciated when it was purchased. Khamsah Mining estimated that about half of this machinery would still be useful when the present mineral resources are exhausted, but that dismantling and removing it would cost about as much as it is worth at that time. The company does not intend to use the machinery elsewhere. The remaining machinery is expected to last until about half of the estimated mineral ore has been removed and will then be worthless. Cost is to be allocated equally between these two classes of machinery.

Khamsah also spent another $126,400 in opening up the mine so that the ore could be extracted and removed for shipping. The company estimates that the site reclamation and restoration costs that it is responsible for by contract when the mine is depleted have a present value of $53,600. Khamsah follows a policy of expensing exploration costs and capitalizing development costs.

Instructions

a. As chief accountant for the company, you are to prepare a schedule that shows the estimated depletion and depreciation costs for each year of the mine's expected life. Round per-tonne calculations to two decimal places and final amounts to the nearest dollar.

b. Prepare the journal entry(ies) to record the transactions for the acquisition of the mining property and related assets during the first year. Also prepare entries to record depreciation and depletion for the first year. Assume that actual production was 5,000 tonnes. Nothing occurred during the year to cause the company engineers to change their estimates of either the mineral resources or the life of the structures and equipment.

c. Assume that 4,500 tonnes of product were processed and sold during the first year of the mine's expected life. Identify all costs mentioned above that will be included in the first-year income statement of Khamsah Mining Ltd.

d. **Auditing** As the auditor of Khamsah Mining Ltd., how would you assess the reasonability of the asset retirement obligations established by the client?

P11.12 Conan Logging and Lumber Company, a small private company that follows ASPE, owns 3,000 hectares of timberland on the north side of Mount Leno, which was purchased in 2008 at a cost of $550 per hectare. In 2020, Conan began selectively logging this timber tract. In May 2020, Mount Leno erupted, burying Conan's timberland under 15 cm of ash. All of the timber on the Conan tract was downed. In addition, the logging roads, built at a cost of $150,000, were destroyed, as well as the logging equipment, with a carrying amount of $300,000.

At the time of the eruption, Conan had logged 20% of the estimated 500,000 cubic metres of timber. Before the eruption, Conan estimated the land to have a value of $200 per hectare after the timber was harvested. Conan includes the logging roads in the depletion base.

Conan estimates it will take three years to salvage the downed timber at a cost of $700,000. The timber can be sold for pulpwood at an estimated price of $3 per cubic metre. The value of the land is unknown, but must be considered nominal due to future uncertainties.

Instructions

a. Determine the depletion cost per cubic metre for the timber that was harvested before Mount Leno erupted.

b. Prepare the journal entry to record the depletion before the eruption.

c. Determine the amount of the estimated loss before income taxes and show how the losses of roads, machinery, and timber and the timber salvage value should be reported in Conan's financial statements for the year ended December 31, 2020.

d. **Digging Deeper** As an investor in Conan Logging and Lumber Company, do you have any concerns about the eruption of Mount Leno?

P11.13 **Finance** Darby Sporting Goods Inc. has been experiencing growth in the demand for its products over the last several years. The last two Olympic Games greatly increased the popularity of basketball around the world. As a result, a European sports retailing consortium entered into an agreement with Darby's Roundball Division to purchase an increasing number of basketballs and other accessories over the next five years.

To meet the quantity commitments of this agreement, Darby had to increase its manufacturing capacity. A real estate firm found an available factory close to Darby's Roundball manufacturing facility, and Darby agreed to purchase the factory and used machinery from Encino Athletic Equipment Company on October 1, 2019. Renovations were needed to convert the factory for Darby's manufacturing use.

The terms of the agreement required Darby to pay Encino $50,000 when renovations started on January 1, 2020, with the balance to be paid as renovations were completed. The overall purchase price for the factory and machinery was $400,000. The building renovations were contracted to Malone Construction at $100,000. The payments made as renovations progressed during 2020 are shown below. The factory began operating on January 1, 2021.

	Jan. 1	Apr. 1	Oct. 1	Dec. 31
Encino	$50,000	$90,000	$110,000	$150,000
Malone		30,000	30,000	40,000

On January 1, 2020, Darby secured a $500,000 line of credit with a 12% interest rate to finance the purchase cost of the factory and machinery and the renovation costs. Darby drew down on the line of credit to meet the payment schedule shown above; this was Darby's only outstanding loan during 2020.

Bob Sprague, Darby's controller, will capitalize the maximum allowable interest costs for this project, which he has calculated to be $21,000. Darby's policy regarding purchases of this nature is to use the land's appraisal value for book purposes and pro-rate the balance of the purchase price over the remaining items. The factory had originally cost Encino $300,000 and had a carrying amount of $50,000, while the machinery originally cost $125,000 and had a carrying amount of $40,000 on the date of sale. The land was recorded on Encino's books at $40,000. An appraisal, conducted by independent appraisers at the time of acquisition, valued the land at $290,000, the factory at $105,000, and the machinery at $45,000.

Angie Justice, chief engineer, estimated that the renovated factory would be used for 15 years, with an estimated residual value of $30,000. Justice estimated that the productive machinery would have a remaining useful life of five years and a residual value of $3,000. Darby's depreciation policy specifies the 200% declining-balance method for machinery and the 150% declining-balance method for the factory. Half a year's depreciation is taken in the year the factory is placed in service and half a year's depreciation is allowed when the property is disposed of or retired.

Instructions

a. Determine the amounts to be recorded on the books of Darby Sporting Goods Inc. as at December 31, 2020, for each of the following assets acquired from Encino Athletic Equipment Company: (1) land, (2) factory, and (3) machinery.

b. Calculate Darby Sporting Goods Inc.'s 2021 depreciation expense, for book purposes, for each of the assets acquired from Encino Athletic Equipment Company.

c. **Digging Deeper** Discuss the arguments for and against the capitalization of interest costs. Why would the treatment of interest costs matter to a shareholder of a public company, for instance?

P11.14 **Finance** Roland Corporation uses special strapping equipment in its packaging business. The equipment was purchased in January 2019 for $10 million and had an estimated useful life of eight years with no residual value. In early April 2020, a part costing $875,000 and designed to increase the machinery's efficiency was added. The machine's estimated useful life did not change with this addition. By December 31, 2020, new technology had been introduced that would speed up the obsolescence of Roland's equipment. Roland's controller estimates that expected undiscounted future net cash flows on the equipment would be $6.3 million, and that expected discounted future net cash flows on the equipment would be $5.8 million. Fair value of the equipment at December 31, 2020, was estimated to be $5.6 million. Roland intends to continue using the equipment, but estimates that its remaining useful life is now four years. Roland uses straight-line depreciation. Assume that Roland is a private company that follows ASPE.

Instructions

a. Prepare the journal entry to record asset impairment at December 31, 2020, if any.

b. Fair value of the equipment at December 31, 2021, is estimated to be $5.9 million. Prepare any journal entries for the equipment at December 31, 2021.

c. Repeat part (b), assuming that on December 31, 2021, Roland's management decides to dispose of the equipment. As at December 31, 2021, the asset is still in use and not ready for sale in its current state. In February 2022, Roland's management will meet to outline an active program to find a buyer.

d. Repeat part (b), assuming that the equipment is designated as "held for sale" as of January 1, 2021, and that the equipment was not in use in 2021 but was still held by Roland on December 31, 2021.

e. For each situation in parts (b), (c), and (d), indicate where the equipment will be reported on the December 31, 2021 balance sheet.

f. Repeat parts (a) and (b), assuming instead that Roland is a public company that prepares financial statements in accordance with IFRS.

g. **Digging Deeper** From the perspective of a financial statement user, discuss the importance of frequent impairment testing in producing relevant and faithfully representative financial statements. Do IFRS and ASPE differ in the required frequency? Explain briefly.

P11.15 The following is a schedule of property dispositions for Shangari Corp.:

SCHEDULE OF PROPERTY DISPOSITIONS

	Cost	Accumulated Depreciation	Cash Proceeds	Fair Market Value	Nature of Disposition
Land	$40,000	—	$31,000	$31,000	Expropriation
Building	15,000	—	3,600	—	Demolition
Warehouse	70,000	$16,000	74,000	74,000	Destruction by fire
Machine	8,000	2,800	900	7,200	Trade-in
Furniture	10,000	7,850	—	3,100	Contribution
Vehicle	9,000	3,460	2,960	2,960	Sale

The following additional information is available:

Land

On February 15, land that was being held mainly as an investment was expropriated by the city. On March 31, another parcel of unimproved land to be held as an investment was purchased at a cost of $35,000.

Building

On April 2, land and a building were purchased at a total cost of $75,000, of which 20% was allocated to the building on the corporate books. The real estate was acquired with the intention of demolishing the building, which was done in November. Cash proceeds that were received in November were the net proceeds from the building demolition.

Warehouse

On June 30, the warehouse was destroyed by fire. The warehouse had been purchased on January 2, 2017, and accumulated depreciation of $16,000 had been properly recorded to the date of the fire. On December 27, the insurance proceeds and other funds were used to purchase a replacement warehouse at a cost of $90,000.

Machine

On December 26, the machine was exchanged for another machine having a fair market value of $6,300. Cash of $900 was also received as part of the deal. The transaction has commercial substance.

Furniture

On August 15, furniture was contributed to a registered charitable organization. No other contributions were made or pledged during the year.

Vehicle

On November 3, the vehicle was sold to Jared Dutoit, a shareholder.

Instructions

a. Prepare the entries to record the transactions and indicate how these items would be reported on the income statement of Shangari Corp. Assume that Shangari follows ASPE, but also indicate if the reporting would be treated differently under IFRS.

b. **Digging Deeper** As a current creditor of Shangari Corp., if you noted that there were several dispositions of property, plant, and equipment, would you have any concerns or questions for management?

(Adapted from AICPA)

P11.16 Sung Corporation, a manufacturer of steel products, began operations on October 1, 2019. Sung's accounting department has begun to prepare the capital asset and depreciation schedule that follows. You have been asked to assist in completing this schedule. In addition to determining that the data already on the schedule are correct, you have obtained the following information from the company's records and personnel:

1. Depreciation is calculated from the first day of the month of acquisition to the first day of the month of disposition.

2. Land A and Building A were acquired together for $820,000. At the time of acquisition, the land had an appraised value of $90,000 and the building had an appraised value of $810,000.

3. Land B was acquired on October 2, 2019, in exchange for 2,500 newly issued common shares. At the date of acquisition, the shares had a fair value of $30 each. During October 2019, Sung paid $16,000 to demolish an existing building on this land so that it could construct a new building.

4. Construction of Building B on the newly acquired land began on October 1, 2020. By September 30, 2021, Sung had paid $320,000 of the estimated total construction costs of $450,000. It is estimated that the building will be completed and occupied by July 2022.

5. Certain equipment was donated to the corporation by a local university. An independent appraisal of the equipment when it was donated estimated its fair value at $30,000 and the residual value at $3,000.

6. Machine A's total cost of $164,900 includes an installation expense of $600 and normal repairs and maintenance of $14,900. Its residual value is estimated at $6,000. Machine A was sold on February 1, 2021.

7. On October 1, 2020, Machine B was acquired with a down payment of $5,740 and the remaining payments to be made in 11 annual instalments of $6,000 each, beginning October 1, 2020. The prevailing interest rate was 8%. The following data were determined from present-value tables and are rounded:

PV of $1 at 8%		PV of an Ordinary Annuity of $1 at 8%	
10 years	0.463	10 years	6.710
11 years	0.429	11 years	7.139
15 years	0.315	15 years	8.559

Sung Corporation
Capital Asset and Depreciation Schedule
For Fiscal Years Ended September 30, 2020, and September 30, 2021

Assets	Acquisition Date	Cost	Residual Value	Depreciation Method	Estimated Life in Years	Depreciation Expense, Year Ended September 30 2020	Depreciation Expense, Year Ended September 30 2021
Land A	Oct. 1, 2019	$ (1)	N/A	N/A	N/A	N/A	N/A
Building A	Oct. 1, 2019	(2)	$40,000	Straight-line	(3)	$17,450	(4)
Land B	Oct. 2, 2019	(5)	N/A	N/A	N/A	N/A	N/A
Building B	Under construction	$320,000 to date	—	Straight-line	30	—	(6)
Donated Equipment	Oct. 2, 2019	(7)	3,000	150% declining-balance	10	(8)	(9)
Machine A	Oct. 2, 2019	(10)	6,000	Double-declining-balance	8	(11)	(12)
Machine B	Oct. 1, 2020	(13)	—	Straight-line	20	—	(14)

N/A = Not applicable

Instructions

a. For each numbered item in the schedule, give the correct amount. Round each answer to the nearest dollar.

b. **Digging Deeper** When would it be appropriate for management to use different depreciation policies as they have done for Machines A and B?

P11.17 Consider the following independent situations.

Situation 1: Ducharme Corporation purchased electrical equipment at a cost of $12,400 on June 2, 2017. From 2017 through 2020, the equipment was depreciated on a straight-line basis, under the assumption that it would have a 10-year useful life and a $2,400 residual value. After more experience and before recording 2021's depreciation, Ducharme revised its estimate of the machine's useful life downward from a total of 10 years to 8 years, and revised the estimated residual value to $2,000.

On April 29, 2022, after recording part of a year's depreciation for 2022, the company traded in the equipment on a newer model, and received a $4,000 trade-in allowance, even though the equipment's fair value was only $2,800. The new asset had a list price of $15,300 and the supplier accepted $11,300 cash for the balance. The new equipment was depreciated on a straight-line basis, assuming a seven-year useful life and a $1,300 residual value.

Situation 2: Malcolm Limited acquired a truck to deliver and install its specialized products at the customer's site. The vehicle's list price was $45,000, but customization added another $10,000 in costs. Malcolm took delivery of the truck on September 30, 2020, with a down payment of $5,000, signing a four-year, 8% note for the remainder, payable in equal payments of $14,496 beginning September 30, 2021.

Malcolm expected the truck to be usable for 500 deliveries and installations. After that, the product's technology would have changed and made the vehicle obsolete. In late July 2023, the truck was destroyed when a concrete garage collapsed. Malcolm used the truck for 45 deliveries in 2020, 125 in 2021, 134 in 2022, and 79 in 2023. The company received a cheque for $12,000 from the insurance company and paid what remained on the note.

Situation 3: A group of new machines was purchased on February 17, 2021, under a royalty agreement with the following terms: The purchaser, Keller Corp., is to pay a royalty of $1 to the machinery supplier for each unit of product that is produced by the machines each year. The machines are expected to produce 200,000 units over their useful lives. The machines' invoice price was $75,000, freight costs were $2,000, unloading charges were $1,500, and royalty payments for 2021 were $13,000. Keller uses the units of production method to depreciate its machinery.

Situation 4: On March 31, 2017, Wayside Corporation purchased a new piece of manufacturing equipment for $323,000. At that time, the estimated useful life of the equipment was five years, with a residual value of $65,000. On August 1, 2020, due to increased competition causing a decreased selling price for its product, Wayside decided to discontinue the product. By December 31, 2020, there was a formal plan in place to sell the equipment, and the equipment qualified for classification as held for sale. At December 31, 2020, the equipment's fair value less costs to sell was $52,000. Due to matters beyond Wayside's control, a potential sale of the equipment fell through in 2021, although consumer confidence in Wayside's product increased significantly because of reported defects in its competitors' products. The equipment remained classified as held for sale at December 31, 2021, when the equipment's fair value less costs to sell increased to $145,000. Wayside uses the straight-line method to depreciate its equipment.

Instructions

a. For situation 1, determine the amount of depreciation expense reported by Ducharme for each fiscal year for the years ending December 31, 2017 to December 31, 2022.

b. For situation 2, prepare all entries that are needed to record the events and activities related to the truck, the note, and its interest, including the depreciation expense on the truck each year. Assume that Malcolm uses an activity approach to depreciate the truck, and bases it on deliveries. Round all amounts to the nearest dollar.

c. For situation 3, prepare journal entries to record the purchase of the new machines, the related depreciation for 2021, and the royalty payment. Round the per-unit charge to the nearest cent.

d. For situation 4, prepare all journal entries required for the years ending December 31, 2020, and December 31, 2021.

e. **Digging Deeper** You are an employee of Wayside Corporation receiving a bonus based on income from continuing operations. If a loss results from the equipment classified as held for sale, how will you be affected under IFRS?

*P11.18 **Finance** Munro Limited reports the following information in its tax files covering the five-year period from 2018 to 2022. All assets are Class 10 with a 30% maximum CCA, and no capital assets had been acquired before 2018.

2018	Purchased assets A, B, and C for $20,000, $8,000, and $1,200, respectively.
2019	Sold asset B for $7,000; bought asset D for $4,800.
2020	Purchased asset E for $5,000; received an investment tax credit of $1,000.
2021	Sold asset A for $9,900 and asset C for $1,800.
2022	Asset D was destroyed by fire and was uninsured; asset E was sold to an employee for $500.

Instructions

a. Prepare a capital cost allowance schedule for Class 10 assets covering the 2018 to 2022 period.

b. Identify any capital gains, terminal losses, or recapture of CCA and indicate how each would be taxed.

c. **Digging Deeper** You have been hired as the tax advisor of Munro Limited. Munro is anticipating low income levels, possibly losses, over the next couple of years due to restructuring. However, management anticipates that income levels will be substantially higher than historical levels in the subsequent three to four years. Munro also anticipates buying a number of new assets at the beginning of fiscal 2028, as management had been told that assets must be purchased in the first half of the year to take advantage of the half-year rule. Munro is a private company following ASPE. Provide advice, if any, with respect to the company's CCA policy.

*P11.19 **Taxation** Kitchigami Limited was attracted to the Town of Mornington by the town's municipal industry commission. Mornington donated a plant site to Kitchigami, and the provincial government provided $180,000 toward the cost of the new manufacturing facility. The total cost of plant construction came to $380,000, and it was ready for use in early October 2020. Kitchigami expects the plant to have a useful life of 15 years before it becomes obsolete and is demolished. The company uses the straight-line method of depreciation for buildings and is required to include the plant in Class 6 (10% rate) for tax purposes.

Instructions

a. Prepare the entry(ies) that are required in 2020 to record the payment to the contractor for the building and the receipt of the provincial government assistance. Assume that the company treats the assistance as a reduction of the asset's cost. Also prepare any adjusting entries that are needed at the company's year ends, December 31, 2020 and 2021, and round all amounts to the nearest dollar.

b. Repeat part (a), but assume instead that the company treats the government assistance as a deferred credit.

c. If Kitchigami reports 2021 income of $79,000 before depreciation on the plant and government assistance, what income before tax will the company report assuming part (a) above? Assuming part (b) above?

d. What is the building's tax value at December 31, 2021?

e. **Digging Deeper** Which method of accounting for government assistance would better represent Kitchigami Limited to a lender? Also, which method would result in higher net income?

Integrated Cases

Refer to the Case Primer on the Student Website and in *WileyPLUS* to help you answer these cases.

(*Hint:* If there are issues here that are new, use the conceptual framework to help you support your analysis with solid reasoning.)

IC11.1 **Auditing** ClubLoop Corporation (CL) is a large owner, operator, and developer of golf courses and resorts. The company is privately owned by several wealthy individuals. During the current year, according to the draft financial statements, revenues increased by 7.2% and net operating income increased by 13% to $22.5 million. Net income dropped from $2.9 million to $822,000. The decrease was largely due to two events: a change in accounting policy and costs related to the settlement of a lawsuit.

One of the company's objectives is to always ensure that capital resources are readily available to meet approved capital expenditures and to take advantage of growth opportunities. According to the draft year-end financial statements, the company has current assets of $12 million and current liabilities of $28 million, resulting in a working capital deficit. Included in the current liabilities are long-term debts that are currently due. The company is working with the financial institutions in question to renew or replace these facilities. CL has received unsolicited expressions of interest from several financial institutions concerning these facilities, and management believes that these facilities will be replaced—hopefully before the current financial statements are issued.

The company owns most of the land on which CL's golf courses are developed. Currently, the company follows a rigorous "weed and feed" program in order to keep the grass on the golf courses in top shape. The chemicals in these fertilizers, herbicides, and insecticides are felt by some people in the local community to be toxic to the environment. The company has met with several community groups and has agreed to study the issue further. In a current meeting of the board of directors, the CEO committed the company to spending $1 million to limit any potential damage. As at year end, none of this amount has yet been spent. There is a concern that the community groups are going to launch legal proceedings and the company feels that this move will help CL's position if there ends up being a lawsuit. Part of the money is for landscaping to limit the spread of the sprayed chemicals and part of it is for advertising to promote the company as a good corporate citizen.

The company is currently developing new golf courses. All direct costs related to the acquisition, development, and construction of these properties, including interest and management costs, are capitalized. For one of the new locations, which was just purchased and developed in the current year, the company has run into a problem. After CL spent several million dollars on development, the planned golf course is being blocked by environmental groups. The costs to develop the land have been capitalized as previously mentioned, on the basis that they would be recoverable from future membership revenues. However, the company has now decided to sell the land to a real estate developer.

On July 1, the government tax department issued notices of assessment to the company regarding a dispute over the recognition of revenues. Although the outcome of an appeal of the assessment cannot be determined, the company believes that it will owe $8.7 million if its appeal is unsuccessful.

Instructions

Adopt the role of the company's auditor and prepare an analysis of the financial reporting issues.

IC11.2 Metropolitan Hydro (MH) is a private company that owns and operates all of the province's electricity generation and transmission systems. It is deciding whether it should follow IFRS or ASPE in the upcoming year. The company must choose now and is looking to analyze the impact of following IFRS or ASPE. Each year, MH must prepare and submit audited financial statements to the government.

The company generates and sells electricity to residential and commercial customers. It is committed to the following:

- Identifying and providing innovative solutions that will improve the reliability and efficiency of electrical delivery
- Sustainability (including not only profitability but also environmental sustainability)—in this regard, MH has a publicly available environmental policy against which the company is measured by the government

The company has just finished a new project to install smart meters in all residential houses. The meters allow residents to track usage and power supply and demand. Each meter is very expensive and will likely become technologically obsolete in three years. MH decided to pursue this strategy nonetheless due to its commitment to sustainability. The company wants all customers to think about using electricity wisely and the meters help with this. The company generally requires a security deposit (amounting to the cost of the meter) when a customer signs up to receive electricity or when the meter is first installed. The value of the meter declines over time and after three years it is worthless. If customers cancel their electricity delivery contract early, they get the full amount back once they return their meters. Otherwise, at the end of three years, MH retains the security deposit and has no obligation to return the cash.

MH is rate-regulated. This means that it must ask for government approval whenever it wants to raise the rates that it charges for electricity. Generally, the government allows the company to recover all costs incurred in generating the electricity plus a reasonable profit margin. Therefore, rates are set as being equal to "cost plus reasonable profit margin." This means that, once approved, the company is able to charge revenues equal to all costs incurred plus a reasonable profit. Under ASPE, special "rate-regulated accounting" exists. One of the features of this special accounting is that companies following rate-regulated accounting are able to defer any losses that are incurred on disposition of assets, on the basis that they can recover these losses from future revenues. IFRS does not allow this.

Sometimes MH signs supply contract agreements with other suppliers of electricity to ensure that power supplies to MH customers are not disrupted. Under the terms of these contracts, MH locks in the quantity and price of electricity. However, the contracts do not explicitly include net settlement provisions. Because electricity is a commodity, the contracts may be bought and sold on the regional commodities exchange.

MH is concerned about maintaining a consistent supply of electricity to its customers, since many of its generating stations are getting very old and the incidence of breakdown and generating station closures due to the age of the equipment is increasing. There is no market for these old generating stations (and MH would probably replace the capacity with newer, greener forms of electricity, such as wind or solar). Often the land that these stations are sitting on is polluted with chemicals. Technically, since this pollution occurred many years ago in most cases, there are no laws in place to force cleanup. Currently, the company is doing a voluntary land assessment and remediation program to identify the extent of this pollution. The company expects that it would recover all of the cleanup costs it might incur from future revenues through increased customer rates. However, there is always the chance that future governments might change the ability to build these costs into the rates charged to customers.

Some of the generating stations are located on lands held by First Nations. The company is negotiating to obtain legal title to the lands but understands that it may have to relocate the assets. The assets in question are material.

MH obtains much of its financing through bonds and commercial paper issuances. Therefore, it is important that it retain its good credit ratings. Currently, it has a very good credit rating, awarded by both S&P and Moody's credit rating agencies. This good rating helps keep costs (and therefore customer rates) down. There are debt covenants in the debt agreements that limit the amount of debt as a percentage of total capitalization (total assets). Debt may not exceed 75% of total assets under these covenants. (Currently, the actual debt to total assets ratio is 65%.)

Instructions

Finance   Assume the role of an accounting consultant hired to determine which set of accounting standards to follow. Discuss the financial reporting issues relating to the above. Use the case analysis framework presented in the Case Primer, including an overview, analysis, and recommendations.

Research and Analysis

RA11.1   **Real World Emphasis**   **Brookfield Asset Management Inc.**

Brookfield Asset Management Inc. is a global publicly traded Canadian company. Obtain a copy of Brookfield's financial statements for the year ended December 31, 2017, through SEDAR (www.sedar.com) or on the company's website.

Instructions

Review the notes to the statements and answer the following questions.

a. What business is Brookfield Asset Management Inc. in?

b. Identify the accounting model or method used for the following Brookfield operating segments' property, plant, and equipment assets: renewable power, infrastructure assets, real estate, and private equity (other) assets. Summarize the changes in each of the types of assets in the property, plant, and equipment group, explaining how the balances changed over the 2017 year. How is the company growing?

c. Comment on the extent to which fair values are used in measuring and reporting property, plant, and equipment assets. What methods and types of assumptions has the company used to determine fair values for these assets measured at fair value?

d. Brookfield also reports significant investment properties on its balance sheet as well as sustainable resources. What measurement models are used for these two types of long-term assets? If any are based on fair value, what methods and types of assumptions are made when measuring them?

e. What other methods are available to determine fair value? Which methods are most reliable from a user's perspective? Base your answer on IFRS 13 and what it indicates about fair value measurement to determine what level of fair value measurement the company has used to determine fair values.

RA11.2 **Real World Emphasis** **Finance** **Canadian Tire Corporation, Limited**

Canadian Tire Corporation, Limited is one of Canada's best-known retailers. Obtain a copy of Canadian Tire's financial statements for each of the years ended December 30, 2017, and December 31, 2016, through SEDAR (www.sedar.com) or on the company's website. To answer the following questions, you may also want to consult the 10-year financial review that is supplementary information in the 2016 annual report.

Instructions

a. **Data Analytics** How significant is Canadian Tire's investment in property, plant, and equipment, including any investment property, compared with its total investment in assets? Compare this with sample companies in other industries, such as financial services (AGF Management Limited), real estate management and development (Brookfield Asset Management Inc.), and technology (The Stars Group Inc.). Comment.

b. Calculate Canadian Tire's total asset turnover for fiscal years 2017, 2016, and 2015.

c. Calculate the company's profit margin for the same three years.

d. Calculate the company's return on assets for the same three years by using the ratios calculated in parts (b) and (c) above.

e. Based on your calculations in part (d), suggest ways in which Canadian Tire might increase the return that it earns on its investment in assets.

RA11.3 **Real World Emphasis** **Canadian National Railway Company and Canadian Pacific Railway Limited**

Two well-known company names in the transportation industry in Canada are Canadian National Railway Company and Canadian Pacific Railway Limited. Go to either SEDAR (www.sedar.com) or each company's website to access the financial statements of these companies for their year ended December 31, 2017.

Instructions

a. How significant are the investments made by these companies in property, plant, and equipment? Express the size of these investments as a percentage of total assets.

b. Compare the types of property, plant, and equipment that each company reports.

c. Do the companies follow similar policies in what they capitalize as part of property, plant, and equipment?

d. What methods of depreciation are used by each company?

e. For assets that are similar at both companies, compare their useful lives or rates of depreciation. Are these similar or would applying them result in differences in the reported results for each year? Explain briefly.

RA11.4 **Ethics** **Changes in Depreciation Policies and Impairment Testing**

Nickel Strike Mines is a nickel mining company with mines in northern Ontario, Colombia, and Australia. It is a publicly traded company and follows IFRS, and has historically followed industry practice and used units of production as its depreciation policy for all of its mines. During 2020, the price of nickel declined significantly, even below the costs of production for the Ontario mines. Consequently, the company has had the Ontario mines closed since early January 2020. It has continued to produce in its Colombian and Australian mines. It is now December 2020 and the controller is trying to decide what accounting issues there are related to the Ontario mines. Since it was a very bad year for the company, and investors are expecting the worst, the controller is considering switching to the declining-balance method of depreciation for the Ontario mines only. This would create a significant depreciation charge for 2020, but in the future, the depreciation costs related to the mines would decrease, resulting in higher net income. In addition, since there were no units produced in the Ontario mines for the year, no depreciation is taken. The controller believes that this is wrong, and that some amount of depreciation should be recorded.

Additionally, the controller is also considering taking as large an impairment loss as possible on all the mines. The controller will do this by assuming a very low nickel price, which will cause the recoverable amounts to be below carrying values for all mines. This impairment loss will likely reverse in the following years, since nickel prices are expected to climb dramatically over the next year, as supplies diminish and as demand from Asian countries increases. With the reversal of the impairment in 2021, this would show a significant improvement in the company's net income.

Instructions

You are a Nickel Strike Mines board member and have just heard the controller's comments on these issues. Comment on the controller's suggestions. Include in your discussion how the impairment test would be completed and the assumptions required. Also discuss the note disclosure that would be required related to all of these issues and any ethical issues that may arise.

RA11.5 Depreciation under ASPE and IFRS

Realtor Inc. is a company that owns five large office buildings that are leased out to tenants. Most of the leases are for 10 years or more with renewal clauses for an additional five years. Currently, Realtor Inc. is a private company that follows ASPE. Recently Rita Mendoza was hired as the controller. Ms. Mendoza has suggested to Habib Ganem, the owner and sole shareholder of the company, that the company should consider switching to IFRS. She explained that under ASPE, the buildings are recorded at cost and then depreciated and tested for impairment when events occur that might indicate a decline in value. However, under IFRS, she explained, the buildings could be classified as investment properties and adjusted to fair value every year. In addition, there is no impact on the income statement, since no depreciation is recorded on the investment properties. Finally, Ms. Mendoza stated that there is no impairment testing required for investment properties under IFRS, so there would never be any impairment losses to be recognized.

Mr. Ganem was intrigued with this idea. He had just been looking at the calculation of the bank loan covenants and had found that the company's debt to asset ratio was very close to the maximum that would be allowed. He wanted to take this year's annual financial statement, once completed, to the bank and ask for revisions on the covenants, since he was also looking at the possible purchase of some new properties. He particularly liked the idea of no depreciation having to be recorded on these assets, which would also improve the company's times interest earned ratio (calculated as Earnings before interest and taxes/Interest expense). Mr. Ganem decided to call his banker to discuss this change and get her thoughts.

Instructions

You are the loans officer at the bank. What comments would you make to Mr. Ganem about the controller's suggestions? In particular, explain the impact on the balance sheet and the income statement under both the cost model and the fair value model and the resulting impact on the existing covenants. From a banker's point of view, which method for reporting the investment properties would be most useful? Make a final recommendation to Mr. Ganem.

RA11.6 `Finance`   PP&E—Transition to IFRS

Howeven Inc. is a private company that expects to "go public" and become publicly traded soon. Accordingly, it expects to be adopting IFRS by 2020. It is a manufacturing company with extensive investments in property, plant, and equipment. The company currently has a profit-sharing plan that is based on 30% of earnings after depreciation, but before interest and taxes. There is also a debt to fixed asset ratio covenant that must be maintained for the bank loan.

The controller has been learning about IFRS and has determined that there are three different treatments that the property, plant, and equipment can have upon the transition to IFRS.

1. The first option is to continue using the cost model, as the company has been doing. The company currently uses the straight-line method of depreciation for all of its assets.

2. The second option is for the company, on transition at January 1, 2020, to elect to revalue all of its property, plant, and equipment to fair value. This is a one-time increase in value that is allowed for first-time adopters of IFRS. The company would still use the cost model to depreciate this new value (which becomes the deemed cost) in subsequent years.

3. The third option is to adopt the revaluation model for just the "property and plant" assets. The company would continue to use the cost model for the equipment, as fair market values are not readily available for this type of asset.

The controller has estimated the following numbers at January 1, 2020 (debt is expected to be $1,700 million):

	Remaining Useful Life	Carrying Amount	Estimated Fair Value at Jan. 1, 2020
Property and plant	25 years	$2,500 million	$3,250 million
Equipment	10 years	$1,300 million	$1,400 million

Instructions

You are the Vice-President Finance and must prepare a memo to the board explaining these options. Using the numbers in the table to assist you, discuss the implications of the three options for the balance sheet, income statement, bonuses, and the debt to fixed asset covenant.

RA11.7 [Real World Emphasis] Air France-KLM Group and Air Canada

Air France-KLM Group and Air Canada are both global airline companies. Both companies report under IFRS. Access the financial statements of Air France-KLM for its year ended December 31, 2017, and Air Canada for the same period, from each company's website.

Instructions

a. What amounts are reported on the statements of financial position for capital assets for Air France-KLM and for Air Canada at December 31, 2017? What percentage of total assets does each company invest in these types of assets? What else might be considered in developing and interpreting these ratios?

b. For Air France-KLM: What types of capital assets does the company report? What does it include in costs? Is interest capitalized? What depreciation methods are used by the company? How are residual values estimated for aircraft?

c. For Air Canada: What types of capital assets does the company report? What is included in costs? Is interest capitalized? What depreciation methods are used by Air Canada? How are residual values estimated for aircraft?

d. Compare the above accounting policies for the two companies. Where are there significant differences between them? What is the likely impact of these differences on the balance sheet and net earnings?

e. For Air France-KLM, how are the assets tested for impairment? Were any impairment losses recorded for the year, and if so, how much? What did these relate to? Was there any reversal of impairment losses from previous years?

f. For Air Canada, how have the assets been tested for impairment and were any impairment losses recognized in 2017?

RA11.8 [Ethics] The Ethical Accountant

Lian Tang, HK Corporation's controller, is concerned that net income may be lower this year. He is afraid that upper-level management might recommend cost reductions by laying off accounting staff, himself included. Tang knows that depreciation is a major expense for HK. The company currently uses the same method for financial reporting as it uses for tax purposes—that is, a declining-balance method—and he is thinking of changing to the straight-line method.

Tang does not want to draw attention to the increase in net income that would result from switching depreciation methods. He thinks, "Why don't I just increase the estimated useful lives and the residual values of the property, plant, and equipment? They are only estimates anyway. These changes will decrease depreciation expense and increase income. I may be able to save my job and those of my staff." Tang calls his professional accounting body's "Ethics Hotline" and reaches the Ethical Accountant for advice.

Instructions

Discuss. Make sure that you, as the Ethical Accountant providing advice to Tang, identify the objectives of depreciation, who the stakeholders are in this situation, what disclosures are required, whether any ethical issues are involved, and what Tang should do.

CHAPTER 12

Intangible Assets and Goodwill

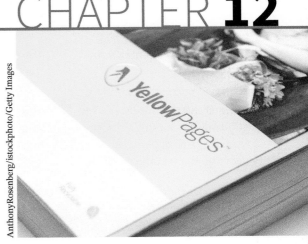

AnthonyRosenberg/istockphoto/Getty Images

Intangible Impairment Is on the Line

The Yellow Pages print directory has been in Canada since 1908, but the phone book's days may be numbered as most Canadians look up businesses online. Yellow Pages Ltd. still prints phone directories, but it has moved into the electronic world with services such as mobile apps to find local restaurants or buy a house. Three quarters of the company's revenues are now digital, but it is struggling to find a successful business model after the company was spun off by Bell Canada in 2002.

In 2017, Yellow Pages Ltd.'s overall revenues dropped by 8.8% from the year before, to $745.9 million, and its print revenues fell by more than 22% from the year before. In January 2018, the company laid off 500 employees, in addition to the 300 positions it cut in October 2015.

The falling value of Yellow Pages is reflected in the company's assessment of the impairment of its goodwill and other intangible assets. In 2016, the company recorded $600 million in impairment of intangible assets and goodwill, and it recorded an impairment loss of another $507 million in 2017, which represented 68% of revenues that year.

IFRS requires goodwill to be tested for impairment annually at the cash-generating unit (CGU) level—the smallest identifiable group of assets that generate cash. "At each reporting date, Yellow Pages Limited determines whether there are any indications that the carrying values of its tangible and intangible assets are impaired. If any such indication exists, the recoverable amount of the asset is estimated in order to determine the extent of the impairment loss, if any," the company says about its accounting policies in the notes to its financial statements.

"As a result of a shortfall in revenues in the Yellow Pages and Other CGUs compared to previous estimates and uncertainty with regards to future long-term trends, the Company revised estimates of future cash flows to reflect recent historical trends as the basis," the company's 2017 annual report states. "In conjunction, the Company recorded an impairment loss of $480 million in the Yellow Pages CGU and an impairment loss of $20 million in a business within the Other CGUs group as the carrying values of these CGUs exceeded their recoverable amounts. The impairment loss was applied to trademarks and non-competition agreements of the Yellow Pages CGU and primarily to goodwill of the Other CGUs."

In 2017, more than half of the impairment writedown, $360.6 million, was for trademarks and domain names. Yellow Pages used to categorize its trademarks as having indefinite lives. But after two consecutive years of impairment losses, and because of uncertainty regarding future cash flows, in 2017 the company reclassified its trademarks as having a finite life, and their useful lives were reduced to 10 years, using straight-line amortization.

Sources: Ross Marowits, The Canadian Press, "Yellow Pages Ltd. Cuts Another 500 Jobs as It Struggles to Survive," CTVNews.ca, January 16, 2018; Yellow Pages Ltd. 2016 and 2017 annual reports; Yellow Pages Ltd. corporate website.

LEARNING OBJECTIVES	CHAPTER OUTLINE	CPA COMPETENCIES
After studying this chapter, you should be able to:	The chapter headings related to the learning objective are:	Competencies addressed by each learning objective are as follows:
1. Understand the importance of goodwill and intangible assets from a business perspective and describe their characteristics.	**The Business Importance and Characteristics of Goodwill and Intangible Assets** • Characteristics of goodwill • Characteristics of intangible assets	**1.1.1, 1.1.2, 1.1.4**
2. Identify and apply the recognition and measurement requirements for purchased intangible assets.	**Recognition and Measurement of Intangible Assets at Acquisition** • Purchased intangibles • Intangibles purchased in a business combination • Prepayments	**1.1.1, 1.1.2, 1.2.1, 1.2.2, 1.2.3**
3. Identify and apply the recognition and measurement requirements for internally developed intangible assets.	**Recognition and Measurement of Internally Developed Intangible Assets** • Identifying research and development phase activities • Accounting for research phase costs • Accounting for development phase costs • Costs included and excluded	**1.1.1, 1.1.2, 1.1.3, 1.2.1, 1.2.2, 1.2.3**
4. Explain how intangible assets are accounted for after initial recognition.	**Recognition and Measurement of Intangible Assets after Acquisition** • Limited-life intangibles • Indefinite-life intangibles	**1.1.1, 1.1.2, 1.2.1, 1.2.2, 1.2.3**
5. Identify and explain the accounting for specific types of intangible assets.	**Specific Intangibles** • Marketing-related intangible assets • Customer-related intangible assets • Artistic-related intangible assets • Contract-based intangible assets • Technology-based intangible assets	**1.1.1, 1.1.2, 1.2.1, 1.2.2**
6. Explain and account for impairment and derecognition of limited-life and indefinite-life intangible assets.	**Impairment and Derecognition** • Impairment of limited-life intangibles • Impairment of indefinite-life intangibles • Derecognition	**1.1.1, 1.1.2, 1.2.1, 1.2.2, 1.2.3**

7. Explain how goodwill is measured and accounted for after acquisition.	**Goodwill—Recognition and Measurement** • Internally generated goodwill • Purchased goodwill • Bargain purchase • Valuation after acquisition	**1.1.1, 1.1.2, 1.2.1, 1.2.2**
8. Explain and account for impairment of goodwill.	**Goodwill—Impairment**	**1.1.1, 1.2.1, 1.2.2, 1.2.3, 1.3.2**
9. Identify the types of disclosure requirements for intangible assets and goodwill and explain the issues in analyzing these assets.	**Presentation, Disclosure, and Analysis** • Presentation and disclosure • Analysis	**1.1.1, 1.1.2, 1.3.2, 1.4.1, 1.4.2, 1.4.4, 5.1.1, 5.1.2**
10. Identify differences in accounting between IFRS and ASPE.	**IFRS/ASPE Comparison** • A comparison of IFRS and ASPE • Looking ahead	**1.1.4**

After studying Appendix 12A, you should be able to:

11. Explain and apply basic approaches to valuing goodwill.	**Appendix 12A: Valuing Goodwill** • Excess-earnings approach • Total-earnings approach • Other valuation methods	**1.1.1, 1.1.2, 1.2.3, 1.2.4, 1.4.4, 1.4.5, 5.4.1, 5.4.2, 5.4.3**

Preview of Chapter 12

The valuation of intangible assets and goodwill is not always clear-cut. For example, in conjunction with the changeover from pre-IFRS GAAP to IFRS, several Canadian companies had very large writedowns relating to goodwill impairment. Goodwill is an asset whose value is typically recognized only when it is acquired in a business combination. This chapter explains the basic conceptual and reporting issues related to intangible assets and their close relative, goodwill.

The Business Importance and Characteristics of Goodwill and Intangible Assets

LEARNING OBJECTIVE 1

Understand the importance of goodwill and intangible assets from a business perspective and describe their characteristics.

Lululemon athletica inc.'s and **Roots Canada**'s most important asset is not their store fixtures, it is their brand image. In lululemon's 2017 annual report, the company notes that it is a "designer, distributor, and retailer of healthy lifestyle inspired athletic apparel ... marketed under the lululemon and ivivva brand names." It discusses the importance of its "premium brand image" and its intellectual property, and states that "distinctive marks that are readily identifiable is an important factor in building our brand image." The annual report also states, "Competition in the athletic apparel industry is principally on the basis of brand image and recognition as well as product quality, innovation, style, distribution, and price" and that "our success depends on the value and reputation of our brand." However, if you look at lululemon's 2017 financial statements, the brand name is not listed as a key part of its $24.7 million in recorded goodwill and intangible assets. The company's financial statements list goodwill and reacquired franchise rights as its two most significant assets of this type.

Similarly, the major asset of **Coca-Cola** is not its plant facilities, it's the secret formula for making Coke. **BCE**'s most important asset is not its Internet connection equipment, it's the subscriber base of almost 21 million customers. Our economy is increasingly dominated by information and service providers, and their major assets are often intangible in nature. Identifying and measuring these intangibles are often difficult. As a result, many intangibles have not been captured on companies' statements of financial position. However, goodwill and intangible assets remain a key focus of companies and standard setters around the globe.

Data Analytics   Although the true value of intangible assets is often not reflected on company financial statements, it does not mean that companies should ignore these assets. For example, many retailers are finding that information from their "bricks and mortar" stores can be used to improve their customers' shopping experience (and spending!). So for example, some companies are using "Big Data" analytics to take advantage of customers' experience both in person and online to identify key trends and behaviours that affect their businesses most. Retailers can assess whether their key performance indicator is driven by weather, in-store promotions, location, supply chain (their ability to fill orders promptly), or other factors by comparing key combinations of category, supplier, and brand day by day or seasonally. In short, data collection and analysis may be a key internally developed intangible asset for retailers and other companies. Perhaps it is no coincidence that **Google** and **Amazon** have two of the three most valuable brands today, as we will discuss later in this chapter.[1]

Characteristics of Goodwill

Goodwill is difficult to imagine because it's not a tangible asset, it can only be recognized when a business is acquired, and it cannot be purchased or sold separately—it can only be sold when a business is sold. **Goodwill** is "an asset representing the future economic benefits arising from other assets acquired in a business combination that are not individually identified and separately recognized."[2]

How is goodwill calculated? In a business combination where **one company purchases 100% of another business**, the fair value of what is given up by the acquiring entity (the **acquirer**) is allocated to the various assets and liabilities it receives.[3] All identifiable assets acquired and liabilities assumed (the **identifiable net assets**) are recognized at their fair values at the acquisition date. **The difference between the fair value of the consideration transferred to acquire the business and the fair value amounts assigned to the identifiable net assets is the amount recognized as goodwill.** This is shown in **Illustration 12.1**.

ILLUSTRATION 12.1

Measurement of Goodwill

> **Fair value of consideration transferred**—any one or a combination of cash, other assets, notes payable at a later date, common or preferred shares or other equity instruments, or contingent consideration
>
> − **Fair value of all identifiable assets acquired and liabilities assumed**, whether or not previously recognized by the acquired entity
>
> = **GOODWILL**

---

[1]Jia Wertz, "Why Brick and Mortar Retailers Need E-Commerce-Style Data Tracking Methods," *Forbes*, December 18, 2017.

[2]*CPA Canada Handbook*, Part II, 1582.03(j) and IFRS 3 Appendix A. Copyright © IFRS Foundation. All rights reserved. Reproduced with permission.

[3]When less than a 100% interest is acquired or the controlling interest is acquired in stages, the calculation of goodwill is more complex. This topic is left to a course in advanced financial accounting.

As you can tell from Illustration 12.1, goodwill is an unidentified excess or residual amount, and it can only be calculated in relation to the business as a whole.

Characteristics of Intangible Assets

What are intangible assets? Broadly defined, intangible assets are identifiable nonmonetary assets that lack physical substance. Intangible assets must have these three characteristics— **identifiability**, **non-physical existence**, and a **nonmonetary nature**—so that only appropriate assets are recognized as intangibles.

1. **Intangible assets are identifiable.** An asset is identifiable if it has at least one of the following characteristics:

   - **Law** It results from contractual or other legal rights.
   - It is separable—it can be separated or divided from the entity and sold, transferred, licensed, rented, or exchanged, either by itself or in combination with another contract, identifiable asset, or liability.[4]

   For example, the right to lease space at a favourable rate arises from a contractual arrangement and the right may or may not be transferable to others. A subscription list of a successful magazine or newspaper has value in contributing to future revenue streams and is saleable. These are examples of identifiable intangibles that are given separate recognition. Note also that, in order to recognize these items as assets, the company has to be able to control access to the future benefits and restrict others' access. One way to control access to the benefits is having legally enforceable rights; another is having the ability to enter into exchange transactions related to the intangible.

   Goodwill and some other non-physical items of value, on the other hand, are not separable from the rest of the entity, and control over the future benefits does not result from contractual or legal rights. For example, the synergies of a combined sales force or a superior management team can be identified as having value. However, these items cannot be recognized separately as intangible assets because they cannot be separated from the entity in order to exchange them with others, nor can they be controlled through contractual or other legal rights. They are therefore considered part of goodwill.

   While it is important to distinguish one identifiable intangible from another, financial reporting objectives are not well met if every identifiable intangible is recognized separately. At a minimum, the ones that have similar characteristics (such as continuity, stability, and risk) are grouped and recognized together. Because knowledge-based and high-technology companies with large investments in such "soft" assets are an important part of our modern economy, how accounting treats such intangibles is a major issue.

2. **Intangible assets lack physical substance.** Unlike assets such as property, plant, and equipment (PP&E), the value of intangible assets comes from the rights and privileges granted to the company using them. Sometimes it is difficult to tell whether a particular asset is tangible and is therefore an item of PP&E, or whether it is intangible and covered by accounting standards for intangible assets. Consider the example of computer software that is used for a key piece of equipment on an assembly line. What is the asset? Is it the intangible software, or is it the related tangible asset of equipment? In general, if the intangible component is needed for the physical component to work, it is treated as an item of PP&E. If the intangible component is not an integral part of the physical object, then it is classified separately as an intangible asset.

3. **Intangible assets are nonmonetary.** Assets such as accounts receivable and long-term loans lack physical substance, but they are not classified as intangible assets. They are monetary assets whose value comes from the right (or claim) to receive fixed or determinable amounts of money in the future. Intangible assets do not contain any such right or claim.

In most cases, items that meet the definition of an intangible asset provide economic benefits over a period of years. The benefits may be in the form of revenue from selling products or services, a reduction in future costs, or other economies. They are normally classified as long-term assets. Examples include such widely varied assets as patents, copyrights,

---

[4]See *Business Combinations* in *CPA Canada Handbook*, Part II, Section 1582.03(k) and IFRS 3, Appendix A.

franchises or licensing agreements, trademarks or trade names, secret formulas, computer software, technological know-how, prepayments, and some development costs. Specific intangibles are discussed later in the chapter.

Recognition and Measurement of Intangible Assets at Acquisition

> **LEARNING OBJECTIVE 2**
>
> Identify and apply the recognition and measurement requirements for purchased intangible assets.

> **Underlying Concept 12.1**
>
> The cost concepts introduced in Chapter 10 for property, plant, and equipment are also appropriate for determining the cost of purchased intangible assets.

The **recognition criteria** for intangible assets are identical to those for PP&E assets and both are **measured at cost** at acquisition as discussed in Underlying Concept 12.1. For example, each type of asset can be recognized only when it meets the same two recognition criteria:

1. It is probable that the entity will receive the expected future economic benefits.
2. The asset's cost can be reliably measured.[5]

In applying these criteria, however, management has to consider that there is often more uncertainty about the future economic benefits associated with intangible assets than with tangible capital assets.

Purchased Intangibles

Intangible assets may be purchased outright, they can be acquired as part of a business combination, or they can be developed internally.

As indicated above, intangible assets purchased from another party are **measured at cost**. Because the amount paid is based on the company's expectations about receiving future economic benefits from the asset, the "probability" criterion for recognition is met. Cost includes the acquisition cost and all expenditures directly associated with making the intangible ready for its intended use—for example, the purchase price, legal fees, and other direct costs to bring it into working condition. Costs that are **not capitalized** are similar to those for property, plant, and equipment assets: they are costs related to product introduction and promotion, conducting business in a new location or with new types of customers, and administration and general overhead. Expenditures incurred after the asset is ready for use as intended and initial operating losses are also excluded.

> **Underlying Concept 12.2**
>
> The basic attributes of intangibles, the uncertainty of their future benefits, and their uniqueness have discouraged valuing them at more than their cost.

Similar to other long-lived assets, when direct costs that meet the recognition criteria are incurred after acquisition of the intangible asset, these costs are accounted for as additions or replacements and are capitalized. This is not as common with intangibles, however.

Cost, as was seen in earlier chapters, is the cash cost, or its equivalent, as discussed below and in Underlying Concept 12.2.

- If there are **delayed payment terms**, any portion of the payments that represents interest is recognized as a financing expense rather than as part of the asset cost.
- If the intangible asset is acquired for shares, cost is measured at an amount equal to the intangible asset's fair value.[6] However, if the fair value of the intangible asset cannot be

---

[5]IAS 38, paragraph 21 and *CPA Canada Handbook*, Part II, Section 3064.21. Copyright © IFRS Foundation. All rights reserved. Reproduced with permission.

[6]IFRS 2 *Share-based Payment* is considerably more complex than is indicated here. In addition, the term "fair value" used in IFRS 2 differs from the definition of fair value in IFRS 13 *Fair Value Measurement*. When applying IFRS 2, an entity measures fair value in accordance with the definition in IFRS 2, not IFRS 13. (See IFRS 2, paragraphs 6A and 16-18.) Copyright © IFRS Foundation. All rights reserved. Reproduced with permission.

measured reliably, then the shares' fair value is used. ASPE is not as prescriptive. It allows the more reliable of the fair value of the intangible asset or the shares to be used.

- If the intangible asset is acquired by giving up **nonmonetary assets**, the cost of the intangible is the fair value of what is given up or the fair value of the intangible asset received, whichever one can be measured more reliably. This assumes that the transaction has **commercial substance** and that fair values can be reliably measured. You may want to review the section in Chapter 10 that discusses this situation and provides examples of transactions and entries for nonmonetary exchanges.

- If the intangible asset is acquired via a government grant, the asset's fair value usually establishes its cost on the books. IFRS does permit a company to recognize a zero or nominal dollar cost in this case. Any other direct costs of acquisition are capitalized into the asset cost, however.

Intangibles Purchased in a Business Combination

When a company purchases an intangible asset as a single asset, such as an acquisition of a specific trademark or patent, the accounting is relatively clear. When several intangibles are bought together in a "basket purchase," the accounting is more complex because the cost has to be allocated to each intangible based on its relative fair value.

A further complication happens when intangibles are acquired in a **business combination**—when one entity acquires control over one or more businesses. This can take place either by directly purchasing the net assets of the business or by acquiring the equity interests (the shares) that control the entity and its net assets. An issue arises because of the variety of assets and liabilities that make up a complete and ongoing business. Even the fact that the business is fully operational instead of being just in the planning stages adds value to it. The entity has to account for all the assets that are acquired, regardless of whether or not they are recognized in the acquired business's accounting records. Many of the assets acquired that contribute to the value of the business are intangible, but only those that are **identifiable** can be separately recognized. Intangibles acquired that are not identifiable assets are considered part of goodwill.

The acquisition cost assigned to each of the identifiable intangible assets acquired as part of a business combination is its fair value.[7] All such assets acquired in this way are recognized, even though they may have been internally generated by the business itself and are not eligible for capitalization under the standards for internally generated intangible assets. Examples include brand names, patents, customer relationships, and **in-process research and development (R&D)**. In-process R&D comes about when one company acquires the business of another company, and one of the identifiable assets acquired is the research work and findings of the acquired company. When the research work and findings meet the requirements for being reported as an asset separate from goodwill, they are recognized as an identifiable intangible.

Prepayments

So far we have seen that, if expenditures for intangibles do not qualify for recognition as an intangible asset or as part of goodwill in a business combination, they must be recognized as an expense when incurred. In some cases, however, a prepaid asset—a **prepaid expense**—can be recognized initially. A prepayment is recognized as an asset only when an entity pays for **goods** before their delivery (or other right of access) or for **services** before receiving those services, as shown in **Example 12.1**. The asset is the right to receive the goods or services. When received, or if the "right to receive" no longer exists, the costs are expensed.

---

[7]If control over the assets is acquired through the acquisition of voting shares, the fair value of all the identifiable assets and liabilities (identifiable net assets) is assigned as their cost through the consolidation process. Refer to Chapter 3 for a discussion of how fair values are determined.

Example 12.1 | Accounting for Prepaid Assets

Facts Beta Limited (BL) places an order for the production of mail-order catalogues by a supplier, and pays $5,000 when the order is placed. When the catalogues are received from the supplier, BL immediately sends them out to its customers.

Instructions How should BL account for the catalogues at the time of initial payment to its supplier, and later when they are received from the supplier?

Solution At the time of payment, BL has a prepayment asset—the right to receive the catalogues from the supplier. The entry to record this exchange is:

Prepaid Expenses	5,000	
Cash		5,000

When the supplier delivers the catalogues, BL immediately sends them to its customers. So, BL no longer has the prepayment asset previously recognized, and it is derecognized.

Because such catalogues are considered a form of advertising and promotion, their cost is expensed. BL makes the following entry:

Advertising Expense	5,000	
Prepaid Expenses		5,000

A	=	L	+	SE
0				

Cash flows: ↓ 5,000 outflow

A	=	L	+	SE
−5,000				−5,000

Cash flows: No effect

Whether intangible assets qualify for recognition or not, they can be quite valuable as illustrated in relation to patents in **What Do the Numbers Mean? 12.1.**

What Do the Numbers Mean? 12.1

Canadian-based **Nortel Networks** filed for bankruptcy protection in January 2009. But unlike many bankrupt companies, Nortel still had some valuable assets to sell: its patents. Two and a half years after declaring bankruptcy, Nortel auctioned off approximately 6,000 patents to **Rockstar**, a company co-owned by **Apple, Microsoft, BlackBerry, Ericsson,** and **Sony,** for $4.5 billion. The patents included products and processes related to 4G wireless networks, Internet and voice technology, semiconductors, and optical equipment. Rockstar filed patent lawsuits against **Google, Samsung, HTC,** and **Huawei** in late 2013 relating to these patents. In November 2014, it was reported that Google and Rockstar agreed to settle the patent litigation. Subsequently, the most valuable patents were distributed among the Rockstar consortium members, with the remaining patents being sold to **RPX,** a patent risk management company, for $900 million. RPX uses the patents acquired from Rockstar and its other patents to provide "sub-licences" to its clients. It considers its patent acquisitions to be a key driver of the value it creates for its clients. With annual revenue of over U.S. $330 million in 2016, the patent business can be a lucrative one!

Sources: RPX Corporation 2016 annual report; Barrie McKenna, "The Ghost of Nortel Continues to Haunt Canada's Tech Sector," *The Globe and Mail*, December 4, 2011; Charles Arthur, "Nortel Patents Sold for $4.5bn," *The Guardian*, July 1, 2011; "Nortel Reports Financial Results for the Fourth Quarter and Full Year 2011," company news release, March 8, 2012; "Nortel Patents at Issue in Suits Against Google, Huawei," CBCNews.ca, November 1, 2013; "Google, Rockstar Agree to Settle Patent Litigation," http://re/code.net, November 20, 2014; "Apple-Backed Rockstar Sells Patents to RPX for $900 Million," http://re/code.net, December 23, 2014.

Recognition and Measurement of Internally Developed Intangible Assets

LEARNING OBJECTIVE 3

Identify and apply the recognition and measurement requirements for internally developed intangible assets.

It is a more challenging task to decide which costs should be capitalized and recognized as intangible assets when an entity develops such assets internally. The difficulty involves the following recognition and measurement issues.

1. Has an identifiable asset been created that will generate expected future cash flows?
2. What costs should be capitalized? Are the costs incurred just day-to-day operating costs or expenditures related to internally generated goodwill (which are expensed), or are they really additional costs of identifiable assets? How reliably can cost be measured?

How costs associated with internally generated intangible assets should be accounted for has been a controversial issue for many years. The following alternatives have been suggested:

a. Recognize the costs as internally generated intangible assets when certain criteria are met, and expense all others.
b. Recognize all costs of internally generated intangible assets as an expense. See Underlying Concept 12.3.
c. Recognize expenditures on all internally generated intangible assets as an expense, with certain specified exceptions.
d. Allow a choice between the accounting treatments in (a) and (b) above.

> **Underlying Concept 12.3**
>
> The Financial Accounting Standards Board (FASB) in the United States has chosen option (b).

IFRS **ASPE** The IASB decided on option (a) in IAS 38 *Intangible Assets* while option (d) was selected in *CPA Canada Handbook*, Part II, Section 3064 *Goodwill and Intangible Assets* for private enterprises.[8] Option (a) is illustrated in the next section. Note that the IFRS requirements for recognizing "self-constructed" intangibles are more stringent than those for property, plant, and equipment assets. This is because of the recognition and measurement uncertainties referred to above.

Identifying Research and Development Phase Activities

To deal with the uncertainty of whether an asset should be recognized, the process of generating the intangible is broken down into two parts: a research phase and a development phase. Research is the planned investigation undertaken with the hope of gaining new

---

[8]IAS 38, *Basis for Conclusions*: BCZ29.

scientific or technical knowledge and better understanding. The investigation may or may not be directed toward a specific practical aim or application. Development, on the other hand, is the translation of research findings or other knowledge into a plan or design for new or substantially improved materials, devices, products, processes, systems, or services before starting commercial production or use.[9]

Research phase and **development phase** activities are interpreted in the accounting standards as broader terms than implied in the definitions of research and development provided. Examples of activities in each of these phases are set out in **Illustration 12.2**.

ILLUSTRATION 12.2

Examples of Research Stage Activities and Development Stage Activities

Activities in the Research Stage	Activities in the Development Stage
Obtaining new knowledge	Designing, constructing, and testing prototypes and models prior to production or use
Searching for, evaluating, and selecting ways to use research findings or knowledge	Designing tools, jigs, moulds, and dies involving new technology
Investigating possible alternatives for existing materials, products, processes, systems, and services	Designing, constructing, and operating pilot plants that are not economically feasible for commercial production
Formulating, designing, evaluating, and choosing possible alternatives for improved or new materials, products, processes, systems, and services	Designing, constructing, and testing chosen alternatives for new or improved materials, products, processes, systems, and services[10]

If there is uncertainty about which phase a particular activity relates to when internally creating an intangible asset, it would be classified as a **research phase** activity.

Accounting for Research Phase Costs

The accounting standards are very clear that costs incurred on research or during the research phase of an internal project do not meet the criteria for recognition as an intangible asset. **All such costs are recognized as expenses when they are incurred.** However, if a company has its own research facility consisting of buildings, laboratories, and equipment that are used for general research activities, it accounts for these assets as capitalized property, plant, and equipment. The depreciation and other costs that are related to such facilities are accounted for as research-related expenses.

Sometimes entities conduct research activities for other companies **under a contractual arrangement**. In this case, the contract usually specifies that all direct costs, certain specific indirect costs, and a profit element will be reimbursed to the entity performing the research work. Because reimbursement is expected, such research costs are recorded as inventory or a receivable.

Accounting for Development Phase Costs

An intangible asset can be recognized from the development stage of an internal project, but only when an entity can demonstrate its technical and financial feasibility and the company's intention and ability to generate future economic benefits from it. **All six of the following specific conditions need to be demonstrated** in order to capitalize costs incurred in the development phase:

1. Technical feasibility of completing the intangible asset
2. The entity's intention to complete it for use or sale

---

[9]Reprinted/adapted with permission from the *CPA Canada Handbook—Accounting* © 2018, Part II, Section 3064.08, by Chartered Professional Accountants of Canada. All rights reserved by the copyright owner.

[10]IAS 38.56 and .59. Copyright © IFRS Foundation. All rights reserved. Reproduced with permission. Reprinted/adapted with permission from the *CPA Canada Handbook—Accounting* © 2018, Part II, Section 3064.39 and .43, by Chartered Professional Accountants of Canada. All rights reserved by the copyright owner.

3. The entity's ability to use or sell it

4. Availability of technical, financial, and other resources needed to complete it, and to use or sell it

5. The way in which the future economic benefits will be generated, including the existence of a market for the asset if it will be sold, or its usefulness to the entity if it will be used internally

6. The ability to reliably measure the costs associated with and attributed to the intangible asset during its development (*CPA Canada Handbook*, Part II, Section 3064.41; IAS 38.57).

Because **all** six criteria must be met, this means that an entity capitalizes development phase costs **only when the future benefits are reasonably certain**. This in turn means that internally generated intangible assets are recognized only in limited situations, and projects may be quite far along in the development stage before all six criteria are met. **Only then do the costs begin to be capitalized.** No expenditures incurred prior to this point and previously expensed are added to the asset's cost, even if the expenditures were in the same accounting period.

Although it is contrary to the usual principles-based approach, several items are specifically identified as not being recognized as internally generated intangible assets. These include brands, mastheads (the front-page or cover banner design of newspapers and magazines), publishing titles, customer lists, and other similar items. They are excluded on the basis that costs incurred to develop them cannot be distinguished from general business development costs. The debate regarding what costs should be expensed vs. capitalized can be considered using "First Principles" as discussed in Underlying Concept 12.4.

> **Underlying Concept 12.4**
>
> The requirement that all research-type and most development-type costs be expensed as they are incurred is an example of the old conflict between relevance and reliability, with verifiability or reliability carrying more weight in this case.

Costs Included and Excluded

The cost of an internally generated intangible begins to be accumulated at the date when the six criteria in the development process are met. From this point forward, the types of expenditures that are capitalized are familiar: all directly attributable costs needed to create, produce, and prepare the intangible asset to operate in the way intended by management. Examples of such direct costs include:

1. Materials and services used or consumed to generate the asset

2. Direct costs of personnel, such as salaries, wages, payroll taxes, and related employee benefit costs

3. Fees needed to register a legal right

4. Amortization of other intangibles needed to generate the new asset

5. Interest or borrowing costs[11]

Specifically **excluded** as capitalized costs are selling, administrative, and other general overhead costs that cannot be directly linked to preparing the asset for use, costs incurred to train employees, and initial operating losses after the intangible is ready for use.

Generally, the costs of start-up activities such as legal and other costs of incorporation (organization costs); pre-opening costs associated with new facilities or businesses; and pre-operating costs for launching new operations, products, or processes are all expensed. Relocation and reorganization costs, and those associated with advertising and promotional activities including mail-order catalogues, are also not capitalized.

To illustrate the accounting treatment of activities associated with intangible items and research and development phases, assume that a company develops, produces, and markets laser machines for medical, industrial, and defence uses. The types of expenditures related to its laser machine activities, along with the recommended IFRS accounting treatment, are listed in Illustration 12.3.

---

[11]Under ASPE, interest or borrowing costs would be included only if this is the accounting policy chosen by the entity. See Chapter 10 for a fuller discussion of the capitalization of borrowing costs.

ILLUSTRATION 12.3

IFRS Sample Expenditures and Their Accounting Treatment

Type of Expenditure	Accounting Treatment
1. Construction of long-range research facility (three-storey, 1,000-square metre building) for use in current and future projects	Capitalize as PP&E assets; depreciate as a research-type expense.
2. Acquisition of research-related equipment for use on current project only	Capitalize as PP&E asset; depreciate as a research-type expense.
3. Purchase of materials to be used on current and future R&D projects	Capitalize as inventory; expense as a research-type expense as consumed.
4. Salaries of research staff designing new laser bone scanner	Expense immediately as a research-type expense.
5. Research costs incurred under contract for customer and billable monthly	Expense as operating expense in period of related revenue recognition.
6. Material, labour, and overhead costs of prototype laser scanner	Capitalize as intangible asset if development criteria are all met; otherwise, expense.
7. Costs of testing prototype and design modifications	Capitalize as intangible asset if development criteria are all met; otherwise, expense.
8. Legal fees to obtain patent on new laser scanner	Capitalize as patent (intangible asset) provided asset meets recognition criteria; amortize to cost of goods manufactured as used.
9. Executive salaries	Expense as operating expense (general and administrative).
10. Cost of marketing research related to promotion of new laser scanner	Expense as operating expense (selling).
11. Engineering costs incurred to advance the laser scanner to full production stage	Capitalize as intangible asset if development criteria are all met; otherwise, expense.
12. Costs of successfully defending patent on laser scanner	Capitalize as intangible asset (patent); amortize to cost of goods manufactured as used.
13. Commissions to sales staff marketing new laser scanner	Expense as operating expense (selling).

Recognition and Measurement of Intangible Assets after Acquisition

LEARNING OBJECTIVE 4

Explain how intangible assets are accounted for after initial recognition.

Items of property, plant, and equipment commonly have parts added to them or replaced, but most intangible assets do not. The nature of intangibles is such that costs incurred after the asset has been acquired are normally made to maintain the asset's benefits and therefore do not meet the recognition criteria for capitalization. Although there are exceptions, most after-acquisition costs are expensed.

IFRS Two models have been put forward for measuring intangible assets after initial recognition: a **cost model (CM)** and a **revaluation model (RM)**. **ASPE** The CM is the most widely used approach by far, and under ASPE, it is the only method allowed.

Why is the RM not widely used? The reason is simply that it can be applied only to intangible assets that have a fair value determined in an active market.[12] This limits its use to situations where the items are homogeneous (interchangeable), there is a good supply of willing buyers and sellers, and the prices are available to the public. An active securities market, such as the Toronto Stock Exchange, exists for equity securities, but active markets do not ordinarily exist for intangible assets. Most intangible assets, such as patents, brands, and trademarks, grant unique rights to the entity that holds them. This results in unique pricing when such assets are bought and sold. There are some exceptions. Examples include the prices of quotas for a variety of agricultural products for which the government sets production limits, such as milk or eggs, or perhaps even bitcoins as discussed later in this chapter. The revaluation model could also be used where there are transferable fishing or taxi licences, which are available in some jurisdictions.

When the RM is chosen for an intangible asset, all the assets in the same class must also apply the same method. Examples of classes include copyrights, patents, computer software, secret recipes, and designs. If there is no active market for the other assets in the class, then the CM is applied to these assets.

Accounting under these two models is the same for intangible assets as for property, plant, and equipment. For both PP&E and intangible assets using the RM, there is no requirement for an annual revaluation, only that the carrying amount reported on the statement of financial position not be materially different from its fair value. Instead of repeating the full coverage of this topic provided in Chapters 10 and 11, we summarize the two methods of accounting for limited-life intangible assets in **Illustration 12.4**.[13] You may want to review the specific examples in the earlier chapters to reinforce this material.

ILLUSTRATION 12.4

Cost Model and Revaluation Model for Limited-Life Intangible Assets

Cost Model (CM)	
At acquisition	Recognized and measured at cost.
After acquisition	Carried at cost less accumulated amortization and any accumulated impairment losses.
On disposal	Difference between asset's carrying amount and proceeds on disposal is gain or loss reported in net income.

Revaluation Model (RM)	
At acquisition	Recognized and measured at cost.
After acquisition	Carried at fair value at the date of the revaluation less any subsequent accumulated amortization and any subsequent loss on impairment.
Revaluation increase	Record credit to Revaluation Surplus (Other Comprehensive Income) unless this reverses a previous decrease recognized in income. If so, recognize the increase in income to the extent of the prior decrease.
Revaluation decrease	Record debit to Revaluation Surplus (Other Comprehensive Income) to the extent there is a balance associated with the same asset. Any remaining amount is recognized as a charge to income.
Revaluation	Apply either the **proportional method** (both asset and accumulated amortization balances continue and are adjusted regularly—for example, every three years—so that the net amount is the asset's new fair value) or the **asset adjustment method** (accumulated amortization is closed periodically to the asset account and begins again at zero; the asset is revalued to the new amount).

(continued)

....

[12]For a fuller discussion, see Chapter 3 regarding fair value measurement and IAS 38.78 regarding active market. Copyright © IFRS Foundation. All rights reserved. Reproduced with permission.

[13]For indefinite-life intangible assets, the same accounting applies except that there would be no amortization or accumulated amortization amounts.

ILLUSTRATION 12.4

(*continued*)

Revaluation Model (RM)	
On disposal	Either (a) adjust the asset to its fair value at the date of disposal, account for the revaluation increase or decrease as above, and recognize no gain or loss on disposal, or (b) recognize a gain or loss on disposal in net income equal to the difference between the proceeds on disposal and the asset's carrying amount on the date of disposal.
Revaluation Surplus account balance	Either transfer amounts directly to Retained Earnings each period (equal to the difference between amortization expense determined on the CM basis and amortization expense determined on the RM basis) or, when the asset is disposed of, transfer the balance remaining in the account directly to Retained Earnings.

As suggested above, intangibles are a diverse mix of assets. Some intangibles have values based on rights that are given legally by contract, statute, or similar means. Examples include a **Tim Hortons** franchise or licences granted by the federal government to broadcasters. Some of these rights have finite or limited legal lives that can be easily renewed; others have lives that are not renewable, and others are renewable only at a significant cost. Some can be sold while others may not be exchangeable. Internally developed intangibles may have a wide range of useful lives. Other intangibles may be granted in perpetuity and have an indefinite life. An **indefinite life** does not mean "infinite"—that the asset will last forever. Instead, it means that, after looking at all relevant factors, there appears to be no foreseeable limit to how long the asset will generate positive net cash flows for the entity.

Accounting standards used to require all intangible assets to be amortized over a period of not more than 40 years. While this simplified the accounting, the reality is that intangibles are diverse, and the approach to their measurement after acquisition should be based on their specific characteristics. Under current standards, if an intangible asset has a finite, or limited, useful life, it is amortized over that useful life. If instead the intangible has an indefinite life, no amortization is taken. The asset is retained in the accounts until it is determined to be impaired or its life becomes limited.

Limited-Life Intangibles

An intangible asset with a **finite** or **limited life** is amortized by systematic charges to expense over its useful life whether using the cost model or the revaluation model. The factors to consider in determining the useful life are similar to the factors for long-lived property, plant, and equipment, and include:

1. The expected use of the asset by the entity, and the expected useful life of other assets that may affect the useful life of the intangible asset (such as mineral rights for depleting assets).

2. Any legal, regulatory, or contractual provisions that may either limit the useful life or allow renewal or extension of the asset's legal or contractual life without the entity having to pay a substantial cost. (If the renewal cost is significant, then the expenditure for the renewal may represent the cost of a new intangible asset.)

3. The effects of obsolescence, demand, competition, and other economic factors. Examples include the stability of the industry, known technological advances, and legislative action that results in an uncertain or changing regulatory environment. For instance, expected future reductions in sales prices of items produced using an intangible asset (such as a patent) could indicate expected commercial or technological obsolescence.[14]

4. The level of maintenance expenditure that is needed to obtain the expected future cash flows from the asset.[15]

---

[14]See IAS 38.92 for further details. Copyright © IFRS Foundation. All rights reserved. Reproduced with permission.

[15]IAS 38.56 and .59. Copyright © IFRS Foundation. All rights reserved. Reproduced with permission. Reprinted/adapted with permission from the *CPA Canada Handbook—Accounting* © 2018, Part II, Section 3064.39 and .43, by Chartered Professional Accountants of Canada. All rights reserved by the copyright owner.

Amortization expense for a limited-life asset should ideally reflect the pattern in which the asset's economic benefits are used up, if that pattern can be reliably determined. For example, assume that Second Wave Inc. has purchased a licence to manufacture a limited quantity of a vaccine called Megadose. Because the life of the licence is reduced with each unit produced, the cost of the licence is amortized following the pattern of production of Megadose—a unit of production approach. If the pattern cannot be determined, the straight-line method is used. The amortization charges are usually reported **as expenses**, and the credits are made to **accumulated amortization** accounts. Note that in the Second Wave Inc. example, the amortization is likely a product cost that is first included in inventory and then expensed on the income statement as part of the cost of goods sold when the product is sold. Effective January 1, 2016, IAS 38.98 was clarified to reflect an underlying assumption that it is inappropriate to use amortization methods based on revenue generated by an activity, including the use of an intangible asset. The standard does allow exceptions, however. An example of an exception would be an intangible asset providing the right to operate a toll road that expires when a preset cumulative toll amount to be collected is reached.

The amount to amortize for an intangible asset is its carrying amount less residual value. Uncertainties about residual values for intangibles are greater than they are for items of property, plant, and equipment. Because of this, an intangible asset's residual value is assumed to be zero. This assumption can be overturned only if the asset is expected to be of use to another entity and a third party commits to purchase the asset at the end of its useful life, or if there is an active market for the asset that is expected to still exist at the end of its useful life to the entity.[16]

There are other similarities between the accounting for limited-life intangibles and property, plant, and equipment assets, as shown in **Illustration 12.5**.

ILLUSTRATION 12.5

Accounting for Intangible Assets with a Limited Life

Transaction or Event	Accounting Treatment for Intangible Assets with a Limited Life	Same as for Most PP&E Assets?
Amortization begins…	…when the asset is in the location and condition to be able to be used as management intends	Yes
Amortization stops…	…at the earlier of when it is derecognized or classified as held for sale	Yes
Review of useful life and amortization method	ASPE: at least annually; IFRS: at least at the end of each financial year	Yes (PP&E is reviewed "regularly")
Change in estimate of useful life, residual value, amortization method	Accounted for prospectively—as a change in accounting estimate	Yes

Indefinite-Life Intangibles

An intangible asset with an indefinite life **is not amortized**. For example, assume that Double Clik Inc. acquires a trademark that is used to distinguish a leading consumer product from other such products. The trademark is renewable every 10 years at minimal cost. After evaluating all relevant factors, the evidence indicates that this trademark product will generate net cash flows for an indefinite period of time. Therefore, it has an indefinite life.

Because of the potential effect on the financial statements, it is important for management to review whether events and circumstances continue to support the assessment of an indefinite life. This is required every accounting period under IFRS (and when circumstances indicate possible impairment under ASPE). If the useful life is later considered to be limited

---

instead of indefinite, the change is considered a change in estimate and past results are not affected. Such an assessment may also indicate that the asset's carrying amount is impaired. The accounting treatment for impairment is discussed later in this chapter.

Specific Intangibles

> **LEARNING OBJECTIVE 5**
> Identify and explain the accounting for specific types of intangible assets.

The many different types of intangible assets are sometimes classified into the following five major categories:[17]

1. Marketing-related
2. Customer-related
3. Artistic-related
4. Contract-based
5. Technology-based

Marketing-Related Intangible Assets

Marketing-related intangible assets are used mainly in the marketing or promotion of products or services and derive their value from the contractual or legal rights that they contain. Examples are trademarks or trade names, Internet domain names, and non-competition agreements.

`Law` A very common form of marketing-related intangible asset is a trademark. A **trademark** or **trade name** is a word, symbol, or design, or combination of these, that is used to distinguish the goods or services of one person or entity from those of others. The terms **brand** and **brand name** are similar but often refer to a group of assets such as a trade name and its related formulas, recipes, and technology. The right to use a trademark or trade name as part of a brand image in Canada is granted by Innovation, Science and Economic Development Canada and the registration system is administered by its Canadian Intellectual Property Office (CIPO).[18] In order to obtain and maintain this right, the owner must have made prior and continuing use of it. Trade names like Kraft Dinner, Pepsi-Cola, and Kleenex, and brand names such as President's Choice and Canadian Tire, create immediate product recognition in our minds, which makes them more marketable. Company names themselves may have value and characteristics that companies are willing to spend money on to develop.[19]

If a mark or name is **purchased**, its capitalizable cost is the purchase price and other direct costs of acquisition. If it is **developed** by the enterprise itself and its future benefits to the company are reasonably assured, the costs may be capitalized, but only from the point in time when all six of the required capitalization criteria are met in its development phase. These costs may include lawyers' fees, registration fees, design costs, consulting fees, successful legal defence costs, expenditures related to securing the mark or name, and other direct development costs. When a trademark, trade name, or brand name's total cost is insignificant

---

[17]This classification framework is used in IFRS 3 *Business Combinations:* Illustrative Examples IE16–IE44 to describe identifiable intangible assets acquired in a business combination. Copyright © IFRS Foundation. All rights reserved. Reproduced with permission.

[18]Canadian Intellectual Property Office: www.ic.gc.ca.

[19]To illustrate how various intangibles might arise from a specific product, consider what the Canadian creators of the highly successful game Trivial Pursuit did to protect their creation. First, they copyrighted the 6,000 questions that are at the heart of the game. Then they shielded the Trivial Pursuit name by applying for a registered trademark. As a third mode of protection, the creators obtained a design patent on the playing board's design because it represents a unique graphic creation.

or all six capitalization criteria have not been met, the costs are expensed. The debate regarding whether intangible assets like brands should be recorded in company financial statements is an important one because, as is discussed in **What Do the Numbers Mean? 12.2**, brands can be very, very valuable!

What Do the Numbers Mean? 12.2

Hoping to promote the management of brands in the same financially robust way as other long-term investments, Brand Finance plc published a report entitled the *Brand Finance Global 500 2017*. The study uses a "royalty relief approach" to value the brands of major companies; that is, the authors determine how much a company would have to pay to license the brand from a third party. The brand's value is the present value of that hypothetical stream of payments.

Google, Apple, and Amazon were ranked as having the three most valuable brands in the world (all having brand values over U.S. $100 billion), with China's ICBC joining Samsung as the only non–U.S.-based companies in the top 10. The most valuable Canadian brand, according to this report, was the Royal Bank of Canada (RBC), with an estimated worth of almost U.S. $12.7 billion. Other major Canadian banks (TD Bank, Bank of Montreal, Scotiabank, and CIBC) were included in the top

500 world brands, together with other well-known companies and brands like Tim Hortons, Bell Canada, Rogers, TELUS, and Brookfield Asset Management. The RBC brand, however, does not appear as an asset on the Royal Bank's balance sheet. Why not? Brand value is a function of marketing, advertising, and public relations spending, including customer loyalty and retention programs, which all result in an increased volume of business, retail sales, and shipments. This type of cost is expensed as it is incurred because it cannot be directly related to future benefits.

In an earlier report, Brand Finance contended that "long-term investment decisions about future promotional expenditures, and the host of other activities that combine to build brand value" are better made when management can articulate the arguments in financial terms, as is done for most other investments.

Source: Brand Finance website, www.brandfinance.com.

Trademark registrations in Canada last for 15 years, and are renewable at a reasonable cost. Although the legal life of such assets **may be unlimited**, in practice they may only provide benefits to the enterprise over a **finite** period. Trademarks can, however, be determined to provide benefits to an enterprise indefinitely. A brand such as Coca-Cola, worth over U.S. $30 billion in 2017, may reasonably be expected to have an indefinite useful life. In this case, the intangible asset is not amortized.

Customer-Related Intangible Assets

Customer-related intangible assets result from interactions with outside parties and their value may be derived from legal-contractual rights, or because they could be sold separately. Examples include customer lists, order or production backlogs, and customer contracts or non-contractual relationships. See **Example 12.2**.

Example 12.2 | Accounting for Customer Lists

Facts   We-Market Inc. acquires the customer list of a large newspaper for $6 million on January 1, 2020. The customer list is a database that includes customer names, contact information, order history, and demographic information. We-Market expects to benefit from the information on the acquired list for 10 years, and it believes that these benefits will be spread evenly over the 10 years. In this case, assume the customer list is a limited-life intangible that should be amortized on a straight-line basis. Customer lists like this one would typically have a limited life due to factors such as people moving into or out of the area and competition from other newspapers and other media sources.

Instructions

a. Provide the journal entries needed to record the purchase of the customer list and its amortization at the end of each year.

b. How would your answer change if We-Market determines that it can sell the list for $60,000 to another company at the end of 10 years?

A	=	L	+	SE
0				

Cash flows: ↓ 6,000,000 outflow

A	=	L	+	SE
−600,000				−600,000

Cash flows: No effect

Solution

a. The journal entries needed are as follows:

January 1, 2020

Intangible Assets—Customer List	6,000,000	
Cash		6,000,000

December 31, 2020, through December 31, 2029

Amortization Expense	600,000	
Accumulated Amortization—Customer List		600,000

b. This example assumes that the customer list has no residual value. If We-Market determines that it can sell the list to another company at the end of 10 years, the residual value ($60,000) would be subtracted from the cost to determine the amortizable amount, but only if there is an active market for customer lists like this or if a third party has committed to purchase the list at the end of the 10 years.

Artistic-Related Intangible Assets

Artistic-related intangible assets involve ownership rights to plays, literary works, musical works, pictures, photographs, and video and audiovisual material. These ownership rights are protected by copyrights and have value because of the legal-contractual nature of the rights as discussed in **What Do the Numbers Mean? 12.3**.

What Do the Numbers Mean? 12.3

Copyrights can be valuable. When Michael Jackson died in mid-2009, he was in dire financial trouble. However, he did have one asset that was extremely valuable: a 50% interest in the **Sony Corp./ATV Music Publishing** joint venture set up in 1995. The partnership owns copyrights to the lyrics and music of tens of thousands of songs by such artists as the Beatles, Roy Orbison, Hank Williams, and Jimi Hendrix. With its 2012 acquisition of EMI Music Publishing, Sony/ATV is said to have become the world's largest publishing company, with over 2 million songs and revenues in excess of U.S. $1.2 billion, and is estimated to be worth more than U.S. $2 billion! Altogether, Sony/ATV Music Publishing owns or administers more than 2 million copyrights for the who's who of the music industry. Sony Corp. acquired Michael Jackson's estate's share of Sony/ATV Music Publishing in 2016, giving it sole ownership of the joint venture.

Law A **copyright** is the exclusive right to copy a creative work or allow someone else to do so. It is a federally granted right that applies to all original literary, dramatic, musical, and artistic works, whatever the mode or form of expression. A copyright is acquired automatically when an original work is created, but it can also be registered with the federal Copyright Office (part of the Canadian Intellectual Property Office). The right is granted for the life of the creator plus 50 years, and gives the owner or heirs the exclusive right to reproduce, sell, communicate, or translate an artistic or published work. Copyrights are not renewable. Like trade names, they may be assigned or sold to other individuals.[20] The costs of acquiring and defending a copyright may be capitalized, but research costs that are associated with them are expensed as they are incurred.

Generally, the copyright's useful life is shorter than its legal life. Its useful life depends on the unique facts and circumstances of each case. Consumer habits, market trends, and prior experience all play a part. Because it is so difficult to determine the period of benefit from a copyright, companies often choose to write these costs off over a short period.

Contract-Based Intangible Assets

Law **Contract-based intangible assets** represent the value of rights that come from contractual arrangements. Examples are licensing arrangements, lease agreements, construction permits, broadcast rights, and service or supply contracts. A very common form of contract-based intangible asset is a franchise.

---

[20]Canadian Intellectual Property Office: www.ic.gc.ca.

When you drive down the street in an automobile purchased from a Toyota dealer, fill your tank at the corner Petro-Canada station, grab a coffee at Tim Hortons, eat lunch at McDonald's, cool off with a Baskin-Robbins cone, work at a Coca-Cola bottling plant, live in a home purchased through a Royal LePage real estate broker, or vacation at a Holiday Inn resort, you are dealing with franchises. A franchise is a contractual arrangement under which the franchisor grants the franchisee the right to sell certain products or services; to use certain trademarks, trade names, or brands; or to perform certain functions, usually within a designated geographic area. Licensing agreements work in a similar way.

After having developed a unique concept or product, the franchisor protects it through a patent, copyright, trademark, or trade name. The franchisee then acquires the right to take advantage of the franchisor's idea or product by signing a franchise agreement. Another type of franchise is the arrangement that is commonly entered into by a municipality or other government body and a business enterprise that uses public property. In this case, a privately owned enterprise is given permission to use public property in performing its services. Examples are the use of public waterways for a ferry service, the use of public land for telephone or electric lines, the use of city streets for a bus line, or the use of the airwaves for radio or TV broadcasting. Such operating rights are frequently referred to as licences or permits, and are obtained through agreements with government departments or agencies.

Franchises and licences may be granted for a definite period of time, for an indefinite period of time, or in perpetuity. The enterprise that acquires the franchise or licence recognizes an intangible asset account titled either Franchise or Licence on its books as soon as there are costs (such as a lump-sum payment in advance or legal fees and other expenditures) that are identified with the acquisition of the operating right. The cost of a franchise or licence **with a limited life** is amortized over the lesser of its legal or useful life. A franchise **with an indefinite life** is not amortized. And a **perpetual franchise** is only amortized if its **useful life** is deemed to be limited.

Annual franchise fees paid under a franchise agreement are recorded as operating expenses in the period in which they are incurred. They do not represent an asset to the enterprise because they do not relate to future rights.

Another contract-related intangible asset is a favourable lease. A lease or leasehold is a contractual understanding between a lessor (property owner) and a lessee (property renter) that grants the lessee the right to use specific property, owned by the lessor, for a certain period of time in return for specific, usually periodic, cash payments. A lease contract is an intangible asset to the extent that the terms are more favourable than the usual market terms for such an arrangement. It could be an asset to the lessor or the lessee.[21]

Technology-Based Intangible Assets

Law Technology-based intangible assets relate to innovations or technological advances. Examples include Nortel's patents that were sold in 2011 (as discussed in What Do the Numbers Mean? 12.1) and patents for technology and trade secrets that are granted by the federal government's Patent Office (also part of CIPO). Patents are granted for products and processes that are new, workable, or ingenious. A patent gives the holder the right to exclude others from making, selling, or using a product or process for a period of 20 years from the date the patent application is filed with the Patent Office. Fortunes can be made by holding patents, as companies such as **BlackBerry**, IMAX, Facebook, and **Google** can attest.[22]

If a patent is purchased from an inventor or other owner, the purchase price represents its cost. Other costs that are incurred in connection with securing a patent, including legal fees and unrecovered costs of a successful lawsuit to protect the patent, are capitalized as part

---

[21]See Chapter 20 for a full discussion of accounting for leases by lessors and lessees.

[22]Consider the opposite result: Sir Alexander Fleming, who discovered penicillin, decided not to use a patent to protect his discovery. He hoped that companies would produce it more quickly to help save sufferers. Companies, however, refused to develop it because they did not have the protection of a patent and, therefore, were afraid to make the investment.

of the patent cost. Most research and development costs incurred that result in an internally generated patent are expensed. Only directly attributable costs incurred in the development phase after the six capitalization criteria are met can be included as part of the asset's cost. For this reason, most research and development costs related to developing a product, process, or idea that is subsequently patented are expensed as they are incurred.

The cost of a patent is amortized over its legal life or its useful life to the entity, whichever is shorter. If a patent is owned from the date it is granted, and it is expected to be useful during its entire legal life, it is amortized over 20 years. If it is expected to be useful for a shorter period, its cost is amortized to expense over that shorter period. Changing demand, new inventions replacing old ones, inadequacy, and other factors often limit the useful life of a patent to less than its legal life. For example, the useful life of patents in the pharmaceutical industry is often less than the legal life because of the testing and approval period that follows their issuance. A typical drug patent has five to 11 years knocked off its 20-year legal life. Why? A drug manufacturer spends one to four years on animal tests, four to six years on human tests, and two to three years for government agencies to review the tests—all after the patent is issued but before the product goes on the pharmacist's shelves.

Legal fees and other costs that are associated with a successful defence of a patent are capitalized as part of the asset's cost because lawsuits establish the patent holder's legal rights. Such costs are amortized along with other acquisition costs over the patent's remaining useful life.

As shown in **Example 12.3**, patent amortization follows a pattern that is consistent with the benefits that are received, if that pattern can be reliably determined. This could be based on time or on units produced.

Example 12.3 | Accounting for Patent Amortization

Facts Assume that on January 1, 2020, Harcott Ltd. either pays $180,000 to acquire a patent or incurs $180,000 in legal costs to successfully defend an internally developed patent. Further, assume that the patent has a remaining useful life of 12 years and is amortized on a straight-line basis.

Instructions What journal entries should be made to record the $180,000 expenditure on January 1, 2020, and amortization at the end of each year?

Solution The required entries are as follows:

A	=	L	+	SE
0				

Cash flows: ↓ 180,000 outflow

A	=	L	+	SE
−15,000				−15,000

Cash flows: No effect

January 1, 2020

Intangible Assets—Patents	180,000	
Cash		180,000

December 31, 2020

Amortization Expense	15,000	
Accumulated Amortization—Patents		15,000

Although a patent's useful life may be limited by its legal life, small modifications or additions may lead to a new patent and an extension of the life of the old patent.[23] In this case, the entity can apply the unamortized costs of the old patent to the new patent if the new patent provides essentially the same benefits. Alternatively, if a patent's value is reduced because, for example, demand drops for the product, the asset is tested for impairment.[24] Overall, as illustrated in **What Do the Numbers Mean? 12.4**, deciding if an intangible asset has an indefinite life or not can be challenging.

---

[23]The Canadian Intellectual Property Office website indicates in its "Guide to Patents" that 90% of patents are for improvements to existing patented inventions.

[24]**Eli Lilly**'s well-known drug Prozac, which is used to treat depression, accounted for 43% of the company's U.S. sales in 1998. The patent on Prozac expired in 2001 and the company was unable to extend its protection with a second-use patent for the use of Prozac to treat appetite disorders. Sales of Prozac went down substantially in 2001 as generic equivalents entered the market.

What Do the Numbers Mean? 12.4

Coca-Cola has managed to keep the recipe for the world's best-selling soft drink under wraps for more than 100 years. How has it done so? The company offers almost no information about its lifeblood. The only written copy of the formula is in a vault in the company's own museum in Atlanta, Georgia. This handwritten sheet is not available to anyone except by vote of the Coca-Cola board of directors.

Why is science unable to offer some clues? Coke contains 17 to 18 ingredients. These include the usual caramel colour and corn syrup, as well as a blend of oils known as 7X—rumoured to be a mix of orange, lemon, cinnamon, and others. Distilling natural products like these is complicated since they are made of thousands of compounds. Although the original formula contained trace amounts of cocaine, this is one ingredient that you will not find in today's Coke. When was it removed? That is a secret, too. Experts suggest that the power of this formula and related brand image account for almost U.S. $56 billion of the company's market capitalization of U.S. $183 billion (as of May 2017).

Sources: Reed Tucker, "How Has Coke's Formula Stayed a, Secret?" *Fortune*, July 24, 2000, p. 42; David Kiley, "Best Global Brands," *Business Week*, August 6, 2007, p. 59; Gavin Allen, "Bad News Pepsi! After 90 Years Coca-Cola's Secret Recipe Is Finally Out of the Bank Vault for Museum Display . . . But Rivals Still Won't Get a Peek at the Ingredients," *The Daily Mail*, December 9, 2011; www.forbes.com/powerful-brands/list/ (accessed January 28, 2018).

Another common technology-based intangible relates to computer software costs, either for internal use or for sale as a product. Costs that are incurred in the development of software as a potential product **for sale** or those directly attributable to the development, betterment, or acquisition of computer software **for internal use** are covered by the same capitalization criteria required for other intangible assets.

Impairment and Derecognition

LEARNING OBJECTIVE 6

Explain and account for impairment and derecognition of limited-life and indefinite-life intangible assets.

Similar to property, plant, and equipment, the carrying amounts of intangible assets and goodwill have to be reviewed to ensure that they do not exceed the economic benefits the assets are expected to provide in the future. If an item is determined to be impaired, its carrying amount will have to be written down and a loss on impairment recognized.

Impairment of Limited-Life Intangibles

The same impairment models and standards that apply to **long-lived tangible assets** also apply to **limited-life intangibles**.[25] As indicated in Chapter 11, under ASPE, long-lived assets that a company intends to hold and use are assessed for potential impairment whenever events and circumstances indicate the carrying value may not be recoverable. Under IFRS, these assets are **assessed for impairment** at the end of each reporting period.

The internal and external sources of information that may indicate an intangible asset is impaired are the same factors described in Illustration 11.5 in Chapter 11 for items of property, plant, and equipment. Of course, evidence of physical damage would not apply in the assessment of an intangible asset! If an assessment indicates there may be impairment, the asset is formally tested by applying the appropriate impairment model.

A summary of the two models and how they are applied is provided in Illustration 12.6. Remember that the cost recovery impairment model is used for **ASPE**, and the rational entity impairment model is used for **IFRS**. If you review the section "Impairment—Recognition and Measurement Models" in Chapter 11, it might help to reinforce your understanding of the details of each model.

---

[25]Reprinted/adapted with permission from the *CPA Canada Handbook—Accounting* © 2018, Part II, Section 3063 Impairment of Long-lived Assets, by Chartered Professional Accountants of Canada. All rights reserved by the copyright owner. See also IAS 36 Impairment of Assets.

ILLUSTRATION 12.6

ASPE **IFRS** **Summary of Impairment Models for Limited-Life Intangible Assets**

Cost Recovery Impairment Model	
Concept	Assumes asset will continue to be used; it is impaired only if the asset's carrying amount is not recoverable from the future undiscounted cash flows from use and eventual sale.
Recoverability test	If undiscounted future cash flows ≥ carrying amount, asset is not impaired.
	If undiscounted future cash flows < carrying amount, asset is impaired. Required to calculate loss on impairment.
Loss on impairment	Asset's carrying amount − fair value = loss on impairment; fair value is a discounted cash flow, market-based concept.

Entry to record loss	Loss on Impairment $XX
	    Accumulated Impairment Losses—
	       Licences (or "—Patents", etc.) $XX

Subsequent amortization	Review carrying amount to be amortized, useful life, and pattern of amortization and determine new periodic amortization charge.
Reversal of loss on impairment	Reversal not permitted. The fair value to which the asset is written down becomes the asset's new cost basis.
If no single-asset identifiable cash flows	Combine with other assets into an asset group, test for impairment, and, if impaired, calculate loss on impairment using same approach as for an individual asset. Allocate loss only to long-lived assets, based on their relative carrying amounts, within limits.
Rational Entity Impairment Model	
Concept	Assumes management will use the asset or dispose of it currently, whichever results in a higher value to the entity. It is impaired only if its carrying amount is not recoverable from the higher of the two options.
Recoverability test	No separate test of undiscounted cash flows.
Loss on impairment	Calculate recoverable amount = **higher of** value in use **and** fair value less costs to sell, both of which are discounted cash flow concepts.
	If recoverable amount ≥ carrying amount, no loss on impairment.
	If recoverable amount < carrying amount, loss on impairment = the difference.

Entry to record loss under cost model	Loss on Impairment $XX
	    Accumulated Impairment Losses—
	       Licences (or "—Patents", etc.) $XX

Subsequent amortization	Review carrying amount to be amortized, useful life, and pattern of amortization and determine new periodic amortization charge.
Reversal of loss on impairment	Reversal of loss is required if estimates underlying recoverable amount have changed. Reversal amount is limited.
If no single-asset identifiable cash flows	Combine with other assets into a cash-generating unit and calculate loss on impairment using same approach as for an individual asset. Allocate loss to assets based on their relative carrying amounts, within limits.

Impairment of Indefinite-Life Intangibles

Accounting for the impairment of intangible assets with an **indefinite life** is a little different than explained above for limited-life intangibles. These differences and the reasons for them are discussed below.

ASPE

An intangible asset with an indefinite life still needs to be tested for impairment only when events and circumstances indicate there might be impairment, but now the test is different. The impairment test for an indefinite-life asset is a **fair value test**. This test compares the **fair value** of the intangible asset with the asset's carrying amount. If its fair value is less than the carrying amount, a loss on impairment equal to the difference is recognized.

Why is there a different standard for indefinite-life intangibles? This one-step test is used because it would be relatively easy for many indefinite-life assets to meet the recoverability test. That is, the undiscounted cash flows would extend many years into the future and the total cash to be recovered tends to add up to a large sum. However, the dollars received in periods far into the future have a much lower value today. **As a result**, **the separate recoverability test is not used**, and the test compares the carrying amount directly with the asset's fair value—a discounted cash flow concept. See **Example 12.4**.

Example 12.4 | Accounting for Impairment of Indefinite-Life Intangibles

Facts   Assume that Space Corp. (SC) purchases a broadcast licence for $4,150,000, and that the licence is renewable every seven years if the company provides appropriate service and does not violate the rules and regulations of the Canadian Radio-television and Telecommunications Commission (CRTC). The licence is then renewed with the CRTC twice at a minimal cost, and because cash flows are expected to last indefinitely, the licence is reported as an indefinite-life intangible asset. Assume that SC is beginning to question whether the asset might be impaired because advertising revenues are expected to drop with changing demographics in the area covered by the licence. The following information has been gathered about the benefits of the licence:

Undiscounted future net cash flows expected from its use	$4,800,000
Discounted future net cash flows, or fair value	$3,950,000

Instructions   Is the licence impaired? If yes, how much impairment should SC record and how should it account for the impairment?

Solution   Yes, the licence is impaired because the carrying amount of $4,150,000 is more than its fair value of $3,950,000, so a loss on impairment of $4,150,000 − $3,950,000 = $200,000 is indicated.

SC may either set up and credit an account called Accumulated Impairment Losses—Licences or credit the asset account itself. The licence is now reported at a net amount of $3,950,000, and this is its new "cost" for subsequent accounting.

IFRS

There is only a minor difference between the IFRS standard for impairment for indefinite-life intangibles and those with limited lives. Assets with an indefinite life are **tested for impairment** by comparing their carrying amount and recoverable value **on an annual basis, whether or not there is any indication of impairment**. Why a stronger standard for these assets? The answer lies in the fact that no expense is being charged against income for such assets on a regular basis. For this reason, the assumption of a continuing recoverable value in excess of book value needs to be regularly tested.

Derecognition

An intangible asset is derecognized when it is disposed of or when its continuing use or disposal is not expected to generate any further economic benefits. Similar to property, plant, and equipment assets, a gain or loss is recognized at this time, equal to the difference between the asset's carrying amount and the proceeds on disposal, if any. The gain or loss on disposal is recognized in income in the period of disposal.

Goodwill—Recognition and Measurement

> **LEARNING OBJECTIVE 7**
> Explain how goodwill is measured and accounted for after acquisition.

Internally Generated Goodwill

Goodwill that is generated internally is not capitalized in the accounts. Measuring the components of internally generated goodwill is simply too complex, and associating costs incurred with future benefits is too difficult. In fact, the future benefits of goodwill may have no relationship to the costs that were incurred to develop it. To add to the complexity, goodwill may even exist when there have been no specific expenditures to develop it. In addition, because no transaction has taken place with outside parties, a great deal of subjectivity—even misrepresentation—might be involved in trying to measure it.

Purchased Goodwill

As previously indicated, goodwill is recognized only when a business combination occurs, because the value of goodwill cannot be separated from a business as a whole. The problem of determining the proper values to assign to identifiable intangible assets in a business combination is complex because of the many different types of intangibles that might be acquired. Because goodwill is a residual amount, every dollar that is assigned to other assets, including identifiable intangible assets, leaves one less dollar to be assigned to goodwill.

Differences between the current fair value and carrying amount are more common among long-term assets, although there can also be significant differences in the current asset category. Cash is obviously not a problem in terms of its value. Receivables are normally fairly close to their current valuation, although adjustments do sometimes need to be made because of inadequate bad debt provisions. The fair values of current and long-term liabilities also are usually close to their recorded book values. However, if interest rates have changed since long-term debt was issued, its value determined using current interest rates may be quite different from the carrying amount. A careful analysis must also be done to ensure that there are no unrecorded liabilities. Example 12.5 explores how fair value of net assets and goodwill is determined in a business combination.

In many cases, the values of long-lived assets such as property, plant, and equipment and intangibles may have increased substantially over the years. This difference could be due to inaccurate estimates of useful lives, continual expensing of small expenditures (say, amounts less than $500), or substantial increases in replacement costs. Alternatively, there may be assets that have not been recognized in the company's books.

Example 12.5 | Purchased Goodwill

Facts To illustrate, assume that Multi-Diversified Inc. decides that it needs a parts division to supplement its existing tractor distributorship. The president of Multi-Diversified is interested in buying Tractorling Ltd., a small company near Edmonton that has an established reputation and is looking to sell its business. Tractorling's current statement of financial position is as follows:

Tractorling Ltd. Statement of Financial Position December 31, 2020			
Assets		**Liabilities and equity**	
Cash	$ 25,000	Current liabilities	$ 55,000
Accounts receivable	35,000	Share capital	20,000
Inventories	42,000	Retained earnings	180,000
Property, plant, and equipment (net)	153,000		
Total assets	$255,000	Total liabilities and equity	$255,000

After considerable negotiation, Tractorling Ltd.'s shareholders decide to accept Multi-Diversified's offer of $400,000. The two companies might agree on a $400,000 cash payment, or $400,000 in value of Multi-Diversified's shares, or other forms of consideration.

Instructions

a. How would the fair value of Tractorling's underlying assets be determined?

b. Why might Multi-Diversified pay an amount in excess of the fair value of the individual assets of Tractorling to acquire the company?

c. How would goodwill, if any, be measured and what does it represent?

d. Provide the journal entry that should be made by Multi-Diversified for its acquisition of Tractorling.

Solution

a. The best way to determine fair value is not obvious. The fair values of Tractorling's identifiable assets and liabilities are not disclosed in its cost-based statement of financial position. It is likely, though, that as the negotiations progressed, Multi-Diversified had a detailed investigation done of Tractorling's underlying assets to determine their fair values. Such an investigation may be done through a purchase audit by Multi-Diversified's auditors, or an independent appraisal from some other source. Let's assume that the result of the analysis of fair values is as follows:

Tractorling Fair Values, December 31, 2020	
Cash	$ 25,000
Accounts receivable	35,000
Inventories	62,000
Property, plant, and equipment (net)	265,000
Patents	18,000
Liabilities	(55,000)
Fair value of identifiable net assets	$350,000

The $20,000 difference between the fair value and carrying amount of Tractorling's inventories ($62,000 − $42,000) could be due to several factors. One explanation might be that Tractorling acquired significant inventories when the prices were lower and uses specific identification or an average cost valuation, in which ending inventory includes inventory at older costs.

In Tractorling's case, let's assume that PP&E includes land that was acquired many years ago and its fair value has increased significantly, and that internally developed patents have not been recognized in the accounts, yet they have a fair value of $18,000.

b. Since the investigation indicates that the fair value of the identifiable net assets is $350,000, why would Multi-Diversified pay $400,000? Tractorling might point to the company's established reputation, good credit rating, top management team, well-trained employees, and so on, as factors that make the value of the business as a whole greater than $350,000. Multi-Diversified places a premium on the future earning power of these attributes as well as the company's current basic asset structure. At this point in the negotiations, Tractorling's total fair value, and price, may be due to many factors; the most important may be sheer skill at the bargaining table.

c. Multi-Diversified labels the difference between the fair value of the consideration paid of $400,000 and the fair value of the identifiable net assets of $350,000 as goodwill. Goodwill is viewed as the unidentifiable values plus the value of the identifiable intangibles that do not meet the criteria for separate recognition. The procedure for valuation shown below is referred to as a master valuation approach, because goodwill is assumed to cover all the values that cannot be specifically associated with any identifiable tangible or intangible asset. Note that this method of accounting for a business combination is a fair value approach rather than one based on the cost of the acquisition and cost allocation. For example, acquisition-related costs associated with a business combination are expensed as incurred and are not capitalized as they would be in a cost-based system.

Determination of Goodwill—Master Valuation Approach		
Fair value of consideration transferred:		$400,000
Fair value of identifiable net assets:		
Cash	$ 25,000	
Accounts receivable	35,000	
Inventories	62,000	
Property, plant, and equipment	265,000	
Patents	18,000	
Liabilities	(55,000)	350,000
Value assigned to goodwill:		$ 50,000

d. Multi-Diversified's entry to record the purchase of Tractorling's net assets, assuming the consideration is $400,000 cash, is as follows:[26]

Cash	25,000	
Accounts Receivable	35,000	
Inventory	62,000	
Property, Plant, and Equipment	265,000	
Intangible Assets—Patents	18,000	
Goodwill	50,000	
Liabilities		55,000
Cash		400,000

*Specific PPE and Liability accounts would be debited and credited as part of this journal entry.

A	=	L	+	SE
+55,000		+55,000		

Cash flows: ▼ 375,000 outflow

Bargain Purchase

A **bargain purchase**, resulting in what is sometimes called **negative goodwill**, arises when the total of the fair value of the identifiable net assets acquired is higher than the fair value of the consideration transferred for those net assets. This situation is a result of market imperfection (or a poor decision by the seller) because the seller would be better off to sell the assets individually than in total. However, situations do occur when the value of what is given up is less than the value of the identifiable net assets that are acquired, and this requires accounting for a goodwill "credit."

How should this credit be handled in the accounts? Should it be an increase to Retained Earnings directly, or Other Comprehensive Income, or included in net income in the year of purchase, or should it be amortized to income over a reasonable future period? The accounting standards over the past 45 years or so have taken a variety of approaches to this "bonus," which shows the difficulty there has been in coming to terms with its conceptual nature.

Current standards require the excess to be recognized **as a gain in net income** in the same period that the combination takes place. However, this cannot be done without a thorough

---

[26]In reality, the Cash amounts would be netted and only $375,000 would be transferred. If Multi-Diversified gained control over Tractorling by buying all of that company's shares instead of buying all the individual assets and liabilities making up the business, the entry would be:

Investment in Subsidiary Company	400,000	
Cash		400,000

When Multi-Diversified prepares consolidated financial statements, the Investment account is removed from the statement of financial position and is replaced with the underlying assets and liabilities that the Investment balance represents. Regardless of the transaction's legal form, the goodwill appears on the investor's consolidated statement of financial position.

reassessment of all the variables, values, and measurement procedures used that resulted in this gain. If a gain still results after the re-examination, then it is recognized in income. While some critics do not agree with recognizing a gain **on the acquisition of assets**, this treatment is not applied lightly and appears to be a practical approach to a situation that rarely occurs.

Valuation after Acquisition

Once goodwill has been recognized in the accounts, how should it be treated in subsequent periods? Three basic approaches have been suggested:

1. **Charge goodwill immediately to expense.** Supporters of this approach justify an immediate write off because the accounting for goodwill is then consistent whether purchased or created internally. Goodwill created internally is not recognized as an asset. Perhaps the best rationale for charging goodwill against income directly is that identifying the periods over which the future benefits are to be received is so difficult that the result is purely arbitrary.

2. **Amortize goodwill over its useful life.** Some believe that goodwill has value when it is acquired, but that its value eventually disappears. Therefore the asset should be charged to expense over the periods that are affected. To the extent that goodwill represents a wasting asset, this method provides a better matching of the costs of the benefits to revenues than other methods, even though the useful life may be difficult to determine.

3. **Retain goodwill indefinitely unless a reduction in value occurs.** Others believe that goodwill can have an indefinite life and should be kept as an asset until a decline in value occurs. Some form of goodwill should always be an asset because the current costs to maintain or enhance the purchased goodwill are being expensed. Also, unless there is strong evidence that a decline in its value has occurred, a write off of goodwill is arbitrary and leads to distortions in net income.

Not so long ago, companies were required to amortize goodwill over a period no longer than 40 years. However, goodwill acquired in a business combination **is now considered to have an indefinite life and is no longer amortized**. Although goodwill may decrease over time, predicting the actual life of goodwill and an appropriate pattern of amortization is extremely difficult. Therefore, it is carried on the statement of financial position at the amount originally recognized in the combination less any subsequent impairment losses. Impairment losses can be challenging to estimate as discussed in **What Do the Numbers Mean? 12.5**. **Income statements are not charged with any amounts paid for the goodwill until the asset is considered impaired.**

What Do the Numbers Mean? 12.5

Duff & Phelps and the Financial Executives Research Foundation prepare an annual Goodwill Impairment Study of U.S. public companies. The 2017 study noted that total goodwill impairment for the companies in their study was cut in half, down to $28.5 billion in 2016. A similar study focused on Canada a few years earlier and included a summary of a survey of members of the Financial Executives International. These members stated that the top challenges for companies when performing goodwill impairment tests were developing cash flow projections, identifying cash-generating units (CGUs), determining the discount rate to be used for estimation, and properly identifying impairment indicators for CGUs.

Goodwill—Impairment

LEARNING OBJECTIVE 8
Explain and account for impairment of goodwill.

Goodwill is not an identifiable asset and cannot generate cash flows independently of other assets. Because it can be acquired only in combination with other assets making up a business, it has to be assigned to a reporting unit or cash-generating unit (CGU) in order to be tested for impairment. An example of a CGU is the Markets division of Thomson Reuters, which, when it adopted IFRS, contributed to the company's goodwill impairment charge of over U.S. $3.0 billion. Other than this specific requirement regarding the reporting unit or CGU, impairment accounting for goodwill is similar to that of intangibles with an indefinite life. Applying the standards in this area can be complex, but we provide a summary of the basic elements in Illustration 12.7 and Examples 12.6 and 12.7, under both ASPE and IFRS.

ILLUSTRATION 12.7

Summary of Accounting for Impairment of Goodwill

	ASPE	IFRS
Apply impairment test…	…when events or changes in circumstances indicate.	…annually, and whenever there is an indication that the CGU may be impaired.
At acquisition date, assign goodwill…	…to a reporting unit: an operating segment or one level below.	…to cash-generating unit: smallest identifiable group of assets where goodwill is monitored for management purposes, and no larger than an operating segment.
There is a loss on impairment…	…when carrying amount of reporting unit including goodwill > fair value of reporting unit. Loss = amount of excess	…when carrying amount of CGU including goodwill > recoverable amount. Loss = amount of excess. Recoverable amount is the higher of value in use and fair value less costs to sell.
Loss on impairment is allocated…	…to goodwill; impairment test for other assets in group is done before goodwill impairment test.	…first to goodwill related to the CGU, then remainder to other assets on a relative carrying amount (proportionate) basis.
Goodwill impairment reversal…	…is not permitted.	…is not permitted.

Example 12.6 | Accounting for Goodwill Impairment

Facts   Assume that Coburg Corporation has three divisions. One division, Pritt Products, was purchased four years ago for $2 million and has been identified as a reporting unit. Unfortunately, it has experienced operating losses over the past three quarters and management is reviewing the reporting unit to determine whether there has been an impairment of goodwill. The carrying amounts of Pritt Division's net assets, including the associated goodwill of $900,000, are listed below. Assume that Pritt's reporting unit is also a cash-generating unit under IFRS.

Pritt Reporting Unit—Carrying Amount of Net Assets Including Goodwill	
Cash	$ 200,000
Receivables	300,000
Inventory	700,000
Property, plant, and equipment (net)	800,000
Goodwill	900,000
Less: Accounts and notes payable	(500,000)
Net assets, at carrying amounts	$2,400,000

Instructions `IFRS` `ASPE` Assume that the fair value of the Pritt Division reporting unit as a whole is estimated to be $2.8 million. Also assume that management determines that the unit's value in use is $2.9 million and that the company would incur direct costs of $50,000 if the unit were sold.

a. Would goodwill be considered impaired under ASPE?

b. Would your answer change under IFRS?

Solution

a. Under **ASPE**, the goodwill is not impaired. The asset group's $2.4-million carrying value is less than its fair value of $2.8 million.

b. Under **IFRS**, goodwill is not considered impaired either. The recoverable amount of the unit is $2.9 million—the higher of its value in use ($2.9 million) and its fair value less costs to sell ($2,800,000 − $50,000)—and this exceeds the unit's carrying amount of $2.4 million.

Example 12.7 | Accounting for Goodwill Impairment with Journal Entries

Facts Assume the same facts as Example 12.6, except assume that the fair value of the Pritt Division unit as a whole is $1.9 million, its value in use is $2.1 million, and the direct costs of selling the unit are $50,000.

Instructions `IFRS` `ASPE`

a. Calculate goodwill impairment under ASPE and under IFRS.

b. Provide the related journal entries, if any, under both ASPE and IFRS, and calculate the net carrying amount for goodwill under ASPE vs. IFRS.

Solution

a. Under **ASPE**, a loss on impairment of $500,000 is indicated as follows:

Carrying amount of unit, including goodwill	$2,400,000
Fair value of unit	1,900,000
Goodwill—loss on impairment	$ 500,000

Under **IFRS**, a loss on impairment of $300,000 is indicated:

Carrying amount of unit, including goodwill		$ 2,400,000
Recoverable amount of unit: higher of		
Value in use	$2,100,000	
and		(2,100,000)
Fair value less costs to sell	$1,850,000	
Goodwill—loss on impairment		$ 300,000

b. The entries to record the losses under ASPE and IFRS are:

	ASPE		IFRS	
Loss on Impairment	500,000		300,000	
Accumulated Impairment Losses—Goodwill		500,000		300,000

A	=	L	+	SE
ASPE				
−500,000				−500,000
IFRS				
−300,000				−300,000

Cash flows: No effect

Because there is a requirement to report the gross amount of goodwill and accumulated impairment losses at the end of the period, the Accumulated Impairment Losses—Goodwill account is credited instead of the Goodwill account so that the required information is retained. The Goodwill's net carrying amount is now $400,000 ($900,000 − $500,000) under ASPE and $600,000 ($900,000 − $300,000) under IFRS.

Impairment tests for various types of assets are summarized in Illustration 12.8.

ILLUSTRATION 12.8

Summary of the Impairment Tests for Intangible Assets and Goodwill

Type of Asset	Impairment Test	
	ASPE	IFRS
Limited-life intangible	Compare carrying amount with undiscounted future cash flows	Compare carrying amount with recoverable amount
Indefinite-life intangible	Compare carrying amount with fair value	Compare carrying amount with recoverable amount
Goodwill	Compare carrying amount of reporting unit with its fair value	Compare carrying amount of CGU with its recoverable amount

Presentation, Disclosure, and Analysis

LEARNING OBJECTIVE 9

Identify the types of disclosure requirements for intangible assets and goodwill and explain the issues in analyzing these assets.

A survey indicates that the most common types of intangible assets reported are broadcast rights, publishing rights, trademarks, patents, licences, customer lists, non-competition agreements, franchises, and purchased R&D.[27] These, along with goodwill, have become an increasingly large proportion of companies' reported assets, making intangibles an important contributor to entity performance and financial position. For example, Corus Entertainment Inc., a Canadian-based media and entertainment company, reported indefinite-life broadcast licences and goodwill at August 31, 2017, that amounted to 71% of its total assets. There were no charges for impairment in either 2017 or 2016, after several periods in a row with impairment charges for these intangibles. For example, the company recognized $130.0 million of impairment losses on these two classes of assets in 2015 ($83.0 million in 2014). The goodwill write off in 2015 represented about 11% of its opening book value, with the impairment being due, in part, to "certain radio clusters (with) actual results and revised cash flow projections that fell short of previous estimates." The CGUs affected by the write offs were predominantly in the radio segments for broadcast licence impairment and also in the radio CGU for goodwill.

Presentation and Disclosure

IFRS ASPE Overview

While there are few required disclosures on the face of the statement of financial position and the statement of comprehensive income, a significant amount of information is required in the notes to the financial statements, particularly those prepared under IFRS. As seen in previous chapters, ASPE disclosures are considerably curtailed because most users of such financial statements can request additional information as needed. The goal of disclosure for publicly accountable entities is basically to allow readers to understand the significance of

[27]Nadi Chlala, Diane Paul, Louise Martel, and Andrée Lavigne, *Financial Reporting in Canada, 2007* (CICA, 2007), p. 343, and Clarence Byrd, Ida Chen, and Joshua Smith, *Financial Reporting in Canada, 2005* (CICA, 2005), p. 256.

intangibles and goodwill to the operations of the business. To that end, this section summarizes some of the major disclosures required.

For each class of intangible asset, and separately for internally generated intangibles and other intangible assets, the following information is required:

- whether their lives are indefinite or finite (limited), useful life, methods and rates of amortization, and the line where amortization is included on the statement of comprehensive income;
- the carrying amount of intangible assets with an indefinite life, and the reasons supporting an assessment of an indefinite life;
- a reconciliation of the opening and ending balances of their carrying amount and accumulated amortization and losses on impairment, separately identifying each reason for an increase or decrease; and
- losses on impairment and reversals of losses on impairment and where they are reported in the statement of comprehensive income.

For each material loss on impairment recognized or reversed in the period, the following is required:

- the circumstances that led to its recognition, the amount recognized, the nature of the asset or cash-generating unit, and information about how the recoverable amount was determined.

For each cash-generating unit or group of units that has a significant amount of goodwill or intangible assets with an indefinite life, the following is required:

- how the unit's recoverable amount was determined, as well as assumptions underlying the calculation of the recoverable amount.

For intangible assets measured using the revaluation model, the following is required:

- their carrying amount, the carrying amounts if the revaluation model had not been applied, the date of the revaluation, the amount of the associated revaluation surplus and changes in that account, and the methods and assumptions used in estimating fair values.

This list identifies only some of the disclosures. The best source of the specific requirements is the standards themselves.

Illustration of Disclosures

Excerpts from the financial statements of Corus Entertainment for its year ended August 31, 2017, are provided in **Illustration 12.9**. These disclosures are based on IFRS, which the company adopted in 2012. This company, reporting in thousands of Canadian dollars, operates through two main lines of business: television and radio. Its 45 specialty television networks include YTV, Treehouse, TELETOON, W Network, and SHOWCASE.

ILLUSTRATION 12.9

Selected Excerpts: Notes on Intangible Assets and Goodwill—Corus Entertainment

3. SIGNIFICANT ACCOUNTING POLICIES

BASIS OF PRESENTATION

The consolidated financial statements have been prepared on a cost basis, except for derivative financial instruments and certain available-for-sale financial assets, which have been measured at fair value. The consolidated financial statements are presented in Canadian dollars, which is also the Company's functional currency and all values are rounded to the nearest thousand, except where otherwise noted.

GOODWILL AND INTANGIBLE ASSETS

Intangible assets acquired separately are measured on initial recognition at cost. Intangible assets acquired in a business combination are measured at fair value as at the date of

(continued)

ILLUSTRATION 12.9
(*continued*)

acquisition. Following initial recognition, intangible assets are carried at cost less accumulated amortization and accumulated impairment charges, if any. Internally generated intangible assets such as goodwill, brands and customer lists, excluding capitalized program and film development costs, are not capitalized and expenditures are reflected in the consolidated statements of income and comprehensive income in the year in which the expenditure is incurred.

Intangible assets are recognized separately from goodwill when they are separable or arise from contractual or other legal rights and their fair value can be measured reliably. The useful lives of intangible assets are assessed as either finite or indefinite.

Intangible assets with finite lives are amortized over their useful economic lives and assessed for impairment whenever there is an indication that the intangible assets may be impaired. The amortization period and the amortization method for intangible assets with finite useful lives are reviewed at least at the end of each reporting period. Changes in the expected useful life or the expected pattern of consumption of future economic benefits embodied in the assets are accounted for by changing the amortization period or method, as appropriate, and are treated as changes in accounting estimates. The amortization expense on intangible assets with finite lives is recognized in the consolidated statements of income and comprehensive income in the expense category, consistent with the function of the intangible assets.

Amortization is recorded on a straight-line basis over the estimated useful life of the asset as follows:

Brand names, trade marks and digital rights	Agreement term
Software, patents and customer lists	3 – 5 years

Intangible assets with indefinite useful lives are not amortized. Broadcast licenses are considered to have an indefinite life based on management's intent and ability to renew the licenses without significant cost and without material modification of the existing terms and conditions of the license. The assessment of indefinite life is reviewed annually to determine whether the indefinite life continues to be supportable. If not, the change in useful life from indefinite to finite is made on a prospective basis.

Goodwill is initially measured at cost, being the excess of the aggregate of the consideration transferred and the amount recognized for non-controlling interest over the net identifiable assets acquired and liabilities assumed. If this consideration is lower than the fair value of the net identifiable assets of the subsidiary acquired, the difference is recognized in the consolidated statements of income and comprehensive income.

After initial recognition, goodwill is measured at cost less any accumulated impairment losses. For the purpose of impairment testing, goodwill acquired in a business combination is, from the acquisition date, allocated to a CGU or group of CGUs that are expected to benefit from the synergies of the combination, irrespective of whether other assets or liabilities of the acquiree are assigned to those units. The group of CGUs is not larger than the level at which management monitors goodwill or the Company's operating segments.

Where goodwill forms part of a CGU and part of the operation within that unit is disposed of, the goodwill associated with the operation disposed of is included in the carrying amount of the operation when determining the gain or loss on disposal of the operation. Goodwill disposed of in this circumstance is measured based on the relative fair value of the operation disposed of and the portion of the CGU retained.

Broadcast licenses and goodwill are tested for impairment annually or more frequently if events or circumstances indicate that they may be impaired. The Company completes its annual testing during the fourth quarter each year.

Broadcast licenses by themselves do not generate cash inflows and therefore, when assessing these assets for impairment, the Company looks to the CGU to which the asset belongs. The identification of CGUs involves judgment and is based on how senior management monitors operations; however, the lowest aggregations of assets that generate largely independent cash inflows represent CGUs for broadcast license impairment testing.

(*continued*)

ILLUSTRATION 12.9

(continued)

CGUs for broadcast license impairment testing

For the Television segment, the Company has determined that there are two CGUs: (1) Managed Brands consisting of conventional television stations, specialty television networks and pay television services (ceased operations February 29, 2016) that are operated and managed directly by the Company; and (2) Other, as these are the levels at which independent cash inflows have been identified.

For the Radio segment, the Company has determined that the CGU is a radio cluster whereby a cluster represents a geographic area, generally a city, where radio stations are combined for the purpose of managing performance. These clusters are managed as a single asset and overhead costs are allocated amongst the cluster and have independent cash inflows at the cluster level.

Groups of CGUs for goodwill impairment testing

For purposes of impairment testing of goodwill, the Company has grouped the CGUs within the Television and Radio operating segments and performs the test at the operating segment level. This is the lowest level at which management monitors goodwill for internal management purposes.

Other intangible assets

Gains or losses on an intangible asset are measured as the difference between the net disposal proceeds and the carrying amount of the asset and are recognized in the consolidated statements of income and comprehensive income when the asset is derecognized.

9. INTANGIBLES

	Broadcast Licenses[1]	Other[2]	Total
Balance—August 31, 2015	956,984	17,631	974,615
Additions	–	122,621	122,621
Acquisitions (note 27)	78,300	987,540	1,065,840
Disposals (note 27)	(50,395)	(2,662)	(53,057)
Amortization	–	(33,782)	(33,782)
Balance—August 31, 2016	984,889	1,091,348	2,076,237
Additions	–	12,439	12,439
Amortizations	–	(42,863)	(42,863)
Balance—August 31, 2017	**984,889**	**1,060,924**	**2,045,813**

[1] Broadcast licenses are located in Canada.
[2] Other intangibles are comprised of brands, trade marks and software.

At August 31, 2017, other intangibles with a finite life consisted of:

	2017	2016
Cost	**258,246**	247,483
Accumulated amortization	**124,125**	82,933
Net book value	**134,121**	164,550

The Company expects that approximately 29% of the net book value of intangible assets with a finite life will be amortized during the year ended August 31, 2018. The Company expects the net book value of intangible assets with a finite life to be fully amortized by August 2022.

Indefinite life intangibles, such as broadcast licenses, are tested for impairment annually as at August 31 or more frequently if events or changes in circumstances indicate that they may be impaired. At August 31, 2017, the Company performed its annual impairment test for fiscal 2017 and determined that there were no impairments for the year then ended on indefinite life intangibles.

Analysis

Missing Values

The requirement that most research and development phase costs incurred for internally developed intangibles be expensed immediately is a conservative, practical solution that ensures consistency in practice and uniformity among companies. But the practice of immediately writing off expenditures that are made in the expectation of benefiting future periods cannot always be justified on the grounds that it is good accounting theory.

Since the 1990s, the conventional financial-accounting model has been increasingly criticized for its inability to capture many of the attributes that give a business value. At the end of third quarter of 2018, for example, Apple Inc. had a total book value of approximately U.S. $115 billion, while its market capitalization (the market value of its outstanding shares) was over U.S. $1.1 trillion.[28] Why such a significant difference?

The answer is that financial accounting does not capture and report many of the assets that contribute to future cash flows, and this is seen by some critics as the greatest challenge facing the accounting profession today. Many of the missing values belong to unrecognized, internally developed intangible assets known as **knowledge assets** or **intellectual capital**. These include the value of key personnel (not only Tim Cook, the CEO successor to Apple co-founder Steve Jobs, but the many creative and technologically proficient employees in general), the investment in products from research and development and their potential, organizational adaptability, customer retention, strategic direction, brands, flexible and innovative management, customer service capability, and effective advertising programs, to name only a few types of knowledge assets. When a company is not allowed to capitalize many of these expenditures, this excludes from its statement of financial position what may be its most valuable assets.

The challenges of proper recording of assets as the economy evolves are significant, as discussed for cryptocurrencies such as bitcoin in **What Do the Numbers Mean? 12.6.**

What Do the Numbers Mean? 12.6

Cryptocurrencies such as bitcoin are difficult to classify. They appear to be a form of cash, but they are not backed by a central bank or intermediary. The lack of backing by a bank or government, and the volatility of their value, implies that bitcoins do not qualify as cash or cash equivalents under IFRS. Similarly, the lack of a contractual right to receive cash or another financial asset implies that bitcoins are not financial instruments. The lack of physical existence or substance implies that bitcoins are not property, plant and equipment.

They are not held for sale in the ordinary course of business for most companies, and a lack of trading activity implies that bitcoins are not likely to be considered inventory. The best choice may be for bitcoins to be considered intangible assets as they are identifiable and separable—they can be separated or divided from the entity and can be sold, transferred or exchanged! Remember that, as we discussed earlier in this chapter, as long as there is an active market for intangible assets (like bitcoins) they can be measured at fair value.[29]

Finance 5.1.1, 5.1.2 These indicators of longer-term value that are created in an organization will ultimately result in realized values through future transactions and, therefore, are relevant information for financial statement readers. Companies increasingly disclose more of this "soft" information in annual reports outside the financial statements, in news releases, and in interviews with market analysts. While some observers believe that standard setters should work to ensure that more of these intangibles are captured on the statement of financial position, others believe that new frameworks for reporting performance need to be developed together with—or to even replace—the current financial reporting model.

Our conventional accounting model captures the results of past transactions. This has been considered a very significant benefit because it is what makes it possible to verify the

---

[28]Based on estimates from Yahoo Finance, which quoted Apple's third quarter (June 30th, 2018) financial statements as compared with its market capitalization on September 5, 2018.

[29]For further discussion of the challenges of classifying cryptocurrency, see "Cracking the cryptocurrency code; or what is a 'bitcoin' anyway?" from PWC's "IFRS news" series, available at www.pwc.lu/ifrs (accessed June 24, 2018).

reported measures and therefore add to the reliability of the financial statements. In most cases, the intellectual capital and knowledge assets identified above cannot be measured in financial terms with enough reliability to give them accounting recognition. Some cannot be included as assets because of the enterprise's inability to control access to the benefits. Investments that are made in employee education and development, for example, can walk out the door when employees leave the company to work elsewhere. Others argue that the amount of costs charged to expense in each accounting period is about the same whether there is immediate expensing or capitalization followed by amortization, because most companies continuously invest in a variety of research, development, and other activities.

Theory Others opposed to increased capitalization of costs point to the decline in market value of technology shares—in particular, from early 2000 to 2001. Microsoft, a key company in the high-tech sector, lost over 60% of its value in this period, bringing it much closer to its book value. Some use this as an argument that the historical cost model still has much to recommend it! The "truth," of course, lies somewhere in between. While inflated market values are not reliable enough to support the recognition of previously unrecognized intangible asset value, the historical-cost, transactions-based model certainly fails to capture many of the things at the heart of corporate value. Much research is being carried out in the search for solutions to the discrepancies between what gets reported as having value on the financial statements and what the capital markets perceive as having value and therefore reflect in share prices.

Comparing Results

When comparing the operating results of companies—either of one company over time or between companies—it is not only important to pay close attention to which set of GAAP each applies. It is also important to examine how deferred charges, intangible assets, and goodwill have been accounted for and how any changes in related accounting policies have been handled. This is important because the standards for intangibles have changed significantly in recent years and may continue to change. Montreal-based communications company **Quebecor Inc.**, for example, like other companies when they first adopted IFRS, was required to review its existing goodwill and was permitted to recognize any impairment as an adjustment to its opening balance of retained earnings. So, when IFRS was first applied, Quebecor recognized a goodwill impairment loss of $2.2 billion—a charge that bypassed the income statement completely and went straight against retained earnings! Quebecor thus took a "big bath" writedown—writing down goodwill that it had previously reported as an asset. This means that these costs will never flow through the company's income statement, and future operating statements are freed from them.[30] Care has to be taken when calculating and interpreting any ratios that include earnings and asset numbers, especially when the results of different years are being compared.

IFRS/ASPE Comparison

LEARNING OBJECTIVE 10
Identify differences in accounting between IFRS and ASPE.

A Comparison of IFRS and ASPE

With a few specific exceptions, accounting for intangible assets and goodwill under IFRS and ASPE is very similar. **Illustration 12.10** identifies the relevant standards that apply to intangible assets and goodwill for both and the areas of difference that exist.

---

[30]A "big bath" in accounting occurs when a company decides that, if a loss has to be reported, it might as well report a very large loss. Any loss is seen as negative but the advantage of reporting a bigger loss is that fewer costs remain in the accounts to be reported as future expenses.

ILLUSTRATION 12.10   **IFRS and ASPE Comparison Chart**

	IFRS—IAS 23, 36, and 38; IFRS 2, 3, and 13	Accounting Standards for Private Enterprises (ASPE)—*CPA Canada Handbook*, Part II, Sections 1582, 3063, 3064, 3475, and 3831	References to Related Examples, Illustrations and Select Brief Exercises
Measurement at acquisition	Borrowing costs directly attributable to the acquisition, construction, or development of qualifying assets are capitalized.	Interest costs directly attributable to the acquisition, construction, or development of an intangible asset, once it meets the criteria to be capitalized, may be capitalized or expensed, depending on the entity's accounting policy.	BE12.3 and BE12.12
	Costs associated with the development of internally generated intangible assets are capitalized when six specific conditions are met in the development stage.	Costs associated with the development of internally generated intangible assets that meet the six specific conditions in the development stage may be capitalized or expensed, depending on the entity's accounting policy.	BE12.8 and BE12.9
Measurement after acquisition	Intangible assets are accounted for under the cost model or the revaluation model. The latter is used only when the asset has an active market fair value.	Intangible assets are accounted for according to the cost model.	Illustration 12.4 BE12.15
Impairment of intangible assets	Assess limited-life intangible assets for potential impairment at the end of each reporting period; for those with an indefinite life, this includes calculating the recoverable amount and comparing it with book value.	Test both limited- and indefinite-life intangibles for potential impairment whenever events and changing circumstances indicate the carrying value may not be recoverable.	Illustration 12.6
	For limited-life intangibles, apply the rational entity impairment model.	For limited-life intangibles, apply the cost recovery impairment model.	Illustrations 12.6 and 12.8 BE12.15, BE12.16, and BE12.17
	For indefinite-life intangibles, apply the rational entity impairment model.	For indefinite-life intangibles, impairment test is comparison of carrying amount with asset's fair value; loss is equal to the difference when fair value is lower.	Example 12.4 Illustration 12.8 BE12.18
	Within limits, losses on impairment are reversed for recoveries related to economic changes.	Losses on impairment are not reversed.	
Impairment of goodwill	Similar to impairment of indefinite-life intangible assets, except that there is no reversal of a loss on impairment for goodwill. See also Illustration 12.7.	Similar to impairment of indefinite-life intangible assets. See also Illustration 12.7.	Examples 12.6 and 12.7 Illustrations 12.7 and 12.8 BE12.20 and BE12.21
Disclosures	Significant disclosures are required including detailed reconciliations between opening and ending balances for each type of intangible and goodwill. Considerable information is also required whenever fair values are used to explain how they are determined, as well as background information about losses on impairment for goodwill and intangibles.	Basic disclosures are required about the balance of intangible assets and goodwill on the balance sheet with additional details by classes and whether or not they are amortized. Details explaining each impairment loss and where each is reported on the income statement are also required.	Illustration 12.9

Looking Ahead

Whether recognized or not, intangible assets are an increasingly important aspect of what gives an entity value, and existing standards do not do a very good job of reporting these assets to users of the financial statements. Current standards significantly restrict the intangibles that can be recognized, and after acquisition, only intangibles with fair values determined in an active market can use the revaluation model under IFRS. Also, there are inconsistent treatments of intangible assets developed internally and those acquired in a business combination, as well as of internally developed property, plant, and equipment assets.

Effective January 1, 2016, IAS 38.98 was clarified via IAS 38.98A such that there is an underlying assumption (which the IASB calls a "rebuttable presumption") that amortization methods based on revenue generated by an activity that includes the use of an intangible asset are inappropriate.

The IASB tentatively decided not to consider reintroducing amortization of goodwill. However, it was considering ways of ensuring that impairment of goodwill is recognized on a timely basis. For example, it was considering simplifying the "value in use" calculation for IAS 36 in its Goodwill and Impairment project, if it could do so without making the impairment test in IAS 36 *Impairment of Assets* less robust. So, in January 2018 the Board announced that it may remove the requirement for companies to exclude cash flows resulting from a future restructuring or a future enhancement from the "value in use" calculation. The next step being considered is a Discussion Paper or Exposure Draft.

Appendix 12A	# Valuing Goodwill

LEARNING OBJECTIVE 11

Explain and apply basic approaches to valuing goodwill.

In this chapter, we discussed the method of measuring and recording goodwill when one entity acquires 100% of another business **as the excess of the fair value of the consideration given up by the acquirer over the fair value of the identifiable assets acquired and liabilities assumed in a business acquisition**. Determining the fair value of the consideration transferred and the fair value of the assets and liabilities acquired is an inexact process, and therefore, so is the calculation of the amount of goodwill. As the chapter suggests, it is usually possible to determine the fair value of specifically identifiable assets, but the question remains, "How does a buyer value intangible factors such as superior management, a good credit rating, and so on?"

Excess-Earnings Approach

`Finance` 5.4.1, 5.4.2, 5.4.3 One method to estimate the amount of goodwill in a business is the **excess-earnings approach**. This approach works as follows:

1. Calculate the average annual "normalized" earnings that the company is expected to earn in the future.

2. Calculate the average annual earnings that the company would be expected to earn if it generated the same return on investment (ROI) as the average firm in the same industry. The return on investment is the percentage that results when income is divided by the net assets or shareholders' equity invested to generate that income.

3. Calculate the excess annual earnings: the difference between what the specific company and the average firm in the industry are expected to earn in the future. The ability to generate a higher income indicates that the business has an unidentifiable value that

provides this greater earning power. This ability to earn a higher rate of return than the industry is considered to be the heart of what goodwill really is.

4. Estimate the value of the goodwill based on the future stream of excess earnings.

This approach is a systematic and logical way to calculate goodwill because its value is directly related to what makes a company worth more than the sum of its parts. We will use the Tractorling Ltd. example referred to in Example 12.5 again here to explain each of the four steps above. As indicated above, we first calculate the average annual "normalized" earnings that the company is expected to earn in the future. Because the past often provides useful information about the future, the past earnings are a good place to start in estimating a company's likely future earnings. Going back three to six years is usually adequate.

Assume that Tractorling's net income amounts for the past five years and the calculation of the company's average earnings over this period are as given in **Illustration 12A.1**. The information in this illustration, and in the discussion that follows it, will provide the basis for our next two examples.

ILLUSTRATION 12A.1

Calculation of Average Past Earnings

Earnings History—Tractorling Limited

2016	$ 60,000
2017	55,000
2018	110,000[a]
2019	70,000
2020	80,000
Total for 5 years	$375,000
Average earnings	$375,000 ÷ 5 years = $75,000

[a] Includes gain on discontinued operation of $25,000

Based on the average annual earnings of $75,000 and the fair value of the company's identifiable net assets of $350,000 from Example 12.5, a return on investment of approximately 21.4% is initially indicated: $75,000 ÷ $350,000. Before we go further, however, we need to know whether $75,000 is representative of Tractorling's **future earnings**. A company's past earnings need to be analyzed to determine whether any adjustments are needed in estimating expected future earnings. This process is often called "normalizing earnings" and the income that results is termed normalized earnings.

First, **the accounting policies applied should be consistent with those of the purchaser**. For example, assume that the purchasing company measures inventory using the FIFO cost formula rather than average cost, which Tractorling uses. Further assume that the use of average cost had the effect of reducing Tractorling's net income by $2,000 each year below a FIFO-based net income. In addition, Tractorling uses accelerated depreciation while the purchaser uses straight-line. As a result, the reported earnings are $3,000 lower each year than they would have been on a straight-line basis.

Second, because the purchaser will pay current prices for the company, **future earnings should be based on the net assets' current fair values** rather than the carrying amount on Tractorling's books. That is, differences between the assets' carrying amounts and fair values may affect reported earnings in the future. For example, internally developed patent costs of $18,000 not previously recognized as an asset would be recognized on the purchase of Tractorling and are included in the $350,000 fair value of identifiable assets. This asset will need to be amortized, say, at the rate of $1,000 per year.

Finally, because we are trying to estimate future earnings, **amounts that are not expected to recur should be adjusted out of our calculations**. The 2018 gain on discontinued operations of $25,000 is an example of such an item. **Example 12A.1** illustrates normalized earnings for a company being acquired.

Example 12A.1 | Calculation of Normalized Earnings

Facts   Illustration 12A.1 provides the earnings history of Tractorling, and the subsequent discussion summarizes differences in Tractorling's accounting policies compared with the company purchasing it (relating to inventory costing, depreciation expense, discontinued operations, and patent amortization).

Instructions   Prepare a calculation of normalized earnings for Tractorling (that is, prepare an estimate of what the purchaser would expect recurring annual future earnings to be).

Solution

Average past earnings of Tractorling (from Illustration 12A.1)		$75,000
Add		
Adjustment for change from average cost to FIFO	$2,000	
Adjustment for change from accelerated to straight-line depreciation	3,000	5,000
		80,000
Deduct		
Gain on discontinued operation ($25,000 ÷ 5)	$5,000	
Patent amortization on straight-line basis	1,000	6,000
Expected future annual earnings of Tractorling		$74,000

Note that it was necessary to divide the gain on the discontinued operation of $25,000 by five years to adjust it correctly. The whole $25,000 was included in the total income earned over the five-year history, but only one fifth of it, or $5,000, is included in the average annual earnings.[31]

Determining the industry's average rate of return earned on net assets requires an analysis of companies that are similar to the enterprise being examined. An industry average may be determined by examining annual reports or data from statistical services. This industry average would typically reflect the level of earnings that is expected from companies in the industry without taking into account any goodwill. We extend the scenario for Tractorling via **Example 12A.2** by taking into account an industry average rate of return.

Example 12A.2 | Estimation of Annual Average Earnings Tractorling Would Generate Based on Industry Average ROI

Facts   Assume that a rate of 15% is found to be average for companies in Tractorling's industry. Consistent with prior examples, assume the fair value of the company's identifiable net assets is $350,000.

Instructions
  a. What would Tractorling's earnings be if they are based on the norm for the industry?
  b. Calculate Tractorling's excess annual earnings: the difference between what the specific company and the average firm in the industry are expected to earn in the future.
  c. Estimate the value of the goodwill based on the future stream of excess earnings discounted at 15% vs. 25%. Discuss how the discount rate should be chosen and how alternate discount periods affect the amount that would be paid for Tractorling.

[31]If you find this unclear, try the following approach: Start with the total earnings of $375,000 over the past five years and make the necessary adjustments. First add 5 × $2,000 for the average cost/FIFO adjustment and 5 × $3,000 for the depreciation, and then deduct 5 × $1,000 for the patent amortization and $25,000 for the gain on discontinued operations. The adjusted total five-year earnings of $370,000 are then divided by 5 to get the expected future annual earnings. The result is $74,000.

Solution

a. An estimate of Tractorling's expected earnings if they were based on the norm for the industry is calculated below:

Fair value of Tractorling's identifiable net assets	$350,000
Industry average rate of return	15%
Tractorling's earnings if no goodwill	$ 52,500

Note that the net assets' fair value—not their carrying amount—is used to calculate Tractorling's level of earnings at the industry average rate of return. Fair value is the relevant measure because the cost of the net identifiable assets to any company that is interested in purchasing Tractorling will be their fair value, not the carrying amount.

b. Excess annual earnings represents how much the company's expected earnings exceed the industry norm. This is what gives the company value in excess of the fair value of its identifiable net assets.

Expected future earnings of Tractorling	$74,000
Tractorling's earnings if no goodwill	52,500
Tractorling's excess annual earnings	$21,500

c. Estimated goodwill based on the future excess earnings: Because excess earnings are expected to continue for several years, they are discounted back to their present value to determine how much a purchaser would pay for them now. A discount rate must be chosen, as well as the length of the discount period.

The choice of discount rate is relatively subjective.[32] The lower the discount rate, the higher the goodwill value and vice versa. To illustrate, assume that the excess earnings of $21,500 are expected to continue indefinitely. If the excess earnings are capitalized at a rate of 25% in perpetuity, for example, the results are:

Capitalization at 25%

$$\frac{\text{Excess earnings}}{\text{Capitalization rate}} = \frac{\$21,500}{0.25} = \$86,000$$

As indicated below, if the excess earnings are capitalized in perpetuity at a somewhat lower rate, say 15%, a much higher goodwill figure results.[33]

Capitalization at 15%

$$\frac{\text{Excess earnings}}{\text{Capitalization rate}} = \frac{\$21,500}{0.15} = \$143,333$$

What do these numbers mean? In effect, if a company pays $86,000 over and above the fair value of Tractorling's identifiable net assets because the company generates earnings above the industry norm, and Tractorling actually does generate these excess profits in perpetuity, the $21,500 of extra earnings per year represents a 25% return on the amount invested. That is, there is a $21,500 return on the $86,000 invested.

---

[32]The following illustrates how the capitalization or discount rate might be calculated for a small business:

	%
Long-term Canadian government bond rate	3
Add: Average premium return on small company shares over government bonds	5
Expected total rate of return on small publicly held shares	8
Add: Premium for greater risk and illiquidity	6
Total required expected rate of return, including inflation component	14
Deduct: Consensus long-term inflation expectation	2
Capitalization rate to apply to current earnings	12

Adapted from Warren Kissin and Ronald Zulli, "Valuation of a Closely Held Business," *The Journal of Accountancy*, June 1988, p. 42.

[33]Why do we divide by the capitalization or discount rate to arrive at the goodwill amount? Recall that the present value of an ordinary annuity is equal to:

$$P\overline{n}|i = [1 - 1 \div (1 + i)^n] \div i$$

When a number is capitalized in perpetuity, $(1 + i)^n$ becomes so large that $1/(1 + i)^n$ essentially equals zero, which leaves $1/i$ or, as in the case above, $21,500/0.25$ or $21,500/0.15$.

If the purchaser invests $143,333 for the goodwill, the extra $21,500 represents a 15% return on investment: $21,500 relative to the $143,333 invested.

Because it is uncertain—risky—that excess profits will continue, a conservative or risk-adjusted rate (higher than the normal rate) tends to be used. Factors that are considered in determining the rate are the stability of past earnings, the speculative nature of the business, and general economic conditions.

As for the discount period, determining the period over which excess earnings are expected to continue is perhaps the most difficult problem in estimating goodwill. The perpetuity examples above assume that the excess earnings will last indefinitely. Usually, however, the excess earnings are assumed to last a limited number of years. The earnings are then discounted over the shorter period.

Assume that the company interested in buying Tractorling's business believes that the excess earnings will last only 10 years and, because of general economic uncertainty, chooses 25% as an appropriate rate of return. The present value of a 10-year annuity of excess earnings of $21,500 discounted at 25% is $76,766.[34] This is the amount that a purchaser should be willing to pay above the fair value of the identifiable net assets—that is, for goodwill—given the assumptions stated.

Total-Earnings Approach

Another way to estimate goodwill that is similar may help to increase your understanding of the process and resulting numbers. Under this approach—the **total-earnings approach**—the value of the company as a whole is determined, based on the total expected earnings, not just the excess earnings. The fair value of the identifiable net assets is then deducted from the value of the company as a whole. The difference is goodwill. The calculations under both approaches are provided in **Example 12A.3**, assuming the purchaser is looking for a 15% return on the amounts it will invest in Tractorling, and the earnings are expected to continue into perpetuity.

Example 12A.3 | Total-Earnings Approach to the Calculation of Goodwill

Facts   Assume that a rate of 15% is the appropriate discount rate for calculating goodwill, and that Tractorling's excess earnings will last indefinitely. Other facts are consistent with Example 12A.2.

Instructions   Estimate the value of the goodwill based on the total-earnings approach, and compare the results with those from the excess earnings approach.

Solution

Assumptions:

Expected future earnings		$ 74,000
Normal or industry-level earnings		52,500
Expected excess future earnings		$ 21,500
Discount rate		15%
Discount period		perpetuity, ∞

Excess-earnings approach:

Goodwill = present value of the annuity of excess future earnings
= present value of annuity of $21,500 ($n = \infty, i = 0.15$)

$$= \frac{\$21,500}{0.15} \qquad = \$143,333$$

---

[34]The present value of an annuity of $1 received in a steady stream for 10 years in the future discounted at 25% is $3.57050. The present value of an annuity of $21,500, therefore, is $21,500 × 3.57050 = $76,765.75.

Total-earnings approach:	Goodwill	= difference between the fair value of the company and the fair value of its identifiable net assets	
	Fair value of company	= present value of the annuity of future earnings	
		= present value of annuity of $74,000 ($n = \infty$, $i = 0.15$)	
		$= \dfrac{\$74,000}{0.15}$	$= \$493,333$
	Fair value of identifiable net assets	= present value of the annuity of industry-level earnings	
		= present value of annuity of $52,500 ($n = \infty$, $i = 0.15$)	
		$= \dfrac{\$52,500}{0.15}$	$= (350,000)$
	Goodwill	=	$\$143,333$

Other Valuation Methods

There are several other methods of valuing goodwill: some are very basic and others are very sophisticated. The methods illustrated here are some of the least complex approaches. Others include simply multiplying excess earnings by the number of years that the excess earnings are expected to continue. This method, often called the **number of years method**, provides a rough measure of goodwill. The approach has the advantage only of simplicity; it does not consider the time value of money because the future cash flows are not discounted.

An even simpler method is one that relies on multiples of average yearly earnings that are paid for other companies in the same industry. If Skyward Airlines was recently acquired for five times its average yearly earnings of $50 million, or $250 million, then Worldwide Airways, a close competitor with $80 million in average yearly earnings, would be worth $400 million.

Finance 5.4.1, 5.4.2, 5.4.3 Another method (similar to discounting excess earnings) is the **discounted free cash flow method**, which involves projecting the company's free cash flow over a long period, typically 10 or 20 years. The method first projects into the future a dozen or so important financial variables, including production; prices; and non-cash expenses such as amortization, taxes, and capital outlays—all adjusted for inflation. The objective is to determine the amount of operating cash flow that will be generated beyond the amount needed to maintain existing capacity. The present value of the free cash flow is then calculated. This amount represents the value of the business.

For example, if Magnaputer Ltd. is expected to generate $1 million a year of free cash flow for 20 years, and the buyer's rate-of-return objective is 15%, the buyer would be willing to pay about $6,260,000 for Magnaputer. (The present value of $1 million to be received for 20 years discounted at 15% is $6,259,330.) The goodwill, then, is the difference between the $6,260,000 and the fair value of the company's identifiable net assets.

In practice, prospective buyers use a variety of methods to produce a valuation curve or range of prices. But the actual price that ends up being paid may be more a factor of the buyer's or seller's ego and negotiating skill.

Valuation of a business—determining how much to pay for it—and its inherent goodwill is at best a highly uncertain process.[35] The estimated value of goodwill depends on a number of factors, all of which are tenuous and subject to bargaining. It ends up accounted for as the difference between the fair value of what you give up to acquire the business and the fair value of the identifiable net assets acquired.

....

[35]Business valuation is a specialist field. The Canadian Institute of Chartered Business Valuators oversees the granting of the specialist designation, Chartered Business Valuator (CBV), to professionals who meet the education, experience, and examination requirements (see cicbv.ca for information).

Review and Practice

Summary of Learning Objectives

1. Understand the importance of goodwill and intangible assets from a business perspective and describe their characteristics.

Our economy is increasingly dominated by information and service providers, and their major assets are often intangible in nature. Identifying and measuring intangible assets tends to be difficult, and as a result many intangibles are not captured on companies' statements of financial position. However, intangible assets and goodwill remain critically important for companies, and are a key focus of standard setters in North America and internationally.

Intangible assets have three characteristics: (1) they are identifiable, (2) they lack physical substance, and (3) they are nonmonetary in nature. Goodwill represents the difference between the fair value of the identifiable assets acquired and liabilities assumed and the consideration given when a company acquires another business.

2. Identify and apply the recognition and measurement requirements for purchased intangible assets.

A purchased intangible asset is recognized when it is probable that the entity will receive the expected future economic benefits and when its cost can be measured reliably. It is measured initially at cost. When several intangibles, or a combination of intangibles and other assets, are acquired in a business combination, the cost of each intangible asset is its fair value. When acquired in a business combination, the identifiable intangibles are recognized separately from the goodwill component.

3. Identify and apply the recognition and measurement requirements for internally developed intangible assets.

No costs are capitalized unless they meet the general recognition criteria concerning future benefits and measurability. Costs incurred in the research phase of developing an intangible asset internally are expensed. Costs incurred in the development phase of a project are also expensed unless the entity can demonstrate that it meets six stringent criteria. These criteria are designed to provide evidence that the asset is technically and financially feasible and that the company has the intent and ability to generate future economic benefits from it. Under ASPE, entities have a choice whether to capitalize or expense development costs that meet the six criteria.

4. Explain how intangible assets are accounted for after initial recognition.

Under ASPE, intangible assets are only accounted for using the cost model. IFRS also allows the revaluation model to be used if the asset's fair value is determined in an active market, but it is not used often. An intangible with a finite or limited useful life is amortized over its useful life to the entity. Except in unusual and specific circumstances, the residual value is assumed to be zero. The amount to report for amortization expense should reflect the pattern in which the asset is consumed or used up if that pattern can be reliably determined. Otherwise, a straight-line approach is used. An intangible with an indefinite life is not amortized until its life is determined to no longer be indefinite. All intangibles are tested for impairment.

5. Identify and explain the accounting for specific types of intangible assets.

Major types of intangibles include the following: (1) marketing-related intangibles that are used in the marketing or promotion of products or services, (2) customer-related intangibles that result from interactions with outside parties, (3) artistic-related intangibles that involve ownership rights to such items as plays and literary works, (4) contract-based intangibles that represent the value of rights that arise from contractual arrangements, and (5) technology-based intangible assets that relate to innovations or technological advances.

6. Explain and account for impairment and derecognition of limited-life and indefinite-life intangible assets.

Under ASPE, impairment is determined and applied by using the cost recovery impairment model. Impairment for *limited-life* intangible assets is based first on a recoverability test. If the carrying amount is higher than the asset's (undiscounted) net recoverable amount, then a loss on impairment must be measured and recognized, based on the asset's fair value. No reversals of such losses are permitted. The procedures are the same as for property, plant, and equipment. *Indefinite-life* intangibles use only a fair value test. Under IFRS, the rational entity impairment model is used. An intangible asset is impaired only if its carrying amount is higher than its recoverable amount. The recoverable amount is defined as the greater of the asset's value in use and its fair value less costs to sell. The loss on impairment is the difference between the carrying amount and the recoverable amount, if lower. The loss may be reversed subsequently if economic conditions change and the recoverable amount increases. The same approach is used for both limited-life and indefinite-life intangible assets.

7. Explain how goodwill is measured and accounted for after acquisition.

Goodwill is unique because, unlike all other assets, it can be identified only with the business as a whole. It is not an identifiable asset. Goodwill is recorded only when a business is purchased. To calculate goodwill in a 100% acquisition, the fair value of the identifiable assets that are acquired and liabilities that are assumed is compared with the fair value of the consideration transferred for the acquired business. The difference is goodwill. After acquisition, it is not amortized but is regularly assessed for impairment.

---

8. Explain and account for impairment of goodwill.

Goodwill is assigned to a cash-generating group or reporting unit and the group/unit is tested for impairment. Under ASPE, a goodwill loss on impairment is recognized if the fair value of the unit is lower than its carrying amount, and the loss is equal to the difference. Under IFRS, there is a goodwill loss on impairment if the recoverable amount of the cash-generating unit is less than its carrying amount. The loss is equal to the difference and is applied to goodwill first. Under **both** ASPE and IFRS, goodwill losses on impairment are not reversed.

---

9. Identify the types of disclosure requirements for intangible assets and goodwill and explain the issues in analyzing these assets.

Disclosures under ASPE are limited because users can typically access additional information. Under IFRS, significant details are required to be disclosed. The disclosures allow a reader to determine how amounts invested in classes of intangibles (and goodwill) have changed over the period, with substantial information provided when fair values are used, such as under the revaluation model and all impairment calculations. For intangibles that are not amortized, companies must indicate the amount of any losses on impairment that have been recognized as well as information about the circumstances that led to the writedown. Goodwill must be separately reported, as must the major classes of intangible assets. Because it is difficult to measure intangibles, some resources, such as intellectual capital and other internally developed intangible assets, do not get captured on the statement of financial position. Other intangibles are recognized, but with a relatively high level of measurement uncertainty. For these reasons, care must be taken when analyzing financial statement information related to earnings and total assets.

---

10. Identify differences in accounting between IFRS and ASPE.

There are few, but significant, differences between ASPE and IFRS regarding intangible assets and goodwill. One major difference is the accounting treatment for costs incurred in the development phase of internally generated intangible assets that meet the six stringent criteria for capitalization. Under ASPE, entities can choose whether to capitalize these costs or expense all such costs. Under IFRS, these costs are capitalized. The other major difference is the impairment models applied: the cost recovery model for ASPE, and the rational entity model for IFRS.

---

11. Explain and apply basic approaches to valuing goodwill.

One method of valuing goodwill is the excess-earnings approach. Using this approach, the value of goodwill is based on discounting expected future earnings in excess of the industry average to their present value. Another method involves determining the total value of the business by capitalizing total earnings, and then deducting the fair values of the identifiable net assets. The number of years method of valuing goodwill simply multiplies the excess earnings by the number of years of expected excess earnings. Another method of valuing goodwill is the discounted free cash flow method, which projects the future operating cash that will be generated over and above the amount needed to maintain current operating levels. The present value of the free cash flows is today's estimate of the firm's value.

Practice Problem

Sky Corp., organized in 2020, provided you with the following information. Sky follows ASPE.

1. Sky purchased a licence for $20,000 on July 1, 2020. The licence gives Sky exclusive rights to sell its services in the province and will expire on July 1, 2028.

2. Sky purchased a patent on January 2, 2021, for $40,000. It is estimated to have a five-year life.

3. Costs incurred to develop an exclusive Internet connection process as of June 1, 2021, were $45,000. The process is expected to have an indefinite life, but Sky is still finalizing its testing of the process to ensure it is technically feasible.

4. On April 1, 2021, Sky purchased a small circuit board manufacturer for $350,000. Goodwill recorded in the purchase transaction was $90,000.

5. On July 1, 2021, legal fees for successful defence of the patent purchased on January 2, 2021, were $11,400.

6. Research and development costs incurred as of September 1, 2021, were $75,000. None of the related projects involved had achieved economic viability.

Instructions

a. Prepare the journal entries to record all the entries related to the patent during 2021.

b. At December 31, 2021, an impairment test is performed on the licence purchased in 2020. It is estimated that the net cash flows to be received from the licence will be $13,000, and its fair value is $7,000. Calculate the amount of impairment, if any, to be recorded on December 31, 2021.

c. (1) What are the amounts to be reported for intangible assets and goodwill on the statement of financial position at December 31, 2020? (2) At December 31, 2021?

Solution

a.

January 2, 2021

Intangible Assets—Patents	40,000	
Cash		40,000

July 1, 2021

Intangible Assets—Patents	11,400	
Cash		11,400

December 31, 2021

Amortization Expense	9,267	
Intangible Assets—Patents		9,267

Calculation of amortization expense for the patent:

$40,000 × 12/60 =	$8,000
$11,400 × 6/54 =	1,267
Total	$9,267

b. Calculation of impairment loss:

Cost	$20,000
Less: Accumulated amortization ($20,000 × 18/96)	3,750
Carrying amount	$16,250

Carrying amount of $16,250 is greater than the undiscounted net cash flows amount of $13,000. Therefore, the licence is impaired. The impairment loss is calculated as follows:

Carrying amount	$16,250
Fair value	7,000
Loss on impairment	$ 9,250

c. (1) Intangible assets as at December 31, 2020:

Licences	$18,750*
*Cost	$20,000
Less: Accumulated amortization ($20,000 × 6/96)	1,250
Net book value	$18,750

(2) Intangible assets and goodwill as at December 31, 2021:

Licences	$ 7,000
Patents ($40,000 + $11,400 − $9,267)	42,133
Goodwill	90,000

All the costs to develop the Internet connection process and the research and development costs are expensed as incurred.

Key Terms

acquirer, p. 12-4
active market, p. 12-13
artistic-related intangible assets, p. 12-18
bargain purchase, p. 12-26
brand, p. 12-16
brand name, p. 12-16
business combination, p. 12-7
computer software costs, p. 12-21
contract-based intangible assets, p. 12-18
copyright, p. 12-18
cost recovery impairment model, p. 12-21
customer-related intangible assets, p. 12-17
development, p. 12-10
development phase, p. 12-9
discounted free cash flow method, p. 12-42
economic benefits, p. 12-5
excess-earnings approach, p. 12-37

favourable lease, p. 12-19
finite life, p. 12-14
franchise, p. 12-19
goodwill, p. 12-4
identifiable, p. 12-5
identifiable net assets, p. 12-4
impaired, p. 12-21
indefinite life, p. 12-14
in-process research and development
    (R&D), p. 12-7
intangible assets, p. 12-5
intellectual capital, p. 12-34
knowledge assets, p. 12-34
lease, p. 12-19
leasehold, p. 12-19
licences, p. 12-19
licensing agreements, p. 12-19

limited life, p. 12-14
marketing-related intangible assets, p. 12-16
monetary assets, p. 12-5
negative goodwill, p. 12-26
normalized earnings, p. 12-38
number of years method, p. 12-42
organization costs, p. 12-11
patent, p. 12-19
permits, p. 12-19
prepaid expense, p. 12-7
rational entity impairment model, p. 12-21
research, p. 12-9
research phase, p. 12-9
technology-based intangible assets, p. 12-19
total-earnings approach, p. 12-41
trademark, p. 12-16
trade name, p. 12-16

Assignment Material

Note: All assignment material with an asterisk (*) relates to the appendix to the chapter.

Unless otherwise indicated, amortization expense should be calculated to the nearest whole month.

Enabling Competencies Completion of this end-of-chapter material will help develop CPA-enabling competencies (such as ethics and professionalism, problem-solving and decision-making, and communication) and technical competencies. We have highlighted selected items with a specific integration word mark and material in *WileyPLUS* has been linked to the competencies. All cases emphasize integration, especially of the enabling competencies. The brief exercises, exercises, and problems generally emphasize problem-solving and decision-making.

Brief Exercises

BE12.1 (LO 1) Wholesome Foods Corporation is a producer of gourmet organic cookies. The company was established three years ago when its founder and president, Martha Spencer, purchased the trademark "Healthy Originals" and its six patented cookie recipes. Martha soon discovered that there was a specialty market for the cookies, and began marketing them as hand-decorated and personalized gourmet organic cookies for special occasions such as birthdays and bridal and baby showers. Nearly all of the company's sales are through its internally developed website where customers can enter personalized orders for batches of individually decorated and wrapped cookies.

a. Provide examples of intangible assets that may appear on the company's statement of financial position.

b. Discuss the importance of the intangible assets to the company's business.

c. Referring to the conceptual framework (discussed in Chapter 2), discuss the importance of recording the intangible assets on the company's statement of financial position.

BE12.2 (LO 1, 2, 3) For each independent scenario outlined below, discuss whether the three criteria required for an asset to be classified as an intangible are fulfilled:

a. Software purchased specifically for a manufacturing machine that cannot operate without that software

b. Software purchased for a hotel reservation system that is not essential to the related ancillary hardware equipment

c. Software developed internally for eventual sale to customers

d. Software purchased for eventual resale to customers

BE12.3 (LO 2, 3, 10) E-Learning Educational Services Inc. incurred the following costs associated with its research facilities. Indicate whether these items are capitalized or expensed in the current year, assuming the company reports under ASPE. Where applicable, indicate how your answer would change under IFRS.

a. Executive salaries

b. Costs of testing prototypes

c. Market research to prepare for the product launch

d. Sales commissions

e. Salaries of research staff investigating alternatives for existing products

f. Borrowing costs directly attributable to the development of a qualifying intangible asset

BE12.4 (LO 2, 3, 4) Azure Industries Ltd. acquired two copyrights during 2020. One copyright was on a textbook that was developed internally at a cost of $36,000. This textbook is estimated to have a useful life of three years from July 1, 2020, the date it was published. The second copyright is for a history research textbook and was purchased from University Press on October 1, 2020, for $54,000. This textbook seems to have an indefinite useful life. How should these two copyrights be reported on Azure's statement of financial position as at December 31, 2020?

BE12.5 (LO 2) Sunny Valley Inc. bought an Internet domain name by issuing a $220,000, five-year, non–interest-bearing note to Ti-Mine Corp. with an effective yield of 12%. The note is repayable in five annual payments of $44,000 made at the end of each year. Prepare the journal entry to record the purchase of the intangible asset. Show calculations using any of the following methods: (a) factor Table A.4, (b) a financial calculator, or (c) Excel function PV. Round final answers to the nearest dollar.

BE12.6 (LO 2, 3, 5) Bountiful Industries Ltd. had one patent recorded on its books as at January 1, 2020. This patent had a book value of $365,000 and a remaining useful life of eight years. During 2020, Bountiful incurred research costs of $140,000 and brought a patent infringement suit against a competitor. On December 1, 2020, Bountiful received the good news that its patent was valid and that its competitor could not use the process Bountiful had patented. The company spent $106,000 to defend this patent. At what amount should the patent be reported on the December 31, 2020 statement of financial position, assuming monthly straight-line amortization of patents? Round amortization amounts to the nearest dollar.

BE12.7 (LO 2, 3) Programming for Kids Ltd. decided that it needed to update its computer programs for its supplier relationships. It purchased an off-the-shelf program and modified it internally to link it to Programming for Kids' other programs. The following costs may be relevant to the accounting for the new software:

Original cost of old software	$10,000
Accumulated amortization of old software	8,000
Purchase price of new software	7,500
Training costs	4,000
General and administrative costs	2,480
Direct cost of in-house programmer's time spent on modifying software	1,480

Prepare the journal entry to record the software replacement.

BE12.8 (LO 2, 3, 5, 10) Indicate whether the following items are capitalized or expensed in the current year, assuming IFRS was used to prepare financial statements. Assume that any items that may qualify for capitalization have met all six "development phase" criteria.

a. The purchase cost of a patent from a competitor

b. Product research costs

c. Organization costs

d. Costs that are incurred internally to create goodwill

e. Costs that are incurred internally to create a secret recipe

f. Legal costs to successfully support trademark

g. Pre-operating costs to launch new products

h. Relocation of manufacturing activities

i. Corporate reorganization costs

j. Costs incurred to develop computer software

How would the answer differ if ASPE were used to prepare financial statements?

BE12.9 (LO 2, 3, 4, 10) Sweet Tooth Inc., a private company that applies ASPE, incurred $15,000 in materials and $12,000 in direct labour costs between January and March 2020 to develop a new product. In May 2020, the criteria required to capitalize development costs were met. A further $45,000 was spent for materials, $15,000 for direct labour costs, $2,000 for borrowing costs, and $72,000 for directly related legal fees. Discuss any options that may be available to Sweet Tooth for recording these expenditures. In addition, prepare the appropriate journal entries. How would your answer change if Sweet Tooth were a public company following IFRS?

BE12.10 (LO 2, 4, 5) Darrien Corporation purchased a trade name, customer list, and manufacturing equipment for a lump sum of $800,000. The fair market values of each asset are $280,000, $290,000, and $320,000, respectively. There were initial operating losses of $14,500 during the first four months after the assets were put into use. Prepare the journal entry to record the treatment of these costs. Do not round intermediate calculations in asset allocations and round final answers to the nearest dollar.

BE12.11 (LO 3) Using the data provided in BE12.10, assume that Darrien also spent $12,500 to promote and launch the product that the manufacturing equipment is used to produce. Explain the accounting for these costs.

BE12.12 (LO 3, 4, 10) Green Earth Corp. has capitalized software costs of $450,000 on a product to be sold externally. During its first year, sales of this product totalled $195,000. Green Earth expects to earn $1,250,000 in additional future revenue from this product, which is estimated to have an economic life of four years. Green Earth is considering capitalizing and amortizing the software based on when the revenue is expected to be generated. Comment on the appropriateness of this approach assuming Green Earth uses IFRS. How would your answer differ under ASPE?

BE12.13 (LO 2, 4) Lakeshore Corporation purchased a patent from MaFee Corp. on January 1, 2020, for $87,000. The patent had a remaining legal life of 16 years. Prepare Lakeshore's journal entries to record the 2020 patent purchase and amortization for the year rounded to the nearest dollar.

BE12.14 (LO 2, 4) Use the information in BE12.13 and assume that in January 2022, Lakeshore spends $26,000 successfully defending a patent suit. In addition, Lakeshore now feels the patent will be useful only for another seven years. Prepare the journal entries to record the 2022 expenditure and amortization for the year rounded to the nearest dollar.

BE12.15 (LO 2, 4, 10) On December 31, 2020, Convenient Cabs Incorporated was granted 10 taxi licences by the City of Somerdale, at a cost of $1,000 per licence. It is probable that Convenient Cabs will receive the expected future economic benefits of the taxi licences. There is an active market for taxi licences in Somerdale.

a. Prepare the journal entry to record the costs incurred.

b. Discuss how the licences are accounted for after initial recognition if Convenient Cabs follows ASPE.

c. Discuss how the licences are accounted for after initial recognition if Convenient Cabs follows IFRS.

BE12.16 (LO 6, 10) Coffee Company Limited has a trademark with a carrying amount of $83,750, and expected useful life of 15 years. As part of an impairment test on December 31, 2020, due to a change in customer tastes, Coffee Company gathered the following data about the trademark for the purposes of an impairment test: fair value $45,000; fair value less costs to sell $40,000; value in use $95,200; and undiscounted future cash flows $125,000. Assume that Coffee Company is reporting under ASPE. Determine if the trademark is impaired on December 31, 2020.

BE12.17 (LO 6, 10) Use the data provided in BE12.16. How would your response change if Coffee Company were a public company reporting under IFRS?

BE12.18 (LO 6, 10) Use the data provided in BE12.16, except assume that useful life is expected to be unlimited. How would your response change if Coffee Company reported under (a) ASPE or (b) IFRS?

 BE12.19 (LO 7) On September 1, 2020, Pipeline Corporation acquired Tunneling Limited for a cash payment of $954,000. At the time of purchase, Tunneling's statement of financial position showed assets of $780,000, liabilities of $420,000, and owners' equity of $360,000. The fair value of Tunneling's assets is estimated to be $1,140,000. Calculate the amount of goodwill acquired by Pipeline.

BE12.20 (LO 8, 10) Using the data from BE12.19, assume that Pipeline Corporation is a public company and that the goodwill was allocated entirely to one cash-generating unit (CGU). Two years later, information about the CGU is as follows: carrying amount $3,740,000; value in use $3,680,000; and fair value less costs to sell $3,575,000. Determine if the goodwill is impaired, and calculate the goodwill loss on impairment, if any.

BE12.21 (LO 8, 10) Using the data from BE12.19, assume that Pipeline Corporation is a private entity. Explain how goodwill will be tested for impairment. If the unit's carrying amount (including goodwill) is $3,581,000 and its fair value is $3,474,000, determine the amount of loss on impairment, if any, under ASPE.

***BE12.22 (LO 11)** **Finance** Nigel Corporation is interested in purchasing Lau Company Ltd. The total of Lau's net income amounts over the past five years is $750,000. During one of those years, Lau reported a gain on discontinued operations of $94,000. The fair value of Lau's net identifiable assets is $690,000. A normal rate of return is 15%, and Nigel wants to capitalize excess earnings at 20%. Calculate the estimated value of Lau's goodwill.

Exercises

E12.1 (LO 2, 5, 10) **(Classification Issues—Intangibles)** The following is a list of items that could be included in the intangible assets section of the statement of financial position:

1. An investment in a subsidiary company
2. Timberland
3. The cost of an engineering activity needed to advance a product's design to the manufacturing stage
4. A lease prepayment (six months of rent paid in advance)
5. The cost of equipment obtained under a capital lease
6. The cost of searching for applications for new research findings
7. Costs incurred in forming a corporation
8. Operating losses incurred in the start-up of a business
9. Training costs incurred in the start-up of a new operation

10. The purchase cost of a franchise

11. Goodwill generated internally

12. The cost of testing in the search for product alternatives

13. Goodwill acquired in the purchase of a business

14. The cost of developing a patent

15. The cost of purchasing a patent from an inventor

16. Legal costs incurred in securing a patent

17. Unrecovered costs of a successful legal suit to protect a patent

18. The cost of conceptual formulation of possible product alternatives

19. The cost of purchasing a copyright

20. Product development costs

21. Long-term receivables

22. The cost of developing a trademark

23. The cost of purchasing a trademark

24. The cost of an annual update of payroll software

25. A five-year advertising contract for rights of advertising by a top hockey player in Canada

26. Borrowing costs specifically identifiable with an internally developed intangible asset

Instructions

a. Indicate which items on the list would be reported as intangible assets on the statement of financial position.

b. Indicate how, if at all, the items that are not reportable as intangible assets would be reported in the financial statements.

c. Identify any differences between ASPE and IFRS with respect to capitalization of such items as intangible assets.

E12.2 (LO 2, 5, 7, 10) (Classification Issues—Intangibles) Selected account information follows for Entertainment Inc. as at December 31, 2020. All the accounts have debit balances. Assume the company uses IFRS when preparing financial statements.

Cable Television Franchises	Film Contract Rights
Music Copyrights	Customer Lists Acquired in a Business Combination
Research Costs	Prepaid Expenses
Goodwill	Covenants Not to Compete
Cash	Brand Names
Accounts Receivable	Notes Receivable
Property, Plant, and Equipment	Investments in Affiliated Companies
Leasehold Improvements	Organization Cost
Annual Franchise Fee Paid	Land
In-Process Research and Development Acquired in a Business Combination	Excess of Purchase Price over Fair Value of Identifiable Net Assets, X Corp.

Instructions

a. Identify which items should be classified as intangible assets. For the items that are not classified as intangible assets, indicate where they would be reported in the financial statements.

b. How would the answer to part (a) differ if ASPE were followed instead of IFRS?

E12.3 (LO 2, 3, 5, 7, 10) Excel (Classification Issues—Intangibles) Berrie Electric Inc. has the following amounts included in its general ledger at December 31, 2020:

Organization costs	$ 34,000
Purchased trademarks	17,500
Development phase activities (meet all six development phase criteria)	29,000
Deposits with advertising agency for ads to promote goodwill of company	8,000
Excess of cost over fair value of identifiable net assets of acquired subsidiary	81,000
Cost of equipment acquired for research and development projects; the equipment has an alternative future use	125,000
Costs of researching a secret formula for a product that is expected to be marketed for at least 20 years	75,000
Payment for a favourable lease; lease term of 10 years	15,000

Instructions

a. Based on the information provided, calculate the total amount for Berrie to report as intangible assets on its statement of financial position at December 31, 2020. Assume Berrie uses IFRS to prepare its financial statements.

b. If an item should not be included in intangible assets, explain the proper treatment for reporting it.

c. Indicate which amounts might be reported differently if ASPE were followed instead of IFRS.

E12.4 (LO 2, 3, 4, 10) **(Intangible Amortization)** Selected information follows for Mount Olympus Corporation for three independent situations:

1. Mount Olympus purchased a patent from Bakhshi Co. for $1.8 million on January 1, 2018. The patent expires on January 1, 2028, and Mount Olympus is amortizing it over the 10 years remaining in its legal life. During 2020, Mount Olympus determined that the patent's economic benefits would not last longer than six years from the date of acquisition.

2. Mount Olympus bought a perpetual franchise from Carmody Inc. on January 1, 2020, for $650,000. Its carrying amount on Carmody's books at January 1, 2020, was $750,000. Assume that Mount Olympus can only provide evidence of clearly identifiable cash flows for 25 years, but thinks the franchise could have value for up to 60 years.

3. On January 1, 2018, Mount Olympus incurred development costs (meeting all required criteria) of $375,000. Mount Olympus is amortizing these costs over five years.

Instructions

a. In situation 1, what amount should be reported in the statement of financial position for the patent, net of accumulated amortization, at December 31, 2020?

b. In situation 2, what amount of amortization expense should be reported for the year ended December 31, 2020?

c. In situation 3, what amount, if any, should be reported as unamortized development costs as at December 31, 2020? How might the accounting treatment change if Mount Olympus were using ASPE?

E12.5 (LO 2, 3, 4, 10) **(Correction of Intangible Asset Account)** As the recently appointed auditor for Daleara Corporation, you have been asked to examine selected accounts before the six-month financial statements of June 30, 2020, are prepared. The controller for Daleara Corporation mentions that only one account is kept for intangible assets. The entries in Intangible Assets since January 1, 2020, are as follows:

Intangible Assets

			Debit	Credit	Balance
Jan.	4	Research costs	1,050,000		1,050,000
	5	Legal costs to obtain patent	45,000		1,095,000
		Payment of seven months' rent on property leased by Daleara (February to August)	49,000		1,144,000
Feb.	11	Proceeds from issue of common shares		296,000	848,000
Apr.	30	Promotional expenses related to start-up of business	157,000		1,005,000
June	1	Development stage costs (meet all six development stage criteria)	215,000		1,220,000
	30	Start-up costs for first six months of operations	316,000		1,536,000

Instructions

Prepare the entry or entries needed to correct this account. Assume that the patent has a useful life of 10 years and that Daleara Corporation follows IFRS.

E12.6 (LO 2, 3, 4, 5) **Excel** **(Recognition and Amortization of Intangibles)** Institute Limited organized late in 2019 and set up a single account for all intangible assets. The following summary shows the entries in 2020 (all debits) that have been recorded in Intangible Assets since then:

Jan.	2	Purchased patent (8-year life)	$ 320,000
Mar.	31	Costs to search for new ways to apply patent that was purchased on Jan. 2	21,000
Apr.	1	Purchased goodwill (indefinite life)	310,000

July	1	Purchased franchise with 10-year life; expiration date July 1, 2030	$ 250,000
	1	Promotional costs to increase the future economic benefit of the goodwill that was purchased on Apr. 1	33,000
Aug.	1	Payment for copyright (5-year life)	140,000
	1	Purchased trademark (3-year life)	15,000
	1	Purchased customer list (2-year life)	10,000
Sept.	1	Research costs	239,000
			$1,338,000

Instructions

a. Prepare the necessary entries to clear the Intangible Assets account and to set up separate accounts for distinct types of intangibles.

b. Make the entries as at December 31, 2020, for any necessary amortization so that all balances are accurate as at that date. Round all amounts to the nearest dollar.

c. Provide the asset amounts reported on the December 31, 2020 statement of financial position.

E12.7 (LO 2, 3, 4, 5) (Accounting for Trade Name)   In early January 2020, FJS Corporation applied for and received approval for a trade name, incurring legal costs of $52,500. In early January 2021, FJS incurred $28,200 in legal fees in a successful defence of its trade name.

Instructions

a. Management determines that this asset has a limited useful life. Identify the variables that must be considered in determining the appropriate amortization period for this trade name.

b. Calculate amortization for 2020; carrying amount at December 31, 2020; amortization for 2021; and carrying amount at December 31, 2021, if the company amortizes the trade name over its 15-year legal life. Round amortization calculations to the nearest dollar.

c. Repeat part (b), assuming a useful life of six years.

d. Assume the trade name is assessed as having an indefinite life upon initial acquisition. Explain the accounting implications.

e. **Digging Deeper**   Assume the role of a potential investor in FJS. Comment on the estimated useful life of the trade name, and its effects on the company's financial statements.

E12.8 (LO 3, 4, 10) (Internally Generated Intangibles)   Oakville Corp. incurred the following costs during 2020 in connection with its research and development phase activities:

Cost of equipment acquired for use in research and development projects over the next five years (straight-line depreciation used)	$240,000
Materials consumed in research projects	61,000
Materials consumed in the development of a product committed for manufacturing in the first quarter of 2021	32,000
Consulting fees paid in the last quarter of 2020 to outsiders for research and development projects, including $4,500 for advice related to the $32,000 of materials used above	95,000
Personnel costs of persons involved in research and development projects	108,000
Indirect costs reasonably allocated to research and development projects	25,000
General borrowing costs on the company's line of credit	12,000
Training costs for a new customer service software program	17,500

Instructions

a. Calculate the amount to be reported as research and development expense by Oakville on its income statement for 2020. Assume the equipment is purchased at the beginning of the year. Assume the company follows IFRS for financial reporting purposes.

b. Explain the treatment of training costs and borrowing costs incurred after the six development phase capitalization criteria are met.

c. Explain how the answer may be the same or differ if ASPE were followed.

E12.9 (LO 3, 4, 5, 10) (Internally Generated Intangibles)   In 2020, Inventors Corp. spent $392,000 on a research project, but by the end of 2020 it was impossible to determine whether any benefit would come from it. Inventors prepares financial statements in accordance with IFRS.

Instructions

a. What account should be charged for the $392,000, and how should it be shown in the financial statements for fiscal 2020?

b. The research project is completed in 2021, and a successful patent is obtained. The research phase costs to complete the project are $71,000. The administrative and legal expenses incurred in obtaining patent number 481-761-0092 on January 3, 2021, total $10,000. The patent has an expected useful life of five years. Inventors Corp. will now begin investigating applications that use or apply the knowledge obtained on this project. Record these costs in journal entry form. Also, record patent amortization for a full year in 2021.

c. In January 2022, the company successfully defended the patent in litigation at a cost of $12,400. The victory extended the patent's life to December 31, 2030. What is the proper way to account for this cost? Also, record patent amortization for a full year in 2022.

d. By early September 2022, and at an additional cost of $101,000, Inventors Corp. had a product design that was technologically and financially feasible. Additional engineering and consulting costs of $66,000 were incurred in October 2022 to advance the design of the new product to the manufacturing stage. Discuss the proper accounting treatment for the 2022 costs incurred.

E12.10 (LO 2, 3, 4, 5, 10) (Accounting for Patents, Franchises, and R&D) Tennessee Corp., reporting under ASPE, has provided the following information regarding its intangible assets:

1. A patent was purchased from Marvin Inc. for $1.2 million on January 1, 2019. Tennessee estimated the patent's remaining useful life to be 10 years. The patent was carried in Marvin's accounting records at a carrying amount of $1,350,000 when Marvin sold it to Tennessee. On January 1, 2020, because of recent events in the field, Tennessee estimates that the remaining life of this patent is only five years from January 1, 2020.

2. During 2020, a franchise was purchased from Burr Ltd. for $290,000. As part of the deal, Burr must also be paid 5% of revenue from the franchise operations. Revenue from the franchise for 2020 was $1.4 million. Tennessee estimates the franchise's useful life to be 10 years and takes a full year's amortization in the year of purchase.

3. Tennessee incurred the following research costs in 2020:

Materials and equipment	$ 81,000
Personnel	111,000
Indirect costs	55,000
	$247,000

Instructions

a. Prepare a schedule showing the intangibles section of Tennessee's statement of financial position at December 31, 2020. Show supporting calculations in good form.

b. Prepare a schedule showing the income statement effect for the year ended December 31, 2020, as a result of the facts above. Show supporting calculations in good form.

c. Explain how the accounting would differ if Tennessee were a public company.

(Adapted from AICPA)

E12.11 (LO 3, 4, 6, 10) (Internally Developed Intangibles) During 2020, Saskatchewan Enterprises Ltd., a private entity, incurred $4.7 million in costs to develop a new software product called Dover. Of this amount, $1.8 million was spent before the company determined that the product was technologically and financially feasible. Dover was completed by December 31, 2020, and will be marketed to third parties. Saskatchewan expects a useful life of eight years for this product, with total revenues of $12 million. During 2021, Saskatchewan realized revenues of $2.7 million from sales of Dover.

Instructions

a. Assuming Saskatchewan reports under ASPE, prepare the journal entries that are required in 2020 to record the above.

b. Prepare the entry to record amortization at December 31, 2021, assuming a straight-line method of amortization.

c. At what amount should the software costs be reported in the December 31, 2021, statement of financial position?

d. Could the net realizable value of this asset at December 31, 2021, affect your answer? Explain how limited-life assets are tested for impairment.

e. How would your response to part (d) change if Saskatchewan Enterprises Ltd. were a public company?

E12.12 (LO 2, 4, 6, 10) (Revaluation Model) Blue and White Town Taxi Incorporated applied for several taxi licences for its taxicab operations in the Town of Somerville and, on August 31, 2020, incurred costs of $12,500 in the application process. The outcome of applying for taxi licences in the town was uncertain, as Somerville has been known to limit the number of issued taxi licences in an effort to encourage use of public transportation.

The application was successful and on June 30, 2021, Blue and White was granted 30 freely transferable taxi licences for a registration fee of $3,750 per licence. According to management, each licence will have a useful life of only five years from the date of registration, because demand for taxi services in Somerville is expected to decrease significantly after the town's subway system is expanded. There is an active market for taxi licences in Somerville.

In 2022, in an effort to decrease traffic congestion in its downtown, the town did not issue any new taxi licences, and the fair value of each taxi licence held by Blue and White was $4,200 as at December 31, 2022. In 2024, due to a severe shortage of taxis in the town, Somerville decreased the registration fee and issued many new taxi licences. As at December 31, 2024, each taxi licence had value in use of $5,400, fair value of $3,800, and costs to sell of $200. Blue and White amortizes intangible assets using the straight-line method, and prepares financial statements in accordance with IFRS.

Instructions

a. Prepare the entry to record the costs incurred on August 31, 2020.

b. Prepare the entry to record the costs incurred on June 30, 2021.

c. Assume that after initial recognition, Blue and White uses the cost model to measure its intangible assets. Prepare the entries required on December 31, 2022, December 31, 2023, and December 31, 2024, and calculate the carrying amount of the intangible asset, if any, as at December 31, 2024.

d. Assume that after initial recognition, Blue and White uses the revaluation model (asset adjustment method) to measure its intangible assets. Prepare the entries required on December 31, 2022, December 31, 2023, and December 31, 2024, and calculate the carrying amount of the intangible asset, if any, as at December 31, 2024. Assume revaluation adjustments are made on December 31, 2022, and December 31, 2024.

e. **Digging Deeper** From the perspective of Blue and White's auditor, discuss the criteria that must be met for the intangible asset to be measured using the revaluation model. Discuss under which financial reporting standards the revaluation model can be applied.

E12.13 (LO 6, 10) (Impairment Testing) At the end of 2020, Dayton Corporation owns a licence with a remaining life of 10 years and a carrying amount of $530,000. Dayton expects undiscounted future cash flows from this licence to total $535,000. The licence's fair value is $425,000 and disposal costs are estimated to be nil. The licence's discounted cash flows (that is, value in use) are estimated to be $475,000. Dayton prepares financial statements in accordance with IFRS.

Instructions

a. Determine if the licence is impaired at the end of 2020 and prepare any related entries that are necessary.

b. Assume the recoverable amount is calculated to be $450,000 at the end of 2021. Determine if the licence is impaired at the end of 2021 and prepare any related entries that are necessary.

c. Explain how the answer to part (b) would change if the licence's fair value were $500,000 at the end of 2021.

E12.14 (LO 6, 10) (Impairment Testing)

Instructions

Repeat E12.13, but now assume that Dayton prepares financial statements in accordance with ASPE, and that the recoverable amount under ASPE (undiscounted future cash flows) is calculated to be $500,000 at the end of 2021.

E12.15 (LO 6, 10) (Impairment Testing)

Instructions

Repeat E12.13, but now assume that the licence was granted in perpetuity and has an indefinite life.

E12.16 (LO 6, 10) (Impairment Testing)

Instructions

Repeat E12.13, but now assume that the licence was granted in perpetuity and has an indefinite life, and that Dayton prepares financial statements in accordance with ASPE.

E12.17 (LO 6, 10) (Intangible Impairment) The following information is for a copyright owned by Lighting Designs Corp., a private entity, at December 31, 2020. Lighting Designs Corp. applies ASPE.

Cost	$4,300,000
Carrying amount	2,150,000
Expected future net cash flows (undiscounted)	2,000,000
Fair value	1,600,000

Assume that Lighting Designs Corp. will continue to use this copyright in the future. As at December 31, 2020, the copyright is estimated to have a remaining useful life of 10 years.

Instructions

a. Prepare the journal entry, if any, to record the asset's impairment at December 31, 2020.

b. Prepare the journal entry to record amortization expense for 2021 related to the copyright.

c. The copyright's fair value at December 31, 2021, is $2.2 million. Prepare the journal entry, if any, to record the increase in fair value.

d. **Digging Deeper** Using the information from part (a), discuss whether the copyright would be amortized in 2020 before the impairment test is conducted. Would the asset be tested for impairment before or after amortizing the copyright in 2020?

E12.18 (LO 6, 10) (Intangible Impairment) Refer to the information provided in E12.17, but now assume that Lighting Designs Corp. is a publicly accountable company. At December 31, 2020, the copyright's value in use is $1,850,000 and its selling costs are $100,000.

Instructions

a. Prepare the journal entry, if any, to record the asset's impairment at December 31, 2020.

b. Prepare the journal entry to record amortization expense for 2021 related to the copyright.

c. The copyright's fair value at December 31, 2021, is $2.2 million. Prepare the journal entry, if any, to record the increase in fair value.

E12.19 (LO 7) (Accounting for Goodwill) Fred Moss, owner of Medici Interiors Inc., is negotiating for the purchase of Athenian Galleries Ltd. The condensed statement of financial position of Athenian follows in an abbreviated form:

Athenian Galleries Ltd.
Statement of Financial Position
As at December 31, 2020

Assets		Liabilities and Shareholders' Equity		
Cash	$118,000	Accounts payable		$ 92,000
Land	70,000	Long-term notes payable		351,000
Buildings (net)	244,000	Total liabilities		443,000
Equipment (net)	185,000	Common shares	$200,000	
Copyright (net)	98,000	Retained earnings	72,000	272,000
Total assets	$715,000	Total liabilities and shareholders' equity		$715,000

Medici and Athenian agree that the land is undervalued by $40,000 and the business equipment is overvalued by $12,000. Athenian agrees to sell the business to Medici for $382,000.

Instructions

Prepare the entry to record the purchase of the business's net assets on Medici's books.

E12.20 (LO 7, 8, 10) (Accounting for Goodwill) On July 1, 2020, Zoe Corporation purchased the net assets of Soorya Company by paying $415,000 cash and issuing a $50,000 note payable to Soorya Company. At July 1, 2020, the statement of financial position of Soorya Company was as follows:

Cash	$ 75,000	Accounts payable	$300,000
Accounts receivable	102,000	Soorya, capital	239,000
Inventory	98,000		$539,000
Land	50,000		
Buildings (net)	75,000		
Equipment (net)	90,000		
Trademarks (net)	49,000		
	$539,000		

The recorded amounts all approximate current values except for land (worth $60,000), inventory (worth $125,000), and trademarks (worthless). The receivables are shown net of an allowance for doubtful accounts of $12,000. The amounts for buildings, equipment, and trademarks are shown net of accumulated amortization of $14,000, $23,000, and $47,000, respectively.

Instructions

a. Prepare the July 1, 2020 entry for Zoe Corporation to record the purchase.

b. Assume that Zoe is a private entity and tested its goodwill for impairment on December 31, 2021. Management determined that the reporting unit's carrying amount (including goodwill) was $500,000 and that the reporting unit's fair value (including goodwill) was $450,000. Determine if there is any impairment and prepare any necessary entry on December 31, 2021. Zoe applies ASPE.

c. Repeat part (a), assuming that the purchase price was $204,000, all paid in cash.

d. Based on part (a), assume now that Zoe is a public entity and tested its goodwill for impairment on December 31, 2021. The cash-generating unit's values (including goodwill) are as follows:

Carrying amount	$500,000
Value in use	475,000
Fair value	450,000
Disposal costs	25,000

Determine if there is any impairment and prepare any necessary entry on December 31, 2021.

e. **Digging Deeper** Based on part (a), discuss factors that Zoe may have considered in deciding to pay total consideration of $465,000 for Soorya.

E12.21 (LO 8, 10) (Goodwill Impairment) The following is net asset information for the Dhillon Division of Klaus Inc.:

Net Assets
As at December 31, 2020
(in millions)

	Book Value	Fair Value Excluding Goodwill
Cash	$ 50	$ 50
Accounts receivable	216	216
Property, plant, and equipment (net)	2,618	2,760
Goodwill	206	
Less: Notes payable	(2,700)	(2,700)
Net assets	$ 390	

The purpose of the Dhillon Division (also identified as a reporting unit or cash-generating unit) is to develop a nuclear-powered aircraft. If successful, travelling delays that are associated with refuelling could be greatly reduced, and operational efficiency would increase significantly.

To date, management has not had much success and is deciding whether a writedown is appropriate at this time. Management has prepared the following estimates for the reporting unit or cash-generating unit:

1. Undiscounted future net cash flows are approximately $400 million.

2. Future value in use is approximately $385 million.

3. Sale of the unit would yield $346 million and selling costs would total $5 million.

Instructions

a. Under ASPE, determine if there is any impairment and prepare any necessary entry on December 31, 2020.

b. On December 31, 2021, it is estimated that the reporting unit's fair value has increased to $400 million. Under ASPE, prepare the journal entry, if any, to record the increase in fair value.

c. Under IFRS, determine if there is any impairment and prepare any necessary entry on December 31, 2020.

d. On December 31, 2021, it is estimated that the cash-generating unit's fair value has increased to $400 million. Under IFRS, prepare the journal entry, if any, to record the increase in fair value.

*E12.22 (LO 11) [Finance] **(Calculation of Normalized Earnings)** Rotterdam Corporation's pre-tax accounting income of $725,000 for the year 2020 included the following items:

Amortization of identifiable intangibles	$147,000
Depreciation of building	115,000
Loss from discontinued operations	44,000
Unusual, non-recurring gains	152,000
Profit-sharing payments to employees	65,000

Ewing Industries Ltd. would like to purchase Rotterdam Corporation. In trying to measure Rotterdam's normalized earnings for 2020, Ewing determines that the building's fair value is triple the book value and that its remaining economic life is double the life that Rotterdam is using. Ewing would continue the profit-sharing payments to employees, with the payments being based on income from continuing operations before amortization and depreciation.

Instructions

Calculate the 2020 normalized earnings amount of Rotterdam Corporation that Ewing would use to calculate goodwill.

*E12.23 (LO 11) [Finance] **(Calculation of Goodwill)** Net income figures for Belgian Ltd. are as follows:

2016—$75,000	2019—$87,000
2017—$53,000	2020—$69,000
2018—$84,000	

Future income is expected to continue at the average amount of the past five years. The company's identifiable net assets are appraised at $460,000 on December 31, 2020. The business is to be acquired by Mooney Corp. in early 2021. The normal rate of return on net assets for the industry is 7%.

Instructions

What amount should Mooney Corp. pay for goodwill, and for Belgian Ltd. as a whole, if:

a. goodwill is equal to average excess earnings capitalized at 23%?

b. a perpetual 18% return is expected on any amount paid for goodwill?

c. goodwill is equal to five years of excess earnings?

d. goodwill is equal to the present value of five years of excess earnings capitalized at 15%? Show calculations using factor Table A.4, a financial calculator, or Excel function PV. Round final amounts to the nearest dollar.

*E12.24 (LO 11) [Finance] **(Calculation of Goodwill)** Aswan Corporation is interested in acquiring Richmond Plastics Limited. Richmond has determined that its excess earnings have averaged approximately $175,000 and feels that such an amount should be capitalized over an unlimited period at a 15% rate. Aswan feels that, because of increased competition, the excess earnings of Richmond Plastics will continue for seven years at the most and that a 12% discount rate is appropriate.

Instructions

a. How far apart are the positions of these two parties? Show calculations using factor Table A.4, a financial calculator, or Excel function PV.

b. Is there really a difference in the two approaches being used by the parties to evaluate Richmond Plastics' goodwill? Explain.

*E12.25 (LO 11) [Finance] **(Calculation of Goodwill)** As the president of Niagara Wineries Corp., you are considering purchasing Grimsby Wine Accessories Limited, whose statement of financial position is summarized as follows:

Current assets	$ 240,000	Current liabilities	$ 210,000
Plant and equipment (net)	825,000	Long-term liabilities	550,000
Other assets	285,000	Common shares	440,000
		Retained earnings	150,000
Total	$1,350,000	Total	$1,350,000

The current assets' fair value is $80,000 higher than their carrying amount because of inventory undervaluation. All other assets and liabilities have book values that approximate their fair value. The normal rate of return on net assets for the industry is 15%. The expected annual earnings for Grimsby are $140,000.

Instructions

Assuming that the excess earnings are expected to continue for five years, how much would you be willing to pay for goodwill, and for the company? Estimate goodwill by the present value method, showing calculations using factor Table A.4, a financial calculator, or Excel function PV.

*E12.26 (LO 11) Finance (**Calculation of Fair Value of Identifiable Assets**) Louvre Inc. bought a business that is expected to give a 25% annual rate of return on the investment. Of the total amount paid for the business, $75,000 was deemed to be goodwill, and the rest was attributed to the identifiable net assets. Louvre Inc. estimated that the annual future earnings of the new business would be equal to the average ordinary earnings per year of the business over the past three years. The total net income over the past three years was $375,000. This amount included a loss on discontinued operations of $25,000 in one year and an unusual and non-recurring gain of $95,000 in one of the other two years.

Instructions

Calculate the fair value of the identifiable net assets that Louvre Inc. purchased in this transaction.

Problems

P12.1 Guiglano Inc. is a large, publicly held corporation. The following are six selected expenditures that were made by the company during the fiscal year ended April 30, 2020. The proper accounting treatment of these transactions must be determined in order to ensure that Guiglano's annual financial statements are prepared in accordance with IFRS.

1. Guiglano spent $3 million on a program that is designed to improve relations with its dealers. Dealers responded well to the project and Guiglano's management believes that it will therefore result in significant future benefits. The program was conducted during the fourth quarter of the 2019–20 fiscal year.

2. A pilot plant was constructed during 2019–20 at a cost of $5.5 million to test a new production process. The plant will be operated for approximately five years. After the five years, the company will make a decision about the economic value of the production process. The pilot plant is too small for commercial production, so it will be dismantled when the test is over.

3. During the year, Guiglano began a new manufacturing operation in Newfoundland, its first plant east of Montreal. To get the plant into operation, the following costs were incurred: (i) $100,000 to make the building fully wheelchair-accessible; (ii) $41,600 to outfit the new employees with Guiglano uniforms; (iii) $12,700 for the reception to introduce the company to others in the industrial mall where the plant is located; and (iv) $64,400 in payroll costs for the new employees while they were being trained.

4. Guiglano purchased Eagle Company for $6 million cash in early August 2019. The fair value of Eagle's net identifiable assets was $5.2 million.

5. The company spent $14 million on advertising during the year. Of that, $2.5 million was spent in April 2020 to introduce a new product to be released during the first quarter of the 2020–21 fiscal year and $200,000 was used to advertise the opening of the new plant in Newfoundland. The remaining expenditures were for recurring advertising and promotion coverage.

6. During the first six months of the 2019–20 fiscal year, $400,000 was spent on legal work on a successful patent application. The patent became effective in November 2019. The patent's legal life is 20 years and its economic life is expected to be approximately 10 years.

Instructions

For each of the six items presented, determine and justify the following:

a. The amount, if any, that should be capitalized and included on Guiglano's statement of financial position prepared as at April 30, 2020.

b. The amount that should be included in Guiglano's statement of income for the year ended April 30, 2020.

P12.2 Information for Naples Corporation's intangible assets follows:

1. On January 1, 2020, Naples signed an agreement to operate as a franchisee of Copy Service Inc., for an initial franchise fee of $75,000. Of this amount, $35,000 was paid when the agreement was signed and the balance is payable in four annual payments of $10,000 each, beginning January 1, 2021. The agreement provides that the down payment is not refundable and no future services are

required of the franchisor. The present value at January 1, 2020, of the four annual payments discounted at 8% (the implicit rate for a loan of this type) is $33,121. The agreement also provides that 5% of the franchisee's revenue must be paid to the franchisor each year. The franchisor requires that Naples provide it with some form of assurance verifying the revenue amount used to determine the 5% payment. Naples's revenue from the franchise for 2020 was $800,000. Naples estimates that the franchise's useful life will be 10 years.

2. Naples incurred $45,000 in experimental costs in its laboratory to develop a patent, and the patent was granted on January 2, 2020. Legal fees and other costs of patent registration totalled $13,600. Naples estimates that the useful life of the patent will be six years.

3. A trademark was purchased from Shanghai Company for $28,600 on July 1, 2017. The legal costs to successfully defend the trademark totalled $8,160 and were paid on July 1, 2020. Naples estimates that the trademark's useful life will be 15 years from the acquisition date.

Assume that Naples reports using ASPE.

Instructions

a. Prepare a schedule showing the intangible assets section of Naples's statement of financial position at December 31, 2020. Show supporting calculations in good form.

b. Prepare a schedule showing all expenses resulting from the transactions that would appear on Naples's income statement for the year ended December 31, 2020. Show supporting calculations in good form.

c. How would your response change under IFRS?

d. **Digging Deeper** What type of report could Naples provide to the franchisor to verify the revenue amount provided?

(Adapted from AICPA)

P12.3 Gelato Corporation, a private entity reporting under ASPE, was incorporated on January 3, 2019. The corporation's financial statements for its first year of operations were not examined by a public accountant. You have been engaged to audit the financial statements for the year ended December 31, 2020, and your audit is almost complete. The corporation's trial balance is as follows:

Gelato Corporation
Trial Balance
December 31, 2020

	Debit	Credit
Cash	$ 57,000	
Accounts receivable	87,000	
Allowance for doubtful accounts		$ 1,500
Inventory	60,200	
Machinery	82,000	
Equipment	37,000	
Accumulated depreciation		26,200
Intangible assets—patents	128,200	
Leasehold improvements	36,100	
Prepaid expenses	13,000	
Goodwill	30,000	
Intangible assets—licensing agreement No. 1	60,000	
Intangible assets—licensing agreement No. 2	56,000	
Accounts payable		93,000
Unearned revenue		17,280
Common shares		300,000
Retained earnings, January 1, 2020		173,020
Sales		720,000
Cost of goods sold	475,000	
Selling expenses	180,000	
Interest expense	29,500	
Totals	$1,331,000	$1,331,000

The following information is for accounts that may still need adjustment:

1. Patents for Gelato's manufacturing process were acquired on January 2, 2020, at a cost of $87,500. An additional $35,000 was spent in July 2020 and $5,700 in December 2020 to improve machinery covered by the patents and was charged to the Intangible Assets—Patents account. Depreciation on

fixed assets was properly recorded for 2020 in accordance with Gelato's practice, which is to take a full year of depreciation for property on hand at June 30. No other depreciation or amortization was recorded. Gelato uses the straight-line method for all amortization and amortizes its patents over their legal life, which was 17 years when the patent was granted. Accumulate all amortization expense in one income statement account.

2. At December 31, 2020, management determined that the undiscounted future net cash flows that are expected from the use of the patent would be $80,000, the value in use was $75,000, the resale value of the patent was approximately $55,000, and disposal costs would be $5,000.

3. On January 3, 2019, Gelato purchased licensing agreement no. 1, which management believed had an unlimited useful life. Licences similar to this are frequently bought and sold. Gelato could only clearly identify cash flows from agreement no. 1 for 15 years. After the 15 years, further cash flows are still possible, but are uncertain. The balance in the Licences account includes the agreement's purchase price of $57,000 and expenses of $3,000 related to the acquisition. On January 1, 2020, Gelato purchased licensing agreement no. 2, which has a life expectancy of five years. The balance in the Licences account includes its $54,000 purchase price and $6,000 in acquisition expenses, but it has been reduced by a credit of $4,000 for the advance collection of 2021 revenue from the agreement. In late December 2019, an explosion caused a permanent 60% reduction in the expected revenue-producing value of licensing agreement no. 1. In January 2021, a flood caused additional damage that rendered the agreement worthless.

4. The balance in the Goodwill account results from legal expenses of $30,000 that were incurred for Gelato's incorporation on January 3, 2019. Management assumes that the $30,000 cost will benefit the entire life of the organization, and believes that these costs should be amortized over a limited life of 30 years. No entry has been made yet.

5. The Leasehold Improvements account includes the following:

   i. There is a $15,000 cost of improvements that Gelato made to premises that it leases as a tenant. The improvements were made in January 2019 and have a useful life of 12 years.

   ii. Movable assembly-line equipment costing $15,000 was installed in the leased premises in December 2020.

   iii. Real estate taxes of $6,100 were paid by Gelato in 2020, but they should have been paid by the landlord under the terms of the lease agreement.

   Gelato paid its rent in full during 2020. A 10-year non-renewable lease was signed on January 3, 2019, for the leased building that Gelato uses in manufacturing operations. No amortization or depreciation has been recorded on any amounts related to the lease or improvements.

6. Included in selling expenses are the following costs incurred to develop a new product. Gelato hopes to establish the technical, financial, and commercial viability of this project in fiscal 2021.

Salaries of two employees who spend approximately 50% of their time on research and development initiatives (this amount represents their full salary)	$110,000
Materials consumed	35,000

Instructions

a. Prepare an eight-column work sheet to adjust the accounts that require adjustment and include columns for an income statement and a statement of financial position. A separate account should be used for the accumulation of each type of amortization. Formal journal entries and financial statements are not required.

b. Prepare Gelato's statement of financial position and income statement for the year ended December 31, 2020, in proper form.

c. Explain how the accounting would differ if Gelato were reporting under IFRS.

(Adapted from AICPA)

P12.4 Monsecours Corp., a public company incorporated on June 28, 2019, set up a single account for all of its intangible assets. The following summary discloses the debit entries that were recorded during 2019 and 2020 in that account:

Intangible Assets—Monsecours

July	1, 2019	8-year franchise; expiration date of June 30, 2027	$ 35,000
Oct.	1	Advance payment on office lease (2-year lease)	25,000
Dec.	31	Net loss for 2019 including incorporation fee, $1,000; related legal fees of organizing, $5,000; expenses of recruiting and training staff for start-up of new business, $3,800	17,000

Feb. 15, 2020	Patent purchased (10-year life)	65,400
Mar. 1	Direct costs of acquiring a 5-year licensing agreement	86,000
Apr. 1	Goodwill purchased (indefinite life)	287,500
June 1	Legal fee for successful defence of patent (see above)	13,350
Dec. 31	Costs of research department for year	75,000
31	Royalties paid under licensing agreement (see above)	2,775

The new business started up on July 2, 2019. No amortization was recorded for 2019 or 2020. The goodwill purchased on April 1, 2020, includes in-process development costs that meet the six development stage criteria, valued at $175,000. The company estimates that this amount will help it generate revenues over a 10-year period.

Instructions

a. Prepare the necessary entries to clear the Intangible Assets account and to set up separate accounts for distinct types of intangibles. Make the entries as at December 31, 2020, and record any necessary amortization so that all balances are appropriate as at that date. State any assumptions that you need to make to support your entries.

b. **Digging Deeper** In what circumstances should goodwill be recognized? From the perspective of an investor, does the required recognition and measurement of goodwill provide useful financial statement information?

P12.5 **Excel** Fields Laboratories holds a valuable patent (No. 758-6002-1A) on a precipitator that prevents certain types of air pollution. Fields does not manufacture or sell the products and processes it develops. Instead, it conducts research and develops products and processes that it patents, and then assigns the patents to manufacturers on a royalty basis. Occasionally it sells one of its patents. The history of Fields patent number 758-6002-1A is as follows.

Date	Activity	Cost
2011 – 2012	Research conducted to develop precipitator	$384,000
Jan. 3, 2013	Design and construction of a prototype	87,600
Mar. 15, 2013	Testing of models	42,000
Jan. 4, 2014	Fees paid to engineers and lawyers to prepare patent application; patent granted January 4, 2014	59,500
Nov. 30, 2015	Engineering activity necessary to advance the design of the precipitator to the manufacturing stage	81,500
Dec. 31, 2016	Legal fees paid to successfully defend precipitator patent	42,000
Apr. 15, 2017	Research aimed at modifying the design of the patented precipitator	43,000
July 31, 2021	Legal fees paid in unsuccessful patent infringement suit against a competitor	34,000

Fields assumed a useful life of 17 years when it received the initial precipitator patent. On January 1, 2019, it revised its useful life estimate downward to five remaining years. The company's year ends December 31. Fields follows IFRS for reporting purposes.

Instructions

Calculate the carrying value of patent No. 758-6002-1A on each of the following dates:

a. December 31, 2014

b. December 31, 2018

c. December 31, 2021

d. How would your answers to parts (a) to (c) differ if ASPE were followed?

P12.6 During 2018, Medicine Hat Tools Ltd., a Canadian public company, purchased a building site for its product development laboratory at a cost of $61,000. Construction of the building started in 2018. The building was completed in late December 2019 at a cost of $185,000 and placed in service on January 2, 2020. The building's estimated useful life for depreciation purposes is 15 years. The straight-line method of depreciation is used and there is no estimated residual value. After the building went into service, several projects were begun and many are still in process.

Management estimates that about 50% of the development projects will result in long-term benefits (for at least 10 years) to the corporation. The other projects either benefited the current period or were abandoned before completion. A summary of the different projects, their number, and the direct costs that were incurred for development activities in 2020 appears in the table that follows.

On the recommendation of its research and development group, Medicine Hat Tools Ltd. acquired a patent for manufacturing rights at a cost of $102,500. The patent was acquired on April 1, 2019, and has an economic life of 10 years.

	Number of Projects	Salaries and Employee Benefits	Other Expenses (Excluding Building Depreciation Charges)
Development of viable products (management intent and capability, financial, technical, and commercial viability criteria were met)	15	$125,000	$ 81,000
Abandoned projects or projects that benefit the current period only	10	87,000	21,000
Projects in process—results uncertain	5	52,500	18,500
Total	30	$264,500	$120,500

Instructions

a. How should the items above that relate to product development activities be reported under IFRS on the company's income statement and statement of financial position at December 31, 2020? Be sure to give account titles and amounts, and briefly justify your presentation.

b. Outline the criteria that would have to be met for any development costs to qualify as an intangible asset.

(Adapted from CMA)

P12.7 In 2020, Aquaculture Incorporated applied for several commercial fishing licences for its commercial fishing vessels. The application was successful and on January 2, 2020, Aquaculture was granted 22 commercial fishing licences for a registration fee of $18,700 per licence. According to management, each licence had a useful life of eight years from the date of registration. After the eight years, further cash flows might still be possible, but they are uncertain. There is an active market for Aquaculture's licences, which are freely transferable.

In 2021, due to an oil spill in the bordering ocean and severe commercial fishing restrictions, the value of Aquaculture's licences decreased. As at December 31, 2021, each licence had a value in use of $9,500, fair value of $8,300, and costs to sell of $200. In 2023, due to much higher demand and restricted issuance of commercial fishing licences, the value of Aquaculture's licences increased. As at December 31, 2023, each licence had a value in use of $14,900, fair value of $17,000, and costs to sell of $200. Aquaculture amortizes intangible assets using the straight-line method, revalues the licences at the end of 2021 and 2023, and prepares financial statements in accordance with IFRS.

Instructions

a. Prepare the entry to record the costs incurred on January 2, 2020.

b. Assume that after initial recognition, Aquaculture uses the revaluation model (asset adjustment method) to measure its intangible assets. Prepare the entries required on December 31, 2021, December 31, 2022, and December 31, 2023, and calculate the carrying amount of the intangible asset, if any, as at December 31, 2023.

c. Assume that after initial recognition, Aquaculture uses the revaluation model (proportionate method) to measure its intangible assets. Prepare the entries required on December 31, 2021, December 31, 2022, and December 31, 2023, and calculate the carrying amount of the intangible asset, if any, as at December 31, 2023. Do not round intermediate calculations but round final amounts to the nearest dollar.

d. **Digging Deeper** Would an investor prefer Aquaculture to use the asset adjustment method or the proportionate method to apply the revaluation model?

P12.8 Meridan Golf and Sports was formed on July 1, 2020, when Steve Powerdriver purchased Old Master Golf Corporation. Old Master provides video golf instruction at kiosks in shopping malls. Powerdriver's plan is to make the instruction business part of his golf equipment and accessory stores. Powerdriver paid $650,000 cash for Old Master. At the time of purchase, Old Master's statement of financial position reported assets of $550,000 and liabilities of $100,000 (shareholders' equity was $450,000). The fair value of Old Master's identifiable assets was estimated to be $700,000. Included in the identifiable assets was the Old Master trade name with a fair value of $15,000 and a copyright on some instructional books with a fair value of $25,000. The trade name had a remaining legal life of five years and can be renewed indefinitely at nominal cost. The copyright had a remaining life of 40 years.

Instructions

Assume that Meridan Golf and Sports is a private company reporting under ASPE.

a. Prepare the intangible assets and goodwill section of Meridan Golf and Sports at December 31, 2020. How much amortization expense is included in Meridan's income for the year ended December 31, 2020? Show all supporting calculations.

b. Prepare the journal entry to record the amortization expense for 2021. Prepare the intangible assets and goodwill section of Meridan Golf and Sports at December 31, 2021. (No impairment needs to be recorded in 2021.)

c. At the end of 2022, Powerdriver is evaluating the results of the instructional business. Due to fierce competition from Internet sites and television, the Old Master reporting unit has been losing money and has a carrying amount (including goodwill) of $450,000 and fair value (including goodwill) of $430,000. Powerdriver has collected the following information about the company's intangible assets:

Intangible Asset	Expected Cash Flows (Undiscounted)	Fair Value
Trade name	$11,000	$ 8,000
Copyright	30,000	25,000

Prepare the required journal entries, if any, to record impairment on Meridan's intangible assets and goodwill. (Assume that amortization for 2022 has been recorded.) Show supporting calculations.

P12.9 Use the data provided in P12.8. Assume instead that Meridan Golf and Sports is a public company. The relevant information for the impairment test on December 31, 2022, is as follows:

	Carrying Amount	Future Net Cash Flows (Undiscounted)	Value in Use	FV–Selling Costs
Trade name	$ 15,000	$ 11,000	$ 7,000	$ 7,500
Copyright	23,438	30,000	27,000	24,000
Cash-generating unit to which goodwill was allocated	450,000	470,000	440,000	420,000

Instructions

Provide the calculations for the impairment test and any associated journal entry.

P12.10 Six examples of purchased intangible assets follow. They are reported on the consolidated statement of financial position of Powers Enterprises Limited and include information about their useful and legal lives. Powers prepares financial statements in accordance with IFRS.

Intangible 1(i) is the trade name for one of the company's subsidiaries. The trade name has a remaining legal life of 16 years, but it can be renewed indefinitely at a very low cost. The subsidiary has grown quickly and been very successful, and its name is well known to Canadian consumers. Powers management has concluded that it can identify positive cash flows from the use of the trade name for another 25 years, and assumes the cash flows will continue even longer.

Intangible 1(ii) is the trade name as identified in 1(i), but assume instead that Powers Enterprises expects to sell this subsidiary in three years, since the subsidiary operates in an area that is not part of Powers's core activities.

Intangible 2 is a licence granted by the federal government to Powers that allows Powers to provide essential services to a key military installation overseas. The licence expires in five years, but is renewable indefinitely at little cost. Because of the profitability associated with this licence, Powers expects to renew it indefinitely. The licence is very marketable and will generate cash flows indefinitely.

Intangible 3 is a magazine subscription list. Powers expects to use this subscriber list to generate revenues and cash flows for at least 25 years. It has determined the cash flow potential of this intangible by analyzing the subscribers' renewal history, the behaviour of the group of subscribers, and their responses to questionnaires.

Intangible 4 is a non-competition covenant. Powers acquired this intangible asset when it bought out a major owner-managed competitor. The seller signed a contract in which he agreed not to set up or work for another business that was in direct or indirect competition with Powers. The projected cash flows resulting from this agreement are expected to continue for at least 25 years.

Intangible 5 is medical files. One of Powers's subsidiary companies owns several dental clinics. A recent purchase of a retiring dentist's practice required a significant payment for the practice's medical files and clients. Powers considers that this base will benefit the business for as long as it exists, providing cash flows indefinitely.

Intangible 6 is a favourable lease. Powers acquired a sublease on a large warehouse property that requires an annual rental amount that is 50% below competitive rates in the area. The lease extends for 35 years.

Instructions

For each intangible asset and situation described above, do the following:

a. Identify the appropriate method of accounting for the asset subsequent to acquisition, and justify your answer.

b. Provide an example of a specific situation that would cause you to test the intangible asset for impairment.

P12.11 In late July 2020, Mona Ltd., a private company, paid $2 million to acquire all of the net assets of Lubello Corp., which then became a division of Mona. Lubello reported the following statement of financial position at the time of acquisition:

Current assets	$ 415,000	Current liabilities	$ 300,000
Non-current assets	1,335,000	Long-term liabilities	265,000
		Shareholders' equity	1,185,000
	$1,750,000		$1,750,000

It was determined at the date of the purchase that the fair value of the identifiable net assets of Lubello was $1.7 million. Over the next six months of operations, the new division had operating losses. In addition, it now appears that it will generate substantial losses for the foreseeable future. At December 31, 2020, the fair value of the Lubello Division is $1,850,000, and the division reports the following statement of financial position information:

Current assets	$ 462,000
Non-current assets (including goodwill recognized in purchase)	2,400,000
Current liabilities	(703,500)
Long-term liabilities	(530,000)
Net assets	$1,628,500

Assume that Mona Ltd. prepares financial statements in accordance with ASPE.

Instructions

a. Calculate the amount of goodwill, if any, that should be recognized in late July 2020.

b. Determine the loss on impairment, if any, to be recognized on December 31, 2020.

c. Assume that the fair value of the Lubello Division on December 31, 2020, is $1.5 million. Determine the loss on impairment, if any, that would be recognized.

d. Prepare the journal entry to record the loss on impairment, if any, in parts (b) and (c) and indicate where the loss would be reported in the income statement.

e. Explain how the accounting would differ under IFRS.

f. **Digging Deeper** Shortly after Mona purchased Lubello, Lubello incurred losses and its future does not look promising. What advice can you provide to Mona's management team for any future acquisitions the company may be considering?

P12.12 On September 1, 2020, Madonna Lisa Corporation, a public company, acquired Jaromil Enterprises for a cash payment of $763,000. At the time of purchase, Jaromil's statement of financial position showed assets of $850,000, liabilities of $430,000, and owners' equity of $420,000. The fair value of Jaromil's identifiable assets is estimated to be $1,080,000.

Instructions

a. Calculate the amount of goodwill acquired by Madonna Lisa.

b. Assume that the goodwill was allocated entirely to one cash-generating unit (CGU), as indicated below. The CGU's value in use at the statement of financial position date was $3,850,000 and the fair value less costs to sell was $4,250,000. Determine if the goodwill is impaired.

	Plant A CGU
Assets (other than goodwill)	$4,500,000
Goodwill	113,000
Total carrying value of CGU	$4,613,000

c. Explain how a future reversal of impairment is accounted for under IFRS.

*P12.13 **Finance** Macho Inc. has recently become interested in acquiring a South American plant to handle many of its production functions in that market. One possible candidate is De Fuentes SA, a closely held corporation, whose owners have decided to sell their business if a proper settlement can be obtained. De Fuentes's statement of financial position is as follows:

Current assets	$125,000
Fair value-net income investments	55,000
Buildings (net)	405,000
Total assets	$585,000
Current liabilities	$ 85,000
Notes payable	105,000
Share capital	225,000
Retained earnings	170,000
Total liabilities and shareholders' equity	$585,000

Macho has hired Yardon Appraisal Corporation to determine the proper price to pay for De Fuentes SA. The appraisal firm finds that the fair value-net income investments have a fair value of $75,000 and that inventory is understated by $40,000. All other assets and liabilities have book values that approximate their fair values. An examination of the company's income for the past four years indicates that the net income has steadily increased. In 2020, the company had a net operating income of $110,000, and this income should increase by 15% each year over the next four years. Macho believes that a normal return in this type of business is 15% on net assets. The asset investment in the South American plant is expected to stay the same for the next four years.

Instructions

a. Yardon Appraisal Corporation has indicated that De Fuentes SA's fair value can be estimated in several ways. Prepare estimates of the value of De Fuentes SA, with the value based on each of the following independent assumptions:

1. Goodwill is based on the purchase of average excess earnings over the next four years.

2. Goodwill is equal to the capitalization of average excess earnings of De Fuentes SA at 30%.

3. Goodwill is equal to the present value of the average excess earnings over the next four years discounted at 15%. Show calculations using factor Table A.4, a financial calculator, or Excel function PV. Round final amounts to the nearest dollar.

4. The value of the business is based on the capitalization of future excess earnings of De Fuentes SA at 16%.

b. De Fuentes SA is willing to sell the business for $1 million. What advice should Yardon Appraisal give Macho in regard to this offer?

c. **Digging Deeper** If Macho were to pay $850,000 to purchase the assets and assume the liabilities of De Fuentes SA, how would this transaction be reflected on Macho's books?

*P12.14 **Finance** The president of Plain Corp., Joyce Lima, is thinking of purchasing Balloon Bunch Corporation. She thinks that the offer sounds fair but she wants to consult a professional accountant to be sure. Balloon Bunch Corporation is asking for $85,000 in excess of the fair value of the identifiable net assets. Balloon Bunch's net income figures for the past five years are as follows:

2016—$67,000	2019—$80,000
2017—$50,000	2020—$72,000
2018—$81,000	

The company's identifiable net assets were appraised at $400,000 on December 31, 2020.

You have done some initial research on the balloon industry and discovered that the normal rate of return on identifiable net assets is 15%. After analyzing such variables as the stability of past earnings, the nature of the business, and general economic conditions, you have decided that the average excess earnings for the past five years should be capitalized at 20% and that the excess earnings will continue for about six more years. Further research led you to discover that the Happy Balloon Corporation, a competitor of similar size and profitability, was recently sold for $450,000, five times its average yearly earnings of $90,000.

Instructions

a. Prepare a schedule that includes the calculation of Balloon Bunch Corporation's goodwill and purchase price under at least three methods.

b. Write a letter to Joyce Lima that includes all of the following:

1. An explanation of the nature of goodwill.
2. An explanation of the different acceptable methods of determining the fair value of goodwill. (Include with your explanation the rationale for how each method arrives at a goodwill value.)
3. Advice for Joyce Lima on how to determine her purchase price.
4. Considerations before relying on the earnings figure used to determine the purchase price.

P12.15 **Excel** On July 31, 2020, Mexico Company paid $3 million to acquire all of the common shares of Conchita Incorporated, which became a division of Mexico. Conchita reported the following statement of financial position at the time of the acquisition.

Conchita Inc.
Statement of Financial Position
As at July 31, 2020

Current assets	$ 800,000	Current liabilities	$ 600,000
Non-current assets	2,700,000	Long-term liabilities	500,000
Total assets	$3,500,000	Shareholders' equity	2,400,000
		Total liabilities and shareholders' equity	$3,500,000

It was determined at the date of the purchase that the fair value of the identifiable net assets of Conchita was $2,750,000. Over the next six months of operations, the newly purchased division experienced operating losses. In addition, it now appears that it will generate substantial losses for the foreseeable future. At December 31, 2020, the Conchita Division reports the following SFP-related information:

Current assets	$ 450,000
Non-current assets (including goodwill recognized in purchase)	2,400,000
Current liabilities	(700,000)
Long-term liabilities	(500,000)
Net assets	$1,650,000

It is determined that the fair value of the Conchita Division as at December 31, 2020, is $1,850,000. The recorded amount for Conchita's net assets (excluding goodwill) is the same as fair value, except for property, plant, and equipment, which has a fair value $150,000 above the carrying value. Assume that Mexico follows ASPE for financial reporting purposes.

Instructions

a. Calculate the amount of goodwill recognized, if any, on July 31, 2020.

b. Determine the loss on impairment, if any, to be recorded on December 31, 2020.

c. Assume that fair value of the Conchita Division is $1,600,000 instead of $1,850,000. Determine the loss on impairment, if any, to be recorded on December 31, 2020.

d. Prepare the journal entry to record the loss on impairment, if any, and indicate where the loss would be reported in the income statement.

Integrated Cases

Refer to the Case Primer on the Student Website and in *WileyPLUS* to help you answer these cases.

(*Hint:* If there are issues here that are new, use the conceptual framework to help you support your analysis with solid reasoning.)

IC12.1 Dr. Gary Morrow, a former surgeon, is the president and owner of Morrow Medical (MM), a private Ontario company that focuses on the design and implementation of various medical and pharmaceutical products. With the recent success of various products put to market by MM, Dr. Morrow has decided that this would be a good opportunity to sell his company and retire to the Arizona desert. Dr. Morrow has found a potential buyer for the business and an agreement has been put in place that would see MM being sold at five times the December 31, 2019 net income. The potential buyer is extremely interested in an MM product that is currently in the development stage—the MM Surgical Drill.

During 2019, MM launched into production a special latex glove for use during surgery. This glove is laced with a special antibacterial agent that significantly reduces the risk of infection during surgery. The product had been in the development phase since 2016, and in early 2018, it was approved by Health Canada for production and use.

Dr. Morrow was pleased with the initial demand for the product after trial runs conducted by surgeons during late 2018. After the success of the trial testing, MM landed contracts with several hospitals in the province and early feedback was favourable. Dr. Morrow was surprised, however, with how small the quantity of orders placed by hospitals actually was. He was certain that hospitals would quickly run out of the gloves and was beginning to fear that they would buy a competitor's product.

Since Dr. Morrow wanted to prevent hospitals from buying elsewhere, as it would result in a loss of sales for MM, for each purchase order received from a hospital, Dr. Morrow shipped several more units than were ordered. He was certain that all of the extra inventory would eventually be consumed and this was MM's way of avoiding the hospitals' running out of inventory. To prevent hospitals from returning the extra inventory, he allowed them eight months to either pay for the entire shipment or return any unused gloves in excess of the initial amount that was ordered. Dr. Morrow's first priority is always getting the product out of the warehouse and into the hospitals. Orders are generally filled and shipped within two days of receipt of a purchase order. Because MM is dealing with hospitals, there is little concern over collectibility.

During 2016, under the supervision of Dr. Morrow, MM began the research and development of a special surgical drill (the MM Surgical Drill mentioned above) that would allow for more precise handling by surgeons than any other drill currently on the market. The development of this product grew from various market surveys conducted in hospitals throughout Ontario that showed that surgeons were unhappy with the drills that were currently available.

The following costs were incurred in 2019:

Cost of setting up production lab	$ 30,000
Testing of Surgical Drill	100,000
Design of the moulds involved in Surgical Drill technology	17,500
Testing to evaluate product alternatives	12,000
Marketing and promotion costs in connection with launching the surgical gloves	15,000

Dr. Morrow intends to capitalize all of these costs for the December 31 year end. In addition, $25,000 of tool design costs that were expensed in 2018 will be capitalized in 2019.

MM has the technical resources available to complete the Surgical Drill project and, since testing to date has been successful, management intends to bring this product to market in early 2021. MM has been faced with cash flow problems in the past few months but hopes that, once MM is sold, additional funding will be available to see this product into its production stage.

In early 2019, an engineer testing the Surgical Drill was severely injured as a result of a product malfunction. This glitch was subsequently identified and fixed. MM has recently been sued. The claim is for $500,000 and alleges that MM was responsible for the engineer's injuries. MM's lawyer's best estimate of what the company will end up paying is $100,000 to $200,000. As the trial does not begin until 2020, MM has no intention of recording this in its December 31, 2019 financial statements.

Instructions

Audit Adopt the role of the auditor hired by MM's potential buyer and analyze the financial reporting issues.

IC12.2 Biofuel Inc. (BI) is a private company that just started up this year. The company's owner, Sarah Biorini, created a process whereby carbon dioxide (CO_2) emissions are converted into biofuel. Specifically, the CO_2 is pumped into a pond where algae are grown. The algae feed on the CO_2 and release oxygen. The algae are harvested, dried, and sold as fuel. The fuel is used by cement manufacturing companies to heat their kilns (ovens). Sarah contributed the prototype and idea to the newly formed company in return for common shares. She estimated that the prototype was worth about $500,000. BI spent the first year developing the idea and by year end was producing and selling the fuel to several cement production companies. Cement companies not only produce large amounts of CO_2, but also need large amounts of fuel to heat their kilns.

One of the critical success factors for BI is that the algae-producing pond should be close to the source of CO_2. This reduces transportation costs. After much consideration, BI decided to build pipelines to pump CO_2 from the source (the cement company) into an adjacent algae-filled pond. The pond is excavated by BI but it sits on the cement company's land (close to the source of CO_2). Once a month, BI harvests the algae and ships it to its manufacturing plant to process into biofuel. It then sells the biofuel back to the cement companies.

The cost of constructing the pipelines is financed by the bank, as is the excavation of the ponds. The construction is done by BI and generally takes about three to six months. The finished biofuel made from the algae is priced to recover patent costs and the cost of building the pipe and the ponds, as well as any other costs. It is sold back to the cement companies. The cement companies are both customers and suppliers of the CO_2.

The bank is quite happy to continue financing additional projects as long as BI sends its financial statements to the bank every quarter, starting next year. In addition, the bank would like to see audited annual financial statements beginning with the current year. The bank and BI have agreed that the debt to equity ratio cannot exceed 3:1, or the loans become immediately due. BI's accountant is looking to produce the annual financial statements for the first year of operations. He has not yet decided whether to follow IFRS or ASPE and is interested in the differences between the two.

Instructions

Assume the role of BI's accountant and discuss the financial reporting issues relating to the above. Use the case analysis framework presented in class, including an overview, analysis, and recommendations.

IC12.3 **Finance** As a recent graduate and newly hired financial analyst for the local branch office of a national brokerage firm, you are excited to get your first assignment, allowing you to use your accounting expertise. Your supervisor provides you with updated data for the most recent quarter for three companies that the firm has been recommending to its clients as "buys." All three companies are publicly traded and use IFRS for financial reporting purposes. Each of the companies made one significant acquisition in the past that expanded their markets in their respective industries. The companies all put a high intrinsic value on the potential that these new markets would bring to the acquiring company. Each of the acquisitions was brought into the acquiring company as a new division. The new acquisitions represent at least 25% of the operations of the companies that acquired them.

The return on assets for each of the companies as a whole has outperformed their industry cohorts in the past. But, given recent challenges in their markets, coupled with unsteady performance overall in the marketplace, there is concern that the companies may experience operating challenges and lower earnings. In particular, each of the acquisitions has not performed as expected and has resulted in quarterly net losses to the companies' bottom line.

As shown by the data summarized below, each newly acquired division's market value is now lower than its corresponding book value. Your supervisor wants to understand what, if any, implications this may have for each company's future prospects, given the significance of the divisions to the overall operations of each company.

The book value reported in the table below includes the carrying value of goodwill assigned to each division at the time of its acquisition. For each company, there has been no impairment of the carrying value of goodwill previously recorded for these divisions.

(All numbers in millions, except return on assets.)

Company Name and Division	Market Value (B)	Book Value (Net Assets) (C)	Carrying Value of Goodwill (D)	Value in Use (E)	Costs to Sell (F)	ROA for the Company (%) (G)
ABC Limited, Division 1	$36,200	$51,500	$30,200	$32,300	$1,000	3.5
DEF Limited, Division H	12,700	22,200	9,000	16,500	500	2.6
XYZ Limited, Division XX	1,800	4,000	900	3,000	200	5.2

Your supervisor suspects that the companies will need to record goodwill impairment for the acquired divisions in the near future, but is unsure about the goodwill impairment rules. She would like to know if it is likely that these companies will recognize impairment. If they will, your supervisor would like you to estimate the amount for each and explain to her where the loss on impairment would be recorded. In addition, she would like to know how this might impact the overall return on assets ratio for each company and the impact on the "buy" recommendations.

Your supervisor would also like to know if these companies can reverse the losses on impairment recorded once the market improves and the prospect of these divisions looks promising. If a reversal is possible, the supervisor has suggested that the current year impairments may have less impact than if no reversal were available.

Your supervisor would like you to respond within two days, as the brokerage firm's clients are nervous about their portfolios and are anxious to hear about any good "buy" recommendations.

Instructions

Adopt the role of the newly hired financial analyst and prepare the report for your supervisor.

Research and Analysis

RA12.1 [Real World Emphasis] **British Airways**

Access the annual report for British Airways Plc (BA) for the year ended December 31, 2017, from its parent company's website (www.iagshares.com). British Airways is now a part of the International Airlines Group. Use the amounts in and notes to BA's group (that is, consolidated) financial statements to answer the following questions.

Instructions

a. Does British Airways Plc report any intangible assets or goodwill in its 2017 financial statements and accompanying notes? Identify all such accounts, describe their nature, their reported balance sheet amounts at December 31, 2017, and the accounting policies that are applied to these assets, including any general impairment policies. Are there any situations where there are discrepancies with IFRS standards?

b. What additions were made to the landing rights and software for 2017? Do you expect the landing rights are mainly for use inside or outside the European Union? Explain briefly.

c. How is goodwill tested for impairment? Provide details on the methods and key assumptions used by the company. Is information provided on the recoverable amounts determined? Were there any losses on impairment recorded in goodwill or other intangible assets in 2017? What assumptions would make the recoverable amount equal to the carrying amount for the network airline operations?

d. Why is the information provided in part (c) considered helpful to users?

RA12.2 [Real World Emphasis] **Rights to Use Sports Celebrities' Names**

Nike, Inc. has had endorsement contracts with some of the world's best-known golfers. For example, Nike has been able to gain the rights to use top golfers' names in advertising promotions and on Nike Golf apparel, footwear, golf balls, and golf equipment. Recently, Rory McIlroy's name has been added to its list.

Instructions

Conduct research on the Internet to determine the nature of the endorsement contracts that Nike has with top athletes, such as Rory McIlroy. What form do Nike's payments for such rights take? Using Nike, Inc.'s most recent financial statements (which can be found in its Form-10K filing), determine how Nike reports the cost of endorsement contracts. Does the cost qualify as an intangible asset under IAS 38? Explain briefly.

RA12.3 Intangible Issues

Kolber Manufacturing Limited designs, manufactures, and distributes safety boots. In January 2020, Kolber purchased another business that manufactures and distributes safety shoes, to complement its existing business. The total purchase price was $10 million in cash paid immediately and another $5 million in cash to be paid in one year's time. The company's current interest cost was 6%. The assets and liabilities purchased include accounts receivable, finished goods inventories, land and plant, manufacturing equipment and office equipment, accounts payable, and a loan that is secured by the manufacturing equipment. In addition, a trademark was included (which has six years remaining on its current legal life), as well as existing customer relationships (although there are no outstanding contracts with these customers), and a non-compete agreement with the existing owners that they will not start any similar business for the next five years. The company reports under IFRS.

Instructions

You are the controller of Kolber and have been given the task of recording the purchase in the company's books.

a. Outline how you might go about determining how to allocate the purchase price to the intangible assets and any goodwill purchased. In addition, consider how each of these assets is subsequently reported and what the effect will be on net earnings in subsequent years given your decisions now.

b. If this company reported under ASPE, explain how the impairment test for goodwill would differ from the IFRS method.

(Adapted from AICPA)

RA12.4 Audit Social Media

Weaver Limited is a company that distributes hard-to-find computer supplies, such as hardware parts and cables. It sells and ships products all over the world. Recently, the board of directors approved the plan and a budget for the company to redesign its web presence. The company previously had a "canned" website with limited general information. Part of the project will involve a redesign of the company's website into two sections. One is for general information (similar to what used to be on its old website) and can be accessed by anyone. On this part of the site, the company has information about what it does and pictures of all the products sold. The other part of the website will be new and is accessible only by logging in. Customers are given passwords to enter this part of the site, where they can place their orders, which are then reviewed by the order clerks and sent on to shipping. Another part of the project will involve setting up a social media presence, including a Twitter account and daily Twitter feeds, as well as a Facebook account with daily content. The IT manager has been put in charge of managing the project and keeping track of and approving all costs incurred.

The company has incurred the following costs to develop the site: the IT manager's salary for the six months required to supervise the project; legal fees to register a new domain name; consulting costs for a feasibility study and communications specialist who will identify a strategy for daily tweets and Facebook posts; purchase of the hardware; software developers to develop the code for the application, installation, and testing of the software; graphic artist to design the layout and colour for the web pages; photographers to take pictures of the products to be shown on the site; staff time to upload all the information to the site, including the company and product descriptions; and the data required to place an order, including prices, data entry screens, and shipping options. Finally, the company has incurred costs to train the employees on using the software and on creating a meaningful media presence. Ongoing costs include updating product prices and content, making daily posts to the company's Twitter and Facebook accounts, adding new functions, and backing up the data.

Instructions

a. You are an external auditor and have been hired by Weaver Limited to explain how these costs should be reported. Using IAS 38 and SIC 32—Intangible Assets—Web Site Costs (an Interpretation under International Financial Reporting Standards that is accessible via an Internet search), discuss the treatment of these costs, referring to the general principles in IAS 38 to support your analysis. Explain how the company must report costs incurred once the website is operating.

b. As Weaver's external auditor, what might you be concerned about in addition to the GAAP financial accounting and reporting of the internally developed intangible asset for social media?

RA12.5 Finance Goodwill

Echo Corp., a retail propane gas distributor, has increased its annual sales volume to a level that is three times greater than the annual sales of a dealer that it purchased in 2019 in order to begin operations. Echo's board of directors recently received an offer to negotiate the sale of the company to a large competitor. As a result, the majority of the board members want to increase the stated value of goodwill on the balance sheet to reflect the larger sales volume that it developed through intensive promotion and the product's current market price. A few of the board members, however, would prefer to eliminate goodwill from the balance sheet altogether in order to prevent possible misinterpretations. Goodwill was recorded properly at the start of fiscal 2019.

Instructions

a. Discuss the meaning of the term "goodwill."

b. Why are the book and fair values of Echo Corp.'s goodwill different?

c. Discuss the appropriateness of each of the following:

    1. Increasing the stated value of goodwill prior to the negotiations

    2. Eliminating goodwill completely from the balance sheet

(Adapted from AICPA)

RA12.6 Real World Emphasis Comparative Analysis

Instructions

From the SEDAR website (www.sedar.com) choose one company from each of four different industry classifications. Choose from a variety of industries, such as real estate (such as **Crombie Real Estate Investment Trust**), food stores—merchandising (such as **Loblaw Companies Limited**), biotechnology and pharmaceuticals (such as **AEterna Zentaris Inc.**), or communications and media (such as **Quebecor Inc.**). From the companies' financial statements for their 2017 fiscal year, identify the year-end amounts reported for goodwill, intangibles, and total assets, and the accounting policies for goodwill and each type of intangible asset reported.

a. What net amounts were reported for goodwill and for intangible assets by each company? What are the amounts of accumulated amortization reported for the intangible assets? Identify any loss on impairment reported in the current period.

b. What percentage of total assets does each company have invested in goodwill and intangible assets?

c. Does the type of intangible assets differ depending on the type of industry? Does the relative size of the investment in this category of asset differ among industries? Comment.

d. Do the policies differ by type of intangible? By type of industry?

e. Describe the type of disclosure provided for those companies that reported losses or reversals of losses on impairment.

RA12.7 Regulatory Assets

When Canadian public companies were required to apply IFRS beginning in 2011, one of the major issues faced by some of them, particularly those whose revenues were regulated by an independent body, concerned the accounting for regulatory assets. This issue remains unresolved.

Instructions

Research the financial accounting issues related to rate regulation, beginning with the IASB website (www.ifrs.org) and the "Projects" and "Work plan" link: look for Rate-regulated Activities. Answer the following questions.

a. Provide a brief history of the IASB's rate regulation project, and explain where the project currently stands and what the future plans are for this issue.

b. Identify the type of companies that are considered rate-regulated, and explain what regulatory assets are.

c. Explain what the current accounting issues were with respect to reporting these assets.

d. What choice, if any, does the IASB have for settling this issue? Identify any progress that has been made since September 2014 in reaching a decision.

Task-Based Simulation and Cumulative Coverage: Chapters 10 to 12

Templates to complete this task-based simulation are available in WileyPLUS *and on the instructor website.*

Fit Fixtures Incorporated (FFI) is a manufacturer of exercise equipment such as treadmills, stair climbers, and elliptical machines. The company has a December 31 year end and uses ASPE. The accounting staff member who normally looks after the capital asset accounts was on maternity leave for the year, and the company put all transactions in a temporary account called Asset Additions and Disposals.

The company policy on calculating depreciation for partial periods of ownership is to take 50% of the normal amount of depreciation in the year of addition or disposal. Due to the staff member's maternity leave, no depreciation or amortization expense has yet been taken in 2020.

1. The company completed construction of a new plant in Saskatchewan on December 15, 2020, to help it better meet the needs of its customers west of Ontario. The costs associated with this construction project were as follows:

Land	$ 500,000
Construction contract: building, 20 years of useful life, residual value	
of $50,000	1,500,000
Equipment	(See below)
Furniture	250,000
Training costs (employees learning to use equipment)	45,000
Avoidable interest calculated at 8% on financing of construction	
project from inception until put in use	75,000

The equipment purchased for the new plant was bought on a deferred payment contract signed on December 1. FFI issued a $5-million, five-year, non–interest-bearing note payable to the equipment supplier at a time when the annual market rate of interest was 6%. The note will be repaid with five equal payments made on December 1 of each year, beginning in 2021. Show calculations using factor Table A.4, a financial calculator, or Excel function PV. Round final amounts to the nearest dollar.

2. FFI purchased a used computer and a printer at an auction for $2,500. The printer needed a new drum. The cost of the new drum was $500. The used computer's fair market value was $2,000 if purchased separately. The printer was worth $1,000 without a drum and $1,500 with the drum replaced.

3. On July 1, 2020, FFI sold a delivery truck for $10,000. The truck originally cost $25,000, and accumulated depreciation on the truck to December 31, 2019, was $10,000. The truck was amortized on a straight-line basis over a five-year period, with no residual value. The sale was recorded as a debit to Cash and a credit to Asset Additions and Disposals. No amortization was recorded in the current year.

4. Due to an office redesign in the Ontario building, FFI traded some old equipment for different equipment with a similar life and value in use. The fair value of the equipment disposed of was $5,000. The cost of this equipment was $7,000, and the accumulated depreciation on the equipment at December 31, 2019, was $3,000. This transaction was not recorded in the books of account. No entry was made to record the exchange.

5. Shortly after the new factory was completed, vandals attacked the building and caused significant damage. The costs to correct the damage, which were not covered by insurance, included:

New paint to cover graffiti	$ 4,000
Glass for broken windows	10,000
Improved security system	25,000

6. During the year, the company developed a new piece of exercise equipment that has a built-in video game. It was the policy to amortize development costs on a straight-line basis over three years, with 50% of the normal amount in the year of development. The costs associated with product development included:

Costs to determine how a video game would work with exercise equipment	$ 50,000
Design, testing, and construction of prototype equipment	350,000
Costs to determine the best production process for the new equipment	40,000
Advertising costs to alert customers about the new product	47,000

7. The company has goodwill and an intangible asset as follows:

Asset	Details	Original Cost as at December 31, 2019	Accumulated Amortization as at December 31, 2019	Amortization Method
Goodwill	Recorded in 2015 when the company took over the business of its predecessor	$500,000	$0	Not applicable
Customer list	Purchased in 2015 when the company took over the business of its predecessor	$250,000	$112,500	Straight-line over 10 years

The customer list has lost value and will not provide benefits through to 2025, as was originally predicted. It is now expected to provide undiscounted future cash flows of $50,000 in total over the next two years. There are no estimated costs to sell the list, as it will not be sold, and the value in use is $46,000. Goodwill has a recoverable value of $700,000 as at December 31, 2020.

Instructions

Part A: New Saskatchewan plant

Determine whether each expenditure related to the new Saskatchewan plant must be capitalized or expensed or whether it could be either (depends on policy choice). Place the dollar amount in the appropriate column in the table below.

	Capitalize	Expense	Policy Choice to Capitalize or Expense
Land			
Building			
Equipment			
Furniture			
Training costs			
Avoidable interest			

Part B: Used equipment purchased at auction

Allocate the expenditure related to the used computer and printer bundle to each component, and identify whether each component must be capitalized or expensed or whether it could be either (depends on policy choice). Place the dollar amount allocated to each component in the appropriate column in the table below.

	Capitalize	Expense	Policy Choice to Capitalize or Expense
Computer			
Printer			

Part C: Delivery truck disposition

Account for the disposition of the delivery truck by preparing a journal entry in good form.

Part D: Office equipment swap

Determine the impact on the company's assets, liabilities, and net income of measuring the transaction with the carrying value versus the fair value. Write "increase," "decrease," or "no impact" in each space.

	Carrying Value	Fair Value
Assets		
Liabilities		
Net income		

Part E: Vandal attack

Determine the impact on the company's assets, liabilities, and net income of the three expenditures related to the vandal attack. Write "increase," "decrease," or "no impact" in each space.

	Paint	Glass	Security System
Assets			
Liabilities			
Net income			

Part F: Research and development costs

Determine whether each expenditure is clearly a research cost or could potentially be a development cost (if the six criteria are met at the point when the costs are incurred). Place the dollar amount of each expenditure in the Research and Other Expenses or Potentially Development cost column.

	Research and Other Expenses	Potentially Development
Costs to determine how a video game would work with exercise equipment		
Design, testing, and construction of prototype equipment		
Costs to determine the best production process for the new equipment		
Advertising costs to alert customers about the new product		

Part G: Intangible assets and Goodwill

Determine whether the assets listed are impaired, and if so, the amount of the writedown. Place an X in the Impaired or Not Impaired column for both assets (only one X per asset). If the asset is impaired, enter the amount of the writedown in the Writedown Required ($) column.

	Not Impaired (X)	Impaired (X)	Writedown Required ($)
Customer list			
Goodwill			

Appendix A

Time Value of Money Tables

Table A.1

FUTURE VALUE OF 1
(FUTURE VALUE OF A SINGLE SUM)

$$FVF_{n,\,i} = (1+i)^n$$

(n) periods	2%	2¹/₂%	3%	4%	5%	6%	8%	9%	10%	11%	12%	15%
1	1.02000	1.02500	1.03000	1.04000	1.05000	1.06000	1.08000	1.09000	1.10000	1.11000	1.12000	1.15000
2	1.04040	1.05063	1.06090	1.08160	1.10250	1.12360	1.16640	1.18810	1.21000	1.23210	1.25440	1.32250
3	1.06121	1.07689	1.09273	1.12486	1.15763	1.19102	1.25971	1.29503	1.33100	1.36763	1.40493	1.52088
4	1.08243	1.10381	1.12551	1.16986	1.21551	1.26248	1.36049	1.41158	1.46410	1.51807	1.57352	1.74901
5	1.10408	1.13141	1.15927	1.21665	1.27628	1.33823	1.46933	1.53862	1.61051	1.68506	1.76234	2.01136
6	1.12616	1.15969	1.19405	1.26532	1.34010	1.41852	1.58687	1.67710	1.77156	1.87041	1.97382	2.31306
7	1.14869	1.18869	1.22987	1.31593	1.40710	1.50363	1.71382	1.82804	1.94872	2.07616	2.21068	2.66002
8	1.17166	1.21840	1.26677	1.36857	1.47746	1.59385	1.85093	1.99256	2.14359	2.30454	2.47596	3.05902
9	1.19509	1.24886	1.30477	1.42331	1.55133	1.68948	1.99900	2.17189	2.35795	2.55803	2.77308	3.51788
10	1.21899	1.28008	1.34392	1.48024	1.62889	1.79085	2.15892	2.36736	2.59374	2.83942	3.10585	4.04556
11	1.24337	1.31209	1.38423	1.53945	1.71034	1.89830	2.33164	2.58043	2.85312	3.15176	3.47855	4.65239
12	1.26824	1.34489	1.42576	1.60103	1.79586	2.01220	2.51817	2.81267	3.13843	3.49845	3.89598	5.35025
13	1.29361	1.37851	1.46853	1.66507	1.88565	2.13293	2.71962	3.06581	3.45227	3.88328	4.36349	6.15279
14	1.31948	1.41297	1.51259	1.73168	1.97993	2.26090	2.93719	3.34173	3.79750	4.31044	4.88711	7.07571
15	1.34587	1.44830	1.55797	1.80094	2.07893	2.39656	3.17217	3.64248	4.17725	4.78459	5.47357	8.13706
16	1.37279	1.48451	1.60471	1.87298	2.18287	2.54035	3.42594	3.97031	4.59497	5.31089	6.13039	9.35762
17	1.40024	1.52162	1.65285	1.94790	2.29202	2.69277	3.70002	4.32763	5.05447	5.89509	6.86604	10.76126
18	1.42825	1.55966	1.70243	2.02582	2.40662	2.85434	3.99602	4.71712	5.55992	6.54355	7.68997	12.37545
19	1.45681	1.59865	1.75351	2.10685	2.52695	3.02560	4.31570	5.14166	6.11591	7.26334	8.61276	14.23177
20	1.48595	1.63862	1.80611	2.19112	2.65330	3.20714	4.66096	5.60441	6.72750	8.06231	9.64629	16.36654
21	1.51567	1.67958	1.86029	2.27877	2.78596	3.39956	5.03383	6.10881	7.40025	8.94917	10.80385	18.82152
22	1.54598	1.72157	1.91610	2.36992	2.92526	3.60354	5.43654	6.65860	8.14028	9.93357	12.10031	21.64475
23	1.57690	1.76461	1.97359	2.46472	3.07152	3.81975	5.87146	7.25787	8.95430	11.02627	13.55235	24.89146
24	1.60844	1.80873	2.03279	2.56330	3.22510	4.04893	6.34118	7.91108	9.84973	12.23916	15.17863	28.62518
25	1.64061	1.85394	2.09378	2.66584	3.38635	4.29187	6.84847	8.62308	10.83471	13.58546	17.00000	32.91895
26	1.67342	1.90029	2.15659	2.77247	3.55567	4.54938	7.39635	9.39916	11.91818	15.07986	19.04007	37.85680
27	1.70689	1.94780	2.22129	2.88337	3.73346	4.82235	7.98806	10.24508	13.10999	16.73865	21.32488	43.53532
28	1.74102	1.99650	2.28793	2.99870	3.92013	5.11169	8.62711	11.16714	14.42099	18.57990	23.88387	50.06561
29	1.77584	2.04641	2.35657	3.11865	4.11614	5.41839	9.31727	12.17218	15.86309	20.62369	26.74993	57.57545
30	1.81136	2.09757	2.42726	3.24340	4.32194	5.74349	10.06266	13.26768	17.44940	22.89230	29.95992	66.21177
31	1.84759	2.15001	2.50008	3.37313	4.53804	6.08810	10.86767	14.46177	19.19434	25.41045	33.55511	76.14354
32	1.88454	2.20376	2.57508	3.50806	4.76494	6.45339	11.73708	15.76333	21.11378	28.20560	37.58173	87.56507
33	1.92223	2.25885	2.65234	3.64838	5.00319	6.84059	12.67605	17.18203	23.22515	31.30821	42.09153	100.69983
34	1.96068	2.31532	2.73191	3.79432	5.25335	7.25103	13.69013	18.72841	25.54767	34.75212	47.14252	115.80480
35	1.99989	2.37321	2.81386	3.94609	5.51602	7.68609	14.78534	20.41397	28.10244	38.57485	52.79962	133.17552
36	2.03989	2.43254	2.88928	4.10393	5.79182	8.14725	15.96817	22.25123	30.91268	42.81808	59.13557	153.15185
37	2.08069	2.49335	2.98523	4.26809	6.08141	8.63609	17.24563	24.25384	34.00395	47.52807	66.23184	176.12463
38	2.12230	2.55568	3.07478	4.43881	6.38548	9.15425	18.62528	26.43668	37.40434	52.75616	74.17966	202.54332
39	2.16474	2.61957	3.16703	4.61637	6.70475	9.70351	20.11530	28.81598	41.14479	58.55934	83.08122	232.92482
40	2.20804	2.68506	3.26204	4.80102	7.03999	10.28572	21.72452	31.40942	45.25926	65.00087	93.05097	267.86355

Table A.2

PRESENT VALUE OF 1

(PRESENT VALUE OF A SINGLE SUM)

$$PVF_{n,i} = \frac{1}{(1+i)^n} = (1+i)^{-n}$$

(n) periods	2%	2½%	3%	4%	5%	6%	8%	9%	10%	11%	12%	15%
1	.98039	.97561	.97087	.96156	.95238	.94340	.92593	.91743	.90909	.90090	.89286	.86957
2	.96117	.95181	.94260	.92456	.90703	.89000	.85734	.84168	.82645	.81162	.79719	.75614
3	.94232	.92860	.91514	.88900	.86384	.83962	.79383	.77218	.75132	.73119	.71178	.65752
4	.92385	.90595	.88849	.85480	.82270	.79209	.73503	.70843	.68301	.65873	.63552	.57175
5	.90583	.88385	.86261	.82193	.78353	.74726	.68058	.64993	.62092	.59345	.56743	.49718
6	.88797	.86230	.83748	.79031	.74622	.70496	.63017	.59627	.56447	.53464	.50663	.43233
7	.87056	.84127	.81309	.75992	.71068	.66506	.58349	.54703	.51316	.48166	.45235	.37594
8	.85349	.82075	.78941	.73069	.67684	.62741	.54027	.50187	.46651	.43393	.40388	.32690
9	.83676	.80073	.76642	.70259	.64461	.59190	.50025	.46043	.42410	.39092	.36061	.28426
10	.82035	.78120	.74409	.67556	.61391	.55839	.46319	.42241	.38554	.35218	.32197	.24719
11	.80426	.76214	.72242	.64958	.58468	.52679	.42888	.38753	.35049	.31728	.28748	.21494
12	.78849	.74356	.70138	.62460	.55684	.49697	.39711	.35554	.31863	.28584	.25668	.18691
13	.77303	.72542	.68095	.60057	.53032	.46884	.36770	.32618	.28966	.25751	.22917	.16253
14	.75788	.70773	.66112	.57748	.50507	.44230	.34046	.29925	.26333	.23199	.20462	.14133
15	.74301	.69047	.64186	.55526	.48102	.41727	.31524	.27454	.23939	.20900	.18270	.12289
16	.72845	.67362	.62317	.53391	.45811	.39365	.29189	.25187	.21763	.18829	.16312	.10687
17	.71416	.65720	.60502	.51337	.43630	.37136	.27027	.23107	.19785	.16963	.14564	.09293
18	.70016	.64117	.58739	.49363	.41552	.35034	.25025	.21199	.17986	.15282	.13004	.08081
19	.68643	.62553	.57029	.47464	.39573	.33051	.23171	.19449	.16351	.13768	.11611	.07027
20	.67297	.61027	.55368	.45639	.37689	.31180	.21455	.17843	.14864	.12403	.10367	.06110
21	.65978	.59539	.53755	.43883	.35894	.29416	.19866	.16370	.13513	.11174	.09256	.05313
22	.64684	.58086	.52189	.42196	.34185	.27751	.18394	.15018	.12285	.10067	.08264	.04620
23	.63416	.56670	.50669	.40573	.32557	.26180	.17032	.13778	.11168	.09069	.07379	.04017
24	.62172	.55288	.49193	.39012	.31007	.24698	.15770	.12641	.10153	.08170	.06588	.03493
25	.60953	.53939	.47761	.37512	.29530	.23300	.14602	.11597	.09230	.07361	.05882	.03038
26	.59758	.52623	.46369	.36069	.28124	.21981	.13520	.10639	.08391	.06631	.05252	.02642
27	.58586	.51340	.45019	.34682	.26785	.20737	.12519	.09761	.07628	.05974	.04689	.02297
28	.57437	.50088	.43708	.33348	.25509	.19563	.11591	.08955	.06934	.05382	.04187	.01997
29	.56311	.48866	.42435	.32065	.24295	.18456	.10733	.08216	.06304	.04849	.03738	.01737
30	.55207	.47674	.41199	.30832	.23138	.17411	.09938	.07537	.05731	.04368	.03338	.01510
31	.54125	.46511	.39999	.29646	.22036	.16425	.09202	.06915	.05210	.03935	.02980	.01313
32	.53063	.45377	.38834	.28506	.20987	.15496	.08520	.06344	.04736	.03545	.02661	.01142
33	.52023	.44270	.37703	.27409	.19987	.14619	.07889	.05820	.04306	.03194	.02376	.00993
34	.51003	.43191	.36604	.26355	.19035	.13791	.07305	.05340	.03914	.02878	.02121	.00864
35	.50003	.42137	.35538	.25342	.18129	.13011	.06763	.04899	.03558	.02592	.01894	.00751
36	.49022	.41109	.34503	.24367	.17266	.12274	.06262	.04494	.03235	.02335	.01691	.00653
37	.48061	.40107	.33498	.23430	.16444	.11579	.05799	.04123	.02941	.02104	.01510	.00568
38	.47119	.39128	.32523	.22529	.15661	.10924	.05369	.03783	.02674	.01896	.01348	.00494
39	.46195	.38174	.31575	.21662	.14915	.10306	.04971	.03470	.02430	.01708	.01204	.00429
40	.45289	.37243	.30656	.20829	.14205	.09722	.04603	.03184	.02210	.01538	.01075	.00373

Table A.3

FUTURE VALUE OF AN ORDINARY ANNUITY OF 1

$$FVF\text{-}OA_{n,\,i} = \frac{(1+i)^n - 1}{i}$$

(n) periods	2%	2½%	3%	4%	5%	6%	8%	9%	10%	11%	12%	15%
1	1.00000	1.00000	1.00000	1.00000	1.00000	1.00000	1.00000	1.00000	1.00000	1.00000	1.00000	1.00000
2	2.02000	2.02500	2.03000	2.04000	2.05000	2.06000	2.08000	2.09000	2.10000	2.11000	2.12000	2.15000
3	3.06040	3.07563	3.09090	3.12160	3.15250	3.18360	3.24640	3.27810	3.31000	3.34210	3.37440	3.47250
4	4.12161	4.15252	4.18363	4.24646	4.31013	4.37462	4.50611	4.57313	4.64100	4.70973	4.77933	4.99338
5	5.20404	5.25633	5.30914	5.41632	5.52563	5.63709	5.86660	5.98471	6.10510	6.22780	6.35285	6.74238
6	6.30812	6.38774	6.46841	6.63298	6.80191	6.97532	7.33592	7.52334	7.71561	7.91286	8.11519	8.75374
7	7.43428	7.54743	7.66246	7.89829	8.14201	8.39384	8.92280	9.20044	9.48717	9.78327	10.08901	11.06680
8	8.58297	8.73612	8.89234	9.21423	9.54911	9.89747	10.63663	11.02847	11.43589	11.85943	12.29969	13.72682
9	9.75463	9.95452	10.15911	10.58280	11.02656	11.49132	12.48756	13.02104	13.57948	14.16397	14.77566	16.78584
10	10.94972	11.20338	11.46338	12.00611	12.57789	13.18079	14.48656	15.19293	15.93743	16.72201	17.54874	20.30372
11	12.16872	12.48347	12.80780	13.48635	14.20679	14.97164	16.64549	17.56029	18.53117	19.56143	20.65458	24.34928
12	13.41209	13.79555	14.19203	15.02581	15.91713	16.86994	18.97713	20.14072	21.38428	22.71319	24.13313	29.00167
13	14.68033	15.14044	15.61779	16.62684	17.71298	18.88214	21.49530	22.95339	24.52271	26.21164	28.02911	34.35192
14	15.97394	16.51895	17.08632	18.29191	19.59863	21.01507	24.21492	26.01919	27.97498	30.09492	32.39260	40.50471
15	17.29342	17.93193	18.59891	20.02359	21.57856	23.27597	27.15211	29.36092	31.77248	34.40536	37.27972	47.58041
16	18.63929	19.38022	20.15688	21.82453	23.65749	25.67253	30.32428	33.00340	35.94973	39.18995	42.75328	55.71747
17	20.01207	20.86473	21.76159	23.69751	25.84037	28.21288	33.75023	36.97371	40.54470	44.50084	48.88367	65.07509
18	21.41231	22.38635	23.41444	25.64541	28.13238	30.90565	37.45024	41.30134	45.59917	50.39593	55.74972	75.83636
19	22.84056	23.94601	25.11687	27.67123	30.53900	33.75999	41.44626	46.01846	51.15909	56.93949	63.43968	88.21181
20	24.29737	25.54466	26.87037	29.77808	33.06595	36.78559	45.76196	51.16012	57.27500	64.20283	72.05244	102.44358
21	25.78332	27.18327	28.67649	31.96920	35.71925	39.99273	50.42292	56.76453	64.00250	72.26514	81.69874	118.81012
22	27.29898	28.86286	30.53678	34.24797	38.50521	43.39229	55.45676	62.87334	71.40275	81.21431	92.50258	137.63164
23	28.84496	30.58443	32.45288	36.61789	41.43048	46.99583	60.89330	69.53194	79.54302	91.14788	104.60289	159.27638
24	30.42186	32.34904	34.42647	39.08260	44.50200	50.81558	66.76476	76.78981	88.49733	102.17415	118.15524	184.16784
25	32.03030	34.15776	36.45926	41.64591	47.72710	54.86451	73.10594	84.70090	98.34706	114.41331	133.33387	212.79302
26	33.67091	36.01171	38.55304	44.31174	51.11345	59.15638	79.95442	93.32398	109.18177	127.99877	150.33393	245.71197
27	35.34432	37.91200	40.70963	47.08421	54.66913	63.70577	87.35077	102.72314	121.09994	143.07864	169.37401	283.56877
28	37.05121	39.85990	42.93092	49.96758	58.40258	68.52811	95.33883	112.96822	134.20994	159.81729	190.69889	327.10408
29	38.79223	41.85630	45.21885	52.96629	62.32271	73.63980	103.96594	124.13536	148.63093	178.39719	214.58275	377.16969
30	40.56808	43.90270	47.57542	56.08494	66.43885	79.05819	113.28321	136.30754	164.49402	199.02088	241.33268	434.74515
31	42.37944	46.00027	50.00268	59.32834	70.76079	84.80168	123.34587	149.57522	181.94343	221.91317	271.29261	500.95692
32	44.22703	48.15028	52.50276	62.70147	75.29883	90.88978	134.21354	164.03699	201.13777	247.32362	304.84772	577.10046
33	46.11157	50.35403	55.07784	66.20953	80.06377	97.34316	145.95062	179.80032	222.25154	275.52922	342.42945	644.66553
34	48.03380	52.61289	57.73018	69.85791	85.06696	104.18376	158.62667	196.98234	245.47670	306.83744	384.52098	765.36535
35	49.99448	54.92821	60.46208	73.65222	90.32031	111.43478	172.31680	215.71076	271.02437	341.58955	431.66350	881.17016
36	51.99437	57.30141	63.27594	77.59831	95.83632	119.12087	187.10215	236.12472	299.12681	380.16441	484.46312	1014.34568
37	54.03425	59.73395	66.17422	81.70225	101.62814	127.26812	203.07032	258.37595	330.03949	422.98249	543.59869	1167.49753
38	56.11494	62.22730	69.15945	85.97034	107.70955	135.90421	220.31595	282.62978	364.04343	470.51056	609.83053	1343.62216
39	58.23724	64.78298	72.23423	90.40915	114.09502	145.05846	238.94122	309.06646	401.44778	523.26673	684.01020	1546.16549
40	60.40198	67.40255	75.40126	95.02552	120.79977	154.76197	259.05652	337.88245	442.59256	581.82607	767.09142	1779.09031

Table A.4

PRESENT VALUE OF AN ORDINARY ANNUITY OF 1

$$PVF\text{-}OA_{n,\,i} = \frac{1 - \dfrac{1}{(1+i)^n}}{i}$$

(n) periods	2%	2½%	3%	4%	5%	6%	8%	9%	10%	11%	12%	15%
1	.98039	.97561	.97087	.96154	.95238	.94340	.92593	.91743	.90909	.90090	.89286	.86957
2	1.94156	1.92742	1.91347	1.88609	1.85941	1.83339	1.78326	1.75911	1.73554	1.71252	1.69005	1.62571
3	2.88388	2.85602	2.82861	2.77509	2.72325	2.67301	2.57710	2.53130	2.48685	2.44371	2.40183	2.28323
4	3.80773	3.76197	3.71710	3.62990	3.54595	3.46511	3.31213	3.23972	3.16986	3.10245	3.03735	2.85498
5	4.71346	4.64583	4.57971	4.45182	4.32948	4.21236	3.99271	3.88965	3.79079	3.69590	3.60478	3.35216
6	5.60143	5.50813	5.41719	5.24214	5.07569	4.91732	4.62288	4.48592	4.35526	4.23054	4.11141	3.78448
7	6.47199	6.34939	6.23028	6.00205	5.78637	5.58238	5.20637	5.03295	4.86842	4.71220	4.56376	4.16042
8	7.32548	7.17014	7.01969	6.73274	6.46321	6.20979	5.74664	5.53482	5.33493	5.14612	4.96764	4.48732
9	8.16224	7.97087	7.78611	7.43533	7.10782	6.80169	6.24689	5.99525	5.75902	5.53705	5.32825	4.77158
10	8.98259	8.75206	8.53020	8.11090	7.72173	7.36009	6.71008	6.41766	6.14457	5.88923	5.65022	5.01877
11	9.78685	9.51421	9.25262	8.76048	8.30641	7.88687	7.13896	6.80519	6.49506	6.20652	5.93770	5.23371
12	10.57534	10.25776	9.95400	9.38507	8.86325	8.38384	7.53608	7.16073	6.81369	6.49236	6.19437	5.42062
13	11.34837	10.98319	10.63496	9.98565	9.39357	8.85268	7.90378	7.48690	7.10336	6.74987	6.42355	5.58315
14	12.10625	11.69091	11.29607	10.56312	9.89864	9.29498	8.24424	7.78615	7.36669	6.98187	6.62817	5.72448
15	12.84926	12.38138	11.93794	11.11839	10.37966	9.71225	8.55948	8.06069	7.60608	7.19087	6.81086	5.84737
16	13.57771	13.05500	12.56110	11.65230	10.83777	10.10590	8.85137	8.31256	7.82371	7.37916	6.97399	5.95424
17	14.29187	13.71220	13.16612	12.16567	11.27407	10.47726	9.12164	8.54363	8.02155	7.54879	7.11963	6.04716
18	14.99203	14.35336	13.75351	12.65930	11.68959	10.82760	9.37189	8.75563	8.20141	7.70162	7.24967	6.12797
19	15.67846	14.97889	14.32380	13.13394	12.08532	11.15812	9.60360	8.95012	8.36492	7.83929	7.36578	6.19823
20	16.35143	15.58916	14.87747	13.59033	12.46221	11.46992	9.81815	9.12855	8.51356	7.96333	7.46944	6.25933
21	17.01121	16.18455	15.41502	14.02916	12.82115	11.76408	10.01680	9.29224	8.64869	8.07507	7.56200	6.31246
22	17.65805	16.76541	15.93692	14.45112	13.16800	12.04158	10.20074	9.44243	8.77154	8.17574	7.64465	6.35866
23	18.29220	17.33211	16.44361	14.85684	13.48857	12.30338	10.37106	9.58021	8.88322	8.26643	7.71843	6.39884
24	18.91393	17.88499	16.93554	15.24696	13.79864	12.55036	10.52876	9.70661	8.98474	8.34814	7.78432	6.43377
25	19.52346	18.42438	17.41315	15.62208	14.09394	12.78336	10.67478	9.82258	9.07704	8.42174	7.84314	6.46415
26	20.12104	18.95061	17.87684	15.98277	14.37519	13.00317	10.80998	9.92897	9.16095	8.48806	7.89566	6.49056
27	20.70690	19.46401	18.32703	16.32959	14.64303	13.21053	10.93516	10.02658	9.23722	8.45780	7.94255	6.51353
28	21.28127	19.96489	18.76411	16.66306	14.89813	13.40616	11.05108	10.11613	9.30657	8.60162	7.98442	6.53351
29	21.84438	20.45355	19.18845	16.98371	15.14107	13.59072	11.15841	10.19828	9.36961	8.65011	8.02181	6.55088
30	22.39646	20.93029	19.60044	17.29203	15.37245	13.76483	11.25778	10.27365	9.42691	8.69379	8.05518	6.56598
31	22.93770	21.39541	20.00043	17.58849	15.59281	13.92909	11.34980	10.34280	9.47901	8.73315	8.08499	6.57911
32	23.46833	21.84918	20.38877	17.87355	15.80268	14.08404	11.43500	10.40624	9.52638	8.76860	8.11159	6.59053
33	23.98856	22.29188	20.76579	18.14765	16.00255	14.23023	11.51389	10.46444	9.56943	8.80054	8.13535	6.60046
34	24.49859	22.72379	21.13184	18.41120	16.19290	14.36814	11.58693	10.51784	9.60858	8.82932	8.15656	6.60910
35	24.99862	23.14516	21.48722	18.66461	16.37419	14.49825	11.65457	10.56682	9.64416	8.85524	8.17550	6.61661
36	25.48884	23.55625	21.83225	18.90828	16.54685	14.62099	11.71719	10.61176	9.67651	8.87859	8.19241	6.62314
37	25.96945	23.95732	22.16724	19.14258	16.71129	14.73678	11.77518	10.65299	9.70592	8.89963	8.20751	6.62882
38	26.44064	24.34860	22.49246	19.36786	16.86789	14.84602	11.82887	10.69082	9.73265	8.91859	8.22099	6.63375
39	26.90259	24.73034	22.80822	19.58448	17.01704	14.94907	11.87858	10.72552	9.75697	8.93567	8.23303	6.63805
40	27.35548	25.10278	23.11477	19.79277	17.15909	15.04630	11.92461	10.75736	9.77905	8.95105	8.24378	6.64178

Table A.5

PRESENT VALUE OF AN ANNUITY DUE OF 1

$$PVF-AD_{n,\,i} = 1 + \frac{1 - \dfrac{1}{(1+i)^{n-1}}}{i}$$

(n) periods	2%	2¹/₂%	3%	4%	5%	6%	8%	9%	10%	11%	12%	15%
1	1.00000	1.00000	1.00000	1.00000	1.00000	1.00000	1.00000	1.00000	1.00000	1.00000	1.00000	1.00000
2	1.98039	1.97561	1.97087	1.96154	1.95238	1.94340	1.92593	1.91743	1.90909	1.90090	1.89286	1.86957
3	2.94156	2.92742	2.91347	2.88609	2.85941	2.83339	2.78326	2.75911	2.73554	2.71252	2.69005	2.62571
4	3.88388	3.85602	3.82861	3.77509	3.72325	3.67301	3.57710	3.53130	3.48685	3.44371	3.40183	3.28323
5	4.80773	4.76197	4.71710	4.62990	4.54595	4.46511	4.31213	4.23972	4.16986	4.10245	4.03735	3.85498
6	5.71346	5.64583	5.57971	5.45182	5.32948	5.21236	4.99271	4.88965	4.79079	4.69590	4.60478	4.35216
7	6.60143	6.50813	6.41719	6.24214	6.07569	5.91732	5.62288	5.48592	5.35526	5.23054	5.11141	4.78448
8	7.47199	7.34939	7.23028	7.00205	6.78637	6.58238	6.20637	6.03295	5.86842	5.71220	5.56376	5.16042
9	8.32548	8.17014	8.01969	7.73274	7.46321	7.20979	6.74664	6.53482	6.33493	6.14612	5.96764	5.48732
10	9.16224	8.97087	8.78611	8.43533	8.10782	7.80169	7.24689	6.99525	6.75902	6.53705	6.32825	5.77158
11	9.98259	9.75206	9.53020	9.11090	8.72173	8.36009	7.71008	7.41766	7.14457	6.88923	6.65022	6.01877
12	10.78685	10.51421	10.25262	9.76048	9.30641	8.88687	8.13896	7.80519	7.49506	7.20652	6.93770	6.23371
13	11.57534	11.25776	10.95400	10.38507	9.86325	9.38384	8.53608	8.16073	7.81369	7.49236	7.19437	6.42062
14	12.34837	11.98319	11.63496	10.98565	10.39357	9.85268	8.90378	8.48690	8.10336	7.74987	7.42355	6.58315
15	13.10625	12.69091	12.29607	11.56312	10.89864	10.29498	9.24424	8.78615	9.36669	7.98187	7.62817	6.72448
16	13.84926	13.38138	12.93794	12.11839	11.37966	10.71225	9.55948	9.06069	8.60608	8.19087	7.81086	6.84737
17	14.57771	14.05500	13.56110	12.65230	11.83777	11.10590	9.85137	9.31256	8.82371	8.37916	7.97399	6.95424
18	15.29187	14.71220	14.16612	13.16567	12.27407	11.47726	10.12164	9.54363	9.02155	8.54879	8.11963	7.04716
19	15.99203	15.35336	14.75351	13.65930	12.68959	11.82760	10.37189	9.75563	9.20141	8.70162	8.24967	7.12797
20	16.67846	15.97889	15.32380	14.13394	13.08532	12.15812	10.60360	9.95012	9.36492	8.83929	8.36578	7.19823
21	17.35143	16.58916	15.87747	14.59033	13.46221	12.46992	10.81815	10.12855	9.51356	8.96333	8.46944	7.25933
22	18.01121	17.18455	16.41502	15.02916	13.82115	12.76408	11.01680	10.29224	9.64869	9.07507	8.56200	7.31246
23	18.65805	17.76541	16.93692	15.45112	14.16300	13.04158	11.20074	10.44243	9.77154	9.17574	8.64465	7.35866
24	19.29220	18.33211	17.44361	15.85684	14.48857	13.30338	11.37106	10.58021	9.88322	9.26643	8.71843	7.39884
25	19.91393	18.88499	17.93554	16.24696	14.79864	13.55036	11.52876	10.70661	9.98474	9.34814	8.78432	7.43377
26	20.52346	19.42438	18.41315	16.62208	15.09394	13.78336	11.67478	10.82258	10.07704	9.42174	8.84314	7.46415
27	21.12104	19.95061	18.87684	16.98277	15.37519	14.00317	11.80998	10.92897	10.16095	9.48806	8.89566	7.49056
28	21.70690	20.46401	19.32703	17.32959	15.64303	14.21053	11.93518	11.02658	10.23722	9.54780	8.94255	7.51353
29	22.28127	20.96489	19.76411	17.66306	15.89813	14.40616	12.05108	11.11613	10.30657	9.60162	8.98442	7.53351
30	22.84438	21.45355	20.18845	17.98371	16.14107	14.59072	12.15841	11.19828	10.36961	9.65011	9.02181	7.55088
31	23.39646	21.93029	20.60044	18.29203	16.37245	14.76483	12.25778	11.27365	10.42691	9.69379	9.05518	7.56598
32	23.93770	22.39541	21.00043	18.58849	16.59281	14.92909	12.34980	11.34280	10.47901	9.73315	9.08499	7.57911
33	24.46833	22.84918	21.38877	18.87355	16.80268	15.08404	12.43500	11.40624	10.52638	9.76860	9.11159	7.59053
34	24.98856	23.29188	21.76579	19.14765	17.00255	15.23023	12.51389	11.46444	10.56943	9.80054	9.13535	7.60046
35	25.49859	23.72379	22.13184	19.41120	17.19290	15.36814	12.58693	11.51784	10.60858	9.82932	9.15656	7.60910
36	25.99862	24.14516	22.48722	19.66461	17.37419	15.49825	12.65457	11.56682	10.64416	9.85524	9.17550	7.61661
37	26.48884	24.55625	22.83225	19.90828	17.54685	15.62099	12.71719	11.61176	10.67651	9.87859	9.19241	7.62314
38	26.96945	24.95732	23.16724	20.14258	17.71129	15.73678	12.77518	11.65299	10.70592	9.89963	9.20751	7.62882
39	27.44064	25.34860	23.49246	20.36786	17.86789	15.84602	12.82887	11.69082	10.73265	9.91859	9.22099	7.63375
40	27.90259	25.73034	23.80822	20.58448	18.01704	15.94907	12.87858	11.72552	10.75697	9.93567	9.23303	7.63805

Appendix B

Specimen Financial Statements

Hudson's Bay Company (HBC)

The following pages contain the financial statements, selected notes, and other information from the 2017 annual financial statements of Hudson's Bay Company. HBC's leading banners across North America and Europe include Hudson's Bay; Lord & Taylor; Saks Fifth Avenue; Gilt; Saks OFF 5TH; Galeria Kaufhof, the leading department store group in Germany; and Belgium's only department store group, Galeria INNO.

The complete annual report is available on the company website and in SEDAR. The corporate profile in the Overview below is taken from the company annual report.

Overview

Our Business

HBC is a diversified global retailer focused on driving the performance of high quality stores and their all-channel offerings, growing through acquisitions and unlocking the value of real estate holdings. Founded in 1670, HBC is the oldest company in North America. HBC's portfolio today includes formats ranging from luxury to premium department stores to off price fashion shopping destinations, with more than 480 stores and over 66,000 employees around the world. It is a leader in the all-channel retail experience with a combination of physical store locations and e-commerce capabilities that enable customers to shop whenever, wherever and however they choose. HBC has a top tier management team comprised of seasoned leaders in the retail sector committed to driving growth and long-term profitability across all banners. The Company has a track record of acquisitions and looks for targets that have great brands, undermanaged retail operations, opportunities for synergies and/or own great real estate locations. The Company is supported by a solid foundation of valuable real estate which enhances its financial flexibility.

INDEPENDENT AUDITOR'S REPORT

To the Shareholders of Hudson's Bay Company

We have audited the accompanying consolidated financial statements of Hudson's Bay Company, which comprise the consolidated balance sheets as at February 3, 2018 and January 28, 2017, and the consolidated statements of loss, consolidated statements of comprehensive loss, consolidated statements of shareholders' equity and consolidated statements of cash flows for the 53 and 52 week periods ended February 3, 2018 and January 28, 2017, and a summary of significant accounting policies and other explanatory information.

Management's Responsibility for the Consolidated Financial Statements

Management is responsible for the preparation and fair presentation of these consolidated financial statements in accordance with International Financial Reporting Standards, and for such internal control as management determines is necessary to enable the preparation of consolidated financial statements that are free from material misstatement, whether due to fraud or error.

Auditor's Responsibility

Our responsibility is to express an opinion on these consolidated financial statements based on our audits. We conducted our audits in accordance with Canadian generally accepted auditing standards. Those standards require that we comply with ethical requirements and plan and perform the audit to obtain reasonable assurance about whether the consolidated financial statements are free from material misstatement.

An audit involves performing procedures to obtain audit evidence about the amounts and disclosures in the consolidated financial statements. The procedures selected depend on the auditor's judgment, including the assessment of the risks of material misstatement of the consolidated financial statements, whether due to fraud or error. In making those risk assessments, the auditor considers internal control relevant to the entity's preparation and fair presentation of the consolidated financial statements in order to design audit procedures that are appropriate in the circumstances, but not for the purpose of expressing an opinion on the effectiveness of the entity's internal control. An audit also includes evaluating the appropriateness of accounting policies used and the reasonableness of accounting estimates made by management, as well as evaluating the overall presentation of the consolidated financial statements.

We believe that the audit evidence we have obtained in our audits is sufficient and appropriate to provide a basis for our audit opinion.

Opinion

In our opinion, the consolidated financial statements present fairly, in all material respects, the financial position of Hudson's Bay Company as at February 3, 2018 and January 28, 2017, and its financial performance and its cash flows for the 53 and 52 week periods ended February 3, 2018 and January 28, 2017 in accordance with International Financial Reporting Standards.

Deloite LLP
Chartered Professional Accountants
Licensed Public Accountants

March 27, 2018
Toronto, Canada

HUDSON'S BAY COMPANY

CONSOLIDATED STATEMENTS OF LOSS

**For the 53 weeks ended February 3, 2018 and 52 weeks ended January 28, 2017
(millions of Canadian dollars, except per share amounts)**

	Notes	February 3, 2018 (Fiscal 2017)	January 28, 2017 (Fiscal 2016)
Retail sales		**14,349**	14,455
Cost of sales	9	**(8,514)**	(8,481)
Selling, general and administrative expenses ("SG&A")		**(5,794)**	(5,692)
Depreciation and amortization	5	**(687)**	(695)
Gain on sale of investments in joint ventures	12	**—**	45
Operating loss		**(646)**	(368)
Finance costs, net	6	**(228)**	(192)
Share of net loss in joint ventures	12	**(85)**	(158)
Dilution gains from investments in joint ventures	12	**10**	24
Loss before income tax		**(949)**	(694)
Income tax benefit	7	**368**	178
Net loss for the year		**(581)**	(516)
Loss per share			
Basic and diluted	20	**(3.04)**	(2.83)

(See accompanying notes to the consolidated financial statements)

HUDSON'S BAY COMPANY

CONSOLIDATED STATEMENTS OF COMPREHENSIVE LOSS

For the 53 weeks ended February 3, 2018 and 52 weeks ended January 28, 2017
(millions of Canadian dollars)

	February 3, 2018 (Fiscal 2017)	January 28, 2017 (Fiscal 2016)
Net loss	**(581)**	(516)
Other comprehensive loss, net of tax as applicable:		
Item that will not be reclassified to earnings or loss:		
Net actuarial gain (loss) of employee benefit plans.............................	**13**	(13)
Items that may be reclassified subsequently to earnings or loss:.....................		
Currency translation adjustment...	**(88)**	(176)
Net gain on net investment hedge	**17**	19
Net gain (loss) on derivatives designated as cash flow hedges	**7**	(9)
Reclassification to non-financial assets of net losses on derivatives designated as cash flow hedges	**6**	4
Reclassification to statement of loss of net (gains) losses on derivatives designated as cash flow hedges	**(11)**	5
Other comprehensive loss	**(56)**	(170)
Total comprehensive loss	**(637)**	(686)

HUDSON'S BAY COMPANY

CONSOLIDATED STATEMENTS OF SHAREHOLDERS' EQUITY

For the 53 weeks ended February 3, 2018 and 52 weeks ended January 28, 2017
(millions of Canadian dollars)

	Notes	Share capital	(Deficit) retained earnings	Contributed surplus	Currency translation adjustment	Employee benefits	Net investment hedge	Cash flow hedges	Total AOCI	Total shareholders' equity
As at January 30, 2016........		**1,420**	**1,029**	**86**	606	11	(56)	3	**564**	**3,099**
Total comprehensive loss		—	(516)	—	(176)	(13)	19	—	(170)	(686)
Share based compensation ..	18	2	—	31	—	—	—	—	—	33
Dividends.............................		—	(36)	—	—	—	—	—	—	(36)
As at January 28, 2017.......		**1,422**	**477**	**117**	430	(2)	(37)	3	**394**	**2,410**
Issuance of preferred shares	19	618	—	—	—	—	—	—	—	618
Total comprehensive loss		—	(581)	—	(88)	13	17	2	(56)	(637)
Share based compensation ..	18	5	—	27	—	—	—	—	—	32
Dividends.............................	19	—	(16)	—	—	—	—	—	—	(16)
As at February 3, 2018........		**2,045**	**(120)**	**144**	342	11	(20)	5	**338**	**2,407**

(See accompanying notes to the consolidated financial statements)

HUDSON'S BAY COMPANY

CONSOLIDATED BALANCE SHEETS

As at February 3, 2018 and January 28, 2017
(millions of Canadian dollars)

	Notes	February 3, 2018 (Fiscal 2017)	January 28, 2017 (Fiscal 2016)
Assets			
Cash	8	70	122
Trade and other receivables	27	388	384
Inventories	9	3,367	3,376
Asset held for sale	4	263	—
Other current assets		214	176
Total current assets		4,302	4,058
Property, plant and equipment	10	5,155	5,284
Intangible assets and goodwill	11	1,629	1,786
Pensions and employee benefits	15	171	175
Deferred tax assets	7	339	301
Investments in joint ventures	12	602	581
Other assets		36	19
Total assets		12,234	12,204
Liabilities			
Loans and borrowings	13	363	418
Finance leases	14	35	24
Trade payables	27	1,422	1,599
Other payables and accrued liabilities	27	1,031	1,046
Deferred revenue		139	128
Provisions		220	167
Other liabilities	16	290	137
Total current liabilities		3,500	3,519
Loans and borrowings	13	2,616	2,744
Finance leases	14	526	499
Provisions		85	59
Pensions and employee benefits	15	714	662
Deferred tax liabilities	7	308	713
Investment in joint venture	12	227	9
Other liabilities	16	1,851	1,589
Total liabilities		9,827	9,794
Shareholders' equity			
Share capital	19	2,045	1,422
(Deficit) retained earnings		(120)	477
Contributed surplus		144	117
Accumulated other comprehensive income		338	394
Total shareholders' equity		2,407	2,410
Total liabilities and shareholders' equity		12,234	12,204

(See accompanying notes to the consolidated financial statements)

HUDSON'S BAY COMPANY

CONSOLIDATED STATEMENTS OF CASH FLOWS

For the 53 weeks ended February 3, 2018 and 52 weeks ended January 28, 2017
(millions of Canadian dollars)

	Notes	February 3, 2018 (Fiscal 2017)	January 28, 2017 (Fiscal 2016)
Operating activities			
Net loss for the year		(581)	(516)
Income tax benefit		(368)	(178)
Dilution gains from investments in joint ventures	12	(10)	(24)
Share of net loss in joint ventures	12	85	158
Finance costs, net	6	228	192
Operating loss		(646)	(368)
Net cash income taxes received (paid)		18	(37)
Interest paid in cash		(198)	(173)
Distributions of earnings from joint ventures	12	216	221
Items not affecting cash flows:			
Depreciation and amortization	5	687	695
Impairment	10, 11	81	174
Net defined benefit pension and employee benefits expense		24	19
Other operating activities		(61)	(24)
Share of rent expense to joint ventures	12	(355)	(367)
Gain on sale of investments in joint ventures	12	—	(45)
Share based compensation	18	36	35
Settlement of share based compensation grants	18	(4)	(2)
Changes in operating working capital	26	(126)	184
Net cash (outflow for) inflow from operating activities		(328)	312
Investing activities			
Capital investments		(903)	(1,085)
Proceeds from landlord incentives		304	428
Capital investments less proceeds from landlord incentives		(599)	(657)
Proceeds from lease terminations and other non-capital landlord incentives		33	34
Deposit for sale of Lord & Taylor Fifth Avenue building	4	96	—
Proceeds on disposal of assets		6	85
Return of capital from joint venture	12	213	6
Acquisition of Gilt Groupe Holdings Inc., net of cash acquired		—	(322)
Proceeds from sale of investments in joint ventures	12	—	65
Investment in joint ventures	12	—	(10)
Other investing activities		(18)	6
Net cash outflow for investing activities		(269)	(793)
Financing activities			
Long-term loans and borrowings:			
Issuance	26	31	522
Repayments	26	(7)	(330)
Borrowing costs		—	(16)
		24	176
Short-term loans and borrowings:			
Net borrowings from asset-based credit facilities	26	(50)	(3)
Borrowing costs		(3)	(13)
		(53)	(16)
Issuance of preferred shares, net of transaction costs paid		615	—
Payments on finance leases	26	(34)	(35)
Dividends paid	19	(16)	(36)
Net cash inflow from financing activities		536	89
Foreign exchange gain on cash		9	7
Decrease in cash		(52)	(385)
Cash at beginning of year		122	507
Cash at end of year		70	122

(See accompanying notes to the consolidated financial statements)

HUDSON'S BAY COMPANY

NOTES TO CONSOLIDATED FINANCIAL STATEMENTS [EXCERPTS]

(For the Year Ended February 3, 2018)
(millions of Canadian dollars unless otherwise stated)

NOTE 1.   GENERAL INFORMATION

Hudson's Bay Company ("HBC" or the "Company") is a Canadian corporation amalgamated under the Canada Business Corporations Act and domiciled in Canada.

On November 26, 2012, the Company completed an initial public offering (the "IPO") of its common shares, which trade on the Toronto Stock Exchange.

On November 4, 2013, the Company acquired Saks Incorporated ("Saks") whereby all of the issued and outstanding shares (other than shares owned by Saks and its subsidiaries) of Saks were purchased through Lord & Taylor Acquisition Inc. ("L&T Acquisition"), a wholly-owned subsidiary of the Company for U.S.$16.00 per share in an all-cash transaction valued at U.S. $2,973 million ($3,097 million), including debt assumed.

On July 9, 2015, the Company and RioCan Real Estate Investment Trust ("RioCan") closed the first tranche of their joint venture, RioCan-HBC Limited Partnership (the "RioCan-HBC JV"). The second tranche of the RioCan-HBC JV closed on November 25, 2015.

On July 22, 2015, the Company and Simon Property Group Inc. ("Simon") closed their joint venture, Simon HBC Opportunities LLC (the "HBC-Simon JV").

On September 30, 2015, prior to the acquisition discussed below, the HBC-Simon JV became a wholly-owned subsidiary of HBS Global Properties LLC (the "HBS Joint Venture").

On September 30, 2015, the Company and the HBS Joint Venture acquired GALERIA Holding GmbH for €2,317 million ($3,490 million) (the "Galeria Kaufhof Acquisition"). The transaction was structured such that effectively, the Company acquired the operating business and certain properties of GALERIA Holding GmbH ("Galeria Kaufhof") while the HBS Joint Venture acquired the property business.

On February 1, 2016, the Company acquired Gilt Groupe Holdings Inc. ("Gilt") for U.S.$237 million ($332 million) (the "Gilt Acquisition") including cash of U.S.$7 million ($10 million) and excluding debt.

On December 6, 2017, the Company issued mandatory convertible preferred shares ("Convertible Preferred Shares") to an affiliate of Rhône Capital LLC for an aggregate purchase price of U.S. $500 million ($638 million) (note 19).

The Company owns and operates department stores in Canada and the United States under Hudson's Bay, Lord & Taylor, Saks Fifth Avenue, Saks Fifth Avenue OFF 5TH, Find @ Lord & Taylor, Gilt and Home Outfitters banners. In Europe, its banners include Galeria Kaufhof, Galeria INNO, Sportarena, Saks Fifth Avenue OFF 5TH Europe and Hudson's Bay Europe, together "HBC Europe". The address of the registered office of HBC is 401 Bay Street, Suite 500, Toronto, ON, M5H 2Y4.

NOTE 2.   SIGNIFICANT ACCOUNTING POLICIES

a)   Statement of compliance

The consolidated financial statements of the Company and its subsidiaries have been prepared in accordance with International Financial Reporting Standards ("IFRS") as issued by the International Accounting Standards Board ("IASB").

The consolidated financial statements for the fifty-three weeks ended February 3, 2018 were authorized for issuance by the Board of Directors of HBC on March 27, 2018.

b)   Basis of presentation

These consolidated financial statements have been prepared on a going concern basis, under the historical cost convention, as modified by the revaluation of financial assets and financial liabilities (including derivative instruments) at fair value through the statements of loss. In accordance with IFRS, the Company has:

- provided comparative financial information; and
- applied the same accounting policies throughout all periods presented

The preparation of financial statements in accordance with IFRS requires the use of critical accounting estimates. It also requires management to exercise judgment in applying the Company's accounting policies. These areas involving a higher degree of judgment or complexity, or areas where assumptions and estimates are significant are disclosed in note 3.

c)   Basis of consolidation

These consolidated financial statements of the Company include the accounts of HBC and its subsidiaries. Inter-company transactions, balances, revenues and expenses have been eliminated.

d)   Fiscal year

The fiscal year of the Company consists of a fifty-two or fifty-three week period. Fiscal year 2017 represents fifty-three weeks ended on February 3, 2018 and fiscal year 2016 represents fifty-two weeks ended on January 28, 2017. References to years in the consolidated financial statements and notes to the consolidated financial statements relate to fiscal years rather than calendar years, unless otherwise noted.

e)   Foreign currency translation

i)   *Functional and presentation currency*

Items included in the financial statements of each of the Company's entities are measured using the currency of the primary economic environment in which the entity operates (the "functional currency"). These consolidated financial statements are presented in Canadian dollars, which is HBC's functional currency and the presentation currency of the Company.

ii)   *Transactions and balances*

Foreign currency transactions are translated into the functional currency using the foreign exchange rates at the dates of the transactions. Foreign exchange gains and losses resulting from the settlement of such transactions and from the translation of monetary assets and liabilities denominated in foreign currencies at balance sheet date foreign exchange rates are recognized in net earnings (loss), except when included in other comprehensive income (loss) as qualifying cash flow or net investment hedges.

iii)   *Foreign operations*

The results and financial position of L&T Acquisition (and its subsidiaries Lord & Taylor Holdings LLC ("L&T"), Saks and Gilt) and HBC Europe, whose functional currencies are not Canadian dollars, are translated into the presentation currency as follows:

- assets and liabilities are translated at the closing foreign exchange rate at the date of each balance sheet;
- revenues and expenses are translated at average foreign exchange rates;
- equity transactions are translated at foreign exchange rates on the date the transactions occur; and
- all resulting foreign exchange translation differences are recognized as a currency translation adjustment in the consolidated statements of comprehensive income (loss).

f)   Business combinations and goodwill

Business combinations are accounted for using the acquisition method.

Consideration transferred is measured at fair value, which is calculated as the sum of the fair value of the assets transferred by the Company (including cash), liabilities incurred by the Company, any contingent consideration and equity interests issued by the Company.

Transaction costs incurred in connection with a business combination are expensed in the period as incurred.

Goodwill is measured as the excess of the consideration paid over the fair value of the identifiable assets acquired and liabilities assumed, all measured as at the acquisition date. Goodwill is not amortized.

After initial recognition, goodwill is measured at cost less any accumulated impairment losses. For the purpose of impairment testing, goodwill is allocated to cash-generating units ("CGUs") or groups of CGUs based on the level at which it is monitored by management. The allocation is made to those CGUs or groups of CGUs that are expected to benefit from the business combination in which the goodwill arose.

Where goodwill forms part of a CGU and part of the operations within that unit are disposed of, the goodwill associated with the operation disposed of is included in the carrying amount of the operation when determining the gain or loss on disposal of the operation. Goodwill disposed of in this circumstance is measured based on the relative fair values of the operation disposed of and the portion of the CGU retained.

g)   Cash

Cash consists of cash on hand, deposits in banks, short-term deposits with maturities of less than 3 months and restricted funds. Restricted cash represents amounts deposited in escrow accounts which are maintained and managed by an independent agent.

h)   Trade and other receivables

Trade and other receivables consisting of credit card issuer, vendor and other receivables are recognized initially at fair value and subsequently measured at amortized cost less allowance for impairment. An allowance for impairment of accounts receivable is established when there is objective evidence that the Company will not be able to collect all amounts due according to the original terms of the receivables.

i)   Inventories

Inventories are valued at the lower of cost and net realizable value. Cost is determined using the weighted average cost method based on individual items. Net realizable value is the estimated selling price determined at the item level using gross profit expectation and historical markdown rates for similar items in the ordinary course of business, less estimated costs required to sell.

Costs comprise all variable costs, and certain fixed costs, incurred in bringing inventories to their present location and condition. Storage and administrative overheads are expensed as incurred. Supplier rebates and discounts are recorded as a reduction in the cost of purchases unless they relate to a reimbursement of specific incremental expenses.

Merchandise that is subject to consignment or licensee (concession) agreements is not included in inventories.

j)   Property, plant and equipment

Property, plant and equipment are carried at cost less accumulated depreciation and any accumulated impairment losses. Freehold land is stated at cost less any impairment loss. Cost includes expenditures that can be directly attributed to the acquisition of the asset and capitalized borrowing costs. Subsequent costs are included in the asset's carrying amount or recognized as a separate asset, as appropriate, only when it is probable that future economic benefits will flow to the Company and the cost can be reliably measured. The carrying amount of the replaced asset is derecognized.

Freehold land and assets under construction are not depreciated. Depreciation commences when the assets are available for use and is recognized on a straight-line basis to depreciate the cost of the assets to their estimated residual value over their estimated useful lives. When significant parts of an asset have different useful lives, they are accounted for as separate components of the asset and depreciated over their respective estimated useful lives.

Estimated useful lives are as follows:

Asset	Amortization Periods
Buildings	up to 50 years
Leasehold improvements	up to 20 years
Fixtures and fittings	up to 20 years
Assets held under finance leases	up to 50 years

Although the table reflects maximum amortization periods, most assets are amortized over shorter periods. The assets' useful lives and residual values are reviewed, and adjusted if appropriate, annually.

In certain cases, HBC is responsible for the construction of leased property on behalf of the landlord, who will provide an allowance covering either all or a portion of the cost of construction. This primarily occurs in situations where the landlord delivers a parcel of vacant land. During the construction period, the Company capitalizes the construction costs incurred as it retains a significant portion of the risks and rewards of ownership. Allowances received from the landlord are deferred and recognized within other liabilities on the consolidated balance sheet and depreciation is not recorded. Upon completion of construction, as the risks and rewards of ownership transfer to the landlord, the Company derecognizes the constructed asset and the related liability. The Company then accounts for the lease on the property in accordance with the accounting policy outlined in note 2(o).

k)   Intangible assets

Intangible assets with finite useful lives are carried at cost less accumulated amortization and impairment losses. These assets are amortized on a straight-line basis or using a declining balance method over their estimated useful lives.

Estimated useful lives are as follows:

Asset	Amortization Period/Rate
Software including internally developed costs	up to 7 years
Banner names	indefinite
Private label brands	indefinite (with exceptions)
Credit cards	up to 5 years
Favourable lease rights	up to 75 years
Customer lists	declining balance at 40%

The assets' useful lives and residual values are reviewed, and adjusted if appropriate, annually.

Costs associated with maintaining computer software programs are recognized as an expense as incurred. Development costs that are directly attributable to the design and testing of identifiable and unique software products controlled by the Company, including employee costs, are recognized as intangible assets.

Private label brands are not amortized except in circumstances where the Company has a formal plan to dispose of certain private label brands. Where such a plan exists, the Company amortizes the remaining cost over the period the brands are expected to be available for use by the Company. Banner names with indefinite lives are measured at cost less any accumulated impairment losses and are not amortized.

l)   Interest in joint ventures

A joint venture is a type of joint arrangement whereby the parties that have joint control of the arrangement have rights to the net assets of the joint venture. Joint control is the contractually agreed sharing of control of an arrangement, which exists only when decisions about the relevant activities require unanimous consent of the parties sharing control.

Gains on contribution of assets to joint ventures that were leased back by the Company are recognized to the extent of the third party ownership interest in the joint ventures. The accounting treatment of the recognized gains is determined based on lease classification, as described in note 2(o).

Investments in joint ventures are accounted for using the equity method. Under the equity method, the investment in a joint venture is initially recognized at cost and adjusted thereafter to recognize the Company's share of the profit or loss and other comprehensive income or loss of the joint venture. When the Company's share of losses of a joint venture exceeds the Company's interest in that joint venture, the Company discontinues recognizing its share of further losses. Additional losses are recognized only to the extent that the Company has incurred legal or constructive obligations or made payments on behalf of the joint venture.

After application of the equity method, the Company determines whether it is necessary to recognize an impairment loss on its investment in its joint venture arrangements. At each reporting date, the Company determines whether there is objective evidence that the investment in its joint ventures is impaired. If there is such evidence, the Company calculates the amount of impairment as the difference between the recoverable amount of the joint venture and its carrying value, and then recognizes the loss as 'Share of net earnings (loss) in joint ventures' in the consolidated statement of income (loss).

The Company has investments in joint ventures that are structured using separate vehicles that give each party to the arrangement rights to the net assets of the joint venture.

The Company reclassifies its share of inter-company rental income from its share of earnings in the joint ventures to rent expense recorded in selling, general and administrative expenses.

m) Impairment of non-financial assets

The carrying amount of property, plant and equipment and intangible assets are reviewed for impairment whenever events or changes in circumstances indicate that the carrying amount may not be recoverable. Indefinite life intangible assets and goodwill are tested for impairment annually, or more frequently, if events or changes in circumstances indicate that the asset may be impaired.

An impairment loss is recognized for the amount by which the asset's carrying value exceeds its recoverable amount. The recoverable amount is the higher of an asset's fair value less costs of disposal ("FVLCD") and value in use. The FVLCD of an asset is assessed, where practicable, by external valuators. Value in use is estimated as the present value of the future cash flows that the Company expects to derive from the asset. For the purposes of assessing impairment, assets are grouped at the lowest level for which there are largely independent cash inflows (CGUs). With the exception of certain corporate assets, which are tested at the entity level, all assets are tested for impairment at the store level asset grouping.

Any impairment loss identified for a particular CGU is allocated to the assets within that unit on a pro-rata basis, except where the recoverable amount of an asset is based on FVLCD, in which case no portion of the impairment loss is allocated to that asset. Any impairment charge is recognized in net income (loss) in the year in which it occurs. Where an impairment loss subsequently reverses due to a change in the original estimate, the impairment loss is reversed but is restricted to increasing the carrying value of the relevant assets to the carrying value that would have been recognized had the original impairment not occurred.

n) Provisions

Provisions are recognized when the Company has a present legal or constructive obligation as a result of past events, it is probable that an outflow of resources will be required to settle the obligation and the amount can be reliably estimated.

Provisions are measured at the present value of management's best estimate of the expenditure required to settle the present obligation at the balance sheet date. Provisions are estimates and the actual costs and timing of future cash flows are dependent on future events. Any difference between expectations and the actual future liability will be accounted for in the period when such determination is made. Recoveries from third parties and other contingent gains are recognized when realized.

o) Leases

Leases in which a significant portion of the risks and rewards of ownership are transferred to the Company are classified as finance leases. All other leases are classified as operating leases.

Finance leases are capitalized at the inception of the lease at the lower of the fair value of the leased property and the present value of the minimum lease payments. The property, plant and equipment acquired under finance leases are depreciated over the lesser of the economic life of the asset or the lease term.

Payments made under operating leases (net of any incentives received from the lessor) are charged to net income (loss) on a straight-line basis over the term of the lease. Income from operating leases is recognized on a straight-line basis over the term of the lease. The lease term includes renewals where management is reasonably certain the renewal option will be exercised.

The accounting treatment of a sale and leaseback transaction depends upon the substance of the transaction and whether the sale price reflects fair value. For sale and finance lease-backs, any gain or loss from the sale is deferred and amortized over the term of the lease. For sale and operating leasebacks, if the transaction is established at fair value, any gain or loss is recognized immediately. If the sale price is below fair value, any gain or loss is recognized immediately except that if the loss is compensated for by future lease payments at below market price, the loss is deferred and amortized in proportion to the lease payments over the term of the lease. If the sale price is above fair value, the excess over fair value is deferred and amortized over the term of the lease.

p)   Income taxes

Deferred income tax is recognized on taxable temporary differences arising from differences between the tax bases of assets and liabilities and their carrying amounts in the consolidated financial statements. Deferred income tax is recognized for all taxable temporary differences, except to the extent where it arises from the initial recognition of an asset or a liability in a transaction that is not a business combination and at the time of the transaction, affects nei-ther accounting profit nor taxable profit. Deferred income tax is determined using income tax rates and laws that have been enacted or substantively enacted at the balance sheet date and are expected to apply when the related deferred income tax asset is realized or the deferred income tax liability is settled.

Deferred income tax assets have been recognized in respect of unused tax losses, unused tax credits and deductible temporary differences giving rise to deferred income tax assets because it is expected that these assets will be recovered by way of reversal of taxable temporary dif-ferences and management's expectation of future taxable profits within the loss expiry period.

Income tax expense or benefit comprises current and deferred income taxes. Income tax is recognized in net income (loss), except to the extent that it relates to items recognized either in other comprehensive income (loss) or directly in equity. The income tax expense or benefit is calculated on the basis of the tax laws enacted or substantively enacted at the date of the consolidated balance sheet.

Deferred tax assets and liabilities are only netted when the Company has a legally enforceable right to offset current tax assets against current tax liabilities and the deferred tax assets and liabilities relate to income taxes levied by the same taxation authority on either the same tax-able entity or different taxable entities which intend to realize or settle current tax assets or liabilities simultaneously in future periods.

q)   Employee benefits

i)   *Short-term employee benefits*

Liabilities for wages, salaries (including non-monetary benefits), vacation entitle-ment and bonuses are measured on an undiscounted basis and are recognized in SG&A as the related service is provided. A liability is recognized for the amount expected to be paid under short-term bonus plans if the Company has a present legal or constructive obligation to this amount as a result of past service provided by the employee and the obligation can be reliably estimated.

ii)   *Post-employment benefits*

Post-employment benefits include pensions (both defined contribution and defined benefit) and non-pension post-retirement benefits (medical and life insur-ance benefits for retirees). The Company reports its obligations under these plans net of any plan assets.

The asset or liability recognized in the consolidated balance sheets in respect of defined benefit pension plans is the present value of the defined benefit obligation at the end of the reporting period less the fair value of plan assets. The defined benefit obligation is calculated annually by independent actuaries using the projected unit credit method. The present value of the defined benefit obligation is determined by discounting the estimated future cash outflows using interest rates of high quality corporate bonds that are denominated in the currency in which the benefits will be paid, and that have terms to maturity approximating the terms of the related pension liability.

Actuarial gains and losses are recognized in other comprehensive income (loss) in the period in which they arise. Past service costs are recognized in SG&A during the year in which they arise. For funded plans, surpluses are recognized only to the extent that the surplus is considered recoverable. Recoverability is primarily based on the extent to which the Company can unilaterally reduce future contributions to the plan.

For defined contribution plans, the Company pays contributions to pension plans on a mandatory, contractual or voluntary basis. The Company has no further payment obligations once the contributions have been paid. Contributions are recognized as employee benefit expenses are incurred, which are as the related employee services are rendered.

iii)   *Other long-term employee benefits*

The Company provides long-term disability benefits to certain employees dependent on the legal employer. The entitlement to these benefits is usually conditional on the completion of a minimum service period. The expected costs of these benefits are recognized when an event occurs that causes the long-term disability. Actuarial gains and losses arising from experience adjustments and changes in actuarial assumptions are recognized in net income (loss) in the period in which they arise. These obligations are calculated annually.

iv)   *Termination benefits*

Termination benefits are recognized as an expense and a liability at the earlier of when the entity can no longer withdraw the offer of the termination benefit and when the entity recognizes any related restructuring costs.

v)   *Share based payments*

The Company operates share based incentive plans under which it receives services from certain employees as consideration. For equity settled awards, the fair value of the grant of equity interests is recognized as an expense over the period that the related service is rendered with a corresponding increase in equity. For cash-settled awards, the fair value of the liability is remeasured at the end of each reporting period, with the change in fair value recognized as an expense over the period that the related service is rendered. Certain awards provide the Company with a choice of settlement in cash or by issuing equity. In these cases, the award is accounted for as a cash-settled award when the Company has a present obligation to settle in cash.

The total amount to be expensed is determined by reference to the fair value of the equity interests granted. The total amount expensed is recognized over the vesting period on a tranche basis, which is the period over which all of the specified vesting conditions are to be satisfied. At each balance sheet date, the estimate of the number of equity interests that are expected to vest is revised. The impact of the revision to original estimates, if any, is recognized in SG&A.

r)   Financial assets

Financial assets have been classified in one of the following categories: at fair value through profit or loss, loans and receivables and held-to-maturity. The classification depends on the purpose for which the financial assets were acquired. Management determines the classification of its financial assets at initial recognition.

i)   Financial assets at fair value through profit or loss

Financial assets at fair value through profit or loss are financial assets held for trading. A financial asset is classified in this category if acquired principally for the purpose of selling in the short-term. Derivatives are also categorized as held for trading unless they are designated as hedges. Assets in this category are classified as current assets.

Financial assets carried at fair value through profit or loss are initially recognized at fair value and transaction costs are expensed immediately to net income (loss). Subsequent changes in the fair value of financial assets at fair value through profit or loss are also recorded in net income (loss).

ii)   Loans and receivables

Loans and receivables are non-derivative financial assets with fixed or determinable payments that are not quoted in an active market. They are included in current assets, except for those with maturities greater than twelve months after the balance sheet date, which are classified as non-current assets. Loans and receivables are measured at amortized cost using the effective interest rate method.

iii)   Held-to-maturity

Held-to-maturity investments are financial instruments with fixed or determinable payments and fixed maturities that the Company has the intention and ability to hold to maturity. They are included in current assets, except for maturities greater than twelve months after the balance sheet date, which are classified as non-current assets. Held-to-maturity investments are measured at amortized cost using the effective interest method.

The Company's non-derivative financial assets are classified and measured as follows:

Asset	Category
Cash	Loans and receivables
Restricted cash	Loans and receivables
Short-term deposits	Held-to-maturity
Trade and other receivables	Loans and receivables

iv)   Impairment

The Company assesses, at each reporting date, whether there is an indicator that a financial asset or group of financial assets is impaired. A financial asset or group of financial assets is deemed to be impaired if, and only if, there is evidence of impairment as a result of one or more events that has occurred after the initial recognition of an asset and that event has an impact on the estimated future cash flows of the financial asset or group of financial assets that can be reliably estimated.

v)   Financial assets carried at amortized cost

For financial assets carried at amortized cost, the Company first assesses whether objective evidence of impairment exists individually for financial assets that are individually significant, or collectively for financial assets that are not individually significant. If the Company determines that no objective evidence of impairment exists for an individually assessed financial asset, whether significant or not, it includes the asset in a group of financial assets with similar credit risk characteristics and collectively assesses them for impairment. Assets that are individually assessed for impairment and for which an impairment loss is, or continues to be, recognized are not included in a collective assessment of impairment.

If there is objective evidence that an impairment loss has occurred, the amount of loss is measured as the difference between the asset's carrying amount and the present value of estimated future cash flows. The present value of the estimated future cash flows is discounted at the financial asset's original effective interest rate.

s)   Financial liabilities

Trade payables and financial liabilities included in other payables and accrued liabilities are recognized initially at fair value, net of transaction costs incurred and subsequently measured at amortized cost using the effective interest method.

Loans and borrowings are recognized initially at fair value, net of transaction costs incurred. Loans and borrowings are subsequently stated at amortized cost; any difference between the proceeds (net of transaction costs) and the redemption value is recognized in net income (loss) as finance costs over the period of the borrowings using the effective interest method, unless related to a qualifying asset (note 2(u)).

Loans and borrowings are classified as current liabilities unless the Company has an unconditional right to defer settlement of the liability for at least twelve months after the balance sheet date.

t)   Derivative financial instruments

Derivatives are initially recognized at fair value on the date a derivative contract is entered into and are subsequently remeasured to their fair value at each balance sheet date. The method of recognizing the resulting gain or loss depends on whether the derivative is designated as a hedging instrument and, if so, the nature of the item being hedged. The Company designates certain derivatives as:

    (a) hedges of the fair value of recognized assets or liabilities or a firm commitment (fair value hedge);

    (b) hedges of foreign currency exposure (net investment hedge); and/or

    (c) hedges of a particular risk associated with a recognized asset or liability or a highly probable forecast transaction (cash flow hedge).

When a derivative financial instrument is not designated in a qualifying hedge relationship, all changes in its fair value are recognized immediately in net income (loss).

The Company documents at the inception of the transaction the relationship between hedging instruments and hedged items, as well as its risk management objectives and strategy for undertaking various hedging transactions. The Company also documents its assessment, both at hedge inception and on an ongoing basis, of whether the derivatives that are used in hedging transactions are highly effective in offsetting changes in fair values or cash flows of hedged items.

The full fair value of a hedging derivative is classified as a non-current asset or liability when the maturity of the remaining hedged item is more than twelve months and as a current asset or liability when the remaining maturity of the hedged item is less than twelve months.

The Company does not use derivatives for trading or speculative purposes. The Company had cash flow hedges and a net investment hedge outstanding as at February 3, 2018 and January 28, 2017.

Cash flow hedges

The effective portion of changes in the fair value of derivatives that are designated and qualify as cash flow hedges is recognized in other comprehensive income (loss). The gain or loss relating to the ineffective portion is recognized immediately in net income (loss) within SG&A. Amounts accumulated in other comprehensive income (loss) are recycled in net income (loss) in the periods when the hedged item affects earnings.

When a forecasted transaction that is hedged results in the recognition of a non-financial asset (for example, inventory or property, plant and equipment), the gains and losses previously deferred in accumulated other comprehensive income (loss) are transferred from equity and included in the initial measurement of the cost of the asset. The deferred amounts are ultimately recognized in cost of sales in the case of inventory or in depreciation in the case of property, plant and equipment.

When a hedging instrument expires or is sold, or when a hedge no longer meets the criteria for hedge accounting, any cumulative gain or loss existing in equity at that time remains in accumulated other comprehensive income (loss) and is recognized when the forecasted transaction is ultimately recognized in net income (loss). When a forecasted transaction is no longer expected to occur, the cumulative gain or loss that was reported in other comprehensive income (loss) is immediately transferred to net income (loss).

Hedges of net investments in foreign operations

Hedges of net investments in foreign operations are accounted for similarly to cash flow hedges. Any gains or losses on the hedging instrument related to the effective portion of the hedge are recognized in other comprehensive income (loss) while any gains or losses related to the ineffective portion are recognized immediately in net income (loss) within SG&A. On disposal of the foreign operation, the cumulative value of any such gains or losses recorded in equity is transferred to the consolidated statements of net income (loss).

Derivatives at fair value through profit or loss

Changes in the fair value of derivatives embedded in a host contract and derivatives that are not distinguished in a hedging relationship are recognized immediately in net income (loss). Embedded derivatives (elements of contracts whose cash flows move independently from the host contract) are required to be separated and measured at their respective fair values unless certain criteria are met. The Company has recorded the fair value of embedded derivatives in HBC's U.S. dollar denominated purchase orders with certain non-U.S. based vendors. The fair value of these embedded derivatives is recorded in financial assets or financial liabilities, depending on the embedded derivative's fair value.

In connection with the acquisition of Saks, the Company also issued warrants. Certain features of the warrants result in their presentation as derivative financial liabilities that are classified as fair value through profit or loss and recorded at fair value.

Offsetting of financial instruments

Financial assets and financial liabilities are offset and the net amount reported in the consolidated balance sheets if:

- There is currently a legally enforceable right to offset recognized amounts; and
- There is an intention to settle on a net basis, or to realize the assets and settle the liabilities simultaneously.

u)   Borrowing costs

Borrowing costs that are directly attributable to the acquisition or construction of qualifying assets are capitalized to the cost of the asset. Qualifying assets are those that necessarily take a substantial period of time to prepare for their intended use. All other borrowing costs are recognized in net income (loss) in the period in which they occur.

v)   Revenue recognition

Revenue comprises the fair value of the consideration received or receivable for the sale of goods and services in the ordinary course of the Company's activities. Revenue is shown net of sales tax and estimated returns.

The Company recognizes revenue when the amount can be reliably measured, it is probable that future economic benefits will flow to the Company and when specific criteria have been met for each of the Company's activities as described below. The Company bases its estimates on historical results, taking into consideration the type of customer, the type of transaction and the specifics of each arrangement.

    i)   Retail merchandise sales

    Revenue consists of sales through retail stores of the banners operated by the Company and includes sales through the Company's e-commerce ("Digital Commerce") operations. Merchandise sales through retail stores are recognized at the time of delivery to the customer which is generally at point of sale. Merchandise sales through Digital Commerce are recognized upon estimated receipt by the customer.

    It is the Company's policy to sell merchandise to the customer with a right to return within a specified period. Accumulated experience is used to estimate and provide for such returns. Where it is determined that the Company acts as an agent rather than a principal in a transaction, revenue is recognized to the extent of the commission.

ii)   Gift cards

Through its retail stores, websites and selected third parties, the Company sells gift cards that have no administrative fee charges or expiration dates. No revenue is recognized at the time gift cards are sold. Revenue is recognized as a merchandise sale when the gift card is redeemed by the customer.

The Company also recognizes income when the likelihood of the gift card being redeemed by the customer is remote ("gift card breakage"). Gift card breakage is estimated based on historical redemption patterns and is recognized in proportion to the redemption of gift card balances.

w)   Credit operations

The Company shares in the income and losses of the credit card program related to private label and co-branded credit cards at Hudson's Bay, Lord & Taylor and Saks. Income related to this program is included in SG&A.

x)   Vendor allowances

The Company receives cash or allowances from vendors, the most significant of which are in respect of markdown allowances and volume rebates. Such amounts are recorded as either a reduction of the cost of purchases or a reduction in cost of sales.

Rebates that are based on specified cumulative purchase volumes are recognized if the rebate is probable and reasonably estimable; otherwise these rebates are recognized when earned. These rebates are applied as a reduction of the cost of purchases.

y)   Loyalty programs

Award credits are accounted for as a separate component of the sales transaction in which they are granted and therefore, part of the fair value of the consideration received is allocated to the award credits. This allocation is reported as deferred revenue until the award credits are redeemed by the customer. The amount deferred is based on points outstanding that the Company estimates will be redeemed by customers and the estimated fair value of those points. The points expected to be redeemed are based on many factors, including an actuarial review, where required, of customers' past experience and trends.

z)   Accounting standards implemented in fiscal 2017

Statement of Cash Flows

In January 2016, the IASB amended IAS 7 – Statement of Cash Flows ("IAS 7") by issuing Disclosure Initiative (Amendments to IAS 7). The amendments require disclosures that enable users of financial statements to evaluate changes in liabilities arising from financing activities, including cash and non-cash changes. The amendments were effective for annual periods beginning on or after January 1, 2017. When an entity first applies these amendments, it is not required to provide comparative information for prior periods. The reconciliation between the opening and closing balances of liabilities arising from financing activities is provided in note 26. Other than the additional disclosure in note 26, the implementation of these amendments did not have an impact on the Company's consolidated financial statements.

aa)   Future accounting standards not yet adopted

Financial Instruments

In July 2014, the IASB issued IFRS 9 – Financial Instruments ("IFRS 9"), which brings together the classification and measurement, impairment and hedge accounting phases of the IASB's project to replace IAS 39 – Financial Instruments: Recognition and Measurement ("IAS 39").

Classification and measurement

Financial assets are classified and measured based on the business model under which they are managed and the contractual cash flow characteristics of the financial assets. Financial liabilities are classified in a similar manner as under IAS 39, except that financial liabilities measured at fair value will have fair value changes resulting from changes in the entity's own credit risk recognized in other comprehensive income (loss) instead of net income (loss).

Impairment

The measurement of impairment of financial assets is based on an expected credit loss model. It is no longer necessary for a triggering event to have occurred before credit losses are recognized. IFRS 9 also includes new disclosure requirements about expected credit losses and credit risk.

Hedge accounting

The new general hedge accounting model more closely aligns hedge accounting with risk management activities undertaken by entities when hedging their financial and non-financial risk exposures. The new model will provide more opportunities to apply hedge accounting to reflect actual risk management activities.

IFRS 9 will be applied retrospectively for annual periods beginning on or after January 1, 2018. Early adoption was permitted, however the Company chose not to. The Company has completed its assessment of the financial and disclosure impact of adopting IFRS 9. Other than the enhanced disclosure requirements, the implementation of this standard is not expected to have a material impact on the Company's results of operations or financial position.

Revenue

In May 2014, the IASB issued IFRS 15 – Revenue from Contracts with Customers ("IFRS 15"), which provides a comprehensive framework for recognition, measurement and disclosure of revenue from contracts with customers, excluding contracts within the scope of the standards on leases, insurance contracts and financial instruments. IFRS 15 is to be applied retrospectively for annual periods beginning on or after January 1, 2018. The Company will adopt IFRS 15 for the 2018 annual fiscal period and expects to do so on a modified retrospective basis without the restatement of prior period results. IFRS 15 is not expected to materially impact the timing or the amounts recognized within the Company's consolidated operating results due to the nature of the contracts it has in place. IFRS 15 is expected to impact the Company's current financial statement disclosures as it contains enhanced disclosure requirements.

Leases

In January 2016, the IASB issued the final publication of IFRS 16 – Leases ("IFRS 16"), which is to replace the current IAS 17 lease accounting standard and related interpretations. IFRS 16 is required to be adopted either retrospectively or by recognizing the cumulative effect of initially applying IFRS 16 as an adjustment to opening equity at the date of initial application. The standard provides a single lessee accounting model, requiring lessees to recognize assets and liabilities for all leases unless the lease term is twelve months or less or the underlying asset has a low value. Lessors continue to classify leases as operating or finance, with the approach under IFRS 16 substantially unchanged from the current IAS 17 lease accounting standard and related interpretations. IFRS 16 is effective for fiscal years beginning on or after January 1, 2019 with earlier adoption permitted if IFRS 15 has also been adopted. The Company has contracted third party advisors to assist with the implementation of this standard. Although the Company is still in the process of assessing the potential impact of IFRS 16, it expects this standard will have a significant impact on its consolidated balance sheet, along with a change to the recognition, measurement, and presentation of lease expenses in the consolidated statement of earnings.

NOTE 3. CRITICAL ACCOUNTING JUDGMENTS AND KEY SOURCES OF ESTIMATION UNCERTAINTY

In the application of the Company's accounting policies, which are described in note 2, and the preparation of the consolidated financial statements, management is required to make judgments, estimates and assumptions about the carrying amounts of assets and liabilities, and reporting of income and expenses, that are not readily apparent from other sources. The estimates and associated assumptions are based on historical experience and other factors that are considered to be relevant. Actual results may differ materially from these estimates.

The estimates and underlying assumptions are reviewed on an ongoing basis. Revisions to accounting estimates are recognized in the period in which the estimate is revised if the revision affects only that period or in the period of the revision and future periods if the revision affects both current and future periods.

The following are the critical judgments and estimations that management has made in the process of applying the Company's accounting policies and that have the most significant effect on the amounts recognized in the consolidated financial statements:

Business combinations

Fair value of assets acquired and liabilities assumed in a business combination is estimated based on information available at the date of acquisition and involves considerable judgment in determining the fair values assigned to property, plant and equipment and intangible assets acquired and liabilities assumed on acquisition. The determination of these fair values involves analysis including the use of discounted cash flows, estimated future margins, future growth rates, market rents and capitalization rates. There is measurement uncertainty inherent in this analysis and actual results could differ from estimates.

Inventory valuation

Inventory is valued at the lower of cost and net realizable value. Current selling price and historical trends for estimating future markdowns are utilized to estimate net realizable value. Inventory valuation also incorporates a write-down to reflect future losses on the disposition of obsolete merchandise.

Inventory is adjusted to reflect estimated losses ("shortage") incurred since the last inventory count. Shortage is estimated based on historical experience as a percentage of sales for the period from the date of the last inventory count to the end of the fiscal year.

Loyalty programs

Where loyalty award credits are issued in connection with a sales transaction that includes the loyalty program, a portion of the revenue has been deferred based on expected redemptions of points outstanding (note 2(y)). The amount of revenue deferred relating to the loyalty programs is sensitive to changes in customer behaviour and the impact of changes in the loyalty programs. Deferred revenue reported in the consolidated balance sheets relates entirely to the loyalty programs.

Impairment and reversal of impairment of long-lived assets

Long-lived assets are subject to impairment and impairment reversal reviews based on whether current or future events and circumstances suggest that their recoverable amount may be more or less than their carrying value. In certain instances, the recoverable amount is based on a calculation of expected future cash flows which includes management assumptions and estimates of future performance.

Impairment of goodwill and indefinite lived intangible assets

The Company uses judgment in determining the grouping of assets to identify its CGUs for the purposes of testing for impairment of goodwill and in determining the level of Company cash flows at which to test its indefinite lived intangible assets. In testing for impairment, goodwill acquired in a business combination is allocated to CGUs that are expected to benefit from the synergies of the business combination. The calculations for impairment testing of the Company's goodwill and indefinite lived intangible assets also involve significant estimates and assumptions. Items estimated include cash flows, discount rates and assumptions on revenue growth rates. These estimates could affect the Company's future results if the current estimates of future performance and fair values change. Judgment is also exercised to determine whether an indication of impairment is present that would require the completion of an impairment test in addition to the annual testing.

Valuation of warrants

In connection with the acquisition of Saks, the Company issued warrants. The classification of these instruments as financial liabilities is an area of significant judgment. The Company records a mark-to-market valuation adjustment on the warrants as finance costs based on a valuation at the end of each reporting period.

Provisions

Provisions have been made for various items including asset retirement obligations, general insurance liability and termination costs. Asset retirement obligations are based on uncertain estimates of remediation and the timing of the remediation. The Company purchases third party insurance for automobile, product, workers' compensation, medical and general liability claims that exceed a certain dollar level and is responsible for the payment of claims below these insured limits. The self-insurance provision is based on claims filed and an estimate of claims incurred but not yet reported.

In the context of provisions for onerous contracts including leases, the Company uses judgment in determining when the expected benefits to be derived by the Company from a contract are lower than the unavoidable costs of meeting its obligations under the contract.

Sales returns

Sales returns are estimated on the basis of historical returns and are recorded so as to allocate them to the same period as the original revenue is recorded.

Share based compensation

The Company operates a share option plan, phantom share plan, restricted share unit plan, performance share unit plan, performance restricted share unit plan and profits interests plan for employees. The grant date fair values are calculated using valuation models, which use a number of assumptions and estimates, including expected volatility, the risk-free interest rate, the dividend yield, the non-marketability discount and the expected life of the grants. Details of these assumptions and estimates are set out in note 18.

Income taxes

The Company recognizes expected liabilities for income taxes based on an estimation of the likely income taxes due, which requires judgment as to the ultimate income tax determination of certain items. In addition, the Company has made estimates of future profitability in relation to an assessment of the recoverability of income tax losses. Details of the income tax benefit and deferred taxes are set out in note 7.

Pensions and employee benefits

The Company operates various defined benefit plans for its employees. The present value of the plans' liabilities recognized at the balance sheet date and net financing charges recognized in net income (loss) are dependent on the interest rate of high quality corporate bonds. Other key assumptions within this calculation are based on market conditions or estimates of future events, including mortality rates, as set out in note 15.

Lease accounting

The Company leases a significant number of store locations as part of its operations. The determination of classification between finance and operating leases requires the exercise of management judgment, including estimates of fair value, the useful and economic lives of the leased assets, the existence of lower than market renewal options and appropriate discount rates. Operating and finance leases are discussed in note 14.

Management judgment is also exercised in the assessment of sale and leaseback transactions, including the determination of leaseback classification between finance and operating leases, the fair value of the leased back property and appropriate discount rates.

Joint ventures

Judgment is used by management when determining what subsidiaries or entities to consolidate in the financial statements. Subsidiaries or entities are consolidated when the Company has control over the entities. In determining if control exists, management considers various factors including whether the Company has the power, directly or indirectly, to govern the financial and operating policies of an entity either through an agreement or by voting rights, exposure or rights to variable returns from the Company's involvement with the entity, and the ability to use its power over the entity to affect the amount of the Company's returns.

The Company holds an 88.0% (January 28, 2017: 88.1%) ownership interest in its joint arrangement with RioCan and 62.4% (January 28, 2017: 63.4%) ownership interest in its joint arrangement with Simon and other non-controlling third party investors. Based on the contractual terms of each arrangement, the Company identified the relevant activities of each joint venture and determined that all significant decisions require the joint consent of both parties to each of the joint arrangements formed. The Company has assessed its rights and obligations arising from the joint arrangements by considering the structure and legal form of the arrangements, the terms agreed by the parties and other facts and circumstances. Based on this assessment, the arrangements have been classified as joint ventures. The Company will reassess the existence of joint control and the joint venture classification should facts and circumstances change. Gains recognized upon the initial contributions into each joint venture were determined based on determinations of fair value that incorporated assumptions from a market participant's perspective under market conditions that existed at the measurement date. Changes in assumptions about these factors could affect the reported fair value of the initial contributions made by HBC into each of the joint venture arrangements formed.

Appendix C

The Accounting Information System

LEARNING OBJECTIVES	APPENDIX OUTLINE	CPA COMPETENCIES
After studying this appendix, you should be able to:	The appendix headings related to the learning objective are:	Competencies addressed by each learning objective are as follows:
1. Understand basic accounting terminology, double-entry rules, and the accounting equation.	**Accounting System Overview** • Basic terminology and double-entry rules • Accounting equation	**1.2.2, 1.3.1**
2. Identify the steps in the accounting cycle and the steps in the recording process.	**The Accounting Cycle and the Recording Process** • Identifying and recording transactions and other events • Journalizing • Posting • Preparing the trial balance	**1.2.2, 1.3.1, 4.1.2**
3. Explain the reasons for, and prepare, adjusting entries.	**Adjusting Entries** • Adjusting entries for prepayments • Alternative method for adjusting prepayments • Adjusting entries for accruals • Adjusting entries for estimated items • Unrealized holding gains or losses (FV-NI and FV-OCI)	**1.2.2, 1.3.1**
4. Explain how the type of ownership structure affects the financial statements.	**Financial Statements and Ownership Structure**	**1.1.1, 1.2.1, 1.2.2, 1.3.1**
5. Prepare closing entries and consider other matters relating to the closing process.	**The Closing Process** • Preparing closing entries • Reversing entries	**1.2.2, 1.3.1**

6. Prepare a 10-column work sheet and financial statements.	**Using a Work Sheet** • Work sheet columns • Completing the work sheet • Preparing financial statements from a work sheet	**1.2.2, 1.3.1**

Preview of Volume 1—Appendix C

This appendix covers bookkeeping systems for capturing and recording transactions. It provides a review of material that is covered in introductory financial accounting courses for most students. The appendix, together with Chapter 0, which is available via *WileyPLUS*, will help ensure that you are ready for the more complex accounting topics that are covered in Chapter 4 and subsequent chapters.

It is important to understand how companies measure and record transactions, update their accounting records, and prepare financial statements. This appendix starts by explaining the features of an accounting information system. It assumes that we are able to measure transactions in a straightforward manner; for instance, where the transaction is a cash transaction, such as the company paying $100 for supplies. However, in other cases, measurement is not so straightforward. For example, how do we measure the value of an asset that is impaired? Refer to Chapter 3 for the tools and techniques that will help you measure more complex financial statement elements. But keep in mind that even as transactions and related measurement issues get more complicated, they will still need to be recorded using the techniques presented in this appendix!

Accounting System Overview

LEARNING OBJECTIVE 1

Understand basic accounting terminology, double-entry rules, and the accounting equation.

The system for collecting and processing transaction data to make financial information available to interested parties is known as the **accounting information system**.

Accounting information systems can be very different from one business to another. Many factors shape these systems, including the type of business and the kinds of transactions it engages in, the firm's size, the amount of data handled, and the kind of information that management and others need to get from the system.

Even though most companies have sophisticated computerized accounting systems, it is still important to understand the mechanics of bookkeeping. How do transactions get captured in the accounting system? How do the accounting records get updated at the end of each period? How and when are the financial statements produced? At the end of the fiscal year, what do we do to ready the books of account to start a new fiscal year and a new accounting cycle? We will address these questions.

Basic Terminology and Double-Entry Rules

Financial accounting is built on a set of concepts (discussed in Chapters 1 and 2) for identifying, recording, classifying, and interpreting transactions and other events relating to enterprises. It is important to understand the **basic terminology** that is used in collecting accounting data. The following terms should be familiar to you from your introductory financial accounting course. Each is defined in the Glossary found at the end of this volume of the textbook (just before the Company Index and the Subject Index). You should refer to the Glossary definitions for any terms that require further explanation.

Basic Terminology

Event   (including an external event or *transaction*).

Account   (including **permanent accounts** and *temporary accounts*).

Ledger[1]   (for example, the **general ledger** or *subsidiary ledger*).

Journal.   (for example, cash disbursements or general journal).

Posting.   (for example, transfer of items from a general journal to general ledger).

Trial balance   (including an **adjusted trial balance** and a **post-closing trial balance**).

Journal entries   (including **adjusting entries, closing entries,** and **reversing entries**).

Financial statements, including (1) the **statement of financial position** (or **balance sheet** under ASPE); (2) the *statement of comprehensive income* (or *income statement* under ASPE); (3) the *statement of cash flows*; and (4) the *statement of changes in shareholders' equity* (alternatively, a *statement of retained earnings* is used under ASPE). These financial statements are discussed further in Chapters 4 and 5. Volume 1, Appendix B, includes an example of recent financial statements for Hudson's Bay Company.

The terms debit and credit refer to the left and right sides of a general ledger account, respectively. They are commonly abbreviated as Dr. for debit and Cr. for credit. These terms do not mean "increase" or "decrease." The terms "debit" and "credit" are used repeatedly in the recording process to describe where entries are made. For example, the act of entering an amount on the left side of an account is called **debiting** the account. Making an entry on the right side is **crediting** the account. When the totals of the two sides are compared, an account will have a debit balance if the total of the debit amounts is more than the credits. Conversely, an account will have a credit balance if the credit amounts exceed the debits. The procedure of having debits on the left and credits on the right is an accounting custom. We could function just as well if debits and credits were reversed. However, the custom of having debits on the left side of an account and credits on the right side (like the custom of driving on the right-hand side of the road) has been adopted for accounting. This rule applies to all accounts.

The equality of debits and credits is the basis for the double-entry system of recording transactions (also sometimes called double-entry bookkeeping). Under the double-entry accounting system, which is used for accounting around the world, the two-sided (dual) effect of each transaction is recorded in the appropriate accounts. This system gives a logical method for recording transactions. It also offers a way to help prove the accuracy of the recorded amounts. Every transaction is recorded with total debits equal to total credits, so the sum of all the debits posted to the accounts must equal the sum of all the credits.

All **asset** and **expense** accounts are increased on the left (or debit side) and decreased on the right (or credit side). Conversely, all **liability** and **revenue** accounts are increased on the right (or credit side) and decreased on the left (or debit side). Shareholders' equity accounts, such as Common Shares, and Retained Earnings, are increased on the credit side, whereas the Dividends account (for dividends paid to shareholders) is increased on the debit side. The basic guidelines for an accounting system are presented in Illustration C.1.

---

[1]Most companies use accounting software systems instead of manual systems. The software allows the data to be entered into a database and various reports can then be generated, such as journals, trial balances, ledgers, and financial statements.

ILLUSTRATION C.1
Double-Entry (Debit and Credit) Accounting System

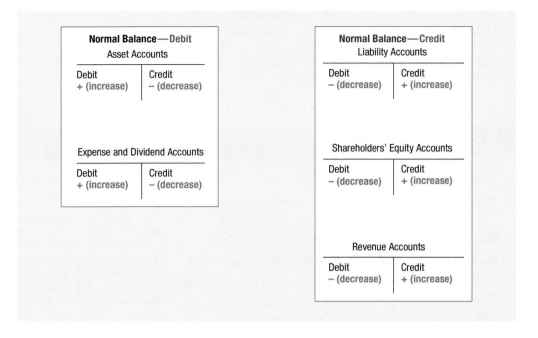

Accounting Equation

In a double-entry system, for every debit there must be a credit, and vice versa. This leads us to the basic accounting equation for corporations shown in **Illustration C.2**.

ILLUSTRATION C.2
The Basic Accounting Equation

Illustration C.3 expands this equation to include shareholders' equity accounts. In addition, it shows the debit/credit rules and effects on each type of account. Study this diagram carefully. It will help you understand the fundamentals of the double-entry system. Like the basic equation, the expanded basic equation must balance. That is, total debits **must** equal total credits.[2]

ILLUSTRATION C.3 **Expanded Basic Equation and Debit/Credit Rules and Effects**

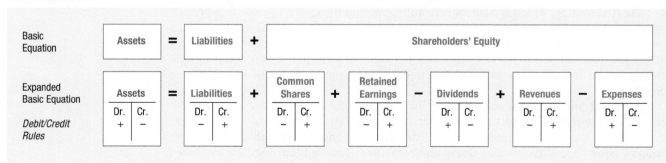

Every time a transaction occurs, the elements in the equation change, but the basic equality of the two sides remains. To illustrate, here are eight different transactions for Perez Inc.:

---

[2] **IFRS** Accumulated Other Comprehensive Income (AOCI) would also be part of the expanded basic equation if the company had Fair Value-OCI Investments (or other items affecting Other Comprehensive Income and Accumulated Other Comprehensive Income). If the AOCI balance represented accumulated gains, it would be added in the equation, similar to retained earnings. If AOCI represented accumulated losses, it would be subtracted.

Transaction	Assets	=	Liabilities	+	Shareholders' Equity
1. Owners invest $40,000 in exchange for common shares	+40,000				+40,000 (shares)
2. Disburse $600 cash for administrative support wages	−600				−600 (expense)
3. Purchase equipment priced at $5,200, giving a 10% promissory note in exchange	+5,200		+5,200		
4. Services are rendered for $4,000 cash	+4,000				+4,000 (revenue)
5. Pay off a short-term liability of $7,000 using cash	−7,000		−7,000		
6. Declare a cash dividend of $5,000			+5,000		−5,000 (dividends)
7. Pay off a long-term liability of $80,000 by issuing common shares			−80,000		+80,000 (shares)
8. Pay $16,000 cash for a delivery van	−16,000 +16,000				

The Accounting Cycle and the Recording Process

LEARNING OBJECTIVE 2

Identify the steps in the accounting cycle and the steps in the recording process.

Illustration C.4 charts the steps in the accounting cycle. These are the accounting procedures normally used by enterprises to record transactions and prepare financial statements.

Identifying and Recording Transactions and Other Events

The first step in the accounting cycle is to **analyze transactions** and other selected events. The problem is determining what to **record**. There are no simple rules for whether an event should be recorded. It is generally agreed that changes in personnel, changes in managerial policies, and the value of human resources, though important, should not be recorded in the accounts. On the other hand, when the company makes a cash sale or purchase—no matter how small—it should be recorded. The treatment relates to the accounting concepts presented in Chapter 2. An item should be **recognized** in the financial statements if it meets the definition of an **element** (such as a liability or asset), and is **measurable**. What happens when there is uncertainty about the future event occurring or not, such as the potential loss from a lawsuit? In that case, the accountant must use all available information to make a neutral decision as to whether the liability/asset exists or not. The accountant would take that uncertainty into account when measuring the element. We discuss recognition and measurement criteria in Chapter 2.

Journalizing

The effects of transactions on the basic business elements (assets, liabilities, and equities) are categorized and collected in accounts. The general ledger then collects all of the asset, liability, shareholders' equity, revenue, and expense accounts.

ILLUSTRATION C.4
The Accounting Cycle

When the steps have been completed, the sequence starts over again in the next accounting period.
Statement preparation per Step 7 uses ASPE statement names (but it also applies under IFRS).

In practice, transactions and other selected events are not first recorded in the ledger. This is because each transaction affects two or more accounts, and since each account is on a different page in the ledger, it would be inconvenient to record each transaction this way. The risk of error would also be greater.[3] To overcome this limitation and to have a complete record of each transaction or other selected event in one place, a journal (the book of original entry) is used. The simplest journal form is a chronological listing of transactions and other events that expresses the transactions and events as debits and credits to particular accounts. This is called a general journal.

Each general journal entry has four parts:

1. The accounts and amounts to be debited (Dr.)

2. The accounts and amounts to be credited (Cr.)

3. A date

4. An explanation

Debits are entered first, followed by the credits, which are slightly indented. The explanation begins below the name of the last account to be credited and may take one or more lines. The Reference column is completed when the accounts are posted.

In most cases, businesses use special journals in addition to the general journal. Special journals summarize transactions that have a common characteristic (such as cash receipts, sales, purchases, and cash payments), which saves time in doing the various bookkeeping tasks.

---

[3]The transition to electronic bookkeeping systems and databases has dramatically changed the way bookkeeping is carried out. Much of the terminology and visual layout of the reports has been retained, however.

Posting

The items entered in a general journal must be transferred to the general ledger. This procedure is called posting and is part of the summarizing and classifying process.

The general journal posting is completed when all the posting reference numbers have been recorded opposite the account titles in the journal. This means that the number in the posting reference column serves two purposes: (1) it indicates the ledger account number of the account involved, and (2) it indicates that the posting has been completed for that item. Each business chooses its own numbering system for its ledger accounts. One practice is to begin numbering with asset accounts and to follow with liabilities, shareholders' equity, revenue, and expense accounts, in that order. Example C.1 illustrates posting using transactions initially recorded in the general journal of Marra Co.

Example C.1 | General Journal, with Sample Entries and Posting

Facts Marra Co. (MC) had these transactions in November 2019:

Nov. 11 Buys a new delivery truck on account from Auto Sales Inc., $22,400.
13 Receives an invoice from the *Evening Graphic* for advertising, $280.
14 Returns merchandise to Canuck Supply for credit, $175.
15 Receives a $95 debit memo from Confederation Ltd., indicating that freight on merchandise purchased from Confederation Ltd. was prepaid by the supplier but is the buyer's obligation.

Instructions

a. Record MC's transactions in its general journal.

b. Discuss how the November 11 transaction would be recorded and explain the posting process that MC would follow to post the transaction to its general ledger (GL).

Solution

a. The November 11 to 15 transactions are shown below in MC's general journal.

General Journal with Sample Entries—Marra Co.

GENERAL JOURNAL PAGE 12

Date 2020	Account Title and Explanation	Ref.	Debit	Credit
Nov. 11	Vehicles	8	22,400	
	Accounts Payable	34		22,400
	(Purchased delivery truck on account)			
Nov. 13	Advertising Expense	65	280	
	Accounts Payable	34		280
	(Received invoice for advertising)			
Nov. 14	Accounts Payable	34	175	
	Purchase Returns and Allowances	53		175
	(Returned merchandise for credit)			
Nov. 15	Freight-in	55	95	
	Accounts Payable	34		95
	(Received debit memo for freight on merchandise purchased)			

The numbers in the Ref. column of the general journal refer to the GL accounts to which the items are posted. For example, the 34 placed in the column to the right of Accounts Payable indicates that this $22,400 item was posted to Account No. 34 in the ledger.

b. The November 11 transaction represents the purchase of a new delivery truck that is recorded with a debit to Vehicles of $22,400 and a credit to Accounts Payable of $22,400. The amount in the debit column would be posted from the journal to the debit side of the GL account Vehicles. The amount in the credit column is posted from the journal to the credit side of the GL account Accounts Payable.

Preparing the Trial Balance

A **trial balance** is a list of general ledger accounts and their balances at a specific time. Customarily, an accountant prepares a trial balance at the end of an accounting period. The accounts are listed in the order in which they appear in the general ledger, with debit balances listed in the left column and credit balances in the right column. The totals of the two columns must agree.

Audit & Assurance 4.1.2 The main purpose of a trial balance is to prove the mathematical equality of debits and credits after posting. Under the double-entry system, this equality will occur when the sum of the debit account balances equals the sum of the credit account balances. A trial balance also uncovers errors in journalizing and posting, and serves as a basic internal control. In addition, it is useful when preparing financial statements. To prepare a trial balance, an entity's accountant:

1. Lists the account titles and their balances.
2. Totals the debit and credit columns.
3. Proves the equality of the two columns.

Illustration C.5 shows the trial balance prepared from the ledger of Pioneer Advertising Agency Inc. (PAAI) at the end of its first month of operations.

ILLUSTRATION C.5

Trial Balance (Unadjusted)

Pioneer Advertising Agency Inc.
Unadjusted Trial Balance
October 31, 2020

	Debit	Credit
Cash	$ 80,000	
Accounts receivable	72,000	
Supplies	25,000	
Prepaid insurance	6,000	
FV-NI investments	10,000	
Equipment	50,000	
Notes payable		$ 50,000
Accounts payable		35,000
Unearned revenue		12,000
Common shares		100,000
Dividends	5,000	
Service revenue		100,000
Salaries and wages expense	40,000	
Rent expense	9,000	
	$297,000	$297,000

Note that the total debits, $297,000, equal the total credits, $297,000. In the trial balance, the account numbers of the account titles are also often shown to the left of the titles.

Adjusting Entries

LEARNING OBJECTIVE 3

Explain the reasons for, and prepare, adjusting entries.

Recall that, under accrual accounting, revenues must be recorded in the period in which they are earned, and expenses must be recognized in the period in which they are incurred, regardless of when payment occurs, and they must match. In order to do this, **adjusting entries** are made at the end of the accounting period. In short, **adjustments are needed to ensure that the revenue recognition principle is followed, proper matching occurs, and estimated items are recorded.**

The use of adjusting entries makes it possible to report on the statement of financial position (or balance sheet) the appropriate assets, liabilities, and shareholders' equity at the statement date and to report on the statement of comprehensive income the proper net income (or loss) and comprehensive income for the period. However, the trial balance—the first pulling together of the transaction data—may not contain up-to-date and complete data. This is true for the following reasons:

1. Some events are **not journalized daily** because it is not efficient to do so. Examples are the consumption of supplies and the earning of wages by employees.

2. Some costs are not journalized during the accounting period because these costs **expire with the passage of time** rather than as a result of recurring daily transactions. Examples of such costs are building and equipment depreciation, rent, and insurance.

3. Some items may be **unrecorded**. An example is a utility service bill that will not be received until the next accounting period.

Adjusting entries are required every time financial statements are prepared. The starting point to preparing adjusting entries is to analyze each trial balance account to determine whether it is complete and up to date for financial statement purposes. The analysis requires a thorough understanding of the company's operations and the relationships between its accounts. Preparing adjusting entries is often a complicated process that requires the services of a skilled professional. In accumulating the adjustment data, the company may need to take inventory counts of supplies and repair parts. It may also be desirable to prepare supporting schedules of insurance policies, rental agreements, and other contractual commitments. Adjustments are often prepared after the end of the period, but the entries are dated as at the statement of financial position date.

Adjusting entries can be classified as one of (1) **prepayments**, (2) **accruals**, or (3) **estimated items** (including fair value estimates).[4] Each of these classes has subcategories as shown in Illustration C.6.

ILLUSTRATION C.6 **Types of Adjusting Entries**

Prepayments	Accruals	Estimated Items
Prepaid expenses. Expenses paid in cash and recorded as assets before they are used or consumed.	**Accrued revenues.** Revenues earned but not yet received in cash or recorded.	**Bad debts.** Expenses for impaired accounts receivable estimated in the period the related revenue is earned.
Unearned revenues. Revenues received in cash and recorded as liabilities before they are earned.	**Accrued expenses.** Expenses incurred but not yet paid in cash or recorded.	**Unrealized gain or loss.** Gain (or loss) on fair value through net income (FV-NI) investments is estimated at the end of an accounting period and recorded as an increase (or decrease) to the investment account with a corresponding gain (or loss) on the statement of comprehensive income.
		Unrealized gain or loss—OCI. Gain (or loss) on fair value through other comprehensive income (FV-OCI) investments is estimated at the end of an accounting period and recorded as an increase (or decrease) to the investment account with a corresponding gain (or loss) in FV on OCI investments in other comprehensive income.

---

[4]Other, less common adjustments, such as revaluation of property, plant, and equipment at the end of an accounting period (Chapter 10), are discussed on a chapter-by-chapter basis.

We give specific examples and explanations of each type of adjustment later in this appendix. Each example is based on the October 31 trial balance of Pioneer Advertising Agency Inc. (Illustration C.5). We assume that PAAI uses an accounting period of one month. Thus, the company will make monthly adjusting entries. The entries will be dated October 31.

Adjusting Entries for Prepayments

As mentioned in Illustration C.6, prepayments are either **prepaid expenses** or **unearned revenues**. Adjusting entries for prepayments are required at the statement date to record the portion of the prepaid expense used or unearned revenue earned in the current accounting period. Assuming an adjustment is needed for both types of prepayments, the asset and liability involved are overstated and the related expense and revenue are understated. For example, in the trial balance, the balance in the asset account Supplies is based on supplies purchased. This asset balance is overstated; the related expense account, Supplies Expense, is understated because the cost of supplies used has not been recognized. Thus, the adjusting entry for prepayments will decrease a statement of financial position account and increase a statement of comprehensive income account. Illustration C.7 shows the effects of adjusting entries for prepayments.

ILLUSTRATION C.7 **Adjusting Entries for Prepayments**

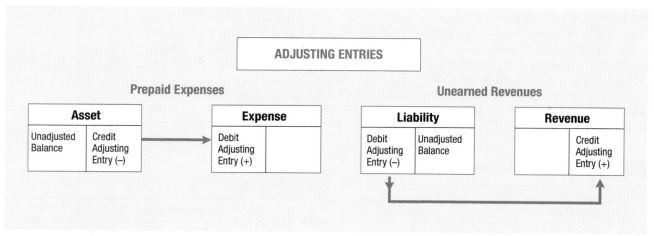

Prepaid Expenses

As shown in Illustration C.6, expenses that have been paid in cash and recorded as assets before they are used or consumed are identified as **prepaid expenses**. When a cost is incurred, an asset account is debited to show the service or benefit that will be received in the future. Prepayments often occur for such things as insurance, supplies, advertising, and rent.

Prepaid expenses expire either with the passage of time (such as rent and insurance) or by being used and consumed (such as supplies). The expiration of these costs does not require an entry each day, which would be unnecessary and impractical. Instead, it is customary to postpone the recognition of such cost expirations until financial statements are prepared. At each statement date, adjusting entries are made to record the expenses that apply to the current accounting period and to show the remaining unexpired costs in the asset accounts.

Before adjustment, assets are overstated and expenses are understated. **Thus, the prepaid expense adjusting entry results in a debit to an expense account and a credit to an asset account**.

Two common types of prepaid items are insurance and depreciation/amortization (where, for example, property, plant, and equipment are purchased and subsequently depreciated over time). The related adjusting entries are discussed next.

Insurance   There are many types of insurance. Most companies have fire and theft insurance on inventory and equipment, personal liability insurance for accidents suffered at company premises, and automobile insurance on company cars and trucks. The cost of insurance protection is the amount paid as insurance premiums. The term (duration) and coverage (what the company is insured against) are specified in the insurance policy. The minimum term is usually one year, but three- to five-year terms may be available and could result in lower annual premiums. Insurance premiums are normally charged to the asset account Prepaid Insurance when they are paid. At the financial statement date, it is necessary to debit Insurance Expense and credit Prepaid Insurance for the cost that has expired during the period, as shown in **Example C.2**.

Example C.2 | Adjusting Journal Entry, Insurance

Facts   On October 4, PAAI paid $6,000 for a one-year fire insurance policy. The coverage began as of October 1. The premium was charged to Prepaid Insurance when it was paid, and this account shows a balance of $6,000 in the October 31 trial balance. An analysis of the policy reveals that $500 of insurance expires each month ($6,000 ÷ 12).

Instructions   Prepare PAAI's adjusting entry for insurance expense.

Solution   The following adjusting entry is made:

	Oct. 31		
Insurance Expense		500	
Prepaid Insurance			500
(To record insurance expired)			

A	=	L	+	SE
−500				−500

Cash flows: No effect

In Example C.2, PAAI's asset Prepaid Insurance would now show a balance of $5,500, which represents the unexpired cost of the 11 months of remaining coverage. At the same time, the balance in Insurance Expense is equal to the insurance cost that has expired in October. **If this adjustment is not made, October expenses will be understated by $500 and net income overstated by $500. Moreover, both assets and shareholders' equity will also be overstated by $500 on the October 31 statement of financial position.**

Depreciation/Amortization   Companies typically own a variety of productive facilities such as buildings, equipment, and motor vehicles. These assets provide a service for many years. The term of service is commonly referred to as the asset's **useful life**. Because an asset such as a building is expected to provide service for many years, it is recorded as an asset, rather than an expense, in the year it is acquired. Such assets are recorded at cost, as required by the historical cost principle. See **Underlying Concept C.1**.

In order to match the cost of the asset with the revenues that it is generating, a portion of the cost of a long-lived asset should be reported as an expense during each period of the asset's useful life. **Depreciation/amortization** is the process of **allocating the cost of an asset** to expense over its useful life in a rational and systematic manner.

From an accounting standpoint, when productive facilities are acquired, the transaction can be viewed as a long-term prepayment for services. Periodic adjusting entries for depreciation are therefore needed for the same reasons described earlier for other prepaid expenses. In other words, it is necessary to recognize the cost that has expired during the period (the expense) and to report the unexpired cost at the end of the period (the asset).

In determining a productive facility's useful life, there are three main causes of depreciation:

1. Actual use
2. Deterioration due to the elements
3. Obsolescence

When an entity acquires an asset, it cannot know the effects of these factors with certainty, so they must instead be estimated. Thus, depreciation is an estimate rather than an

> **Underlying Concept C.1**
>
> The historical cost principle requires that depreciable assets be recorded at cost. Matching allows this cost to be allocated to periods of use.

exact measurement of the cost that has expired. A common procedure in calculating depreciation expense is to divide the asset's cost by its useful life. For example, if the cost is $10,000 and the useful life is expected to be 10 years, annual depreciation is $1,000. **Example C.3** illustrates this.

Example C.3 | Adjusting Journal Entry, Depreciation

Facts   For PAAI, depreciation on the equipment is estimated at $4,800 a year (cost of $50,000 less a residual value of $2,000 divided by a useful life of 10 years), or $400 per month.

Instructions   Prepare PAAI's adjusting entry for depreciation expense for October.

Solution   Depreciation for October is recognized by the following adjusting entry:

Oct. 31

Depreciation Expense	400	
Accumulated Depreciation—Equipment		400
(To record monthly depreciation)		

A	=	L	+	SE
−400				−400

Cash flows: No effect

After the adjusting entry illustrated in Example C.3 is posted, the balance in the relevant accumulated depreciation account will increase by $400 each month. Therefore, after journalizing and posting the adjusting entry at November 30, the balance in the accumulated depreciation account will then be $800.

Accumulated Depreciation—Equipment is a contra asset account. A **contra asset account** is an account that is offset against an asset account on the statement of financial position. In the case of accumulated depreciation, this account is offset against Equipment on the statement of financial position and its normal balance is therefore a credit. This account is used instead of crediting Equipment so that the equipment's original cost and the total cost that has expired to date can both be disclosed. In the statement of financial position, Accumulated Depreciation—Equipment is deducted from the related asset account (which is normally a debit), as shown below.

Equipment	$50,000
Less: Accumulated depreciation—equipment	400
	$49,600

The difference between any depreciable asset's cost and its related accumulated depreciation is known as its book value. As shown above, the equipment's book value, or **carrying amount**, at the statement of financial position date is $49,600. It is important to realize that the asset's **book value and market value are generally two different values**.

Note also that depreciation expense identifies that portion of the asset's cost that has expired in October. What would happen if PAAI did not make an adjusting entry for this? As in the case of other prepaid asset adjustments, **if this adjusting entry is not made, then total shareholders' equity and net income will be overstated and the expense will be understated**.

If additional equipment is involved, such as delivery equipment or furniture, or if the company has buildings, depreciation expense is recorded on each of these items. Related accumulated depreciation accounts also are created. These accumulated depreciation accounts would be described in the ledger as follows: Accumulated Depreciation—Vehicles, Accumulated Depreciation—Furniture, and Accumulated Depreciation—Buildings.

Unearned Revenues

As shown in Illustration C.6, revenues that have been received in cash and recorded as liabilities before they are earned are called **unearned revenues**. Items such as rent, magazine subscriptions, and customer deposits for further service may result in unearned revenues. See **What Do the Numbers Mean? C.1**.

What Do the Numbers Mean? C.1

Companies that receive revenue before providing a service include sports teams, live theatres, and transportation companies. Airlines such as **Air Canada** and **WestJet** treat receipts from the sale of tickets as unearned revenue until the flight service is provided. (For example, "Advance Ticket Sales" totalled $695.1 million on WestJet's December 31, 2017 financial statements.) The growth in advance ticket sales of $68.5 million (or 10.9% as compared with

2016) was part of the reason WestJet's cash flow from operating activities totalled over $1.0 billion in 2017. In fact, one of the ratios that WestJet tracks is cash and cash equivalents on hand divided by advance ticket sales, which was 1.65 in 2017 (as compared with 2.43 in 2016). This is a key indicator that the company continues to have sufficient cash on hand to meet its liabilities as they come due.

Tuition fees received by a university before the start of a semester are also considered unearned revenue. Unearned revenues are the opposite of prepaid expenses. Indeed, unearned revenue on the books of one company is likely to be a prepayment on the books of the company that has made the advance payment. For example, if identical accounting periods are assumed, a landlord will have unearned rent revenue when a tenant has prepaid rent.

When the payment is received for services that will be provided in a future accounting period, an unearned revenue account (a liability) should be credited to recognize the obligation that exists. Unearned revenues are later earned by performing the service for the customer (which discharges the liability). During the accounting period, it may not be practical to make an entry each day that the revenue is earned. In such cases, the recognition of earned revenue is delayed until the adjustment process. At that time, an adjusting entry is then made to record the revenue that has been earned and to show the liability that remains. Typically, liabilities are overstated and revenues are understated prior to adjusting unearned revenue. Thus, the adjusting entry for unearned revenues results in a debit (decrease) to a liability account and a credit (increase) to a revenue account. Let's look at an example of unearned revenues for PAAI in **Example C.4**.

Example C.4 | Adjusting Journal Entry, Unearned Revenues

Facts   PAAI received $12,000 on October 2 from R. Knox for advertising services that PAAI expected to complete by December 31. The payment was credited to Unearned Revenue, and this account shows a balance of $12,000 in the October 31 trial balance.

Instructions   Prepare PAAI's adjusting entry if PAAI determines that $4,000 of the advertising services provided to R. Knox have been earned in October.

Solution   PAAI would make the following adjusting entry:

Oct. 31

Unearned Revenue	4,000	
Service Revenue		4,000
(To record revenue for services provided)		

A	=	L	+	SE
		−4000		+4000

Cash flows: No effect

After the adjusting entry from Example C.4 is posted, the Unearned Revenue account now shows a balance of $8,000, which represents the remaining advertising services that PAAI expects to perform in the future. At the same time, Service Revenue shows total revenue earned in October of $104,000. **If this adjustment is not made, revenues and net income will be understated by $4,000 in the statement of comprehensive income. Moreover, liabilities will be overstated and shareholders' equity will be understated by $4,000 on the October 31 statement of financial position.**

Alternative Method for Adjusting Prepayments

So far, the assumption has been that an asset (such as prepaid rent) or liability (such as unearned revenue) is recorded when the company initially pays or receives the cash. An alternative treatment is to record the initial entry through the related income statement account and adjust it later. **Example C.5** illustrates this type of adjusting entry for Prepaid Insurance. The same type of adjustment could be done for other prepayments, such as supplies and rent.

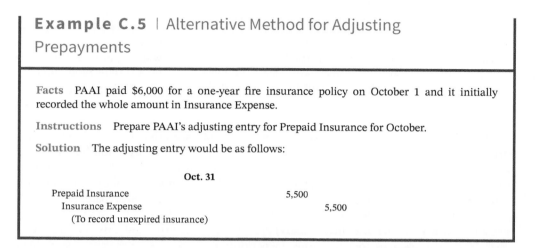

Example C.5 | Alternative Method for Adjusting Prepayments

Facts   PAAI paid $6,000 for a one-year fire insurance policy on October 1 and it initially recorded the whole amount in Insurance Expense.

Instructions   Prepare PAAI's adjusting entry for Prepaid Insurance for October.

Solution   The adjusting entry would be as follows:

Oct. 31

Prepaid Insurance	5,500	
Insurance Expense		5,500
(To record unexpired insurance)		

A	=	L	+	SE
+5,500				+5,500

Cash flows: No effect

Adjusting Entries for Accruals

Another category of adjusting entries is **accruals**. Adjusting entries for accruals are needed to record revenues earned and expenses incurred in the current accounting period that have not been recognized through daily entries. If an accrual adjustment is needed, the revenue account (and the related asset account) and/or the expense account (and the related liability account) are understated. Thus, adjusting entries for accruals will increase both a statement of financial position and a statement of comprehensive income account. Adjusting entries for accruals are shown in **Illustration C.8**.

ILLUSTRATION C.8   **Adjusting Entries for Accruals**

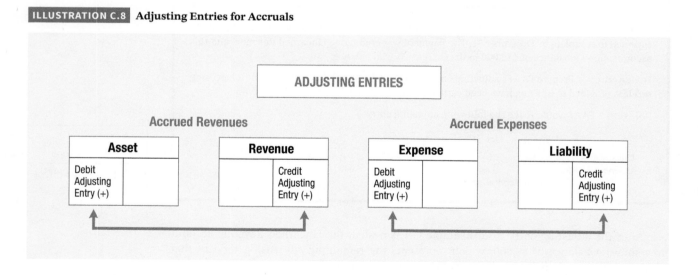

Accrued Revenues

As shown in Illustration C.6, revenues that have been **earned but not yet received** in cash or recorded at the statement date are **accrued revenues**. There are two common types of accrued revenues.

1. Accrued revenues may **accumulate (accrue) with the passing of time**, as in the case of interest income and rent revenue. These types of accrued revenues are unrecorded because earning interest and rent does not involve daily transactions.

2. Accrued revenues may also result from **services that have been performed but neither billed nor collected**, as in the case of commissions and fees. These types of accrued revenues may be unrecorded because only a portion of the total service has been provided.

An adjusting entry is required to show the receivable that exists at the statement of financial position date and to record the revenue that has been earned during the period. Before adjustment, both assets and revenues are understated. Accordingly, an adjusting entry for accrued revenues results in a debit (increase) to an asset account and a credit (increase) to a revenue account. Let's look at an example of accrued revenues for PAAI in Example C.6.

Example C.6 | Adjusting Journal Entry, Accrued Revenues

Facts   In October, PAAI earned $2,000 for advertising services that were not billed to clients before October 31. Because these services have not yet been billed, they have not been recorded in any way.

Instructions   Prepare PAAI's adjusting entry to accrue revenues for advertising services.

Solution   The adjusting entry would be as follows:

Oct. 31

Accounts Receivable	2,000	
Service Revenue		2,000
(To record revenue for services provided)		

A	=	L	+	SE
+2,000				+2,000

Cash flows: No effect

After the adjusting entry from Example C.6 is posted, the asset Accounts Receivable shows that $74,000 is owed by clients at the statement of financial position date. The balance of $106,000 in Service Revenue is the total revenue earned during the period ($100,000 + $4,000 + $2,000). If the adjusting entry is not made, assets and shareholders' equity on the statement of financial position, and revenues and net income on the statement of comprehensive income, will all be understated.

Accrued Expenses

As indicated in Illustration C.6, expenses that have been incurred but not yet paid or recorded at the statement date are recorded as **accrued expenses**. See Underlying Concept C.2. Examples of possible accrued expenses are interest, rent, taxes, and salaries. Accrued expenses result from the same causes as accrued revenues. In fact, an accrued expense on the books of one company may be accrued revenue for another company. For example, the $2,000 accrual of service revenue by PAAI is an accrued expense to the client that received the service.

Adjustments for accrued expenses are needed to record the obligations that exist at the statement of financial position date and to recognize the expenses that apply to the current accounting period. Before adjustment, both liabilities and expenses are understated. Therefore, the adjusting entry for accrued expenses results in a debit (increase) to an expense account and a credit (increase) to a liability account. Example C.7 illustrates PAAI's accrued interest expense.

> **Underlying Concept C.2**
>
> Accrual accounting requires that expenses be accrued when they are incurred.

Example C.7 | Adjusting Journal Entry, Accrual of Interest Expense

Facts   PAAI signed a three-month note payable for $50,000 on October 1. The note requires interest at an annual rate of 6%. The interest to be paid is determined by three factors:

1. The note's face value
2. The interest rate, which is always expressed as an annual rate
3. The length of time the note is outstanding

Instructions

a. How much interest would be due when the note payable matures? Show details of the calculation.

b. Provide the related journal entry to accrue interest for the month of October.

Solution

a. The total interest due on the $50,000 note at its due date three months later would be $750 ($50,000 × 6% × $^3/_{12}$), or $250 for one month. The formula for calculating interest and how it applies to PAAI for the month of October is shown below.

$$\begin{array}{c} \text{Face Value} \\ \text{of Note} \end{array} \times \begin{array}{c} \text{Annual} \\ \text{Interest} \\ \text{Rate} \end{array} \times \begin{array}{c} \text{Time} \\ \text{in Terms of} \\ \text{One Year} \end{array} = \text{Interest}$$

$$\$50,000 \quad \times \quad 6\% \quad \times \quad \frac{1}{12} \quad = \quad \$250$$

Note that the time period is expressed as a fraction of a year.

b. The accrued expense adjusting entry at October 31 is as follows:

	Oct. 31		
Interest Expense		250	
Interest Payable			250
(To record interest on notes payable)			

A	=	L	+	SE
		+250		−250

Cash flows: No effect

The Interest Expense in Example C.7 shows the interest charges that apply to the month of October. The amount of interest owed at the statement date is shown in Interest Payable. It will not be paid until the note comes due at the end of three months. The Interest Payable account is used instead of crediting Notes Payable in order to disclose the two types of obligations (interest and principal) in the accounts and statements. **If this adjusting entry is not made, liabilities and interest expense will be understated, and net income and shareholders' equity will be overstated.**

Accrued Salaries Some types of expenses, such as employee salaries and commissions, are paid for after the services have been performed. **Examples C.8** and **C.9** illustrate the adjusting entries for PAAI's accrued salaries at the end of October, and the related payment in November.

Example C.8 | Adjusting Journal Entry, Accrual of Salaries

Facts At PAAI, salaries were last paid on October 22; the next payment of salaries will not occur until November 4. Six working days remain in October (October 23, 26, 27, 28, 29, and 30).

At October 31, the salaries for these days represent an accrued expense and a related liability to PAAI. The employees receive total salaries of $10,000 for a five-day workweek, or $2,000 per day.

Instructions Prepare the adjusting entry for PAAI's accrued salaries at October 31.

Solution PAAI's accrued salaries are $12,000 ($2,000 × 6), and the adjusting entry is:

	Oct. 31		
Salaries and Wages Expense		12,000	
Salaries and Wages Payable			12,000
(To record accrued salaries)			

A	=	L	+	SE
		+12,000		−12,000

Cash flows: No effect

After this adjustment, the balance in Salaries and Wages Expense of $44,000 (22 days × $2,000) is the actual salary expense for October. The balance in Salaries and Wages Payable of $12,000 is the amount of liability for salaries owed as at October 31. **If the $12,000 adjustment for salaries is not recorded, PAAI's expenses will be understated by $12,000, and its liabilities will be understated by $12,000.**

Example C.9 | Journal Entry, Payment of Accrued Salaries

Facts   At PAAI, salaries are payable every two weeks, on every second Thursday. Consequently, continuing with Example C.8, assume that the next payday is November 5, when total salaries of $20,000 will again be paid.

Instructions   Prepare the journal entry for payment of PAAI's accrued salaries at PAAI's next payday, November 5.

Solution   The payment on November 5 consists of $12,000 of salaries and wages payable at October 31 plus $8,000 of salaries and wages expense for November (4 working days in November × $2,000). Therefore, PAAI makes the following entry:

Nov. 5

Salaries and Wages Payable	12,000	
Salaries and Wages Expense	8,000	
Cash		20,000
(To record November 5 payroll)		

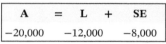

A	=	L	+	SE
−20,000		−12,000		−8,000

Cash flows: ▼ 20,000 outflow

The journal entry shown in Example C.9 eliminates the liability for Salaries and Wages Payable that was recorded in the October 31 adjusting entry and records the proper amount of Salaries and Wages Expense for the period November 1 to November 5.

Adjusting Entries for Estimated Items

The third category of adjusting entries is **estimated items**. Adjusting entries for estimated items are required in order to record expenses, gains, and losses incurred in the current accounting period that have not been recognized through daily entries. If an estimated adjustment is needed for anticipated bad debts, the expense account is understated. So, the adjusting entry will often increase both a contra account on the statement of financial position and an income statement account. Similarly, an adjusting entry for fair value through net income investments for an unrealized gain would increase an investment account and affect unrealized gains on the statement of comprehensive income. Adjusting entries for estimated items are shown in **Illustration C.9**.

Bad Debts

An estimate of bad debts should be recorded as an expense of the period in which the revenue was earned. It should not be recorded in the period when the accounts or notes are written off. This is done so that expenses are properly matched with revenues. Estimated uncollectible receivables should be recognized so that the receivable balance shows its proper value. Proper valuation therefore require an adjusting entry and leads to matching of revenues and expenses.

At the end of each period, an estimate is made of the amount of current period revenue on account that will later be uncollectible as illustrated in **Example C.10**. The estimate is based on the amount of bad debts experienced in past years, general economic conditions, how long the receivables are past due, and other factors that indicate the likelihood of collection. Often the

ILLUSTRATION C.9
Adjusting Entries for Estimated Items

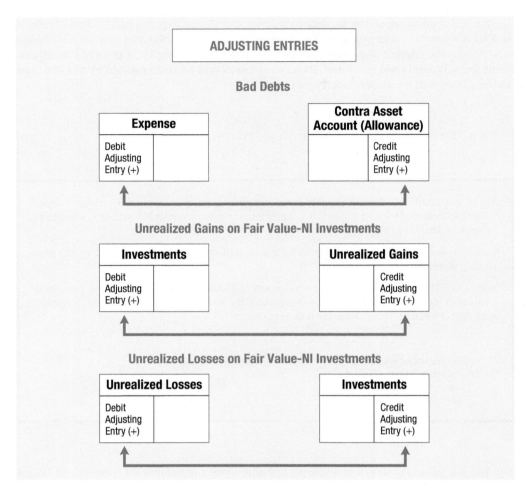

ILLUSTRATION C.9
Adjusting Entries for Estimated Items

estimate is expressed as a percentage of revenue each month, followed by a detailed analysis at the end of the fiscal year. As we see in Chapter 7, the Allowance for Doubtful Accounts contra account may also be calculated by applying different percentages to the aged trade accounts receivable and trade notes receivable balances at the end of the period.

Example C.10 | Adjusting Journal Entry, Bad Debts

Facts Assume that experience shows that a reasonable estimate for bad debt expense for the month is $1,600.

Instructions Prepare the adjusting entry for bad debts.

Solution

Oct. 31

Bad Debt Expense	1,600	
Allowance for Doubtful Accounts		1,600
(To record monthly bad debt expense)		

A	=	L	+	SE
−1,600				−1,600

Cash flows: No effect

Unrealized Holding Gains or Losses (FV-NI and FV-OCI)

An unrealized gain or loss must be recorded in the statement of comprehensive income at the end of the reporting period. This is done to adjust FV-NI and FV-OCI investments to their fair values.

At the end of each period, an estimate is made of the fair value of investments held in the fair value through net income (FV-NI) and fair value through other comprehensive income (FV-OCI) categories. FV-NI investments could include equity investments or investments in debt securities.[5] See **Example C.11**.

Example C.11 | Adjusting Journal Entries, FV-NI and FV-OCI Investments

Facts   Assume that $10,000 of common shares were acquired as an equity investment on October 1, 2020. On October 31, 2020, the shares' fair value had increased to $11,500.

Instructions   Prepare the adjusting entry, assuming that the investments are classified as FV-NI. How would your journal entry change if the investment was considered fair value-OCI?

Solution   The adjusting entry, if the investments are classified as FV-NI, would be:

	Oct. 31		
FV-NI Investments		1,500	
Unrealized Gain or Loss			1,500
(To record holding gain on FV-NI investments)			

A	=	L	+	SE
+1,500				+1,500

Cash flows: No effect

Alternatively, if the investment was being held in the fair value-OCI category, the adjusting entry would be as follows:

	Oct. 31		
FV-OCI Investments		1,500	
Unrealized Gain or Loss-OCI			1,500
(To record holding gain on FV-OCI investments)			

A	=	L	+	SE
+1,500				+1,500

Cash flows: No effect

The impact on the basic accounting equation and cash flows for the FV-OCI journal entry shown in the second part of Example C.11 would be the same as in the FV-NI part.

Financial Statements and Ownership Structure

LEARNING OBJECTIVE 4

Explain how the type of ownership structure affects the financial statements.

After the adjusting entries have been prepared and posted, an adjusted trial balance is prepared. The adjusted trial balance greatly helps when preparing the financial statements. Where are the various financial statement elements reported?

1. Assets and liabilities are reported on the statement of financial position, often grouped into current and non-current classifications.
2. Common shares, retained earnings, and accumulated other comprehensive income are reported in the shareholders' equity section of the statement of financial position.
3. Dividends are reported on the statement of changes in shareholders' equity (IFRS) or the statement of retained earnings (ASPE).

---

[5]Fair value-OCI investments are not permitted under ASPE. All fair value investments would typically be treated as FV-NI investments under ASPE. See Chapter 9 for a full discussion of accounting for investments.

4. Revenues and expenses are reported on the statement of income (ASPE) or the statement of comprehensive income (IFRS). Revenues and expenses are eventually transferred to retained earnings at the end of the period while other comprehensive income is transferred to **accumulated other comprehensive income**.[6]

The relationships within shareholders' equity are shown in **Illustration C.10**.

ILLUSTRATION C.10   **Financial Statements and Shareholders' Equity Classifications**

The type of ownership structure that a business enterprise uses determines the types of accounts that are part of the equity section or that affect it. In a **corporation, Common Shares, Contributed Surplus, Dividends, Retained Earnings**, and **Accumulated Other Comprehensive Income** are commonly used accounts.[7] In a **proprietorship** or **partnership**, an **Owners' Capital** account is used to indicate the investment in the company by the owner(s). An **Owners' Drawings** or withdrawal account may be used to indicate withdrawals by the partners. These two accounts are grouped or netted under **Owners' Equity**. We focus on the corporate organization structure in this text. Companies may use a work sheet to facilitate the preparation of financial statements. We summarize the use of a work sheet for the preparation of corporate financial statements later in this appendix.

The Closing Process

LEARNING OBJECTIVE 5

Prepare closing entries and consider other matters relating to the closing process.

---

[6]Accumulated Other Comprehensive Income is a statement of financial position (SFP) account that is the total of all past charges and credits to OCI to the SFP date. It is similar to the Retained Earnings account.

[7]Corporations are incorporated under a government act such as the Canada Business Corporations Act. The main reason for incorporation is to limit the liability for the owners if the corporation gets sued or goes bankrupt. When companies are incorporated, shares are issued to owners and the company becomes a separate legal entity (that is, it is distinct from its owners).

The **closing process** reduces the balances of temporary accounts to zero in order to prepare the accounts for the next period's transactions. In the closing process, all of the revenue and expense account balances (the statement of comprehensive income items) are transferred to a clearing account called **Income Summary**, which is used only at year end. The net result of this matching of revenues and expenses is the net income or net loss for the period. This is then transferred to a shareholders' or owners' equity account. For a corporation, this would be Retained Earnings or, for OCI items, an Accumulated Other Comprehensive Income (AOCI) account. For proprietorships and partnerships, this would normally be the capital accounts or owners' equity accounts.

Preparing Closing Entries

Closing entries are journal entries that close the temporary accounts in order to prepare for the start of a new financial reporting period. All closing entries are posted to the appropriate general ledger accounts.

For example, assume that Collegiate Apparel Shop Inc. (CASI) has three revenue accounts, after adjustments, at year end. CASI would close these accounts by making the following closing journal entry:

Sales Revenue	280,000	
Rent Revenue	27,000	
Interest Income	5,000	
Income Summary		312,000
(To close revenue accounts to Income Summary)		

A	=	L	+	SE
				−312,000
				+312,000

Cash flows: No effect

Similarly, CASI's expense accounts would be closed and the balances transferred through the following closing journal entry:

Income Summary	289,000	
Cost of Goods Sold		206,000
Selling Expenses		25,000
Administrative Expenses		40,600
Interest Expense		4,400
Income Tax Expense		13,000
(To close expense accounts to Income Summary)		

A	=	L	+	SE
				−289,000
				+289,000

Cash flows: No effect

The Income Summary account now has a credit balance of $23,000, which is net income. **The net income is then transferred to retained earnings by closing the Income Summary account to Retained Earnings,** as follows:

Income Summary	23,000	
Retained Earnings		23,000
(To close Income Summary to Retained Earnings)		

A	=	L	+	SE
				−23,000
				+23,000

Cash flows: No effect

IFRS Any items posted to Other Comprehensive Income would similarly be closed out to Accumulated Other Comprehensive Income, which acts like a second retained earnings account for certain gains and losses booked to Other Comprehensive Income. Assuming CASI had holding gains on Fair Value through Other Comprehensive Income investments of $12,000, the holding gain would be closed to Accumulated Other Comprehensive Income as follows:

Unrealized Gain or Loss—OCI	12,000	
Accumulated Other Comprehensive Income		12,000
(To close unrealized gains on FV-OCI investments to Accumulated Other Comprehensive Income)		

A	=	L	+	SE
				−12,000
				+12,000

Cash flows: No effect

Assuming that dividends of $7,000 were declared and distributed during the year, the Dividends account is closed directly to Retained Earnings, as follows:

Retained Earnings	7,000	
Dividends		7,000
(To close Dividends to Retained Earnings)		

A	=	L	+	SE
				−7,000
				+7,000

Cash flows: No effect

After the closing process is completed, each statement of comprehensive income account has a zero balance and is ready to be used in the next accounting period.

Inventory and Cost of Goods Sold

The closing procedures we just showed assume that an entity uses a perpetual inventory system. With a perpetual inventory system, purchases and sales are recorded directly in the Inventory account as they occur. Therefore, the balance in Inventory should represent the ending inventory amount, and no adjusting entries are needed to update the inventory account. To be sure that the inventory amount is accurate, a **physical count** of the items in the inventory is generally done each year.

In the perpetual inventory system, since all purchases are debited directly to the Inventory account, there is no separate Purchases account. However, a Cost of Goods Sold account is used to accumulate what is issued from inventory. That is, when inventory items are sold, the cost of inventory being sold is credited to Inventory and debited to Cost of Goods Sold.

What about entities using a periodic inventory system? In that case, a Purchases account is used, and the Inventory account is unchanged during the period. The Inventory account therefore represents the beginning inventory amount throughout the period. At the end of the accounting period, the Inventory account must be adjusted by **closing out the beginning inventory amount and recording the ending inventory amount**. The company determines ending inventory by physically counting the items on hand and valuing them at cost or at the lower of cost and net realizable value. Under the periodic inventory system, cost of goods sold is therefore determined by adding the beginning inventory to net purchases and deducting the ending inventory.

To illustrate how cost of goods sold is calculated with a periodic inventory system, let's assume that Collegiate Apparel Shop Inc. has a beginning inventory of $30,000, purchases of $200,000, freight in of $6,000, purchase returns and allowances of $1,000, purchase discounts of $3,000, and ending inventory of $26,000. CASI would close out each of these accounts to Cost of Goods Sold (as illustrated in the end-of-period entries in Chapter 8) and then would close the Cost of Goods Sold account to the Income Summary account.

Post-Closing Trial Balance

We already mentioned that a trial balance is taken after the period's regular transactions have been entered and that a second trial balance (the adjusted trial balance) is taken after the adjusting entries have been posted. A third trial balance may be taken after posting the closing entries. The trial balance after closing, often called the post-closing trial balance, shows that equal debits and credits have been posted to the Income Summary account. The post-closing trial balance consists only of asset, liability, and shareholders' equity accounts (that is, the permanent accounts).

Reversing Entries

After the financial statements have been prepared and the books have been closed, it is often helpful to reverse some of the adjusting entries before recording the next period's regular transactions. Such entries are called reversing entries. A reversing entry is made at the beginning of the next accounting period and is the exact opposite of the related adjusting entry made in the previous period. The recording of reversing entries is an optional step in the accounting cycle that may be done at the beginning of the next accounting period. The purpose of reversing entries is to make it easier to record transactions in the next accounting period. The use of reversing entries does not change the amounts reported in the previous period's financial statements.

Reversing entries are usually used for reversing two types of adjusting entries: accrued revenues and accrued expenses. They are also sometimes used for prepayments. See **Example C.12**.

Example C.12 | Reversing Entries

Facts Assume that Your Company (YC) is considering using reversing entries for accrued expenses, and provides you with following sample transaction and adjustment data:

1. Period to October 22 (initial salary entries): $400,000 of salaries and wages expense has been incurred from the start of the year to Thursday, October 22, and was fully paid.

2. October 31 (adjusting entry): $12,000 of salaries and wages expense is incurred between October 23 and October 31. This will be paid in the November 5 payroll.

3. November 5 (subsequent salary entry): $20,000 of salaries and wages expense is paid. Of this amount, $12,000 applies to accrued salaries and wages payable at October 31 and $8,000 was incurred between November 1 and November 5.

Instructions Compare and contrast the journal entries that YC would make regarding its salaries and wages accounts if it used reversing entries vs. not using reversing entries.

Solution YC would make the following entries for its salaries and wages accounts, depending whether it used or did not use reversing entries. YC's year-end is October 31.

Reversing Entries Not Used			Reversing Entries Used		
Adjusting Entry			**Adjusting Entry**		
Oct. 31 Salaries and Wages			Oct. 31 Salaries and Wages		
Expense	12,000		Expense	12,000	
Salaries and			Salaries and		
Wages Payable		12,000	Wages Payable		12,000
Closing Entry			**Closing Entry**		
Oct. 31 Income Summary	412,000		Oct. 31 Income Summary	412,000	
Salaries and			Salaries and		
Wages Expense		412,000	Wages Expense		412,000
Reversing Entry			**Reversing Entry**		
Nov. 1 No entry is made.			Nov. 1 Salaries and Wages		
			Payable	12,000	
			Salaries and		
			Wages Expense		12,000
Subsequent Salary Entry			**Subsequent Salary Entry**		
Nov. 5 Salaries and Wages			Nov. 5 Salaries and Wages		
Payable	12,000		Expense	20,000	
Salaries and Wages			Cash		20,000
Expense	8,000				
Cash		20,000			

Although reversing entries reduce potential errors and are therefore often used, they do not have to be used. Many accountants avoid them entirely. Reversing entries add an extra step to the bookkeeping process. Also, there may be instances where it does not make sense to use them. As an example, assume a company with a December 31 year end has accrued six months' worth of interest on a bond that pays interest annually (June 30 interest payment date) at year end. If the company releases financial information monthly, it would not make sense to reverse the entry in January because this would show a credit balance when the monthly reports are prepared.

We have now completed our summary of the steps in the accounting cycle. Refer back to Illustration C.4 to ensure that you are comfortable with the entire accounting cycle, including preparing journal entries, adjusting entries, and financial statements.

Using a Work Sheet

> **LEARNING OBJECTIVE 6**
>
> Prepare a 10-column work sheet and financial statements.

In Illustration C.4, we discuss the accounting cycle, including the preparation of a trial balance, adjustments, and financial statements. Companies will often use a **work sheet** to make the end-of-period (monthly, quarterly, or annual) accounting and reporting process easier. A work sheet is a spreadsheet that managers use to adjust the account balances and prepare financial statements. Using a work sheet helps accountants prepare financial statements on a timelier basis. They do not need to delay preparing the financial statements until the adjusting and closing entries are journalized and posted. The **10-column work sheet** shown later in this appendix (Illustration C.11) has columns for the first trial balance, adjustments, an adjusted trial balance, the statement of comprehensive income, and the statement of financial position.

The work sheet does not replace the financial statements. Instead, it is an informal tool for accumulating and sorting the information that is needed for the financial statements. Completing the work sheet makes it more certain that all of the details of the end-of-period accounting and statement preparation have been brought together properly. **Example C.13**

Example C.13 | Adjustments to Be Entered on Uptown Cabinet Corp.'s Work Sheet

Facts The following items are the adjusting entries that Uptown Cabinet Corp. plans to make before completing its work sheet and financial statements:

a. Equipment is amortized at the rate of 10% per year based on an original cost of $67,000.

b. Estimated bad debts are 0.25% of sales ($400,000).

c. Prepaid insurance of $360 expired during the year.

d. Interest of $800 is accrued on notes receivable as at December 31.

e. The Rent Expense account contains $500 of rent paid in advance, which is applicable to next year.

f. Property taxes of $2,000 are to be accrued to December 31.

g. The Fair Value through Other Comprehensive Income (FV-OCI) Investments account is based on the original cost of $12,000 of an equity investment acquired on July 1. On December 31, the fair value of the investment is $15,000. We will cover tax calculations for OCI items in Chapter 18. To simplify matters for this example, assume that unrealized changes in fair value for FV-OCI investments are non-taxable.

Instructions Prepare Uptown Cabinet Corp.'s adjusting journal entries.

Solution The adjusting entries required for Uptown Cabinet Corp.'s December 31, 2020 work sheet are as follows:

a. Depreciation Expense	6,700	
Accumulated Depreciation—Equipment		6,700
b. Bad Debt Expense	1,000	
Allowance for Doubtful Accounts		1,000
c. Insurance Expense	360	
Prepaid Insurance		360
d. Interest Receivable	800	
Interest Income		800
e. Prepaid Rent	500	
Rent Expense		500
f. Property Tax Expense	2,000	
Property Tax Payable		2,000
g. FV-OCI Investments	3,000	
Unrealized Gain or Loss-OCI		3,000

provides the adjusting entries that are combined with the trial balance information in a work sheet for Uptown Cabinet Corp., a retail company. The work sheet information is provided in Illustration C.11, and is used to complete the company's financial statements.

Uptown Cabinet Corp.'s adjusting entries are transferred to the work sheet's Adjustments columns and each adjustment can be named by letter. The accounts that are set up from the adjusting entries and that are not already in the trial balance are listed below the totals of the trial balance, as shown on the work sheet. The Adjustments columns are then totalled and balanced.

Work Sheet Columns

The 10-column work sheet for Uptown Cabinet Corp. is shown in Illustration C.11. Each of the columns is explained below.

Trial Balance Columns

Data for the trial balance are obtained from the ledger balances of Uptown Cabinet Corp. at December 31. The amount for Inventory, $40,000, is the year-end inventory amount under a perpetual inventory system.

Adjustments Columns

After entering all adjustment data on the work sheet, verify that the total amounts in each adjustment column are equal. Then extend the balances in all accounts to the adjusted trial balance columns.

Adjusted Trial Balance Columns

The adjusted trial balance shows the balance of all accounts after adjustment at the end of the accounting period. For example, the $2,000 shown opposite Allowance for Doubtful Accounts in the Trial Balance Cr. column is added to the $1,000 in the Adjustments Cr. column. The $3,000 total is then extended to the Adjusted Trial Balance Cr. column.

Similarly, the $900 debit opposite Prepaid Insurance is reduced by the $360 credit in the Adjustments column. The result, $540, is shown in the Adjusted Trial Balance Dr. column.

Statement of Comprehensive Income and Statement of Financial Position Columns

IFRS **ASPE**   All the debit items in the Adjusted Trial Balance columns are extended into the Statement of Comprehensive Income or Statement of Financial Position columns to the right. All the credit items are also extended. The next step is to total the Statement of Comprehensive Income columns; the amount that is needed in order to balance the debit and credit columns is the total of the pre-tax income or loss for the period and OCI. The income (before tax plus OCI) of $18,640 is shown in the Statement of Comprehensive Income Dr. column because revenues and gains exceeded expenses and losses by that amount. The Unrealized Gain or Loss-OCI would eventually be closed out to Accumulated Other Comprehensive Income, whereas all other revenue and expense accounts would be closed to Retained Earnings.

Completing the Work Sheet

Income Taxes

The federal and provincial income tax expense and related tax liability are calculated next (item [h] in Illustration C.11). We will assume that Uptown Cabinet Corp. uses a tax rate of 25% to arrive at $3,910. (To simplify the example, no allocation is made for deferred taxes on Other Comprehensive Income.) This adjustment is entered in the Statement of Comprehensive Income Dr. column as Income Tax Expense and in the Statement of Financial Position Cr. column as Income Tax Payable. The following adjusting journal entry is recorded on December 31, 2020, posted to the general ledger, and then entered on the work sheet:

(h) Income Tax Expense	3,910	
Income Tax Payable		3,910
(To record income tax expense on income before tax; 15,640 × 25% = 3,910)		

ILLUSTRATION C.11 **Work Sheet**

	A	B		C		D		E		F	
1				**UPTOWN CABINET CORP.** **Ten-Column Work Sheet** **For the Year Ended December 31, 2020**							
2											
	Accounts	**Trial Balance**		**Adjustments**		**Adjusted Trial Balance**		**Statement of Comprehensive Income**		**Statement of Financial Position**	
		Dr.	**Cr.**	**Dr.**	**Cr.**	**Dr.**	**Cr.**	**Dr.**	**Cr.**	**Dr.**	**Cr.**
3	Cash	1,200				1,200				1,200	
4	Notes receivable	16,000				16,000				16,000	
5	Accounts receivable	41,000				41,000				41,000	
6	Allowance for doubtful accounts		2,000		(b) 1,000		3,000				3,000
7	Inventory	40,000				40,000				40,000	
8	Prepaid insurance	900			(c) 360	540				540	
9	FV-OCI investments	12,000		(g) 3,000		15,000				15,000	
10	Equipment	67,000				67,000				67,000	
11	Accumulated depreciation—equipment		12,000		(a) 6,700		18,700				18,700
12	Notes payable		20,000				20,000				20,000
13	Accounts payable		13,500				13,500				13,500
14	Bonds payable (due June 30, 2025)		30,000				30,000				30,000
15	Common shares		50,000				50,000				50,000
16	Retained earnings, Jan. 1, 2020		26,200				26,200				26,200
17	Sales revenue		400,000				400,000		400,000		
18	Cost of goods sold	316,000				316,000		316,000			
19	Salaries and wages expense	20,000				20,000		20,000			
20	Advertising expense	2,200				2,200		2,200			
21	Selling expense	8,000				8,000		8,000			
22	Office expense	19,000				19,000		19,000			
23	Telephone & internet expense	600				600		600			
24	Rent expense	6,800			(e) 500	6,300		6,300			
25	Property tax expense	1,300		(f) 2,000		3,300		3,300			
26	Interest expense	1,700				1,700		1,700			
27	**Totals**	**553,700**	**553,700**								
28	Depreciation expense			(a) 6,700		6,700		6,700			
29	Bad debt expense			(b) 1,000		1,000		1,000			
30	Insurance expense			(c) 360		360		360			
31	Interest receivable			(d) 800		800				800	
32	Interest income				(d) 800		800		800		
33	Prepaid rent			(e) 500		500				500	
34	Property tax payable				(f) 2,000		2,000				2,000
35	Unrealized gain or loss-OCI				(g) 3,000		3,000		3,000		
36	**Totals**			**14,360**	**14,360**	567,200	567,200	385,160	403,800		
37	Income (before tax) plus OCI							18,640			
38	**Totals**							**403,800**	**403,800**		
39	Income (before tax) plus OCI								18,640		
40	Income tax expense			(h) 3,910		3,910		3,910			
41	Income tax payable				(h) 3,910		3,910				3,910
42	Net income plus OCI							14,730			14,730
43	**Totals**					**571,110**	**571,110**	**18,640**	**18,640**	**182,040**	**182,040**

Net Income

Next, the Statement of Comprehensive Income columns are balanced with the income taxes included. The $14,730 difference between the debit and credit columns in this illustration represents the total of net income plus OCI, or comprehensive income. The comprehensive income of $14,730 is entered in the Statement of Comprehensive Income Dr. column to achieve equality and in the Statement of Financial Position Cr. column.

Preparing Financial Statements from a Work Sheet

The work sheet gives the information needed to prepare financial statements without referring to the ledger or other records. In addition, the data have been sorted into appropriate columns, which makes it easier to prepare the statements. The financial statements being prepared using this work sheet are for a corporation that follows IFRS. The work sheet could also be used to prepare financial statements of a corporation following ASPE, or the financial statements for a sole proprietorship or partnership.

The financial statements prepared from the 10-column work sheet are as follows: **statement of comprehensive income for the year ended December 31, 2020 (Example C.14), statement of changes in shareholders' equity for the year ended December 31, 2020 (Example C.15), and statement of financial position as at December 31, 2020 (Example C.16).**

Example C.14 | Statement of Comprehensive Income

Facts   Uptown Cabinet Corp.'s financial data have been sorted into appropriate columns in the work sheet provided in Illustration C.11. Salaries and wages are assumed to relate to selling. Earnings per share is based on net income (not comprehensive income). (See also Chapter 4, where we covered earnings per share in more detail.) It is calculated assuming that 10,000 shares were outstanding for all of 2020.

Instructions   Prepare Uptown Cabinet Corp.'s statement of comprehensive income for the year ended December 31, 2020, using the work sheet information (see Column E).

Solution

Uptown Cabinet Corp.		
Statement of Comprehensive Income		
For the Year Ended December 31, 2020		
Sales revenue		$400,000
Cost of goods sold		316,000
Gross profit on sales		84,000
Selling expenses		
Salaries and wages expense	$20,000	
Advertising expense	2,200	
Selling expense	8,000	
Total selling expenses	30,200	
Administrative expenses		
Office expense	$19,000	
Telephone & internet expense	600	
Rent expense	6,300	
Property tax expense	3,300	
Depreciation expense	6,700	
Bad debt expense	1,000	
Insurance expense	360	
Total administrative expenses	37,260	
Total selling and administrative expenses		67,460

(continued)

Income from operations	16,540
Other revenues and gains	
Interest income	800
	17,340
Other expenses and losses	
Interest expense	1,700
Income before income taxes	15,640
Income tax expense	3,910
Net income	11,730
Other comprehensive income	3,000
Comprehensive income	$ 14,730
Earnings per share	$ 1.17

The statement of comprehensive income in Example C.14 is for a trading or merchandising (retailing) business. If Uptown were a manufacturing business, it would use three inventory accounts: raw materials, work-in-process, and finished goods in its SFP (below).

The net income earned by a corporation may be retained in the business or distributed to shareholders by paying dividends. In Example C.15, Uptown's net income is added to the balance of Retained Earnings on January 1, increasing the balance to $37,930 on December 31. Uptown did not declare any dividends during the year. A statement of changes in shareholders' equity is required for public companies such as Hudson's Bay Company (see Appendix B). Only a statement of changes in retained earnings is required for companies following ASPE.

Example C.15 | IFRS Statement of Changes in Shareholders' Equity—Uptown Cabinet Corp.

Facts   Uptown Cabinet Corp.'s financial data have been provided in the work sheet in Illustration C.11.

Instructions   Prepare Uptown Cabinet Corp.'s statement of changes in shareholders' equity for the year ended December 31, 2020, using the work sheet information.

Solution   The statement of changes in shareholders' equity includes changes in all equity accounts, including Accumulated Other Comprehensive Income, Retained Earnings, and Common Shares. We covered this type of statement in more detail in Chapter 4.

Uptown Cabinet Corp. Statement of Changes in Shareholders' Equity For the Year Ended December 31, 2020				
	Total	**Common Shares**	**Retained Earnings**	**Accumulated OCI**
Beginning, Jan. 1, 2020	$76,200	$50,000	$26,200	$ –0–
Net income for 2020	11,730		11,730	

Other
  comprehensive
  income
	3,000			3,000

Comprehensive income				
Ending balance, **Dec. 31, 2020**	**$90,930**	**$50,000**	**$37,930**	**$3,000**

The statement of financial position prepared from the 10-column work sheet in Example C.16 has new items, such as property tax payable, created by year-end adjusting entries. Interest receivable, prepaid insurance, and prepaid rent are included as current assets. These assets are considered current because they will be converted into cash or consumed in the ordinary routine of the business in a relatively short period. The amount of Allowance for Doubtful Accounts is deducted from the total of accounts, notes, and interest receivable because it is estimated that only $54,800 of the $57,800 will be collected in cash. If the allowance relates only to Accounts Receivable, it could be set up as a contra account for just Accounts Receivable. The Fair Value-OCI Investments are typically considered a non-current (or long-term) asset, which we discuss in Chapter 9.

In the property, plant, and equipment section, accumulated depreciation is deducted from the cost of the equipment; the difference in the two amounts is the book value or carrying amount of the equipment.

Example C.16 | Statement of Financial Position (SFP)

Facts Uptown Cabinet Corp.'s financial data have been sorted into appropriate columns in the work sheet in Illustration C.11.

Instructions Prepare Uptown's SFP as at December 31, 2020, using the work sheet information (see Column F) and discuss the proper financial statement presentation of property tax payable, bonds payable, and accumulated other comprehensive income (AOCI) on the SFP.

Solution The 2020 property tax payable is shown as a current liability because it is an obligation that is payable within a year. Other short-term accrued liabilities would also be shown as current liabilities.

The bonds payable, due in 2025, are non-current liabilities and are shown in a separate section. (Interest on the bonds was paid on December 31.) AOCI is included in the shareholders' equity section.

Uptown Cabinet Corp.'s statement of financial position for 2020 follows:

Uptown Cabinet Corp. **Statement of Financial Position** **As at December 31, 2020**			
Assets			
Current assets			
Cash			$ 1,200
Notes receivable	$16,000		
Accounts receivable	41,000		
Interest receivable	800	$57,800	
Less: Allowance for doubtful accounts		3,000	54,800
Inventory			40,000
Prepaid insurance			540
Prepaid rent			500
Total current assets			97,040
Non-current assets			
Long-term investments			
Fair value-OCI investments			15,000
Property, plant, and equipment			
Equipment		67,000	
Less: Accumulated depreciation		18,700	
Total property, plant, and equipment			48,300
Total assets			$160,340
Liabilities and Shareholders' Equity			
Current liabilities			
Notes payable			$ 20,000
Accounts payable			13,500
Property tax payable			2,000
Income tax payable			3,910
Total current liabilities			39,410

(continued)

Non-current liabilities		
Bonds payable, due June 30, 2025		30,000
Total liabilities		69,410
Shareholders' equity		
Common shares, issued and outstanding,		
10,000 shares	$50,000	
Retained earnings	37,930	
Accumulated other comprehensive income	3,000	
Total shareholders' equity		90,930
Total liabilities and shareholders' equity		$160,340

Review and Practice

Summary of Learning Objectives

1. Understand basic accounting terminology, double-entry rules, and the accounting equation.

It is important to understand the following terms: (1) event, (2) transaction, (3) account, (4) permanent and temporary accounts, (5) ledger, (6) journal, (7) posting, (8) trial balance, (9) adjusting entries, (10) financial statements, (11) closing entries, and (12) reversing entries.

The left side of any account is the debit side; the right side is the credit side. All asset and expense accounts are increased on the left or debit side and decreased on the right or credit side. Conversely, all liability and revenue accounts are increased on the right or credit side and decreased on the left or debit side. Shareholders' equity accounts Common Shares and Retained Earnings are increased on the credit side, whereas the shareholders' equity Dividends account is increased on the debit side as dividends are declared.

In a double-entry accounting system, for every debit there must be a credit, and vice versa. This leads us to the basic accounting equation: Assets = Liabilities + Shareholders' Equity. The effect of individual transactions on the statement of financial position can be explained using the basic accounting equation. The shareholders' equity portion of the equation can also be expanded to illustrate the effect of transactions on components of equity such as common shares and retained earnings. Whenever a transaction occurs, the elements of the equation change, but the equality of the two sides of the equation remains unaffected.

2. Identify the steps in the accounting cycle and the steps in the recording process.

The basic steps in the accounting cycle are (1) identification and measurement of transactions and other events, (2) journalizing, (3) posting, (4) unadjusted trial balance preparation, (5) adjustments, (6) adjusted trial balance, (7) statement preparation, and (8) closing. The first three steps in the accounting cycle form the basis of the recording process used by most medium-sized companies on a daily basis. The simplest journal form is a chronological listing of transactions and events that are expressed as debits and credits to particular accounts. The items entered in a general journal must then be transferred (posted) to the general ledger.

To help prepare financial statements, an unadjusted trial balance should be prepared at the end of a specific period (usually a month, quarter, or year) after the entries have been recorded in the journals and posted to the general ledger.

3. Explain the reasons for, and prepare, adjusting entries.

Adjustments achieve an accurate statement of the end-of-the-period balances in assets, liabilities, and shareholders' equity accounts and also achieve a proper matching of expenses and revenues, to determine the correct net income for the current period. When preparing adjusting journal entries, you must first determine how the original transaction was recorded. For example, was an asset created earlier in the fiscal year (such as prepaid rent) when the initial payment was made? If so, an adjustment for the related expense is required. Alternatively, if an income statement account was used initially, an adjustment may be required to set up the proper statement of financial position account at the end of the period.

4. Explain how the type of ownership structure affects the financial statements.

The type of ownership structure that a business uses determines the types of accounts that are part of the equity section. In a corporation, ordinary or common shares, contributed surplus, retained earnings, and accumulated other comprehensive income are commonly shown separately on the statement of financial position. In a proprietorship or partnership, an owner's capital account is used to indicate the investment in the company by the owner(s). An owner's drawings or withdrawal account may be used to indicate withdrawals by the owner(s). These two accounts are grouped or netted under owner's equity.

5. Prepare closing entries and consider other matters relating to the closing process.

In the closing process, all of the revenue and expense account balances (income statement items) are transferred to a clearing account called Income Summary, which is used only at the end of the fiscal year. Revenues and expenses are matched in the Income Summary account. The net result of this matching, which represents the net income or net loss for the period, is then transferred to a shareholders' equity account (Retained Earnings for a corporation and capital accounts for proprietorships and partnerships). Reversing entries may be used for reversing accrued revenues and accrued expenses. Prepayments may also be reversed if the initial entry to record the transaction is made to an expense or revenue account.

6. Prepare a 10-column work sheet and financial statements.

The 10-column work sheet provides columns for the first trial balance, adjustments, adjusted trial balance, statement of comprehensive income, and statement of financial position. The work sheet does not replace the financial statements. Instead, it is the accountant's informal device for accumulating and sorting the information that is needed for the financial statements.

Key Terms

account, p. C-3
accounting cycle, p. C-5
accounting information system, p. C-2
accrued expenses, p. C-9
accrued revenues, p. C-9
accumulated other comprehensive income, p. C-20
adjusted trial balance, p. C-22
adjusting entries, p. C-8
balance sheet, p. C-9
book value, p. C-12
carrying amount, p. C-12
closing entries, p. C-21
closing process, p. C-21
contra asset account, p. C-12
credit, p. C-3

debit, p. C-3
depreciation/amortization, p. C-11
double-entry accounting, p. C-3
event, p. C-5
financial statements, p. C-3
general journal, p. C-6
general ledger, p. C-5
income statement, p. C-3
journal, p. C-6
journal entries, p. C-3
periodic inventory system, p. C-22
permanent accounts, p. C-22
perpetual inventory system, p. C-22
post-closing trial balance, p. C-22
posting, p. C-7
prepaid expenses, p. C-9

reversing entries, p. C-22
special journals, p. C-6
statement of cash flows, p. C-3
statement of changes in shareholders' equity, p. C-3
statement of comprehensive income, p. C-3
statement of financial position, p. C-9
statement of retained earnings, p. C-3
subsidiary ledger, p. C-3
temporary accounts, p. C-3
transaction, p. C-3
trial balance, p. C-8
unearned revenues, p. C-9
useful life, p. C-11
work sheet, p. C-24

Assignment Material

Note: Completion of this exercise and problem material will help develop CPA-enabling competencies (such as ethics and professionalism, problem-solving and decision-making, and communication) and technical competencies. We have highlighted selected items with a specific integration word mark and material in *WileyPLUS* has been linked to the competencies. The brief exercises, exercises, and problems generally emphasize problem-solving and decision-making.

Brief Exercises

BEC.1 (LO 1) Plant Inc. uses the following accounts in its trial balance:

1. Sales

2. Investment Income or Loss

3. Dividends

4. Salaries and Wages Payable

5. Fair Value-OCI Investments

6. Cost of Goods Sold

7. Accumulated Other Comprehensive Income

8. Allowance for Doubtful Accounts

9. Fair Value-Net Income Investments

10. Retained Earnings

11. Interest Receivable

12. Unrealized Gain or Loss-OCI

Indicate whether each account is (a) a permanent account or a temporary account; and (b) an asset, contra asset, liability, revenue, expense, gain, loss, or shareholders' equity account.

BEC.2 (LO 1) Kothari Ltd. made the following transactions:

1. Payment of a $200 invoice on account
2. Increase in the fair value of a Fair Value-Net Income Investment by $250
3. Sale on account for $100
4. Purchase of equipment paid for with $500 cash and a $1,000 note payable
5. Increase in the fair value of a Fair Value-OCI Investment by $150
6. Repayment of a $2,000 bank loan

Indicate the effect of each of the transactions on (a) the basic accounting equation and (b) the expanded basic accounting equation.

BEC.3 (LO 2, 3) One Wiser Corp. had the following transactions during the first month of business. Journalize the transactions.

Aug.	2	Invested $12,000 cash and $2,500 of equipment in the business in exchange for common shares.
	7	Purchased supplies on account for $600. (Debit asset account.)
	12	Performed services for clients, collecting $1,300 in cash and billing the clients $670 for the remainder.
	15	Paid August rent, $600.
	19	Counted supplies and determined that only $270 of the supplies purchased on August 7 were still on hand.

BEC.4 (LO 2, 3) On August 1, Secret Sauce Technologies Inc. paid $12,600 for an insurance policy that is for two years and is effective August 1. Prepare two sets of journal entries for Secret Sauce, with each set of journal entries recording the August 1 journal entry and the December 31 adjusting entry. (a) Treat the expenditure as an asset in a first set of journal entries. (b) Treat the expenditure as an expense in a second set of journal entries.

BEC.5 (LO 2, 3) Store-it-Here owns a warehouse. On September 1, it rented storage space to a lessee (tenant) for six months for a total cash payment of $12,000 received in advance. Prepare two sets of journal entries for Store-it-Here, with each set of journal entries recording the September 1 journal entry and the December 31 adjusting entry. (a) Treat the receipt of cash as a liability in a first set of journal entries. (b) Treat the receipt of cash as a revenue in a second set of journal entries.

BEC.6 (LO 3) Included in Carville Corp.'s December 31, 2020 trial balance is a note payable of $20,000. The note is an eight-month, 12% note dated October 1, 2020. Prepare Carville's December 31, 2020 adjusting entry to record the accrued interest, and June 1, 2021 journal entry to record payment of principal and interest due to the lender.

BEC.7 (LO 3) Jerry Holiday is the maintenance supervisor for Ray's Insurance Co. and has recently purchased a riding lawn mower and accessories that will be used in caring for the grounds around corporate headquarters. He sent the following information to the accounting department:

Cost of mower and accessories	$9,600	Date purchased	July 1, 2020
Estimated useful life	8 years	Monthly salary of groundskeeper	$1,100
		Estimated annual fuel cost	$150

Calculate the amount of depreciation expense (for the mower and accessories) that should be reported on Ray's Insurance Co.'s December 31, 2020 income statement. Assume straight-line depreciation and no residual value.

BEC.8 (LO 3, 5) Pelican Inc. made a December 31 adjusting entry to debit Salaries and Wages Expense and credit Salaries and Wages Payable for $2,700. On January 2, Pelican paid the weekly payroll of $5,000. Prepare Pelican's (a) January 1 reversing entry, (b) January 2 entry (assuming the reversing entry was prepared), and (c) January 2 entry (assuming the reversing entry was not prepared).

BEC.9 (LO 5) Willis Corporation, which follows ASPE, has Beginning Inventory $76,000; Purchases $486,000; Freight In $16,200; Purchase Returns and Allowances $5,800; Purchase Discounts $5,000; and Ending Inventory $69,500. Calculate Willis's cost of goods sold.

BEC.10 (LO 5) Tiger Inc. has the following year-end account balances: Sales Revenue $928,900; Interest Income $17,500; Cost of Goods Sold $406,200; Operating Expenses $129,000; Income Tax Expense $55,100; and Dividends $15,900. Prepare the year-end closing entries.

BEC.11 (LO 4, 5) Active Consulting, a proprietorship, has the following year-end account balances: Service Revenue $426,500; Salaries and Wages Expense $219,000; Rent Expense $74,000; Utilities Expense $33,000; and Owner's Drawings $65,000. Prepare the year-end closing entries.

Exercises

EC.1 (LO 2, 3, 4)   (Transaction Analysis—Service Company)   Bill Rosenberg recently opened his legal practice as a sole proprietorship. During the first month of operations, the following events and transactions occurred:

Apr.	2	Invested $15,000 cash along with equipment valued at $10,000 in the business.
	2	Hired an administrative assistant at a salary of $480 per week payable monthly.
	3	Purchased $1,200 of supplies on account. (Debit an asset account.)
	7	Paid office rent of $750 for the month.
	11	Completed the preparation of a will and billed the client $1,500 for services rendered. (Use the Service Revenue account.)
	12	Received cash of $4,200 in advance of performing services.
	17	Received cash of $2,900 for services completed for Botticelli Limited.
	21	Paid insurance expense of $180.
	30	Paid the administrative assistant $1,920 for the month.
	30	A count of supplies indicated that $220 of supplies had been used during the month.
	30	Purchased a new computer for $4,100 paid for with personal funds. (The computer will be used only for business purposes.)

Instructions

Journalize the transactions in the general journal.

EC.2 (LO 2, 6) **Excel**   **(Trial Balance)**   The trial balance of Mis-Match Inc. on June 30, 2020, is as follows:

	Debit	Credit
Cash	$ 2,870	
Accounts receivable	3,231	
Supplies	800	
Equipment	3,800	
Accounts payable		$ 2,666
Unearned revenue		1,200
Common shares		6,000
Retained earnings		2,795
Service revenue		2,380
Salaries and wages expense	3,400	
Office expense	940	
	$15,041	$15,041

The following transactions took place in July 2020:

1. Payments received from customers on account amounted to $1,320.

2. A computer printer was purchased on account for $500.

3. Services provided to clients and billed on account amounted to $3,890.

4. In July, $400 of supplies was purchased on account, and a physical count on July 31 showed that there was $475 of supplies on hand on July 31.

5. When the Unearned Revenue account was reviewed, it was found that $825 of the balance was earned in July.

6. Salaries and Wages Expense of $670 related to employee services provided in July was not yet recorded as at July 31 (will be paid in August).

7. Payments to suppliers on account amounted to $2,125.

8. Received invoices totalling $1,160 related to office expenses incurred in July.

9. Declared a dividend of $575 on July 31.

Instructions

Prepare the trial balance as at July 31, 2020, assuming that Mis-Match did not record closing entries at the end of June 2020. (*Note:* It may be necessary to add one or more accounts to the trial balance.) Use a work sheet to record and summarize transactions and balances.

EC.3 (LO 2, 3) **(Transactions of a Corporation, Including Investment and Dividend)** LD Driving Range Inc. was opened on March 1 by Phil Woods. The following selected events and transactions occurred during March:

Mar.	1	Invested $80,000 cash in the business in exchange for common shares.
	3	Purchased Mickey Mickelson's Golf Land for $70,500 cash. The price consists of $2,500 for March rent that was already paid on a storage warehouse; land, $20,000; buildings, $32,000; and equipment, $16,000.
	5	To advertise the new driving range, LD sponsored and paid for an open house costing $6,800.
	6	Paid $2,400 cash for a one-year insurance policy.
	10	Purchased golf equipment for $5,500 from Rory Ltd., payable in 30 days.
	18	Earned fees of $3,700, which were billed on account.
	25	Declared and paid a $1,500 cash dividend.
	28	Incurred and paid salaries and wages expense of $1,900.
	30	Paid rent for the month of April in the amount of $2,500.
	31	Received fees of $750 related to a golf tournament that will take place in April.

Woods uses the following accounts for his company: Cash; Prepaid Insurance; Prepaid Rent; Land; Buildings; Equipment; Accounts Payable; Unearned Revenue; Common Shares; Dividends; Service Revenue; Advertising Expense; Rent Expense; and Salaries and Wages Expense.

Instructions

a. Journalize the March transactions.

b. Identify any adjusting entries that should be recorded before preparing financial statements for the month of March.

EC.4 (LO 2, 3) **(Alternative Treatment of Prepayment)** At Sugarland Ltd., prepaid costs are debited to expense when cash is paid and unearned revenues are credited to revenue when the cash is received. During January of the current year, the following transactions occurred.

Jan.	2	Received $11,100 for services to be performed in the future.
	2	Paid $3,600 for casualty insurance protection for the year.
	10	Paid $5,700 for supplies.

On January 31, it is determined that $3,500 of the service revenue has been earned and that there is $2,800 of supplies on hand.

Instructions

a. Journalize and post the January transactions. Use T accounts.

b. Journalize and post the adjusting entries at January 31. Use T accounts.

c. Determine the ending balance in each of the T accounts.

d. How would account balances on January 31 be affected if Sugarland records prepayments by debiting an asset when prepaid costs are paid in cash, and crediting a liability when unearned revenues are collected in advance?

EC.5 (LO 3) **Excel** **(Adjusting Entries)** Alex Roddick is the new owner of Ace Computer Services. At the end of August 2020, his first month of ownership, Roddick is trying to prepare monthly financial statements. Below is some information related to unrecorded expenses that the business incurred during August.

1. At August 31, Roddick owed his employees $1,900 in wages that will be paid on September 1.

2. At the end of the month, he had not yet received the month's utility bill. He estimated the bill would be approximately $600.

3. On August 1, Roddick borrowed $30,000 from a local bank on a 15-year mortgage, with the principal being repaid at the end of 15 years. The annual interest rate is 8%.

4. A telephone bill in the amount of $117 covering August charges is unpaid at August 31.

Instructions

Prepare the adjusting journal entries as at August 31, 2020, suggested by the information above.

EC.6 (LO 3) **(Adjusting Entries)** The ledger of Rainy Day Umbrella Ltd. on March 31 of the current year includes the following selected accounts before quarterly adjusting entries have been prepared:

	Debit	Credit
Prepaid Insurance	$ 3,600	
Supplies	2,800	
Equipment	25,000	
FV-OCI Investments	150,000	
Accumulated Depreciation—Equipment		$ 8,400
Notes Payable		20,000
Unearned Rent Revenue		9,300
Rent Revenue		60,000
Interest Expense	–0–	
Salaries and Wages Expense	14,000	

An analysis of the accounts shows the following:

1. The equipment depreciation is $350 per month.

2. One half of the unearned rent was earned during the quarter.

3. Interest of $300 has accrued on the notes payable.

4. Supplies on hand total $950.

5. Insurance expires at the rate of $300 per month.

6. The FV-OCI Investments were purchased for $150,000 on March 1. No investments were purchased or sold after that date. The fair value on March 31 was $170,000.

Instructions

a. Prepare the adjusting entries at March 31, assuming that adjusting entries are made quarterly. Additional accounts are Unrealized Gain or Loss-OCI; Depreciation Expense; Insurance Expense; Interest Payable; and Supplies Expense.

b. If the notes payable have been outstanding since January 1 of the current year, what is the annual interest rate on the notes payable?

EC.7 (LO 3) (Adjusting Entries) The trial balance for Hanna Resort Limited on August 31 is as follows:

Hanna Resort Limited
Trial Balance
August 31, 2020

	Debit	Credit
Cash	$ 6,700	
Prepaid insurance	3,500	
Supplies	1,800	
Land	20,000	
Buildings	142,000	
Accumulated depreciation—buildings		$ 20,448
Equipment	16,000	
Accumulated depreciation—equipment		4,320
Accounts payable		4,800
Unearned rent revenue		4,600
Notes payable		77,000
Common shares		81,000
Retained earnings		4,680
Dividends	5,000	
Rent revenue		68,002
Salaries and wages expense	43,200	
Insurance expense	12,250	
Interest expense	3,080	
Utilities expense	7,720	
Repairs and maintenance expense	3,600	
	$264,850	$264,850

Additional information:

1. The balance in Prepaid Insurance includes the cost of four months premiums for an insurance policy that will expire on September 30, 2020.

2. An inventory count on August 31 shows $650 of supplies on hand.

3. Buildings and equipment are depreciated straight-line. From the date of purchase, the buildings have an estimated useful life of 25 years, and the equipment has an estimated useful life of 10 years. For both asset categories, residual value is estimated to be 10% of cost.

4. (i) Rent revenue includes amounts received for September rentals in the amount of $8,000. (ii) Of the unadjusted Unearned Rent Revenue of $4,600, one half was earned prior to August 31.

5. Salaries of $375 were unpaid at August 31.

6. Rental fees of $800 were due from tenants at August 31. Use Accounts Receivable.

7. The note payable interest rate is 8% per year, and the note has been outstanding since December 1, 2019. No principal repayments are due. Interest is paid twice per year (on June 1 and December 1).

Instructions

a. Journalize the adjusting entries on August 31 for the three-month period from June 1 to August 31.

b. Prepare an adjusted trial balance as at August 31.

EC.8 (LO 3, 5) **(Adjusting and Reversing Entries)** On December 31, adjusting information for Big & Rich Corporation is as follows:

1. Estimated depreciation on equipment is $3,400.

2. Property taxes amounting to $2,525 have been incurred but are unrecorded and unpaid.

3. Employee wages that have been earned by employees but are unpaid and unrecorded amount to $3,900.

4. The Service Revenue account includes amounts that have been paid by customers for services that have not yet been completed. The amount has been determined to be $5,500.

5. Interest of $200 on a $25,000 note payable has not been recorded or paid.

Instructions

a. Prepare the adjusting entries.

b. Prepare the reversing entries, where appropriate.

EC.9 (LO 3, 5) **(Closing and Reversing Entries)** On December 31, the adjusted trial balance of Domino Inc. shows the following selected data:

Accounts receivable	$ 9,700	Service revenue	$110,000
Interest expense	12,800	Interest payable	6,400

Analysis shows that adjusting entries had been made, and included above, for (1) $9,700 of services performed but not billed, and (2) $6,400 of accrued but unpaid interest.

Instructions

a. Prepare the closing entries for the temporary accounts at December 31.

b. Prepare the reversing entries on January 1.

c. Enter the adjusted trial balance data in the four accounts using T accounts, and post the entries in parts (a) and (b).

d. Prepare the entries to record (1) collection of the service revenue on January 10, and (2) the $6,400 payment of interest due on January 15.

e. Post the entries in part (d) to the temporary accounts.

EC.10 (LO 3, 5) **(Adjusting and Reversing Entries)** A review of the accounts of Tucker and Wu Pan Accountants reflected the following transactions, which may or may not require adjustment for the year ended December 31, 2020.

1. The Prepaid Rent account shows a debit of $7,200 paid October 1, 2020, for a one-year lease that started on that day.

2. On November 1, 2020, Service Revenue was credited for $2,400 that was paid by a client for audit services to be performed in January.

3. On June 1, 2020, a cheque in the amount of $6,000 was issued for a two-year insurance policy starting on June 1, 2020. The amount was charged to Insurance Expense.

4. Interest of $1,270 has accrued on notes payable.

Instructions

Prepare (a) the adjusting entry for each item and (b) the reversing entry for each item, where appropriate.

EC.11 (LO 5) (Closing Entries) Selected accounts for Winslow Inc., a private company following ASPE, as at December 31, 2020, are as follows:

Inventory	$ 60,000	Sales Returns and Allowances	$ 2,000
FV-NI Investments	22,000	Cost of Goods Sold	222,700
Retained Earnings	45,000	Administrative Expenses	31,000
Dividends	18,000	Income Tax Expense	30,000
Sales Revenue	390,000	Investment Income	3,000
Sales Discounts	5,000		

Instructions

Prepare closing entries for Winslow Inc. on December 31, 2020.

EC.12 (LO 5) (Finding Missing Amounts—Periodic Inventory) Financial information follows for four different companies, all following ASPE:

	Pamela's Cosmetics Inc.	Scheibli Grocery Inc.	Berthault Wholesalers Ltd.	Kaiserman Supply Ltd.
Sales Revenue	$98,000	$ (c)	$144,000	$120,000
Sales Returns and Allowances	(a)	5,000	12,000	9,000
Net Sales Revenue	74,000	101,000	132,000	(g)
Beginning Inventory	21,000	(d)	44,000	24,000
Purchases	63,000	105,000	(e)	90,000
Purchase Returns and Allowances	6,000	10,000	8,000	(h)
Ending Inventory	(b)	48,000	30,000	28,000
Cost of Goods Sold	64,000	72,000	(f)	72,000
Gross Profit	10,000	29,000	18,000	(i)

Instructions

Determine the missing amounts for parts (a) to (i). Show all calculations.

EC.13 (LO 6) (Work Sheet) Selected accounts follow for Kings Inc., a private company following ASPE, as reported in the work sheet at the end of May 2020:

	Adjusted Trial Balance		Income Statement		Statement of Financial Position	
Accounts	**Dr.**	**Cr.**	**Dr.**	**Cr.**	**Dr.**	**Cr.**
Cash	9,000					
Inventory	80,000					
Accounts payable		26,000				
Sales revenue		480,000				
Sales returns and allowances	10,000					
Sales discounts	5,000					
Cost of goods sold	290,000					
Salaries and wages expense	62,000					
Interest income		12,000				

Instructions

Extend the amounts reported in the adjusted trial balance to the appropriate columns in the work sheet. Do not total individual columns.

EC.14 (LO 6) (Work Sheet Preparation) The trial balance of Airbourne Travel Inc. on March 31, 2020, is as follows:

Airbourne Travel Inc.
Trial Balance
March 31, 2020

	Debit	Credit
Cash	$ 1,800	
Accounts receivable	2,600	
Supplies	600	
Equipment	6,000	
Accumulated depreciation—equipment		400
Accounts payable		1,100
Unearned revenue		500
Common shares		6,400
Retained earnings		600
Sales revenue		2,600
Salaries and wages expense	500	
Miscellaneous expense	100	
	$11,600	$11,600

Additional information:

1. A physical count reveals only $520 of supplies on hand.
2. Equipment is depreciated at a rate of $100 per month.
3. Unearned revenue amounted to $100 on March 31.
4. Accrued salaries are $850.

Instructions

Enter the trial balance on a work sheet and complete the work sheet, assuming that the adjustments relate only to the month of March. (Ignore income taxes.)

EC.15 (LO 6)   (Work Sheet and Statement of Financial Position Presentation)   The adjusted trial balance of North Bay Corporation is provided in the following work sheet for the year ended December 31, 2020.

North Bay Corporation
Work Sheet (Partial)
For the Year Ended December 31, 2020

Account Titles	Adjusted Trial Balance		Statement of Comprehensive Income		Statement of Financial Position	
	Dr.	Cr.	Dr.	Cr.	Dr.	Cr.
Cash	117,600					
FV-NI investments	42,150					
Accounts receivable	56,720					
Prepaid rent	11,000					
FV-OCI investments	33,990					
Equipment	219,000					
Accumulated depreciation— equipment		81,000				
Accounts payable		54,470				
Interest payable		4,800				
Notes payable		60,000				
Common shares		100,000				
Retained earnings		133,440				
Service revenue		211,190				
Salaries and wages expense	73,090					
Rent expense	66,000					
Depreciation expense	27,000					
Bad debt expense	5,250					
Interest expense	5,100					
Investment income		5,800				
Unrealized gain or loss-OCI		6,200				

Instructions

The note payable is due in four months. Complete the work sheet and prepare a statement of financial position as illustrated in this appendix.

Problems

PC.1 Transactions follow for Emily Cain, D.D.S., a proprietorship following ASPE, for the month of September:

Sept. 1   Cain begins practice as a dentist and invests $32,000 of her own cash.
2   Purchases dental equipment on account from Dig Deep Drill Limited for $12,500.
4   Pays rent for office space, $1,300 in total for the months of September and October (that is, $650 per month).
4   Employs a receptionist, Wanda Micelli.
5   Purchases dental supplies for cash, $900.
8   Receives cash of $1,960 from patients for services performed and $1,600 for referrals to specialists.
10   Pays miscellaneous expenses, $680.
14   Bills patients $4,740 for services performed.
18   Pays Dig Deep Drill Limited on account, $6,300.
19   Withdraws $2,000 cash from the business for personal use.
20   Receives $2,100 from patients on account.
25   Bills patients $2,780 for services performed.
30   Pays the following expenses in cash: salaries and wages, $1,400; and miscellaneous expense, $85.
30   Dental supplies used during September amount to $330.

Instructions

a. Enter the transactions in appropriate T accounts, using the following account titles: Cash; Accounts Receivable; Prepaid Rent; Supplies; Equipment; Accumulated Depreciation—Equipment; Accounts Payable; Owner's Drawings; Service Revenue; Rent Expense; Miscellaneous Expense; Salaries and Wages Expense; Supplies Expense; Depreciation Expense; Income Summary; and Owner's Capital. Allow 10 lines for the Cash and Income Summary accounts, and five lines for each of the other accounts that are needed. Record depreciation on the equipment using the straight-line method, with a five-year useful life, and no residual value.

b. Prepare an adjusted trial balance.

c. Prepare an income statement, statement of financial position, and statement of owner's equity.

d. Prepare a post-closing trial balance at September 30.

PC.2 **Excel** Mason Advertising Agency Inc. was founded in January 2017. Presented below are adjusted and unadjusted trial balances as at December 31, 2020.

Mason Advertising Agency Inc.
Trial Balance
December 31, 2020

	Unadjusted		Adjusted	
	Dr.	Cr.	Dr.	Cr.
Cash	$ 11,000		$ 11,000	
Accounts receivable	20,000		23,500	
Supplies	8,400		3,000	
Prepaid insurance	3,350		2,500	
Equipment	60,000		60,000	
Accumulated depreciation—equipment		$ 28,000		$ 33,000
Accounts payable		5,000		5,000
Interest payable		–0–		150
Notes payable		5,000		5,000
Unearned revenue		7,000		5,600
Salaries and wages payable		–0–		1,300
Common shares		10,000		10,000
Retained earnings		3,500		3,500
Service revenue		58,600		63,500
Salaries and wages expense	10,000		11,300	
Insurance expense			850	
Interest expense	350		500	
Depreciation expense			5,000	
Supplies expense			5,400	
Rent expense	4,000		4,000	
	$117,100	$117,100	$127,050	$127,050

Instructions

a. Journalize the annual adjusting entries that were made. (Omit explanations.)

b. Prepare an income statement and a statement of retained earnings for the year ending December 31, 2020, and an unclassified statement of financial position at December 31.

c. Answer the following questions.

    1. If the note has been outstanding three months, what is the annual interest rate on that note?

    2. If the company paid $12,500 in salaries and wages in 2020, what was the balance in Salaries and Wages Payable on December 31, 2019?

PC.3 A review of the ledger of Rolling Resort Inc. at December 31 produces the following data for the preparation of annual adjusting entries:

1. Salaries and Wages Payable, $0. There are eight salaried employees. Five employees receive a salary of $1,200 each per week, and three employees earn $800 each per week. Employees do not work weekends. All employees worked two days after the last pay period and before December 31.

2. Unearned Rent Revenue, $415,200. The company began leasing condos in its new building on November 1. Each tenant has to make a $5,000 security deposit that is not refundable until occupancy is ended. At December 31, the company had the following rental contracts that were paid in full for the entire term of the lease:

Date	Term (in months)	Monthly Rent	Number of Leases
Nov. 1	6	$ 4,100	5
Dec. 1	6	$10,300	4

3. Prepaid Insurance, $16,200. This balance consists of payments on two policies. The terms of the policies are as follows:

Policy	Effective Date	Amount	Number of Months Coverage
A650	May 1	$7,200	12
B974	Oct. 1	9,000	24

4. Notes Payable, $80,000. This balance consists of a one-year, 9% note that is dated June 1.

Instructions

a. Prepare the adjusting entries at December 31. (Show all calculations.)

b. **Digging Deeper** Rolling Resort is preparing for a meeting with potential investors. What is the net effect of the adjusting entries on net income? Explain why Rolling Resort's potential investors should be willing to wait for Rolling Resort to complete its year-end adjustment process before deciding whether or not to invest in the company.

PC.4 Second-Hand Almost New Department Store Inc., a private company following ASPE, is located near a shopping mall. At the end of the company's fiscal year on December 31, 2020, the following accounts appeared in two of its trial balances:

	Unadjusted	Adjusted
Accounts payable	$ 79,300	$ 79,300
Accounts receivable	95,300	95,300
Accumulated depreciation—buildings	42,100	52,500
Accumulated depreciation—equipment	29,600	42,900
Buildings	190,000	190,000
Cash	68,000	68,000
Common shares	160,000	160,000
Cost of goods sold	412,700	412,700
Depreciation expense	–0–	23,700
Dividends	28,000	28,000
Equipment	110,000	110,000
Insurance expense	–0–	7,200
Interest expense	3,000	11,000

(continued)

	Unadjusted	Adjusted
Interest income	$ 4,000	$ 4,000
Interest payable	–0–	8,000
Inventory	75,000	75,000
Mortgage payable	80,000	80,000
Prepaid insurance	9,600	2,400
Property tax expense	–0–	4,800
Property tax payable	–0–	4,800
Retained earnings	16,600	16,600
Salaries and wages expense	108,000	108,000
Sales commission expense	11,000	14,500
Sales commission payable	–0–	3,500
Sales returns and allowances	8,000	8,000
Sales revenue	718,000	718,000
Utilities expense	11,000	11,000

Analysis reveals the following additional information:

1. Insurance expense and utilities expense are 60% selling and 40% administrative.

2. In the next year, $20,000 of the mortgage payable will be due for payment.

3. Property tax expense and depreciation on the building are administrative expenses; depreciation on the equipment is a selling expense; and $32,000 of the salaries and wages expense related to office salaries and the remainder related to sales salaries. Depreciation expense includes $10,400 relating to the building and $13,300 relating to equipment.

Instructions

a. Prepare a multiple-step income statement, statement of retained earnings, and classified statement of financial position. (*Hint:* Use Example C.14 as a model or look to Chapter 4 to see what a multiple-step income statement is.)

b. Journalize the adjusting entries that were made.

c. Journalize the closing entries that are necessary.

PC.5 The following accounts appeared in the December 31 trial balance of the Majestic Theatre:

	Debit	Credit
Equipment	$960,000	
Accumulated depreciation—equipment		$120,000
Notes payable		186,000
Sales revenue		750,000
Rent expense	62,000	
Salaries and wages expense	80,000	
Interest expense	9,000	

Instructions

a. From the account balances above and the information that follows, prepare the annual adjusting entries necessary on December 31. Round amounts to the nearest dollar.

1. The equipment has an estimated life of 16 years and a residual value of $40,000. (Use the straight-line method.)

2. The note payable is a 90-day note given to the bank on October 20 and bearing interest at 10%. (*Hint:* Use number of days in your calculation.)

3. In December, 2,000 coupon admission books were sold at $25 each. They can be used for admission any time after January 1.

4. Of the Rent Expense balance, $1,100 is paid in advance.

5. Salaries accrued but unpaid are $11,800.

b. What amounts should be shown for each of the following on the income statement for the year?

1. Interest expense

2. Sales revenue

3. Rent expense

4. Salaries and wages expense

PC.6 Excel The trial balance and other information for consulting engineers Mustang Rovers Consulting Limited follow:

Mustang Rovers Consulting Limited
Trial Balance
December 31, 2020

	Debit	Credit
Cash	$ 83,700	
Accounts receivable	81,100	
Allowance for doubtful accounts		$ 750
Supplies	1,960	
Equipment	85,000	
Accumulated depreciation—equipment		6,250
Notes payable		7,200
Common shares		35,010
Retained earnings		161,100
Service revenue		100,000
Rent expense	9,750	
Salaries and wages expense	28,500	
Insurance expense	18,500	
Utilities expense	1,080	
Miscellaneous expense	720	
	$310,310	$310,310

Additional information:

1. Service revenue includes fees received in advance from clients of $6,900.

2. Services performed for clients that were not recorded by December 31 totalled $7,300.

3. Bad debt expense for the year is $6,300.

4. Insurance expense includes a premium paid on December 31 in the amount of $6,000 for the period starting on January 1, 2021.

5. Equipment is depreciated on a straight-line basis over 10 years. Residual value is $15,000.

6. Mustang gave the bank a 90-day, 12% note for $7,200 on December 1, 2020.

7. Rent is $750 per month. The rent for 2020 and for January 2021 has been paid.

8. Salaries and wages earned but unpaid at December 31, 2020, are $2,598.

9. Dividends of $80,000 were declared on December 15, 2020 for payment on February 1, 2021.

Instructions

a. From the trial balance and other information given, prepare annual adjusting entries as at December 31, 2020. Round amounts to the nearest dollar.

b. Prepare an adjusted trial balance for Mustang Rovers as at December 31, 2020.

c. Prepare an income statement for 2020, a statement of financial position as at December 31, 2020, and a statement of retained earnings for 2020.

d. Explain how the financial statements in part (c) would change if Mustang Rovers operated as a sole proprietorship, rather than a corporate ownership structure.

PC.7 The following information relates to Joachim Anderson, Property Manager, at the close of the fiscal year ending December 31:

1. Joachim paid a storage locker facility $335 for next January's rent on a locker and charged it to Rent Expense.

2. On November 1, Joachim signed a three-month, 10% note to borrow $15,000 from Yorkville Bank.

3. The following salaries and wages are due and unpaid at December 31: sales, $1,420; office clerks, $1,060.

4. Interest of $500 has accrued to date on a note that Joachim holds from Grant Muldaur.

5. The estimated loss on bad debts for the period is $1,560.

6. Stamps and stationery are charged to the Office Expense account when purchased; $110 of these supplies remain on hand.

7. Joachim has not yet paid the December rent of $1,000 on the building his business uses.

8. Insurance was paid on November 1 for one year and charged to Prepaid Insurance, $1,170.

9. Property tax accrued, $1,670.

10. On December 1, Joachim accepted Alana Zipursky's two-month, 15% note in settlement of her $6,000 account receivable.

11. On October 31, Joachim received $2,580 from Tareq Giza in payment of six months' rent for Giza's office space in the building and credited Unearned Rent Revenue.

12. On September 1, Joachim paid six months' rent in advance on a warehouse, $8,300, and debited the asset account Prepaid Rent.

13. The bill from Light & Power Limited for December has been received but not yet entered or paid, $510.

14. The estimated depreciation on equipment is $1,400.

Instructions

Prepare annual adjusting entries as at December 31. Round amounts to the nearest dollar.

PC.8 The trial balance follows of the Masters Golf Club Inc. as at December 31. The books are closed annually on December 31.

Masters Golf Club Inc. Trial Balance December 31	Debit	Credit
Cash	$ 115,000	
Accounts receivable	63,000	
Allowance for doubtful accounts		$ 9,000
Land	350,000	
Buildings	600,000	
Accumulated depreciation—buildings		40,000
Equipment	300,000	
Accumulated depreciation—equipment		120,000
Prepaid insurance	12,000	
Common shares		880,000
Retained earnings		152,000
Sales revenue		413,000
Rent revenue		44,000
Utilities expense	74,000	
Salaries and wages expense	90,000	
Repairs and maintenance expense	54,000	
	$1,658,000	$1,658,000

Instructions

a. Enter the balances in ledger accounts. Allow five lines for each account.

b. From the trial balance and the information that follows, prepare annual adjusting entries and post to the ledger accounts:

   1. The buildings have an estimated life of 30 years with no residual value. (The company uses the straight-line method.)

   2. The equipment is depreciated at 10% of its year-end carrying value per year.

   3. Insurance expired during the year was $5,300.

   4. The rental revenue is the amount received for 11 months for dining facilities. The December rent of $4,000 has not yet been received. A Rent Receivable account is used.

   5. It is estimated that 24% of the accounts receivable will be uncollectible.

   6. Salaries and wages earned but not paid by December 31 amounted to $3,600.

   7. Sales revenue included dues paid in advance by members and totalled $9,900.

c. Prepare an adjusted trial balance.

d. Prepare closing entries and post to the ledger.

PC.9 The unadjusted trial balance of Clancy Inc., a private company following ASPE, at December 31, 2020, is as follows:

	Debit	Credit
Cash	$ 17,740	
Accounts receivable	103,000	
Allowance for doubtful accounts		$ 3,500
Inventory	60,000	
Prepaid insurance	4,620	
Bond investment at amortized cost	40,000	
Land	30,000	
Buildings	154,000	
Accumulated depreciation—buildings		12,400
Equipment	33,600	
Accumulated depreciation—equipment		5,600
Goodwill	16,600	
Accounts payable		101,050
Bonds payable (20-year, 7%)		180,000
Common shares		121,000
Retained earnings		21,360
Sales revenue		200,000
Rent revenue		10,800
Rent expense	22,500	
Supplies expense	10,800	
Purchases	98,000	
Purchase discounts		900
Salaries and wages expense	53,500	
Interest expense	12,250	
	$656,610	$656,610

Additional information:

1. Actual rent costs amounted to $1,500 per month. The company has already paid for rent for the first quarter of 2021.

2. The building was purchased and occupied on January 1, 2018, with an estimated useful life of 20 years, and residual value of $30,000. (The company uses straight-line depreciation.)

3. Prepaid insurance contains the premium costs of several policies, including Policy A, cost of $2,640, one-year term, taken out on April 1, 2020; and Policy B, cost of $1,980, three-year term, taken out on September 1, 2020.

4. A portion of Clancy's building has been converted into a snack bar that has been rented to the Ono Food Corp. since July 1, 2019, at a rate of $7,200 per year payable each July 1 in advance.

5. One of the company's customers declared bankruptcy on December 30, 2020. It is now certain that the $2,700 the customer owes will never be collected. This fact has not been recorded. In addition, Clancy estimates that 4% of the Accounts Receivable balance on December 31, 2020, will become uncollectible.

6. An advance of $600 to a salesperson on December 31, 2020, was charged to Salaries and Wages Expense.

7. On November 1, 2018, Clancy issued 180 $1,000 bonds at par value. Interest is paid semi-annually on April 30 and October 31.

8. The equipment was purchased on January 1, 2018, with an estimated useful life of 12 years, and no residual value. (The company uses straight-line depreciation.)

9. On August 1, 2020, Clancy purchased at par value 40 $1,000, 9% bonds maturing on July 31, 2022. Interest is paid on July 31 and January 31.

10. The inventory on hand at December 31, 2020, was $90,000 after a physical inventory count.

Instructions

a. Prepare adjusting and correcting entries for December 31, 2020, using the information given. Record the adjusting entry for inventory using a Cost of Goods Sold account.

b. Indicate which of the adjusting entries could be reversed.

PC.10 The unadjusted trial balance of Imagine Ltd., a private company following ASPE, at December 31, 2020 is as follows:

	Debit	Credit
Cash	$ 10,850	
Accounts receivable	56,500	
Allowance for doubtful accounts		$ 750
FV-NI investments	8,600	
Inventory	58,000	
Prepaid insurance	2,940	
Prepaid rent	13,200	
FV-OCI investments	14,000	
Bond investment at amortized cost	18,000	
Land	10,000	
Equipment	104,000	
Accumulated depreciation—equipment		18,000
Accounts payable		9,310
Bonds payable		50,000
Common shares		100,000
Retained earnings		103,260
Sales revenue		223,310
Rent revenue		10,200
Purchases	170,000	
Purchase discounts		2,400
Freight out	9,000	
Freight in	3,500	
Salaries and wages expense	31,000	
Interest expense	6,750	
Miscellaneous expense	890	
	$517,230	$517,230

Additional information:

1. On November 1, 2020, Imagine received $10,200 rent from its lessee for a 12-month lease beginning on that date. This was credited to Rent Revenue.

2. Imagine estimates that 7% of the Accounts Receivable balances on December 31, 2020, will be uncollectible. On December 28, 2020, the bookkeeper incorrectly credited Sales Revenue for a receipt of $1,000 on account. This error had not yet been corrected on December 31.

3. After a physical count, inventory on hand at December 31, 2020, was $77,000.

4. Prepaid insurance contains the premium costs of two policies: Policy A, cost of $1,320, two-year term, taken out on April 1, 2020; Policy B, cost of $1,620, three-year term, taken out on September 1, 2020.

5. The regular rate of depreciation is 10% of cost per year. Acquisitions and retirements during a year are depreciated at half this rate. There were no retirements during the year. On December 31, 2019, the balance of Equipment was $90,000.

6. On April 1, 2020, Imagine issued at par value 50 $1,000, 11% bonds maturing on April 1, 2024. Interest is paid on April 1 and October 1.

7. On August 1, 2020, Imagine purchased at par value 18 $1,000, 12% Legume Inc. bonds, maturing on July 31, 2022. Interest is paid on July 31 and January 31.

8. On May 30, 2020, Imagine rented a warehouse for $1,100 per month and debited Prepaid Rent for an advance payment of $13,200.

9. Imagine's FV-NI investments consist of shares with total market value of $9,400 as at December 31, 2020.

10. The FV-OCI investment is an investment of 500 shares in Yop Inc., with current market value of $25 per share as at December 31, 2020.

Instructions

a. Prepare the year-end adjusting and correcting entries for December 31, 2020, using the information given. Record the adjusting entry for inventory using a Cost of Goods Sold account.

b. Indicate which of the adjusting entries could be reversed.

PC.11 Mona Kamaka, CPA, was retained by Downtown TV Repair Ltd. to prepare financial statements for the month of March 2020. Mona accumulated all the ledger balances from the business records and found the following:

Downtown TV Repair Ltd.
Trial Balance
March 31, 2020

	Debit	Credit
Cash	$ 7,200	
Accounts receivable	3,500	
Supplies	900	
Equipment	15,000	
Accumulated depreciation—equipment		$ 3,000
Accounts payable		5,950
Salaries and wages payable		600
Unearned revenue		1,500
Common shares		10,000
Retained earnings		4,160
Service revenue		8,000
Salaries and wages expense	3,600	
Advertising expense	800	
Utilities expense	310	
Depreciation expense	700	
Repairs and maintenance expense	1,200	
	$33,210	$33,210

Mona reviewed the records and found the following errors:

1. Cash received from a customer on account was recorded as $570 instead of $750.

2. The purchase, on account, of equipment that cost $900 was recorded as a debit to Supplies and a credit to Accounts Payable for $900.

3. A payment of $30 for advertising expense was entered as a debit to Utilities Expense, $30, and a credit to Cash, $30.

4. The first salary payment this month was for $1,800, which included $600 of salaries and wages payable on February 28. The payment was recorded as a debit to Salaries and Wages Expense of $1,800 and a credit to Cash of $1,800. The business does not use reversing entries.

5. A cash payment for Repairs and Maintenance Expense on equipment for $90 was recorded as a debit to Equipment, $90, and a credit to Cash, $90.

Instructions

a. Prepare an analysis of each error that shows (1) the incorrect entry, (2) the correct entry, and (3) the correcting entry.

b. Prepare a corrected trial balance.

PC.12 Samuels Corp. began operations on January 1, 2020. Its fiscal year end is December 31. Samuels has decided that prepaid costs are debited to an asset account when paid, and all revenues are credited to revenue when the cash is received. During 2020, the following transactions occurred.

1. On January 1, 2020, Samuels bought supplies for $4,100 cash. A physical count at December 31, 2020, revealed $1,900 of supplies still on hand.

2. Samuels bought a $6,000, one-year insurance policy for cash on August 1, 2020. The policy came into effect on this date.

3. On November 15, 2020, Samuels received a $1,200 advance cash payment from a client for services to be provided in the future. As at December 31, 2020, one third of these services had not been performed.

4. On December 1, 2020, Samuels rented out excess office space for a six-month period starting on this date, and received a $1,100 cheque for the first and last month's rent.

Instructions

a. For each of the above transactions, prepare the journal entry for the original transaction and any adjusting entry required at December 31, 2020.

b. Digging Deeper In a business where accounting is performed at several divisions or office locations, is it possible that prepayments would be treated as assets in some offices and as expenses
in others when initially recorded? Why or why not? Does the business have to have a consistent
approach in all of its offices? Why or why not?

PC.13 Below are the completed financial statement columns of the work sheet for Canned Heat Limited:

Canned Heat Limited
Work Sheet
For the Year Ended December 31, 2020

Account No.	Account Titles	Statement of Comprehensive Income		Statement of Financial Position	
		Dr.	Cr.	Dr.	Cr.
101	Cash			18,000	
112	Accounts receivable			42,000	
130	Prepaid insurance			1,800	
140	FV-OCI investments			25,500	
157	Equipment			98,000	
167	Accumulated depreciation— equipment				28,600
201	Accounts payable				31,600
212	Salaries and wages payable				7,200
301	Common shares				80,000
306	Retained earnings				60,000
400	Service revenue		142,000		
622	Repairs and maintenance expense	13,200			
711	Depreciation expense	28,800			
722	Insurance expense	18,800			
726	Salaries and wages expense	106,600			
732	Utilities expense	3,500			
801	Unrealized gain or loss-OCI		6,800		
	Totals	170,900	148,800	185,300	207,400
	Net loss plus OCI		22,100	22,100	
		170,900	170,900	207,400	207,400

Instructions

a. Prepare a statement of comprehensive income, statement of changes in equity, and statement of
financial position. During 2020, Canned Heat's shareholders invested $24,000 in exchange for com-
mon shares. Accumulated other comprehensive income had a balance of $0 on January 1, 2020.

b. Prepare closing entries for the year ended December 31, 2020, and a post-closing trial balance. Income Summary is account number 350 and Accumulated Other Comprehensive Income is account
number 310.

c. Briefly discuss how the financial statements in part (a) would change if Canned Heat followed ASPE
rather than IFRS.

d. Assume that Canned Heat operates as a partnership. What additional changes, beyond those discussed in part (c), would affect the financial statements prepared in part (a)?

PC.14 The trial balance of Slum Dog Fashion Centre Inc., a private company following ASPE, contained
the following accounts at November 30, the company's fiscal year end:

Slum Dog Fashion Centre Inc.
Trial Balance
November 30, 2020

	Debit	Credit
Cash	$ 29,200	
Accounts receivable	82,000	
Inventory	105,000	
Supplies	8,600	
Equipment	225,000	

(continued)

	Debit	Credit
Accumulated depreciation—equipment		$ 86,000
Vehicles	$ 128,000	
Accumulated depreciation—vehicles		39,000
Notes payable		85,000
Accounts payable		78,500
Common shares		300,000
Retained earnings		38,000
Sales revenue		950,200
Sales returns and allowances	24,200	
Cost of goods sold	611,500	
Salaries and wages expense	150,000	
Advertising expense	46,400	
Utilities expense	24,000	
Repairs and maintenance expense	32,100	
Travel expense	46,700	
Rent expense	64,000	
	$1,576,700	$1,576,700

Adjustment data:

1. Supplies on hand totalled $3,100.

2. Depreciation is $40,000 on the store equipment and $30,000 on the delivery trucks.

3. Interest of $9,000 is accrued on notes payable at November 30.

Additional information:

1. Salaries and wages expense is 60% selling and 40% administrative.

2. Rent expense and utilities expense are 90% selling and 10% administrative.

3. Of the notes payable, $35,000 is due for payment next year.

4. Repairs and maintenance expense is 100% administrative.

5. Expenses pertaining to travel, advertising and supplies are 100% selling.

6. The income tax rate for the company is 20%. No taxes have been accrued or paid during the year.

Instructions

a. Enter the trial balance on a work sheet and complete the work sheet.

b. Prepare a multiple-step income statement and statement of retained earnings for the year, and a classified statement of financial position as at November 30, 2020. (*Hint:* Look to Chapter 4 to see what a multiple-step income statement is.)

PC.15 Tudor Services Ltd., a private company following ASPE, has an August 31 fiscal year end. The company's trial balance prior to adjustments follows:

Tudor Services Ltd.
Trial Balance
August 31, 2020

	Debit	Credit
Cash	$ 35,420	
Supplies	6,000	
Equipment	140,000	
Accumulated depreciation—equipment		$ 42,000
Vehicles	110,000	
Accumulated depreciation—vehicles		48,125
Accounts payable		7,950
Notes payable		60,000
Common shares		20,000
Retained earnings		55,750
Dividends	36,000	
Service revenue		200,525
Supplies expense	28,038	
Insurance expense	9,500	

(continued)

	Debit	Credit
Interest expense	3,392	
Rent expense	21,000	
Salaries expense	45,000	
	$434,350	$434,350

Additional data:

1. The equipment has an expected useful life of 10 years. The vehicles' expected useful life is eight years.

2. A physical count showed $2,000 of supplies on hand at August 31, 2020.

3. Accrued salaries payable at August 31, 2020, were $2,550.

4. Interest on the 5.5% note payable is payable at the end of each month and $10,000 of the principal must be paid on December 31 each year. Interest payments are up to date as at July 31, 2020.

5. During 2020, additional common shares were issued for $3,000 cash.

Instructions

a. Enter the trial balance on a work sheet and complete the work sheet. (*Hint:* Consider writing out the adjusting journal entries at August 31, 2020.) Ignore income taxes.

b. Prepare an income statement and a statement of retained earnings for the year ended August 31, 2020, and a balance sheet as at August 31, 2020.

c. Prepare closing entries.

d. Explain how the financial statements in part (b) would change if Tudor operated as a sole proprietorship, rather than a corporation.

Appendix D

Coverage of the CPA Competency Map Knowledge Supplement—The following table maps the knowledge reference list from the CPA Competency Map Knowledge Supplement as "issued and revised for clarification in 2018, retaining original effective date of 2013" (per www.cpacanada.ca) to *Intermediate Accounting, Twelfth Canadian Edition* (Volumes 1 and 2). We focus on Section 1: Financial Reporting of the Knowledge Supplement. However, the course also partially covers some of the other sections of the Knowledge Supplement.

SECTION 1: FINANCIAL REPORTING

Introduction to Accounting	Chapters
• Objectives and fundamental accounting concepts and principles (qualitative characteristics of accounting information, basic elements)	1, 2
• Ethical professional judgement	2 and all chapters
• Objectives of financial reporting	1, 2
• Methods of measurement	2, 3
• Difference between accrual accounting and cash accounting	3, 4A
• Framework of standard setting (IFRS and ASPE)	1, 2
• Financial statement users and their broad needs, standard setting, and requirement for accountability	1, 2
• Accounting information systems	Volume 1, App. C
• The role of information technology in the reporting of information, including real-time access, remote access to information, dashboard, spreadsheet, report generator, and XBRL (eXtensible Business Reporting Language)	23
• Emerging trends in accounting standards and recent updates	All chapters
• Legislation that has an impact on accounting (Sarbanes-Oxley Act, Bill 198)	1

Financial Statements—Process, Design, and Preparation	
• The accounting cycle	Volume 1, App. C
• Internal control and cash (bank reconciliation, control over cash receipts and disbursements)	7, 7A
• Interim reporting	23
• Segment reporting	23
• Financial statements in accordance with applicable standards	All chapters
• Routine disclosure requirements (notes to financial statements)	All chapters
• Complex disclosure requirements (notes to financial statements)	All chapters
• Role and composition of the MD&A	23

Issues Regarding Items in Financial Statements (under various GAAPs)	
The appropriate accounting treatment for the following:	
• Cash and cash equivalents	7
• Receivables	7
• Inventories	8
• Property, plant, and equipment	10
• Goodwill and intangible assets	12
• Depreciation, amortization, impairment, and disposition/derecognition	11, 12
• Provisions, contingencies, and current liabilities	13
• Long-term liabilities	14
• Owners'/shareholders' equity	Volume 1, App. C, 15, 16
• Earnings per share (basic, diluted)	4, 17
• Financial instruments	7, 9, 14, 15, 16
• Investments in associates/significant influence	9
• Investment property	10
• Revenue recognition/revenue from contracts with customers, and accounting for revenue and related expenses	6, 6A

Issues Regarding Items in Financial Statements (under various GAAPs) (continued)	Chapters
• Government assistance	10
• Leases	20
• Changes in accounting policies and estimates, and errors	21
• Foreign currency transactions	16
• Accounting for income taxes	18
• Events after the reporting period	5, 23
• Uncommon capital assets (e.g., natural resources, exchanges of assets, decommissioning costs)	10, 11, 13
• Pension plans and other employee future benefits	19
• Assets held for sale and discontinued operations	4
• Fair value and cash flow hedges	16, 16A
• Foreign currency translation	NA
• Business combination	12
• Consolidated statements on date of acquisition	NA
• Consolidated financial statements subsequent to acquisition date	NA
• Joint arrangements	NA
• Share-based payments	10
• Related party transactions	23
• Nonmonetary transactions	6, 10
• Complex financial instruments (e.g., perpetual debt, convertible debt, derivatives)	16

Financial Statement Analysis	
• Vertical and horizontal analysis	23
• Ratios and benchmarking	5A, 23, and all chapters
• Financial statement results for various users	5A, 23, and all chapters
• Pro forma statements	NA
• Impact of financial results on the whole organization	5A, 23, and all chapters

Meeting Financial Reporting Technical Competencies in the CPA Competency Map—The following table maps the financial reporting technical competencies from the CPA Competency Map to *Intermediate Accounting, Twelfth Canadian Edition* (Volume 1). The textbook in its entirety covers the Financial Reporting competencies as noted below. Detailed mapping of specific CPA Financial Reporting competencies to specific textbook Learning Objectives is provided in the charts at the beginning of each chapter. Coverage of other technical competencies (that is, Strategy and Governance, Management Accounting, Audit and Assurance, Finance, and Taxation competencies) has also been identified in the charts at the beginning of each chapter and in the end-of-chapter material. Selected enabling competencies have also been identified throughout.

FINANCIAL REPORTING

1.1 Financial Reporting Needs and Systems	Chapters
1.1.1 Evaluates financial reporting needs	1, 2, 4, 5, 6, 7, 8, 9, 10, 11, 12, Volume 1, App. C
1.1.2 Evaluates the appropriateness of the basis of financial reporting	1, 2, 3, 4, 5, 6, 7, 8, 9, 10, 11, 12
1.1.3 Evaluates reporting processes to support reliable financial reporting	3, 8, 12
1.1.4 Explains implications of current trends and emerging issues in financial reporting	2, 3, 4, 5, 6, 7, 8, 9, 10, 11, 12
1.1.5 Identifies financial reporting needs for the public sector	10
1.1.6 Identifies specialized financial reporting requirements for specified regulatory and other filing requirements	NA

1.2 Accounting Policies and Transactions	
1.2.1 Develops or evaluates appropriate accounting policies and procedures	1, 2, 3, 4, 5, 6, 7, 8, 9, 10, 11, 12, Volume 1, App. C
1.2.2 Evaluates treatment for routine transactions	2, 3, 4, 5, 6, 7, 8, 9, 10, 11, 12, Volume 1, App. C
1.2.3 Evaluates treatment for non-routine transactions	2, 3, 4, 5, 6, 7, 8, 9, 10, 11, 12
1.2.4 Analyzes treatment for complex events or transactions	7, 8, 10, 12

1.3 Financial Report Preparation	
1.3.1 Prepares financial statements	1, 4, 5, 6, Volume 1, App. C
1.3.2 Prepares routine financial statement note disclosure	4, 5, 6, 7, 8, 9, 10, 11, 12

1.4 Financial Statement Analysis	
1.4.1 Analyzes complex financial statement note disclosure	4, 5, 7, 8, 9, 11, 12
1.4.2 Evaluates financial statements including note disclosures	4, 5, 7, 8, 9, 11, 12
1.4.3 Analyzes and provides input in the preparation of the management communication (e.g., management discussion and analysis (MD&A))	5
1.4.4 Interprets financial reporting results for stakeholders (external or internal)	4, 5, 7, 8, 9, 11, 12
1.4.5 Analyzes and predicts the impact of strategic and operational decisions on financial results	3, 4, 5, 6, 7, 8, 9, 12

A Summary of the Case Primer*

Framework for Case Analysis

Decision-making must be done in the context of the situation at hand. We have to consider the accounting body of knowledge (*CPA Canada Handbook*, accounting methods, etc.) and must do this within a specific scenario. Who is in charge of preparing the financial information? Who will be using the information (and for what purpose)? Are there any circumstances either inside the company or outside it that may lead to bias?

Stages

Case analysis can be seen as having three main stages:

1. Assessment of the reporting environment/framework/overview
2. Identification and analysis of the financial reporting issues
3. Recommendations

A short version of the case primer follows. A more detailed version is available in *WileyPLUS* and on the Student Website <www.wiley.com/go/kiesocanada> accompanying *Intermediate Accounting*, Twelfth Canadian Edition.

1. **Assessment of the reporting environment/framework/overview**

   a. **Potential for bias** (Look for sensitive numbers and/or financial statement items. Identify and articulate the bias and related key numbers.)

      i. **Users and the decisions they are making.** Who is using the information and for what purpose? Are there any key numbers/ratios that will be the focus of these users? Are there any contracts that refer to the financial reporting (such as debt covenants, payout ratios, etc.)?

      ii. **Financial statement preparers.** Consider management compensation such as bonuses that are based on net income, stock options that are based on the value of the stock (and are affected by the financial information), the need to obtain financing, etc.

      iii. **Business/economic reporting environment.** Is the company experiencing a decline in profitability or cash flows due to increased competition, less demand for services, internal problems, etc.? What are the key numbers/ratios that users focus on to assess the financial health of the company?

   b. **GAAP constraint** If the company's shares trade on a stock exchange, there is normally a legal requirement to follow IFRS. Otherwise, the GAAP constraint depends on what the users want from the statements. GAAP statements, by definition, are reliable, relevant, comparable, consistent, and understandable. Private entities may choose to follow ASPE or IFRS.

   c. **Overall conclusion on financial reporting objective** Based on your role in the case and the above information, conclude on whether the financial reporting will be more aggressive or conservative or somewhere in between. Note that aggressive accounting tends to overstate net income/assets and present the company in the best light. Conservative accounting ensures that net income/assets are not overstated and that all pertinent information (positive or negative) is disclosed.

2. **Identification and analysis of the financial reporting issues**

   a. **Issue identification** Read the case and look for potential financial reporting issues. To do this, you need to know the accounting principles and rules and have an understanding of the business and the business transactions. Issues are usually about deciding whether or not to **recognize** something, deciding how to **measure** financial statement elements, or how to **present/disclose** these items in the financial statements.

   b. **Ranking issues** Focus on the more important issues. In other words, focus first on the issues that are material to the users of the information (those that are more complex and/or those that affect any of the key numbers or ratios identified above). You should identify what you consider to be material.

   c. **Analysis** The analysis should consider both qualitative and quantitative aspects. It should also look at the issue from different perspectives. For example, in a revenue recognition issue, should the revenue be recognized now or later? Consider only the relevant alternatives.

   Qualitative:

   - Each perspective must be supported by making reference to GAAP and accounting theory (including the conceptual framework). For example, recognize the revenue now because…or recognize it later because…
   - Make sure the analysis is case specific—i.e., that it refers to the facts of the specific case.
   - Make strong arguments for both sides of the discussion. If the issue is a real issue, there is often more than one way to account for the transaction or event.
   - Make sure that the analysis considers the substance of the transaction from a business and economic perspective.

   Quantitative:

   - Calculate the impact of the different perspectives on key financial statement numbers/ratios. Would this decision be relevant to users?
   - Calculate what the numbers might look like under different accounting methods, if they are relevant.

3. **Recommendations**

   After each issue is analyzed, conclude on how to account for the items. Your conclusion should be based on your role and the financial reporting objective that you identified earlier.

This primer is a summary of the case primer document on the Student Website and in WileyPLUS.

Some conventions to note when using this glossary: Terms listed but **not** defined refer to *defined synonyms* as "See...." Terms listed and defined refer to *listed synonyms* as "Also known as" with the synonyms in italics. Terms listed and defined refer to *unlisted synonyms* as "Also known as" with the synonyms in quotation marks.

Accelerated amortization A depreciation method that creates a higher depreciation expense in the earlier years and lower charges in the later periods. An example is the *Diminishing balance method.*

Account An individual accounting record of increases and decreases in a specific asset, liability, shareholders' equity or income statement item.

Accounting cycle A series of steps followed by accountants in preparing financial statements.

Accounting information system The system of collecting and processing transaction data and communicating financial information to interested parties.

Accounting Standards Advisory Forum A forum established in 2013 to provide technical advice to the IASB, consisting of representatives from national standard setters from around the world.

Accounting Standards Board (AcSB) The group primarily responsible for setting GAAP in Canada, which publishes the *CPA Canada Handbook* and other authoritative documents.

Accounting Standards for Private Enterprises (ASPE) The financial reporting standards applicable to private entities in Canada. Private entities may also use IFRS.

Accounting Standards Oversight Council (AcSOC) The group that provides oversight to AcSB activities such as setting the agenda, reporting to the public, and raising funds for standard setting.

Accrual basis The most commonly used basis of accounting whereby revenue is recognized when it is earned and expenses are recognized in the period incurred, without regard to the time of receipt or payment of cash. Also known as *Accrual-basis accounting.*

Accrual-basis accounting See *Accrual basis.*

Accrued expenses Expenses incurred, but not yet paid at the statement date.

Accrued revenues Revenues earned, but not yet received in cash at the statement date.

Accumulated other comprehensive income The cumulative total of all past charges and credits to OCI up to the statement of financial position date. It is similar to retained earnings, but it is for OCI items.

Acquirer A company that purchases another business.

Active market A level of trading of a particular security or asset where there is a good supply of willing buyers and sellers.

Activity method A method of calculating depreciation whereby depreciation is determined as a function of the use or productivity of the asset.

Activity ratios Ratios that measure how effectively a company uses its assets, and the liquidity of certain assets such as inventory and receivables.

Additions Increases or extensions of existing assets.

Adjunct account An account that increases either an asset, a liability, or an owners' equity account.

Adjusted trial balance A list of all open accounts in the ledger and their balances taken immediately after all adjusting entries have been posted.

Adjusting entries Journal entries made at the end of the accounting period to ensure that the revenue recognition and matching principles are followed.

Adverse selection A result of information asymmetry whereby the capital marketplace may attract the wrong types of companies (such that companies with higher-quality products may choose not to enter the market).

Aggressive accounting A bias that exists in financial reporting that focuses more on the positive information about a company and its financial position and operations; for example, a company may overstate net income or net assets.

Aging method A method of estimating the percentage of outstanding receivables that will become uncollectible based on past experience using the percentage-of-receivables approach.

Aging schedule A schedule to organize accounts receivable that indicates which accounts require special attention for collection based on the age of such accounts receivable.

Agricultural produce The produce that is harvested from biological assets.

All-inclusive approach An income measurement approach that indicates that most items, including irregular ones, are recorded in income.

Allowance method A method of estimating uncollectible accounts receivable whereby bad debt expense is recorded in the same period as the sale to obtain a proper matching of expenses and revenues, and to achieve a proper carrying value for accounts receivable.

Amortization The process of allocating the cost of an asset to expense over its useful life in a rational and systematic manner. Also known as *Depreciation.*

Amortized cost The acquisition cost adjusted for the amortization of the discount or premium.

Amortized cost model A model applied to investments in debt securities and long-term notes and loans receivable that measures the difference between the initial amount recognized and the maturity value and allocates it to income over time.

Arm's-length transaction A transaction that has been carried out between parties that are not related (resulting in terms that are fairly bargained and that represent market terms).

Artistic-related intangible assets Ownership rights over the reproduction of a creative work. They are protected by copyright and have value because of their legal-contractual nature.

Asset group See *Cash-generating unit (CGU).*

Asset retirement costs Costs recognized at the same time that the liability associated with the retirement of an asset is recognized.

Asset turnover ratio A measurement of how efficiently a company uses its total assets to generate revenue. It is calculated by dividing net sales by average total assets.

Asset-backed financing The use of receivables as collateral to generate immediate cash for a company, either through secured borrowings or sales of receivables.

Asset-backed securities Securities that represent ownership claims to a pool of individual loans that have been securitized; that is, repackaged into asset pools in which ownership interest has been sold.

Asset-liability approach A revenue recognition approach that focuses on changes in contractual rights and contractual obligations created by contracts with customers.

Assets Economic resources which are controlled by the company and result from past transactions or events.

Associate An entity that an investor has significant influence over that is neither a subsidiary nor a joint venture.

Assurance-type warranty A type of warranty that provides assurance as to the quality of the product sold at the point of sale and for a reasonable period thereafter.

Average days to sell inventory A variable of the inventory turnover ratio that represents the average age of the inventory on hand based on the number of days it takes to sell inventory once purchased.

Avoidable borrowing costs The actual borrowing costs that would not have been incurred by a company borrowing funds to finance a specific qualifying asset if the expenditures for the qualifying asset had not been made.

Bad debts A charge for impaired trade receivables. Also known as "uncollectible accounts."

Balance sheet A financial statement that shows a company's financial condition at the end of a period. Also known as *Statement of financial position.*

Bank overdrafts What occurs when cheques are written for more than the amount in the cash account.

Bank reconciliation A schedule explaining any differences between the bank's and the company's records of cash.

Bargain purchase The purchase of an investment or asset at a price that is lower than its fair value.

Barter transactions Transactions where few or no monetary assets are received as consideration when goods or services are purchased or sold. Also known as *Nonmonetary transactions.*

Basic elements Financial reporting terms that constitute the language of accounting and business, such as "assets," "liabilities," and "equity."

Basic loan features Contractual terms that result in cash flows that are payments of principal and interest.

Basket purchase The purchase of a group of units with different characteristics at a single lump-sum price.

Bearer plants Plants that produce agricultural produce such as grapes or apples.

Beneficial interest A debt or equity claim to the cash flows of the party that acquired the receivables, arising when a company sells a receivable.

Bill-and-hold arrangement A type of business arrangement where goods are sold but the seller does not deliver the goods right away.

Biological assets Any living asset, such as livestock or trees.

Book value The amount at which an asset is recognized in the statement of financial position. Also known as *Carrying amount.*

Boot The payment or receipt of a significant amount of cash or other monetary asset when assets are exchanged or traded in.

Borrowing costs Interest and other costs that a company incurs in connection with the borrowing of funds.

Brand A group of assets such as a trade name and its related formulas, recipes, and technology that are used to distinguish a particular company or product.

Brand name See *Brand.*

Breakage Unredeemed points in loyalty programs.

Bright-line tests Quantitative thresholds in financial reporting standards that act as a benchmark to dictate how something is to be accounted for.

Bundled sales Contracts involving the sale of multiple goods and/or services for one price. Also known as *Multiple deliverables.*

Business combination What results when one entity acquires control over the net assets of another business, either by acquiring the net assets directly, or by acquiring the equity interest representing control over the net assets.

Business model The manner in which a company adds value. Different business models include manufacturing, retail selling, providing services, exploration and development, and others.

Canadian Institute of Chartered Accountants (CICA) The predecessor organization of Chartered Professional Accountants Canada (CPA Canada).

Canadian Public Accountability Board (CPAB) The regulatory oversight body that oversees audit quality for Canadian firms performing auditing work.

Capital allocation The process by which accounting enables investors and creditors to assess the relative returns and risks associated with investment opportunities and thereby channel resources effectively.

Capital approach A method of accounting for donated assets from an owner where the increase in assets is credited to Contributed Surplus - Donated Capital (it is not included in net income).

Capital cost allowance (CCA) The amount of depreciation allowed to be deducted for tax purposes in tax returns.

Capital cost allowance method The method used in calculating depreciation for tax purposes and calculating the tax value of an asset by Canadian businesses, regardless of the method used for reporting purposes.

Capital expenditure An expenditure that increases an asset's useful life, increases the quantity of units produced from the asset, or enhances the quality of units produced.

Capital gain The result when the proceeds on disposal of a capital asset are greater than the original cost of the asset.

Capitalization period The time period during which interest may be capitalized. It begins when three conditions are present: (1) expenditures for the asset have been made, (2) activities that are necessary to get the asset ready for its intended use are in progress, and (3) interest cost is being incurred.

Capitalization rate A weighted-average borrowing rate on general borrowings, used to determine avoidable borrowing costs on non–asset-specific debt.

Capitalized Recorded in asset accounts and then depreciated, as is appropriate for expenditures for items with useful lives greater than one year.

Carrying amount The amount at which an asset is recognized in the statement of financial position. Also known as *Book value.*

Cash Cash on hand and demand deposits.

Cash and cash equivalents Cash, demand deposits, and short-term highly liquid investments that are readily convertible into known amounts of cash and that are subject to insignificant risk of changes in value.

Cash debt coverage ratio A long-run measure of financial flexibility that indicates a company's ability to repay its liabilities from net cash provided by operating activities, without having to liquidate the assets used in its operations.

Cash discounts Sales discounts that are offered to induce prompt payment.

Cash equivalents Short-term, highly liquid investments that are readily converted to known amounts of cash and are subject to an insignificant risk of change in value.

Cash-generating unit (CGU) The smallest identifiable group of assets that generates cash inflows that are largely independent of the cash flows from other assets or groups of assets (IFRS). Similar to an "asset group" (ASPE).

Change in accounting principle A change that occurs when an accounting principle adopted is different from the one previously used.

Chartered Professional Accountants of Canada (CPA Canada) The main professional accounting body for professional accountants in Canada that also has primary responsibility for setting GAAP in Canada through the Accounting Standards Board.

Closing entries The journal entries that close the temporary accounts in order to start a new financial reporting period. After closing revenue and expense accounts, the related Income Summary amounts are posted to retained earnings.

Closing process The procedure generally followed to reduce the balance of temporary accounts to zero in order to prepare the accounts for the next period's transactions.

Commercial substance A term referring to the validity of a transaction from a business perspective.

Comparability What occurs when information that has been measured and reported in a similar manner for different companies is considered comparable.

Compensating balances That portion of any demand deposit (or any time deposit or certificate of deposit) maintained by a company that constitutes support for existing borrowing arrangements of the company with a lending institution.

Completed-contract method The revenue recognition method in which revenues and gross profit are recognized only when the contract is completed.

Completeness The quality of accounting information that makes it reliable by including all information necessary to provide an accurate portrayal of events and transactions.

Component of an enterprise A part of an entity being disposed of where the operations, cash flows, and financial elements are clearly distinguishable from the rest of the entity.

Componentization Decisions regarding which fixed asset components to recognize separately.

Compound interest Interest that is earned on the principal amount invested and on any accrued interest.

Comprehensive income A measure of income under IFRS that includes net income plus other comprehensive income.

Computer software costs A technology-based intangible asset, either developed for internal use or for sale as a product.

Conceptual framework A coherent system of interrelated objectives and fundamentals that can lead to consistent standards and that prescribes the nature, function, and limits of financial accounting and financial statements.

Conservatism The exercise of caution where making decisions under conditions that are uncertain. Also known as *prudence*.

Conservative accounting A bias that exists in financial reporting that ensures that, where uncertainty exists and judgement is needed, net income and/or net assets are understated rather than being overstated.

Consigned goods Goods that are sold on consignment yet remain the consignor's property and therefore must be included in inventory.

Consignee The party in a consignment arrangement that displays goods for sale (where legal title remains with the supplier/consignor).

Consignment A type of transaction where one party, who does not have legal title to goods, presents them to customers for sale and earns a commission when the customer buys the goods.

Consignor The party in a consignment arrangement that has legal title to goods for sale but allows the goods to be displayed for sale by another party (consignee).

Consistency What occurs when a company applies the same accounting treatment to similar events from period to period.

Consolidation The process of presenting both parent and subsidiary companies as a single economic entity.

Constructive obligation A type of performance obligation that is created through a past practice or by signalling something to potential customers, such as a "100% satisfaction guaranteed" policy.

Contingency "An existing condition or situation involving uncertainty as to a possible gain or loss to an enterprise that will ultimately be resolved when one or more future events occur or fail to occur," as defined under ASPE.

Contra account An account on the statement of financial position that reduces an asset, a liability, or an owners' equity account.

Contra asset account An account that is offset against an asset account on the statement of financial position.

Contract A legally binding arrangement between two or more parties.

Contract assets Assets that arise through contractual rights.

Contract liability Liabilities that arise through contractual obligations.

Contract modification When the contract terms of an ongoing contract are changed.

Contract-based intangible assets The value of rights that arise from contractual arrangements, such as licensing agreements, lease agreements, and broadcast rights.

Contractual yield basis A model of managing a long-term receivables contract involving the holding of instruments for their principal and interest flows.

Control Under ASPE, the continuing power to determine the strategic operating, financing, and investing policies of another entity without the co-operation of others. Under IFRS, the power to direct the activities of another entity to generate returns, either positive or negative, for the investor.

Conversion costs A type of product cost that includes labour and variable production overhead costs incurred in processing materials into finished goods.

Copyright A federally granted right that all authors, painters, musicians, sculptors, and other artists have in their creations, whatever mode or form of expression. It is an exclusive right to reproduce and sell an artistic or published work.

Cost All expenditures needed to acquire an item of property, plant, and equipment and bring it to its location and ready it for use.

Cost formula A method of assigning inventory costs incurred during the accounting period to inventory that is still on hand at the end of the period. The three acceptable formulas are specific identification; first-in, first-out (FIFO); and weighted average cost.

Cost model (CM) The model that measures property, plant, and equipment assets after acquisition at their cost, less accumulated depreciation and any accumulated impairment losses.

Cost of goods available for sale or use The total of (1) the cost of goods on hand at the beginning of the period and (2) the cost of the goods acquired or produced during the period.

Cost of goods manufactured The total cost of items that have been manufactured including raw materials and related processing costs.

Cost of goods sold The difference between the goods available for sale during the period and those on hand at the end of the period.

Cost recovery impairment model A model of measuring impairment losses whereby a long-lived asset is impaired only if a company cannot recover the asset's carrying amount from using the asset and eventually disposing of it.

Cost reduction method An income approach method for accounting for government assistance, whereby the asset cost and future depreciation are reduced by the amount of government assistance received.

Cost-benefit relationship A constraint of financial reporting that the costs of obtaining and providing information should not be higher than the benefits that are gained by providing it.

Cost-to-cost basis The process by which the percentage-of-completion is measured by comparing costs incurred to date with the most recent estimate of the total costs to complete the contract.

Cost-to-retail ratio A ratio used in the retail inventory method determined by dividing goods available for sale at cost, by the goods available for sale at retail.

Coupon rate See *Stated interest rate*.

Coverage ratios Ratios that measure the degree of protection for long-term creditors and investors. Also known as *Solvency ratios*.

CPA Canada Handbook A set of principles and guidelines for accounting and assurance.

Credit The right side of a general ledger account.

Credit risk The likelihood of loss because of the failure of the other party in a transaction to fully pay the amount owed.

Current assets Cash and other assets ordinarily realizable within one year from the date of the balance sheet or within the normal operating cycle where that is longer than a year.

Current cash debt coverage ratio The ratio of net cash provided by operating activities to average current liabilities, indicating how well a company can address its current obligations from internally generated cash flow.

Current liabilities Amounts due within one year from the date of the statement of financial position or within the normal operating cycle, where this is longer than a year.

Current operating performance approach An income measurement approach that argues that the most useful income measure will reflect only regular and recurring revenue and expense elements.

Current ratio The ratio of total current assets to total current liabilities.

Customer-related intangible assets Intangible assets that occur as a result of interactions between company employees and systems with outside parties interested in buying goods and services.

Cut-off schedule A schedule prepared by the accountant for the period end to ensure that goods received from suppliers and shipped to customers around the end of the year are recorded in the appropriate period.

Data analytics A study of data sets, using special software and systems, to make deductions about the information that they possess. This information obtained from the data sets is used to make better decisions in business and science.

Debit The left side of a general ledger account.

Debt instruments Financial instruments that have contractual cash flows including principal and interest.

Debt securities Financial instruments that have contractual cash flows including principal and interest whose prices are generally quoted in an active market.

Decision-usefulness Approach to financial reporting whereby the amount and types of information to be disclosed and the format in which information should be presented are determined based on which alternative provides the most useful information for decision-making purposes.

Declining-balance method A depreciation method that uses a depreciation rate that remains a constant percentage throughout the asset's useful life and uses book value each year to determine depreciation expense.

Decreasing charge method A depreciation method that provides for a higher depreciation expense in the earlier years and lower charges in the later periods on the basis that more depreciation should be charged in earlier years if that is when the asset offers the greatest benefits.

Deferral method The method of recording the amount of government assistance received as a deferred credit, amortizing it to revenue over the life of the related assets.

Deferred income tax assets The future tax consequence due to deductible temporary differences. Also known as *Future income tax assets* under ASPE.

Deferred income tax liabilities The future tax consequences associated with taxable temporary differences. Also known as *Future income tax liabilities* under ASPE.

Depletion The amortization of natural resources.

Depletion base A natural resource's capitalized costs of acquisition, exploration, development, and restoration.

Deposits in transit End-of-month deposits of cash recorded in the depositor's books one month and received and recorded by the bank the following month.

Depreciable amount The difference between the asset's cost, or revalued amount if the revaluation model is being used, and its residual value.

Depreciation The cost of tangible capital assets allocated to the accounting periods benefiting their use; generally used to describe tangible assets. Also known as *Amortization*.

Derecognition The process of removing an item from a company's statement of financial position or income statement.

Derecognized What happens to an asset after all of its related items have been removed from a company's accounts.

Development The translation of research findings or other knowledge into a plan or design for new or substantially improved materials, devices, products, processes, systems, or services prior to the start of commercial production or use.

Development phase A broad category of development activities where costs are capitalized only when future benefits are reasonably certain.

Diminishing balance method A depreciation method that applies a constant percentage rate to net book value to calculate depreciation expense over the useful life of the asset. A type of *Accelerated amortization*.

Direct write-off method A method for recording uncollectible accounts receivable where no entry is made until a specific account has definitely been established as uncollectible.

Discontinued operations The operations of an identifiable business segment that has been sold, abandoned, shut down, or otherwise disposed of, or that is the subject of a formal plan for disposal.

Discount What occurs when a bond sells at less than face value.

Discounted cash flow model A model for measuring fair value that deals with uncertainty and the time value of money. It has two approaches: the traditional approach and the expected cash flow approach.

Discounted free cash flow method A method to value goodwill that involves a projection of the company's free cash flow over a long period.

Double-declining-balance method A depreciation method that uses a rate (which is the straight-line percentage rate multiplied by two) that is applied to the net book value every year, resulting in a declining depreciation expense year after year.

Double-entry accounting System of accounting requiring the equality of debits and credits

when recording transactions, which helps prove the accuracy of the recorded amounts.

Due process A method used in standard setting in order to ensure that standard-setting bodies operate in full view of the public by giving those who are interested ample opportunity to make their views known.

Earnings approach An approach to revenue recognition whereby revenues are recognized when performance is substantially complete and collection is reasonably assured.

Earnings management The process of targeting certain earnings levels (whether current or future) or desired earnings trends and working backward to determine what has to be done to ensure that these targets are met.

Earnings multiple A number calculated by dividing the market price of a share by earnings per share.

Earnings per share (EPS) Net income available to common shareholders divided by the weighted average number of common shares outstanding.

Economic benefits Benefits provided by assets, such as increased revenues from sales of products or services and reductions in future costs.

Economic entity assumption An assumption that a company's business activity can be kept separate and distinct from its owners and any other business units. Economic activity can therefore be identified with a particular degree of accountability.

Economic substance The underlying economic reality reported on a representationally faithful document.

Effective interest method A method of amortization whereby the current market rate of interest at the time of investment is used to calculate interest income by applying it to the carrying amount (book value) of the investment for each interest period. The note's carrying amount changes as it is increased by the amount of discount amortized.

Effective interest rate The interest rate actually earned. Also known as *Market rate* or *Yield rate*.

Efficient markets hypothesis A theory that states that, if information is available, it will be incorporated into decisions made by market participants.

Elements of financial statements Basic items that are presented in the financial statements.

Entity perspective The viewpoint that companies are viewed as separate and distinct from their owners and therefore financial reporting should focus on the needs of the main users and not just the owners.

Equitable obligations Commitments that arise from moral or ethical considerations.

Equity The residual interest in the assets of a company that remains after deducting its liabilities.

Equity instruments Any contract that evidences a residual interest in the assets of a company after deducting all of its liabilities; examples are common and certain preferred shares.

Equity method A method of accounting for investments where a significant influence relationship is acknowledged between the investor and the investee. The investment is originally recorded at its cost, but is subsequently adjusted each period for changes in the investee's net assets.

Equity pickup What occurs when an investor "picks up" its share of income or loss under the equity method.

Ethical dilemmas Problems where there are no set guidelines to follow in order to resolve a situation. These are the grey areas where one has to ask "Is it morally right or wrong?"

Event Something of consequence that happens, which is generally the source of changes in asset, liability, and equity balances. An event may be internal or external.

Excess-earnings approach A method used to value goodwill that calculates the "normal" earnings generated by companies in the same industry. If a company earns a higher rate of return than the industry average, this excess is goodwill.

Existence uncertainty Uncertainty as to whether an element exists or not (for instance, a liability).

Exit price A measure of fair value that represents the amount that a company would receive on selling an asset or transferring a liability.

Expected cash flow approach An approach to the discounted cash flow model where a risk-free discount rate is used to discount cash flows that have been adjusted for uncertainty. The discount rate is the risk-free rate and the cash flow uncertainty is dealt with by using probabilities.

Expected loss impairment model A model of accounting for impairment where estimates of future cash flows used to determine the present value of the investment are made on a continuous basis.

Expected value The probability-weighted amount where there is a range of possible amounts.

Expenses Decreases in economic resources, either by outflows or reductions of assets or incurrence of liabilities resulting from a company's ordinary revenue-generating activities.

Face rate See *Stated interest rate*.

Face value The value of an interest-bearing note or loan receivable when the stated interest rate is equal to the effective (market) rate.

Factoring receivables When a company sells its accounts receivable to banks or finance companies that buy receivables from businesses for a fee and then collect the remittances directly from the customers.

Fair value An estimate of the price a company would have received if it had sold the asset or would have paid, if it had been relieved of the liability, on the measurement date in an arm's-length exchange motivated by normal business considerations.

Fair value hierarchy A model that categorizes inputs to valuation methods (and the items being valued) by quality of information.

Fair value loss impairment model A model of impairment whereby the impairment loss is the difference between the asset's fair value and its current carrying amount assuming the fair value is less than the carrying amount.

Fair value model (FVM) A method of accounting for investment property, under which it is recognized on the statement of financial position after acquisition at its fair value.

Fair value option The option given to companies allowing them to use fair value for most financial instruments. Under IFRS, certain conditions must be met.

Fair value principle The GAAP principle that provides guidance regarding how to measure financial statement elements using best estimates of market values.

Fair value through net income (FV-NI) A method of measuring the fair value of financial instruments where the carrying amount is adjusted to its current fair value at each reporting date such that all holding gains and losses are reported in net income along with any dividends or interest income earned. Also known as *Fair value through profit or loss (FVTPL)*.

Fair value through other comprehensive income (FV-OCI) A model where the carrying amount of each FV-OCI investment is adjusted to its current fair value at each reporting date, and the holding gains and losses are recognized in other comprehensive income.

Fair value through profit or loss (FVTPL) See *Fair value through net income (FV-NI)*.

Favourable lease A lease that is considered an intangible asset when the terms are more favourable than the usual market terms.

Feedback/confirmatory value The notion that relevant information helps users confirm or correct prior expectations.

Financial accounting The process that culminates in the preparation of financial reports for the company as a whole for use by both internal and external parties. Also known as *Financial reporting*.

Financial Accounting Standards Board (FASB) The major standard-setting body in the United States.

Financial asset A receivable that represents contractual rights to receive cash or other financial assets from another party. May also be cash, a derivative or investment.

Financial components approach A method of recording a sale of receivables transaction whereby each party to the sale of an account receivable recognizes the components (assets and liabilities) that it controls after the sale and derecognizes the assets and liabilities that were sold or extinguished.

Financial engineering A process whereby a business arrangement or transaction is structured legally such that it meets the company's financial reporting objective (for example, to maximize earnings, minimize a debt-to-equity ratio, or other).

Financial flexibility The measurement of a company's ability to take effective actions to alter the amounts and timing of cash flows so it can respond to unexpected needs and opportunities.

Financial instruments Contracts that give rise to both a financial asset for one party and a financial liability or equity instrument for another.

Financial reporting The process that culminates in the preparation of financial reports for the company as a whole for use by both internal and external parties. Also known as *Financial accounting*.

Financial statements The principal means through which financial information is communicated to those outside a company. They provide a company's history, quantified in money terms.

Financing activities Activities resulting in changes in the size and composition of the company's equity capital and borrowings.

Finished goods inventory The reporting of the costs associated with the completed but unsold units at the end of the fiscal period.

Finite life A term referring to the life of an asset where there is a foreseeable limit to its useful life. Also known as *Limited life*.

First principles Foundational principles from which decisions stem, making decisions theoretically consistent if they stem from the same foundational reasoning.

First-in, first-out (FIFO) cost formula The method that assigns costs to inventory assuming that goods are used in the order in which they are purchased.

Fixed assets Tangible capital assets that are acquired for use in operations and not for resale, are long-term in nature, are usually subject to depreciation, and possess physical substance. Also known as *Plant assets* or *Property, plant, and equipment*.

f.o.b. destination Shipping designation meaning that the legal title of an asset does not pass to the buyer until the goods reach the customer's location.

f.o.b. shipping point Shipping designation meaning that the legal title of an asset belongs to the buyer when the goods leave the shipping company's dock.

Franchise A contractual arrangement under which the franchisor grants the franchisee the right to sell certain services, to use certain trademarks or trade names, or to perform certain functions, usually within a designated geographical area. Also known as a *Licensing agreement*.

Free cash flow An indicator of financial flexibility that uses information provided on the cash flow statement. Free cash flow is net operating cash flows reduced by dividends and the capital expenditures needed to sustain the current level of operations.

Freedom from error A measure of the reliability of reported information, assuring that the relevant information is accurate and unaffected by the opinions of stakeholders.

Fulfillment costs The costs that will be incurred to complete a contract.

Full cost method A method of accounting for natural resource properties in which oil and gas companies capitalize all of their exploration costs, even those representing "dry holes" that do not contain oil and gas reserves. Each year, they assess the net capitalized costs to determine whether it is likely that the costs will be recovered in the future.

Full disclosure principle Financial reporting of information significant enough to influence the judgement of an informed reader.

Function (of expense) Using the type of activity, such as cost of goods sold, selling and distribution, and research and development as a way of classifying and presenting expenses on the statement of income.

Future income tax assets The future tax consequences due to deductible temporary differences. Also known as *Deferred income tax assets* under IFRS.

Future income tax liabilities The future tax consequences associated with taxable temporary differences. Also known as *Deferred income tax liabilities* under IFRS.

GAAP hierarchy Guidance that notes that primary sources of GAAP should be used first, followed by other relevant and reliable sources, including the conceptual framework and professional judgement.

Gains Increases in equity (net assets) from a company's peripheral or incidental transactions and from all other transactions and other events and circumstances affecting the company during a period, except those that result from revenues or investments by owners.

General journal A chronological listing of transactions and other events expressed in terms of debits and credits to particular accounts.

General ledger A collection of all asset, liability, shareholders' equity, revenue, and expense accounts and their respective balances.

General-purpose financial statements Basic GAAP financial statements that provide information that meets the needs of external users (normally investors and creditors).

Generally accepted accounting principles (GAAP) The common set of standards and procedures used to prepare financial statements with the expectation that the majority of users' needs will be met.

Going concern assumption The assumption that the company will continue to operate for at least 12 more months.

Goodwill An asset representing the future economic benefits acquired in a business combination that are not individually identified or separately recognized.

Gross profit method A method for estimating inventory where taking a physical count is impractical or impossible. It is based on three premises: (1) the beginning inventory plus purchases equal total goods to be accounted for; (2) goods not sold must be on hand; and (3) when the net sales, reduced to cost, are deducted from the total goods to be accounted for, the result is the ending inventory.

Gross profit percentage The gross profit expressed as a percentage of sales.

Half-year rule A requirement of the income tax regulation that in the year a capital asset is acquired, only half the usual capital cost allowance can be claimed for tax purposes.

Held for sale The characteristic of assets where a formal, detailed plan exists to sell the assets, normally within a year.

Highest and best use A concept for valuing assets that assumes the highest value that the market would place on the asset, considering uses that are possible, legally permissible, and financially feasible.

Historical cost principle An accounting principle that provides guidance on how to measure transactions and balances on the basis of acquisition price.

Identifiable (intangible asset) A characteristic of intangible assets that either results from contractual or other legal rights, or can be separated and divided from the company and sold, transferred, licensed, rented, or exchanged, either by itself or with another contract, identifiable asset, or liability.

Identifiable net assets What arise when a company's purchase price is allocated among all the assets and liabilities to which a value can be attributed; refers to all net assets except goodwill.

IFRS Advisory Council A group that provides strategic advice to the IASB (International Accounting Standards Board).

IFRS Discussion Group (IFRS DG) A subcommittee of the AcSB that provides a forum for the discussion of issues arising in Canada because of implementing IFRS. It also provides recommendations to the AcSB for referral to the IFRS Board.

IFRS Foundation A group that raises finances and provides strategic direction and oversight to the IASB.

Impaired The state when a long-lived asset's carrying amount is higher than its future economic benefits to the company.

Impairment loss The amount by which the asset's carrying amount exceeds its fair value.

Impairments A decrease in the carrying value of a long-term asset to an amount that is less than the amount shown under the cost principle.

Implicit interest rate The discount rate that corresponds to the lessor's internal rate of return on the lease.

Imprest system A petty cash system where the custodian is responsible for the amount of funds on hand at all times, whether the amount is in cash or signed receipts.

Imputed interest rate The actual interest rate realized on a bond, which is different from the stated rate when there is a discount or premium.

In-process research and development (R&D) An identifiable intangible asset involving the research work and findings of a company, acquired when the company purchases another. It must be separable from goodwill to be reported separately.

Income An increase in assets or decrease in liabilities resulting from transactions or events other than those relating to shareholder contributions.

Income approach A method to account for contributions of assets that requires the amount received to be deferred and recognized over the period that the related assets are employed.

Income statement A report that measures the success of a company's operations used for a specific time period (under ASPE). Also known as *statement of financial performance*, *Statement of income/earnings*, or *Statement of profit or loss*.

Incurred loss impairment model A model where investments are recognized as impaired when there is no longer reasonable assurance that the future cash flows associated with them will be collected in their entirety when due. It accounts for credit losses triggered by specific events that occurred by the balance sheet date.

Indefinite life An asset's useful life where there appears to be no foreseeable limit to how long the asset will generate positive net cash flows to the company.

Information asymmetry The state that exists when one party (such as management) has access to more information than the other party (for example, investors).

Information overload The phenomenon that too much information may result in a situation where the user is unable to digest or process the information.

Information symmetry The state that exists when both parties have access to the same information.

Input measures Costs incurred that measure efforts devoted to a contract.

Inspection An organized formal evaluation of property, plant, and equipment that is considered a type of recurring cost after acquisition.

Institutional investors Large corporations or corporate investors such as pension funds or mutual funds.

Intangible assets Nonmonetary assets that lack physical substance and usually have a higher degree of uncertainty concerning their future benefits.

Intellectual capital See *Knowledge assets.*

Interest-bearing notes Notes that have a stated rate of interest that is payable over and above the face value of the note.

International Accounting Standards Board (IASB) The group responsible for setting IFRS with the goal of increasing the transparency of financial reporting by achieving a single, global method of accounting.

International Financial Reporting Standards Interpretations Committee (IFRIC) A committee that studies and provides recommendations on issues not covered by the IASB.

International Financial Reporting Standards (IFRS) The internationally recognized common set of financial reporting standards and procedures.

International Integrated Reporting Committee (IIRC) A group that looks at a broader view of financial reporting that includes management information, governance and compensation, and sustainability reporting.

Intraperiod tax allocation The approach to allocating taxes within the financial statements of the current period.

Inventories Assets that are held for sale in the ordinary course of business.

Inventory turnover ratio A ratio that measures the number of times, on average, the inventory was sold during the period.

Investing activities Activities covering the acquisition and disposal of long-term assets and other investments not included in cash equivalents.

Investment property Property held to generate rentals and/or appreciate in value rather than to sell in the ordinary course of business or to use in production, administration, or supplying goods and services.

Joint cost A single cost of purchasing or producing multiple items.

Joint venture A type of equity investment characterized by joint control, rather than unilateral control by one party.

Journal The book of original entry where transactions and selected other events are initially recorded.

Journal entries The means by which transactions are recorded in the general ledger. Includes adjusting, closing and reversing entries

Knowledge assets Unrecognized intangible assets related to the creativity and knowledge of key employees that create value for a company. Also known as *Intellectual capital.*

Laid-down costs Any cost incurred to get the asset in place and ready for use (whether it is for sale or to generate income through use). Also known as "out-of-pocket costs."

Last-in, first-out (LIFO) cost formula A method no longer permitted under ASPE and IFRS that assigns inventory costs on the basis that the cost of the most recent purchase is the first cost to be charged to cost of goods sold.

Lease A contractual agreement between a lessor (property owner) and a lessee (property renter) that gives the lessee the right to use specific property, owned by the lessor, for a specified time in return for stipulated, and generally periodic, cash payments (rents). Also known as *Leasehold.*

Leasehold See *Lease.*

Leasehold improvements Improvements made to the leased property by the lessee.

Legal title A right meaning that a good is legally owned; not the same as possession.

Liabilities Duties or responsibilities (to transfer economic resources) which result from past transactions or events.

Licences Operating rights obtained through agreements with governmental units or agencies, such as the use of airwaves for radio or television broadcasting. Also known as *Permits.*

Licensing agreement A contractual arrangement under which a government body or a business entity grants a business enterprise the right to sell certain services, to use certain trademarks or trade names, or to perform certain functions, usually within a designated geographical area. Also known as a *Franchise.*

Limited life See *Finite life.*

Liquidating dividend A dividend greater than accumulated net income, which represents a return of a shareholder's investment rather than profits of the company.

Liquidity A company's ability to convert assets into cash to pay off its current liabilities in the ordinary course of business.

Liquidity ratios Ratios that measure the company's short-run ability to pay its maturing obligations.

Loans and receivables Financial assets that result from the delivery of cash or other assets by a lender to a borrower in return for a promise to pay an amount on specified dates or on demand, usually with interest.

Loans receivable An agreement where one party advances cash or other assets in exchange for a promise to be repaid later.

Long-term liabilities Obligations that are not reasonably expected to be liquidated within the greater of one year or the normal operating cycle, but instead are payable at some date beyond that time.

Losses Decreases in equity (net assets) from a company's peripheral or incidental transactions and from all other transactions and other events and circumstances affecting the company during a period, except those that result from expenses or distributions to owners.

Lower of cost and net realizable value (LC&NRV) standard A principle used for ensuring that inventory is not overstated by comparing carrying cost and the amount that could be received if the inventory were disposed of and measuring the inventory at the lower of the two.

Lump-sum price The price paid when several assets are purchased together for a single price.

Major overhauls Substantial repairs or replacements of equipment, or renovations to property. Treated as a recurring component of cost after acquisition.

Management best estimate Assumptions made by management in light of their knowledge and familiarity with the company, the industry, and the economy.

Management bias The presentation by management of information about their company in its best light in order to make their company look as successful as possible.

Management stewardship A concept whereby management is charged with protecting and enhancing the capital of a company.

Managerial accounting The process of identifying, measuring, analyzing, and communicating financial information to internal decision-makers.

Markdown A decrease in price below the original selling price.

Markdown cancellations What occurs when markdowns are offset by an increase in the prices of goods that had been previously marked down.

Market rate The interest rate actually earned. Also known as *Effective interest rate* or *Yield rate.*

Marketing-related intangible assets Intangible assets related primarily to the marketing or promotion of products or services.

Markup An increase in the price above the original selling price.

Markup cancellations What occurs when markups are offset by a decrease in the prices of goods that had been previously marked up.

Markup on cost What occurs when the selling price is determined by a rate being equal to the gross profit as a percentage of cost.

Matching The accounting principle that dictates that efforts (expenses) be matched with accomplishments (revenues) whenever reasonable and practicable.

Material rights Rights that a customer has in a sales contract that are significant.

Materiality The concept that relates to an item's impact on a company's overall financial operations. An item is material if its inclusion or omission would influence or change the judgement of a reasonable person.

Measurement uncertainty What occurs when there is a variance between the recognized amount and another reasonably possible amount.

Merchandise inventory Inventory purchased in a form ready for sale.

Mineral resource properties Capitalized costs that are associated with the acquired rights, and the exploration, evaluation, and development of these minerals.

Mineral resources Mining and oil and gas resources that do not regenerate. Also known as "wasting assets."

Minority interest The percentage of a subsidiary's net assets not owned (reported as a liability on the balance sheet), or the percentage of the net income that does not accrue to the parent company (reported as a deduction from the combined net income on the income statement). Also known as *Noncontrolling interest.*

Modified cash basis A mixture of cash basis and accrual basis accounting often followed by professional service firms.

Monetary assets Money or claims to future cash flows that are fixed in amount and timing by contract or other arrangement.

Monetary unit assumption The assumption that money is the common denominator of economic activity and provides an appropriate basis for accounting measurement and analysis.

Moral hazard The risk that certain parties who have additional information not accessible to others will act in their own self-interest.

Most advantageous market A concept used for measuring fair value that considers the value based on the market that would pay the most for the asset.

Most likely amount The single amount in a range of outcomes that is most likely to occur.

Moving-average cost formula An inventory pricing method that prices inventory items based on the moving-average cost of the goods available for sale in the period.

Multiple deliverables See *Bundled sales.*

Multiple-step income statement An income statement format that recognizes a separation between operating transactions and non-operating transactions and matches the relevant costs and expenses with their related revenues.

Nature (of expense) The type of expense, such as payroll, depreciation, and cost of raw materials, as classified and presented on the statement of income.

Negative goodwill See *Bargain purchase.*

Net income Revenues less expenses (including gains and losses) other than those defined under IFRS as other comprehensive income.

Net markdowns Markdowns less markdown cancellations.

Net markups Markups less markup cancellations.

Net realizable value (NRV) The net amount expected to be received in cash for an asset.

Neutrality The quality of accounting information that ensures faithful representation by being factual, truthful, and unbiased.

Non-current investments Long-term investments that will not be realized within one year or during the current operating cycle.

Non-GAAP earnings An adjusted net income number derived from GAAP net income plus or minus any nonrecurring or non-operating items.

Non–interest-bearing notes Notes that include interest, equal to the difference between the amount borrowed (the proceeds) and the face amount paid back. Also known as *Zero-interest-bearing notes.*

Non-reciprocal transfers Transfers of assets in one direction only, such as donations, gifts, or government grants, where no assets are given in exchange.

Noncontrolling interest The percentage of the net assets not owned (reported as a liability on the balance sheet), or the percentage of the net income that does not accrue to the parent company (reported as a deduction from the combined net income on the income statement). Also known as *Minority interest.*

Nonmonetary assets Items whose value in terms of the monetary unit may change over time.

Nonmonetary, non-reciprocal transactions A type of transaction where there is no exchange (such as a donation), making it difficult to determine cost or fair value.

Nonmonetary transactions Transactions where few or no monetary assets are received as consideration when goods or services are purchased or sold. Also known as *Barter transactions.*

Nontrade receivables Written promises entitling a company to receive a certain sum of money, arising from a variety of transactions that are not part of normal business operations.

Normal production capacity The usual amount of goods that a company can produce in a year, and the basis for allocating fixed production costs.

Normalized earnings Adjusted past earnings that reflect expected annual future earnings.

Not-sufficient-funds (NSF) cheque A cheque that is written or deposited and the corresponding money for payment does not exist at the time of the deposit.

Notes receivable Written promises entitling a company to receive a certain sum of money on a specified future date.

Notes to financial statements Information that is linked to the financial statements that generally amplifies or explains the items presented in the main body of the statements in order to complete the picture of a company's performance and position.

Number of years method A method of valuing goodwill whereby the excess earnings are multiplied by the number of years they are expected to continue.

Objective of financial reporting The goal "to communicate information that is useful to investors, members, contributors, creditors, and other users in making their resource allocation decisions and/or assessing management stewardship," per the *CPA Canada Handbook.*

On margin Investments in shares where the investor pays only part of the purchase price to acquire the shares, and the broker finances the difference.

Onerous contract A contract where the unavoidable costs of completing the contract are higher than the benefits expected from receiving the contracted goods or services. A loss provision is recognized for such a contract under IFRS, though such a provision is not stipulated under ASPE.

Ontario Securities Commission (OSC) A group that regulates companies listed on the Toronto Stock Exchange (TSX) by reviewing and monitoring their financial statements with a view to assessing whether the statements present fairly the financial position and results of operations.

Operating activities "The enterprise's principal revenue-producing activities and other activities that are not investing or financing activities," as defined under IFRS and ASPE.

Operating income Income from ongoing revenues after deducting expenses.

Ordinary repairs Expenditures made to maintain plant assets in operating condition, which are charged to an expense account in the period in which they are incurred.

Organization costs Costs incurred in the formation of a corporation.

Other assets Assets that are not included in any other category and are generally not individually material.

Other comprehensive income (OCI) Items of revenues, expenses, gains, and losses that are required by IFRS to be included in comprehensive income, but excluded from net income.

Outcome uncertainty Uncertainty surrounding future cash inflows or outflows relating to assets and liabilities.

Output measures The output of a contract, or the process that is used to measure results.

Outstanding cheques Cheques written by a depositor and recorded when written but that are not recorded or cleared by the bank until a following month.

Owners' equity The residual amount, or net assets, of a company, composed of capital shares, contributed surplus, retained earnings, and accumulated other comprehensive income.

Patent A right to use, manufacture, and sell a product or process for a period of 20 years from the date of application without influence or infringement by others.

Percentage-of-completion method A revenue recognition method that recognizes revenue, costs, and gross profit as progress is made toward completion of a long-term contract.

Percentage-of-receivables approach The process whereby the allowance for doubtful accounts for receivables is estimated based on the expected uncollectible percentage.

Percentage-of-sales approach A method of estimating bad debt expense.

Performance obligation An obligation that arises when a company promises to deliver something or provide a service in the future.

Period costs Costs, such as selling and administrative, that are not considered directly related to the acquisition or production of goods and, therefore, are not considered a part of inventory.

Periodic inventory system The inventory recording system where a Purchases account is used and the Inventory account is unchanged during the period. Cost of goods sold is determined by adding the beginning inventory to the net purchases and deducting ending inventory.

Periodicity assumption The accounting assumption that implies that a company's economic activities can be divided into artificial time periods.

Permanent accounts All of the asset, liability, and equity accounts that appear on the balance sheet. Also known as "real accounts."

Permits Operating rights obtained through agreements with governmental units or agencies. Also known as *Licences*.

Perpetual inventory system The inventory recording system where purchases and sales are recorded in the Inventory account as they occur.

Petty cash A method of keeping cash on hand to cover small amounts where it would not be practical to issue cheques, such as for office supplies and taxi fares.

Plant assets Tangible capital assets that are acquired for use in operations and not for resale, are long-term in nature, are usually subject to depreciation, and possess physical substance. Also known as *Fixed assets* or *Property, plant, and equipment*.

Possession The physical control over a good, but not necessarily the legal title to the good.

Post-closing trial balance A trial balance taken immediately after closing entries have been posted.

Posting The process whereby items entered in a general journal are transferred to the general ledger.

Predictive analytics A branch of data analytics that uses statistics, artificial intelligence, data mining, and other techniques to analyze data sets in order to predict future trends and patterns.

Predictive value A characteristic of accounting information that helps users make predictions about the ultimate outcome of past, present, and future events.

Premium What occurs when a bond sells at more than face value.

Prepaid expenses Expenses paid in cash and recorded as assets before they are used or consumed.

Price risk The risk that the value of an asset will change due to changes in market conditions.

Principal market The market that the company normally uses to buy and sell or transfer things, used for measuring fair value.

Principal-agent relationship The fact that companies act either as principals or agents in selling transactions. When acting as a principal, the company generally has the risks and rewards of ownership of the item being sold. When acting as an agent, the company does not.

Product costs Those costs that "attach" to the inventory and are recorded in the Inventory account.

Professional judgement The process by which professional accountants with significant education and experience apply the *CPA Canada Handbook*'s "general principles" appropriately as they see fit, which is important in Canada because IFRS and ASPE are based primarily on general principles rather than specific rules.

Profit margin ratio A ratio that indicates how much is left over from each sales dollar after all expenses are covered.

Profitability ratios Ratios that measure the financial performance of a given company or division for a given period of time.

Promissory note A written promise that supports a note receivable to pay a certain sum of money at a specified future date.

Property, plant, and equipment Tangible capital assets that are acquired for use in operations and not for resale, are long-term in nature, are usually subject to depreciation, and possess

physical substance. Also known as *Fixed assets* or *Plant assets*.

Proprietary perspective The viewpoint that financial reporting should focus on the needs of the owners of the company.

Provincial securities commissions The groups that oversee and monitor the provincial capital marketplaces. They ensure that the participants in the capital markets adhere to securities legislation, and that the marketplace is fair.

Provision A liability that has an uncertain timing or amount (under IFRS).

Provision matrix A matrix-based calculation that multiplies age-based groupings of accounts receivable by the historical observed default rates over the expected life of the trade receivables. The default rates used are adjusted at each reporting date for changes in forward-looking estimates due to matters such as changes in economic conditions.

Prudence The exercise of caution in making decisions where uncertainty exists. See also *Conservatism*.

Public Company Accounting Oversight Board (PCAOB) The regulatory oversight body in the United States that ensures that certain standards are met regarding quality controls and independence.

Purchase commitments Arrangements under which a company agrees to buy inventory weeks, months, or even years in advance.

Qualifying assets Assets that require substantial time to get ready for sale or their intended use and qualify for capitalization of interest.

Qualitative characteristics The characteristics defined by the conceptual framework that distinguish more useful information from less useful information for decision-making purposes.

Quality of earnings How well reported earnings reflects the sustainability of earnings and underlying business fundamentals without bias.

Rate of return on assets (ROA) Net income expressed as a percentage of average total assets.

Ratio analysis An analysis based on relationships among selected financial statement data.

Rational entity impairment model A model for measuring impairment losses that assumes that an entity makes rational decisions in managing its long-term assets and therefore it compares the asset's book value with a recoverable amount that differs depending on what leads to a higher return for the entity.

Raw materials inventory The costs assigned to goods and materials on hand, but not yet placed into production.

Realizable (revenue) Revenue from assets received or sold that can be readily converted into cash or claims to cash.

Realized (revenue) Revenue from products (goods or services), merchandise, or other assets that is received in cash.

Rearrangement and reinstallation costs Expenditures intended to benefit future periods and to facilitate future production by the movement of assets from one location to another.

Recapture The recovery of capital cost allowance when, after deducting the appropriate amount from the class on disposition of the last asset, a negative amount is left as the undepreciated capital cost balance.

Receivables turnover ratio A ratio calculated to evaluate the liquidity of a company's accounts receivable. It measures the number of times, on average, the receivables balance is collected during the period.

Reciprocal exchange A two-way exchange.

Recognition The process of recording a transaction in a company's statement of financial position or income statement.

Recoverability test A test to determine whether an impairment loss needs to be recognized for a long-lived asset.

Recoverable amount The higher of an asset's value in use and its fair value less costs to sell (IFRS).

Related party transaction A transaction in which one of the transacting parties has the ability to significantly influence the policies of the other, or in which a nontransacting party has the ability to influence the policies of the two transacting parties.

Relative sales value method A method used to apportion a total cost or sales amount to individual components using fair values. Commonly used whenever there is a joint product cost that needs to be allocated or in a "basket" purchase or sale.

Relevance A qualitative characteristic of accounting information that indicates that it must make a difference in a decision.

Replacement The substitution of one asset for a similar asset.

Representational faithfulness A qualitative characteristic of accounting information that represents economic reality. It is transparent, complete, neutral, and free from material error and bias.

Repurchase agreements Arrangements between a company and customer where a sale is completed but the company also agrees to repurchase the items sold at a later date.

Research A planned investigation undertaken with the hope of gaining new scientific or technical knowledge and understanding.

Research phase A broad category of research activities where costs are recognized as expenses when they are incurred.

Residual value An estimate of the amount that a company would obtain from the disposal of a fixed asset at the end of its useful life.

Restricted cash Cash that is segregated from "regular" cash for reporting purposes because it needs to be set aside for a particular purpose.

Retail inventory method A method of valuing inventory when necessary, where inventory taken at its selling price (retail) can be converted to inventory at cost by applying the cost-to-retail formula.

Revaluation model (RM) A model for accounting for a long-lived asset that carries the asset at its fair value at the date of revaluation less any subsequent accumulated depreciation and impairment losses.

Revenue expenditure An expenditure where the benefit is in the period in which the expenditure occurred.

Revenue recognition principle The accounting principle that sets guidelines as to when revenue should be reported.

Revenues Increases in economic resources, either by inflows or other enhancements of a company's assets or settlement of its liabilities resulting from its ordinary activities.

Reversing entry A journal entry made at the beginning of the next accounting period that is the exact opposite of the related adjusting journal entry made in the previous period.

Right of return A right given by a company to a customer that allows the customer to return items that have been purchased.

Risk management The identification, assessment, and mitigation of potential risks to a company.

Risk/return trade-off An economic concept that notes that the higher the risk, the greater the return or compensation that is required to take that risk.

Sales discounts Cash discounts that are offered by the seller to induce prompt payment.

Sales returns and allowances An amount representing sales items returned by customers or, for example, where customers receive a credit for damaged goods. These should be anticipated and recognized in the period of the sale to avoid distorting the current period's income statement.

Salvage value A fixed asset's estimated net realizable value at the end of its life.

Secured borrowing When a creditor requires that a debtor designate (assign) or pledge receivables or other assets as security for the loan, but the assets remain under the control of the borrowing company.

Securities and Exchange Commission (SEC) The U.S. counterpart of the Ontario Securities Commission, which regulates the U.S. capital markets and supports the FASB by indicating that financial statements conforming with FASB standards will be presumed to have substantial authoritative support.

Securitization When a pool of assets is taken, such as credit card receivables, mortgage receivables, or car loan receivables, and shares are sold in these pools of interest and principal payments. The effect is to create securities backed by these pools of assets.

Self-constructed assets Assets built by a company and assigned all relevant costs to be capitalized.

Service-type warranty A type of warranty whereby the company agrees to fix or replace products that subsequently break or cease to work over an extended period.

Servicing asset component An asset that is recognized if the benefits of servicing (such as servicing fees under contract and late charges) are greater than the estimated cost of the obligation.

Servicing liability component An obligation that is recorded if the transferor receives no reimbursements for servicing the receivables, or receives less than the estimated cost of doing so.

Significant influence What an investor has when it owns roughly 20% to 50% of a company and/or there is investor representation on the board of directors, participation in policy-making processes, material inter-company transactions, interchange of managerial personnel, or provision of technical information.

Simple interest Interest paid or received on only the initial investment (the principal).

Single-step income statement A simplified income statement that lists all income first followed by all expenses.

Solvency A company's ability to pay its debts and related interest.

Solvency ratios Measures of the degree of protection for long-term creditors and investors or a company's ability to meet its long-term obligations. Also known as *Coverage ratios*.

Special journals Journals that summarize transactions possessing a similar characteristic.

Specific identification A cost formula whereby each inventory item is identified separately, the costs of the specific item sold are included in cost of goods sold, and the cost of the specific items on hand is included in inventory.

Stakeholders Parties who rely on and use financial statements and other financial documents to make decisions.

Stand-alone selling price The amount that a company is able to sell a particular product or service at.

Standard cost system A system that predetermines unit costs for material, labour, and manufacturing overhead based on costs that should be incurred at normal levels of efficiency and capacity.

Stated interest rate   The interest rate written in the terms of a bond indenture. Also known as *Coupon rate* or *Face rate*.

Statement of cash flows   A financial statement that provides information about the cash inflows (receipts) and outflows (payments) for a specific period of time. It is divided into operating activities, investing activities, and financing activities, and allows users to assess a company's capacity to generate cash and cash equivalents and its needs for cash resources.

Statement of changes in equity   The financial statement that reconciles the balance of the Retained Earnings account, common shares, and other shareholders' equity accounts from the beginning to the end of the period (under IFRS).

Statement of comprehensive income   The financial statement that reconciles net income to comprehensive income; reconciling items include unrealized gains and losses on certain financial instruments, and other transactions not recognized in net income (under IFRS). Some companies provide a combined statement of income and comprehensive income.

Statement of financial performance   Also known as Income statement, Statement of income/earnings or Statement of profit or loss.

Statement of financial position   The financial statement that shows a company's financial condition at the end of a period. Also known as *Balance sheet* under ASPE.

Statement of income/earnings   The main financial statement that reports a company's financial performance during the period. Also known as *Income statement, Statement of financial performance*, or *Statement of profit or loss*.

Statement of profit or loss   Also known as *Income statement, Statement of financial performance*, or *Statement of income/earnings*.

Statement of retained earnings   The financial statement that reconciles the balance of the Retained Earnings account from the beginning to the end of the period (under ASPE).

Stewardship   Management's responsibility to manage assets with care and trust, which is described as its fiduciary relationship.

Straight-line method   A method of depreciation (or amortization) where depreciation is considered a function of the passage of time.

Strict cash basis   A basis of reporting whereby revenues and expenses are recorded only when cash is received or paid out.

Subsequent events   Events that occur after the balance sheet date, but before the financial statements are issued.

Subsidiary   A corporation that is controlled by another corporation.

Subsidiary ledger   A ledger that contains the details related to a given general ledger account.

Successful efforts method   A method of accounting for natural resource properties

where oil and gas companies initially capitalize exploration costs until the drilling activities for each oil field are complete. If the drilling activities are not successful and no proven reserves are found, the costs are written off to expense as a "dry hole."

Sum-of-the-years'-digits method   A decreasing charge depreciation method where the depreciable amount is multiplied each year by a decreasing fraction related to the number of years in the asset's useful life.

Supplementary information   Information that may include details or amounts that present a different perspective from that adopted in the financial statements.

Tangible capital assets   Assets that are acquired for use in operations and not for resale, are long-term in nature, are usually subject to depreciation, and possess physical substance.

Tax basis   See *Tax value*.

Tax value   The amount that will be deductible for tax purposes when the carrying amount of the asset is recovered or the liability settled. Also known as *Tax basis*.

Technology-based intangible assets   Innovations or technological advances such as patented technology and trade secrets.

Temporary accounts   Revenue, expense, and dividend accounts; except for dividends, they appear on the statement of comprehensive income. Temporary accounts are closed at the end of each fiscal year; permanent accounts are left open. Also known as "nominal accounts."

Terminal loss   What occurs when the disposition of the last asset in its class results in a positive balance remaining in the capital cost allowance class.

Timeliness   A characteristic of relevance that states that information should be available for decision-makers before it loses its capacity to influence their decisions.

Toronto Stock Exchange (TSX)   The largest stock exchange in Canada.

Total-earnings approach   A method of valuing goodwill where the value of the company as a whole is determined based on the total expected earnings, not just the excess earnings.

Trademark   One or more words, or a series of letters or numbers, or a design or shape that distinguishes a particular company or product. Also known as a *Trade name*.

Trading   The act of buying and selling for profit in the short term.

Trade discounts   A reduction in the catalogue price used to avoid frequent changes in catalogues, to quote different prices for different quantities purchased, or to hide the true invoice price from competitors.

Trade name   One or more words, or a series of letters or numbers, or a design or shape that

distinguishes a particular company or product. Also known as a *Trademark*.

Trade receivables   Amounts owed by customers for goods and services rendered as part of the normal course of business operations.

Traditional discounted cash flow approach   An approach to the discounted cash flow model where the discount rate reflects all risks in the cash flows but the cash flows are assumed to be certain. The stream of contracted cash flows is discounted, and the discount rate is adjusted to accommodate their riskiness.

Transaction   An external event involving a transfer or exchange between two or more entities or parties.

Transaction costs   Costs associated with the acquisition of financial instruments, such as fees, commissions, or transfer taxes.

Transaction price   The amount of consideration that a company expects to receive from a customer.

Transparency   A goal of financial reporting such that the information provided reflects the underlying transactions and events and their effects on a company. It is one of the characteristics of representational faithfulness.

Trial balance   A list of all open accounts in the general ledger and their balances.

Undepreciated capital cost (UCC)   The amount of a class of assets' cost less total capital cost allowance (for tax purposes).

Understandability   The quality of information that permits reasonably informed users to perceive its significance.

Unearned revenues   Revenues received in cash and recorded as liabilities until they are earned.

Unit of measure/account   The level at which an asset such as property, plant, and equipment is recognized (that is, the extent to which separate components are measured and recorded).

Units of production method   A method of calculating depreciation whereby depreciation is determined as a function of use or productivity of the asset.

Unrealized holding gains or losses   The difference between the fair value and cost (carrying amount) of an asset still held (owned) by the investor.

Upfront fees   Amounts collected from a customer in advance of the goods or services being shipped or provided.

Useful life   The term of service provided by a capital asset, often many years long.

Value in use   The present value of the future cash flows expected to be derived from an asset's use and subsequent disposal. It is an entity-specific measure.

Verifiability The quality of information that demonstrates that independent measurers, using the same measurement methods, obtain similar results.

Volume rebate/discount A retroactive discount on goods if the buyer meets certain criteria, such as purchasing a target quantity within a year.

Warranty An arrangement with a customer to replace or fix goods with deficiencies that have been sold.

Weighted average cost formula A cost formula that determines the average cost of inventory weighted by the number of units purchased at each unit cost. It is calculated as the cost of goods available for sale divided by the number of units available for sale.

Weighted-average accumulated expenditures A calculation of construction expenditures that is weighted by the amount of time that interest cost could be incurred on the expenditure.

With recourse The characteristic of receivables sold via a third party, where the transferor guarantees payment to the seller if the customer fails to pay.

Without recourse The characteristic of receivables sold via a third party, where the buyer assumes the risk of collection and absorbs any credit losses.

Work sheet A spreadsheet that is used to adjust the account balances and prepare the financial statements.

Work-in-process inventory The cost of the raw materials on which production has been started but not completed, plus the direct labour cost applied specifically to this material, and an applicable share of manufacturing overhead costs.

Working capital The excess of total current assets over total current liabilities.

Yield rate The interest rate actually earned. Also known as *Effective interest rate* or *Market rate*.

Zero-interest-bearing notes See *Non-interest-bearing notes*.

Zero-profit method A method for recognizing revenues under IFRS where the company is unable to measure the percentage complete. Recoverable revenues equal to costs are recognized.

Company Index

A

Accounting Standards Advisory Forum, 1-15
Accounting Standards Board (AcSB), 1-12, 1-13, 1-14, 1-21, 2-3, 2-5, 2-8, 2-11, 6-48, 7-42
Accounting Standards Oversight Council (AcSOC), 1-14
AcSB. *See* Accounting Standards Board (AcSB)
AcSOC. *See* Accounting Standards Oversight Council (AcSOC)
Adelphia Communications Corp., 10-29
AEterna Zentaris Inc., 12-69
AGF Management Limited, 11-70
Agrium Inc., 7-19, 8-4
Air Canada, 2-7, 3-9, 5-9–5-10, 5-25, 6-12, 6-45, 9-7, 10-63, 11-5, 11-7, 11-72, AP-39
Air France-KLM Group, 11-72
Airbnb, 4-1
Airbus Group S.E., 6-85, 8-4
Alacer Gold, 11-13
Alta Vista Ventures Ltd., 1-1
Amazon, 8-1, 12-4, 12-17
American Accounting Association, 2-33
American Institute of Certified Public Accountants, 2-33
Andrew Peller Limited, 7-52, 8-82
ANZ Bank, 3-1
Apple Inc., 4-1, 12-8, 12-17, 12-34
Arthur Andersen, 1-3
Atlas Cold Storage Income Trust, 10-29
Atmosphere, 7-73
ATV Music Publishing, 12-18

B

Bank of Montreal, 4-69, 12-17
BBB, 7-32
BCE Inc., 4-69–4-70, 6-85, 7-33, 7-37–7-39, 7-52, 10-42, 12-4
Becker Milk Company Limited, 7-59
Bell Aliant, 7-5
Bell Canada, 12-17
BHP Billiton plc, 10-75
BlackBerry, 12-8, 12-19
Bombardier Inc., 5-69, 6-11–6-12, 6-55
BP plc, 10-33–10-34
Brand Finance plc, 12-17
Brick Brewing Company Limited, 4-27–4-28, 4-29
British Airways plc, 5-9, 11-5, 12-68
British Columbia Securities Commission, 1-17
Brookfield Asset Management Inc., 10-1–10-2, 10-27, 10-75, 11-69, 11-70, 12-17
Brookfield Office Properties Inc., 4-68
Brookfield Property Partners, L.P., 5-11

C

Cameco Corporation, 4-25–4-26, 4-34–4-35
Canada Life Financial Corporation, 9-6–9-7, 9-41–9-43

Canada Pension Plan Investment Board (CPPIB), 1-8–1-9
Canada Revenue Agency (CRA), 4-30, 5-67, 8-30, 8-32, 8-48, 9-10, 11-12
Canadian Institute of Chartered Accountants (CICA), 1-13
Canadian Intellectual Property Office (CIPO), 12-16, 12-18, 12-19, 12-20
Canadian National Railway Company, 11-70
Canadian Natural Resources Limited (CNRL), 4-5–4-6
Canadian Pacific Railway Limited (CP Railway), 11-16, 11-34, 11-70
Canadian Public Accountability Board (CPAB), 1-20
Canadian Radio-television and Telecommunications Commission (CRTC), 7-1
Canadian Securities Administrators (CSA), 1-20, 1-24, 4-69, 5-1, 11-12
Canadian Securities Exchange (CSE), 1-1
Canadian Tire Bank, 7-30
Canadian Tire Corporation, Limited, 5-11, 7-19–7-20, 7-30, 7-32, 7-33, 7-73, 8-18, 8-82, 11-70
Canadian Utilities Limited, 7-39–7-40, 10-8–10-9
Canopy Growth Corporation, 8-39–8-40, 8-44
Carestream Health, 4-20
Cendant, 1-19
Centerra Gold Inc., 7-8–7-9
CGI, 6-51
Chapters, 8-13
Chartered Professional Accountants of Canada (CPA Canada), 1-13, 2-19, 2-30, 4-38, 10-4
CIBC, 5-67–5-68, 7-7, 12-17
CICA. *See* Canadian Institute of Chartered Accountants (CICA)
Cicis, 4-20
CIPO. *See* Canadian Intellectual Property Office (CIPO)
ClubLink, 9-7
Coca-Cola Company, 6-86, 12-4, 12-17, 12-21
Coles, 8-13
Committee of Sponsoring Organizations of the Treadway Commission (COSO), 2-33–2-34
Copyright Office, 12-18
Corus Entertainment Inc., 12-30, 12-31–12-33
CP Railway. *See* Canadian Pacific Railway Limited (CP Railway)
CPA Canada. *See* Chartered Professional Accountants of Canada (CPA Canada)
CPAB. *See* Canadian Public Accountability Board (CPAB)
CPPIB. *See* Canada Pension Plan Investment Board (CPPIB)
CRA. *See* Canada Revenue Agency (CRA)

Crombie Real Estate Investment Trust, 12-69
CRTC. *See* Canadian Radio-television and Telecommunications Commission (CRTC)
CSA. *See* Canadian Securities Administrators (CSA)
CSE. *See* Canadian Securities Exchange (CSE)

D

Dental Digital, 4-20
Duff & Phelps, 12-27

E

EADS NV. *See* European Aeronautic Defence and Space Company (EADS NV)
Eastman Kodak Company, 5-5–5-6
Easton, 5-37
ECT Merchant Investments Corp., 2-11
EDGAR, 4-70
Eli Lilly and Company, 8-5, 12-20
EMI Music Publishing, 12-18
Empire Company Limited, 5-19–5-20, 7-10–7-11, 7-74, 8-47–8-48, 8-82–8-83, 9-7, 10-74–10-75
Enron Corporation, 1-3, 1-19, 2-11, 2-21, 2-32, 5-67, 5-68
Ericsson, 12-8
European Aeronautic Defence and Space Company (EADS NV), 6-85
European Financial Reporting Advisory Group, 1-21

F

Facebook, 6-1, 12-19
Fairfax Financial Holdings Limited, 5-37
Falconbridge Ltd., 11-20
FASB. *See* Financial Accounting Standards Board (FASB)
FGL Sports, 7-73
Financial Accounting Standards Board (FASB), 1-12, 1-13, 1-16, 1-23, 2-4, 6-1, 7-41, 7-42
Financial Executives International, 2-33, 12-27
Financial Executives Research Foundation, 12-27
Financial Reporting in Canada, 12-30
Find @ Lord & Taylor, AP-12
Ford Motor Corporation, 8-57

G

GALERIA Holding GmbH, AP-12
Galeria INNO, AP-6, AP-12
Galeria Kaufhof, AP-6, AP-12
General Mills, 6-42
Geodis, 8-1
Gilt, AP-6, AP-12, AP-13
Gilt Groupe Holdings Inc., AP-12
Glacier Credit Card Trust, 7-32
Glencore PLC, 8-36–8-37
Global UAV Technologies, 1-1
Goldcorp Inc., 5-70
Google, 12-4, 12-8, 12-17, 12-19

Google Wallet, 6-1
Government of Alberta, 11-19
Great Canadian Gaming Corporation, 4-24, 4-25

H

HBC. *See* Hudson's Bay Company (HBC)
HBS Global Properties LLC, AP-12
The Hershey Company, 11-31–11-32
Hollinger International Inc., 11-12
Home Outfitters, AP-12
HTC, 12-8
Huawei, 12-8
Hudson's Bay Company (HBC), 3-39, 4-6, 4-8, 5-69, 6-85, 7-4, 8-4, 8-45, 8-47, 8-81, 9-77–9-78, AP-6–AP-26, AP-29, AP-54
Hudson's Bay Europe, AP-12, AP-13
Husky Energy Inc., 11-14, 11-20

I

IASB. *See* International Accounting Standards Board (IASB)
IASC. *See* International Accounting Standards Committee (IASC)
IBI Group Inc., 5-12–5-13
ICBC, 12-17
IFRIC. *See* IFRS Interpretations Committee (IFRIC)
IFRS Advisory Council, 1-15
IFRS DG. *See* IFRS Discussion Group (IFRS DG)
IFRS Discussion Group (IFRS DG), 1-14, 6-24
IFRS Foundation, 1-15
IFRS Interpretations Committee (IFRIC), 1-15, 1-18
IFRS Taxonomy Consultative Group, 1-24
IIRC. *See* International Integrated Reporting Committee (IIRC)
IMAX, 12-19
Imperial Metals Corporation, 10-8
Indigo Books & Music Inc., 8-13, 9-7
Innovation, Science and Economic Development Canada, 12-16
Institute of Internal Auditors, 2-33
Institute of Management Accountants, 2-33
International Accounting Standards Board (IASB), 1-7, 1-12, 1-13, 1-14–1-16, 1-18, 1-21, 1-22, 1-23, 1-24, 2-1, 2-4–2-5, 2-7, 2-8, 2-11, 2-34–2-35, 3-13, 3-28, 4-39, 5-38–5-39, 6-10–6-11, 6-13, 6-14, 7-41, 7-42, 8-38, 9-3, 9-32–9-33, 9-48, 10-36, 11-12, 11-36, 12-9, 12-37, AP-12, AP-22, AP-23
International Accounting Standards Committee (IASC), 1-14
International Financial Reporting Standards Foundation (IFRSF), 6-11
International Integrated Reporting Committee (IIRC), 1-24
Intertape Polymer Group Inc., 11-12
iTunes, 4-1

J

The Jean Coutu Group (PJC) Inc., 8-4
JELD-WEN, 4-20

K

Kirkland Lake Gold Ltd., 4-68
Kobo Inc., 8-13
KPMG, 6-12–6-13
KraussMaffei, 4-20

L

Linamar Corporation, 5-13–5-14
Livent Inc., 1-19, 2-22, 10-29
Loblaw Companies Limited, 2-10, 5-28–5-29, 5-40, 6-42, 7-74, 8-21, 8-82–8-83, 10-74–10-75, 11-33, 12-69
Lord & Taylor, AP-6, AP-12, AP-22
Lord & Taylor Acquisition Inc., AP-12, AP-13
lululemon athletica inc., 12-3–12-4
Lyft, 4-1

M

Magna International Inc., 7-4, 10-74
Mainstreet Equity Corp., 4-68
Manufacturers Hanover Trust Co., 7-42
Maple Leaf Foods Inc., 3-39–3-40, 5-69, 7-72
Mark's Work Wearhouse, 7-73
MasterCard, 7-31
McDonald's, 4-21
Microsoft, 12-8, 12-35
MiningWatch Canada, 11-1

N

National Association of Accountants, 2-33
Netflix, 4-1
New York Stock Exchange (NYSE), 1-16, 4-22
Newfield Exploration, 10-75
Nike, Inc., 12-68
Nortel Networks, 12-8, 12-19
Nutrien Ltd., 7-19, 8-4
NYSE. *See* New York Stock Exchange (NYSE)

O

OECD. *See* Organisation for Economic Co-operation and Development (OECD)

Office of the Superintendent of Financial Institutions, 5-67
Onex Corporation, 4-17–4-20, 4-22, 4-23
Ontario Power Generation (OPG), 11-4
Ontario Securities Commission (OSC), 1-12, 1-13, 1-17, 4-36, 4-37
Open Text Corporation, 11-33–11-34
OPG. *See* Ontario Power Generation (OPG)
Organisation for Economic Co-operation and Development (OECD), 9-1
Orphan Well Association, 11-1
OSC. *See* Ontario Securities Commission (OSC)

P

Patent Office, 12-19
PayPal, 6-1, 7-42
PCAOB. *See* Public Company Accounting Oversight Board (PCAOB)
Pembina Institute, 11-1
PepsiCo, 6-86
Performance Sports Group, 5-37
PetroCanada, 7-4, 10-21
P&G. *See* The Procter & Gamble Company (P&G)
Potash Corporation of Saskatchewan Inc., 7-19, 8-4, 9-78
The Procter & Gamble Company (P&G), 6-85–6-86
Public Company Accounting Oversight Board (PCAOB), 1-19
Public Sector Accounting Board, 10-4

Q

Quebecor Inc., 5-70, 12-35, 12-69

R

Rakuten Inc., 8-13
Rhône Capital LLC, AP-12
RioCan-HBC Limited Partnership, AP-12, AP-26
RioCan Real Estate Investment Trust, AP-12
Ripple Brand Collective, LLC, 11-31
Rite-Aid, 1-19
Rockstar, 12-8

Rogers Communications, 6-13, 12-17
Roots Canada, 12-3
Royal Bank of Canada (RBC), 4-68, 4-69, 9-5–9-6, 9-78, 12-17
RPX, 12-8–12-9

S

Sagard Holdings Inc., 5-37
Saks, 3-39, AP-13, AP-21, AP-22
Saks Fifth Avenue, AP-6, AP-12
Saks Fifth Avenue OFF 5TH, AP-6, AP-12
Saks Fifth Avenue OFF 5TH Europe, AP-12
Saks Incorporated, AP-12
Saks OFF 5TH, AP-6
Samsung, 12-8, 12-17
Scotiabank, 12-17
SEC. *See* Securities and Exchange Commission (SEC)
Securities and Exchange Commission (SEC), 1-12, 1-16, 1-23, 2-34, 3-1, 4-70, 5-6, 5-67
SEDAR, 4-69, 4-70, 5-69, 5-70, 6-85, 7-72, 7-73, 7-74, 8-82, 9-78, 10-75, 11-69, 11-70, 12-69, AP-6
Shopify Inc., 5-20–5-21
Shoppers Drug Mart, 11-33
Shortcovers, 8-13
SHOWCASE, 12-31
Simmons & Company International, 11-14
Simon HBC Opportunities LLC, AP-12
Simon Property Group Inc., AP-12
Sitel Worldwide, 4-20
SmithBooks, 8-13
Sobeys Inc., 5-20, 9-7
Sony, 12-18
Sony/ATV Music Publishing, 12-18
Sony Corp., 12-18
Sport Chek, 7-73
Sportarena, AP-12
Sports Experts, 7-73
Standard & Poor's, 4-31
Standards Interpretation Committee (SIC), 1-18
Stantec Inc., 7-19
The Stars Group Inc., 11-70
Stora Enso Oyj, 8-81–8-82, 10-74
Sunbeam, 1-19
Suncor Energy, 7-4–7-5

T

TD Bank, 12-17
TELETOON, 12-31
TELUS Corporation, 4-22, 4-23–4-24, 6-85, 7-1, 7-3, 7-70, 12-17
Thomson Reuters Corporation, 5-70, 12-28
Tim Hortons, 12-14, 12-17
Toronto Stock Exchange (TSX), 1-1, 1-17, 3-11, 3-12, 4-22, 7-8, 12-13, AP-12
Torstar Corporation, 4-29–4-30
Toyota Motor Corporation, 3-40, 8-4
TransAlta Corporation, 10-8, 11-19
Treehouse, 12-31
TripAdvisor Inc., 3-40
TSX. *See* Toronto Stock Exchange (TSX)
TWC Enterprises Limited, 5-16, 9-7

U

Uber, 4-1
U.S. Federal Reserve, 5-67
U.S. Justice Department, 5-67
USI, 4-20

V

Valeant Pharmaceuticals International, 5-17
Visa, 7-31

W

W Network, 12-31
The Wall Street Journal, 7-42
Walmart Stores Inc., 2-10, 3-1, 4-5, 4-6, 8-1, 8-47, 8-57
WestJet, AP-39
Whitewing, 2-11
WorldCom Inc., 1-3, 10-29

Y

Yellow Pages Ltd., 12-1
YTV, 12-31

Z

Zynga Inc., 6-1

Subject Index

A

abnormal shortages, 8-50
abnormal terms, 6-7
accelerated amortization, 11-10
account, AP-29
    see also specific types of accounts
    contra account, 7-12
    crediting the account, AP-29
    debiting the account, AP-29
    writing off an account, 7-18
account sales, 6-41
accountants' role, 2-33
accounting

accrual-basis accounting, 1-8, 2-23, 4-39–4-44
aggressive accounting, 1-11
and capital allocation, 1-4–1-5
challenges and opportunities, 1-19–1-25
conservative accounting, 1-11
defined, 1-3
essential characteristics of, 1-3
financial accounting, 1-3
goals and purposes, 2-4
language of, 2-12
managerial accounting, 1-3

accounting cycle, AP-31, AP-32
    adjusting entries, AP-34–AP-45
    adjustments. *See* adjusting entries
    closing process, AP-46–AP-49
    financial statements, AP-45–AP-46
    identification of transactions and other events, AP-31
    journalizing, AP-31–AP-32
    ownership structure, AP-45–AP-46
    posting, AP-33
    recording transactions and other events, AP-31
    reversing entries, AP-48–AP-49
    trial balance, AP-34

accounting equation, AP-30–AP-31
    basic accounting equation, AP-30
    expanded basic equation, AP-30
accounting guidelines, 1-18
accounting information system, 1-24, AP-28
    see also accounting cycle
    accounting equation, AP-30–AP-31
    basic terminology, AP-28–AP-30
accounting oversight board, 1-19
accounting policies, 4-35, 5-23
accounting policy changes, 4-33

accounting standards, 1-12
   see also Accounting Standards for
      Private Enterprises (ASPE);
      International Financial
      Reporting Standards (IFRS);
      standard setting
   conceptual framework, 2-5
   private entities, 2-11–2-12
Accounting Standards for Private
   Enterprises (ASPE), 1-13
   see also generally accepted
      accounting principles (GAAP);
      IFRS-ASPE comparison
   accounting policy changes, 4-33
   amortization method not specified,
      7-23
   asset retirement costs, 10-9
   associates, investments in, 9-32–9-38,
      9-43–9-44
   bank overdrafts, 7-8
   basic presentation requirements,
      4-21
   biological assets and agricultural
      produce, 8-37–8-38
   borrowing costs, 8-19, 10-8
   buildings, 10-20
   capitalization of costs, 10-7
   cash equivalents, 7-8
   collectibility, 6-14
   completed-contract method,
      6-49, 6-56
   components, 10-6, 11-5
   comprehensive income and other
      comprehensive income, 2-16
   contingencies, 5-19, 5-22
   contract criteria, 6-14
   contract modification, 6-15
   control, 2-20, 9-38, 9-40
   cost model, 9-9–9-10, 10-23, 12-13
   cost recovery impairment model,
      11-21–11-22, 11-25, 11-26, 12-21
   current assets, 9-40
   depreciation, 11-5
   derecognition of receivables,
      7-33–7-34, 7-35, 7-41
   disclosure, 12-30–12-31
   earnings approach, 6-11, 6-35–6-36,
      6-47–6-48
   expenses, 4-28–4-29
   fair value, 2-28–2-29
   fair value option, 2-28–2-29
   financial assets, 7-14
   financial instruments, 5-8
   financial statements, names of,
      AP-29
   full cost method, 10-22
   future income tax assets, 5-18
   goodwill, 12-28–12-30, 12-30–12-31
   held for sale, 4-16, 11-27–11-28
   impairment, 9-26–9-27, 9-31, 11-21
   income, 4-12
   income statement, 4-22
   income statement approach, 2-21
   incurred loss impairment model,
      9-26
   indefinite life, 12-15
   indefinite-life intangibles, 12-23
   intangible assets, 12-30–12-31
   inventory, 8-7
   inventory cost, 8-17
   investment measurement
      models, 9-47
   investment property, 10-21
   investments, 9-8, 9-15
   liabilities, recognition of, 5-23
   limited-life intangibles, 12-21
   long-term contracts, 6-49

other comprehensive income
   items, 4-13
principles-based approach, 1-23,
   2-32
"probable," 2-18
product costs, 8-18
professional judgement, 1-19
rearrangement and reinstallation
   costs, 10-33
receivables, 7-33–7-34, 7-35, 7-37
recoverability test, 11-22
replacements, major overhauls, and
   inspections, 10-32
retained earnings statement,
   4-32–4-34
revenue recognition, 6-20
revenues, 2-15
sales returns and allowances,
   7-12–7-13
sales revenues, and returns, 6-23
share-based payments, 10-13
significant influence, 9-33, 9-37, 9-40
straight-line method, 7-26–7-27,
   7-28, 9-13
subsidiaries, investments in, 9-38–9-39
transaction costs, 6-21, 7-23
accounting theory, 1-10
accounts receivable, 5-7, 7-9–7-11
   see also receivables
   aging method, 7-15
   aging schedule, 7-15
   allowance method, 7-16–7-18
   cash discounts, 7-12
   direct write off method, 7-20
   effects on accounts, 7-18–7-20
   estimating uncollectible trade
      accounts receivable, 7-14–7-16
   expected credit losses, 7-41
   extensive accounts receivable, 7-4
   gross average accounts receivable
      (GAAR), 7-19
   impairment, 7-14–7-20
   lifetime expected credit losses, 7-14
   management of, 7-5
   measurement, 7-11–7-14
   measurement after acquisition, 7-14
   monitoring, 7-5
   net realizable value (NRV), 7-15
   nonrecognition of interest element,
      7-13–7-14
   percentage-of-receivables approach,
      7-15
   percentage-of-sales approach, 7-17
   previously written off account, 7-18
   provision matrix, 7-15
   recognition, 7-11–7-14
   sales discounts, 7-12
   sales returns and allowances,
      7-12–7-13
   securitization, 7-1
   trade discounts, 7-12
   types of, 7-4
   written off, 7-18
accrual basis, 4-39
   see also accrual-basis accounting
accrual-basis accounting, 1-8, 2-23
   accrued expenses, AP-41–AP-43
   conversion from cash basis,
      4-41–4-43
   equity method, 9-33
   and estimates, 4-8
   expense calculation, 4-42–4-43
   revenue calculation, 4-41–4-42
   vs. cash basis accounting, 4-39–4-41
accruals, AP-35
   accrued expenses, AP-35,
      AP-41–AP-43

accrued revenues, AP-35,
   AP-40–AP-41
   adjusting entries, AP-40–AP-43
   reversing entries, AP-48–AP-49
accrued expenses, AP-35, AP-41
   accrued interest, AP-41–AP-42
   accrued salaries, AP-42–AP-43
   adjusting entries, AP-41–AP-43
accrued interest, AP-41–AP-42
accrued revenues, AP-35, AP-40
accrued salaries, AP-42–AP-43
Accumulated Depreciation account,
   10-24–10-25
accumulated other comprehensive
   income, 4-32, 5-20, AP-46
Accumulated Other Comprehensive
   Income account, 4-14, AP-47
acid-test ratio, 5-5, 5-41
acquirer, 12-4
acquisition cost, 2-26, 10-19
active market, 12-13
activity methods of depreciation,
   11-11–11-12
activity ratios, 5-5, 5-40, 5-41
actual use, AP-37
additions, 10-29, 10-30
adjunct account, 5-26
adjusted market assessment approach,
   6-29
adjusted trial balance, AP-29
adjusting entries, AP-29, AP-34–AP-45
   accruals, AP-35, AP-40–AP-43
   estimated items, AP-35, AP-43–AP-44
   prepayments, AP-35, AP-36–AP-39
   types of, AP-35
   when required, AP-35
   work sheet, AP-51–AP-52
advances, 7-10
adverse selection, 1-10–1-11, 2-5
aggressive accounting, 1-11
aging method, 7-15
aging schedule, 7-15
agricultural produce, 8-37–8-40, 8-52
all-inclusive approach, 4-12
allocation technique, 2-22
allowance account, 7-17–7-18
allowance for loans receivable, 7-20
allowance method, 7-16–7-18, 8-33
amortization, 10-5, 11-4, AP-37
   see also depreciation
   accelerated amortization, 11-10
   accumulated amortization, 12-15
   expenses, 12-15
   finite or limited life, 12-14
   intangible assets, 11-5, 12-14
   prepaid expenses, AP-37
amortized cost, 7-23
amortized cost model, 9-9–9-15, 9-47
   debt instruments of other entities,
      9-11–9-15
   income under, 9-11–9-14
   sale of investments, 9-14–9-15
analysis
   accounting policies, 4-35
   cash flow statement, 4-36
   comparison of operating results, 12-35
   financial statements, 4-36
   goodwill, 12-34–12-35
   income statement, 4-36
   information-rich analysis, 5-40
   intangible assets, 12-34–12-35
   investments, 9-44
   measurement uncertainty, 4-36
   missing values, 12-34–12-35
   notes to financial statements, 4-36
   property, plant, and equipment,
      11-32–11-35

ratio analysis. *See* ratio analysis
receivables, 7-39–7-40
statement of financial position,
   4-36, 5-4
of transactions, AP-31
annuities, 3-20–3-22
arm's-length transaction, 2-26, 6-5
articles, 1-18
artificial time periods, 2-25
artistic-related intangible assets, 12-18
ASPE. *See* Accounting Standards for
   Private Enterprises (ASPE)
asset account, AP-29
asset adjustment method, 12-13
asset-backed financing, 7-31
asset-backed securities, 7-32
asset class, 11-39–11-41
asset exchanges, 10-14–10-18
asset groups, 11-25–11-27
asset-liability approach, 6-10–6-13,
   6-47–6-48, 10-33
   allocation of transaction price
      to separate performance
      obligations, 6-28–6-31
   determination of transaction price,
      6-21–6-28
   example, 6-11–6-12
   identification of separate
      performance obligations,
      6-16–6-20
   identification of the contract with
      customers, 6-13–6-16
   recognition of revenue when
      each performance obligation
      satisfied, 6-32–6-35
   summary of process, 6-35
asset retirement costs, 8-18, 10-9
asset retirement obligations, 11-1
asset turnover, 5-41
assets, 2-12–2-13
   see also specific types of assets
   biological assets, 6-48, 8-37–8-40,
      8-52, 10-22, 10-27
   classes, 10-23
   classification in statement of
      financial position, 5-7
   contract assets, 6-42–6-44
   contractual rights, 2-12–2-13
   contractual rights to receive
      cash, 5-8
   contributed assets, 10-18–10-19
   current assets, 5-10–5-15, 11-20
   current vs. non-current
      classification, 2-26
   deferred income tax assets, 5-18
   definition, 2-12–2-13
   disposal of assets. *See* disposition
   exploration and evaluation
      assets, 11-14
   financial assets, 5-8, 5-13, 7-6
   fixed assets, 10-4
   function, 5-7
   future income tax assets, 5-18
   held for sale, 4-15–4-16
   historical cost, 5-6
   identifiable, 12-5
   identifiable net assets, 12-4
   impairment, 3-7
   intangible assets. *See* intangible
      assets
   knowledge assets, 12-34
   liquidation approach, 2-26
   long-lived assets, 11-27–11-28
   monetary assets, 5-7–5-8, 10-14, 12-5
   net assets, 5-8
   nonmonetary assets, 5-7–5-8, 10-14,
      12-5

assets (continued)
other assets, 5-17–5-18
plant assets, 10-4
property, plant, and equipment. *See* property, plant, and equipment
qualifying assets, 10-37
recognized from costs incurred to fulfill a contract, 6-44
right, vs. physical asset, 2-12–2-13
on statement of financial position, 5-8
tangible capital assets, 3-5, 10-4
that become liabilities, 11-1
useful life, AP-37
wasting assets, 10-21
associates, 9-32–9-38, 9-43–9-44
assurance-type warranty, 6-18, 6-48
asymmetric prudence, 2-1
audit, 1-5
audit committees, 1-20
auditing standards, 2-7
auditors, 1-5, 2-7
authorized plan to sell, 4-15–4-16
available for sale investments, 9-7, 9-20
see also fair value through other comprehensive income (FV-OCI)
average days to sell inventory, 8-45
avoidable borrowing costs, 10-8, 10-38, 10-39–10-40

B

bad debt expense, 7-17–7-18
bad debts, 7-14, AP-35, AP-43–AP-44
balance sheet, 1-3, 5-4, AP-29
see also statement of financial position (balance sheet)
balance sheet approach, 2-21
bank accounts, 7-42–7-43
bank charges, 7-45
bank credits, 7-45
bank drafts, 7-6
bank errors, 7-45
bank overdrafts, 7-7–7-8, 7-9
bank reconciliation, 7-45–7-47
bargain purchase, 12-26–12-27
barter transactions, 2-26–2-27, 6-6
basic elements, 2-12
basic terminology, AP-28–AP-30
basket purchase, 8-19, 12-7
beginning inventory, AP-48
beneficial interests, 7-36
benefits, 2-12
benefits of ownership, 6-36
best-quality fair value measure, 3-12
bias
in financial reporting, 1-11, 4-8, 6-10
management bias, 1-11, 1-20–1-21
motivation to bias information, 1-11
revenue numbers, biased, 6-10
"big bath" writedown, 12-35
Big Data, 3-1
bill-and-hold arrangement, 6-7, 6-42
biological assets, 6-48, 8-37–8-40, 8-52, 10-22, 10-27
bona fide, 6-6
bonds, 5-18
bonuses, 1-20
book value, AP-38
book value per share, 5-41
boot, 10-15
borrowing costs, 8-19, 10-8–10-9, 10-37–10-42
brand, 12-16
brand name, 12-16
bright-line tests, 1-23

brokerage commissions, 9-8
budgets, 2-33
buildings, 10-20
bundled sales, 6-4–6-5
burden, 10-7
business combination, 12-7
business environment, 2-33
business models, 4-3–4-7, 4-20, 5-39
business perspective, 6-4
depreciation, 11-3–11-4
disposition, 11-3–11-4
impairment, 11-3–11-4
property, plant, and equipment, 10-4
sales transaction, 6-4
statement of cash flows, 5-3–5-4
statement of financial position (balance sheet), 5-3–5-4
business risks, 5-39–5-40
buyback agreements, 8-9

C

Canadian dollar, 7-7
cannabis industry, 1-1
capital
allocation of, 1-4–1-5
and financial reporting, 1-1–1-2
sources of capital, 1-4–1-5
Capital account, AP-46, AP-47
capital allocation, 1-4–1-5
capital allocation process, 1-4–1-5
capital approach, 10-18
capital cost allowance (CCA), 11-37
capital cost allowance method, 11-37–11-41
additions to an asset class, 11-39–11-40
basic CCA and UCC example, 11-38–11-39
half-year rule, 11-38
recapture, 11-40
retirements from asset class, continuation of class, 11-40
retirements from asset class, elimination of class, 11-40–11-41
terminal loss, 11-40–11-41
undepreciated capital cost (UCC), 11-38, 11-39
capital expenditure, 10-29
capital gain, 11-40
capital-intensive, 5-16
capital maintenance, 11-28
capital market risks, 5-40
capital marketplace
oversight in, 1-19–1-20
signals to, 2-29
capital markets, 1-10
capital shares, 5-20
capitalization of costs, 10-6–10-7, 10-37–10-42
capitalization period, 10-38
capitalization rate, 10-39
capitalized, 10-5
carrying amount, 9-18, 9-40, AP-38
cash, 5-11–5-12, 5-34, 7-6–7-7
bank overdrafts, 7-7–7-8, 7-9
classification, 7-9
compensating balances, 7-9
control of, 7-4
see also cash controls
as financial asset, 5-8
in foreign currencies, 7-7
IFRS-ASPE comparison, 7-41
management, 2-5, 7-4
see also cash controls
measurement, 7-6–7-9

net cash provided by operating activities, 5-32
and operations, 4-7
recognition, 7-6–7-9
and recurring obligations, 7-7
reporting cash, 7-7–7-9
restricted cash, 7-7
summary of cash-related items, 7-9
cash and cash equivalents, 5-11–5-12
see also cash; cash equivalents
cash basis accounting
conversion to accrual basis, 4-41–4-43
modified cash basis, 4-41
strict cash basis, 4-39
theoretical weaknesses of, 4-44
vs. accrual basis accounting, 4-39–4-41
cash controls, 7-42–7-47
bank accounts, 7-42–7-43
imprest petty cash system, 7-43–7-44
internal control, 7-42
physical protection of cash balances, 7-44
reconciliation of bank balances, 7-45–7-47
cash cost, 10-10
cash crunch, 5-35
cash debt coverage ratio, 5-35, 5-41
cash discounts, 6-24, 7-12, 10-10
cash equivalents, 7-8–7-9
cash flow per share, 5-38
cash flow statement, 1-3, 4-36
see also statement of cash flows
cash flows
cash flow patterns, 5-35–5-36
discounting the future cash flows, 3-16
estimates, 3-5
free cash flow, 5-36–5-37
interest cash flows, 7-27
prospects, 1-8
cash-generating unit (CGU), 11-25–11-27, 12-27–12-28
cash inflows, 5-27
cash outflows, 5-27
cash payments
ending prepaid expenses, 4-42
expenses, conversion to accrual basis, 4-42–4-43
revenue, conversion to accrual basis, 4-41–4-42
cash price equivalent, 10-11
cashier's cheques, 7-6
cause and effect relationship, 2-22
CCA rate, 11-37
certificates of deposit, 7-6
certified cheques, 7-6
challenges for accounting profession, 1-19–1-25
change funds, 7-6
changes in accounting principle, 4-33
checks and balances, 1-6
cheques
not-sufficient-funds (NSF) cheques, 7-45
outstanding cheques, 7-45
postdated cheques, 7-6, 7-9
classified statement of financial position (balance sheet), 5-9–5-10, 5-10–5-22
see also statement of financial position (balance sheet)
clearing account, AP-47
closing entries, AP-29, AP-47–AP-48
closing process, AP-46–AP-49
inventory and cost of goods sold, AP-48

post-closing trial balance, AP-48
preparation of closing entries, AP-47–AP-48
code of ethics, 1-20
codification project, 1-23
collectibility, 6-14, 6-38
collection float, 7-42
collections received in advance, 5-18
combined statement of income/comprehensive income, 4-22–4-24
commercial paper, 7-8
commercial substance, 6-6, 10-14–10-15, 10-16, 12-7
commissions, 6-41
commodity broker-traders, 8-52
Common Shares account, AP-46
communication of information about performance, 4-7
comparability, 2-10, 2-32
compensating balances, 7-7, 7-9
completed-contract method, 6-48, 6-56
completeness, 2-8
component of an enterprise, 4-14–4-15
componentization, 10-6, 11-5
compound interest, 3-15–3-16
comprehensive income, 2-16, 4-12, 4-38
computer software costs, 12-21
conceptual framework, 1-18, 1-19, 2-3, 4-14
assets, 2-12–2-13
current values, 2-24
development of, 2-3–2-5
elements of financial statements, 2-4, 2-12–2-16
expanded conceptual framework, 2-31
Exposure Drafts (EDs), 2-34, 4-39
foundational principles, 2-16–2-31
historical costs, 2-24
objective of financial reporting, 2-4, 2-5
overview of, 2-4
prudence, 2-1
qualitative characteristics, 2-6–2-12, 4-8
rationale for, 2-3
universally accepted conceptual framework, 2-3
"Conceptual Framework for Financial Accounting and Reporting: Elements of Financial Statements and Their Measurement" (FASB), 2-4
concessionary terms, 6-7–6-8
condensed financial statements, 4-27–4-28
conditional right to receive consideration, 6-43
confirmatory value, 2-6
see also feedback
conservatism, 2-1, 2-27
conservative accounting, 1-11
consideration, 6-5, 6-15
conditional right to receive consideration, 6-43
noncash consideration, 6-27
paid or payable to customers, 6-27–6-28
present value of, 10-11
unconditional right to receive consideration, 6-42
variable consideration, 6-21–6-25, 6-48
consigned goods, 8-9
consignee, 6-40

consignments, 6-40–6-41, 6-42
consignor, 6-40
consistency, 2-11, 2-32, 4-33
consolidation, 2-20, 9-39
constructive obligations, 2-14,
    6-9–6-10
contingencies, 5-19, 5-22–5-23
contingent gains, 5-23
contra account, 5-26, 7-12
contra asset account, AP-38
contra items, 5-25–5-26
contract, 6-13
    basic accounting, 6-14–6-15
    consideration. *See* consideration
    contract modification, 6-15–6-16
    contractual rights, 2-12–2-13
    costs to obtain and/or fulfill a
        contract, 6-44–6-45
    criteria for revenue guidance, 6-14
    with customers, 6-46
    executory contract, 8-10
    financing component, 6-26
    long-term contracts, 6-49–6-54
    new and separate contract,
        6-15–6-16
    non-cancellable purchase contracts,
        8-10
    onerous contract, 8-10
    performance, need for, 6-14
    profitable contracts, 6-57–6-58
    unprofitable contract, 6-58–6-59
contract assets, 6-42–6-44
contract-based approach. *See* asset-
    liability approach
contract-based intangible assets,
    12-18–12-19
contract law, 6-9
contract liability, 6-43
contract modification, 6-15–6-16
contractual obligations to pay, 5-8
contractual rights to receive cash, 5-8
contractual situations, 5-23–5-24
contractual yield basis, 7-23
contributed assets, 10-18–10-19
contributed surplus, 5-20
Contributed Surplus account, AP-46
control, 2-12, 2-18–2-21, 6-12, 6-32,
    6-36, 9-38
control of cash. *See* cash controls
conversion costs, 8-18
copyright, 12-18
corporate scandals, 1-19
corporate strategy, 9-5
corporation, 2-19
    equity section accounts, AP-46
    shareholders' equity account, AP-47
cost-based measures, 3-3
cost-benefit relationship, 2-11
cost formulas, 5-13, 8-23–8-30
    choice of, 8-6, 8-29
    first-in, first-out (FIFO) cost
        formula, 8-27–8-29, 8-50
    last-in, first-out (LIFO) cost formula,
        2-10, 8-29–8-30
    moving-average cost formula, 8-26
    specific identification, 8-24–8-25
    weighted average cost, 8-26–8-27
cost model, 9-9–9-15, 9-47, 10-23,
    11-20, 12-13
cost of goods available for sale or
    use, 8-6
cost of goods manufactured, 8-12–8-13
cost of goods sold, 8-6
cost recovery impairment model,
    11-21–11-22, 11-24–11-25,
    12-21–12-22
cost reduction method, 10-19

cost-to-cost basis, 6-34, 6-51
cost-to-retail ratio, 8-47
costs, 10-6
    acquisition cost, 2-26, 10-21
    asset retirement costs, 8-18, 10-9
    borrowing costs, 8-19, 10-8–10-9,
        10-37–10-42
    capitalization of, 6-45, 10-6–10-7
    cash cost, 10-10
    change in estimated costs, 6-53
    computer software costs, 12-21
    conversion costs, 8-18
    current costs, 2-24
    demolition cost, 10-20
    development phase costs,
        12-10–12-11
    directly attributable costs, 10-7–10-8
    dismantling costs, 10-9–10-10
    excluded from inventory, 8-19
    flow of costs, 8-12–8-13
    freight costs, 8-50
    general and administrative costs,
        6-44
    historical cost principle, 2-24,
        2-26–2-27, AP-37
    historical costs, 10-23
    IAS 16 definition, 10-11
    incremental costs, 6-44
    inventory costs. *See* inventory costs
    joint cost, 8-19–8-20
    kinds of costs, 2-11
    laid-down costs, 2-26
    to obtain and/or fulfill a contract,
        6-44–6-45, 6-46
    organization costs, 12-11
    period costs, 2-22, 8-19
    product costs, 2-22, 8-18–8-20
    property, plant, and equipment,
        10-6–10-10
    rearrangement and reinstallation
        costs, 10-29, 10-33
    replacement cost, 8-30–8-31
    research phase costs, 12-10
    restoration costs, 10-9–10-10
    of service providers' work in
        progress, 8-19
    that expire with passage of time,
        AP-35
    transaction costs, 7-23, 9-8
coupon rate, 7-23
coupons, 6-27
covenants, 5-19
coverage ratios, 5-5, 5-40, 5-41
CPA Canada Handbook, 1-13, 1-18,
    8-7, 10-5, 12-9
    see also Accounting Standards for
        Private Enterprises (ASPE)
credible financial statements, 2-9
credit, AP-29
credit policy, 6-7
credit rating agencies, 1-5
credit risk, 6-6, 7-1, 7-14, 7-23
crediting the account, AP-29
creditors, 1-6, 5-34
creditworthiness, 5-4
critical event, 6-36
cross-references, 5-25–5-26
current assets, 5-10–5-15, 11-20
    cash, 5-11–5-12
    inventories, 5-13–5-14
    prepaid expenses, 5-15
    receivables, 5-12–5-13
    short-term investments, 5-12
current cash debt coverage ratio, 5-5,
    5-35, 5-41
current cost, 2-24

current liabilities, 5-18
current operating performance
    approach, 4-12
current ratio, 5-5, 5-9, 5-41, 8-14, 8-15
current values, 2-24
customer acceptance conditions, 6-7
customer-related intangible assets,
    12-17–12-18
cut-off schedule, 8-9

D
data analytics, 3-1, 7-17, 8-5, 11-9, 12-4
debit, AP-29
debit/credit rules and effects, AP-30
debiting the account, AP-29
debt
    debt covenants, 5-19
    long-term debt, 5-18–5-20
debt instruments, 9-4, 9-11–9-15
debt market, 1-4
debt securities, 9-4
debt to equity ratios, 5-9
debt to total assets, 5-41
decision usefulness, 2-6
decision-usefulness approach, 1-7
declining-balance method, 11-10
decreasing charge methods, 11-10
deferral method, 10-19
deferred income tax assets, 5-18
deferred income tax liabilities, 5-19
deferred payment terms, 10-11–10-12
deficit, 5-20
deflation, 2-25
delayed payment terms, 7-10, 12-6
demolition cost, 10-20
depletion, 10-5, 11-5, 11-13
    estimate of recoverable reserves,
        11-14–11-15
    liquidating dividend, 11-15
    pattern of depletion, 11-13–11-14
depletion base, 10-22
depletion expense, 11-13
depositor errors, 7-45
deposits in transit, 7-45
depreciable amount, 11-6
depreciation, 3-3, 10-5, 11-4, AP-37
    see also amortization
    activity methods, 11-11–11-12
    allocation methods, 11-7–11-12
    asset components, 11-5
    assets held for sale, 11-27
    business perspective, 11-3–11-4
    calculation, 11-7–11-12
    declining-balance method, 11-10
    depreciable amount, 11-6
    depreciation period, 11-7
    diminishing balance methods,
        11-10–11-11
    double-declining-balance method,
        11-11, 11-19
    estimate, 11-5
    factors considered in depreciation
        process, 11-5–11-7
    IFRS-ASPE comparison, 11-35–11-36
    and income tax, 11-37–11-41
    as means of cost allocation, 11-4
    partial periods, 11-16–11-17
    prepaid expenses, AP-37
    and replacement of assets,
        11-32–11-33
    residual value, 11-6
    revalued amount, 10-24, 10-42
    revision of depreciation rates,
        11-18–11-19
    salvage value, 11-6
    straight-line method, 11-9–11-10
    sum-of-the-years'-digits method, 11-10

tax purposes, 11-12
    units of production method,
        11-11
derecognition, 2-18
    disposition, 11-28–11-30
    IFRS-ASPE comparison, 7-41
    intangible assets, 12-24
    receivables, 7-30–7-37
derivatives, 3-5, 5-18
deterioration due to elements, AP-37
development, 12-10
development phase, 12-9–12-11
differentiation strategy, 4-7
digital economy, 6-1
diminishing balance methods,
    11-10–11-11
direct method, 5-33, 8-33
direct write off method, 7-20
directly attributable costs, 10-7–10-8
disclosure
    accounting methods, 4-8
    assets recognized from costs
        incurred to fulfill a contract,
        6-46
    borrowing costs, 10-42
    contra items, 5-25–5-26
    contract with customers, 6-46
    cross-references, 5-25–5-26
    of date financial statement
        authorized for issue, 5-38
    disaggregation of revenue, 6-46
    disclosure problem, 2-34–2-35
    estimates, use of, 5-23
    full disclosure principle, 2-29–2-31,
        4-21, 5-19, 6-9
    goodwill, 12-30–12-33
    greater disclosures, 1-20
    IASB research project, 2-34–2-35
    increased disclosure under
        IFRS, 2-30
    intangible assets, 12-30–12-33
    inventories, 8-43–8-44
    investments, 9-39–9-43
    Management Discussion and
        Analysis (MD&A), 2-30
    measurement, 3-9
    note disclosures, 1-4
    notes to financial statements,
        4-36, 5-25
    operations income, 4-26
    parenthetical explanations,
        5-24–5-25
    property, plant, and equipment,
        11-30–11-32
    receivables, 7-37–7-39
    reconciliation of contract balances,
        6-46
    remaining performance obligations,
        6-46
    restatement of, 1-20
    revenue recognition, 6-45–6-46
    sale of receivables, 7-36–7-37
    significant judgements, 6-46
    supporting schedule, 5-26
    techniques, 5-24–5-26
discontinued operations, 4-14–4-20
    assets held for sale, 4-15–4-16
    component of an enterprise,
        4-14–4-15
    measurement, 4-16–4-20
    presentation, 4-16–4-20
    separate component, 4-14
discount, 6-27, 6-31, 7-28
    cash discounts, 6-24, 7-12, 10-10
    employee discounts, 8-50
    prompt settlement discounts, 6-24
    purchase discounts, 8-50

discount (*continued*)
sales discounts, 7-12, 8-50
trade discounts, 7-12
volume discounts, 6-23–6-24
volume rebates, 8-17–8-18
discount period, 12-41
discount rate, 3-6, 6-48, 12-40
discounted cash flow model, 3-6
discounted free cash flow method,
12-42
discounting the future cash flows, 3-16
discrete earnings process, 6-36
discussion papers (DPs), 1-16
dismantling costs, 10-9–10-10
disposal costs, 11-23
disposition, 4-14
see also sale
business perspective, 11-3–11-4
derecognition, 11-28–11-30
donations of capital assets, 11-29
held for sale, 11-27–11-28, 11-29
IFRS-ASPE comparison,
11-35–11-36
involuntary conversion, 11-29
long-lived assets to be disposed of by
sale, 11-27–11-28
other issues, 11-30
sale of property, plant, and
equipment, 11-28–11-29
dividends, 11-15
Dividends account, AP-46
dividends receivable, 7-10
donations of capital assets, 11-29
double-declining-balance method,
11-11, 11-19
double-entry accounting, AP-29
double-entry bookkeeping, AP-29
due process, 1-14

E
earnings
all-inclusive approach, 4-12
earnings process, 2-21
higher-quality earnings, 4-9
non-GAAP earnings, 4-36
normalized earnings, 12-38
presentation, 4-9
quality of, 4-7–4-12, 5-4
retained earnings, 5-20
sustainability of, 4-9
earnings approach, 6-11, 6-35–6-38,
6-47–6-48
earnings before interest, taxes,
depreciation, and amortization
(EBITDA), 11-12
earnings management, 4-10–4-11,
10-29
earnings multiple, 4-37–4-38
earnings per share (EPS), 4-12, 4-14,
4-31–4-32, 5-41
earnings process, 6-36
economic activity, 2-18–2-19
economic benefits, 2-13, 12-5
economic consequences argument, 2-9
economic entity, 2-20, 9-39
economic entity assumption,
2-18–2-21
economic environment, 2-33
economic factors, 11-7
economic resources, 2-15, 5-8
economic substance, 2-8
economic theory, 1-10
economics of sales transactions,
6-4–6-8
effective interest method, 3-3, 7-25–7-26,
9-12, 9-13
effective interest rate, 7-23

efficiency of asset use, 11-33–11-35
efficient markets hypothesis, 1-10
efficient use of resources, 1-4
elements of financial statements, 2-4,
2-12–2-16, AP-31
assets, 2-12–2-13
basic elements, 2-12
equity, 2-15
expenses, 2-15
fair value, measurement of, 3-9–3-13
gains, 2-15
liabilities, 2-13–2-15
losses, 2-16
measurement of, 3-2–3-9
present value-based accounting
measurements, 3-5
recognition, 2-17–2-22
revenues, 2-15
valuation techniques, 3-3–3-7
value in use measurements, 3-7–3-8
emerging fields, 1-1
employee discounts, 8-50
enforceable promise, 6-9
enhancing qualitative characteristics,
2-10–2-11
entity concept, 2-18
entity perspective, 1-7
entity-specific measure, 2-27, 3-7
environmental liabilities, 3-5, 11-1
E.O.M. (end of the month), 7-12
equipment, 10-21
equitable obligations, 2-14–2-15
equity, 2-15, 5-8
equity claims, 9-39
equity instruments, 5-7, 5-8, 9-4
equity investments, 7-8
equity market, 1-4
equity method, 9-33–9-37, 9-38
equity securities, 9-18
error
bank or depositor errors, 7-45
freedom from material error, 2-9
inventory errors, 8-14–8-16
estimated items, AP-35
adjusting entries, AP-43–AP-44
bad debts, AP-35, AP-43–AP-44
unrealized holding gain or loss,
AP-44–AP-45
estimates
and accrual accounting, 4-8
cash flow estimates, 3-5
change in, 6-53
depreciation, 11-5
disclosure of use of, 5-23
for income measurement, 4-8
inventories, 8-40–8-43
recoverable reserves, 11-14–11-15
in statement of financial position, 5-6
uncollectible trade accounts
receivable, 7-14–7-16
for unperformed work, 6-56
useful life, 11-7
variable consideration, 6-21–6-25
ethical dilemmas, 1-20–1-21
ethical sensitivity, 1-21
ethics
accountant's judgement, 5-23–5-24
biased information, 2-9, 6-10
centrality of ethics, 1-20–1-21
code of ethics, 1-20
correct amounts, determination
of, 8-16
cost deferrals, 2-22
earnings management, 4-10, 10-29
earnings quality, 5-4
economic or business environment,
2-33

ethical dilemmas, 1-20–1-21
ethical sensitivity, 1-21
fair values, ability to measure, 10-15
financial engineering, 2-32
fraudulent financial accounting,
2-33
principles-based GAAP, 2-32
and professional judgement,
5-23–5-24
revenue recognition, 6-10
event, AP-29
see also transaction
excess-earnings approach, 12-37–12-41
exchange price, 7-12, 10-11
executory contract, 8-10
existence uncertainty, 2-18, 2-23
exit price, 2-27
expansion expenses, 5-16
expected cash flow approach, 3-6
expected cost plus a margin, 6-29
expected credit losses, 7-41
expected loss impairment model,
9-27–9-31, 9-31
expected present value technique, 3-7
expected value, 6-21
expenditures, major types of,
10-29–10-34
expense account, AP-29
expenses, 2-15
see also specific expenses
accrued expenses, AP-35,
AP-41–AP-43
calculation of, 4-42–4-43
expansion expenses, 5-16
function, 4-28–4-30
IFRS-ASPE comparison, 4-38–4-39
nature, 4-28–4-30
operating expenses, 5-16
prepaid expenses, 5-15, AP-35,
AP-36–AP-39
presentation, 4-28–4-30
in single-step income statements, 4-24
supplementary schedules, 4-27
exploration and evaluation assets, 11-14
Exposure Drafts (EDs), 1-16
conceptual framework, 2-34, 4-39
extended payment terms, 6-26
extended warranties, 6-19
extensible business reporting language
(XBRL), 1-24
external users, 1-3
extractive industries, 10-37, 11-36

F
face rate, 7-23
face value, 7-23–7-24
factoring receivables, 7-31
fair value, 2-24, 10-24, 11-21
best-quality fair value measure, 3-12
"cost" on the books, 10-18
estimate of, 2-26
less costs of disposal, 11-23
less costs to sell, 10-22, 10-27
loans receivable, 7-23, 7-30
measurement, using IFRS 13,
3-9–3-13
nonmonetary transactions, 10-15
not equal to cash consideration, 7-30
notes receivable, 7-23
property, plant, and equipment, 10-24
relative fair value, 6-48
and revenue recognition, 6-27
fair value hierarchy, 3-11
fair value less costs to sell, 8-38–8-39
fair value loss impairment model, 9-31
fair value model (FVM), 10-23,
10-27–10-28, 10-28, 10-32

fair value option, 2-28, 5-8, 9-47
fair value principle, 2-27–2-29
fair value standard, 10-14–10-15
fair value test, 12-23
fair value through net income (FV-NI),
9-15–9-19, 9-47, AP-45
fair value through other
comprehensive income (FV-
OCI), 4-13, 9-20–9-26, 9-47,
AP-45
income from FV-OCI investments
(debt instruments), 9-23–9-25
income from FV-OCI investments
(shares), 9-21–9-22
investments in debt instruments of
other entities, 9-23–9-26
investments in shares of other
entities, 9-21–9-23
with recycling, 9-21
sale of FV-OCI investments (debt
instruments), 9-25–9-26
sale of FV-OCI investments (shares),
9-22–9-23
without recycling, 9-21
favourable lease, 12-19
feedback, 2-6, 4-7
feedback value, 4-12, 4-26
financial accounting, 1-3
conceptual framework, 2-4
derecognition of receivables,
7-41–7-42
nonmonetary exchange, 10-14
performance reporting project, 4-39
financial assets, 5-8, 5-12–5-13, 7-6, 7-14
financial calculators, 3-19–3-20, 3-23
financial components approach, 7-35
financial crisis, 1-7, 1-19
financial engineering, 2-32
financial flexibility, 5-5, 5-7, 5-19, 5-35
financial institutions, 1-4, 1-7
financial instruments, 5-8, 8-52
financial ratios. *See* ratio analysis
financial reporting, 1-3
bias in, 1-11, 4-8, 6-10
conceptual framework. *See*
conceptual framework
decision-usefulness approach, 1-7
economic or business environment,
2-33
entity perspective, 1-7
financial engineering, 2-32
fraudulent financial reporting,
2-33–2-34
integrated reporting, 1-24
issues, 2-31–2-34
objective of financial reporting,
1-7–1-9, 2-31–2-32
other pressures, 2-33–2-34
proprietary perspective, 1-8
"prudent" approach, 2-1
and raising capital, 1-1–1-2
stakeholders, 1-5–1-7
well-reasoned and supported
analysis, 2-33
financial risks, 5-40, 9-41
financial statements, 1-3, 2-29, AP-29,
AP-46
see also specific types of financial
statements
analysis. *See* analysis
basic elements, 2-12
basic presentation requirements,
4-21–4-22
condensed financial statements,
4-27–4-28
consolidation, 2-20, 9-39
credible financial statements, 2-9

elements of financial statements, 2-4, 2-12–2-16, 3-2–3-9, AP-31
general-purpose financial statements, 1-7, 2-4
measurement of financial statement elements, 3-2–3-9
note disclosures, 1-4
notes to financial statements, 2-29–2-30, 4-36
as point estimates, 4-8
preparation from work sheet, AP-53–AP-56
presentation. See presentation
specimen financial statements, AP-6–AP-26
supplementary information, 2-30
users, 1-3, 1-5, 2-5, 6-4
financial technology industry, 1-1
financing activities, 4-3, 5-27, 5-32
finished goods inventory, 8-5
finite life, 5-17, 12-14
first-in, first-out (FIFO) cost formula, 8-27–8-29, 8-50
first principles, 2-32
five-step revenue recognition process
 allocation of transaction price to separate performance obligations, 6-28–6-31
 determination of transaction price, 6-21–6-28
 example, 6-11–6-12
 identification of separate performance obligations, 6-16–6-20
 identification of the contract with customers, 6-13–6-16
 recognition of revenue when each performance obligation satisfied, 6-32–6-35
 summary of, 6-35
fixed assets, 10-4
 see also property, plant, and equipment
flexibility, 2-32
f.o.b. destination, 6-9, 8-8
f.o.b. shipping point, 6-9, 8-8
foreign currencies, 7-7
formal plan to sell, 4-16
forms of organization, 2-19
foundational principles, 2-16–2-31
 measurement, 2-23–2-29
 presentation and disclosure, 2-29–2-31
 recognition and derecognition, 2-17–2-22
franchise, 12-19
fraudulent financial reporting, 2-33–2-34
Fraudulent Financial Reporting: 1998-2007, 2-33–2-34
Freakonomics (Levitt and Dubner), 1-10
free cash flow, 5-36–5-37
freedom from material error, 2-9
freight costs, 8-50
fulfilment value, 2-24
full cost method, 10-22
full disclosure principle, 2-29–2-31, 4-21, 5-19, 6-9
function, 4-28–4-30, 5-7
fundamental qualitative characteristics, 2-6–2-9
future income tax assets, 5-18
future income tax liabilities, 5-19
future value, AP-1, AP-3
FV-OCI model. See fair value through other comprehensive income (FV-OCI)

G
GAAP. See generally accepted accounting principles (GAAP)
GAAP hierarchy, 1-17–1-18
gains, 2-15
 contingent gains, 5-23
 realized, 9-8
 unrealized holding gains or losses, 9-8, AP-35
 unusual gains, 4-21
 vs. revenues, 4-21
general and administrative costs, 6-44
general and administrative expenses, 8-19
general chequing account, 7-43
general journal, AP-32, AP-34
general ledger, AP-29, AP-31
general-purpose financial statements, 1-7, 2-4
generally accepted accounting principles (GAAP), 1-6, 1-12–1-13
 see also Accounting Standards for Private Enterprises (ASPE)
 in absence of specific GAAP guidance, 2-32
 comprehensive income, 4-12
 conceptual framework, 1-18
 consolidated statements, 2-20
 CPA Canada Handbook, 1-13, 1-18
 disclosure of accounting methods, 4-8
 entities responsible for GAAP, 1-13
 GAAP hierarchy, 1-17–1-18
 under IFRS, 1-18
 not always optimal, 4-8
 other sources of GAAP, 1-18
 primary sources, 1-18, 2-16
 principles-based approach, 1-23, 2-32
 principles vs. rules, 1-22
 professional judgement, 1-19
 rational and systematic allocation policy, 2-22
 rules-based approach, 1-22
 sources of GAAP, 1-18
 U.S. GAAP, 1-16, 1-23, 8-30
gift cards, 6-27–6-28
going concern assumption, 2-25–2-26
goods, 6-4
 consigned goods, 8-9
 distinct goods, 6-15
 included in inventory, 8-8–8-13
 sale of goods, 6-36–6-37
  see also sales transaction
 substantially the same, 6-20
 vs. sales of services, 6-4
goods in transit, 8-8–8-9
goodwill, 5-17, 12-4–12-5
 after mergers and acquisitions, 5-1
 analysis, 12-34–12-35
 bargain purchase, 12-26–12-27
 business importance, 12-3–12-4
 characteristics, 12-3–12-4
 disclosure, 12-30–12-33
 discounted free cash flow method, 12-42
 excess-earnings approach, 12-37–12-41
 IFRS, effects of, 12-1
 IFRS-ASPE comparison, 12-36
 impairment, 12-27–12-30
 internally generated goodwill, 5-17, 12-24
 measurement, 12-4, 12-24–12-27
 negative goodwill, 12-26
 number of years method, 12-42
 present value-based accounting measurements, 3-5

 presentation, 12-30–12-33
 purchased goodwill, 12-24–12-26
 recognition, 12-24–12-27
 total-earnings approach, 12-41–12-42
 valuation after acquisition, 12-27
 valuation of goodwill, 12-27, 12-37–12-42
government grants, 10-18–10-19
Great Depression, 1-12
gross average accounts receivable (GAAR), 7-19
gross margin percentage, 8-42
gross method, 7-12
gross profit margins, 4-28
gross profit method, 8-41–8-43
gross profit percentage, 8-42–8-43

H
half-year rule, 11-38
hard numbers, 2-10, 4-8, 5-6
held for sale, 4-15–4-16, 11-27–11-28, 11-29, 11-36
held for trading instruments, 9-7
held to maturity instruments, 9-11
highest and best use, 3-10
historical cost-based model, 2-27
historical cost measures, 3-3
historical cost principle, 2-24, 2-26–2-27
 depreciable assets, AP-37
 on statement of financial position, 5-6
historical costs, 10-23
holder, 7-31
human behaviour, 1-10
hyperinflation, 2-25

I
identifiable, 12-5
identifiable net assets, 12-4
IFRS. See International Financial Reporting Standards (IFRS)
IFRS-ASPE comparison
 see also Accounting Standards for Private Enterprises (ASPE); International Financial Reporting Standards (IFRS)
 accounting changes, 4-39
 cash and cash equivalents, 7-41
 cash flow per share information, 5-38
 current vs. non-current liabilities, 5-38
 depreciation, 11-35–11-36
 derecognition, 7-41
 disclosure, property, plant, and equipment, 11-36
 disclosure of date financial statement authorized for issue, 5-38
 discontinued operations, 4-38
 earnings per share, 4-38
 expenses, 4-38
 fundamental similarities, 2-34–2-35
 goodwill, 12-36
 held for sale, 11-36
 impairment, 7-41, 9-46, 11-35–11-36
 intangible assets, 12-35–12-37
 inventories, 8-45–8-46
 investments, 9-44–9-47
 measurement issues, 3-27–3-28, 9-46
 other comprehensive income/comprehensive income, 4-38, 9-46
 "probable," and recognition of losses and liabilities, 2-18

 property, plant, and equipment, 10-34–10-37
 receivables, 7-41
 revenue recognition, 6-47–6-48
 significant influence investments, 9-47
 statement of cash flows, 5-38
 statement of changes in shareholders' equity, 4-39
 statement of financial position (balance sheet), 5-38
 statement of income/comprehensive income (income statement), 4-38–4-39
 statement of retained earnings, 4-39
impaired, 11-20
impairment, 11-19–11-27
 accounts receivable, 7-14–7-20
 asset groups, 11-25–11-27
 business perspective, 11-3–11-4
 cash-generating unit (CGU), 11-25–11-27
 cost recovery impairment model, 11-21–11-22, 11-24–11-25, 12-21–12-22
 goodwill, 12-27–12-30
 IFRS-ASPE comparison, 7-41, 9-46, 11-35–11-36
 indefinite-life intangibles, 12-23
 indicators of impairment, 11-20–11-21
 intangible assets. See intangible assets
 limited-life intangibles, 12-21–12-22
 rational entity impairment model, 12-21–12-22
 rational entity model, 11-21, 11-22–11-25
 recognition and measurement models, 11-21–11-25
 recoverable amount, 11-22
 in value, equity method, 9-37
impairment loss, 9-27, 11-21–11-22, 11-24, 11-26–11-27
impairment models, 9-26–9-31
 expected loss impairment model, 9-27–9-31, 9-31
 fair value loss impairment model, 9-31
 incurred loss impairment model, 9-26–9-27, 9-31
 summary of, 9-31
implicit interest rate, 7-24
imprest bank accounts, 7-43
imprest system, 7-43–7-44
imputation, 7-29
imputed interest rate, 7-29
in-process research and development (R&D), 12-7
incidental transactions, 2-15, 2-16, 4-26
income
 all-inclusive approach, 4-12
 under amortized cost model, 9-11–9-14
 comprehensive income, 2-16, 4-12
 measurement, 4-8, 4-12–4-14
 multiple view of income, 4-14
 net income. See net income
 nonrecurring income or losses, 4-26
 numbers, and accounting methods, 4-8
 operating income, 4-7, 4-12
 operations income, 4-26
 other comprehensive income. See other comprehensive income (OCI)
 sustainability of, 4-9
income approach, 10-18

income models, 3-3–3-4
income statement, 1-3, 4-3, 4-36, AP-29
  see also statement of income/
    comprehensive income (income
    statement)
Income Summary account, AP-47
Income Tax Act, 11-37
income taxes
  capital cost allowance method,
    11-37–11-41
  depreciation, 11-37–11-41
  work sheet, AP-51–AP-52
incremental costs, 6-44
incurred loss impairment model,
  9-26–9-27, 9-31
indefinite life, 5-17, 12-14, 12-15–12-16,
  12-19, 12-23, 12-27
indirect method, 5-32–5-33, 8-33
industries, 4-3–4-7
industry practice, 1-18
inflation, 2-25
inflation accounting, 2-25
information
  integrity of, 4-9
  quality of, 4-7–4-12
  useful information, 2-18
information asymmetry, 1-9–1-11, 2-5
  adverse selection, 1-10–1-11, 2-5
  moral hazard, 1-11, 2-5
information overload, 2-29
information symmetry, 1-9
input measures, 6-33, 6-50
inspections, 10-29, 10-30–10-32
institutional investors, 1-8–1-9, 9-1–9-2
insurance, 5-15, AP-37
insurance claims, 7-10
intangible assets, 5-17, 12-5
  at acquisition, 12-6–12-7
  after acquisition, 12-12–12-16
  after mergers and acquisitions, 5-1
  amortization, 11-5, 12-14
  analysis, 12-34–12-35
  artistic-related intangible assets, 12-18
  business combination, 12-7
  business importance, 12-3–12-4
  characteristics, 12-5–12-6
  contract-based intangible assets,
    12-18–12-19
  customer-related intangible assets,
    12-17–12-18
  derecognition, 12-24
  development phase, 12-9–12-11
  disclosure, 5-1, 12-30–12-33
  finite life, 5-17
  IFRS-ASPE comparison, 12-35–12-37
  impairment, generally, 12-1
  impairment of indefinite-life
    intangibles, 12-23
  impairment of limited-life
    intangibles, 12-21–12-22
  indefinite life, 5-17, 12-14,
    12-15–12-16, 12-23
  internally developed intangible
    assets, 5-17, 12-6
  limited-life intangibles, 12-14–12-15,
    12-21–12-22
  marketing-related intangible assets,
    12-16–12-17
  measurement, 12-6–12-16
  measurement difficulties, 5-17
  prepayments, 12-7–12-9
  presentation, 12-30–12-33
  purchased intangibles, 12-6–12-7
  recognition, 12-6–12-16
  research phase, 12-9–12-10
  technology-based intangible assets,
    12-19–12-21

useful life, 5-17
  valuation difficulties, 5-17
integrated reporting, 1-24
intellectual capital, 12-34
interest, 10-11
  accrued interest, AP-41–AP-42
  capitalization of interest, 10-8
  compound interest, 3-15–3-16
  nature of, 3-13–3-14
  nonrecognition of interest element,
    7-13–7-14
  notes receivable, 7-21
  simple interest, 3-15
interest-bearing investment, 9-11
interest-bearing notes, 7-21, 7-27–7-29
interest rates
  calculation of, 3-25–3-26
  effective interest rate, 7-23
  implicit interest rate, 7-24
  imputed interest rate, 7-29
  market rate, 7-23, 7-27, 7-29
  present value calculations, 3-24
  stated interest rate, 7-23, 7-27, 7-29
  yield rate, 7-23
interest receivable, 7-10
internal control, 7-42
internal control systems, 1-20
internal users, 1-3
International Accounting Standards
  (IAS), 1-18
  see also International Financial
    Reporting Standards (IFRS)
  agriculture, 8-37, 10-22
  biological assets and agricultural
    produce, 6-48, 8-46
  borrowing costs, 10-8
  cost, 10-11
  depreciation, 11-12
  disclosure, 8-44
  fair value through other
    comprehensive income, 4-13
  hyperinflation, 2-25, 10-23
  impairment of assets, 12-36
  intangible assets, 12-9, 12-14, 12-37
  inventories, 8-38, 8-45–8-46
  investment property, 10-21, 10-28
  markdowns, 8-50
  property, plant, and equipment,
    10-5, 10-21, 11-28
  provisions, contingent liabilities,
    and contingent assets, 8-10
  statement of cash flows, 5-38
International Accounting Standards
  Board (IASB), 1-12, 1-14–1-15,
  1-16, 1-21, 1-22
  see also International Financial
    Reporting Standards (IFRS)
  adoption date for IFRS 15, 6-48
  conceptual framework, 2-4–2-5,
    2-34, 3-28, 4-14
  derecognition of receivables, 7-42
  disclosures, 2-34–2-35
  extractive industries, 10-36–10-37
  financial statement presentation, 5-38
  intangible assets, 12-37
  materiality, 2-34
  Primary Financial Statements
    Project, 4-39
  revenue recognition, 6-10–6-11
International Financial Reporting
  Standards (IFRS), 1-13
  see also generally accepted accounting
    principles (GAAP); IFRS-ASPE
    comparison; International
    Accounting Standards (IAS);
    International Accounting
    Standards Board (IASB)

accounts receivable, 7-14
accumulated other comprehensive
  income, 5-20, 9-20
all-inclusive approach, 4-12
asset impairment, 3-7
asset-liability approach, 6-10–6-11,
  6-35, 6-47–6-48
asset retirement costs, 10-9–10-10
associates, investments in, 9-33, 9-43
balance sheet approach, 2-21
bank overdrafts, 7-8
basic presentation requirements,
  4-21
biological assets and agricultural
  produce, 8-38
borrowing costs, 8-19, 10-8
capitalization of costs, 10-7
cash equivalents, 7-8
combined statement of income/
  comprehensive income,
  4-22–4-24
components, 10-6, 11-6
comprehensive income, 2-16
control, 2-20, 9-38, 9-40
cost model, 10-23
current assets, 9-40
depreciation, 11-6, 11-18
derecognition, 7-33–7-34, 7-35
disclosure, 12-30–12-31
effective interest method, 7-23,
  7-25, 9-12
evolution of a new or revised IFRS,
  1-15
existence uncertainty, 2-18, 2-23
expected loss impairment model,
  9-27
expenses, 4-28, 4-29
fair value, 2-27, 3-7, 3-9–3-13, 10-24,
  10-27, 11-22–11-23, 12-36
fair value option, 2-28–2-29
financial assets, 7-14, 9-47–9-48
financial instruments, 5-8
GAAP under IFRS, 1-18
goodwill, 12-1, 12-28–12-30,
  12-30–12-31
held for sale, 4-16, 11-27–11-28
impairment, 7-41, 9-26, 9-27,
  9-28–9-29, 9-31, 9-41, 11-21
income, 2-15, 4-12
increased disclosure, 2-30
indefinite life, 12-15
indefinite-life intangibles, 12-23
intangible assets, 12-9, 12-11–12-12,
  12-30–12-31
inventory, 2-10, 8-7, 8-44
inventory cost, 8-17
investment measurement models,
  9-47–9-48
investment property, 10-21, 10-23
investments, 9-8, 9-15, 9-23
liabilities, recognition of, 5-23
lifetime expected credit losses,
  7-14, 9-29
limited-life intangibles, 12-21–12-22
long-term contracts, 6-49–6-50
measurability and, 2-18
mineral resources, 10-36–10-37
monetary unit, stability of, 2-25
other comprehensive income, 2-16,
  4-12–4-14, 4-31, 5-20, 9-20, 10-24
price-level change, 2-25
principles-based approach, 1-23, 2-32
probability and, 2-18
"probable," 2-18
product costs, 8-18
professional judgement, 1-19
property, plant, and equipment, 5-15

provisions, 5-19, 5-23
prudence, 2-1
rational entity impairment model,
  11-22, 11-23, 11-26,
  12-21–12-22
receivables, 7-33–7-34, 7-35, 7-37, 7-41
refund liability, 7-13
replacements, major overhauls, and
  inspections, 10-32
revaluation model, 10-42,
  12-13–12-14
revenue from contracts with
  customers, 2-21, 6-10
revenue recognition, 6-32, 6-38, 6-45
sales revenue, 7-12
share-based payment, 10-13
significant influence, 9-37, 9-40
statement of changes in equity, 4-32,
  4-34–4-35
statement of income/comprehensive
  income, 4-22–4-24, 4-28, 4-29
subsidiaries, investments in,
  9-38–9-39
transaction costs, 7-23
United States, and IFRS, 1-23
vs. U.S. GAAP, 1-23
zero-profit method, 6-49, 6-55
Internet, 1-10, 1-24
intraperiod tax allocation, 4-30–4-31
inventories, 8-7–8-8
  accounting definition, 8-7–8-8
  analysis, 8-44–8-45
  basket purchases and joint product
    costs, 8-19–8-20
  beginning inventory, AP-48
  categories, 8-4–8-5
  change in control, 8-11–8-12
  companies with inventory, 8-4
  consigned goods, 8-9
  and cost of goods sold, AP-48
  costs. *See* inventory costs
  as current asset, 5-13–5-14
  disclosure, 8-43–8-44
  ending inventory, 8-14–8-15, AP-48
  estimates, 8-40–8-43
  finished goods inventory, 8-5
  goods in transit, 8-8–8-9
  goods included in inventory,
    8-8–8-13
  IFRS-ASPE comparison, 8-45–8-46
  information for decision-making,
    8-5–8-6
  inventory errors, 8-14–8-16
  inventory tracking, 8-1
  last-in, first-out (LIFO) cost formula,
    2-10
  manufacturing inventory, 5-13
  measurement, 8-6, 8-16–8-20
  merchandise inventory, 8-4
  physical count, AP-48
  planning and control, 8-5
  presentation, 8-43–8-44
  purchase commitments, 8-10–8-11
  purchases and inventory misstated,
    8-15–8-16
  raw materials inventory, 8-5
  recognition of physical goods
    included in inventory, 8-7–8-13
  repurchase agreements, 8-9–8-10
  risks and rewards, 8-11–8-12
  types of inventory, 8-51–8-52
  understatement of, 8-9
  vendor rebate, 8-18
  volume rebates, 8-17–8-18
  vs. property, plant, and equipment,
    10-5
  work-in-process inventory, 8-5

inventory accounting systems
  periodic inventory system, 8-21,
    8-28, 8-33, AP-48
  perpetual inventory system, 8-21,
    8-26, 8-28, 8-33, AP-48
  quantities only system, 8-23
inventory costs, 8-16–8-20, 8-47–8-51
  borrowing costs, 8-19
  cost formula. See cost formulas
  cost of service providers' work in
    progress, 8-19
  costs excluded from inventory, 8-19
  exceptions to lower of cost and
    net realizable value model,
    8-35–8-40
  fair value less costs to sell, 8-38–8-39
  flow of costs, 8-12–8-13
  lower of cost and market (LCM),
    8-30
  lower of cost and net realizable
    value, 8-30–8-35
  net realizable value, 8-35–8-36
  product costs, 8-18–8-20
  retail inventory method, 8-47–8-51
  standard cost system, 8-19
inventory errors, 8-14–8-16
inventory turnover ratio, 5-41, 8-44
investee, 9-5
investing activities, 4-4, 5-27, 5-33,
  5-36
investment property, 10-21, 10-23
investments
  amortized cost model, 9-11–9-15
  analysis, 9-44
  application of accounting models,
    9-9
  associates, investments in, 9-32–9-38,
    9-43–9-44
  available for sale, 9-7
  cost model, 9-9–9-15
  in debt instruments of other entities,
    9-23–9-26
  disclosure, 9-39–9-43
  equity investments, 7-8
  expected loss impairment model,
    9-27–9-31, 9-31
  fair value loss impairment model,
    9-31
  fair value model, 10-28
  fair value through net income
    (FV-NI), 9-15–9-19
  fair value through other
    comprehensive income
    (FV-OCI), 9-20–9-26
  held for trading, 9-7
  held to maturity investments, 9-11
  IFRS-ASPE comparison, 9-44–9-47
  impairment models, 9-26–9-31
  incurred loss impairment model,
    9-26–9-27, 9-31
  information for decision-making, 9-7
  long-term investments, 5-15
  on margin, 9-8
  measurement, overview, 9-7–9-9
  non-current investments, 5-15
  present value-based accounting
    measurements, 3-5
  presentation, 9-39–9-43
  recoverable amount, 9-37
  returns, 9-5
  in shares of other entities, 9-21–9-23
  short-term investments, 5-12, 7-6
  significant influence investments,
    9-32
  strategic investments, 9-32–9-39
  subsidiaries, investments in,
    9-38–9-39

types of companies, 9-5–9-7
types of investments, 9-3–9-5
  without significant influence or
    control, 9-40–9-43
investors, 1-6, 1-8–1-9, 9-5
involuntary conversion, 11-29
IOUs, 7-6, 7-9
irregular activities, 4-26
irregular items, 4-12, 4-30
item-by-item approach, 8-33

J
joint cost, 8-19–8-20
joint venture, 9-33
journal entries, AP-29
  see also specific journal entries
journalizing, AP-31–AP-32
journals, 1-18, AP-29
  general journal, AP-32, AP-34
  special journal, AP-32
judgement. See professional
  judgement

K
knowledge assets, 12-34

L
laid-down costs, 2-26
language of accounting and business,
  2-12
last-in, first-out (LIFO) cost formula,
  2-10, 8-29–8-30
leasehold, 12-19
leasehold improvements, 10-20
leases, 12-19
  favourable lease, 12-19
  present value-based accounting
    measurements, 3-5
ledger, AP-29
  general ledger, AP-29, AP-31
  subsidiary ledger, AP-29
legal control, 9-32
legal entity, 2-19–2-20
legal life, 11-7
legal title, 6-4, 6-7, 6-9, 6-37, 8-9
lenient return or payment policy, 6-7
liabilities, 2-13–2-15
  assets that become liabilities, 11-1
  classification in statement of
    financial position, 5-7
  contract liability, 6-43
  contractual obligations to pay, 5-8
  current liabilities, 5-18
  current vs. non-current
    classification, 2-26
  deferred income tax liabilities,
    5-19
  environmental liabilities, 3-5, 11-1
  and financial flexibility, 5-7
  future income tax liabilities, 5-19
  historical cost, 5-6
  liquidation approach, 2-26
  monetary liabilities, 5-7–5-8
  nonmonetary liabilities, 5-7–5-8
  potential liability, 2-13–2-14
  recognition, 5-23
  on statement of financial position,
    5-8
liability account, AP-29
licences, 12-19
licensing agreements, 6-34, 12-19
lifetime expected credit losses, 7-14,
  9-29
limited liability partnerships (LLPs),
  2-19
limited life, 12-14–12-15, 12-19,
  12-21–12-22
limited resources, 1-4

liquidating dividend, 11-15
liquidation approach, 2-26
liquidity, 1-12, 5-4, 5-5, 5-9, 5-35
liquidity ratios, 5-5, 5-6, 5-40, 5-41
liquidity risk, 5-6
loans, 7-10, 7-23
loans receivable, 7-4, 7-10
  see also notes receivable
  fair value, 7-23, 7-30
  long-term loans receivable,
    7-22–7-30
  short-term loans receivable,
    7-21–7-22
  transaction costs, 7-23
lockbox accounts, 7-43
long-lived assets, 11-27–11-28
long-term contracts, 6-49–6-54
  completed-contract method, 6-56
  examples of, 6-49–6-50
  loss in current period, 6-57–6-58
  loss on unprofitable contract,
    6-58–6-59
  losses on, 6-57–6-59
  percentage-of-completion method,
    6-49–6-54
  progress billings, 6-49
  treatment under IFRS 15, 6-49–6-50
long-term debt, 5-18–5-20
long-term investments, 5-15
long-term liabilities, 5-18–5-20
long-term loans receivable, 7-22–7-30
long-term notes receivable, 7-22–7-30
longer-term returns, 9-5
loss events, 9-26–9-27
losses, 2-16
  allowance for loans receivable, 7-20
  in current period, on profitable
    contract, 6-57–6-58
  in current period, on unprofitable
    contract, 6-58–6-59
  on long-term contracts, 6-57–6-59
  nonrecurring income or losses, 4-26
  on profitable contract, 6-57–6-58
  realized, 9-8
  terminal loss, 11-40–11-41
  on unprofitable contract, 6-58–6-59
  unrealized holding gains or losses,
    9-8, AP-35
  unusual losses, 4-21
low-cost/high-volume strategy, 4-6
lower of cost and market (LCM), 8-30
lower of cost and net realizable value,
  8-30–8-35, 8-50, 8-51–8-52,
  11-20
lower of cost and net realizable value
  (LC&NRV) principle, 8-31–8-35
lump-sum price, 10-12

M
major overhauls, 10-29, 10-30–10-32
maker, 7-21
management best estimate, 2-9
management bias, 1-11, 1-20–1-21
Management Discussion and Analysis
  (MD&A), 2-30
managerial accounting, 1-3
manufacturing inventory, 5-13
markdown cancellations, 8-48
markdowns, 8-48
market, 8-30
  capital markets, 1-10
  debt market, 1-4
  efficient markets hypothesis, 1-10
  equity market, 1-4
  most advantageous market, 3-10
  principal market, 3-10–3-11
market-based measure, 2-27

market models, 3-4
market participant view, 3-7
market rate, 7-23, 7-27, 7-29
market valuation model, 2-27
market value, AP-38
marketing-related intangible assets,
  12-16–12-17
markup, 8-48
markup cancellations, 8-48
markup on cost, 8-42
matching, 2-21–2-22
  and adjusting entries, AP-35
  depreciable assets, AP-37
  depreciation, 11-7
  estimate of bad debts, AP-43
  percentage-of-sales approach, 7-17
material right, 6-17–6-18
materiality, 2-6–2-7, 2-34, 4-21,
  6-9, 10-29
MD&A: Guidance on Preparation and
  Disclosure (CICA), 2-30
measurement, 2-23–2-29
  accounts receivable, 7-11–7-14
  cash, 7-6–7-9
  choice of tool used, 2-24
  of company performance, 1-4
  at cost, 12-6
  cost/amortized cost model, 9-9–9-15
  cost-based measures, 3-3
  and cost formulas, 8-23–8-30
  current value measures, 3-3
  disclosures, 3-9
  discontinued operations, 4-16–4-20
  entity-specific measure, 2-27, 3-7
  fair value principle, 2-27–2-29
  fair value through net income (FV-
    NI), 9-15–9-19
  fair value through other
    comprehensive income (FV-
    OCI), 9-20–9-26
  of fair value using IFRS 13, 3-9–3-13
  financial assets, 7-14
  going concern assumption,
    2-25–2-26
  goodwill, 12-4, 12-24–12-27
  historical cost principle, 2-26–2-27
  hybrid measures, 3-3
  IFRS-ASPE comparison, 3-27–3-28,
    9-46
  impairment, 11-21–11-25
  impairment models, 9-26–9-31
  of income, 4-12–4-14
  income measurement, 4-8
  intangible assets, 5-17, 12-6–12-16
  inventory, 8-6
  of inventory, 8-16–8-20
  and inventory accounting systems,
    8-20–8-23
  investments, 9-7–9-31
  items recognized in financial
    statements, AP-31
  long-term loans receivable, 7-22–7-30
  long-term notes receivable, 7-22–7-30
  and lower of cost and net realizable
    value, 8-30–8-35
  market-based measure, 2-27
  measurement uncertainty, 2-23, 2-27
  monetary unit assumption, 2-25
  non-GAAP measures, 4-36–4-37
  other key measures, 4-37–4-38
  periodicity assumption, 2-25
  present value-based accounting
    measurements, 3-5
  property, plant, and equipment—
    after acquisition, 10-23–10-28
  property, plant, and equipment—
    cost, 10-10–10-19

receivables, 7-11–7-14
and recognition, 2-23–2-29
remeasurement, 4-16
of revenue, 6-10–6-11
short-term loans receivable,
7-21–7-22
short-term notes receivable,
7-21–7-22
tools, 2-23
transactions, at contract inception,
6-38
and uncertainty, 2-24–2-25
value in use measurements, 3-7–3-8
measurement uncertainty, 2-23, 2-27,
4-36
merchandise inventory, 8-4
mineral resource properties,
10-21–10-22, 10-36–10-37
see also depletion
mineral resources, 10-21
see also depletion
minority interest, 9-39
mixed valuation model, 2-27
modified cash basis, 4-41
monetary assets, 5-7–5-8, 10-14, 12-5
monetary liabilities, 5-7–5-8
monetary unit assumption, 2-25
money, 5-12
money-market funds, 7-6, 7-8
money orders, 7-6
moral hazard, 1-11, 2-5
most advantageous market, 3-10
most likely amount, 6-21
moving-average cost formula, 8-26
multiple deliverables, 6-4
multiple performance obligations,
6-17, 6-29–6-31
multiple-step income statement,
4-24–4-27

N
natural resources, 10-21–10-22
see also mineral resources
nature, 4-28–4-30
negative goodwill, 12-26
negotiable instruments, 7-6
net assets, 5-8
net carrying amount, 11-6
net cash inflows, 4-7
net income, 2-25, 4-12, 5-34
accrual-based net income, 4-44
income approach, 10-18
losses, AP-35
significantly higher than cash flows
from operations, 5-4
work sheet, AP-53
net income per share. *See* earnings per
share (EPS)
net markdowns, 8-48
net markups, 8-48
net method, 7-12
net realizable value (NRV), 2-26, 7-15,
8-30–8-35, 8-35–8-36
net working capital, 5-18
neutrality, 2-8, 2-32, 11-8
non-cancellable purchase contracts,
8-10
non-current investments, 5-15
non–GAAP earnings, 4-36
non–GAAP measures, 4-36–4-37
non–interest-bearing investment,
9-11, 9-17
non–interest-bearing notes, 7-21–7-22
non-operating transactions, 4-25
non-reciprocal transfers, 10-18
noncash consideration, 6-27
noncontrolling interest, 9-39

nonmonetary, non-reciprocal
transactions, 2-26
nonmonetary assets, 5-7–5-8,
10-14, 12-7
nonmonetary exchanges, 10-10–10-19
nonmonetary liabilities, 5-7–5-8
nonmonetary transactions, 2-26, 6-6,
10-14–10-18
nonrecurring income or losses, 4-26
nontrade receivables, 7-4, 7-10
normal business practices, 6-8
normal production capacity, 8-18
normal selling terms, 6-7–6-8
normal shortages, 8-50
normalized earnings, 12-38
Norwalk Agreement, 1-16
not–sufficient-funds (NSF) cheques,
7-45
note disclosures, 1-4
notes receivable, 5-7, 7-10
see also loans receivable
face value, 7-23–7-24
fair value, 7-23
interest-bearing notes, 7-21,
7-27–7-29
long-term notes receivable, 7-22–7-30
non–interest-bearing notes,
7-21–7-22
received for property, goods, or
services, 7-29–7-30
short-term notes receivable,
7-21–7-22
transaction costs, 7-23
zero-interest-bearing notes, 7-21,
7-24–7-27
notes to financial statements, 2-29–2-30,
4-36, 5-25
present value-based accounting
measurements, 3-5
number of years method, 12-42

O
objective of financial reporting, 1-7–1-9,
2-4, 2-5, 2-31–2-32
obsolescence, 11-7, 11-20, AP-37
off–balance sheet, 5-6
oil and gas properties, 10-22,
10-36–10-37
on margin, 9-8
one-line consolidation, 9-37
onerous contract, 8-10
operating activities, 4-4, 5-27, 5-31–5-33,
5-34
operating expenses, 4-42–4-43, 5-16
operating income, 4-7, 4-12
operating items, 4-12
operating risk, 5-40
operating segments, 5-1
operating transactions, 4-25
operations income, 4-26
opportunities, 4-4
opportunities for accounting
profession, 1-19–1-25
ordinary activities, 2-15, 4-21
ordinary enterprise operations, 5-19
ordinary repairs, 10-33
ordinary revenue-generating activities,
2-15
ordinary trade accounts, 5-12
organization costs, 12-11
original oil in place, 11-14
other assets, 5-17–5-18
other comprehensive income (OCI),
2-16, 4-12–4-14
accumulated other comprehensive
income, AP-46
IFRS-ASPE comparison, 4-38, 9-46

unrealized holding gain or loss,
AP-35
outcome uncertainty, 2-23
output measures, 6-50
outstanding cheques, 7-45
overhead, 10-7
oversight in capital marketplace,
1-19–1-20
Owners' Drawings account, AP-46
owners' equity, 5-20–5-21, AP-46,
AP-47
ownership
ownership interest, 2-15
ownership structure, AP-45–AP-46
risk of, 6-36

P
parent corporation, 9-38
parenthetical explanations, 5-24–5-25
parking transactions, 8-9
partial periods, and depreciation,
11-16–11-17
partnership, 2-19, AP-46, AP-47
past events, 2-12, 2-13, 2-14
patent, 12-19–12-20
payee, 7-21
payment policy, 6-7
payout ratio, 5-41
pensions, 3-5
percentage markup, 8-42
percentage-of-completion method,
6-48, 6-49–6-54
percentage-of-receivables approach, 7-15
percentage-of-sales approach, 7-17
performance
business models, 4-3–4-7
communication of information
about performance, 4-7
industries, 4-3–4-7
quality of earnings/information,
4-7–4-12
performance obligations, 2-21, 6-16
allocation of transaction price,
6-28–6-31
identification of, 6-16–6-20
multiple performance obligations,
6-17, 6-29–6-31
remaining performance obligations,
6-46
satisfaction of, 6-32–6-35
single performance obligation, 6-17
period costs, 2-25, 8-19
periodic inventory system, 8-21, 8-28,
8-33–8-34, AP-48
periodic payment, 3-26–3-27
periodicity assumption, 2-25
peripheral activities, 4-21
peripheral transactions, 2-15, 2-16
permanent account, AP-29
permits, 12-19
perpetual franchise, 12-19
perpetual inventory system, 8-21, 8-26,
8-28, 8-34, AP-48
petty cash, 7-7, 7-9, 7-43–7-44
physical count, AP-48
physical factors, 11-7
physical life, 11-7
plant assets, 10-4
see also property, plant, and
equipment
point of delivery, 6-36
political environment, standard setting
in, 1-21–1-22
possession, 2-13, 6-4, 6-9, 6-37
post-closing trial balance, AP-29, AP-48
post-retirement benefits, 3-5
postage on hand, 7-9

postdated cheques, 7-6, 7-9
posting, AP-29, AP-33
predictive value, 2-6, 2-27, 4-7, 4-9,
4-12, 4-26
preferred shares, 7-8
premium, 7-29
prepaid expenses, 5-15, 12-7, AP-35
adjusting entries, AP-36–AP-39
depreciation/amortization,
AP-37–AP-38
expiration of, AP-36
insurance, AP-37
vs. unearned revenues, AP-38–AP-39
prepayments, AP-35
adjusting entries, AP-36–AP-39
alternative method for adjusting,
AP-39–AP-40
as current assets, 5-15
intangible assets, 12-7–12-9
prepaid expenses, 12-7–12-9, AP-35,
AP-36–AP-39
unearned revenues, AP-35, AP-36,
AP-38–AP-39
present obligations, 5-8
present value, 3-13–3-27
calculation methods, 3-16–3-25
compound interest, 3-15–3-16
of consideration, 10-11
exchange price, 10-11
expected present value technique,
3-6
financial assets, 7-14
financial calculators, 3-19–3-20, 3-23
fundamental variables, 3-14–3-16
interest, nature of, 3-13–3-14
interest rate calculation, 3-25–3-26
interest rates and time periods, 3-24
notes, 7-23, 7-25
periodic payment, calculation of,
3-26–3-27
present value formula, 3-17–3-18,
3-21–3-22
present value tables, 3-18–3-19,
3-22–3-23
series of future cash flows
(annuities), 3-20–3-22
simple interest, 3-15
single future amount, 3-16–3-20
spreadsheets, 3-20, 3-23–3-24
tables, AP-2, AP-4, AP-5
value in use, 3-7–3-8
present value-based accounting
measurements, 3-5
present value factor, 7-25
presentation, 2-29–2-31
basic presentation requirements,
4-21–4-22
contract assets, 6-42–6-44
discontinued operations, 4-16–4-20
of earnings, 4-9
expenses, 4-28–4-30
goodwill, 12-30–12-33
intangible assets, 12-30–12-33
inventories, 8-43–8-44
investments, 9-39–9-43
issues, 5-37
multiple-step income statement,
4-24–4-27
ordinary vs. peripheral activities, 4-21
percentage-of-completion method,
6-52–6-53
property, plant, and equipment,
11-30–11-32
receivables, 7-37–7-39
revenues and revenue recognition,
6-42–6-46
single-step income statements, 4-24

statement of cash flows, 5-29–5-33
statement of changes in equity, 4-34–4-35
statement of financial position (balance sheet), 5-9–5-10, 5-10–5-22
statement of income/comprehensive income, 4-21–4-32
statement of retained earnings, 4-32–4-34
price
 cash price equivalent, 10-11
 exchange price, 7-12, 10-11
 lump-sum price, 10-12
 stand-alone selling price, 6-28
 transaction price, 6-21–6-28, 6-26, 6-27, 6-28–6-31
price earnings ratio, 4-38, 5-41
price-level change, 2-25
price risk, 6-7
primary sources of GAAP, 1-18, 2-16, 8-37
principal-agent relationship, 6-39–6-40, 6-42
principal market, 3-10–3-11
principles-based approach, 1-23, 2-32
principles vs. rules, 1-22–1-23
private companies, 1-14
private entity GAAP. See Accounting Standards for Private Enterprises (ASPE)
pro forma numbers, 11-12
product costs, 2-22, 8-18–8-20
product market risks, 5-40
professional corporations, 2-19
professional judgement, 1-19, 2-31, 5-6, 5-23–5-24, 6-46
profit margin on sales, 5-41
profit margin ratio, 11-34
profit margins, 4-26, 4-28
profitability ratios, 5-40, 5-41
profitable contracts, 6-57–6-58
profits, 1-20
promise, 6-9
promissory note, 7-20, 7-22
 see also loans receivable; notes receivable
prompt settlement discounts, 6-24
pronouncements, 1-18
property, plant, and equipment, 5-15–5-16, 10-5
 additions, 10-29, 10-30
 analysis, 11-32–11-35
 asset exchanges, 10-14–10-18
 assets classified as, 10-5
 biological assets, 10-22
 borrowing costs, 10-8–10-9
 buildings, 10-20
 business perspective, 10-4
 cash discounts not taken, 10-10
 characteristics, 10-4–10-6
 contributed assets, 10-18–10-19
 cost elements, 10-6–10-10
 cost model (CM), 10-23–10-24
 costs associated with specific assets, 10-19–10-22
 costs incurred after acquisition, 10-29–10-34
 deferred payment terms, 10-11–10-12
 depreciation. See depreciation
 disclosure, 11-30–11-32
 dismantling and restoration costs, 10-9–10-10
 disposal. See disposition
 economic benefits, 11-3

efficiency of asset use, 11-33–11-35
equipment, 10-21
expenditures, major types of, 10-29–10-34
fair value model (FVM), 10-23, 10-27–10-28, 10-32
fair value standard, 10-14–10-15
government grants, 10-18–10-19
IFRS-ASPE comparison, 10-34–10-37
impairment. See impairment
inspections, 10-29, 10-30–10-32
investment property, 10-21
leasehold improvements, 10-20
lump-sum purchases, 10-12–10-13
major overhauls, 10-29, 10-30–10-32
measurement after acquisition, 10-23–10-28
natural resource properties, 10-21–10-22
net basis, 5-32
nonmonetary exchanges, 10-10–10-19
nonmonetary transactions, 10-14–10-18
presentation, 11-30–11-32
rearrangement and reinstallation costs, 10-29, 10-33
recognition principle, 10-5–10-6
repairs, 10-29, 10-33–10-34
replacement of assets, 11-32–11-33
replacements, 10-29, 10-30–10-32
return on investment, 11-33–11-35
revaluation adjustment, 4-22, 10-25–10-26
revaluation model (RM), 10-23, 10-24–10-27, 10-32
sale of, 11-28–11-29
self-constructed assets, 10-7–10-8
share-based payments, 10-13
vs. inventory, 10-5
proportional method, 12-13
proprietary perspective, 1-7
provincial securities commissions, 1-12, 1-17
provision matrix, 7-15
provisions, 5-19, 5-23
prudence, 2-1
public companies, 1-14
Public Sector Accounting Handbook, 10-4
purchase allowances, 8-50
purchase commitments, 8-10–8-11
purchase discounts, 8-50
purchase returns, 8-50
purchasers of receivables, 7-31

Q
quadrophobia, 4-10
qualifying assets, 10-37, 10-38–10-39
qualitative characteristics, 2-6–2-12, 4-8
 comparability, 2-10
 cost-benefit relationship, 2-11
 elements of financial statements, 2-4
 enhancing qualitative characteristics, 2-10–2-11
 fundamental, 2-6–2-9
 relevance, 2-6–2-7, 2-11
 representational faithfulness, 2-6, 2-8–2-9, 2-11
 timeliness, 2-10
 trade-offs, 2-11–2-12
 understandability, 2-10–2-11
 verifiability, 2-10
quality of earnings, 4-7–4-12, 5-4
quantitative data, 2-25

quantitative factors, 2-7
quantities only system, 8-23
quick ratio, 5-5, 5-41

R
radio-frequency identification (RFID), 8-1
rate of gross profit/rate of gross margin, 8-42
rate of markup, 8-42
rate of return on assets (ROA), 5-41, 11-34
rate of return on common share equity, 5-41
ratio analysis, 4-37–4-38, 5-40
 acid-test ratio, 5-5, 5-41
 activity ratios, 5-5, 5-40, 5-41
 asset turnover, 5-41
 average days to sell inventory, 8-45
 benchmarking, 5-41–5-42
 book value per share, 5-41
 business risks, 5-39–5-40
 cash debt coverage ratio, 5-35, 5-41
 cost-to-retail ratio, 8-47
 coverage ratios, 5-5, 5-40, 5-41
 current cash debt coverage ratio, 5-5, 5-35, 5-41
 current ratio, 5-5, 5-9, 5-41, 8-14, 8-15
 debt to equity ratios, 5-9
 debt to total assets, 5-41
 earnings per share (EPS), 4-12, 4-14, 4-31–4-32, 5-41
 inventory turnover ratio, 5-41, 8-45
 liquidity ratios, 5-5, 5-6, 5-40, 5-41
 major types of ratios, 5-40
 misclassification, effect of, 5-37
 payout ratio, 5-41
 price earnings ratio, 4-38, 5-41
 profit margin on sales, 5-41
 profit margin ratio, 11-34
 profitability ratios, 5-40, 5-41
 quick ratio, 5-5, 5-41
 rate of return on assets (ROA), 5-41, 11-34
 rate of return on common share equity, 5-41
 receivables turnover ratio, 7-39–7-40
 solvency ratios, 5-6
rational entity impairment model, 12-21–12-22
rational entity model, 11-21, 11-22–11-25
ratios. See ratio analysis
raw materials inventory, 8-5
real-time financial information, 2-25
realizable (revenue), 2-21
realized (gains and losses), 9-8
realized (revenue), 2-21
rearrangement and reinstallation costs, 10-29, 10-33
reasonable knowledge, 2-10
rebates, 6-21, 8-17–8-18
recapture, 11-40
receivables, 7-9–7-11
 see also accounts receivable
 analysis, 7-39–7-40
 as current asset, 5-12–5-13
 definition, 7-9–7-10
 derecognition, 7-30–7-37
 disclosure, 7-36–7-37, 7-37–7-39
 estimated uncollectible receivables, AP-43
 factoring receivables, 7-31
 IFRS-ASPE comparison, 7-41
 loans receivable. See loans receivable

measurement, 7-11–7-14
nontrade receivables, 7-4, 7-10
notes receivable. See notes receivable
presentation, 7-37–7-39
recognition, 7-11–7-14
with recourse, 7-35–7-36
reporting, 7-11
sale of receivables, 7-31–7-36
sale without recourse, 7-35
secured borrowings, 7-31
trade receivables, 7-4, 7-10
receivables management, 7-5
receivables turnover ratio, 5-41, 7-39–7-40
reciprocal exchange, 2-26
reciprocal transaction, 6-5–6-7
reclassification adjustment, 9-22
reclassified items, 4-13
recognition, 2-17–2-22
 accounts receivable, 7-11–7-14
 cash, 7-6–7-9
 control, 2-18–2-21
 economic entity assumption, 2-18–2-21
 estimated uncollectible receivables, AP-43
 goodwill, 12-24–12-27
 impairment, 11-21–11-25
 intangible assets, 12-6–12-16
 inventory, physical goods included in, 8-7–8-13
 liabilities, 5-23
 long-term loans receivable, 7-22–7-30
 long-term notes receivable, 7-22–7-30
 matching principle, 2-21–2-22
 and measurement, 2-23–2-29
 property, plant, and equipment, 10-5–10-6
 realized and realizable, 2-21
 receivables, 7-11–7-14
 revenue recognition. See revenue recognition
 short-term loans receivable, 7-21–7-22
 short-term notes receivable, 7-21–7-22
 when to recognize an item, AP-31
reconciliation of bank balances, 7-45–7-47
recording process
 adjusting entries, AP-34–AP-45
 closing process, AP-46–AP-49
 identification of transactions and other events, AP-31
 journalizing, AP-31–AP-32
 posting, AP-33
 recording transactions and other events, AP-31
 reversing entries, AP-48–AP-49
 trial balance, AP-34
recoverability test, 11-21, 11-22, 12-23
recoverable amount, 11-22
recoverable reserves, 11-14–11-15
recycled items, 4-12–4-13
recycling, 9-21
refund liability, 7-13
regular activities, 4-26
regular-way purchase or sale, 9-8
reinstallation, 10-29, 10-33
related party transactions, 2-26, 5-12
relative fair value, 6-48
relative sales value method, 8-20
relevance, 2-6–2-7, 2-11, 2-18, 4-21
rental real estate, 10-21
repairs, 10-29, 10-33–10-34

replacement cost, 8-30–8-31
replacements, 10-29, 10-30–10-32, 11-32–11-33
reporting entity, 2-20
representational faithfulness, 2-6, 2-8–2-9, 2-11, 2-18, 4-4, 10-23
repurchase agreements, 6-38–6-39, 6-42, 8-9–8-10
research, 12-9–12-10
research phase, 12-9–12-10
research studies, 1-18
reserves, 4-10
residual approach, 6-29
residual interest, 2-15, 5-8
residual value, 11-6, 11-11
residual value method, 6-48
resources
    allocation of, 1-4, 2-5, 2-10
    economic resources, 2-15, 5-8
    efficient use of resources, 1-4
    evaluations of alternatives, 2-10
    successful use of, 4-26
    transfer of, 1-5
restoration costs, 10-9–10-10
restricted cash, 7-7
restrictions, 5-19
retail inventory method, 8-47–8-51
    evaluation of, 8-51
    special items, 8-50–8-51
    terminology, 8-48–8-50
retained earnings, 5-20
Retained Earnings account, AP-46, AP-47
retrospective restatement, 4-33, 4-34
return on investment, 9-5, 11-33–11-35
return policy, 6-7
returnable items, 7-10
revaluation adjustment on property, plant, and equipment, 4-22, 10-25–10-26
revaluation model (RM), 10-23, 10-24–10-27, 10-32, 10-42–10-43, 11-20, 12-13–12-14
Revaluation Surplus account, 10-24, 10-26–10-27
revenue account, AP-29
revenue constraint, 6-25
revenue expenditure, 10-29
revenue recognition
    approaches to, 2-10–2-13
    asset-liability approach, 6-10–6-13
    bill-and-hold arrangement, 6-39, 6-42
    consignments, 6-40–6-41, 6-42
    disclosure, 6-45–6-46
    earnings approach, 6-10–6-11, 6-35–6-38
    five-step revenue recognition process, 6-10–6-35
    gross basis, 6-40
    IFRS-ASPE comparison, 6-47–6-48
    key concepts, 6-11
    licensing type arrangements, 6-34
    long-term contracts, 6-49–6-54
    misrepresentation in financial statements, 6-10
    net basis, 6-40
    presentation, 6-42–6-45
    principal-agent relationship, 6-39–6-40, 6-42
    repurchase agreements, 6-38–6-39, 6-42
    revenue recognition principle, 2-21, AP-35
    right of return, 6-22–6-23
    satisfying performance obligation over time, 6-33
    situations, 6-16

substantially the same goods and services, 6-20
    upfront fees, 6-19–6-20
    warranties, 6-18–6-19
revenue recognition principle, 2-21, 6-38, AP-35
revenues, 2-15
    accrued revenues, AP-35, AP-40–AP-41
    basic revenue transaction, 6-15
    biased revenue numbers, 6-10
    calculation of, 4-41–4-42
    collectible revenues, 2-21
    contract assets and liabilities, 6-42–6-44
    from contracts with customers, 2-21
    costs to obtain and/or fulfill a contract, 6-44–6-45, 6-46
    disaggregation of revenue, 6-46
    measurement, 6-10–6-11
    and operations, 4-7
    presentation, 6-42–6-45
    realizable (revenue), 2-21
    realized (revenue), 2-21
    recognition. See revenue recognition
    reconciliation of contract balances, 6-46
    remaining performance obligations, 6-46
    sales revenues, 7-12
    in single-step income statements, 4-24
    unearned revenues, AP-35, AP-38–AP-39
    vs. gains, 4-21
reversing entries, AP-29, AP-48–AP-49
rewards of ownership, 6-36
right of return, 6-22–6-23, 6-48
risk, 4-4
    of bankruptcy, 5-5
    business model, and various related risks, 5-39
    business risks, 5-39–5-40
    capital market risks, 5-40
    credit risk, 6-6, 7-1, 7-14, 7-23
    financial risks, 5-40, 9-41
    inputs to income models, 3-5
    liquidity risk, 5-6
    operating risk, 5-40
    of ownership, 6-36
    price risk, 6-7
    product market risks, 5-40
    risks and rewards, 2-21
risk-free discount rate, 3-6
risk management, 4-4
risk profile, 6-6–6-7
risk/return trade-off, 4-4
ROA. See rate of return on assets (ROA)
royalty relief approach, 12-17
rules-based approach, 1-22

S

sale
    of goods, 6-36–6-37
    see also sales transaction
    property, plant, and equipment, 11-28–11-29
    of receivables, 7-31–7-36
    regular-way purchase or sale, 9-8
    of services, 6-37
sales discounts, 7-12, 8-50
sales returns and allowances, 7-12–7-13, 8-50
sales revenues, 7-12–7-13
sales transaction
    business perspective, 6-4
    concessionary terms, 6-7–6-8
    constructive obligation, 6-9–6-10

contract law, 6-9
    economics of, 6-4–6-8
    fundamentals of understanding sales transactions, 6-4–6-5
    information for decision-making, 6-10
    legalities of, 6-9–6-10
    reciprocal nature, 6-5–6-7
    revenue recognition. See revenue recognition
salvage value, 11-6
Sarbanes-Oxley Act (SOX), 1-19–1-20
secured borrowings, 7-31, 7-33
Securities Act, 1-20
securitization, 1-7, 7-1, 7-32, 7-40
self-constructed assets, 10-7–10-8
self-interest, 1-6
selling expenses, 8-19
selling transactions. See sales transaction
sensitive numbers on financial statements, 2-7
service contracts, 6-4
service life. See useful life
service-type warranty, 6-18–6-19
services, 6-4
    additional services, 6-7
    distinct services, 6-16
    ongoing services, 6-7
    performance of the service, 6-37
    sale of services, 6-37
    substantially the same, 6-20
    virtual services, 6-1
    vs. sales of goods, 6-1
servicing asset component, 7-36
servicing liability component, 7-36
share-based payments, 10-13
shared advertising, 6-27
shareholders' equity, 5-20–5-21
short-term financing, 5-18
short-term investments, 5-12, 7-6
short-term liquidity ratios, 5-5
short-term loans receivable, 7-21–7-22
short-term notes receivable, 7-21–7-22
short-term paper, 7-6, 7-9
short-term returns, 9-5
significant influence, 9-32–9-33
significant influence investments, 9-32, 9-47
significant judgements, 6-46
simple interest, 3-15
single-step income statements, 4-24
soft numbers, 2-10, 2-23, 4-8, 5-6
sole proprietorship, 2-19, AP-46, AP-47
solvency, 1-12, 5-5, 5-9
solvency ratios, 5-5, 5-6, 5-40
special journal, AP-32
special purpose entity (SPE), 1-7, 2-21
specific identification, 8-24–8-25
spreadsheets, 3-20, 3-23–3-24
stable dollar, 2-25
stakeholders, 1-5–1-7
stand-alone selling price, 6-28–6-29
standard cost system, 8-19
standard setting
    challenge for, 1-23
    and conceptual framework, 2-3
    funding, 1-22
    need for standards, 1-12
    parties involved in standard setting, 1-12–1-17
    in political environment, 1-21–1-22
    provincial securities commissions, 1-17
standard-setting organizations, 1-12
stated interest rate, 7-23, 7-27, 7-29
statement of cash flows, 4-36, 5-27, AP-29

cash flow patterns, 5-35–5-36
    cash inflows and outflows, 5-28
    content, 5-26–5-29
    direct method, 5-33
    financial flexibility, 5-35
    financing activities, 5-27, 5-31–5-33, 5-33
    format, 5-26–5-29
    free cash flow, 5-36–5-37
    IFRS-ASPE comparison, 5-38
    indirect method, 5-32–5-33
    investing activities, 5-27, 5-33
    liquidity, 5-35
    operating activities, 5-27, 5-31–5-33
    perspectives, 5-35–5-37
    preparation of, 5-29–5-33
    purpose, 5-27
    usefulness from business perspective, 5-3–5-4
    usefulness of, 5-34–5-37
statement of changes in equity, 1-3, 4-32, 4-34–4-35
    see also statement of retained earnings
statement of changes in shareholders' equity, AP-29, AP-54
statement of comprehensive income, 4-3, AP-29
    see also income statement
    preparation from work sheet, AP-53–AP-54
    unrealized holding gain or loss, AP-44–AP-45
statement of financial position (balance sheet), 1-3, 5-4–5-5, AP-29
    accounting policies, 5-23
    additional detail, 5-24
    analysis of, 5-4
    assets, 5-8
    cash, 5-11–5-12
    classification, 5-7–5-10
    classified statement of financial position, 5-9–5-10, 5-10–5-22
    comparative, 5-30
    contingencies, 5-22–5-23
    contra items, 5-25–5-26
    contractual situations, 5-23–5-24
    cross-references, 5-25–5-26
    current assets, 5-10–5-15
    current liabilities, 5-18
    disclosure techniques, 5-24–5-26
    elements of, 5-8–5-10
    financial assets, 5-12–5-13
    financial instruments, 5-7–5-10
    format, 5-21–5-22
    IFRS-ASPE comparison, 5-38
    intangible assets, 5-17
    inventories, 5-13–5-14
    leaving out items of relevance, 5-6
    liabilities, 5-8
    limitations, 5-6
    long-term investments, 5-15
    long-term liabilities, 5-18–5-20
    monetary vs. nonmonetary assets and liabilities, 5-7–5-8
    non-current investments, 5-15
    notes to financial statements, 5-25
    off-balance sheet, 5-6
    other assets, 5-17–5-18
    other required disclosures, 5-22–5-24
    owners' equity, 5-20–5-21
    parenthetical explanations, 5-24–5-25
    prepaid expenses, 5-15
    preparation from work sheet, AP-53–AP-56

preparation of, 5-9–5-10, 5-10–5-22
property, plant, and equipment,
    5-15–5-16
provisions, 5-23
receivables, 5-12–5-13
short-term investments, 5-12
standard format, 5-8
subsequent events, 5-24
supporting schedule, 5-26
terminology, 5-26
usefulness, 5-5–5-6
statement of income/comprehensive
    income (income statement), 1-3,
    4-5–4-6
see also income statement
basic presentation requirements,
    4-21–4-22
combined statement of income/
    comprehensive income,
    4-22–4-24
condensed, 4-27–4-28
continuing operations, 4-26–4-27
conversion of statement of cash
    receipts and disbursements to
    income statement, 4-4
detail, level of, 4-27
discontinued operations, 4-14–4-20,
    4-27
earnings per share, 4-31–4-32
expenses, 4-28–4-30
IFRS-ASPE comparison, 4-38–4-39
income tax section, 4-27
intraperiod tax allocation, 4-30–4-31
multiple-step income statement,
    4-24–4-27
non-operating section, 4-27
operating section, 4-26
ordinary vs. peripheral activities,
    4-21
other comprehensive income, 4-27
as point estimates, 4-8
presentation, 4-21–4-32
sections, 4-26–4-27
single-step income statements,
    4-24
statement of income/earnings, 4-3
see also income statement; statement
    of income/comprehensive
    income (income statement)
statement of retained earnings, 1-3,
    4-32–4-34, AP-29
see also statement of changes in
    equity
Statements of Financial Accounting
    Concepts, 2-4
stewardship, 1-11, 2-5
stock market crash, 1-12
straight-line amortization, 9-13
straight-line method, 7-26–7-27, 7-28,
    9-13, 11-9–11-10
strategic investments, 9-32–9-39
    associates, investments in, 9-32–9-38
    equity method, 9-33–9-37, 9-38
    subsidiaries, investments in,
        9-38–9-39
strategy
    corporate strategy, 9-5
    differentiation strategy, 4-7

low-cost/high-volume strategy, 4-6
strict cash basis, 4-39
structured entity, 7-32
structured financings, 2-32
studies, 1-18
subjective values, 2-27
subprime mortgages, 1-7
subsequent events, 5-24
subsidiary, 9-38–9-39
subsidiary ledger, AP-29
substantial completion or
    performance, 6-36
substantially the same goods or
    services, 6-20
successful efforts method, 10-22
sum-of-the-years'-digits method, 11-10
supplementary information, 2-30
supplementary schedules, 4-27
supporting schedule, 5-26

T

tangible capital assets, 3-5, 10-4
    see also property, plant, and
        equipment
tax basis, 11-39
tax rebates receivable, 7-10
tax value, 11-39
taxation
    capital cost allowance. *See* capital
        cost allowance (CCA); capital
        cost allowance method
    capital gain, 11-40
    deferred income tax assets, 5-18
    deferred income tax liabilities, 5-19
    and depreciation, 11-37–11-41
    future income tax assets, 5-18
    future income tax liabilities, 5-19
    income taxes, AP-51–AP-52
    intraperiod tax allocation, 4-30–4-31
technology, impact of, 1-23–1-24
technology-based intangible assets,
    12-19–12-21
telecom companies, 7-1
temporary account, AP-29
temporary use of land during
    construction, 10-7
10-column work sheet, AP-50
terminal loss, 11-40–11-41
textbooks, 1-18
time periods, 3-24
time value concepts, 3-13, 7-21
    see also present value
time value of money, 3-5, 6-25–6-26,
    AP-1–AP-5
timeliness, 2-10
times interest earned, 5-41
total-earnings approach, 12-41–12-42
trade discounts, 7-12
trade-in allowance, 10-15
trade name, 12-16
trade-offs, 2-11–2-12
trade receivables, 7-4, 7-10
trademark, 12-16
trading, 9-5
traditional discounted cash flow
    approach, 3-6
transaction, AP-29
    see also event

analysis of, AP-31
arm's-length transaction, 2-27, 6-5
barter transactions, 2-26, 6-6
incidental transactions, 2-15,
    2-16, 4-26
nonmonetary, non-reciprocal
    transactions, 2-26
nonmonetary transactions, 2-26,
    6-6
peripheral transactions, 2-15, 2-16
related party transactions, 2-26
revenue transaction, 6-15
sales transaction. *See* sales
    transaction
transaction costs, 7-23, 9-8
transaction price, 6-21–6-28, 6-25,
    6-27–6-28, 6-28–6-31, 6-48
transfers in, 8-50
transparency, 2-8
travel advances, 7-9
treasury bills, 7-8
treasury stock, 5-20
trial balance, AP-29, AP-34
trigger events, 9-26–9-27
tuition fees, AP-39
turnover ratio, 5-5
typical business activities, 4-21

U

uncertainty
    acceptable level of uncertainty,
        2-25
    existence uncertainty, 2-18, 2-23
    inputs to income models, 3-5
    level of, 2-25
    measurement uncertainty, 2-23,
        2-27, 4-36
    outcome uncertainty, 2-23
uncollectible accounts, 7-14
    see also bad debts
uncollectible trade accounts
    receivable, 7-14–7-16
unconditional right to receive
    consideration, 6-42
undepreciated capital cost (UCC),
    11-38, 11-39
understandability, 2-10–2-11
unearned revenues, AP-35, AP-36
    adjusting entries, AP-38–AP-39
    vs. prepaid expenses, AP-38–AP-39
unit of accountability, 2-18
unit of measure, 10-5–10-6
United States, and IFRS, 1-23
units-of-delivery method, 6-33
units of production method, 11-11
unprofitable contract, 6-58–6-59
unrealized holding gains or losses, 9-8,
    AP-35, AP-44–AP-45
unrecorded items, AP-35
unusual gains and losses, 4-21
unusual items, 5-12
upfront fees, 6-19–6-20
U.S. dollar, 7-7
U.S. GAAP, 1-16, 1-23, 8-30
    last-in, first-out (LIFO) accounting,
        2-10
U.S. stock markets and exchanges,
    1-16

useful life, 5-17, 10-6, 11-7, 12-14,
    12-19, AP-37
users of financial information, 1-3,
    1-5, 2-5, 6-4

V

valuation
    goodwill, 12-27, 12-37–12-42
    intangible assets, 5-17
valuation premise, 3-10
valuation techniques, 3-3–3-7
    choice of model, 3-4–3-5
    discounted cash flow model,
        3-6
    income models, 3-3–3-4
    inputs, 3-5
    market models, 3-4
    quality of the measurement,
        3-6
value in use, 2-24, 11-23
value in use measurements,
    3-7–3-8
variable charge approach, 11-11
variable consideration, 6-21–6-25,
    6-48
vendor rebate, 8-18
verifiability, 2-10, 10-23
virtual services, 6-1
volume discounts, 6-23–6-24
volume rebates, 6-21, 8-17–8-18

W

warranties, 5-19, 6-5, 6-18–6-19, 6-48
wasting assets, 10-21
weighted-average accumulated
    expenditures, 10-38
weighted average cost, 8-26–8-27
with recourse, 7-35–7-36
without recourse, 7-35
work-in-process inventory, 8-5
work sheet, AP-50
    adjusted trial balance columns,
        AP-51
    adjustments, AP-50–AP-51
    adjustments columns, AP-51
    columns, AP-51
    completion of, AP-51–AP-53
    income taxes, AP-51–AP-52
    net income, AP-53
    preparation of financial statements,
        AP-53–AP-56
    statement of comprehensive income
        columns, AP-51
    statement of financial position
        columns, AP-51
    10-column work sheet, AP-50
    trial balance columns, AP-51
    using a work sheet, AP-50–AP-56
working capital, 5-18, 5-23, 8-14
writing off an account, 7-18

Y

yield rate, 7-23

Z

zero-interest-bearing notes, 7-21,
    7-24–7-27
zero-profit method, 6-50, 6-55